ST. JAMES
ENCYCLOPEDIA OF
LABOR HISTORY
WORLDWIDE

ST. JAMES ENCYCLOPEDIA OF LABOR HISTORY WORLDWIDE

Major Events in Labor History and Their Impact

VOLUME 2
N–Z

With Introductions by

Willie Thompson, Northumbria University
and
Daniel Nelson, University of Akron

Neil Schlager, Editor

PRODUCED BY SCHLAGER GROUP

**ST. JAMES
PRESS®**

Detroit • New York • San Diego • San Francisco • Cleveland • New Haven, Conn. • Waterville, Maine • London • Munich

St. James Encyclopedia of Labor History Worldwide: Major Events in Labor History and Their Impact

Schlager Group Inc. Staff

Neil Schlager, editor

Vanessa Torrado-Caputo, assistant editor

Project Editor
Margaret Mazurkiewicz

Editorial
Erin Bealmear, Joann Cerrito, Jim Craddock, Stephen Cusack, Miranda H. Ferrara, Peter M. Gareffa, Kristin Hart, Melissa Hill, Carol Schwartz, Christine Tomassini, Michael J. Tyrkus

Permissions
Shalice Shah-Caldwell

Imaging and Multimedia
Robert Duncan, Leitha Etheridge-Sims, Mary Grimes, Lezlie Light, Daniel Newell, David G. Oblender, Christine O'Bryan, Kelly A. Quin

Product Design
Cynthia Baldwin

Manufacturing
Rhonda Williams

Library of Congress Cataloging-in-Publication Data

St. James encyclopedia of labor history worldwide : major events in labor history and their impact / Neil Schlager, editor ; with introductions by Daniel Nelson and Willie Thompson.
     p. cm.
        Includes bibliographical references and index.
        ISBN 1-55862-542-9 (set : alk. paper) — ISBN 1-55862-559-3 (Vol. 1) —
        ISBN 1-55862-560-7 (Vol. 2)
        1. Labor movement—History—Encyclopedias. 2. Labor unions—
        History—Encyclopedias. I. Schlager, Neil, 1966-

HD4839.S74 2003
331.8'03—dc21
2003000294

Printed in the United States of America
10 9 8 7 6 5 4 3 2 1

CONTENTS

EDITOR'S NOTE

Overview

Welcome to the *St. James Encyclopedia of Labor History Worldwide*. Our aim is to provide a scholarly, encyclopedic treatment of the labor movement during the past 200 years. The encyclopedia covers 300 key events in labor history, from the struggle to abolish slavery both in the British Empire and in the United States during the 1800s; to the rise of trade unions later in the century; to the often violent clashes between labor and management in the early twentieth century; and to the onset of globalization toward the end of the twentieth century. Throughout the encyclopedia, events are placed in the context of the labor movement as a whole and related to societal change and development worldwide.

Scope and Coverage

The encyclopedia includes 300 events from period from 1800 to 2000. Two-thirds of the articles focus on U.S. labor history and one-third are devoted to international history. Because of this distribution, international events in particular were chosen for their relevance to larger social movements and their impact on development of the labor movement in a country or region. The entries were selected by an advisory board of expert labor historians, whose names and affiliations are listed elsewhere in this frontmatter; more information about the advisers is available in the "Notes on Advisers and Contributors" section at the back of Volume 2. The entries were written by labor historians, freelance writers, librarians, and journalists.

Format of Volumes, Entries

In response to feedback from public and academic librarians, we have arranged the volumes alphabetically by entry title. An alphabetical listing of the entry titles is included in the frontmatter. In addition, readers may also wish to consult the chronological listing of entries elsewhere in the frontmatter as well as the detailed index at the back of Volume 2.

Within each entry, readers will find the following format:

* Entry title, location, and date. Although the location is typically the country where the event occurred, in some cases it refers to the place where an organization or movement was founded.
* Synopsis: Brief overview of the event.
* Event and Its Context: In-depth discussion of the event and its impact.
* Key Players: Brief biographical notes on people who figured prominently in the event.
* Bibliography: List of sources used to compile the entry.
* Additional Resources: Other sources that readers may wish to consult.

In addition, each entry contains a chronology of key events in world history, so that readers may better understand the historical context in which the event occurred. At the end of most entries, readers will find cross references to other entries in the encyclopedia that may be of interest.

Other Features

In addition to the main text, the encyclopedia features two lengthy introductions, one of which discusses international labor history and another that covers U.S. labor history. In addition, users will find a glossary of labor terms; a general chronology consisting of key events in world history combined with important labor events; a reading list covering English-language sources devoted to labor history; and a subject index. The encyclopedia also includes more than 350 photographs as well as nearly 50 sidebars that provide information on other subjects of interest.

Acknowledgements

The editors wish to thank the following individuals for their assistance in preparing the encyclopedia: Judson Knight, who compiled all of the sidebar material in addition to the chronologies; Caryn E. Neumann, who prepared the glossary; and Willie Thompson and Daniel Nelson, who wrote the introductory pieces.

—Neil Schlager
Editor

INTRODUCTION: INTERNATIONAL LABOR, 1800–2000

The worldwide labor movement that was a central social reality of the nineteenth and twentieth centuries was formed from many and diverse sources and traditions. Its development and history coincided with that of the growth and spread of factory industry and of similar forms of capitalist and public enterprise, such as transport, primary production, and the many divisions of labor in societies economically connected to mass markets and advanced public utilities.

This labor movement originated in Europe. However, its spread around the world was determined less by imitation of the European model (although that played its part) as by similar responses from industrial or quasi-industrial workforces to equivalent problems of the workplace and living environment, and above all by conflict with employers.

Given the character of modern production, it was inevitable that organizations of workers aiming to defend their members' interests would emerge sooner or later, unless repressively prevented, but the shape of the labor movement and its precise nature and development were the outcome of contingent circumstances and actions that might well have taken place under other situations. There was nothing inevitable about the structure of more-or-less nationally unified labor unions supporting labor parties, which evolved as the general rule (outside the United States), not only in the original centers of modern industry, but also in what was later to be termed the Third World.

Early Trade Associations

The decades of the late eighteenth and early nineteenth centuries were eras of economic, social, and political transition and upheaval. In Western Europe and Britain, protocapitalist market forces (developing in Britain since the previous century, if not earlier) made growing inroads into traditional standards and practices. Handicraft artisans found themselves increasingly threatened with deskilling, reduced incomes, and tighter subordination to the mercantile elements on whom they were dependent for supply and marketing, and they protested vigorously as a result. The French revolutionary government of 1790 regarded workers' coalitions as troublesome enough to outlaw them under the Le Chapelier law, and at the turn of the century, the Parliament of Britain, where there had already been workers' riots leading to fatalities, reinforced the already existing prohibition against "combinations in restraint of trade" by means of the notorious Combination Acts of 1799 and 1800.

Combinations nevertheless continued, both in Britain and elsewhere. They were feared by the propertied classes, not only on account of their immediate objectives, but for the possibility they could be infected by the democratic virus of the French Revolution, which, although defeated, continued to inspire many at the bottom of the social pyramid.

By the 1820s, with the accelerating penetration of steam-powered machinery into the production process, a further development became apparent—concentrated masses of factory operatives in expanding urban areas. The growing reliance upon coal required new factories to be sited in towns for ease of transport, first by canal and subsequently by railway. The latter generated entire industries, and coal mining also expanded prodigiously.

The Emergence of Modern Labor Movements

In these circumstances, a European labor movement of a more recognizably modern type began to evolve. A new social layer of workers entirely dependent upon minimal subsistence wage payments as their sole source of income, lacking any alternative resources of land or capital, multiplied in the new industrial centers of the United Kingdom, France, Belgium, and Germany. Although divided by age, gender, occupation, and cultural traditions, these workers shared the miseries of overcrowded slums bereft of space, sanitation, clean water, and access to adequate diet or medical care. Plagued by adulterated foodstuffs, alcoholism, crime, violence, and the narcotic substances of the time, they were also subject at unpredictable intervals to a total loss of income, whenever economic depression or an overstocked labor market produced long-term unemployment.

These circumstances, together with memories of the French Revolution—or rather its image of mighty elites overthrown and social equality enforced for all citizens—combined to determine the shape of the European labor movement. Out of that revolution in its later stages had been born the idea of socialism, with its core idea that the enormous productive forces that new technologies were releasing should be collectively owned and operated for the common good rather than private profit. However, it was not predestined that socialism would come to dominate the consciousness of European labor in the nineteenth century, for other options were available. Socialist ideas did not prevail among labor in the United States, and only by the narrowest of margins did they become the accepted mainstream ideology of British labor in the twentieth century. It was even less inevitable that the Marxian variety would emerge as the prominent form of socialism in most European countries, yet by the turn of the century, with the notable exception of Britain, it indeed had.

Marxism and Labor

The Manifesto of the Communist Party (1847), was written by the young revolutionaries Karl Marx and Frederick Engels. The *Manifesto* sketched their vision of historical development, rational and purportedly scientific, which denoted the bourgeoisie as the revolutionary class that through technology and market relations had transformed the world so that the society of universal abundance had moved from the realm of utopia to that of the possible. Having acclaimed the historical role of capital, Marx and Engels went on to condemn its current reality as an obstacle to the great possibilities it had created. They pronounced that it was both necessary and inevitable that the proletariat should displace the bourgeoisie and institute its own rule, making the transition to a society of abundance feasible. Their text thus provided both inspiration and confidence that a historic role awaited the proletariat, indeed the most momentous role of all time—in abolishing capitalism, this social class would abolish itself and all class-based society. Marx's analysis of economic relationships in the first volume of *Capital* (written in 1867, but not published until 1887) was equally important. This analysis claimed to demonstrate how, under the misleading guise of freedom and equality, the wage contract was inherently exploitative, and the wage worker, although not bound like a serf to any individual capitalist, was just as tightly bound to capitalists as a class.

It took time, however, for Marx's influence to make itself felt. After the social and political traumas of early industrialization, which had been marked by massive economic slumps along with intense discontent, the 25 years following the failed European revolutions of 1848 were years of comparative social peace, underpinned by relatively consistent high growth rates both in Britain and the continent (the large-scale construction of railway systems had a lot to do with this). During this period Marx's theoretical impact became evident, and labor organizations that based their programs on his analysis began to emerge.

Challenges to Marx

Marx's theoretical superiority did not go unchallenged. It was contested by representatives of the anarchist movement, particularly the French reformer Pierre Joseph Proudhon, in the 1840s, and Mikhail Bakunin, the Russian revolutionist, in the 1860s. Anarchism established a strong presence among workers in Switzerland, Italy, Spain (especially), and to a lesser extent, France. The movement was attractive principally to independent artisans and small farmers rather than factory workers, a reflection of the different positioning of these classes in relation to the state. A more substantial rival to Marx appeared in Germany. The radical lawyer Ferdinand Lassalle, a brilliant demagogue, admired Marx and claimed he could recite the *Manifesto* by heart. However, Lassalle was the first leader of a successful German workers' movement, the German Workers' Association, which he founded in 1863 in opposition to the exiled Marx. Lassalle supported reform, rather than revolution, and was willing to make deals with the landlord-dominated Prussian state led by Bismarck in opposition to the big capitalists. Given that Prussia was developing into the most industrialized society on the continent, with an attendant growing factory proletariat, and would soon amalgamate with smaller German states in 1866 and 1871 to create the mighty *Kaiserreich,* this workers' movement represented the greatest obstacle to Marx's intellectual hegemony.

Marxism Takes Hold

Lassalle's death in 1864, without any significant political heir, left the field clear for Marx's followers, who succeeded in bringing the rapidly growing German labor movement under their aegis. They absorbed the dead leader's very considerable following, establishing the Social Democratic Party of Germany (SPD) in 1875. It was not, however, historical accidents like Lassalle's death in a duel that determined Marx's ascendancy, but the depth and coherence of his comprehensive theoretical undertaking, which provided a ready-made understanding of the social world and a guide to action.

Marx was the moving spirit behind the establishment of the International Workingmens' Association (IWMA) in 1864. Known as the First International, the IWMA was an attempt to bring together political and trade union movements from a number of European countries to concert their actions, especially against strikebreaking. In reality, although it alarmed a number of governments—particularly after the Paris Commune, the bloody insurrection of 1871 for which the IWMA was in no way responsible—it remained small and marginal. Internal wrangles, above all between the followers of Marx and of Mikhail Bakunin, wrecked the organization and brought about its dissolution in 1874. Matters were very different when a successor organization, the Socialist, or Second

International, was set up in Paris on the centenary of the French Revolution in 1889. By this time, significant labor movements, the majority and most important basing themselves on Marx's ideas, were well established throughout western and central Europe. The Socialist International benefited from the fact that it was a loosely structured organization and that its headquarters in Amsterdam served a coordinating, rather than executive, function. This reduced friction between its constituent parts that a more centralized organization would have found difficult to handle.

The Influence of the SPD

The flagship of the Socialist International was its German component, the SPD, with a million and a half voters. Although it had been outlawed in 1878, and in 1889 was still formally illegal in its own country, the SPD was nonetheless thriving. It was clear that the ban could not long be maintained, and it was lifted in 1890. The SPD was more than a political party, more even than a political-industrial organization. With its multiplicity of journals, its attached women's and youth organizations, its cultural and athletic societies, its cooperative retail network, and of course its mighty trade union arm, it provided an alternative subculture for the working masses. The SPD had rivals in the Catholic and Liberal workers' unions, but these were a pale shadow of its own dominant strength. No other labor movement in Europe could claim this breadth of support combined with depth of cultural penetration.

Historians generally agree that the main consideration behind the hegemony of the SPD in the German workers' movement was that the dominant classes and parties in the state disdained the working class and its organizations and provided no alternative avenues for their political participation. This state of affairs was very different from that prevailing in other parts of western Europe, including the United Kingdom, where labor parties were much less hegemonic among their working classes. There is also general agreement that everywhere the SPD succeeded in establishing itself, the labor movement—although only occasionally imposing formal discrimination upon women—was institutionally misogynist (not unlike other societies of its time and since). How far that attitude toward women retarded its progress is impossible to guess, but probably a good deal.

Labor Movements Outside Western Europe

By the time the International was founded, embryonic labor movements had already been established in North America and the British settlement colonies, and were starting to appear in eastern Europe, Asia, and Latin America, where modern industry was beginning to be introduced. These embryonic organizations were frequently subject to persecution, often clandestine, and sometimes more forcefully revolutionary than their formally Marxist (but generally pacific) counterparts in Western Europe, North America, and Australasia. By the end of the 1890s they had become embedded in the working classes, combining trade union activities and political propagandizing. By the beginning of the twentieth century, trade union organizations were beginning to form in India, and in Japan, socialist ideas, albeit rather eclectic ones strongly influenced by Christianity, were appealing to circles of intellectuals.

Labor in the Twentieth Century

The Early Twentieth Century

At the beginning of the twentieth century, existing labor movements with an orientation toward political action as the long-term solution to labor's problems—with socialism as their ultimate goal—were facing a serious rival in the form of syndicalism (the name is derived from the French word for trade union). This trend of thought regarded political approaches, whether reformist or revolutionary, as inadequate to the vital interests of the workers. Instead, syndicalists envisaged taking direct action to overthrow capitalism. This action would involve the formation of wide-embracing industrial unions, followed by a general strike as the final act leading to the establishment of workers' power. As frustration grew with the existing unions and labor parties in the United States, Western Europe, the United Kingdom, and the British settlement colonies, the influence of syndicalism, taking as its icon the physically powerful male industrial worker, proliferated and strengthened. Its most effective and successful component was the organization called the Industrial Workers of the World (IWW), popularly styled the "Wobblies." The IWW put down strong roots in many trade unions, becoming dominant, for example, among the Welsh miners, produced many notable agitators, and left behind a heritage of labor movement songs and legends.

The years between 1873 and 1914 were a period of long-term economic recession (although never of negative growth) punctuated by short-lived inflationary episodes of boom conditions. This period also saw the introduction and initial development of major new technologies, from electrical apparatus to motor vehicles. Industrial workforces increased in number and spread to new parts of the world, as did workers' organizations and working-class ideologies, along with dramatic working-class struggles. The climax of European imperialism was reached with the partitioning of Africa and "opening" of China. Working classes in the imperial countries, their unions and parties, were inevitably drawn into these developments, for the most part giving them a qualified approval. Increasingly frenetic imperial rivalry brought with it the threat of general European war. The danger was foreseen, and on more than one occasion the Socialist International at its congresses committed its member parties to spare no effort in bringing such armed conflict to a stop. Regrettably, when the long-predicted war finally arrived in 1914, these resolutions were consigned to oblivion, and the International shattered. Various International sections in France, Germany, and Britain, along with labor movements, parties, and trade unions, with few exceptions, enthusiastically gave their governments all the support they could by voting war credits, suppressing strike action, encouraging recruitment, and the like. When the chips were down, each national component of the International, whatever its reservations, viewed its existing national state as the best guarantor of its future.

The Rise of the Bolsheviks

This outcome was to have reverberations for global labor movements and for world politics during the remainder of the twentieth century. Up to that point, the labor mainstream had been more and more accommodating to the realities of capitalist market economies, the concern (in spite of bitter industrial struggles and ceremonial revolutionary rhetoric) being to obtain for labor a tolerable niche in terms of material resources and social opportunity within the structures of a capital-dominated universe. Certainly there were elements like the Wobblies and some small parties who seriously envisaged the total overthrow of the existing state and complete social overturn, but these were marginal groups, either politically or geographically or both. Among the latter were the Russian Bolsheviks, one of the factions of what had been intended to be a unified Russian socialist (Social Democratic and Labor) party, but immediately upon its foundation in 1903 had splintered over policy and organizational issues, reflecting support for or disagreement with the unbending revolutionary will to power of the Bolshevik leader Vladimir Ilich Ulyanov, who had adopted the pseudonym "Lenin."

By the late nineteenth century, capitalist industry was developing strongly in parts of Russia amid the most miserable conditions for its workforce (employers tended to pay minimal wages irregularly, whenever it suited their convenience). Illegal workers' organizations soon sprung up, and these were encouraged and guided by circles of Marxist-influenced intellectuals. These same Marxists promptly fell into bitter disputes regarding the correct interpretation of Marxism and its implications for revolutionary strategy in the Russian Empire. The division in 1903 was a reflection of these disagreements; nevertheless, the Bolsheviks (the name means "majority people") and their principal rivals, the Mensheviks ("minority people") were both part of the International, which vainly struggled to reconcile their differences.

Lenin concluded that the collapse of the International's parties into what he termed "social-patriotism" following the outbreak of World War I took place because leaders at all levels of the European working classes had been seduced and debauched by profits derived from imperial exploitation, but that the murderous European war now in progress would shortly open the eyes of the masses to the way in which they had been deceived. Accordingly, from his place of exile in Switzerland, Lenin set out to establish a new genuinely revolutionary International. In the circumstances it appeared to be a completely harebrained scheme, but the outbreak of revolution in Russia in February and March 1917 transformed realities. Seven months later the Bolsheviks had taken control of the Russian state.

The revolution of October and November 1917 was one of the workers, the only example in history. The Russian workers had transferred their political allegiance to the Bolsheviks, not because of mass conversion to Marxism, but because that party promised an end to the war and the resolution of the urban supply crisis. The Bolsheviks also temporarily won the approval of the peasantry by endorsing their seizure of the landlords' estates, and that of the conscripted soldiers by promising peace. The revolution was contingent on a series of contingent events, a very unlikely outcome in historical perspective, but it set the agenda for most of the remainder of the century. Revolutionaries everywhere, especially Marxist ones, now had what they had previously lacked, a model and a point of reference, as well as the material support of an established state. For the Bolshevik leaders, the revolution in Russia was merely the initial episode in a workers' world revolution that they regarded as imminent, and in the midst of a desperate civil war to retain power, they established in 1919 a new, revolutionary International, the Third (Communist) International, or Comintern.

According to Lenin, the Comintern was to function as the general staff of the world anticapitalist revolution, and its first imperative was to establish Bolshevik-style parties in as many parts of the world as possible. The principal strategy for accomplishing this was to hive off the more revolutionary elements from the existing labor movements and parties and form these into communist parties subject to the discipline of the International, although in a number of countries the Comintern had to settle for amalgamating a number of small radical, left-wing sects to form its communist party.

The Failure of the Global Labor Movement

Overall this strategy was only moderately successful. Although within a few years communist parties made their appearance in most countries and major colonies around the world, Lenin's expectations were not realized, and no new revolution emerged out of these developments. Instead the global labor movement was disastrously and irrevocably split; bitter hatred and rivalry, including bloodshed, became the prevailing relationship between the social democrat and communist contenders for the workers' allegiance. A turning point arrived in Germany in 1919 when the working class there solidly supported the Social Democrat government (it had taken office upon the Kaiser's downfall) in using military elements of the old regime to crush communist revolutionaries led by Rosa Luxemburg and Karl Liebknecht, who were both murdered thereafter. The Bolsheviks/Communists now rejected the Social Democrat name they had accepted up to that point and left it to their constitutionalist labor movement rivals.

The experience of Soviet Russia (from 1924 the Union of Soviet Socialist Republics, or USSR), which emerged from the Revolution and Civil War, demonstrated that whether or not a workers' state was a feasible project, it certainly was not practicable in the circumstances of an isolated and devastated Russia. Even before Lenin's death in 1924, the regime had fallen into the control of a largely unaccountable bureaucracy and the labor organizations reduced to ciphers, their main remit being to exhort their members to intensified production. The world revolution had been expected to make limitless resources available for Soviet Russia's desperately needed reconstruction. When the revolution failed to materialize, Lenin's successors quarreled fiercely among themselves over what should be done. The hitherto unimpressive Josef Stalin took advantage of this to quietly accumulate power through the party's administrative apparatus. He displaced and exiled his main opponent, Leon Trotsky, and by 1929 Stalin had established his own personal dictatorship.

The Interwar Years

The working classes in the developed economies of western Europe and the British white Dominions, where they were most numerous and best organized, preferred in the main to trust their political fortunes to parties that worked within the guidelines of the constitutional politics of representative democracy and to unions that conducted industrial relations according to accepted constraints on the behavior of both sides, stretched though these bounds might be from time to time. The balance on the whole remained in favor of the employers in the 1920s, as chronic recession and high unemployment greatly impeded industrial militancy, and workers had to compromise on the best terms they could get. Their parties also tended on the whole to be weak and on the defensive within imperfectly democratic structures. In the 1930s, the situation worsened, except in Scandinavia (especially Sweden), where social democrat governments and strong union movements were able to establish a regime that combined greater levels of welfare than existed anywhere else in Europe, combined with a centralized system of wage bargaining not too disadvantageous to the unionized workforce.

However, even Scandinavia suffered from the economic hurricane that struck the world in October 1929, beginning with the collapse of the U.S. stock market. Elsewhere in the world the effects were catastrophic, both socially and politically. Italy had already provided an indicator of what was to come, with the total destruction in the 1920s of political democracy and workers' movements. In the 1930s, the political system of fascism, which Italy's elites had pioneered to mobilize terrified lower middle-class masses against the left, spread throughout Europe in even more virulent forms, and analogous types of politics appeared elsewhere around the globe, from Argentina to Japan. The years following 1929 were particularly calamitous for labor movements everywhere except for Scandinavia (less Finland) and the United States.

A considerable part of the disaster was due to the policy laid down by the Comintern as a reflection of developments in the USSR, where the workers of the workers' state were being reduced to near-serf conditions in the breakneck industrialization demanded by Stalin. According to the Comintern, the capitalist world was entering the paroxysms of a final crisis (an analysis superficially confirmed by the crash of the U.S. stock market), and capitalism was ripe for overthrow. Social democracy, allegedly deceiving the workers, was stigmatized as the last obstacle to victorious revolutionary advance ("social fascists" indeed) and targeted as the deadliest enemy of the Communists and proletariat. The real fascists were dismissed as a near irrelevance. The unbridgeable antagonisms and divisions caused by this viewpoint greatly undermined the labor movement everywhere it had once flourished, and in Germany produced unparalleled disaster, contributing in no small measure to the success of Adolph Hitler. Thus abstruse expositions of Marxist theory in the councils of the state and the Comintern produced calamitous consequences for workers on the ground almost everywhere throughout Europe and perhaps further afield. Following these manifest catastrophes, the policy began to be relaxed (although without any admission of fault) and in 1935, at the final congress of the Comintern, it was replaced by the policy of the "Popular Front," a complete reversal that called for antifascist unity among all democrats, not merely among organizations of the working class.

The embryonic labor movements of the Third World were also attacked and repressed during the interwar years. Throughout their colonial sphere from Jamaica to Malaya, and especially in India, the British crushed labor unions and jailed trade unionists (although a general strike in the British Caribbean in 1938 won some concessions). The authoritarian military government in Japan, entering into a project of aggressive military expansion, outlawed what had earlier been a significant labor movement. In China, the workforce organizations of the coastal cities were annihilated and the workers massacred when the nationalist general Chiang Kai-Shek turned against his communist allies. The Communist Party, however, survived by abandoning its urban base and turning itself into a peasant movement, and after many traumatic episodes embedded itself among the villagers of remote northwestern China, where its military forces controlled an extensive territory.

Labor During the Cold War

Most labor movements were destroyed or driven deep underground in the years leading up to World War II and the period of Nazi occupation. With the total defeat of the Axis powers in 1945, however, their situation was transformed. It would hardly be an exaggeration to suggest that in the brief period between the Allied victory and the onset of the Cold War, the world was moving to a labor agenda, and communist parties (on account of their resistance records) were popular with wide sections of the liberated European electorate, as reflected in their votes in the elections of that period. Social Democrats were also popular, and even surviving conservative parties such as the Christian Democrats in Germany and Italy were at pains to distance themselves from unregulated capitalism. A unified world trade union movement, the World Federation of Trade Unions (WFTU), was established in 1945.

Matters changed once the Cold War became an unmistakable reality from 1947, and the developed world was divided into two hostile camps, with the labor movements in the Third World assiduously courted by both sides, with varying outcomes. In 1949 China was swept by communist revolution brought from the countryside to the cities, and its urban labor movements, paralyzed since 1927, came under state control as part of the communist bloc. The same happened to labor movements in eastern Europe, when in 1947 and 1948 the continent became divided between the spheres of the United States and the USSR. Not surprisingly, the international labor movement also split, when trade union centers aligned with the West broke away from the Soviet-dominated WFTU to form the International Confederation of Free Trade Unions (ICFTU) in 1949. In Western countries, such as Italy and France, where significant communist movements survived, the parties and their associated unions and labor organizations became isolated in a political ghetto, although they continued to exercise political leverage in legislatures, to control local authorities, and to carry out the routine union functions of collective bargaining with employers.

The period of the Cold War was also an era of decolonization, as European empires disintegrated around the world. Economic development there, modest though it was by "first world" standards, resulted in the formation and development of trade unions, except in cases where they were forcibly suppressed. The trade unions participated in the independence struggles, although only very occasionally, as in Kenya, were trade union leaders also major political figures. Paradoxically, once independence was achieved, trade unionists, and industrial workers in general, tended to count among the privileged classes of the post-colonial regime, enjoying higher incomes and living standards than the mass of the rural peasantry. During the Chinese Cultural Revolution of 1966–1970, wage demands by urban workers were denounced by the Maoist Red Guards—in a state theoretically led by the working-class vanguard—as "sugar-coated bullets."

Since 1945, where workers' uprisings or even insurrections have occurred, they were directed against the supposed workers' governments of the Soviet bloc, from East Berlin in 1953 (and the less well-known simultaneous industrial unrest in Czechoslovakia), through to the strikes in Poland in 1956, the Hungarian armed insurrection immediately afterwards, and to the mass strikes along the Baltic coastline in 1970, 1975, and finally 1980. Of necessity, these actions, provoked by material, political, and national grievances, were spontaneous and inchoate, for the official trade union organizations were under tight regime control, and represented the government to the workers, not the other way round.

During the 25 years or so following World War II, trade union organizations in Western Europe (even those controlled by communists) and in the Western sphere generally enjoyed unparalleled strength, prosperity, and prestige in what was later referred to as the world "long boom." With a labor market favoring the organized workforce, income levels reached unprecedented heights, and the consumer society blossomed. Governments, even conservative ones, were careful to take account of labor demands and aspirations. Social policy fell into a recognizably social democratic mode. Full employment and welfare characterized Western society during the 1950s and 1960s.

Great changes occurred after the onset of a long-term recession following the fuel crisis of 1973. Although unions in Britain were to overthrow a Conservative government in 1974, and in France the Socialist and Communist Parties entered government in coalition in 1981, the overall trend was toward a triumphant reassertion of neoliberal values, reduced taxation, and curtailed welfare, combined with an intensification of corporate business power. Unions found their membership declining as unemployment rose, business grew more hostile, and governments moved to curb their legal powers. Social democratic parties (and electorates) increasingly accepted the new climate of low taxation, market values, and minimum social intervention by government.

The End of the Cold War and Beyond

In eastern Europe, the peaceful revolt by the Polish workforce beginning in the Gdansk shipyards in 1980, although temporarily suppressed, proved to be the overture to the collapse of the Soviet bloc and the USSR itself. With this collapse went not only the command economy and the all-embracing state ruling ostensibly in the name of the working class, but the entire tradition of the October Revolution (even among the purportedly communist parties that survived). Unregulated market capitalism became the order of the day, and full employment and the basic welfare structure of these states were repudiated. In the less-developed of these countries, including Russia, the living standards of the industrial workforce, despite their now-free trade unions, plunged catastrophically.

At the beginning of twenty-first century, labor movements around the world, whether industrial or political, were not facing happy or promising circumstances. Nevertheless, they still retained very considerable assets—human, material, organizational, and intangible—and the rise of the Workers' Party in Brazil beginning in the 1980s demonstrated that their potential was far from exhausted. Of one thing it was possible to be sure: their future role and success would be determined by how far labor movements succeeded in imaginatively facing up to the new challenges that confronted them—the recomposition of workforces everywhere, the reality of globalization, and the environmental issues that increasingly dominated the beginning of the twenty-first century.

The history of the labor movement is extraordinarily convoluted, with more than its share of tragedy and horror as well as achievement and triumph. This volume is intended to highlight, recount, and explain in context the central episodes of that process and to serve as a reference work for the benefit of scholars, of people who participated, and those of the general public who want to be better informed about this remarkable social and political phenomenon.

—Willie Thompson

INTRODUCTION: LABOR IN THE UNITED STATES, 1800–2000

As the American labor force grew from perhaps three million at the beginning of the nineteenth century to nearly 200 million at the beginning of the twenty-first century, the character of the work it performed changed as dramatically as the numbers. In 1800 most American workers were farmers, farm laborers, or unpaid household workers. Many were bound (as slaves in the southern states and indentured servants in the North). Most of the others were proprietors of family businesses. The majority were of British, German, or African origins. Many workers received housing, food, and goods as part of their pay. A large percentage were unaware of labor market conditions in other states or regions and had no reason to take a greater interest: competition was limited by geography, slow and costly transportation, and seemingly unchanging technologies.

Two hundred years later, farm labor had become insignificant, employees vastly outnumbered the self-employed, bound labor had disappeared, and child and unpaid household labor had declined greatly. Family and other social ties had become less important in finding work or keeping a job, large private and public organizations employed more than a third of all workers and set standards for most of the others, the labor force had become more ethnically diverse, labor productivity and real wages were many times higher, wage contracts and negotiated agreements covering large groups were commonplace, and workplace disputes were subject to a web of laws and regulations. Increasingly American workers competed with workers in Mexico, Southeast Asia, or China.

Technology

The changing character of work was closely related to the classic technological innovations of the nineteenth century. Changes in energy use were particularly influential. Thanks to the availability of numerous waterpower sites in New England and the mid-Atlantic region, American industry developed rapidly after the American Revolution. By the 1820s, the massive, water-powered Waltham Mills of northern Massachusetts and southern New Hampshire were among the largest factories in the world. By midcentury, steam power had become widespread in manufacturing as well as transportation, and steam-powered factories had become the foundation of the industrial economy. The advent of electrical power at the turn of the twentieth century had an even greater impact, making possible the giant manufacturing operations of the early twentieth century; the smaller, more specialized plants that became the rule after the 1920s; the great versatility in machine use that characterized the second half of the twentieth century; and the mechanization of stores, offices, and homes.

Steam and electrical power and related innovations in machine technology not only made it feasible to create large organizations but also gave them an economic advantage over small plants and shops. Workers in the new organizations were wage earners, usually not family members, and often were not even acquainted outside the plant. They rejected payment in kind or in services (company housing and company stores in isolated mining communities became a persistent source of grievances), started and stopped at specific times (the factory bell tower remained a powerful symbol of the new era), and became accustomed to rules defining their responsibilities and behavior. Mechanization was also a stimulus to specialization. Elaborate hierarchies of pay and status grew out of the new ways of work.

The industrial model soon spread to the service sector. Railroad corporations created hierarchical, bureaucratic structures with even stricter lines of authority and more specialized tasks. Insurance companies, department stores, mail-order houses, and large banks followed this pattern, though they typically used simple, hand-operated machines. The growth of regional and national markets (a result of technological innovations in transportation and communication as well as the expanding economy) made the hierarchical, bureaucratic organization profitable even when power-driven machines played little role in production.

Free Labor

Although almost one-fifth of the U.S. population was not free at the beginning of the nineteenth century, the institutions and practices that had made unfree labor economically advantageous in earlier centuries soon came under attack. Indentured servitude was a victim of changing market conditions and falling transport costs. It had barely survived the turmoil surrounding the American and French Revolutions and died in the 1820s as immigrants who financed their own transportation replaced bound servants. Slavery was more entrenched and continued to be profitable to many slave owners through the first half of the century. Northern states abolished slavery with minimal controversy, but southern cotton, rice, and sugar growers remained intransigent. They devised elaborate rationales for slavery and used their political power to thwart reform, foreclosing the possibility of a repetition of the northern experience. Antislavery agitators succeeded in making abolition an increasingly important and contentious political cause. More moderate opponents stressed the ill effects of slavery on free labor. By the end of the 1850s the impasse between proslavery and antislavery groups had produced a political and constitutional crisis that quickly degenerated into war.

The Thirteenth Amendment to the Constitution (1865) formally abolished slavery in the United States, but neither it nor the Reconstruction measures that accompanied it effectively addressed the social and economic legacies of slavery. As a result, the South remained an isolated, economically stagnant region, and most southern workers, white and black, remained significantly poorer and less mobile than workers of other regions until the twentieth century.

Immigration

Most workers who filled nonexecutive positions in the new industrial organizations of the nineteenth century were European immigrants or their children. The rapid growth in the demand for labor (interrupted by periodic economic downturns and mass unemployment, notably in the 1870s, 1890s, and 1930s) attracted a swelling tide of newcomers. At first it included many skilled workers from the British Isles and Germany, but by the latter decades of the century most immigrants were from the economic and technological backwaters of Europe and filled the low-skill jobs that better-situated workers, native and immigrant, scorned. By the early twentieth century more than a million people were arriving each year, the majority from eastern and southern Europe.

An obvious question is why ill-paid American agricultural workers, especially those in the South, did not respond to the opportunities of industrial and service employment. Several factors apparently were involved. The regional tensions between North and South and the post–Civil War isolation of the South discouraged movement to northern industrial centers. Racial prejudice and lifestyle decisions were also important. In the midwestern states, where industry and agriculture developed in close proximity, farm workers were almost as reluctant to take industrial or urban service jobs. Consequently, a paradox emerged: American farm workers seemed content to make a modest living in the country, while European agricultural workers and their U.S.-born children filled new jobs in industry and the services.

Mass immigration was socially disruptive. Immigrants faced many hazards and an uncertain welcome. Apart from the Scandinavians, they became highly concentrated in cities and industrial towns. By the early twentieth century, most large American cities were largely immigrant enclaves. With few exceptions, immigrants and their children made up more than 60 percent of the population, and in extreme cases, such as Milwaukee, the total was over 80 percent. To visitors from the countryside, cities were alien places with a hodgepodge of different languages and mores. It is hardly surprising that observers and analysts bemoaned the effects of immigration and especially the shift from "old" northern and western European to "new" southern and eastern European immigrants.

In the workplace, native-immigrant tensions took various forms. The concentration of immigrants in low-skill jobs created a heightened sense of competition—of immigrants driving out old stock or "old" immigrant workers—and led to efforts to restrict immigrant mobility. One other result of these divisions may have been a lack of solidarity in industrial disputes. The relatively low level of labor organization and the particular character of the American labor movement often have been explained in part as the consequences of a heterogeneous labor force.

The end of traditional immigration during World War I and the low level of immigration during the interwar years eased many of these tensions and encouraged the rise of "melting pot" interpretations of the immigrant experience. World War I also saw the first substantial movement of southern workers to the North and West, a process that seemed to promise a less tumultuous future. In reality, the initial phases of this transition increased the level of unrest and conflict. Part of the problem—repeated in the early years of World War II—was the excessive concentration of war-related manufacturing in a few congested urban areas. The more serious and persistent irritant was racial conflict, with the poorest of the "new" immigrants pitted against African-American migrants from the South. Though the violence waned after 1921, tensions lingered. In most northern cities African-American immigrants were more likely than any immigrant group to live in ethnically homogeneous neighborhoods.

By midcentury most Americans looked back at immigration as a feature of an earlier age and celebrated the ability of American society to absorb millions of outsiders. Yet at the same time, a new cycle of immigration was beginning. It had the same economic origins and many similar effects. Most of the post–World War II immigrants came from Latin America and Asia rather than Europe. By the 1990s the movement of Hispanics into the labor force was reminiscent of the turn-of-the-century influx of eastern Europeans. They settled overwhelmingly in the comparatively vacant Southwest and West, areas that had grown rapidly since World War II. In contrast, the Northeast and Midwest, traditional centers of industrial activity, attracted fewer immigrants. Most of the newcomers were poorly educated and filled low-skill positions, but there were exceptions. Among the Asian immigrants were many well-educated engineers, technicians, and professionals, who quickly rose to important positions, a development that had no nineteenth-century parallel.

Employer Initiatives

Though managers of large organizations had enormous power vis-à-vis their employees, they also were dependent on them. Turnover, absenteeism, indifferent work, and outright sabotage were significant threats to productivity and profits. Conversely, highly motivated employees could enhance a firm's performance. Uncertain about how to respond, nineteenth-century employers experimented widely. A handful introduced elaborate benefits, such as company towns; others devised new forms of "driving" and coercion. Most simply threw up their hands, figuratively, and delegated the management of employees to first-line supervisors, who became responsible for hiring, firing, and other personnel functions. The results were wide variations in wages, working conditions, and discipline; abuses of authority; and high turnover rates. Friction between supervisors and wage earners became a common cause of labor unrest.

Growing public anxiety over industrial conflict resulted in numerous policy initiatives. In the last quarter of the nineteenth century, state governments began to impose restrictions on employers, especially employers of women and children. By 1900 most northern and western states regulated the hiring of children, the hours of labor, health and sanitation, and various working conditions. During the first third of the twentieth century, they tightened regulations, extended some rules to male workers, and introduced workers compensation, the first American social insurance plans. The federal government was slow to act until the 1930s, when it embraced collective bargaining (principally via the Wagner Act of 1935), created a social security system based on old age pensions and unemployment insurance, set minimum wages, defined the workday and workweek, and restricted child labor. Nearly all of this legislation, both state and federal, was designed to set and uphold minimum standards (the "safety net" metaphor of later years was apt) rather than to supercede private decision making or to create a welfare state. It reflected both a distrust of government and a belief that individuals could and should work out better arrangements for themselves.

Many employers also responded to the problems of the new industrial economy. Beginning at the turn of the century, a few of them, mostly large, profitable corporations, introduced policies designed to discourage turnover and improve morale. One example that spread rapidly was the personnel department, which centralized and standardized many of the supervisor's personnel functions. By the 1920's, most large industrial and service corporations had personnel departments whose functions and responsibilities expanded rapidly. Also popular were employee benefit plans that provided medical, educational, recreational, or other services. The employment crisis of the 1930s gave renewed impetus to these activities. The largest employers (often responding to union-organizing campaigns or collective bargaining demands) created even more elaborate benefit programs, and smaller and less generous companies introduced rudimentary programs. The spread of collective bargaining and a more prosperous postwar economy further reinforced this trend. The years from the early 1940s to the mid-1970s would be the heyday of welfare capitalism.

The American Labor Movement

As noted earlier, the growth of industrial and service employment in the nineteenth century introduced new forms of unrest and protest. The years from the 1870s to the 1940s witnessed waves of strikes, which were widely viewed as a perplexing and troubling feature of modern society. Yet strikes were only the most visible examples of the tensions and conflicts that characterized industrial employment. In essence, dissatisfied wage earners could quit and search for more satisfying jobs, or they could try to improve their current jobs through the use of their collective "voice," that is, through protests, complaints, and negotiations. Most workers concluded that quitting was easier than trying to organize and sustain a union, the most obvious form of institutional "voice." Still, the history of organized labor (because it has been carefully documented) is the best available valuable measure of the tensions associated with modern employment and the ability of workers to express themselves.

Nineteenth-Century Unions

The American labor movement began in the early nineteenth century, grew fitfully during the antebellum decades, became an important force during the inflationary prosperity of the 1860s, and flourished during the boom years of the 1880s. The people most likely to organize were "autonomous" workers, those who had substantial independence in the workplace. Most, but not all, were highly skilled and highly paid. In any case, they were indispensable workers who could increase their influence through collective action. Their strategic roles also made employers wary of antagonizing them, another critical factor in union growth. Regardless of their particular jobs, workers were more likely to organize successfully in prosperous times and when they could count on sympathetic public officials. Prosperity and a favorable political climate were critical determinants of union growth; recession conditions and state repression often made organization impossible.

Two groups dominated the nineteenth-century labor movement. Miners were autonomous workers who, though not highly skilled or highly paid, worked alone or in small groups and faced extraordinary hazards. Organization was a way to express a sense of solidarity, increase or maintain wages, reduce the cut-throat competition that characterized their industries, and restrict the entrance of less skilled, lower-wage workers. Miners' unions began in the 1840s, flourished in both anthracite and bituminous coal fields in the 1860s and early 1870s, and emerged in the western "hard rock" industry in the 1870s. After numerous conflicts and setbacks during the recession of the mid-1870s, miners' organizations became stronger than ever. Their success was reflected in the emergence of two powerful unions, the United Mine Workers, formed in 1890, and the Western Federation of Miners, which followed in 1892. They differed in one important respect: the UMW was committed to collective bargaining with the goal of regional or even national contracts, while the WFM favored workplace activism over collective bargaining.

The second group consisted of urban artisans, led by construction workers and industrial workers, such as printers and molders. Having established the legal right to organize in the 1820s and 1830s, they became a powerful force in the rapidly growing cities of the antebellum period. Unions maximized opportunities for some workers and created buffers against excessive competition. They also played an influential role in urban politics, adding a worker's voice to local government deliberations. Citywide coalitions appeared as early as the 1820s, but neither the individual groups nor the coalitions were able to withstand the ups and downs of the economy.

In this turbulent environment, highly skilled workers had obvious advantages. The railroad workers were a notable example. Engineers and other skilled operating employees formed powerful unions in the 1860s and 1870s. The Brotherhood of Locomotive Engineers became the most formidable and exclusive organization of that era. Through collective bargaining, the engineers and the other railroad "brotherhoods" were able to obtain high wages, improved working conditions, and greater security, but they made no effort to organize the vast majority of railroad workers who lacked their advantages. Most railroad managers reluctantly dealt with the skilled groups, though the Burlington Railroad strike of 1888 demonstrated that even the BLE was not invincible.

The limitations of this approach inspired efforts to organize other employees. The notable example was the Knights of Labor, which grew rapidly in the late 1870s and 1880s and briefly became the largest American union. The Knights attempted to organize workers regardless of skill or occupation. Several successful strikes in the mid-1880s created a wave of optimism that the Knights might actually succeed, and membership rose to more than 700,000 in 1886. But employer counterattacks, together with the Knights' organizational shortcomings, brought this activity to an abrupt halt. The Haymarket massacre of 1886, at the height of the Knights' popularity, underlined its vulnerability. By 1890 the Knights of Labor had lost most of its members; it never again enjoyed the kind of success it had experienced in the preceding decade.

In 1893 Eugene V. Debs, an officer of the Brotherhood of Locomotive Firemen, and a handful of followers undertook another campaign to create a more inclusive organization. The American Railway Union, an industrial union of railroad workers, enjoyed a few initial successes but suffered a fatal defeat in the infamous Pullman strike of 1894. The ARU's failure was largely a result of the anti-union policies of the federal government, which so outraged Debs that he henceforth devoted himself to the cause of political change, notably as a candidate of the Socialist Party.

In the meantime, most of the established unions banned together to form a new labor federation, the American Federation of Labor, which took a pragmatic approach to the issues of organizational structure and jurisdiction. Although the AFL initially consisted of craft organizations that were hostile to the Knights of Labor and the American Railway Union, it soon demonstrated sufficient flexibility to become the locus of union activity. Dominated by President Samuel Gompers of the Cigar Makers, the AFL thereafter guided relations between unions and between organized labor and government. It also maintained a staff of organizers who aided individual unions.

In its early years the AFL confronted a strong employer backlash and a deteriorating economy. One of the most powerful AFL organizations, the Amalgamated Association of Iron and Steel Workers, lost a decisive battle against the industry's largest employer, the Carnegie Steel Company, in 1892. The failure of the famous Homestead strike sealed the fate of the Amalgamated Association and unionism in the steel industry until World War I. Other defeats followed as the severe recession of 1893–1897 encouraged employers to reject union contracts and agreements and reduce employment opportunities. The Pullman strike and a 1897 United Mine Workers strike against most of the coal industry illustrated the plight of organized labor.

Twentieth-Century Unions

As the economy recovered, the labor movement began a long period of expansion and growing influence. Autonomous workers groups, led by the coal miners and construction workers, dominated organized labor for the next third of a century. The debate over tactics was decisively resolved in favor of collective bargaining, though a dissenting group, the Industrial Workers of the World, originally an outgrowth of the Western Federation of Miners, rallied critics with some success before World War I. This decision was effectively institutionalized during World War I, when the federal government endorsed collective bargaining as an antidote to wartime unrest. The other major development of this period was the revival of the AFL. Under Gompers, who proved to be a wily and articulate leader, the AFL promoted autonomous worker groups while professing to speak for all industrial workers. Gompers and his allies disavowed socialism and efforts to create an independent political party, policies that led to an erroneous perception (encouraged by their many critics) of indifference or hostility to political action. On the contrary, Gompers closely aligned the AFL with the Democratic Party and created aggressive lobbying organizations.

Labor's political activism seemed to pay off during World War I, when President Woodrow Wilson appointed Gompers to a high post in the mobilization effort and the federal government directly and indirectly encouraged organization. The greatest gains occurred in the railroad industry, which was almost completely organized by 1920. Government efforts to limit unrest and strikes also resulted in inroads in manufacturing, notably in steel, shipbuilding, and munitions. In 1920 union membership totaled five million, twice the prewar level.

These gains proved to be ephemeral. The end of wartime regulations, the defeat of the Democrats in the 1920 national elections, the spread of the anti-union "American Plan" in many industries, and the severe recession of 1920–1922 completely reversed the situation of 1915–1920 and put all unions on the defensive. Membership contracted. The disastrous 1919–1920 steel strike, which restored the open shop in most firms, was only the first of many setbacks. The decline of the coal and railroad industries in the 1920s was an additional blow. By the late 1920s union membership was back to its prewar level. The one positive feature of the postwar decade was the rapid growth of service sector unionism.

The dramatic economic downturn that began in 1929 and continued with varying severity for a decade set the stage for the greatest increase in union membership in American history. Why? Recessions and unemployment typically reduced the appeal of anything likely to provoke employer reprisals. This was true of the 1930s, too. Union membership declined precipitously between 1930 and 1933, as unemployment rose. It also plunged in 1937–1938, when a new recession led to sweeping layoffs. Union growth occurred in 1933–1937 and in the years after 1938, when employment was increasing. Yet even the generally unfavorable economic conditions of the early 1930s had important indirect effects. Harsh economic conditions produced a strong sense of grievance among veteran workers who lost jobs, savings, and status. They also turned many voters against Republican office holders. The 1932 election of Franklin D. Roosevelt, who had strong progressive and activist credentials as governor of New York, proved to be a turning point in the history of the twentieth-century labor movement.

Union growth after 1933 reflected these factors, particularly in the early years. Roosevelt's New Deal was only intermittently prounion, but it effectively neutralized employer opposition to organization and, with the passage of the Wagner Act in 1935, created a mechanism for peacefully resolving representation conflicts and introducing collective bargaining. Though the goal of the legislation was to foster dispute resolution and increase wages, it indirectly promoted union growth by restricting the employer's ability to harass union members. In the meantime, industrial workers, notably workers in the largest firms in steel and automobile manufacturing, reacted to the new political environment with unprecedented enthusiasm. A wave of organizing in 1933–1934 surprised employers and public officials alike. Defeats in a series of spectacular, violent strikes in 1934 and other setbacks in 1935 seemingly had little effect. One expression of the workers' determination was the growing popularity of the sit-down strike, notably in the Goodyear Tire and Rubber strike of 1936 and the General Motors strike of 1937. Though most sit-downs were union-led, they represented a degree of shop-floor militancy that shocked many employers and not a few outside observers. Another important expression of the changing industrial landscape was the emergence of the Congress of Industrial Organizations, a new federation of unions devoted to aggressive organizing, especially in manufacturing. John L. Lewis, the creator of the CIO, was the veteran president of the United Mine Workers who had presided over the decline of that once formidable organization in the 1920s. Whatever his shortcomings, Lewis grasped the possibilities of the moment. By the end of the decade he was closely identified with both the revival of organized labor and the increasingly bitter relations between the CIO and AFL.

Although the Wagner Act (and other related legislation designed for specific industries) most clearly and explicitly addressed the industrial relations issues of the 1930s, other New Deal measures complemented it. The move to regulate prices and production n the transportation, communications, and energy industries, which dated from the National Industrial Recovery Act of 1933 and continued with a variety of industry-specific measures between 1935 and 1938, created additional opportunities for unions. Regulated corporations had powerful incentives to avoid strikes and cooperate with unions. As a result, about one-third of union membership growth in the 1930s occurred in those industries. If the United Auto Workers and United Steel Workers were symbols of the new militancy in manufacturing, the equally dramatic growth of the Teamsters symbolized the impact of government regulation in the service sector.

Government regulations were more directly responsible for the even more dramatic growth in union membership that occurred during World War II, when aggregate membership rose from 10 million to 15 million members. Most new jobs during the war years were in manufacturing companies that had collective bargaining contracts and, in many cases, union security provisions that required new hires to join unions. War mobilization thus automatically created millions of additional union members, including large numbers of women and African Americans. Organized labor, in turn, opposed strikes, cooperated with the government's wage-and-price-control programs, and promoted the war effort. By 1945 the labor movement had become a respected part of the American establishment.

Postwar Labor

By the mid-1940s full employment, high wages, and optimism about the future, based on a sense that government now had the ability to manage prosperity (together with awareness of the safety net that government had created since the mid-1930s), replaced the depressed conditions of the 1930s. Most workers' experiences in the 1940s and 1950s seemed to confirm the lessons of the New Deal era. With the exception of a few mild recession years, jobs were plentiful, real wages rose, and public and private benefit programs became more generous. The labor movement also continued to grow, but with less dynamism than in the 1940s. Optimists viewed the 1955 merger of the AFL and CIO as a likely stimulus to new gains.

In retrospect, however, those lessons were often misleading. The striking feature of the economy of the 1950s and 1960s was the degree to which the character of work and the characteristics of the labor force changed. Farming and other natural resource industries declined at an accelerated rate, industrial employment leveled and then began to decline, and service industry employment boomed. Formal education became even more critical to success. Married women entered the labor force in unprecedented numbers. Civil rights laws adopted in the early 1960s banned racial and other forms of discrimination in employment decisions.

One other major development also was little noticed at the time: organized labor stopped growing. Contrary to most predictions and popular impressions, the labor movement lost momentum in the 1950s and 1960s and faced a host of obstacles by the 1970s. Three problems, in reverse order of importance, were particularly notable. First were the unions' internal difficulties. Adapting to an expanded membership and larger public presence was inevitably challenging, but it also could be damaging, as two well-publicized incidents suggest. At the end of World War II the CIO included numerous (mostly small) communist-dominated unions. Though the CIO soon expelled them and supported U.S. cold war policies, it was unable to prevent anti-union demagogues from loudly portraying it, and by implication unions in general, as subversive.

Even more harmful was the mounting evidence of union corruption and especially of abuses involving the now giant Teamsters organization. Revelations of Teamster misdeeds led to the U.S. Senate's McClellan Committee investigation of 1957–1958 and the subsequent passage of the Landrum-Griffin Act (1959), designed to protect union members from dishonest officials. Whether the act was warranted or effective was beside the point: the scandals devastated the unions' public image.

A more fundamental cause of union decline was organized labor's association with industries (manufacturing, mining, transportation) that were growing slowly, if at all, and its tardiness in recognizing the overwhelming importance of the service economy in the postwar era. Labor's one significant breakthrough came in the 1970s and early 1980s, when it won collective bargaining rights for most state and municipal employees. By the end of the 1980s unions increasingly were associated with public rather than private employment.

Finally, employer counterattacks grew more effective in the postwar years. Though some employer groups sought to challenge unions directly (for example, in the Taft-Hartley Act of 1947 and state right-to-work legislation), others adopted a more subtle approach, attacking union power in the regulatory agencies and the courts and promoting employment policies that reduced the benefits of membership. These attacks gained momentum during the presidency of Dwight D. Eisenhower. One additional tactic, locating new plants in southern or western states, where there was no tradition of organization, also helped isolate organized workers.

The impact of these varied trends became inescapable in the 1970s, when the economy experienced its most severe downturns since the 1930s. Major recessions in 1973–1975 and 1979–1982 led to thousands of plant closings in traditional industrial areas. Unemployment reached levels that rivaled the 1930s. Productivity declined, and real wages stagnated. Exploiting anxiety over the future of the economy, Republican Ronald Reagan ran successfully for president on a platform that attacked government assistance to the poor and support for collective bargaining. Reagan left no doubt about his intentions when, in 1981, he fired air traffic controllers for striking in violation of federal law.

The experiences of the 1970s created a labor force that was more diverse in composition and overwhelmingly engaged in service occupations. The return of favorable employment conditions in the 1980s was almost entirely a result of service sector growth. Formal education, together with antidiscrimination laws and affirmative action policies, opened high-paying jobs to ethnic and racial minorities, including a growing number of immigrants. At the same time, industry continued its movement into rural areas, especially in the South and West, and unions continued to decline. Indeed, by the mid-1990s, the private sector of the American economy was largely union free.

The decline of organized labor was associated closely with three other ominous developments. The first was a slowing in real-wage increases, especially among low-income workers. The purchasing power of most manufacturing and service employees remained largely unchanged between the 1970s and 1990s, eliminating an important source of social mobility. Second was a gradual decline in welfare capitalism. A new generation of nonunion firms that paid high wages but provided few or no benefits initiated this trend. Other firms followed, arguing that cost reductions were necessary for survival. Other employers reacted to the rising cost of medical insurance and to the lower costs of defined-contribution retirement plans (as opposed to the traditional defined-benefit plans). Even the tight labor market conditions of the mid-1990s to late 1990s, which led to real-wage increases, did not result in expanded benefit programs.

Third was the accelerating globalization of economic activity. The growth of international trade and investment were partly a consequence of the transfer of industrial technology to economically disadvantaged countries. It also was a result of a series of legal and regulatory changes, such as the North American Free Trade Agreement of 1993, which liberalized economic relations between countries and encouraged international activity. These changes had the potential to raise living standards, but their immediate effects were often painful, as employers moved some or all of their operations to lower-wage countries. Already many American manufacturers had moved labor-intensive assembly operations to Mexican border towns to take advantage of lower wages and other low costs. In most cases Mexican employees replaced American workers. And while the Mexican employees earned more than most of their neighbors, their jobs were extremely insecure. Indeed, by 2000 manufacturers were increasingly moving their operations from Mexico to China and other Asian countries, where wages were even lower.

The results of these complex developments were at least superficially contradictory. On the one hand, by the 1990s many workers enjoyed expanded opportunities and high wages. Severe labor shortages in some industries attracted a flood of immigrants and made the United States a magnet for upwardly mobile workers. On the other hand, many other workers, especially those in agriculture or industry or who had little formal education, found that the combination of economic and technological change, a less activist government, and union decline depressed their wages and made their prospects bleak. A recession that began in 2000 created additional uncertainties. At the beginning of the new century the labor force, and American society, were divided in ways that would have seemed unlikely or even impossible only a few decades earlier.

—Daniel Nelson

ADVISERS

Michael Hanagan, PhD
Senior Lecturer
New School University

Alice Kessler-Harris, PhD
R. Gordon Hoxie Professor of
    American History
Columbia University

Andrew H. Lee, PhD
Tamiment Librarian
New York University

Daniel Nelson, PhD
Emeritus Professor of History
University of Akron

Colleen O'Neill, PhD
Assistant Professor of Ethnic
    Studies
California Polytechnic State
    University-San Luis Obispo

Marcel van der Linden, PhD
Research Director
International Institute of Social
    History

Zaragosa Vargas, PhD
Associate Professor of History
University of California, Santa
    Barbara

CONTRIBUTORS

Don Amerman
William Arthur Atkins

Kimberley Barker
Bill Barry
Elizabeth A. Bishop
Lawrence Black
Mary H. Blewett
Timothy G. Borden
Jeffrey Bortz
John Boughton
Valeria Bruschi
William E. Burns
Dieter K. Buse

Robert Cassanello
Olivier Compagnon
Sylvie Contrepois
Richard Croucher

Evan Daniel
Jonathan Darby
Ralph Darlington
Hendrik Defoort
Dennis Deslippe
Thomas Dublin
Linda Dynan

Beth Emmerling
Lisa Ennis

Katrina Ford
Carol Fort
Kimberly F. Frederick
Paul Frisch

Kevin M. Gannon
Roberta Gold
Juan José Gómez Gutiérrez
Tom Goyens

Michael Hanagan
Jennifer Harrison
Jane Holzka
Roger Horowitz
Nik Howard

Lisa Kannenberg
Karla Kelling
Brett Allan King
Steven Koczak

Paul Le Blanc
James G. Lewis
David Lewis-Colman
Darren G. Lilleker

Martin Manning
Soe Tjen Marching
Joseph McCartin
David Lee McMullen
Lee McQueen
Greg Miller
Carl Mirra
Paul Misner

David Nack
Miriam C. Nagel
Daniel Nelson
Caryn E. Neumann
Mitchell Newton-Matza

Melanie Nolan

Jaime Ramon Olivares
Michael J. O'Neal
Melissa Ooten

Lee Ann Paradise
Linda Dailey Paulson
Luca Prono
Sean Purdy

Jonathan Rees
David Renton
Markku Ruotsila

Courtney Q. Shah
Emily Straus

Willie Thompson
Rebecca Tolley-Stokes
Patricia Toucas-Truyen

Marcel van der Linden
Michael T. Van Dyke
Geert Van Goethem
Yanic Viau

Joel Waller
Peter Waterman
Elizabeth Willis

Ronald Young

ST. JAMES ENCYCLOPEDIA OF LABOR HISTORY WORLDWIDE

LIST OF EVENTS

Abolition of Serfdom, Russia
Abolition of Slavery, British Empire
Abolition of Slavery, United States
Act to Encourage Immigration, United States
AFL, CIO Merge, United States
AFL-CIO Expels Key Unions, United States
AFSCME Strike, United States
Age Discrimination in Employment Act, United States
Agriculture Workers Strike, Italy
Alliance for Labor Action, United States
All-India Trade Union Congress, India
Amalgamated Society of Engineers, Great Britain
American Association for Labor Legislation, United States
American Federation of Labor, United States
American Plan, United States
Anarchists Lead Argentine Labor Movement, Argentina
Anthracite Coal Strike, United States
Apex Hosiery Co. v. Leader, United States
Arbitration Act of 1888, United States

Bans on Labor Unions Lifted, Germany
Barcelona Workers' Rebellion, Spain
Battle of the Overpass, United States
Bituminous Coal Strike, United States
Black Codes, United States
Bloody Sunday, Russia
Boston Police Strike, United States
Bracero Program, United States and Mexico
Brotherhood of Locomotive Engineers, United States
Brotherhood of Railroad Trainmen, United States
Brotherhood of Sleeping Car Porters, United States
Bureau of Labor Established, United States
Burlington Railroad Strike, United States
Byrnes Act, United States

Calcutta General Strike, India
Cananéa Strike, Mexico
Carlisle Indian School, United States
Charleroi Confrontation Between Miners and the Military, Belgium
Charter of Amiens, France
Chartist Movement, Great Britain
Chiang Kai-shek Purges Communists, China
Child Labor Amendment, United States
Chinese Exclusion Act, United States
Chinese Rail Workers Strike, United States
Christian Trade Unionists Conference, Switzerland
CIO Anticommunist Drive, United States
CIO Expelled from AFL, United States
CIO Joins, AFL Rejects WFTU, United States
Civil Rights Act of 1964, United States
Civilian Conservation Corps, United States
Clayton Antitrust Act, United States
Clifton-Morenci-Metcalf Strike, United States
Coal Mine Contract Signed, United States
Coalition of Labor Union Women, United States
Colored Farmers' Alliance, United States
Colored National Labor Union, United States
Combination Acts, Great Britain
Committee for Industrial Organization, United States
Commonwealth v. Hunt, United States
Communist Manifesto Published, England
Confederación de Trabajadores de América Latina, Latin America
Confederación Obrera Pan-Americana, Western Hemisphere
Confédération Générale du Travail, France
Congress of Industrial Organizations, United States

Congress of South African Trade Unions, South Africa
Coronado Coal v. UMWA, United States

Davis-Bacon Act, United States
Department of Commerce and Labor, United States
Department of Labor, United States
Dockers' Strike, Great Britain
Dorr Rebellion, United States
Dover Textile Strike, United States

Eight-hour Day Movement, United States
Employee Retirement Income Security Act, United States
Equal Pay Act, United States
Equal Rights Amendment and Protective Legislation, United States
Equal Rights Party, United States
Erdman Act, United States
European Strike Wave, Europe
European Trade Union Confederation, Europe

Factory Act, Great Britain
Factory Girls' Association, United States
Fair Employment Practice Committee, United States
Fair Labor Standards Act, United States
Federal Employees Gain Union Rights, United States
Federation of Organized Trades and Labor Unions of the United States and Canada (FOTLU), United States and Canada
First International, Great Britain
Five-Year Plan, USSR
Foran Act, United States
Forced Labor, Germany
Forced Labor, USSR
Ford-UAW Contract, United States
Ford-UAW SUB Agreement, United States
Free Soil Party, United States
French Labor, World War II, France

CHRONOLOGICAL LIST OF EVENTS

1799-1800	Combination Acts, Great Britain
1799-1827	Owen Model Communities, Great Britain, United States
1800	Gabriel's Rebellion, United States
1811-1813	Luddites Destroy Woolen Machines, Great Britain
1814	Power Loom Invented, United States
1819	Peterloo Massacre, Great Britain
1820s-1850s	Ten-Hour Day Movement, United States
1823-1836	Lowell Industrial Experiment, United States
1824	Pawtucket Textile Strike, United States
	Repeal of Combination Acts, Great Britain
1825	United Tailoresses Society, United States
1827	Mechanics' Union of Trade Associations, United States
	Tailors' Strike, United States
1828	Dover Textile Strike, United States
	Workingmen's Party, United States
1831	*Liberator* Founded, United States
1831, 1834	Silk Workers' Revolts, France
1833	General Trades' Union, United States
	Factory Act, Great Britain
1834	Abolition of Slavery, British Empire
	National Trades Union, United States
1834-1836	Factory Girls' Association, United States
1836	Equal Rights Party, United States
	London Workingmen's Association, Great Britain
1838	Chartist Movement, Great Britain
1840	Strikes of Journeymen and Workers, France
1842	*Commonwealth v. Hunt*, United States
	Dorr Rebellion, United States
1844	Weavers' Revolt, Silesia
1845-1851	Potato Famine, Ireland
1848	June Days Rebellion, France
	Communist Manifesto Published, England
	Revolutions in Europe, Europe
1848-1854	Free Soil Party, United States
1851	Amalgamated Society of Engineers, Great Britain
1852	National Typographical Union, United States
1853-1854	Lancashire Textile Strikes, Great Britain

1859	National Union of Iron Molders, United States
	Harpers Ferry Raid, United States
1860	Shoemaker's Strike, United States
1860-1879	Molly Maguires, United States
1860s-1900s	Eight-hour Day Movement, United States
1861	Abolition of Serfdom, Russia
1861-1869	Bans on Labor Unions Lifted, Germany
1863	Working Women's Protective Union, United States
	Brotherhood of Locomotive Engineers, United States
1863-1865	Abolition of Slavery, United States
1864	Strike Ban Lifted, France
	Act to Encourage Immigration, United States
	First International, Great Britain
1865	European Strike Wave, Europe
1865-1877	Black Codes, United States
1866	National Labor Union, United States
1867	Second Reform Act, Great Britain
	Chinese Rail Workers Strike, United States
1867, 1869	St. Crispin Organizations, United States
1868	Charleroi Confrontation Between Miners and the Military, Belgium
	Trades Union Congress, Great Britain
	Workingman's Benevolent Association, United States
1869	Knights of Labor, United States
	Colored National Labor Union, United States
1870	Coal Mine Contract Signed, United States
1871	Trades Union Act, Great Britain
	Paris Commune, France
1873	Panic of 1873, United States
1874	Union Label Movement, United States
	Tompkins Square Rally, United States
1875-1902	Organized Labor Established, Argentina
1876	Workingmen's Party of the United States, United States
	Workers' Congress, Mexico
1877	Railroad Strike of 1877, United States
1878	International Labor Union, United States
1878-1911	Taylor and Scientific Management, United States

Memorial Day Massacre, United States

CIO Expelled From AFL, United States

1938 Confederación de Trabajadores de América Latina, Latin America

Fair Labor Standards Act, United States

Congress of Industrial Organizations, United States

1939 Hatch Act, United States

1940 *Apex Hosiery Co. v. Leader*, United States

1940-1944 French Labor, World War II, France

1941 March on Washington Movement, United States

Ford-UAW Contract, United States

No-strike Pledge, World War II, United States

Fair Employment Practice Committee, United States

1941-1945 World War II Labor Measures, United States

1942 United Steelworkers of America, United States

1942-1964 Bracero Program, United States and Mexico

1945 CIO Joins, AFL Rejects WFTU, United States

World Federation of Trade Unions, France

1945-1946 Strike Wave, United States

1945-1960 Japanese Labor After World War II, Japan

1946 Miners' Strike, South Africa

Perón Elected President, Argentina

Socialist Unity Party of Germany, East Germany

1947 *United States v. United Mine Workers of America*, United States

Taft-Hartley Act, United States

1947-1962 General Agreement on Tariffs and Trade, Worldwide

1948, 1950 General Motors-United Auto Workers Landmark Contracts, United States

1949 International Confederation of Free Trade Unions, Worldwide

1949-1950 CIO Anticommunist Drive, United States

1950 Salt of the Earth Strike, United States

1951 Organización Regional Inter-americana de Trabajadores, Western Hemisphere

1952 Steel Seizure Case, United States

Meany and Reuther Lead AFL, CIO, United States

1953 Calcutta General Strike, India

1954 Guatemalan Coup Orchestrated by CIA, Guatemala

1955 Ford-UAW SUB Agreement, United States

AFL, CIO Merge, United States

1956 Poznan Workers' Riots, Poland

Hungarian Revolution and Workers Councils, Hungary

International Confederation of Arab Trade Unions, Egypt

1957 AFL-CIO Expels Key Unions, United States

1959 Landrum-Griffin Act, United States

1960s Maquiladoras Established, Mexico

1962 Federal Employees Gain Union Rights, United States

1963 Equal Pay Act, United States

1964 Civil Rights Act of 1964, United States

1965-1970 Grape Pickers' Strike, United States

1966 National Organization for Women, United States

1967 Taylor Law, United States

Age Discrimination in Employment Act, United States

1968 General Strike, France

1969 Alliance for Labor Action, United States

Philadelphia Plan, United States

Hot Autumn, Italy

1970 Postal Workers' Strike, United States

Hawaii Collective Bargaining Law, United States

Occupational Safety and Health Act, United States

1970-1973 Popular Unity, Chile

1973 European Trade Union Confederation, Europe

Steelworkers Experimental Agreement, United States

Washington Union Shop Law, United States

1974 Coalition of Labor Union Women, United States

Employee Retirement Income Security Act, United States

1975 AFSCME Strike, Pennsylvania, United States

Navajos Occupy Fairchild Plant, United States

1980 Solidarity Emerges, Poland

1981 PATCO Strike, United States

1985 Congress of South African Trade Unions, South Africa

1985-1986 Hormel Strike, United States

1985-1987 Watsonville Canning Strike, United States

1987 General Motors Introduces Team Concept, United States

1991 USSR Collapse, USSR

1992 North American Free Trade Agreement, North America

1995 Unions Plan Merger, United States

Sweeney Elected President of AFL-CIO, United States

1999 World Free Trade Conference Demonstrations, United States

N

National Child Labor Committee

United States 1904

Synopsis

To combat labor practices that trapped children in a cycle of poverty by interfering with their schooling and physical development, progressive reformers established the National Child Labor Committee (NCLC) in 1904. Under the leadership of Felix Adler and Alexander McKelway, the nonpartisan organization focused its energies on the businesses that employed large numbers of children under the age of 15 in hazardous tasks, including midwestern coal mines, New England glass factories, Gulf Coast canneries, and southern textile mills. The committee also objected to the large numbers of children in the street trades, holding jobs such as selling newspapers and providing messenger services. The NCLC successfully used photographs of children, most taken by Lewis Hine, to stimulate public debate about the issue of child labor, but the committee failed to muster enough support for nationwide laws banning labor practices harmful to children.

Timeline

1884: At the Berlin Conference on African Affairs, 14 nations (including the United States) discuss colonial expansion in Africa and call for an end to slavery and the slave trade.

1890: Congress passes the Sherman Antitrust Act, which in the years that follow will be used to break up large monopolies.

1894: War breaks out between Japan and China. It will end with China's defeat the next year, marking yet another milestone in China's decline and Japan's rise.

1897: Zionist movement is established under the leadership of Theodor Herzl.

1900: China's Boxer Rebellion, which began in the preceding year with attacks on foreigners and Christians, reaches its height. An international contingent of more than 2,000 men arrives to restore order, but only after several tens of thousands have died.

1902: Second Anglo-Boer War ends in victory for Great Britain. It is a costly victory, however, resulting in the loss of more British lives (5,774) than any conflict between 1815 and 1914. The war also sees the introduction of concentration camps, used by the British to incarcerate Boer civilians.

1904: The 10-hour workday is established in France.

1904: Russo-Japanese War, which lasts into 1905 and results in a resounding Japanese victory, begins. In Russia, the war is followed by the Revolution of 1905, which marks the beginning of the end of czarist rule; meanwhile, Japan is poised to become the first major non-Western power of modern times.

1908: Ford Motor Company introduces the Model T.

1911: In China, revolutionary forces led by Sun Yat-sen bring an end to more than 2,100 years of imperial rule.

Event and Its Context

The Problem

The industrialization of the United States brought a number of changes that adversely affected workers. Jobs required more machines and fewer skills, thereby enabling managers to replace expensive skilled labor with workers who could be paid comparatively little and trained in a few hours. With few adult industrial workers able to earn enough to support and educate a family, children were compelled by necessity to enter the work force. By 1900 about 1.7 million children labored in American industries, more than double the number in 1870. In the 10 to 15 year old age group, 18.2 percent were employed, with just under half working in nonagricultural trades such as mining and manufacturing.

Cheap to employ and with small, nimble fingers, children were well suited to performing the repetitious, small tasks that American industry now demanded, but their labor came at a high price. Breaker boys in coal mines sorted coal from slate and developed hunched-over backs along with a pallor. Snapping-up boys in glass factories suffered eye damage from bright, glaring light as they handled molten glass and lung damage from inhaling glass dust. Children of both genders cracked open sharp oyster shells and shelled shrimp in canneries, then soaked their bleeding hands in a strong alum solution to toughen the skin and help heal the wounds. Mill children lost fingers or limbs to machinery, and boys and girls who peeled apples or shelled peas often slipped with the knife and injured themselves.

At the same time, as more children entered the workforce, new ideas about child development also emerged. Americans began to see childhood as a series of stages, each with specific physical and psychological demands that had to be satisfied for the child to progress into a healthy adult able to fulfill his or her potential. Children who spent crucial years at labor would progress into "human junk," as one poster proclaimed, adults doomed to become burdens upon society because of weakened bodies and uncultivated minds. Halting child labor would help to end the cycle of poverty, reduce crime, and ensure the preservation of democracy. On this rising tide of sentiment for child labor reform, the NCLC emerged.

Formation of the NCLC

The first call for an organized anti–child labor movement came from Edgar Gardner Murphy, a progressive Episcopal

1

Young boy working in glass factory. © Bettmann/Corbis. Reproduced by permission.

clergyman from Montgomery, Alabama, who lived close to a textile mill. After listening to the factory whistles call children to work at 4:45 A.M., Murphy saw ill-clad, pallid, often maimed boys and girls tramp home long after dusk. Horrified by the poor state of the children, he subsequently likened child labor to slavery in a series of articles designed to drum up support for the abolition of child labor. Murphy made several appearances before the Alabama state legislature to press for the adoption of a 12-year minimum age for factory work, but opponents successfully neutralized his efforts by painting the native southerner as a tool of New England industrialists determined to destroy the South's prosperity by closing its textile mills. In 1901 Murphy created the Alabama Child Labor Committee, the first such

organization in the United States, and soon tasted success. In 1903 Alabama set the highest child labor standards of any southern industrial state by specifying a 12-year age limit and a 66-hour week. In 1902–1903, 15 other states placed child labor statutes on the books, but Murphy believed that the general movement would be more successful with central organization. He had become acquainted with leading reformers as the executive secretary of the New York City-based Southern Education Board, and he used his connections to found the NCLC at a meeting of National Conference of Charities and Correction in Atlanta in 1903.

While Murphy mobilized in Alabama, other progressives were attacking the child labor problem in New York. In 1902

Teenage boys at work in coal mines of West Virginia. AP/Wide World Photos. Reproduced by permission.

Florence Kelley and Lillian D. Wald founded the New York Child Labor Committee, the second such body in the country. Both Kelley and Wald were long-time social reformers. A former labor bureau statistician, Kelley sought to make government more responsive to the needs of the working class. Wald had abandoned an affluent life to combat poverty and suffering as a public health nurse. Founder of the famed Henry Street Settlement, Wald recognized that she could accomplish little to better the lives of immigrants without legislation and spent much of her time lobbying elected officials for labor and health reforms. At the suggestion of Felix Adler, a Columbia University professor, the New York Child Labor Committee joined with Murphy and a few other reformers to set up a national commit-

tee based in New York City to take aggressive measures to protect children from premature employment. The drafting committee invited all interested people to a meeting convened at Carnegie Hall on 15 April 1904.

At this first meeting of the NCLC, Adler stated the need for an organization to serve as a moral force against greed and warned of barbaric conditions that placed children in danger. He would serve as the first president of the organization, with Murphy holding the post of the NCLC's general secretary for only one month before resigning. The first permanent general secretary would be Samuel McCune Lindsey, an industrial relations expert and sociology professor at the University of Pennsylvania. Lindsey handled day-to-day activities, and an executive committee determined policy and legislative goals. By 1912 the NCLC had a membership of over 6,400 and an annual budget of $13,500.

First NCLC Activities

Most Americans, firm in the belief that children learned valuable skills and discipline by laboring next to their parents, did not realize that the majority of child workers were no longer engaged in the invigorating farm work of years past. The NCLC did not oppose children occasionally working for wages outside the home or doing chores on the family farm or around the house. It objected to the employment of children at monotonous tasks under unhealthful conditions for 10 or 12 hours a day, week in and week out. This work made it next to impossible for children to attend school regularly. To put laws into place that would protect children, the NCLC had to convince Americans that a problem existed.

The first step of the NCLC involved gathering data about child labor, as very few studies of the practice had been conducted. This proved to be a challenge, as NCLC investigators were run out of hotels and forbidden to enter factories. If factory owners did allow entrance, the children were hidden, as many youths later gleefully reported to the NCLC men. Some mill towns even posted signs at the outer limits requiring visitors to get permission before entering.

After managing to collect information despite these obstacles, the NCLC embarked on a public relations crusade to educate Americans about the causes of the problem and possible solutions to it. In its first year of operation, the NCLC distributed more than two million pages of printed matter, much of which went to the nation's newspapers and little of which had any significant impact.

Deciding to capitalize on the emotional power of pictures, the NCLC became the first organization to sponsor documentary photography and the first to use images to influence public opinion. Factory owners had often claimed that the NCLC statistics were lies, but the same charge of fraud could not be lodged against photographs. The NCLC hired photographer Lewis Hine in 1906 to document the realities and consequences of child labor. Hine, who became one of the best-known Progressive Era photographers because of his work for the NCLC, gathered a major portion of the information. He talked to the child laborers, learned their ages and work histories, and presented his findings in the captions, lectures, and poster displays that accompanied the photos on tours throughout the United States. He discovered that employers, parents, and government officials persistently disregarded the few existing child labor laws, especially in regard to the age of children. Hine would continue to work for the NCLC until 1918, traveling over 50,000 miles to study child workers in New York tenements, Colorado beet farms, Connecticut cranberry fields, Pennsylvania coal mines, and Gulf Coast canneries, as well as glass, tobacco, and textile manufacturers scattered throughout the country. Despite harassment from factory owners and a lack of cooperation from many parents who were dependent on the labor of their offspring, Hine managed to capture ill-fed, ill-clad children in dangerous, dead-end jobs. His photographs made it impossible to deny that children were being misused in what

anti-child labor advocates commonly characterized as "child slavery," and his photographs played a crucial role in rousing public opinion against child labor.

Along with bombarding Americans with the facts about child labor, the NCLC decided to attempt a state-by-state promotion of child labor laws. Southerners in the organization had advised such a solution in the belief that states' rights proponents would react to a federal statute with a great deal of resentment and opposition. Accordingly, the NCLC encouraged the formation of state and local child labor committees and helped to coordinate their activities. By 1910, 25 of these committees had formed.

First Successes

After scouting several states, the committee elected to focus on the industries with the most outrageous labor practices: the anthracite coal mines in Pennsylvania, widely scattered glass factories, and southern cotton mills. The street trades and coastal canneries would be subsequent targets. The first state target of the NCLC would be Pennsylvania.

A heavily industrialized state, Pennsylvania had developed industries that heavily employed children, including coal, glass, cotton, and silk, with coal in particular utilizing more children than any other branch of mining or quarrying. After heavy pressure by the NCLC, particularly by chief lobbyist and publicist Alexander McKelway, Pennsylvania enacted laws to afford children some protection. In 1909 the state began to require documentary proof of age. By mandating the presentation of a birth certificate or similar proof of age, the state could thwart parents who often lied about the ages of their children to secure jobs for them. Pennsylvania also prescribed educational standards, and in 1911 the state extended a 16-year age limit to mine workers.

In 1910 the NCLC drew up a Uniform Child Labor Law based on the best features of the Massachusetts, New York, and Illinois child labor statutes and sought to get it passed in the various states. The bill prescribed a minimum working age of 14 in manufacturing and 16 in mining, quarrying, and other dangerous trades; a maximum working day of eight hours; no night work (covering the hours of 7 P.M. to 6 A.M.) for children under 16; and documentary proof of age. The organization also wanted effective enforcement of the existing child labor laws. Although the NCLC also desired compulsory school attendance, it never devoted much energy to this issue. By 1914, 35 states prohibited the employment of children aged less than 14 years and mandated a maximum eight-hour day for workers less than 16 years old. Thirty-six states employed factory inspectors and established more potent mechanisms for enforcing child labor laws.

Southern Problems

These successes came chiefly in the North and West, with the NCLC unable to gain much of a foothold in the South despite McKelway's best efforts. In response to the charge that he was an agent of New England textile manufacturers seeking to destroy southern industry, he demonstrated that northern manufacturers owned many southern mills and actually opposed child labor laws in the South. Despite this successful defense, the NCLC had enormous troubles with the South. To help dispose of the charge that it was sectional in aim and support, the NCLC incorporated in 1907 but never made much headway against southern child labor. As McKelway recognized, structural problems in the South forced families to send children to work. Under the auspices of the NCLC, he would consistently push southern legislatures for reforms that would influence the supply of child labor such as unemployment insurance, public schools, and workers' compensation.

Federal Child Labor Law

Southerners like McKelway believed that the solution to the child labor problems lay with state legislatures, and at first, most other members of the NCLC went along with them. Lindsay, Kelley, and Jane Addams, a founding member and the most famous female social reformer of the era, continued to staunchly advocate federal legislation. By 1912 the slow progress of state legislation led most of the NCLC executive committee, including McKelway and Adler, to conclude that federal assistance was necessary. The bill drafted by the committee in 1913 punished the employers of child labor for violating its provisions. The Keating-Owen law, the bill eventually passed by Congress in 1916 after three years of battles, targeted interstate carriers of child-made goods instead of employers but included the principal standards of the Uniform Child Labor Law. The executive committee characterized Keating-Owen as the NCLC's greatest single accomplishment, but their delight was short-lived as the Supreme Court overturned it in a 5–4 decision in 1918 for interfering with commerce. The law had only been in effect for nine months.

The rise in child labor occasioned by World War I and the close Supreme Court decision led the NCLC to try again for a federal child labor law. After failing to get support for its own draft, the NCLC supported an amendment by Ohio senator Atlee Pomerene to the Revenue Act that taxed the employment of children. The provision passed in 1919, but the Supreme Court also threw out this second federal law in 1922 for violating states' rights by regulating local labor conditions. The NCLC would spend the next several decades working to raise state legislative standards.

End of the Problem

Child labor disappeared for the same reasons that it had appeared: changes in the structure of the economy. In the 1930s and 1940s jobs required more skills, the numbers of working women grew, organized labor grew in strength, minimum-wage legislation became law, and the real income of the working class rose. All of these factors combined to reduce the need for families to send children to work and to lessen the demand for unskilled workers. The NCLC, greatly weakened from its heyday, remains in existence to educate children about the world of work and to prevent their exploitation.

Key Players

Adler, Felix (1851–1933): The German-born Adler held a professorship in political and social ethics at Columbia University from 1902 until his death. His interest in social reform led to many honorific positions including chair of the NCLC (1904–1921).

Hine, Lewis Wickes (1874–1940): A Wisconsin native, Hine taught nature study at the Ethical Culture School in New York City. His position put him in touch with prominent social reformers, and he joined the NCLC in 1906 to photograph child laborers. As its staff photographer, he spent 12 years touring the United States investigating, documenting, and publicizing the issues that surrounded child labor.

Kelley, Florence (1859–1932): A socialist from Philadelphia, Kelley authored the 1889 pamphlet *Our Toiling Children* as well as a number of anti–child labor articles in popular magazines. During a decade-long stay at Chicago's Hull House, she earned a law degree from Northwestern University and collected data on the garment industry as a special agent for the Illinois Bureau of Labor Statistics. She served as chief factory inspector for Illinois (1893–1896), then headed the New York–based National Consumers' League (1899–1932).

McKelway, Alexander Jeffrey (1866–1918): A North Carolina Presbyterian minister, McKelway helped found the NCLC and, beginning in 1905, served as a full-time lobbyist and publicist for the organization. He succumbed to a heart attack just before the federal child labor law for which he had fought was ruled unconstitutional.

Murphy, Edgar Gardner (1869–1913): Born in Arkansas, Murphy served as an Episcopal minister in several southern states before ending his career in Montgomery, Alabama. He headed the Southern Education Board from 1903 to 1908. His interests included race relations, the education of African Americans, and the availability of public schools for all children. Murphy authored several pamphlets about child labor, including two in opposition to a federal child labor bill.

Wald, Lillian (1867–1940): A public health nurse who founded the Henry Street Settlement on New York City's Lower East Side, Wald provided medical care to her neighbors in their homes. Unable to improve significantly the lives of the working class, she lobbied for government legislation to clean the streets, improve housing, and reform labor conditions.

See also: *Keating-Owen Act.*

BIBLIOGRAPHY

Books

Curtis, Verna Posever, and Stanley Mallach. *Photography and Reform: Lewis Hine and the National Child Labor Committee.* Milwaukee: Milwaukee Art Museum, 1984.

National Child Labor Committee. *Twenty-fifth Anniversary of the National Child Labor Committee, 1904–1929.* New York: National Child Labor Committee, 1929.

———. *The Work of the National Child Labor Committee, 1904–1929.* New York: National Child Labor Committee, 1929.

Sklar, Kathryn Kish. *Florence Kelley and the Nation's Work: The Rise of Women's Political Culture, 1830–1900.* New Haven: Yale University Press, 1995.

Trattner, Walter I. *Crusade for the Children: A History of the National Child Labor Committee and Child Labor Reform in America.* Chicago: Quadrangle Books, 1970.

Periodicals

Doherty, Robert J., Jr. "Alexander J. McKelway: Preacher to Progressive." *Journal of Southern History* 24 (May 1958): 177–190.

Other

National Child Labor Committee [cited 7 October 2002]. <http://www.kapow.org/nclc.htm>.

ADDITIONAL RESOURCES

Books

Bailey, Hugh C. *Edgar Gardner Murphy: Gentle Progressive*. Coral Gables, FL: University of Miami Press, 1968.

Davidson, Elizabeth H. *Child Labor Legislation in the Southern Textile States*. Chapel Hill: University of North Carolina Press, 1939.

Felt, Jeremy. *Hostages of Fortune: Child Labor Reform in New York State*. Syracuse, NY: Syracuse University Press, 1965.

Murphy, Edgar Gardner. *The Federal Child Labor Bill: A Criticism*. Montgomery, AL: Paragon Press, 1907.

—Caryn E. Neumann

John Mitchell. © Archives Photos, Inc. Reproduced by permission.

National Civic Federation

United States 1900

Synopsis

The roots of the National Civic Federation (NCF) are found in the response to the Panic of 1893, with its massive unemployment and social dislocation. Late in 1893 in Chicago, Illinois, William T. Stead, an English evangelical clergyman and editor with a local following, and Ralph Montgomery Easley, an energetic young newspaperman, founded a civic federation. By 1894 the Chicago Civic Federation (CCF), aimed at improving municipal government, ameliorating social evils and slums, and relieving the poor, had focused on industrial conciliation. Its tripartite board of conciliation, comprised of representatives of business, labor, and the professions, unsuccessfully attempted to mediate the Pullman Strike of 1894; the board concluded that legal reform was needed and determined to work for the passage of an industrial arbitration law. The CCF sponsored conferences on issues such as industrial arbitration, primary elections, foreign policy, and the trust question. The early activities of the CCF presaged those of the National Civic Federation (NCF), which Easley organized in 1900. The NCF played a significant role from 1900 to 1916 in bringing representatives of American capital and labor together and in serving as a clearinghouse for ideas of reform that aimed at preserving the social order while addressing social problems engendered by industrial capitalism.

Timeline

1880: Completed Cologne Cathedral, begun 634 years earlier, with twin spires 515 feet (157 m) high, is the tallest structure in the world, and will remain so until 1889, when it is surpassed by the Eiffel Tower. (The previous record for the world's tallest structure lasted much longer—for about 4,430 years following the building of Cheops's Great Pyramid in c. 2550 B.C.)

1885: Sudanese capital of Khartoum falls to forces under the Mahdi Mohammed Ahmed, whose forces massacre British General Charles "Chinese" Gordon and his garrison just before a British relief expedition reaches the city.

1890: U.S. Congress passes the Sherman Antitrust Act, which in the years that follow will be used to break up large monopolies.

1893: Wall Street stock prices plummet on 5 May, precipitating a market collapse on 27 June. In the wake of this debacle, some 600 banks and 15,000 other businesses fail. The nationwide depression will last for four more years.

1898: United States defeats Spain in the three-month Spanish-American War. As a result, Cuba gains it independence, and the United States purchases Puerto Rico and the Philippines from Spain for $20 million.

1900: China's Boxer Rebellion, which began in the preceding year with attacks on foreigners and Christians, reaches its height. An international contingent of more than 2,000 men arrives to restore order, but only after several tens of thousands have died.

1900: Commonwealth of Australia is established.

1900: The first zeppelin is test-flown.

1900: Sigmund Freud publishes *The Interpretation of Dreams.*

1900: German physicist Max Planck develops Planck's constant, a cornerstone of quantum theory.

1903: Henry Ford establishes the Ford Motor Company.

1907: U.S. markets experience a financial panic.

1910: Neon lighting is introduced.

Event and Its Context

The NCF was headquartered in New York City and conceived as its purpose "to organize the best brains of the nation in an educational movement seeking the solution of some of the great problems related to social and industrial progress." Its National Committee on Conciliation and Arbitration, also founded in 1900, declared its purpose to be "to enter into active service in the cause of peace and harmony in the industrial world" and to prevent ". . . those most threatening of all industrial disturbances, the strike and the lock-out."

Holding the highest regard for "harmony in the industrial world" and cross-class collaboration, the NCF favored conservative leaders of the American Federation of Labor (AFL) and their acceptance of industrial capitalism. The NCF opposed radicalism, socialism, and after 1905 the Industrial Workers of the World (IWW) and others pursuing the politics of class conflict. An NCF statement, published in 1905, attacked both the individualistic hostility toward labor expressed by employer associations, such as the National Association of Manufacturers, and the revolutionary objectives of socialists. The document asserted, "The division of the people into classes is against the spirit of democratic institutions." The NCF dedicated itself "to prevent the . . . revolution threatened by extremists and to promote industrial peace." Easley worked successfully to encompass within the NCF both top labor leaders, like Samuel Gompers, president of the AFL, and John Mitchell, president of the United Mine Workers (UMW), and important business leaders, such as the industrialist Republican powerhouse and Ohio senator, Marcus Alonzo Hanna, and the New York banker, urban railway (subway) magnate, and conservative Democrat, August Belmont.

Early Years: Industrial Conciliation and Trade Agreements

Hanna, the first president of the NCF, was proud of his willingness to negotiate with unions at his own coal and iron businesses and was active in the field of industrial conciliation. Hanna's term marked the high water mark of NCF conciliation efforts and sponsorship of industry-wide trade agreements between employer associations and AFL unions. Such agreements did expand following his presidency, but the NCF and AFL unions soon encountered limitations to this growth.

Employers preferred to negotiate with conservative national union officers rather than often intractable and militant local union representatives, but only if they were able to maintain discipline over the rank and file on the shop floor. When national union leaders were unable to exert such control, employers

Marcus Alonzo Hanna.

repudiated trade agreements with alacrity. Perhaps the best example of this was the contract between the International Association of Machinists (IAM) and the National Metal Trades Association after a successful strike in Chicago metalworking shops in 1900 won laborers the nine-hour workday. In the Murray Hill Agreement, named for the New York hotel in which it was negotiated, the IAM agreed to halt the myriad practices machinists employed to limit production, and not to insist on the closed shop, in return for the shortened workday. When metal trades employers found to their consternation that the Murray Hill Agreement spurred worker militancy in the shops, rather than contained it, they declared war. Murray Hill became a dead letter after a protracted IAM strike in 1901, and in historian David Montgomery's words, "soon practically the entire business world [became convinced] of the folly of the NCF philosophy of business relations."

Later Civic Federation Activities

With the death of Hanna in 1904, the presidency of the NCF passed to the less union-friendly August Belmont. This signaled a change in NCF policy away from promoting industry-wide trade agreements and focusing more on other social problems. Conservative labor leaders still found value in the NCF's conciliation and safety work, however, and they used its mediation capabilities up until its role in this area was supplanted by the Federal Mediation and Conciliation Service after 1914. The NCF turned to researching and reporting on issues related to immigration, utility regulation, women, and most especially what was often referred to as "the trust question." NCF goals were consistent throughout: to reform the social order while preserving it—molding traditional, individualistic, American liberalism and reverence for the rights of private property to fit the social conditions wrought by the new and expanding industrial capitalism. Government was seen as a positive agency for change so long as the values of individualism and self-sufficiency were retained, though the economy had placed the actual achievement of such goals beyond the reach of most people.

As president of the UMW, John Mitchell made extensive use of the NCF's conciliation staff to curtail sympathy strikes and the spontaneous rank-and-file militancy such strikes bred within his own union. In 1908 he left his post in the UMW to become a full-time officer of the NCF's Trade Agreement Department. Here he quickly became frustrated with employer resistance to unionization and commitment to the open shop. His "highly ideological support" for the "labor peace movement" naturally attracted the attention of socialists, radicals, and militants within the ranks of labor, not least within his own union. In 1911 the UMW's convention passed a resolution prohibiting union members from belonging to the NCF, and Mitchell, forced to choose, resigned his position with the NCF. This watershed event marked the growing antagonism between the NCF's efforts to quell class conflict and those in organized labor who desired to subdue not the conflict engendered by the workings of the capitalist economy, but the egregious wrongs they perceived it to inflict on the working class. The UMW was not alone in proscribing members from affiliating with the NCF.

The NCF in a Time of War and Revolution

With the onset of the Woodrow Wilson administration (1913) and the passage of the legislation embodying his "New Freedom" reforms, the NCF's focus gradually shifted once again. During World War I the NCF concerned itself first with military preparedness issues, and after the United States entered the war in April 1917 on the side of the Allies, it supported the prosecution of the war to the fullest extent possible.

Even before the war the NCF's Woman's Department, coordinated by Gertrude S. Beeks, who later became the wife of Ralph Easley, covertly infiltrated the Consumer's League to report on the activities of suffragists and socialists who were active in that organization. This activity increased as the nation moved toward war, and Gompers, having eschewed his former labor pacifism, became increasingly concerned with the peace agitation and activities of socialists, the IWW, pacifists, and actual German agents, believing them to be cultivating strikes and sabotage in American industry. Together with Easley he procured the services of onetime New York City chief of police Theodore Bingham, who assisted the NCF in forming an espionage bureau. The agents of this bureau infiltrated pacifist organizations, attended labor conferences, interviewed union officials, and on at least one occasion persuaded such an individual to cease all peace work. The NCF's extensive subversive activities files were likely made available to the Military Intelligence Division of the U.S. Army in 1917.

With the end of World War I, the coming of the Russian Revolution and the rise of bolshevism, and the establishment of an international Communist Party movement, the NCF moved to the forefront of professional anticommunist and antiradical

organizations. Its heyday as a prominent reform organization seeking to bring together labor and capital and ameliorate social conditions while preserving the social order quickly passed. By the time Easley died, nearly penniless, in 1939, he had become a severe critic of President Franklin D. Roosevelt's New Deal. Although his wife attempted to carry on his work until her own death in 1944, the NCF was well on its way to oblivion. The vehement anticommunism for which it stood, however, lived on in such NCF-affiliated labor leaders as Matthew Woll, and this political tradition was carried forward and further developed by leaders of the AFL, and subsequently the AFL-CIO, such as George Meany and Lane Kirkland.

Key Players

Easley, Ralph Montgomery (1856–1939): Founding member and moving spirit behind the National Civic Federation, Easley began his career as a teacher and newspaperman in Hutchinson, Kansas. As an organizer and promoter of the NCF he worked to foster labor-management cooperation, produce NCF publications, and oppose radical movements. He became a confidant of Samuel Gompers.

Hanna, Marcus Alonzo (1837–1904): Businessman, senator from Ohio, and Republican Party architect of William McKinley's successful presidential campaigns of 1896 and 1900, Hanna served until his death as the first president of the NCF. He prided himself on his willingness to negotiate with unions in his own enterprises and encouraged other employers to do the same.

Mitchell, John (1870–1919): Mitchell worked as a coal miner and joined the Knights of Labor in 1885 and the United Mine Workers of America in 1890. He held a number of offices in the UMW, including its presidency from 1899 to 1908. Known for his leadership of the 1902 Pennsylvania Anthracite Strike, Mitchell went on to work as chairman of the NCF's trades agreement department from 1908 to 1911, and then to serve on public bodies dealing with labor relations in both New York City and the state of New York.

See also: *American Federation of Labor; Industrial Workers of the World; Panic of 1893; Pullman Strike.*

BIBLIOGRAPHY

Books

Croly, Herbert D. *Marcus Alonzo Hanna.* New York: Chelsea House, 1912, 1983.

Cyphers, Christoper J. *The National Civic Federation and the Making of a New Liberalism, 1900-1915.* Westport, CT: Praeger Publishers, 2002.

Foner, Philip S. *History of the Labor Movement in the United States,* Volume III: *The Policies and Practices of the American Federation of Labor, 1900–1909.* New York: International Publishers, 1964.

Gompers, Samuel. *Seventy Years of Life and Labor.* New York: E. P. Dutton & Co. 1925, 1926.

Green, Marguerite. *The National Civic Federation and the American Labor Movement, 1900–1925.* Washington, DC: The Catholic University of America Press, 1956.

Montgomery, David. *The Fall of the House of Labor.* New York: Cambridge University Press, 1987.

Ramirez, Bruno. *When Workers Fight.* Westport, CT: Greenwood Press, 1978.

Periodicals

Tompkins, Stephen G. "In 1917, Spy Target Was Black America," *The Commercial Appeal,* Memphis (Tennessee), 21 March 1993.

ADDITIONAL RESOURCES

Easley, Ralph M., and Gertrude S. Beeks. "Papers." Papers, Rare Book, and Manuscript Division, New York Public Library, New York City.

Hanna, Marcus Alonzo. *Labor and Capital.* Springfield, OH: Chautauqua Press, 1902[?]. Pamphlet Collection, State Historical Society of Wisconsin, Madison, Wisconsin.

Nack, David. "The American Federation of Labor Confronts Revolution in Russia and Early Soviet Government, 1905 to 1928: Origins of Labor's Cold War." Ph.D. diss., Rutgers University, 1999.

National Civic Federation 1905. Pamphlet Collection, State Historical Society of Wisconsin, Madison, Wisconsin.

National Civic Federation. Pamphlet Collection (1900–1944). Library of Congress, Washington, DC

National Civic Federation. "Papers." Papers, Rare Book, and Manuscript Division, New York Public Library, New York City.

—David Nack

National Congress of German Trade Unions

Germany 1892

Synopsis

The decade from 1890 to 1900 was a crucial period of redevelopment in the German labor movement. Following the repeal of the Anti-Socialist Law in 1890, workers had more freedom to organize for economic and political purposes. The form and direction that the labor movement should take, however, was uncertain. In particular, the trade unions, which had been an important source of working-class organization during the years when organizing had been illegal, stood at a crossroads. The trade unionist Carl Legien argued that a centralized union movement, independent from the German Social Democratic Party (SPD), was needed. The 1892 National Congress of German Trade Unions accepted Legien's plans and led to the official establishment of a national trade union organization. The relationship between the trade unions and the SPD, however, continued to be a source of tension. The direction taken by the trade union movement in the early 1890s would have important consequences for the future of the German labor movement as a whole.

Timeline

1872: The Crédit Mobilier affair, in which several officials in the administration of President Ulysses S. Grant are accused of receiving stock in exchange for favors, is the first of many scandals that are to plague Grant's second term.

1877: In the face of uncertain results from the popular vote in the presidential election of 1876, the U.S. Electoral Commission awards the presidency to Rutherford B. Hayes despite a slight popular majority for his opponent, Samuel J. Tilden. The election of 1876 will remain the most controversial in American history for the next 124 years, until overshadowed by the race between George W. Bush and Al Gore in 2000.

1882: Agitation against English rule spreads throughout Ireland, culminating with the assassination of chief secretary for Ireland Lord Frederick Cavendish and permanent undersecretary Thomas Burke in Dublin's Phoenix Park. The leader of the nationalist movement is Charles Stewart Parnell, but the use of assassination and terrorism—which Parnell himself has disavowed—makes clear the fact that he does not control all nationalist groups.

1885: German engineer Karl Friedrich Benz builds the first true automobile.

1888: Serbian-born American electrical engineer Nikola Tesla develops a practical system for generating and transmitting alternating current (AC), which will ultimately—and after an extremely acrimonious battle—replace Thomas Edison's direct current (DC) in most homes and businesses.

1890: U.S. Congress passes the Sherman Antitrust Act, which in the years that follow will be used to break up large monopolies.

1891: French troops open fire on workers during a 1 May demonstration at Fourmies, where employees of the Sans Pareille factory are striking for an eight-hour workday. Nine people are killed—two of them children—and sixty more are injured.

1893: Henry Ford builds his first automobile.

1893: New Zealand is the first nation in the world to grant the vote to women.

1894: French army captain Alfred Dreyfus, a Jew, is convicted of treason. Dreyfus will later be cleared of all charges, but the Dreyfus case illustrates—and exacerbates—the increasingly virulent anti-Semitism that pervades France.

1896: First modern Olympic Games are held in Athens.

1900: The first zeppelin is test-flown.

Event and Its Context

Early Attempts at Centralization

With the partial legalization of unions during the 1860s came the first attempts to organize them on a national basis. In

1868 the leader of the Lassallean Party, Johann Baptist von Schweitzer, set up the General Federation of German Workers. The federation was intended as an umbrella organization for unions associated with the Lassallean Party. Many of the leaders of the emerging trade unions, however, were opposed to von Schweitzer's highly autocratic leadership and his subordination of the unions to the political party. One such leader was Theodore York, whose ideas about the organization of the trade unions would be influential in later decades. York recognized the need for an independent centralized trade union movement. However, several factors worked together to prevent York's ideas from reaching fruition. Police harassment, the split in the social democratic movement, and suspicion from within both the union movement and the socialist movement all prevented the creation of a national trade union organization. Many of these obstacles would appear again in the early 1890s when new attempts were made to unite and centralize the union movement.

Unions Under the Anti-Socialist Law

From 1878, with the passing of Otto von Bismarck's Anti-Socialist Law, attempts to create a national organization were put aside in the struggle to keep the union movement alive. Although the law was ostensibly aimed at preventing social democrat, socialist, and communist agitation, in practice it was also used to attack the workers' right of association and combination. In the first few weeks following the passing of the Anti-Socialist Law, the authorities dissolved 17 trade unions, 63 local associations, and 116 workers' friendly societies. By the end of the year, almost all trade union activity had come to a halt. Some organizations, such as the Printers' Union, did manage to survive, but only by renouncing any connection with the social democratic movement and abandoning militant trade union aims. This was exactly what Bismarck had hoped to achieve. By 1880, however, the union movement began to stir again. The most common form of activity involved occupational craft associations organized at a local level. These groups were the basis for the spread of socialist ideas in the years when the political party was forced into exile. From the late 1880s, strike waves indicated that Bismarck's Anti-Socialist Law had failed to crush the labor movement in Germany.

Trade Unionism After 1890

The German government repealed the Anti-Socialist Law in 1890. However, the workers' right to association and combination was far from assured. The authorities were still determined to make trade union organization as difficult as possible. In addition, employer resistance to bargaining with unions had hardened in the face of strikes in the late 1880s and early 1890s. Employers had created their own national associations to oppose organized labor. The position of the trade unions also was weakened by renewed economic recession in the early 1890s. As a result, several strikes in a number of different industries ended in total failure, sapping the morale and financial resources of the unions and resulting in falling membership numbers.

The weakness of the union movement in the early 1890s could be interpreted in two ways. One argument saw the crisis as proof that the union movement was generally ineffective. In-stead of being engaged in futile attempts to bargain with the capitalists for better wages and conditions, the labor movement therefore should concentrate on the political struggle. Another position saw the strike defeats as evidence that the union movement needed to be organized according to a centralized, federalist plan. The strongest champion of the latter position was the chairman of the German Association of Turners, Carl Legien.

The General Commission and the First Congress

In 1890 Legien was the main force behind the establishment of the General Commission of German Trade Unions. The main task of the General Commission was the drafting of an organizational plan for the trade unions. Legien was a powerful advocate for a strong, centralized union movement that would focus on the economic struggle between the workers and their employers. As the laws regarding association prevented the unions from being involved in politics, Legien believed it was best for the union movement to be independent of the SPD. In other words, the political and industrial wings of the labor movement should organize separately.

The plan that was eventually drafted by the General Commission was an echo of that formulated by Theodore York 20 years earlier. The existing craft associations would be centralized to create *Zentralverband*, or central associations, for each trade. The central associations of related trades, such as those for woodworkers or metalworkers, would then link up to form a mixed union. The General Commission would preside over these unions and take responsibility for the concerns common to all the unions, such as direction of agitation and organization in nonunionized areas, production of a union newspaper, and in urgent cases, supply of funds for strike action. The plan called for this to be funded by a levy placed on all the members of the affiliated craft associations.

This plan went up for a vote at the first National Congress of German Trade Unions, held in Halberstadt, 14–18 March 1892. At this congress, Legien presented his vision for the future of the trade union movement. He argued that the role of the unions was crucial because they contributed to the workers' struggle for freedom. The battle for improvements in wages and working conditions was legitimate because it encouraged the development of class consciousness among the workers. As most workers in Germany were not unionized, the focus of the trade unions should be on agitation and recruitment. According to Legien, this was best done through the craft organizations, as there was still a great deal of craft consciousness amongst workers. The trade unions could build upon organizational forms that were already in place. Legien reminded the union delegates that to avoid harassment under the laws of association, the trade unions should focus on economic struggle and remain politically neutral while still committed to the labor cause.

Legien's plan did not meet with complete agreement. Among his opposition were those who favored local associations affiliated to the SPD over a separate centralized union organization. To Legien, however, the nationalization and centralization of the unions seemed to be the most logical step, especially given the direction of industrial development. As companies grew and expanded to include more varieties of workers in different localities, union organization that was limited to the local level could not hope to be effective. The heated debate over the form to be taken by the union organization was a reflection of some more fundamental conflicts over the role of the unions and the direction of the labor movement. The localists focused on the political struggle, as opposed to improvements in wages and working conditions, and espoused a more radical, revolutionary form of trade unionism. Opposition to Legien's plan also came from those who were skeptical about using the occupational craft associations as the basis for union organization. This faction instead preferred industrial unions comprising both skilled and unskilled workers. These debates about the ideal form of union organization were not resolved before World War I, and different types of unions continued to exist side by side.

Legien did succeed in gaining acceptance for the plan of the General Commission, albeit in slightly modified form. The congress passed a resolution recognizing the centralized craft association as the basis of union organization. However, it only recommended that these should be grouped into centralized unions. The delegates agreed on most of the other functions of the General Commission, but they did not agree to the provision of a centralized strike fund. Again, there was resistance to placing too much power in the hands of the General Commission. Despite the dilution of Legien's plan, the first national trade union organization in Germany had been officially created.

The Trade Unions versus the SPD

The SPD was no longer the only national organization claiming to represent the interests of the workers. Thus, the congress had created a separate sphere of influence in the German labor movement. Understandably, this was cause for some concern within the SPD, and the General Commission came under attack in the SPD newspaper, *Vorwarts*. The SPD leadership, including August Bebel, was decidedly lukewarm in its support for Legien's efforts to strengthen the unions. Most of the SPD leaders truly believed, in the midst of the economic depression of the early 1890s, that the fall of the capitalist system was imminent. Union efforts to improve wages and working conditions therefore seemed at best irrelevant, and at worst, a dangerous distraction from the approaching struggle. Legien was sharply criticized at the 1893 party conference when he tried to get a stronger endorsement for the union movement from the party hierarchy. Bebel warned that the work of the trade unions should never be seen as a substitute for the true proletarian struggle. It was quite clear that many in the party were suspicious of Legien's long-term ambitions for the independence of the trade union movement. As the trade union movement grew in strength from the mid-1890s, the balance of power between the party and the unions shifted. The SPD hierarchy was therefore forced to reevaluate its attitude toward Legien's aims and tactics. This conflict between the approach of the trade unions and the policies of the party was the central theme in the German labor movement prior to World War I.

Key Players

Bebel, August (1840–1913): Bebel was the leader of the German Social Democratic Party. Although Bebel supported the trade union movement as a recruiting ground for the socialist movement, he regarded union goals as subordinate to those of the party. He was therefore opposed to any attempt to supplant the SPD's leadership of the German labor movement and was clearly suspicious of Legien's intentions.

Legien, Carl (1861–1920): Chairman of the General Commission of German Trade Unions, Legien was the dominant force in the trade union movement from 1890 until his death in 1920. His vision and leadership shaped the direction of the labor movement, a direction that was vindicated by the growth of the trade union movement from the mid-1890s.

York, Theodore (1830–1874): German trade union leader during the 1860s and 1870s. York's plan for the centralization of the German trade unions was the blueprint for union organization during the 1890s.

BIBLIOGRAPHY

Books

Grebing, Helga. *History of the German Labour Movement*. Rev. ed. Leamington Spa, UK: Berg Publishers Ltd., 1985.

Guttman, W. L. *The German Social Democratic Party, 1875–1933: From Ghetto to Government*. London: George Allen & Unwin, 1981.

Moses, John A. *Trade Unionism in Germany from Bismarck to Hitler, 1869–1933*. Vol. 1, *1869–1918*. London: George Prior Publishers, 1982.

Schneider, Michael. *A Brief History of the German Trade Unions*. Bonn, Germany: Verlag J. H. W. Dietz Nachf., 1991.

ADDITIONAL RESOURCES

Books

Maehl, William Harvey. *August Bebel: Shadow Emperor of the German Workers*. Philadelphia: The American Philosophical Society, 1980.

—Katrina Ford

National Industrial Recovery Act

United States 1933

Synopsis

The National Recovery Administration, or NRA, was instituted in the wake of the passage of the National Industrial Recovery Act (NIRA) into law in 1933. The NIRA was one of the earliest efforts by President Franklin D. Roosevelt and his administration to ease the economic depression into which the

NRA Day parade, New York City, 1933. AP/Wide World Photos. Reproduced by permission.

United States had been plunged when the stock market crashed in 1929. The purpose of the NIRA was to encourage the formation of industrial cartels. Supposedly, the existence of cartels would put a stop to the cutthroat price-cutting that was integral to competitive business practices at the time yet would still allow businesses a reasonable profit; with these profits, they could afford to employ greater numbers of workers. In exchange, however, businesses had to set up a code, one of whose provisions, Section 7a, granted workers in that industry the right to bargain collectively "with representatives of their own choosing." Once the government cracked the door on collective bargaining, it was soon knocked down by labor organizers, who

convinced workers that the president was essentially calling on them to join unions.

Timeline

1919: With the formation of the Third International (Comintern), the Bolshevik government of Russia establishes its control over communist movements worldwide.

1924: In the United States, Secretary of the Interior Albert B. Fall, along with oil company executives Harry Sinclair and Edward L. Doheny, is charged with conspiracy and bribery in making fraudulent leases of U.S. Navy oil reserves at Teapot Dome, Wyoming. The resulting Teapot Dome scandal clouds the administration of President Warren G. Harding.

1929: On "Black Friday" in October, prices on the U.S. stock market, which had been climbing wildly for several years, suddenly collapse. Thus begins the first phase of a world economic crisis and depression that will last until the beginning of World War II.

1931: Financial crisis widens in the United States and Europe, which reel from bank failures and climbing unemployment levels. In London, armies of the unemployed riot.

1934: Austrian chancellor Engelbert Dollfuss, who aligns his nation with Mussolini's Italy, establishes a fascist regime in an attempt to keep Austria out of the Nazi orbit. Austrian Nazis react by assassinating Dollfuss.

1934: Dionne sisters, the first quintuplets to survive beyond infancy, are born in Canada.

1937: Japan attacks China, and annexes most of that nation's coastal areas.

1939: After years of loudly denouncing one another (and quietly cooperating), the Nazis and Soviets sign a non-aggression pact in August. This clears the way for the Nazi invasion of Poland, and for Soviet action against Finland. (Stalin also helps himself to a large portion of Poland.)

1942: Axis conquests reach their height in the middle of this year. The Nazis control a vast region from Normandy to the suburbs of Stalingrad, and from the Arctic Circle to the edges of the Sahara. To the east, the Japanese "Co-Prosperity Sphere" encompasses territories from China to Burma to the East Indies, stretching deep into the western Pacific.

1945: April sees the death of three leaders: Roosevelt passes away on 12 April; the Italians execute Mussolini and his mistress on 28 April; and Hitler (along with Eva Braun, propaganda minister Josef Goebbels, and Goebbels's family) commits suicide on 30 April.

1949: Establishment of North Atlantic Treaty Organization (NATO).

Event and Its Context

Economic Crisis in the United States

When Franklin D. Roosevelt (1882–1945) was sworn in as president in 1933, the economy of the United States was near total collapse. After declaring a bank holiday, Roosevelt and his administration set about creating policy to stimulate the economy. The Roosevelt administration was not the sole actor on this stage, however; at the instigation of the American Federation of Labor (AFL), Senator Hugo Black (1886–1971) of Alabama introduced legislation in April 1933 to decrease the workweek to 30 hours, a law that the Senate promptly approved. Roosevelt's advisors were opposed to this unilateral adjustment of wages and hours, however. They believed that it was bad policy

NRA member holds promotional poster. AP/Wide World Photos. Reproduced by permission.

for the government to arbitrarily set wages and hours; moreover, they were convinced that the United States Supreme Court would find such legislation unconstitutional. Therefore, the president's advisers sought to create mechanisms that facilitated a planned adjustment of factory output, hours, and wages based upon the rationalization of competitive conditions. Rather than oppose the Black bill, however, the administration proposed to replace it with another piece of legislation that would utilize this idea of rationalizing business competition.

Theoretical Basis of the National Recovery Act

The National Industrial Recovery Act, passed early in the summer during the famous First Hundred Days of the administration, was planned to "encourage national industrial recovery, to foster fair competition, and to provide for the construction of certain useful public works." In fact, the purpose of the act was to help steady the economy. The intent was to foster confidence on the part of the American public by stabilizing wages and creating more full-time jobs in which to earn these wages. President Roosevelt and Labor Secretary Frances Perkins (1882–1965) were less interested in supporting unionism than in raising labor standards. However, to gain the support of organized labor for the bill, Section 7a was added at the insistence of AFL president William Green (1873–1952), who thought the clause would guarantee workers the right to bargain collectively, which had long been a goal of the AFL.

To achieve these ends, advisors to Roosevelt proposed to allow the creation of a number of cartels, which were to be self-regulating and would allow members to control output, prices, and wages within the industry. When Roosevelt assumed the office of the presidency, fully 25 percent of American workers were without jobs, and many of those who had retained jobs were working only part-time. Advisors close to the president placed much of the blame for this condition upon the competitive nature of capitalism, in which companies tried both to increase sales of their product by cutting prices, and to control the costs of doing business by cutting wages.

To end this trend, members of the "brain trust" (an informal group of advisors consisting of Raymond Moley, Rexford G. Tugwell, and Adolph A. Berle, Jr.) proposed to allow industries to form cartels and regulate output among themselves, which would also allow them to regulate the wages of their workers at a higher rate than was the current practice at the time. Although Roosevelt's cousin (and political idol) Theodore Roosevelt made his reputation through his "trust-busting" activities, he had in fact broken up only those trusts that he determined were "bad" for the country. Rather than break up monopolies, however, the younger Roosevelt proposed to encourage their growth, as long as these cartels agreed to abide by certain conditions. Firms wishing to form a cartel had to submit their code to the administration for approval. These firms also had to pledge that they would not engage in monopolistic practices, especially those practices concerned with consumer prices, which would have to be submitted to the government for its approval. Members of a cartel were also restrained from prohibiting other firms within the industry from joining the cartel. Members within each cartel also had to agree to abide by Section 7a of the act, which guaranteed employees the rights of organization and collective bargaining.

To monitor this legislation, a new government agency was mandated, the National Recovery Administration (NRA). The NRA was led by a retired brigadier general, Hugh Johnson (1882–1942), who had served as the War Department representative on the War Labor Board during World War I. After resigning his commission in 1919, Johnson worked for financier Bernard Baruch and as an executive with Moline Plow. From his experience with government planning in World War I, Johnson became firmly convinced of the desirability of a government-business partnership in the management of the country's economy. Because of his service with the War Labor Board, Johnson also realized that the cooperation of labor was required in this endeavor, and to that end he recruited a leading labor lawyer, Donald Richberg, to assist him in the administration of the agency.

For the administration's point man in the Senate, Robert Wagner (1877–1953), Section 7a was the heart of the bill; indeed, he stated that he could not support the bill without its inclusion. Wagner had long been an advocate of legislative and administrative action to achieve fundamental social change. Wagner had been frustrated during the Hoover years (1928–1932) and complained that the potential of law to play a constructive role was limited by the belief that its role was to prevent certain behaviors, rather than to encourage others. Senator Wagner viewed the NIRA as a means of freeing the law from these fetters.

Passage of the NIRA into Law

In what was to become typical Roosevelt fashion, several different groups both within and without the administration were working on recovery legislation. Once the groups had developed plans, Roosevelt called them into the White House to work together to prepare the bill he would submit to Congress.

The group that advised Roosevelt on recovery legislation consisted of Secretary of Labor Frances Perkins, Director of the Budget Lewis W. Douglas, Rexford G. Tugwell, assistant Secretary of Commerce John Dickinson, Senator Robert Wagner, and General Hugh Johnson and Donald Richberg from the proposed NRA. This group worked out a bill that the president submitted to Congress on 17 May; by 13 June the NIRA was passed by both houses of Congress, and the president signed it into law three days later.

Differing Attitudes of Labor and Management Toward the NIRA

Labor enthusiastically embraced Section 7a of the legislation. William Green, president of the AFL, described the section as a "Magna Carta" for labor, and Daniel Tobin, president of the International Brotherhood of Teamsters (IBT), declared the bill as "about as good, or better, than we expected." Most famously, organizers from John L. Lewis's United Mine Workers (UMW) used Section 7a to appeal to unorganized workers, telling them, "The President wants you to join the union." Workers in the second half of 1933 and 1934 responded to these appeals in huge numbers, not only in mine work and other already established craft unions, but also in industries that had heretofore been unorganized, particularly automobile, rubber, and electrical manufacturing.

Management, on the other hand, was not enthusiastic about reintroducing labor unions into their businesses, particularly after just having rid themselves of most of them in the early 1920s. To maintain the appearance of worker representation (part of the "American Plan" proposed to members by the National Association of Manufacturers), many companies had adopted the practice of hosting company unions. Through these paternalistic organizations, companies were able to control most areas of employer/employee relations, while at the same time denying workers the right to collective bargaining. Because Section 7a did not outlaw company unions but merely stated that workers had the right to choose a union, companies attempted to "encourage" workers to choose the company union as their bargaining representative. Many workers resisted this ploy, however, and sought representation from unions affiliated with the AFL. Workers employed in unorganized sectors of the manufacturing economy were particularly adamant in seeking out independent unions, even though the AFL had no craft union for them to join. Workers in the automobile and rubber industries were particularly insistent. Workers in the Firestone and Goodyear Rubber plants formed federal unions, as did automobile workers in Cleveland and Toledo, Ohio, and other minor automobile manufacturing centers around the Midwest. (Federal unions were a kind of protoindustrial union, where the AFL organized workers while negotiating jurisdictional control of the workers organized.)

Legacy of the NIRA

As a result, the various industrial boards set up to administer price and production controls spent much of their time adjudicating labor-management disputes instead. The resultant backlog discouraged not only management but also the labor unions, which had been the greatest proponents of the NIRA. The ultimate result was that the legislation was in fact a dead issue even before the United States Supreme Court administered the coup de grâce in 1935 by declaring the act unconstitutional. Despite what may be termed the failure of the NIRA, however, the legislation introduced institutions that remained a part of the government-labor-business sphere during the remainder of the New Deal era and beyond. The most important aspect of the NIRA that remained was the National Labor Board, which was transformed slightly by the Wagner Act of 1935 and remains the major institution at the government level handling labor-management disputes to this day. Perhaps most importantly, the NIRA signaled a change in government policy towards labor-management disputes, in that it could no longer be assumed that the federal government would merely allow business to use the courts to control their labor problems.

Key Players

Green, William (1870–1952): The second president of the American Federation of Labor, this former coal miner was the conservative voice of labor during the New Deal years. Green supported the NIRA and the agency that the legislation created, the National Recovery Administration, but quickly became disenchanted with the lack of results.

Johnson, Hugh (1882–1942): In 1933 President Franklin D. Roosevelt appointed Johnson as the person to lead the National Recovery Agency that had been created by the National Industrial Recovery Act. Johnson was responsible for leading the agency's effort to organize industries under the fair trade codes that trade associations set up by companies within these industries. Both industry and labor quickly became disenchanted with the agency, however, and had stopped supporting the agency well before the Supreme Court declared it unconstitutional in 1935. Johnson later became an administrator with the Works Progress Administration, before leaving government to work for the Scripps-Howard newspaper chain.

Lewis, John L. (1880–1969): Lewis was long-time president of the United Mine Workers (1920–1960). Autocratic in his methods, Lewis saw the well-being of his union threatened by the antiunion drives of the 1920s. With the passage of the NIRA in 1933, particularly Section 7a, Lewis instructed his organizers to tell miners that "the President wants you to join the Union."

Roosevelt, Franklin Delano (1882–1945): Following in the footsteps of his cousin Theodore Roosevelt, Franklin Roosevelt assumed the office of the presidency in 1933, during the depths of the Great Depression. Roosevelt was swayed by arguments that one of the causes for the depression was cutthroat competition by businesses, which caused overproduction. Roosevelt's disappointment with the Supreme Court decision abolishing the NRA led him to "pack" the Supreme Court with justices whose viewpoints aligned with his own.

Wagner, Robert F. (1877–1953): A native of Germany, Wagner served in the New York legislature and as a Supreme Court justice in that state. In 1926 Wagner was elected to the United States Senate, were he became labor's strongest advocate in that body. In 1933 Wagner helped write the National Industrial Recovery Act and insisted upon the clause known as Section 7a, which granted workers the right to join a union "of their own choosing." Franklin D. Roosevelt appointed Wagner as the first chairman of the National Recovery Administration.

See also: *American Federation of Labor; Stock Market Crash; Wagner Act.*

BIBLIOGRAPHY

Books

Badger, Anthony J. *The New Deal: The Depression Years, 1933–1940.* New York: Noonday Press, 1989.

Brinkley, Alan. *The End of Reform: New Deal Liberalism in Recession and War.* New York: Alfred A. Knopf, 1995.

Fine, Sidney. *The Automobile Under the Blue Eagle: Labor, Management, and the Automobile Manufacturing Code.* Ann Arbor, MI: University of Michigan Press, 1963.

Tomlins, Christopher L. *The State and the Unions: Labor Relations, Law, and the Organized Labor Movement in America, 1880-1960.* New York: Cambridge University Press, 1985.

—Gregory M. Miller

National Labor Relations Act: *See* **Wagner Act.**

National Labor Union

United States 1866

Synopsis

The first congress of the National Labor Union (NLU) was held in Baltimore, Maryland, on 20–23 August 1866. The purpose of the NLU was to bring together disparate labor unions to work for common goals important to all working men and women. Its primary concern was to reduce the 10-hour workday to eight hours.

One of the NLU's most outstanding accomplishments was the passage of labor reform for federal government workers, including attainment of the eight-hour day. The NLU was also largely responsible for the creation of the Department of Labor.

Timeline

1846: American inventor Elias Howe patents his sewing machine.

1851: Britain's Amalgamated Society of Engineers applies innovative organizational concepts, including large contributions from, and benefits to, members, as well as vigorous use of direct action and collective bargaining.

1856: British inventor Henry Bessemer introduces his process for producing steel cheaply and efficiently.

William Sylvis. © Bettmann Archive. Reproduced by permission.

1859: Building of the Suez Canal begins.

1862: Though Great Britain depends on cotton from the American South, it is more dependent on grain from the North and therefore refuses to recognize the Confederacy.

1864: George M. Pullman and Ben Field patent their design for a sleeping car with folding upper berths.

1866: Austrian monk Gregor Mendel presents his theories on the laws of heredity. Though his ideas will be forgotten for a time, they are destined to exert enormous influence on biological study in the twentieth century.

1866: Dynamite and the Winchester repeating rifle are invented.

1866: Prussia defeats Austria in the Seven Weeks' War.

1868: Congressional efforts to impeach President Andrew Johnson prove unsuccessful, but they do result in his removal from any direct influence on Reconstruction policy, and ensure his replacement by Ulysses S. Grant as the Republican presidential candidate later that year.

1872: The Crédit Mobilier affair, in which several officials in the administration of President Ulysses S. Grant are accused of receiving stock in exchange for favors, is the first of many scandals that are to plague Grant's second term.

1876: Alexander Graham Bell introduces the telephone.

Event and Its Context

William Sylvis was a labor organizer who believed that the best way to achieve common goals was to bring together as many unions as possible. Sylvis met with representatives of the

New York coachmakers union and the printers union in February 1866 to begin the process of organizing the first National Labor Union (NLU) congress for August of that year.

The first congress convened on 20 August in the Front Street Theater in Baltimore. To welcome the delegates, organizers hung a banner on Baltimore Street that read, "Welcome Sons of Toil—From North and South, East and West." Sylvis was ill and unable to attend but sent in his place a trusted colleague, Isaac Neil. The congress was called to order by William Cather, president of the Trade Assembly of Maryland. Cather nominated John Hinchcliffe, who represented several unions in Illinois, for president and J. D. Ware of Pennsylvania as secretary. The motions passed, and the congress was officially under way. J. C. C. Whaley became president and C. W. Gibson assumed the post of secretary.

Mr. Rand of the Boston Bookbinders Union opened the day with a call for an eight-hour day, an issue of common interest to all attendees. Sylvis had laid out his personal belief about the ills of the 10-hour workday. His ideology was common among the delegates at the congress. The organizers considered the eight-hour workday crucial for workers' intellectual, social, and physical growth. Working all day bred ignorance because it left no time for reading or for education. Socially, an eight-hour day was important, as the extra hours in the day could be spent in pursuit of cultural enlightenment and with family and friends. Physically, the eight-hour day was crucial, because working too long took too much of a toll on the human body and shortened workers' life spans.

The congress also addressed the high rents that the companies charged the workers for company-owned housing. This burden ensured that the workers would have to work long days to meet their financial obligations. The delegates decided not to use strikes in the attempt to gain the eight-hour workday.

Rand spoke about his own commitment to the attainment of the eight-hour workday. He shared his views that the NLU should also work toward the implementation of year-round work for all workers rather than the seasonal work that left so many workers destitute for part of the year. Rand refered to the labor gains that had been made possible because of the strength of the labor movement in Great Britain. "As long as we are united we cease to be weak," Rand said to rally the crowd, according to the 21 August 1866 edition of the *Baltimore Sun*.

Harding, one of the organizers of the congress, urged workers to fight for the eight-hour day and, according the *Baltimore Sun*, stated his belief that the congress would "lay the foundation of future strength for the workingmen of America." Hinchcliffe said that although this congress was not as large as some that had been held, it was of great historical importance because it affected the well-being of millions of men and women workers. The organization would be the first national labor federation.

Additional Demands

As the congress went into its second and third days, the delegates voiced and voted on other demands. Hinchcliffe stated his hope that political affiliations would not get in the way of the larger, more important labor goals. This point would be reiterated several times over the remaining two days.

National Labor Union Statement of Purpose

In our organization we make no discrimination as to nationality, sex, or color. Any labor movement based upon such discrimination and embracing a small part of the great working masses of the country, while repelling others because of its partial and sectional character, will prove to be of very little value. Indeed, such a movement, narrow and divisional, will be suicidal, for it arrays against the classes represented by it all other laboring classes which ought to be rather allied in the closest union, and avoid these dissensions and divisions which in the past have given wealth the advantage over labor.

We would have "the poor white man" of the South, born to a heritage of poverty and degradation like his black compeer in social life, feel that labor in our organization seeks the elevation of all its sons and daughters; pledges its united strength not to advance the interests of a special class; but in its spirit of reasonableness and generous catholicity would promote the welfare and happiness of all who "earn their bread in the sweat of their brow."

With us, too, numbers count, and we know the maxim, "in union there is strength," has its significance in the affairs of labor no less than in politics. Hence our industrious movement, emancipating itself from every national and partial sentiment, broadens and deepens its foundations so as to rest thereon a superstructure capacious enough to accommodate at the altar of common interest the Irish, the Negro and the German laborer; to which, so far from being excluded, the "poor white" native of the South, struggling out of moral and pecuniary death into life "real and earnest," the white mechanic and laborer of the North, so long ill taught and advised that his true interest is gained by hatred and abuse of the laborer of African descent, as well as the Chinaman, whom designing persons, partially enslaving, would make in the plantation service of the South the rival and competitor of the former slave class of the country, having with us one and the same interest, are all invited, earnestly urged, to join us in our movement, and thus aid in the protection and conservation of their and our interests.

In the cultivation of such spirit of generosity on our part, and the magnanimous conduct which it prompts, we hope, by argument and appeal addressed to the white mechanics, laborers and trades unions of our country, to our legislators and countrymen at large, to overcome the prejudices now existing against us so far as to secure a fair opportunity for the display and remuneration of our industrial capabilities.

We launch our organization, then, in the fullest confidence, knowing that, if wisely and judiciously managed, it must bring to all concerned, strength and advantage, and especially to the colored American as its earliest fruits that power which comes from competence and wealth, education and the ballot, made strong through a union whose fundamental principles are just, impartial and catholic.

Source: Philip S. Foner and Ronald L. Lewis, eds. *The Black Worker: A Documentary History from Colonial Times to the Present.* Philadelphia: Temple University Press, 1978.

—Judson Knight

Sylvis believed that land monopoly was the source of great tyranny in the United States, and his opinion was circulated at the congress. The meeting also articulated demands for appropriate governmental disbursement of public lands. Public lands, the delegates held, should be given to settlers who would live on and work the land, rather than allocating large tracts of land and thus permitting the formation of monopolies among wealthy individuals and companies that had been accumulating these lands. The delegates were not satisfied by a simple statement of intent, however, and voted to include a demand that the government provide every man a farm and support until that farm was self-sufficient. Only in this way did the delegates and Sylvis believe that workers could gain control of their labor and their lives.

The delegates resolved that the government should create the demand for railroads by making the lands that were accessible to them available for settlers, fixing a minimal price for them, and then granting the proceeds of that land for the building of the railroads.

The congress also addressed the issue of taxes. The NLU voted to work toward the abolition of income taxes for everyone, which would free working men and women from the unfair burden that these taxes imposed on the working class. To compensate for the money lost, the NLU suggested that the government should tax landowners exclusively. Another issue of concern was the national debt, and the delegates agreed to demand that the wealthy should be taxed directly to pay it off.

The congress also protested the ill treatment of women who worked in factories. This was quite unusual, as women's rights in the workplace were of little concern to anyone besides the women themselves. The delegates passed a resolution to support the Sewing Women's Union and other working women in exchange for the women's support.

Women were not the only group that the 1866 NLU congress resolved to support. Although Sylvis was personally prejudiced against African Americans, he did allow them to join the NLU when the congress resolved that "all workingmen be included within its rank, without regard to race or nationality." Sylvis and the NLU recognized that to accomplish their agenda they must collaborate with *all* unions. This spirit would eventually lead the NLU to accept membership from all trade unionists, eight-hour champions, women's rights advocates, immigrants, African Americans, and farmers. Unity for many groups was achieved at a price. Each group wanted its own agenda to be considered, but that was not feasible, so compromises were made for the good of the NLU agenda, in particular the eight-hour day.

The congress closed with the committed delegates vowing to return to their homes and work toward the achievement of the agenda that had been set forth. They believed that with the combination of organization and agitation that they could change the lives of working men in the United States. Sylvis felt that although the congress was a step in the right direction, there was still not a strong organizational frame that would allow union members enough support to accomplish the agreed-upon agenda.

The Second Congress

The second NLU congress convened in Chicago in August 1867. Sylvis attended along with 71 delegates representing 64 organizations. Other notable union leaders present were A. C. Cameron of the Illinois State Workingmen's Convention, Richard Trevellick from the Detroit Trades' Assembly, John Bingham from the American Miners' Association, and Harding and Hinchliffe. Sylvis focused on the social reforms that he wanted to see implemented. He had a talent for organization, and he brought this to the NLU and to the second congress. An article in the women's labor journal, *The Revolution*, stated that skillful leadership had finally emerged to lead the union.

The NLU in Action

The NLU's agenda continued to expand under Sylvis's direction. Social reforms such as cooperative enterprise, decent housing to replace the squalor of tenements, the end of convict labor, labor reforms for working women, the establishment of mechanics institutes, and the creation of a central government agency (the Department of Labor) to oversee labor statistics and to regulate trade unions and other labor bodies were all credited to him.

Sylvis and other NLU speakers worked tirelessly to get their message out to working men and women throughout the country. They toured the South, lecturing and meeting members of southern trade unions to invite them to join forces with the NLU. They printed fliers and articles and disseminated them throughout the South. They also wrote to many organizations in cities and states. All of this activity increased the NLU's visibility and membership.

Women's Rights

The second congress solidified the NLU stand on the inclusion of working women, as it moved to include women's demands for equal pay for equal work. The delegates subsequently urged elected officials to support this item, and state conventions throughout New England and New York adopted this resolution. Men in the NLU did not adopt the notion of equal pay for equal work because they were inherently concerned with women achieving equal rights; rather, it was an act of self-preservation. If women received the same pay as men, companies, they theorized, would hire men instead.

The second congress also passed a resolution to encourage women to learn skills, get involved in business activities, join men's unions or form their own unions for protection, and use every reasonable method available to convince employers to give them fair wages for fair work. At the time, women's wages were approximately one-fourth of men's.

At the 1868 congress Sylvis emerged as prosuffrage. The NLU admitted four women as delegates: Susan B. Anthony and Mary Kellogg from the New York Working Women's Protective Labor Union of Mount Vernon, New York; Elizabeth Cady Stanton, secretary of the National Woman's Suffrage Association; and Kate Mullaney, head of the Troy Collar Laundresses Union. There was some controversy over whether Stanton should be seated because she was a delegate from the suffrage movement rather than from a labor union. In the end she was allowed to attend. Mullaney was elected second vice president of the NLU. Although she was later declared ineligible on a technicality, this does not change the fact that for the first time a national federation of labor unions admitted a woman to the upper ranks.

Politics

Sylvis believed that the surest route to achieving equity for working men and women was through politics. In the beginning he believed that the NLU should place labor candidates on political tickets, but in the election of 1868, only 1,500 votes were cast for labor. This changed Sylvis' strategy. He now prompted the NLU to seek to convince politicians from the two major parties to address labor needs. Richard Trevellick, an NLU member, proved to be an effective lobbyist and convinced many congressmen to make labor concerns their own. It was in part thanks to Trevellick's lobbying activities that the NLU attained its greatest victory. In 1868 the U.S. Congress passed a law that gave government employees an eight-hour day. This was the first eight-hour day legislation, and it was seen as a huge victory by the NLU.

Government officials were not pleased with the new law, and they reacted by threatening to reduce their employees' pay to reflect the two-hour differential between the eight- and 10-hour day. The two sides reached a compromise in which it was agreed that the workers would do 10 hours' worth of work in eight hours. The issue of pay reduction versus work increase remained a topic of dissent for several years.

In 1869 the NLU was dealt what came to be a fatal blow with the sudden death of Sylvis. With Sylvis gone, the men no longer tolerated female delegates from suffrage organizations. The organization asked Susan B. Anthony to leave the congress. The union had become splintered when the political faction began to break off from the reform faction. By 1870 the division was official, and in 1872 the political branch renamed itself the Labor Reform Party. The 1873 and 1875 NLU congresses saw the remaining members trying valiantly to save the badly fractured group. Without anyone who could replicate Sylvis' organizational genius, the NLU was dead.

Legacy

The NLU advanced the cause of labor in several important ways. The adoption of the eight-hour day for governmental employees; the repeal of the Contract Labor Act, which outlawed the influx of immigrants who would work to repay their passage to America; and the organization of many trade unions that brought the labor movement closer to the creation of a permanent national federation of labor were all crucial gains, as were the inclusion of women and African Americans.

Key Players

Anthony, Susan B. (1820–1906): Anthony was a labor activist and served as a delegate to the NLU congress in 1868. She published a union newspaper, *The Revolution*, which in 1868 called for equal pay for equal work and for an eight-hour day. In 1870 Anthony became president of the Workingwomen's Central Association. In the 1890s she was elected president of the National American Woman Suffrage Association. In this position she sought the support of labor unions. She remained a labor and suffrage activist until her death.

Mullaney, Kate (1845–1906): Mullaney was the head of the Troy Collar Laundry Union, second vice president of the NLU, and the first woman to hold an office in a national labor union.

Sylvis, William (1828–1869): Sylvis was the primary force in the formation of the NLU. His visions for labor and political reform were merged into the NLU, and upon his death the union fragmented and soon was disbanded.

Trevellick, Richard (1830–1895): Trevellick was a member of the Detroit Trades' Assembly and an excellent lobbyist. He was instrumental in the passage of the eight-hour day for government employees and remained devoted to lobbying for the eight-hour day for all working men and women throughout his life.

See also: *Act to Encourage Immigration; Department of Labor; Eight-hour Day Movement.*

BIBLIOGRAPHY

Books

Commons, John R., et al., eds. *History of Labour in the United States*, Vol. 1. New York: The Macmillan Company, 1921.

Grossman, Jonathan. *William Sylvis, Pioneer of American Labor: A Study of the Labor Movement During the Civil War*. New York: Octagon Books, 1973.

Powderly, Terence Vincent. *Thirty Years of Labor, 1859–1924, in Which the History of the Attempts to Form Organizations of Workingmen for the Discussion of Political, Social and Economic Questions Is Traced.* Columbus, OH: Excelsior Publishing House, 1890.

Rayback, Joseph G. *A History of American Labor*. New York: The Macmillan Company, 1959.

Todes, Charlotte. *William H. Sylvis and the National Labor Union*. Westport, CT: Hyperion Press, 1975.

Periodicals

The Baltimore Sun, 20–24 August 1866.

Grob, Gerald N. "Reform Unionism: The National Labor Union." *The Journal of Economic History* 14, no. 2 (spring 1954): 126–142.

Other

America's Story from America's Library. Reconstruction, 1866–1877. *National Labor Union Requested an Eight-Hour Workday, August 20, 1866* [cited 28 September 2002]. <http://www.americaslibrary.gov/jb/recon/jb_recon_workday_1.html>.

Detroit Historical Museums and Society. *Frontiers to Factor* [cited 24 August 2002]. <http://www.detroithistorical.org/exhibits/index.asp?MID=1&EID=4&ID=65>.

Lause, Mark. Lause's Links. *National Labor Reform Party* [cited 29 August 2002]. <http://www.geocities.com/CollegePark/Quad/6460/dir/872nlr.html>.

Library of Congress Online. American Memory. *Today in History* [cited 7 September 2002]. <http://memory.loc.gov/ammem/today/aug20.html>.

National Park Service. Parknet. *Places Where Women Made History: The Kate Mullaney House*. 30 March 1998 [cited 24 August 2002]. <http://www.cr.nps.gov/nr/travel/pwwmh/ny18.htm>.

Public Employees Federation. *Kate Mullaney, A True Labor Pioneer* [cited 27 September 2002]. <http://www.pef.org/katemullaney.htm>.

Susan B. Anthony House Web site. *Biography of Susan B. Anthony* [cited 13 August 2002]. <http://www.susanbanthonyhouse.org/biography.html>.

—Beth Emmerling

National Organization for Women

United States 1966

Synopsis

Unionists played a prominent role in forming the National Organization for Women (NOW) in October 1966, but middle-class, professional women dominated NOW in its early years. Unlike radical feminists of the period, NOW members sought change through the political system. One of their first campaigns was to get the Equal Employment Opportunity Commission (EEOC) to enforce Title VII of the Civil Rights Act of 1964's ban on sex discrimination. NOW argued that protective laws for women no longer served women's best interests.

Women union leaders differed with NOW's position on key issues. They were ambivalent about Title VII's strong enforcement and sought to retain at least some protective measures for women. Although NOW was one of the chief supporters of the Equal Rights Amendment, unionists struggled to explain how its enactment might harm women in low-wage service and industrial jobs. They charged that NOW did not consider the needs of working-class women. Moreover, unionists opposed NOW when it sought to safeguard the recently won employment gains of women and minorities in the face of a deep recession in the mid-1970s by calling for a modification of the traditional seniority concept of "last hired, first fired." The Coalition of Labor Union Women argued that such a change would be divisive to workers and punish veteran employees unfairly.

The two organizations grew considerably closer by the later 1970s, when NOW began to devote more resources to economic concerns such as the minimum wage and full-employment legislation. Reacting to pressure from rank-and-file women unionists who sought gender equality, union leaders reversed their long-standing opposition to the ERA.

Gloria Steinem (front left), participating in "Fight the Right" march, San Francisco, California, 1996. AP/Wide World Photos. Reproduced by permission.

Betty Friedan, at Equal Rights Amendment rally, linking hands with (l-r) Liz Carpenter, Rosalyn Carter, Betty Ford, Elly Peterson, Jill Ruckelshaus, and Bella Abzug. © Bettmann/Corbis. Reproduced by permission.

Timeline

1946: First true electronic computer, the Electronic Numerical Integrator and Computer (ENIAC), is built.

1951: Julius and Ethel Rosenberg are convicted and sentenced to death for passing U.S. atomic secrets to the Soviets.

1956: Workers revolt against communist rule in Poland, inspiring Hungarians to rise up against the Soviets. Soviet tanks and troops crush these revolts.

1959: Vice President Richard Nixon and Soviet leader Nikita Khrushchev engage in their famous "kitchen debate" in Moscow. Later in the year, Khrushchev visits the United States, signaling an improvement in U.S.-Soviet relations.

1962: Publication of Rachel Carson's *Silent Spring* heightens Americans' awareness of environmental issues. A year later, *The Feminine Mystique* by Betty Friedan helps to usher in a feminist revolution.

1966: As a result of the Supreme Court's decision in *Miranda v. Arizona,* law officers are now required to inform arrestees of their rights.

1966: In August, Mao Zedong launches the "Great Proletarian Cultural Revolution," which rapidly plunges China into chaos as armed youths plunder the countryside, rooting out suspected foreign collaborators and anti-Chinese elements. Along with rifles and other weapons, these Red Guards are armed with copies of Mao's "Little Red Book."

1969: Assisted by pilot Michael Collins, astronauts Neil Armstrong and Edwin E. "Buzz" Aldrin become the first men to walk on the Moon on 20 July.

1971: *Pentagon Papers,* based on a secret Defense Department study of the Vietnam War, are published.

1976: Striking a blow in favor of affirmative action, the U.S. Supreme Court rules that minorities are entitled to retroactive job seniority. The Court also holds that the death penalty is not necessarily cruel or unusual punishment, thus reversing a decade-old ruling.

1981: President Reagan nominates Sandra Day O'Connor of Arizona to become the first female Supreme Court justice.

Event and Its Context

NOW's Stance on Employment Issues in Its Early Years

The wider, national battle for gender equality gathered political force only with the emergence of the second-wave feminist movement in the late 1960s. Unionists played a fundamental role in defining the shape and character of this movement. Union women, joining with upper-class women from the small, conservative National Woman's Party (NWP), and younger, liberal activists, formed the National Organization for Women (NOW) in October 1966. The Equal Pay Act and the report of the President's Commission on the Status of Women, both of which appeared in 1963, and Title VII of the Civil Rights Act of 1964 energized this new wave of feminists to protest what its members viewed as the EEOC's unwillingness to provide equal employment conditions for women. Among its founding members were unionists Aileen Hernandez, Dorothy Haener, Caroline Davis, Betty Talkington, and others. Despite the presence of these unionists in the early years of NOW, the organization was dominated by middle-class, professional women who were often at odds with unionists over such issues as continued enforcement of protective laws, the Equal Rights Amendment (ERA), and maintaining union seniority systems. NOW and labor movement leaders viewed each other warily: the former were hostile to unions, often viewing them as nothing more than bastions of male supremacy; the latter saw feminists as unappreciative of the importance unions played in the lives of working women. Some key figures in NOW, such as Betty Friedan, had radical union and left-wing pasts, but they did not make feminist claims as unionists.

In general, mainstream feminists considered women's economic status in a gender rather than in a class context. Unlike the radical feminists of the period, NOW members sought to use the political system to effect reform. There was cause for optimism in the heady days of the 1960s. Responding to NOW pressure, for example, President Lyndon Johnson in 1967 amended an executive order banning discrimination on the basis of race by government contractors to include a prohibition on sex discrimination as well. More than any other issue at the time, feminists sought a full enforcement of Title VII. They argued that the protective laws for women, many of which dated back to the early twentieth century, hindered the ability of women workers to gain access to equal pay, seniority, and job assignment with men. The EEOC's commissioners balked, maintaining that some protective laws might override Title VII's seemingly clear mandate that there be no discrimination.

Despite pressure on EEOC officers to reevaluate their Title VII guidelines, feminists were unable to meet with most commissioners. The two identifiably feminist commissioners at the EEOC, Aileen Hernandez and Richard Graham, left in 1966. These were temporary setbacks, however. By 1968 the cumulative effect of EEOC data pointing to the prevalence of sex discrimination and the pressure of feminists forced the recalcitrant commission to modify its policies. Commissioners returned to their original practice of determining the legality of protective laws on a case-by-case basis instead of ignoring the issue altogether; they ruled that separate retirement ages for men and women violated Title VII. Separate want ads became unlawful. The next year, EEOC policymakers finally bowed to pressure and released new guidelines mandating that Title VII superseded all state protective laws for women.

NOW and Organized Labor

The relationship between NOW and the labor movement during NOW's first decade of existence was characterized by distrust. Whereas rank-and-file women were in accord with many of NOW's positions, older female union activists continued into the 1970s to argue the need for protective laws. They underestimated the new economic and social forces that were shaping working women's lives. Most of these unionists were approaching middle age by 1969; they had been out of the workforce for at least a decade, often in appointed union staff positions in Washington, D.C.

Rank-and-file women unionists, however, rejected protective laws and fully embraced Title VII. The nearly 2,500 women charging sex discrimination against their unions and employers during the EEOC's first year alone (27 percent of the total complaints) did not create a formal association. They helped to change the labor movement's stance on gender equality and to legitimize NOW's efforts by unloosing an avalanche of discrimination charges. A minority of older activists joined them in their quest for equality, most notably EEOC commissioner Aileen Hernandez. Before her appointment to the commission, Hernandez had been the West Coast education director for the International Ladies Garment Workers Union. After she left the EEOC, Hernandez was elected NOW president.

NOW's championing of the Equal Rights Amendment (ERA) put it at odds with most of labor's leadership as well. The ERA had existed in one form or another since the 1920s but had failed to gather significant support when it came up for annual renewal in Congress. Most reform groups and labor unions opposed it on the grounds that it would negate protective laws and threaten the economic status of working women. When it reappeared in the late 1960s, it found new life as a key component in the battle for gender equality. With the passing of the pro-ERA baton from the NWP to a new generation of feminists, the amendment took on a different meaning in the context of second-wave feminism. For the vast majority of feminists, the ERA was the centerpiece of their agenda, the ultimate expression of gender equality. The EEOC and judicial decisions against protective laws, the failure to interest courts in testing the Fourteenth Amendment as a substitute for the ERA, and the Nixon administration's Women's Task Force energized receptive feminists. For the first time the ERA gained grassroots support, passed the U.S. Senate (1972), and went to the states for ratification.

Union leaders did not flood the pro-ERA camp during this period, and many came to back the amendment by the mid-1970s reluctantly, and some not at all. They resisted supporting the ERA long past the point at which it had become clear that state protective laws for women were invalid. They risked alienating longtime allies over the matter, arguing that justice for working women came in the form of protective laws, not in measures demanding equal treatment. Despite evidence to the contrary, union activists continued to view the ERA as the work of conservative NWP members. Those having the most to lose from the elimination of protective laws for women rejected the ERA in the fiercest manner. This was especially true for unionists in organizations with a high percentage of women members, such as the Garment Workers, Amalgamated Clothing Workers, and the Hotel and Restaurant Workers unions. They presented their case against the ERA in what they asserted were practical terms: their members needed at least some of the protective measures to make their difficult working lives a bit easier.

Rank-and-file women unionists used public protests and worked through their own unions and ultimately proved decisive in bringing their labor organizations to back the ERA. At hearings in 1970, most labor leaders present testified against the ERA while women from various unions protested their unions' stance at a press conference. Labor leaders gave their approval to the amendment: by the time the AFL-CIO convention delegates backed a resolution approving the ERA in 1973, most large labor unions had made the ERA's passage a their goal.

Although they were in accord with middle-class feminists on key issues and at odds with their own leaders, NOW seemed to win few working-class members in this period, however. What little research there is on rank-and-file women unionists' relationship with NOW indicates that, with the exception of local chapters such as one in Chicago, there was little working-class support for NOW. Union women saw it as too removed from their own concerns and communities. Union leaders criticized NOW's efforts on behalf of women workers through the 1970s. They charged that NOW did not expend enough resources on economic issues affecting lower-paid working women. When they did—for example, advocating strong EEOC enforcement—they ignored the valuable role labor played in educating its members on equality and offering the grievance procedure as a tool to fighting discrimination. The debate over seniority and affirmative action points to the fault lines among union women and NOW leaders in the mid-1970s. With the massive layoffs during the economic recession, the EEOC, NOW, and other liberal and civil rights organizations proposed that the traditional collective bargaining guarantee of "last-hired, first-fired" be suspended so as to preserve the recent hiring gains of women and minorities. This plan met with scorn from male and female unionists alike on the grounds that it would undercut labor's already diminished strength.

NOW and unionists averted a damaging break over the issue with the Supreme Court's *Franks v. Bowman Transportation* ruling in 1976, in which the justices left the traditional seniority system intact but ordered that measures be taken to provide a "rightful-place" remedy (i.e., retroactive seniority to the date of discrimination) for victims of unequal treatment. The Coalition of Labor Union Women (CLUW), formed in 1974 by industrial, service, skilled trades, and government unionists, and NOW worked together on the ERA and comparable-worth campaigns. For their part, CLUW delegates supported abortion rights at their 1977 convention. With an even greater number

of women in the workforce, NOW leaders gave greater attention to workplace issues such as minimum wage legislation and National Labor Relations Act reform, two items of key importance to organized labor.

Key Players

Friedan, Betty (1921–): Friedan, who is best known as the author of *The Feminine Mystique* and was NOW's first president, was a labor journalist in the 1940s and early 1950s. She began writing under her maiden surname Goldstein while at Smith College; she later worked for the United Electrical Workers, a left-wing union.

Haener, Dorothy (1917–2001): Haener was a high-level staff member in the United Automobile Workers' (UAW) Women's Bureau in the 1960s and a founding member of NOW. Along with fellow UAW member Caroline Davis, she lobbied the EEOC for full enforcement of Title VII of the Civil Rights Act of 1964.

Hernandez, Aileen (1926–): Hernandez was a union organizer and West Coast Education Director of the International Ladies Garment Workers Union before being appointed as the only woman commissioner of the EEOC in 1965. She was the only African American woman serving as a commissioner until the arrival of Eleanor Holmes Norton in the late 1970s. Hernandez was a founding member of NOW and the organization's president in the late 1960s.

See also: *Civil Rights Act of 1964; Coalition of Labor Union Women; Equal Pay Act; Equal Rights Amendment and Protective Legislation.*

BIBLIOGRAPHY

Books

Deslippe, Dennis A. *"Rights, Not Roses": Unions and the Rise of Working-Class Feminism, 1945–80.* Urbana: University of Illinois Press, 2000.

Gabin, Nancy F. *Feminism in the Labor Movement: Women and the United Auto Workers, 1935–1975.* Ithaca, NY: Cornell University Press, 1990.

Harrison, Cynthia. *On Account of Sex: The Politics of Women's Issues, 1945–1968.* Berkeley: University of California Press, 1988.

Hartmann, Susan M. *The Other Feminists: Activists in the Liberal Establishment.* New Haven, CT: Yale University Press, 1998.

Horowitz, Daniel. *Betty Friedan and the Making of "The Feminist Mystique": The American Left, The Cold War, and Modern Feminism.* Amherst: University of Massachusetts Press, 1998.

ADDITIONAL RESOURCES

Other

"Step by Step: Building a Feminist Movement, 1941–1977." Joyce Follet, producer; Mimi Omer, coproducer. Close-captioned video. Worthington, MA: Step-by-Step, 1998.

—Dennis A. Deslippe

Immigrants arrive at Ellis Island. The Library of Congress.

National Origins Act

United States 1924

Synopsis

The National Origins Act, sometimes referred to as the Johnson-Reed Act, represented the culmination of early twentieth-century anti-immigration sentiment. The act sharply restricted the total number of immigrants who could come to the United States and established quotas for various nationality groups. The chief purpose of the act was to limit the number of "less desirable" immigrants from southern and eastern Europe and from Japan, many of whom had played a vital role in the nation's industrial development.

Timeline

1909: Robert E. Peary and Matthew Henson reach the North Pole.

1914: On 28 June in the town of Sarajevo, then part of the Austro-Hungarian Empire, Serbian nationalist Gavrilo Princip assassinates Austrian Archduke Francis Ferdinand and wife Sophie. In the weeks that follow, Austria declares war on Serbia, and Germany on Russia and France, while Great Britain responds by declaring war on Germany. By the beginning of August, the lines are drawn, with the Allies (Great Britain, France, Russia, Belgium, Serbia, Montenegro, and Japan) against the Central Powers (Germany, Austria-Hungary, and Turkey).

1919: Treaty of Versailles is signed by the Allies and Germany but rejected by the U.S. Senate. This is due in part to rancor between President Woodrow Wilson and Republican Senate leaders, and in part to concerns over Wilson's plan to commit the United States to the newly established League of Nations and other international duties. Not until 1921 will Congress formally end U.S. participation in the war, but it will never agree to join the League.

1921: As the Allied Reparations Commission calls for payments of 132 billion gold marks, inflation in Germany begins to climb.

1923: Conditions in Germany worsen as inflation skyrockets and France, attempting to collect on coal deliveries promised at Versailles, marches into the Ruhr basin. In November an obscure political group known as the National Socialist German Workers' Party attempts to stage a coup, or putsch, in a Munich beer hall. The revolt fails, and in 1924 the party's leader, Adolf Hitler, will receive a prison sentence of five years. He will only serve nine months, however, and the incident will serve to attract attention for him and his party, known as the Nazis.

1924: V. I. Lenin dies, and thus begins a struggle for succession from which Josef Stalin will emerge five years later as the undisputed leader of the Communist Party and of the Soviet Union.

1924: In the United States, Secretary of the Interior Albert B. Fall, along with oil company executives Harry Sinclair and Edward L. Doheny, is charged with conspiracy and bribery in making fraudulent leases of U.S. Navy oil reserves at Teapot Dome, Wyoming. The resulting Teapot Dome scandal clouds the administration of President Warren G. Harding.

1927: Charles A. Lindbergh makes the first successful solo nonstop flight across the Atlantic, and becomes an international hero.

1929: On "Black Friday" in October, prices on the U.S. stock market, which had been climbing wildly for several years, suddenly collapse. Thus begins the first phase of a world economic crisis and depression that will last until the beginning of World War II.

1934: Austrian chancellor Engelbert Dollfuss, who aligns his nation with Mussolini's Italy, establishes a fascist regime in an attempt to keep Austria out of the Nazi orbit. Austrian Nazis react by assassinating Dollfuss.

_____

Event and Its Context

"Give Me Your Tired, Your Poor, Your Huddled Masses"

Prior to 1890, most U.S. immigrants came from such northern European countries as England, Ireland, Germany, Holland, and the Scandinavian countries, although on the West Coast a significant number were Chinese. Around 1890, however, the face of America began to change as many Slavs, southern Italians, Hungarians, Greeks, Rumanians, Lithuanians, Lebanese, and eastern European Jews began coming to the United States, many of them intending to work in the mines and mills. For many, their goal was to save enough money to return to their native lands and buy a farm or business. Between 1892 and 1914, 17 million immigrants—as many as a million a year—passed through Ellis Island, most from eastern and southern Europe. By 1910 the foreign-born represented 13 percent of the U.S. population, and they and their American-born children made up 40 to 50 percent of the population.

During these years the popular press was filled with pictures of exotic-looking immigrants. It was not long before many "old immigrants"—those of northern European stock—began to decry the influx of these new immigrants, who conjured images of dirt, disease, and crime. Leading the assault on immigration were many Boston Brahmins, including Senator Henry Cabot Lodge. They gathered in 1894 to form the Immigration Restriction League (IRL), based on eugenic views of the superiority of the "Nordic races" and the corresponding inferiority of Slavs, Italians, and Jews. The IRL repeatedly urged Congress to restrict immigration by requiring a literacy test for admission to the United States, in the mistaken belief that most of the new immigrants would not be able to pass it. Grover Cleveland was the first of three presidents to veto such bills, and many Americans believed that the United States should remain a haven for the poor and oppressed.

Organized labor joined in the public debate. Skilled workers expressed contempt for their unskilled brethren from foreign countries. Many workers believed that industrialists were actually bringing in foreign labor to drive down wages. The American Federation of Labor and its leader, Samuel Gompers, were growing increasingly convinced that cheap foreign labor threatened the interests of the labor movement. Labor also believed that the shallow roots of the new immigrants made them resistant to unionization, although the success of the International Ladies Garment Workers Union and the Amalgamated Clothing Workers of America, many of whose members were Jewish, in part refuted this notion.

The gathering storm clouds of World War I intensified the effort to restrict immigration as a wave of patriotism and "Americanism" swept the nation. In the context of war, virtually any foreigner was regarded as suspect, leading Tennessee senator Kenneth McKellar to declare in April 1917, "From now on there can be but two classes of people in the country—Americans and traitors." In 1917 the anti-immigrationists finally got their literacy test, which Congress approved over Woodrow Wilson's veto.

Fueling the animosity toward immigrants was the Russian Revolution. In the minds of many Americans, Slavs and Jews were nothing more than "dirty Bolsheviks" who threatened

American security. This view was strengthened by the violent steel strike of 1919, during which many Slavs, Hungarians, Lithuanians, and other immigrant nationalities enthusiastically supported the position of the National Committee for Organizing Iron and Steel Workers and walked off their jobs. On the heels of this strike, the infamous case of Nicola Sacco and Bartolomeo Vanzetti, anarchists who were convicted of murder and robbery in 1920, confirmed negative stereotypes about southern Europeans and further polarized the critics and defenders of immigration.

The Emergency Immigration Act of 1921

Calls for immigration restriction peaked in 1920 and 1921 as the economy softened and the labor unions and others argued that immigrants were no longer providing much-needed labor. Instead, they argued, the United States was becoming a "dumping ground" for Europe's "refuse" and the nation needed to act immediately to prevent its shores from being overrun with refugees from war-torn Europe. The anti-immigrationists had a strong ally in Congress in Representative Albert Johnson, a member of the Asiatic Exclusion League and chairman of the House Committee on Immigration.

The House adopted Johnson's call for a two-year suspension of immigration in 1921, but slightly cooler heads prevailed in the Senate, which called for limiting immigration to 5 percent of the number of foreign born of each nationality living in the United States in 1910. In conference the House and Senate agreed to a bill, the Emergency Immigration Act, which limited the number to 3 percent, with a maximum of 357,803 immigrants per year. These figures considerably favored those from the "old immigrant" countries and granted them 200,000 slots. The law was supposed to remain in effect for one year, but in 1922 it was extended until 1924.

Many business leaders, including the U.S. Chamber of Commerce and the National Association of Manufacturers, opposed passage of the 1921 law, pointing to the contributions of immigrant labor in the coal, steel, meat-packing, textile, and other industries that were responsible for America's industrial might. After the act was passed, however, many reevaluated their attitudes and crept into the restrictionist camp, arguing that improvements in technology were reducing the need for unskilled labor, that the migration of African Americans from the South was alleviating labor shortages in the industrial North, and that Mexicans, who were exempt from the act, were filling labor shortages in the industrial Midwest. Adversity can make strange bedfellows, for the AFL agreed: closing America's gates would drive up wages in many industries. Labor found an advocate for its position in Secretary of Labor James J. Davis, a proponent of Nordic superiority who referred to the new immigrants as "rat people."

Closing the Gates

With the 1921 act due to expire in 1924, Congress felt a sense of urgency to pass a bill that would even further restrict immigration. Johnson and the Committee on Immigration devised a formula that would cut immigration to just over 161,000, with each nation's quota cut to 2 percent of its numbers according to the 1890 census; using the census of that year would ensure that the numbers of Slavic, eastern European, and

Jewish immigrants would be drastically reduced, with those from such countries as Germany and the United Kingdom would be only modestly reduced. Thus, for example, Hungary's quota would be reduced from 5,638 (under the 1921 act) to 474, Poland's from 21,076 to 5,156, and Italy's from 42,057 to 3,912. In contrast, Germany's quota would be cut from 67,607 to 51,299 and the United Kingdom's from 77,342 to 62,458. The committee also attached a provision that excluded Japanese immigrants.

The committee bill passed easily in the House, but when it reached the Senate, David A. Reed of Pennsylvania was concerned that the use of the 1890 census would be perceived as too discriminatory. He thus proposed restricting immigration to 150,000 per year but using the 1920 census to establish quotas, a provision he believed would largely accomplish the goals of the House version; after 1927, quotas would be based on the results of a survey of the national origins of the American population. The Reed bill won handily in the Senate, and after the two bills went to a joint House-Senate committee, it was the Senate version that was approved. Thus, the Johnson-Reed Act went to President Calvin Coolidge, who signed the bill despite his misgivings over irritating Japan. Although hope persisted in some quarters that the act would in time be repealed, it would provide the basic framework for American immigration policy into the 1960s.

The Effects of the National Origins Act

The National Origins Act met with a storm of protest. Newspapers published by Italians, Poles, Jews, Armenians, and other ethnic groups denounced the law, which identified them as inferior races. Romania chastised the United States for assigning it a quota of 831. Even the fabric of Nordic unity frayed: Congressman Knud Wefald of Minnesota denounced the "breach of faith" that favored people from "British slums" over "farmer lads and skilled laborers" from Scandinavia.

The National Origins Act had far-reaching effects, many of which its proponents could not have anticipated. Denied entry between 1924 and 1929 were 300,000 Jews from eastern Europe, some of whom were aboard ship at the time the act was passed and many of whom might have been saved from the Nazi Holocaust. Japan took the act as "the culminating act of rejection by the United States." Ultimately the act soured relations between the two countries and added to the climate of tension that led to World War II and the internment of Japanese Americans during the war. Because Western Hemisphere countries were exempt from the act, during the 1920s a half a million Mexicans crossed the border, where they were welcomed as a source of cheap labor in agriculture, mining, the railroads, and the steel and auto industries. Ironically, the act indirectly aided the Congress of Industrial Organizations (CIO) during its organizing drives of the 1930s. First-generation immigrants had in fact generally not been receptive to unionization efforts; the ethnic groups tended to distrust one another, many workers did not speak English, and many intended to return to their home countries. Their sons and daughters, however, embraced the union movement and contributed enormously to the CIO's growth after 1930.

Key Players

Davis, James J. (1873–1947): Born in Wales, Davis immigrated to the United States at age eight. He worked as a "puddler" in the steel industry at age 11 and later became active in the Amalgamated Association of Iron, Steel, and Tin Workers. After serving as secretary of labor for three presidents, he was elected to the U.S. Senate (1930–1945).

Johnson, Albert (1869–1957): Johnson was born in Springfield, Illinois, and began his career as a newspaper reporter and, later, news editor at the *Washington Post* and editor of the *Tacoma News*. He was elected to the U.S. House of Representatives as a Republican from Washington and served from 1913 to 1933.

Lodge, Henry Cabot (1850–1924): Lodge began his career as a faculty member at Harvard until he was elected to the U.S. House of Representatives (1887–1893) and the Senate (1893–1824). He is best remembered for his staunch opposition to the treaty ending World War I and President Wilson's linking it to U.S. entry in the League of Nations.

Reed, David Aiken (1880–1953): Born in Pittsburgh, Pennsylvania, Reed was an attorney and a veteran of World War I. He was originally appointed to the Senate, but he won reelection in his own right and served from 1922 to 1935. Although he was a conservative and an opponent of the New Deal, he was a strong supporter of Franklin Roosevelt's defense policies.

See also: *Congress of Industrial Organizations; International Ladies Garment Workers Union.*

BIBLIOGRAPHY

Books

Archdeacon, Thomas. *Becoming American: An Ethnic History*. New York: Free Press, 1983.

Daniels, Roger. *Coming to America*. New York: HarperCollins, 1990.

Goldberg, David J. *Discontented America: The United States in the 1920s*. Baltimore, MD: Johns Hopkins University Press, 1999.

Lane, Thomas. *Solidarity or Survival? American Labor and European Immigrants, 1830–1924*. Westport, CT: Greenwood Press, 1987.

—Michael J. O'Neal

National Trades' Union

United States 1834

Synopsis

Even before the United States' first true labor strike in 1786, unionism developed in the ranks of journeymen. Low

President Andrew Jackson. The Library of Congress.

wages and unreasonable hours, among other complaints, were common problems. To combat this, one of the workers' greatest weapons was the ability to strike with the support of their union. In addition to support during a strike, union representatives negotiated with the employers for better conditions. The early results of such action were usually far from positive. Employers mounted heavy resistance to unions, and legislation often favored their position. As unionism became more prevalent, employers began to band together to combat the trade societies. Until the late 1820s, because of the fear of employer reprisal, employees kept their union memberships private, and trade unions operated as virtual secret societies.

Despite the opposition, trade unions established themselves in the labor force and began making headway for improvements. Legislative changes encouraged union membership, and enrollments grew tremendously. One of the most important developments, however, was the establishment of national trade unions. It became apparent that an effective unification of the numerous trade unions would provide them with greater strength against their centralized opposition. A significant step toward solidarity came in August 1834 with the formation of the National Trades' Union (NTU): the first national labor union in United States history. Headed by John Commerford, the NTU played a vital role in the establishment of a 10-hour workday for navy yard workers. The NTU engaged in research and open discussion of labor issues. It pushed for social changes to better the lives of working men and women, including the establishment of public libraries. The organization became a vic-

Nicholas Biddle. The Library of Congress.

tim of difficult times and did not survive a period of economic turmoil called the "panic of 1837."

Timeline

1811: Worst earthquakes in U.S. history occur near New Madrid, Missouri, greatly altering the topography of a million-square-mile region.

1816: American Colonization Society is formed, in an attempt to ease racial tensions by sending freed slaves to Africa.

1821: Mexico declares independence from Spain.

1826: Friction or "Lucifer" matches are invented in England.

1830: Mormon Church is founded by Joseph Smith.

1834: British mathematician Charles Babbage completes drawings for the "analytic engine," a forerunner of the modern computer that he never builds.

1835: American inventor and painter Samuel F. B. Morse constructs an experimental version of his telegraph, and American inventor Samuel Colt patents his revolver.

1836: In Texas's war of independence with Mexico, the defenders of the Alamo, among them Davy Crockett and Jim Bowie, are killed in a siege. Later that year, Texas wins the Battle of San Jacinto and secures its independence.

1837: Coronation of Queen Victoria takes place in England.

1842: Scientific and technological advances include the development of ether and artificial fertilizer; the identification of the Doppler effect (by Austrian physicist Christian Johann Doppler); the foundation of biochemistry as a discipline; and the coining of the word *dinosaur*.

1846: The United States declares war on Mexico and adds California and New Mexico to the Union.

1848: Women's Rights Convention in Seneca Falls, New York, launches the women's suffrage movement.

Event and Its Context

The Roots of Trade Unionism

According to Florence Peterson in her book *American Labor Unions*, "The earliest labor organizations . . . were established in the skilled handicraft trades. The first organizations of labor in [the United States] appeared among the carpenters, shoemakers, printers, and tailors in the East Coast cities during the 1790s." Indeed, the first official labor strike occurred in 1786 when Philadelphia printers protested for a minimum wage of $6 a week. The country's second labor strike occurred five years later when carpenters in Philadelphia protested for a 10-hour workday. The growth of unionism in the trade community proceeded quickly between 1790 and 1820, despite strong opposition from employers, the master-craftsmen (or "masters"). The strongest and most durable unions were in the printing and shoemaking industries.

The growth of unionism in the trades is significant in light of the fact that workers in industries such as cotton and textiles suffered far worse conditions. By the turn of the nineteenth century, journeymen had far better working conditions than most laborers in the United States, relatively speaking. Even so, long hours and low wages remained the norm. What differentiated the journeymen from other laborers was their experience and education. As "skilled" laborers, they could expect and essentially demand higher wages and better working conditions. The economic climate, however, hindered them greatly.

One major factor in the growth of unionism came near the turn of the century. Mechanization had become prevalent in the production of goods. This, in turn, increased competition in the marketplace, and small masters were forced to cut production costs, including wages, to survive. This trend made it more difficult and expensive for journeymen to establish their own businesses. Thus, highly skilled journeymen were unable to rise to the master class and became trapped in a "wage" position. Over the years, the division between journeymen and masters continued to broaden. This division increased as the number of semi-skilled journeymen expanded in the printing and building industries, allowing employers to hire workers for lower wages. It became obvious to trade laborers that something needed to be done.

Early Trade Unions

In response to the trade industry's labor problems, journeymen began forming unions. These "trade societies," as they were called at the time, gathered wage earners together into organized groups. Striking became their weapon of choice. When employees expressed dissatisfaction with their working conditions, a union representative would relay the membership's demands to the employer, and if they were not met, a strike typically took place. The unions used members' dues to maintain the workers during strikes.

One problem created by trade societies involved the increased separation between journeymen and masters, as well as between journeymen and semiskilled laborers. Most labor groups refused membership to masters in the belief that an employer's interests were in opposition to those of the journeymen. In addition, apprentices were barred from union membership because employers could easily replace trained journeymen with semiskilled and women laborers. As such, workers were required to finish their apprenticeship before they could join unions or work in union shops. This separation proved a disservice to the union's goals. Masters experienced deep bitterness against union involvement in their shops. This stemmed from wage disputes and from limitations placed on their businesses by the unions, including the limitation of apprentice hiring and the formation of "closed shops." Employers formed their own masters' associations to combat the trade societies, both through the courts and negative campaigning.

The early trade societies soon found themselves facing an unsympathetic community. Although most strikes were peaceful, violent protests such as the 1806 Philadelphia shoemakers strike gained the trade societies a bad reputation. The beatings of strikebreakers or "scabs" and the property damage caused by strikers did little to improve their public image. Criminal conspiracy trials held between 1806 and 1815 against "closed shops" typically found for the employers rather than the trade societies.

The end of the Napoleonic era marked another setback when foreign products began to flood the U.S. marketplace after trade embargoes were lifted. Competition among employers became fierce. The depression effectively ended trade unionism, and journeymen's societies only survived by uniting together. In many ways, this period provided unionists with the concept of joint unions and began the idea of national representation. The brief depression also foreshadowed how the Panic of 1837 would affect future trade unions.

Birth of the NTU

By 1820 the depression's hold on the nation had faded. Almost immediately, journeymen once more engaged in union activities. By that time a democratic movement had begun to overtake the nation. Unions were forming in all industries, not only in the trades. Labor publications such as Robert Owen's *Free Inquiry* and New York's *Workingman's Advocate* helped fuel the flames of unionism. By 1827 the American labor movement had truly begun. That same year several trade organizations united to form a citywide union in Philadelphia, also known as the Mechanics' Union of Trade Associations. This attempted federation of trade societies was the first in the United States, if not the world. The trend of unifying local trade associations was repeated in several U.S. cities between 1827 and 1837.

In addition to demands for wage increases and a 10-hour workday, unions sought social changes and legislative changes

affecting workers' rights. For example, laborers required liens on their work for wages and the establishment of free public schools. Other goals included the abolishment of conspiracy statutes that interfered with cooperative effort and collective bargaining and changes to the compulsory militia service (nonattendance could result in fines and imprisonment). The practice of imprisonment for debt became a key issue for unions. Citizens in debt could face jail time, even for shockingly small debts. In his book *A History of Trade Unionism in the United States*, Selig Perlman cited "an astounding case of a widow whose husband had lost his life in a fire while attempting to save the property of the man who later caused her imprisonment for a debt of 68 cents." He further explained, "In 1829 . . . about 75,000 persons were annually imprisoned for debt in the United States."

By 1829 the timing for such changes was right as the United States entered the Jacksonian era, also known as the "Age of the Common Man." President Andrew Jackson felt that the government should be for all the people, rather than the elite. The government became more sympathetic to the plight of journeymen and the trade societies. Over the next few years, workers won several victories, including the abolition of debtors' prison, free public schooling, a mechanics' lien law, and positive changes to labor conditions. One of the most important accomplishments was overcoming solidarity issues and combining the numerous trades toward the common good. On 14 August 1833 the first true "trades' union" organized in New York City. Several cities, including Baltimore, Boston, Philadelphia, and Washington, D.C., followed New York's example in the ensuing months, forming their own trade unions. It soon became common for other trades to lend their support when a specific trade group, such as carpenters, went on strike.

This concept of trade unity was taken one step further only a year later. Impressed with the successes gained by citywide trade unions, the General Trades' Union of New York invited delegates from several cities to meet to discuss the concept of a nationally based trade union. In late August 1834 representatives from Boston, Brooklyn, Newark, New York, Philadelphia, and Poughkeepsie attended the proposed labor convention. According to Philip Foner in his book *History of the Labor Movement in the United States*, delegates believed that "the rights of each [trade union member] would be sustained by every workingman in the country, whose aggregate wealth and power would be able to resist the most formidable apposition." At the convention's conclusion, the delegates had founded the NTU, America's first national labor organization. Ely Moore, a congressional labor candidate and editor of the labor paper *National Trades' Union*, became president of the organization. In addition, John Commerford, a journeyman chairmaker, headed the new federation of city trade unions.

The NTU

Success came quickly for the NTU, and by 1836 its affiliation had grown to 300,000 members. The NTU began organizing committees to discuss and plan labor reforms such as the first trade union program for women. These discussions expanded during annual conventions. For example, during its 1835 convention, the NTU passed a resolution that pushed for a national uniform wage policy with the right to engage in a general strike should employers unify against the movement. The NTU also urged its affiliations to campaign for the establishment of public libraries, perhaps one of the first such movements in the United States. The organization's national voice remained strong in the U.S. government as it prompted reforms in public education, factory legislation, and prison labor. Formed from the ranks of NTU, the Workingmen's Party became the world's first labor-oriented political party.

One of the NTU's greatest successes involved the 10-hour day legislation for government workers. The NTU formed a committee to collect data and research the problem of extended hours. According to Foner, the NTU tried to prove that "violent and unremitting bodily exertion for 12 or 14 hours a day, while it is exceedingly injurious to the health of the employed, [was] accompanied with no particular advantage to the employer." Essentially, a 12-hour employee would only accomplish the same amount of work as a 10-hour employee because of sheer exhaustion; thus the extra work hours served no purpose. In 1835 the NTU's representative, New York Representative Ely Moore, presented the committee's findings to Congress. The response was less than cordial: the matter was deemed unworthy of legislation. Undaunted, the NTU pushed forward. In 1836 a navy yard strike in Philadelphia gained the attention of President Jackson. Having previously supported Jackson's fight with the United States Bank, the NTU called in a favor and appealed to the president to enact a 10-hour system.

After reviewing the data collected by the NTU committee, Jackson established a 10-hour workday for government employees. However, the enactment applied only to the areas affected by the strike and those with existing trade unions. Outside of these areas, 12-hour and 14-hour workdays continued. Unsatisfied, the NTU continued to pressure the president to extend his enactment on a national level. It took another four years and another president before the 10-hour workday was established for government work on 31 March 1840. However, despite its role in achieving this monumental labor reform, the NTU would not be able to enjoy the victory. Like almost all trade unions, the NTU no longer existed in 1840, having become one of the many victims of the panic of 1837.

The Panic of 1837

Even as the NTU and other trade unions grew in strength, the chain of events culminating in their downfall had already begun. By 1837 the United States plunged into a deep depression. These troubled times crippled trade unions, and few survived the economic woes.

The reasons for the panic of 1837 were many, but chief among them was Jackson's "war" on the Bank of the United States. According to William Sumner in *The Forgotten Man*, "The chief purposes of which the Bank of the United States had been founded in 1816 were to provide a sound and uniform paper currency convertible with specie [money in coin], of uniform value throughout the Union, and to act as fiscal agent for the government." Unfortunately, from its inception in 1816 up to 1823, the bank's operations were wholly inefficient and, in some cases, illegal. Fortunately, in 1823, Nicholas Biddle took over as the bank's president. Under his guidance and over the next five years, the bank regained its efficiency and stability. However, this would not soothe President Jackson's animosity

for the bank. This resentment stemmed from Jackson's belief that the bank was unconstitutional and working for the upper classes at the expense of the working class. Despite strong opposition, Jackson's first attack removed all government deposits and distributed them among the state banks. Even after this action caused confusion and turmoil in the industrial sector, Jackson continued his attacks on the bank. When Biddle attempted to renew its charter four years ahead of schedule, Jackson went so far as to use one of his vetoes to crush the bank once and for all. Despite Biddle's best efforts, the Bank of the United States expired in 1836.

Meanwhile, numerous state banks that had been given government monies from the Bank of the United States began engaging in "wildcat" activities. The banks flooded the market with paper money and engaged in unregulated land speculation often involving federal lands. The import of foreign products, paid for with credit, increased drastically. New banks, with the same wildcat intentions, sprang up everywhere. Concerned about the growing trend of paper money being distributed without proper specie to back it, Jackson issued his infamous Specie Circular on 11 July 1836. The executive order required that the payment of federal land be made with only gold and silver. Although well intended, the Specie Circular threw the money market into a tailspin. Banks called in loans, and investors hurried to exchange paper money for hard currency. Already unsettled by the collapse of the Bank of the United States, which had held vast credit with Europe, foreign banks called in their loans as well. Foreign merchants, especially those in England, refused to export products without guaranteed payment in hard currency. Suddenly, hard currency virtually disappeared. In response, banks began calling in more loans from their customers just to survive. Caught between the banks and foreign creditors, businesses floundered. Things came to a head on 10 May 1837 when the New York banks suspended specie. This trend spread like wildfire throughout most of the nation. Over 300 banks completely failed and closed forever.

Financial panic and widespread bankruptcy ensued. Inflation swept through the United States, and wages were nearly cut in half. Unemployment soared to staggering levels. According to Reginald McGrane in his book *The Panic of 1837*, "Six thousand masons and carpenters and other workmen connected with building had been discharged" during 1837 just in New York City. One-third of American workers were unemployed by the fall of 1837, and the majority of others had only part-time work. Even those who kept their jobs were still plunged into dire financial straits. Hundreds of thousands worried about surviving the rapidly approaching winter.

Trade unions, local and national, quickly collapsed during the resulting depression. Among those to fade away was the NTU. The first blow of the panic struck the trade unions financially. Workers hardly had the money to feed themselves, let alone to pay union dues. Without these funds, the unions crumbled. The second and perhaps more deadly blow struck their bargaining power. For years, the strike was the unions' greatest threat. During the panic, tens of thousands of workers were eager to take any job they could get. Employers slashed wages by 30 and 50 percent, and workers did not complain. Those who did were easily replaced by the masses of unemployed laborers. Strikes essentially doomed the protesters to losing their jobs. In addition, with little or no income, the unions could do little to support their members during a strike. Their power had completely vanished. The trade unions and the NTU disappeared.

Trade Unionism After the Panic of 1837

Trade unionism continued to suffer during the mid-nineteenth century, troubled by the Panic's economic fallout and the Civil War. It would not be until the "Greenback" period of 1862 to 1879 that a true labor movement would begin again. During its short existence, however, the NTU had proven that the concept of national trade unions could work. That belief brought life to several national trade unions during the 1850s and 1860s, including the National Labor Union in 1866. The principles set by early trade unionists would live on, despite setbacks like the panic of 1837.

Key Players

Biddle, Nicholas (1786–1844): An American financier from Philadelphia, Biddle became the president of the Bank of the United States. The battle between his bank and the Jackson administration was one of the contributing factors to the Panic of 1837.

Commerford, John: A journeyman who specialized in chair and cabinet making, Commerford headed the National Trades' Union in 1834.

Jackson, Andrew (1767–1845): Born in Waxhaw, South Carolina, Jackson served as the United States' seventh president between 1829 and 1837. President Jackson's economic policies of the period contributed to the Panic of 1837.

Moore, Ely (1798–1860): Moore served as editor of the *National Trades Union*, a labor newspaper that perhaps inspired the naming of the NTU. During his presidency of the NTU, Moore also served as a New York representative in Congress, a position he used to help improve labor relations.

Van Buren, Martin (1782–1862): Vice president during the 1833–1837 period of the Jackson administration, Van Buren became the United States' eighth president in 1837. Because the Panic of 1837 began at the start of his administration, Van Buren was blamed for it, albeit unfairly. Van Buren's poor political response only enflamed the issue.

See also: *Mechanics' Union of Trade Associations; National Labor Union; Ten-hour Day Movement; Workingmen's Party (1828).*

BIBLIOGRAPHY

Books

Bullock, Edna, comp. *Selected Articles on Trade Unions.* New York: H. W. Wilson Company, 1916.

McGrane, Reginald C. *The Panic of 1837.* New York: Russell & Russell, 1965.

Perlman, Selig. *A History of Trade Unionism in the United States.* New York: MacMillan Company, 1923.

Peterson, Florence. *American Labor Unions.* New York: Harper & Brothers Publishers, 1952.

Sumner, William G. *The Forgotten Man, and Other Essays.* Freeport, NY: Yale University Press, 1919.

Other

Bancroft, Hubert H. *The Great Republic by the Master Historians.* Vol 3. 2002 [cited 14 October 2002]. <http://www.publicbookshelf.com/public_html/The_Great_Republic_By_the_Master_Historians_Vol_III/thepanic_ce.html>.

Flaherty, Edward. "A Brief History of Banking in the United States, 1816–1836." *The American Revolution—An.HTML Project.* 1997 [cited 14 October 2002]. <http://odur.let.rug.nl/~usa/E/usbank/bank04.htm>.

Gilder Leherman History Online. The Roots of American Economic Growth: Labor Protests (1820–1860) [cited 14 October 2002]. <http://www.gliah.uh.edu/database/article_display.cfm?HHID=610>.

Jossman, J. "Labor Day, Celebrating the Achievements of the American Labor Movement." Paper presented at the annual meeting of the Unitarians and Universalists Amalgamated, AFL-CIO. 2 September 2001.

Trask, H. A. "The Panic of 1837 and the Contraction of 1839–43: A Reassessment of Its Causes from an Austrian Perception and a Critique of the Free Banking Interpretation." Paper read at the Ludwick von Mises Institute, March 2002.

—Lee Ann Paradise

National Typographical Union

United States 1852

Synopsis

The groundwork for formation of the National Typographical Union was laid at a meeting in New York City on a chilly evening in early December 1850. Gathered together in Stoneall's Hotel on Fulton Street, 18 printers, representatives from local typographical associations in New York, New Jersey, Pennsylvania, Maryland, and Kentucky, discussed standards of craftsmanship, union discipline, and apprenticeship guidelines. They also explored the possibility of a national union and formed a temporary national leadership panel, headed by John F. Keyser of Philadelphia, who acted as chairman. Before going their separate ways, the delegates agreed to meet again in convention in Baltimore in September 1851. At the Baltimore convention, delegates resolved to form a national union. That union, the National Typographical Union, was formally organized at yet another convention, this one held in Cincinnati, Ohio, on 3 May 1852. The first national labor organization to endure to the present, the National Typographical Union in 1869 was renamed the International Typographical Union (ITU). Although the ITU merged into the Communication Workers of America (CWA) in 1987, it survives as a distinct unit within the CWA called the Printing, Publishing, and Media Workers Sector.

Timeline

1831: Unsuccessful Polish revolt is waged against Russian rule.

1837: British inventor Isaac Pitman devises his shorthand system.

1842: Scientific and technological advances include the development of ether and artificial fertilizer; the identification of the Doppler effect (by Austrian physicist Christian Johann Doppler); the foundation of biochemistry as a discipline; and the coining of the word *dinosaur*.

1847: Patenting of the first successful rotary press replaces the old flatbed press, in the United States.

1848: Scottish mathematician and physicist William Thomson, Lord Kelvin, introduces the concept of absolute zero, or the temperature at which molecular motion ceases. This value, -273°C, becomes 0K on his Kelvin scale of absolute temperature.

1851: Britain's Amalgamated Society of Engineers applies innovative organizational concepts, including large contributions from, and benefits to, members, as well as vigorous use of direct action and collective bargaining.

1852: Emigration from Ireland to the United States reaches its peak.

1852: France's Second Republic ends when Louis Napoleon declares himself Napoleon III, initiating the Second Empire.

1852: American inventor Elisha Graves Otis introduces the "safety" elevator, which has a safety brake to keep it from falling even if the cable holding it is completely cut.

1854: "The Charge of the Light Brigade" by Alfred Lord Tennyson and *Walden* by Henry David Thoreau are published.

1858: British explorer John Hanning Speke locates Lake Victoria, which he correctly identifies as the source of the Nile.

1862: American Richard Gatling invents the first practical machine gun.

Event and Its Context

Early Efforts at Organization

Workers in the printing trades were among the first American laborers to organize trade unions. Even before the end of the eighteenth century, a number of local unions had been formed within the printing industry, and in 1776 a group of New York City printers went on strike to press their demands for higher wages and better working conditions. In the wake of increased trade union activity during the 1820s and early 1830s, delegates from a handful of these local unions convened in Washington, D.C., in November 1836 to form a national union, the National Typographical Society (NTS).

The NTS, which had local unions in at least eight cities, was very short-lived, collapsing under the weight of the economic recession that followed the financial panic of 1837. Most of the local unions that had been members of the NTS survived, however. Once the economic contraction had ended in 1843, organizational activities within the print trades resumed with a vengeance. On 2 December 1850 delegates from local printing unions in Kentucky, Maryland, New York, New Jersey, and Pennsylvania, met at Stoneall's Hotel on Fulton Street in lower Manhattan (New York City). The 18 printers present at the meeting discussed such common concerns as union discipline, apprenticeship regulations, and standards of craftsmanship. They also looked at the possibility of forming a national umbrella organization to link their individual unions. Unable to tackle the complex task of putting together a national organization in just one meeting, delegates voted to convene the first-ever national printers' convention the following year in Baltimore, Maryland, to continue their discussions. Before returning home, they also formed a temporary national organization, naming John F. Keyser of Philadelphia, Pennsylvania, as chairman and F. J. Ottarson of New York City as secretary.

Formation of National Union

Printers reconvened in Baltimore on 12 September 1851. Presiding over the convention were the president, John W. Peregoy of Baltimore; two vice presidents, George E. Green of Louisville, Kentucky, and M. C. Brown of Philadelphia; and two secretaries, F. J. Ottarson of New York and John Hartman of New Jersey. As one of the first orders of business, printers set up an executive committee composed of three delegates from each state represented. Members of the executive committee were responsible for enforcing all resolutions passed by the convention, gathering information on matters of interest to the printing trade, and making arrangements for the next convention. Among the resolutions passed at the Baltimore convention was one providing for the formation of a union local in every town or city where six or more journeymen printers were employed. However, by far the most important resolution to come out of Baltimore was one calling for the formation of a national union. Delegates also agreed to hold their next convention in Cincinnati, Ohio, in May 1852.

The National Typographical Union was formally organized at the printers' national convention in Cincinnati on 3 May 1852. The initial membership of the new national union consisted of locals from 14 cities, most of them clustered in the eastern part of the United States. After a number of locals from Canada affiliated with the union during the following decade, the union's name was officially changed to the International Typographical Union (ITU) in 1869. Upon its formation, the national union represented workers from a number of crafts within the printing industry. These included pressmen, stereotypers and electrotypers, bookbinders, photoengravers, and compositors, the last of which dominated the membership. Over the years that followed, several of these specialized crafts broke away from the ITU in order to gain recognition for and better address their special needs.

Breakaway Groups from Within the ITU

The first of the special craftsmen to strike out on their own were the pressmen. Although the advance of technology had done little to change the work process of the compositors, who made up the largest segment of the ITU membership, half a century of mechanization had radically changed the nature of the pressmen's job. When the pressmen failed to convince the ITU leadership to recognize their specialized skills by adding "pressmen" to the union's name, they decided to establish a union of their own. That union, the International Printing Pressmen's Union (IPPU), was formed in October 1889 but in 1896 changed its name to International Printing Pressmen and Assistants' Union (IPPAU). Next to leave the ITU fold were the bookbinders, whose jobs were being mechanized in the 1890s. Their separate union, the International Brotherhood of Bookbinders (IBB), was formed in 1892.

Stereotypers and electrotypers, although relatively few in number, eventually grew unhappy within the ITU and in 1902 formed the International Stereotypers and Electrotypers Union (ISEU) in Cincinnati. Membership in the ISEU, representing a highly specialized trade, had reached only 5,400 by 1920. Last to quit the ITU were the photoengravers, most of whom worked in the newspaper industry. Trade-shop engravers had already formed their own independent unions. Both groups of engravers came together in 1904 to form the International Photoengravers Union (IPU), bringing an end to jurisdictional conflicts. These four craft unions that had broken away from the ITU, along with the Amalgamated Lithographers of America (ALA), were eventually united under the umbrella of the Graphic Communications International Union (GCIU), which received its charter on 1 July 1983.

Women in the ITU

Women had been employed in the printing industry since the second quarter of the nineteenth century, but the ITU at first was reluctant to admit women fully into the ranks of the union. In 1868 a separate local union of women typographers was established under a charter from the ITU in New York City. Augusta Lewis Troup, a typesetter with the *New York Era* and *New York World,* played a major role in establishing the Women's Typographical Union (WTU) No. 1 and served as its president for a decade. The following year Troup was also elected corresponding secretary of the ITU, the first woman to be elected to a national union office. From within the mostly male ITU, she worked tirelessly to bring women into full equality with men, while at the same time she helped swell the ranks of the WTU. Eventually the ITU agreed in 1878 to disband the WTU and admit rank and file women typographers to membership in the union. Another influential female leader in the ITU was Maud O'Farrell Swartz, who in 1913 joined ITU Local No. 6. She served as secretary of the Women's Trade Union League, New York, from 1917 to 1921 and as president of the National Women's Trade Union League from 1922 until 1926.

The ITU Gains Authority

When first organized, the ITU was little more than a loose confederation of local printing trade unions, all of which enjoyed a great deal of autonomy. That began to change in 1884 when the union's international leadership introduced a more centralized administration and hired a full-time organizer. Centralization advanced further in 1888 when the positions of international president and secretary-treasurer were made full-time, salaried jobs. That same year the ITU established a defense fund to assist striking locals. In the following years, the grip of the international organization over local unions was further strengthened. The international leadership won the right to withhold funds from dissident locals, and the union's growing corps of full-time representatives made it easier to monitor the activities of local unions. Although such steps greatly increased central control, collective bargaining continued to be conducted at the local level.

An early and passionate supporter of national labor unity, the ITU played a major role in the founding of the Federation of Organized Trades and Labor Unions of the United States and Canada in 1881. The federation was a predecessor to the American Federation of Labor (AFL). Ironically, it was the growing awareness of different crafts reflected in the formation of the AFL that promoted dissension within the ranks of the ITU. Many of the smaller crafts represented by the ITU began to chafe under the domination of the compositors. This growing discomfort eventually led many of the crafts to break away from the ITU and form their own unions. By the end of the first decade of the twentieth century, the membership of the ITU had been trimmed down, leaving it basically a craft union of typesetters.

The ITU's "Union Bug"

The ITU first began using the union label in the final two decades of the nineteenth century. The purpose of the label, also known as a "union bug," was five-fold: (1) a protection against nonunion print shops that might claim to provide union working conditions; (2) a part of a campaign to persuade customers to buy union-made products; (3) a sign that the product was produced with quality standards and good workmanship; (4) a means of attracting new members; and (5) a warning against trespass by competing unions. The ITU adopted its first bug in 1886. One of its earliest appearances was atop an editorial column in the 15 October 1891 edition of the union's publication, *Typographical Journal.* In 1897 the ITU, now made up almost exclusively of compositors, reached an agreement with the breakaway pressmen and bookbinders on a design for a new Allied Printing Trades Council bug. By 1911 all five major unions in the printing trade (the ITU, IBB, ISEU, IPU, and IPPAU) came together to form the International Allied Printing Trades Council (IAPTC), an interunion agency designed to control and promote use of the union label. By 1939 the bug of the IAPTC enjoyed general use throughout the printing industry, largely replacing the individual labels of the five craft unions.

Not surprisingly, early opposition to the printing unions' use of the label came from management. Print shop owners in the late 1880s organized the United Typothetae of America (UTA) to represent their collective interests, particularly in management's dealings with labor. In 1899 the UTA passed a resolution opposing use of the label by its member shops, which were strongly urged to stop putting the union bug on work produced in their shops.

Social Services Provided by the ITU

In the late nineteenth century the ITU, along with a handful of other unions, began to show an interest in developing a safety net for members through such benefits as pension plans to see members through old age, as well as plans to cover the costs of funerals. In 1892 the union opened the Union Printers' Home in Colorado Springs, Colorado. Originally planned as a home for aged and indigent union members, the facility was later expanded to encompass a hospital and a sanitarium for tuberculosis patients.

The early years of the ITU's existence were marred by conflict with rival unions. In 1873 a union of printers employed by German-language U.S. newspapers, active in several major cities of the United States, was established. Any threat that might have been posed by the German-American Typographia evaporated after 1894 when it agreed to amalgamate with the ITU under an agreement that preserved much of its autonomy. Less easily resolved was a jurisdictional dispute with the International Association of Machinists (IAM) that arose after the introduction of typesetting machinery. The IAM claimed that it should represent workers employed to operate such machinery, a claim the ITU bitterly contested. The printers union eventually prevailed, but only after a lengthy and bitter struggle with the IAM.

The ITU and the Formation of the Congress of Industrial Organizations

In the mid-1930s the ITU and its president, Charles Perry Howard, played a major role in the formation of the Committee for Industrial Organization, which was later to become the Congress of Industrial Organizations (CIO). The ITU, with Howard at its helm, joined with seven other unions—United Mine Workers of America, Amalgamated Clothing Workers of America, International Ladies' Garment Workers Union, United Textile Workers of America, Oil Field, Gas Well and Refinery Workers of America, United Hatters, Cap, and Millinery Workers International Union, and International Mine, Mill, and Smelter Workers—to form the committee. The Committee for Industrial Organization was originally conceived as part of the AFL but became an independent organization when most of the unions involved were expelled from the AFL in 1936. The ITU never affiliated with the CIO but continued to support the coalition of breakaway unions, a policy that eventually drew the wrath of the AFL leadership. In 1939 the AFL suspended the ITU for its opposition to a special AFL assessment to fund an organizing campaign to fight the CIO. The typographical union was not reinstated by the AFL until 1944. Despite their differences, the AFL and CIO eventually reached an understanding and merged in 1955 to form the AFL-CIO.

Opposition to the Taft-Hartley Act

The ITU was one of the most outspoken opponents of the Taft-Hartley Act, enacted by Congress in 1947. The statute outlawed the closed shop and permitted union shops only when approved by a majority of a shop's employees. The act also prohibited jurisdictional disputes and secondary boycotts. The legislation was anathema to the ITU, which had long placed great emphasis on the closed shop and the strict enforcement of its seniority system. Led by Woodruff Randolph, the union's president at the time, the ITU directed much of its spending to a campaign to change what it considered the most undesirable features of the act.

Merger with the Communication Workers of America

In 1979 the International Mailers Union merged with the ITU. However, in the years that followed, dramatic changes in the printing industry greatly weakened the union. In 1987 the ITU affiliated with the Communication Workers of America (CWA). Recognizing the unique nature of the work performed by its ITU members, the CWA created a new Printing, Publishing, and Media Workers Section (PPMWS), giving it a certain degree of autonomy within the CWA.

Key Players

Howard, Charles Perry (1879–1938) Born in Harvel, Illinois, Howard worked as a boy in the railroad and mining industries before finally becoming involved in the printing trade. He joined an ITU local in Tacoma, Washington, in 1907 and quickly became heavily involved in union affairs. In 1922 he was elected vice president of the ITU, succeeding to the presidency the following year. In the 1930s he aligned himself with the AFL industrial union splinter group led by John L. Lewis. After the formation of the CIO, Howard was named secretary, although the ITU never formally joined the CIO.

Swartz, Maud O'Farrell (1879–1937): Born in Ireland, Maud O'Farrell immigrated to the United States after spending some time in Germany and France, where she was educated in convent schools. In America she worked as a typesetter. She was married briefly to fellow printer Lee Swartz. She became active in the Women's Trade Union League, serving as its president from 1922 to 1926.

Troup, Augusta Lewis (1848–1920): Orphaned in infancy, "Gussie" Lewis went to work as a reporter and typesetter, eventually becoming involved in establishing the Women's Typographical Union (WTU) No. 1. She served as president of the WTU from its inception in 1868 until it was disbanded a decade later by the ITU. Troup also served as corresponding president of the ITU, becoming the first women elected to a national union office.

See also: *Congress of Industrial Organizations; Federation of Organized Trades and Labor Unions of the United States and Canada; Taft-Hartley Act.*

BIBLIOGRAPHY

Books

Fink, Gary M., ed. *Labor Unions.* The Greenwood Encyclopedia of American Institutions Series. Westport, CT: Greenwood Press, 1977.

Taylor, Paul F. *The ABC-CLIO Companion to the American Labor Movement.* Santa Barbara, CA: ABC-CLIO, 1993.

Other

Birth of the International Typographical Union. Discovery Press [cited 30 October 2002]. <http://www.discoverypress.com/itu/ITU-history.html>.

The GCIU Story. Graphic Communications International Union [cited 30 October 2002]. <http://www.gciu.org/histtemp.shtml>.

Proposal for Inclusion of Union Label Description in Bibliographic and Archival Cataloging Guidelines.

School of Information Management & Systems, University of California, Berkeley [cited 30 October 2002]. <http://www.sims.berkeley.edu/~lcush/ UnionBug.htm>.

ADDITIONAL RESOURCES

Books

Lipset, Seymour Martin, Martin A. Trow, and James S. Coleman. *Union Democracy: The Internal Politics of the International Typographical Union.* New York: Free Press, 1956.

—Don Amerman

William Howard Sylvis. © Corbis. Reproduced by permission.

National Union of Iron Molders

United States 1859

Synopsis

In 1859 the National Union of Iron Molders (sometimes shortened to National Molders Union) was formed in Philadelphia, Pennsylvania, as a loose federation of existing local unions. William Howard Sylvis was the prominent leader of the union; some historians call him an important pioneer of the early American labor union movement. The unions of local iron molders retained nearly total independence and authority at the inception of the National Molders Union. In fact, the national body was only given authority in the areas of the "union card" and the collection of contributions for striking members. However, with the guidance and organizational abilities of Sylvis, the national union gained more central authority to direct the locals, and in the process gained the ability to finance its operations. The National Union of Iron Molders was eventually disbanded at the beginning of the Civil War but was reorganized two years later as the International Union of Iron Molders. Sylvis again was instrumental in its reformation and, ultimately, in its successful operation.

Timeline

1839: England launches the First Opium War against China. The war, which lasts three years, results in the British gaining a free hand to conduct a lucrative opium trade, despite opposition by the Chinese government.

1844: American artist and inventor Samuel F. B. Morse successfully sends the first message via telegraph: a series of dots and dashes that conveys the phrase, "What hath God wrought?," across a circuit between Baltimore, Maryland, and Washington, D.C.

1849: Harriet Tubman escapes from slavery in Maryland. Over the next eight years, she will undertake at least 20 secret missions into Maryland and Virginia to free more than 300 slaves through the so-called Underground Railroad.

1852: *Uncle Tom's Cabin* by Harriet Beecher Stowe, though far from a literary masterpiece, is a great commercial success, with over half a million sales on both sides of the Atlantic. More important, it has an enormous influence on British sentiments with regard to slavery and the brewing American conflict between North and South.

1855: *Leaves of Grass* is published by Walt Whitman.

1859: Building of the Suez Canal begins.

1859: Charles Darwin publishes *On the Origin of Species by Means of Natural Selection,* sparking enormous controversy with an account of humankind's origins that differs markedly from the Bible.

1859: Retired American railroad conductor Edwin L. Drake drills the first successful oil well in the United States, at Titusville, Pennsylvania.

1861: Within weeks of Abraham Lincoln's inauguration, the U.S. Civil War begins with the shelling of Fort Sumter. Six states secede from the Union, joining South Carolina to form the Confederate States of America (later joined by four other states) and electing Jefferson Davis as president. The first major battle of the war, at Bull Run or Manassas in Virginia, is a Confederate victory.

1865: U.S. Civil War ends with the surrender of General Robert E. Lee to General Ulysses S. Grant at Appomattox, Virginia. More than 600,000 men have died, and the South is in ruins, but the Union has been restored.

1869: The first U.S. transcontinental railway is completed.

Event and Its Context

As early as the 1820s, iron molders (workers who build iron objects, called castings, by pouring molten iron into a hollow mold) in the United States were complaining of such problems as low wages, long working hours, and partial payments required to be made to company stores. Many tried to remedy their problems by forming fraternal and social organizations to help ailing members; buying and operating their own cooperative foundries; and other, mostly ineffectual, measures. The first real hint of organized activity that could rightfully be called an iron molders union was within a Philadelphia, Pennsylvania, iron foundry (a workplace for casting metal such as iron) in 1833. Other local unions soon followed in that same year in the cities of Boston, Massachusetts, and Pittsburgh, Pennsylvania.

First Temporary Iron Molders Organizations

The industrial depression that occurred in 1837 had precipitated the reduction of wages of iron molders, along with other U.S. workers. Because work was scarce, employers possessed the upper hand with regards to employment. As a result, an ineffective society was formed in Philadelphia; it was composed of molders from several foundries. It survived for only a short period of time, and no unions were established for the next 10 years.

In 1847 the molders in the stove foundries of Cincinnati, Ohio, were organized to counter the attempt by management to reduce wages. The labor organization was successful in preventing the wage cut, but once the problem was solved, the organization disbanded. Other new organizations were later established in New York City, in Cincinnati, and, again, in Philadelphia. All of these unions were essentially social in nature, with only traces of economic interests. They disappeared as quickly as they were formed.

First Permanent Local Union

The iron molders of Philadelphia organized a union in 1853 called the Journeymen Iron Molders Association. Then, on 16 July 1855 the first permanent iron molders union was organized in Philadelphia: the Stove and Hollowware Molders Union of Philadelphia (commonly shortened to the Philadelphia Molders Union). The constitution of the new economic organization pledged members to secure employment for other union members in preference to nonmembers, prohibited members from undercutting a standard union wage of $10 a week, and provided benefits for men on authorized strikes.

Sylvis First Appears

The most prominent leader of iron molders during this time was William Howard Sylvis. He did not, however, join the Philadelphia Molders Union until 1857, when a strike to prevent a wage reduction occurred at the foundry where he worked. After his fiery temper caught the attention of union members, he joined on 5 December 1857 and was quickly elected recording secretary of the union. Sylvis soon became active in union activities, helping to strengthen the union with his aggressive participation. The panic of 1857 and the depression that followed eliminated many trade unions, while others survived only by combining with similar organizations in the same trade. The condition of the Philadelphia Molders Union, like others of that era, became desperate.

Iron Market Expands

The decade preceding the Civil War (1861–1865) was especially good for the Philadelphia Molders Union due primarily to the expansion of the iron market in the northeastern United States and the Ohio River area between Louisville, Kentucky, and Cincinnati, Ohio. The expansion was fueled by the railroad industry, which had recently quadrupled its number of rails to 30,000 miles. Because the growth in the railroads cheapened freight costs, iron products were in huge demand.

The good times for iron molders did not last, however, as foundries saw the opportunity to increase their profits by eliminating the competition through mass production. Consequently, skilled molders found themselves working alongside many unskilled workers in order to increase production. Additionally, ironworkers were often required to provide their own tools, purchase their family needs at company-owned stores, and sign contracts that withheld part of their wages until their contract was completed. As a result of these unfair conditions, unions rapidly grew during this period. As companies increased their shares of the national market, the leaders of the local unions felt bargaining powers shrink. They were ineffective in bringing about major reforms because most employers paid their workers the wage that was paid by the cheapest producer in the industry.

First National Union

Though he had only four months of union experience, Sylvis encouraged the Philadelphia union to coordinate activities with the other local unions. Sylvis himself communicated with the other molders' organizations about supporting each other in matters such as regulating their trade and preventing strikebreaking. On 14 December 1858 Sylvis introduced a resolution at the Philadelphia meeting to appoint a committee to investigate the organization of a national convention. Sylvis became the secretary of the committee. Support for a national organization developed primarily due to bitter strikes between molders and foundries. Soon a national convention, coordinated primarily by the efforts of Sylvis, met on 5 July 1859 in Philadelphia. The delegation was composed of 35 delegates representing 12 local unions. The convention formed a provisional organization and drew up a tentative constitution.

A second convention was held in Albany, New York, from 10 to 14 January 1860. The representatives of more than 1,000 molders—46 delegates from 18 unions—officially agreed to form the National Union of Iron Molders. The members elected Isaac J. Neall as the union president; Sylvis was subsequently elected as national treasurer and played the leading role at the convention. Sylvis voiced the words "Resolved, that this Convention do now resolve itself into a National Union." Because of his dedication in organizing the conventions and his carefully planned agenda at the convention, many labor historians regard Sylvis as actually having founded the National Union of Iron Molders.

Constitution

The original constitution of the National Molders Union gave limited power to the president and executive committee. Only advice could be given to local unions out on strike. Little empowerment was given to the national union by the local unions; for instance, it could do little to prevent the numerous strikes that occurred annually within the local organizations. During the second convention in 1860 the national union recommended that all strikes be discontinued. The resolution was not approved, and the National Molders Union could only urge the locals to strike after all other remedies had been tried and failed.

The National Molders Union grew in members and financial strength over the next few years. In fact, by the beginning of the Civil War it was one of the best-organized and most powerful trade unions in the country. Much of the credit for this success goes to Sylvis, who worked unselfishly to promote the union's positions. Also during this time, control of union activities began to transfer from the local unions to the central National Molders Union. Sylvis is widely regarded as the person most responsible for initiating actions to transform the loosely knit federation of local unions into a powerful central body. Strikes for better wages and improved conditions of employment became more frequent, and the outcomes were more positive for the employees.

Disbanded in 1862

Important victories in 1859 and 1860 had increased the national union's power, and it used that power to instigate strikes to preserve the rights and dignity of its workers. The large numbers of strikes eventually depleted the union's financial reserves. The chaos created by the Civil War also caused deterioration to both the local and national unions as foundry owners were forced to cut back on production in order to survive.

In 1862 the national union was too weak to hold its scheduled convention in July. Sylvis no longer held a position within the union. He watched helplessly as the union he had so arduously worked for disintegrated, partially from the economic chaos and strikes during the Civil War, but also from a lack of effective management. Sylvis vowed he would rebuild an organization that would become strong enough to survive any crisis.

Recreated as an International Union

The National Molders Union became virtually extinct during the Civil War, though some local unions continued to communicate with one another, which led to talk of another national union. However, union leaders had either been killed in the war or were busy with other affairs. But Sylvis was still adamant about reviving the national union. With the endorsement of the Philadelphia molders, he called a Pittsburgh convention for 6 January 1863. Although turnout was light, with only 21 delegates from 15 cities, Sylvis was elected unanimously as president of the new union.

The organization's name was now the International Union of Iron Molders (commonly shortened to International Molders Union), acknowledging the Canadian locals that were now represented. From the start it was an upward battle for Sylvis because the new international union was a mere shell with little power. But Sylvis coordinated the organization of all the committees in order to make the union an active voice of the molders. During 1863 he visited more than 100 cities with foundries that were organized at the local level. He spoke at union meetings, explained the principles of trade unionism, sold subscriptions to the labor papers, and pleaded with local union members

to support the common cause of the international union. The organizing tour increased membership and created new local unions. He also met with employers who were at odds with iron molder employees. He gained union recognition from many of these employers through a mixture of threats and conciliatory proposals.

Sylvis also established the *Iron Molders Journal,* a monthly newspaper containing such articles as synopses of communications between local unions and editorials. Sylvis contended that the publication provided a means for strengthening the International Molders Union and giving a voice to labor.

At this time Sylvis was widely recognized as the best-known labor leader in the country. At the 1866 convention, Sylvis reported that the International Molders Union consisted of 137 local unions with nearly 10,000 members, about nine-tenths of the journeymen iron molders in the United States. Because of this nearly absolute control of the iron molders trade, the International Molders Union was highly respected in the union community.

Accomplishments

The period during which the National Molders Union (and subsequently the International Molders Union) served its iron molder members was a critical one in the history of American trade unionism. Accomplishments of the National Molders Union included higher wages, shorter working days, job security through elimination of cheap labor competition, and status in the community for the workingman commensurate with his importance to society. Under the leadership of Sylvis, the National Union of Iron Molders challenged the power of the iron foundry owners. In 1868 the *New York Sun* declared that because of his tireless efforts at directing and organizing a national labor union, and his abilities at bringing together labor leaders, the name of Sylvis "is familiar as a household word."

Before the National Molders Union, the activities of national unions had yet to be established, and the ideas of a centralized national trade union were still not known. Local unions had been largely self-governing, fearful of giving a national union any authority. The National Union of Iron Molders laid the foundation for a nationwide movement of centralized trade unions.

Key Players

Sylvis, William Howard (1828–1869): Organizer of the National Molders Union and the International Molders Union, Sylvis was also president of the National Labor Union (1868–1869). During his lifetime, Sylvis earned a reputation as a defender of the rights of laborers and as a devoted and capable leader of all working people. His determination and dedication made him a popular national labor leader during the Civil War period.

BIBLIOGRAPHY

Books

Austin, Aleine. *The Labor Story: A Popular History of American Labor 1786–1949.* New York: Coward-McCann, Inc., 1949.

Commons, John R., et al. *History of Labour in the United States.* New York: The Macmillan Company, 1921.

Dulles, Foster Rhea, and Melvyn Dubofsky. *Labor in America: A History.* Arlington Heights, IL: Harlan Davidson, Inc., 1993.

Grossman, Jonathan. *William Sylvis, Pioneer of American Labor: A Study of the Labor Movement During the Era of the Civil War.* New York: Columbia University Press, 1945.

Taft, Philip. *Organized Labor in American History.* New York: Harper & Row, 1964.

OTHER

Images of Pittsburgh Historic Labor Sites [cited 19 October 2002]. <http://www.pittsburghaflcio.org/tourfoto.html>.

William H. Sylvis Collection. Special Collections and University Archives, Manuscript Collections, Indiana University of Pennsylvania [cited 19 October 2002]. <http://www.lib.iup.edu/spec_coll/mg99.html>.

—William Arthur Atkins

William Howard Taft. The Library of Congress.

National War Labor Board

United States 1918–1919

Synopsis

With growing labor unrest and incidents of strikes increasing throughout the United States during World War I, government advisors and labor leaders insisted that President Woodrow Wilson create a more direct national labor policy. Wilson instructed the Department of Labor to formulate a policy to address the nation's growing labor concerns. William B. Wilson, secretary of labor, created a War Labor Conference Board (WLCB) composed of representatives from business and labor interest. The WLCB was to recommend to the Department of Labor specific labor policies. The WLCB recommended the creation of a federal agency to enforce federal labor policy and formulate recommendations. In April 1918, with these recommendations in hand, President Wilson created the National War Labor Board (NWLB). Throughout its short life, the NWLB insisted that all strikes and lockouts cease until the end of the war. In addition, the agency supported the principles of collective bargaining, an eight-hour work day, and equal pay for men and women as well as encouraging union growth. Although the federal government believed that the NWLB was an effective avenue by which to curb labor unrest, the end of the war and demobilization made the NWLB obsolete. Thus by 1919 the federal government dismantled the NWLB.

Timeline

1898: United States defeats Spain in the three-month Spanish-American War. As a result, Cuba gains it independence, and the United States purchases Puerto Rico and the Philippines from Spain for $20 million.

1903: Russia's Social Democratic Party splits into two factions: the moderate Mensheviks and the hard-line Bolsheviks. Despite their names, which in Russian mean "minority" and "majority," respectively, Mensheviks actually outnumber Bolsheviks.

1910: Revolution breaks out in Mexico and will continue for the next seven years.

1914: On 28 June in the town of Sarajevo, then part of the Austro-Hungarian Empire, Serbian nationalist Gavrilo Princip assassinates Austrian Archduke Francis Ferdinand and wife Sophie. In the weeks that follow, Austria declares war on Serbia, and Germany on Russia and France, while Great Britain responds by declaring war on Germany. By the beginning of August, the lines are drawn, with the Allies (Great Britain, France, Russia, Belgium, Serbia, Montenegro, and Japan) against the Central Powers (Germany, Austria-Hungary, and Turkey).

1916: Battles of Verdun and the Somme are waged on the Western Front. The latter sees the first use of tanks, by the British.

1918: The Bolsheviks execute Czar Nicholas II and his family. Soon civil war breaks out between the communists and their allies, known as the Reds, and their enemies, a collection of anticommunists ranging from democrats to czarists, who are known collectively as the Whites. In March, troops from the United States, Great Britain, and France intervene on the White side.

1918: The Second Battle of the Marne in July and August is the last major conflict on the Western Front. In November, Kaiser Wilhelm II abdicates, bringing an end to the war.

1918: Upheaval sweeps Germany, which for a few weeks in late 1918 and early 1919 seems poised on the verge of communist revolution—or at least a Russian-style communist coup d'etat. But reactionary forces have regained their strength, and the newly organized Freikorps (composed of unemployed soldiers) suppresses the revolts. Even stronger than reaction or revolution, however, is republican sentiment, which opens the way for the creation of a democratic government based at Weimar.

1918: Influenza, carried to the furthest corners by returning soldiers, spreads throughout the globe. Over the next two years, it will kill nearly 20 million people—more than the war itself.

1921: As the Allied Reparations Commission calls for payments of 132 billion gold marks, inflation in Germany begins to climb.

1925: European leaders attempt to secure the peace at the Locarno Conference, which guarantees the boundaries between France and Germany, and Belgium and Germany.

Woodrow Wilson. The Library of Congress.

Event and Its Context

Origins

The NWLB existed because of the unique circumstances of World War I and the growing influence of labor within the Wilson administration. Throughout the nineteenth century the federal government had a *laissez-faire* interest in labor relations. Before 1900, if government intervened in a dispute between labor and management, it was usually in support of management by helping to put down a strike. President Theodore Roosevelt deviated from this policy by intervening in the 1902 anthracite coal strike, which resulted in the miners and their union winning some concessions. His successor, President William Howard Taft, laid the foundation for the creation of the Department of Labor and the Commission on Industrial Relations. Even with limited attention directed toward labor by the executive branch during the Progressive Era, federal policymakers were still apathetic at best to the concerns and the demands of American workers. President Woodrow Wilson was the first president to appear concerned for the plight and the vote of American workers. To gain the support and appreciation of labor unions and the American Federation of Labor, President Wilson appointed William B. Wilson as the first secretary of labor. By appointing Wilson, who was a former official in the United Mine Workers, as secretary of labor, President Wilson

gave labor its greatest voice in the federal government up to that point in time.

Early in the war, President Wilson intervened in a series of strikes that threatened wartime production. He then decided to create a more direct national labor policy. Wilson issued an executive order in January of 1918 to create the War Labor Administration, which was to be headed by Secretary Wilson. President Wilson gave the War Labor Administration the power to reorganize existing labor agencies. Soon after its creation the War Labor Administration created the War Labor Conference Board (WLCB), which would be responsible for establishing an all-encompassing labor agency to recommend and support federal labor policy. William Howard Taft and Frank P. Walsh, a successful and influential labor attorney, cochaired the WLCB. The members of the board were split evenly between promanagement and prolabor interests. Although the members came from different perspectives concerning labor disputes, all of the members of the board agreed that an end to the labor strife would be best for the country during wartime. From January to March 1918, the WLCB formulated labor policies and submitted a report of those recommendations to President Wilson. By April, Wilson publicly supported those polices and reassembled the WLCB and its members into a new agency known as the National War Labor Board (NWLB).

Principles, Policies, and Framework

The WLCB report that was submitted to Wilson would be the foundation of the labor policy that the NWLB would spearhead. The NWLB rallied around one guiding principle: no strikes or lockouts during the war. The NWLB would also agree to support eight measures to quell labor tensions. The measures included collective bargaining; support of the status quo within the workplace with regard to open shop; protective labor laws; union shops; equal pay for men and women; eight-hour workdays where proscribed by law (they were open to negotiation in other places); measures that delayed or reduced production; and a program to allow the war industries to have access to skilled workers in high demand. The NWLB also would also take into consideration preexisting labor and wage conditions when formulating policies concerning wages, hours, and conditions. Finally, the NWLB supported the principle of a "living wage." Although both labor and management were represented on the NWLB, labor made tremendous gains through these measures, whereas business interests were not equally represented through policy or action. All agreed that these policies would help to settle the labor unrest. Even though the NWLB supported all these progressive labor policies, it was still only a voluntary association with no legal authority within the private sector. When confronted with a strike or a lockout, the NWLB procedure was to send investigators to research the incident and eventually hold hearings to determine a decision. If both sides agreed to meet with the NWLB, then it could bind both parties to its decision. If the NWLB could not get both sides to agree to meet, then it would publish its decision and hope that popular opinion would persuade both sides to agree to a settlement.

Investigations and Rulings

In April 1918 a conflict involving the Commercial Telegraphers Union of America (CTUA) became the first real case to be addressed by the NWLB. The president of the Western Union Company fired 800 employees who had joined the CTUA. The CTUA mobilized for a strike before the NWLB stepped in to avert a shutdown of the nation's communication systems. Management at Western Union decided not to work with the NWLB, and in fact the president of the company, Newcomb Carlton, even rejected the moderate voices on the board. Partly because of Carlton's intransigence, Taft, who represented the probusiness members of the board, decided to side with Walsh and recommend a reinstatement of the fired employees. Carlton chose not to adhere to the board's recommendations. In response, President Wilson nationalized the telegraph lines, giving legitimacy to the new agency and symbolically demonstrating to employers that the administration would punish companies that refused to cooperate with the NWLB.

Another important decision by the NWLB was in response to a strike by machinists in Waynesboro, Pennsylvania. On 23 May 1918, 3,000 machinists went on strike in response to employers' use of semiskilled workers in skilled positions. The strikers believed that dependence on unskilled and semiskilled labor kept wages down. The NWLB immediately investigated and soon concluded that workers in Waynesboro deserved a minimum wage set at 40 cents an hour. This was an important decision because it cemented support for the idea of a "living wage" within the federal government.

At the same time as the Waynesboro decision, the NWLB handed down another important ruling. This time machinists with the Worthington Pump Company in Cambridge, Massachusetts, demanded that their job classifications be protected from their employer who chose not to recognize certain skills associated with specific positions. Industry utilized this tactic to keep skilled wages down. The NWLB found in favor of the local union and sent federal agents to classify jobs at the plant.

In these early decisions, the NWLB recognized the grievances of labor over management. In fact, issues such as job classification and a "living wage" had been confined previously to workers and their unions, but as the NWLB favored these policies, these issues found more legitimacy outside the labor movement.

NWLB and Worker Organizing

Although the NWLB had a direct impact on federal labor policy during the war, it also enjoyed an indirect impact on worker activism and organizing. One of the first NWLB cases in this arena was its decision against General Electric. The Pittsfield Metal Trades Council brought this case to the attention of the board. Workers for General Electric in Pittsfield, Massachusetts, went on strike to protest the use of "yellow-dog contracts." Before hiring workers, employers would force them to sign these contracts, which forbade them from joining a union during their tenure with the company. Earlier in 1917, the Supreme Court had handed down the decision in *Hitchman Coal and Coke Company v. Mitchell et al.,* which recognized the constitutionality of the yellow-dog contracts. The NWLB decided to suspend the use of these contracts for the duration of the war, not only for the workers in Pittsfield, but for also for similar incidents that came before the board. Not only did the NWLB strike down the yellow-dog contracts, but it also supported the peaceful participation of workers in strikes and banned the use of the military draft to intimidate union members or potential union members. Because the NWLB supported the rights of unions and of organizing, the board had significant influence over the increase of union activity and activism throughout the war. Membership in unions increased throughout the board's tenure, as did strikes and grievances filed with the board itself. NWLB actions led workers to believe that the federal government was supportive of their rights and grievances within the work place. Many employers, on the other hand, believed that labor unions used the NWLB as a tool to promote their own agendas.

In other cases the NWLB facilitated labor organizing. The NWLB organized war industry workers into committees for the purpose of collective bargaining. Previously, shop committees had been exclusive to a certain skill, thus several committees could exist within a single factory. By introducing one overall committee to negotiate collectively with a single employer, the NWLB united workers who previously had been divided within the workplace. Union members dominated these committees. Typically, if nonunion representatives were elected to a committee, they soon became members. Unions used these shop committees to push union issues and bring them to the attention of the employers. They also used their position and influence in the shop committees to promote union membership and activities. Shops that the NWLB helped to organize constituted over 45 percent of the cases brought before the board.

Not only did the NWLB shop committees help to organize different skilled workers within a single workplace, but they also helped to organize skilled and unskilled workers. Usually when skilled union members initiated a strike, the strikers approached the NWLB to ask for intervention. The board would then organize a shop committee made up of a handful of skilled workers. The skilled workers rose to prominence within the shop committee, and eventually they would organize unskilled labor under them. Thus the ranks of union membership rose as a direct consequence of NWLB action.

The NWLB and African American Workers

African American workers did not gain the same influence within federal labor policy as did their white counterparts. Walsh wanted to hire an African American representative to address cases involving African American workers, but the other members of the board did not agree with this approach. Instead, Walsh hired many white liberals to staff the NWLB. Many of those he hired had had previous success in organizing interracial unions in the Midwest. Walsh hoped that these agents would be successful in organizing both black and white workers in the South. This southern strategy was not popular with southern white politicians who complained about the influence of the NWLB on African Americans in the South. For example, Sidney Catts, then governor of Florida, compared federal labor agents to "carpetbaggers" who had in some views incited otherwise content southern blacks.

No case illuminates the relationship the of NWLB with African American workers better than that of the New Orleans Streetcar Drivers and Mechanics. The NWLB decided to establish a 42-cent minimum wage for all workers in the company. Local politicians and white union leaders demanded that the NWLB reconsider, because with such a high minimum wage, there would be more pay parity between black and white workers within the company, and blacks within the company would make more than whites in other industries in the city. To maintain the "Jim Crow" system in the South, the streetcar owners believed they would have to increase the pay of whites within the company and thus pay for it through higher ticket prices. Taft favored lowering the minimum wage to maintain racial hegemony within the city. Walsh caved in and the board recommended only a 38-cent minimum wage. Although the NWLB offered a glimmer of hope to African Americans that the federal government was interested in their grievances, nothing tangible materialized by way of policy for black workers.

Women in the Wartime Workplace

During wartime, women workers joined the workforces more than ever before. A large number of women entered the war industries. Labor unions reacted negatively to this because many employers hired women at a lower salary than men, thus unions and male workers feared that women in the workplace would drive them from their jobs. The NWLB reacted to this fear by supporting the policy of equal pay for men and women performing the same task. The board believed that if men and women received the same pay, then employers would be discouraged from hiring women over men in the workplace. At a time when women did not enjoy suffrage in the national political culture, they participated actively in shop committee elec-

tions. In fact, many agents noted that it was not unusual for women to vote in larger numbers than men in workplace elections. This newfound political agency was also evident in workplaces in which women were not allowed to vote. In those cases women demanded that the NWLB nominate women as representatives on the shop committees.

The NWLB employed many women who wanted to move beyond the issue of voting within the workplace and demanded that the board address issues of equality on the job. Not only did these women demand equal pay, but they also demanded proportional representation on the committees that negotiated collective bargaining. Although the sense of organizing and activism transcended gender, women made superficial gains within the board itself. Throughout most of its existence female labor activists demanded that the president name at least two women to the NWLB. Both President Wilson and Walsh rebuffed these efforts by claiming that the board was qualified to address the concerns of women in the workplace. Activists engaged in a long hard struggle to convince the NWLB to establish a policy whereby women would be represented on shop committees in positions traditionally held by men.

The Continuing Impact

During its existence, the NWLB settled only 72 of the 847 cases that it heard. With the Armistice of 1918, business leaders quickly began to clamor for the end of the NWLB. They believed that the board incited labor agitation, which business leaders were willing to address as part of the war measure but not as a precedent for postwar labor relations. Walsh and his assistant, Basil Manly, tried feverishly to create some kind of policy that would allow for a transition of the board into postwar America. Their recommendations to maintain some spirit of the board after the war met with deadlock. Taft and probusiness interests did not want the board extended and quickly rallied to put an end to the board altogether. Discouraged, Walsh resigned as cochair. Manly replaced him in that position, and the board decided to stop hearing cases by the end of 1918. In December 1918 the board voted to disband.

The NWLB had a great impact during its time as well as after. Throughout its tenure, membership in unions increased with a simultaneous sharp increase in the frequency of strikes. In fact, the NWLB had encouraged labor activism. Ninety percent of the complaints filed with the board came from workers. As a result of the influence of the NWLB, relations between the government, workers, and big business would never be the same. This wartime style of mediation had a lasting effect on the nature of mediation in American labor.

Key Players

Manly, Basil (1886–1950): Manly was an assistant and close advisor to Frank P. Walsh, cochair of the NWLB. Walsh and Manly worked closely on NWLB policies. When Walsh resigned his position with the NWLB late in its tenure, Manly replaced him as cochairman.

Taft, William Howard (1857–1930): Taft served one term as president before Woodrow Wilson. President Wilson appointed him cochair of the NWLB along with Frank P. Walsh.

Walsh, Frank P. (1864–1939): Walsh was a lawyer and labor advocate. President Wilson appointed Walsh chairman of the United States Commission on Industrial Relations during his first term. When Wilson created the NWLB, he appointed Walsh cochair along with former president William Howard Taft.

Wilson, Woodrow (1856–1924): Wilson was president of the United States during World War I. To combat the possibility of disruptions in wartime production, Wilson created the NWLB to solve labor disputes during the war.

See also: *Department of Labor; Jim Crow Segregation and Labor.*

BIBLIOGRAPHY

Books

Conner, Valerie Jean. *The National War Labor Board: Stability, Social Justice, and the Voluntary State in World War I.* Chapel Hill: University of North Carolina Press, 1983.

Gitlow, Abraham L. *Wage Determination Under National Boards.* New York: Prentice Hall, 1953.

McCartin, Joseph A. "An American Feeling: Workers, Managers, and the Struggle over Industrial Democracy during the World War I Era." In *Industrial Democracy in America: The Ambiguous Promise*, edited by Nelson Lichtenstein and Howell John Harris. New York: Cambridge University Press, 1993.

———. *Labor's Great War: The Struggle for Industrial Democracy and the Origins of Modern American Labor Relations, 1912–1921.* Chapel Hill: University of North Carolina Press, 1997.

Periodicals

McCartin, Joseph A. "Abortive Reconstruction: Federal War Labor Policies, Union Organization, and the Politics or Race, 1917–1920." *Journal of Policy History* 9 (spring 1997): 155–183.

———. "Using the Gun Act: Federal Regulation and the Politics of the Strike Threat during World War I." *Labor History* 33 (fall 1992): 519–528.

—Robert Cassanello

National Women's Trade Union League

United States 1903

Synopsis

Beginning with the Industrial Revolution, the American workforce had a female presence. Like their male counterparts, women laborers suffered intolerable working conditions, low wages, and long hours. Unlike their male counterparts, however, they did not possess the same rights or respect in the workforce. Therefore, their interests were not represented with the same vigor as men, and women rarely held positions of union leadership.

Although female members of the American Federation of Labor (AFL) assumed an active role in union activities, the women's efforts were often met with resistance. After an AFL meeting in Boston, it became clear that the organization did not intend to embrace women in leadership roles. If women did not want to continue to be under-represented, therefore, they would have to take a bold new step. This step resulted in the formation of the National Women's Trade Union League (WTUL) in 1903. Uniting women from all classes, the WTUL was the first national association dedicated to organizing women workers. In the spirit of the social settlement, the league successfully focused on providing women with educational opportunities as well as improved working conditions through legislation and union organization.

Timeline

1883: Foundation of the League of Struggle for the Emancipation of Labor by Marxist political philosopher Georgi Valentinovich Plekhanov marks the formal start of Russia's labor movement. Change still lies far in the future for Russia, however: tellingly, Plekhanov launches the movement in Switzerland.

1893: Henry Ford builds his first automobile.

1899: Start of the Second Anglo-Boer War, often known simply as the Boer War.

1903: Anti-Jewish pogroms break out in Russia.

1903: Henry Ford establishes the Ford Motor Company.

1903: Russia's Social Democratic Party splits into two factions: the moderate Mensheviks and the hard-line Bolsheviks. Despite their names, which in Russian mean "minority" and "majority," respectively, Mensheviks actually outnumber Bolsheviks.

1903: Polish-born French chemist Marie Curie becomes the first woman to be awarded the Nobel Prize.

1903: One of the earliest motion pictures, *The Great Train Robbery,* premieres.

1903: United States assumes control over the Panama Canal Zone, which it will retain until 1979.

1903: Wright brothers make their first flight at Kitty Hawk, North Carolina. Though balloons date back to the eighteenth century and gliders to the nineteenth, Orville Wright's twelve seconds aloft on 17 December mark the birth of practical human flight.

1906: Founding of the British Labour Party.

1913: Two incidents illustrate the increasingly controversial nature of the arts in the new century. Visitors to the 17 February Armory Show in New York City are scandalized by such works as Marcel Duchamp's cubist *Nude Descending a Staircase,* which elicits vehement criticism, and theatergoers at the 29 May debut of Igor Stravinksy's ballet *Le Sacré du Printemps* (*The Rite of Spring*) are so horrified by the new work that a riot ensues.

Event and Its Context

For many working-class women in the late nineteenth century, employment outside the home did not constitute a rebellion against their roles as wives and mothers. They worked out of necessity to escape the poverty they suffered and hoped to achieve some modicum of economic freedom. Such financial independence was often hard to find and certainly not encouraged for white married women, especially given the strength of the patriarchy. Working-class families also depended on the largely unpaid labor provided by wives and mothers, which included endless hours of sewing, cleaning, laundering, cooking, childrearing, and, in some unfortunate cases, even scavenging in the street. In fact, only a small percentage of white married women, between 3 and 5 percent, entered the labor force in the nineteenth century, and they did so primarily in response to dire circumstances such as the desertion, injury, or death of their husbands. Nonetheless, working outside the home served as more than an extension of the family economy; it helped to create informal female peer groups, women's "work space" cooperatives, and mutual support networks.

Banding together in mutual support was not uncommon for women of the time. They helped each other routinely in their domestic lives, living "simultaneously in an expressive world of female support rituals and networks and a repressive world of male-superior/female-subordinate routines." As historian Carol Smith-Rosenberg wrote, "Women revealed their deepest feelings to one another, helped one another with the burdens of housewifery and motherhood, nursed one another's sick, and mourned for one another's death. It was a world in which men made only a shadowy appearance." Certainly Smith-Rosenberg is not denying the "importance of women's relations with particular men," but there is plenty of evidence from diaries, for example, to suggest that women's relationships with one another differed dramatically in "emotional texture."

Indeed, the social norms encouraged separate roles for men and women; however, some women questioned this logic. Certainly this was true of the activists who attended a convention in Seneca Falls, New York, in 1848 to discuss the social, civil, and religious condition of women. Recognized by many historians as the official start of the women's rights movement, the gathering served as a forum for the exchange of ideas regarding the roles of women in society. Embracing the idea that women should be afforded the same rights as men, Elizabeth Cady Stanton wrote a treatise that called for women to have the legal right to vote. Many of her statements, considered radical at the time, became the root structure of today's definition of egalitarian liberal feminism, which correlates female subordination with the legal constraints that interfere with the ability of women to enter or succeed in the "public world." Many nineteenth-century feminist leaders believed, as do some modern feminists, that "gender justice" depends on making the rules of the game

Jane Addams. The Library of Congress.

fair, and ensuring that no class of people is systematically excluded from the race for goods or stature in society.

By the late 1880s new patterns of leadership were developing that embraced inclusion rather than exclusion; the social language used to communicate ideas was shaped and redefined, allowing feminist theory to emerge anew. Women wanted access to birth control and the freedom to explore their sexual natures. They wanted to escape the confines of patriarchal language and define themselves in terms that embraced their own self-awareness. This sometimes required new modes of thinking that were outside traditional frameworks. Inherent in this female consciousness was the idea that women should have the same opportunities as men and that women should be able to define their own goals.

In this spirit, affluent and college-educated women opted not to marry and instead carved out professional careers for themselves. These "New Women" were socially controversial because their claims of rights and privileges that had been reserved traditionally for middle- and upper-class men also rejected the conventional female roles. Yet, conversely, what Susan B. Anthony said in an 1893 speech still rang true for many women. She hypothesized that there were not more suffragettes "because women have been taught always to work for something else than their own personal freedom and the hardest thing

Second biennial convention, National Womens Trade Union League, Chicago, Illinois. © Corbis. Reproduced by permission.

in the world is to organize women for the one purpose of securing their political liberty and political equality."

By the end of the nineteenth century, increased access to education allowed women access to different types of employment. The advent of the typewriter prompted a shift from male clerks to female. Unwilling to remain quietly in their homes, more middle-class women began to participate in social reform activities. Immigrant women helped to support their families by working in sweatshops, and industrialization brought women into factories and realigned some jobs along gender lines. Women of color faced racial discrimination as well as gender bias. The variety among women's situations created a need for new leadership and a diversity of organizations.

Unfortunately, women who belonged to the American Federation of Labor (AFL) were rarely chosen for leadership positions. Many historians point out that the AFL chartered "ladies'" federal unions for "women's jobs," but according to historian James J. Kenneally, most affiliated unions "were not sympathetic to their needs. Some excluded women or made them feel uncomfortable or negotiated for inferior pay scales." The gender prejudice that permeated women's domestic lives was ever present in their professional lives as well. Indeed, the highly influential AFL labor leader Samuel Gompers had forged a limited agenda as far as the female workforce was concerned. His primary goal was to "organize the organizable," which meant a preference for "skilled workers who possessed leverage in the work place." Therfore, Gompers did not think it was sensible to "pour energies into enrolling less skilled, easily replaced workers." Because many female workers were unskilled and were paid significantly less than men, they were not valued in the same way as male members. Union dues were often set too high for the women. Male organizers also complained that organizing women was difficult, as social propriety inhibited them from speaking to women in private or discussing moral or sanitary issues.

The half-hearted support that was given to Mary Kenney, the AFL's first female organizer, was a testament to the AFL's unwillingness to embrace female leadership. Despite Gompers's public rhetoric that every energy would be exhausted to unite trade unions and "federate their effort without regard to . . . sex," the limited support for women in leadership roles was, according to historian Alice Kessler-Harris, "tinged with the conviction and perhaps the hope that women would get out of the work force altogether." Furthermore, although Gompers and others conceded that women should be given the "full and free opportunity to work whenever and wherever necessity requires," the slippery slope is evident in the word "requires." This wording implied that need was the only valid reason for women to work outside the home, thus erasing professional ambition from the equation.

Whether women's leaders aligned themselves with feminist ideology or not, they all recognized an urgent need to protect working women and children, which facilitated the creation of coalitions that worked together on the issue. Although the needs of self-supporting professional women tended to be complex and ambiguous, the demands of working-class women were more straightforward. They needed income stability, legitimacy for unions, legal protection against exploitation and hazardous working conditions, and some reversal of negative stereotypes in the media regarding the morality of working women. Some women workers, especially immigrants, worked in sweatshops or as domestic help and were subject to frequent indignities, such as sexual harassment and insults regarding their morality and heritage. Certainly immigrant women faced additional hurdles because of language barriers and cultural differences.

To deal with these problems, it was evident that women needed to be their own advocates, because they alone understood the complexities of their work environment and the indignities they sometimes suffered. It became clear at a 1903 Boston meeting that the AFL did not intend to include women as full members in its ranks or to work effectively on their behalf. In response, labor leaders Mary Kenney O'Sullivan and Leonora O'Reilly and settlement workers Lillian Wald and Jane Addams helped form the National Women's Trade Union League (WTUL), which was the first national association dedicated to organizing women workers. In a broadminded alliance, women from all classes united in the common pursuit of better and more equitable working conditions. With its strong reformist agenda, the WTUL was founded in the spirit of the social settlement; it strived to provide women with educational opportunities as well as improved working conditions through legislation and union organization. By 1904 the WTUL had branches in Chicago, New York, and Boston and had identified some specific focus areas such as the need for work hour and wage legislation.

Having chosen Minerva, the Roman goddess of wisdom and war, as their symbol, the WTUL managed to secure protective legislation, organize women into trade unions, and educate the public about the needs of working-class women. The WTUL presidency of Margaret Dreier Robins (1907–1922) fostered many of the league's most notable achievements, including its effective support of garment industry strikes in New York and Chicago from 1909 to 1911. During the strikes, settlement house workers provided support and encouragement, women's club matrons provided money, and working-class young women provided the pickets. Help could be found on an individual or group basis, with union members, regardless of class, marching side by side to lend support. When the clothing manufacturers refused to settle with the strikers, wealthy members of the league boycotted their clothing until a settlement was reached. Robins and the WTUL were pivotal in the development of arbitration methods at Hart Schaffner and Marx, a men's clothing company in Chicago, which introduced a groundbreaking level of industrial equality.

The WTUL published its own journal, *Life and Labor,* and successfully combined feminist theory and reform unionism. The support it provided, especially in the early twentieth century, had an empowering effect on women. In fact, there was a new consciousness regarding self-supporting women at all levels of society, which found expression not only in the WTUL and the ranks of settlement house workers, but also in the public image of the New Woman. Feminist ideology was being openly articulated and began to define the relationships between women and society in ways that broadened the cultural concept of liberty to encompass independence as economic self-support, artistic self-expression, freer sexual development, and conscious choice between career or marriage.

Even the language changed to reflect the progress of women in society. Early activists used the singular term *woman* to symbolize the identity and unity of the female gender, but twentieth-century activists increasingly used the plural term *women* to denote the united diversity of their causes. Harriet

Stanton Blanch, the daughter of Elizabeth Cady Stanton, noted that the basis of unity among women had shifted to the workplace and their numerous roles in it. Equal rights activists found themselves at home in the WTUL. Having learned successful ways to lobby elected officials, propose referenda, and conduct publicity campaigns, some WTUL members married their collective skills to promote causes other than work-related reform, such as the suffrage campaign.

Interestingly, in 1923, three years after the Nineteenth Amendment gave women the right to vote, the AFL officially acknowledged competition as a primary motivating factor for organizing women. According to the AFL, "Unorganized [women] constitute a menace to standards established through collective action. Not only for their protection, but for the protection of men . . . there should be organization of all women." So, in other words, according to the AFL, women needed to be controlled and guided or they might interfere with the status quo. This prejudicial way of thinking was unacceptable to women activists who knew that self-organization and female leadership would empower them to accomplish work reform that specifically benefited their gender.

The torch of leadership within the WTUL soon passed to a new generation of women, and the established generation took up the role of mentor. The WTUL embraced a form of social feminism by concentrating on "unity and integration." To WTUL president Robins's credit, she made a point of recruiting members from all sectors of the community without regard to class standing. It was therefore not surprising that by the mid-1920s, the WTUL's leadership had transitioned from affluent middle-class women to those with working-class backgrounds. Although financial difficulties associated with the Great Depression took their toll on the league, it stayed solvent primarily from member resources until it was dissolved in 1950.

Key Players

Addams, Jane (1860–1935): After founding Hull House with Ellen Gates Starr, Addams became a vocal suffragette. She was later the vice president of the National Women's Suffrage Association. She also helped to establish the Women's Trade Union League (WTUL) and was a founding member of the National Association for the Advancement of Colored People (NAACP). An accomplished author and pacifist, Addams wrote several books about peace, democracy, and her experiences at Hull House. She received the Nobel Peace Prize in 1931.

Anthony, Susan B. (1820–1906): A political writer and social reformer, Anthony worked closely with Elizabeth Cady Stanton to champion women's rights. Unafraid to question authority, she was often the target of abuse by the press. Nevertheless, she worked zealously to improve the status of women, especially with regard to their marital and political rights. She believed strongly that women should strive for personal freedom and gender justice.

O'Sullivan, Mary Kenney (1864–1943): In 1892 Samuel Gompers, president of the AFL, appointed Kenney as the AFL's first female general organizer. Highly motivated, Kenney successfully organized garment workers in New York and shoemakers, weavers, and printers in Massachusetts. She was a cofounder of the WTUL and a champion of women's rights in the workplace.

Robins, Margaret Dreier (1868–1945): As president of the WTUL from 1907 to 1922, Robins was extremely effective. She helped to organize numerous strikes against the garment industry. Robins believed strongly that women were suited for positions of leadership. She played a pivotal role in developing a highly successful training program for women leaders and served as the editor of the league's journal, *Life and Labor.*

Stanton, Elizabeth Cady (1815–1902): Stanton, a social reformer and suffragette, is considered by some to be the mother of the women's rights movement. Considered radical in her day, Stanton worked tirelessly in pursuit of social and political reforms for the equality of women. In 1848, at the famous women's rights convention in Seneca Falls, New York, she presented the Declaration of Sentiments, which was modeled after the Declaration of Independence. In her treatise, she called for sweeping social reform, including legislation that would give women the right to vote.

See also: *American Federation of Labor.*

BIBLIOGRAPHY

Books

Kessler-Harris, Alice. "Where Are the Organized Women Workers?" In *A Heritage of Her Own,* edited by Nancy F. Cott and Elizabeth Pleck. New York: Simon & Schuster, 1979.

Kinneally, James J. "Women in the United States and Trade Unionism." In *The World of Women's Trade Unionism: Comparative Historical Essays,* edited by Norbert C. Soldon. Westport, CT: Greenwood Press, 1985.

Licht, Walter. *Industrializing America: The Nineteenth Century.* Baltimore, MD: The Johns Hopkins University Press, 1995.

Paulson, Ross Evans. *Liberty, Equality, and Justice: Civil Rights, Women's Rights, and the Regulation of Business, 1865–1932.* Durham, NC: Duke University Press, 1997.

Smith-Rosenberg, Carol. *Disorderly Conduct: Visions of Gender in Victorian America.* New York: Alfred A. Knopf, 1985.

———. "The Female World of Love and Ritual: Relationships Between Women in Nineteenth-Century America." In *A Heritage of Her Own,* edited by Nancy F. Cott and Elizabeth Pleck. New York: Simon & Schuster, 1979.

Tong, Rosemary. *Feminist Thought.* Boulder, CO: Westview Press, 1989.

Other

"Women's Trade Union League, 1903–1950, Organization." Women in American History. *Encyclopedia Britannica.* 1998 [cited 19 October 2002]. <http://www2.britannica.&d8;com/women/articles/Women's_Trade_Union_League.html>

—Lee Ann Paradise

Navajos Occupy Fairchild Plant

United States 1975

Synopsis

Fairchild Camera and Instrument Corporation was the largest employer on the Navajo Reservation in the 1970s. The tribal council actively courted industry to improve the employment situation of its people. Members of the American Indian Movement (AIM) occupied the plant to protest the layoff and treatment of 140 Navajo workers. They objected to what they considered exploitation by Fairchild and demanded the rehiring of all 140 workers who had been laid off. AIM also had several other concerns related to conditions in both the Navajo and Hopi tribes.

Tribal leaders intervened minimally during the eight-day occupation of the plant. Their hope was that at the end of the siege, the company would continue to operate the plant. After the plant closed, an analysis found that the tribe and government had expended much more in keeping Fairchild in the area than the company had returned to the agencies or community.

Timeline

1955: African and Asian nations meet at the Bandung Conference in Indonesia, inaugurating the "non-aligned" movement of Third World countries.

1965: Power failure paralyzes New York City and much of the northeastern United States on 9 November.

1969: Assisted by pilot Michael Collins, astronauts Neil Armstrong and Edwin E. "Buzz" Aldrin become the first men to walk on the Moon (20 July).

1972: On 5 September, Palestinian terrorists kill eleven Israeli athletes and one West German policeman at the Olympic Village in Munich.

1975: Pol Pot's Khmer Rouge launch a campaign of genocide in Cambodia unparalleled in human history. By the time it ends, with the Vietnamese invasion in 1979, they will have slaughtered some 40 percent of the country's population. Cambodia is not the only country to fall to communist forces this year: the pro-Western governments of South Vietnam and Laos also succumb, while Angola and Mozambique, recently liberated from centuries of Portuguese colonialism, align themselves with the Soviet Bloc.

1975: U.S. *Apollo* and Soviet *Soyuz* spacecraft link up in space.

1975: Two assassination attempts on President Ford in September.

1978: Terrorists kidnap and kill former Italian premier Aldo Moro. In Germany, after a failed hijacking on behalf of the Red Army Faction (RAF, better known as the Baader-Meinhof Gang), imprisoned RAF members commit suicide.

1980: In protest of the Soviet invasion of Afghanistan, President Carter keeps U.S. athletes out of the Moscow Olympics.

1985: In a year of notable hijackings by Muslim and Arab terrorists, Shi'ites take a TWA airliner in June, Palestinians hijack the Italian cruise ship *Achille Lauro* in October, and fundamentalists take control of an Egyptian plane in Athens in November.

1995: Bombing of the Alfred P. Murrah Federal Building in Oklahoma City, Oklahoma, kills 168 people. Authorities arrest Timothy McVeigh and Terry Nichols.

Event and Its Context

The Navajo Invitation

The tribal council and tribal leader Raymond Nakai had taken pains to attract Fairchild Camera and Instrument Corporation and other industry to the reservation. Until Fairchild located a plant on the reservation, the Navajo had been badly in need of employment. Unemployment at that time was about 40 percent. Alcoholism was rampant among the unemployed. Unemployed Navajos often gathered at the trading posts to sell blankets and wool, but were otherwise idle. The Navajo Nation knew it needed to attract businesses that could guarantee jobs with futures. They wished to get away from mining and subsistence ranching or farming.

Beginning in 1963, the tribal leadership worked hard to bring industry to the area. With Nakai's persistence and leadership, the council issued a resolution 3 March 1964 extending an invitation to private investors "to develop the extensive natural and human resources of the Navajo Reservation." The document also suggested that assistance to relocating companies from the tribe would be forthcoming if substantial employment opportunities were made available to Navajo. The tribe upped the ante by earmarking $1 million of its assets for development.

Several companies took advantage of the program. Fairchild, attracted by the promise of cheap labor, had been the largest private employer to take advantage of the offer. At its peak some 1,200 Navajos worked for the company. Other companies including General Dynamics, Cardinal Plastics, Armex Corporation, and Westward Coach Corporation also opened facilities on the Navajo Reservation.

At the time of the siege, Fairchild had been operating in Shiprock for 10 years. The company had invested about $1 million to get the plant operational. They had significant help from the Navajo Nation, which constructed the plant. The facility was used to assemble integrated circuits. An estimated 470 Navajo worked at the plant. The weekly payroll was estimated at $55,000; typical wages were $85 per week. During this period, Fairchild had also helped to construct a 250-unit housing project.

Defense, Economy Prompt Layoffs

Neither Fairchild management nor the tribe had factored into the equation a slump in defense spending and a poor national economy beginning in 1970. "This is a business venture, not a charitable activity," said Paul W. Driscoll, the plant's manager. "We are here because it makes sense economically for

Peter MacDonald. AP/Wide World Photos. Reproduced by permission.

us and for the Navajos." Fairchild officials acknowledged that the government provided job training, but pointed to a critical need for more education and management training.

Layoffs occurred at Fairchild, which was a nonunion plant, and at General Dynamics. The abrupt nature of the additional 140 layoffs in 1975 caused escalated bitterness and prompted AIM's involvement in what had been a local issue.

Members of AIM, about half Navajo but including no Fairchild employees, occupied the plant. The point of the strike was to register their objection to what they considered exploitation by Fairchild. AIM demanded that all 140 workers laid off be rehired. The action was also conducted to publicize and protest other local problems in both the Navajo and Hopi communities. AIM demanded a halt to strip mining and renegotiation of lease agreements with companies including Arizona Public Service Co., operators of the Four Corners power plant near Shiprock.

A day into the occupation, Fairchild executives stopped trying to negotiate and gave AIM a deadline for discontinuing the occupation. They left it to the tribe to get the AIM members off their property. Within hours of the missed deadline, local management handed out statements announcing the suspension of Shiprock operations.

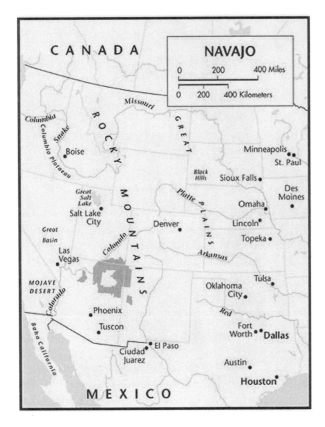

Map showing the location of Navajo lands in the Four Corners region. © Maryland Cartographics.

Parting Shots

When the occupation ended, both AIM and Fairchild Semiconductor left Shiprock. Damage was incurred to the plant, company property, and inventory. Fairchild executives were upset at the way the tribe had handled the event. The Fairchild employees blamed intertribal politics. Peter MacDonald, who had replaced Nakai as Navajo tribal leader in 1970, had failed to either come to Shiprock or to contact Fairchild representatives during the eight-day seige. Local residents supported Nakai, which may have influenced the tribal council's approach to negotiating with the American Indian Movement (AIM). Local residents had, in fact, supported his successor in tribal elections. MacDonald promised AIM that the tribe would ask for employees to be rehired and that they would ask for an investigation of employment practices at the plant, including an audit of federal payments made to Fairchild. The tribal council also granted unconditional amnesty to those involved in the takeover.

There had been hopes within the community that the plant would reopen. With no assurance from the tribal leadership that this sort of action would never happen again, the plant remained closed. The protest over the loss of 140 jobs resulted in a loss of almost 500 jobs.

Russell Means, one of those AIM members who had occupied the plant, told *The Navajo Times* that Fairchild's departure was a forgone conclusion. "They [plant owners] were going overseas to Korea. They were leaving this area. They were leav-

ing the Navajo Nation," he said. "Fairchild used that as an excuse and who got the blame? The victims."

The tribe's attempts to court new business to the plant were unsuccessful. The protest tainted Shiprock. Local residents, including former employees, were rightfully upset. Some resented AIM's actions, saying the group did not represent their views. Area business slowed significantly by as much as 60 percent according to some estimates. Some local businesses were forced to halt new construction or expansion. Investors that had planned to locate to the area went elsewhere.

John Trudell, AIM national chairman, called the event a success. It had ended peacefully. "Fairchild can no longer openly and quietly exploit Indian people," he said. Indeed, according to an Economic Development Administration analysis, the cost of creating jobs—both to the tribe and government—had been $5,672 per employee. The rate of return for these investments was a paltry 1 percent. According to author Peter Iverson, "Given the isolation of the Navajo country and the knowledge that the tribe would be less extravagant in its inducements to companies, company officials tended to shy away from locating on the reservation. In some ways, the closing of the Fairchild plant in Shiprock may have set the tone for this period."

Key Players

Anderson, Larry: Anderson was AIM national treasurer and one of the AIM leaders during the takeover of the Fairchild plant.

Curtis, Mercer E., Jr.: Curtis was the Fairchild Shiprock plant manager during its occupation by AIM.

Driscoll, Paul: A former Fairchild Shiprock plant manager, Driscoll had been recognized for his work on business development within the community for which he received an award in 1970 from *Business Week*.

Johnson, Fred: Member of the tribal council, Johnson acted as intermediary between the tribe and the AIM group during the Fairchild plant occupation.

MacDonald, Peter (1928–): A 1957 graduate of the University of Oklahoma, MacDonald was chairman of the Navajo Tribal Council at the time of the siege at Shiprock. He had been elected in 1970 as director of the Office of Navajo Economic Opportunity. Among his political deals, one in particular was struck that, in a roundabout way, gave AFL-CIO union organizers entrée to organize on the reservation. Despite attempts to modernize the Navajo Nation, he was reportedly dismissed with the nickname "Peter MacDollars, Shah of the Navajo." Opinions about MacDonald within the community were extremely polarized.

Means, Russell Charles (1939–): A Lakota Sioux, Means was one of the 20 armed AIM protestors who occupied the Shiprock Fairchild plant for eight days in February 1975. To this day, Means contends the group was asked to take action by the Diné (Navajo) AIM. He has been taken to task for not mentioning his participation in this event in his autobiography. Means says he is no longer an AIM member.

Nakai, Raymond (1918–): Nakai was the tribal chairman initially responsible for attracting industry to the Navajo reservation. He served as Navajo Tribal Council chairman between 1963 and 1970. He is credited with helping to develop a variety of employment opportunities within the Navajo Nation, particularly for his efforts in attracting Fairchild to the reservation. Shiprock area residents backed Nakai in the 1970 tribal elections, but Peter MacDonald succeeded him.

Trudell, John (1947–): A Dakota Sioux, Trudell was the national chairman for American Indian Movement at the time of the occupation of the Fairchild Shiprock plant. He was first involved with the Indians of All Tribes organization during the native American occupation of Alcatraz Prison in California and, immediately after that event, he became active in AIM.

BIBLIOGRAPHY

Books

Benedek, Emily. *The Wind Won't Know Me: A History of the Navajo-Hopi Land Dispute.* New York: Alfred A. Knopf, 1992.

Iverson, Peter. *The Navajo Nation.* Westport, CT: Greenwood Press, 1981.

Malinowski, Sharon, ed. *Notable Native Americans.* George H. J. Abrams, consulting editor and author of foreword. New York: Gale Research, 1995.

Weyler, Rex. *Blood of the Land: The Government and Corporate War Against the American Indian Movement.* New York: Everest House Publishers, 1982.

Periodicals

Atchison, Sandra D. "Letter from Shiprock." *Business Week* (15 September 1975).

Brenner, Malcolm. Review of "Where White Men Fear to Tread," by Russell Means. *The Gallup Independent,* (n.d.).

"Will Fairchild Really Pull Out of Shiprock?" *Business Week* Industrial Edition, Employment (17 March 1975): 28.

Other

American Indian Movement Web Site. [cited 6 August 2002]. <http://www.aimovement.org>.

Tohtsoni, Nathan J. "American Apartheid: Russell Means Defends His Case Against Navajo Nation Courts." *The Navajo Times.* 15 February 2001 [cited 6 August 2002]. <http://www.thenavajotimes.com/Tribal_News/Means/means.html>.

—Linda Dailey Paulson

New Orleans General Strike

United States 1892

Synopsis

From 24 October 1892 to 11 November 1892, the city of New Orleans came to a virtual standstill as the city's employees challenged their employers for union recognition, collective bargaining, shorter workdays, increased salaries, and a closed shop, which guaranteed that union workers would be hired ahead of nonunion workers. Inspired by the streetcar drivers' successful strike earlier in the year, workers throughout New Orleans organized and lobbied for their demands. Of the striking workers, the most important group was the racially diverse Triple Alliance. As the relationship between the employees and the employers deteriorated, the unions called for a general strike. After being twice postponed, the general strike began on 8 November. Though the action lasted only three days, the workers won wage and hour concessions but failed to secure the important closed shop.

Timeline

1872: The Crédit Mobilier affair, in which several officials in the administration of President Ulysses S. Grant are accused of receiving stock in exchange for favors, is the first of many scandals that are to plague Grant's second term.

1877: In the face of uncertain results from the popular vote in the presidential election of 1876, the U.S. Electoral Commission awards the presidency to Rutherford B. Hayes despite a slight popular majority for his opponent, Samuel J. Tilden. The election of 1876 will remain the most controversial in American history for the next 124 years, until overshadowed by the race between George W. Bush and Al Gore in 2000.

1882: Agitation against English rule spreads throughout Ireland, culminating with the assassination of chief secretary for Ireland Lord Frederick Cavendish and permanent undersecretary Thomas Burke in Dublin's Phoenix Park. The leader of the nationalist movement is Charles Stewart Parnell, but the use of assassination and terrorism—which Parnell himself has disavowed—makes clear the fact that he does not control all nationalist groups.

1885: German engineer Karl Friedrich Benz builds the first true automobile.

1888: Serbian-born American electrical engineer Nikola Tesla develops a practical system for generating and transmitting alternating current (AC), which will ultimately—and after an extremely acrimonious battle—replace Thomas Edison's direct current (DC) in most homes and businesses.

1890: U.S. Congress passes the Sherman Antitrust Act, which in the years that follow will be used to break up large monopolies.

1891: French troops open fire on workers during a 1 May demonstration at Fourmies, where employees of the Sans Pareille factory are striking for an eight-hour workday. Nine people are killed—two of them children—and sixty more are injured.

1893: Henry Ford builds his first automobile.

1893: New Zealand is the first nation in the world to grant the vote to women.

1894: French army captain Alfred Dreyfus, a Jew, is convicted of treason. Dreyfus will later be cleared of all charges, but the Dreyfus case illustrates—and exacerbates—the increasingly virulent anti-Semitism that pervades France.

1896: First modern Olympic Games held in Athens.

1900: The first zeppelin is test-flown.

Event and Its Context

In May 1892 New Orleans streetcar drivers struck and forced arbitration on its employers. The workers won a shorter workday, reduced from 16 to 10 hours, and a closed shop, which meant that union members would be hired in preference to nonunion applicants. As a result of the streetcar drivers' seemingly easy victory, workers flocked to the American Federation of Labor (AFL) in huge numbers. Thirty new unions were chartered in New Orleans, bringing the total number of unions in the city to 95. The Workingmen's Amalgamated Council, which represented over 20,000 workers, and the Triple Alliance were formed. The more powerful of the two was the Triple Alliance, which served the AFL unions of teamsters, scalesmen, and packers, which had both black and white members. Because the Triple Alliance performed labor essential to New Orleans' success as a commercial port, its members were in a potentially advantageous position. The bulk of the South's cotton export and a good deal of the Midwest's agricultural goods traveled down the Mississippi River and through New Orleans.

The success of the streetcar drivers' strike and the confidence gained from joint action inspired the Triple Alliance to strike on 24 October, at the peak of the business season, for 10-hour days, overtime pay, and—most importantly—a closed shop. The Workingmen's Amalgamated Council immediately supported the strike. The council's president, James Leonard, firmly believed that the survival and success of unionism depended on extending the closed shop. The council and Triple Alliance founded a labor committee of five men from the oldest unions to run the strike. Ironically, none of the five men were from the Triple Alliance.

The New Orleans employers were also unified and had strong allies, including the press. In addition to raising several thousand dollars in a defense fund, the employers enlisted four railroads; the clearing house; and the cotton, sugar, rice, mechanics', and dealers' exchanges to their side. They received offers from industrialists from other regions for both support and money. The employers formed a committee of five members from the Board of Trade to deal with the strike, petitioned the

governor to send the militia, and refused to enter negotiations for the first week. The Board of Trade also attempted to use race to foster divisiveness in the racially mixed Triple Alliance. The board said it would sign a contract with the white unions but not the black Teamsters. The scalesmen and packers refused to sign anything without the Teamsters. The resulting stalemate practically paralyzed the city.

The labor committee, motivated by its angry constituency and the stalemate, called for a general strike. With the threat of a general strike looming, the employers whose employees had not yet struck pressured the Board of Trade to meet with union leaders. An agreement was made that called for employees to return to work while a final settlement was reached, and the order to strike was rescinded. However, the situation between the Board of Trade and the union leaders grew gradually worse in the hours after the agreement.

Some workers refused to return to work, and some employers refused to give back jobs now filled by other workers. Both sides grew angrier and accused each other of bad faith, making both groups even more frustrated, suspicious, and stubborn. On the defensive, the merchants now refused to even begin arbitration until the workers returned to their jobs. In response, the workers again called for a general strike.

This second call for a general strike was postponed in response to a plea from the mayor, John Fitzpatrick, and City Council. In a last ditch attempt at reconciliation, Fitzpatrick brought the two sides together. The attempt was a miserable failure, and the merchants labeled Mayor Fitzpatrick a labor politician. Although the unions were ready and willing to negotiate, the Board of Trade still refused to do anything until the strike was canceled. In response, the general strike was scheduled for Monday, 7 November. Over the weekend unions held meetings to poll members who were overwhelmingly in favor of the striking. The original complaint of the Triple Alliance had evolved into a citywide effort to establish the preferential closed shop and collective bargaining throughout New Orleans.

The labor committee worked to avoid the strike and even pushed back the walk-out time in the hopes the governor, Murphy James Foster, would intervene, but on Tuesday, 8 November, the general strike occurred. It included over 20,000 workers from 42 unions and half of the organized crafts in New Orleans. Each union involved had its own demands, which usually included recognition, closed shop, wage increases, and shorter workdays. Nonindustrial workers, such as musicians and hat, shoe, and clothing clerks, joined the strike in support of the others. Public utility workers also struck. Governor Foster asked the labor committee to send utility workers back to work since they performed jobs essential to the basic operation of the city. Union leaders complied with the request, but the utility employees refused to return to work. Of the workers who already had union contracts, only the streetcar drivers and printers broke their contracts to join the strike. The Cotton Exchange, for example, remained in operation, although its workers did not overtly cooperate with the Board of Trade. The strike brought the city to a standstill.

The merchants appealed to Mayor Fitzpatrick to call in special deputies to run the city's utilities, but Fitzpatrick refused, saying he could only use his authority to preserve peace and order, not to force people to work. Fitzpatrick was unwilling to use the police as strikebreakers or as a means to frighten the strikers. The merchants, with the help of their railroad allies, brought in strikebreakers from cities in other states such as Birmingham and Mobile, Alabama; Memphis, Tennessee; and Galveston, Texas. With the threat of violence growing and under pressure from the governor, Fitzpatrick finally issued a call for special deputies, but only 59 people volunteered. Merchants then trained their own clerks for riot control and told the governor they would pay all the costs for the state militia if he would agree to dispatch it.

With the potential for violence increasing, Foster issued a proclamation outlawing public gatherings and threatened to call in the militia if the strike continued. Fearing bloodshed and a clash with the militia, the labor committee called an end to the strike on its third day, 11 November. Workers were restored to jobs still open and the unions won a ten-hour workday, overtime pay, and adjusted salaries, but the employers refused to grant recognition to the various unions and New Orleans remained an open shop.

Once the strike was over, the merchants organized themselves in a stronger, more permanent way, and the labor committee worked to find jobs for the blacklisted strikers. Another repercussion of the strike was a lawsuit brought in Federal Circuit Court against 44 union leaders for violation of the Sherman Antitrust Act for conspiracy to restrain trade. The suit was thrown out.

The New Orleans general strike is largely considered a failure. It arguably weakened unions in New Orleans for years. There were no strikes in Louisiana in the next two years, and the number of unions in New Orleans dropped. However, the strike is one of the most dramatic demonstrations of interracial and interunion cooperation in the late 1800s and the first general strike in American history to show that skilled and unskilled workers and black and white workers could work together for a common goal, even in the Deep South.

Key Players

Fitzpatrick, John (1844–1919): New Orleans mayor (1892–1896). Fitzpatrick entered politics at an early age. He holds the distinction of being the only New Orleans mayor to be impeached; he was not convicted.

Foster, Murphy James (1849–1921): Served as Louisiana state senator (1880–1892), governor (1892–1900), and United States Senator (1900–1912). A native of Louisiana, Foster attended law school at Tulane University.

Gompers, Samuel (1850–1924): London-born Gompers immigrated to New York and became a cigar maker. In 1874 he became active in trade unions and eventually became president of the AFL (1886–1894 and 1896–1924).

See also: *American Federation of Labor.*

BIBLIOGRAPHY

Books

Filippelli, Ronald L. "New Orleans General Strike of 1892." In *Labor Conflict in the United States: An Encyclopedia.* New York: Garland, 1990.

Periodicals

Cook, Bernard A. "The Typographical Union and the New Orleans General Strike of 1892." *Louisiana History* 24 (1983): 377–388.

Shugg, Roger Wallace. "The New Orleans General Strike of 1892." *Louisiana Historical Quarterly* 21 (1937): 547–560.

ADDITIONAL RESOURCES

Books

Brecher, Jeremy. *Strike.* San Francisco: Straight Arrow Books, 1972.

—Lisa A. Ennis

No-strike Pledge, World War II

United States 1941

Synopsis

The entry of the United States into World War II in December 1941 brought near-total unanimity among the varying factions of the American labor movement in their support of the war effort. The AFL and CIO, two of the country's largest and most influential unions, were bitter enemies before the war, with antagonism over such ideals as craft (skilled) versus industrial (semiskilled and unskilled) unionism. Although not without conflicts during the war, leaders from both unions joined together and promised "no-strike pledges" for the duration of hostilities.

Even though the country stood united against the Nazi regime in Germany and the Imperial Japanese government, the no-strike pledge complicated the lives of union workers. The initial shock of being attacked on U.S. territory by Japanese forces, along with early Allied military setbacks, helped to control any pre-existing tensions in the workplace. Beginning in 1943, however, as Allied forces gradually gained superiority in the war, disputes within labor, from the rank and file as well as from the leaders, became more apparent. Union leaders, especially within the AFL and CIO, were stuck in the middle, on the one hand as allies of the government and corporations, and on the other as representatives of their members.

Timeline

1921: Washington Disarmament Conference limits the tonnage of world navies.

1925: European leaders attempt to secure the peace at the Locarno Conference, which guarantees the boundaries between France and Germany, and Belgium and Germany.

1931: Financial crisis widens in the United States and Europe, which reel from bank failures and climbing unemployment levels. In London, armies of the unemployed riot.

1936: Germany reoccupies the Rhineland, while Italy annexes Ethiopia. Recognizing a commonality of aims, the two totalitarian powers sign the Rome-Berlin Axis Pact. (Japan will join them in 1940.)

1941: German troops march into the Balkans, conquering Yugoslavia and Greece. (Bulgaria and Romania, along with Hungary, are aligned with the Nazis.)

1941: In a move that takes Stalin by surprise, Hitler sends his troops into the Soviet Union on 22 June. Like his hero Napoleon, Hitler believes that by stunning Russia with a lightning series of brilliant maneuvers, it is possible to gain a quick and relatively painless victory. Early successes seem to prove him right, and he is so confident of victory that he refuses to equip his soldiers with winter clothing.

1941: Japanese bombing of Pearl Harbor on 7 December brings the United States into the war against the Axis. Combined with the attack on the Soviet Union, which makes Stalin an unlikely ally of the Western democracies, the events of 1941 will ultimately turn the tide of the war.

1941: The United States initiates the Manhattan Project to build an atomic bomb and signs the Lend-Lease Act, whereby it provides aid to Great Britain and, later, the Soviet Union.

1941: Great films of the year include *The Maltese Falcon, Sullivan's Travels, Meet John Doe, How Green Was My Valley,* and a work often cited as one of the greatest films of all time: Orson Welles's *Citizen Kane.*

1946: Winston Churchill warns of an "Iron Curtain" spreading across Eastern Europe.

1951: Introduction of color television.

1956: First aerial testing of the hydrogen bomb at Bikini Atoll. The blast is so powerful—the equivalent of 10 million tons of TNT—that it actually results in the infusion of protons to atomic nuclei to create two new elements, einsteinium and fermium, which have atomic numbers of 99 and 100, respectively.

Event and Its Context

World War II had an immense and long-lasting impact upon the American labor movement. This was especially true with regard to the two largest unions: the American Federation of Labor (AFL) and the Congress of Industrial Organizations (CIO).

Membership Expansion and Limited Union Activities

For the American workforce, the Great Depression of the 1930s was an extremely tough time rife with high unemployment, low wages, and monetary deflation. By 1939 war in both Europe and Asia increased demand for American products and brought the United States out of the depression, resulting in a high demand for workers to fill new jobs. America's subsequent entrance into World War II resulted in a dramatic increase in union membership. By the end of World War II unions had nearly 15 million members combined, up from about 8.5 million members in 1940. However, during the war the activities of organized labor were dramatically curtailed by governmental restrictions and regulations.

With the dramatic increase in union membership came positives and negatives for both labor and management. On the positive side, the surge of new employees helped companies produce wartime products and increased membership helped unions strengthen their positions. On the negative side, wartime patriotism was sometimes dampened by the volatile nature of labor relations that resulted from excessive government control during the war. The elaborate mechanism established by the administration of President Franklin D. Roosevelt to control labor became a central point of aggravation for both unions and employees. In addition, many new employees had no training at working in factories and no experience at being members of organized labor. New employees often took their grievances directly to management without going through formal union grievance procedures. Often, new union members paid little attention to union affairs or to traditional work rules. New union members were often not good union "team players."

AFL and CIO

During the years prior to the United States' involvement in World War II, there were distinct hostilities between the AFL and the CIO. From its establishment in 1881, the AFL emphasized organization of skilled workers into craft unions (composed of a single occupation, skill, or trade, such as plumbers), as opposed to industrial unions (composed of all workers in a particular industry, such as automobile). It was a relatively conservative political force within the labor movement of the late nineteenth and early twentieth centuries.

Over the years, radicals within the AFL had pressured the organization to expand its organizing efforts to the unskilled industrial sector. Lead by John L. Lewis, president of the United Mine Workers, these radicals took their demands to the 1935 AFL convention, where they formed the Committee of Industrial Organizations, the original CIO, within the AFL. A special organizing fund was established and AFL president William Green approved charters for the aluminum, cement, automobile, radio, rubber, and steel unions. The groups immediately launched organizing drives in the basic mass-production industries and assigned them to existing or new industrial unions. Their successes, especially in the automobile and steel industries, strengthened the prestige of the relatively new CIO to the point that it seriously challenged the AFL's leadership within organized labor.

A majority of the AFL unions did challenge the CIO's organizing efforts. Because of continuing disagreements over this type of organizing, the AFL suspended 10 national unions of the CIO in 1936. As a result, the CIO broke off from the AFL and formed its own labor federation in 1938, changing its name to the Congress of Industrial Organizations (CIO). In reaction, AFL president Green declared, "We will fight against a movement [the CIO] which has vowed to destroy us and wipe us off the face of the earth." With the war approaching, great rivalry was ever present between these two powerful unions.

Wartime factory workers, New Britain, Connecticut. © Archive Photos/Anthony Potter Collection. Reproduced by permission.

Roosevelt Deals with Unions

Before the United States entered World War II, the CIO supported government defense efforts because it offered a concrete chance for its members to benefit from substantial wage increases and other worker benefits that were essential for the welfare of its members. The AFL was the more pacifistic of the two unions, wanting the United States to remain strictly neutral with regard to the war in Europe. It supported providing aid to free labor groups in Europe and assisting England and its allies as long as it did not jeopardize the country's position of neutrality. However, as the United States moved toward war in 1941,

the Roosevelt administration became anxious about the volatility of labor unions and placed heavy pressure on union leaders to prevent disruption of war production.

At the same time, many workers and union activists viewed the war buildup as an opportunity to win as many concessions as possible from management. Throughout 1941 the determination of unions to expand their respective organizations and to improve wages triggered hundreds of strikes. Led by the CIO, whose members constituted 70 percent of the total number of strikers, 2.36 million workers conducted work stoppages that year. Around 4,200 strikes represented one of the highest annu-

Workers leave factory at end of workday, 1941. © Getty Images. Reproduced by permission.

al strike counts in American history. The huge 1941 strike wave featured a conflict at the North American Aviation plant in Inglewood, California, which threatened to slow down President Roosevelt's defense efforts.

A walkout by 4,000 workers occurred in June 1941 at the North American Aviation plant. It was the largest strike in California since the maritime general strike of 1934. The workers did not resort to a sit-down strike because the Supreme Court had earlier declared such actions illegal; instead, they organized a mass picket line that surrounded the factory. With the approval of the Roosevelt administration, military troops broke up the mass picket lines around the plant and imposed martial law in the surrounding area. In breaking up the strike with troops and threatening strikers with induction into the army, Roosevelt sent a strong message to AFL and CIO leaders that their organizations were at risk if they allowed disruption of his war programs.

Even though the government prevented and eliminated many strikes in the several years before the war, key gains in 1940 and 1941 laid the foundation for better wage rates, equitable disciplinary procedures, better work rules, guidelines for promotions, and seniority that, in all, made for stronger and better contracts on the side of labor. One radical organizer declared

that "the worst evil—the total submissiveness of worker to boss" had been eliminated.

Entering the War

The Japanese attack on Pearl Harbor on 7 December 1941 brought together government, labor, and management in a common cause. To defeat the Axis powers, the United States would have to mount a massive war production program. President Roosevelt called labor and business leaders to a White House conference to study the new wartime problems in order to "reach a unanimous agreement to prevent the interruption of production." In an attempt to establish a basis for wartime labor-management cooperation and to assure the greatest possible production, the AFL and CIO outlined a program that was subsequently accepted by President Roosevelt. It was agreed that:

• There would be no strikes or lockouts in defense industries.

• A National War Labor Board would be established by the president to peacefully settle all labor-management controversies and grievances.

• The president would appoint members of the board.

On 24 December 1941 President Roosevelt announced a no-strike pledge by the AFL and CIO that would last for the duration of the war. The AFL and the CIO gave the country a "no strike" promise to which most workers faithfully adhered. Some strikes did, of course, occur, but only a very small number of working hours between 1941 and 1944 were lost because of strikes.

One of the sacrifices made by most unions led by the AFL and the CIO was to pledge to forego strikes throughout the war. Philip Murray, who had succeeded Lewis as CIO president, said in September 1944 that "on the 17th day of December, 1941, ten days after our country had become involved in the war . . . without formal request upon the part of the President of the United States, we all voluntarily agreed to give our Commander-in-Chief, and through him to the people of our country our No Strike commitment."

The no-strike pledge was a voluntary agreement made by AFL and CIO leaders to forego work stoppages for the duration of the war. The unions gained immediate approval from the public and support from the government. However, veteran unionists and social militants argued that for labor organizations to give up the right to strike was to deny them the ability to negotiate in good faith with employers that could be backed up with the threat of strike if their demands were not met. One such critic, Mechanics Educational Society of America President Matthew Smith, said of the no-strike policy, "The AFL and CIO did not sell out their membership, they gave them away."

It must be noted, however, that Smith was the only union official who did not publicly support the no-strike pledge. Also union leaders, although unwilling to publicly acknowledge such a fact, were willing to sacrifice labor's basic rights and just demands in support of the war. Third, although labor gave up many of its basic rights, management was not forbidden to secure war profits from their newly found war businesses. During the war the slogan "equality of sacrifice" was used to convince labor that it needed to sacrifice its peacetime union conditions and wage standards for the sake of the war. Capitalists, at the same time, agreed to restrictions on their right to produce civilian goods while expanding war production at "guaranteed" profits—a no-lose situation. However, many companies declined the guaranteed profits during the war and turned over profits to the government.

Other critics wondered why—in light of the seeming lack of power of organized labor with respect to resolving employer-employee disputes—independent workers would join unions or current union members would continue to pay their dues. Thousands of patriotic workers who in theory agreed with the no-strike pledge became resentful when they found that in specific cases involving their own wages or work rules, their own unions could not support their legitimate needs and goals. This was borne out when workers found that their union could function as a disciplinary agent (involving severe union sanctions) against its own members for those who did go out on strike in violation of the no-strike pledge.

With the U.S. entry into the war, CIO President Murray stated that its five million members were ready to defend the country against the "outrageous aggression" of Hitler and Japa-

nese imperialism. Murray stated, "Everyone who works for a living has burned into his very soul the full appreciation of what this war is about." Like the AFL, the CIO acted to discipline militant workers' struggles within its ranks in exchange for increased membership and recognition. In turn, Roosevelt pressured steel and other major U.S. industries during the war to permit the unionization of their work forces. The war itself acted as the major disciplining force for the U.S. working class by sending off young, potentially militant U.S. workers to fight overseas. The government also encouraged industry, generating an output rise of nearly 90 percent between 1941 and 1945 and making possible such achievements as the production of 300,000 airplanes, 71,000 naval vessels, 45,000,000 tons of merchant shipping, 2,700,000 machine guns, 2,500,000 trucks, and 86,000 tanks.

Union Security

Unfortunately, some employers perceived the no-strike pledge as an opportunity to reduce (and sometimes eliminate) the gains of the labor movement. The no-strike pledge created a crisis for AFL and CIO union leaders. They were afraid that no workers would voluntarily belong to a union that was unwilling to fight for its members. Before the war, grievances had been settled by direct methods. With a no-strike pledge in place, however, management had less incentive to make concessions on labor issues. The case of the United Electrical Workers local at Walker-Turner in New Jersey illustrates the problem. After Hitler's invasion of Russia in June 1941, saving the Soviet Union from Hitler's advancing armies was more important, in the eyes of some political groups, than fighting for the interests of American workers. Thus, leadership of the Walker-Turner local had abandoned efforts to improve wages or fight management on other issues. By late 1941 the local had lost 25 percent of its members and most of the remaining members were delinquent in their dues.

The no-strike pledge thus threatened to undermine worker support for the CIO and the AFL and to erode the unions' ability to collect membership dues. To enforce a no-strike policy, the Roosevelt administration was forced to offer the unions some substitute way that could be represented as a court of appeals for workers' grievances. The National War Labor Board (NWLB) was thus established on 12 January 1942 as a way to resolve war industry disagreements. The tripartite agency had 12 members, four each from (as it was called) "Big Business," "Big Labor," and "Big Government." It originally incorporated labor leaders George Meany and George M. Harrison from the AFL, and Philip Murray and Thomas Kennedy from the CIO.

The cooperation of the AFL and CIO with the federal government increased during World War II. Union leaders traded a wartime no-strike pledge (sometimes ignored by workers) for the federal government's help in increasing the stability of union membership. One of the first acts of the NWLB was to devise a policy for "maintenance-of-membership" to give security to unions that had voluntarily relinquished their right to strike during the war. The maintenance-of-membership policy required that if a union had a contract with an employer, then all newly hired workers would automatically become dues-paying members after their first 15 days on the job. If they did not want to join, they had to declare that intention before the end of the 15-day period. If they did not exercise this option, the worker would be subject to discharge from employment. Employers hated this rule because they were forced to discharge employees. This policy helped to assure unions that their growth would not be stunted by their willingness to forego their right to strike.

With regard to labor disputes, workers often could only watch in frustration as an overworked NWLB slowly processed over 20,000 wage dispute cases. Workers facing harsh discipline or unfair work assignments often had to endure punishment or an unpleasant or dangerous job for months while their grievance was awaiting review. This condition was detrimental to some workers during the war. In general, the AFL, CIO, and other labor unions cooperated with the NWLB and enforced even unpopular rulings (even though they privately criticized government policy).

Wildcat Strikes

U.S. workers experienced the realities of state-enforced war rationing, severity of discipline, and obligatory military service. Because of this, they sometimes took advantage of the industrial expansion during this period. Despite the no-strike pledges, workers oftentimes used "wildcat strikes" as their frustration mounted with high inflation, low wages, and uncomfortable and sometimes hazardous working conditions. (A wildcat strike is a sudden strike not authorized by the strikers' labor union.)

There were numerous wildcat strikes outside of, and often against, the leadership of both the AFL and the CIO. Some wildcat strikes threatened to paralyze essential industries such as transportation. In 1942 there were only 2,970 work stoppages involving 840,000 workers, down drastically from the 4,200 strikes involving 2.36 million workers in 1941. By 1943 the number of strikes rose to over 3,700, with 1.98 million workers participating, and another 2 million workers engaged in some 5,000 strikes in 1944. A total of 3.5 million workers struck in 1945. In total, some 14,000 strikes and around 8.32 million workers (about a fourth of the workforce) struck during the four war years.

When it could, the federal government cooperated with the AFL and CIO with negotiated reforms such as increased pay and better benefits taken from businesses' war profits. In spite of such balancing efforts, during the war U.S. business experienced record profits, much to the frustration of labor. In reality, the federal government used its power to crush the more militant union actions as well as the wider wildcat workers' movement because such actions and movements were seen as threatening the war effort. The employer was obviously more protected than the employee.

After the War

The final victory over the Japanese in the Pacific ended the no-strike pledge. The labor movement hoped to continue the economic and political power that it had gained over the past several years. Returning veterans and those who had remained on the home front to work long, exhausting hours to produce what the soldiers needed to win the war, all hoped for better times after living through the Great Depression and then World War II. In reality, industrial workers became frustrated over the lack of organized labor's progress during the war and fearful that another depression would happen after the war. They unleashed their pent-up frustrations from the war years in a wave of postwar work stoppages. During the six-month period after 1 September 1945, more workers went out on strike for longer periods than ever before (or since) in American history.

At the end of 1945, the U.S. labor movement was composed of 14.5 million members, estimated at 35.8 percent of the (nonagricultural) civilian labor force. The AFL claimed over 10 million members, and the CIO, the smaller of the two unions, had 4.5 million members. Although rough times seemed to lie ahead, especially without the comfort of the no-strike pledge, the labor movement, spearheaded by the AFL and the CIO, realized hard-won gains by a vigorous and imaginative labor movement in the ensuing years.

Key Players

Green, William (1873–1952): Green became a member of the United Mine Workers of America (UMW) in 1890 and moved quickly to a leadership position. From 1910 to 1913 Green served two terms as a Democrat in the Ohio State Senate, where he secured passage of the Ohio Workmen's Compensation Law and other labor measures. In 1913 Green was appointed to the Executive Council of the American Federation of Labor (AFL), and in 1924 he succeeded Samuel Gompers as AFL president, a position he held until his death. He was a member of several federal government bodies, including the Labor Advisory Council of the National Recovery Administration in 1935–1937, and he also served on the governing board of the International Labor Organization.

Lewis, John L. (1880–1969): Lewis settled in Panama, Illinois, in 1906. He served, successively, as president of the Panama local of the United Mine Workers of America, lobbyist for the UMW, organizer for the AFL, and vice president of the UMW. In 1920 Lewis was elected president of the UMW, a post he held until 1960, when he retired and was named president emeritus. In 1935 Lewis was one of the labor leaders who formed the Committee for Industrial Organization (CIO). Three years later he became the first president of the newly independent CIO. Lewis resigned in 1940, withdrew his union from the CIO in 1942, led it back into the AFL in 1946, and withdrew it again in 1947.

Murray, Philip (1886–1952): Murray was an American labor leader who advocated moderate reform policies and avoided radicalism. In 1920 Murray became international vice president of the United Mine Workers, and in 1935, when the Committee for Industrial Organization was formed within the AFL, he was named to head the organizing committee of the steelworkers. This committee led to the formation of the United Steelworkers of America in 1940. He was elected its first president and in the same year succeeded labor leader John L. Lewis as president of the CIO.

Roosevelt, Franklin D. (1882–1945): Roosevelt was the 32nd president of the United States, serving from 1933 to his death in 1945. Roosevelt guided the United States through the Great Depression (which lasted from the end of 1929 to the early 1940s) and initiated a series of "New Deal" programs to help bring the country back to prosperity and through World War II.

See also: *American Federation of Labor; CIO Expelled from AFL; Committee for Industrial Organization; Congress of Industrial Organizations; Strike Wave, United States.*

BIBLIOGRAPHY

Books

Buhle, Paul. *Taking Care of Business: Samuel Gompers, George Meany, Lane Kirkland, and the Tragedy of American Labor.* New York: Monthly Review Press, 1999.

Goldberg, Arthur J. *AFL-CIO: Labor United.* New York: McGraw-Hill Book Company, Inc., 1956.

Merkel, Muriel. *The Labor Union Handbook.* New York: Beaufort Books, Inc., 1983.

Preis, Art. *Labor's Giant Step: Twenty Years of the CIO, 1936–1955.* New York: Pathfinder Press, 1972.

Schnapper, M. B. *American Labor: A Pictorial Social History.* Washington, DC: Public Affairs Press, 1972.

Taft, Philip. *The A. F. of L: From the Death of Gompers to the Merger.* New York: Harper & Brothers Publishers, 1959.

Zieger, Robert H. *American Workers, American Unions, 1920–1985.* Baltimore, MD: The Johns Hopkins University Press, 1986.

—William Arthur Atkins

Norris–La Guardia Act

United States 1932

Synopsis

The Norris–La Guardia Anti-Injunction Act (hereafter referred to as Norris–La Guardia) is a federal law passed in 1932 in an attempt to forbid court injunctions from being used to undermine or halt labor union activities. Under the law, federal courts were not allowed to invoke an injunction to stop any labor activity, including boycotts, pickets, and strikes. Also banned under the law were yellow-dog contracts. These documents were signed statements wherein workers, as a condition of employment, agreed not to join or support a union.

Timeline

1917: Russian revolutions.

1922: Inspired by the Bolsheviks' example of imposing revolution by means of a coup, Benito Mussolini leads his blackshirts in an October "March on Rome," and forms a new fascist government.

1927: Charles A. Lindbergh makes the first successful solo nonstop flight across the Atlantic, and becomes an international hero.

The Harlan County War of 1931–1932

Harlan County, Kentucky, has been the site of numerous strikes and conflicts between miners and management. Most well-known among these was the 1973 Brookside Mine strike, depicted both in the documentary *Harlan County, U.S.A.* (1973) and the 2000 Showtime movie *Harlan County War,* starring Holly Hunter. But more than four decades before those events was another conflict—one that may have been even more bitter, because it occurred against the backdrop of more desperate times.

In the aftermath of World War I, demand for coal was high, but with the end of the 1920s boom and the increased use of other energy sources, the market for coal tightened. Companies began laying off workers, and even when a miner was fortunate enough to have work, he faced economic exploitation that dramatically reduced an already meager paycheck. The coal companies in Harlan County applied the familiar practice of paying miners, not in cash, but in scrip that was good only at the company store—where prices were as much as 50 percent higher than other stores. Companies also deducted money for rent, doctor bills (a mandatory payment, even if the miner did not go to a doctor), burial funds, and "mine expenses." The last of these covered costs of mining that most certainly should have been the company's to bear—costs associated with fuel, explosives, and the maintenance of the miners' tools.

Fed up with this situation, the Harlan County miners formed a local chapter of the United Mine Workers of America (UMWA) in 1931. However, the UMWA had an antistrike policy in effect at the time and refused to support the miners, so they turned to the communist-affiliated National Miners Union (NMU). Although the NMU would ultimately let them down as well, initially it provided assistance.

Faced with demands that they begin treating workers fairly, the coal companies responded by burning down houses and dynamiting soup kitchens. They also put Sheriff John Henry Blair (made infamous in the song "Whose Side Are You On?" by Florence Reece) in charge of strike-breaking gangs. More than a dozen miners were killed, and many more lost their homes. Jesse Wakefield, a lawyer who attempted to defend the miners, also found her home dynamited as well. By January 1932 the miners, cowed by threats of violence and starvation, gave up the strike.

Source: John W. Hevener. *Which Side Are You On? The Harlan County Coal Miners, 1931–39.* Urbana: University of Illinois Press, 1978.

—Judson Knight

1929: On "Black Friday" in October, prices on the U.S. stock market, which had been climbing wildly for several years, suddenly collapse. Thus begins the first phase of a world economic crisis and depression that will last until the beginning of World War II.

1932: When Ukrainians refuse to surrender their grain to his commissars, Stalin seals off supplies to the region, creating a manmade famine that will produce a greater death toll than the entirety of World War I.

1932: A "Bonus Army" of unemployed veterans marches on Washington, D.C. Many leave after Congress refuses their demands for payment of bonuses for wartime service, but others are forcibly removed by General Douglas MacArthur's troops. Also participating are two other figures destined to gain notoriety in the next world war: majors Dwight D. Eisenhower and George S. Patton.

1932: In German elections, Nazis gain a 37 percent plurality of Reichstag seats, raising tensions between the far right and the far left. On a "bloody Sunday" in July, communists in Hamburg attack Nazis with guns, and a fierce battle ensues.

1932: Charles A. Lindbergh's baby son is kidnapped and killed, a crime for which Bruno Hauptmann will be charged in 1934, convicted in 1935, and executed in 1936.

1935: Second phase of New Deal begins with the introduction of social security, farm assistance, and housing and tax reform.

1937: Italy signs the Anti-Comintern Pact, signed by Germany and Japan the preceding year. Like the two others before it, Italy now withdraws from the League of Nations.

1942: Axis conquests reach their height in the middle of this year. The Nazis control a vast region from Normandy to the suburbs of Stalingrad, and from the Arctic Circle to the edges of the Sahara. To the east, the Japanese "Co-Prosperity Sphere" encompasses territories from China to Burma to the East Indies, stretching deep into the western Pacific.

1947: Establishment of the Marshall Plan to assist European nations in recovering from the war.

Event and Its Context

Purpose of an Injunction

An injunction is a court order that forbids either an individual or a group from pursuing a course of action deemed harmful or destructive, especially towards property. The idea is to prevent an injury before it happens, rather than try to provide a remedy after the act is committed. Injunctions come in different forms, although temporary injunctions are the kind most commonly used. Individuals or organizations that think their property might be at risk due to the actions of another may petition a court for relief. Courts often grant a restraining order, or a temporary injunction, in such instances, to be followed by a hearing. Both parties are given the chance to present their side of the story at the hearing. If the presiding judge holds that the petitioner is correct in fearing for the property in question, the judge may issue a permanent injunction, which forbids the defendant to take any action against the property or person of the plaintiff. Defendants who refuse to adhere to the terms of the injunction may be ruled in contempt of court, which puts them at risk of a prison sentence.

Even though injunctions are meant to reduce crimes against property and prevent violence, conflicting issues and opinions swirl round effective use of this legal tool. Two complaints merit discussion. First, an injunction is law decreed by a single person, a judge, for no juries are used in such instances. Second, even though a temporary injunction is simply a holding pattern and does not indict one side or the other, the defendants against whom the injunction has been issued have no recourse or relief until the hearing is held. Regardless of the circumstances, they must either obey the injunction or face the legal consequences.

History of the Injunction

The court injunction has a very long history. The use of the injunction in modern times is based upon English common law. Under this system, in keeping with the definition of the term *injunction,* the monarch was empowered to forbid persons or groups from pursuing specific courses of action. As absolute monarchical rule gradually gave way to civil authority in England, courts of chancery assumed the role of issuing injunctions.

In the United States, courts of equity played the same role, although no one knows for certain when injunctions were first used to try to break the emerging power of the labor movement. What is certain is that the definition of property, the very thing meant to be protected by an injunction, evolved over time. At first property referred only to a physical structure, such as a home, factory, or warehouse. In time property came to include various means of transportation, such as railroads or ships. As the nineteenth century progressed, and with it the Industrial Revolution, owners of industry and capital began to classify their businesses as property. As the meaning of the word broadened, so did attempts to protect property, especially in the emerging capitalist world.

The first injunctions known to be issued against labor in the United States were used against striking railroad workers in 1877. Leaders in the labor movement viewed management's use of the injunction as difficult at best, if not destructive and devastating as well, at least in terms of achieving their goals. The most formidable tool of the labor movement, the strike, demands swift, decisive action at exactly the right moment in order to win a conflict or achieve a more advantageous bargaining position. By using the legal tool of the injunction, management defended its right to conduct business; however, labor lost its edge in the process. Even worse, if labor chose to ignore the injunction, leaders and sometimes members of the rank and file were subject to a fine or prison sentence. Any hope of ameliorating the conditions that led to contemplating a strike or other labor action in the first place was greatly diminished in such a situation.

The Pullman Strike of 1894

Although use of the injunction varied from state to state and even from court to court, the event that brought it to nationwide attention was the infamous Pullman Strike of 1894, which started in Chicago, Illinois, in the midst of an economic depression. George Pullman, who helped to revolutionize long-distance rail travel, manufactured luxury railway cars. In order to maintain control over the workers who labored in his manufacturing plants, Pullman constructed a company town. Here his employees could live close to work, provided that they paid the rents he controlled, patronized his stores, and purchased his utilities. During the economic downturn, Pullman cut the wages of his workers, but he did not reduce the price of living in his town.

Led by Eugene V. Debs and his newly created American Railway Union (ARU), workers initiated a boycott against the Pullman Palace Car Company. The effects of this boycott and ensuing strike were spectacular and widespread, as within a mere two weeks the railway system throughout the Midwest and in some areas of the rest of the United States ground to a halt. By 1894 the country was heavily dependent on railways, so getting them running again engaged the best efforts of federal officials as well as railway management. In searching for a way to break the strike, a federal court issued an injunction against the strikers. They were charged with interfering with the mail and delaying interstate commerce through their actions. Debs, the ARU, and the strikers ignored the injunction.

President Grover Cleveland dispatched federal troops on the spot, which prompted an outburst of violence. Since he had blatantly ignored the injunction, Debs was cited with contempt of court and jailed. When the U.S. Supreme Court upheld the injunction, many labor leaders and ordinary workers realized that management now had access to a new and dangerous means of combating labor activities. Employers were not afraid to turn to the injunction, and courts were more than willing to issue them.

Disputes Arising from Use of the Injunction

After the Pullman Strike, the use of the injunction was hotly disputed, with no shortage of opinions on the matter. Laborers and their leaders viewed the injunction as a way to curb their constitutional rights to free speech and assembly. This was true, as many injunctions were "blanket injunctions," which placed all members of a union or other labor organization under their directives, regardless of their knowledge or participation in a labor dispute. Moreover, many courts refused to adhere to the guidelines of first issuing a temporary injunction and then moving forward to a hearing. Instead, without hearing both sides, they simply ordered the injunction requested by employers. Those who owned a business or industry, however, also had rights. They viewed the injunction as a means to prevent labor unrest, which could potentially destroy not only their property but also their livelihoods.

At the center of this issue was whether or not unions had the right to conduct strikes, boycotts, or other labor actions. In 1842 the U.S. Supreme Court ruled in *Commonwealth v. Hunt* that unions did indeed have the legal right to strike. However, the ruling stopped short of defining what kind of strike was legal, and subsequent judicial decisions propounded the ambiguity, since they conflicted with one another. Therefore, no single legal precedent supported the use of the injunction to quell disruptive labor activities.

Clayton Antitrust Act of 1914

Debate ranged beyond the anger and frustration felt within the labor movement and entered the political realm. The Democratic Party condemned any move toward anti-injunction legislation in the 1896 election, so attempts to enact legal restrictions on management's use of the injunction languished for years at the federal level. Finally, however, Congress passed the Clayton Antitrust Act in 1914. The federal government was following in the footsteps of six states that had enacted similar legislation prior to this time. The Clayton Act was intended to strengthen the earlier Sherman Antitrust Act and eased the restrictive use of the injunction. According to the act, labor activities such as peaceful picketing, boycotts, and strikes were both legal and immune to the labor injunction, unless plaintiffs could prove that property might be irreparably damaged. Employers were also required to give unions notice prior to the issuance of an injunction.

Truax v. Corrigan

For a few years the truce among labor, management, and the injunction held. In the 1921 U.S. Supreme Court case *Truax v. Corrigan,* however, an Arizona law that was based on the Clayton Act was declared unconstitutional. At issue was a picketed boycott of a restaurant, and in striking down the law, the Court argued that the owner's right to do business was protected by both the Fourteenth Amendment and the due process clause. In the wake of this decision, state legislatures throughout the country used the language of *Truax v. Corrigan* to rewrite their anti-injunction laws, many of which passed state constitutional review.

Iterations of Anti-Injunction Legislation

The torch passed once again to the federal government to enact an anti-injunction law that would pass court review, and Congress began to investigate the matter seriously. First, in order to create acceptable legislation, they called specialists to testify in committees and to work with them to write the law in such a way that it would pass constitutional muster in the courts. In 1927, even while states were busy reworking their laws following the *Truax v. Corrigan* decision, Congress prepared to send an anti-injunction bill to the floor for consideration. Introduced by Senator Henrik Shipstead of Minnesota, the bill revised the meaning of property. In March 1928 a Senate committee, led by George Norris, began hearings on the bill. Organized labor considered the bill ineffective. Even Shipstead himself was not committed to the act, and when the committee decided to rewrite the measure altogether, he did not object.

In May 1928 Norris submitted a new bill. The proposed law banned yellow-dog contracts and gave labor the legal authority to organize and to engage in collective bargaining. Except in specific circumstances, which were clearly outlined in the bill, federal courts no longer had jurisdiction to issue injunctions. Courts could no longer require labor to stop a lawful, peaceful strike, nor could they prevent workers from assembling to discuss, plan, or encourage a strike. The bill removed the stigma of "unlawful conspiracy" from workers engaged in a labor dispute, and labor leaders could no longer be held responsible for the actions of the rank and file. However, if authorities determined that a situation was unlawful or that irreparable injury to property or persons was imminent, courts were empowered to offer relief in the form of an injunction.

Norris–La Guardia Becomes Law

During the debate, revisions were made to the bill, and a new version was again ready for consideration in 1930. Because of various political roadblocks and sidetracking, however, the Senate's Judiciary Committee did not vote on the bill until 1932. Following their favorable vote, the bill moved to the Senate floor for consideration and was overwhelmingly approved. Norris himself delivered a copy of the Senate bill to Fiorello La Guardia of New York, a member of the House of Representatives. La Guardia presented the bill on the House floor, which made him a cosponsor; therefore, his name was appended to the title. The measure received an overwhelmingly positive reception, and the House quickly passed it. On 23 March 1932 President Herbert Hoover signed the bill into law.

Provisions of Norris–La Guardia

Despite the many revisions and changes made to the measure between 1928 and 1932, the power of Norris–La Guardia was not diminished. Federal courts were forbidden to issue injunctions in the case of labor disputes. Workers were permitted to strike, or merely begin a work stoppage, and the courts were not allowed to prevent these actions. Furthermore, unions could assist striking workers and their families with subsistence funds, something some courts in the past had prevented through injunctions.

Additionally, provided that there was no evidence of violence or fraud, workers could lawfully publicize the strike, boycott, or picket. They could also encourage workers still on the job to support the action by joining forces with the strikers. Most importantly, employers could no longer make workers choose between having a job and joining a union, since courts of law could no longer enforce yellow-dog contracts. However, Norris–La Guardia balanced labor's gains with provisions for employers, who could still bring suit against unions in civil court. Moreover, swift prosecution awaited anyone, labor or management, involved in criminal actions under the guise of a labor activity or management response to it.

Norris–La Guardia represented a victory for labor, but the bill's becoming law coincided with some of the darkest years of the Great Depression. Thousands of people were out of work, and while the injunction issue mattered, many other concerns garnered workers' attention as well. The election of Franklin D. Roosevelt to the presidency and the beginnings of the New Deal assured labor's achieving even greater gains, especially in the realm of collective bargaining. Labor-management relations remained cordial throughout the World War II years, as everyone was focused on the war effort.

Norris–La Guardia After World War II

The end of the war, however, marked a backlash against the gains labor had won during the previous two decades. In 1947 the Taft-Hartley Act was passed over President Harry S Truman's veto. Taft-Hartley rolled back many of labor's hard-won gains. For example, the law banned the closed shop and allowed employers to sue a union if the company incurred any sort of damages, especially monetary, due to a strike.

The injunction issue never completely disappeared and is still contentious from time to time today. However, use of the injunction no longer provokes the controversy it did in the early years of the twentieth century. Passage of the Norris–La Guardia Act was a milestone in labor history. From the battles begun on the state level to the eventual passage of federal legislation, the injunction issue was a major rallying cry for workers who were being prevented from exercising their constitutional rights of free speech and assembly. Moreover, Norris–La Guardia was the logical precursor to the much more extensive National Labor Relations Act (also known as the Wagner Act), the most important single piece of labor legislation enacted in the United States in the twentieth century.

Key Players

La Guardia, Fiorello Henry (1882–1947): Greatly loved and respected mayor of New York City (1933–1945). A coalition with La Guardia as its standard bearer unseated the Tammany Hall regime in New York City, ending years of corrupt machine politics. Prior to his leadership role in New York City, La Guardia served in the House of Representatives briefly in 1916. He left this post to serve as a pilot during World War I. He was reelected to the House in 1922 and served four terms, during which time he supported the right of women to vote and laws governing child labor. He opposed Prohibition and cosponsored the Norris–La Guardia Act.

Norris, George (1861–1944): Although born in Ohio, Norris eventually moved to Nebraska, where he served as prosecuting attorney, district judge, congressman from 1903 to 1918, and then eventually senator from 1913 to 1942, during which time he worked indefatigably to secure passage of a federal anti-injunction act.

See also: *Clayton Antitrust Act; Commonwealth v. Hunt; Pullman Strike; Taft-Hartley Act; Traux v. Corrigan; Wagner Act.*

BIBLIOGRAPHY

Books

Bernstein, Irving. *The Lean Years: A History of the American Worker, 1920–1933.* Boston, MA: Houghton Mifflin, 1960.

Frankfurter, Felix, and Nathan Greene. *The Labor Injunction.* New York: Macmillan, 1930.

Friedman, Lawrence. *A History of American Law.* New York: Simon & Schuster, 1985.

Taylor, Albion Guilford. *Labor Problems and Labor Law.* New York: Prentice Hall, 1938.

Taylor, Benjamin, and Fred Witney. *U.S. Labor Relations Law: Historical Development.* Englewood Cliffs, NJ: Prentice Hall, 1992.

Periodicals

Newton-Matza, Mitchell. "The Crack of the Whip: The Chicago Federation of Labor Battles Against the Labor Injunction in the 1920s." *Journal of the Illinois State Historical Society* 93 (spring 2000): 82–107.

—Mitchell Newton-Matza

North American Free Trade Agreement

North America 1992

Synopsis

After two years of negotiations, the North American Free Trade Agreement (NAFTA) was signed on 17 December 1992 by President Bush of the United States, President Salinas of Mexico, and Prime Minister Mulroney of Canada. NAFTA took effect on 1 January 1994. The act immediately lifted the majority of tariffs on goods exported among the three countries, with the remaining barriers to free trade of goods and services to be phased out over a period of 15 years. Additional provisions included in NAFTA cover environmental and labor concerns. The agreement also provides for future regional and multilateral cooperation to expand free-trade areas in the Americas.

Timeline

1973: Signing of peace accords in Paris in January ends the Vietnam War.

1978: U.S. Senate approves a measure presented by President Carter the year before, to turn the Panama Canal over to Panama by 2000.

1982: Argentina invades the Falkland Islands, a British possession, and Great Britain strikes back in a ten-week war from which Britain emerges victorious.

1986: In November, the scandal variously known as Iran-Contra, Irangate, and Contragate breaks, when it is revealed that the Reagan administration agreed to sell arms to Iran in exchange for hostages, and to divert the funds from the arms sales to support the anti-Sandinista Contras in Nicaragua.

1991: The United States and other allies in the UN force commence the war against Iraq on 15 January. By 3 April the war is over, a resounding victory for the Allied force.

1992: Trouble begins after the Yugoslav Federation breaks up in January. Soon Yugoslavia, now dominated by Serbia, is at war in several former Yugoslav republics, and in September, the United Nations expels Yugoslavia.

1992: Former Panamanian leader General Manuel Noriega is convicted on drug charges in a U.S. court and is sentenced to forty years in prison.

1992: Four Los Angeles police officers are acquitted in April on federal civil rights charges stemming from the 1991 beating of motorist Rodney King, an incident captured on videotape. Following the announcement of the verdict, Los Angeles erupts with rioting and looting.

1992: U.S. military forces depart the Philippines, ending nearly a century of American presence in that country.

1992: Despite a campaign fraught with controversy involving the candidate's evasion of the draft, his extramarital affairs, and allegations of shady financial dealings, Bill Clinton wins election as President of the United States. The election marks a changing of the guard in several respects: not only does it end twelve years of Republicans in the White House, but Clinton is the first baby boomer elected president.

1998: Scandal engulfs the White House amid allegations that President Clinton instructed former White House intern Monica Lewinsky to lie about their sexual affair. Clinton's fortunes begin to improve, however, late in the summer, after rumors circulate that his filmed deposition, scheduled to be televised, reveals damning evidence. In fact the deposition presents him in a positive light, and he appears as the victim of unfair scrutiny. Thenceforth, Clinton and his damage-control team have the upper hand, and in the end, it will be House Speaker Newt Gingrich, not Clinton, who is forced to step down.

Event and Its Context

NAFTA's Beginning

The negotiations that ultimately led to the North American Free Trade Agreement, NAFTA, began in August 1990 when the U.S. trade representative, Carla A. Hills, and the Mexican secretary for commerce and industrial development, Jamie Serra Puche, recommended to their respective presidents that formal negotiations should begin on a comprehensive free trade agreement. Shortly after that recommendation, President Salinas of Mexico sent a formal proposal to President Bush suggesting the negotiations should begin as soon as possible for a free trade agreement between the U.S. and Mexico in accordance with each country's official legal procedures.

The Canada–United States Free Trade Agreement, FTA, had been in place between the United States and Canada since 1 January 1989. The FTA had the general provisions for the gradual elimination of tariffs and the reduction of nontariff trade barriers on goods that were later incorporated into NAFTA in 1992. There were some improvements to FTA, however, when it was replaced by NAFTA. The main change was that NAFTA included Mexico and expanded free trade into such areas as investment, services, intellectual property, competition, the cross-border movement of business persons, and government procurement.

In September 1990 President Bush sent a formal notification to the chairman of the Committee on Ways and Means in accordance with the existing Omnibus Trade and Competitiveness Act of 1988 that negotiations were to begin with Mexico. He also noted that the Canadian government asked to participate in the negotiations with the intentions of getting an agreement among the three countries.

In March 1991 President Bush asked Congress to apply fast-track legislation to the proposed North American Free Trade Agreement and Congress agreed. Fast track is an expeditious procedure to get important legislation processed. The fast track procedure was included in the Trade Act of 1974. It provides for a strict timetable, a limit to the time spent on debate, and prohibition on adding amendments to the bill or resolution.

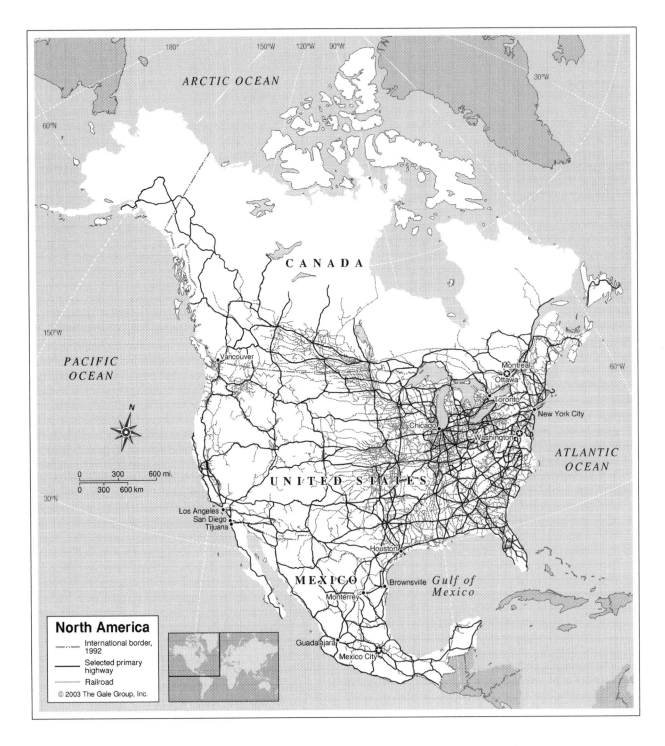

Fast track provides for a 90-day window between the time the president notifies Congress and the date he actually signs the agreement.

On 12 August 1992 President Bush announced that the negotiations were completed for the North American Free Trade Agreement between Mexico, Canada, and the United States. On 7 October 1992 President Bush, President Salinas, and Prime Minister Mulroney met in San Antonio, Texas, where they made a commitment to adopt NAFTA in 1993 with an effective date of 1 January 1994. The actual signing of the Agreement

was on 17 December 1992 when Bush, Salinas, and Mulroney each signed it in their respective capitals. The date was the last date President Bush could sign the agreement under the fast track provision.

By the time NAFTA was actually signed, President Bush had lost his bid for reelection to President-elect Clinton, but Clinton declared his support for NAFTA, with some reservations regarding issues he considered still needed to be addressed. These included the environment, workers, and special safeguards for unexpected surges in imports. NAFTA had be-

President Bill Clinton signs add-on chapters 27 and 28 to the North American Free Trade Agreement, applauding from left, vice president Al Gore, House Minority Leader Bob Michel, and House Speaker Thomas Foley, Mellon Auditorium, Washington, D.C. AP/Wide World Photos. Reproduced by permission.

come a hotly debated issue during the presidential campaign, particularly by a third-party candidate, Ross Perot, who declared in a heated presidential debate that the real effect of NAFTA would be a "giant sucking sound" caused by millions of jobs moving across the U.S. border to Mexico.

The Benefits of NAFTA

The 500-plus page NAFTA document is a complex legal agreement that spells out in great detail all aspects related to a free trade zone that represented a combined economy of $6.5 trillion and 370 million people in 1992. The North American Free Trade Agreement created the world's largest integrated market for goods and services. NAFTA also was designed to serve as a guide for the liberalization of trade throughout the Western Hemisphere.

Foremost in the agreement is the gradual elimination of all tariffs on North American-made goods. Because the United States and Canada already had a free-trade pact, the principal benefit of NAFTA was the increased trade opportunities with Mexico, which at the time was the second largest importer of

U.S.-manufactured goods and the third largest importer of U.S. agricultural products.

Before NAFTA, Mexican tariffs were about two and a half times comparable to U.S. duties. NAFTA eliminated tariffs on more than half of the 9,000 goods traded between Mexico and the U.S., with about 15 percent more to be eliminated in the next five years. The tariffs on the rest were scheduled to be removed at intervals of between two and 15 years after the start of NAFTA. Product sensitivity determines the tariff removal schedule. Each country has some products that it feels need a longer period of protection to adjust to a free market. Sensitive products for Mexico include agricultural products such as orange juice, sugar, and corn. Textiles are another example. Approximately 65 percent of U.S. industrial and agricultural exports were either tariff free at the start of NAFTA or would be free within five years. The existing schedule for tariff reductions between the U.S. and Canada remained the same as it was in the 1989 Free Trade Agreement.

The principal benefits of NAFTA are outlined at the start of the agreement. They are then elaborated more specifically through sections on principles and rules that include national

Some Statistics on Violence in the Workplace from the Late 1980s to the Early 1990s

From 1987 to 1992, nearly 875,000 eight-hour shifts, along with the company profits associated with them, were lost because of workplace violence.

During 1992, there were 1,004 workplace homicides in the United States. Of these, 33 percent were technical, sales, or administrative support employees; 22 percent were in service occupations; 20 percent were operators, fabricators, or laborers; 18 percent were managers or professionals; and 7 percent were in other jobs.

In 1993, more secretaries were killed on the job than policemen and bartenders—two high-risk groups—combined.

Of all professions, nursing aides were the workers most likely to be assaulted on the job in 1993.

On average, three workers died each day due to violence in the workplace.

Contrary to popular belief, the postal service had less workplace violence than most industries. The overall homicide rate was 0.8 deaths per 100,000 workers, whereas the U.S. Postal Service had 0.52 deaths per 100,000 workers.

Source: *Safe Jobs: Promises Kept, Promises Broken: 25 Years of Worker Safety and Health in the United States.* Washington, DC: AFL-CIO, 1996.

—Judson Knight

treatment and Most-Favored-Nation treatment. The United States changed the name "Most-Favored Nation" in 1998 to "Normal Trade Relations." Nearly all U.S. trading partners have Normal Trade Relations, which does not mean that they are free of tariffs.

As presented in the agreement under Article 102, NAFTA's objectives are to eliminate barriers to trade and facilitate the cross-border movement of goods and services, promote fair competition, increase investment opportunities in the countries governed by the agreement, protect and enforce intellectual property rights, create procedures for the implementation and administration of the agreement and for the resolution of disputes; and to establish a framework for cooperation in the expansion and enhancement of the benefits of the agreement.

The terms of the agreement dictate that NAFTA will prevail in the case of any conflict between it and other agreements that are in place. The exceptions to this are specific trade obligations that are set out in the *Convention on International Trade in Endangered Species of Wild Fauna and Flora*, the *Montreal Protocol on Substances that Deplete the Ozone Layer*, and the *Basel Convention on the Control of Transboundary Movements of Hazardous Wastes and Their Disposal*.

NAFTA also provides for continuing adherence to two preexisting agreements: an agreement signed in 1983 between the United States and Mexico related to environmental concerns for the protection and improvement in the border area, and one signed in 1986 between the United States and Canada that governs the transboundary movement of hazardous waste.

Rules of Origin

NAFTA covers North American-made goods. This sounds straightforward, but it is not. A great many goods, particularly autos and automotive goods, are made in part or whole from materials of foreign origin. Textiles, another sensitive area, required incorporation of special Rules-of-Origin in the Agreement because they may be manufactured with foreign materials. Among the many regulations in NAFTA is one that stipulates that manufacturers of finished goods that are exported from a *maquiladora* (manufacturing plant) in Mexico to the U.S or Canada have 60 days from the date of export to pay Mexico import duties on non-NAFTA parts contained in the goods.

The FTA with Canada already covered automobiles and automotive parts, and U.S. automotive parts manufacturers were already in Mexico for a number of years before NAFTA. With NAFTA, the Mexican-U.S. tariffs were being phased out to the advantage of all three countries. This raised concern for the possibility that European and Japanese automobile and automotive parts manufacturers would establish businesses in Mexico to get their products into the United States using the tariff advantages of NAFTA.

Rules-of-Origin is such a complex issue that the U.S. Department of Commerce (DOC) lists it as one of the most commonly misunderstood issues. DOC therefore suggests that exporters should seek legal assistance or an advanced ruling from the Customs Administration in the country to which they are exporting if they are unsure of the answers in filling out a NAFTA Certificate of Origin. When foreign components or raw materials are used in the manufactured products, it may be necessary to get a customs ruling on each item in them to get a NAFTA tariff benefit on the finished product.

Maquiladoras

A maquiladora is a Mexican manufacturing plant that operates with foreign capital and management to produce goods for export. The program is a "value added" operation named after the payment given to millers by farmers for the service of grinding corn into meal. The foreign assembly operations are sometimes simply called *maquilas*. Mexico started permitting foreign assembly plants in 1965 to get some of the off-shore business that was going to Taiwan and Singapore and other foreign countries as U.S. companies were using lower cost labor to remain competitive in world markets. Maquiladoras may be simple assembly plants that use foreign parts or they may be in the business to manufacture products from raw materials through to finished products. They have also expanded into nonindustrial operations such as data-processing and packaging.

In 1989 the Mexican government published a Decree for Development and Operation of the Maquiladora Industry that outlines maquila program application procedures and requirements and the special provisions that apply to running one. The provisions of the Decree are incorporated in the text of NAFTA with timetables for bringing in line any inconsistencies. For example, NAFTA includes a provision that gives Mexico until 1 January 2004 to maintain the decree as it applies to the development and modernization of the automotive industry; at that point Mexico must bring any inconsistent provisions into conformity with other provisions in NAFTA.

The maquiladora program started slowly in the 1960s but grew rapidly once the Mexican government made the first revisions to regulations early in the 1980s. Those regulations were replaced by the 1989 decree. The maquiladora movement has created a population migration to the border region, particularly in the Matamoros, Mexico/Brownsville, Texas, region and the Tijuana, Mexico/San Diego, California, region. The maquiladoras may be located anywhere in Mexico, but congestion and existing industrial development prompted a mandate that the maquiladoras must be located away from major urban areas such as Mexico City, Guadalajara, and Monterrey. The border region is favored because it is closest to the point of export.

NAFTA: More Than a Trade Agreement

NAFTA covers more than trade in goods. It also covers services such as engineering, construction, accounting, tourism, land transportation, architecture, education, health care, management, and environmental services. In 1992 the Mexican combined services market was estimated to be worth $146 billion. At the time, the U.S. share was about 5 percent of that.

NAFTA requires each country to treat foreign service providers no less favorably than it treats its own service providers. Also, no country may require a foreign service provider to maintain a local office or enterprise as a condition of cross-border provision of a service. The agreement spells out a timetable for the negotiation or liberalization of local laws that do not comply.

NAFTA covers banking, insurance, investment, and intellectual property issues as well as services and trade in goods. The agreement specifically addresses financial services by financial institutions in the banking, insurance, and securities sectors and spells out the requirements in detail. As a result of the agreement, U.S. banks and securities firms were able to establish wholly owned subsidiaries in Mexico for the first time in 50 years. Although there are limits on the market share, the opening of the Mexican banking and financial market is significant part of the agreement. There are similar agreements in place with Canada from the Canada–U.S. Free Trade Agreement, and under NAFTA, Canada-Mexico financial services and institutions will be similarly structured.

NAFTA's intellectual property stipulations require each country to provide the same effective enforcement of the rights to the protection of copyright, patent, trademark, plant breeders' rights, industrial designs, trade secrets, integrated circuits, and geographical indications to foreign intellectual property that it provides to its own citizens. The copyright protection extends to all types of computer programs as literary works. Throughout NAFTA there are provisions to handle dispute resolution.

NAFTA Add-ons: Environment and Labor

Chapters 27 and 28 were added to NAFTA after President Clinton came to office in 1993, but they were part of the agreement when it came into effect on 1 January 1994. Chapter 27,

the North American Agreement on Environmental Cooperation (NAAEC), is designed to promote sustainable development based on supportive environmental and economic policies.

Among the issues that prompted the addition of environmental cooperation to NAFTA was a growing recognition of the long-range air transport of persistent pollutants that cross borders on what are described as continental pollutant pathways. Other concerns included the deterioration of the environment in border areas where expanding maquiladoras meant burgeoning populations. One of the objectives of NAAEC is to promote pollution prevention policies and practices without creating trade distortions or new trade barriers.

As with all of NAFTA, each country's laws govern actions within its own borders. The levels of domestic environmental protection and environmental development policies and priorities are a local prerogative, but the parties have agreed to ensure high levels of environmental protection and to improve laws and regulations. The local laws and regulations must be published. When a country bans a pesticide or toxic substance, the export into that country of the banned substance is prohibited.

NAFTA created the Commission for Environmental Cooperation (CEC) to establish programs that foster the development of regional information and the sharing of technical expertise. CEC also addresses issues related to the conservation of wildlife and natural ecosystems in North America, such as that of the monarch butterfly.

Chapter 28, the North American Agreement on Labor Cooperation (NAALC), recognizes that NAFTA was created to expand and secure markets for goods and services and to enhance the competitiveness of each country's businesses in global markets. It also was intended to create new employment opportunities while improving working conditions and living standards in each country's respective environment. Basic worker rights were to be protected and enhanced.

The labor component of NAFTA added a resolution to invest in continuous human resource development, promote employment security, and strengthen labor–management cooperation. NAALC prompted the creation of cooperative programs and technical exchanges between the countries on industrial relations, health and safety, child labor, gender, and migrant worker issues.

Unfortunately, as the respect for basic labor standards increases in Mexico, the cost of labor is making the maquiladoras less competitive on the global level. The Ross Perot complaint that there would be a "giant sucking sound" as U.S. companies went south for cheaper labor is now a concern in Mexico, as U.S. companies are looking to countries such as China for cheap labor.

Free Trade Area of the Americas (FTAA)

In 1994 conferees at a Summit of the Americas initiated a process designed to integrate the economies of all of the democratic countries of the Western Hemisphere into a single free trade agreement. In accordance with one of the objectives of NAFTA, Canada, the United States, and Mexico have been active in negotiations that may open the world's largest market to free trade.

Key Players

Mulroney, Martin Brian (1939–): Mulroney was prime minister of Canada between 1984 and 1993. He was a strong promoter of the North American Free Trade Agreement and signed NAFTA for Canada in 1992.

Perot, H. Ross (1930–): Perot was a candidate for the office of president of the United States in 1992 when NAFTA was being negotiated. He was not in favor of the agreement and in a public debate among the candidates declared that there would be a "giant sucking sound" as jobs moved to Mexico if NAFTA were approved. Perot, a Texan, was the founder of Electronic Data Systems.

Salinas de Gortari, Carlos (1948–): Salinas was president of Mexico between 1988 and 1994. He was a major promoter of NAFTA and signed the North American Free Trade Agreement for Mexico in 1992.

See also: *Maquiladoras Established.*

BIBLIOGRAPHY

Books

Glick, Leslie Alan. *Understanding the North American Free Trade Agreement.* Boston: Kluwer Law & Taxation Publishers, 1993.

Periodicals

Greider, William. "A New Giant Sucking Sound." *The Nation* (31 December 2001): 22–24.

"NAFTA'S Scorecard: So Far, So Good." *Business Week* (9 July 2001): 54–56.

Other

Foreign Trade Information System (SICE). "Free Trade Areas of the Americas—FTAA" [cited 1 August 2002]. <http://www.sice.oas.org/ftaa_e.asp>.

Issues 2000. "Ross Perot on Free Trade." 2000 [cited 1 August 2002]. <http://www.issues2000.org/Ross_Perot_Free_Trade.htm>.

North American Free Trade Agreement. NAFTA Trilateral Customs Web Site. "Chapter 4: Rules of Origin" [cited 1 August 2002]. <http://www.customs.gov/nafta/docs/us/chap04.html>.

North American Free Trade Agreement. NAFTA Trilateral Customs Web Site. "Public Law 103-182" [cited 1 August 2002].<http://www.customs.gov/nafta/agreement.htm>.

U.S. Department of Commerce. Trade Information Center. "NAFTA Update." Created 20 December 1999; last modified 17 January 2002 [cited 1 August 2002]. <http://tradeinfo.doc.gov>.

United States Trade Representative. "NAFTA: The Agreement" [cited 1 August 2002]. <http://www.ustr.gov/regions/whemisphere/nafta.shtml>.

ADDITIONAL RESOURCES

Books

Folsom, Ralph H. *NAFTA in a Nutshell.* Eagan, MN: West Group, 1999.

Mayer, Frederick. *Interpreting NAFTA: The Science and Art of Political Analysis.* New York: Columbia University Press, 1998.

Orme, William. *Understanding NAFTA: Mexico, Free Trade, and the New North America.* Austin, TX: University of Texas Press, 1996.

Other

"Research Guide on the North American Free Trade Agreement (NAFTA)" Vanderbilt University Alyne Queener Massey Law Library [cited 1 August 2002]. <http://law.vanderbilt.edu/library/research/nafta.html>.

—M. C. Nagel

O

Occupational Safety and Health Act

United States 1970

Synopsis

A tragic byproduct of the Industrial Revolution was an alarming rate of death, serious injury, and illness among the generally young, poorly trained, and often immigrant workers. By the 1960s, 14,000 workers were dying on the job each year. Individual states and the U.S. government were making disjointed efforts to provide safer and healthier workplaces, but labor, politicians, and the general public all recognized that a federal agency was needed to coordinate efforts. A bill was promoted in President Lyndon B. Johnson's administration but it died in Congress. The legislature quickly introduced a new bill, and in December 1970, President Richard M. Nixon signed into law the Occupational Safety and Health Act, which established OSHA, the Occupational Health and Safety Administration, and two other supportive agencies.

Timeline

1950: North Korean troops pour into South Korea, starting the Korean War.

1955: Signing of the Warsaw Pact by the Soviet Union and its satellites in eastern Europe.

1959: Alaska and Hawaii become the last states added to the Union.

1965: Arrest of the Rev. Martin Luther King, Jr., and more than 2,600 others in Selma, Alabama. Three weeks later, in New York City, Malcolm X is assassinated.

1967: Arabs attack Israel, launching the Six-Day War, which results in an Israeli victory.

1970: After thirty-two months of civil war in Nigeria, Biafran secessionists surrender in January.

1970: Nixon sends U.S. troops into Cambodia on 30 April. Four days later, National Guardsmen open fire on antiwar protesters at Kent State University in Ohio. By 24 June antiwar sentiment is so strong that the Senate repeals the Gulf of Tonkin resolution. On 29 June, Nixon orders troops back out of Cambodia.

1970: Gamal Abdel Nasser, father of Arab nationalism and mentor of younger leaders such as Libya's Muammar al-Qaddafi, dies.

1973: Signing of peace accords in Paris in January ends the Vietnam War.

1975: Pol Pot's Khmer Rouge launch a campaign of genocide in Cambodia.

1980: In protest of the Soviet invasion of Afghanistan, President Carter keeps U.S. athletes out of the Moscow Olympics.

1985: A new era begins in the USSR as Konstantin Chernenko dies and is replaced by Mikhail Gorbachev, who at fifty-four years old is the youngest Soviet leader in decades.

Event and Its Context

The Williams-Steiger Occupational Safety and Health Act of 1970

The Occupational Safety and Health Act of 1970 that established the Occupational Safety and Health Administration (OSHA) was signed into law on 29 December 1970 by President Richard M. Nixon. To some it is known as the Williams-Steiger Occupational Safety and Health Act in honor of Congressman Harrison A. Williams Jr. of New Jersey and Senator William A. Steiger of Wisconsin, who led the fight to get the act passed from the time a similar bill was defeated in President Johnson's administration in 1968. The act has also been called the Safety Bill of Rights.

In the Introduction to Public Law 91–596, 91st Congress, S.2193, 29 December 1970—as the document is titled—under the simple heading, "An Act," it states the purpose of the bill is "to assure safe and healthful working conditions for working men and women; by authorizing enforcement of standards developed under the Act; by assisting the States in their efforts to assure safe and healthful working conditions; by providing for research, information, education, and training in the field of occupational safety and health; and for other purposes."

The law required the formation of three different permanent agencies to carry out the mandates of the bill. The first and key agency is the Occupational Safety and Health Administration, the official OSHA. This agency comes under the Labor Department with an assistant secretary of labor for occupational safety and health as the head. OSHA sets and enforces workplace safety and health standards. When it was formed, OSHA was given two years to set up federal and consensus standards. Many standards were first adopted from respected organizations such as the American National Standards Institute, the National Fire Protection Association (popularly known as NFPA), and the American Conference of Governmental Industrial Hygienists. OSHA is also involved in education and outreach programs aimed at accident prevention.

The second agency is the National Institute for Occupational Safety and Health (NIOSH), which was initially part of the Department of Health, Education and Welfare (HEW), a cabinet-level department created by President Eisenhower in 1953. In 1980, HEW was renamed the Department of Health and Human Services. NIOSH is part of the Centers for Disease Control and Prevention in the Department of Health and Human

President Richard M. Nixon signing Occupational Safety and Health Act, Washington, D.C. AP/Wide World Photos. Reproduced by permission.

Services where it is responsible for research on occupational safety and health matters.

The third agency created is the Occupational Safety and Health Review Commission (OSHRC). This independent federal agency handles disputes between the Department of Labor and employers regarding OSHA enforcement actions. OSHRC is not part of any other federal department. The purpose of this approach was to enable OSHRC to provide impartial judgments. There are two levels of adjudication. If the first level judge does not resolve the case, it is reviewed by the agency's Commissioners for final settlement.

The Long Struggle

The industrial revolution in the nineteenth century brought more than mass production of material goods. It produced misery for common workers in the form of industrial accidents. After the Civil War in the United States factories proliferated and with them chemicals, dusts, and unguarded machinery and a workforce that was generally young and inadequately trained; many were new immigrants. As the number of grisly accidents and deaths grew, so did a labor movement devoted to convincing states to pass safety and health laws. Massachusetts passed the first factory inspection law in 1877. By 1890 eight more states had factory inspections, 13 required machine guarding, and 21 had some regulations for health hazards.

The start of the twentieth century is sometimes called the Progressive Era for the group in American society who worked for a better and safer lifestyle. Newspapers and national magazines were widely circulated. In 1907 a coal mine disaster in West Virginia killed 362 miners. The tragic news was carried across the country. The public outcry led to the formation of the U.S. Bureau of Mines in 1910 to promote mine safety. News of the working hazards in the steel industry, where about 1200 out of every 10,000 workers were killed or seriously injured, led to the formation of the National Safety Council in 1915. Two years earlier the U.S. Congress created a Department of Labor with the secretary of labor specifically commissioned to report on industrial disease and accidents.

In 1933, President Franklin D. Roosevelt appointed Frances Perkins secretary of labor. She was the first woman cabinet member in the U.S. Perkins brought experience in occupational safety and health from her earlier work in New York. The U.S. Public Health Service began funding programs that were run by state health departments. The Fair Labor Standards Act of 1938 included provisions to bar workers under 18 from hazardous occupations. Perkins led the Department of Labor until 1945.

Unfortunately by the 1950s the federal-state partnerships were inadequate to protect workers. The secretary of labor was given power to prosecute willful violators for the workers cov-

Mexican farm worker labors in bin full of cotton, Palacios, Texas. © James A. Sugar/Corbis. Reproduced by permission.

ered under an amendment to the 1958 Workers' Compensation Act. In 1960, the Department of Labor acquired more authority and began applying occupational safety and health regulations to a wide range of industrial settings, but those efforts were not well received. Business protested that the rules were too restrictive, and there was growing resentment that the federal regulations were replacing state efforts.

By 1965 pollution in the environment had become an added public concern. The Public Health Service produced a report, "Protecting the Health of Eighty Million Americans," that cited dangers from the rapidly growing use of technology and new chemicals. The AFL-CIO labor unions called on President Johnson to support the major national occupational health and safety efforts suggested in the report. A mining tragedy again brought action. This was not as dramatic as the coal mine disaster, but it was a major public concern as it revealed the high death rate in the uranium industry. Conflicting opinions regarding safe levels of exposure and who had responsibility precipitated Secretary of Labor Willard Wirtz's announcement of standards.

At the start of 1968 President Johnson asked Congress to develop an occupational safety and health program that was essentially the same as the one that the Department of Labor had put in place. Wirtz led the first hearings and pointed out that there were two casualty lists in America: one from the Vietnam War and one from industrial accidents. The Labor Department pushed hard for legislation. The booklet "On the Job Slaughter," published by the Labor Department, featured horrendous pictures of accident victims, but unfortunately the pictures were old and the publicity backfired. The Johnson-supported legislation never came to a vote.

In 1969, in spite of considerable disagreement on who should be leading occupational safety and health measures, the legislature introduced new bills similar to the Johnson general health and safety bill. In that year it was estimated that every month while the debates of who is responsible continued, 1,100 U.S. workers would die.

Labor leader George Meany, president of AFL-CIO, supported the bill. Also, activist groups such as those led by consumer advocate Ralph Nader kept fighting for a number of causes including occupational safety. Their work is credited with contributing to the formation of OSHA. Nader's efforts also are credited as influential in the formation of the Environmental Protection Agency (EPA).

A Rough Start in Troubled Times

OSHA was conceived and began operation in a period of political turmoil. The hopelessness of the Vietnam War drove President Johnson to not seek another term in 1969. Fortunately, the Occupational Safety and Health Act survived and became law in President Nixon's first year in office. Nixon had a goal he called New Federalism to establish new working partnerships between the federal government and the states. However, that policy was not pushed with OSHA. The spotty history of occupational health and safety in the hands of states had prompted the creation of the federal agency. The law does provide for state programs that offer workers protection "as effective as" what is provided in the federal program. Among OSHA's responsibilities is oversight of the state programs.

The first head of OSHA was George Guenther. He had been the head of a family hosiery manufacturing firm and also brought to the position experience in the Pennsylvania Department of Labor and Industry. Guenther described his philosophy for the agency as one of striving to be "responsive and reasonable." An early decision to seek voluntary compliance by companies was well received by business. Limited resources required OSHA to target investigation of catastrophic accidents and employer compliance in the most dangerous and unhealthy work environments. The first standard that was set by OSHA was for asbestos fiber exposure. In 1969, an asbestos-related illness expert, Dr. Irving J. Selikoff of Manhattan's Mount Sinai Hospital, predicted that 40 percent of the nation's 36,000 insulation installers could die of asbestos-related cancer.

In spite of Guenther's goal to be reasonable, OSHA rushed to enforce rules immediately in 1971 rather than take the two years allowed in the law, a policy that was very poorly received. Counting on states to be far more active in OSHA's goals than they were, Guenther had underestimated the need for enforcement staff. Adding to these troubles, a very damaging internal memo surfaced during the 1974 Watergate investigations. The memo indicated that Nixon was looking for ways to tailor OSHA's programs to increase business support for his reelection campaign in 1972. There is no evidence that Guenther acted on the memo, but the revelation tarnished the agency's reputation at the time.

Meany and Nader both began speaking out for the full implementation of the Occupational Safety and Health Act. Nader prepared a condemning report titled *Occupational Epidemic*. Business leaders gave mixed reviews. Small businesses opposed OSHA; large organizations mostly tolerated it, but some challenged the competence of OSHA inspectors. Bills were entered in Congress in 1972 to limit OSHA's powers, principally to exempt small employers. Several bills made their way to Nixon's desk but were stopped with a presidential veto.

Nixon replaced most of his political appointees in 1972, including Guenther. With the political problems in Washington, D.C., it is not surprising that OSHA continued to be an agency in crisis. Nixon had just appointed a new secretary of the Department of Labor when there were two serious workplace accidents: first, an explosion of a large liquefied natural gas tank in New York that killed 40, and three weeks later, a high-rise building under construction near Washington collapsed killing more than a dozen, just as John H. Stender, an official on the Boilermakers Union, was appointed the new head of OSHA.

As a labor leader, Stender seemed an ideal choice for the job, but he had little administrative experience. Under his leadership a number of new standards were put into place, including one for vinyl chloride in 1974 when an epidemic of liver cancer was discovered among workers. That same year, Senator Williams' labor subcommittee charged the agency with being "shackled by administrative ineptitude." Stender is not blamed for the crises, but the agency was being seriously criticized by labor and big business, as well as Congress, by the time he left in 1975.

OSHA Finally Gets Respect

When President Nixon resigned in August 1974 and President Gerald R. Ford came into office, OSHA was a distressed agency. Ford appointed a new secretary of labor, John Dunlop, who recognized that getting OSHA on the right track should be a priority. At about this time, Nicholas Ashford of the Massachusetts Institute of Technology published a Ford Foundation study on the politics and economics of job safety. The study concluded that occupational safety and health was too big a task for any government agency to handle alone. It required the cooperation of all involved. The study was a blueprint for reform.

An interim team of OSHA leaders directed OSHA to concentrate on the most dangerous and unhealthy workplaces, the 30 percent which reported workplace casualties. They started with focusing on foundries, metal casting, and stamping operations. The program included special training for inspectors and assistance to state governments, industry, unions, and others to get voluntary compliance.

The appointment in 1975 of Morton Corn, a professor of occupational health and chemical engineering at the University of Pittsburgh, to lead OSHA was a major step in the right direction. Corn brought professionalism to the job. He was appreciated by business because he stressed cooperation among the groups involved in occupational safety and health. He was also soon tested on the job. On 1 January 1976 the news broke that 29 workers at a small chemical plant in Virginia had been exposed to a pesticide that sent them to the hospital with nerve damage. One worker had tried earlier to contact OSHA, but there had been no follow-up.

Corn quickly reformed the agency, hiring qualified inspectors and improving the competence of those on the job. He established a data center to provide quick technical information. He proposed a number of important standards including one for coke ovens and an improved standard for cotton dust. He worked to improve relations with NIOSH.

AFL-CIO president George Meany at one point challenged the OSHA for being slow to issue new standards on asbestos, ammonia, lead, arsenic, cotton dust, and other substances, but he was appeased with some voluntary guidelines for lead, mercury, and silica until permanent standards could be issued.

There was considerable political wrangling between President Ford and the secretary of labor, who resigned in January

1976. Corn stayed on and a new secretary was appointed. When President Carter was elected at the end of 1976, Corn was not retained, although overall OSHA was more respected for all the reform and professionalism that Corn brought to the agency during his brief tenure.

Overview of OSHA

Thirty years after OSHA was created, in the spring of 2001, the agency published a review of its three decades of progress in their newsletter *JSHQ* (*Job Safety and Health Quarterly*). The responsibilities of OSHA have increased tremendously over the years. When the agency was set up in 1971 it was responsible for 56 million workers in 3.5 million workplaces. Thirty years later OSHA had responsibility to provide guidance for the occupational safety and health of 105 million workers at 6.9 million workplaces. During those 30 years, workplace fatalities have been reduced by half, and injury and illness rates decreased by 40 percent of the 1971 rate. Particularly in light of the increases in workers and workplaces, these are significant achievements.

OSHA still considers its size as a government agency small. There were 2,370 OSHA employees in 2001 but OSHA also had 2, 948 partners in state agencies. That is an outstanding statement of cooperation that developed in spite of the agency being founded at a very troubled time in America's political history. OSHA's strategy for success has evolved through the years. In 2001 OSHA concentrated its attention on highly hazardous industries and sites with high injury rates. However, if a death occurs in a workplace anywhere, the employer must report it to OSHA within eight hours.

Education and outreach programs to promote health and safety have become an integral part of OSHA. In Des Plains, Illinois, OSHA operates its Training Institute, which was established in 1972. OSHA also encourages companies with exemplary safety and health records through the Voluntary Protection Programs. Free consultations were begun in 1975.

Most of OSHA's early standards for the safe handling of hazardous materials were adopted from respected agencies that were already involved in safety. Some standards that OSHA sites as particular milestones include: a 1978 cotton dust standard intended to prevent as many cases of "brown lung" as possible; lead standards (also in 1978); grain handling (in 1987) to protect workers at nearly 24,000 grain elevators from the dangers of explosion and fire; and in 1991, standards for occupational exposure to blood-borne pathogens to protect 5.6 million workers against AIDS, hepatitis B, and other diseases.

Key Players

Guenther, George Carpenter (1931–): Guenther was the first assistant secretary of labor to head the Occupational Safety and Health Administration. Prior to that position, he had been the director of the Bureau of Labor Standards in the Department of Labor.

Meany, George (1894–1980): Meany served as the first president of the combined unions, AFL-CIO (American Federation of Labor and Congress of Industrial Organizations). He was influential in the establishment of the Occupational Health and Safety Administration. He also played a major role in the AFL–CIO's international activities.

Nader, Ralph (1934–): Nader, a lawyer, has made a career of consumer advocacy. Among the groups he founded are the Center for Responsive Law and the Public Interest Research Group. Nader was influential in the establishment of both OSHA and the Environmental Protection Agency (EPA).

Wirtz, William Willard (1912–): Wirtz was secretary of the Labor Department from 1962–1969. He strongly supported the first bill to establish an agency to coordinate occupational safety and health that was introduced in the Johnson administration.

See also: *Department of Labor; Fair Labor Standards Act.*

BIBLIOGRAPHY

Periodicals
Fleming, Susan Hall. "OSHA at 30: Three Decades of Progress in Occupational Health and Safety." In *JSHQ* 12, no. 3 (spring 2001): 23–32.
"Industrial Safety: The Toll of Neglect." *Time* (7 February 1969): 76–77.

Other
MacLaury, Judson. "The Job Safety Law of 1970: Its Passage Was Perilous." *DOL History In-Depth*. 2002 [cited 18 July 2002]. <http://www.dol.gov/asp/programs/history/osha.htm>.
U.S. Department of Labor. "Dunlop/Corn Administration, 1975–1977: Reform and professionalism." *DOL History In-Depth Research 3*. 2002 [cited 18 July 2002]. <http://www.dol.gov/asp/programs/history/osha13corn.htm>.
———. "John Stender Administration, 1973–1975: OSHA Becomes an Agency in Crisis." *DOL History In-Depth Research 2*. 2002 [cited 18 July 2002] <http://www.dol.gov/asp/programs/history/osha13stender.htm>.
———. "OSHA Act 1970" *DOL History In-Depth Research*. 2002 [cited 18 July 2002]. <http://www.osha.gov/pls/oshaweb/owasrch.search_form?p_doc_type=OSHACT&p_toc_level=0&p_keyvalue=>.
———. "Overview of the Nixon-Ford Administration at the Department of Labor, 1969-1977." *DOL History In-Depth Research*. 1977 [cited 18 July 2002]. <http://www.dol.gov/asp/programs/history/webid-nixonford.htm>.

ADDITIONAL RESOURCES

Other
MacLaury, Judson. "A Brief History: The U.S. Department of Labor." *DOL History Annals of the Department*. 2001 [cited 18 July 2002]. <http://www.dol.gov/asp/programs/history/dolhistoxford.htm>.
U.S. Department of Labor. "Eula Bingham Administration, 1977–1981: Of Minnows, Whales and 'Common Sense'." *DOL History In-Depth Research 4*. 2002 [cited 18 July 2002]. <http://www.dol.gov/asp/programs/history/osha13bingham.htm>.

———. "Thorne Auchter Administration, 1981–1984: 'Oh, What a (Regulatory) Relief'." *DOL History In-Depth Research 5.* 2002 [cited 18 July 2002]. <http://www.dol.gov/asp/programs/history/osha13auchter.htm>.

—M. C. Nagel

Organización Regional Inter-americana de Trabajadores

Western Hemisphere 1951

Synopsis

In the years after World War II, labor organizations in the United States began to take a renewed interest in Latin America. In particular, the American Federation of Labor (AFL) hoped to establish a hemispheric labor body that it could control so as to counter the role of the left-leaning *Confederación de Trabajadores de América Latina* (CTAL). To this end, in 1947 the AFL hired Serafino Romualdi as its "labor ambassador" to Latin America, a post that he held until 1965. After touring Latin America in 1946–1947 to gain support for a regional labor confederation, Romualdi helped to establish the *Confederación Inter-Americana de Trabajadores* (CIT) in 1948. In 1951 this organization became the *Organización Regional Inter-Americana de Trabajadores* (ORIT).

In general, ORIT ideology was similar to that of the AFL. In the context of the cold war, one of ORIT's main goals was to fight against communism and to promote democratic trade unionism. The leaders of ORIT looked to U.S. labor relations as a model and sought to reform the role of labor within the capitalist system. Rather than encourage class conflict, ORIT leaders hoped to strengthen the position of labor as an interest group. Although ORIT claimed to be a nonpolitical organization, it clearly followed the lead of the U.S. government. ORIT had close ties to the U.S. State Department and supported U.S. policies and actions in Latin America and opposed any leftist activity such as the Cuban Revolution.

Timeline

1932: Charles A. Lindbergh's baby son is kidnapped and killed, a crime for which Bruno Hauptmann will be charged in 1934, convicted in 1935, and executed in 1936.

1937: Stalin uses carefully staged show trials in Moscow to eliminate all rivals for leadership. These party purges, however, are only a small part of the death toll now being exacted in a country undergoing forced industrialization, much of it by means of slave labor.

1942: Signing of the Declaration of the United Nations in Washington, D.C.

1945: On 7 May, Germany surrenders to the Allied powers. Later in the summer, the new U.S. president, Harry Tru-

man, joins Churchill and Stalin at Potsdam to discuss the reconstruction of Germany. (Churchill is replaced in mid-conference by Clement Attlee as Labour wins control of the British Parliament.)

1947: Establishment of the Marshall Plan to assist European nations in recovering from the war.

1949: Soviets conduct their first successful atomic test. This heightens growing cold war tensions, not least because the sudden acquisition of nuclear capabilities suggests that American spies are passing secrets.

1952: Among the cultural landmarks of the year are the film *High Noon* and the book *The Invisible Man* by Ralph Ellison.

1952: George Jorgenson travels to Copenhagen and returns as Christine Jorgenson. (This is not the first sex-change operation; however, it is the first to attract widespread attention.)

1955: Signing of the Warsaw Pact by the Soviet Union and its satellites in Eastern Europe.

1957: Soviets launch *Sputnik,* the world's first artificial satellite. This spawns a space race between the two superpowers.

1962: As the Soviets begin a missile buildup in Cuba, for a few tense days in October it appears that World War III is imminent. President Kennedy calls for a Cuban blockade, forcing the Soviets to back down and ultimately diffusing the crisis.

1967: Racial violence sweeps America's cities, as Harlem, Detroit, Birmingham, and other towns erupt with riots.

Event and Its Context

The United States and Latin American Labor in the Late 1940s and the Founding of the CIT

In the years following World War II, Latin America was largely unimportant in U.S. foreign policy. With the emergence of the cold war, the U.S. government concentrated on Europe and Asia. When U.S. government officials did take Latin American issues into account, they were often accepting of right-wing governments that were anticommunist. In contrast, U.S. convictions saw the traditionally left-leaning Latin American labor movement as a potential enemy. The U.S. government did not approve of Latin American labor's support of economic nationalism and protectionism. The United States occasionally tried to influence the region's working classes through the International Labor Organization (ILO), programs that brought Latin American labor leaders to the United States, and the labor attachés at U.S. embassies. All of these efforts failed to affect the Latin American labor movement.

It was in this context of U.S. government failure and inaction that the AFL took the initiative to influence and mold the labor movement in Latin America. To this end, the AFL sought to create a rival for the CTAL by founding the *Confederación Inter-America de Trabajadores* (CIT) in 1948. The AFL was able to take advantage of the fact that CTAL was losing support, especially as the position of its leader, Vicente Lombardo Toledano, in his native Mexico declined and a number of CTAL affiliates defected. Many noncommunist unions in Latin America had grown unhappy with the increasing communist influence on CTAL. In addition, in the late-1940s there were numerous splits in the national labor confederations in various Latin American countries. In general, these splits took the form of a divide between communists and their former left-wing allies such as socialists, populists, and nationalists. Thus, groups emerged that were willing to work with the AFL to create a new inter-American labor federation. For example, in Chile a split between the communists and socialists prompted socialist leader Bernardo Ibañez to call for the creation of a new inter-American labor confederation and for increased contact with the AFL. In Peru a split between the communists and *Alianza Popular Revolucionaria Americana* (APRA) led the latter to seek a closer relationship with the AFL. In Venezuela a coup led by the military and the *Acción Democrática* (AD) party produced a flurry of union activity and opened the door for AFL inroads. In light of this situation, the AFL sent Romualdi to seek allies in Latin America.

In January 1948 the AFL succeeded in establishing the CIT as a more conservative counterweight to the traditionally leftist CTAL. The founding conference took place in Lima, Peru. Some 150 delegates from 16 countries participated in the conference.

The new inter-American labor organization was weak and short-lived. Its weakness resulted from a number of factors, including lack of support from the U.S. government, opposition by the Congress of Industrial Organizations (CIO), and weak allies in Latin America. Indeed, many Latin American unions chose not to join CIT. In addition, there was a significant divide between the goals of the AFL and those of the Latin American labor movement. The AFL sought to promote an integrated world economy, whereas many Latin American labor leaders preferred economic nationalism. Furthermore, the AFL opposed political activity by labor organizations, but many in Latin America criticized the AFL for its lack of political participation. These factors would contribute to the rapid demise of CIT.

The Founding of ORIT

The transformation of the CIT to ORIT was a result of international labor developments. By 1949 the World Federation of Trade Unions (WFTU) had split as many noncommunist affiliates withdrew. Many of the unions that left the WFTU joined with both the AFL and CIO to found a new international labor organization known as the International Confederation of Free Trade Unions (ICFTU). In light of these events, at its second congress the leaders of the CIT decided to disband their organization in favor of forming a new inter-American labor confederation that would be an affiliate of the ICFTU.

The founding convention of ORIT convened in January 1951 in Mexico City. The first two days of the conference went smoothly, as labor leaders made speeches, held elections, carried out committee work. On the third day, however, dissension quickly became evident. The main cause of disagreement was a dispute over the participation of Argentina's *Confederación General de Trabajo* (CGT). The leader of Mexico's *Confedera-*

ción Regional Obrera Mexicana (CROM) wanted to include members of the Argentine confederation in the meeting. Representatives from the United States agreed that the Argentines could be present, but only as guests and not as official delegates. This attitude was a result of the U.S delegates' dislike for Argentine president Juan Peron and the accusation that his government exercised too much control over the country's labor movement. Both the AFL and CIO opposed the entrance of the CGT, and the CIO's Jacob Potofsky even went so far as to say that his confederation would withdraw if the CGT was admitted. When the convention's delegates failed to vote formally in the Argentine confederation, a number of Latin American representatives were unhappy. Fidel Velázquez Sanchez, leader of Mexico's *Confederación de Trabajadores de México* (CTM), resigned his post as president of the convention and claimed that ORIT was simply an instrument of the U. S. State Department and that it was manipulated by U.S. labor groups. His CTM withdrew from the CIT. Also in response, CROM formed its own Latin American labor organization known as the *Asociación de Trabajadores Latino Americanos* (ATLAS).

Organization of ORIT

Organizationally, ORIT was divided into three parts. The administrative committee, located in Mexico City, received reports from the secretary general and heard from official missions from countries of the hemisphere. The executive board, which met in different cities throughout the hemisphere, dealt with administrative and policy questions. For example, in March 1951, at the executive board meeting in Havana, ORIT leaders sent a statement to the Organization of American States. This statement outlined many of the organization's main concerns. It also handled the organization's budget and expenditures. Finally, ORIT's congresses, which generally met biennially, discussed hemispheric activities, such as the economic integration of the hemisphere, the repudiation of communism, amnesty for democratic political prisoners, freedom for trade unions, and regular democratic elections. For example, ORIT's major concern in its early days was the plight of labor under military dictatorships in countries such as Venezuela, Peru, Argentina, and the Dominican Republic. ORIT called on democratic nations, especially the United States, to support oppressed workers in such countries. This attitude, however, would not always continue in practice, as ORIT leaders later supported military regimes as anticommunism became more important in the organization's ideology.

After its formation, ORIT carried out several activities. One of the organization's activities was education. ORIT shared information and spread its message through publications such as the *Inter-American Labor Bulletin* and *Facts and Figures*. It also sponsored workers' seminars to train leaders. ORIT also offered correspondence courses for union leaders.

A second function of ORIT was to provide aid for labor organizations, helping those in need and creating new organizations where they were lacking. ORIT aid was both advisory and material. Sometimes the organization sent experts to countries where labor organization was weak or nonexistent. For example, ORIT leaders began an organizing drive in Central America and the Caribbean, where the organization was weakest. Also, drawing on ICFTU funds, ORIT provided material aid such as office equipment to Latin American unions. Furthermore, among ORIT's other early activities was providing aid to labor leaders in exile. To this end, it lodged human rights complaints wit the ILO, the OAS, and the UN.

ORIT's third function was to inform workers in the American hemisphere about economic and political issues, and to find solutions to such problems. Thus, ORIT missions often dealt with issues such as low living standards, poor working conditions, and unemployment.

ORIT's Role in Latin America

ORIT played a significant role in the labor movement in Latin American countries on a number of occasions. For example, in Guatemala, ORIT became involved in events that brought about the overthrow of President Jacobo Arbenz in 1954. The AFL in particular opposed the Arbenz government, as seen in Romualdi's description of the Guatemalan president as "procommunist." Labor organizing had begun in earnest with the 1944 revolution in the country and continued under Arbenz, who won the 1950 presidential election. In October 1951 many Guatemalan unions merged into the *Confederación Central de Trabajadores de Guatemala*. The new confederation soon came to be dominated by communists. Romualdi went so far as to describe the situation as a "veritable communist trade union dictatorship." Indeed, there was persecution of the old labor leaders and of noncommunists unionists.

In response, ORIT and the AFL helped to create the *Unión Nacional de Trabajadores Libres* (UNTL) in 1953, which organized both urban industrial workers and agricultural laborers. This new organization claimed to oppose government control of the labor movement and the interference of political parties. UNTL faced much oppression, and in January 1954 there was a violent assault on its headquarters. Many UNTL leaders then played a role in the 1954 movement to overthrow President Arbenz. Later, ORIT was influential in helping to organize Guatemalan unions in the post-Arbenz period.

In keeping with its anticommunist stand, ORIT opposed the Cuban Revolution and the government of Fidel Castro that came to power in 1959. ORIT leaders were unhappy that Castro replaced the old leaders of Cuba's *Confederación de Trabajadores Cubanos* (CTC). Originally, communists controlled the CTC, which Cuban labor leaders formed in 1938. In 1947 more conservative elements led by Eusebio Mujal drove the communists out of the CTC. In 1949 Mujal became secretary general of the CTC and subsequently had the Cuban confederation withdraw from CTAL. In turn the CTC, now linked to the Batista government, became friendly with the AFL and soon began to participate in ORIT. After the Cuban Revolution and the removal of the old leaders, ORIT claimed that the Cuban labor movement was no longer free. In response to these accusations, in late 1959 the CTC withdrew from ORIT, calling the organization a tool of the U.S. State Department.

ORIT also played a significant role in Brazil. In 1961 Brazilian president Jânio Quadros resigned and vice president João Goulart became president. Along with groups such as the Brazilian military and the United States, ORIT leaders felt that the Goulart government was overly influenced by communism. ORIT feared the new Brazilian regime would threaten its influence in the labor movement and would allow for the spread of communism.

In response, ORIT sent a mission to Brazil, established programs there, and brought a team of 33 Brazilian labor leaders to Washington, D.C., to learn more about democratic trade unions. In 1963 ORIT led a major push to gain control of the Brazilian labor movements. Two developments in particular upset the ORIT leaders. First, at an inter-American conference of labor leaders, the Brazilian delegation took a decidedly anti-U.S. stand and criticized the Alliance of Progress. Second, many ORIT leaders were concerned about the desire by some in Brazil to create a single national trade union center and feared that it would be dominated by left-wing labor leaders. ORIT leaders such as Romualdi saw such developments as a prelude to a communist takeover in Brazil.

Then in 1964 the U.S. government basically gave the Brazilian military a green light by announcing that it would not oppose military regimes if they seemed to offer a stable government. So in April 1964 the military overthrew the Goulart government. Some of the 33 labor leaders who had gone to the United States under the auspices of ORIT participated in the coup. ORIT leaders initially praised the new military government, as they felt that Goulart had allowed the communists to gain control of the major labor unions in Brazil. The new government, however, proved to be antilabor, and it purged many unions of those workers considered to be "subversive" and closely monitored all labor activity, tolerating no labor dissent.

As in Brazil, the labor movement in the Dominican Republic also came under strict government control. Dictator Rafael Leonidas Trujillo, who came to power in 1930, had dominated the Dominican labor movement. Upon coming to power, Trujillo eliminated many labor leaders, and the *Confederación Dominicana del Trabajo* was subordinate to the dictator. In 1956 the ICFTU, to which ORIT belonged, denounced the Dominican leader before the ILO. Furthermore, when the ICFTU sent a mission to the Dominican Republic in 1958, it found that Dominican unions did not operate independently of government control and that collective bargaining was nonexistent.

The AFL-CIO supported sanctions against Trujillo that had been called for by the Organization of American States. It also called on ORIT member unions to do the same. Then, in 1961 Trujillo was assassinated. In the aftermath of the dictator's death, ORIT sought to gain control of the Dominican labor movement, sending Andrew McLellan to carry out this goal and to unify the three Dominican labor organizations that had been formed in 1961. They attempted to do so through FOUPSA–LIBRE, using the specter of communism as a tool to make inroads into the country's labor movement. ORIT leaders organized the first FOUPSALIBRE national convention in November 1962, took control of the organization, and replaced it with the new *Confederación Nacional de Trabajadores Libres*.

As these examples show, ORIT took an active role throughout Latin America after its creation in 1951. This inter-American labor organization supported those unions and governments that shared a similar ideology and opposed those that ORIT leaders considered to be procommunist or that exerted too much control over a particular country's labor movement.

Key Players

Jáuregui Hurtado, Arturo (1920–): Born in Lima, Peru, Jáuregui was influential in the creation of both the CIT and

ORIT. As a teenager he became a factory worker and was active in organizing unions and asserting workers rights. Jáuregui also became of a member of Peru's *Alianza Popular Revolucionaria Americana* (APRA) political party and later a key national labor leader in Peru. He served as secretary treasurer of the CIT. He held high-ranking positions in ORIT until 1958, when he temporality left the organization. He later served as the secretary general of ORIT starting in 1961.

McLellan, Andrew: Born in Scotland, McLellan later moved to the United States and became involved in organized labor. He served as the inter-American representative of the International Union of Food and Allied Workers. He was also the first ORIT organizer in Central America. In 1961 he took over Romualdi's post as the AFL-CIO's inter-American representative. McLellan soon became the most powerful figure within ORIT. He was influential in the organization's efforts against Cheddi Jagan in British Guinea and João Goulart in Brazil.

Monge, Luis Alberto (1925–): Costa Rican labor leader who served as the secretary-general of ORIT starting in 1952. Monge had been an organizer of CIT and also was the chief of the ILO's Latin American Trade Union Division. Later, from 1982 to 1986, he served as president of Costa Rica.

Romualdi, Serafino: As the AFL's labor ambassador in Latin America, Romualdi was influential in establishing ORIT. He worked closely with the U.S. State Department, briefing new U.S. ambassadors to Latin America on labor issues. This role reflects the traditional cooperation between the AFL and the State Department that dates back to Samuel Gompers. The State Department aided Romuladi in hopes of countering the activities of CTAL. Thus, Romuladi's main concern was anticommunism and maintaining the strength of traditional powers in Latin America. He played a role in British Guiana, Guatemala, Brazil, the Dominican Republic, and Cuba. After 1958 U.S. representatives in ORIT took a more active role, and Romualdi played a smaller part. By 1961 he had been replaced by Andrew McLellan.

Velázquez Sanchez, Fidel (1900–1997): Mexican labor leader who headed that country's CTM for more than 50 years. Velásquez served as the president of the founding convention of ORIT, although he resigned over a dispute involving the Argentine CGT. After initially withdrawing his CTM from ORIT, it later rejoined ORIT. Velásquez was a member of Mexico's dominant PRI political party and twice served as a senator in his country.

See also: *American Federation of Labor; Confederación de Trabajadores de América Latina; Congress of Industrial Organizations; International Labor Federation; World Federation of Trade Unions.*

BIBLIOGRAPHY

Books

Alexander, Robert J. *Organized Labor in Latin America.* New York: The Free Press, 1965.

Hawkins, Carroll. *Two Democratic Labor Leaders in Conflict: The Latin American Revolution and the Role of the Workers.* Lexington, MA: D. C. Heath and Company, 1973.

Levenstein, Harvey A. *Labor Organizations in the United States and Mexico: A History of Their Relations.* Westport, CT: Greenwood Publishing, 1971.

Poblete Troncoso, Moisés, and Ben G. Burnett. *The Rise of the Latin American Labor Movement.* New York: Bookman Associates, 1960.

Romualdi, Serafino. *Presidents and Peons: Recollections of a Labor Ambassador in Latin America.* New York: Funk and Wagnalls, 1967.

Spalding, Hobart. *Organized Labor in Latin America: Historical Case Studies of Workers in Dependent Societies.* New York: New York University Press, 1977.

Torrence, Donald R. *American Imperialism and Latin American Labor, 1959–1970: A Study of the Organización Regional Interamericana de Trabajadores (ORIT) in the Latin American Policy of the United States.* Ph.D. Diss. Northern Illinois University, 1975.

Welch, Christopher. *Searching for Allies: The United States and Latin American Labor, 1945–1951.* Ph.D. Diss. American University, 1998.

—Ronald Young

Organized Labor Established

Argentina 1875–1902

Synopsis

Argentina gained its independence from Spain in 1810. By the middle of the 1800s, workers had started organizing mutual aid societies. Beginning in the 1870s, the Argentine labor movement gradually established its presence with the development of important trade unions. As economic development spread across Argentina in the last half of the nineteenth century, trade unions had to change with the changing times. Most members of the labor movement had originated as immigrant workers from Spain, Italy, Portugal, Germany, and other European countries. Many of these workers had been affiliated both with trade unions and with radical political groups in their native countries. As a result, socialists and anarchist philosophies played important roles in the establishment of Argentina's first national congress of Argentinean trade unions and the founding of the *Federación Obrera de la República Argentina* (Workers' Federation of the Argentine Republic, or FORA), during 1901–1902.

Timeline

1860: South Carolina secedes from the Union.

Bartolomé Mitre. The Library of Congress.

General Julio Argentino Roca. The Library of Congress.

1866: Prussia defeats Austria in the Seven Weeks' War. In the next year, the dual monarchy is established in Austria-Hungary.

1867: Meiji Restoration in Japan ends 675 years of rule by the shoguns.

1870: Beginning of Franco-Prussian War. German troops sweep over France, Napoleon III is dethroned, and France's Second Empire gives way to the Third Republic.

1871: Franco-Prussian War ends with France's surrender of Alsace-Lorraine to Germany, which proclaims itself an empire under Prussian king Wilhelm, crowned Kaiser Wilhelm I.

1873: The gold standard, adopted by Germany in 1871 and eventually taken on by all major nations, spreads to Italy, Belgium, and Switzerland. Though the United States does not officially base the value of its currency on gold until 1900, an unofficial gold standard dates from this period, even as a debate over "bimetallism" creates sharp divisions in American politics.

1874: As farm wages in Britain plummet, agricultural workers go on strike.

1882: The Chinese Exclusion Act, a treaty between the United States and China, provides for restrictions on immigration of Chinese workers.

1886: Bombing at Haymarket Square, Chicago, kills seven policemen and injures numerous others. Eight anarchists

are accused and tried; three are imprisoned, one commits suicide, and four are hanged.

1894: Thousands of unemployed American workers—a group named "Coxey's Army" for their leader, Jacob S. Coxey—march on Washington, D.C. A number of such marches on the capital occurred during this period of economic challenges, but Coxey's march was the only one to actually reach its destination.

1899: Polish-born German socialist Rosa Luxemburg rejects the argument that working conditions in Europe have improved and that change must come by reforming the existing system. Rather, she calls for an overthrow of the existing power structure by means of violent international revolution.

1904: The 10-hour workday is established in France.

Event and Its Context

Between Europe and Argentina

The process of modernization in Argentina began during the second half of the nineteenth century. Probably one of the first events that helped to bring economic development to Argentina was the overthrow of dictator Juan Manuel de Rosas in 1852. After this time, Presidents Bartolomé Mitre (1862–1868) and Domingo F. Sarmiento (1868–1874) initiated processes to encourage the use of new techniques for farming and ranching, the development of education, the expansion of trade, the improvement of transportation such as the construction of railroads and ports, and the use of immigration to bolster the workforce. As the government made these improvements, the labor movement also grew in strength. Both developments occurred, for the most part, in response to what was happening in Europe at this time.

As the countries of Europe experienced the Industrial Revolution, they began to rely increasingly on the countries of Latin America for many products. Argentina was especially important for the export of wool, meats, and cereals to Europe. As a result, transportation facilities along with secondary industries emerged to support the major export industries. As the economy expanded, people from Europe immigrated to Argentina to fulfill the ever-growing need for labor. This often-uncontrollable migratory flow was a concern of the early labor movement, as employers had an excess of workers and often had little need to entertain the demands of labor. Buenos Aires, as the center of the industrial complex, experienced one of the greatest inflows of immigrants. In 1869 immigrants represented more than 49 percent of the city's inhabitants (which totaled 177,787 inhabitants); they increased to almost 53 percent of the total in 1887 (by that time, totaling 433,375 inhabitants). Between 1857 and 1914, and especially during the expansion decades of the 1880s and 1900s, more than two million immigrants permanently settled in Argentina.

1850s–1860s: The Protective Organizations

By the 1850s industrial workers—primarily Spanish and Italian immigrants but also English, German, Polish, and Swiss—had started to form protective organizations, such as mutual aid societies. One of the earliest such unions was the Printing Trades Workers' Union of Buenos Aires, which was founded in 1853. It was originally formed as a mutual-benefit society whose purpose was to provide social programs such as sick and death benefits for its members. Within a decade, however, the organization had evolved into a trade union, and it conducted negotiations with employers and led strikes against those same employers when negotiations failed.

In 1864 Argentine workers established the International Workingmen's Association to help coordinate activities among various workers' organizations. Unfortunately, hostile actions by the government and internal disputes between socialist and anarchist factions doomed the association's effectiveness. The limited successes of these organizations did not discourage the labor movement. By the end of the nineteenth century, records indicate that some 79 Italian and 57 Spanish mutual aid societies existed in Argentina.

1880s: The Decade of Development

The decade of the 1880s is considered to be the beginning of the first great period of economic development for Argentina. The majority of modernization in Argentina took place in the city of Buenos Aires (located on the western shore of the Río de la Plata, inland from the Atlantic Ocean). Two important events occurred during this time that helped to shape Argentina's future. One event was the establishment in 1880 of the stable government under General Julio A. Roca. During his presidency, the city of Buenos Aires was established as the Federal

District and as the national capital; the eastern half of Tierra del Fuego (located at the southern tip of Argentina) was acquired from Chile; and about 65,000 square kilometers (25,000 square miles) of land bordering Brazil was awarded to Argentina. The other significant event was the development of the refrigerated ship, which permitted Argentina to sell its meats to the rapidly expanding European market.

As has happened repeatedly in other lands and cultures, in the midst of an industrial revolution, the capitalists in Argentina frequently exploited its workers and failed to provide a safe and healthy working environment. Such was the case when Adolfo Dorfman reported in the newspaper *La Nación* on 28 August 1887 that when "the first industrial machines began operating" they were "in general, primitive, inadequate, and dangerous." Accidents were frequent, working hours long, and penalties and fines numerous when workers disobeyed.

The Modern Labor Movement

Argentine labor historians generally agree that the period between the last third of the 1870s and 1900 was a time of transformation of a primitive labor movement into a modern one. Because Buenos Aires was the center of growth for industrialization, it also was the area where most of the progress of the labor movement occurred. The foreign-born immigrants who arrived in Argentina primarily from Europe in large measure headed the labor movement. Although native Argentine workers joined the labor unions, they did so as a minority to the immigrant workers, and were for the most part participating in nonleadership roles. The typical immigrant was a Spanish or Italian farmer or a skilled or semiskilled laborer who was employed in a small factory or shop. Most of the immigrants were located in the eastern provinces of Argentina, especially in the cities of Buenos Aires and Rosario (located northwest of Buenos Aires).

As industrial progress unfurled in the decade of the 1880s, some of the oldest unions of present-day Argentina were starting to become established, such as unions for shipbuilding craftsmen, building trades workers, and hotel and restaurant employees. One such union was organized in 1885 with the help of a railroad delegation from the United States. Because of the efforts of this delegation, a union of locomotive engineers, firemen, and washers, known as *La Fraternidad* (the Brotherhood), was established.

In 1889 the working-class organizations of Buenos Aires cooperated in the establishment of the International Working Committee (*Comité Internacional Obrero*, or CIO). This organization was a revolutionary-type group with socialist leadership. The CIO was able to organize what is generally considered the country's first labor federation, the Federation of Workers of the Argentina Region (*Federación de Trabajadores de la Región Argentina*, FTRA). The FTRA dissolved after little more than a year of operations after being weakened by a lack of support from the anarchists and an economic downturn in the country. The socialists organized other labor organizations during the 1890s, including the International Socialist Workers' Party, which was renamed the Argentine Socialist Party in 1895.

Between 1877 and 1887 there were only 15 recorded strikes in Argentina. The most frequent worker demands concerned wage increases, along with back pay, the length of the workday, and general working conditions. However, the situation changed in 1888 when an economic recession prompted a reduction in wages. This resulted in a series of strikes that continued midway through 1890. More than 30 strikes took place during this two-year period, which doubled the total number of strikes that occurred in the previous 10 years. The strikes during this time, along with the early process of trade union formation, formed the basis of Argentine labor's giant advances during the last decade of the nineteenth century and the first decade of the twentieth century.

The Long Route to Permanence for the FORA: 1890 to 1902

During the late 1880s, both the socialists and the anarchists were weakened by the economic downturn that took place in Argentina. Although rivals during the previous several decades, the socialists and the anarchists joined forces in 1890 to establish the Argentine Workers' Federation (*Federación Obrera Argentina*, FOA), which was the precursor to the Workers' Federation of the Argentine Republic (*Federación Obrera de la República Argentina*, FORA) and the first national congress of Argentinean trade unions.

The FOA was first organized following a meeting on the first annual celebration of May Day in Buenos Aires in 1890. The FOA was later officially established in mid-1891 by five unions that were based in Buenos Aires and a few federations from the interior provinces of Argentina. The organization's objectives were to seize political power and place it in the hands of the working class; to socialize all means of production in the country; and to achieve social and political equality for all. However, the FOA failed to survive the economic depression. One legacy of the FOA began in 1890 when it founded Argentina's first labor journal, called *El Obrero* (The Worker). The journal was expressly written to help workers understand the complex social and political situation in Argentina. In 1894 the FOA was revived, but it soon disappeared again.

The Argentine economy began to recover in 1895. This coincided with an increase the number of strikes and with the formation of new trade unions. Between 1895 and 1896 more than 40 strikes occurred. These were generally staged to support wage demands but also centered on a reduction of working hours. In 1896 several trade union organizations collaborated to form the *Convención Obrera* (Workers' Convention). The joint effort ended up being only a fairly loose agreement among various unions. The anarchists, who established the Workers' Convention, did not participate in another attempt to establish the FOA in 1897. The upsurge in strike activity did not last beyond 1897, as unemployment increased in the country. The situation reversed itself by 1899, however, as trade unions began to spread widely across Argentina and as workers began their first attempts at broad-scale strike actions.

Argentine socialists again revived the FOA in 1900, but the effort was not supported by the anarchists and therefore failed. However, important strikes protesting unemployment in the country, along with further organization and consolidation of trade unions, brought together the socialists and the anarchists. This unity reestablished the FOA once again. On 25 May 1901 the journal *La Organización* and a group of trade unions launched the FOA. The congress, the first national congress of Argentinean trade unions, was attended by 27 socialist-led resistance societies including 15 from Buenos Aires and 12 from the provinces. After the continuing labor struggles of the workers of Argentina over the previous few decades, the anarchists finally accepted the objectives of the FOA. Anarchist leaders Pedro Gori and Antonio Pellicer Paraire and socialist leader Adrian Padroni played a prominent role in the founding of the FOA. During the first congress the delegation discussed the use of strikes, arbitration of industrial disputes, the viewpoints of labor legislation, and the types of union organizations. Much compromise was needed as anarchists and socialists were together for one of the first times. For a year the FOA remained an active and effective organization without being crippled by too many disputes.

However, at the FOA's second congress in April 1902, the organization's members argued over the seating of the delegates. The socialist delegates walked out of the congress. The anarchists immediately took over control and converted it into a political organization called the *Federación Obrera de la República Argentina* or Workers' Federation of the Argentine Republic, FORA). The anarchists who led the FORA adopted a program based on the partisan ideas of Pellicer Paraire and by 1905 supported the political philosophy of anarchist communism. They eliminated all nonanarchists members of FORA.

Conclusion

In the 50 years following 1880, Argentina made remarkable economic and social progress. During the first decade of the twentieth century, Argentina emerged as one of the leading nations of South America. At the first congress of the FOA in 1901, the leaders and delegates identified and discussed many topics that were important to the labor movement. However, with the takeover of the FOA by the very militant anarchists and the subsequent founding of the FORA, the labor movement in 1902 adopted a revolutionary stand and maintained that attitude for the rest of the 1900s. The anarchists' labor organizations favored liberal use of the general strike. From 1902 to 1910 the anarchists dominated the labor movement of Argentina. Rather than negotiating through collective bargaining, anarchist labor organizations commonly used direct action to reach their goals. These actions often involved sabotage, solidarity strikes, and general walkouts.

Key Players

Gori, Pietro (1865–1911): Gori was an internationally known Italian anarchist, as well as a poet, lawyer, and criminologist. Gori encouraged anarchist participation in the early Argentina labor movement.

Mitre, Bartolomé (1821–1906): Mitre was an Argentine statesman, military leader, and historian. After being exiled in Chile, Bolivia, and Peru, Mitre returned to Argentina in 1852 and participated in the overthrow of President Juan Manual Rosas by General Justo José Urquiza. In 1853 Mitre was appointed minister of war in the Buenos Aires provincial government. Mitre was made governor of Buenos Aires Province in 1860 and defeated Urquiza at the Battle of Pavon in 1861. In 1862 Mitre was elected to a six-year term as president of the republic. He was defeated for the presidency in 1874 and again in 1891. Mitre founded the influential newspaper *La Nación* (The Nation) in 1870. His writings include histories of South America and Argentina.

Paraire, Antonio Pellicer (1851–1916): Paraire was a Spanish printer who immigrated to Argentina in 1891. In 1900 Paraire published a series of articles on labor organizations in which he put forward the basic principles for a labor federation.

Roca, Julio Argentino (1843–1914): Roca was Argentine general and president from 1880 to 1886 and 1898 to 1904. He left school to fight with the Argentine Confederation and, later, in the Paraguayan War. President Roca introduced a single legal currency throughout Argentina, settled boundary disputes with Brazil and Chile, and in later years served as minister of the interior and as ambassador to Brazil and France.

Sarmiento, Domingo Faustino (1811–1888): Sarmiento was Argentine president from 1868 to 1874. In 1835 he went into exile in Chile. At that time, he worked in journalism and education and in 1845 published *Facundo: Civilización o Barbarie*, a discussion of barbarism and civilization as a regular theme in Latin American literature. In 1842 Sarmiento was appointed director of a new teacher-training institution in Santiago, Chile. Three years later, the Chilean government sent him to Europe and the United States to study educational systems. Sarmiento was Argentine minister to the United States from 1864 to 1868. After his presidential years, Sarmiento became director of schools in Buenos Aires, where he reorganized the school system.

See also: *Anarchists Lead Argentine Labor Movement.*

BIBLIOGRAPHY

Books

Alexander, Robert Jackson. *An Introduction to Argentina.* New York: Praeger, 1969.

———. *Organized Labor in Latin America.* New York: The Free Press, 1965.

Baily, Samuel L. *Labor, Nationalism, and Politics in Argentina.* New Brunswick, NJ: Rutgers University Press, 1967.

Munck, Ronaldo. *Argentina from Anarchism to Peronism: Workers, Unions and Politics, 1855–1985.* London: Zed Books Ltd., 1987.

Other

Oved, Yaacov. "The Uniqueness of Anarchism in Argentina." Tel Aviv University [cited 4 December 2002]. <http://www.tau.ac.il/eial/VIII_1/oved.htm>.

—William Arthur Atkins

Osborne Judgment

Great Britain 1909

Synopsis

The finances of the Labour Party (founded in 1900 as the Labour Representation Committee) depended on contributions from affiliated trade unions, which were acquired by a compulsory political levy on the subscriptions of their membership. In 1907 Walter Osborne, a member of the Amalgamated Society of Railway Servants (ASRS), began legal action against his union's political levy; in 1909, the House of Lords (the highest court in the land) declared the levy unlawful. The ruling struck a serious blow against the Labour Party and against the broader political and nonindustrial activities of the unions themselves. The impact of the ruling was mitigated in 1911 by the introduction of payment for Members of Parliament (MPs) and largely overturned by the 1913 Trade Union Act, which established a new legal basis for the unions' political funds and political levy.

Timeline

1889: Flooding in Johnstown, Pennsylvania, kills thousands.

1893: Wall Street stock prices plummet on 5 May, precipitating a market collapse on 27 June. In the wake of this debacle, some 600 banks and 15,000 other businesses fail. The nationwide depression will last for four more years.

1898: Bayer introduces a cough suppressant derived from opium. Its brand name: Heroin.

1902: The *Times Literary Supplement,* a weekly review of literature and scholarship, begins publication in London.

1905: Russian Revolution of 1905. Following the "bloody Sunday" riots before the Winter Palace in St. Petersburg in January, revolution spreads throughout Russia, in some places spurred on by newly formed workers' councils, or soviets. Among the most memorable incidents of the revolt is the mutiny aboard the battleship *Potemkin.*

1909: Robert E. Peary and Matthew Henson reach the North Pole.

1909: Founding of the National Association for the Advancement of Colored People (NAACP) by W. E. B. Du Bois and a number of other prominent black and white intellectuals in New York City.

1909: William Cadbury's *Labour in Portuguese West Africa* draws attention to conditions of slavery in São Tomé and Principe.

1911: Revolution in Mexico, begun the year before, continues with the replacement of the corrupt Porfirio Diaz, president since 1877, by Francisco Madero.

1915: A German submarine sinks the *Lusitania,* killing 1,195, including 128 U.S. citizens. Theretofore, many Americans had been sympathetic toward Germany, but the incident begins to turn the tide of U.S. sentiment toward the Allies.

1919: Formation of the Third International (Comintern), whereby the Bolshevik government of Russia establishes its control over communist movements worldwide.

Event and Its Context

Background of the Case

The Labour Representation Committee, which was established in 1900 to further the independent representation of labor in parliament, was a federal body formed by socialist organizations and sympathetic trade unions. Trade union support had risen markedly after the Taff Vale case; around 90 percent of Labour Party income derived from trade union contributions financed by the political levy.

In 1905, Walter Osborne, an active Liberal and secretary of the Walthamstow (North Londo) branch of the ASRS, threatened legal action against his union's political fund, which was used to support the parliamentary candidatures under Labour auspices of the union's general secretary, Richard Bell, and three others. Osborne resented his union dues going to a political party which he alleged was under socialist control. The ASRS responded by holding a successful ballot of members to sanction its political expenditure but Osborne pursued the matter.

In 1906 Osborne wrote a letter to the *Daily Express* to solicit funds; in the following year he launched legal action against the ASRS, claiming that it was acting unlawfully. As was expected, Osborne lost his initial hearing—the courts had recently sanctioned political spending by unions in the case of *Steele vs. the South Wales Miners*—but he raised additional funds and appealed the decision. The three Court of Appeal judges found in his favor. They asserted that the 1875 Trade Union Act provided a "limiting and restrictive definition" of trade union functions that did not permit political activity. Two judges lamented the plight of an "unwilling minority" of union members who were forced to support financially "objects of which they may heartily disapprove." The Labour Party pledge, which required that its MPs vote as determined by the majority of its parliamentary representatives, provided a further point of legal attack as it was held to contravene the public interest in requiring that MPs subordinate their individual judgment in favor of a party line. In brief, the judges argued that if the unions acted beyond their statutory powers, the unions could not expect to enjoy the immunities granted by the 1906 Trade Disputes Act. The union appealed the case to the House of Lords, which one year later upheld the Appeal Court verdict: three judges found against the union on *ultra vires* grounds (that the union was acting beyond its statutory powers) and two condemned the Labour Party pledge.

Significance of the Case

The nature of the verdict and its background in a series of damaging court cases seemed plausibly to evidence the hostility of the British legal establishment to the labor movement. The implication of the ruling for the Labour Party in particular was stark: the party's financial lifeline of trade union finance had been cut. Responses varied. Some unions carried on as if nothing had happened, and a few got away with this approach. By November 1910, however, some 25 injunctions preventing unions expending monies for political purposes had been brought successfully. Other unions sought to make political contributions voluntary. In some areas (for example, among South Wales miners), this approach worked satisfactorily, but overall there was a sharp drop in contributions. The Labour Party coped in the two general elections of 1910 by financing the bulk of its candidatures from its own financial reserves, but the number of standing Labour candidates fell from 78 in the January election to 58 in December. (Conversely, the number returned rose from 40 to 42, so in some respects the Party may have fared better by concentrating its forces.)

Overall, it appears that the political impact of the Osborne Judgement may have been less immediately damaging than anticipated, but the longer-term implications remained severe. The Miners' Federation, for example, lost some £27–28,000 a year in political funding, and the political fund of the Derbyshire Miners' Federation fell £1600 into debt. The ASRS itself was losing £3000 to £3500 a year in uncollected political levies. On a local level, the ruling's implied ban on union support for trades councils (the bodies that coordinated the labor movement's local political campaigns) led to the dissolution of a number of such organizations and a significant weakening of the Labour Party's still fledgling grassroots network. Furthermore, the threat of further injunctions loomed large. Such considerations became influential in Labour's willingness to accept the Liberal reform that was eventually proposed.

For the unions, the verdict had a twofold significance. Ideologically, its values seemed to undercut the collectivist beliefs and practices of the union movement. Both as a matter of principle and in terms of practical effectiveness, the unions held that majority decisions should be determinant and enforceable. If dissenting minorities were to be allowed to flout collectively agreed upon union policies, the unions would be powerless to wage effective strike action or discipline members who contravened union rules. More specifically, the judgement's strict interpretation of the 1875 Act might prohibit a wide range of the unions' nonindustrial functions such as financial backing of education, labor newspapers, and the Trades Union Congress (the unions' national coordinating body).

The Labor and Government Response

In 1910 the labor movement campaigned hard for reform, but it faced obstacles from within its own ranks and without. Many union members voted Liberal (and some Conservative). Many others believed that the whole reform matter was irrelevant to their practical concerns as rank and file trade unionists. Both groups were unsympathetic to the levy, and union activists, therefore, had to tread warily in promoting the issue. In this light, Osborne may be considered as a genuine workers' voice and not merely as the tool of wealthy interests, as sometimes portrayed at the time and since. Although he did receive financial and legal backing from upper-class opponents of labor, the evidence suggests that he also found support among ordinary workers. The ballots held to authorize the unions' newly legalized political funds after 1913 provided further evidence of the lack of Labour sympathies of many workers. In the first 63 ballots, 37 percent of voters opposed political expenditure by their unions, many presumably because such spending would benefit the Labour Party.

In the broader politics of the time, the issue paled into insignificance when placed against the constitutional crisis caused by the House of Lords' rejection of the 1909 Liberal budget and the Liberals' proposal to limit the powers of the Upper House. The Liberals themselves possessed mixed feelings on the question of post-Osborne reform. Pragmatically, the weakening of a growing rival to their own working-class constituency was not unwelcome. Ideologically, Liberalism's individualist core values favored the rights of the individual union members against the majoritarian and collectivist principles espoused by labor leaders. After the hung elections of 1910, the Liberals' dependence on Labour's parliamentary support was offset by the Parliamentary Labour Party's support of the Liberal reform agenda and its desperate wish to avoid a further general election. Such an election might threaten both the return of an ideologically unsympathetic Conservative government and Labour's own parlous finances. On the other hand, many Liberals were disquieted by the broader implications of the judgment and were struck by powerful opposition by both Labour interests and from amongst their own ranks by the so-called Lib-Labs (working-class representatives elected under Liberal auspices who were also affected by the Osborne ruling).

In late 1910, the Liberal leader, Herbert Asquith, proposed a reform that would legalize political spending by the unions and enable union members who objected to their unions' political activity to withhold a proportion of their dues. Labour rejected this compromise but, in February 1911, it facilitated the process of reform by abandoning the parliamentary pledge that required its MPs to vote with the party majority. In August 1911, a parliamentary motion was passed agreeing to payment of MPs. The same year, Labour grudgingly accepted as the best they could achieve a bill to overturn Osborne. This bill was withdrawn in response to pressure of parliamentary business, but the Trade Union bill became law in 1913.

The 1913 act permitted unions to allocate money to political purposes provided that a separate political fund was established and endorsed by ballot by a majority of union members. Members who wished to opt out of political contributions were to be allowed to do so without penalty. In the following 15 months, 63 unions organized ballots. In 60, a majority of union members supported the creation of political funds and, in practice, their support of the Labour Party. By requiring that unions create a specific account for political spending, the act may actually have benefited the Labour Party by countering the unions' reluctance to draw money from their general funds. By April 1916, some 100 unions had established political funds; by the time of the 1918 General Election, the Labour Party enjoyed an unprecedentedly strong financial and organizational position that reflected both the legal protection afforded to union politics and the massive increase in unionism during the First World War.

Trade union support for Labour was to remain a controversial issue. The Conservative Government took the pretext offered by the 1926 General Strike to pass legislation that union members *contract in* to the unions' political funds rather than specifically withhold their contributions as had been the case after 1913. Income from the political levy fell by one-third,

largely it seems as a result of the inertia of union members rather than any active or new-found opposition to Labour. The Labour government of 1945 restored the principle of *contracting out*, with the result that political contributions rose by one-third. Margaret Thatcher's Conservative government renewed the offensive against trade union funding of the Labour Party in a law passed in 1984 that required that unions ballot their members every 10 years to assess their membership's continued support for their political funds. In 1985–86, all 38 unions voted to retain their funds with the "yes" vote averaging 82 percent. Subsequently some 12 other unions voted to establish political funds for the first time.

Key Players

Bell, Richard (1859–1930): Born in South Wales, he became an active member of the ASRS and was elected the union's general secretary in 1898. He served as Labour MP for Derby from 1900 to 1910 but remained essentially a Liberal in his politics. He worked for the Government Board of Trade from 1910 to 1920.

Osborne, Walter (1870–1950): Foreman porter at Clapton Station, north London, and secretary of the Walthamstow branch of the Amalgamated Society of Railway Servants. Once a member of the Social Democratic Federation, he became a strong anti-socialist and was elected a Progressive member of his local council in 1906. After the judgment, he left railway employment to become clerk to the British Constitutional Association and wrote *Sane Trade Unionism* (1913).

BIBLIOGRAPHY

Books

Clegg, H. A. *A History of British Trade Unions Since 1889.* Volume II, *1911–1933.* Oxford: Clarendon Press, 1985.

Clegg, H. A, Alan Fox, and A. F. Thompson. *A History of British Trade Unions Since 1889.* Volume I, *1889–1910.* Oxford: Clarendon Press, 1964.

Periodicals

Klarman, Michael J. "Osborne: A Judgement Gone Too Far?" *English Historical Review* 103, no. 406 (1988): 21–39.

———. "Parliamentary Reversal of the Osborne Judgement." *The Historical Journal* 32, no. 4 (1989): 893–924.

Pelling, Henry. "The Politics of the Osborne Judgment." *The Historical Journal* 25, no. 4 (1982): 889–909.

ADDITIONAL RESOURCES

Books

Adelman, Paul. *The Rise of the Labour Party, 1880–1945.* 3rd ed. London, New York: Longman, 1996.

Pelling, Henry. *A Short History of the Labour Party.* 11th ed. New York: St. Martin's Press, 1996.

—John Boughton

Robert Owen. © Getty Images. Reproduced by permission.

Owen Model Communities

Great Britain, United States 1799–1827

Synopsis

Robert Owen, reacting to the brutalities of industrial capitalism, attempted to establish cooperative communities that would serve as models for a new pattern of life. Often categorized as a utopian and the father of British socialism, he encouraged laborers to pursue the happiness of all instead of the few, refused to exploit workers under his command, and pushed for communal alternatives to the family system. By turning his cotton mill at New Lanark, Scotland, into a successful example of communitarianism and amassing a large fortune in the process, Owen hoped to demonstrate that the changes wrought by capitalism were not permanent and that nonrevolutionary alternatives could still be created. Conflicts with his partners pushed Owen out of New Lanark and prompted him to establish a model town in New Harmony, Indiana, in 1825. He never attracted more than a small group of followers in the United States and returned to Britain in 1827.

Timeline

1800: The world's population reaches 870 million.

1801: French National Convention makes the metric system, established in 1799, compulsory throughout French-occupied western and central Europe.

1806: Noah Webster publishes his first *Compendious Dictionary of the English Language*.

1810: Revolts begin in South America, initiating the process whereby colonies will win their freedom from Spain and other European colonial powers.

1815: Napoleon returns from Elba, and his supporters attempt to restore him as French ruler, but just three months later, forces led by the Duke of Wellington defeat his armies at Waterloo. Napoleon spends the remainder of his days as a prisoner on the island of St. Helena in the south Atlantic.

1815: Congress of Vienna establishes the balance of power for post-Napoleonic Europe, and inaugurates a century of British dominance throughout most of the world.

1818: In a decisive defeat of Spanish forces, soldier and statesman Simón Bolívar leads the liberation of New Granada, which includes what is now Colombia, Panama, Venezuela, and Ecuador. With Spanish power now waning, Bolívar becomes president and virtual dictator of the newly created nation of Colombia.

1825: Britain's Stockton and Darlington Railway introduces the world's first passenger rail service.

1828: Election of Andrew Jackson as president begins a new era in American history.

1829: Overturning of the last of the "penal laws" imposed by the English against the Catholics of Ireland since 1695.

Event and Its Context

In the early nineteenth century, English socialists argued that reformers had made little impact on the poverty, oppression, and gross inequality of wealth that plagued modern society. Arguing that the liberal doctrine of individualism had degenerated into selfish egoism that harmed community life and challenging the laissez-faire belief that the elimination of poverty and suffering ran contrary to the natural order, socialists demanded the creation of a new society based on cooperation rather than competition. The man who emerged as the leading socialist, the manufacturer Robert Owen, aimed to demonstrate the practicality and profitability of communitarianism by putting his theories into practice.

Robert Owen

Owen's experience as a worker gave him enormous sympathy for the lives of laborers as well as credence among the working class. The son of a saddler and ironmonger, Owen left school at the age of nine to learn a trade. After a year, he briefly joined a brother in London, then found work in Lincolnshire as a draper's apprentice. In 1785, having completed his term of service, Owen headed to London to widen his experience and obtain a post as an assistant in a large drapery shop on London Bridge. The long hours and poor working conditions of this job took a toll on Owen's health, and after several months he headed to Manchester for a fresh start. This bustling city would turn Owen into a reformer.

With accessible supplies of coal and good transportation, Manchester had become the burgeoning hub of the new textile industry and, in effect, of the Industrial Revolution. It also be-

Tenement buildings provided by Robert Owen for his cotton mill workers, New Lanark, Scotland. © Hulton/Getty Images. Reproduced by permission.

came a testament to the evils of rapid industrial development. Manchester's cotton mills attracted a flood of workers to the city, and its population exploded during the 13 years of Owen's residence. Smoke from the mills established a permanent haze throughout the city, and soot coated everything including every man, woman, and child. Living and working conditions were horrendous, with the result that Manchester became a hotbed of radicalism.

In Manchester in 1789, Owen joined a friend in the manufacture of spinning machines. The partnership did not last long, and Owen set up as a cotton spinner with three employees. This venture prospered and enabled him to obtain a job as manager of a large mill. Only 20 years old, he found himself in charge of a steam-powered mill employing 500 people. He soon mastered the art of cotton spinning and earned a considerable reputation as a producer of fine cotton. His career prospered, and eventually he became a partner in the Chorlton Twist Company. As a respected businessman, Owen received an invitation to join the Manchester Literary and Philosophical Society. He began to voice publicly his theories about universal happiness and industrialization. Not surprisingly, he advocated a model other than that found in Manchester.

New Lanark

In 1799 Owen and his partners bought the cotton mills at New Lanark, just outside Glasgow, and shortly afterwards he moved to New Lanark to serve as the sole manager and dominant partner of what would become the largest and most prosperous cotton spinning establishment in Britain. The mills would bring Owen an immense fortune, but profit was not his sole concern. From the start, Owen resolved to modernize the mill and improve both the working and social conditions of his

workers. Along the way, he would test his communitarian theories.

In sharp contrast to Manchester, New Lanark was isolated and rural. The village consisted of a cluster of mills and row after row of gray granite four-story stone houses huddled along the wooded bank of the River Clyde just below its falls. A tunnel had been cut through a hillside to provide water to power the mill machinery. The simplicity of the village strongly appealed to Owen, and he hoped that its very primitiveness would allow New Lanark to preserve the spirit of community that had been lost in the larger city. He would later claim that because he could not make a fresh start, his experiment had been seriously compromised from the beginning.

At the time that Owen assumed control of the mill, it employed between 1,500 and 2,000 people, including 500 pauper children. These children, many younger than 10 years, had been removed from parish workhouses and employed as apprentices in conditions that often permanently compromised their health. The children worked 13-hour days and, although they were well fed, well clothed, and well housed, Owen argued in testimony before Parliament that their minds and growth had been materially injured by their employment. His testimony gave Owen a reputation as a child labor reformer, but his attempts to institute reforms at his mills ran into considerable opposition from his business partners. Although he would have preferred to accept no children younger than 12 for full employment, his associates forced him to compromise by taking children 10 and older. Owen did succeed in banning the use of pauper children, accepting only those child laborers who could be supervised by their parents.

Although wages were low at New Lanark in comparison with other mills, the treatment accorded to the workers compensated for the disparity. Refusing to exploit his workers, Owen offered housing at a moderate rent, free medical services, and a contributory sickness and retirement fund. All children were strongly encouraged to attend village schools and, because only a nominal fee was charged, families could afford to educate their offspring. The company store sold food, clothing, and household goods at cost.

While improving upon the typical factory colony, Owen also embarked upon efforts to establish a utopian society. Problems with alcoholism were limited by the absence of a tavern in the village and the imposition of fines for drunkenness. Fines were also imposed for illegitimate births with both the mother and father required to make weekly payments to a poor fund.

Owen aimed to reduce the hours that people spent in disagreeable or heavy labor. Machines were used not to displace workers but to protect and assist the laborers in the performance of necessary tasks. In accord with this philosophy, Owen also tried to reduce the work burden placed upon women. Children as young as two years were encouraged to attend school. Families could take advantage of communal dining rooms and kitchens, thereby freeing women from household drudgery. There is no evidence, though, that the dining rooms and kitchens were actually used. When Owen departed for the United States, the areas were still under construction.

Although New Lanark made a considerable amount of money and Owen received much acclaim for reducing longstanding social problems such as drunkenness, the experiment collapsed in controversy. After launching attacks on the church for encouraging oppression, Owen saw sympathy for his views among wealthy philanthropists and the middle class slowly ebb away. In spite of this, his denunciation of the competitive economy gave him enormous popularity among the working class. Increasing opposition from his partners added to Owen's determination to make a fresh start elsewhere. By 1824 he had concluded that a cotton mill was a poor location to begin a social revolution and that progress in Britain would be interminably slow. He left New Lanark and would never return.

New Harmony

In 1825 Owen bought the 20,000-acre settlement of New Harmony, on the Wabash River in Indiana, from a German religious sect under the leadership of George Rapp. Owen's involvement with this former Rappite village marked the end of his long association with the world of business and his establishment as a radical social reformer. Like other millennial sects, Owenites believed that they needed to withdraw from the world so as to live according to their principles and precepts, for only in an isolated community could alternatives to the evils of the world be developed and honed.

By starting with New Harmony, Owen took advantage of an already established settlement. A tannery, silk factory, woolen mill, sawmill, brickyard, brewery, distillery, and shops were in operation along with orchards, vineyards, and farms cut out of the wilderness. Although Owen in theory sought to unite manufacturing and agriculture, in practice agriculture became the major community pursuit. No attempt was made to establish factory production on the scale of New Lanark. The small industries and farms did no more than meet the needs of the residents and, further emphasizing the importance of agriculture,

all men were required to perform two hours of chores every afternoon under the command of a leader.

Owen's ideas for social reform and cooperative communities had been well received in America, and settlers flocked to New Harmony. Unfortunately, the enthusiasm of these pioneers could not compensate for their lack of mechanical and farming skills. These practical difficulties soon led to conflict among the settlers and the subsequent division of New Harmony into five settlements. Labor notes, first proposed by Owen in 1820 as a standard of value and representing hours of time, were introduced to facilitate trading between these bickering communities. A committee assigned value to goods according to the number of hours judged to be necessary for their production plus the cost of raw materials. This labor exchange eventually became a depot where individuals and trade unions exchanged their products without the use of money.

The conflict that rent the community never entirely abated. Owen made a final unsuccessful attempt to reorganize New Harmony in 1827 and then departed for Great Britain. At this point, the experiment essentially came to an end as the New Harmonites abandoned communitarianism and embraced individualism. Owen never attempted to lead another community and elected instead to spend his remaining years writing and lecturing.

Key Players

Owen, Robert (1771–1858): The Welsh-born Owen apprenticed as a draper, worked as a shop assistant, then set up as a manufacturer of cotton spinning machinery. When New Harmony failed, he returned to Britain and discovered that Owenite ideas had come to dominate the British working-class movement. In 1834 Owen briefly headed the Grand National Consolidated Trade Union, an umbrella association of unions that formed upon his suggestion.

BIBLIOGRAPHY

Books

Claeys, Gregory. *Machinery, Money, and the Millennium: From Moral Economy to Socialism, 1815–1860*. Princeton, NJ: Princeton University Press, 1987.

Donnachie, Ian L., and George Hewitt. *Historic New Lanark: The Dale and Owen Industrial Community Since 1785*. Edinburgh, Scotland: Edinburgh University Press, 1993.

Harrison, J. F. C. *Robert Owen and the Owenites in Britain and America*. New York: Charles Scribner's Sons, 1969.

Other

The Robert Owen Museum. 1999 [cited 7 November 2002]. <http://robert-owen.midwales.com/>

ADDITIONAL RESOURCES

Books

Butt, John, ed. *Robert Owen: Aspects of His Life and Work. A Symposium*. New York: Humanities Press, 1971.

Donnachie, Ian. *Robert Owen: Owen of New Lanark and New Harmony*. East Linton, Scotland: Tuckwell, 2000.

Morton, A. L. *The Life and Ideas of Robert Owen*. London: Lawrence and Wishart, 1962.

Owen, Robert. *The Life of Robert Owen: By Himself*. London: G. Bell, 1920.

Royle, Edward. *Robert Owen and the Commencement of the Millennium: A Study of the Harmony Community*. New York: St. Martin's Press, 1998.

Periodicals

Carmony, Donald F., and Josephine M. Elliott. "New Harmony, Indiana: Robert Owen's Seedbed for Utopia." *Indiana Magazine of History* 76 (September 1980): 161–261.

—Caryn E. Neumannc

P

Pan-American Federation of Labor: *See* Confederación Obrera Pan-Americana.

Panic of 1873

United States 1873

Synopsis

After the economic devastation wrought by the panic of 1837, unions remained unable to regain their former power for several decades. Although scattered national unions took root during the 1850s, they faded quickly during the Civil War. The beginning of the "Greenback" era in 1862 also marked the renewed growth of unionism in America. The government flooded the marketplace with paper currency. Extreme levels of inflation immediately resulted, and prices continued to rise unchecked. Wage increases did not rise in proportion to the rate of inflation. This caused dissatisfaction within the labor force, which in turn resulted in a renewed interest in unionism.

Mimicking the same progression as its previous growth at the beginning of the nineteenth century, this new labor movement began with the formation of local trade unions. By the end of 1862, virtually every trade possessed a representing union in its city. These quickly transformed into citywide trade assemblies and eventually expanded into national trade unions. A brief depression near the end of the 1860s crippled many of these fledgling organizations, but the aspirations for unionism remained strong. As the 1870s began, national unions regained their strength and membership numbers. A new wave of successes in labor relations owed much to lessons learned in the previous growth of unionism.

However, despite their brief recuperation, national unions would once more be struck down by economic strife. Like the panic of 1837, the panic of 1873 stripped unions of their influence and power, particularly of the threat of strikes. The unions that were not crushed almost immediately lost the majority of their membership. The depression caused by the panic of 1873 continued to hinder the growth of unionism, and national trade unions would not recover for several years.

Timeline

1854: Republican Party is formed by opponents of slavery in Michigan.

1859: American abolitionist John Brown leads a raid on the federal arsenal at Harpers Ferry, Virginia. His capture and hanging in December heighten the animosities that will spark the Civil War sixteen months later.

1864: General William Tecumseh Sherman conducts his Atlanta campaign and his "march to the sea."

1867: Establishment of the Dominion of Canada.

1870: Beginning of Franco-Prussian War. German troops sweep over France, Napoleon III is dethroned, and France's Second Empire gives way to the Third Republic.

1872: The Crédit Mobilier affair, in which several officials in the administration of President Ulysses S. Grant are accused of receiving stock in exchange for favors, is the first of many scandals that are to plague Grant's second term.

1874: As farm wages in Britain plummet, agricultural workers go on strike.

1874: Discovery of gold in the Black Hills of South Dakota.

1874: Norwegian physician Arrnauer Gerhard Henrik Hansen discovers the bacillus that causes leprosy. This marks the major turning point in the history of an ailment (now known properly as Hansen's disease) that afflicted humans for thousands of years and was often regarded as evidence of divine judgment.

1876: General George Armstrong Custer and 264 soldiers are killed by the Sioux at the Little Big Horn River.

1882: The Chinese Exclusion Act, a treaty between the United States and China, provides for restrictions on immigration of Chinese workers.

1884: Chicago's Home Life Insurance Building, designed by William LeBaron Jenney, becomes the world's first skyscraper.

Event and Its Context

Unionism During the Long Depression

Since the tragic times caused by the panic of 1837, unionism had seen little growth within the labor community. In addition, during this time, America suffered another economic downturn in 1857 and the horrors of the Civil War (1861–1865). Twenty-five years of confusion, conflict, and repeated depressions hindered all attempts by workers to organize with any success. Strike movements in key industrial sectors such as New England and Pennsylvania were plagued with continued failures. The aggressive methods used by the majority of unions from the 1830s were ineffective against the challenges of the 1840s and 1850s. In response, workers began changing their philosophies on how to effect changes in labor conditions.

Several "intellectuals" headed the new labor movement. This gathering of educated men and women began to focus their efforts on changing social conditions rather than on the simple accumulation of wealth in the form of wages. The "cooperative" approach headed their reform strategy, empowering the workers and consumers. In an era of depression, this philosophical method had far greater success than trade unionism. Since

Officials close doors of New York Stock Exchange, Panic of 1873. © Getty Images. Reproduced by permission.

Crowds gather in streets after close of New York Stock Exchange, Panic of 1873. © Getty Images. Reproduced by permission.

the first cooperative shop had opened in Philadelphia in 1791, producer cooperation had seen success in numerous industries. As strikes began to fail more regularly during and after the panic of 1837, cooperatives became increasingly popular. This popularity was compounded by the humanitarian call for changes to labor conditions of women and children. Several trade societies began to adopt the cooperative approach, including the New England Protective Union in 1845.

Agrarianism also found popularity among trade unions during this time. Many union leaders fully supported the movement and engaged in lobbying for its inception. They even went so far as to offer incentives to wage earners, such as paying for travel and startup expenses. The reason for their strong support of this movement was obvious. The depression after the panic of 1837 had created an overwhelming number of unemployed wage earners. As a result, trade unions lost their striking power because employers had an enormous workforce from which to choose. Employers could, and did, hire laborers for virtually nothing with little opposition. By sending these laborers westward with the homesteaders, the excess workforce could be thinned out. With fewer laborers to hire, employers would have to offer better wages and hours. In addition, trade unions would regain their influential striking power. Despite protracted lobbying attempts, Congress did not pass the Homestead Law to encourage westward migration until 1862.

With the exception of two growth spurts in the early and mid-1850s, trade unionism made little progress before the 1860s. The period did, however, inspire new ways of thinking in unionism and the labor movement. Labor leaders learned from previous mistakes with unions and from the cooperative and agrarianism movements. Resulting refinements to the concept of national unionism, which had died out with the panic of 1837, allowed trade assemblies to build the support system they would need in the future. The nationals were among the only labor organizations to survive the economic strife caused by the Civil War.

The "Greenback" Era Begins

The "Greenback" era marked the return of the national trade unions to the U.S. labor community. In 1862 and 1863 the U.S. government signed the Legal Tender Acts. These acts authorized the issue of just over $1 billion in paper currency or "greenbacks." This massive influx of paper currency into the market resulted in a period of inflation that fluctuated over the following 16 years. Also at the heart of this striking inflation rate were speculation and supplying the army. According to Selig Perlman in his book *A History of Trade Unionism in the United States*, "In July 1863, retail prices were 43 percent above those of 1860. . . In July 1874, retail prices rose to 70 percent. . .and in July 1865, prices rose to 76 percent [above those of 1860]." As inflation soared, however, wage rates remained relatively unchanged. By July 1863 wages had increased by only 12 percent over their 1860 level, less than half the rate of inflation. By July 1865 wage increases were only two-thirds that of the inflation rate (50 percent as compared to 76 percent). This difference between wages and price increases renewed laborers' interest in unionism.

As in the 1830s, the number of unions began to grow in the United States. By the summer of 1862, almost every major city in America had a local union representing each trade. These locals collaborated with other trade unions to create trade assemblies. In 1863 the first trades' assembly formed in Rochester, New York. Thereafter trade assemblies began to appear in nearly every industrial center. As with the formation of the National Trades Union in 1834, interest in creating national unions was soon to follow. National unions that had formed before the Civil War, such as the National Typographical Union and the Iron Molders' Union, immediately found renewed interest in their organizations and reported decisive jumps in the number of charters. This trend expanded to include new organizations as well.

By the 1860s the marketplace had changed dramatically. In the early nineteenth century, "national" referred mostly to the eastern industrial centers. By 1862 expansionism had created a truly national marketplace. Industrial centers competed against one another for products. Many trade assemblies quickly realized that their activities could undermine unions in other areas if competitive balances were not established. As such, national organizations with set regulations governing strikes and trade rules appealed to these assemblies. A national presence could also benefit strictly local trade unions that faced the problem of migratory workers, who created competition with resident tradesmen. In addition, employers had begun to form associations to combat local unions. With national support, local unions could withstand the assault of these employer associations with greater success. In the period between 1863 and 1873, 26 national trade unions formed. Combined with the six prewar organizations, the 32 national trade unions had a collective membership of 300,000, with some estimates claiming as high as 600,000.

The National Labor Movement

Despite a brief depression between 1866 and 1869, national trade unions continued to prosper and take shape throughout the United States. During this time, several labor organizations formed with the purpose of reforming work conditions in the United States. These groups believed that having a strong presence in government would benefit their common causes. After overcoming initial rivalries, delegates from the various trade assemblies, national unions, and reform organizations held a convention in Baltimore on 20 August 1866. From this convention came the formation of the National Labor Union (NLU). The NLU became the successor of the National Trades' Union and the predecessor of the American Federation of Labor (AFL). Issues discussed during the convention included the eight-hour workday, public domain, women in industry, and unemployment problems caused by the Civil War.

Of these issues, the eight-hour workday became the focus of the NLU's efforts. Before that time, Ira Steward, a Boston

machinist, and his associates had been fighting for eight-hour workday legislation. Steward believed that improving a worker's standard of living resulted in increasing wages, as employers could not drop wages below the standard of living. An eight-hour workday would provide workers with more leisure time and thus increase their needs; this, in turn, would fuel a change in the standard of living. Steward also pointed out that a decrease in work hours would not decrease work output because longer hours led to exhaustion and inefficiency. Inspired by Steward's work, the NLU approached the federal government to legislate an eight-hour workday bill for government employees. They believed that if eight-hour legislation were achieved for government employees then it would take hold in private industry as well. During the summer of 1866, an NLU delegation met with President Andrew Johnson to discuss the issue. Although impressed with their presentation, Johnson refused to make any promises. He finally signed the eight-hour bill into law on 29 June 1868. The resulting legislation did not work as well as the NLU would have liked, but amendments four years later greatly improved the bill. Following in the footsteps of the federal government, state legislatures passed eight-hour bills in California, Connecticut, Illinois, Missouri, New York, and Wisconsin. These bills, however, did not restrict longer hours being assigned to workers willing to sign a contract. In addition, and perhaps worse, there were no powers of enforcement behind the laws.

After their relative success with the eight-hour bill, the NLU shifted its focus toward "greenbackism." Essentially, this social movement meant to empower those without capital, placing them on a level equal to that of their wealthy competitors. Supporters of this movement believed they could thus create an industrial democracy. At that time, however, the NLU began a descent into political bickering and stagnation. Wage earners, already disappointed with the results of legislation and political dealings, returned their support to the national trade unions as the source of a solution to their problems. The workers believed that direct interaction with employers would bring greater success than attempts to deal with the government. This trend continued until 1873; by then the NLU had become a hollow shell of its former self.

By 1869 the industrial sector had recovered from the brief depression and entered a period of prosperity. The negative perception of strikes had all but disappeared, which fueled support for national trade unions. Unionists were learning from their mistakes and gaining ground. An attribute that set these national trade unions apart from their counterparts from the 1830s was consistency. When they developed trade rules, the unions remained steadfast to them even during periods of industrial plenty. By maintaining this "status quo," the trade unions maintained or improved their position and that of other organizations. This philosophy brought them surprising success over the next few years. With the signing of the Trade Union Act, which provided trade unions with legal status, the future appeared bright for trade unionism. Despite their successes, however, national trade unions remained wholly unprepared for the financial devastation that was soon to hit the country. Even as they attempted to create the National Industrial Congress, a national labor federation solely based on trade-union ideals, the panic of 1873 would put an end to all their efforts.

The Panic of 1873

The panic of 1873 came as a result of both national and international economic problems. During and after the Civil War, the United States began selling government bonds to European investors. This created much-needed capital inflow into America. The proceeds from the sale and redemption of these bonds were, in turn, invested into the growing railways. After 1866, however, repeated wars, banking difficulties, and poor agricultural yields set off an economic reversal in European countries. As the depression in Europe worsened, this source of capital grew perilously thin. By 1870 the U.S. Treasury's attempt to refinance increasing debt by selling more government bonds to European investors failed. Currency grew scarce and paper money depreciated considerably. United States banks looked to national investors to solve their monetary problems.

The expansion of the railways continued to be the focus of investment during this period. Railway companies had been given lands to accommodate the progression of the railroads. Realizing that the land surrounding these railway lines was extremely valuable, the railroad owners began to sell it to investors. In response came a wave of rash speculation and increased the development of a high credit/low currency economy. As had the United States before the panic of 1837, the industrial community became financially unstable. A crash would require only a simple catalyst.

That catalyst came in the form of Jay Cooke and Company, a banking firm in Philadelphia. The financial growth of the company had stemmed from its sale of government war bonds. Cooke's innovative approach to selling to the general public rather than only to prominent investors provided his firm with considerable financial clout. Indeed, the company was considered one of the most prominent investment firms in the United States. The company's 1869 decision to engage in the railroad industry surprised no one. However, the firm's late entrance into the business meant they had little investment leeway. All of the financially stable railroads had already been purchased. Taking a financial risk, Cooke raised $100 million and bought the Northern Pacific Railroad, which ran from Seattle to Minneapolis. Cooke quickly discovered that he had invested poorly. The land surrounding the railway line could not be used for farming. Even the presence of a railway would not inspire settlers to move there. Investors had no incentive to buy the land. The problem began to worsen as construction costs rapidly outweighed the influx of investment funds. Desperate, Cooke sent out publicity agents to lie about the value of the land. In another stroke of bad luck, the truth about Cooke's shady dealings became public and investors immediately pulled out. Overextended and without viable income, Jay Cooke and Company faced financial ruin. On 18 September 1873 the company collapsed and closed it doors. The death of one of America's most prominent financial institutions put investors into a selling frenzy. The panic of 1873 had begun.

The New York Stock Exchange closed on 20 September and remained so for the next 10 days. Other financial firms such as Fisk and Hatch and numerous banks began to close daily. Thousands of businesses went bankrupt as lending agencies demanded immediate payment on loans. Credit became nonexistent and foreclosures grew increasingly common. Unemployment soared to unprecedented levels, stretching charitable organizations well beyond their means. By the winter of 1873, 25 percent of New York workers were unemployed. By 1878 more than three million people had joined the ranks of the unemployed nationwide. Antagonism against the president and government grew as workers blamed the economic tragedy on their mismanagement. Worker demonstrations such as the 1874 Tompkins Square protest became common. Some of these protests were so violent that many major cities built armories.

As with the panic of 1837, national unions were devastated by the panic of 1873. Their financial resources dried up almost immediately, preventing them from operating or funding members during strikes. In addition, the sheer number of unemployed workers had abolished their striking strength. Strikers were replaced by the masses of workers who were literally begging for jobs. Local trade unions failed one after the other, and the national organizations crumbled. They would not recover from this economic disaster for several years.

National Unions after the Panic

As devastating as the panic of 1873 was to the national union movement, it also fueled the fires of unionism. When financial stability began to return, so too did the unions. Strikes and protests increased in frequency. The Great Strike of 1877, among others, reflected the animosity of workers toward bankers and employers. Following in the steps of the Knights of Labor, unions stopped operating in secrecy. Rather than buckling under the tragedy of the panic, unionism began to flourish. Learning from their predecessors, the new national unions became stronger and more successful. They would begin making landmark accomplishments in labor relations and conditions. The strife they had experienced in the panic of 1873 would serve them well in the new century and beyond.

Key Players

Cooke, Jay (1821–1905): Founder of Jay Cooke and Company, Cooke transformed his company into one of the strongest financial firms in America. After the purchase of the Northern Pacific Railroad, however, Cooke's firm immediately ran into financial difficulties. The closing of Jay Cooke and Company's doors began the economic disaster known as the panic of 1873.

Grant, Ulysses S. (1822–1885): America's eighteenth president (1869–1877), Grant received public blame for the panic of 1873.

Johnson, Andrew (1808–1875): The seventeenth president (1865–1869), Johnson met with the National Labor Union to discuss eight-hour day legislation. He signed into law the eight-hour workday bill for government employees in 1868.

Steward, Ira (1831–1883): Leader of the Machinists' and Blacksmiths' International Union during the Civil War, Steward fought for eight-hour day legislation. His writings inspired the National Labor Union toward this goal. In 1877 Steward helped with the formation of the International Labor Union.

See also: *Eight-hour Day Movement; National Trades Union; National Typographical Union; National Union of Iron Molders.*

BIBLIOGRAPHY

Books

Commons, John R., David Saposs, Helen Sumner, E. B.
    Mittelman, H. E. Hoagland, John Andrews, et al. *History
    of Labour in the United States*, vol. 2. New York:
    Augustus M. Kelly Publishers, 1966.

Perlman, Selig. *A History of Trade Unionism in the United
    States*. New York: MacMillan Company, 1923.

Sumner, William G. *The Forgotten Man and Other Essays*.
    Freeport, NY: Yale University Press, 1919.

White, Eugene N., ed. *Crashes and Panics: The Lessons
    from History*. New York: New York University Press,
    1990.

Other

"The Financial Panic of 1873." Excerpted from *The Great
    Republic by the Master Historians*. Vol. 3, edited by
    Hubert H. Bancroft. Public Bookshelf Web Site. 2002
    [cited 17 October 2002]. <http://www.publicbookshelf.
    com/public_html/The_Great_Republic_By_the_
    Master_Historians_Vol_III/panicof1_hd.html>.

Lause, Mark. Lause's Links. "Post-war Social Conflicts."
    American Labor History [cited 17 October 2002]. <http://
    www.geocities.com/CollegePark/Quad/6460/AmLabHist/
    1870.html>.

Online Highways. U-S-history.com. "The Grant Admin-
    istration: Panic of 1873." 2002 [cited 17 October 2002].
    <http://www.u-s-history.com/pages/h213.html>.

                                                    —Lee Ann Paradise

William Jennings Bryan. The Library of Congress.

Panic of 1893

United States 1893

Synopsis

A financial panic in May 1893 led the United States into the worst economic depression it had experienced up to that point in its history. Following the collapse of several Wall Street brokerage houses, over 600 banks and 16,000 businesses failed by the end of the year. National unemployment reached an estimated 20 percent in the first year of the crisis, and only a few cities managed to provide relief of any kind. The agricultural sector, already experiencing a slump, also felt the aftereffects of the panic. As thousands of farmers lost their land, the Populist Party gained momentum as a voice of reform and government intervention in the economy. The party reached a peak in 1896 when it endorsed the Democratic candidate for president, William Jennings Bryan, for office. Although he lost the election, Bryan's "Cross of Gold" speech in support of a free silver monetary policy became the most electrifying moment in the campaign. Shortly after Bryan's defeat in the election of 1896, the economy began to improve as prices for American crops began to climb. The four-year depression finally lifted but not before giving impetus to a new era of political and economic reforms.

Timeline

1890: U.S. Congress passes the Sherman Antitrust Act, which in the years that follow will be used to break up large monopolies.

1891: Construction of Trans-Siberian Railway begins. Meanwhile, crop failures across Russia lead to widespread starvation.

1895: German physicist Wilhelm Roentgen discovers X rays.

1896: First modern Olympic Games held in Athens.

1897: In the midst of a nationwide depression, Mrs. Bradley Martin, daughter of Carnegie Steel magnate Henry Phipps, throws a lavish party at New York's recently opened Waldorf-Astoria Hotel, where she has a suite decorated to look like Versailles. Her 900 guests, dressed in Louis XV period costumes, consume 60 cases of champagne.

1898: United States defeats Spain in the three-month Spanish-American War. As a result, Cuba gains it independence, and the United States purchases Puerto Rico and the Philippines from Spain for $20 million.

1899: U.S. Secretary of State John Hay proposes an "Open Door" policy—meaning that all foreign powers with an economic interest in China should have an equal share

Jacob Coxey's Army of unemployed workers march from Masillon, Ohio, to Washington, D.C. © Corbis. Reproduced by permission.

in the benefits. This meets with the agreement of other nations involved, including western European countries and Japan.

1900: China's Boxer Rebellion, which began in the preceding year with attacks on foreigners and Christians, reaches its height. An international contingent of more than 2,000 men arrives to restore order, but only after several tens of thousands have died.

Event and Its Context

In Gilded Age America, there were few financial controls and little government oversight of the business sector. Although reformers had fought for the Interstate Commerce Act (1887) and the Sherman Antitrust Act (1890), both measures were quickly co-opted by businessmen to serve their own interests. Antitrust laws were rarely applied to business trusts; instead, corporations invoked them to break up labor unions. The apparent collusion of big business and the federal government also riled farmers who were convinced that the railroads were taking

Coxey's Army

In 1894 thousands of unemployed American workers marched on Washington. A number of such marches on the capital occurred during this period of economic challenges, but a group from Ohio, known as "Coxey's Army" for their leader, Jacob Sechler Coxey, was the only one to actually reach its destination. As an industrialist, Coxey might have seemed an unlikely advocate of the working man—but this was far from his only unusual quality.

At age sixteen, Coxey went to work at an iron mill and moved up to the position of stationary engineer before starting his own scrap-iron business in 1878. After three years, 27-year-old Coxey moved to Massillon, Ohio, and started a company that processed silica, a mineral used by industry. The silica company would be his chief money-making enterprise, and the proceeds from this would help him to pursue a second career in politics.

As a result of the financial recession that followed the panic of 1893, Coxey was forced to lay off 40 laborers. This pained him greatly, and he wished he could do something for his workers. Around this time, he joined forces with Carl Browne, a former radical politician and cartoonist from California who dressed like a cowboy and claimed that he and Coxey were both parts of Christ's brain. Together they organized "Coxey's Army," a group of unemployed men who set out for Washington on Easter Sunday, 25 March 1894.

Coxey, who gained the nickname "General Coxey," predicted that his "Army" would eventually number in the thousands. Yet only about 100 men started out with him, and by the time they got to the capital on 1 May, their numbers had grown to only about 500. In Washington they did not gain an audience with President Grover Cleveland, and Coxey was arrested.

Although Coxey's Army did not have an enormous direct impact in their 1894 march on Washington, it inspired other similar armies of the unemployed, who undertook their own cross-country marches. In part because of Coxey's effort, which gained national attention as a curiosity if not as a political movement to be taken seriously, marches on Washington would become a part of American political life for the next century. Notable examples included the 1932 march of the unemployed "Bonus Army"; the labor marches on Washington in the early 1940s (an elderly Coxey re-created his own march on its fiftieth anniversary in 1944); and the 1963 march led by black labor organizer A. Philip Randolph.

Source: Donald Le Crone McMurry, *Coxey's Army: A Study of the Industrial Army Movement of 1894.* Boston: Little, Brown, 1929.

—Judson Knight

advantage of them with high shipping rates and monopolistic practices. In response, Kansas farmers formed the first People's Party chapter in 1890. Two years later a St. Louis convention established a national People's (or Populist) Party to fight for a host of reforms. Chief among the Populists' demands were the unlimited coinage of silver to increase the money supply, direct elections of senators, a national income tax, and government ownership of the railroads and telephone and telegraph companies. Populist candidate James B. Weaver received over a million votes in the presidential election of 1892, taking 8.5% of the total vote and 22 electoral votes.

The Panic of 1893

The Populists' criticism of corrupt eastern elites seemed to be justified in the financial crisis that began in early May 1893. On 3 May a trust that controlled the production and sale of twine declared bankruptcy. The announcement triggered a panic on the stock market, particularly among companies that had indulged in overproduction and investors who had engaged in speculation and profiteering. By the end of the year, 642 banks had collapsed, wiping out their depositors' savings, and about 16,000 individual businesses failed. As many as one in five people in a working population of 15 million was without a job. The railroad sector was particularly hard hit, with over 150 companies holding 30,000 miles of track and worth an estimated $2.5 billion going bankrupt in the first year of the financial crisis alone.

In the absence of state relief programs for the unemployed, many looked to the federal government for help. At least 17 workers' marches on Washington occurred in 1894, including the one led by Jacob Sechler Coxley.

The Pullman Strike

Even more dramatic than Coxey's march on Washington was the Pullman Strike by the American Railway Union in 1894. That spring, workers at the Pullman Car Works near Chicago announced a strike to protest wage cuts that had reduced incomes by between one-third and one-half since the previous year. Many of the workers lived in Pullman, Illinois, a company-owned town with rents, utility rates, and food prices set by the company. After the company refused to reduce the prices of these goods, employees began to circulate plans for a strike. After the Pullman Company fired three workers' representatives on 11 May 1894, the company's entire workforce walked off the job. Although Eugene V. Debs, president of the American Railway Union (ARU), was hesitant to support the strike, the union nevertheless agreed to ask its members to refrain from handling any Pullman cars on the rail lines. The boycott went into effect on 26 June 1894 and quickly stalled rail traffic across the United States.

Claiming that the strike interfered with the delivery of the U.S. mail, the Cleveland administration obtained an injunction against the strike on 3 July 1894. An estimated 2,000 federal troops and 5,000 federal marshals arrived in Pullman on the same day on the pretext of putting down any violence. On 4 July 1894 the troops clashed with the strikers; the violence left 13 strikers dead and more than 50 wounded. Over the next week, the death toll rose to 34, and the ARU was forced to admit defeat on 12 July. Debs and other union officials were subsequently arrested for refusing to follow the injunction. Debs served a term in jail from June to November 1895.

Political Deadlock

The use of brute force by the federal government against the Pullman strike did little to enhance the image of President Cleveland, who had taken office just before the Panic of 1893. Cleveland also faced a scandal when the public learned that he had ordered the government to replenish its depleted gold supply in an agreement with financier J. P. Morgan in 1895. Under the terms of the deal, the government issued bonds to Morgan in exchange for about $129 million in gold reserves held by New York City banks. When Morgan turned around and resold the government bonds for an $18 million profit, the public was outraged.

President Cleveland also faced criticism from Populists over the issue of monetary standards. A supporter of the gold standard, Cleveland believed that the free coinage of silver would lead to inflation and economic instability. By contrast, supports of free silver believed that inflation would allow farmers to pay off their debts more quickly and fuel an economic recovery. In 1894 Cleveland convinced Congress to repeal the Sherman Silver Purchase Act of 1890, which had forced the government to buy silver each month even if it did not coin it. The action only served to contract the money supply further and deepen the depression that had started in 1893.

The Election of 1896

Public discontent with the country's economic and political scandals reached a peak in the presidential race of 1896, one of the most pivotal elections in American history. The Democrats spurned Cleveland's policies and nominated William Jennings Bryan as the prosilver Democratic candidate. Bryan also gained the endorsement of the Populist Party, in large part because of the "Cross of Gold" speech he gave in support of free silver coinage at the Democratic National Convention. Republican William McKinley upheld the gold standard in the election and argued that only a sound monetary policy based on gold would restore business confidence in the country. McKinley won the election with 52 percent of the vote and would win against Bryan again in 1900 by about the same margin.

After McKinley took office, the depression of the 1890s gradually lifted as agricultural disasters in other countries increased the demand for American products. The recovery of the agriculture sector led the way for other business sectors. The basic platform of the Populists was not forgotten, however, and Progressive Era reforms saw the enactment of several of the party's demands. In 1913 the Sixteenth Amendment legalized a federal income tax and the Seventeenth Amendment mandated the direct election of senators.

Key Players

Bryan, William Jennings (1860–1925): Trained as a lawyer, Bryan entered politics in 1890 when he won a seat representing Kansas in the U.S. House of Representatives. He won the Democratic nomination for president in 1896 after giving the "Cross of Gold" speech in support of a free silver monetary policy. His 1896 bid was unsuccessful, as were his subsequent runs in 1900 and 1908. In 1925 Bryan represented the creationist side in the Scopes Monkey Trial in Tennessee.

Cleveland, Grover (1837–1908): Cleveland worked as a lawyer in Buffalo, New York, and started his political career by winning the sheriff's office in 1870. He then served as Buffalo's mayor and New York's governor in subsequent years. For his stand against political corruption, Cleveland gained a reputation as a reformer. Nominated for the presidency by the Democrats in 1884, he won a close election over James G. Blaine. He lost against Benjamin Harrison in the presidential race in 1888 but returned to office in 1892, shortly before the Panic of 1893.

Coxey, Jacob (1854–1951): The owner of a sandstone quarry in Massillon, Ohio, Coxey was dismayed by the lack of efforts to help unemployed workers after the panic of 1893. Hoping to convince the federal government to implement a program of public works, Coxey organized a group of about 100 men and began a march to Washington, D.C. By the time "Coxey's Army" reached the capital, its numbers had reached about 500 men. After Coxey's men tried to demonstrate on the grounds of the U.S. Capitol, federal troops removed them by force. Coxey remained active in politics for the rest of his life and served as mayor of Massillon from 1931 to 1933.

Debs, Eugene (1855–1926): A railroad worker by profession, Debs organized his colleagues into several different union locals before helping to found the American Railway Union in 1893. One of the most famous labor leaders during the Depression of 1893–1897, Debs joined the Socialist Party in 1897. He ran for president five times and conducted his last campaign from behind bars, where he was serving time for speaking out against World War I.

Morgan, John Pierpont (1837–1913): The most prominent financier of his era, J. P. Morgan was accused of setting up monopolies to guarantee a high rate of return from his investments. Even his critics admitted, however, that Morgan was a genius at putting together complex financial deals such as the creation of U.S. Steel. Morgan's input was vital in easing the financial crises of 1893 and 1907.

See also: *People's Party; Pullman Strike.*

BIBLIOGRAPHY

Books

Brodsky, Alyn. *Grover Cleveland: A Study in Character.* New York: Truman Talley Books, 2000.

Montgomery, David. *Citizen Worker: The Experience of Workers in the United States with Democracy and the Free Market During the Nineteenth Century.* New York: Cambridge University Press, 1993.

Salvatore, Nick. *Eugene V. Debs: Citizen and Socialist.* Urbana: University of Illinois Press, 1992.

Wiebe, Robert H. *The Search for Order, 1877–1920.* New York: Hill and Wang, 1967.

—Timothy G. Borden

Paris Commune

France 1871

Synopsis

In March 1871 the citizens of the city of Paris rejected the authority of the French national government at Versailles. The immediate origins of this revolt against the central government lay in the Franco-Prussian War and the four-month siege of Paris. Fuelled by intense patriotism and isolation from the rest of France, radical and socialist elements came to the fore among the Parisian lower classes. With the end of the siege and the defeat of France, the Parisian population felt betrayed. In the face of open defiance from the Parisian National Guard, the government withdrew from Paris. In its place, municipal elections created the Paris Commune, which instigated some social reforms. The Commune was eventually defeated, resulting in the massacre of approximately 25,000 people in one of the worst periods of violence in French history. In the immediate aftermath, the labor movement in France was destroyed, and the international socialist movement faced repression. However, the Paris Commune raised the profile of socialism, and in its failure, became an important example to socialists worldwide.

Timeline

1851: Britain's Amalgamated Society of Engineers applies innovative organizational concepts, including large contributions from, and benefits to, members, as well as vigorous use of direct action and collective bargaining.

1853: Crimean War begins in October. The struggle, which will last until February 1856, pits Russia against the combined forces of Great Britain, France, Turkey, and Sardinia-Piedmont. A war noted for the work of Florence Nightingale with the wounded, it is also the first conflict to be documented by photojournalists.

1861: Unification of Italy under Sardinian king Victor Emmanuel II.

1864: Foundation of the International Red Cross in Geneva.

1867: Dual monarchy established in Austria-Hungary.

1871: Franco-Prussian War ends with France's surrender of Alsace-Lorraine to Germany, which proclaims itself an empire under Prussian king Wilhelm, crowned Kaiser Wilhelm I.

1871: U.S. troops in the West begin fighting the Apache nation.

1871: Boss Tweed corruption scandal in New York City.

1871: Chicago fire causes 250 deaths and $196 million in damage.

1873: Financial panic begins in Vienna and soon spreads to other European financial centers as well as to the United States.

1876: Alexander Graham Bell introduces the telephone.

1880: Completion of Cologne Cathedral, begun 634 years earlier. With twin spires 515 feet (157 m) high, it is the tallest structure in the world, and will remain so until 1889, when it is surpassed by the Eiffel Tower. (The previous record for the world's tallest structure lasted much longer—for about 4,430 years following the building of Cheops's Great Pyramid in c. 2550 B.C.)

Event and Its Context

The Siege of Paris

The immediate seeds of the revolt that created the Paris Commune lay in the Franco-Prussian War. In particular, four months of siege isolated Paris from the rest of France. With the defeat and capture of Napoleon III at Sedan, the victors declared a republic on 4 September 1870. However, the new moderate provisional government was more concerned with neutralizing the threat of radical revolution than with fighting the Prussians. As a result, it tried to negotiate peace with Otto von Bismarck as quickly as possible while simultaneously claiming to be committed to the defense of Paris. The Parisian population, including a well-armed National Guard, became increasingly frustrated at the inaction and apparent duplicity of the government.

Intense republican patriotism and isolation from central authority proved to be a heady mixture. In the working-class districts of the city, committees and clubs formed and began making increasingly radical demands. Most significantly, many people began to request municipal elections. In French, the term *commune* refers to the municipal authority in major cities. However, the Paris Commune had a revolutionary history that gave it particularly radical overtones. It had played an important role in the most radical stage of the French Revolution. Therefore, the demand for a Paris Commune elected through direct democracy was ominous. The government managed to stall most of these demands, but its control over the population became increasingly fragile.

Finally, the siege of Paris ended on 28 January. In its eagerness to end the war, the French government acceded to most of Bismarck's demands. Over the next two months, Paris became increasingly alienated from the central government. National elections returned a National Assembly that was even more conservative than the provisional government. The new regime, led by Adolphe Thiers, was insensitive to the suffering of the Parisian lower classes and passed a series of measures that inflicted further economic hardship. This succeeded in uniting the working and lower middle classes of Paris against the government.

The Paris Commune

The standoff between Paris and the National Assembly, then based at Versailles 25 miles to the southwest of the city, came to a head on 18 March. Thiers was determined to take strong action against the increasingly defiant Parisian National Guard. Therefore, he sent in troops to take possession of the National Guard's cannons. However, the people of Paris firmly resisted the attempt. In the working-class district of Montmartre, women and children defied the troops, who refused to fire on the crowd. With this open rejection of central power, Thiers

Rioters, Paris Commune, Paris, France. © Hulton-Deutsch Collection/Corbis. Reproduced by permission.

called for the evacuation of the government from Paris. The army and most of the bureaucracy abandoned the city and fled to Versailles. Control of Paris had fallen to its citizens.

The recently formed National Guard Central Committee emerged as the main authority in the wake of the government's hasty retreat. The committee's immediate concern was to hold municipal elections and transfer power as quickly as possible to the Commune. The elections, held on 26 March, returned a Paris Commune that was far to the left of the National Assembly at Versailles. Most districts elected representatives who were opponents of the Versailles government. Significantly, 35 out the 91 representatives were manual laborers, mainly crafts-

men from small workshops. One of the Commune's first and most effective measures was to abolish the back payment of rents accumulated during the siege. This was a huge relief to the lower classes of the city and helped to rally support for the Commune.

However, such decisive action proved to be rare. With no obvious leader, the Commune consisted of shifting factions with different political and social agendas. Jacobins motivated by the ideals of the French Revolution clashed with the supporters of Louis-August Blanqui, Pierre Joseph Proudhon, and other socialist theorists. The lack of clear leadership or direction meant that the Commune was often paralyzed by conflict. The constant feuding alienated many people, and the Commune struggled to develop new forms of authority. At the outset, decentralized, federalist principles were emphasized. However, as the military situation grew more desperate, the Committee of Public Safety, a central authority modeled on the French Revolution, formed. Many representatives rejected the committee, fearing its dictatorial overtones. Some of the more zealous members favored repressive measures to stifle criticism and pursue opponents of the regime within Paris. Such activities eroded support for the Commune.

Despite these problems, some interesting social reforms were attempted. The Commission of Labor and Exchange dealt with the organization of labor. Workers' cooperatives were a strong part of French socialist thought, and during the Commune, 43 producers' cooperatives were set up in the city's craft industries. In support of this, the Commune decreed that abandoned workshops could be taken over by trade unions to form cooperatives, and 10 factories were occupied as a result. Many of these looked to the Commune to provide work at reasonable prices, thus challenging the competitive basis of the capitalist system of production. Education was another area in which reforms were attempted. Schools were set up to replace those run by the church, according to a policy of free secular public education.

Most of this reform occurred at the grassroots level. In many of the working-class districts, people worked to create new organizations and institutions. On the boulevards and in the cafés of Paris, the lower classes gathered to meet and discuss these issues. There was a strong sense of celebration during the weeks of the Commune, to the extent that it has been referred to as "a festival of the oppressed." Despite the limitations of the Commune, for the first time, the lower classes were allowed an active part in running their city and creating social forms and relations that answered their needs. Most historians agree that the reform measures taken by the Commune were not socialist. There was no move to attack the principle of private property or to nationalize the assets of the Bank of France, which extended credit to the Commune. However, with its reforms, the Commune was responding to long-term concerns of the French workers' movement.

The Civil War

In the days after Thiers's withdrawal from Paris, some of the rebels advocated an immediate attack on Versailles. However, the National Guard Central Committee was unwilling to take such drastic action. Therefore, Thiers had time to reorganize his demoralized and mutinous army. The release of French officers captured during the Franco-Prussian War was particularly significant in restoring discipline. The Versailles government also used propaganda to encourage the army, portraying the Commune as a group of madmen, criminals, and foreign *agents provocateurs*. The government forces first attacked on 2 April. In response, the National Guard launched a major assault towards Versailles the next day. The Parisian forces were routed, and many of those taken prisoner were executed. This was the only offensive military move made by the Commune. Thiers's troops closed in and placed Paris effectively under a second siege. The decentralized nature of the Commune, with its emphasis on localized authority, made the war effort difficult to

coordinate. Even the National Guard Central Committee struggled to impose discipline on the individual National Guard units.

Defeat and Repression

Inevitably, on 21 May the Versailles forces began entering the city. Centrally organized defense of the city or of strategic points became impossible as the National Guard reverted to defending its own districts against the invaders. However, the chaotic war effort of the previous two months was forgotten, as those who still supported the Commune fought on the barricades to defend it. This became known as *semaine sanglante*, the bloody week, in which indiscriminate slaughter occurred on both sides. Responding to the bestial portraits painted of the Communards over the previous two months, the Versailles troops shot men, women, and children in working-class areas. In response, the Communards began shooting their prisoners, including the Archbishop of Paris. By this stage, much of the center of Paris was in flames, set alight by the retreating Communards and Versailles artillery.

Legacy

The immediate consequence of the fall of the Paris Commune was the utter decimation of the French labor movement. The death toll on the side of those supporting the Commune was approximately 25,000, most of which occurred during the last week of frenzied bloodshed. A further 40,000–50,000 were arrested, and many were sentenced to long imprisonment or deportation. Some 3,300 fled into exile overseas. However, amnesty was granted to the exiles in 1880, and many of them returned to France. The repression following the Commune affected the whole European labor movement, eventually contributing to the collapse of the First International.

However, the Paris Commune did raise the profile of the socialist movement. After its defeat, Karl Marx wrote a brilliant polemic against Thiers and the republican government, which acknowledged the Commune as the first example of a workers' government. This brought Marx notoriety and made the International appear to be a more influential organization than it really was. Following the Commune, interest in Marx's socialist theory increased, and several new editions of the *Communist Manifesto* were published, although none of those involved in the Commune could be described as followers of Marx. The example of the Commune was important to the refinement of Marx's ideas about the socialist revolution. In turn, Marx's writings on the Commune were very influential in the development of Lenin's revolutionary strategy and the Bolshevik revolution. More generally, the Commune became an important symbol of heroic sacrifice for the socialist movement.

Key Players

Blanqui, Louis-August (1805–1881): French revolutionary socialist. Blanqui played an important in leading socialist opposition to the provisional government in 1870–1871. While he was imprisoned on the eve of the Paris Commune, his followers played a prominent role in it.

Delecluze, Charles (1809–1871): French republican journalist. Delecluze was a major figure in the Commune, although he was hampered by poor health as the result of long imprisonment. Delecluze took over the position of war delegate in the final days of the Commune and died on the barricades.

Thiers, Adolphe (1797–1877): French conservative politician. As first president of the Third Republic, Thiers was the architect of the defeat of the Paris Commune.

Vaillant, Edouard (1840–1915): Labor activist. Vaillant emerged as an important leader during the Paris Commune, especially in the area of educational reform. With the defeat of the Commune, he escaped to London, returning to France in 1880.

See also: *Communist Manifesto Published; First International.*

BIBLIOGRAPHY

Books

Edwards, Stewart. *The Paris Commune, 1871.* London: Eyrie and Spottiswood, 1971.

Lindemann, Albert S. *A History of European Socialism.* New Haven, CT, and London: Yale University Press, 1983.

Magraw, Roger. *France 1815–1914: The Bourgeois Century.* London: Oxford, 1983.

Smith, William C. *Second Empire and Commune: France 1848–1871.* 2nd ed. London & New York: Longman, 1996.

Other

"Marxist History: The Paris Commune, March–May, 1871" [cited 6 November 2002]. <http://www.marxists.org/history/france/paris-commune/index.htm>

ADDITIONAL RESOURCES

Books

McLellan, David. *Karl Marx: His Life and Thought.* London: Macmillan, 1973.

Williams, Roger L. *The French Revolution of 1870–1871.* New York: Norton, 1969.

—Katrina Ford

PATCO Strike

United States 1981

Synopsis

Following failed efforts to reach a contract agreement, the Professional Air Traffic Controllers Organization (PATCO), a union affiliate of the AFL-CIO, polled its members for a strike vote on 31 July 1981. Ninety-five percent of the air traffic con-

trollers voted to strike. PATCO president Robert Poli set the strike date at 3 August if union demands were not met. The Federal Aviation Administration (FAA), the employer of the air traffic controllers, refused to change the last offer to the union. President Ronald Reagan, who had been supported by PATCO in his bid for election less than a year before, announced on 3 August that if the strikers did not return to work within 48 hours, their jobs would be terminated. Reagan decertified the union and fired 11,359 air traffic controllers for not returning to work. The move enforced a 1955 regulation that denied federal employees the right to strike. His forceful action against the strikers set the tone for labor-management relations for a generation. This quick and decisive action established Reagan's image as a tough president. Congressional and other investigations later determined that the principal cause for the strike was autocratic management by the FAA, which had added to an already stressful employment for air traffic controllers who had the responsibility for safety at the nation's airports. They were trained for that one job and essentially had no other employment options.

Timeline

1975: Two assassination attempts on President Ford in September.

1977: Newly inaugurated U.S. President Jimmy Carter pardons Vietnam draft dodgers.

1979: After years of unrest, the Shah of Iran leaves the country, and Islamic fundamentalist revolutionaries under the leadership of Ayatollah Ruhollah Khomeini take control. Later in the year, militants seize control of the U.S. embassy in Teheran and take more than 50 Americans hostage.

1981: In an act calculated to strike one last blow at Carter, Iran releases the 52 remaining U.S. hostages on the day Reagan is inaugurated as the new president.

1981: John David Hinckley, a young man with a history of obsession and mental imbalance, shoots and wounds President Reagan on 30 March. Also seriously wounded are Reagan's press secretary, James Brady (who will be confined to a wheelchair thereafter), and two law-enforcement officers. Six weeks later, on 14 May, a Turkish gunman wounds Pope John Paul II.

1981: Reagan nominates Sandra Day O'Connor of Arizona to become the first female Supreme Court justice.

1981: Pathologists identify a new type of disease, known as acquired immunodeficiency syndrome, or AIDS.

1981: Launch of the first space shuttle, *Columbia.*

1981: In a storybook wedding witnessed by millions on television, Lady Diana Spencer weds Prince Charles of Great Britain.

1984: As retaliation for the U.S. refusal to participate in the Summer Olympics in Moscow four years earlier, the Soviet Union and other members of the communist bloc stay away from the Olympic Games in Los Angeles.

1989: The Ayatollah Khomeini, soon to die himself, puts out a death warrant on author Salman Rushdie for his book

PATCO strikers, City Hall Plaza, Boston, Massachusetts. AP/Wide World Photos. Reproduced by permission.

The Satanic Verses, which flirts with the idea that the prophet Muhammad had doubts about his mission on earth.

1999: Though the House has voted along party lines in December to impeach U.S. President Bill Clinton on two charges—perjury and obstruction of justice—the vigor has gone out of the entire case by the time it reaches the Senate, which acquits him of all charges on 12 February.

Event and Its Context

Prelude to the Strike

In 1962 President John F. Kennedy granted by executive order the right of federal employees to join unions and engage in collective bargaining. By that time, stress was becoming an issue for air traffic controllers as air traffic was on the rise. By the early 1960s the controllers grew further discontented because they were not involved in important decision-making. This inspired a group of New York–based controllers to form the Professional Air Traffic Controllers Organization (PATCO)

President Ronald Reagan with Attorney General William French Smith addresses striking federal air traffic controllers, Washington, D.C. © Bettmann/Corbis. Reproduced by permission.

in 1968. It started as a professional society but later became a labor union affiliated with the AFL-CIO.

In 1967 the FAA became a part of the newly established U.S. Department of Transportation. The FAA had the sole responsibility for developing and maintaining air traffic and employed the controllers. FAA-PATCO relations were adversarial by 1970, when PATCO ordered "Operation Air Safety," which declared that controllers should adhere to established standards for air traffic separation and thus caused air traffic slowdowns. In the early years of PATCO, in response to the FAA's involuntary transfers of union activists, about 3,000 controllers participated in a "sickout" in an effort to get better pay, training, staffing retirement benefits, and reduced work hours.

Under the leadership of union president John Leyden, a relatively peaceful period followed these early actions. During that period, air controllers gained wage and retirement benefits, but demands for improved working conditions were not addressed. In January 1980 PATCO leadership passed to Robert Poli, who was more responsive to the growing dissatisfaction with working conditions among air controllers. Within a few months, the union distributed to members an "educational package" that provided information on how to establish communication networks and committees on security, welfare, and picketing. It also outlined how to prepare for lost wages during a job

action. The FAA considered the document a strike plan. PATCO staged a one-day slowdown at Chicago's O'Hare International Airport in August 1980 over a wage dispute.

PATCO was one of the few labor unions that had publicly supported presidential candidate Ronald Reagan in the fall of 1980, a clear response to the union's contention that President Jimmy Carter was ignoring serious safety problems that jeopardized the air traffic controller system. Reagan wrote to PATCO President Robert Poli, "You can rest assured that if I am elected president, I will take whatever steps are necessary to provide our air traffic controllers with the most modern equipment available and to adjust staff levels and work days so that they are commensurate with achieving a maximum degree of public safety."

Some small safety improvements were made at the start of Reagan's term under his newly appointed secretary of the Department of Transportation, Andrew L. (Drew) Lewis. In March 1981 the three-year labor agreement between PATCO and the FAA expired. The provisions of the old contract were allowed to remain with one exception: the provision for immunity under National Aeronautic and Space Administration's (NASA's) Aviation Safety Reporting System, which had been arbitrarily canceled in 1979. The immunity provision allowed controllers and pilots to report errors without risk of penalty so that solutions to problems could be addressed. At about this time the FAA administration changed and J. Lynn Helms, who had a long history in aviation, took over.

Negotiations for a new contract stalled in April 1981, when the Office of Management and Budget opposed PATCO's demands for a 32-hour workweek and a separate federal pay scale for air traffic controllers. In June 1981 a telephone poll of members indicated that less than 80 percent of air traffic controllers at the largest 80 percent of facilities voted to strike (the 80/80 requirement for agreement to strike), so Poli tentatively accepted a "final" offer for a contract from transportation secretary Drew Lewis. The agreement met some of the pay demands but not those for a reduced workweek. The proposed contract also did not address a provision that gave supervisors the right to require controllers to eat lunch on the job during periods of heavy air traffic, an issue that controllers cited as contributing to their stress levels. Meanwhile, the FAA was expanding some safety equipment, such as the Traffic Alert and Collision Avoidance system, but it was not enough to please controllers.

PATCO Strike Begins

In spite of the results of the June poll, by early July 1981 the PATCO executive board unanimously recommended that controllers reject the contract offer. Hoping this time to get the 80/80 agreement numbers, the union in fact got more than 95 percent of the members to reject the FAA offer. The vote was 13,495 to 616. On 31 July 1981 Robert Poli announced that the union would strike on 3 August unless PATCO's demands were met. The talks failed and the walkout started as schedule at 7 A.M. eastern standard time. Almost 13,000 of the 17,500 members of PATCO went on strike.

That same day at the White House, President Reagan, who strongly admired Calvin Coolidge, read a handwritten statement to his advisers that he had prepared the night before. Quoting Coolidge, he declared, "There is no right to strike the public safety by anybody, anywhere, anytime." He said to reporters in the Rose Garden that if the strikers did not return to work within 48 hours, their jobs would be terminated. From his point of view, he was not firing them. If they did not return they were giving up their jobs; 11,359 air traffic controllers were subsequently dismissed. Reagan also gave orders to the FAA to reduce the level of air traffic to what they could handle safely with the supervisors and controllers who were still on the job.

The number of controllers was down about 74 percent, although about 1,300 strikers did return to work, making a total of approximately 2,000 nonstriking air traffic controllers. The FAA had a contingency plan to reduce scheduled flights by 50 percent during peak hours, and it shut down about 60 small airport towers. They also called in 900 military controllers and used 3,000 supervisors as air traffic controllers to supplement those left on the job. To the surprise of almost everyone and the distress of the strikers, the FAA's plan functioned smoothly. With the cooperation of the Air Line Pilots Association, which took on extra monitoring efforts, air traffic soon returned to about 80 percent of normal operation. The FAA also set out to increase the number of trainees at their Oklahoma City air traffic control school's 17–21 week course from 1,500 to 5,500. Within four weeks of 3 August, the FAA had 45,000 applicants for training.

Reagan had the backing of Drew Lewis and FAA administrator J. Lynn Helms for his actions. He also had the legal right to take this action. At the time of the strike, the 1955 government regulation known as 5 U.S.C section 7311 stated that an "individual may not accept or hold a position in the Government of the United States . . . if he . . . participates in a strike, or asserts the right to strike against the government of the United States." The regulation also disqualified persons who engaged in these types of actions from the job for three years. This prompted President Reagan's 9 December 1981 memorandum, which stated, "The Office of Personnel Management has established the position that the former air traffic controllers who were discharged for participating in a strike against the Government initiated on August 3, 1981 shall be debarred from federal employment for a period of three years. Upon deliberation I have concluded that such individuals, despite their strike participation should be permitted to apply for federal employment outside the scope of their former employing agency." Years later, Reagan wrote of the PATCO strike, "I supported unions and the rights of workers to organize and bargain collectively, but no president could tolerate an illegal strike by Federal employees."

Consequences of the Strike

An immediate consequence of the strike was the destruction of PATCO. At the start of the strike, a federal court impounded PATCO's $3.5 million strike fund and another federal judge imposed on the union fines totaling $4.75 million. On 4 August federal judge Thomas C. Platt in New York fined PATCO $100,000 an hour for defying a 1970 injunction against striking.

AFL-CIO President Lane Kirkland expressed outrage at President Reagan, who was described as engaging in "union-busting" by labor leaders. There was some truth to their claims. For years after the PATCO strike unions lost ground. The hiring of permanent replacements for strikers became a common tactic of corporations.

Reagan's decisive action against the strike was legal, and it set the tone for labor-management relations for a generation.

On 22 October 1981 the Federal Labor Relations Authority decertified the union. Although an appeals court temporarily stayed the order, it became final on 27 October. In December, Robert Poli resigned as president of PATCO. By July 1983 PATCO declared bankruptcy. PATCO was finished.

On the positive side, the FAA published a 450-page document, the National Airspace System Plan, which outlined an ambitious 20-year blueprint for upgrading the air traffic control system, including replacement of aging and unreliable mainframe computers, consolidation of facilities, addition of Doppler weather radio, and an ambitious plan to install 1,250 microwave landing system sites by the year 2000.

The airlines suffered considerable financial losses during the strike. Some of the major carriers reported losses of $30 million a day at the start of the strike. It was no coincidence that the strike occurred at their busiest time of the year. The airlines were forced to cut back service and lay off workers, and management took pay cuts. Ground transportation services benefited for a while. Media reports that did not support the strike and the inconvenience suffered by the public made the strike unpopular. Most of the reports on the workers' complaints centered on pay increases and demands for a shorter workweek. The FAA offer sounded generous to the general public. Although the air traffic controllers were largely driven to action by stress on the job, few in the media, and therefore in the public, sympathized with them.

Analysis of the Causes of the Strike

Congress, the FAA, and even PATCO investigated the air traffic control strike. In spite of public perception to the contrary, hearings and interviews that followed the strike revealed that the controllers' demands focused on stress and safety as the chief issues. In fairness to the media, some publications did see these issues as part of the reason for striking. On 17 August 1981 *Time* published an article titled "Turbulence in the Tower" that said PATCO's demand for a 32-hour workweek was "a reduction that the controllers seem to want more than the pay increases. . . . Most PATCO members see this issue as the key to lowering their on-the-job anxieties and enhancing safety."

The deep-rooted underlying cause for the ongoing tensions between the air traffic controllers and the FAA was frustration with labor-management relations, a frustration that had been recognized as far back as 1968. In April 1968 the secretary of transportation commissioned the Corson Committee Report. The report, issued in January 1970, cited significant employee morale problems among the air traffic controllers and indicated that the problems might be serious enough to affect public safety. The report put most of the blame on the FAA for poor management techniques.

Another report issued in 1972 cited the autocratic management style of the FAA as the source of the serious job stress among air traffic controllers. Morale became worse in 1979 when FAA administrator Langhorne Bond arbitrarily terminated the immunity provision that had been included in the 1978 three-year FAA/PATCO contract. The immunity program allowed air traffic controllers, pilots, and administrators to share information so each could learn from common errors and not fear retribution. An outside disinterested committee under NASA processed these reports and circulated the data as a learning tool. The impact of the termination of the immunity provision was that incidents were seldom reported.

In addition to eliminating the protection of immunity, the FAA demanded that air traffic controllers handle higher traffic loads than were allowed by their own standards. When the controllers complained, the FAA changed the standards instead of hiring more controllers. In addition, during this same period the FAA hired additional managers. Some described FAA managers as militaristic, and many of them did in fact come from the military. The lack of management training for FAA supervisors as well as a management philosophy of top-down control further added to the friction between controllers and management.

Out of the Ashes: A New Union Forms

Following the demise of PATCO, the air traffic controllers made several efforts to organize a new bargaining unit. Finally, in September 1986 delegates ratified a constitution for the National Air Traffic Controllers Association (NATCA). They also signed an affiliation agreement with the Marine Engineers' Beneficial Association (MEBA). PATCO had been first affiliated with MEBA. In January 1998 NATCA sent a request for a national charter to join the AFL-CIO. The executive council of the AFL-CIO voted unanimously to accept NATCA as a direct affiliate of the union. In 1998, after a year of negotiating, the union and the FAA signed a five-year, $1.6 billion collective bargaining agreement. The contract was accepted by 92 percent of the union members.

Key Players

Dole, Elizabeth H. (1936–): Appointed 7 February 1983 by President Reagan to succeed Drew Lewis as secretary of transportation. She served until 30 September 1987. Dole had been a White House assistant for public liaison at the time she was nominated for the Department of Transportation position.

Helms, J. Lynn (1925–): Helms was the administrator of the Federal Aviation Administration (FAA) from 22 April 1981 to 31 January 1984. He had a long history working in the aviation industry prior to his appointment as the head of FAA. Among his prior positions, he had been chairman of the board of Piper Aircraft Corporation and president of the Norden Division of United Technologies; he also had been a fellow in the American Institute of Aeronautics Association.

Lewis, Andrew L. ("Drew," 1931–): Lewis was secretary of the U.S. Department of Transportation from 23 January 1981 to 1 February 1983. He worked with the FAA to draft the National Airspace System Plan to modernize air traffic control after the PATCO strike.

See also: *AFL, CIO Merge.*

BIBLIOGRAPHY

Books

Reagan, Ronald. *Ronald Reagan: An American Life*. New York: Simon & Schuster, 1990.

Periodicals

Magnuson, R. et al. "Turbulence in the Tower," *Time*, 17 August 1981.

Other

A Brief History of Federal Agencies Regulating Aviation. Appendix A, FAA Regulations [cited 26 July 2002]. <http://www.fire.tc.faa.gov/pdf/handbook/00-12_apA.pdf.>

"Detailed Chronology, 1926–96." FAA History Information and Resources [cited 26 July 2002]. <http://www.faa.gov/apa/history/HISTORY.htm.>

Pels, Rebecca. "The Pressures of PATCO: Strikes and Stress in the 1980s." *Essays in History* 37, Corcoran Department of History at the University of Virginia, 1995 [cited 26 July 2002]. <http://etext.lib.virginia.edu/journals/EH/EH37/Pels.html.>

Ronald Reagan Presidential Library, University of Texas. "Statement on Federal Employment of Discharged Air

Traffic Controllers," 9 December 1981 [cited 26 July 2002]. <http://www.reagan.utexas.edu/resource/speeches/1981/120981a.htm.>

ADDITIONAL RESOURCES

Books

Nordlund, Willard J. *Silent Skies: The Air Traffic Controllers' Strike.* Westport, CT: Greenwood Publishing Group Incorporated, 1998.

Shostak, Arthur, and David Skocik. *The Air Controllers Controversy: Lessons from the PATCO Strike.* Norwell, MA: Kluwer Academic Publishers, 1986.

—M. C. Nagel

Pawtucket Textile Strike

United States 1824

Synopsis

The textile strike in Pawtucket, Rhode Island, was the first strike of women workers in the United States. Female loom workers joined with male weavers to protest the attempt by mill owners in Pawtucket to reduce wages by 25 percent and increase the length of the workday. Largely because of community support in the village, mill owners were forced to rescind the proposed wage cut, as well as the attempt to increase the workday, until they were able to consolidate their political position within the village and in the state of Rhode Island. This strike was the result of deeper concerns than a wage reduction and increase in the workday, however; it also reflected the growing concern of workers over the increasing influence of factory owners and the workers' own change in status as they were forced to work harder for their wages.

Timeline

1800: The United States moves its federal government to Washington, D.C.

1805: Napoleon defeats a combined Austrian and Russian force at the Battle of Austerlitz.

1811: Prince Aleksandr Borosovich Kurakin, Russian ambassador to Paris, introduces the practice of serving meals *à la Russe*—in courses.

1814: Napoleon's armies are defeated by an allied force consisting of Austria, Britain, Portugal, Prussia, Russia, and Sweden. Napoleon goes into exile on the isle of Elba, off the Italian coast, and Bourbon king Louis XVIII takes the throne in France.

1819: First production of chocolate for eating (as opposed to cooking), in Switzerland.

1823: U.S. President James Monroe establishes the Monroe Doctrine, whereby the United States warns European

Samuel Slater. The Library of Congress.

nations not to interfere in the political affairs of the Western Hemisphere.

1824: Ludwig van Beethoven composes his Ninth Symphony.

1824: French engineer Sadi Carnot describes a perfect engine: one in which all energy input is converted to energy output. The ideas in his *Reflections on the Motive Power of Fire* will influence the formulation of the Second Law of Thermodynamics—which shows that such a perfect engine is an impossibility.

1824: Cherokee scholar Sequoyah perfects his 85-letter Cherokee alphabet.

1826: French inventor Joseph-Nicéphore Niepce makes the first photographic image in history.

1835: American inventor and painter Samuel F. B. Morse constructs an experimental version of his telegraph.

1842: Scientific and technological advances include the development of ether and artificial fertilizer; the identification of the Doppler effect (by Austrian physicist Christian Johann Doppler); the foundation of biochemistry as a discipline; and the coining of the word *dinosaur*.

Event and Its Context

In the years before 1824, Pawtucket was the location of a variety of manufacturing concerns. Located on the falls of the Blackstone River at the northern edge of the tidewaters of the

Narragansett Bay, the village was strategically placed to develop a variety of manufacturing enterprises. Artisans in Pawtucket ran a gristmill, a tannery and bark mill, a linseed oil mill, three fulling mills, three snuff mills, and a clothier's works. Pawtucket had been an iron working center since the mid-seventeenth century, and by the time of the introduction of textile manufacturing anchors, it also produced cannons, hollow ware, nails, and screws for linseed and fish oil presses. The village was also home to a sizable shipbuilding industry, which provided jobs not only for approximately 20 ship's carpenters, but also provided a market for many of the iron works in the town. Because of the other businesses and industries that had been established in Pawtucket, the town had no need for paternalistic institutions such as company housing and company stores that closely followed the establishment of textile mills in other locations, most notably in Lowell, Massachusetts. The artisans in Pawtucket also maintained close relationships with farmers in the area, who provided the artisans both with raw materials with which to manufacture their products, as well as much of the market for the finished products the artisans produced. This kind of relationship was eventually changed by the introduction of textile mills and the factory discipline that these factory owners and managers demanded of their workers.

The location of the town of Pawtucket made it attractive to early capitalists for locating factories as the location provided both an inexpensive power supply and ready access to markets. This made Pawtucket an attractive site for textile factories, which was the earliest industry to begin to mechanize (that is, to use machines in the production of manufactured goods). Textile factory owners attempted to enforce a new kind of work discipline on the workers that they hired for their factories. Before the rise of the factory system, artisans and laborers often worked irregular hours. Workers only produced "bespoken" products—that is, products that a customer had ordered before it was produced. If no customer orders were outstanding, there was no need for workmen to put in a full day's work. Even with pressing business, an artisan did not feel compelled to put in an 8-, 10-, or 12-hour day at work, because his family may have needed him to supplement their diet by his hunting or fishing skills—or the artisan may have just felt that he deserved a day off from work. Oftentimes, the artisans consumed copious quantities of alcohol during the workday, as well. This usually occurred during a mid-morning break from work, lunch, and a mid-afternoon break. The usual work schedule for preindustrial artisans was a five-and-a-half day week, with Saturday afternoon usually given over to heavy drinking with coworkers. This drinking often carried over to heavy drinking on Sunday as well, which itself often left workers less than eager to return to a full work schedule on Monday. This in turn meant that workers often honored "St. Monday" or "blue Monday," with the day given over to sharpening tools and preparing materials and supplies for the rest of the week. This was largely a male-dominated work world, with workers having to prove their "manliness" not only through the consumption of large amounts of alcohol, but also by "treating" fellow workers (to drinks of alcohol), and by resisting efforts by management (personified in the person of the master craftsman in this time period) to enforce a more rigorous work discipline.

The introduction of machines spurred many factory owners to attempt to change these old work patterns. To use machinery

most efficiently, owners felt the need to have machine tenders at work every scheduled workday—generally six days a week. The manufacture of machinery in the textile industry occurred first in England, and the government there jealously tried to prevent the export of machinery to other countries, and also to prevent the emigration of persons who had the knowledge to build that machinery. Despite these efforts, however, mechanically inclined Americans did manage to visit textile mills in England and then reproduce those machines and factories back in the United States. England was just as unsuccessful in preventing those persons with specialized knowledge from emigrating from the country. In the early 1790s, English immigrant Samuel Slater, who had been a machinist in textile mills in England, settled in Rhode Island and introduced the Arkwright system of carding and spinning to the United States. Smith Brown, with business partner William Almy (both relatives of Quaker Moses Brown, a Providence merchant who made his fortune in the slave trade), joined with Slater to establish the earliest textile mill in Pawtucket, the Slater Mill, which began operating in 1793. In the next 20 years, seven other mills opened in Pawtucket. Among the largest and most important were the White Mill (established in 1800 and expanded in 1813), the Yellow Mill (established in 1805 and expanded in 1813), and the Wilkinson Mill (opened in 1811). By the early 1830s, Pawtucket was home to approximately 14,000 spindles and 350 looms and employed nearly 500 workers. This made Pawtucket perhaps the most important industrial village of that period.

The earliest workers in the mills in Pawtucket were children; in fact, by 1820 children comprised approximately 70 percent of the workforce. Many farm families provided workers for the textile factories. The factory managers prized large families, because they felt that the fathers were able to discipline their broods more effectively. In fact, many of these fathers were reluctant to allow factory management to discipline their children, and after 1820 young females replaced children as unskilled operatives. Mill owners thought it easier to enforce factory discipline on female workers, because the women had no inclination to demonstrate "manly" behavior, and it was thought that the women would adjust better to the demands for punctuality. Women were placed in positions of machine tenders, largely with the spinning mules, which were used to turn raw cotton into thread. The demand for skilled work was less, and many of the women had learned the little skill needed (tying knots to join pieces of broken thread) at home. The textile manufacturing process was not entirely mechanized; both hand picking (opening the cotton bolls and removing excess dirt and seeds) and hand looming were still performed at area farm homes; this was all changed by 1824, however, with the introduction of mechanical pickers and power looms. This further removed textile work from the home, decreased the need for skilled workers, and increased the demand for female workers and for the pace of work to be determined by machines.

Unlike the later mill towns (such as Lowell, for example), the female workers in Pawtucket were drawn from the town itself and from the immediate surrounding area. This meant that the women were not forced to live in company-provided housing but stayed with their families in the area or at independent boarding houses. The ties to the Pawtucket area became even more important when industrial conflict erupted in late May 1824.

On 24 May an organized group of factory owners announced that on 1 June they planned to lengthen the workday by one hour and cut the wages of female handloom weavers by almost 25 percent. These owners pointed out that the handloom weavers in Pawtucket earned more than their counterparts in other sections of the country and that the depressed price for cotton cloth had cut their profit margins. Upon learning of this proposed action, the handloom weavers walked off their jobs; other mill workers, who decided that all mill workers should refrain from working until mill owners rescinded their proposal, quickly joined them. Other workers in Pawtucket, including skilled artisans, joined the mill hands in their protest. This large group of workers gathered in the streets to vent their frustrations, and it was decided that the workers would visit the homes of each of the mill owners to make their feelings known. In response to this protest, the mill owners shut down all of the mills in the town. Five days into this lockout, the Yellow Mill in Pawtucket was the site of an apparent arson attempt; although damage was relatively minor, the incident did spur mill owners to reach an agreement with the strikers. Details of the settlement are sketchy; however, it seems likely that the mill owners agreed to rescind or modify the wage cut and length of workday proposals.

As a result of this conflict, mill owners began to move into local politics to protect their economic interests, although they were not able to consolidate their position in local politics until the 1850s. Workers in Pawtucket continued to resist mill owner hegemony, pooling their money to buy a town clock with a bell to keep time in the town. Owner control of the political process, however, eventually meant that mill owners were able to use the force of law to assert their "property rights" over the interests of workers.

Key Players

Slater, Samuel (1768–1835): Slater immigrated to the United States in 1789, bringing with him the experience and knowledge of the textile industry as it was being developed in England. After first settling in New York, Slater became acquainted with the early factories being run in Pawtucket by Moses Brown and William Almy. After visiting the Brown and Almy factory, Slater realized the improvements he could institute and offered his services. From this partnership grew the "Rhode Island system" of factory organization.

See also: *Lowell Industrial Experiment.*

BIBLIOGRAPHY

Books

Kulik, Gary, Roger Parks, and Theodore Z. Penn, eds. *The New England Mill Village, 1790–1860*. Cambridge, MA: MIT Press, 1982.

Tucker, Barbara M. *Samuel Slater and the Origins of the American Textile Industry, 1790–1860*. Ithaca, NY: Cornell University Press, 1984.

Wertheimer, Barbara M. *We Were There: The Story of Working Women in America*. New York: Pantheon Books, 1977.

Periodicals

Kulik, Gary. "Pawtucket Village and the Strike of 1824: The Origins of Class Conflict in Rhode Island." *Radical History Review* 17 (spring 1978): 5–37.

—Gregory M. Miller

People's Party

United States 1892

Synopsis

The People's Party was formed in St. Louis in 1892 to represent working people, particularly farmers, against entrenched financial interests: the two major political parties, bankers and financiers, railroad magnates, corporations, agricultural processors, grain-elevator operators, and anyone allied with such interests. The party ran presidential candidates in 1892 and 1896, but its inability to forge a coalition with eastern industrial workers, coupled with internal divisions and rising farm prices in the late 1890s, undermined the party and led to its collapse. The terms "People's Party" and "Populist Party" are often used interchangeably, although "Populist" tends to refer to the national party, whereas "People's" is the name by which the party was known in some states.

Timeline

1872: The Crédit Mobilier affair, in which several officials in the administration of President Ulysses S. Grant are accused of receiving stock in exchange for favors, is the first of many scandals that are to plague Grant's second term.

1877: In the face of uncertain results from the popular vote in the presidential election of 1876, the U.S. Electoral Commission awards the presidency to Rutherford B. Hayes despite a slight popular majority for his opponent, Samuel J. Tilden. The election of 1876 will remain the most controversial in American history for the next 124 years, until overshadowed by the race between George W. Bush and Al Gore in 2000.

1882: Agitation against English rule spreads throughout Ireland, culminating with the assassination of chief secretary for Ireland Lord Frederick Cavendish and permanent undersecretary Thomas Burke in Dublin's Phoenix Park. The leader of the nationalist movement is Charles Stewart Parnell, but the use of assassination and terrorism—which Parnell himself has disavowed—makes clear the fact that he does not control all nationalist groups.

Ex-slave Horace Bailey sitting on porch, Hope Farm, Natchez, Mississippi. © Corbis. Reproduced by permission.

1885: German engineer Karl Friedrich Benz builds the first true automobile.

1888: Serbian-born American electrical engineer Nikola Tesla develops a practical system for generating and transmitting alternating current (AC), which will ultimately—and after an extremely acrimonious battle—replace Thomas Edison's direct current (DC) in most homes and businesses.

1890: U.S. Congress passes the Sherman Antitrust Act, which in the years that follow will be used to break up large monopolies.

1891: French troops open fire on workers during a 1 May demonstration at Fourmies, where employees of the Sans Pareille factory are striking for an eight-hour workday. Nine people are killed—two of them children—and sixty more are injured.

1893: Henry Ford builds his first automobile.

1893: New Zealand is the first nation in the world to grant the vote to women.

1894: French army captain Alfred Dreyfus, a Jew, is convicted of treason. Dreyfus will later be cleared of all charges, but the Dreyfus case illustrates—and exacerbates—the increasingly virulent anti-Semitism that pervades France.

1896: First modern Olympic Games held in Athens.

1900: The first zeppelin is test-flown.

Event and Its Context

Background

After the U.S. Civil War, the nation's farm sector grew dramatically as hundreds of thousands of farmers followed the nation's expansion and settled in the Great Plains, the Rocky Mountain West, and the West Coast. Additionally, thousands of ex-slaves became sharecroppers on small farms in the South. At the start of the Civil War, there were about two million farmers in the United States, but by 1916 that number had more than tripled, rising to 6.4 million. During the same years,

Thomas Wilson Dorr and the First People's Party

Half a century before the formation of the People's Party in 1892, another organization known by that name crusaded for voting rights in Rhode Island. At that time, there was no question of suffrage for women or non-whites; instead, the short-lived organization built by Thomas Wilson Dorr (1805–1854) fought merely to secure the vote for white men with limited personal property.

In Rhode Island during the first half of the nineteenth century, a man had to possess at least $200 worth of real estate in order to secure voting rights for himself and his eldest son. Dorr, a representative in the state legislature with the Federalist Party, supported another legislator's proposed amendment that would extend the franchise to men with $250 worth of property of any kind. When this resolution failed to pass, Dorr proposed a more radical alterative: for every $134 in real estate a man possessed, he could qualify one of his sons to vote. This amendment, too, failed to pass.

Though he switched from the Federalist to the Democratic Party in 1836 and successfully introduced legislation limiting the power of banks in the state, Dorr had meanwhile organized what came to be known as the People's Party. At a mass meeting in Providence on 5 July 1841, members called for a state constitutional convention, which was held in October and which—according to party members—earned approval from a majority of the state's eligible voters. A suffragist election in March 1842 chose Dorr as governor, but two months later, the officially recognized state elections returned incumbent Samuel Ward King to the governor's seat.

Faced with the prospect of an illegal shadow government, King called for martial law, and when Dorr tried unsuccessfully to seize control of the state arsenal, the governor placed a reward of $1,000 for his capture. The amount was raised to $5,000 after an armed conflict broke out in July 1842 between the People's Party and a group called "the Law and Order Party." Arrested in June 1843, Dorr stood trial for treason before the state supreme court and was sentenced to life imprisonment with hard labor.

In 1845 the Rhode Island general assembly released all prisoners convicted of treason against the state. Nine years later, at the time of Dorr's death in 1854, the legislature voted to completely annul the state supreme court's ruling against him. As a result of Dorr's work, Rhode Island ultimately adopted a constitution that granted virtual universal manhood suffrage.

Source: Marvin E. Gettleman. *The Dorr Rebellion: A Study In American Radicalism, 1833–1849*. New York: Random House, 1973.

—Judson Knight

the total number of acres under cultivation more than doubled, from 407 million to 879 million, and improvements in the technology of planting, cultivating, and harvesting increased the yield of this acreage.

It should have been a golden age for farmers, but it was not. The post–Civil War period was marked by a general decrease in prices, a problem exacerbated in the farm sector by the huge surpluses the farmers were producing. The result was that many farmers were failing, or at least sinking into a quagmire of debt, and many lost their land. The problem became especially acute after the financial panic of 1873, which many people, especially farmers, blamed on the financial manipulations of eastern moneyed interests. Workers and farmers believed that an expansion of the U.S. paper money supply would benefit them and that the United States maintained a currency backed by specie, such as gold, because it served the interests of the rich—especially creditors such as banks, which stood to lose by any expansion of the money supply, for they would be paid back in dollars that were not worth as much as the dollars they had loaned. Out of this conflict the Greenback Party emerged in 1876 to advocate repeal of the Specie Resumption Act of 1875, which put the nation's currency on the gold standard. The party attracted few voters in the 1876 elections, but in the congressional elections of 1878, almost a million voters cast ballots for Greenbackers and sent 14 to Congress. One of those was James B. Weaver, who would later gain prominence in the 1892 presidential election.

The Farmers' Alliance

The Greenback Party faded from sight, but the discontent of farmers did not, particularly after a severe drought hit the wheat-growing regions of the Plains and the price for southern cotton sank to new lows. Thus, a second step toward the emergence of the People's Party was the formation of the Farmers' Alliance in the 1880s. The alliance was a loosely knit confederation of farmers in two principal geographical areas, with the National Farmers' Alliance (Northern Alliance) dominating the Plains states, and the National Farmers' Alliance and Industrial Union (Southern Alliance) dominating the South, particularly Arkansas, Louisiana, and Texas. These groups supported a network of cooperatives and sponsored lectures, published newspapers, and provided farmers with a sense of solidarity. They agitated for railroad reform, tax reform, and the unlimited coinage of silver. They were outspoken in their disdain for the entrenched economic and political interests that seemed indifferent to their inability to make a decent living, though they lent their support to major-party candidates who promised to come to their aid. The alliances grew rapidly, attracting a quarter of a million members by 1888.

By 1889 efforts were being made to form a coalition of the two Alliances, the Knights of Labor, and the Colored Farmers' Alliance, but these organizations were unable to put aside their prejudices and sectional differences and work toward common goals. The Southern Alliance began to expand into a nationwide organization, with a presence ultimately in 43 states. It was becoming increasingly clear, however, that the organizations could not succeed without reform legislation, and the major-party candidates they had supported were proving unreliable.

Talk thus began to center on the formation of a new farm-labor political party, particularly at the Farmers' Alliance 1890 convention in Ocala, Florida. Out of this convention emerged the so-called Ocala Demands—essentially a threat to politicians in the major parties that the alliance would form its own political party if the parties did not meet its demands. Included in the Ocala Demands were calls for free coinage of silver (a move that would inflate the money supply, thereby helping indebted farmers), the direct election of U.S. senators, and low tariffs. Additionally, the alliance called for the formation of a "subtreasury" system—a massive government warehouse-building program that would allow farmers to store their crops until prices rose; in the meantime, the government would grant loans to farmers, with the stored crops as collateral.

The Populist Party

After the Ocala convention, the Southern Alliance continued to try to operate within the Democratic Party, but many members of the Northern Alliance formed a third party in the Plains states. Kansas took the lead, and in 1890 Populists seized control of the state legislature and sent to Washington the party's first U.S. senator, William Peffer. Although Peffer was an object of ridicule by eastern journalists and politicians, the party continued to gain support in western and southern states until many Farmers' Alliance members called for the formation of a national party.

Their call was answered in February 1892 when the Farmers' Alliance and the Knights of Labor convened in St. Louis to form the People's Party, intended to be an alliance of agricultural workers in the South and West and industrial workers in the North. Triggering their actions was the waffling of the two major-party presidential candidates (Republican Benjamin Harrison and Democrat Grover Cleveland) over the currency issue. In July the new party convened in Omaha, Nebraska, where it nominated James B. Weaver, a former Union general from Iowa, for president; the vice presidential nominee was James Field, an ex-Confederate from Virginia.

In the preamble to its platform, written by Ignatius Donnelly of Minnesota, the party made its position clear: "We have witnessed for more than a quarter of a century the struggles of the two great political parties for power and plunder, while grievous wrongs have been inflicted upon the suffering people. We charge that the controlling influences dominating both these parties have permitted the existing dreadful conditions to develop without serious effort to prevent or restrain them. Neither do they now promise us any substantial reform." Donnelly further wrote that "they propose to drown the outcries of a plundered people with the uproar of a sham battle over the tariff, so that capitalists, corporations, national banks, rings, trusts, watered stock, the demonetization of silver and the oppression of the usurers may be lost sight of."

The platform went on to call for free coinage of silver, abolition of national banks, a subtreasury system, a graduated income tax, an expanded supply of paper money, government ownership of transportation and communication (especially the railroads), direct election of U.S. senators and term limits for the president and vice-president, the repatriation of land currently owned by foreigners, civil service reform, an eight-hour workday, postal banks, pensions for ex-Union soldiers, revision of the law of contracts, and reform of the immigration system (which "opens our ports to the pauper and criminal classes of

the world and crowds out our wage-earners"). The convention also offered its full support to the Knights of Labor in its labor dispute with the "tyrannical combine of clothing manufacturers of Rochester."

Weaver and Field made a respectable showing, polling over one million votes and actually carrying five western states (22 electoral votes); from the Civil War to the beginning of the twenty-first century, only Teddy Roosevelt, Strom Thurmond, and George Wallace had won more electoral votes as third-party candidates, and only four third-party candidates—Roosevelt, Wallace, Robert LaFollette, and H. Ross Perot—exceeded Weaver's 8.5 percent of the popular vote. In some parts of the country the ticket won up to 45 percent of the vote, but it made a disappointing showing in the North, where it was able to attract little support from nonfarm voters. In the South, racial divisions, sectional loyalties, election fraud, and even violence ensured the solid control of the Democratic Party. Nonetheless, the People's Party grew, and in the 1894 congressional elections the party's candidates polled more than 1.5 million votes.

The Decline of the People's Party

The decline and collapse of the People's Party began as the 1896 presidential election approached. The party was in turmoil, riven by two factions. One faction, which included the party's national chairman, Herman E. Taubeneck, consisted of "fusion Populists." This faction sought to drop the Omaha platform and fuse with the Democrats, believing that a regional party could never achieve national prominence and that it would be more expedient to exert influence within a major political party. In Kansas the Populist Party had already fused with the Democrats, prompting cries from bitter opponents of the move that the party had sold out.

The other faction, generally referred to as "mid-roaders," believed that the Democrats wanted to destroy the threat of a third party and that fusion would play right into their hands. This group wanted to stay "in the middle of the road" between the two major parties—though this phrase fails to suggest the sweeping changes desired by the mid-roaders. The mid-roaders tried to schedule the party's nominating convention before the conventions of the two major parties, but the fusionists succeeded in scheduling the convention afterwards in the hope that a "silver" Democrat they could support would win his party's nomination in Chicago.

The fusionists realized their hopes when William Jennings Bryan, a former congressman from Nebraska, won the Democratic Party nomination after electrifying the convention with his famous "Cross of Gold" speech ("You shall not crucify mankind on a cross of gold") in opposition to the firm commitment to the gold standard on the part of the Republican nominee, William McKinley.

The mid-roaders were in a tight spot. They had hoped actually to capture the White House, believing that the "gold voters" would split between the two major parties and that the People's Party would appeal to a growing corps of "silver voters." When the Democrats nominated Bryan, however, they faced a dilemma: they could either nominate Bryan themselves and ensure silver coinage, in the process losing their identity as a distinct party, or they could nominate their own candidate and wind up splitting the silver vote. Relations between the fusionists and the mid-roaders were tense. The fusionists were in communication with Bryan's campaign manager; the mid-roaders' most eloquent spokesman, the fiery Tom Watson of Georgia, stayed at home, sensing disaster. When the convention endorsed Bryan—putting him in the unique position of being the presidential candidate of two political parties—the mid-roaders tried to rally, but the lights in the convention hall mysteriously went out. They just as mysteriously came back on 15 minutes after the mid-roaders had given up and dispersed.

The People's Party platform in 1896 was essentially the same as the 1892 platform. In contrast to the "sound money" platform of the Republicans, party members continued to place their faith in silver coinage and an expanded money supply. Additionally, they called for abolition of the electoral college, recognition of Cuba as a free and independent state, home rule in the territories and the District of Columbia, early admission of the territories as states, and a public-works system to put "idle labor" to work during times of industrial depression.

To try to salvage some independence, the mid-roaders did manage to defeat the nomination of Arthur Sewall, Bryan's Democratic running mate and an antilabor conservative. Instead, for vice president they chose Watson, the editor of the *People Party's Paper* and a dedicated Populist who had received death threats from Georgia Democrats who feared the rise of the People's Party. Thus, voters could choose between a Bryan-Sewall ticket or a Bryan-Watson ticket. Watson accepted the nomination only because he was led to believe that Bryan had promised the party's leadership that he would renounce Sewall. Bryan, however, had given no such promise, so Watson refused to campaign for him; Bryan, for his part, virtually ignored the People's Party. Out of this bitterness and confusion the Republicans were able to portray the Populists and the silver Democrats as ignorant "hayseeds" and "anarchists." In the election, McKinley won 7.1 million votes and 271 electoral votes, and Bryan won 6.5 million votes and 176 electoral votes. Bryan carried no industrial state in the North and even lost the agricultural states of Iowa, Minnesota, and North Dakota.

Disillusion and Dissolution

Many members of the People's Party were disillusioned by Bryan's defeat, and rising farm prices in the 1890s took much of the fire out the party. After 1896 many joined the Democratic Party, believing that the Democrats were the best hope for unseating conservative, antilabor Republicans. Some joined a new party, the Social Democratic Party, which nominated Eugene V. Debs for president in 1900. Others clung to the People's Party and ran candidates primarily in state and local elections, though they did nominate Wharton Barker for president in 1900 and Tom Watson in both 1904 and 1908. Neither of these candidates won nearly the number of votes that Weaver had in 1892.

Although the People's Party died, its ideals lived on, and many of its proposals eventually became realities. President Theodore Roosevelt expanded federal regulation of business corporations, and under his leadership the Progressive Party's 1912 platform echoed that of the People's Party. In 1912 Congress passed a constitutional amendment that provided for direct election of U.S. senators. In the 1930s the government began to provide aid to farmers and public works programs to help unemployed workers during the depression. In recent years the issue of term limits for elected officials has been widely discussed.

Key Players

Bryan, William Jennings (1860–1925): Born in Salem, Illinois, Bryan practiced law before being elected to the U.S. House of Representatives (1891–1895) from Nebraska. After leaving office, he turned to lecturing and journalism, then ran for president in 1896, 1900, and 1908. In 1913 President Woodrow Wilson appointed him secretary of state, but he resigned in 1915 to protest Wilson's belligerence toward Germany. In 1920 he moved to Florida, where he made a fortune in the real estate boom. His last major public appearance was in the 1925 Scopes "monkey trial," where he spoke for the prosecution.

Peffer, William (1831–1912): Peffer was born in Cumberland County, Pennsylvania. He began his career as a school teacher, but later he migrated throughout the country. He made money in the California gold rush; farmed in Missouri and Illinois; served in the Civil War; practiced law in Tennessee; and then moved to Kansas to practice law, establish two newspapers, and purchase a third, the *Kansas Farmer*. In 1874 he was elected to the state senate as a Republican. In 1890 he joined the Farmers' Alliance and was elected to the U.S. Senate, where he served one term (1891–1897).

Watson, Tom (1856–1922): Watson, the firebrand of the Populist movement, was born on a small plantation near Thomson, Georgia. After prospering as a lawyer and landowner, he entered politics and was elected to the Georgia legislature in 1882 and resigned in 1884. In 1890 he was elected to Congress as a Democrat, but he supported the existence of a third party and helped found the Populist Party in Georgia in 1892. In addition to running for vice president in 1896, he ran for president in 1904 and 1908 and was elected to the U.S. Senate in 1920. Late in life he became a virulent racist, anti-Semite, and anti-Catholic.

Weaver, James B. (1833–1912): Weaver was born near Dayton, Ohio, and grew up in Iowa. He practiced law until he joined the Union Army during the Civil War, rising to the rank of brevet brigadier general. After the war he was elected district attorney and was appointed federal assessor of internal revenue, a post he held until 1873. Throughout the 1870s and 1880s, Weaver was active in third-party politics, and in 1878 he was elected to Congress as a member of the Greenback Party (1878–1880, 1884–1888). After running for president in 1892, he returned to Iowa, where he served as mayor of Colfax.

See also: *Colored Farmers' Alliance; Knights of Labor.*

BIBLIOGRAPHY

Books

Beals, Carleton. *The Great Revolt and Its Leaders*. New York: Abelard-Schuman, 1968.

Hofstadter, Richard. *The Age of Reform.* New York: Random House, 1955.

McGrath, Robert C., Jr. *American Populism: A Social History, 1877–1898.* New York: Hill and Wang, 1993.

Peffer, William. *Populism: Its Rise and Fall.* Lawrence: University Press of Kansas, 2000.

Pollack, Norman, ed. *The Populist Mind.* New York: Macmillan, 1967.

———. *The Just Polity: Politics, Law, and Human Welfare.* Champaign: University of Illinois Press, 1987.

Other

Edwards, Rebecca. "People's Party Platform" (1896). Vassar Collage Web site. 2000 [cited 8 October 2002]. <http://iberia.vassar.edu/1896/peoplesplatform.html>.

W. W. Norton and Company. *The Essential America.* "Populist Party Platform (1892)." From "People's Party Platform," *Omaha Morning World-Herald*, 5 July 1892 [cited 8 October 2002]. <http://www.wwnorton.com/eamerica/media/ch22/resources/documents/populist.htm>.

—Michael J. O'Neal

Secretary of Labor Frances Perkins. © AP/WideWorld Photos. Reproduced by permission.

Perkins Becomes Secretary of Labor

United States 1933

Synopsis

Frances Perkins was the first woman to serve in a presidential cabinet position. She became secretary of labor in 1933 after Franklin Delano Roosevelt was elected president. This position allowed her to bring about sweeping changes with regard to social reform and labor conditions. She served in the position for the entirety of Roosevelt's term in office, 1933–1945, making her the longest-serving secretary of labor in the nation's history. Among her achievements in office were three hugely influential pieces of social legislation: the Social Security Act (1935), the National Labor Relations Act (1935), and the Fair Labor Standards Act (1938).

Timeline

1917: Russian revolutions.

1922: Inspired by the Bolsheviks' example of imposing revolution by means of a coup, Benito Mussolini leads his blackshirts in an October "March on Rome," and forms a new fascist government.

1927: Charles A. Lindbergh makes the first successful solo nonstop flight across the Atlantic, and becomes an international hero.

1929: On "Black Friday" in October, prices on the U.S. stock market, which had been climbing wildly for several years, suddenly collapse. Thus begins the first phase of a world economic crisis and depression that will last until the beginning of World War II.

1932: When Ukrainians refuse to surrender their grain to his commissars, Stalin seals off supplies to the region, creating a manmade famine that will produce a greater death toll than the entirety of World War I.

1932: A "Bonus Army" of unemployed veterans marches on Washington, D.C. Many leave after Congress refuses their demands for payment of bonuses for wartime service, but others are forcibly removed by General Douglas MacArthur's troops. Also participating are two other figures destined to gain notoriety in the next world war: majors Dwight D. Eisenhower and George S. Patton.

1932: In German elections, Nazis gain a 37 percent plurality of Reichstag seats, raising tensions between the far right and the far left. On a "bloody Sunday" in July, communists in Hamburg attack Nazis with guns, and a fierce battle ensues.

1932: Charles A. Lindbergh's baby son is kidnapped and killed, a crime for which Bruno Hauptmann will be charged in 1934, convicted in 1935, and executed in 1936.

1935: Second phase of New Deal begins with the introduction of social security, farm assistance, and housing and tax reform.

1937: Italy signs the Anti-Comintern Pact, signed by Germany and Japan the preceding year. Like the two others before it, Italy now withdraws from the League of Nations.

1942: Axis conquests reach their height in the middle of this year. The Nazis control a vast region from Normandy to the suburbs of Stalingrad, and from the Arctic Circle to the edges of the Sahara. To the east, the Japanese "Co-Prosperity Sphere" encompasses territories from China to Burma to the East Indies, stretching deep into the western Pacific.

1947: Establishment of the Marshall Plan to assist European nations in recovering from the war.

Event and Its Context

Educational Background and Early Career

Frances Perkins was born on 10 April 1880. After graduating from Mt. Holyoke College in 1902 with a degree in social work, Perkins knew that change was necessary to obtain social justice. Her postgraduate work in 1903 began in Worchester, Massachusetts, where she offered her services to help female factory workers. In 1904, after accepting a teaching post at a girl's prep school in Lake Forest, Illinois, Perkins met Dr. Graham Taylor, from whom she learned a great deal about trade unionism. She met other social reform leaders such as Jane Addams and Ellen Gates Starr, cofounders of Hull House. Progressive thinking abounded at Hull House. Its leaders started a kindergarten and encouraged mothers to share their thoughts with each other on equal footing. The free lectures offered by university professors and their students served to empower women. Operating from a profoundly articulated aesthetic that encompassed humanitarian objectives through social and political activities, Perkins lived at Hull House for a time. This marriage of her professional and personal experiences with her naturally pragmatic mindset would served her well at Hull House and throughout her career.

The social climate of the time was an enormous influence on Perkins. Women still had not obtained the right to vote, and much work remained to be done with regard to women's rights. Women who took leadership roles faced great challenges and had to fight for their rightful place in society. As true in the early 1900s as today, a solid education opened professional doors. Understanding this, Perkins studied economics and sociology at the Wharton School of Finance and accepted a fellowship at the New York School of Philanthropy. While Perkins was pursuing her master's degree in political science at Columbia University, which she obtained in 1910, Pauline Goldmark, the head of the School of Philanthropy, asked her to survey Hell's Kitchen on the West Side of New York. Refusing to be passive in the process, Perkins decided that to help a slum family she had met, she would need to solicit the support of Timothy J. McManus, a state senator and the infamous Tammany Hall boss of Hell's Kitchen. Given the patriarchal nature of the political world during that era, Perkins's arguments must have been convincing, as McManus agreed to help. The experience allowed Perkins to demonstrate her powers of persuasion and also served to prepare her for her future role as secretary of labor—a role that would require her to understand thoroughly the political machinery of the time and to use it to achieve social reform.

By 1910 Perkins was able to put her wealth of education and experience to good use by becoming the secretary of the New York Consumer's League. Florence Kelley, the league's national director, served as a role model to Perkins and helped direct her emotional and intellectual passage into a world of political maneuvers and social reform. It was, after all, the league's mission to "spread information about harmful industrial conditions and lobby for protective legislation"; in this regard, Perkins became a recognized expert after conducting detailed surveys of filthy bakeries, unsafe laundries, and overcrowded textile mills. Having learned from Kelley to "look behind the immediate conditions and search for the real causes of safety and health problems in industry," Perkins developed a multilevel social awareness that married statistics with her moral convictions.

An avid reader, Perkins was profoundly influenced by the writing of investigative journalists such as Upton Sinclair, author of *The Jungle*, an international bestseller that focused attention on the deplorable conditions in Chicago's stockyards. Controversial in its socialist message, *The Jungle* profoundly affected people who could relate to the suffering of the poor, even if they did not necessarily embrace all of the book's political statements.

The period marked a major shift of consciousness in the American psyche. The early 1900s saw a public outcry for social justice that included demands for better labor conditions and new policies designed to aid the poor. The idea that "poverty is preventable" and that its existence in the "midst of potential plenty is morally unacceptable" must have been central to Perkins's belief system and at least in part formed the foundation of her staunch positions on labor reform and the elimination of slum conditions. She firmly believed that in order to achieve lasting social reform, new protective legislation would need to be enacted.

Early Government Service

On 25 March 1911 the Triangle Shirtwaist Company in New York caught fire. The accident resulted in 146 deaths, most of which were young girls and immigrant women. Girls as young as seven years of age were employed to cut thread, and teenagers and young women sat behind sewing machines in narrow rows with aisles that were blocked by huge piles of flammable linen. With no consideration for employee safety, Triangle's owners implemented the despicable policy of locking the doors to avoid unnecessary bathroom breaks and the unlikely event of employee theft. When the fire broke out, it spread so quickly that many of the workers were unable to escape and died at their machines. Some women attempted to take the fire escape, but it was rusty and in need of repair. When it suddenly collapsed, many women fell to their death, leaving the remainder of the women with no way out. Perkins's resolve was profoundly deepened after witnessing the tragedy first-hand. Perkins, along with the crowd that had begun to gather, watched in horror as young girls jumped from eighth-story windows, either in pairs or alone, and crashed to their death on the pavement below. For Perkins, it was a defining moment about which she would later write in her book *The Roosevelt I Knew*. She cited the experience as having fueled her lifelong commitment to regulate wages and work hours as well as ensure factory safety through legislation.

Perkins became executive secretary of the Committee on Safety that formed after the fire. In that capacity, she met New

York assemblyman Al Smith. Together they actively engaged in helping to achieve the goals set by the Factory Investigating Committee, which had been created by the New York state legislature that "reviewed the entire scope of job safety and health conditions." Perkins not only testified on the conditions she witnessed, but she managed to persuade legislators to come with her to see firsthand the terrible conditions endured by many laborers. At a visit to a cannery, they witnessed young children shelling peas at 4:00 A.M.

When Smith became governor of New York in 1919, he appointed Perkins to the State Industrial Commission. Smith's faith in her was not unfounded as she was steadfast in her work, articulate under pressure, and respected in her field. Later, when Smith appointed Perkins chairman of the Industrial Board of the State Labor Department, Perkins was able to reduce the work week for women to 54 hours.

Perkins Joins Presidential Cabinet

When Franklin Delano Roosevelt replaced Smith as governor in 1929, Roosevelt appointed Perkins to be New York's Industrial Commissioner. Later in 1933, after Roosevelt was elected U.S. president, he appointed her secretary of labor, making her the first woman in history to be named to a cabinet position. This position allowed her to bring about sweeping social reforms and improvements in labor conditions.

Perkins knew that Roosevelt trusted her to help restore public confidence and return people to work. She played a key role in many aspects of Roosevelt's New Deal. Indeed, in the whirlwind first year of Roosevelt's administration, over 15 major laws were enacted. Roosevelt, who had a tendency to "think big," as Perkins wrote in 1946, often left the details to others. For example, the Civilian Conservation Corps, created in 1933, recruited approximately 2 million unemployed men to help repair environmental damage. Its success was made possible only after Perkins faced and ultimately overcame the objections by some trade unions that feared that unemployed workers would be exploited.

A perfectionist by nature, Perkins worked diligently to make the Department of Labor more efficient. Her ability to recognize talent in others allowed Perkins to compile a team that was considered one of the best in government. She streamlined the Bureau of Immigration and increased the responsibilities of the Bureau of Labor Statistics.

Unwavering in her belief that working Americans had a right to benefits at retirement age, Perkins delivered hundreds of speeches in a relentless quest to create a social security program that would pass the scrutiny of Congress and meet the needs of the people. Her efforts paid off with the 1935 passage of the groundbreaking Social Security Act. Perkins also collaborated with Senator Robert F. Wagner to pass the National Labor Relations Act (NRLA) in 1935 and the Fair Labor Standards Act (FLSA) in 1938. According to Perkins, Wagner deserved all the credit for the NRLA, because he had uncovered unfair practices that employers had used to prevent unionization. Wagner sought to enact legislation to address the abuses. The bill had limitations; it did not, as Perkins noted, "attempt to draw up a comprehensive code of ethical behavior in labor relations." Therefore, with Roosevelt's support, she took Wagner's idea one step further and suggested that labor leaders hungry for recognition develop the code and submit it for consideration. The act established maximum working hours and minimum wages. It also prohibited child labor in any form of interstate commerce and limited the labor of children between 16 and 18 years of age in hazardous occupations.

Perkins's interests and influence exceeded the realm of labor issues. A champion of privacy rights, she counseled Roosevelt against FBI director J. Edgar Hoover's plan to fingerprint and keep a file on every citizen. In addition, she was a proponent of state sovereignty, which was in keeping with her belief that the decision-making process should be kept as close to the people as possible. She believed wholeheartedly in mobilizing the "woman power" of the country for national defense, a conviction she shared with First Lady Eleanor Roosevelt.

Perkins remained the secretary of labor until 1945 when Roosevelt died; she was appointed to the United States Civil Service by President Harry Truman and later taught at Cornell University. She died on 14 May 1965.

Key Players

Addams, Jane (1860–1935): Having founded Hull House with Ellen Gates Starr, Addams was a vocal suffragette and later became the vice president of the National Woman Suffrage Association. She helped to establish the Women's Trade Union League and was a founding member of the National Association for the Advancement of Colored People (NAACP). An accomplished author and pacifist, Addams wrote several books about peace, democracy, and her experiences at Hull House. She was awarded the Nobel Peace Prize in 1931.

Kelley, Florence (1859–1932): Having graduated from Cornell University in 1882, Kelley later attended Northwestern University's law school and was subsequently admitted to the bar. A strong supporter of women's suffrage and African American rights, Kelley helped establish the National Consumers League. A former mentor to Frances Perkins, Kelley strongly advocated for minimum wage laws and work hour reform as well as the elimination of child labor. Kelley teamed up with Upton Sinclair and Jack London to form the Intercollegiate Socialist Society in 1905 and later was a member of the Woman's Peace Party. Kelley was the author of several books such as *Some Ethical Gains Through Legislation* and *The Supreme Court and Minimum Wage Legislation*.

Roosevelt, Franklin Delano (1882–1945): Elected before there were term limits, Roosevelt served as president of the United States for three consecutive terms. He oversaw the passage of groundbreaking New Deal policies and led the nation through the Great Depression and World War II.

Sinclair, Upton (1878–1968): Sinclair penned over 90 books in his lifetime and won a Pulitzer Prize for his novel *Dragon's Teeth*. One of his best-known works, *The Jungle*, greatly influenced many people, including Frances Perkins, and was an international bestseller.

Smith, Al (1873–1944): Smith served as governor of New York for four terms. Committed to ending child labor and improving factory laws, Perkins and Smith became political allies. While Smith was governor of New York, he appointed Perkins chairman of the Industrial Board of the State Labor Department.

Wagner, Robert (1877–1953): After becoming a justice of the New York Supreme Court, Wagner was elected to the Senate. Appointed by Franklin Roosevelt as the first chairman of the National Recovery Administration, Wagner is probably best known for his work regarding the National Labor Relations Act, which is commonly referred to as the Wagner Act.

See also: *Civilian Conservation Corps; Fair Labor Standards Act; Sinclair Publishes* The Jungle; *Social Security Act; Triangle Shirtwaist Fire; Wagner Act.*

BIBLIOGRAPHY

Books

Davis, Kenneth S. *FDR: The War President, 1940–1943*. New York: Random House, Inc., 2000.

Perkins, Frances. *The Roosevelt I Knew*. New York: Viking Press, 1946.

Other

Berg, Gordon. " *Be Ye Steadfast": The Life and Work of Frances Perkins*. U.S. Department of Labor. 2002 [cited 14 October 2002]. <http://www.dol.gov/opa/frances/frances.htm>.

Spartacus Educational. *Frances Perkins*. 2002 [cited 14 October 2002]. <http://www.spartacus.schoolnet.co.uk/USARperkins.htm>.

Spartacus Educational. *Upton Sinclair*. 2002 [cited 14 October 2002]. <http://www.spartacus.schoolnet.co.uk/Jupton.htm>.

—Lee Ann Paradise

Perón Elected President

Argentina 1946

Synopsis

Juan Domingo Perón ranks as the most important figure in the political life of twentieth-century Argentina. First elected to the Argentine presidency in 1946 as an economic populist, Perón retained his popularity with the majority of workers by inaugurating massive social spending schemes, many of which were sponsored in the name of his wife, Eva Perón. His years in office also entailed widespread political repression as he stifled his opponents and kept a firm grip on his trade union supporters. Eva Perón's death, coupled with deteriorating economic conditions, contributed to Perón's ouster in 1955, when he

fled to Spain. Even after Perón went into exile, Perónism lived on with massive government outlays on public projects, even as the economy failed to keep pace with Argentina's Latin American neighbors. Perónism's political legacy included a series of military coups that prevented democracy from taking hold in the country, including reinstallation of Perón as president in 1973–1974. Perón died in office and was succeeded by his third wife, Isabel Perón, who was subsequently overthrown in a military coup in March 1976.

Timeline

1926: Britain paralyzed by a general strike.

1931: Financial crisis widens in the United States and Europe, which reel from bank failures and climbing unemployment levels. In London, armies of the unemployed riot.

1936: The election of a leftist Popular Front government in Spain in February precipitates an uprising by rightists under the leadership of Francisco Franco. Over the next three years, war will rage between the Loyalists and Franco's Nationalists. The Spanish Civil War will prove to be a lightning rod for the world's tensions, with the Nazis and fascists supporting the Nationalists, and the Soviets the Loyalists.

1941: Japanese bombing of Pearl Harbor on 7 December brings the United States into the war against the Axis. Combined with the attack on the Soviet Union, which makes Stalin an unlikely ally of the Western democracies, the events of 1941 will ultimately turn the tide of the war.

1946: Winston Churchill warns of an "Iron Curtain" spreading across Eastern Europe.

1946: Three months after the first meeting of the United Nations General Assembly in London in January, the all-but-defunct League of Nations is officially dissolved.

1946: At the Nuremberg trials, twelve Nazi leaders are sentenced to death, and seven others to prison.

1946: Building of the first true electronic computer, the Electronic Numerical Integrator and Computer (ENIAC).

1951: Six western European nations form the European Coal and Steel Community, forerunner of the European Economic Community and the later European Union.

1956: Elvis Presley appears on Ed Sullivan's *Toast of the Town,* where he performs "Hound Dog" and "Love Me Tender" before a mostly female audience. Nationwide, 54 million people watch the performance, setting a new record.

1961: President Eisenhower steps down, warning of a "military-industrial complex" in his farewell speech, and 43-year-old John F. Kennedy becomes the youngest elected president in U.S. history. Three months later, he launches an unsuccessful invasion of Cuba at the Bay of Pigs.

**Juan Domingo Perón travels along Avenida de Mayo to Government House to assume presidency of Argentina.
© Hulton/Getty Images. Reproduced by permission.**

Event and Its Context

Juan Domingo Perón was born on 8 October 1895 in Lobos, about 60 miles southwest of Argentina's capital, Buenos Aires. His father was a rancher who relocated the family several times. The younger of two sons, Perón left home to study in Buenos Aires when he was nine years old and entered the Army's Military College in 1911. Commissioned as a second lieutenant in 1913, Perón rose steadily through the ranks. Perón kept himself relatively aloof from the characteristically turbulent realm of Argentine politics, and his career was unremarkable through the late 1930s.

After the death of his first wife, Aurelia, from cancer in 1938, Perón departed on a two-year fact-finding mission to Europe. He spent most of his tour in Italy, where he was greatly impressed by the public rallies held by President Benito Mussolini. He also took note of the Fascist Party's co-optation of Italy's trade unions as a power base, a tactic he also witnessed in Nazi Germany. After his return to Argentina in late 1940, Perón was promoted to colonel and started to consolidate his own power base through a secret cabal of military officers known only by its initials, "GOU," which was probably an acronym for *Grupo de Oficiales Unidos*, or Group of United Officers.

After playing a minor role in a military coup in June 1943, Perón used his political and propaganda skills and emerged as one of the leaders of the new government. In October 1943 he became secretary of labor and welfare at the country's National Labor Department. He immediately began courting the Confederación General del Trabajo (General Labor Confederation, or CGT) for its support. Founded in 1930, the association gradually had been drawn into politics by its Socialist leadership but had been largely shut out of the political process. Although he had rarely espoused any concrete views on labor in the years prior to his appointment, Perón recognized the CGT's value in serving as his power base. In his capacity as secretary of labor and welfare, Perón authorized government-paid pensions to unions in return for their political support. He also intervened through the newly created system of labor courts on behalf of friendly unions. With the GOU and CGT solidly behind him, Perón attained the position of minister of war in February 1944. The position was one of the most important offices in Argentina, as the country remained neutral in World War II until the final months of the war, when it finally sided with the Allies. Just prior to leading the Ministry of War, Perón made another political alliance that proved decisive to the development of Perónism when he met Eva Duarte, who would become his second wife.

Evita and Perónism

Born illegitimate in 1919 in the Argentine interior town of Los Toldos, María Eva Ibarguren Duarte pursued a career as a film and radio actress in Buenos Aires starting at the age of 15. By 1943 Eva Duarte was a radio celebrity who headed the Association of Argentine Radio and had close ties to several government officials. After meeting Colonel Perón at a benefit concert for earthquake victims on 22 January 1944, the couple began sharing adjoining apartments in Buenos Aires. In September 1945 Perón was forced out of office and briefly jailed in an abortive military coup. In the month after the attempted coup, Perón rallied enough support from the military establishment and organized labor to make a triumphant return to power. His appearance at Casa Rosada, the president's official residence, on 17 October 1945 before a crowd of 200,000 supporters marked the beginning of Perón's domination of Argentine politics for the next 10 years.

Juan Perón and Eva Duarte married in a civil ceremony on 22 October 1945 and set off together on the campaign trail for the presidential elections set for May 1946. Eva Perón's appearances marked the first time that a candidate's wife had taken an active role in the political arena in the country. Using her performing skills as a passionate orator and striking public figure, Eva Perón became the country's biggest celebrity. Perón won the May 1946 presidential election with over 52 percent of the vote and a commanding victory in the electoral college.

Although she never took an official title, Eva Perón chaired the Department of Labor and Welfare in her husband's administration. Her work demonstrated a commitment to improving the lives of the poorest segments of Argentine society and symbolized the idealism of Perónism. Fueled in part by memories of her own mistreatment during her youth and employing a political shrewdness that capitalized on her husband's support by the country's working classes, Perón championed the cause of the descamisados (literally, the "shirtless ones"). She established the María Eva Duarte de Perón Foundation in 1948, which subsequently spent an estimated three billion pesos on new houses, hospitals, clinics, and household items for the poor. The fact that the foundation's funds came from other government programs and in some cases, outright extortion of businesses, fueled charges that the Perónist government was corrupt. To critics of Perónism, the couple's actions seemed calculated merely to increase the power of the regime at the expense of any sustainable long-term reforms or democratization.

Eva Perón was gravely ill with uterine cancer by the time her husband was sworn in to a second term as president in June of 1952. Although her illness had been reported in general terms in the media, her death on 16 July 1952 plunged Argentina into a period of unprecedented national mourning. It also initiated the gradual erosion of support for the Perón government. Whereas the Peróns' projects had been feasible during the economic boom of the postwar years—when Argentina's export products found ready buyers in war-ravaged countries—as Europe recovered, the country increasingly fell victim to Perón's shortsighted economic policies. Wage gains of 37 percent for industrial workers between 1943 and 1948 made Argentina's products more expensive than those of its Latin American rivals, and government-built housing and vacation resorts sapped the national treasury. Political liberties also were repressed during Perón's years in office; although the CGT became one of the most powerful institutions in the country, with 2.3 million members in 1954, it largely served to stifle dissent within labor's ranks to serve the goals of Perónism. Not long into its second term, Perón's administration was finally overwhelmed by economic problems, and he was overthrown by a military coup in September 1955.

The Legacy of Perónism

Even after Perón went into exile, Perónism lived on. Massive government outlays on hydroelectric plants; a national airline and shipping fleet; and newly nationalized railroad lines, telephone companies, and power plants continued to drain the federal coffers. In the 1950s Venezuela surpassed Argentina in per capita income, and Brazil became the leading export nation in South America. Although there were periodic upswings in the Argentine economy, growth in annual trade averaged just 1 percent per year through the 1950s and 1960s, in contrast to a global growth rate of 7.8 percent. The political arena also bore the legacy of Perónism, with 12 separate governments taking power in Argentina in the period from 1955 to 1976.

Perón's party, the Partido Justicialista (PJ), returned to power in 1988 with the election of Carlos Saul Menem to the presidency. Menem's two terms in office, from 1989 to 1999, represented a rare period of political stability in the country, but his critics accused him of continuing the failed political and economic policies that had plagued Argentina for years. As governor of La Rioja province, Menem had doubled the number of employees on the public payroll, even though the action meant that the province had to circulate state bonds in place of currency after the government ran out of money for its payroll. During his terms as president, Menem presided over a foreign debt that climbed to $142 billion. As Menem left office, Argentina's gross domestic product growth rate plunged into negative territory and a period of intense political upheaval ensued, leading to renewed calls to break with the country's legacy of Perónism and undertake fundamental economic and political reforms.

Key Players

Menem, Carlos Saul (1930–): President of Argentina from 1989 to 1999, Menem became the most important political figure in Argentina since Juan Perón. A member of Perón's Partido Justicialista since his university days, Menem served as governor of La Rioja province from 1973 to 1989 before assuming the presidency. Although his two terms in office marked a period of relative political stability in Argentina, Menem's political career has been dogged by scandal, and many have blamed him for the economic crisis that plagued his country after he left office.

Perón, Juan Domingo (1895–1974): Perón began his military career in 1915 and rose to the rank of colonel at the end of 1941. After taking part in a military coup in June 1943, Perón became minister of war, and he was later elected to the presidency in May 1946. He ruled until 1955, when he was overthrown in a military coup; he returned to power in 1973, holding the office until his death in 1974.

Perón, María Eva Ibarguren Duarte de ("Evita," 1919–1952): Evita Perón worked as a film and radio actress before marrying General Juan Domingo Perón in 1945. She served as an unofficial representative of Argentina's Department of Labor and Welfare after her marriage and served as the chair of the María Eva Duarte de Perón Foundation from 1948 until her death in 1952.

BIBLIOGRAPHY

Books

Castañeda, Jorge G. *Utopia Unarmed: The Latin American Left After the Cold War.* New York: Alfred A. Knopf, 1993.

Crassweller, Robert. *Perón and the Enigmas of Argentina.* New York: W.W. Norton & Company, 1987.

Fraser, Nicholas and Marysa Navarro. *Evita: The Real Life of Evita Perón.* New York: W.W. Norton & Company, 1996.

Guillermoprieto, Alma. *Looking for History: Dispatches from Latin America.* New York: Pantheon Books, 2001.

Lewis, Paul H. *The Crisis of Argentine Capitalism.* Chapel Hill: University of North Carolina Press, 1990.

Marchak, Patricia. *God's Assassins: State Terrorism in Argentina in the 1970s.* Montreal: McGill–Queen's University Press, 1999.

Newton, Ronald C. *The "Nazi Menace" in Argentina, 1931–1947.* Stanford: Stanford University Press, 1992.

Ortiz, Alicia Dujovne. *Eva Perón: A Biography.* New York: St. Martin's Press, 1995.

Page, Joseph. *Perón: A Biography.* New York: Random House, 1983.

Perón, Eva. *In My Own Words.* Reprint, New York: New Press, 1996.

Rock, David. *Argentina 1516–1987: From Spanish Colonization to Alfonsín.* Berkeley: University of California Press, 1987.

—Timothy G. Borden

Peterloo Massacre

Great Britain 1819

Synopsis

The Peterloo Massacre took place at St Peter's Fields, Manchester, England, on 16 August 1819. (The name was an ironic reference to the Battle of Waterloo four years earlier.) A large meeting comprising 50 to 60,000 men, women, and children had assembled to demand reform of Britain's archaic and elitist political system. The meeting was to be addressed by the leading radical figure of the day, Henry "Orator" Hunt, among others. Local magistrates, fearful of disorder, ordered the arrest of Hunt and other platform speakers. As the yeomanry charged into the crowd to effect the arrests, panic ensued. Eleven people were killed and some 400 injured. The episode aroused fierce anger among both working-class radicals and the more liberal upper classes, but Lord Liverpool's Government endorsed the action of the magistrates and passed a series of repressive measures (the "Six Acts") to suppress further protest.

Timeline

1798: British parson Thomas Malthus publishes *An Essay on the Principle of Population,* in which he maintains that populations increase geometrically or exponentially, whereas food production increases only arithmetically. Accordingly, he holds that overpopulation and a world food crisis are inevitable, and opposes social welfare programs.

1801: United Kingdom of Great Britain and Ireland is established.

1802: British Parliament passes the Health and Morals of Apprentices Act, an early piece of child-labor legislation, which prohibits the employment of children under nine years of age and limits a child's workday to twelve hours.

1809: Progressive British industrialist Robert Owen proposes an end to employment of children in his factories. When his partners reject the idea, he forms an alliance with others of like mind, including philosopher Jeremy Bentham.

1810: Revolts begin in South America, initiating the process whereby colonies will win their freedom from Spain and other European colonial powers.

1815: Congress of Vienna establishes the balance of power for post-Napoleonic Europe and inaugurates a century of British dominance throughout most of the world.

Yeomantry charges crowds during bread riots, Peterloo Massacre, Manchester, England. © Hulton/Getty Images. Reproduced by permission.

1818: In a decisive defeat of Spanish forces, soldier and statesman Simón Bolívar leads the liberation of New Granada, which includes what is now Colombia, Panama, Venezuela, and Ecuador. With Spanish power now waning, Bolívar becomes president and virtual dictator of the newly created nation of Colombia.

1819: First production of chocolate for eating (as opposed to cooking), in Switzerland.

1820: In the Missouri Compromise, Missouri is admitted to the Union as slave state, but slavery is prohibited in all portions of the Louisiana Purchase north of 36°30' N.

1825: British Parliament enacts a law permitting workers to join together in order to secure regulation of wages and hours; however, other provisions in the law effectively deny the right to strike.

1829: Overturning of the last of the "penal laws" imposed by the English against the Catholics of Ireland since 1695.

1833: British Parliament passes the Slavery Abolition Act, giving freedom to all slaves throughout the British Empire.

Event and Its Context

Radical Criticisms

Britain's unreformed political system had been condemned by middle-class reformers and a growing working-class radical movement, which was influenced by the late eighteenth century writings of Thomas Paine and the American and French Revolutions. Complex franchise arrangements essentially restricted the vote to upper-class male property holders. Furthermore, constituency arrangements dating back to the Middle Ages ensured that many newly emergent towns, the products of Britain's recent industrial growth, were unrepresented in parliament while virtually depopulated centers ("rotten boroughs") retained their historic right to elect Members of Parliament (MPs).

Radicalism condemned what it saw as an essentially parasitic system that was dominated by the landed aristocracy and the Church, which controlled political power. The radicals construed that the ruling elite had suppressed the ancient constitutional rights of the "free-born Englishman" and had systematically expropriated the wealth of the "producing classes" (conceived as comprising both middle-class entrepreneurs and respectable workingmen). However, the growing extremism of the French Revolution, which culminated in the Terror of

1793–1794, anti-French patriotic sentiment during the wars with France, and fierce government repression, quashed these early protests.

Post-War Discontent and Ideology

The end of the French Wars in 1815 brought about the revival of popular discontent and organized radical protest. Demobilization, industrial and agricultural depression, and severe inflation created widespread hardship. Lord Liverpool's Tory Government further alienated reforming opinion. Income Tax was abolished in 1816 and government revenues came to depend heavily on indirect taxation (i.e., duties on consumables), which hit the poor hardest. The 1815 Corn Laws banned the import of corn until it had reached the price of 80 shillings a quarter (approximately 500 pounds). The apparent intent was to protect domestic agriculture but the impact of the law was to create high and fluctuating grain prices and confirm the impression of a land-owning class governing in its own self-interest. The wartime enclosure of common land (i.e., conversion of land held by the peasantry to private ownership by the gentry) and punitive Game Laws (1816), which prescribed seven years "transportation" for poaching, added to popular grievance.

William Cobbett's journalism became influential, and organized protest recommenced with the Hampden Club, which was established by Major John Cartwright in London in 1812. Cartwright's tour of the provinces by 1816 had influenced the formation of a number of similar societies in the industrial towns of northern England. The clubs demanded universal manhood suffrage, equal electoral districts, annual parliaments, and a secret ballot.

The essence of working-class radical ideology lay in a deep constitutionalism. Reformers argued that political reform would *restore* traditional liberties and stressed that their tactics—the mobilization and exercise of popular opinion through petitioning and mass meetings—were peaceful and legal. This apparently passive strategy contained a double-edged challenge to the ruling class. It implied the threat of sheer force of numbers, as emphasized by the deliberately menacing platform rhetoric of leading radical spokesmen. The strategy further challenged the government to act in a restrained and constitutional way in that an overtly repressive response from the government would demonstrate its illegitimacy and would, moreover, justify defensive violence.

Popular Protest

The first mass reform meeting took place in November 1816 in Spa Fields, London, where Henry Hunt addressed a crowd of around 10,000 people. At a second meeting in December, a portion of the crowd, incited by the more radical followers of Thomas Spence, launched a futile attack on the Tower of London. In the following month, a delegate meeting of radicals met in London to forward a reform petition to Parliament, but an attack on the Prince Regent's coach ensured that the government responded only with the most severe repression. The government re-enacted wartime laws that banned seditious speech and organization and in March 1817 suspended for one year the law of *habeas corpus* (which requires that all detainees be properly charged or released). In the same month, mass arrests broke up the March of the Blanketeers—a procession from

Manchester to London of textiles workers, each carrying a blanket and a reform petition. The apparent futility of peaceful reform methods and the brutality of government action persuaded some that the time for violent resistance had come. The evidence is clouded by the secretive nature of the planning and greatly complicated by the provocative role of government spies, but the Pentridge Rising in Derbyshire in June 1817 seems to have been part of a wider revolutionary conspiracy. In the event, a well-informed government made pre-emptive arrests well before there was any possibility of the sympathetic uprisings for which the rebels had hoped.

Peterloo

Agitation revived in 1819 in response to a series of mass meetings held in Birmingham, Leeds, and London. Formed in March 1819, the Manchester Patriotic Union Society organized a mass meeting to be addressed by Richard Carlile and Henry Hunt at St. Peter's Fields, Manchester, on 16 August. The meeting was planned as a gala day, attended by women and children, to demonstrate the respectability of the reform movement. Crowds from Manchester and environs began to gather at midmorning. Local magistrates, fearful of the threat of disturbance, watched apprehensively as numbers grew and determined that Hunt, Carlile, and local radical leaders on the platform should be arrested. The Manchester Yeomanry, a local militia comprising middle-class tradesmen and shopkeepers, most of whom were fiercely antagonistic to the reform movement and some allegedly drunk, surged into the crowd with sabers swinging to force a path to the platform. In the ensuing mêlé, 11 were killed and around 400 injured. Carlile escaped but Hunt and a number of local radical leaders, including Samuel Bamford, were detained.

Reforming Opinion

Reforming opinion, even among the moderate middle classes, was outraged by these actions. Highly critical reports circulated rapidly and a series of protest meetings followed. The government, while privately disconcerted by the magistrates' intemperate behavior, gave them public support. Hunt was sentenced to 30 months' imprisonment. Bamford and two others were sentenced to 12 months each. To prevent any further upsurge in protest, the government clamped down in a series of measures (the "Six Acts") passed in December 1819 that banned military drilling, gave magistrates the power to search property or persons for arms, prohibited public assemblies of more than 50 people without official permission, tightened the taxation of radical journals, and sought to expedite the legal process and strengthen punishment for "blasphemous and seditious libels." Cartwright, Carlile, and other leading reformers were also arrested and imprisoned in 1820.

Peterloo effectively marked the end of the first phase of working-class radical protest. A group of extreme radicals, followers of Thomas Spence, attempted to assassinate the Cabinet at a private dinner party in February 1820. The plot was known to the government's spy network, however, and the so-called Cato Street Conspiracy was foiled with the arrest of the conspirators and subsequent execution of its five ringleaders. Reforming opinion seized on the exclusion of Queen Caroline from the coronation of her estranged husband, George IV, in 1820 as a means of embarrassing a reactionary government and culpable monarchy, but the next major upsurge of protest did not occur until 1829.

Government repression and Home Office spies had wreaked havoc on the radical movement, and an upturn in the economy quelled more immediate discontents. Radical leaders were, in any case, unsure and divided as to how to proceed. Most believed that the mass of working-class opinion would not—or should not—be led into further, possibly bloody, confrontation with a determinedly repressive government. The program and strategy that underlay Peterloo remained the staple of radical politics into the period of reform agitation of the early 1830s and once more in early Chartism, but its essential dilemmas—how to wrest reform from an obdurate and powerful ruling elite and when the much-vaunted right of popular self-defense might be mobilized—remained unsolved.

Key Players

Bamford, Samuel (1788–1872): A Lancashire weaver and moderate reformer. On his release from prison after Peterloo, he became a journalist and memoirist. His *Passages in the Life of a Radical* (1843) and *Early Days* (1849) were influential in subsequent interpretations of the working-class movement, but Bamford himself urged working-class respectability and became estranged from later radical politics, which he criticized for its extremism.

Carlile, Richard (1790-1843): Radical London journalist and publisher, Carlile was imprisoned after Peterloo for seditious libel (for his report on the massacre) and blasphemy (for his publication of Paine's *Age of Reason*). His wife and sister were also jailed for their roles in the unstamped press and Carlile became an advocate of women's political and personal rights and a campaigner against child labor. Jailed in 1830 for his support of protesting agricultural laborers, Carlile died in poverty.

Cartwright, Major John (1740–1824): English landowner and former naval officer, discharged for his support of the American rebels. He wrote *Take Your Choice* (1776), which outlined a radical political reform program and subsequently formed the Society for Constitutional Information. The Hampden Club network of radical societies, which he helped establish in 1812, played a significant role in the postwar upsurge of radicalism. Cartwright sought to engineer an alliance of middle- and working-class radicals.

Cobbett, William (1763–1835): A self-taught journalist whose homespun, direct style in the *Political Register* (published from 1802) made him the most powerful voice of English working-class radicalism. Cobbett himself looked back to an idealized rural past but his eloquent critique of the contemporary political corruption became the mainstay of radical analysis. He served a brief, unsuccessful stint as MP for Oldham from 1832–1835.

Hunt, Henry ("Orator," 1773–1835): A landed gentleman converted to radical politics in 1800 and subsequently an inspirational and demagogic speaker at reform rallies. Elected MP for the popular constituency of Preston in 1831, he lost his seat in 1835 for his opposition to the 1832 Reform Act, which he believed did not go far enough.

Paine, Thomas (1737–1809): A former exciseman who emigrated from England to America and became, through his pamphlet, *Common Sense* (1776), a leading advocate of U.S. independence. Back in Europe, *The Rights of Man* (1791), which defended the French Revolution and condemned hereditary rule, sold 1.5 million copies in his lifetime. Paine became a French citizen but, after a brief imprisonment, he returned to the U.S. where he died. Paine's lively coruscating style made him one of the most influential radical writers of his day.

Spence, Thomas (1750–1814): Newcastle schoolmaster, radical journalist and pamphleteer. Spence was unusual in advocating women's rights and sweeping economic reform including parochial ownership of land, the rents of which were to provide for public education. He favored a decentralized revolutionary organization to harness and foment popular discontent and incite insurrection.

Thistlewood, Arthur (1774–1820): An ex-soldier and failed farmer, Thistlewood moved to London in 1811 where he became active as a follower of Thomas Spence and advocate of insurrection. An instigator of the Spa Fields riot in 1816 and an organizer of protests after Peterloo, Thistlewood led the attempt to assassinate the Cabinet at Cato Street in 1820, but he and four others were arrested before the attack on the evidence of a government spy and executed for high treason.

BIBLIOGRAPHY

Books

Marlow, Joyce. *The Peterloo Massacre*. London: Rapp and Whiting, 1970.

Thompson, E. P. *The Making of the English Working Class*. London: Penguin, 1991

Periodicals

Belchem, John. "'Orator' Hunt, 1773–1835: A British Radical Reassessed." *History Today* (March 1985): 21–27.

Hewitt, Martin. "Radicalism and the Victorian Working Class: The Case of Samuel Bamford." *The Historical Journal* 34, no. 6 (1991): 873–892.

ADDITIONAL RESOURCES

Books

Belchem, John. *"Orator" Hunt: Henry Hunt and English Working-class Radicalism*. Oxford and New York: Clarendon Press and Oxford University Press, 1985.

Read, Donald. *Peterloo, the Massacre and Its Background*. Manchester: Manchester University Press, 1985.

Reid, Robert. *The Peterloo Massacre*. London: Heinemann, 1989.

Other

"Peterloo." *Spartacus Educational*. 30 June 2002 [cited 11 July 2002]. <http://www.spartacus.schoolnet.co.uk/peterloo.html>.

"The Peterloo Massacre." *Cotton Times* [cited 11 July 2002].
    <http://www.cottontimes.co.uk>.

—John Boughton

Philadelphia Plan

United States 1969

Synopsis

With the implementation of the Philadelphia Plan in 1969, President Richard M. Nixon's administration changed the federal government's stance on affirmative action. For the first time, a specific industry was required to articulate a plan for hiring minority workers. Presidents John F. Kennedy and Lyndon B. Johnson had identified affirmative action as necessary to redress the effects of racism. During their administrations, policies were created to facilitate both equal employment opportunities for African Americans and equal accommodations in the workplace. Yet the Civil Rights Act of 1964 had limited the type of remedies possible by forbidding any form of discrimination. This was interpreted to include preferential hiring, which was seen as compensatory discrimination.

Despite this limitation, the Nixon administration used the power of the federal purse to create specific hiring goals in the highly segregated construction industry. Designed by the Department of Labor during the Johnson administration, the Philadelphia Plan was revived by George Shultz, Nixon's labor secretary, and Arthur Fletcher, his assistant secretary. The plan required Philadelphia government contractors in six construction trades to set goals and timetables for the hiring of minority workers or risk losing the valuable contracts. No quotas were set. This left businesses a fair amount of autonomy in determining how to meet the goals. As a result, the Philadelphia Plan withstood a court challenge and growing public hostility to affirmative action.

Timeline

1954: The French military outpost at Dien Bien Phu falls to the communist Vietminh.

1959: Vice President Richard Nixon and Soviet leader Nikita Khrushchev engage in their famous "kitchen debate" in Moscow.

1964: On 7 February, in the midst of both a literal and figurative winter in America following Kennedy's assassination, the Beatles arrive at New York's newly renamed JFK Airport.

1966: In August, Mao Zedong launches the "Great Proletarian Cultural Revolution," which rapidly plunges China into chaos as armed youths plunder the countryside, rooting out suspected foreign collaborators and anti-Chinese elements.

President Richard Milhous Nixon. The Library of Congress.

1969: Richard M. Nixon sworn in as president of the United States. In June he pulls 25,000 troops from Vietnam. From this point, America is no longer trying to win the war but to keep from losing it.

1969: Assisted by pilot Michael Collins, astronauts Neil Armstrong and Edwin E. "Buzz" Aldrin on 20 July become the first men to walk on the Moon.

1969: Some 400,000 people attend the Woodstock Music and Arts Festival in August. Also in the world of popular culture, the year is notable for several outstanding movies: *Midnight Cowboy, Butch Cassidy and the Sundance Kid,* and *Easy Rider.*

1969: At the orders of Charles Manson, members of his "Family" kill seven adults and one unborn child (Sharon Tate's) in a pair of grisly L.A. murders. Other crimes are also in the news: authorities learn that in March 1968, an army platoon led by Lieutenant William Calley massacred 567 villagers in the South Vietnamese hamlet of Mylai.

1969: U.S. Department of Defense puts its Arpanet, forerunner of the Internet, online.

1972: In June, police apprehend five men attempting to burglarize Democratic Party headquarters at the Watergate Hotel in Washington, D.C.

1974: On 30 July the House Judiciary Committee adopts three articles of impeachment for President Nixon, but rather than undergo a lengthy trial, Nixon on 8 August becomes the first president in U.S. history to resign.

1979: After years of unrest, the Shah of Iran leaves the country, and Islamic fundamentalist revolutionaries under the leadership of Ayatollah Ruhollah Khomeini take control.

Event and Its Context

Affirmative Action: Developing the Concept

The Philadelphia Plan makes sense in three contexts: the history of civil rights, the history of labor regulation, and the history of the exercise of state power in the United States. The plan may be seen as one of the last steps in a trend toward growing government activism that ranged from the end of the Civil War until 1980. The coalition that opposed the Philadelphia Plan formed the basis of the opposition to government activism that characterized the subsequent period.

Affirmative action has a long history in discussion of both civil rights and labor rights in the United States. The concept of affirmative action to compensate for the harm done to African Americans by slavery has existed since Reconstruction. The term was applied to labor by the Wagner Act of 1935, which stated that it was not enough to stop unfair labor practices; it was also necessary "to take such affirmative action" to redress them. In 1945 New York became the first state to pass an antidiscrimination law that used "affirmative action" in the context of remedies for discrimination.

Use of the term for federal policy to address employment discrimination against African Americans may be traced to President Kennedy. His Executive Order 10925 in 1961 ordered public employers to "take affirmative action to ensure that applicants are employed and employees are treated during their employment without regard to race, creed, color or national origin." Executive Order 10925 was drafted by a committee that included the Memphis lawyer Abe Fortas, Labor Secretary Arthur Goldberg, and a young African American lawyer from Detroit named Hobart Taylor, Jr. Taylor used the term "affirmative action," he explained later, "because it was alliterative." In adopting this usage, the committee linked a history of public discussion of compensation for African Americans with a history of government action to produce fair employment. The order created the President's Committee on Equal Employment Opportunity. Its chief weapon was the power to cancel federal contracts of businesses who refused to comply with the president's order. No contracts were ever actually cancelled, but discriminatory practices were stopped in workplaces around the country.

Many factors encouraged the battle for civil rights in the 1960s. A long-standing tradition of organizing efforts among African Americans had received modest success with the integration of the armed forces by President Harry Truman in 1946. A generation of mature, well-educated African American activists was poised to push for further gains. Postwar economic growth demanded a growing industrial working class. The great migration of African Americans who had moved to the more industrialized parts of the country expanded the potential labor pool. In addition, the cold war with the Soviet Union made America's institutionalized racism an international embarrassment. From the cold war perspective, it was worth addressing issues of race to ensure U.S. rhetoric about freedom would be taken seriously.

In 1963 President Kennedy proposed the civil rights bill that was still being debated in Congress when he was assassinated. Among the objections raised in the debate was the concern that quotas would take away jobs from white people. This was a specific form of the generalized fear that extending rights to African Americans would necessitate taking them away from whites. The new president, Lyndon Johnson, had years of experience in the Senate working with the core group of southern legislators who objected to the bill. Johnson took up the battle for the civil rights bill and oversaw both the creation of many compromises and the bill's passage in 1964. The act provided for equal public accommodations and required employers to provide equal employment opportunities. Projects receiving federal funds could lose those funds if they failed to provide equal employment opportunity. Although the act created an Equal Employment Opportunity Commission (EEOC), in its final form it excluded any stated quotas or enforcement powers. The EEOC was to respond to citizen complaints, not defend the public interest in eliminating patterns of discrimination.

The Johnson Years

While many African Americans found well-paid factory jobs in the 1960s, many more were part of the chronically underemployed class waiting in the wings for more expansive times. Following the passage of the Civil Rights Act, Johnson moved to create a "war on poverty." A host of new programs was initiated to address both rural and urban poverty. Under the Johnson administration, the Department of Labor developed federally funded jobs for urban blacks. Manpower programs, such as the Neighborhood Youth Corps, which employed 1.5 million high school students, and the Work Incentive Program, were developed in an attempt to shift workers from the welfare rolls to low-income employment.

President Johnson issued Executive Order 11246 on 24 September 1965. This order created the Labor Department's Office of Federal Contract Compliance (OFCC, later the OFCCP). The new agency was given specific responsibilities for enforcing antidiscrimination laws among federal contractors. Although originally the order only pertained to discrimination against minorities, it was amended in 1967 to include discrimination against women. The creation of the OFCC took affirmative action out of the White House and placed it in the Department of Labor with a staff designated for enforcement. Between 1965 and 1968 the OFCC designed a plan to address the racist hiring practices that were endemic in the construction industry.

What factors made the construction industry a bastion of racism? In part it was the nature of the work, where employers bid on contracts and hired workers just for the duration of the contract. Construction crafts had been at the center of the American Federation of Labor (AFL) from its inception. These craft unions were characterized by master-apprentice relationships bolstered by family and ethnic ties. Although the merger of the AFL with the Congress of Industrial Organizations (CIO) brought more African Americans into the organization, few of them came in the skilled trades. Contractors who employed members of the craft trade unions generally did not themselves control whom they hired, but got workers through union hiring systems that depended largely on seniority. In this situation, where there was no direct link between the agency allocating federal construction funds and the actual workers performing the labor, coordinating enforcement of antidiscrimination policies proved difficult.

Thus, the Johnson administration had to face the irony that billions of dollars of urban renewal money were paying white construction workers in jobs inaccessible to African Americans. When ghetto residents in Watts, Newark, Detroit, and smaller cities across the country rioted in the mid-1960s, they expressed how little they felt like stakeholders in society. In this context, the federal government was pressured to respond to specific calls for more construction jobs for African Americans. The riots created a sense of urgency that called for a more proactive federal government.

The first head of the OFCC was Edward Sylvester, an African American. One of Sylvester's goals was to figure out how to assure compliance with the Labor Department's affirmative action standards in federally funded construction. He worked out a method of retaining funds awarded to successful low bidders until they submitted evidence that they were in compliance. Such efforts were tried in St. Louis, San Francisco, and Cleveland with limited success. In Philadelphia, Sylvester found an already existing regional coordinating agency called the Federal Executive Board (FEB). The board had surveyed local hiring patterns in the construction trades and had found clear patterns that African Americans were excluded. They proposed having the FEB not award contracts until it had determined that the "apparent low bidder" had hired sufficient minorities to be in compliance.

Both organized labor and contractors objected to the new requirements. The AFL-CIO objected that the plan threatened all of labor's gains in collective bargaining since the 1930s. Contractors, represented by the U.S. Chamber of Commerce and the National Association of Manufacturers, objected that the requirement set no definitive minimum numbers of minorities to be hired and thus left bidders in the dark about what the job would eventually entail. Furthermore, if the plan did address the contractors' concerns and provided specific goals, it would be illegal under the Civil Rights Act of 1964, which prohibited preferential treatment on the basis of race, sex, and ethnicity. When Nixon was elected in 1968 the plan seemed to have died.

The Nixon Administration

President Nixon selected George Shultz, an economist and the former dean of the business school at the University of Chicago, as his labor secretary. The free-market ideology of the Chicago school of economics may have predisposed Shultz to move against the hiring practices of the construction unions. A personal belief in racial integration may have encouraged him to make fighting job discrimination a priority for the administration. Whatever Shultz's motives, according to most accounts he was the adviser who persuaded Nixon to support the Philadelphia Plan.

Shultz appointed Arthur Fletcher as the assistant labor secretary to re-tool the Philadelphia Plan. Fletcher stated that it was necessary to have specific goals for percentages of minority employees to redress America's history of segregation. To avoid the issue of quotas, Fletcher sought to make the goals a target

range rather than an absolute number. A secondary issue was which groups qualified for protection. In 1969 most Americans meant African Americans when they said "minorities," but other groups also had claims to inclusion. Fletcher's revision listed "Negro, Oriental, American Indian and Spanish-surnamed Americans." Even though women had already been added to the list of protected groups in 1967, they were not included in the Philadelphia Plan.

Fletcher announced the administration's intention to put the new plan into effect as soon as possible. The implementation order was issued on 23 September 1969. It included the following trades: steamfitters, ironworkers, sheetmetal workers, electricians, elevator construction workers, and plumbers and pipefitters. OFCC area coordinators in all cities were to issue a target range of minority employees for each trade, expressed as a percentage of workers hired. The 23 September memorandum set target ranges for Philadelphia for the next five years. Contractors did not need to meet the goals exactly; they merely had to demonstrate that they had made a good faith effort to do so.

The next problem was how to define what constituted a good faith effort on the part of contractors. It was not sufficient to blame union hiring procedures for any problems contractors might encounter in finding minority workers. They needed to prove they had contacted community organizations, maintained a list of minority workers, and used job training programs as potential sources for workers. A contractor whose efforts did not meet the OFCC requirements would be disqualified from the bidding on the relevant job. If a pattern of failure to meet OFCC requirements existed, a contractor could be dropped from the list of potential contractors.

The plan faced stiff opposition from within the government. The General Accounting Office (GAO) opposed the plan on the grounds that it violated Title VII of the 1964 Civil Rights Act by requiring employment practices aimed at meeting a minority quota. The Nixon administration fought this battle with a report from Attorney General John Mitchell that presidential authority overrode the power of the GAO. Nixon had just released an executive order directing all federal agencies to maintain a "continuing affirmative program" of equal opportunity for federal employees.

A Senate judiciary subcommittee heard testimony against the Philadelphia Plan, while the GAO drafted a rider to a bill denying congressional appropriations "to finance, either directly or indirectly or through any Federal aid or grant, any contract or agreement which the Comptroller General of the U.S. holds to be in contravention of any Federal statute." Civil rights liberals joined with the Nixon administration to oppose the rider, while labor and southern Democrats supported it. The rider was defeated, giving the Nixon administration the latitude to implement the plan.

Conclusion

Nixon later stated, "Getting the plan written into law turned out to be easier than implementing the law." The plan faced continued resistance from the construction trades, from contractors who found compliance challenging, and from growing public opposition to affirmative action. It survived a court challenge from the Contractor's Association and remained policy. Yet the Nixon administration became increasingly ambivalent about its enforcement. The ambivalence reflected the political exigencies of Nixon's position.

In John Ehrlichman's words, the Philadelphia Plan enabled Nixon to get the "AFL-CIO and the NAACP [National Association for the Advancement of Colored People] locked in combat over one of the passionate issues of the day," leaving the Nixon administration "in the sweet and reasonable middle." Since President Franklin D. Roosevelt's New Deal, trade unionists and African Americans had been part of the Democratic Party coalition. In the 30 years since the Great Depression, Nixon was only the second Republican to be elected to the presidency. He faced a Democratic majority in Congress. Breaking apart the alliance at the heart of the Democrats' constituency made sense from his perspective.

In his memoir, Nixon explained it somewhat differently. He took credit for identifying the problem that major labor unions were excluding minorities and asking Shultz to "see what could be done." What Nixon did not explain was that increasingly he needed labor unions as part of his constituency. Perhaps his biggest accomplishment in the Philadelphia Plan struggle was creating an alliance between southern conservatives and organized labor.

Other factors were already creating such an alliance. The civil rights coalition had included organized labor, but the rise of black separatism had already threatened large numbers of white liberals and had driven them to more conservative politics. The Vietnam War also had a divisive effect on the traditional liberal constituency. The Philadelphia Plan did not so much create a new alliance as give it one more unifying principle. From its beginnings in 1961, affirmative action had looked like preferential treatment to a significant segment of the white population. In opposing the Philadelphia Plan, that segment merely increased its working-class constituency.

Key Players

Ehrlichman, John (1925–1999): Influential domestic affairs adviser to President Richard Nixon who resigned in 1973 when he was implicated in the Watergate break-in. In 1975 he was convicted of obstruction of justice, perjury, and conspiracy and served for 18 months in federal prison.

Fletcher, Arthur A. (1924–): As a school teacher in Kansas in 1954, Fletcher helped to raise money for the *Brown v. Board of Education* desegregation lawsuit. He held many appointments in Republican administrations through the 1970s and 1980s. As the assistant secretary of labor in 1969, he wrote the orders that initiated the goals and timetables phase of affirmative action. Referring to himself as the "father of affirmative action," he sought nomination to be the Republican presidential candidate in 1996 on a pro–affirmative action platform.

Nixon, Richard Milhous (1913–1994): Thirty-seventh president of the United States from 1969 to 1974. Nixon also served as a congressman and senator from California as well as the vice president under President Dwight D. Eisenhower. Nixon's presidency ended with his resignation following the investigation of a break-in at Democratic Party headquarters that occurred during the 1972 presidential campaign in the Watergate building in Washington, D.C.

Shultz, George Pratt (1920–): Formerly a professor of industrial relations, Shultz held three major posts in the Nixon administration: secretary of labor, first director of the newly created Office of Management and Budget, and treasury secretary from 1972 to 1974. As the secretary of labor, he oversaw the implementation of the Philadelphia Plan for affirmative action. From 1982 to 1989 he served as the secretary of state under presidents Ronald Reagan and George Bush.

See also: *AFL, CIO Merge; Civil Rights Act of 1964; Wagner Act.*

BIBLIOGRAPHY

Books

Ehrlichman, John. *Witness to Power: The Nixon Years.* New York: Simon and Schuster, 1982.

Graham, Hugh Davis. *The Civil Rights Era: Origins and Development of National Policy, 1960–1972.* New York: Oxford University Press, 1990.

———. *Civil Rights and the Presidency: Race and Gender in American Politics, 1960–1972.* New York: Oxford University Press, 1992.

Haldeman, H. R. *The Haldeman Diaries: Inside the Nixon White House.* New York: G. P. Putnam's, 1994.

Hoff, Joan. *Nixon Reconsidered.* New York: Basic Books, 1994.

Kotlowski, Dean J. *Nixon's Civil Rights: Politics, Principle, and Policy.* Cambridge, MA: Harvard University Press, 2001.

Kull, Andrew. *The Color-blind Constitution.* Cambridge, MA: Harvard University Press, 1992.

Nixon, Richard M. *RN: The Memoirs of Richard Nixon.* New York: Grosset and Dunlap, 1978.

Panetta, Leon E., and Peter Gall. *Bring Us Together: The Nixon Team and the Civil Rights Retreat.* Philadelphia: Lippincott, 1971.

Sitkoff, Harvard. *The Struggle for Black Equality, 1954–1992.* New York: Hill and Wang, 1993.

Stern, Mark. *Calculating Visions: Kennedy, Johnson, and Civil Rights.* New Brunswick, NJ: Rutgers University Press, 1992.

Periodicals

Ginsburg, Ruth Bader. "A Considered Opinion: Affirmative Action as an International Human Rights Dialogue." *Brookings Review,* 18, no. 1 (winter 2000): 2–3.

—Jane Holzka

Popular Front

France 1934–1938

Synopsis

Alarmed by the expanding fascist menace both at home and abroad, the main components of the bitterly divided French left—that is, the radicals of the Radical Socialist Party, the socialists of the *Section Française de l'Internationale Ouvrière* (French Chapter of the International Workers' Party or SFIO), and the communists (*Parti Communist Français*, PCF)—began in early 1934 to discuss proposals for united action. These discussions resulted in an electoral alliance (the *Front Populaire* or Popular Front) and victory in the 1936 parliamentary elections. The communists supported the formation of a coalition government of radicals and socialists, with the socialist Léon Blum as prime minister.

In the wake of the election result, sit-in strikes occurred all over France, to the terror of employers and the propertied classes in general. In June 1936 agreements, reinforced by the new government's legislation and signed by the employers' representatives, made numerous concessions. In the following months, however, a combination of internal and external pressures divided the components of the Front, permitted an employers' counterattack, and eventually led to the fall of Blum's government in June 1937. This constituted the effective end of the Popular Front, but its memory remained a rallying symbol for the French labor movement.

Timeline

1920: League of Nations, based in Geneva, holds its first meetings.

1925: European leaders attempt to secure the peace at the Locarno Conference, which guarantees the boundaries between France and Germany, and Belgium and Germany.

1930: Naval disarmament treaty signed by the United States, Great Britain, France, Italy, and Japan.

1933: Newly inaugurated U.S. president Franklin D. Roosevelt launches the first phase of his New Deal to put depression-era America back to work.

1935: Italians invade Ethiopia, and the response by the League of Nations—which imposes sanctions but otherwise fails to act—reveals the impotence of that organization.

1935: Second phase of New Deal begins with the introduction of social security, farm assistance, and housing and tax reform.

1936: Germany reoccupies the Rhineland, while Italy annexes Ethiopia. Recognizing a commonality of aims, the two totalitarian powers sign the Rome-Berlin Axis Pact. (Japan will join them in 1940.)

1936: The election of a leftist Popular Front government in Spain in February precipitates an uprising by rightists under the leadership of Francisco Franco. Over the next three years, war will rage between the Loyalists and Franco's Nationalists. The Spanish Civil War will prove

Léon Blum. The Library of Congress.

to be a lightning rod for the world's tensions, with the Nazis and fascists supporting the Nationalists, and the Soviets the Loyalists.

1937: Japan attacks China, and annexes most of that nation's coastal areas.

1937: Stalin uses carefully staged show trials in Moscow to eliminate all rivals for leadership. These party purges, however, are only a small part of the death toll now being exacted in a country undergoing forced industrialization, much of it by means of slave labor.

1940: Hitler's troops sweep through Western Europe, annexing Norway and Denmark in April, and in May the Low Countries and France. At the same time, Stalin—who in this year arranges the murder of Trotsky in Mexico—takes advantage of the situation to add the Baltic republics (Latvia, Lithuania, and Estonia) to the Soviet empire, where they will remain for more than half a century.

1945: April sees the death of three leaders: Roosevelt passes away on 12 April; the Italians execute Mussolini and his mistress on 28 April; and Hitler (along with Eva Braun, propaganda minister Josef Goebbels, and Goebbels's family) commits suicide on 30 April.

Event and Its Context

Prelude to the Popular Front

The Popular Front of the mid-1930s emerged from a conjunction of French historical circumstances and broader European developments. The French Third Republic, though it had survived for over 60 years, was an unstable political entity that was torn by bitter political and social divisions. It was hated by the extreme right, which loathed democracy on principle, and was detested no less by the extreme left, which dreamed of a Soviet-style republic.

The bedrock of the republic was the independent lower middle class—peasant farmers, shopkeepers, small independent producers, civil servants, and lower-ranking professionals (although not all of these were committed republicans)—which was mainly represented by the Radical Party (also known by its formal title, the Radical Socialist Party), a politically diverse group that contained both right- and left-wing elements. Its supporters were said to "wear their hearts on the left and their wallets on the right." Only on the condition that their leaders could control the republic did the moderate right, which passed under a variety of political guises, accept the republic (although with no great enthusiasm). The moderate right drew its support from some of the same social elements as did the radicals, together with the majority of the upper bourgeoisie. They had the support of all the major national daily newspapers.

Of the industrial workforce, the greater part was nonunionized. The unions themselves were divided into two rival federations, the socialist *Confédération Générale du Travail* (CGT) and the communist *Confédération Générale du Travail Unitaire* (CGTU). The division was the outcome of the split in French socialism in 1920, when the PCF was formed; the movement's non-Bolsheviks, continuing to adhere to social democracy, formed the Socialist Party. This attracted the majority of the industrial workforce as well as a minority of left-wing middle class elements.

Initially, France was affected less than other industrially developed nations by the Great Depression, but by the mid-1930s, economic depression was increasingly evident in rising unemployment and plummeting agricultural prices. This created conditions favorable for political advance by both the extreme left and the extreme right. The extreme right, moreover, had its morale and confidence improved by events abroad, especially with Adolf Hitler's assumption of power in Germany in January 1933.

The fascist-minded right was organized in paramilitary leagues, rather than in political parties. One of these, the *Croix de Feu* (Cross of Fire), possessed a substantial supply of arms, motor vehicles, and even some aircraft. On 6 February 1934 a demonstration by the leagues became an attempt to storm the Assembly building. The police repulsed the attack with great difficulty and considerable bloodshed. Less than a week later, the Austrian socialists were crushed by military force, and a clerical-fascist regime was imposed on that country. The French left was galvanized by these events, and a massive, spontaneously unified demonstration was staged in Paris on 12 February. Before any effective long-term joint action could be possible, however, a major obstacle had to be surmounted.

The Communists and the Comintern

The PCF's first loyalty was to the Communist International or Comintern, which by the late 1920s meant, in effect, Moscow and Stalin. Considerations that were in reality specific to Soviet developments caused the Comintern to demand in 1928 that its parties pursue a strategy of "class against class" by vehemently attacking and denouncing all other working-class parties. This action was fueled by the expectation that the proletarian masses would then rally to the communists. Social democrats were even pilloried as "social fascists." Such policies practiced in Germany assisted, if not ensured, Hitler's ultimate victory.

The developments of early 1934 brought about a reassessment on the part of Soviet and Comintern leaders. In addition, Stalin, finding that Hitler spurned his initial efforts to continue German-Soviet cooperation, concluded that the latter was an implacable enemy of the USSR and began to seek rapprochement with Britain and France. In May 1935 the USSR and France signed a mutual assistance pact (to the consternation of the right wing), and in July the Seventh and final Comintern Congress marked a total turnaround in policy (though it was never acknowledged as such). There is reason to believe that the French events and the French communists provided the major impetus behind the reversal in policy. The PCF leader, Maurice Thorez, dwelt at length on his party's work after February 1934 and noted that the disasters of the previous three years had been caused by "the isolation of . . .and division in the working class." He went on to declare that "we have formulated definite demands, but we have not hesitated to take over those that were launched by other organizations, even those hostile to the Communist Party." It was not only divisions within the working class that needed repair; all democrats were invited to rally to the antifascist struggle.

All was thus changed utterly. The detested republic—once characterized as the seedbed of fascism—and the tricolor were now embraced passionately. The PCF rank and file appeared to have little difficulty in adjusting to the switch and indeed approved it. As historians Bernard and Dubief have noted, "It was as if a long-suppressed patriotism burst out with extraordinary force, to the immense satisfaction and relief of the militant rank and file, happy to leave their isolation."

Formation of the Popular Front

Starting in February 1934, a series of developments culminated in the political coalition of early 1936. As early as July 1934, communist and socialist leaders signed a pact for electoral cooperation. An enormous show of unity on the streets at the 1935 Bastille Day celebrations included some of the Radical Party leaders. In the autumn the more left-wing elements prevailed inside the Radical Party, and Edouard Daladier, their principal spokesperson, took over as party leader. At the end of that year and beginning of 1936, the centrist government then in office, responding to public pressure, set about the suppression of the fascist paramilitary gangs. The three parties concluded an agreement on an electoral alliance in January 1936. This comprised a fairly minimalist program with parameters set by the radicals rather than either of the other two parties. In the event of the Front's widely expected victory, it would most likely be the radicals who would lead the new administration.

Central to the platform was the protection of democracy by suppression of fascist leagues, reform of the antidemocratic press, and strengthening the secular character of the education system (though the communists had been making overtures even to the Catholic church). Other elements of the platform included raising the age for leaving school to 14, reform of the Bank of France to make lending easier, and nationalization of key war industries. Social measures included reduction of the working week, institution of public works to reduce unemployment, and enhancement of agricultural prices by creating an *Office Interprofessional du Blé* (denounced by the right wing as "agricultural Bolshevism") to handle the marketing of wheat. Proposed financial reforms took aim at the "200 Families" that were said to control the existing system and to be holding all honest citizens to ransom. The communists, anxious to secure agreement at all costs, backed the Radical Party at every turn against the bolder economic preferences of the socialists.

When the rival trade unions restored their unity in March 1936, an event with long-term significance, it illustrated a similar accommodating disposition on the part of the PCF. The CGTU conceded to all of the demands of the CGT. The reunified federation drew its top leaders from the noncommunist side and retained the CGT title. It looked like a complete capitulation for the sake of unity, but the communists, thanks to their superior discipline and commitment (and the popular surge behind them), in due course secured their dominance of the reunified organization. Their unstated agenda was to do the same to the SFIO, so here too they pressed for organizational unity. The socialist leaders, however, were well aware of the likely outcome and avoided drawing any closer to their new allies.

The Popular Front Government and the General Strike

The results of the elections, held at the end of April and beginning of May (in a two-round system with the two leading candidates from the first round contesting the second), conformed to expectations in producing a decisive victory for the left. The distribution of votes and seats between the partners of the Popular Front was more unexpected. The Radical Party, far from coming out ahead, suffered significant losses in both votes and seats. This left the socialists as the largest component. The communists gained most spectacularly with a leap from 12 to 72 deputies. There were also a number of smaller groupings in the alliance. Overall the left held 376 seats. The combined representation of the center-right by contrast shrank from 259 to 222, with votes and seats shifting from the center to the right.

The socialists thus became the senior partners in the Front. Their leader, Léon Blum, assumed the premiership and took office on 5 June with Daladier as his deputy. Blum invited the communists to participate in government but they declined, preferring to give their support from the floor of the Assembly. They chose this approach so that they could share the credit for the government's achievements yet remain free to criticize it for any unpopular measures.

During May, however, events ran far ahead of anything that had been anticipated by the party leaderships. A series of sit-in strikes, commencing in several aircraft factories, spread throughout most of French industry. The strikers, fired with hopes of dramatic improvements to their life conditions, took spontaneous action to pressurize their employers. The strikes took place in a carnival atmosphere, with the public bringing in food and other resources and all sorts of impromptu cultural events being staged inside the occupied premises. Notions that the PCF was responsible were unfounded, though the communists hastened to acclaim the action and organize it where they could. Union membership rocketed from around a million to about five million, with 80 percent of these in the CGT. PCF

membership expanded from fewer than 50,000 to more than 350,000.

On 7 June at the Hôtel Matignon, the premier's residence, Blum met four terrified employers' representatives, who hastened to make unprecedented concessions. The parties reached an agreement to implement wage increases from 7 to 15 percent, and they agreed on trade union recognition, a 40-hour week (with exceptions), and holidays with pay. In the following weeks bills to entrench the concessions in law were voted through the Assembly and Senate. Above all, as the historian Braunthal has commented, the "aim was to smash the absolute rule of the employers in the factories." Ending the strikes once these concessions were made was not easy, and Thorez had to work very hard indeed to persuaded the strikers that "it is necessary to know when to end a strike as much as when to begin it."

That event was the peak of the Popular Front's success; thereafter it was downhill all the way. The parties in the front were united only by antifascism. In every other respect their agendas were wholly divergent. The radicals remained committed to private property and the free market, given the support of small businesses; the socialists aimed at pervasive state control of the economy. The communists continued to support the radicals against the SFIO, to soothe middle class fears. The government restructured the management of the Bank of France and nationalized railways and some armaments manufacture as per the platform and the Grain Office recommendations.

Difficulties, Decline, and Aftermath

Within weeks the new administration was beset by unmanageable internal and external problems. Once the crisis was over, the employers recovered their nerve, got rid of the representatives who had signed the agreements, and, with support in the indirectly elected and conservative-dominated Senate, set out to regain as much of their lost authority as they could. Strikes ensued as the workforce resisted. The workforce's gains did not, contrary to many hopes, reinvigorate the economy. Instead, increasing production costs put the economy under additional strain. Unemployment increased, and in the autumn the government was, contrary to its initial promises, forced to devalue the currency (admittedly overvalued in the first place).

By far the worst problem emerged in foreign relations. Spain had elected a Popular Front government of a similar complexion to that in France. In July right-wing military officers, led by General Francisco Franco, commenced a revolt against it and soon engulfed Spain in a three-year civil war. Blum's initial impulse to send military aid to his Spanish counterpart evoked the utmost fury among the French right wing and, because the British government was also hostile to the Spanish Republic, he felt obliged to promote a "non-intervention" policy that was intended to deny arms to both sides. The rebels' ideological soulmates, the Italian and German dictatorships, promptly agreed to this approach and just as promptly disregarded it by sending massive amounts of military supplies and reinforcements to support Franco.

The issue created extreme dissension within France and within the Popular Front. The communists vehemently criticized the nonintervention policy, but Blum, though he agonized over it, felt that to change it could provoke civil war in France itself. By the end of the year the Popular Front was in disarray, and in June 1937 Blum, being refused special powers by the Senate to tackle the economic crisis, resigned. His radical colleague, Camille Chautemps, took over. This marked the effective end of the Front's rule, though on paper it continued into late 1938 (Blum even briefly returned to office). In November of that year, further sit-in strikes in defense of the gains of 1936 broke out. Daladier, by then premier and signatory of the Munich agreement, smashed them by military force.

Failure appeared complete, but the episode had important consequences. It raised the PCF to a standing in French politics that it would retain for 50 years. The year 1936 retained an iconic status on the French left in the manner of the commune or the Jacobin republic before it, as a foretaste of what might once more become possible. Suggestions that it might have been the opportunity for a real social revolution, however, are misplaced. The strikers and occupiers were not looking for the establishment of proletarian power. To have pushed further would have splintered the Popular Front immediately and most likely would have led to civil war on the Spanish model, in which the left would have been hopelessly disadvantaged.

Key Players

Blum, Léon (1872–1950): A lawyer by profession, Blum became leader of the Socialists after the split with the Communists in 1920. Being of Jewish extraction, he was ferociously loathed by the right-wing extremists. He survived imprisonment by the Nazis during the war, continued as the Socialist leader after the liberation, and headed a brief caretaker administration in 1946–1947.

Daladier, Edouard (1884–1970): Lawyer and leader of the Radical Party starting in 1927. He held various ministry offices and was premier several times during the 1930s, and, most notoriously, signatory of the Munich Pact. Foreign minister at the fall of France, Daladier survived imprisonment but played no further political role.

Thorez, Maurice (1900–1964): A miner and very able orator, Thorez became general secretary of the Parti Communiste Français (PCF) by devoted adherence to the Moscow line. A great deal of his energy was occupied in restraining the enthusiasm of his rank and file, both at the time of the Popular Front and following the liberation. He took part in the post-liberation coalition government until it was ended in 1947 by the onset of the cold war.

See also: *French Labor, World War II.*

BIBLIOGRAPHY

Books

Bernard, P., and H. Dubief. *The Decline of the Third Republic, 1914–1938.* Translated by Anthony Forster. Cambridge; New York: Cambridge University Press; Paris: Maison des Sciences de l'Homme, 1985.

Braunthal, Julius. *History of the International*, Vol. 2: *1914–1943.* New York: Praeger, 1967.

Brower, D. *The New Jacobins: The French Communist Party and the Popular Front.* Ithaca, NY: Cornell University Press, 1968.

Greene, N. *Crisis and Decline: The French Socialist Party in the Popular Front Era.* Ithaca: Cornell University Press, 1969.

Marcus, John T. *French Socialism in the Crisis Years, 1933–1936: Fascism and the French Left.* New York: F. A. Praeger, 1958.

Warwick, P. *The French Popular Front: A Legislative Analysis.* Chicago: University of Chicago Press, 1977.

Werth, Alexander. *The Destiny of France.* London: H. Hamilton, 1937.

ADDITIONAL RESOURCES

Claudin, F. *The Communist Movement: From Comintern to Cominform.* New York: Monthly Review Press, 1975.

Graham, Helen, and Paul Preston, eds. *The Popular Front in Europe.* New York: St. Martin's Press, 1987.

Other

VII Congress of the Communist International: Abridged Stenographic Report of Proceedings. Moscow: 1939.

—Willie Thompson

Popular Unity

Chile 1970–1973

Synopsis

Nearly 11 years after the Cuban Revolution, the socialist Salvador Allende was elected through a democratic process as president of the Republic of Chile to head a left-wing coalition called Popular Unity. His economic and social platform aimed to decrease Chile's dependence on other nations and the social inequality that dominated the country. Weakened by internal and external strife, by dissension within its own party ranks, and by grassroots demonstrations in the streets, the Popular Unity government faced a particularly adverse economic situation and had only implemented a part of its program three years after the election. On 11 September 1973 the government was ousted in a coup d'état that brought General Augusto Pinochet Ugarte to power and neoliberalism to Chile.

Timeline

1955: African and Asian nations meet at the Bandung Conference in Indonesia, inaugurating the "non-aligned" movement of Third World countries.

1960: Congo, along with several other African nations, becomes independent. But as the province of Katanga secedes and pro-Soviet Prime Minister Patrice Lumumba disappears (he is later murdered), the country devolves into civil war. Soon, UN troops will arrive to restore order.

1965: Arrest of the Rev. Martin Luther King, Jr., and more than 2,600 others in Selma, Alabama. Three weeks later, in New York City, Malcolm X is assassinated.

1967: Biafra secedes from Nigeria, starting a three-year civil war.

1970: Gamal Abdel Nasser, father of Arab nationalism and mentor of younger leaders such as Libya's Muammar al-Qaddafi, dies.

1971: East Pakistan declares its independence, as the new nation of Bangladesh, from East Pakistan (now simply known as Pakistan); civil war, exacerbated by famine and a cholera epidemic in Bangladesh, ensues.

1972: On 5 September, Palestinian terrorists kill 11 Israeli athletes and one West German policeman at the Olympic Village in Munich.

1973: Completion of the twin towers of the World Trade Center in New York City, built at a cost of $750 million. The 110-story buildings are the world's tallest, but by year's end they will be eclipsed by the Sears Tower in Chicago.

1976: In a daring raid on an Air France plane hijacked by supporters of the Palestinians, Israel commandoes rescue 103 passengers at Entebbe Airport in Uganda.

1978: U.S. Senate approves a measure presented by President Carter the year before, to turn the Panama Canal over to Panama by 2000.

1983: A Palestinian terrorist drives an explosive-laden truck into the U.S. Marine compound in Beirut, killing 237 marines.

1988: Pakistan's Benazir Bhutto becomes the first female prime minister of a Muslim country.

Event and Its Context

The June 1954 overthrow of the reform government of the socialist Jacobo Arbenz in Guatemala was ordered by the United States, which saw its economic interests threatened by the agrarian reform program. The overthrow opened a new era in Latin American left-wing history. All attempts to reform social conditions by legal means were apparently destined to failure; it appeared that the only hope of introducing socialism was by revolutionary means. In January 1959 the Cuban Revolution seemed to many activists to confirm this hypothesis. Shortly after, the United States embarked on a policy of "preventive coup d'état" that aimed to crush any further left-wing victories in their Latin American backyard. The 4 September 1970 electoral victory of Allende in Chile (with 36.3% of the votes, against 34.9% for the conservative right-wing candidate, Jorge Alessandri, and 27.8% for the Christian-Democrat Radomiro Tomic) therefore came as a surprise. That victory illustrated the strategy of nonviolent transition toward socialism as defined by the Twentieth Congress of the Communist Party of the Soviet Union in 1956. In his victory speech, Allende insisted that his ascendance was both democratic and revolutionary and was going to benefit the Chilean people: "I won't be just another president. I will be the first president of the first really democratic, popular, national and revolutionary government in the history of Chile."

Two months of political negotiation testified to the anxiety inspired by Popular Unity in Chile as well as abroad. Allende then assumed office on 4 November 1970. He announced the creation of a coalition government comprising four socialists, three communists, three radicals, two social-democrats, two independent members, and one member of the Christian left. For the first time in Chile's history, four ministers were former workers: the communist José Oyarce, minister of work and social planning; Américo Zarilla, minister of finance; Pascual Barraga, minister of public works and transport; and Carlos Cortés, minister of housing and urbanism. In one of his first public addresses, Allende aimed to reassure the industrial and financial sector as well as the country's economic partners. He expressed his commitment to using only legal measures in his bid to transform Chilean society and even claimed that his reforms were a continuation of those of his predecessor, the Christian Democrat Eduardo Frei Montalva, who had, he argued, only gone part of the way. Popular Unity had presented its electoral platform in December 1969; its most significant social and economic measures included the continuation and acceleration of agrarian reform, the complete nationalization of the copper mining industry and of the banks and the strategic production sector, increased wages, and broader social security coverage. These were to be the key features of "Chile's road to socialism" as presented by the new president in his first speech to congress in May 1971.

When Allende came to power, however, the economic and social situation was critical. A huge debt had been left by the Frei administration, including a foreign debt of over $2 billion and a budgetary deficit of $150 million. The election period had been difficult, production was partially paralyzed, and a huge drain of capital out of the country exacerbated the symptoms of crisis in a country that already had galloping inflation and rising unemployment. In its first weeks in power, the government implemented important measures to calm social unrest and to increase employment: in November 1970 it granted amnesty to political prisoners, restored diplomatic relations with Cuba, withdrew a proposed electricity price increase, granted social security rights to all part-time workers, implemented an emergency plan providing for the construction of 120,000 residential buildings, resumed payment of pensions and grants, and allocated 3,000 scholarships to Mapuches children in a bid to integrate the native minority into the educational system. The following month, the government signed a protocol agreement with the United Centre of Workers (CUT) granting workers representational rights on the funding board of the Social Planning Ministry; created a central commission to oversee a tripartite payment plan in which equal place was given to government, employees, and employers; sent 55,000 volunteers to the south of the country to teach writing and reading skills and provide medical attention to a sector of the population hitherto ignored; and fixed bread prices.

Apart from these emergency measures aimed at the poorest section of the population, the government presented a broad outline for structural reform. The first element was a Keynesian-based economic recovery plan initiated by Minister for the Economy Pedro Vuskovic, a sort of Chilean New Deal based on redistribution of wealth and an attempt to freeze partially the rising commodity prices (the 1970 price increase was 35%). If one takes into account the salary increases introduced on 1 January 1971 and the bonuses and increases in welfare benefits, the salaries of the lowest-paid workers and peasants may have risen by as much as 100%. The consequences were immediate: a spending fever hit the lowest income groups and industrial production suddenly took off again (production increased by 10% a year in 1971 and 1972), commercial activity revived, and unemployment dropped off. To boost the increase in production and avoid a commodity shortage that might have escalated prices, the government took various measures to help small- and medium-sized industries: on 3 February 1971, for instance, the government lowered interest rates on loans to the productive sector from 24% to 18%. The results were rapid: within a few months, inflation dropped to 20% and unemployment dropped to below 4%.

The second element of Allende's social and economic policy was the furthering of agrarian reform. Using Frei's law of 1967, the new government appropriated and redistributed within six months nearly as many properties as the Christian Democrat government had in six years. Between 1970 and 1973, six million hectares were distributed among approximately 100 thousand peasant families who became property owners, and the state took control of larger holdings henceforth to be run on a cooperative basis. At the same time new peasant councils meant that the peasant population was to be integrated into the decision-making process on rural development. Participation in the political process was thereby opened up in a country where access to political power had been limited to a small elite.

The last facet of this groundbreaking policy was an ambitious program of nationalization along the lines sketched out in the Popular Unity platform to eradicate monopoly capitalism at home and abroad. The program began in December 1970 in the textile industry with the appropriation of Bellavista Tome, a company whose directors had almost ceased production when Allende's victory had been announced in September. The following year it was the turn of the banking and chemical sector and, spurred on sometimes by striking workers, the iron, steel, and coal industries. Finally, in July 1971 a constitutional amendment unanimously voted by the Congress provided a legal basis for the nationalization of the copper industry. In October, Allende presented a bill on the *areas de la economía y participación de los trabajadores* that defined the three types of property (private, social or state, and mixed) that would form the basis of Chile's socialism.

All of these reforms provoked dissent, which slowed down the social reconstruction of the country. The United States felt that its interests in Chilean industry was threatened by the nationalization policy and silently set in place an embargo on Chilean goods. In September 1971 Allende reneged on the principle of compensation for the appropriated foreign companies (such as Kennecott and Anaconda in the copper sector) on the grounds that they had made enormous profits previously and had thereby aggravated the economic war waged by the Nixon administration and decreased foreign investment even further. On the other hand, the financial and industrial sectors teamed up with representatives of North American businesses such as Ford and ITT and formed a liberal right-wing, and sometimes extreme right-wing, nucleus of opposition to Popular Unity. Finally, a segment of public opinion and some members of the coalition government remained convinced that the country could only be radically transformed and socialism introduced by armed conflict. This was the position of the *Movimiento de Izquierda Revolucionaria* (MIR) activists, whose charismatic leader, Miguel Enriquez, advocated physical elimination of the most hard-core opponents.

The increasing number of strikes organized either by employers opposed to nationalization (notably the truck drivers' strikes in October 1972 and August 1973, led by Leon Vilarín) or by workers demanding that the socialization of the economy be speeded up (for example, El Teniente miners in April 1973 insisted that the promised wage increases be introduced) slowed down economic recovery in the first year and helped bring back high inflation. Further, the global market impeded recovery: the international market price of copper dropped, depriving Chile of essential financial resources and preventing Allende from furthering his socialist policies. The attempt to integrate military men such as General Carlos Prats into the government and to open the coalition to the more progressive elements of the Chilean church did not assuage tensions. In July and August 1973 the economy was so seriously paralyzed that inflation reached 320% and the budget deficit amounted to 115% of the state's receipts. Any attempt on the part of the government to boost economic revival became illusory in the context of such hostility to the Popular Unity and its inability to maintain public order: these were the grounds on which the armed forces would justify the coup d'état of 11 September.

Popular Unity was a hybrid of ideological positions, an attempt to pursue the Marxist-Leninist tradition within constitutional norms combined with an ad-hoc Keynesianism, and a mystique of revolution of the Castro/Guévara variety. Because it was of such short duration and because the regime that followed undid all the structural changes that it had introduced, it left hardly any trace in Chilean society. Nevertheless it continues to perpetuate a golden legend of popular government and peaceful transition toward socialism, an image of the hope to which it gave rise in its own time not only in Latin America but also in Europe. In the late 1970s numerous left-wing leaders took inspiration from Popular Unity on how to get into power on the basis of a large left-wing coalition, from the Italian communist Enrico Berlinguer, who pursued a historic compromise with the Christian Democrats, to the French socialist François Mitterrand, who worked with the Communist Party on a joint platform. A political myth whose ramifications go far beyond the Chilean borders, Popular Unity still awaits from historians the nonpartisan analysis and appraisal to which it could never aspire in its own time and has rarely been granted since.

Key Players

Allende Gossens, Salvador (1908–1973): After running unsuccessfully in 1952, 1958, and 1964, Allende was elected president of Chile in 1970. The first socialist to be elected to the office of president in Chile, he held his position until 1973, when he was overthrown during a military coup d'état directed by General Augusto Pinochet Ugarte. Although Allende was given the opportunity to flee Chile and live in exile, he declined, refusing to leave the presidential offices, where he was found dead on 11 September 1973. Allende's government introduced broad economic and social changes in Chile, including the nationalization of many businesses as well as land reform initiatives that aimed to redistribute the ownership of land. Allende sought to establish socialist reforms while maintaining existing democratic institutions.

Pinochet Ugarte, Augusto (1915–): Rising through the ranks of the Chilean army, Pinochet became an army general in 1971 and was named chief major general of the army in 1972. He was named commander in chief of the army on 23 August 1973. In September that year he led the four-man military junta that planned and executed the coup d'état that overthrew Salvador Allende. In 1974 Pinochet assumed the role of president, a position he held until 1990, when he was ousted by Christian Democrat Patricio Aylwin after a general election. Pinochet kept his position as commander in chief of the army until 1998, when he was named to a life term as senator. Pinochet was arrested during a trip to London in 1998, after appeals by the Spanish government that sought to have him extradited to Spain to face charges of murder and terrorism. In 1999 a British court decided to grant Pinochet's extradition to Spain, a decision that was then appealed.

See also: *Guatemalan Coup Orchestrated by CIA.*

BIBLIOGRAPHY

Books

Angell, Allan. "Chile Since 1958." In *The Cambridge History of Latin America*, vol. VIII, edited by Leslie Bethell. Cambridge, MA: Cambridge University Press, 1991.

Collier, Simon, and Willian F. Sater. *A History of Chile, 1808–1994*. Cambridge, MA: Cambridge University Press, 1996.

Garces, Joan. *Allende et l'Expérience Chilienne*. Paris: Ed. Fondation Nationale des Sciences Politiques, 1976.

Jocelyn-Holt Letelier, Alfredo. *El Chile Perplejo. Del Avanzar sin Transar al Transar sin Parar*. Santiago, Chile: Ed. Planeta, 1998.

Joxe, Alain. *Le Chili sous Allende*. Paris: Ed. Gallimard/Julliard, 1974.

Labrousse, Alain. *L'expérience Chilienne*. Paris: Ed. du Seuil, 1974.

Moulian, Tomás. *Conversación Ininterrumpida con Allende*. Santiago, Chile: Ed. LOM, 1998.

del Pozo José. *Rebeldes, Reformistas y Revolucionarios: Una Historia Oral de la Izquierda Chilena en la Época de la Unidad Popular*. Santiago, Chile: Ed. Documentas, 1992.

del Pozo, José, and Jacob André. *Le Chili de 1970 à 1990: de l'Unité Populaire à l'Aprés Pinochet*. Quebec, Canada: Ed. VLB, 1994.

Seguel-Boccara, Ingrid. *Les Passions Politiques au Chili Durant l'Unité Populaire, 1970–1973: Essai d'Analyse Socio-historique*. Paris: Ed. L'Harmattan, 1997.

de Vylder Stephan. *Allende's Chile: The Political Economy of the Rise and Fall of the Popular Unity*. Cambridge, MA: Cambridge University Press, 1976.

—Olivier Compagnon

Populist Party: *See* **People's Party.**

Postal Workers' Strike

United States 1970

Synopsis

In March 1970 the first nationwide strike of federal employees occurred in New York City. Plagued by persistent problems, the most important being low wages, the postal carriers of New York's local number 36 walked out on 17 March 1970. Within two days the New York strikers were joined by mail carriers throughout the Northeast. The postmaster general obtained an injunction ordering postal carriers back to work, but the federal government was unwilling to enforce the injunction so early in the strike. Because the majority of the country's financial correspondence traveled through New York, the postal strike was of national concern. After failed attempts to fashion an agreement, President Richard Nixon finally stepped in and ordered the use of troops, enforced injunctions, and stated that no negotiations would be held until the postal workers went back to work. This pressure worked, and postal carriers returned to work. The two sides eventually agreed on a two-part settlement that raised salaries and addressed the concerns of postal reorganization. President Nixon signed the resulting Postal Reorganization Act on 12 August 1970.

Timeline

1950: North Korean troops pour into South Korea, starting the Korean War.

1955: Signing of the Warsaw Pact by the Soviet Union and its satellites in eastern Europe.

1959: Alaska and Hawaii become the last states added to the Union.

1965: Arrest of the Rev. Martin Luther King, Jr., and more than 2,600 others in Selma, Alabama. Three weeks later, in New York City, Malcolm X is assassinated.

1967: Arabs attack Israel, launching the Six-Day War, which results in an Israeli victory.

1970: After 32 months of civil war in Nigeria, Biafran secessionists surrender in January.

1970: Nixon sends U.S. troops into Cambodia on 30 April. Four days later, National Guardsmen open fire on antiwar protesters at Kent State University in Ohio. By 24 June antiwar sentiment is so strong that the Senate repeals the Gulf of Tonkin resolution. On 29 June, Nixon orders troops back out of Cambodia.

Letter carriers picket the main post office, St. Paul, Minnesota. AP/Wide World Photos. Reproduced by permission.

1970: Gamal Abdel Nasser, father of Arab nationalism and mentor of younger leaders such as Libya's Muammar al-Qaddafi, dies. His funeral in Cairo is the largest in history.

1973: Signing of peace accords in Paris in January ends the Vietnam War.

1975: Pol Pot's Khmer Rouge launch a campaign of genocide in Cambodia unparalleled in human history.

1980: In protest of the Soviet invasion of Afghanistan, President Carter keeps U.S. athletes out of the Moscow Olympics.

1985: A new era begins in the USSR as Konstantin Chernenko dies, and is replaced by Mikhail Gorbachev, who at 54 years old is the youngest Soviet leader in decades.

Event and Its Context

During the 1960s a number of problems in the postal service created an environment of militancy and discontent among postal workers and led to the first nationwide strike of federal employees. The problems plaguing the postal services were varied and complex. Among these problems was the issue of fa-

Picketers prevent mail truck from passing during wildcat postal strike, Rincon Annex post office, San Francisco, California. AP/Wide World Photos. Reproduced by permission.

cility and location obsolescence. Many of the post office's facilities were outdated and too small to handle the increasing mail volume. The management structure of the post office was largely ineffective and cumbersome. Further, the post office's union adopted the organizational structure of the post office, which created the same difficulties within the union that existed in the post office itself.

The most immediate problem, however, was the pay scale. In New York, where the strike started, postal carriers were unable to support their families without supplementing their pay with either a second job or welfare. Also in New York, the top pay for a postal carrier with 21 years of service was several thousand dollars below what the government determined as the salary needed to maintain a moderate standard of living in New York.

As early as 1968, postal carriers at the United Federation of Postal Clerks convention and the National Postal Union convention voted to remove no-strike clauses from their organizations. In New York the letter carriers tried unsuccessfully to pass a "right-to-strike" resolution. When the letter carriers received word in 1970 that their July pay increases might be postponed, they demanded a strike. National Association of Letter

Carriers (NALC) president James Rademacher complied by stating if the pay matter was still unresolved by 15 April, he would call for a nationwide strike.

On 12 March the House Post Office and Civil Service Committee passed a reform pay package that Rademacher favored, but the union membership remained displeased. Also on 12 March, New York's Local number 36, composed of almost 7,000 members from the Bronx and Manhattan, held its scheduled monthly meeting. When the president of the local, Gustave Johnson, reported on the reform pay package, the members insisted on setting a date for a strike. Over Johnson's objection, the members set the strike date for 17 March. Picket lines were in place that morning, even though most union leaders, including Rademacher, were not in favor of a strike. The movement spread very quickly as support for Local 36 grew. By 19 March the strike had spread to such cities as Akron, Ohio; Boston, Massachusetts; Pittsburgh, Pennsylvania; Houston, Texas; and Detroit, Michigan. The wildcat strike was hugely effective.

The response from the federal government was a court injunction ordering the carriers back to work, but the rank and file ignored the injunction as well as requests from union leaders to return to work. The postmaster general, Winton M. Blount, placed strikers on nonpay status, issued mail embargo orders, and suspended the postal monopoly for New York City. Everyone realized the importance of the financial papers, such as paychecks, bills, bonds, and stocks, that moved through New York City. A prolonged strike would devastate the national economy.

The union leaders were also afraid that the strike was moving beyond their control. The letter carriers struck without the approval of the national unions, and the longer the strike continued, the harder it was to keep others from joining. Union leaders asked Secretary of Labor George Shultz for help. Shultz found Blount and others very resistant to a meeting while an illegal strike was in progress, so he initially refused to intervene. However, Assistant Secretary of Labor William J. Usery convinced Shultz to help, and together they convinced Blount to meet with union leaders. This meeting was scheduled for 20 March, the same day that the emergency conference of letter carriers was meeting to vote on a national strike.

The Shultz meeting reached several agreements. First, union leaders agreed to request that everyone return to work. Once service was restored, the appropriate officials would meet and discuss all the issues raised. When the issues had been addressed and agreed upon, the unions and the postal administration would then send a united proposal to Congress. The union leaders pitched the agreement to their members, but it was rejected. The rank-and-file postal carriers viewed the agreement as a sellout that was too similar to past broken promises.

Instead of making things better, the negotiations worsened the situation. Union officials realized that to remain in power they had to take control of the strike and lead it instead of trying to settle it. Rademacher also lost his standing and authority in his attempts to settle the strike. He was hung in effigy at several union meetings. With union leaders poised to lead the strike, Rademacher losing influence, and the threat of more walk-outs, President Nixon finally stepped into the fray.

Nixon declared that if the mail service was not restored by 23 March, he would meet his "Constitutional obligation to see that the mails go through." Nixon also made it clear that no negotiations would occur until the postal workers initiated a back-to-work movement. If there was no such movement, then the president would authorize the use of troops to enforce the court injunctions.

When the deadline passed without action, Nixon authorized the use of military troops. The Defense Department plan allowed for the deployment 115,000 troops in 36 cities. On 24 March, Nixon decided to send 2,500 federal troops and 16,000 National Guardsmen into New York to fill the void left by 57,000 postal workers. The soldiers were charged with moving the mail. They entered New York wearing fatigues, not battle gear, and were unarmed. The troops were not to confront or arrest any protestors, and they did not attempt any home delivery of mail. The soldiers mainly sorted mail, loaded and unloaded trucks, and sold stamps. The use of troops was more of a symbolic act asserting the power and authority of the federal government than a determined effort to resume normal postal services.

Federal marshals also served Gustave Johnson and several other New York union leaders with papers ordering them to appear in federal court to demonstrate why they should not be charged with contempt. Similar injunctions were also issued in other cities. The combination of the troops and the enforcement of the injunctions spurred a back-to-work movement that began on 25 March.

After the postal employees went back to work, negotiations began. Union officials had drawn up an agreement that provided for a 12 percent pay raise retroactive to October 1969 and that paid health benefits. The agreement reduced the length of service required for top pay from 20 to eight years, based wages on cost-of-living indices, gave amnesty to the strikers, and allowed for collective bargaining and arbitration. This package went to the negotiations to be held in Washington, D.C.

As a result of these negotiations, on 30 March the union and post office officials finished a proposal for a two-part agreement. The revised agreement included an immediate six percent raise retroactive to January 1970 for all government and military employees and joint sponsorship of postal reorganization. This would mean another six percent raise for postal carriers on the congressional enactment date, top pay for eight years of service, collective bargaining on future issues, and no disciplinary action for strikers until the conclusion of amnesty talks. The first part of the settlement was announced on 2 April. It quickly passed both houses of Congress, and President Nixon signed the bill, with an eight percent raise, on 15 April 1970.

At the same time, union and postal officials continued to work on postal reorganization. In the final version of part two of the agreement, the unions adopted a collective bargaining structure in place of their traditional structure. The parties reached agreement on this second part of negotiations on 16 April. Congress acted much more slowly on this agreement than on the first, but after a threatened filibuster and talk of another strike, the agreement passed with amendments to address new concerns.

The majority of postal workers accepted the settlement, but enough workers were dissatisfied that Local 36 threatened another walkout. There were basically two problems. The first was that New York workers believed they would receive area wage differentials, prepaid health insurance, and a longer period of retroactivity. The second was that neither the National Postal Union nor the National Alliance of Postal and Federal Employees were allowed to participate in the negotiations. The amendments that were added protected minority unions and prevented a union shop. The Postal Reorganization Act passed Congress on 6 August, and Nixon signed the act into law on 12 August 1970.

Key Players

Blount, Winton M. (1921–): Blount, a native of Alabama, graduated from the University of Alabama and during World War II flew B-29 bombers. After the war he and his brother created a successful general contracting business. Active in civil affairs, Blount eventually rose through the ranks and served as postmaster general from 1969 to 1971.

Rademacher, James: President of the National Association of Letter Carriers (NALC) from 1969 to 1976. Rademacher successfully negotiated three collective bargaining agreements.

Shultz, George Pratt (1920–): Shultz served in a number of political positions including secretary of labor (1968), head of the Office of Management and Budget (1970), secretary of the treasury (1973), and as President Ronald Reagan's secretary of state (1982–1989).

BIBLIOGRAPHY

Books

Filippelli, Ronald L. "Postal Strike of 1970." In *Labor Conflict in the United States: An Encyclopedia*, edited by Ronald L. Filippelli. New York: Garland, 1990.

Periodicals

Shannon, Stephen C. "Work Stoppage in Government: The Post Strike of 1970." *Monthly Labor Review* 101 (1978): 14–22.

Woolf, Donald A. "Labor Problems in the Post Office." *Industrial Relations* 9 (1969): 27–35.

ADDITIONAL RESOURCES

Books

Walsh, John, and Garth Mangum. *Labor Struggle in the Post Office*. New York: M. E. Sharpe, Inc., 1992.

—Lisa A. Ennis

Potato Famine

Ireland 1845–1851

Synopsis

The Irish potato famine killed one million people and led 2.5 million people to emigrate, making it one of the worst famines in modern European history. The Irish potato famine dealt a devastating blow to landless labor in Ireland but contributed an important element to the wage-labor force in the rest of the English-speaking world. In Australia, the United States, and England, famine refugees assumed a large role in the casual and domestic labor force. With their arrival, nationality and religion—most of the new migrants were Catholics—began to play a much more important role in working-class politics in the English-speaking world.

"Famine" refers to mass starvation stemming from a failure of food entitlements. In Ireland in 1846 and early 1847, there was a genuine food shortage, but hundreds of thousands of lives could have been saved if Irish resources had been used more efficiently. Most importantly, the food resources of the United Kingdom, of which Ireland was a component part, were more than adequate for famine relief. The fact that hundreds of thousands starved in a United Kingdom successfully emerging from the era of the Industrial Revolution must be seen as a triumph of the principles of political economy over the idea that governments are responsible for preserving the lives of those whom they rule.

Timeline

1825: British Parliament enacts a law permitting workers to join together in order to secure regulation of wages and hours; however, other provisions in the law effectively deny the right to strike.

1833: British Parliament passes the Slavery Abolition Act, giving freedom to all slaves throughout the British Empire.

1842: British forces in the Afghan capital of Kabul are routed, experiencing one of the first major defeats of a European force by a non-European one in modern times.

1844: Samuel Laing, in a prize-winning essay on Britain's "National Distress," describes conditions in a nation convulsed by the early Industrial Revolution. A third of the population, according to Laing, "hover[s] on the verge of actual starvation"; another third is forced to labor in "crowded factories"; and only the top third "earn[s] high wages, amply sufficient to support them in respectability and comfort."

1845: The United States formally annexes Texas.

1846: The United States declares war on Mexico, and adds California and New Mexico to the Union.

1847: Liberia, colonized since 1821 by freed American slaves, declares itself a republic and becomes the first independent nation in Africa.

1848: Scottish mathematician and physicist William Thomson, Lord Kelvin, introduces the concept of absolute

Starving peasants clamor at gates of workhouse during Irish potato famine. © Hulton/Getty Images. Reproduced by permission.

zero, or the temperature at which molecular motion ceases. This value, -273°C, becomes 0K on his Kelvin scale of absolute temperature.

1851: With a population of 2.37 million, London is the world's most populous city.

1852: Publication of *Uncle Tom's Cabin* by Harriet Beecher Stowe. Though far from a literary masterpiece, it is a great commercial success, with over half a million sales on both sides of the Atlantic. More important, it has an enormous influence on British sentiments with regard to slavery and the brewing American conflict between North and South.

1861: Emancipation of the serfs in Russia.

Event and Its Context

The Famine and Its Causes

In 1845 some areas of continental Europe and Ireland felt the potato blight, *Phytophthora infestans,* but the first sign of unusual hardship did not appear until 1846, when the blight hit again on a larger scale. As is often the case in large-scale fam-

ines, epidemic disease in Ireland accompanied famine and intensified its effects. Hungry people took to the road hoping to find relief in less affected areas, and epidemic diseases, particularly typhus, spread quickly among the malnourished bands swelling the highways. In turn, typhus not only increased the mortality toll on its own but further weakened rural society's famine defenses. In times of hardship, Irish peasants had long depended upon reciprocity and mutual aid. Fear of disease undermined their participation in the ordinary social relationships that promoted solidarity among the poor.

The famine was long and its magnitude was great. In comparison with the other major nineteenth- and twentieth-century famines, it lasted a very long time. Hitting some areas in full strength year after year, striking some regions episodically, ignoring other areas entirely, the famine dominated the Irish countryside between the autumn of 1846 to the autumn of 1851. In Irish folk memory, "Black '47" dated the worst of the famine. The winter of 1846 to 1847 was unusually cold, and bad weather exacerbated the famine's effects by making it difficult or impossible to work outdoors, the major form of government relief. The maize imports that would save many lives did not begin to arrive until the spring and summer of 1847. Still, many communities reached rock bottom in the winter of 1848 or the summer of 1849.

Funeral procession during Irish potato famine, Skibbereen, County Cork, Ireland. © Hulton/Getty Images. Reproduced by permission.

The famine also would not have taken so great a toll if Irish agriculture had not been so terribly dependent on the potato. Since the eighteenth century, potatoes had spread rapidly throughout the island. They thrived in the damp Irish climate, required minimum investment, and provided a nutritious diet. Ironically, although Irish cultivators had long lamented that the potato did not bear long storage, they generally regarded it as an unusually reliable crop. The spread of the "conacre system" had both ratified and reinforced the potato's hold on Irish agriculture. In the golden era of Irish agriculture during the Napoleonic wars, landlords were desperate for laborers; for a landlord class chronically short of capital, conacre provided an easy way of paying workers. Under the conacre system, in place of money wages, the poorest sections of the Irish laboring classes were given access to fertilized fields for growing potatoes.

Despite the length of the famine and the exceptional dependence on a single crop, reinforced by the conacre system, mass starvation would not have occurred if political authorities had acted aggressively. Effective suggestions for dealing with the famine were not wanting. In the last months of 1845, the great Irish political leader Daniel O'Connell called for a series of emergency measures. These included the ending of distilling and brewing in Ireland (which consumed vast quantities of grain), prohibition of the export of food products, opening of Irish ports to receive food directly from foreign countries, and imposition of a tax on landlords to subsidize the distribution of food to the needy. But by this time O'Connell was already a spent force in British politics and his old opponent Robert Peel was the prime minister. Peel insisted that welfare was a local responsibility and successfully sought the repeal of the Corn Laws in 1846 to lower the cost of grain; cheap grain would enable Irish landlords to afford the relief of the starving population.

The Irish authorities and the voluntary committees that administered relief certainly bear a heavy share of responsibility for the famine disaster. Although the potato crop had failed disastrously, other crops had not, and the continued export of food from a starving island made a lasting impression on the Irish memory. If the income from wheat and livestock exports had been used to finance famine relief, it might have been looked upon differently, but the landlord class did not respond to the famine in a unified way. Some landlords drew heavily on their resources to help their starving laborers and tenants. Many were already deeply in debt and the cost of famine relief was the final blow to long-weakened fortunes. Landlords who bought up these bankrupted estates as well as many established landlords responded to the famine by clearing the land of the unemployed and evicting tenants in arrears. Mass evictions, which often meant starvation for those who were turned out, were part of the famine legend. Some landlords offered tenants tickets to North America in exchange for a clear title to the land and so helped to swell the migratory wave departing Ireland. Remittances from kin and state assistance allowed some famine migrants to reach Australia.

While the failure of Irish administrative efforts contributed to the severity of the famine, the failure of England to act to save its subjects was pivotal. A famine extending so long and affecting so many required strong action from the national government. The famine must be seen in a British context, for the 1800 Act of Union had incorporated Ireland into the United Kingdom. While the revolution of 1798 had shown the dangers of maintaining Ireland with its own governing institutions, British preoccupation with Ireland had largely stemmed from political struggles over Catholic emancipation and compulsory tithes. British governments had made relatively little effort to integrate Ireland economically or socially into the realm. In re-

From a Letter to the Editor of the London *Times* on the Irish Famine (15 April 1846)

Sir, From the eloquent and powerful articles you occasionally write in favour of this unfortunate country, I think you will not hesitate to expose the heartless proceedings of the Government, or their agents, with respect to the distribution, or rather non-distribution, of the Indian corn meal so prudently imported, about which so loud a flourish of trumpets was made in the House, and for which paternal care the English press appears to think we are so astoundingly ungrateful.

The Irish are not ungrateful, and the poor are the least ungrateful of all; but with all their quickness and acute perception, they are yet to learn for what they are expected to list the dust. They have heard of such things as a birthright bartered for a noggin of stirabout; but it seems they are expected to give up the one without getting the other in exchange, and they are to throw their gratitude to boot into the bargain. We ask for bread, and you give us a stone. Can you wonder if we put it in our sleeve to hurl it at you in your time of utmost need? for the day will come despite all your greatness in which I rejoice, and of all your glory, in which I take pride, when you will need us, hungry and helpless though we are, and despised though we seem to be. . . .

If Ireland is fed, England need have no fears of her fidelity, or of her gratitude. But coercion bills will not do it, nor will the speeches of the Knights of Netherby perform it, and least of all will free trade relieve a people who have so little to trade in.

Let England beware, not of us, but of herself. If she will not, then let her beware of both; for she is making bad subjects of the best in Ireland.

I am, Sir, your most obedient servant,

J. CRAIG

32, South-mall, Cork, April 11

Source: *Interpreting the Irish Famine, 1846–1850.* http://www.people.virginia.edu/~eas5e/Irish/Famine.html.

—Judson Knight

---

sponse to 1837 legislation, Poor Law unions were only beginning to be constructed in Ireland, while many areas of the west and south were still isolated and unreachable by dependable roads.

England's initial response to the Irish famine was a generous outpouring of private contributions; even Peel, in the end, provided government aid. But the English contributions were seen as aid to a distressed neighbor rather than as entitlements of citizenship. As the famine wore on, English impatience increased and the modern phenomenon known as donor fatigue appeared. Stories of Irish laziness and fraud were widely publicized, and Irish political protest was seen as base ingratitude. The government's decision to play a passive role was rein-

forced by a monetary crisis in the English financial markets and rising food prices throughout Europe, which made providing relief more costly.

Just at the moment when the famine began to worsen, in the summer of 1846, Lord John Russell's ministry came to power. Even more than Peel, Russell was an advocate of laissez-faire policies who was determined to make Irish landlords pay for the crisis. Whig suspicions of the landlords were not unmerited; many Irish relief committees ceased to function, not because the famine had subsided but because ratepayers could no longer stand the burden. Yet the Russell government's insistence on local responsibility ignored the urgency of the case and the magnitude of the need. However culpable they may have been for the plight of Irish agriculture, local landlords simply did not have the money to relieve the famine and were often resistant to paying any money at all. The conflict between the central government and local relief officials chiefly had the consequences of relieving the national government of any responsibility and of slowing famine relief. Assistant secretary of the treasury Charles Trevelyan refused to open the national government's purse strings, consoling a local relief inspector, "We must do all we can and leave the rest to God."

The dilemma facing treasury officials like Trevelyan was not new. Nineteenth-century British social policy was torn between the demands of political economy and the claims of citizenship. Political economists were determined to prevent dependency and feared that aid, even for the needy and deserving, would undermine work incentive. In England, the indignities and cruelties of the Poor Law were designed so that only men and women actually on the edge of starvation would avail themselves of poor relief. But when very survival was at stake, claims of English citizenship, claims that no member of the English polity could be allowed to starve, outweighed those of political economy. In his 1798 essay on human population, Thomas Malthus suggested starvation as a natural check on improvidence, but his contemporaries refused to allow even improvident Englishmen to perish. To prevent Irish famine, the British government would have had to violate the principle that local government was responsible for poverty relief and contributed a very large sum of money—a fraction of what Britain spent on any major nineteenth-century war, but still a large sum. When the English government regarded Ireland, political economy trumped citizenship.

Some historians have used the racism and anti-Catholicism of many English politicians to paint the famine as an attempt at genocide—an effort to remove the thorny Irish problem from the British agenda by removing the Irish from the face of the earth. Such an interpretation wrongly imposes twentieth-century policies on nineteenth-century politicians. While English racism and anti-Catholicism were real and contributed importantly to the famine tragedy, charges of genocide are wide of the mark. Even the most pernicious measures were taken in the belief that they were for the ultimate good of the Irish population. It is worth pondering the point that laissez-faire policies ruthlessly carried out and unmitigated by any sense of the responsibilities of citizenship could have the same practical effects as conscious programs of racial genocide.

Results of the Famine

In the end, the Irish potato famine was the greatest human disaster in nineteenth-century Europe. Deaths occurred in every region and among a wide variety of occupational groups, but fatalities were worst among the Gaelic-speaking day laborers in the west and south whose participation in the conacre system had made them fatally dependent on potatoes. The famine was the beginning of the end for the day-laboring class and the death knell for a Gaelic-speaking Ireland already in long retreat. The famine finally forced a massive reconversion of Irish agriculture. In succeeding decades, day laborers were replaced by tenants who came to dominate an Irish agriculture increasingly based on raising livestock.

The famine accelerated the migration of Irish villagers in areas of the country outside the north and in sections of the population, particularly the Catholic population, that were only beginning to migrate in the 1830s. Famine refugees arriving in foreign ports sometimes discovered that their ordeal was not over. In England, Irish migrants were sometimes deported by communities that refused to bear the burden of their relief. In Canada, England, and the United States, famine refugees might be greeted by riotous crowds fearful that Irish migrants were carrying epidemic diseases. The willingness of famine refugees to work for low wages also excited concern among many workers. Many large cities like Liverpool and Philadelphia opened their welfare institutions to Irish immigrants and played an essential role in helping peasants become urbanites.

The largest number of famine migrants ended up in the United States, although the real extent of the migration is unknown. Many took advantage of the cheaper tickets to Canada; an unknown but quite large number of these emigrants may have subsequently moved to the United States. Although the famine Irish followed some of the same paths as those of preceding waves of Irish immigrants, there were some important differences. Having few resources but manual labor, Irish migrants avoided destinations where they might be forced to compete directly with unfree labor. Only a small number of Irish famine migrants went to the U.S. South, a favorite destination of previous Irish migrants. The Cape Colony in South Africa also attracted few new Irish migrants. Those who brought a little money or acquired some rapidly in North America established farms along the Ohio River or in the Great Plains of the U.S. Midwest. Following the Ohio River westward, they joined an older generation of Irish migrants in establishing farms. But the great mass of famine migrants settled in rapidly growing U.S. cities such as Boston, Chicago, New York, and Philadelphia. The Irish migration was unusual in the large proportion of women, many of them single women, who crossed the ocean, many to enter domestic service in North America.

In Scotland, the United States, and the United Kingdom, many Irish migrants became wage laborers and contributed significantly to the lowering of wages for the least skilled portions of the labor force. In the United States, the Irish sometimes competed with African Americans for less skilled jobs. The Irish often won such struggles, because although theories of a separate and inferior Celtic race were common, the Irish migrants were seldom the victims of the virulent racism visited on African Americans. While many Irish Protestants styled themselves as "Scots Irish" to distinguish themselves from the famine migrants, the size and importance of this migration made the Celtic race card difficult to play. Those threatened by the new wave of Irish migrants were more likely to seize upon their Catholicism.

The presence of Catholic Irish migrants in labor markets made anti-Catholicism a major issue in the English-speaking, working-class world during the mid-nineteenth century. Despite the campaigns of American Know-Nothings and the grumbling of Canadian Orange Lodges, Catholic Irish migrants acquired citizenship in the United States and British colonies on the same terms as earlier Irish migrants. Many Irish migrants already spoke English, and this enabled them to accept jobs in government and to participate in politics almost as soon as they got off the boat.

In the 1850s and 1860s, Catholic workers began to play an important role in many trade unions within the English-speaking world. Famine migrants contributed substantially to the trade union movement. Toward the end of the nineteenth century and the beginning of the twentieth, Irish migrants and their children provided some of the foremost working-class leaders, including James Connolly, Elizabeth Gurley Flynn, William Z. Foster, Mother Jones, Terence Powderly, James Sexton, and John Wheatley. Famine migrants and their children also involved themselves in Irish questions and trade unions, with large numbers of Catholics often endorsing Irish Home Rule. In the United States, Irish migrants, many of them Civil War veterans, played an important role in the Fenian movement of the 1860s, which endorsed using force to gain Irish independence from England. In both the United States and the United Kingdom, Irish migrants provided critical support for the Home Rule campaigns of Charles Stewart Parnell in the 1870s and 1880s.

The tide of Irish migration that grew up during the 1840s continued its flow for decades. The potato crop failed in later decades of the nineteenth century without producing mass starvation. While Irish dependence on the potato never again became as total as it had in the 1840s, emigration became the Irish solution to crop failure. Famine emigration established networks of kin and family in foreign countries who relieved Irish hardship by sending tickets to the United States or Australia.

Perhaps the most tragic aspect of the Irish potato famine is that British policymakers learned so little from it. In India between 1897 and 1899, millions died as a result of a great drought caused by a change in world weather patterns. Making no effort to maintain traditional state-sponsored grain stores, British governors struggled to unchain market forces while millions starved. The reasons for British inaction were the same as in Ireland: a commitment to laissez-faire principles combined with a colonial relationship that made the governed less than full citizens. In India as in Ireland, British administrators were unwilling to spend large sums of money to save the lives of their colonial subjects.

Key Players

O'Connell, Daniel (1775–1847): Founder and leader of the Catholic Association—the driving force in the struggle for Catholic emancipation, which finally was achieved in 1829.

Unable to win concessions for Ireland by his coalition with the Whigs between 1835 and 1839, O'Connell embarked on a campaign for Irish Home Rule that rallied Ireland but failed to make any headway in British politics. By 1844 O'Connell was a defeated figure, unable to use his many political connections to affect famine policy.

Russell, John, First Earl (1792–1878): Scion of one of the great Whig aristocratic families, Russell championed both electoral reform and Catholic emancipation. He was committed to liberal reform and was an ardent advocate of laissez-faire principles.

BIBLIOGRAPHY

Books

Akenson, Donald Harman. *Small Differences: Irish Catholics and Irish Protestants, 1815–1922: An International Perspective.* Kingston, Ontario: McGill-Queen's University Press, 1988.

Bielenberg, Andy, ed. *The Irish Diaspora.* Harlow, U.K.: Longman, 2000.

Davis, Mike. *Late Victorian Holocausts: El Niño Famines and the Making of the Third World.* London: Verso, 2001.

Gallman, J. Matthew. *Receiving Erin's Children: Philadelphia, Liverpool, and the Irish Famine Migration, 1845–1855.* Chapel Hill: University of North Carolina Press, 2000.

Gráda, Cormac Ó. *Black '47 and Beyond: The Great Irish Famine in History, Economy, and Memory.* Princeton, NJ: Princeton University Press, 1999.

Miller, Kerby A. *Emigrants and Exiles: Ireland and the Irish Exodus to North America.* New York: Oxford University Press, 1985.

Post, John D. *The Last Great Subsistence Crisis in the Western World.* Baltimore, MD: Johns Hopkins University Press, 1977.

Sen, Amartya. *Poverty and Famines: An Essay on Entitlement and Deprivation.* New York: Oxford University Press, 1981.

Other

An Gorta Mor: The Great Irish Famine. University of Wales Swansea History Department. <http://www.swan.ac.uk/history/teaching/teaching%20resources/An%20Gorta%20Mor/>.

Irish Famine: 1845–1850. University of Virginia. <http://www.people.virginia.edu/~eas5e/Irish/Famine.html>.

—Michael P. Hanagan

Power Loom Invented

United States 1814

Synopsis

The textile industry in the United States entered a new era in 1814 when Francis Cabot Lowell created the first successful American power loom in Waltham, Massachusetts. Lowell copied successful designs of power looms that had been in use in England and invented an improved version of the power loom and other related devices for use in the United States. These inventions revolutionized the organization of all the technical processes by which cloth was made. For the first time mass production of finished textile products became possible.

Lowell and his brother-in-law, Patrick Tracy Jackson, incorporated their business in 1814 with one brick structure, six stories tall. They added a second mill in 1818 and a third one in 1820. First using water to power his machines, Lowell located his factory on the Charles River at Waltham. It was the first successful power-driven textile mill in the world. It was here that the entire process of transforming raw cotton into cloth was gathered within the same building for the first time. Lowell used the new power loom, along with effective mill organization and mass production, to make textile manufacturing a successful operation in the United States.

Timeline

1789: George Washington sworn in as first U.S. president in New York City.

1793: Eli Whitney patents his cotton gin—a machine that, by making cotton profitable, spurs the expansion of slave labor in the southern United States.

1796: British engineer and inventor Joseph Bramah develops the first practical hydraulic press, a machine that will have numerous industrial applications

1800: Italian physicist Alessandro Volta develops the voltaic cell, an early form of battery.

1810: German art publisher Rudolph Ackerman invents the differential gear, which enables wheeled vehicles to make sharp turns.

1812: The War of 1812, sparked by U.S. reactions to oppressive British maritime practices undertaken in the wake of the wars against Napoleon, begins in June.

1814: British engineer George Stephenson builds the first practical steam locomotive.

1814: War of 1812 ends with the Treaty of Ghent in December—before General Andrew Jackson, unaware of the treaty, leads American troops to victory in the Battle of New Orleans.

1820: In the Missouri Compromise, Missouri is admitted to the Union as a slave state, but slavery is prohibited in all portions of the Louisiana Purchase north of 36°30' N.

1825: Opening of the New York Stock Exchange.

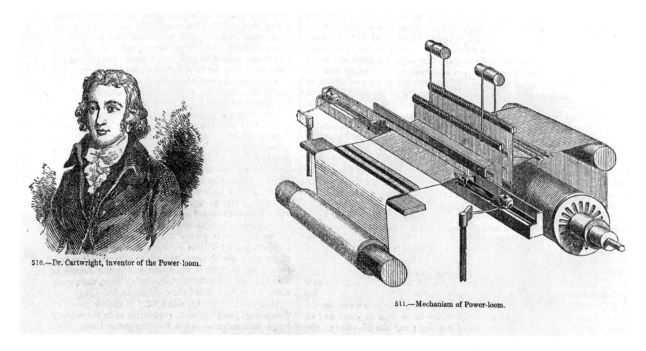

510.—Dr. Cartwright, inventor of the Power-loom.

511.—Mechanism of Power-loom.

Edmund Cartwright with blueprint of power loom. © Hulton/Getty Images. Reproduced by permission.

1834: American inventor Cyrus H. McCormick patents his reaper, a horse-drawn machine for harvesting wheat.

1839: Invention of the bicycle in Scotland.

Event and Its Context

People are known to have weaved as far back as the eighth millennium B.C., during what historians call the Neolithic Period of the Stone Age. By the time of the ancient Egyptians (over 6,000 years ago), the making of cloth was established as a regular activity to provide clothing and other materials. During the Middle Ages (from about A.D. 400 to 1400) people wove cloth in homes on hand looms, hand-powered machines that interweave yarns or other fibers into fabrics.

Mechanization Advances

During the early eighteenth century with the use of looms in factories, an industrial revolution spread across England. People began to work in factories rather than from homes. Eventually, factories replaced the domestic or "cottage" system and became the standard method of cloth production in industrial countries. Due to the size of the looms, children, some as young as nine years old, were often better suited to performing some of the operations. The use of children along with poor working conditions and extremely long work hours were common during these years. By 1835 the British Factory Act limited working hours and improved conditions within the factories.

The factory system began to develop seriously in the late eighteenth century following a series of inventions that transformed the British textile industry and heralded the beginning of the Industrial Revolution. One of the more important of these inventions was the "flying shuttle" patented in 1733 by British

inventor John Kay. It consisted of a lever mechanism that drove the shuttle across the loom along a track. The flying shuttle greatly increased the speed of weaving and permitted "picking" (an operation that opens the fleece) to be performed by one person. In 1745 Jacques de Vaucanson produced a loom in France, which was further developed by his countryman Joseph-Marie Jacquard, on which intricate patterns could be achieved.

In 1764 Englishman James Hargreaves invented the "spinning jenny," which could produce thread from animal and plant fibers. This made available large supplies of yarn and forced the development of faster weaving techniques to keep up with increased demand. In 1769 Sir Richard Arkwright invented the "water frame" for spinning, and in 1779 Samuel Crompton invented the "spinning mule." Such inventions mechanized many of the hand processes involved in weaving and made it possible to produce textiles much more quickly and cheaply. As these new machines became larger and more costly, it became necessary to operate them in factories. Even greater technological advances would soon be possible when power was applied to the loom.

The Power Loom

A power loom is a machine that at least partially mechanizes the weaving of cloth. It is powered by means other than human effort. In a power loom, precise movements that were once coordinated through human hands and eyes were duplicated by intricate interactions of cams, gears, levers, and springs. Because these movements required precision and intense coordination, weaving was the final step to be mechanized in the textile mills.

One of the major technological breakthroughs early in the Industrial Revolution was the invention in 1712 of the first practical steam engine by English inventor Thomas Newcomen.

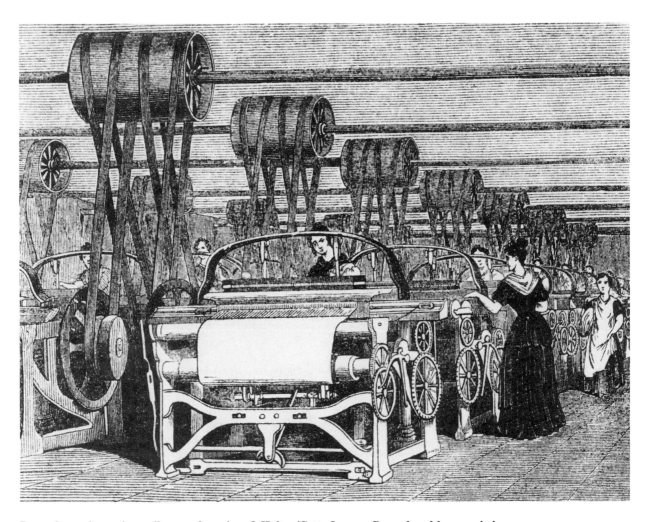

Power looms in use in textile manufacturing. © Hulton/Getty Images. Reproduced by permission.

While making improvements to the Newcomen engine, the Scottish engineer and inventor James Watt developed a series of inventions (the first one patented in 1769) that made possible the modern steam engine. When textile factories first became mechanized, only waterpower was available to operate the machinery. The factory owner was forced to locate the manufacturing facility near a water supply, sometimes in an inconvenient or isolated region far away from the labor supply. After 1785, when a steam engine was first installed in a cotton factory, steam began to replace water as the recommended power supply for the new machinery. Manufacturers could then build factories closer to labor supplies and to markets for the textile goods produced.

Edmund Cartwright's Loom

English clergyman Edmund Cartwright invented the first successful power loom in 1785. Although not the first power loom, Cartwright's power loom was the first practical design that could weave wide cloth (such as calico) in a mass manufacturing process. It was similar to a standard loom except that many of the working parts took the place of human hands and feet. Cartwright's development of the power loom allowed operations to be faster and more efficient. It permitted a semi-

skilled worker with little experience to produce the same amount of cloth as a professional hand weaver. Using waterpower to operate various functions, Cartwright's loom could weave automatically much more quickly than a skilled worker operating a standard loom.

In 1787 Cartwright opened a textile mill in Doncaster, England, and two years later began using steam engines manufactured by James Watt and Matthew Boulton to drive his looms. Improving upon the previous designs of looms, Cartwright's steam-powered machines made the textile manufacturing process much more efficient and popular—and therefore profitable—to factory owners. The earlier method, powered by the water wheel, nearly disappeared as the steam engine became the preferred power supply. The power loom became not only quicker but also more precise. All operations that had been performed previously by the weaver's hands and feet could now be operated mechanically.

Power Loom Improvements

In 1802 English cotton manufacturer William Horrocks of Stockport patented an improved power loom. It featured a better way to wind the woven cloth onto a rear beam on the loom. During the next 20 years further improvements appeared. Early in the nineteenth century a vast number of English factory owners began to use Cartwright's power loom, which had been modified with basic design improvements from Horrocks and other inventors. By 1818 in the areas surrounding Manchester, there were 14 factories with a combined total of 2,000 power looms. Three years later the number of northern English factories had increased to 32 mills and with 5,732 power looms in use. By 1850 over 250,000 cotton power looms were used in Great Britain, of which nearly 177,000 were in Lancashire county.

Looms in the United States

Former British textile apprentice Samuel Slater introduced the Arkwright method of spinning into the United States in 1790 when he started a factory in Pawtucket, Rhode Island. Yet the manufacture of cotton did not grow rapidly because the southern states had not yet found a quick method of removing seeds from cotton fiber.

In 1793 Massachusetts teacher Eli Whitney, who was then living in Georgia, invented a machine that he called the "cotton gin." This new machine could clean at least 300 pounds of cotton each day, a remarkable improvement of the rate of about one pound per day by hand. Whitney's cotton gin solved the problem of mass production and manufacture of cotton. Ten years after the machine had gone into operation, the United States was exporting over 100,000 bags of cotton, or more than 40,000,000 pounds, and enormous increases occurred every year hence. Up to that time, and much later, the cotton yarn spun in U.S. mills was mostly woven into cloth by hand in family homes. The invention of the cotton gin and the power loom led to the rise of the cotton industry as mechanized textile mills sprang up mostly in the northeastern portion of the United States.

Successful power looms were in operation in England by the early 1800s, but those made within the United States were poorly designed for factory production. American industrialist Francis Cabot Lowell of Massachusetts realized that the U.S. needed to develop a practical power loom to manufacture cotton on a large scale. To do so, Lowell borrowed British technology to establish a cotton factory. While touring English textile mills, Lowell memorized the construction and workings of the different types of power looms that he observed. Lowell was determined to build a large cotton factory that could produce cloth similar to that made in the latest English weaving system. Returning home, Lowell recruited master mechanic Paul Moody to help him recreate and develop what he had observed. In 1814 they succeeded in adapting the British design and constructed the first successful power loom operated by waterpower in the United States. Lowell was also the first person in the United States to produce cloth and thread with a power loom in a factory.

What Lowell built in 1814 at Waltham was no less than the first textile mill in the world where all the steps of the industrial process were combined under one roof: the cotton entered the factory as raw fiber (straight from Whitney's cotton gin), was spun into thread, woven into cloth, and exited as finished goods ready to be sold. The technicians at the machine shop that was established at the Waltham mills by Lowell and Moody continued to make improvements to the loom. With the introduction

of a dependable power loom, the emerging American textile industry was underway. The power loom revolutionized the organization of all the technical processes by which cloth was made. For the first time mass production of finished goods in the United States became possible. The power loom, along with the combination of all processes under one roof, effective mill organization, and mass production, combined to make textile manufacturing successful and profitable. Lowell's operation greatly reduced the amount of loss from wasted time, labor, and materials, and in the process forever altered the American textile industry.

Soon textile mills sprang up along the rivers of the states in New England and transformed the landscape, the economy, and society in general. Initially, daughters of local farmers performed the textile work. In later years, recently arrived immigrants became the main source of mill employees. Prior to the U.S. Civil War (1861–1865), textile manufacturing was the most important American industry. After the death of Lowell in 1817, the great cotton-manufacturing city of Lowell, Massachusetts, was named in his honor.

Key Players

Arkwright, Richard (1732–1792): Arkwright was born in Preston, England. As a young man, Arkwright was a barber's apprentice but had a strong ambition to operate his own company. In 1762 Arkwright started a wig-making business. During this time, Arkwright learned about new machines that were being developed for the textile industry. Arkwright employed John Kay, a clockmaker from Warrington, and other local craftsmen to help him make a "spinning frame" that was able to produce a thread that was far stronger than that made by other devices. In 1769 Arkwright formed a partnership with Jedediah Strutt and Samuel Need to build a factory using the spinning frame. In 1771 the three men set up a large factory powered by water from the River Derwent in Cromford, Derbyshire. Arkwright's machine then became known as the "water frame." Arkwright's textile factories were quite profitable. Later, Arkwright made improvements in a "carding" machine and in 1775 took out a patent for a new "carding engine."

Cartwright, Edmund (1743–1823): Cartwright was a British inventor who was born in Nottinghamshire, England, and educated at the University of Oxford. After spending several years as a clergyman, Cartwright invented the first successful power loom in 1785, upon which he subsequently made major improvements. Cartwright took out a patent for a wool-combing machine in 1789 and secured patents for numerous other machines. In 1797 he patented an alcohol-powered steam engine. Cartwright also helped U.S. inventor Robert Fulton with experiments involving a steamboat. Cartwright retired to a farm in Kent, England, and spent the rest of his life inventing improvements for farm machinery.

Crompton, Samuel (1753–1827): Crompton invented a "spinning mule" in 1775. Its unusual name was an indication that it was a hybrid that combined features of two earlier inventions, the "spinning jenny" and the "water frame" (mules are a cross between a horse and a donkey, hence the moniker). The mule produced a soft but strong yarn that could be used in all kinds of textiles, especially muslins. Crompton sold his rights to a Bolton, England, manufacturer. Eventually, a large number of factory owners purchased Crompton's "mules," but because he had sold the rights to his machine, Crompton made no money. Crompton was granted a reward for his invention from the British House of Commons. He used the money to invest in a cotton factory, but the business failed.

Hargreaves, James (1720–1778): Hargreaves was one of many weavers who owned and operated his own spinning wheel and loom while living in the village of Stanhill, England, during the 1760s. Some historians claim that his daughter Jenny accidentally knocked over the family spinning wheel. When the tipped-over spindle continued to revolve, Hargreaves got the idea that a complete line of spindles could be worked off one wheel. In 1764 Hargreaves invented a machine that used eight spindles onto which the thread was spun from one wheel. He named it the "spinning jenny" after his daughter. Hargreaves later moved to Nottingham, England, where he built a small spinning mill.

Kay, John (1704–1764): Kay was a clockmaker from Warrington, England. He also was an inventor who developed a flying shuttle in 1733 for textile manufacture, and an improved combing, or carding, device. Associations of weavers kept Kay from profiting by his inventions, and he died in poverty in France.

Lowell, Francis Cabot (1775–1817): Lowell was born in Newburyport, Massachusetts. He was a businessman, merchant, and trader from Boston who founded in Waltham, Massachusetts, America's first successful power-driven textile mill. The increasing demands for textile goods prompted the building a series of canals to supply the largest group of water-powered textile mills ever built in a localized area. After Lowell's death, this new industrial area became a city that was named in his honor.

See also: *Lowell Industrial Experiment.*

BIBLIOGRAPHY

Books

Bryant, David. *Wheels and Looms: Making Equipment for Spinning and Weaving*. London: Batsford, 1987.

Hills, Richard Leslie. *Power in the Industrial Revolution*. New York: A. M. Kelley, 1970.

Lord, P. R., and M. H. Mohamed. *Weaving: Conversion of Yarn to Fabric*. Durham, England: Merrow Publishing Company, 1976.

Smelser, Neil J. *Social Change in the Industrial Revolution: An Application of Theory to the Lancashire Cotton Industry, 1770–1840*. London: Routledge & Paul, 1959.

Other

"The Power Looms." HistoryWiz. 1999, updated 5 August 2002 [cited 13 August 2002]. <http://www.historywiz. com/powerloom.htm>.

"Textile Industry." Spartacus Educational [cited 13 August 2002]. <http://www.spartacus.schoolnet.co.uk/Textiles. htm>.

—William Arthur Atkins

Poznan Workers' Riots

Poland 1956

Synopsis

On the morning of 28 June 1956, about 16,000 factory workers in Poznan, Poland, walked off their jobs and staged an impromptu street march to protest their low wages. The action quickly turned into a mass protest by 100,000 citizens of Poznan against the communist regime that governed the country under the close supervision of the Soviet Union. The mass protests were put down by violent repression that left an estimated 80 demonstrators dead. The incident also led to a power struggle within the Polish United Workers' Party (*Polska Zjednoczona Partia Robotnicza*, PZPR), which governed the country as its only recognized political entity. In the end, public pressure plus the support of some key PZPR officials brought Wladyslaw Gomulka, who had been silenced in 1951, back into power in October 1956. The appointment was at first opposed by Soviet Premier Nikita Khrushchev, who allowed it to go forward only after he was convinced of Gomulka's willingness to keep Poland firmly within the Soviet orbit. Gomulka's ascension to power on the basis of public support was a stunning development for the Soviet Bloc and influenced the abortive Hungarian Revolution that began on 23 October 1956. It also led to reforms within Poland, as Gomulka eased censorship and other repressive measures against the populace.

Timeline

1936: Germany reoccupies the Rhineland, while Italy annexes Ethiopia. Recognizing a commonality of aims, the two totalitarian powers sign the Rome-Berlin Axis Pact. (Japan will join them in 1940.)

1941: Japanese bombing of Pearl Harbor on 7 December brings the United States into the war against the Axis. Combined with the attack on the Soviet Union, which makes Stalin an unlikely ally of the Western democracies, the events of 1941 will ultimately turn the tide of the war.

1946: Winston Churchill warns of an "Iron Curtain" spreading across Eastern Europe.

1951: Julius and Ethel Rosenberg are convicted and sentenced to death for passing U.S. atomic secrets to the Soviets.

1953: The people of East Berlin revolt against communist rule, but the uprising is suppressed by Soviet and East German tanks.

1956: Elvis Presley appears on Ed Sullivan's *Toast of the Town,* where he performs "Hound Dog" and "Love Me Tender" before a mostly female audience. Nationwide, 54 million people watch the performance, setting a new record.

1956: By now firmly established as the Soviet leader, Nikita Khrushchev denounces the crimes of his predecessor and mentor, Josef Stalin.

1956: First aerial testing of the hydrogen bomb at Bikini Atoll. The blast is so powerful—the equivalent of 10 million tons of TNT—that it actually results in the infusion of protons to atomic nuclei to create two new elements, einsteinium and fermium, which have atomic numbers of 99 and 100, respectively.

1956: Egypt seizes control of the Suez Canal, and Israel attacks Egypt on the Sinai Peninsula. Britain and France intervene against Egypt and only relent under U.S. pressure.

1961: President Eisenhower steps down, warning of a "military-industrial complex" in his farewell speech, and 43-year-old John F. Kennedy becomes the youngest elected president in U.S. history. Three months later, he launches an unsuccessful invasion of Cuba at the Bay of Pigs.

1966: In August, Mao Zedong launches the "Great Proletarian Cultural Revolution," which rapidly plunges China into chaos as armed youths plunder the countryside, rooting out suspected foreign collaborators and anti-Chinese elements. Along with rifles and other weapons, these Red Guards are armed with copies of Mao's "Little Red Book."

1971: East Pakistan declares its independence, as the new nation of Bangladesh, from East Pakistan (now simply known as Pakistan); civil war, exacerbated by famine and a cholera epidemic in Bangladesh, ensues.

Wladyslaw Gomulka. © Hulton/Getty Images. Reproduced by permission.

Event and Its Context

At the Yalta Conference in February 1945, Soviet Premier Josef Stalin declared to his Western allies that free elections would take place in Poland after the end of World War II. It was an empty promise; the Soviets quickly engineered a series of rigged elections, combined with outright repression, that eliminated their political opposition. After the democratic and Western-oriented Polish Peasant Party (PSL) was crushed in rigged elections on 19 January 1947, a one-party system under the Polish United Workers' Party—as the Polish Workers Party was called after absorbing the Polish Socialist Party in 1948—governed the state without question. The PZPR would remain in power until 1989.

The chairman of the PZPR, Boleslaw Bierut, faced a host of problems in rebuilding Poland after the devastation of World War II. With six million casualties, over 15 percent of the country's population had perished during the war. Two-fifths of the country's production capacity had been destroyed along with a third of the nation's wealth. Most of its major cities lay in ruins. The Soviet-backed Temporary Government of National Unity

moved to nationalize production immediately, and industrial operations with more than 50 employees came under direct state control in January 1946. The PZPR also started a collectivization program in agriculture; although such efforts in Poland always lagged behind other Eastern-bloc countries, about one-quarter of the country's land was collectivized by 1955. To staunch political and grassroots opposition to its programs for industry and agriculture, the PZPR expanded its secret police force to 200,000 agents by the early 1950s.

Stalinist Poland

The PZPR injected itself into civil society on an unprecedented scale in postwar Poland. Pro-Soviet propaganda influenced all levels of education, and university instruction in English was abolished save for one program at Warsaw University. Although funding for the arts expanded, cultural programs were used to glorify the communist worker-hero, the friendship and guidance of the Soviet Union, and the great gains made by Poland under the PZPR. The Roman Catholic Church was banned from conducting activities in the nation's schools and in 1953 the state demanded loyalty oaths from all clergy. For his opposition to the plan, the PZPR jailed Poland's religious leader, Primate and Archbishop Stefan Wyszynski.

In emulation of the Soviet Union, Poland implemented its first Six-Year Plan for industrial production in 1950 under

PZPR official Hilary Minc. Like the Soviet-style command economy, Poland's blueprint for progress emphasized investment in heavy industries such as steel and iron works over the production of consumer items. Results were measured in production figures, and success was gauged by meeting established quotas; quality and productivity gains were not factored into the equation. The regime's proudest accomplishment was the construction of the massive Lenin Steel Works at Nowa Huta, a planned suburb adjacent to the university and cultural center of Krakow. The site was supposed to bring peasant workers fully into the industrial age but instead became a symbol of the alienation and inefficiency of a centrally planned economy.

After the death of Stalin in March 1953, demonstrations broke out in neighboring Czechoslovakia and the German Democratic Republic. To forestall violence within Poland, the PZPR cautiously allowed some popular discontent to surface. Some censorship controls were lifted and articles critical of the Soviets began to appear in the press. A few hard-liners in the PZPR were ousted from office, and others who had previously been purged were released from jail. In January 1955 the PZPR even released a public critique of the excesses committed during the previous 10 years. The criticism increased after Bierut's death, which occurred while he was attending the 20th Congress of the Soviet Communist Party in Moscow on 12 March 1956. The PZPR took advantage of Bierut's demise by blaming him for much of the popular discontent; it also began circulating copies of Soviet Premier Nikita Khrushchev's secret speech that denounced Stalinism before the Congress.

The Poznan Uprising

Following Bierut's death, the PZPR immediately installed Edward Ochab as its new leader. Ochab was soon engulfed in the first widespread protests that the regime had experienced in the postwar era. On 28 June 1956 nearly 16,000 workers at the Hipolit Cegielski engineering plant (also known as the ZISPO works) walked off the job to demand higher wages and lower production quotas. Workers in the part of the plant that produced locomotives had led the grievances; with parts delivered to their section late and incomplete, meeting their production quota had been impossible that month. After a workers' delegation to Warsaw had been rejected, strikers marched to the city's center on the morning of 28 June. The crowd grew to include about 100,000 Poznan citizens, a full third of its population. Many in the crowd carried the national flag, sang religious songs, and chanted the impromptu slogan of the march, "Bread and Freedom," as they massed in Wolnosci Square.

Riots broke out when some of the demonstrators attacked a radio station that was jamming broadcasts of Radio Free Europe and the BBC; others attacked the city jail and freed the prisoners. The scene turned violent when part of the crowd attacked the PZPR headquarters and built a bonfire out of police files; the secret police fired into the crowd and turned them back. For the next several hours, various battles broke out throughout the city, with the police sometimes siding with the demonstrators in protest against the regime and its policies. Estimates of the final death toll that day ranged from 53 to 80 victims, with at least 300 injured. The fighting continued through the next day and was finally extinguished in the early morning hours of 30 July.

Once the army had quashed the uprising, the PZPR moved to place the blame for the incident on secret agents in league with Poland's capitalist enemies. It abruptly changed course, however, and in the weeks following the Poznan uprising announced that workers' councils would take a more active role in managing their factories, wages would rise, and industrial production goals would be revised. The split in the PZPR's outlook also affected its leadership, with reformist elements arguing for a return to power of Wladyslaw Gomulka. Gomulka had previously lost to Bierut in a power struggle and was jailed between 1951 and 1953. A committed communist, Gomulka was nevertheless viewed as more independent-minded than other PZPR leaders. His commitment to a "Polish Road to Socialism" was disturbing to the country's Soviet handlers.

Realizing that they had little chance of electing Gomulka to the PZPR chairmanship, his supporters conducted a public campaign for his elevation through the workers' councils that they controlled in factories across the nation. The workers' meetings spilled over into carefully staged, public mass rallies in support of Gomulka's leadership. In this tense atmosphere, the PZPR met for its Eighth Plenum on 19 October 1956. Khrushchev and other Soviet leaders also attended the meeting, which took place as the Soviets massed their tanks on the Polish border for a possible invasion. Other Soviet troops within the country started to head toward Warsaw. After Khrushchev expressed his rage that the PZPR had tried to change its leadership without consulting with him, he met privately with Gomulka throughout the night. After Gomulka convinced the Soviet leader of his sincerity in keeping Poland in the Soviet bloc, Khrushchev backed down from his threats. Gomulka was elected first secretary of the party on 21 October 1956, concluding a dramatic shift in Poland's political fortunes. It was the first time that popular opinion had proved decisive in a change of leadership in the Eastern bloc.

The "Polish October"

The Poznan uprising and "Polish October" also influenced events throughout the region. Just as Gomulka was being confirmed as Poland's leader, a protest in support of Poland's defiance took place in Budapest. A huge crowd in the Hungarian capital paid homage to a statue of General Jozef Bem, a Pole who had fought for Hungarian independence in 1848. On 24 October 1956 the demonstrations grew violent, and the Hungarian Revolution had begun. It was crushed by Soviet tanks on 4 November and served as a reminder to Gomulka how close his nation had been to invasion.

The Polish October of 1956 resulted in few concrete reforms. Capitalizing on his political momentum, Gomulka secured an agreement from the Soviets to repatriate Polish war prisoners who were still being held. Gomulka also managed to send some of the worst of the hard-line advisors back to the Soviet Union. Cardinal Wyszynski was released from jail in October 1956, and censorship was applied with a lighter hand than in other Eastern-bloc nations. Yet the country's centrally planned economy remained hopelessly inefficient, and wage gains were soon wiped out by inflation. Civil liberties remained largely repressed; combined with the economic mismanagement of the country, Poland witnessed another round of disturbances in 1968 and 1970, when Gomulka was thrown out of office.

Key Players

Bierut, Boleslaw (1892–1956): After Bierut led the Polish Communist Party resistance effort during World War II, Josef Stalin chose him to become Poland's first postwar leader in rigged elections. Bierut's leadership prompted the rebuilding of a substantial portion of the country's housing and infrastructure; however, the period also witnessed the gradual restriction of political freedom through a series of rigged elections and outright repression. Bierut's death while attending the 20th Congress of the Soviet Communist Party in Moscow in March 1956 led to a year of political instability that culminated in the "Polish October" of that year.

Gomulka, Wladyslaw (1905–1982): Gomulka became secretary of the Polish Communist Party in 1943. He lost out to Bierut in a power struggle in 1951 and served two years in prison. Gomulka later returned to power after Bierut's death when the Polish United Workers' Party (PZPR) named him secretary of the party in response to calls for reform during the Polish October of 1956. Gomulka enjoyed some genuine support in the 1950s and early 1960s as he eased censorship and other restrictions on civil liberties in Poland. Faced with renewed protests against the regime from 1968 to 1970, however, Gomulka ordered reprisals that made him a reviled figure. He was ousted from office in 1970.

Wyszynski, Cardinal Stefan (1901–1981): Ordained as a Catholic priest in 1924, Wyszynski served in the underground resistance during World War II. In 1946 he was appointed bishop of Lublin and in 1949 became the primate of Poland and archbishop of Gniezno and Warsaw. After Wyszynski was named a cardinal in 1953, Poland's Communist rulers jailed him for speaking out against government interference in church affairs and the spiritual life of the nation. Wyszynski served three years and was released after Wladyslaw Gomulka came to power in 1956. Wyszynski remained a voice of the opposition until his death in 1981.

See also: *Hungarian Revolution and Workers Councils; Solidarity Emerges.*

BIBLIOGRAPHY

Books

Asherson, Neal. *The Struggles for Poland.* New York: Random House, 1987.

Bethell, Nicholas. *Gomulka: His Poland, His Communism.* New York: Holt, Rinehart, and Winston, 1969.

Davies, Norman. *God's Playground: A History of Poland, Volume II: 1795–Present.* New York: Columbia University Press, 1982.

Goodwyn, Lawrence. *Breaking the Barrier: The Rise of Solidarity in Poland.* New York: Oxford University Press, 1991.

Lukowski, Jerzy, and Hubert Zawadzki. *A Concise History of Poland.* Cambridge: Cambridge University Press, 2001.

Schöpflin, George. "Destalinization." In George Schöpflin, *Politics in Eastern Europe.* Oxford, UK, Cambridge, MA: Blackwell, 1993

Zamoyski, Adam. *The Polish Way: A Thousand-Year History of the Poles and Their Culture.* New York: Franklin Watts, 1988.

—Timothy G. Borden

Profintern: *See* **Red International of Labor Unions.**

Protocol of Peace

United States 1910

Synopsis

The 1910 Protocol of Peace was a historic compromise between the International Ladies Garment Workers Union and the major employers of women's garment industry centered in New York City. The protocol resulted from the peculiarities of the garment industry and from the remarkable combativeness of the garment workers. It represented—under the somewhat misleading label of "industrial democracy"—a union-inspired regulation of the garment business and a business-inspired regulation of the unions. The agreement was seen as a far-reaching partnership of the garment industry and the garment workers' union. It cannot be understood apart from the bitter and hard-fought strikes of 1909 and 1910 that made it possible. Some of the underlying dynamics that generated those strikes were never resolved and ultimately led to the decline of the protocol on the eve of World War I. The spirit of the protocol, however, continued to come to the fore at various times in future years within the garment industry and as a powerful impulse within the larger labor movement and political economy of the United States.

Timeline

1889: Flooding in Johnstown, Pennsylvania, kills thousands.

1893: Wall Street stock prices plummet on 5 May, precipitating a market collapse on 27 June. In the wake of this debacle, some 600 banks and 15,000 other businesses fail. The nationwide depression will last for four more years.

1898: Bayer introduces a cough suppressant, derived from opium. Its brand name: Heroin.

1902: The *Times Literary Supplement,* a weekly review of literature and scholarship, begins publication in London.

1905: Russian Revolution of 1905. Following the "bloody Sunday" riots before the Winter Palace in St. Petersburg in January, revolution spreads throughout Russia, in some places spurred on by newly formed workers' councils, or soviets. Among the most memorable incidents of the revolt is the mutiny aboard the battleship *Potemkin.* Suppressed by the czar, the revolution brings an end to liberal reforms, and thus sets the stage for the larger revolution of 1917.

Members of International Ladies Garment Workers Union participate in Labor Day parade, New York City.
© Bettmann/Corbis. Reproduced by permission.

1909: Robert E. Peary and Matthew Henson reach the North Pole.

1909: Founding of the National Association for the Advancement of Colored People (NAACP) by W. E. B. Du Bois and a number of other prominent black and white intellectuals in New York City.

1909: William Cadbury's *Labour in Portuguese West Africa* draws attention to conditions of slavery in São Tomé and Principe.

1911: Revolution in Mexico, begun the year before, continues with the replacement of the corrupt Porfirio Diaz, president since 1877, by Francisco Madero.

1915: A German submarine sinks the *Lusitania,* killing 1,195, including 128 U.S. citizens. Theretofore, many Americans had been sympathetic toward Germany, but the incident begins to turn the tide of U.S. sentiment toward the Allies.

1919: Formation of the Third International (Comintern), whereby the Bolshevik government of Russia establishes its control over communist movements worldwide.

Event and Its Context

The garment industry has historically been marked by instability, mobility, and volatility. In addition to dramatic fluctuations that are endemic to the market, this labor-intensive industry with relatively light capital outlays has generated a cutthroat competitiveness among entrepreneurs. Businesses in the industry are often on the edge of bankruptcy and are always seeking to increase profit margins by subjecting their workers to intensified exploitation and innumerable indignities. The larger and more substantial manufacturers were historically supplemented by a vast network of smaller sweatshops, whose low wages and abysmal working conditions always acted as a drag to the workers in the "better" establishments.

This reality shaped the development of the International Ladies Garment Workers Union (ILGWU) and undermined the union's initial gains. These same conditions prompted explosive struggles, including the "rising of the 20,000" in 1909 and "the great revolt" of 1910. These bitter and hard-fought strikes inspired great heroism and won partial victories that secured the survival of the ILGWU. Yet the intensive class struggle set the stage for an experiment in class collaboration through the Protocol of Peace that was signed by the union and the employers' association.

Women protestors during Ladies Tailors Strike, Manhattan, New York, 1910. © Corbis. Reproduced by permission.

Rising of the 20,000

In October 1909 Samuel Gompers, president of the American Federation of Labor (AFL), joined with socialist lawyer Meyer London and other prominent speakers to address an October 1909 agitational meeting of 3,000 shirtwaistmakers at New York City's Cooper Union. A young worker named Clara Lemlich challenged the assembly: "I have listened to all the speakers, and I have no further patience for talk. I am one who feels and suffers from the things pictured. I move we go on a general strike!" The electrified crowd voted to strike and raised their hands in the Hebrew oath: "If I turn traitor to the cause I now pledge, may this hand wither from the arm I now raise."

The demands included a union shop, a 52-hour workweek, limitations on forced overtime, a uniform price scale for piecework to be negotiated in each shop, the elimination of unfair penalties and charges for equipment and materials, and the end of the subcontracting system.

The ILGWU could count on the support of the AFL as well as the Socialist Party, the Women's Trade Union League, and an impressive array of social reformers, feminists, and intellectuals. There were also many who denounced the strike, with hired thugs and unsympathetic police introducing the element of violence and intimidation. The strikers held firm. The newly formed employers association was finally prepared to accept many of the demands (bargaining with the union's all-male negotiating team), but not the union shop or the elimination of nonunion subcontractors. The breakdown of negotiations with the employers' association and the erosion of AFL support caused the ILGWU leadership to end to strike in February 1910. Only weak contracts could be signed with individual shops, but 339 of the 353 firms in the employers' association signed union contracts.

Although many of the problems that had generated the strike remained unresolved, there was now an upsurge in ILGWU membership and a new vitality in the union. Out of this struggle, a number of female figures became prominent (if not powerful) in the ILGWU: in addition to Clara Lemlich, Pauline Newman, Rose Schneiderman and Fannia Cohn were among the best known. In this struggle and in the strike to follow, a number of men also distinguished themselves. One of the best known men in the confrontation was a former IWW dissident and tough-minded street fighter, Morris Sigman, whose later conservatism never eroded his base of support, especially among anarchist currents within the ILGWU.

Revolt of 1910

The struggle was resumed with less spontaneity and more careful organization with the "great revolt" of the cloakmakers on 7 July 1910. Men were in the forefront of this action, and the ranks of the strikers swelled to 60,000. "Many of our devoted workers wept tears of joy seeing their long years of work and sacrifice crowned with success," recalled ILGWU president Abraham Rosenberg. "To me it seemed that such a spectacle had happened before only when the Jews were led out of Egypt." Union ranks soared from about 20,000 to almost 75,000.

The demands included a 40-hour workweek, a hike in the minimum wage, ending charges for equipment and materials, elimination of the subcontracting system, and employment only of union members. The strike was solid and massively effective, with scores of newly trained union cadres mobilizing thousands in workplace shut downs, picketing, rallies, and mass meetings, and the action won widespread community support.

Whereas more than 300 smaller manufacturers caved to the demands, the larger firms in the Cloak, Suit, and Skirt Manufacturers Protective Association held firm. They continued to mobilize their considerable resources, including enlisting the aid of local officials for mass arrests and court injunctions against the efforts of the ILGWU. "We offer no apology for the general strike," proclaimed Socialist orator Meyer London, who was also a union lawyer and negotiator. "If at all we should apologize to the tens of thousands of the exploited men and women for not having aroused them before." He added: "This general strike is greater than any union. It is an irresistible movement of the people. It is a protest against conditions that can no longer be tolerated."

Upper-class Progressives intervened to mediate the conflict, foremost among them the future Supreme Court Justice Louis D. Brandeis, who enjoyed a significant degree of confidence on both sides. Largely through his efforts, the sides negotiated a "Protocol of Peace" that brought an end to the strike on 2 September.

The Protocol

The protocol set forth both immediate and long-range components. Employers agreed to a 50-hour workweek, 10 paid legal holidays, payment of time-and-a-half for overtime, an increase in the minimum wage, establishment of mechanisms to oversee prices for piece work, and the abolition of inside contracting. Moreover, the agreement included a qualified acceptance of the union shop. Also out of the protocol there arose the Union Health Center designed to provide health care to union members who could not afford to buy it individually.

The long-range components of the protocol involved the establishment of three new institutions. A Joint Board of Sanitary Control, with representatives of union and industry, was to wipe out the remnants of the sweatshop by seeing that shops established a sanitary work environment. A Board of Grievances, also with representatives of both sides, "replaces the strike," as ILGWU secretary–treasurer John Dyche put it bluntly. All disputes that the Board could not resolve would pass on to the third institution. The Board of Arbitration, made up of representatives of the "public" accepted by both sides, would be chaired by Brandeis.

According to Brandeis, "It was the purpose of the Protocol to introduce into the relations of the employer and the employee a whole new element; that is the element of industrial democracy." By this, however, he did not mean the socialist notion of "rule by the people" over the industries. Instead the agreement established "a joint control" of industry by the employers' association (representing the handful of wealthy owners) and the union (speaking in the name of the masses of workers) that functioned as equal partners "with joint control." This would eliminate those conditions that "prevented the employers and the employee alike from attaining that satisfactory living within the industry which it must be the aim of all effort in business to secure."

Samuel Gompers' comment that future wage increases would come as "adjustments on a scientific basis" suggested that there would be a common union–employer interest in the productivity and profitability of the garment industry.

Decline and Legacy of the Protocol

Although the protocol brought great public acclaim and some obvious improvements for the workers, it did not directly address a myriad of problems and tensions that continued to divide workers and bosses, despite all the rhetoric about "industrial democracy" and "social harmony." The agreement also contained profound ambiguities, especially for the more militant trade unionists, socialists, and anarchists in the union's ranks and who dominated the powerful Cloakmakers Joint Board in New York City. Many grievances began to pile up, and not everything could be arbitrated quickly or, from the workers' standpoint, appropriately. Powerful ILGWU leader John Dyche was a devoted supporter of the protocol, fully prepared to help enforce protocol provisions designed to control the union ranks, and he helped to break now-illegal strikes of union members.

The Joint Board brought in from Chicago the practical-minded but principled radical Abraham Bisno to head its dealings with employers. Bisno's efforts to interpret, apply, and expand the protocol in ways that would enhance the position and power and of the workers soon ran into dogged opposition both from the employers association and ILGWU president Dyche. Bisno was soon replaced by Dr. Isaac Hourwich, a highly respected academic with a legal background, long associated with the union, whose socialism was widely known to be of the most moderate variety. Hourwich also generated antagonism from the employers and from some union sectors (including public attacks from Dyche) as he rigidly insisted on his own authority to interpret and redesign the protocol on a more rational and equitable basis. Talk of "industrial democracy" had not allowed for actual worker control of the workplaces and their own conditions, nor did it even permit the union too much power in relation to the power of the employers. Hourwich finally went the way of Bisno.

In 1911 a disaster hit the Triangle Shirtwaist Company, which had been one of the focal points of the 1909 uprising. Unsafe conditions had persisted at the plant and finally resulted in workers being trapped (and many leaping to their deaths) when a fire broke out. The death toll was 146 women and men. "I can't talk fellowship to you who are gathered here," said Rose Schneiderman at a memorial meeting. "Too much blood has been spilled." She spoke the feelings of many workers as she added, "I know from my experience it is up to the working people to save themselves. The only way they can save themselves is by a strong working-class movement." There was no mention of the protocol here, and a rising tide of anger, frustration, and militancy ultimately culminated in the 1914 replacement of Rosenberg and Dyche with socialist Benjamin Schlesinger as president and militant strike leader Morris Sigman as secretary-treasurer.

Yet the spirit of the protocol persisted in the 1920s under Schlesinger and Sigman, and even more under David Dubinsky beginning in the 1930s. Legislation such as the National Labor Relations Act (NLRA) of 1935, which placed the authority of the U.S. government behind guarantees of union recognition by employers and compelled union enforcement of workers' contract obligations and industrial peace (with the government representing the interests of the "public" as central arbiter) drew on the principles of the protocol.

The spirit of the protocol also could be found in the post–World War II compact between dominant sectors of the U.S. business community and the labor movement. Unions would be accepted under the modified structure of the NLRA. The unions would act on concerns for the profit margins and productivity of the employers, with workers' wage increases and other benefits "scientifically" linked to the success of the capitalist enterprise, and a working-class commitment to a regulated capitalist economy that would provide decent living standards with extensive health and social services. Only in the 1980s did the underlying economic developments and class tensions lead to the erosion and partial collapse of this latter-day triumph of the protocol principles.

Key Players

Bisno, Abraham (1866–1929): Working in the garment trades from the time his family arrived in the United States from Russia in 1881, Bisno became involved in anarchist and socialist currents in Chicago and union organizing efforts.

Prominent among union leaders in the Chicago garment workers, he became a founder and leader of the ILGWU, though was often too militant for the organization's top leadership. He left the ILGWU in 1917 and went into real estate but maintained his labor and radical sympathies.

Dyche, John A. (1867–1938): Emigrating from Russia to England, and then to the United States in 1901, Dyche began as a socialist critical of outside "meddlers" in the labor movement. Dyche was hostile to trade union militancy and left-wing influence, knowledgeable about the garment industry, and inclined to collaborate with employers to secure the best deal for his members. He was ILGWU secretary-treasurer from 1903 until 1914.

Hourwich, Isaac (1860–1924): Arriving in 1890 from Russia to the United States, Hourwich became a professor with expertise in economics, law, and statistics. In 1912 he supported Theodore Roosevelt's Bull Moose Progressive, thus alienating many of his socialist comrades. In the same year he published his classic study, *Immigration and Labor*. Long associated with the ILGWU, in 1913 the New York Cloakmakers' Joint Board enlisted Hourwich to help oversee the protocol. He left this position a year later amid fierce controversy.

Lemlich, Clara (1886–1982): Leaving Russia in 1903, Lemlich became immersed in the socialist milieau and became a militant union organizer and leader among the garment workers, especially during the rising of the 20,000. Active in the Women's Trade Union League and in woman suffrage struggle, she married a Russian immigrant worker (Joseph Shavelson, with whom she had three children) and became an early member of the Communist Party. She was active for many years in consumer struggles, tenants rights struggles, community struggles, and more. In later years she once again became a garment worker and rank-and-file member of the ILGWU.

London, Meyer (1871–1926): Coming to the United States from Russia in 1891, London switched from the Socialist Labor Party to the Socialist Party of America at the beginning of the new century. London was a lawyer who devoted his energies to serving the unions in the garment trades. As a Socialist, he was elected to Congress from New York City's Lower East Side in 1914, 1916, and 1920.

Newman, Pauline (1888?–1986): Newman emigrated from Russia to the U.S. in 1901. An activist in the Socialist Party and a garment worker, she was centrally involved in the rising of the 20,000. She worked for many years in the ILGWU in labor education and workers' health. In the 1920s she served as a director of the ILGWU Health Center, with which she was closely connected for much of her career. She was also active in the Women's Trade Union League.

Rosenberg, Abraham (1870–1935): Coming to the United States from Russia in 1883, Rosenberg was involved in the garment workers union beginning in 1890 and gained a widespread popularity among the union ranks. As president of the ILGWU from 1907 to 1914, he closely identified with the moderate policies pursued by the powerful secretary-treasurer John Dyche.

Schlesinger, Benjamin (1876–1932): A Lithuanian immigrant coming to the United States in 1891, Schlesinger became involved with the Socialist Labor Party and as an activist among garment workers, then with the *Jewish Daily Forward* and the Socialist Party of America. He was a capable organizer and leader of the ILGWU, for which he served as president in 1903–1904, 1914–1923, and 1928–1932.

Schneiderman, Rose (1882–1972): Schneiderman immigrated to the United States from Poland in 1890 and began working in the garment industry at the age of 13. In the early 1900s she joined the Socialist Party, in which she remained active until the 1920s, when she shifted to the Democratic Party. A leader in the rising of the 20,000, she became an organizer for the ILGWU, although much of her energy was focused in the Women's Trade Union League, in which she was prominent for many years. She had close ties to the New Deal administration of Franklin D. Roosevelt in the 1930s, and she served as secretary of the New York Department of Labor from 1937 to 1943.

Sigman, Morris (1880–1931): Going from Russia to England in 1901 and then to the United States a year later, Sigman got a job as a cloak presser and soon became a leading activist in the Industrial Workers of the World. He first challenged the ILGWU then switched over to it in 1907. He allied himself with socialists in the union and became secretary-treasurer in 1914, first vice president in 1920, and president in 1923, a position he held for five years during a "civil war" that broke Communist Party influence in the union.

See also: *American Federation of Labor; International Ladies Garment Workers Union (ILGWU); Triangle Shirtwaist Fire; Wagner Act.*

BIBLIOGRAPHY

Books

Epstein, Melech. *Jewish Labor in U.S.A., 1882–1952.* New York: KTAV Publishing House, 1969.

———. *Profiles of Eleven.* Lanham, MD: University Press of America, 1987.

Fink, Gary, ed. *Biographical Dictionary of American Labor.* Westport, CT: Greenwood Press, 1984.

Foner, Philip S. *Women and the American Labor Movement: From the First Trade Unions to the Present.* New York: Free Press, 1982.

Hardy, Jack. *The Clothing Workers: A Study of the Conditions and Struggles in the Needle Trades.* New York: International Publishers, 1935.

Herochik, Shelly G. "Uprising of the 20,000 of 1909." In *Labor Conflict in the United States, an Encyclopedia,* edited by Ronald L. Filipelli. New York: Garland Publishers, 1990.

Kessler-Harris, Alice. "Organizing the Unorganizable: Three Jewish Women and Their Union." In *The Labor History Reader,* edited by Daniel J. Leab. Urbana: University of Illinois Press, 1985.

———. "Rose Schneiderman and the Limits of Women's Trade Unionism." In *Labor Leaders in America,* edited by Melvyn Dubofsky and Warren Van Tine. Urbana: University of Illinois Press, 1987.

Levine, Louis. *The Women's Garment Workers: A History of the International Ladies Garment Workers Union.* New York: B. W. Huebsch, 1924.

Schappes, Morris U. "Introductory Comments: Remembering the Waistmakers General Strike, by Clara Lemlich Shavelson." In *Jewish Currents Reader, 1976-1986,* edited by Louis Harap. New York: Jewish Currents, 1987.

Scheier, Paula. "Clara Lemlich Shavelson." In *The American Jewish Woman, A Documentary History,* edited by Jacob Rader Marcus. New York: KTAV Publishing House, 1981.

Schneider, Dorothy and Carl J. Schneider. *The ABC–CLIO Companion to Women in the Workplace.* Santa Barbara, CA: ABC-CLIO, 1993.

Schofield, Ann. "Pauline Newman: A Voice of the Less Articulate." In *To Do and To Be: Portraits of Four Women Activists, 1893–1986,* edited by Ann Schofield. Boston: Northeastern University Press, 1997.

———. "The Uprising of the 20,000: The Making of a Labor Legend." In *A Needle, a Bobin, a Strike: Women Needleworkers in America,* edited by Joan M. Jensen and Sue Davidson. Philadelphia: Temple University Press, 1984.

Stein, Leon, ed. *Out of the Sweatshop: The Struggle for Industrial Democracy.* New York: Quadrangle/New York Times, 1977.

Stolberg, Benjamin. *Tailor's Progress: The Story of a Famous Union and the Men Who Made It.* Garden City, NY: Doubleday, Doran and Co., 1944.

Tax, Meredith. *The Rising of the Women: Feminist Solidarity and Class Conflict, 1880–1917.* New York: Monthly Review Press, 1980.

Tyler, Gus. *Look for the Union Label: A History of the International Ladies' Garment Workers Union.* Armonk, NY: M. E. Sharpe, 1995.

—Paul Le Blanc

Public Contracts Act

United States 1936

Synopsis

The Public Contracts Act (also known as the "Walsh-Healey Act") of 1936 was one of several important federal labor laws that Congress enacted during the mid-1930s. The act requires vendors who supply goods or services to the United States government to treat their employees "fairly and decently." The "fair and decent" labor practices required by the act include: paying prevailing minimum wages as determined by the secretary of labor, including overtime pay; not employing children or prison inmates; and providing safe and sanitary working conditions. The act also bars the government from dealing with vendors who are not manufacturers or regular dealers of the items to be supplied.

Timeline

1921: As the Allied Reparations Commission calls for payments of 132 billion gold marks, inflation in Germany begins to climb.

1926: Britain paralyzed by the general strike.

1931: Financial crisis widens in the United States and Europe, which reel from bank failures and climbing unemployment levels. In London, armies of the unemployed riot.

1933: Adolf Hitler becomes German chancellor, and the Nazi dictatorship begins.

1936: Germany reoccupies the Rhineland, while Italy annexes Ethiopia. Recognizing a commonality of aims, the two totalitarian powers sign the Rome-Berlin Axis Pact. (Japan will join them in 1940.)

1936: The election of a leftist Popular Front government in Spain in February precipitates an uprising by rightists under the leadership of Francisco Franco. Over the next three years, war will rage between the Loyalists and Franco's Nationalists. The Spanish Civil War will prove to be a lightning rod for the world's tensions, with the Nazis and fascists supporting the Nationalists, and the Soviets the Loyalists.

1936: Hitler uses the Summer Olympics in Berlin as an opportunity to showcase Nazi power and pageantry, but the real hero of the games is the African American track star Jesse Owens.

1939: Britain and France declare war against Germany after the 1 September invasion of Poland, but little happens in the way of mobilization.

1944: Allies land at Normandy on 6 June, conducting the largest amphibious invasion in history.

1951: Six western European nations form the European Coal and Steel Community, forerunner of the European Economic Community and the later European Union.

Event and Its Context

In the late nineteenth century, the American labor market was transformed by rapid industrialization. The jobs created by the industrial revolution drew workers away from farms to cities and transformed self-reliant agriculturists and artisans to wage-earning factory hands and laborers. Despite increasing the availability of consumer goods, the Industrial Revolution contributed to the misery of millions of workers. Women and children were tied to factories for long hours, often under brutal conditions. Men and boys were employed in hazardous, hard-labor industries such as mining and rail construction. Further, industrialization increased enormously the number of workers dependent on wages for their livelihood. Because of their relative interchangeability, however, individual workers lacked the

Frances Perkins. The Library of Congress.

bargaining power necessary to extract favorable terms of employment from the captains of industry who controlled their jobs.

Beginning in the nineteenth century, workers sought to ameliorate their situation, primarily using labor organizing and collective bargaining. Progressive Era (1890s–1920s) reformers battled both the business lobby and the Supreme Court to obtain limited state and federal legislative protection of workers. During the New Deal era (1933–1939), the U.S. Congress overcame the resistance of the Supreme Court and enacted a series of important federal statutes that permanently changed employer-employee relations. The Public Contracts Act of 1936, one statute in this series, improved the lot of some workers by prohibiting the federal government from contracting with private sector employers who did not adhere to certain "fair and decent" labor standards.

Before the 1936 act took effect, the U.S. government generally purchased needed goods and services from the lowest "responsible" bidder. In practice, any bidder who posted a bond guaranteeing fulfillment of the contract was deemed a "responsible" bidder. Several abusive practices emerged. Under "bid brokering" (or "vest-pocket dealing"), unscrupulous "bid brokers" secured government contracts by placing low bids, then subcontracting the work to sweatshops that relied on child labor or other substandard labor practices. In another practice known as the "kick-back" system, contractors nominally paid their employees a reasonable wage, but required employees to return a portion of their pay.

Ethel M. Johnson, chairperson of New Hampshire Wage Committee, signs compact providing for minimum standards for women and minorities in industry. John G. Winant, governor of New Hampshire, stands behind her, with other New England states representatives. AP/World Wide Photos. Reproduced by permission.

The Public Contracts Act sought to end such practices by establishing standards for fair labor practices in government contracting. The provisions of the act generally prohibit the U.S. government from contracting to purchase goods or services from any private vendor who: (1) pays its employees less than the "prevailing minimum wage" as determined by the secretary of labor; (2) works its employees more than 40 hours per week without paying overtime; (3) employs boys younger than 16 years or girls younger than 18 years; (4) employs prison inmates; (5) fails to provide a safe and sanitary work environment; or (6) does not manufacture or regularly deal in the type of goods or services to be supplied.

If a vendor who has contracted to supply goods or services to the federal government fails to honor the Public Contracts Act's labor practice requirements, the government may cancel the contract and fulfill it elsewhere. In that event, the violating vendor is liable to reimburse the government for any costs incurred in consequence of switching vendors. The vendor may also be blacklisted from receiving any further government contracts for a period of three years.

Labor Standards Pre-Lochner: 1800–1905

From 1800 to 1840 many trade unions representing skilled craftsmen and artisans bargained successfully with employers

to obtain a 10-hour workday for their members. On 31 March 1840 President Martin Van Buren, persuaded by the National Trades Union, issued an executive order establishing a 10-hour workday for laborers and mechanics employed by the federal government.

During the 1860s eight-hour leagues, beginning in Boston, spread to numerous cities. The National Labor League, a combination of various trades advocating eight-hour days, met in Baltimore in 1867. Subsequently, eight states passed advisory eight-hour day legislation. On 25 June 1868 Congress enacted a National Eight-Hour Law applicable to federal government employees.

In 1874 Massachusetts enacted the first enforceable maximum hours law that covered private sector employees. The law set a maximum of 60 hours per week for female workers. Other states soon followed suit. In *Holden v. Hardy* (1898), the U.S. Supreme Court upheld a Utah state law that restricted the maximum daily working hours of men engaged in hazardous mining and smelting industries to eight. In *Muller v. Oregon* (1908), the Court upheld an Oregon law that restricted the maximum working hours of working women.

In the 1905 case of *Lochner v. New York*, however, the Supreme Court cast doubt on the constitutionality of state maximum hours laws by striking down a state law that restricted bakers to a 10-hour workday. The Court held that the restriction violated the "liberty of contract" purportedly protected against state government interference by the due process clause of the Fourteenth Amendment.

Lochner to the Public Contracts Act: 1905–1936

Before the twentieth century, the U.S. Congress never sought to regulate the wages or working conditions of private sector employees. By 1910, however, Congress felt increasing pressure to take action in response to a wave of fatal industrial accidents. Mining disasters claimed more than 3,000 lives in 1907 alone. Influenced by the progressive political activists of the era, Congress established several specialized administrative agencies, such as the Bureau of Mines (1910), to investigate industrial conditions and recommend legislative initiatives that might be needed to protect specific labor groups.

In 1912 Congress enacted the Federal Public Works Act, which required the inclusion of an eight-hour day clause in every U.S. government contract. In 1915 the La Follette Seaman's Act regulated safety, living conditions, working hours, payment terms, and food standards for maritime workers. The 1916 Adamson Act granted rail workers an eight-hour day and overtime pay. By 1920 the Supreme Court had upheld both the Seaman's Act and the Adamson Act as valid exercises of Congress's constitutional authority to regulate interstate commerce.

Between 1913 and 1918, 16 states had separately enacted minimum wage laws on behalf of women and minors, and Congress enacted a minimum wage law for women working in the District of Columbia. However, in *Adkins v. Children's Hospital* (1923), the U.S. Supreme Court found the D.C. women's minimum wage law to be unconstitutional. The Adkins decision, combined with the Court's earlier decision in *Lochner* striking down a state maximum hours law, diminished the prospects for successful implementation of any wide-reaching state or federal legislation governing labor standards.

In 1916 Congress enacted the Keating-Owen Act, the first national child labor law. By that time, almost every state had passed some form of child labor law, varying on issues of age, industries covered, and conditions. The national legislation established minimum acceptable child labor standards. The Supreme Court, however, ruled the Keating-Owen Act unconstitutional in *Hammer v. Dagenhart* (1918) on the grounds that congressional power to regulate interstate commerce did not extend to the conditions of labor. Congress responded to the *Dagenhart* decision by enacting the federal Child Labor Tax Law of 1919, which imposed a special excise tax on the profits of companies that employed children younger than 14 year in mills, workshops, or manufacture, or children younger than 16 in mines or quarries. The Supreme Court declared this law unconstitutional in 1922. Following these judicial reversals, efforts were mounted for a constitutional amendment to allow Congress to regulate child labor.

The onset of the Great Depression (1929–1940) exacerbated the harms caused by the abusive employment practices (e.g., substandard wages, excessive hours, unsafe working conditions, child and convict labor) that Congress and the state legislatures had been fighting since the beginning of the twentieth century. Although such employment practices had always been harmful to the welfare of workers who labored under them, their additional harms to the national economy were amplified by two interrelated economic problems that erupted during the Great Depression: widespread unemployment and diminished aggregate consumer demand. In particular, national unemployment rates rose when employers largely ignored President Herbert Hoover's call to reduce excessive work hours and "spread the work around." The unemployment problem was further exacerbated by employment of child and convict laborers as low-wage alternatives to the employment of adult men. At the same time, substandard wages harmed the national economy by preventing workers from earning income sufficient to stimulate consumer demand.

To combat these harms, without waiting for any constitutional amendment, President Franklin Roosevelt and his allies in Congress enacted a comprehensive package of "New Deal" legislation during the 1930s, including a series of statutes that extended wage and hour protection and to an ever-expanding portion of the American labor force. The Public Contracts Act was one in that series of statutes and an important precursor to the Fair Labor Standards Act of 1938 (FLSA).

The first important "New Deal" labor statute enacted during the Great Depression was the Davis-Bacon Act of 1931, which required employers who won U.S. government contracts to construct, maintain or repair public works to pay their construction workers the prevailing minimum wage at the work site, as determined by local union contracts. These workers were protected by eight-hour days but not by 40-hour weeks. In enacting the Davis-Bacon Act, Congress relied on the authority of *Atkin v. Kansas* (1903), in which the Supreme Court had sustained a state law that prohibited private vendors working to fulfill state government contracts from requiring employees to work more than eight hours per day. Five years later, the Public Contracts Act would expand the Davis-Bacon Act's protections to all workers whose employers held government contracts.

In 1932 Senator Hugo Black (D-AL) introduced the Black-Connery bill, which would have mandated a 30-hour week for most U.S. laborers. The bill passed the Senate but died in the House of Representatives when both organized labor and the president shifted their support to the National Industrial Recovery Act (NIRA). NIRA, enacted in 1933, was a comprehensive labor law that vested organized labor with an ongoing role in setting legally enforceable labor standards on an industry-by-industry basis. Under share-the-work provisions of these codes, maximum working hours per week were generally set at 35 to 40 hours and minimum wages at $12 to $15 per week. In *Schechter Poultry v. United States* (1935), however, the Supreme Court struck down the NIRA as unconstitutional.

In 1936 the American Federation of Labor (AFL) called for minimum wage legislation for women and children—but not for men. Many union men preferred to secure their wages through collective bargaining, maintaining that "the minimum tends to become the maximum." That same year however, the Supreme Court in *Morehead v. NY ex rel Tipaldo* undermined the momentum toward enactment of such legislation when it held that neither the states nor the federal government could enact a general minimum wage law applicable to private sector employees.

Public Contracts Debate

The restrictive decisions of the Supreme Court in *Schechter Poultry* (1935) and *Tipaldo* (1936) did not surprise President Roosevelt or his secretary of labor, Frances Perkins. Rather, in anticipation of the *Schechter* decision, Perkins suggested reenactment of a more limited bill that would codify the labor standards that had been promulgated under the National Recover Administration (NRA; created under the NIRA). This time, however, the law would apply only to employees of private vendors working to fulfill federal contracts. Perkins's proposal was adopted in a bill introduced by Senator David Walsh (D-MA). An amended Walsh bill, introduced in the House of Representatives in 1936 by Representative Arthur Daniel Healey (D-MA), was more narrowly drafted and did not rely on the NRA codes.

Two principal objections to the Public Contracts bill were raised during floor debate in the House of Representatives. First, Representative Earl C. Michener (R-MI), joined by Representative James W. Wadsworth Jr. (R-NY), claimed that the bill was a rear-guard effort to reinstate the NIRA, which had recently been declared unconstitutional. These legislators claimed that the two laws differed only in that the secretary of labor would determine industry codes under Public Contracts, whereas the NIRA had allowed each industry to determine its own code, subject to presidential approval. Representative Thomas Lindsay Blanton (D-TX) also characterized the Public Contracts bill as "another NRA in the miniature." Representative Clarence Hancock (R-NY) argued that the "meat in the coconut" of the Public Contracts bill was maximum hour and minimum wage legislation and that the bill would vest the secretary of labor with too much discretionary power to "unduly interfere with and harass businessmen." In Michener's words, "We want as few inspectors as possible from Washington swarming about the country, snooping into everybody's business and telling the honest community businessman just what he must do."

In defense of the bill, Representative William M. Citron (D-CT) countered that the bill did not regulate industry, interfere with business, or harass anyone. "It merely says that before anyone can make money out of the Government, or dip his fingers in the Government till, he shall maintain certain standards." Healey, the bill's sponsor, noted that it merely extended the prevailing minimum wage provisions of the 1931 Davis-Bacon Act to a wider class of employees of government contractors. He argued that the administration of the Public Contracts bill would be no more onerous than administration of Davis-Bacon, which had worked well.

Second, Wadsworth objected that 18 was too old a cut-off for defining child labor. Blanton claimed "the minimum age in the NRA bill was 16 years, and that was bad enough. . . . I have been the main breadwinner of a family ever since I was 10 years old, and I am proud of it." Representative John William Wright Patman (D-TX) argued that the precise age determination should be left up to the states.

Representative Walter (Clift) Chandler (D-TN) responded to these objections by proclaiming that "Boys and girls are not employed in factories because they are better workmen. It is because they are cheaper workmen and are paid less." Representative William P. Connery (D-MA) introduced an amendment to prohibit employment of males under 16 and females under 18. This amendment was adopted and remains in effect.

Despite these objections, Healey's amended Walsh bill passed Congress fairly easily. President Roosevelt signed the Public Contracts Act into law on 30 June 1936.

Administration of the Act

The Public Contracts Act vests the secretary of labor with power to make all rules, regulations, findings, and decisions under the act. Under a 1952 amendment, the secretary's actions are subject to judicial review.

The act had the immediate effect of smoothing a path for the broader FSLA legislation, although it eventually had an impact on the conditions of workers under employers with federal contracts. The FLSA became law in 1938 after the Supreme Court in *West Coast Hotel Co. v. Parrish* (1937) reversed its earlier decisions declaring state minimum wage laws unconstitutional. The FLSA extended maximum hours and minimum wages protections to most industrial workers employed in the private sector. It was sustained by the Supreme Court in *United States v. Darby Lumber Company* (1941).

After FLSA was enacted, the secretary of labor consolidated the administration of the Public Contracts Act into the Wage and Hour Division of the Employment Standards Bureau, which was created within the Department of Labor by the FLSA. Yet, despite the similarity of the FLSA provisions for hours, wages, and working conditions to those of the Public Contracts Act, organized labor supported retention of the Public Contracts Act as a separate law. The Public Contracts Act was seen as setting a national example of the government's commitment to fair labor practice, specifically in its own contracts.

Efforts to expand fair labor practices since the enactment of the Public Contracts Act have continued. Major post–New Deal landmarks include the Work Hours Act (1962), which ensures time-and-a-half pay for hours worked over 40; the Occupational Safety and Health Act (1970); and Executive Order 13126: Prohibition of Acquisition of Products Produced by Forced or Indentured Child Labor (12 June 1999). In Executive Order 13126, President Bill Clinton formally interpreted the Public Contracts Act to bar the U.S. government from contracting to purchase goods and services produced outside the United States from vendors whose employment practices in foreign jurisdictions do not conform to the act's standards. The FLSA, in contrast, does not govern the terms or conditions of any employment outside U.S. geographic territory.

Key Players

Healey, Arthur Daniel (1889–1948): Born in Somerville, Massachusetts, Healey was elected as a Democrat to the 73rd Congress and to the four succeeding congresses (1933–1942). He then accepted an appointment as judge of the United States District Court for Massachusetts. Healey served as a federal district judge until his death in 1948. Healey introduced the Public Contracts bill in the House of Representatives in 1936.

Perkins, Frances (1882–1965): U.S. secretary of labor from 1933 to 1945. Originally from Massachusetts, Perkins graduated from Mount Holyoke College and trained as a social worker. She worked in settlement houses in Chicago and Philadelphia and was involved in reform efforts after the 1911 Triangle Shirtwaist Factory fire in New York City. She was the first female state Industrial Commissioner under New York governor Franklin Roosevelt, who later appointed her secretary of labor, making her the first female cabinet member. She championed labor and progressive reforms throughout the New Deal and until her death in 1965.

Walsh, David Ignatius (1872–1947): Born in Worcester County, Massachusetts, Walsh was elected as a Democrat to the U.S. Senate and served from 1919 to 1925. After failing to be reelected in 1924, Walsh was elected to the U.S. Senate in 1926 to fill the vacancy caused by Henry Cabot Lodge's death. Walsh retook his seat on 6 December 1926, and was reelected in 1928, 1934, and 1940 for the term ending in January 1947. He died in Boston in 1947. Walsh introduced the Public Contracts bill in the Senate in 1935.

See also: *Davis-Bacon Act; Eight-hour Day Movement; Fair Labor Standards Act; Keating-Owen Act; La Follette Seamen's Act; Lochner v. New York; Muller v. Oregon; National Industrial Recovery Act; Occupational Safety and Health Act (OSHA).*

BIBLIOGRAPHY

Books
Bernstein, Irving. *A Caring Society: The New Deal, the Worker, and the Great Depression.* Boston: Houghton-Mifflin, 1985.

Periodicals
"The Determination of Prevailing Minimum Wages under the Public Contracts Act." *The Yale Law Journal,* 48, no. 610 (1939).
Fuller, Raymond G. "Child Labor and Federal Legislation." *American Review of Reviews,* 66 (July 1922).
Samuel, Howard D. "Troubled Passage: The Labour Movement and the Fair Labor Standards Act." *Monthly Labor Review,* 12 (1 December 2000).

Other
Congressional Record 10001–10026. 18 June 1936. Washington, D.C.
Zwick, Jim, ed. "The Campaign to End Child Labor." 1995–2002 [cited 10 October 2002]. <http://www.boondocksnet.com/>.

—Linda Dynan

Public Employee Fair Employment Act: *See* **Taylor Law.**

Eugene Victor Debs. The Library of Congress.

Pullman Strike

United States 1894

Synopsis

The Pullman strike—also known as the Chicago strike, Pullman boycott, Debs Revolution, or the American Railway Union strike—was the most dramatic U.S. labor challenge to the power of capital in the 1890s. A local strike that expanded into a national boycott and strike, it grew to include outright class warfare. A turning point for the U.S. labor movement, especially the American Federation of Labor, it was also an economic and political turning point for the United States as a whole. While labor suffered a resounding defeat, the strike lent impetus to both radical labor currents and more moderate social reformers and led directly to what has become known as the Progressive Era of 1900 to 1920.

Timeline

1876: General George Armstrong Custer and 264 soldiers are killed by the Sioux at the Little Big Horn River.

1880: Completion of Cologne Cathedral, begun 634 years earlier. With twin spires 515 feet (157 m) high, it is the tallest structure in the world and will remain so until 1889, when it is surpassed by the Eiffel Tower. (The previous record for the world's tallest structure lasted much longer—for about 4,430 years following the building of Cheops's Great Pyramid in c. 2550 B.C.)

1885: Belgium's King Leopold II becomes sovereign of the so-called Congo Free State, which he will rule for a

Striking workers sabotage railroad tracks during Pullman Strike. © Getty Images. Reproduced by permission.

quarter-century virtually as his own private property. The region in Africa, given the name of Zaire in the 1970s (and Congo in 1997), becomes the site of staggering atrocities, including forced labor and genocide, at the hands of Leopold's minions.

1891: French troops open fire on workers during a 1 May demonstration at Fourmies, where employees of the Sans Pareille factory are striking for an eight-hour workday. Nine people are killed—two of them children—and 60 more are injured.

1894: French army captain Alfred Dreyfus, a Jew, is convicted of treason. Dreyfus will later be cleared of all charges, but the Dreyfus case illustrates—and exacerbates—the increasingly virulent anti-Semitism that pervades France.

1895: German physicist Wilhelm Roentgen discovers X-rays.

1895: Brothers Auguste and Louis Lumière show the world's first motion picture—*Workers Leaving the Lumière Factory*—at a café in Paris.

1895: Guglielmo Marconi pioneers wireless telegraphy, which in the next three decades will make possible the use of radio waves for commercial broadcasts and other applications.

1895: German engineer Rudolf Diesel invents an engine capable of operating on a type of petroleum less highly refined, and therefore less costly, than gasoline.

1898: Marie and Pierre Curie discover the radioactive elements radium and polonium.

1901: U.S. President William McKinley is assassinated by Leon Czolgosz, an anarchist. Vice President Theodore Roosevelt becomes president.

1905: In the industrial Ruhr region in Germany, 200,000 miners go on strike.

Event and Its Context

The Pullman strike in Chicago, Illinois, was part of a nationwide crisis, generated by the social turbulence of the industrialization process that had been dramatically transforming the United States since the end of the Civil War. The rail strike of 1877 and the eight-hour uprising of 1886, culminating in the violence of the Haymarket affair in Chicago, had ended in defeats for the working class. However, these incidents were harbingers of deeper, better-organized, and more sustained challenges to the new industrial order that emerged in the final decade of the nineteenth century.

Intensifying Confrontation

The economic depression of the1890s (following similar downturns in the 1870s and 1880s) intensified the rise of radical populism among insurgent small farmers and many urban workers, while at the same time increasingly pushing industrialists to centralize and rationalize production to restore and enhance profit margins. In response, there was a growing trend among skilled workers to forge alliances with less skilled workers in more inclusive organizations. Industrial unions made their appearance among certain sectors of the working class: miners, garment workers, and railway workers, for example.

In the face of the growing power of business interests that many saw as profiteering "robber barons," increasing numbers of organized workers turned to more militant forms of collective action. For example, in 1877 Eugene V. Debs— then a prominent member of the Brotherhood of Locomotive Firemen—agreed with other railway labor leaders that the railroad corporation was "the architect of progress" and that the 1877 strikes represented "anarchy and revolution" to be rejected by the railway brotherhoods. By 1893, however, he was calling for "all railway employees to meet upon common ground and there unite forces for the protection of all" through the American Railway Union (ARU). He added that "such an army would be impregnable" to the assaults of the corporations that "trample on the divine declaration 'that all men are created equal.'" He had also come to believe that "the strike is the weapon of the oppressed, of men capable of appreciating justice and having the courage to resist wrong and contend for principle."

Debs's shifting outlook reflects a broader radicalization of the American working class. After completing an extensive speaking tour through the United States in 1887, Eleanor Marx, the daughter of Karl Marx, commented on the prevalence of "unconscious socialism" among workers and others she encountered. She called the workers "grievously misled by capitalist papers and capitalist economists and preachers" about what socialism actually means, and therefore hostile to it, but in fact embracing its essential ideas and values. "[Many] persons, finding . . . that Socialism does not mean equal division of property, nor application of dynamite to capitalists, nor anarchy, have . . . declared, 'Well, if that is Socialism we are Socialists.'"

While relatively few American workers saw themselves as socialists, a significant number, particularly among organized workers, embraced a popular ideology of labor radicalism (what some historians have dubbed "producerism"). This radicalism blended the labor theory of value ("labor creates all wealth") and inclusive labor solidarity ("an injury to one is an injury to all") with a vision of American society being transformed into a new order of economic justice and social democracy. Outside of the working class, a growing number of intellectual, political,

and cultural figures—including writer Henry Demarest Lloyd, social worker Jane Addams, lawyer Clarence Darrow, Governor John Peter Altgeld of Illinois, and others—were challenging the dominant social and economic orthodoxies of laissez-faire capitalism and social Darwinism.

Local Strike

In the early spring of 1894, after winning an 18-day strike against the Great Northern Railroad, the ARU found itself with 150,000 members—60,000 more than all the railroad brotherhoods put together, and only 25,000 fewer than the combined unions of the American Federation of Labor (AFL). While this dynamic new force inspired hostility from leaders of the old craft brotherhoods and uneasiness on the part of AFL president Samuel Gompers, the organization was a magnet for the employees of the Pullman Company involved in an escalating dispute with their employer.

Pullman was a 600-acre "model town" of roughly 12,000 residents founded in 1880 by luxury sleeping car manufacturer George Pullman. Annexed by the city of Chicago in 1889, in 1894 it housed over 3,000 Pullman Company wage earners, as well as a large number of laid-off Pullman workers. The company owned every inch of property in Pullman, including the town's only church. An experiment in labor and public relations, the town's brick construction, careful design, order, cleanliness, amenities, and lack of saloons both advertised the Pullman Palace Car Company and represented a bold, innovative attempt to preempt class conflict.

During the depression of 1893, the utopian town proved spectacularly unsustainable. Pullman residents had long been dissatisfied with Pullman's paternalism, which many characterized as industrial feudalism. One resident is reported to have stated that "we are born in a Pullman house, fed from the Pullman shop, taught in a Pullman school, catechized in the Pullman church, and when we die we shall be buried in the Pullman cemetery and go to the Pullman hell." Likewise, employees had standing grievances against corrupt, incompetent, and arbitrary foremen. By April 1894 the ARU had enlisted about 4,000 members in Pullman.

During the winter of 1893–1894 the company had slashed wages by an average of 25 percent. The company also reduced commercial rents paid by shopkeepers; yet, the town's retail prices and high residential rents remained unchanged. Moreover, management accepted no cuts in salary or personnel, and the company did not reduce dividends paid to investors. On 7 and 9 May committees of Pullman workers presented their demands to Pullman management: either lower rents or return to the wage levels of May 1893.

The company responded by firing three local union leaders, so Pullman workers voted to strike on 10 May 1894. The ARU, which was holding its first annual convention in Chicago 9–26 June, received appeals for help. Debs, fearing that the ARU had not developed sufficient organization or alliances for a major confrontation, urged caution. On 21 June, nevertheless, moved by the testimony of "girls' union" president Jennie Curtis, the ARU determined to stop handling Pullman cars on 26 June unless the company agreed to arbitration. Likewise, the powerful Chicago Trades and Labor Assembly, itself representing 150,000 members, pledged its support, though setting its own strike date of 11 July in order to give Pullman an opportunity to accept arbitration.

Instead of replying to the ARU, the company consulted with the General Managers Association (GMA). The association, which represented at least 24 railroads terminating in or passing through Chicago, vowed to fire and replace any worker who participated in the ARU boycott of Pullman cars. It also worked single-mindedly to secure government support, particularly that of President Grover Cleveland, in the campaign to break the strike.

A Nationwide Strike

This boycott changed the struggle from a local dispute into what Debs called "a contest between the producing classes and the money power of the country." Starting on 26 June, the boycott of Pullman cars led immediately to a nationwide strike against the GMA, as ARU locals walked off the job whenever a switchman was fired for boycotting a Pullman car.

By the end of June, most of the nation's train traffic—and virtually all of it to the west of Chicago—had been shut down. In some cases crowds of 2,000 or more gathered to encourage or require switchmen to disengage Pullman trains. Approximately 260,000 railroad workers were involved in the strike, almost half of them not affiliated with the ARU, and the boycott spread to 26 states, idling about 500,000 workers from California to Maine.

The association responded cunningly, reassigning mail cars to trains containing Pullman cars in order to create a rationale for federal intervention. The GMA also responded brutally, assembling a private army to subdue the strikers. Over 1,000 unsupervised, newly deputized U.S. marshals employed and armed by the railroads assumed duty on 30 June—in some cases firing, with fatal consequences, into unarmed crowds.

Class War

On 2 July U.S. attorney general Richard Olney obtained an indictment against the strikers under the Sherman Antitrust Act of 1890. (This was the first time the Sherman Act, supposedly a curb on corporate monopolies, had been applied.) Simultaneously, 2,000 federal troops were dispatched to Chicago by order of President Cleveland. Debs and three other ARU officials were arrested, charged with interrupting the mails and with various vague "conspiracy" charges, and then released under $10,000 bail.

The arrival of troops in Chicago and the imprisonment of the principal officers of the ARU escalated the level of destruction and violence associated with the strike. Debs's dream of peaceful, nonprovocative action—a reality in Pullman, which reported no property destruction whatsoever—became a nightmare of riot and reprisal. Trains were overturned and fires were set. Chicago, specifically the Blue Island junction, remained the epicenter of the conflict: roughly 14,000 armed men maintained "order" for the railroads, ransacking union offices, arresting hundreds of strikers and union sympathizers, and killing dozens. No one was indicted for any of these murders, and strikers and their allies suffered all reported fatalities. The vast American West was an equally significant battleground, and it took 12,000 federal troops—roughly half of the U.S. standing army—to repress the strike.

The strike had earned significant, though far from unanimous, labor solidarity and community support. Some local and national representatives of the middle class also supported the strikers. Attorney Clarence Darrow represented the ARU, while a young Methodist minister, William Carwardine, served as an influential strike leader in Pullman. The populist senator from Kansas, William A. Peffer, denounced Pullman from the floor of the U.S. Senate. The Chicago Civic Association, led by social worker Jane Addams, offered to mediate; Debs was receptive, but the Pullman Company responded that "there is nothing to arbitrate." Chicago mayor John Hopkins supported the strikers materially as well as politically. Most appreciated by the strikers, Illinois governor Peter Altgeld strenuously opposed the introduction of federal troops, insisting in a 5 July telegram to President Cleveland that "so very little actual violence has been committed."

Public sympathy for the strike, initially strong, diminished over the course of the boycott. Consumers were inconvenienced by the disruption of transportation and the resulting rise in the price of commodities, especially perishable food. As the Pullman conflict grew to national proportions, a shift in press coverage (partly reflecting the political and economic differences between local and national opinion making) influenced public perceptions as well. Initially scornful of the company's refusal to negotiate and of the GMA's dependence on a reportedly lawless and drunken private army of deputy marshals, journalists tended to become more critical of "King Debs" and the ARU as the disruption continued.

Defeat and Legacy

Force of arms got the trains running again by 9 July—a situation not reversed by the one-day Chicago general strike of 11 July. Debs urgently reached out to the AFL for assistance. Gompers and his colleagues backed away, saluting the ARU's "impulsive, vigorous protest against the gathering, growing forces of plutocratic power and corporation rule," but considering it "folly" to join the ARU in being destroyed. The AFL committed only $1,000 to Debs's defense and even refused to act as a liaison between the ARU and the GMA.

On 17 July, Debs and other ARU officers were arrested again, this time for contempt of court. (Finally sentenced in January 1895, they served six months.) Most troops were withdrawn from the rail lines by 19 July. On 2 August the Pullman works reopened. Returning workers were forced to sign an oath repudiating the ARU, and many were blacklisted. Though never officially ended, the strike's last gasps came as the United States celebrated its first national Labor Day, which was signed into law by a president anxious to counteract the taint of being a strikebreaker.

The Pullman strike was a blow from which the ARU never recovered. Yet the strike also discredited Pullman's attempt to merge urban planning and labor relations, and it split the Democratic Party (with such key figures as Cleveland and Altgeld at loggerheads), resulting in the party's shift to radical populism in 1896.

Under the impact of the defeat of labor radicalism and industrial unionism in 1894—with the Pullman defeat as well as the bituminous miner's strike that nearly destroyed the United Mine Workers of America—labor's mainstream shifted in a very different direction from Debs's open embrace of socialism. Gompers accelerated his turn away from labor radicalism. He asserted that the AFL should focus on building strong craft unions with a "pure and simple" orientation that explicitly accepted capitalism and further maintained that "responsible" labor leaders should forge alliances with "liberal-minded" businessmen.

The Pullman strike contributed to the rise of a major new force in American life: the progressivism that flourished in the next two decades. The trajectory of writer and social critic Henry Demarest Lloyd encapsulated the shift in thought. Initially hopeful over the prospects of the emergence of a mass socialist workers' movement in the 1890s (to be led by Gompers), Lloyd was bitterly disappointed by the workers' defeat and, with many other reformers, concluded that a less radical, cross-class, urban "progressivism" held more promise for the country. In response to the arbitrary powers of employers and judges, as well as to the unpredictable behavior of aggrieved workers, progressives pursued policies to make government power a neutral intermediary in the conflict between the classes.

Perhaps the most enduring legacy of the strike was the seeming miracle of a powerful working-class solidarity that shook the structures of power. Debs affirmed, "This act will shine forth in increasing splendor long after the dollar worshipers have mingled with the dust of oblivion."

Key Players

Curtis, Jennie (*ca.* 1875–*ca.* 1927): Played a central role in the organization of workers at Pullman, especially women. Through her consultation with Debs, her speech to the ARU convention, and perhaps also her legendary dance with Chicago mayor Hopkins at a strike-support fundraiser, Curtis stands out as a significant leader of the early phases of the strike. She was interviewed by the U.S. Strike Commission on 16 August 1894.

Debs, Eugene Victor (1855–1926): Active in the Brotherhood of Locomotive Firemen and by 1880 the editor of its national journal. By the early 1890s Debs had become convinced of the necessity of a more industrial unionism and helped to form the American Railway Union (ARU). After its destruction in the Pullman strike, and after imprisonment for his role in that strike, Debs became a prominent socialist, helping to form the Socialist Party of America in 1901 and running five times as the socialist candidate for president of the United States. He helped to form the Industrial Workers of the World, although he also favored supporting AFL unions. He was imprisoned again for his opposition to U.S. involvement in World War I.

Gompers, Samuel (1850–1924): Prominent in the Cigar Makers Union, Gompers became the long-time (1886–1924)

and increasingly conservative president of the American Federation of Labor, a spokesman for the "pure and simple union" orientation initially developed by his colleague Adolph Strasser. In his later years he became an outright opponent of socialism, though he never lost his admiration for Karl Marx, whose outlook he viewed as consistent with his own "pure and simple" unionism.

See also: *American Federation of Labor; Eight-hour Day Movement; Haymarket Riot; Panic of 1893; Railroad Strike of 1877; Sherman Antitrust Act.*

BIBLIOGRAPHY

Books

Boyer, Richard O., and Herbert M. Morais. *Labor's Untold Story.* New York: United Electrical, Radio, & Machine Workers of America, 1975.

Brecher, Jeremy. *Strike!* Boston, MA: South End Press, 1997.

Carwardine, William H. *The Pullman Strike.* Chicago, IL: Charles H. Kerr & Company, for the Illinois Labor History Society, 1971.

Foner, Philip S. *History of the Labor Movement in the United States.* Vol. 2: *From the Founding of the American Federation of Labor to the Emergence of American Imperialism.* New York: International Publishers, 1988.

Lindsey, Almont. *The Pullman Strike: The Story of a Unique Experiment and of a Great Labor Upheaval.* Chicago, IL: University of Chicago Press, 1942.

Manning, Thomas G., ed. *The Chicago Strike of 1894: Industrial Labor in the Nineteenth Century.* New York: Henry Holt and Company, 1960.

Marx, Eleanor, and Edward Aveling. *The Working-Class Movement in America,* edited by Paul Le Blanc. Amherst, NY: Humanity Books, 2000.

Salvatore, Nick. *Eugene V. Debs: Citizen and Socialist.* Urbana, IL: University of Illinois Press, 1982.

Schneirov, Richard, Shelton Stromquist, and Nick Salvatore, eds. *The Pullman Strike and the Crisis of the 1890s: Essays on Labor and Politics.* Urbana, IL: University of Illinois Press, 1999.

Stromquist, Shelton. *A Generation of Boomers: The Pattern of Railroad Labor Conflict in Nineteenth-Century America.* Urbana, IL: University of Illinois Press, 1987.

Warne, Colston E., ed. *The Pullman Boycott of 1894 and the Problem of Federal Intervention.* Boston, MA: D.C. Heath and Company, 1955.

—Paul Le Blanc/Joel Woller

R

Railroad Strike of 1877

United States 1877

Synopsis

In 1877 an explosion of working-class protest rocked the United States. Initiated as a more or less spontaneous railway workers strike, it became generalized into a nationwide crescendo of street protests and pitched battles. Millions of dollars of property was destroyed, more than a hundred lives were lost, with many more injuries. Pittsburgh, Pennsylvania, was at the explosive center of this historic upsurge, but similar confrontations and struggles wracked cities throughout the eastern and midwestern portions of the country. The uprising was systematically repressed but helped to generate future labor struggles.

Timeline

1857: In its Dred Scott decision, the U.S. Supreme Court rules that a slave is not a citizen.

1862: Major Civil War battles include Shiloh, Second Bull Run (Manassas), and Antietam. During the latter battle, 17 September is the bloodiest day in American history, with nearly 5,000 dead, and more than 20,000 wounded.

1867: Establishment of the Dominion of Canada.

1870: Beginning of Franco-Prussian War. German troops sweep over France, Napoleon III is dethroned, and France's Second Empire gives way to the Third Republic.

1877: In the face of uncertain results from the popular vote in the presidential election of 1876, the U.S. Electoral Commission awards the presidency to Rutherford B. Hayes despite a slight popular majority for his opponent, Samuel J. Tilden. The election of 1876 will remain the most controversial in American history for the next 124 years, until overshadowed by the race between George W. Bush and Al Gore in 2000.

1877: In part as a quid pro quo demanded by southern legislators in return for their support of the Republican Hayes over the Democrat Tilden, the new president agrees to end the period of martial law in the South known as Reconstruction.

1877: Surrender of Nez Perce leader Chief Joseph to federal troops.

1877: Great Britain's Queen Victoria is proclaimed the empress of India.

1877: Debut of Peter Ilych Tchaikovsky's ballet *Swan Lake*.

1879: Thomas Edison invents the incandescent electric light.

1883: Brooklyn Bridge completed.

1887: Heinrich Hertz proves the existence of electromagnetic waves, which are propagated at the speed of light.

Event and Its Context

In the era of dramatic industrialization following the Civil War, the most powerful of the big business corporations were the railroad companies. During the economic depression that had begun in 1873, the companies reduced the pay of railroad workers by 10 percent. In 1877 they announced another 10 percent reduction in the workers' pay, and also insisted that railroad employees use company hotels when away from home, which meant a further reduction in real wages. Workforce reductions meant unemployment for some and intensified labor for those remaining. This generated fierce resentment among rail workers and their families, and also within the laboring population generally.

Eruption

In Allegheny City (now Pittsburgh's north side), workers held meetings in early June to organize a national Trainmen's Union that was designed to include all railway workers and to organize a general rail strike for 27 June. Information provided by company spies resulted in the firing of many union members, and the strike was cancelled, but the anger and discontent deepened. On 16 July a spontaneous strike erupted in Martinsburg, West Virginia, and quickly spread to cities including St. Louis, Chicago, New York City, and Baltimore; it hit Pittsburgh on 19 July.

Pittsburgh Massacre

Despite rising passions, the Pittsburgh strikers sought to maintain a peaceful but effective work stoppage that halted all rail traffic. Rallies and meetings explained their goals to a largely approving public. Railroad officials and state authorities, however, soon pushed events onto a different track.

State militia units from Philadelphia were ordered to Pittsburgh. (Militia units from Pittsburgh were deemed unreliable because they sympathized with the strikers.) On 21 July 600 troops arrived from Philadelphia. Led by Superintendent Robert Pitcairn of the Pennsylvania Railroad and a posse of constables with arrest warrants for the strike leaders, they found themselves confronted by crowds of men, women, and children. The crowds, loudly protesting the troops' presence and expressing support for the strikers, sought to prevent military action. The militiamen responded with a bayonet charge that resulted in injuries and provoked a hail of rocks from some sections of those assembled. The troops opened fire on the unarmed crowd, scattering them and leaving at least 20 dead (including one woman and three small children) and 29 wounded.

As word of the massacre spread, thousands of workers rushed to the scene, many of them armed. The militia retreated into the roundhouse and considered using Gatling guns against the now violent crowds, but decided at the last minute that such a move would be unwise. As it was, the enraged crowds broke every window in the roundhouse and some went on to set fire to the rail yards. The fire destroyed 39 buildings of the Pennsyl-

Railroad strike, Pittsburgh, Pennsylvania, 1877. © Getty Images. Reproduced by permission.

vania Railroad, 104 engines, 46 passenger cars, and over 1,200 freight cars. All buildings on Penn and Liberty Avenues from Union Depot to 28th Street were consumed. It is estimated that more than $4 million in damage was done.

From Allegheny City, the Trainmen's Union sought to maintain order, working to maintain an effective strike on a nonviolent basis. Union leader Robert Ammon—who had worked as a brakeman—coordinated protection of remaining company property and even oversaw the conduct of passenger traffic on the Pennsylvania Railroad for a few days. In the same period, other workers in the Pittsburgh area, including thousands of iron and steel workers and coal miners, were inspired to go out on strike. Workers from other cities and towns in Pennsylvania joined in the strikes or in rallies and meetings supporting the strike.

On 26 July, however, regular troops of the U.S. Army joined with state militia units to take control of the city and re-open all railroad operations in Pittsburgh and Allegheny City. This was the first time in U.S. history that federal troops were utilized against strikers and labor protests. In western Pennsylvania a military force of 10,000 was deployed to secure the re-opening of rail service from the Pittsburgh area to Harrisburg.

A National Working-Class Uprising

Dozens of cities throughout the Northeast and Midwest experienced some version of these confrontations and conflicts. Many newspapers and magazines interpreted the upsurge along the lines articulated by Allan Pinkerton, head of the Pinkerton Detective Agency, an "expert" who made a career of working with employers and the government to undermine and destroy labor organizations. Pinkerton saw it all as a case of "ignorant workingmen being gulled and deceived" into rebellion by "communistic scoundrels who in stealth and secret continue their conspiracies against civilization."

Pointing to the influence of the International Workingmen's Association (the First International) headed by Karl Marx, the detective chieftain asserted that "all manner of labor unions and leagues have been forming [that were] animated by the vicious dictation" of the International and that "no manufacturing town, nor any city, has escaped this baleful influence." Pinkerton further pointed out that because of worsening economic conditions, increasing numbers of workers "have become discontented and embittered," and in 1877 "by these dangerous communistic leaders were made to believe that the proper time for action had come." He pointed to the example of Chicago, where "the rantings of a young American communist named Parsons" had precipitated violent riots.

In fact, the role of Albert Parsons and other members of the socialist Workingmen's Party of the United States (WPUS) in the Chicago strike and street battles of 23–27 July were almost the opposite of that attributed to them by Pinkerton. Believing that the time was ripe not for revolution but for such things as trade unions, increased wages, socialist election campaigns, and struggles for an eight-hour workday, Parsons and his comrades eloquently shared this message with the 15,000 workers who attended a WPUS rally on 21 July. Two days later, the socialists of Chicago found that they could exercise little control over the masses of workers and enraged crowds that were engaged in pitched battles with the police. Urging moderation, they proved irrelevant to the violence swirling past them.

The only place where the WPUS was consistently in the leadership of the struggle was in St. Louis during the events of 23–28 July. Such WPUS leaders as Albert Currlin and Laurence Gronlund formed and served on a strike executive committee that helped to channel the upsurge into a nonviolent and powerfully effective general strike. This action was punctuated by impressive and spirited mass demonstrations and rallies and characterized by the executive committee functioning with a quasigovernmental authority to maintain order while advancing the workers' demands. The mingling of African American and white workers was disconcerting for some, however, and because of racist anxieties the mass demonstrations were discontinued. Nor did the strike leaders have a clear program for victory. Violent assaults by police and troops, followed by mass arrests, brought an end to what had been dubbed the "St. Louis Commune."

More typical were the events of 19–16 July in Baltimore, where the deployment of militia to break the strike generated a furious response from thousands of indignant working people. Jeers and stones from the crowds were matched by bullets from the troops. "The streets were quickly deserted and the detachment passed by," wrote an eyewitness reporter of the *Baltimore Sun*, "still firing random shots over their shoulders with apparent recklessness." The dead and wounded were pulled into nearby saloons and drugstores, where the floors soon "looked like a butcher's pen." Riots and arson soon overshadowed the efforts of the strike committee, which was swept aside with scorn as soon as federal troops arrived to restore order.

Insurgent crowds that included women, children, and adolescent boys surged through many cities but only a substantial minority of railroad workers participated in the rioting. Among the participants were skilled and unskilled workers, white-collar employees, professionals, and small proprietors; there was also significant ethnic and racial diversity. The crowds in these cities were responding in part to the damage done to them by unbridled industrialization and economic hard times, and many were also mobilizing against the destructive impact that the railroad companies were having on their lives.

The railroad companies were the most powerful of the big business corporations that were coming to dominate the rapidly industrializing economy. They were in the forefront of a process that was degrading not only the lives of railroad workers, but also the communities and the environments of working-class America. A major factor in the explosion was the long-

standing resentment of urban residents over the railroad's impact on urban space. Streets lined with retail stores, schools, churches, saloons, and homes were impacted by the filth and noise and sometimes danger that came with frequent train traffic. The angry crowds were, in part, engaging in community uprisings in defense of their streets and neighborhoods.

In all of this, some gains were made but—in the opinion of Friedrich Sorge, the old warhorse of the First International with extensive labor contacts—two severe limitations turned potential victories into defeat. First was the "cowardice" of railway workers in New York City and New England, "whose participation would have made the strike undefeatable." Second, the workers lacked the organization to capitalize on their many victories. The backlash of the employers, who could count on powerful support by the state and national governments, was consequently triumphant.

Legacy

The strikes certainly had global impact. Karl Marx commented in London to his friend Frederick Engels that although these early efforts would be suppressed, they might indeed "form the point of origin" of a true workers' party. Marx further noted that President Rutherford B. Hayes' policies would make African Americans and the dissatisfied farmers of the West into allies of the organizing workers. Yet this fusion of rebellious forces did not take place: for the most part, African Americans and whites did not unite, and the farmers' who organized in the Grange (which soon culminated in the massive populist rebellion) remained separate from the fleeting wave of labor party efforts that swept much of the country from the late 1870s to the late 1880s.

In fact, the utter defeat of the workers through the use of U.S. troops was a key aspect of the triumph of American capitalism. This becomes clear when it is seen in the larger context of the period. Troops had just been withdrawn from the South as part of the dismantling of Reconstruction, which involved an understanding that the reestablishment of white power regimes in that region (at the expense of African American rights) would harmonize with a continuation of industrial development policies that had been advanced by the Republican Party through the 1860s and early 1870s.

Troops were deployed to the West to subdue various Native American peoples who were resisting the invasion and conquest of their homeland by railroads and white settlers. The troops were also deployed, of course, in the cities that had been rocked by working-class uprisings. In less than two decades troops would be deployed overseas when the United States (which was, by the 1890s, already the world's foremost manufacturing nation) moved to become a major world power, particularly in Latin America and Asia, beginning with the Spanish-American War.

The 1877 events highlighted the inability of local and state militia units to guarantee the law and order required for a healthy business climate in the United States. The need to create a more effective basis for the operation of troops in such circumstances resulted in the construction of a substantial number of strong armories in larger U.S. cities. In addition, the courts and state legislatures in much of the country increasingly equated labor organizing with criminal conspiracy, which initiated a wave of rulings and laws directed against labor. Although the workers' defeat of 1877 was the most dramatic indication during the Gilded Age of the power of the rising big businesses over the working class, the uprising itself was immensely powerful and helped to inspire future struggles.

Key Players

Ammon, Robert A. (1852–1915): College-educated son of a well-to-do insurance man, Ammon traveled around the country (including serving a stint in the U.S. Cavalry) before the age of 21. With a wife and child, he got a job as a railroad brakeman in 1876, but was fired in 1877 for his role in organizing the Trainmen's Union. During the 1877 strike he sought to protect company property and maintain order but was arrested and jailed when the strike was broken. After his release he moved to California and was briefly involved in anti-Chinese activity of that state's labor movement. In 1887 he moved to New York City, went into business and law, and became a prosperous figure on Wall Street.

Gronlund, Laurence (1846–1899): Under the name of Peter Lofgreen, Danish-born Gronlund (who worked at various times as a teacher, a clerk, and a journalist) was a leader of the St. Louis WPUS. He was later author of the first substantial popularization of Marxist ideas in the U.S., the 1884 classic *The Cooperative Commonwealth*. After drifting out of the SLP, he became a leading activist in the Nationalist Clubs initiated by Edward Bellamy, author of the best-selling utopian novel *Looking Backward*.

Parsons, Albert (1848–1887): Parsons was a Confederate war veteran in Texas who fell in love with and married a woman of color (Lucy Gonzales, at least partly African American, perhaps also Indian and Mexican). Parsons subsequently became a radical Republican; with the collapse of Reconstruction in Texas, he fled with his wife to Chicago, where they both become active in radical labor activities. Active in the Typographical Workers Union, he was blacklisted after 1877 when he became a full-time labor and socialist activist. Editor of the revolutionary paper *The Alarm* in the 1880s, and a leader of the radical wing of the eight-hour movement, he was victimized as one of the Haymarket martyrs and executed in 1887.

See also: *Panic of 1873; Workingmen's Party of the United States.*

BIBLIOGRAPHY

Books

Bruce, Robert V. *1877: Year of Violence*. Indianapolis: Bobbs Merril, 1959.

Burbank, David T. *Reign of the Rabble: The St. Louis General Strike of 1877*. New York: Augustus M. Kelley, 1966.

Commons, John R., and Associates. *History of Labor in the United States*, Vol. II. New York: Macmillan, 1918.

Foner, Philip S. *The Great Labor Uprising of 1877*. New York: Monad Press, 1977.

Gompers, Samuel. *Seventy Years of Life and Labor*. New York: E. P. Dutton, 1925.

Hacker, Louis M. *The Triumph of American Capitalism*. New York: Columbia University Press, 1947.

Pinkerton, Allan. *Strikers, Communists, Tramps, and Detectives*. New York: G. W. Dillingham and Co., 1878.

Sorge, Friedrich A. *Labor Movement in the United States*. Edited by Philip S. Foner and Brewster Chamberlin. Westport, CT: Greenwood Press, 1977.

Stowell, David O. *Streets, Railroads, and the Great Strike of 1877*. Chicago and London: University of Chicago Press, 1999.

—Paul Le Blanc

Railway Labor Act

United States 1926

Synopsis

The Railway Labor Act (RLA) of 1926 was the most important piece of labor legislation "and the most significant attempt by the federal government to foster and regulate collective bargaining" prior to the New Deal. The RLA was the result of many years of effort to find a labor relations policy for U.S. railroads that would minimize labor unrest and avoid potentially crippling blockages of the nation's main arteries of transportation and commerce. The law provided for the creation of a mediation apparatus and empowered the president of the United States to seek a cooling-off period for parties to a railroad labor dispute. The act encouraged collective bargaining and forbade employers from interfering in workers' selection of their representatives. Subsequent judicial interpretations prevented employers from forcing workers to bargain through company-dominated unions, an important legal breakthrough that presaged elements of New Deal labor policy. In later years the RLA was revised and extended to cover the U.S. air transport system as well. While the freedom to strike was circumscribed by the RLA's provisions, unions gained security under its regulatory regime, and national rail strikes of the sort that periodically erupted during the half century prior to the RLA's enactment did not recur after 1926.

Timeline

1911: In China, revolutionary forces led by Sun Yat-sen bring an end to more than 2,100 years of imperial rule.

1917: On both the Western Front and in the Middle East, the tide of the war begins to turn against the Central Powers. The arrival of U.S. troops, led by General Pershing, in France in June greatly boosts morale and reinforces exhausted Allied forces. Meanwhile, Great Britain scores two major victories against the Ottoman Empire as T.

E. Lawrence leads an Arab revolt in Baghdad in March, and troops under Field Marshal Edmund Allenby take Jerusalem in December.

1922: Inspired by the Bolsheviks' example of imposing revolution by means of a coup, Benito Mussolini leads his blackshirts in an October "March on Rome," and forms a new fascist government.

1924: V. I. Lenin dies, and thus begins a struggle for succession from which Josef Stalin will emerge five years later as the undisputed leader of the Communist Party, and of the Soviet Union.

1927: Stalin arranges to have Trotsky expelled from the Communist Party.

1927: Charles A. Lindbergh makes the first successful solo nonstop flight across the Atlantic and becomes an international hero.

1927: American inventor Philo T. Farnsworth demonstrates a working model of the television, and Belgian astronomer Georges Lemaître proposes the Big Bang Theory.

1927: *The Jazz Singer,* starring Al Jolson, is the first major motion picture with sound. Within a few years, silent movies will become a thing of the past.

1927: Babe Ruth hits 60 home runs, establishing a record that will stand until 1961.

1930: Naval disarmament treaty signed by the United States, Great Britain, France, Italy, and Japan.

1932: When Ukrainians refuse to surrender their grain to his commissars, Stalin seals off supplies to the region, creating a manmade famine that will produce a greater death toll than the entirety of World War I.

1937: Japan attacks China, and annexes most of that nation's coastal areas.

Event and Its Context

American Railway Labor Policy before 1926

Four factors conspired to make railroads a uniquely fruitful laboratory for American labor law in the era before the New Deal. Railroads occupied a unique place in the American economy in the pre-depression era. Most of the nation's market commerce depended upon railroads. Assurance of a maximum degree of labor stability on rail lines was therefore deemed important by law makers. Second, the reach of most railroads across state lines made them subject to federal regulation in a way that many other businesses of their era were not. Even when the U.S. Supreme Court read the commerce clause of the Constitution most narrowly, "as in exempting manufacturing from federal regulation as it did through the 1895 *United States v. E.C. Knight* decision," the courts always recognized the federal government's power to regulate railways. Third, railroad workers were among the first employees of interstate corporations to organize unions. Locomotive engineers formed their union in 1863. Conductors followed in 1868, firemen in 1876, and trainmen in 1883. The railroad brotherhoods were among the strongest unions in the United States in the late nineteenth

Calvin Coolidge. The Library of Congress.

and early twentieth centuries. Finally, the intense competition that characterized the industry, as well as the degree to which its fortunes were hostage to fluctuations in the health of the larger economy, meant that railroad workers often found their work threatened by instability or erosion of work standards. Railroad workers fought hard to defend themselves against such threats. For example, in 1877 a massive strike that eventually spread to a dozen states erupted when employees of the Baltimore and Ohio railroad protested a wage cut imposed upon them in the midst of a depressed economy. Federal troops were mobilized in Pittsburgh, Pennsylvania, and other cities in order to quell the strike.

Such conditions set the stage for federal regulation of railway labor relations. The first effort to provide such regulation came in 1888 with the passage of the Arbitration Act. This act empowered the president to appoint investigatory boards in cases of work stoppages and encouraged voluntary arbitration between the parties to a labor dispute, yet it failed to forestall labor–management conflict on the railways. Nothing illustrated this failure more clearly than the massive Pullman Boycott of 1894, in which members of the American Railway Union (ARU) refused to handle trains that pulled Pullman sleeping cars until the Pullman Company dealt fairly with its employees. As the boycott shut down rail traffic across wide swaths of the nation, President Grover Cleveland established an investigatory board. Voluntary arbitration did not settle the strike, however; federal intervention did. Troops were again mobilized to facilitate strike-breaking, and Attorney General Richard Olney won

Wright v. Universal Maritime Service Corp., et al. (1998): Collective-Bargaining Agreements and the Americans with Disabilities Act

By 1998, more than seven decades after the Railway Labor Act, collective-bargaining agreements (CBAs) prevailed in a number of industries. Such an agreement had been reached by the International Longshoremen's Association, an AFL-CIO union that also had a seniority plan. Both the seniority plan and the CBA had arbitration clauses. The CBA between the union and the South Carolina Stevedores Association (SCSA), which represented stevedore companies, stated that "Matters under dispute which cannot be promptly settled between the Local and an individual Employer shall, no later than 48 hours after such discussion, be referred in writing covering the entire grievance to a Port Grievance Committee."

Ceasar Wright had been working as a longshoreman in Charleston, South Carolina, since 1970, and was a member of Local 1422 of the International Longshoremen's Association. On 18 February 1992, while working for Stevens Shipping and Terminal Company, he injured his right heel and back. He sought compensation directly from Stevens for permanent disability under the Longshore and Harbor Workers' Compensation Act, and ultimately settled a claim for $250,000, plus $10,000 in attorney's fees. Some time later, his doctor told him he could go back to work, and in January 1995 he went to the union hiring hall asking for a job. Wright subsequently went to work for four different companies before one of them, realizing that he had already settled a claim for permanent disability, informed the union that they would not accept him for employment since a person certified as permanently disabled was no longer qualified to work under the terms of the CBA.

Wright filed a suit against the company under the terms of the Americans with Disabilities Act (ADA). A lower court recommended that the case be dismissed without prejudice, because Wright had failed to apply the remedies outlined in the CBA. The U.S. Circuit Court of Appeals for the Fourth Circuit affirmed, but the U.S. Supreme Court overturned this judgment. Delivering an opinion for a unanimous Court, Justice Antonin Scalia maintained that the CBA's general arbitration clause did not require Wright to use the arbitration procedure for alleged violation of the ADA.

Scalia wrote that "The Fourth Circuit's conclusions that the CBA arbitration clause encompassed a statutory claim under the ADA and was enforceable bring into focus the tension between two lines of this Court's case law." These two lines were represented by *Alexander v. Gardner-Denver Co.* (415 U.S. 36) on the one hand, and *Gilmer v. Interstate/Johnson Lane Corp.* (500 U.S. 20) on the other. In any event, "it is unnecessary to resolve the question of the validity of a union-negotiated waiver of employees' statutory rights to a federal forum, since it is apparent, on the facts and arguments presented here, that no such waiver has occurred."

Source: Leonard D. Polletta. "What's Left after Wright?" *Dispute Resolution Journal,* November 1999, pp. 48–58.

—Judson Knight

---

an injunction against the ARU, which resulted in the arrest and imprisonment of the union's leader, Eugene V. Debs.

In 1898 Congress replaced the moribund Arbitration Act with new legislation, the Erdman Act, a significant improvement over the 1888 law. Erdman strengthened the voluntary arbitration provisions of the Arbitration Act, outlined a clear mediation and conciliation process, and declared discrimination against workers on the basis of union membership illegal. However, the relief anticipated under the Erdman Act was short-lived. In 1908 the Supreme Court declared the Erdman Act's antidiscrimination provision unconstitutional in the case of *Adair v. United States.*

The next foray into the regulation of railway labor relations came in 1913 with the passage of the Newlands Act. This particular piece of President Woodrow Wilson's New Freedom legislation established a permanent, three-person board of mediation while retaining the voluntary arbitration procedures that had characterized previous legislative efforts in this area. It was not the Supreme Court but rather the railway brotherhoods themselves that overrode this act. In 1916, on the eve of U.S. entrance into World War I, the brotherhoods threatened a national strike unless their demands for an eight-hour workday were met. President Wilson quickly signed the Adamson Act into law, granting the workers' demands.

During World War I, the government was drawn still deeper into railway labor relations. In order to deal with extreme burdens that the war emergency placed on the nation's railways, President Wilson placed private railroad corporations under federal control by creating the Railway Labor Administration, headed by his son-in-law, Secretary of the Treasury William Gibbs McAdoo. From his new office, McAdoo promptly issued General Order No. 8, which forbade discrimination against railway union members. At the same time, McAdoo promoted collective bargaining and created arbitration boards that rendered judgements on labor disputes. Although strikes were never formally outlawed, this mandatory grievance procedure served to reduce wartime work stoppages on the rails. Their rights to organize now recognized by the federal government, railway workers flocked to unions as never before, and union membership soared along the rails. So encouraged were railway workers by the improvement in their wartime conditions that a powerful movement demanding that government control of the railroads be made permanent arose by the war's end. This movement eventually coalesced around an idea for nationalizing the nation's railroads called the Plumb Plan. However, the wave of political reaction that followed the war doomed the Plumb Plan. Rather than nationalizing the railroads, Congress returned them to private control and crafted new labor regulations through the Esch-Cummins Transportation Act of 1920. The act created a Railway Labor Board (RLB) made up of three railway representatives, three employee representatives, and three public representatives. The board was authorized to investigate disputes and publish decisions, the enforcement of which would rely on the force of public opinion.

Origins and Structure of the 1926 Railway Labor Act

In 1922 the Transportation Act was put to the test by a massive strike that exposed its flaws, ultimately forcing the revision of railway labor law in 1926. The 1922 strike was triggered when employers sought to exploit their strong postwar position by displacing established unions with company unions and engaging in other tactics to weaken the unionized railway crafts. The RLB provided no relief to workers. Indeed, it even ruled in favor of a wage reduction during the recession of 1921. Unions of railway shop craft workers fought back against deteriorating working conditions with a huge national strike in 1922. The largest railway strike in U.S. history, it was broken in large part by the intervention of the federal government. The administration of Warren G. Harding, through Attorney General Harry Daugherty, sought and received a sweeping injunction that prohibited virtually any action by workers in furtherance of their work stoppage.

In the aftermath of the bitter 1922 strike, neither carriers nor railway labor unions were satisfied with the RLB. The railway unions were the first to try to achieve an alternative. During 1922 those unions helped form the Conference for Progressive Political Action, endorsing candidates committed to labor reform in the off-year elections of 1922. In 1923 the shop craft unions joined with the operating unions in a committee that sought the abolition of the RLB and the drafting of alternative railway labor legislation. This committee worked with Representative Alben Barkley (D-KY) and Senator Robert Howell (R-NE) on legislation that was introduced in 1923. The premise of the Howell-Barkley bill recognized unions as workers' representatives in collective bargaining. It failed to pass, in part due to White House opposition, but the effort caused great concern to Calvin Coolidge, who succeeded to the presidency upon the death of Warren G. Harding in 1923. Coolidge was determined to avoid a repeat of the split between the Republican old guard and Progressives that had elected Wilson in 1912. Consequently, Coolidge called upon railway carriers and unions to work out a legislative compromise that would bring labor stability to the nation's rails. In 1925 negotiations between the unions and the carriers, facilitated by Secretary of Commerce Herbert Hoover, produced a compromise. That compromise was embodied in the bills proposed by two Republican legislators, Senator James Eli Watson of Indiana and Representative James S. Parker of New York, which resulted in the Watson-Parker Railway Labor Act (RLA). President Coolidge signed the act into law on 20 May 1926.

The 1926 act represented the culmination of a process of nearly a half-century of experimentation with federal railway labor legislation. The 1926 act included many features embodied in previous legislation; the difference was its emphasis on collective bargaining as a means of settling labor disputes. The 1926 legislation continued to rely on voluntary settlement procedures, and it lacked criminal penalties for noncompliance, but it did include stronger mandatory arbitration provisions that could be invoked in some situations.

The act made the following provisions: first, it empowered the president to appoint a nonpartisan board of mediation that had the authority to invite the parties in a labor dispute to negotiate a solution to their differences. If this process failed, the board was empowered to request both parties to submit their dispute to arbitration. If both parties agreed to arbitration, then the awards issued by the arbitration process were legally binding. Should one or both parties refuse arbitration, the board of mediation could request the president to appoint an emergency board of investigation. If the president did so, the board was required to submit a report on the dispute to the president within 30 days. During that initial 30-day interval, and for another 30 days afterward, the parties in the dispute were forbidden to change the status quo. However, parties were not required to adhere to the findings of the board of investigation. And after the expiration of 60 days following the president's appointment of the emergency board, both parties were free to exercise their right to enforce a strike or lockout. If the president chose not to appoint an emergency board of investigation, parties could still be required to refrain from strike or lockout actions for 30 days. Yet at the end of that period, they were also free to act in their perceived best interests. The "cooling-off" periods stipulated in the 1926 act were obviously meant to discourage parties from taking actions that could lead to large-scale shutdowns of portions of the nation's commercial arteries.

The 1926 act was less desirable for labor than the Barkley-Howell bill had been in two ways. First, it did not explicitly recognize unions as the workers' representatives; workers could choose the representation they desired. This in effect allowed workers to choose company unions to represent them. Second, the cooling-off periods prescribed by the 1926 act were more likely to disadvantage unions than employers. Indeed, unions traditionally have opposed legislation that enforces cooling-off periods, because such laws can be used to deny workers the power to strike when strike action might achieve the greatest leverage.

Despite these problems, however, labor supported the enactment of the 1926 law. First, the RLB system was so unsatisfactory that, in the minds of most union leaders, the new legislation was preferable to the status quo. Second, unions gained significant concessions that counterbalanced whatever problems they perceived in the act's elaborate mediation mechanism. The most significant concession came in the third part of Section 2 of the act, which was the first significant piece of federal legislation that directly limited employer use of company unions as vehicles through which to weaken unions. This portion of the act allowed each side in the negotiation of a dispute to select its own representatives free of "interference, influence, or coercion" by the other side. Unions read the provision as forbidding employers from forcing company unions upon their employees as a condition of collective bargaining. The U.S. Supreme Court agreed. In the 1930 case of *Texas and New Orleans Railroad Company v. Brotherhood of Railway and Steamship Clerks* (281 U.S. 548), the court upheld an injunction issued against a railway company when a union complained that it was being forcibly supplanted by a company-sponsored union. The decision stated clearly that "As the carriers subjected to the Act have no constitutional right to interfere with the freedom of employees to make . . . selections, they cannot complain of the statute on constitutional grounds." The effect of the act and its judicial interpretation was to promote collective bargaining in which workers were represented by independent unions, a precedent of huge magnitude.

The RLA did not forbid strikes, yet it clearly lessened their severity, as only one national rail strike followed in the years after its passage. That strike came when engineers and trainmen walked off the job in 1946 only to return to work when President Harry S Truman threatened to conscript them. The lack of national railroad strikes did not mean that workers or unions were entirely satisfied with the RLA. By the end of World War II, for example, the Brotherhood of Railroad Trainmen was complaining that it sometimes took as long as six to nine years to resolve grievances under the law. In one case, the union alleged that a pay claim filed against the Central New England Railway in July 1932 was not settled until March 1945. On balance, however, the act worked to the benefit of railway unions, and those unions resisted efforts to scrap the act.

Evolution of the Railway Labor Act

The RLA was amended or expanded on four occasions: 1934, 1936, 1951, and 1966. The general thrust of the first three revisions of the RLA responded to the concerns of workers and unions. The 1934 legislation made three major amendments to the act. It introduced criminal penalties in the case of violation of the act's provisions related to collective bargaining. It provided for a certification process through which workers chose their collective bargaining representation. It also created a National Railroad Adjustment Board (NRAB) and strengthened the Board of Mediation created in 1926 by reconstituting it as a National Mediation Board (NMB). The National Mediation Board was composed of three members, no more than two of whom could be members of the same political party. It was empowered to adjudicate representation questions, to foster mediation of disputes, and to propose arbitration in cases where mediation failed. The National Railway Adjustment Board was made up of 34 members, with equal halves representing carriers and unions. The NRAB was itself made up of four divisions, corresponding to different classifications of railroad employees. In the event of a dispute, a section of the NRAB could hear the facts and attempt to render a judgement. If the NRAB itself deadlocked on the dispute, the NMB was empowered to appoint a neutral umpire to break the deadlock. The RLA was further strengthened by the Supreme Court's 1937 decision in the case of *Virginia Railway Company v. System Federation No. 40* (300 U.S. 515), which permitted judicial enforcement of the "duty to bargain" that was embodied in the 1934 amendments.

The 1936 legislation extended the act to cover common air carriers of both interstate and foreign commerce and transporters of the U.S. mail. This ensured that the RLA would remain an important component of American labor law in the decades that followed, as the railroads declined and airlines expanded robustly. The 1951 amendment of the act revised that portion of the original law that outlawed union security arrangements, allowing unions to bargain for union shops and dues checkoff arrangements.

The sweeping 1966 revision of the RLA made awards of the National Railroad Adjustment Board final and binding. While it provided parties the opportunity to seek court review of an unfavorable NRAB decision, it ensured that the grounds upon which such a review could be undertaken would be narrow. An NRAB award could be overturned only if the NRAB itself failed to comply with the provisions of the RLA; if the order exceeded the scope of the board's jurisdiction; or if there was evidence of fraud or corruption of a member of the NRAB.

By the end of the twentieth century, there were many calls for scrapping or drastically revising the Railway Labor Act by those who felt that a 1926 law was no longer suitable in an era of global commerce. Yet the RLA outlived its critics. The longest-lasting major piece of federal labor legislation, the RLA continued to influence American labor relations at the beginning of the twenty-first century.

Key Players

Coolidge, Calvin (1872–1933): Republican president known for having broken the Boston police strike as governor of Massachusetts in 1919. As president, he signed the RLA into law in 1926.

Hoover, Herbert C. (1874–1964): Secretary of commerce in the administrations of Warren G. Harding and Calvin Coolidge. He facilitated and encouraged the negotiations between railway unions and carriers that resulted in compromise provisions that were embodied in the RLA.

Howell, Robert (1864–1933): Republican senator from Nebraska. In his first term in office in 1923, he introduced legislation to scrap the Railroad Labor Board. His unsuccessful effort to pass this legislation pressured President Coolidge and the conservative Republican old guard in the Congress to write their own version of railway labor legislation, which they did in 1926.

Parker, James S. (1867–1933): Republican representative from New York. As chairman of the House Committee on Interstate and Foreign Commerce, he drafted the House version of the RLA.

Watson, James Eli (1864–1948): Republican senator from Indiana, and a member of the party's conservative old guard. He drafted the Senate's version of the RLA.

See also: *Arbitration Act of 1888; Erdman Act; Pullman Strike; Railroad Strike of 1877; Texas and NOR v. Brotherhood of RSC.*

BIBLIOGRAPHY

Books

Davis, Colin J. *Power at Odds: The 1922 National Railroad Shopmen's Strike.* Urbana, IL: University of Illinois Press, 1997.

Dubofsky, Melvyn. *The State and Labor in Modern America.* Chapel Hill, NC: University of North Carolina Press, 1994.

O'Brien, Ruth Ann. *Workers' Paradox: The Republican Origins of New Deal Labor Policy, 1886–1935.* Chapel Hill, NC: University of North Carolina Press, 1998.

Twomey, David P. *Labor Law and Legislation.* Cincinnati, OH: Southwestern Publishing Company, 1980.

Zieger, Robert H. *Republicans and Labor, 1919–1929.* Lexington, KY: University of Kentucky Press, 1969.

—Joseph A. McCartin

Willie Gallacher. AP/Wide World Photos. Reproduced by permission.

Red Clyde Strike

Scotland 1919

Synopsis

The events of Bloody Friday, 31 January 1919, in George Square, Glasgow, have become symbolic of the conflict between the workers and the state that took place in the Clydeside region of Lanarkshire, Scotland. The demonstration by around 60,000 striking workers who were demanding shorter working hours and subsequent violent retaliation by the police resulted from ongoing tensions that had emerged between the workers, their families, and the factory owners who were backed by the British government. Throughout the previous nine years, sporadic mass protests had been held to oppose infringements on workers' rights, rent increases, and Britain's participation in World War I. The context was a marked shift away from moderate Liberal politics toward support for Marxist political groups or the British Labour Party. The effects of growth in left-wing activism and the successful use of direct action to promote the workers' struggle were to characterize the relationship between workers and the state in Britain for the next 65 years and created the Scottish political character that still exists today.

Timeline

1900: China's Boxer Rebellion, which began in the preceding year with attacks on foreigners and Christians, reaches its height. An international contingent of more than 2,000 men arrives to restore order, but only after several tens of thousands have died.

1907: U.S. markets experience a financial panic.

1912: *Titanic* sinks on its maiden voyage, from Southampton to New York, on 14 April. More than 1,500 people are killed.

1915: At the Second Battle of Ypres, the Germans introduce a terrifying new weapon: poison gas.

1917: The intercepted "Zimmermann Telegram" reveals a plot by the German government to draw Mexico into an alliance against the United States in return for a German promise to return the southwestern U.S. territories taken in the Mexican War. Three months later, in response to German threats of unrestricted submarine warfare, the United States on 6 April declares war on Germany.

1919: Formation of the Third International (Comintern), whereby the Bolshevik government of Russia establishes its control over communist movements worldwide.

1919: Treaty of Versailles signed by the Allies and Germany, but rejected by the U.S. Senate. This is due in part to rancor between President Woodrow Wilson and Republican Senate leaders, and in part to concerns over Wilson's plan to commit the United States to the newly established League of Nations and other international duties. Not until 1921 will Congress formally end U.S. participation in the war, but it will never agree to join the League.

1919: Ratification of the Eighteenth Amendment, which prohibits the production, sale, distribution, purchase, and consumption of alcohol throughout the United States.

1919: In India, Mahatma Gandhi launches his campaign of nonviolent resistance to British rule.

1919: In Italy, a former socialist of the left named Benito Mussolini introduces the world to a new socialism of the right, embodied in an organization known as the "Union for Struggle," or Fasci di Combattimento. Composed primarily of young war veterans discontented with Italy's paltry share of the spoils from the recent world war (if not with their country's lackluster military performance in the conflict), the fascists are known for their black shirts and their penchant for violence.

171

1921: As the Allied Reparations Commission calls for payments of 132 billion gold marks, inflation in Germany begins to climb.

1925: European leaders attempt to secure the peace at the Locarno Conference, which guarantees the boundaries between France and Germany, and Belgium and Germany.

1929: On "Black Friday" in October, prices on the U.S. stock market, which had been climbing wildly for several years, suddenly collapse. Thus begins the first phase of a world economic crisis and depression that will last until the beginning of World War II.

Event and Its Context

Background

Historians have often attempted to downplay the extent to which Red Clydeside was indeed "Red" or Marxist-Leninist inspired. This is due to the largely organic nature of the unrest; as each dispute developed from specific grievances experienced by the Clydeside workers over a 30-year period. Across industrial Scotland, trade unionism had grown since the late nineteenth century; strikes were often called but had often been broken by force or threat of dismissals. The watershed occurred in 1911.

The introduction of limited automation to the Singer Sewing Machine plant at Clydebank led to an increase in workload but a reduction in the use of skills and so a decrease in wages. Twelve female cabinet polishers called a strike in protest and in two days 11,000 of their colleagues had joined them in support. The increased solidarity caused by shared grievances and involvement of political groups such as the Independent Labour Party (ILP) led to initial successes. However, Singer's threat to close the works and move production to Europe led to an unconditional return to work on 10 April 1911. Systematic dismissals of the strike leaders, however, particularly those active in the ILP, the Socialist Labour Party (SLP), and the Industrial Workers of Great Britain, meant tensions remained high. Trade union membership increased, as did membership in the Marxist political parties, and throughout Lanarkshire workers learned that unless "all the workers supported all the workers" then the factory and pit owners would always win.

John MacLean was instrumental in spreading the notion of worker solidarity. MacLean ran classes in Marxist economics and industrial history throughout Lanarkshire and was charged and imprisoned for sedition several times during World War I. MacLean encouraged workers to unite within trade unions and behind the Marxist parties (the ILP, SLP, and the British Socialist Party, which would later be re-formed as the Communist Party of Great Britain). His teachings inspired a generation of Scottish socialists including Willie Gallacher, James Maxton, Harry McShane, James Messer, Neil MacLean, and Emmanuel Shinwell, all of whom were instrumental in the Red Clydeside movement. During the 1920s, many of them entered parliament. The coming of World War I—which was, in socialist eyes, the "great imperialist war"—and its effects on the Clydeside workers and their families, gave a practical dimension to MacLean's teaching.

World War I

Industrial centers such as Govan and Partick became key production centers for Britain's war machine. Thousands of workers who had been brought into the munitions industry were rehoused on Clydeside. The demand for housing led to rent increases, and it was the women, many of whose husbands had volunteered or been conscripted, who created Tenants Strike Committees. By mid-1915, at the height of the rent strikes, 20,000 tenants across Glasgow were involved in the nonpayment campaign. British Prime Minister Lloyd George, afraid of the effects on munitions production, introduced legislation to cap rents. In practice, the Rent Restrictions Act (1915) standardized rents at prewar levels. The victory showed that collective action of entire communities, backed by the skilled workers and guided by the political leadership of the Marxist groups, was a winning formula. The act became symbolic of what could be achieved and the strikes became the blueprint for future action.

Industrial disputes and opposition to the war grew apace. The trade union leaders, however, were often conservative when faced with government pressure. The Labour Withholding Committee (LWC) formed following the collapse of the 1915 Engineer's Dispute, which had been caused by the dissembling of the Amalgamated Society of Engineers leaders. This organization passed control over industrial disputes directly into the hands of the workers, agitators, and political activists. The first battle staged by the LWC was in response to the Munitions of War Act, referred to as "the slavery act" by Clydeside workers. This act made it unlawful for a worker to leave the service of an employer without the employer's consent; a new position in a factory could not be refused, regardless of the rate of pay; overtime became mandatory; and tribunals, usually consisting of employers, were created to deal with transgressors. Inevitably agitators were sacked, blacklisted from working elsewhere, and often imprisoned for refusing the terms of the act. Threats of industrial action resulted in few victories and, on the whole, workers were too scared of losing their jobs to support strike action.

The fact that trade union leaders had participated in drafting the Munitions of War Act and were complicit in the dilution policy, which allowed employers to "import" unskilled, cheap labor to do work previously performed by skilled workers, meant that union support waned. The LWC, renamed the Clyde Workers Committee (CWC), expanded its membership and became the only organization to represent the workers. The CWC also enjoyed the backing of all the Marxist parties, many of the leaders of which sat on the Committee. The Dilution Committee, a government body set up to coordinate the placement of the new workforce, refused to recognize the CWC as a legitimate trade union. CWC shop stewards were banned from recruiting the imported dilutees and were threatened with dismissal if they were caught trying. A new weapon against the political agitators, the Defense of the Realm Act (1915), reinforced these rules. Attempts to recruit dilutees resulted in deportation to Edinburgh and placement under curfew of a number of shop stewards. John MacLean was arrested in February 1916 and imprisoned for sedition for delivering anticonscription speeches. MacLean's arrest was closely followed by arrests of Willie Gallacher, chairman of the CWC, and Walter Bell, manager of the Socialist Labour Press. John Muir, editor of "The Worker's Freedom of Speech," was found inimical to the Defense of the Realm Act and throughout 1916 socialists across Britain were imprisoned. The movement was also given a martyr when James Connolly, an Irish socialist and ally of the Clydesiders, was executed for taking part in the Easter Rising.

A number of Peace Conventions were held throughout Britain during the summer of 1917. The largest, held in June at Leeds, was inspired by the Russian Revolution but borrowed largely from Leninist rhetoric. Willie Gallacher and a number of MacLean's students were in attendance and calls were made for the release of political prisoners. MacLean was released shortly after, and inspired by the Bolshevik revolution of October 1917, he continued his teachings. His successes and his close contacts with the Leninist government led to his appointment as Consul for Soviet Affairs in Great Britain by Lenin. This was unofficial: his office was based in Glasgow rather than London and his activities led once again to his arrest on sedition charges. During his trial in Edinburgh, MacLean said, "I am not here as the accused. I am here as the accuser of capitalism, dripping with blood from head to foot." His sentence of five years inspired nationwide demonstrations, which gained him a royal pardon on 3 December 1918. Characteristically, MacLean denounced the pardon, arguing it was the workers who had secured his release by threatening revolution. In speeches following his return to Clydeside, he told the king that his days as monarch were numbered.

Black Friday and Its Legacy

The main reason that the "Red" influence is played down is the reliance placed on parliamentary representation by the majority of the Clydesiders. Many of the CWC leaders stood in 1918, however, despite electoral reforms and extension of suffrage; only Neil MacLean was elected in the discredited "Khaki" Election. The inefficiency of applying the new electoral rules and the fact that many discharged servicemen found themselves disenfranchised contributed to the failure of the Marxist parties. The result was met with widespread dissatisfaction and increased the reliance on direct action as a means to effect the will of the workers.

The key concern for the Clydeside workers in 1918–1919 was the increasing levels of unemployment that would inevitably lead to reduced job security. Calls were made to reduce the weekly working hours to 40 to enable discharged servicemen to find employment. The lack of response led the CWC to call a strike and, by 30 January 1919, despite the lack of concern from the government or trade union leaders, 40,000 workers in engineering and shipbuilding and 36,000 miners from the Lanarkshire and Stirlingshire coalfields had set down their tools. The organizers deployed flying pickets and planned marches and rallies. The police led a violent and unprovoked attack on the largest march, which converged on George Square, Glasgow the next day to hear the Lord Provost's reply to their demands. Many of the CWC leaders were arrested and in two days English troop battalions were deployed to prevent the situation escalating into revolution. By 10 February the strike was called off. The strike did not achieve its stated goal of a 40-hour workweek, but the parties reached a negotiated settlement. Thus the power of direct action was again shown to be a force for exacerbating change.

Although Clydeside did not turn "Red," the 1922 ballot saw the election of many CWC leaders, most of whom represented the ILP or the Labour Party. The industrial regions of Scotland remained a source of radical left-wing and nationalist ideas. Willie Gallacher became the longest-serving communist member of Parliament (MP; 1935–1950). In broader terms direct action as a tool of the workers was established as a mode by which government policy could be changed until the 1980s, when trade union power in Britain was finally broken. The Clydesiders would again act decisively in ending British intervention in the Russian Civil War. In fact as long as industry was based on the banks of the river Clyde, the workers as a force would remain endowed with the spirit of 1919. As one Clydesider of the 1970s recalled, "We were a state within the United Kingdom. A little Bolshevik center that would always fight till the end. They could only destroy our power by closing the yards and the mines."

Key Players

Barbour, Mary (1875–1958): Barbour formed the Glasgow Women's Housing Association and was instrumental in coordinating the rent strikes. In 1920 she became the first female councillor in Glasgow.

Gallacher, Willie (1881–1965): Gallacher worked as an apprentice engineer at Albion Motor Works and became the political leader of the Clyde Workers Committee. He helped form the Scottish branch of the Communist Party and became the longest standing Communist MP, representing East Fife from 1935 to 1950. He wrote an account of Red Clydeside (*Revolt on the Clyde*, 1936).

MacLean, John (1879–1923): Taught classes on Marxism across industrial Scotland and was the chief ideological influence behind the event. MacLean's antiwar agitation after 1914 led to several arrests for sedition. Some 20,000 Clydeside workers attended his funeral; his eulogy declared him the champion of the laboring classes. Historians since have named MacLean the leading revolutionary of the 1910–1922 era.

BIBLIOGRAPHY

Books

Duncan, Robert, and Arthur McIvor, eds. *Militant Workers: Labour and Class Conflict on the Clyde 1900–1950.* Edinburgh: John Donald, 1992.

Gallacher, Willie. *Revolt on the Clyde.* London: Lawrence & Wishart, 1936.

Kenefick, William, and Arthur McIvor, eds. *The Roots of Red Clydeside, 1910–1914.* Edinburgh: John Donald, 1996.

Kirkwood, Davie. *My Life of Revolt.* London: Harrap & Co. Ltd, 1935.

MacLean, Ian. *The Legend of Red Clydeside.* Edinburgh: J. Donald, 1983.

Shinwell, Emmanuel. *Conflict without Malice.* London: Oldhams, 1955.

Young, John D. *The Very Bastards of Creation: Scottish International Radicalism, 1707–1995*. Glasgow: Clydeside Press, 1997.

Periodicals

Foster, John. "Strike Action and Working Class Politics on Clydeside 1914–1919." *International Review of Social History,* 25 (1990): 33–70.

Melling, Joseph. "Whatever Happened to Red Clydeside?" *International Review of Social History,* 35 (1990): 3–32.

Other

"Red Clydeside." Glasgow Digital Library, University of Strathclyde, Scotland. 7 May 2002 [cited 22 July 2002]. <http://gdl.cdlr.strath.ac.uk/prototype/redclyde/index.html>

ADDITIONAL RESOURCES

Other

The John MacLean Resource Archive. <http://www.marxists.org/archive/maclean/macl-idx.htm>

—Darren G. Lilleker

Grigory Zinoviev. © Hulton-Deutsch Collection/Corbis-Bettmann. Reproduced by permission.

and Czechoslovakia, the RILU only really succeeded outside western Europe. The organization, which effectively became an adjunct of the Russian-dominated Comintern, finally dissolved in 1937.

Red International of Labor Unions

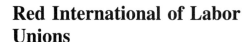

Russia 1921

Synopsis

During 1919–1920 the inspiration of the Russian Revolution, combined with the conditions of economic and political crisis that accompanied the end of World War I, produced a wave of mass strikes and revolutionary struggle that swept across the world. The formation of the Red International of Labor Unions (RILU), or Profintern, was both a product of this dramatic situation and a response to it.

RILU was one of the most important of the subsidiary organizations that was established under the auspices of the Third (Communist) International. Communist leaders saw it as providing a focal point for the world's revolutionary trade unionists and anarcho-syndicalists that could rival the reformist-led International Federation of Trade Unions (IFTU). The founding congress took place in Moscow on 3–19 July 1921 with 380 delegates from 41 countries.

Bitter political arguments with syndicalist delegates undermined the organization's potential support, however, and optimistic expectations of rapid communist advance were soon to be confounded by the partial stabilization of the European economy, the ebbing of working-class struggle, and the continued strength of social democracy. Many existing trade union centers remained loyal to Amsterdam and, with the exception of France

Timeline

1906: Founding of the British Labour Party.

1911: Revolution in Mexico, begun the year before, continues with the replacement of the corrupt Porfirio Diaz, president since 1877, by Francisco Madero.

1916: Battles of Verdun and the Somme on the Western Front. The latter sees the first use of tanks, by the British.

1918: The Second Battle of the Marne in July and August is the last major conflict on the Western Front. In November, Kaiser Wilhelm II abdicates, bringing an end to the war.

1921: As the Allied Reparations Commission calls for payments of 132 billion gold marks, inflation in Germany begins to climb.

1921: Canadian scientists Frederick Banting and Charles Herbert Best isolate insulin, an advance that will alter the lives of diabetics and greatly reduce the number of deaths associated with the disease.

1921: Washington Disarmament Conference limits the tonnage of world navies.

1921: In a controversial U.S. case, Italian-born anarchists Nicola Sacco and Bartolomeo Vanzetti are tried and convicted of armed robbery and murder. Despite numerous protests from around the world, they will be executed six years later.

1924: V. I. Lenin dies, and thus begins a struggle for succession from which Stalin will emerge five years later as the undisputed leader of the Communist Party, and of the Soviet Union.

1928: Discovery of penicillin by Alexander Fleming.

1931: Financial crisis widens in the United States and Europe, which reel from bank failures and climbing unemployment levels. In London, armies of the unemployed riot.

1936: Germany reoccupies the Rhineland, while Italy annexes Ethiopia. Recognizing a commonality of aims, the two totalitarian powers sign the Rome-Berlin Axis Pact. (Japan will join them in 1940.)

Event and Its Context

RILU was one of the most important of the subsidiary organizations established under the auspices of the Third (Communist) International, known as the Comintern. The Comintern, formed in Moscow 1919, set itself the task of winning over that section of the working class that had been disillusioned by social democracy by encouraging and sponsoring the building of revolutionary communist parties of the Bolshevik type. Unlike the Second International, which had been a loose federal body that allowed varying degrees of independence for its national sections, the Comintern sought to be a single centralized and exclusively communist world party. The Comintern's structure reflected a conception of the world as a single battlefield on which to wage the class war with one army and one high command; the aim was to ensure that the 1914 collapse of the Second International into reformism and nationalism was never repeated. Against a background of revolutionary upheaval, a number of newly radicalized militants from the rapidly growing communist parties and others from antiparliamentary syndicalist traditions made the journey to Moscow to participate in the Comintern's deliberations.

At the Comintern's second Congress in June 1920, Grigory Zinoviev, the president of the Comintern, offered a proposal that was supported by the All-Russian Congress of Trade Unions to form a new revolutionary trade union international that would operate alongside the party-structured Comintern. Communist leaders viewed the proposal as providing a focal point for attracting the world's revolutionary trade unionists and syndicalists that could rival the reformist-led International Federation of Trade Unions (IFTU), generally known as the Amsterdam International after the location of its headquarters. Despite the Amsterdam International's recent growth, the authority of its reformist leaders had been severely damaged by their conduct during the war in renouncing prior internationalist commitments. On the expectation of renewed social explosions and working-class revolutions in the coming years, a new "Red" trade union international, it was believed, could woo national trade unions to break from their allegiance to the IFTU and affiliate to Moscow.

Provisional International Council

During the Comintern Congress, a group representing the Russian, Italian, and Bulgarian trade union delegations, and

some members of the British delegation, met to give their general approval to the Russian initiative. However, syndicalist delegates who insisted on trade union independence from political organizations rejected Zinoviev's proposal that the new union body be constituted as a trade union section of the Comintern. Their counterproposal was an invitation to all unions who supported the Comintern's revolutionary anticapitalist platform to attend a broader conference that would decide how to structure and launch the new trade union international. The congress elected a Provisional International Council of Trade and Industrial Unions (*Mezhsovprof*) composed of Solomon Lozovsky (Russia) as president and Tom Mann (Britain) and Alfred Rosmer (France) as vice presidents. The provisional council was responsible for organizing the founding congress of the Red International to be held in May 1921.

Founding Congress

The inaugural congress of the Russian-sponsored Red International of Labor Unions (*Krasnyi internatsional professionalnykh soyuzov* or Profintern), took place in July 1921. The meeting was scheduled to coincide with the Comintern's Third Congress. Some 380 delegates from 41 countries, composed of different syndicalist currents and the trade union fractions of communist parties, represented minority groups within the unions. For two weeks it thrashed out the basic principles of the new international, in the process revealing a serious division of opinion. The first argument was whether revolutionaries should stay inside the existing reformist unions. American delegates from the Industrial Workers of the World, supported by some syndicalists from Europe, argued that, because the existing unions, such as the AFL, had betrayed the cause of workers, new revolutionary union bodies should be set up to replace them. By contrast, the Bolshevik leaders, supported by most communist delegates, argued that rather than abandoning the unions to their reactionary leaders and in turn isolating themselves from the working class, revolutionaries should enter the unions and attempt to win them to their cause.

The question of the relationship between the new international and the Comintern became the major debate. The Russians favored an "organic" connection between them and a similar connection at the national level between communist parties and national sections of the Red International. Sections of the French, German, Italian, and Spanish delegations, however, continued to oppose any connection with political movements. Many syndicalists were worried that the RILU would simply become a subordinate appendage of the Comintern and that the trade unions would be transformed into subsidiary organizations under the control of the communist parties. After a long and bitter debate, a large majority voted to accept an alternative resolution that the new international be structured as a separate organization linked to the Comintern by fundamental political agreement. The resolution also affirmed the need for a "close and real connection" between the revolutionary unions and the communist parties in applying the joint decisions of the RILU and Comintern. Yet it proved to be a Pyrrhic victory. News of the decisions taken at the RILU congress elicited a storm of protest from the syndicalist movement in the West, including the Spanish Anarcho-Syndicalist Trade Union Confederation (CNT) and Italian Syndicalist Union (USI), who subsequently broke away to establish their own separate syndicalist international.

Activity and Organization

The newly formed Red International produced a *Programme of Action* that called for the worldwide overthrow of capitalism and the establishment of an international republic of soviets on the Russian model. It detailed the strategy and tactics to be followed by "Red Trade Unions." All trade union action was to be seen as leading to mass actions: demonstrations, factory occupations, and ultimately armed insurrection. Amalgamation, though local, district, and national trade union machinery would be the key tool for attaining industrial unionism. Members of the national RILU sections were to form factory cells and press for workers' control of production and the organic unity of the Communist Party and the revolutionary trade unions. The leadership reaffirmed hostility toward Amsterdam in the most militant terms, although the older unions in the West proposed the tactic of conquering from within using cell-building tactics, rather than repudiation, restructuring, or abandonment.

The basic organizational structure institutionalized Russia's pre-eminent position within the RILU in the arrangements for finance and in provision for extra Russian membership in its executive organs. By 1923 the organization and chain of command of the new trade union international were firmly established. The supreme governing body was the annual RILU Congress. Between congresses an executive bureau, consisting of representatives of the various national sections, was to decide policy. The RILU failed to organize annual congresses, and only four more occurred between 1922 and 1930. The executive bureau became a deliberate assembly and met only occasionally. The driving force of the organization was its full-time secretariat, notably Russian general secretary Losovsky. In practice the organization became little more than an adjunct of the Comintern.

Failure and Demise

The RILU's optimistic expectations of rapid communist advance were soon confounded by the partial stabilization of the European economy, the ebbing of working-class struggle, and the continued strength of social democracy. Working-class retreat was symbolized by the failure of the "March Action" in Germany and of the French, Italian, and British communist parties to win mass support. At the Fifth Comintern Congress in 1924, Zinoviev admitted that the RILU had been founded at a time when the movement was on the ascendant and looked as if it could win over the trade unions *en masse,* whereas in fact the movement had ebbed and developments were much slower than anticipated.

After just one year the RILU claimed a total membership of 17 million worldwide, but this figure failed to distinguish between affiliated unions and revolutionary minorities within the reformist unions and did not account for the continued connection of some individual unions with the Amsterdam International. The RILU was in fact far smaller, with the 6.5 million Russian trade unionists providing a solid core, but with the communists able to bring only party trade union fractions into the new international. Many existing British, German, and

French trade unions remained loyal to Amsterdam and, with the exception of France (where the communists set up their own confederation) and Czechoslovakia, the RILU only really succeeded outside western Europe.

The failure of the RILU, however, was also related to the ambiguous nature of its structure. British shop steward leader J. T. Murphy claimed that the slightest suggestion of splitting the trade unions would have denied the effort the support of the labor movement. Yet as other participants pointed out, it proved totally contradictory to work within the Amsterdam unions on a national level, while at the same time attempting to split them from Amsterdam in favor of an alternative revolutionary trade union body based in Moscow on an international level. Ironically, as soon as the RILU was founded, the Comintern, faced with the decline in revolutionary struggle, adopted new "united front" tactics that required it to cooperate with the very body that it had been set up to destroy. From November 1922 to 1927, the communists unsuccessfully attempted to bring about a merger of the RILU and the Amsterdam International before pushing it into a disastrous Stalin-inspired ultraleft phase between 1928 and 1934, and then finally dissolving the discredited international in 1937.

Key Players

Lozovsky, Solomon (1878–1952): Dissident Bolshevik starting in 1903, Lozovsky played an important part in the Soviet trade unions and was general secretary of the RILU from its inception in 1920 to its dissolution in 1937. He was a prolific orator and pamphleteer and author of *Marx and the Trade Unions* (1935). In 1949 he was arrested and died in a prison camp.

Mann, Tom (1856–1941): British trade union organizer and leader of the prewar Industrial Syndicalist Education League, Mann became a founding member of the Communist Party and chairman of the British Bureau of the RILU.

Murphy, J. T. (1888–1965): Wartime shop stewards' leader and founding member of the British Communist Party, Murphy was a key figure on the International Trade Union Council that set up the RILU. Murphy was later elected to the executive committee of the Comintern but was expelled from the Communist Party in 1932.

Rosmer, Alfred (1877–1964): A French revolutionary syndicalist, Rosmer played a leading role in Moscow establishing the RILU and winning other syndicalists to the Comintern. He was appointed to the leadership of the French Communist Party in 1921 but was expelled after becoming a supporter of Trostky's Left Opposition.

Zinoviev, Grigory (1883–1936): One of Lenin's closest Bolshevik Party collaborators from 1903 until 1917, he became president of the Communist International. In 1923 he joined with Stalin and Kamenev against Trotsky; in 1925 he broke with Stalin and formed the Joint Opposition with Trotsky, and in 1927 Zinoviev capitulated to Stalin but was one of the main defendants in the 1935 show trial, after which he was shot.

See also: *First International; Industrial Workers of the World; International Federation of Trade Unions; Russian Revolutions; Second International.*

BIBLIOGRAPHY

Books

Carr, E. H. *Socialism in One Country, 1924–1926*, Vol. 3, Part 1. London: Macmillan, 1964.

———. *The Bolshevik Revolution, 1917–1923*. Vol. 3. London: Macmillan, 1966.

Cliff, T., and D. Gluckstein. *Marxism and Trade Union Struggle: The General Strike of 1926*. London: Bookmarks, 1986.

Degras, J., ed. *The Communist International, 1919–1943: Documents*. 3 vols. London: Open University Press, 1956–1965.

Riddell, J., ed. *Workers of the World and Oppressed Peoples, Unite! Proceedings and Documents of the Second Congress, 1920*. New York: Pathfinder Press, 1991.

Rosmer, A. *Lenin's Moscow*. London: Pluto Press, 1971.

Thorpe, W. *"The Workers Themselves": Revolutionary Syndicalism and International Labour, 1913–1923*. Dordrecht: Kluwer Academic Publishers, 1989.

Periodicals

Swain, G. "Was the Profintern Really Necessary?" *European History Quarterly,* 17, no. 1 (1987): 57–77.

Thorpe, W. "Syndicalist Internationalism and Moscow, 1919–1922: The Breach." *Canadian Journal of History,* 14 (1979): 199–234.

Other

Constitution of the Red International of Labour Unions, Adopted at the First World Congress Held in Moscow, July 1921. Moscow, 1921.

Murphy, J. T. *The "Reds" in Congress: Preliminary Report of the First World Congress of the Red International of Trade and Industrial Unions.* (Pamphlet.) London: British Bureau of RILU, 1921.

Resolutions and Decisions of the First International Congress of Revolutionary Trade and Industrial Unions. Chicago: The American Labor Union Educational Society, 1921.

Tosstorff, R. "'Moscow or Amsterdam'? The Red International of Labour Unions 1920/1–1937." Ph.D. diss. Johannes Gutenberg University, Germany, 1999.

ADDITIONAL RESOURCES

Books

Adibekow, G. M. *Die Rote Gewerkschafts-International: Grunriss der Geschichte der RGI.* Berlin: Tribune, 1973.

Broué, P. *Historie de l'Internationale Communiste, 1919–1843.* Paris: Fayard, 1997.

Resis, A. "Comintern Policy Towards the World Trade Union Movement: The First Year." In *Essays in Russian and Soviet History,* edited by J. S. Curtiss. New York: Columbia University Press, 1963.

Sworakowski, W. S. *The Communist International and Its Front Organisations: A Research Guide and Checklist of Holdings in American and European Libraries.* Stanford, CA: Hoover Institution, 1965.

Other

Manifesto of the Provisional International Council of Trade and Industrial Unions to the Organised Workers of Great Britain, January 1921 (signed by M. Tomsky, A. Rosmer and J. T. Murphy). London: British Bureau of the Provisional International of Trade and Industrial Unions, 1921.

Murphy, J. T. *Stop the Retreat! An Appeal to Trade Unionists.* (Pamphlet.) London: Red International of Labour Unions, 1922.

Second World Congress: Resolutions and Decisions 19 November to 2 December 1922. London: Red International of Labour Unions, 1923.

The Tasks of the International Trade Union Movement: Resolutions and Decisions of the Third World Congress of the RILU, Moscow, July 1924. London: National Minority Movement, 1924.

Williams, G. *The First Congress of the Red Trades Union International at Moscow.* (Pamphlet.) Chicago: Industrial Workers of the World, 1922.

—Ralph Darlington

Red Week

Italy 1914

Synopsis

Red Week (or, in Italian, *Settimana Rossa*) was the popular term eventually used for the violent uprising that occurred across Italy after a general strike in the city of Ancona on 7 June 1914 resulted in the killing of three demonstrators by the police. For years, workers had become increasingly vocal about miserable working conditions, poor wages, and police coercion. As a result of the Red Week activities—in which rioters destroyed shops and tore apart telegraph lines and railroad tracks—many communities declared themselves independent communes, while other regions proclaimed themselves independent republics. More than 100,000 soldiers were brought in before order was restored.

Timeline

1894: Thousands of unemployed American workers—a group named "Coxey's Army" for their leader, Jacob S. Coxey—march on Washington, D.C. A number of such marches on the capital occurred during this period of economic challenges, but Coxey's march was only one to actually reach its destination.

1899: Start of the Second Anglo-Boer War, often known simply as the Boer War.

1904: The ten-hour workday is established in France.

1911: Turkish-Italian War sees the first use of aircraft as an offensive weapon. Italian victory results in the annexation of Libya.

1914: On 28 June in the town of Sarajevo, then part of the Austro-Hungarian Empire, Serbian nationalist Gavrilo Princip assassinates Austrian Archduke Francis Ferdinand and wife, Sophie. In the weeks that follow, Austria declares war on Serbia, and Germany on Russia and France, while Great Britain responds by declaring war on Germany. By the beginning of August, the lines are drawn, with the Allies (Great Britain, France, Russia, Belgium, Serbia, Montenegro, and Japan) against the Central Powers (Germany, Austria-Hungary, and Turkey).

1914: On the Western Front, the first battles of the Marne and Ypres establish a line that will more or less hold for the next four years. Exuberance is still high on both sides but will dissipate as thousands of German, French, and British soldiers sacrifice their lives in battles over a few miles of barbed wire and mud. The Eastern Front is a different story: a German victory over Russia at Tannenberg in August sets the stage for a war in which Russia will enjoy little success, and will eventually descend into chaos that paves the way for the 1917 revolutions.

1914: Official opening of the Panama Canal.

1914: U.S. Congress passes the Clayton Antitrust Act, and establishes the Federal Trade Commission.

1914: Intervening in Mexico's civil war to protect American financial assets and other U.S. interests, U.S. Marines occupy the city of Veracruz.

1916: Battles of Verdun and the Somme on the Western Front. The latter sees the first use of tanks, by the British.

1920: League of Nations, based in Geneva, holds its first meetings.

1924: V. I. Lenin dies, and thus begins a struggle for succession from which Stalin will emerge five years later as the undisputed leader of the Communist Party, and of the Soviet Union.

Event and Its Context

The Giolitti Period

The events leading up to Red Week in Italy can be traced to the leadership of the progressive liberal Giovanni Giolitti, who first entered the Italian parliament in 1882. Later, Giolitti held the position of minister of finance from 1889 to 1890 and was appointed premier at five various times between 1892 and 1921. Historians sometimes call this era in Italian political history the Giolitti period.

Under Giolitti's dominant leadership, Italy experienced political, social, and economic modernization; workers experienced dramatic increases in real income, and the economy expanded at an unprecedented pace. According to government statistics, Italy's rate of industrial growth during this time was 87 percent, and workers' wages grew by more than 25 percent, despite new employee benefits such as a shortened workday and the introduction of a guaranteed day of rest. However, Italian historians often criticize Giolitti for political corruption, including such activities as interfering with and controlling the electoral process, tolerating trade protectionism, dominating the organizations of coalitions, and creating a near-total parliamentary dictatorship.

Giovanni Giolitti. The Library of Congress.

On the other hand, some of the same historians who find fault with Giolitti's methods also applaud him as the architect of modern Italy. One of the more important accomplishments of his tenure was the introduction of a number of protective and social labor legislation reforms. The right of workers to strike for higher wages was recognized; changes in electoral law greatly increased male suffrage; members of the Roman Catholic clergy were drawn into Italy's political life; and the first major legislation on behalf of the economically depressed South was passed. For the first time, the labor movement could openly organize, bargain, and strike in an atmosphere of freedom without fear of government suppression.

But for the all the good Giolitti introduced, the Italian worker still suffered under poor working and living conditions. As the country experienced prosperous times, the division between the wealthy land- and business-owners and the poverty-stricken laborers grew. In addition, industrialization was concentrated in the North, leaving the southern section mostly agricultural, with few hopes for prosperity. Despite the progress made, Italy still suffered from governmental policies that hindered economic growth.

Workers realized that they had a common interest in fighting for a better life. For this reason, as industrialization grew rapidly in the late nineteenth century, by the 1880s trade unions appeared as an outgrowth of existing mutual aid organizations.

However, in spite of the newly formed unions, workers found themselves powerless against employers who would resort to force to keep their workers in line. Workers were therefore readily inclined to go out on strike and to support sympathy strikes with fellow workers in order to win economic concessions.

Tensions: Workers and Government

The strikes caused additional tensions between the Italian government and the labor movement. A local strike against the high cost of living would bring the police, who frequently used excessive force, including bloodshed and arrests, to control and disperse the protesting workers. Sympathy strikes would then result in protest to police brutality. The strikes left the protestors with a hatred for the wealthy in power. In 1904 an Italian syndicalist theory emerged; the most militant strike leaders thought the workers should not strike against the capitalists but rather take over the factories, operate them, and remove the capitalists all together. Without strong leadership, little was done to carry out this plan, but the idea was planted in the minds of Italian workers.

Three Worker Factions

During the next 10 years, three major forces dominated the Italian worker movement: (1) *reformist social democracy*, which believed that Giolitti's social welfare legislation was the best course for the working class and supported by the General Confederation of Labor (CGL), which was established in 1906 (similar to the unions in England, Germany, and the United States); (2) *syndicalism*, which appealed to the revolutionary workers, who modeled themselves after their French counterparts who voiced their opinions for social revolution and urged workers to aid other workers in the form of sympathy and solidarity strikes; and (3) *revolutionary socialism*, which shared some syndicalist notions but insisted on the necessity of parliamentary political action. Worker attitudes in this period can best be described as reformist but conservative in nature, with an active minority of revolutionary syndicalists.

When the Socialist Party Congress met in 1912, the revolutionary socialists were able to gain control of the party. Benito Mussolini was its chief spokesman, through the official socialist daily newspaper *Avanti!* The control of the Socialist Party by the revolutionaries created serious labor relations problems with the trade union movement, which was controlled by the reformists and which resisted revolutionary attempts to create general strikes and dictate union policy. However, the use of the strike as a weapon of political pressure and demonstration purposes gained support from many worker groups. The period between 1912 and 1914 saw innumerable local demonstration strikes. For example, the revolutionary railway union demanded an increase in wages, but the government and workers eventually agreed to compromise. These local general demonstration strikes culminated in the national general strike of June 1914 that came to be known as Red Week.

The 1914 Socialist Party Congress held at Ancona in April 1914 (two months before Red Week) consolidated the predominance of the revolutionaries in the party. With war looming over all of Europe, a strong resolution was adopted attacking militarism and urging antimilitarist activity and propaganda both on a national and an international level.

Benito Mussolini. The Library of Congress.

The Beginning of Red Week

At the same time, the moderate conservative premier, Antonio Salandra, was forming a new government (after Giolitti temporarily lost his premiership), and various radicals vocally resisted taxation, demanded wage increases, and opposed militarism. At the beginning of June 1914, tensions, which had been increasing since 1911, were extremely high between capital and labor. Plans were made by worker organizations throughout the country to use Sunday, 7 June 1914, which was Italy's National Day, to demonstrate against militarism (including the special punishment battalions in the army), against the government, for the release of Augusto Masetti (who was imprisoned for defying his colonel), and for a better quality of life.

The government, now headed by Salandra, moved to prohibit the demonstration planned for the east-central coastal city of Ancona (within the region of Marche) by anarchists (persons believing in a state of disorder due to absence or nonrecognition of authority), syndicalists (persons believing that ownership and control of the means of industrial production and distribution should be transferred to workers' unions), and republicans (persons believing in a republican form of government). The CGL, which was officially aligned with the Socialist Party of Italy (PSI), sanctioned the strike. Anarchists and the anarchosyndicalist trade union Italian Workers Union (USI, or *Union Sindacale Italiana*, founded in 1912 by Italian anarchist militant Ettore Bonometti) led the strike.

Prime Minister Salandra sent troops against the demonstrations but did not deter the workers, headed by veteran revolutionaries Enrico Malatesta and Pietro Nenni, from proceeding. Malatesta wanted to use this general strike to popularize the idea of an armed insurrection. Incited by antimilitants like Mussolini, then editor of a socialist newspaper in the northern city of Milan, in the Lombardy region, the strikers and rebels provoked gunfire from the police; three workers were killed.

Spreading Strike

The Ancona shootings ignited the growing resentment of the working class. The news immediately precipitated general insurrectionary incidents and strikes throughout the country. Rebels held Ancona for 10 days, and as a result, roadblocks went up in all the big cities. In the regions of Marche (in the east-central part of Italy) and Emilia-Romagna (north of Marche), rebellious landless laborers confronted strikebreakers hired by local landowners. Bologna was taken over by dissidents. Ancona and nearby towns proclaimed themselves independent communes; other areas, particularly in the north-central region of Emilia-Romagna and the adjoining southeast area of Marche, established autonomous republican governments. The cities of Ferrara and Ravenna (both located in Emilia-Romagna) surrendered to the rebels.

The syndicalists saw the strike as an occasion to launch the social revolution. Eventually, more than 100,000 soldiers were called into action before order was restored. The mass uprising, initiated by a local strike, came to be known as Italy's Red Week.

Aftermath

In spite of its widespread support, the Red Week general strike lacked national coordination. Consequently, though the government acted hesitantly when confronted with the strike—apparently it hoped the strike would end on its own—the organized leadership of the workers' movement took no offensive actions toward transforming the general strike into a full-scale rebellion in key industrial cities. The government was never in danger of losing overall authority, although it did lose control of parts of central Italy for a short time. There were also no signs of mass defections of soldiers. The lack of direction of the general strike showed plainly, after a few days, that it was going nowhere. The strike had expressed the workers' protest against the shootings at Ancona. The movement soon collapsed after the Italian Socialist Party's union wing called off the strike, but it took 10,000 troops to regain control of Ancona.

By early July 1914 Italy—despite its alliance with Germany and Austria—was so preoccupied with trying to remain neutral in the face of impending war in Europe that the problems of its laborers were temporarily shelved. The real importance of the June general strike came a month and a half later with the outbreak of World War I. The PSI demanded Italian neutrality, especially opposing the country' commitment to the Triple Alliance (the defensive union of Germany, Austria-Hungary, and Italy). It even threatened to call a general antiwar strike should the government intervene on the side of Austria-Hungary. The events of Red Week showed the government that the PSI's commitment to an antiwar strike was substantial. Nonetheless, when Italy finally entered the war on the side of the Triple Entente (France, England, and Russia) in May 1915, no efforts were made to call a general strike against the war despite the opposition of the PSI.

Key Players

Bonometti, Ettore (1872–1961): Bonometti was an Italian anarchist militant who was imprisoned several times between 1892 and April 1895, then forced into exile in France, England, and Switzerland. He was eventually allowed to return to Italy but was held under house arrest. However, he used his home for secret antifascist activities and the recruitment of fighters for the underground partisan movement. In 1912 he helped found the anarcho-syndicalist trade union, *Unione Syndicale Italiana* (USI).

Giolitti, Giovanni (1842–1928): Giolitti graduated from the law school at the University of Turin in 1861 and was first elected to parliament in 1882. He recognized the workers' right to strike during his first term as prime minister (1892–1893) but was forced to resign after being implicated in a banking scandal. He returned as prime minister four times: 1903–1905, 1906–1909, 1911–1914, and 1920–1921. He used corruption and manipulation to influence government members and elections. He introduced laws for a national insurance act and for universal male suffrage. From 1911 to 1912 Giolitti waged a war with the Ottoman Empire that resulted in the annexation of Libya, Rhodes, and the Dodecanese Islands. In his last term as prime minister he faced economic problems, including severe inflation. Violence from the Fascist Party, led by Benito Mussolini, increased. In 1920 Giolitti formed the National Bloc, a coalition of Liberals, Democrats, Catholics, and fascists designed to defeat the socialists. In 1921 the National Bloc's coalition disintegrated, and Giolitti lost his majority in parliament.

Malatesta, Enrico (1853–1932): Malatesta was an important Italian anarchist militant and thinker, and a member of the Naples branch of the International Working Men's Association (IWMA). In 1873 he began to spread internationalist propaganda. He was imprisoned many times for his revolutionary activities and repeatedly forced into exile to avoid imprisonment. In 1876 he helped develop a theory of anarchist communism, and the next year took part in the short-lived uprising of Benevento in the Neapolitan mountains. He published the first serious anarchist newspaper in Italy, *La Questione Sociale* in Florence in 1883–1884, and resumed its publication in Argentina (1885–1889) and again in the United States (c. 1900). He opposed the Marxists at the London International Socialist Conference of 1896. He edited *Umanità nova Milan/Rome* (1920–1921) and *Pensiero e Volontà* (1924–1926). He spent the last years of his life held in house arrest by the fascist government.

Mussolini, Benito (1883–1945): Mussolini became an Italian schoolmaster in 1901. He moved to Switzerland the next year but, unable to find a permanent job, was arrested for vagrancy and later expelled and returned to Italy to perform military service. Mussolini joined the staff of a newspaper in the Austrian town of Trento in 1908. He was jailed for his opposition to Italy's war in Libya (1911–1912). Soon after, he was named editor of *Avanti!*, the Socialist Party newspaper in Milan. When World War I began in 1914, he first denounced it as "imperialist" but soon reversed himself and called for Italy's entry on the Allied side. Expelled from the Socialist Party, he started his own Milan newspaper, *Il Popolo d'Italia* (*The People of Italy*), which later became the voice of the fascist movement. He was the premier-dictator of Italy from 1922 to 1943 and the founder and leader of Italian fascism. He attempted to create an Italian empire in alliance with Hitler's Germany. The defeat of Italy in World War II led to his downfall.

Nenni, Pietro (1891–1980): Nenni was a political agitator by the age of 17. While he was editor of *Avanti!* in 1926, the fascists exiled him. He became secretary-general of the Italian Socialist Party in 1944 and served as vice premier in the Gasperi coalition cabinet (1945–1946) and foreign minister (1946–1947). In 1963 Nenni became deputy prime minister of a coalition government that included social democrats and socialists. He succeeded in his longstanding aim of uniting the two groups as the United Socialist Party in 1966, but in the 1968 elections the socialists withdrew from the coalition. He became foreign minister in a new coalition from December 1968.

See also: *Strike Wave, Italy.*

BIBLIOGRAPHY

Books

Goodstein, Phil H. *The Theory of the General Strike from the French Revolution to Poland.* Boulder, CO: East European Monographs, 1984.

Horowitz, Daniel L. *The Italian Labor Movement.* Cambridge, MA: Harvard University Press, 1963.

Neufeld, Maurice F. *Italy: School for Awakening Countries.* Ithaca, NY: Cayuga Press, 1961.

Roberts, David D. *The Syndicalist Tradition and Italian Fascism.* Chapel Hill: University of North Carolina Press, 1979.

Other

Hacken, Richard. "Salandra, Antonio, Premier (1853–1931)." Harold B. Lee Library, Brigham Young University [cited 7 February 2003]. <http://www.lib.byu.edu/~rdh/wwi/bio/s/salandra.html>

"Labor Uprising in Italy 1914." War.com [cited 7 February 2003]. <http://www.onwar.com/aced/data/india/italy1914.htm>

"Towards a History of Anarchist Anti-imperialism." FlagBlackened.net [cited 7 February 2003]. <http://flag.blackened.net/revolt/issues/war/afghan/pamwt/antiimp.html>

—William Arthur Atkins

Robert Peel. © Archive Photos, Inc. Reproduced by permission.

Repeal of Combination Acts

Great Britain 1824

Synopsis

The English Combination Acts forbade workers to organize for the purpose of obtaining higher wages or controlling workplace conditions. The acts were repealed in 1824 as the result of a campaign led by the radical London tailor and political agitator Francis Place and the radical member of Parliament (MP) Joseph Hume. The social basis of the campaign was the skilled artisan class, particularly in London, rather than factory workers or laborers. A wave of strikes following repeal aroused organized opposition from manufacturers, and a new version of the Combination Act was passed in 1825. The new act, although it severely restricted the activities permitted to workers' groups, did allow trade unions a legal existence.

Timeline

1800: The United States moves its federal government to Washington, D.C.

1805: Napoleon defeats a combined Austrian and Russian force at the Battle of Austerlitz.

1811: Prince Aleksandr Borosovich Kurakin, Russian ambassador to Paris, introduces the practice of serving meals *à la Russe*—in courses.

1814: Napoleon's armies are defeated by an allied force consisting of Austria, Britain, Portugal, Prussia, Russia, and Sweden. Napoleon goes into exile on the isle of Elba,

William Huskisson. © Getty Images. Reproduced by permission.

off the Italian coast, and Bourbon king Louis XVIII takes the throne in France.

1819: First production of chocolate for eating (as opposed to cooking), in Switzerland.

1823: U.S. President James Monroe establishes the Monroe Doctrine, whereby the United States warns European nations not to interfere in the political affairs of the Western Hemisphere.

1824: Ludwig van Beethoven composes his Ninth Symphony.

1824: French engineer Sadi Carnot describes a perfect engine: one in which all energy input is converted to energy output. The ideas in his *Reflections on the Motive Power of Fire* will influence the formulation of the Second Law of Thermodynamics—which shows that such a perfect engine is an impossibility.

1824: Cherokee scholar Sequoyah perfects his 85-letter Cherokee alphabet.

1826: French inventor Joseph-Nicéphore Niepce makes the first photographic image in history.

1835: American inventor and painter Samuel F. B. Morse constructs an experimental version of his telegraph.

1842: Scientific and technological advances include the development of ether and artificial fertilizer; the identification of the Doppler effect (by Austrian physicist Christian Johann Doppler); the foundation of biochemistry as a discipline; and the coining of the word *dinosaur*.

Event and Its Context

The Movement for Repeal

The campaign that eventually resulted in the repeal of the Combination Acts began in 1814, when Francis Place began organizing, collecting information, and using the press to express opposition to the acts. The basis of Place's criticism was that the acts, by rendering workers' organizations illegal, embittered relations between workers and employers (although it did not actually prevent the formation of combinations or unions). Place himself was not a great supporter of workers' combinations, which he believed were essentially useless in increasing wages. A follower of classical political economy, Place believed that wages were influenced by the supply and demand for labor rather than by organization. He also believed that it would be better for workers to be free to form combinations and then realize their weakness for themselves rather than be forbidden to form them.

The social base of the campaign against the Combination Acts was not factory workers but London artisans, particularly those in the skilled trades. A short-lived but influential newspaper aimed at London artisans, the *Gorgon*, which had been founded in 1818 by John Wade with the backing of Place's friend, utilitarian philosopher Jeremy Bentham, joined the campaign against the Combination Acts. More successful periodicals that campaigned against the acts included Thomas Wooler's radical weekly *Black Dwarf*, which organized a petitioning campaign in support of repeal in January 1824, and Joseph Robertson and Thomas Hodgskin's three-penny monthly, *Mechanics' Magazine*. Using Hodgskin as an intermediary, Place won the support of the influential Edinburgh political economist John McCulloch, who wrote an article in the January 1824 *Edinburgh Review* that influenced the thinking of MPs and others among the elite.

Joseph Hume presented large numbers of petitions calling for reform of the Combination Acts and gained approval in principle from government leaders. The situation was complicated by the introduction of an alternative bill supported by the Midlands leader of framework-knitters, Gravener Henson. Henson's bill would have abolished not just the Combination Acts themselves, but many other acts against combination, some of which had become dead letters. Because many of the legal actions taken against workers' groups rested not on the Combination Acts themselves but on other laws or an interpretation of common law that forbade unions as conspiracies in restraint of trade, Place and other activists recognized the need to go beyond merely repealing the Combination Acts of 1799 and 1800. The difference between the bill Place and Hume planned to introduce and Henson's bill was that Henson would not only have abolished all laws pertaining to combination, but also would have set up an elaborate machinery to govern labor relations, regulate wages, and settle disputes. Henson gained the support of a Whig MP, Peter Moore of Coventry, who introduced the bill in 1823. Place believed that Henson's and Moore's bill had no chance to pass and merely provoked opposition to repeal of the Combination Acts among MPs and the government. Place and Hume also disagreed with Henson's approach on philosophical grounds, as both believed in orthodox "political economy" with minimal regulation of both capital and labor.

Parliament and the Select Committee

At the opening of Parliament in 1824, Place and his parliamentary allies moved to preempt Henson and Moore and promote their own version of repeal by creating and stacking a parliamentary select committee. Hume moved for the creation of the committee, with the task of investigating the Combination Acts along with other economically restrictive laws, the bans on the export of machinery, and emigration of workmen. Hume chaired the new committee and Place provided witnesses to give testimony against the acts. Place's witnesses excluded both radical trade unionists and the most reactionary employers. There was significant popular support for repeal, as evidenced by workers' meetings, the lobbying of MPs, and petitioning. The committee ended by proposing a series of resolutions rather than a report, and Hume introduced three bills based on the committee's work. One repealed the ban on worker emigration and another consolidated and modified laws on arbitration. The third was the repeal of the Combination Acts. It went further than merely repealing the laws of 1799 and 1800, though, and further than the committee had envisioned. It repealed laws against combination that dated back to the middle ages and also made unions immune from prosecution as conspiracies at common law. It retained the provision for summary trial of those charged with using violence or intimidation to force adherence to a combination. All three bills passed without serious opposition and with the advantage of surprise. Both the prime minister, Lord Liverpool, and the president of the Board of Trade, William Huskisson, later admitted that they had not been aware of the provisions of the act when it was passed.

The Combination Act of 1825

Although some warned workers that attempts to exploit the new legal situation to win higher wages would result in new combination laws, the British economy was booming, the cost of living was rising sharply, and upward pressure on wages was high. Repeal was followed by a wave of strikes, particularly in Lancashire, much to Hume's disgust. The Lancashire manufacturers and Thames shipbuilders, whose shipwrights were on strike, lobbied Parliament for the reinstatement of the combination laws, or for new and even more restrictive laws against combination. Newspapers aimed at the middle and upper classes, such as the *London Times*, attacked what they claimed was trade union criminality and violence. This pressure resulted in Huskisson's taking action. On 28 March 1825 Parliament appointed a Select Committee on the Combination Laws. It was chaired by one of the government's economic experts, the master of the mint, Thomas Wallace. The new committee's mission was to develop very quickly a bill that would satisfy the demands of employers. The committee spent little time on hearings or studying the effects of the 1824 bill. The committee was also strongly biased toward employers and refused to hear trade union representatives, but they paid the expenses of witnesses who would testify against trade unions and charge them with violence and intimidation.

The organized workers met the new committee with massive lobbying efforts, led by Place and the leader of the London shipwrights, John Gast, who was one of the country's leading trade unionists. On 18 April, Gast arranged for the formation of a committee comprising two delegates apiece from many London trades including shipwrights, hatters, brassfounders, silk weavers, carpenters, ladies' shoemakers, and ropemakers. Similar developments were occurring outside London. In Manchester, a meeting of members of different trades on 14 April led to the formation of a Manchester Artisans' General Committee that worked with the Londoners. Groups of artisans in different trades also formed in Birmingham, Sheffield, and Sunderland. Place encouraged provincial workers' organizations to send delegates to London; these included Thomas Hodgson, Henry Woodruffe, and John Beveridge of the Shields and Sunderland seamen and Thomas Worsley of the Stockport cotton-spinners. Others arrived from as far away as Glasgow. The London trade union group met at the Red Lion in Parliament square. Their efforts to win a hearing before the committee were usually frustrated, although eventually the committee heard some representatives from the London shipwrights and coopers. Another petition drive led to the presentation of 97 petitions containing over 100,000 signatures against reimposing the combination laws. These far outweighed the manufacturers' petitions that favored a new combination law. The trades also sponsored the printing and distribution of a pamphlet by Place that attacked a speech by Huskisson.

The government was less concerned with the use of collective bargaining on wages and working conditions than on restrictions on labor mobility and mechanization. The government was also worried about the growth of nationwide labor federations that clearly had a mission outside individual workplaces. The bill presented by the attorney general on 17 June did not restore the original Combination Acts. Instead, it made combinations illegal with the exception of those that met solely for the purpose of determining wages, prices, or working hours. Although this exception recognized the legitimacy of trade union activity, it was followed by a clause that forbade the intimidation of any worker by a combination. This clause interpreted any action against workers who undercut union rates as an offense. The act made such charges easy to bring and prosecute and provided for summary jurisdiction by a magistrate rather than trial by jury. Workers were also concerned by the exclusion of matters such as apprenticeship from those that could be legitimately discussed by combinations. The act seemed to limit combinations to a single trade or workplace and endangered the legality of organizations based on delegates from different trades or workplaces. Place, Hume, and others secured an agreement that these problems would be remedied in the final version of the bill, and in turn he and Place agreed to work against public opposition to the bill.

Robert Peel, a Tory politician working with the London shipbuilders torpedoed initial prospects of a compromise. The shipwrights were still on strike, and Peel threatened that if they did not go back to work, he would modify the bill to once again make combinations prosecutable. The shipwrights did not end their strike. Late June was marked by intense and rather nasty debates, with Peel championing the employers and Hume the workers. The radical Westminster MPs, John Cam Hobhouse and Sir Francis Burdett, supported Hume. There was a see-saw parliamentary struggle over the intimidation clause, with the supporters of the employers seeking to define the forbidden behavior with vague terms such as "insult," which would open the doors for very broad interpretations of what workers were not allowed to do. Place and Gast organized opposition and lobbied both in the House of Commons and the House of Lords. The bill in its final form met some of the demands of the trade unions, including providing more safeguards for workers accused of intimidation. Although the bill definitely marked a step backward from 1824, it was not as bad for workers' groups as many had anticipated and was generally accepted.

The struggles over the 1824 and 1825 bills were important for the development of English trade unionism. They brought home to workers the importance of cooperation between different trades and between London and provincial workers. Out of the struggle was born the *Trades Newspaper*, which was launched in July 1825, edited by Robertson, and in practice dominated by Gast. Actions of organized workers at this time were also a great leap forward in the effective lobbying of Parliament. The most important institutional effect of the new laws was that they protected the legal existence of trade unions, which operated under a variety of restrictions on what they could discuss and what methods they could use to promote solidarity. Many of these restrictions would be subjects of further struggle in the nineteenth century.

Key Players

Gast, John (1772–1837): Gast was the leader of Thames shipwrights in the early nineteenth century. He founded the Hearts of Oak Society, a benefits society for shipwrights that erected almshouses for retired shipwrights, and the Thames Shipwrights' Provident Union, one of the first groups of workers anywhere to use the word union to describe themselves. Gast was a leader in the attempt to form a general union of London's skilled workers, the "Philanthropic Hercules." He was also active in radical London politics and religion.

Henson, Gravener (1785–1852): Henson was a leader of the framework-knitters movement in the Midlands and the author of *History of the Framework-Knitting and Lace Trades* (1831). He tried to bring an action against the masters under the Combination Act in 1811, but the magistrates refused to take action. He lobbied Parliament unsuccessfully to pass legislation to benefit the framework-knitters in 1812. Henson was rumored to be connected with the Luddites and was imprisoned during the suspension of *habeas corpus* from 1817 to 1818.

Hodgskin, Thomas (1783–1869): A retired naval lieutenant, Hodgskin was a colleague of Joseph Robertson in the *Mechanics' Magazine* and the founding of the London Mechanics' Institution. He wrote *Labour Defended against the Claims of Capital* (1825) under the pseudonym "A Labourer" and *Popular Political Economy* (1827). He was one of the earliest English writers to advocate the overthrow of capitalism in the interest of the laborers.

Hume, Joseph (1777–1855): Hume was a radical London member of Parliament but tended to support the doctrines of orthodox political economy, emphasizing the evil of government restraints on trade. For this reason, he opposed the movement for a 10-hour workday.

Huskisson, William (1770–1830): Huskisson was a politician and economic expert in the Tory Party. He served as president of the Board of Trade and treasurer of the navy from 1823 to 1827 and as secretary for war and the colonies from 1827 to 1828.

Peel, Robert (1788–1850): Peel was a Conservative politician who served as prime minister from 1834 to 1835 and 1841 to 1846. He was active in the repeal of the Corn Laws.

Place, Francis (1771–1854): Place was a leader in London radicalism for decades, organizing a strike in 1793 and agitating against the sinking fund from 1816 to 1823. Despite his strong anticlerical and antiaristocratic opinions, he was never a revolutionary or a democrat. Place served as an intellectual point of contact between working-class movements and the world of middle-class utilitarian reformers. Along with Robertson and Hodgskin, he was a leader in the 1823 founding of the London Mechanics' Institution, devoted to scientific and technical education. Place had a prominent role in organizing popular support, even to the point of insurrection, for the Reform Bill of 1832, and assisted in the drafting of the People's Charter.

Robertson, Joseph: Robertson, along with Thomas Hodgskin, launched the *Mechanics' Magazine* in 1823. Robertson was an advocate and organizer of the London Mechanics Institution, although he and Place disagreed about the program of the Institution and became bitter rivals. Robertson was the first editor of the *Trades Newspaper*.

Wade, John (1788–1875): Wade was a woolsorter by profession and founder in 1818 of the *Gorgon*, the first newspaper to cover extensively the affairs of trade unions. Although it only lasted until 1819, it defended striking Manchester cotton workers and drew upon Utilitarian philosophy and working-class experience to make detailed analyses of the position of different trades. Wade later wrote *History of the Middle and Working Classes* (1835).

Wooler, Thomas (1786–1853): Wooler was a printer from Yorkshire who founded and managed the *Black Dwarf* (1817–1824), one of the most popular papers among British radicals. He consistently supported open radical organization aimed at peacefully taking power over violent and clandestine organizations.

See also: *Combination Acts.*

BIBLIOGRAPHY

Books

Pelling, Henry. *A History of British Trade Unionism*, 3rd ed. Harmondsworth, UK: Penguin Books, 1976.

Prothero, Iorwerth. *Artisans and Politics in Early Nineteenth-Century London: John Gast and His Times*. Baton Rouge: Louisiana State University Press, 1979.

Thompson, E. P. *The Making of the English Working Class*. New York: Pantheon Books, 1964.

Woodward, Llewellyn. *The Age of Reform: England, 1815–1870*. 2nd ed. Oxford: Oxford University Press, 1962

ADDITIONAL RESOURCES

Books

Miles, Dudley. *Francis Place, 1771–1854: The Life of a Remarkable Radical*. New York: St. Martin's Press, 1988.

Repeal of the Combination Acts: Five Pamphlets and One Broadside. New York: Arno Press, 1972.

Rice, John, ed. *British Trade Unionism, 1750–1850: The Formative Years*. London: Longman, 1988.

Periodicals

Thompson, W. S. "Francis Place and Working-Class History." *Historical Journal* 5 (1962): 61–70.

—William E. Burns

Revolutions in Europe

Europe 1848

Synopsis

Revolutions swept much of Europe in 1848. The revolutions were a response to the dislocations of the Treaty of Vienna, the growth of centralized states with unchecked royal power, and the largely indirect effects of the Industrial Revolution. Although old quarrels played an important role in creating an unparalleled revolutionary situation on the European continent, the fall of established governments opened the way for new contenders on the political stage. In France particularly, artisans threatened by technology, hard pressed by competition from mechanized industry, and exploited by small masters entered the urban political arena. In 1848 in France, the labor movement asserted itself as an independent political entity on the European continent for the first time. European labor had previously been part of a broadly republican movement. The events of 1848 revealed previously concealed antagonisms between labor and the republican movement.

Timeline

1824: French engineer Sadi Carnot describes a perfect engine: one in which all energy input is converted to energy output. The ideas in his *Reflections on the Motive Power of Fire* will influence the formulation of the Second Law of Thermodynamics—which shows that such a perfect engine is an impossibility.

1833: British Parliament passes the Slavery Abolition Act, giving freedom to all slaves throughout the British Empire.

1838: As crops fail, spawning famine in Ireland, Britain imposes the Poor Law. Designed to discourage the indigent from seeking public assistance, the law makes labor in the workhouse worse than any work to be found on the outside, and thus has the effect of stimulating emigration.

Louis Blanc. The Library of Congress.

1842: In *Sanitary Conditions of the Labouring Population of Great Britain,* British reformer Edwin Chadwick draws attention to the squalor in the nation's mill town slums, and shows that working people have a much higher incidence of disease than do the middle and upper classes.

1845: From Ireland to Russia, famine plagues Europe, killing some 2.5 million people.

1846: Height of the Irish potato famine.

1848: Mexican War ends with the Treaty of Guadalupe Hidalgo, in which Mexico gives up half of its land area, including Texas, California, most of Arizona and New Mexico, and parts of Colorado, Utah, and Nevada. In another treaty, with Great Britain, the United States sets the boundaries of its Oregon Territory.

1848: Discovery of gold at Sutter's Mill in California starts a gold rush, which brings a tremendous influx of settlers—and spells the beginning of the end for California's Native Americans.

1848: Women's Rights Convention in Seneca Falls, New York, launches the women's suffrage movement.

1850: German mathematical physicist Rudolf Julius Emanuel Clausius enunciates the Second Law of Thermodynamics, stating that heat cannot pass from a colder body to a warmer one, but only from a warmer to a colder body. This will prove to be one of the most significant principles of physics and chemistry, establishing that a perfectly efficient physical system is impossible, and that all physical systems ultimately succumb to entropy.

Louis-Napoleon Bonaparte.

1854: In the United States, the Kansas-Nebraska Act calls for decisions on the legality of slavery to be made through local votes. Instead of reducing divisions, this measure will result in widespread rioting and bloodshed, and will only further hasten the looming conflict over slavery and states' rights.

1858: In a Springfield, Illinois, speech during his unsuccessful campaign for the Senate against Stephen Douglass, Abraham Lincoln makes a strong case against slavery, maintaining that "this Government cannot endure permanently half-slave and half-free."

Event and Its Context

Origins of Revolution

The revolutions of 1848 began as efforts to undo the settlements of 1815 brought about by the Treaty of Vienna. At that time, all of Europe was exhausted by war and most of it was tired of French domination. As French armies had retreated, all of Europe was glad to see them go. Rapacious, venal, intolerant, and brutal were among the kindest words used to describe them. Yet by early 1848, in most of continental Europe, some of Europe's best and brightest young men and women and some of its most skilled workers sported tricolor cockades and shouted for a republic.

The persistence and extension of state centralization, the expansion of market society, and the beginnings of industrial-

ization account for this dramatic transformation and made it impossible to return to the old ways. Yet European rulers' fears of revolution led them to discount all efforts at reform. Within individual countries and regions of western and central Europe, networks of middle-class patriots formed during the years of the French Republic. The Empire served as the leaven for the development of new national political cultures and for the spread of revolutionary ideals. Together with regional opposition to centralization, middle-class hostility to absolutism and artisanal and peasant economic grievances provided the tinder for revolution.

Purged of many of its republican and imperial administrators, the state structures introduced by the French remained intact even as their armies withdrew, and so did many elements of their legal code and the social reforms that they had introduced. Restored governments in Bavaria, Naples, Savoy, Tuscany, the Joint Kingdom of the Netherlands, and Württemberg kept most of the administrative apparatus left to them by the French, and the Napoleonic Civil Code remained in force in most of the Prussian Rhine province.

The Napoleonic threat also accelerated existing trends toward centralization in nations that had never been subjected fully to French rule. Before 1789, Fredrick II in Prussia and Marie-Theresa and Joseph II in the Austrian lands already had made great strides toward central administration. They built on past precedents: the restructuring of Prussia between 1807 and 1815 was stimulated by French successes and influenced by French examples, as was the Austrian General Civil Code of 1811 and the administrative system installed in Lombardy and Venetia in 1815.

The advance of state centralization increased the ability of European states to tax their subjects, conscript their soldiers, and intervene in local affairs. Although the states' ability to extract resources grew, their subjects received nothing in return. In France and the states run by French administrations, state centralization and enhanced state power had been counterbalanced by citizenship rights, including the right to trial by jury, religious toleration, freedom of the press, the end of legally privileged corporations, and the abolition of noble titles. More importantly, many males—the number varied according to different election laws—received the right to vote. In contrast, under the various restoration regimes, Europeans paid the price of the centralized states without receiving any of the benefits of citizenship.

The Vienna settlement had focused on strengthening the states bordering France by merging smaller states into more powerful ones. Such mergers, however, created new religious and economic tensions. Ardently Catholic Rhinelanders became subjects of the very Protestant Prussian monarch; liberal Protestants in the Rhenish Palatinate became subjects of a devoutly Catholic Bavarian king. Where mercantile states had been incorporated into agrarian empires, many merchants were dissatisfied. Merchants in Lombardy and Venetia who had formerly traded with France rued the prohibitive tariffs that tied them to stagnant Austrian markets. A Cologne businessman who, learning that his city had been given to Prussia, summed up the mercantile response to such mergers in his remark, "We have married into a poor family." Even in the case of the solidly commercial Dutch state, many in the Austrian Netherlands (modern day Belgium) resented having to pay off the enormous debts the Dutch state had accumulated under revolutionary rule.

Memories of the 25 years of French dominance proved hard to eradicate. Even when official amnesties were granted for past actions, in France, Italy, and Spain, many aristocrats and clergymen found it difficult to forgive or forget those who had purchased church property and confiscated familial estates. Those French businessmen and administrators who had rallied to Napoleon during the Hundred Day period when he returned from Elba found themselves in an especially exposed situation. Authorities were particularly unforgiving to these men who had banded together to support their country while Napoleon fought their foreign enemies. No matter whether they willed a permanent break or not, their actions had linked them irretrievably to the revolutionary era and, unable to escape this label, many embraced it.

The impact of Industrial Revolution and the implementation of French legislation in the economic arena, combined with unfavorable conditions in agriculture, provided further fuel for a revolutionary conflagration. The growing impact of market forces produced a new self-confidence and demand for recognition on the part of businessmen and financiers. Between 1815 and 1848, industrialization only indirectly affected the continent. The growth of an industrial proletariat played only a relatively minor role. Before 1848 only Belgium, parts of France, a few areas in Germany, and a portion of Bohemia had really begun to adopt the new English industrial technologies. Large-scale coal production was confined to the Liège basin in Belgium and the Stéphanois basin in France. The Upper Silesian coalfields were in production in both Prussia and Bohemia, but transportation costs limited the yield to local purposes. Of all the technologies of the Industrial Revolution, before 1848 only textiles had spread across the European continent from Barcelona to Lodz. As in Lancashire, cotton textiles gathered a workforce of mainly unskilled workers, largely women and children, into cities that lacked all social and health amenities. Cotton textile towns such as Barmen, Elberfeld, Elbeuf, Ghent, Mulhouse, and Verviers more or less replicated the miserable living conditions of their English urban contemporaries, and wool spinning towns such as Aachen, Liberic, and Tourcoing were as bad or worse.

The true impact of industrialization's contribution to social revolution, however, was indirect. Industrialization had its most dramatic effect in those areas where the legal code of the French Revolution had struck down guilds, privileged monopolies, and corporations and where it abolished the legal jurisdiction of towns over their surrounding countryside. In Berlin, Düsseldorf, Paris, and Turin, subcontracting and domestic work increasingly menaced the livelihood of tailors, shoemakers, and cabinetmakers. In Cologne, ready-to-wear clothing threatened masters more than did machinery. Masters complained that journeymen and apprentices had become insubordinate and more inclined to set up their own shops before completing their training. By 1848 the capital cities were tinderboxes, filled with skilled workers who possessed strong traditions of solidarity and organizing and a growing sense of frustration and rage. The expansion of a discontented domestic workforce in the countryside also contributed to rural unrest. In Solingen, low paid domestic metalworkers replaced urban craft workers in the less

skilled metal trades, but the living standards of domestic workers steadily declined as their charcoal-fired steel products were exposed to competition from English blast furnaces.

Economic crises in 1829 and 1846–1847 also increased the pressure on the working classes. Massive grain purchases to offset the failure of the potato and rye crops in northern Europe raised the price of bread and put further pressure on the living standards of artisans and rural outworkers.

The Revolution

There is a certain sameness to the events that opened the revolution of 1848 in different European cities. Imagine this scene: a serious political crisis occurs that brings people into the street of the capital city. The army is called out. Noisy crowds taunt uneasy and frightened troops. Violence erupts to the sounds of gunfire. Panicked, the soldiers fire on the crowd. Barricades arise, manned largely by skilled artisans. Columns of troops sent into the narrow streets of the preindustrial city find themselves surrounded and subjected to murderous crossfire and sniper bullets. Often the middle-class national guard or militia refuses to reinforce the regular troops, which then are pulled out of the city. Alternatively, a national guard or civil militia group forms in response to demands, and the hastily established group demands social reforms. In any case, leading oppositional politicians with no connection to the insurrection in the streets bring a series of demands, including one for a new constitution, to the ruler or his representative. Under pressure from the crowd, these politicians influence the selection of a temporary government that will rule until elections are carried out for a representative body that will write a new constitution. With minor modifications, the setting could be Milan, Munich, Palermo, Paris, Venice, or Vienna in 1848. Together, barricades, armed confrontation between militia men, and constitution-making constituted the repertoire of protest in 1848.

Workers in the Revolution of 1848

If there was a great similarity to the opening of revolutionary situations in key capital cities in February and March of 1848, divergences quickly appeared. From the young Karl Marx to the middle-aged Alexis de Tocqueville, social commentators were struck by the entry of organized workers on to the national political stage. In Paris, for the first time in 1848, an organized labor movement put forward in the national political arena demands that were explicitly class-related. Between 1815 and 1848, Paris had been in the political vanguard of revolutionary Europe: the middle classes and artisans had accumulated considerable revolutionary experience and had come to reject monarchism. In France alone, a significant section of politically active, middle-class liberals—men such as Alphone de Lamartine, a minority certainly—were committed to a democratic republicanism, that is, to a government without a king and to something approaching universal manhood suffrage.

Also in France, an artisanal working class, thrown into contact with these democratic republicans, combined republican political ideals and its own work-based feelings of solidarity to produce a new sense of class consciousness. These workers developed the core concepts of central state intervention, citizenship, and nationality to put forward their own political demands. Requests for government funds to implement workers' control at the workplace profoundly shocked the French middle class, even its republican members. In the 1840s the growth of trade unionism among highly skilled workers also threw workers into conflict with the state; trade unions were illegal and shared the shadows with secret political societies.

New rights only barely envisaged in 1793–1796 became the focus of political struggles in Paris in the months after February 1848. Organized workers presented their demands to the hastily established provisional government formed of mostly middle-class political leaders. Workers possessed leverage because many had joined the national guard and had acquired arms. At the same time, the army was demoralized, its embittered generals reticent to involve themselves in politics. The neutrality of the army and the deep divisions within the national guard, split between workers and the lower middle classes, constituted the enduring dual power situation that finally surfaced in June 1848. The demands of workers for a "right to work," their organized presence in the streets, and their determination to pressure the provisional government to recognize their demands produced glaring divisions with the republican camp.

Meanwhile the speed with which national elections were called gave very limited opportunity for educative political discussion; outside the urban political debate, peasants cast their votes for familiar names, which usually meant members of the landed elite. As a result, the new Constituent Assembly that met in early May 1848 had a monarchical majority. Only international divisions among the monarchist factions and the rise of a new authoritarian political figure, Louis-Napoleon Bonaparte, prevented a restoration. This conservatized political environment made it increasingly unlikely that middle-class republicans would continue to yield to working-class pressures, while a trade depression, prolonged by the revolutionary turmoil, made workers all the more desperate for state employment.

While consolidating its political hold, the government temporized. It attempted to coopt workers by enrolling them in "national workshops" and in a citizens' militia, the *Garde Mobile*. The title *national workshops* came from a celebrated pamphlet by the socialist Louis Blanc. Instead of the state-funded collectives of skilled workers envisaged by Blanc, however, the national workshops became the traditional outdoor manual public workers' programs long used by French governments in times of high unemployment. Workers felt betrayed but enrolled in the national workshops for lack of other recourse. In June of 1848, when the workshops in Paris were abolished by the reactionary legislature, the unemployed revolted and, with guns obtained in the National Guard, rebuilt their barricades. Here the tense situation that had existed since February, when the French army had collapsed, finally reached its climax in armed conflict. The counter-revolutionary workers organized in the *Garde Mobile* subdued the revolutionary workers in the national workshops. The repression of these workers opened the way for a general smashing of left-wing opposition and, in the end, the defeat of the workers removed a key prop that had been supporting an already rickety republic. With the organized workers defeated and the republican camp in a shambles, the way was paved for the rise of Louis-Napoleon, the first of the plebiscitarian dictators.

Although the main action in 1848 involved artisanal workers, middle-class male republicans, and reactionary legislators, other social movements also began to develop in the public space created by the revolution. In 1848 women's rights activists claimed a portion of that space to argue that women should be admitted into full citizenship in the republic. Their demands attracted less attention than those of workers because they lacked the more powerful weapons possessed by male workers. Secret societies, national guards, trade unions, and most of the national workshops were strictly male preserves. Many of the political clubs that organized after February of 1848 did not admit female members. Some feminist scholars have suggested, plausibly, that the term "fraternity" in the revolutionary slogan referred to "male solidarity," its literal meaning, and entailed the exclusion of females. Yet women took advantage of the de facto freedom of assembly to organize their own clubs and used the language of universal rights to appeal for admission into citizenship. After June, the general suppression of opposition eliminated the organs of feminist claim-making just as thoroughly as they eliminated that of organized workers.

Key Players

Blanc, Louis (1811–1882): Published in 1840, Blanc's book *Organization of Labor* popularized socialist ideas. His idea of state-funded workers' cooperatives had great appeal to Parisian artisanal workers. During the heady days of the revolution, the provisional government appointed Blanc as a minister without portfolio and head of the Luxembourg Commission to study labor conditions. It soon became clear that this move was intended only to coopt a figure who had been popular among the working-classes. As soon as the working-class movement was defeated, Blanc was forced to flee into exile.

Blanqui, Louis-Auguste (1805–1881): Blanqui was famous throughout Europe for his conspiratorial activities and a brand of radical republicanism that touched on socialism. Blanqui organized secret societies intended to overthrow European monarchies and establish a dictatorship. Under the republican dictatorship, the people would be inculcated with republican antireligious views that would enable them to build a socialist order.

Bonaparte, Louis-Napoleon (1808–1873): The cousin of Napoleon Bonaparte, Louis-Napoleon was an adventurer who used his great name to become president of France (10 December 1848). Louis-Napoleon appealed to both popular and elitist segments of French society. To the elite, he was a man of order. To the impoverished, he was a man who favored social reform. Once established in the presidency, Louis-Napoleon at once began the quest to extend his term, engineering a coup d'etat in 1851 and becoming the Emperor Napoleon III. He lost his throne after defeat in the Franco Prussian War (1870–1871).

de Lamartine, Alphone (1790–1869): A great French poet who proved a mediocre political figure. Lamartine's romantic political rhetoric managed to carry along many, both middle class and artisan, in the exciting early days of the revolution. He was the de facto head of the provisional government that emerged after the February revolution. His attempt to paper over the increased conflict between middle classes and artisans finally led to his political fall. Beloved in February 1848, he was rejected by everyone when he ran for president in December 1848, polling last in a field of five.

See also: *June Days Rebellion.*

BIBLIOGRAPHY

Books

Harsin, Jill. *Barricades: The War of the Streets in Revolutionary Paris, 1830–1848.* New York: St. Martin's Press, 2002.

Sperber, Jonathan. *The European Revolutions, 1848–1851.* Cambridge, MA: Cambridge University Press, 1994.

Tilly, Charles. *European Revolutions, 1492–1992.* Oxford, UK: Basil Blackwell, 1993.

Traugott, Mark. *Armies of the Poor: Determinants of Working-Class Participation in the Parisian Insurrection of June 1848.* Princeton, NJ: Princeton University Press, 1985.

—Michael Hanagan

Russian Revolutions

Russia 1917

Synopsis

Historians largely agree that revolution was inevitable in Russia after 1861. The maintenance of strict authoritarian rule and the growing separation of people from state created a situation in which any increase in the hardship endured by the Russian workers, soldiers, and peasants could initiate a violent uprising. The revolution of 23–27 February 1917, as denoted by the Julian calendar, began in a bread queue. Following the abdication of Czar Nicholas II, a parliamentary democracy was established, but the state Duma was weak from inception and plagued with attempts at overthrow from both the right and the left. Democracy lasted only eight months. Between 24 and 25 October the Bolsheviks led an armed insurrection supported by a broad coalition of workers and soldiers. This ushered in a new regime that would effect radical change across the economic, political, and social spheres of Russian life. For many, however, life continued much the same as under czardom: punctuated by hardship and repression.

Timeline

1897: Establishment of the Zionist movement under the leadership of Theodor Herzl.

1902: Second Anglo-Boer War ends in victory for Great Britain. It is a costly victory, however, resulting in the loss of more British lives (5,774) than any conflict between 1815 and 1914. The war also sees the introduction of concentration camps, used by the British to incarcerate Boer civilians.

1911: In China, revolutionary forces led by Sun Yat-sen bring an end to more than 2,100 years of imperial rule.

1915: A German submarine sinks the *Lusitania,* killing 1,195, including 128 U.S. citizens. Theretofore, many Americans had been sympathetic toward Germany, but the incident begins to turn the tide of U.S. sentiment toward the Allies.

1917: The intercepted "Zimmermann Telegram" reveals a plot by the German government to draw Mexico into an alliance against the United States in return for a German promise to return the southwestern U.S. territories taken in the Mexican War. Three months later on 6 April, in response to German threats of unrestricted submarine warfare, the United States declares war on Germany.

1917: On both the Western Front and in the Middle East, the tide of the war begins to turn against the Central Powers. The arrival of U.S. troops, led by General Pershing, in France in June greatly boosts morale and reinforces exhausted Allied forces. Meanwhile, Great Britain scores two major victories against the Ottoman Empire as T. E. Lawrence leads an Arab revolt in Baghdad in March, and troops under Field Marshal Edmund Allenby take Jerusalem in December.

1919: Formation of the Third International (Comintern), whereby the Bolshevik government of Russia establishes its control over communist movements worldwide.

1923: Conditions in Germany worsen as inflation skyrockets and France, attempting to collect on coal deliveries promised at Versailles, marches into the Ruhr basin. In November an obscure political group known as the National Socialist German Workers' Party attempts to stage a coup, or putsch, in a Munich beer hall. The revolt fails, and in 1924 the party's leader, Adolf Hitler, will receive a prison sentence of five years. He will only serve nine months, however, and the incident will serve to attract attention for him and his party, known as the Nazis.

1927: Stalin arranges to have Trotsky expelled from the Communist Party.

Event and Its Context

The Long-term Causes of Revolution

Russians had attempted revolution prior to 1917, and the fear of an uprising dogged the czarist regime after the French Revolution. Czar Nicholas I had faced a limited rebellion in 1825, which led him to abandon reforms that had been inspired by the influence of revolutionary France. Alexander II, despite introducing sweeping reforms, was assassinated in 1881 by a terrorist bomb, and his successors resorted to the traditional forms of societal control: repression and fear. The Russian political system thus followed the strict autocratic model. Dissent

Vladimir Ilich Lenin and Leon Trotsky. © Hulton/Getty Images. Reproduced by permission.

was dealt with swiftly and severely, and any reforms that were introduced were only considered in order to bolster the position of the czar.

The reforms of the 1860s, however, reduced the state's ability to control the masses. The emancipation of the serfs and industrial revolution had allowed the peasants to leave the village communes and seek work in the industrial centers. The working class that this created did not find any greater prosperity. The industrial workers were housed in damp, drafty barracks; wages were low; and the workday was long. In practical terms they had swapped land slavery for wage slavery. They worked to afford their rent and food alone. The diminished number of landed peasants had to work harder as many of the young men migrated to the cities. They had fewer mouths to feed but they still had to meet the redemption payments through which land had passed from the nobility to the communes. The workers and peasants, therefore, had little in the way of security and were no freer than they had been as rural serfs.

The greatest single cause of Russia's problems was economic mismanagement. Agricultural production had plummeted following emancipation. The nobility purchased the majority of commune surpluses and neglected their own arable land. Food crops were largely imported. Food prices in the cities were high at a time when wages needed to be kept low. The low wages were the result of the backward state of Russian industry. Most of the production equipment was imported, as were specialists who trained the workers. Communication links were vastly improved, incredible growth rates were achieved, and an industrial base and a corporate structure were created, both of which expanded exponentially between 1880 and 1910. Output, however, remained low and of poor quality, and these conditions prevailed throughout the czarist period.

With economic instability and extreme hardship as a backdrop, a revolutionary movement flourished. The leaders emerged from, and were denoted as, the intelligentsia. This highlights the division between revolutionaries and the people. The peasants and workers largely sought amelioration by appealing to the czar, not by instituting a change of government. The trade unions, which formed around the major industrial centers, stood as the chief foci for anti-czarist activity. These groups circulated the speeches of Lenin and Leon Trotsky and Lenin's Marxist newspaper, *Iskra* (*The Spark*). As economic conditions worsened, exacerbated by wars against the Ottoman Empire and Japan, the force of the revolutionaries' arguments were strengthened.

Short-term Causes, 1905–1917

The event that most significantly damaged the position of the czar in Russian society also led to the failed revolution of 1905. Czarist soldiers fired on a peaceful protest march, led by Father Gapon, outside the Winter Palace. More than a hundred died and became martyrs for the Octobrist cause, a political group whose October Manifesto demanded democratic reforms. Although the revolution was soon suppressed, the Octobrists tried to use the threat of revolution to effect reform, while reminding the people that those killed on Bloody Sunday in 1905 were murdered on the orders of the czar. The ensuing combination of reform and fierce repression paved the way for the events of 1917.

Following the suppression of the mass demonstrations in 1905, Czar Nicholas II attempted to regain control over the Russian people. His first targets were the "disloyal" non-Russians. He used pogroms and educational reforms to attempt the Russification of the various minorities of the Russian Empire. Poles, Finns, and Jews suffered particularly, and many escaped Russia for Britain and the United States. Nicholas II also broke up the communes to reduce collective identity. He created the *kulak* class of peasant smallholders who had to compete with one another for land and trade. Some complied voluntarily; however, the majority of rural peasants grouped behind the *Trudovik* or Labour Party to oppose the Stolypin reforms, named after Piotr Stolypin (minister of the interior 1904–1907 and prime minister after 1907). Compliance was enforced brutally among those who resisted. By 1907 the Russian countryside was decorated with "Russia's peasants wearing the neckties awarded by Stolypin,"—in other words, peasants hung on main routes between villages as an example for others considering revolt against reform.

The revolutionary parties were quick to voice their support for the peasants and often campaigned on behalf of the Jews. Their support of the miners and shipbuilders, however, provided a practical dimension for the Marxist arguments of groups such as the Octobrists and the Bolsheviks. Brutality against striking workers fuelled the agitation. One event particularly marked a watershed in political agitation. In March 1912 advancing troops forced over 100 striking miners at the Lena goldfield into a mineshaft entrance and massacred them. The role of the Bolsheviks after any such event was to spread their account of the repression throughout trade union membership. Lenin and Trotsky often toured the industrial centers teaching the workers in Marxist economics and convincing them of their role in the impending revolution.

The major dissatisfaction for the majority of political groups was that, despite having become a constitutional monarchy, the czar was still able to exert autocratic power. On 23 April 1906 the czar agreed to the Octobrist demand of political reform. This transformed the czar's state council into a semiappointed upper house whose membership was supplemented by representatives from the land owning and corporate classes. The move also created a lower house, the state Duma, that would be elected by popular suffrage. Other reforms of the time included rights of free expression and assembly and the right to form a trade union. Article 87 of the new constitution, however, gave the czar the power to dissolve the Duma and legislate alone. Therefore the traditional power of the czar was retained as the Duma was in practice only allowed to pass laws with which the czar agreed.

By March 1907 two Dumas had collapsed because of differences with the czar and his upper house. Nicholas constantly attempted to ensure that the Duma had a conservative majority. This contrasted sharply with popular choice, as it was the left-wing revolutionary groups that largely benefited from the elections. The government found some level of stability under Stolypin, and the third Duma managed to survive until 1912. Stolypin failed to get the Duma and the state council to agree on reform designed on the Bismarkian model, but he managed to maintain his image as a reformer while also bolstering the position of the czar. In reality though, this made him the sworn enemy of both right and left. In September 1911 he was assassinated by a Social Revolutionary turned police agent, possibly under the orders of Czar Nicholas II. Historians agree that Stolypin's power over the Duma, coupled with his popularity among the nobility, made him appear a threat to the czar's power. His death led to a vacuum that could only be filled by

the left wing. Following the Lena massacre, Bolshevik activism increased, and the left made considerable advances in the 1912 election. Divisions between the left-wing factions, however, allowed the nationalist *Kadets*, who at that time supported the czar, to control the Duma. The stagnation of social reforms fed the dissatisfaction within Russian society; war and its associated hardships would spell the end for czarist Russia.

War and Revolution

Russia's position as the policeman of postrevolutionary Europe meant that the nation's entry into World War I was inevitable. Despite contrary advice from his closest advisors, the czar pledged to honor his contract with Britain and France. This led Russia into a war that the nation was economically unable to support and that the czar himself was ill-equipped to lead.

Nicholas II, however, saw himself as the only person capable of leading Russia into war. In his opinion the people had elected those least capable of running a nation, thus he squandered the initially patriotic mood by suspending the Duma and relying increasingly on the advice of his wife, who was of German extraction, and her confidant, the monk Grigory Rasputin. This alienated him from the people, the Russian armed forces, and from large sections of the nobility. Czarina Alexandria became known as "the German woman" or "the German whore." Stories abounded about the debauched lifestyle of Rasputin, as did rumors that Rasputin had the czar and czarina under a demonic spell. These stories compounded to suggest that the czar was personally responsible for Russia losing the war.

Hardships faced by ordinary Russian people increased opposition to the czar. Munitions were scarce and basic food supplies were rationed. Prices for bread spiraled out of control, and few could afford an adequate diet. Famine threatened all the major cities by January 1917.

Even so, only a small minority within the moderate social democratic party openly opposed the war, though the Bolsheviks later claimed that they supported the war because of the opportunities it offered for revolution. Notably, few questioned the course of the nation's policy. In 1915 the liberals formed the Progressive bloc to demand that power be returned to the Duma, though this was largely to coordinate delivery of food supplies. Contemporary accounts express little fear of revolution. The revolutionaries themselves were either in exile or deep underground. By late 1916 the liberals were demanding that the "dark, treasonable elements be removed from court and a constitutional government put in charge of our nation." Their demands were preempted. Rasputin, chief among those seen as dark and treasonous, was assassinated by a group of young nobles led by Prince Yusupov, the czar's cousin. This was symptomatic of the increasingly united opposition to czardom among the upper echelon of society across Russia. Conscription drives were met with violent resistance, troops often deserted, and even the police appeared unwilling to enforce czarist law. Civil war seemed the most likely outcome.

The February Revolution

By December 1916 there were clear signs that order was breaking down. Police officers, facing continual demonstrations

Demonstrators, Russian Revolution, Petrograd, now St. Petersburg, Russia. © Hulton/Getty Images. Reproduced by permission.

against food shortages, warned that "preventative measures are no longer practical." This was proven correct. On 23 February 1917 a group of St. Petersburg (later Petrograd) housewives marked International Women's Day by organizing a demonstration against the price of bread. The march also coincided with calls from de facto Bolshevik leader Joseph Stalin for a national strike and a march on St. Petersburg. For two days demonstrations escalated, and by 25 February the troops were mobilized against the Russian people. On 26 February, a day of prolonged rioting, a Volhynian regiment of the czar's personal guard opened fire and killed over 50 demonstrators. Appalled by their own actions, on the following day regiments of domestic guards

joined the demonstrators. The central headquarters of the police was razed to the ground, czarist ministers were arrested, and the government in St. Petersburg was dissolved. Similar demonstrations took place across Russia, and many local government centers were attacked and their occupants killed.

The czar dissolved the Duma on 27 February, declared a state of emergency, and attempted to bring troops back from the front to restore order. The Duma deputies ignored Nicholas II's orders and reconvened to establish the Provisional Duma Committee. This represented all the mainstream parties in the previous Duma. The revolutionary groups, in opposition to the "Pro-

Battleship Potemkin

It is a quirk of film history that the two most widely acclaimed silent pictures were propaganda films of the extreme right and extreme left respectively. D. W. Griffith's *Birth of a Nation* (1915) portrayed freed slaves in the American South of the Reconstruction as raping, looting savages abetted by the villains of the occupation forces—and opposed by the brave knights of the Ku Klux Klan. Protested at the time of its release by the recently formed National Association for the Advancement of Colored People (NAACP), *Birth of a Nation* helped spawn the twentieth-century resurrection of the Klan.

At the other end of the political spectrum was *Battleship Potemkin* (1925) by Soviet director Sergei Eisenstein, which depicts a 1905 naval uprising. Though the *Potemkin* mutiny is today viewed in light of Russia's Revolution of 1905, it was to some extent an isolated incident, sparked by unbearable conditions aboard ship. The sailors' revolt, joined by the people of Odessa, led to an assault by government troops, portrayed in one of the most memorable (and oft-imitated) sequences in film history: the "Odessa Steps" scene. As Eisenstein portrayed it, the czar's soldiers press forward so relentlessly that not even a baby in a carriage is safe from their ruthlessness.

In contrast to Griffith's movie, Eisenstein's does not as immediately strike the viewer as propaganda, since the year of the film's setting prevents the portrayal of Bolsheviks in the story. (The Bolshevik wing of the Social Democratic Party was formed in 1903, but in 1905 it had little impact on events in Russia.) Rather, the propagandistic aspect of the film is more implicit, since it clearly aligns the freedom-loving sailors of the *Potemkin* with the future rulers of Soviet Russia.

Interestingly, the Bolsheviks themselves in 1921 faced a mutiny by sailors aboard the *Kronstadt* in Petrograd. Whereas the *Potemkin* mutineers demanded only better food and living conditions, the *Kronstadt* sailors wanted free elections, freedom of speech, and freedom of association. Leon Trotsky crushed the uprising with a brutality that would have impressed the czarist troops. Even years later, when he was on the run from Stalin in Mexico, he dismissed the revolt of the Kronstadt sailors as "counterrevolutionary."

Source: Edward Murray. *Ten Film Classics: A Reviewing.* New York: F. Ungar, 1978.

—Judson Knight

The composition of the Provisional government was almost identical to that of the Progressive bloc. The only addition was socialist Alexander Kerensky, minister of justice. Prime Minister Prince Lvov surrounded himself with members of the Kadet Party, supporters of a constitutional monarchy. Despite the ambiguity of the legitimacy of the government and its liberal conservative composition, it initially enjoyed widespread popularity after ending all forms of repression and discrimination. The problem of the war, however, remained. It was in this area that the Soviet should have controlled policy. The workers and soldiers had all pledged loyalty to the Soviet, yet the leaders failed to take the initiative over policy.

The Soviet was happy to condemn Provisional government policy. The government, in turn, made little attempt to meet the demands of the Soviet. In effect there was a stalemate between the competing loci of power. The government hid behind its self-ordained provisionality, arguing that necessary fundamental changes should be postponed until the election of a constituent assembly. The election date was set but constantly postponed while parts of Russia were under enemy occupation; this meant continuing with the war until the Germans were forced into a retreat. The major national concerns—reallocation of land, economic reorganization, and industrial reforms—were sidelined. Lvov showed his enthusiasm for continuing Russian participation in the war by pledging on 6 March 1917 to "unswervingly carry out the agreements made with our allies." This set the tone for the Provisional government's policy and indicated that there was little hope of middle ground between the government and the Soviet.

With freedom of speech and assembly restored, the left wing was able to mobilize in spite of the lack of social reforms. The left also gained a new leader in April when Lenin returned from exile. The Bolsheviks, led in Lenin's absence by Stalin and Lev Kamenev, had become increasingly moderate. At their conference on 29 March 1917, a delegate calling for Bolshevik seizure of power was declared out of order. Lenin, however, reversed this stance. He argued that they should embark on a program of propaganda to convince the workers to prepare for a proletarian dictatorship. Trotsky returned to Russia in May and joined Lenin. Between them they led the campaign to the people under the slogans of "Peace, Bread and Land" and "All Power to the Soviets."

Circumstances favored the Bolsheviks. Despite the Soviet calling for "peace without annexation or indemnity," the Provisional government declared support for annexing territory and imposing reparations on defeated combatants. This represented a serious misreading of the public mood, and St. Petersburg again witnessed mass demonstrations by workers and soldiers. General Kornilov suggested to Lvov that the government must use force to restore order, and Lvov agreed. The Soviet, however, ordered all troops to remain in their barracks, and a political crisis ensued. Lvov and the majority of Kadets resigned from government.

By 16 June the most senior member still in government was Kerensky, minister of war. He decided that the only way to win back public support was to mount a new and successful offensive against the Germans. The resulting defeat and rout of the Russian army added further credibility to the Bolshevik arguments. Discipline collapsed, millions of soldiers took their

visionals," formed the St. Petersburg Soviet. The Soviet pledged to pave the way for a socialist revolution, but it was ill-placed to assume control of Russia. Instead it agreed that the Provisionals, the bourgeoisie, should form a government. Largely, the Provisional government, as it became known, existed only as long as the Soviet agreed that it could.

weapons and deserted, and demonstrations escalated. Delays of the promised elections increased tensions. Despite the fact that the moderate left had taken control over the government, policy remained in stasis.

Kerensky used those troops who remained loyal to the government to crush demonstrations staged on 3–5 July and to seize the leading Bolsheviks. Lenin fled to Finland, denounced as a German spy; Trotsky was arrested for treason. Kornilov, with the agreement of Kerensky, began an advance on St. Petersburg with the intention of establishing a military dictatorship. Kornilov had to march his troops on foot, however, as the railway workers refused to transport them. Troops loyal to the Soviet met them on the outskirts of the capital and, rather than fighting, the regiments fraternized. Most of Kornilov's army abandoned his cause. Kornilov arrived in St. Petersburg virtually alone and was arrested. Although this could have been seen as a victory for democracy, without Kornilov's troops, the Provisional government was powerless. The troops ignored Kerensky's orders to return to the front, and on 16 October, in direct opposition to Kerensky's government, the Soviet formed the Military Revolutionary Committee to defend St. Petersburg against counterrevolution. The remaining Bolsheviks held the majority on the committee, which prompted the Mensheviks and social revolutionaries to refuse to participate; clearly there was little to stop them from seizing power.

Bolshevik Rule

From his exile in Finland, Lenin pressed the Bolsheviks to seize power. On 10 October the central committee of the party approved Lenin's policy. Two weeks later, on 24–25 October, Trotsky led the forces under the Military Revolutionary Committee in a coup. The workers and soldiers seized the main government and administrative buildings and arrested those who opposed them. On the afternoon of 25 October, Trotsky announced the end of the Provisional government; the majority of ministers were already under arrest.

At the Congress of Soviets, which met on 25 October, 390 (60 percent) of 650 delegates were Bolsheviks. The debate centered on the legality and character of the coup. The moderate left voiced their opposition to the Bolsheviks, doubting their motives, and withdrew. Only a small group of left-wing Social Revolutionaries remained to form a short-lived coalition. At the second congress on 8 November, Lenin took control. He declared that they should "proceed to the construction of the socialist order." In practice this meant immediately withdrawing from the war, embarking on a reorganization of the economic basis of society, and establishing a dictatorship consisting of workers and soldiers' deputies. Whether his intention was to establish a permanent dictatorship is unknown; the civil war that ensued defined the character of the Soviet regime as much as the ideology.

The Treaty of Brest-Litovsk, signed on 3 March 1918, marked Russia's exit from World War I and emasculated the Bolshevik state. The Baltic states, Finland, Poland, and the Ukraine were ceded. Within Russia, czarist supporters rallied to attempt to overthrow the Bolsheviks. With the aid of American, British, and French forces, the "White Army" was able to mount a serious challenge to Lenin's "Red" forces. International support eroded, largely due to trade union pressure, and by 1920 the White Army was defeated.

With civil war and external interference as a backdrop, the "Red Terror" began. Strikes and peasant uprisings, protesting hardships and attempts by the state to exert control over industry and seize the land, were put down with similar force and brutality as had been employed by the czars. Lenin retreated somewhat from introducing socialism by force and launched the New Economic Policy in 1921. His incapacitation and death, however, paved the way for Stalin to reintroduce repressive methods for reorienting society. By the late 1920s the government had greater control and used fear more effectively than had the czarist regime. Thus the revolutions achieved little to ameliorate the hardships of the Russian people.

The revolutions, particularly the Bolshevik coup, changed the course of history. Not only did Marxist socialism become a viable alternative to capitalism, it was also seen as a threat by the Western world. Beyond the final three years of World War II in 1942–1945, the Western powers tried to contain Bolshevik influence, which led to the cold war. Despite a propaganda campaign, few could reconcile the tales of Soviet achievement with the reports of purges and state repression. The popular culture thus characterized the USSR as the "evil empire" until its fall in 1990. Within modern Russia the old hark back to the glory days of Stalinism; however, to the majority, Bolshevism was a tragedy for the Russian people.

Key Players

Kerensky, Alexander (1882–1970): Lvov's successor as head of the Provisional government who attempted unsuccessfully to reunite the Russian people behind the war. When the Bolsheviks took over, he fled to the United States and became a professor of politics.

Lenin (orig. Vladimir Ilich Ulyanov, 1870–1924): Revolutionary theorist and leader of the Bolshevik party. He founded the Soviet Union as an ideological state based on his writings, *What Is to Be Done* (1902) and *The State and Revolution* (1917).

Lvov, Georgy Yevgenyevich (1861–1925): Prince who was head of the Provisional government (March–July 1917) and architect of the zemstvo system of peasant self-government. After his resignation he emigrated to Paris.

Nicholas II (1868–1918): Emperor of all Russia (1894–1917). His refusal to accept the will of the people and to devolve some of his power caused a deep fissure between the royal leaders and the people. The Bolsheviks executed him and his family during the Russian Civil War.

Rasputin, Grigory (1869 or 1872–1916): A "holy man" who had great influence in the court of Czar Nicholas II because of his ability to treat the czarevitch's hemophilia. He was assassinated by members of the czar's family.

Stalin, Joseph (orig. Iosif Vissarionovich Dzhugashvili, 1879–1953): Revolutionary guerrilla (1905–1917) who became a trusted servant of the Bolshevik leaders. He succeeded Lenin as leader of the Soviet Union and redesigned Marxist-Leninism as socialism in a single country.

Trotsky, Leon (1879–1940): Revolutionary theorist and influential leader of revolutionary cells in the Russian army in 1917. Although he was Lenin's chosen successor as leader of the Soviet Union, he failed to stop Stalin, went into exile, and was assassinated by Stalinist agents. He wrote a critique of Stalinism, *The Revolution Betrayed* (1936), and an autobiography, *My Life* (1930).

See also: *Abolition of Serfdom; Bloody Sunday; Forced Labor: Soviet Union.*

BIBLIOGRAPHY

Books

Acton, Edward. *Rethinking the Russian Revolution*. London: Edward Arnold, 1990.

———, Vladimir Iu Cherniaev, and William G. Rosenberg, eds. *Critical Companion to the Russian Revolution, 1914–1921*. London: Arnold, 1997.

Ferro, Marc. *The Russian Revolution of February 1917*. Translated by J. L. Richards; notes and bibliography translated by Nicole Stone. London: Routledge and Kegan Paul, 1972.

Figes, Orlando. *A People's Tragedy: The Russian Revolution, 1891–1924*. London: Jonathan Cape, 1996.

Fitzpatrick, Sheila. *The Russian Revolution, 1917–1932*. Oxford: Oxford University Press, 1982.

Hill, Christopher. *Lenin and the Russian Revolution*. Harmondsworth: Penguin, 1971.

Keep, John L. H. *The Russian Revolution: A Study in Mass Mobilization*. New York: Norton, 1976.

Reed, John. *Ten Days That Shook the World*. Harmondsworth: Penguin, 1966.

Rothnie, Niall. *The Russian Revolution*. Basingstoke: Macmillan, 1990.

Simkin, John, ed. *The Bolshevik Revolution*. Brighton: Spartacus Educational, 1986.

Steinberg, Mark D., and Vladimir M. Khrustalëv. *The Fall of the Romanovs: Political Dreams and Personal Struggles in a Time of Revolution*. New Haven: Yale University Press, 1995.

Trotsky, Leon. *The History of the Russian Revolution*. Translated by Max Eastman. London: Victor Gollancz, 1934.

Wood, Alan. *The Origins of the Russian Revolution, 1861–1917*. 2nd ed. London: Routledge, 1993.

—Darren G. Lilleker

S

St. Crispin Organizations

United States 1867, 1869

Synopsis

Massachusetts shoemakers organized the International Knights of St. Crispin (KOSC) in the mid-nineteenth century to oppose the worst effects of industrialization on the work of shoemaking and to preserve the values of their equal rights ideology based on artisan culture. Industrialization centralized production of boots and shoes in factories. The introduction of steam-powered machinery increasingly divided jobs by specialization. Resistance to the growing power of industrial capitalism required factory workers to organize and confront their employers as trade unionists. Resisting both wage cuts and seeking control of work processes as mechanization continued, the activities of the KOSC, led by the craft lodges in Massachusetts, expanded into emerging shoe centers in the American Northeast and Canada.

The sexual division of labor and the mechanization of sewing light leather also introduced women shoeworkers into shoe factories. With the goal of protecting women who moved among Northeastern shoe centers in search of higher wages, the national Daughters of St. Crispin (DOSC) sought to represent the economic interests and political rights of migratory female shoeworkers and those resident in shoe towns. Led by women workers, the DOSC operated separately from the Knights but cooperated in strikes and in pressuring employers to arbitrate wages and grievances.

Timeline

1860: South Carolina secedes from the Union.

1861: Within weeks of Abraham Lincoln's inauguration, the U.S. Civil War begins with the shelling of Fort Sumter. Six states secede from the Union, joining South Carolina to form the Confederate States of America (later joined by four other states) and electing Jefferson Davis as president. The first major battle of the war, at Bull Run or Manassas in Virginia, is a Confederate victory.

1862: Though Great Britain depends on cotton from the American South, it is more dependent on grain from the North, and therefore refuses to recognize the Confederacy.

1862: Victor Hugo's *Les Misérables* depicts injustices in French society, and Ivan Turgenev's *Fathers and Sons* introduces the term *nihilism.*

1863: President Lincoln issues the Emancipation Proclamation, freeing all slaves in Confederate territories, on 1 January. Thus begins a year that sees the turning point of the Civil War, with decisive Union victories at Gettysburg, Vicksburg, and Chattanooga. Thereafter, the

Confederacy is almost perpetually on the defensive, fighting not to win but to avoid losing.

1864: General William Tecumseh Sherman conducts his Atlanta campaign and his "march to the sea."

1865: Civil War ends with the surrender of General Robert E. Lee to General Ulysses S. Grant at Appomattox, Virginia. More than 600,000 men have died, and the South is in ruins, but the Union has been restored.

1865: Ratification of the Thirteenth Amendment to the U.S. Constitution, which prohibits slavery.

1866: Introduction of the Winchester repeating rifle.

1867: United States purchases Alaska from Russia for $7.2 million.

1868: Congressional efforts to impeach President Andrew Johnson prove unsuccessful, but they do result in his removal from any direct influence on Reconstruction policy, and ensure his replacement by Ulysses S. Grant as the Republican presidential candidate later that year.

1869: Black Friday panic ensues when James Fisk and Jay Gould attempt to control the gold market.

Event and Its Context

Borrowing the patron saint and preindustrial rituals from English cordwainers, the Knights of St. Crispin in the United States and Canada transferred the political and cultural values of their artisan training into the environment of the emerging post–Civil War shoe factory. These male factory workers organized the most successful union of industrial workers in the 1870s. The KOSC represented various jobs, including skilled lasters and teams of shoeworkers called *bottomers.* Native-born Massachusetts residents, migratory Yankee workers from Maine and New Hampshire, and Irish immigrants joined the Crispin movement, which reflected the interests of about half of all American shoeworkers in 1870. At the same time the activism of artisan-trained shoeworkers in Canadian factories in southern Ontario and Quebec provinces made the KOSC organization international.

Efforts by large New England manufacturers to dominate sectors of the American shoe market through higher productivity and lower costs confronted shoeworkers with intensifying mechanization, wage cuts, and concentrated, intense seasons of production. As employers defined labor costs as just another commodity in their calculations, shoeworkers experienced downward pressures on piece rates. Manufacturers blamed the forces of supply and demand during the busy seasons of shoe production for cuts in wages, while shoeworkers struggled to support their families. A former Massachusetts shoemaker in Milwaukee founded the KOSC in 1867. In 1868 Lynn shoeworkers organized the first KOSC craft lodge in Massachusetts to control the pace of work and gain better wages. Crispins feared that wealth and power were being concentrated into a few hands and undermining their fair share of the value created by factory labor. They contended that their labor was not a commodity to be buffeted by market forces; supply and demand could not justify unfair wages for exhausting effort. Crispinism was both a general critique of industrial capitalism and a labor organization. KOSC members also organized to prevent migratory shoeworkers called green hands from overcrowding the labor market and being introduced into teams of experienced workers. Unless the Crispins were able to stabilize wage levels, manufacturers would use green hand labor to cut wages.

By 1869 the Crispin organization in Massachusetts, spearheaded by activists in Lynn, Worcester, and Brockton, claimed 30,000 members or sympathizers. In 1870, 2000 Lynn lasters organized Unity Lodge of the KOSC to seek a citywide wage scale protected by procedures for arbitration of grievances. A Mutual Lodge of 500 factory workers quickly backed this move. A strike timed to interrupt the beginning of the busy fall production season backed their demands to negotiate with their employers on an equal basis. Many smaller manufacturers, wishing to stabilize wage levels, agreed to arbitration. While unfilled orders piled up, KOSC negotiated a one-year citywide wage scale. Five Crispins and five manufacturers formed a joint board of arbitration to avoid the rigors of intense industrial competition on both production and wages. This agreement stabilized wages in 1870 and was renewed in 1871. As the leading center of shoe production in New England, Lynn factories, joined by others throughout Essex County in Massachusetts, set the scale of wages for the Crispin organization, which was expanding in shoe centers such as Utica, New York, and Philadelphia. Similar agreements stabilized wages in Toronto and Hamilton, Ontario, although Canadian Crispins left the international order in 1873.

The Knights of St. Crispin in Massachusetts pushed for labor reform, linking up with a statewide movement to restrict hours of factory work and involve the Commonwealth in protecting labor from the degradations of industrialization. In 1869, reacting to outrage over the state legislature's refusal to grant a charter for their union, local workers formed a Labor Reform club. Labor Reform Party candidates for state offices won Lynn elections. In 1878, the Workingmen's Party candidate and long-time Crispin activist beat the incumbent mayor, a large manufacturer and key opponent of the KOSC. In 1869 Crispin leaders encouraged the organization of women shoeworkers in the Daughters of St. Crispin and endorsed women's rights including suffrage. The Crispin movement also advocated cooperative shoe factories as a fairer alternative to industrial capitalism. After the destruction in 1870 of the KOSC in North Adams, Massachusetts, by Asian strikebreakers, the KOSC used politics and strikes to oppose Chinese immigration.

The Lynn strike of 1878 signaled the decline of Crispinism in Massachusetts and undermined KOSC lodges in other shoe centers but not the impetus for future union activity among shoeworkers. Shoeworkers had faced hard times during the depression of 1873, which undercut their organization and agreements on wages. A strike in 1872 failed to renew the citywide wage scale. Small manufacturers closed their factory doors; larger firms dominated production and set wages. Cutthroat competition worsened in 1874 and 1875, and wages dropped.

Crispinism began to revive to oppose the worst practices and conditions of the depression years. Led by the lasters of Unity Lodge who struck against further wage cuts in 1875, Lynn Crispins denounced "injurious competition" and sought the support of manufacturers who were sick of industrial chaos. Arbitration of wages and grievances revived in a search for stability. Between 1875 and 1878, arbitration in Lynn settled strikes, protected profits, and maintained wages for union men. This ended in 1878.

The large Lynn manufacturers, eager to sustain their dominant position in the reviving national shoe market, targeted local Crispin activism. Destroying the Crispin arbitration system in Lynn meant undermining wage levels in the key center of American production of popular ladies high-buttoned shoes. Eliminating arbitration would allow cuts in labor costs and sharpen their competitive edge against competitors outside of New England. In 1878 most Lynn firms insisted on direct negotiations with their workers and thus isolated the Crispin board. In response, the Lynn KOSC lodges struck all firms that had cut the previous year's wage scale. The manufacturers fired Crispin members and recruited strikebreakers from the depression-era labor market. After five weeks of extreme tension, the Lynn Crispins lost the right to arbitration but not the right to organize in lodges. Without a negotiated citywide wage scale, their fight to sustain wages against competitive pressures failed. Still the KOSC developed effective trade unionism to mount opposition to the power of industrial capitalism. After the defeat of arbitration, men's wages in 1879 declined as much as one-third from 1872 levels. Supply and demand determined wages in shoe factories until American and Canadian shoeworkers reasserted the spirit of Crispinism in the Knights of Labor in the 1880s and later in trade unionism.

Daughters of St. Crispin

In late 1868 young female workers in Lynn shoe factories organized Central Lodge No. 1 of the Daughters of St. Crispin (DOSC) to prevent manufacturers from lowering costs through wage cuts. Meeting in Lynn during the summer of 1869, 31 female delegates from local DOSC lodges met to form the national association, which stretched from lodges in Maine to California and south to Philadelphia and Baltimore. The persistence of the sexual division of labor in post-Civil War shoe production, even with the advent of stitching uppers by machine, meant that there was no serious competition with men over jobs. Male Crispins encouraged and supported the movement, but women shoeworkers organized themselves. Labor reformers Jennie Collins and Elizabeth Daniels of Boston attended the organizing convention to promote the involvement of the DOSC in broader activities on behalf of the rights of workingwomen.

The DOSC represented skilled women shoe stitchers, many of whom were unmarried, self-supporting boarders in shoe towns. The organization also included women resident in shoe centers who lived in male-headed families. The leadership of the Lynn and Stoneham lodges provided many national officers between 1869 and 1874. Emma A. Lane of Central Lodge, the wife of a Lynn shoeworker and a strong supporter of Crispinism, became the First Grand Directress. Martha Wallbridge of Excelsior Lodge, an unmarried, self-supporting boarder from New York state who stitched shoes in Stoneham, Massachusetts, was elected Second Grand Directress. Other officers came from Maine and New York. They represented the self-supporting boarding stitcher and the female head of family to a greater extent than residents living in male-headed families. In late 1869, 24 lodges formed with the largest in Rochester, New York. The combined efforts of the Knights and Daughters won strikes in Syracuse, New York, and Baltimore in 1871. The KOSC and the DOSC cooperated, but they held separate meetings and conventions and chose different newspapers for public statements. Stitchers' wages did not appear on citywide KOSC wage scales of 1870 and 1871 in Lynn, nor were they discussed at arbitration meetings.

In the summer of 1869, shortly after Samuel Cummings participated in the DOSC's organizational convention, he and Martha Wallbridge represented the Crispins at the National Labor Union convention. They, along with other New England delegates and over the objections of trade unionists, voted to seat Susan B. Anthony of the Woman Suffrage Association as a delegate to the NLU, but Anthony's ideas were unpopular and she was ejected from the convention. Martha Wallbridge also attended the 1870 NLU convention as the First Grand Directeress of the DOSC, having just defeated Emma Lane, who opposed women's suffrage. At this NLU convention Wallbridge reiterated Anthony's call for equal pay for equal work and for equal access by women to all trades. Whether equal rights for working women should include both economic rights as workers and political rights as women citizens remained a divisive issue for the DOSC.

Wage cuts in 1871 became the primary issue for Crispin shoeworkers and prompted the KOSC and the DOSC to join forces. During the busy season, Lynn employers who ran shops that subcontracted stitching for large manufacturers attempted to stop the turnover of skilled working women who left to seek higher wages elsewhere. The manufacturers imposed the requirement of either a week's notice backed by a wage deposit or the disgrace of a "dishonorable discharge." Denouncing these "obnoxious rules" and exposing them as a ruse to cut wages, the infuriated stitchers insisted that their rights as "free-born women" would not be infringed. They rejected the requirements and struck the subcontract shops. The DOSC and the KOSC in Lynn quickly backed these women workers and helped win the strike. The action forced the employers to agree that if the stitcher were dissatisfied with their wages, they could leave the shop without penalty. The settlement protected the mobility of skilled, experienced workingwomen who were important to the DOSC organization.

Wages for stitching stabilized for part of in 1872. Women shoeworkers held the enviable position as the highest paid female industrial workers in Massachusetts next to women typesetters in Cambridge and Boston. In 1872, the large shoe manufacturers targeted these high wages and the citywide KOSC wage scale in Lynn. That year DOSC women shoeworkers in Stoneham and Danvers struck against wage cuts. Enlisting the support of the local KOSC lodge was crucial to success in Danvers but failed in Stoneham. The DOSC in Lynn faced downward pressure on wages with the collapse of the KOSC citywide wage agreement. The wages of skilled women shoeworkers declined 10 percent as Lynn manufacturers cut labor costs to dominate the national market in the production of high-buttoned la-

dies shoes. The fine quality of the finished product often depended on the expert stitching on uppers executed on sewing machines by experienced workers, but lower production costs determined market dominance. Wage cuts became commonplace in shoe centers during the depression years of 1873–1878, which reduced demand for fancy styles and crowded the labor markets.

Only Central Lodge No. 1 survived the disappearance of the national DOSC in 1874. When the Crispin lasters revived KOSC wage arbitration in Lynn in 1876, the reawakened local DOSC in Lynn sought to stabilize stitching wages. When the stitchers refused a KOSC offer to arbitrate in 1876, they lost their strikes as underemployed and desperate women returned to work at lower wages. The depression undermined the DOSC's effectiveness. Women shoeworkers did not participate in the last important strike by the KOSC in 1878, which destroyed the men's organization. Efforts to organize Liberty Lodge in Lynn faded in 1879.

Diversity within the DOSC produced both strengths and divisions. Civil War losses and westward migration had pushed single women in the Northeast into paid work, postponing marriage and creating a pool of migratory, self-supporting working-women. High wages in shoe factories attracted them. Intensifying seasons of shoe production encouraged geographical mobility; this phenomenon explains why the DOSC became the first national women's union to organize successful resistance to employers. Many of these workingwomen believed their rights included the right to vote. Cooperation with resident workingwomen in shoe centers, who were loyal to family and more interested in Crispinism than in female political rights, sustained effective organization. The DOSC lodges tried to represent this political diversity during the years of postwar prosperity and high wages, but, as the depression years undermined the wage scale, competition among working women over jobs made diversity a source of weakness.

Key Players

Cummings, Samuel P.: A native-born resident of Danvers, Massachusetts, and International Grand Secretary, Cummings became the key leader of the KOSC organization in Massachusetts (1869–1874). He pushed for craft union recognition, labor reform legislation, cooperative shoe factories, and the arbitration of wages. As a KOSC delegate to the 1869 National Labor Union convention in New York City, Cummings strongly supported labor reform politics, the organization of women shoeworkers, and equal rights for women including suffrage. Cummings represented the interests of shoeworkers on the executive board of the NLU.

Litchman Charles H.: A native-born resident of Marblehead, Massachusetts, and factory worker, Litchman was the First Grand Scribe of the International Knights of St. Crispin. During the 1878 lockout against the Lynn Crispins, Litchman secretly organized an association of 8,000 men who later formed 11 assemblies in the Knights of Labor. As a Master Workman Litchman successfully linked the Crispins with a new nationwide organization to advocate the rights of workingmen.

Wallbridge, Martha: An unmarried native of New York state who worked as a shoe stitcher and boarded in Stoneham, Massachusetts. In 1869 at age 30, Wallbridge became an organizer of the DOSC and its leader from 1870 to 1874. As DOSC delegate, Wallbridge represented self-supporting migratory women workers and chaired the Committee on Female Labor at the 1869 National Labor Union convention in 1869. She argued for equal access for women to the trades and backed the controversial presence of delegate Susan B. Anthony from the Woman Suffrage Association.

See also: *National Labor Union; Panic of 1873.*

BIBLIOGRAPHY

Books

Blewett, Mary H. *Men, Women, and Work: Gender, Class, and Protest in the New England Shoe Industry, 1780–1910.* Urbana: University of Illinois Press, 1988.

———. *We Will Rise in Our Might: Workingwomen's Voices from Nineteenth-Century New England.* Ithaca, NY: Cornell University Press, 1991.

Dawley, Alan. *Class and Community: The Industrial Revolution in Lynn.* Rev. ed. Cambridge, MA: Harvard University Press, 2001.

Lescohier, Don D. *The Knights of St. Crispin, 1867–1874: A Study of the Industrial Causes of Trade Unionism.* New York: Arno, 1969. Original work published 1910.

Palmer, Bryan. *A Culture in Conflict: Skilled Workers and Industrial Capitalism in Hamilton, Ontario, 1860–1914.* Montreal: McGill–Queen's University Press, 1979.

Periodicals

Commons, John R. "American Shoemakers, 1648–1895: A Sketch of Industrial Evolution." *Quarterly Journal of Economics,* 24 (November 1909): 39–83.

Hall, John Philip. "The Knights of St. Crispin in Massachusetts, 1869–1879." *Journal of Economic History,* 18 (June 1958): 161–75.

Kealey, Gregory. "Artisans Respond to Industrialism: Shoemakers, Shoe Factories and the Knights of St. Crispin." *Historical Papers*, Canadian Historical Association (June 1973): 137–57.

ADDITIONAL RESOURCES

Other

K.O.S.C Monthly Journal, constitutions and by-laws of various lodges of the Knights of St. Crispin, convention proceedings, rituals, see scattered copies and dates (1868–1870). Crispin newspapers in Lynn, *Little Giant* (1870–1873) and *Vindicator* (1878–1879).

—Mary H. Blewett

Salt of the Earth Strike

United States 1950

Synopsis

In October 1950, after several months of unsuccessful bargaining with Empire Zinc, the members of Local 890 of the International Union of Mine, Mill, and Smelter Workers (IUMM-SW, or Mine-Mill) went on strike in Hanover, New Mexico. Neither side was willing to back down, and the strike lasted for 15 months. The strike sometimes became violent, as local authorities attempted to arrest picketers or strikebreakers tried to push through the picket lines. Finally, in January 1952 the sides negotiated a settlement in which both the company and workers made concessions.

The strike, which became known as the "Salt of the Earth" strike, was important on a number of levels. It took place in the context of the cold war, and the issue of communism was always present. In fact, the IUMMSW had been dispelled from the Congress of Industrial Organizations (CIO) because it was seen as being overly influenced by communism. After the strike, several blacklisted Hollywood filmmakers made a film about the strike. The film, however, was suppressed because of the anticommunist sentiment prevalent in Hollywood at the time. Ethnic relations in the United States also played a role in the strike, as most of the miners were Mexican American. One of the workers' complaints was that Mexican American workers were not paid as much as white workers. The strike also was important for the role played by women. Although the miners were all men, women took part in the strike and the picketing.

Timeline

1931: Financial crisis widens in the United States and Europe, which reel from bank failures and climbing unemployment levels. In London, armies of the unemployed riot.

1935: Second phase of New Deal begins with the introduction of social security, farm assistance, and housing and tax reform.

1940: Hitler's troops sweep through Western Europe, annexing Norway and Denmark in April, and in May the Low Countries and France.

1945: On 7 May, Germany surrenders to the Allied powers in World War II.

1950: United States begins developing hydrogen bomb.

1950: North Korean troops pour into South Korea, starting the Korean War. Initially, the communists make impressive gains, but in September the U.S. Marines land at Inchon and liberate Seoul. China responds by sending in its troops.

1950: Senator Joseph McCarthy launches his campaign to root out communist infiltrators.

1955: Over the course of the year, a number of key ingredients are added to the pantheon of American culture: the 1955 Chevrolet, the first of many classic models; Tennessee Williams's *Cat on a Hot Tin Roof*; Marilyn Monroe's performance in *The Seven-Year Itch*; Disneyland; and Bill Haley and the Comets' "Rock Around the Clock."

1960: When an American U-2 spy plane piloted by Francis Gary Powers is shot down over Soviet skies, this brings an end to a short period of warming relations between the two superpowers. By the end of the year, Khrushchev makes a scene at the United Nations, banging his shoe on a desk. As for Powers, he will be freed in a 1962 prisoner exchange.

1965: Arrest of the Rev. Martin Luther King, Jr., and more than 2,600 others in Selma, Alabama. Three weeks later, in New York City, Malcolm X is assassinated.

Event and Its Context

The IUMMSW and the Cold War

The Salt of the Earth strike must be understood in the larger context of the cold war. The anticommunist sentiment that was so common throughout the United States in the years after World War II affected the labor movement. Big labor was relatively conservative and followed the main currents of the time. Both the American Federation of Labor (AFL) and CIO were anticommunist. Thus in 1950 the CIO, once much more concerned with issues of social equality, purged its organization of communist influence, expelling 11 unions and affecting more than one million workers. Most of these unions were outside of the mainstream, and the CIO likely considered them unimportant.

One of the expelled unions was the IUMMSW. The IUMMSW grew out of the Western Federation of Miners (WFM), which had organized miners in the 1890s and was part of the Industrial Workers of the World (IWW). In 1916 the WFM became the IUMMSW and was a pioneer in organizing female and minority workers. Despite its sometimes radical positions, it did become an affiliate of the AFL. The IUMMSW later left the AFL to join the CIO. The organization's leaders included many left-wingers, including communists. Communism, however, was much less important among the rank-and-file members.

The IUMMSW membership included many Mexican Americans, in part because of its record on civil rights and racial equality. The organization also promoted Anglo-Chicano solidarity. Many of the white workers were from Oklahoma, Texas, and Arkansas and were discriminated against just as were the Mexican American workers. One of the IUMMSW's strongholds was New Mexico, where there was much discrimination against Chicano workers. Indeed, there was de facto segregation. Furthermore, Empire Zinc only hired Mexican Americans for underground work.

During the cold war, the IUMMSW took a number of controversial stands. Its leaders opposed both the Truman Doctrine and the Marshall Plan. They refused to sign the noncommunist affidavits of the Taft-Hartley Act of 1947. Furthermore, the IUMMSW opposed participation in the Korean War. Soon, the union found itself expelled from the CIO and suffering from raids on its membership.

Local 890 and Empire Zinc

In July 1950 Mine-Mill Local 890 of Hanover, New Mexico, opened talks with the management of Empire Zinc. Juan Chacón and Ernesto Velásquez led local 890. In addition, the IUMMSW sent Clinton Jencks to aid in the discussions. The union entered the negotiations with two disadvantages. One was the union's radical reputation. The other was the depression in the metals industry. Indeed, half of Grant County's 2,000 or so mineworkers were unemployed at the time. The basic demand of the union was economic equality. The IUMMSW claimed that Empire Zinc maintained wage differentials so as to create ethnic tensions among workers. Also, the workers demanded "collar-to-collar" pay, which meant that miners would be paid for all of their time underground. In 1944 the War Labor Board had directed all companies to do so. However, Empire Zinc was allowed to maintain an unpaid lunch and keep an 8.5-hour day in exchange for higher wages. In addition, the workers were concerned with issues of paid holidays, working conditions, pensions, and benefits.

Empire Zinc refused to negotiate on the issue of collar-to-collar pay, claiming that the issue had already been settled. Company officials offered no proposals of their own until September, when they suggested a company-controlled pension plan instead of wage increases. When the union made a counteroffer, the company rejected it with no discussion and withdrew their own offer.

The Strike Begins

By October the two sides had reached an impasse. Empire Zinc took on a very militant, antiunion attitude. When the company refused to continue the talks in October, the union went on strike. Local 890 established a strike committee to determine policy and set up two picket posts around the company's property. The pickets had three shifts each of six men, creating a 24-hour presence. The company seemed to have the advantage in the strike. It spent more than $1 million in an attempt to maintain production and break the strike. The workers had some money in their own strike fund and also received funds from the IUMMSW, which issued food rations to the strikers and paid their utility bills. However, Local 890 was no financial match for Empire Zinc. The company's resources allowed it to wait while the workers' resources declined.

As the strike progressed, the leaders of the IUMMSW grew worried. They were concerned with the negative publicity that accompanied the strike and also were beginning to doubt that the leaders of Local 890 could end the deadlock. Indeed, the local union was showing some signs of division. Thus, after 18 weeks of the strike, the IUMMSW took control of the strike. This action in turn worried the local labor leaders, who felt that they were losing control of the struggle. At this time, some worker defections began, with some men deserting to find work elsewhere. Other strikers requested releases to find other work, although the strike committee generally rejected these requests. Those who did receive releases complained about the 25 percent kickback that they had to pay into the strike fund. By May 1951 some workers even had signed a back-to-work petition that was circulated by the company.

Women Join the Strike, and Violence Increases

In June 1951 Empire Zinc announced that it would reopen with nonunion labor. The company had assurances from Sheriff Leslie Goforth and the district attorney that the highway leading into company property would be open. This decision prompted the union to increase its picketing. Then in reaction to increased worker activity, the police took a more active role and made several arrests on the picket lines. The building tension led a federal district judge to prohibit picketing by union members. Despite the order, the union continued to picket, although with a change in tactics. The workers voted to authorize women to play a greater role in the strike and proposed that they take up picketing. This allowed the workers to avoid the prohibition on union members picketing, as the women were not union members. Women had already been increasingly involved in various support roles, including writing letters and providing the public with information on the strike. In particular, the militant roles played by Virginia Jencks and Virginia Chacón gave the strike a boost.

At first, Goforth was reluctant to deal with the female picketers. However, on 15 June arrest warrants were issued for six women charged with assault and battery. The issuance of these warrants led to a confrontation on 16 June. Goforth went to arrest the six women and to escort strikebreakers. The picketers, however, refused to allow the sheriff and strikebreakers through their line. In response, an angry Goforth ordered his deputies to arrest anyone who stood in their way. The deputies began to arrest the women picketers. However, others soon took their places. The situation became more confrontational, and the sheriff and his deputies used tear gas when the strikebreakers tried to go through and around the picket line. In all, authorities arrested 45 women and 17 children, including a 16-week-old baby. They were taken to the local jail designed to hold only 24 people. This event drew national attention to the strike. In the aftermath of this confrontation, the Federal Mediation and Conciliation Service offered arbitration. Mine-Mill accepted, but Empire Zinc refused.

In August the strike became more violent as the number of incidents between the strikers, authorities, company employees, and strikebreakers increased. The worst incident took place on 23 August. On that day Goforth arrived at the picket line with 10 deputies and 9 armed, nonunion workers. Goforth argued with the strikers, but the picketers, who numbered about 75, refused to move. The strikebreakers then forced their way through the picket with their vehicles, striking three of the female picketers. The sheriff's men then fired shots at the strikers, wounding one man. The violent incident led to a general strike of the entire mining district, as workers from other mines joined the Local 890 strikers.

The End of the Strike

The end of the strike finally came in January 1952. On 21 January a new negotiating session opened. At this point, both sides made concessions. The company was able to keep the 8.5-hour day that it preferred. However, the company agreed to raise wages for the extra half hour. Instead of the paid holidays that the workers sought, they received an increased hourly wage. They also received an insurance program and pension plan. The company, however, was able to strengthen its no-

strike clause in the contract. Furthermore, it still pressed charges against some of the strike leaders, some of whom served jail time. The union also had to pay a fine.

Key Players

Chacón, Juan: One of the leaders of the International Union of Mine, Mill, and Smelter Workers (IUMMSW, or Mine-Mill) Local 890, Chacón had a reputation as a hard bargainer. The son of a Mexican immigrant miner, he entered the mines himself at age 18. After serving in the merchant marine during World War II, Chacón returned to the mines in 1946. He rose from shop steward to vice president of Local 1890 and then became its president in 1953. Chacón was a strong believer in class solidarity and racial equality. He played the lead in *Salt of the Earth*, the film version of the strike.

Jencks, Clinton: A highly religious man from Colorado, Jencks was a political activist. After serving in the air force during World War II, he returned to organize veterans in Denver. He later joined the IUMMSW. He served as the union's representative during the Salt of the Earth strike in 1950. He was highly regarded by the local workers because he lived in the community and encouraged the Mexican American leaders.

See also: *American Federation of Labor; Congress of Industrial Organizations; Taft-Hartley Act; Western Federation of Miners.*

BIBLIOGRAPHY

Books

Cargill, Jack. "Empire and Opposition: 'The Salt of the Earth' Strike." In *Labor in New Mexico: Unions, Strikes, and Social History since 1881*, edited by Robert Kern. Albuquerque: University of New Mexico Press, 1983.

Lorrence, James J. *The Suppression of* Salt of the Earth: *How Hollywood, Big Labor, and Politicians Blacklisted a Movie in Cold War America.* Albuquerque: University of New Mexico Press, 1999.

Salomon, Larry R. *Roots of Justice: Stories of Organizing in Communities of Color.* Berkeley, CA: Chardon Press, 1998.

—Ronald Young

Seattle General Strike

United States 1919

Synopsis

The Seattle strike of 1919 was the first large-scale general strike in the United States. Although sparked by wage griev-

Striking workers, Seattle General Strike, Seattle, Washington, 1919. © Bettmann/Corbis. Reproduced by permission.

ances of shipyard workers, the strike quickly grew into a larger showdown between the city's American Federation of Labor (AFL) movement and local politicians, business interests, and federal war agencies, all of whom saw it as a crucial test of the power that organized labor would wield in the wake of World War I. For four days during the strike, labor reigned. Some 65,000 workers walked off their jobs. Strikers served food, supplied hospitals, and kept peace in the streets with astonishing organization and efficiency. Under pressure from the mayor, federal troops, and unsupportive AFL internationals, however, the walkout collapsed.

The strike left an ambivalent legacy. The failure of such a massive action to raise shipyard wages—let alone ward off the union-busting and red-hunting that followed—showed the limits of local labor's power against state-supported, antiunion capital. Yet the memory of a moment when working people not only shut down an entire city but ran a successful system of essential services along syndicalist lines also offered hope. In the short run it fueled Seattle's vibrant union-affiliated cooperative movement. In the long run it inspired generations who dreamed of building a labor-based social order.

Timeline

1900: China's Boxer Rebellion, which began in the preceding year with attacks on foreigners and Christians, reaches its height. An international contingent of more than 2,000 men arrives to restore order, but only after several tens of thousands have died.

1907: U.S. markets experience a financial panic.

1912: *Titanic* sinks on its maiden voyage, from Southampton to New York, on 14 April. More than 1,500 people are killed.

1915: At the Second Battle of Ypres, the Germans introduce a terrifying new weapon: poison gas.

1917: The intercepted "Zimmermann Telegram" reveals a plot by the German government to draw Mexico into an alliance against the United States in return for a German promise to return the southwestern U.S. territories taken in the Mexican War. Three months later, in response to German threats of unrestricted submarine warfare, the United States on 6 April declares war on Germany.

1919: Formation of the Third International (Comintern), whereby the Bolshevik government of Russia establishes its control over communist movements worldwide.

1919: Treaty of Versailles signed by the Allies and Germany but rejected by the U.S. Senate. This is due in part to rancor between President Woodrow Wilson and Republican Senate leaders, and in part to concerns over Wilson's plan to commit the United States to the newly established League of Nations and other international duties. Not until 1921 will Congress formally end U.S. participation in the war, but it will never agree to join the League.

1919: Ratification of the Eighteenth Amendment, which prohibits the production, sale, distribution, purchase, and consumption of alcohol throughout the United States.

1919: In India, Mahatma Gandhi launches his campaign of nonviolent resistance to British rule.

1919: In Italy, a former socialist of the left named Benito Mussolini introduces the world to a new socialism of the right, embodied in an organization known as the "Union for Struggle," or Fasci di Combattimento. Composed primarily of young war veterans discontented with Italy's paltry share of the spoils from the recent world war (if not with their country's lackluster military performance in the conflict), the fascists are known for their black shirts and their penchant for violence.

1921: As the Allied Reparations Commission calls for payments of 132 billion gold marks, inflation in Germany begins to climb.

1925: European leaders attempt to secure the peace at the Locarno Conference, which guarantees the boundaries between France and Germany, and Belgium and Germany.

1929: On "Black Friday" in October, prices on the U.S. stock market, which had been climbing wildly for several years, suddenly collapse. Thus begins the first phase of a world economic crisis and depression that will last until the beginning of World War II.

Event and Its Context

Seattle in 1919 was an auspicious stage for labor's critical fight. The port city's workers were among the most organized in the nation, with solid union presence in building, longshore, transport, retail, and other trades by the mid-1910s. Although most locals were affiliated with the AFL, both their membership and their institutional linkages departed in important ways from the AFL's elite craft archetype. Seattle's craft locals forged industrial ties through trade councils that coordinated such fields as Metal and Building, and they maintained a citywide coalition through the Seattle Central Labor Council (CLC). They also stretched the usual AFL boundaries by organizing in such "unskilled" fields as waitressing and longshore work. Finally, many Seattle unionists stood well to the left of the AFL mainstream in political ideology. Socialists (and, to a lesser extent, Wobblies) formed substantial minorities in some unions and occupied a number of leadership positions. Rank and filers enjoyed

a flourishing working-class culture and associational life embodied in such institutions as the widely circulated labor-owned daily, *The Union Record*; the popular leftist speaker circuit; and an array of consumer and producer cooperatives. In some respects, however, the standard AFL exclusivity prevailed: as in California, the AFL in Seattle grew from a movement among white working men to drive out Chinese labor. As in much of the United States, AFL locals in Seattle barred people of color—the city was home to several thousand Japanese, Chinese, and African American working people—as well as, in most cases, women.

Having laid this complex groundwork by the middle teens, Seattle's AFL movement gained a powerful advantage from labor market changes generated by the world war. The war cut off American access to European fleets and created a sudden need for merchant vessels to sustain the nation's commerce. Congress responded by creating an Emergency Fleet Corporation (EFC) that was authorized to fund new construction at private shipyards. EFC orders placed with Seattle yards in 1917 made the city a boomtown. Overnight, owners sought to hire 35,000 new workers, and men thronged to Puget Sound to earn the high shipyard wages. Union organizing thrived in this seller's market and the shipyard locals won a concession of both practical and symbolic importance: the closed shop. Led by the exponentially expanding metal trades, which filled the yards that built steel-bottomed ships, Seattle's union ranks grew from 15,000 to 60,000 in three years. Moreover, many new shipyard unionists were Wobblies and Socialists from the outlying timber camps who brought militancy as well as numbers to the Seattle movement.

If the latter 1910s looked propitious for local labor, they also held ominous signs. Class-inflected upheavals in America and Europe—including the Bolshevik revolution of 1917—stoked fears of radical upsurge and sparked a U.S. crackdown on the left. Meanwhile, the 1918 armistice spelled trouble for an American labor movement that was built on war production. By January 1919 Seattle's wooden shipyards were closed and metal yards were facing steep cuts.

Against this stormy political-economic sea, Seattle's shipyard workers and the EFC charted a course toward conflict. They first clashed in the summer of 1917, when the EFC established a Shipbuilding Labor Adjustment Board (known as the Macy board after its chair, Everit Macy) to handle wage and other labor questions during the war. The Macy board quickly angered Seattle's metal trades workers when it set uniform shipbuilding wages below those prevailing in the expensive port city. EFC general manager Charles Piez provoked the workers further when he reneged on his promise to let Seattle locals negotiate directly with yard owners rather than be bound by board rates. The locals struck, then yielded to patriotic calls and returned to work. They did so with their grievances unsettled; they looked forward to armistice when they could win back what they saw as just wages and rights. Within days of the November 1918 peace, the Metal Trades Council requested direct negotiation, and members authorized a strike to back up their demands. Bargaining stalled when the owners, having offered a small increase to the elite crafts, refused to discuss raises for the underpaid lesser-skilled workers. More outrageous to the unions, Piez tried to intervene in the new peacetime negotiations by wiring the owners to stand firm or lose their steel ration. Through a messenger boy's "mistake" the telegram reached union rather than employer offices. It confirmed labor's fears that more than shipyard wages were at stake: government and capital were out to drive back labor's wartime gains, including the closed shop. On the morning of 21 January 1919, Seattle's shipyard workers walked silently off the job.

The silence did not last. Citywide, labor felt itself under attack, as grocers cut off strikers' credit and police raided the offices of the union-based Cooperative Food Producers, which had stepped in to fill the credit gap. The Metal Trades Council asked the Central Labor Council to propose a general sympathy strike. The ensuing debate showed clearly that both sides saw the conflict through a broad lens. "We knew that if the metal trades were forced to their knees our turn would come next," said a plasterer explaining his local's prostrike vote. Moreover, "If Seattle gets away with this, the war will be carried further than the confines of Seattle," the widely respected CLC secretary James Duncan forecast. On the managers' side, an observer noted, "It appears as if the federal government was using Seattle as an experimental station to find out just how much radicalism and unrest there is in labor." A strong majority of union members and locals voted to strike. The CLC set a date of 6 February.

On that morning, labor was jubilant. So solidly did 65,000 organized workers hit the streets that 40,000 nonunion employees were also idled by lack of transport and work. (In a bittersweet vein of solidarity, segregated Japanese American locals struck as well and were rewarded with second-class labor citizenship, allowed to attend but not to vote at CLC meetings.) Yet arguably labor's greatest achievement was not in idling private industry but in organizing alternative public provisions. To feed the 30,000 single men who depended on restaurant meals every day, striking cooks prepared and striking teamsters carried hot food to labor halls that set up makeshift "eating stations." To supply other vital needs, the General Strike exemptions committees dispatched teamsters to haul milk cans and hospital laundry. To maintain public order, labor's war veterans patrolled the streets unarmed to "persuade" fellow citizens to keep peace and to avoid clashes with the National Guard troops that the Secretary of War had ordered to the city on 6 February.

These measures won much sympathy. On another public service front, however, antiunion forces dealt the CLC a powerful blow. The issue was Seattle City Light. The CLC had decided that electricity was not a vital necessity for the public at large and refused to let the utility run at full capacity. Mayor Ole Hanson, under strong pressure from business leaders, declared the strike a Bolshevik action and on 7 February issued an ultimatum: run City Light or it will be operated by the National Guard. The press decried the CLC's intransigence, and the threat of armed federal strikebreakers raised fears of bloodshed. Meanwhile, AFL international officers, afraid that Seattle's conflict would scuttle organizing efforts in the east, declared the strike an unauthorized action, withheld support funds, and threatened to revoke striking locals' charters. Thus attacked on both flanks, the strike gave way. A trickle of strikers went back to work on Saturday, 8 February, and by Monday virtually all had returned. The CLC officially ended the action the next day.

The fallout of the strike was mixed. From a shop floor perspective, the strike was a defeat, as the shipbuilders lost their wage bid. Moreover, true to labor's fears, Seattle industrialists soon launched a successful offensive against the closed shop. Within local labor ranks, criticism over the strike led to the ouster of militant leaders and the end of "Duncanism," the earlier state of tolerance between craft and industrial unionists. Government repression also intensified. Federal agents arrested local Wobblies and *Union Record* editors on charges of criminal syndicalism and sedition in what would later appear to be a curtain-raiser for the Palmer Raids. Mayor Hanson became a national hero for facing down Bolshevism.

From a labor consumer perspective, however, the strike was a success. Although it did not break capitalists' control of waged work, it did demonstrate that working people could circumvent capitalism in the consumer sphere by organizing cooperative modes of production and distribution. This cooperativist branch of Seattle's labor movement did not die in February 1919; indeed, it grew dramatically in the months after the strike until it included stevedoring, butchering, barbering, and savings establishments as well as numerous grocery and dry goods stores and the increasingly popular *Union Record*. Many Socialists whom red-baiters drove from the party took up cooperative work instead and so stayed active on the left for years.

From a longer historical perspective, the strike marked a watershed between labor's wartime bargaining strength and its bitter postwar struggles in basic industries (mining, steel) and politics (the Red Scare). Less a tactical failure than a last stand, the Seattle strike left a memory of worker solidarity and social vision that far outlasted 1919.

Key Players

Ault, Harry (b. 1884): Founding editor of the *Union Record*, Ault grew up on the Equity cooperative near Bellingham, Washington. Ault was active in the Socialist Party and preceded Duncan as Central Labor Council (CLC) secretary. He used his paper to advocate for progressive and cooperativist labor projects.

Duncan, James (b. 1879): A Scottish-born marine engineer, Duncan was CLC secretary in 1919. A socialist, he was a respected "progressive" labor leader in Seattle through the early twenties and ran strongly but unsuccessfully for mayor in 1920.

Hanson, Ole (1874–1940): Hanson, a real estate investor, was elected mayor of Seattle in 1918. Having billed himself as a moderate before the strike, he subsequently embraced his status as American hero, resigned from office, and enjoyed a career as handsomely paid lecturer on law and order.

Piez, Charles (1866–1933): A German-born engineer and businessman, Piez was operative head of the Emergency Fleet Corporation (EFC) during the strike.

Strong, Anna Louise (1885–1970): Feature editor of the *Union Record* from 1918 to 1921. Her February 1919 editorial "No One Knows Where" became an anthem of the strike's radical aspirations. Later Strong traveled and lectured widely, reported on the Soviet Union and other European countries, and spent the last decade of her life in China as an honored guest of Mao Zedong.

See also: *American Federation of Labor; Russian Revolutions.*

BIBLIOGRAPHY

Books

Frank, Dana. *Purchasing Power: Consumer Organizing, Gender, and the Seattle Labor Movement, 1919–1929.* New York: Cambridge University Press, 1994.

Friedheim, Robert L. *The Seattle General Strike.* Seattle: University of Washington Press, 1964.

————. *Papers 1919–64.* Special Collections, University of Washington Libraries, Seattle, WA.

History Committee of the General Strike Committee. "The Seattle General Strike: An Account of What Happened in Seattle, and Especially in the Seattle Labor Movement during the General Strike, February 6 to 11, 1919." Seattle: Seattle Union Record Pub. Co., 1919.

Other

James Gregory, ed., "The Seattle General Strike Project." Harry Bridges Center for Labor Studies, University of Washington. Updated 14 May 2002 [cited 15 August 2002]. <http://faculty.washington.edu/gregoryj/strike/strikehome.htm>.

—Roberta Gold

Second International

France 1889

Synopsis

On 14 July 1889 over 1,000 representatives of the socialist movement met in Paris to establish the Second International. It had been 17 years since the First International had dissolved at the Hague Congress in 1872. In that time, scattered groups of socialists had developed into organized parties in many countries. In Germany, despite persecution by the government, socialism had evolved into a mass working-class political movement. The time was right to demonstrate again international solidarity against the capitalist system that exploited workers everywhere. At the very moment of its foundation, however, the fractured nature of the socialist movement, which had caused the demise of the First International, returned to cause confusion and acrimony in the Second. In particular, the divisions between reformist and revolutionary socialism and between anarchists and Marxists created complications. The founding congress also demonstrated the organization and strength of the German socialists and indicated the extent to which they would dominate the Second International for the next 25 years.

Timeline

1869: Black Friday panic ensues when James Fisk and Jay Gould attempt to control the gold market.

1874: Norwegian physician Arrnauer Gerhard Henrik Hansen discovers the bacillus that causes leprosy. This marks the major turning point in the history of an ailment (now known properly as Hansen's disease) that afflicted humans for thousands of years and was often regarded as evidence of divine judgment.

1882: Agitation against English rule spreads throughout Ireland, culminating with the assassination of chief secretary for Ireland Lord Frederick Cavendish and permanent undersecretary Thomas Burke in Dublin's Phoenix Park. The leader of the nationalist movement is Charles Stewart Parnell, but the use of assassination and terrorism—which Parnell himself has disavowed—makes clear the fact that he does not control all nationalist groups.

1885: Belgium's King Leopold II becomes sovereign of the so-called Congo Free State, which he will rule for a quarter-century virtually as his own private property. The region in Africa, given the name of Zaire in the 1970s (and Congo in 1997), becomes the site of staggering atrocities, including forced labor and genocide, at the hands of Leopold's minions.

1887: John Emerich Edward Dalbert-Acton, a leader of the opposition to the papal dogma of infallibility, observes, in a letter to Cambridge University professor Mandell Creighton, that "Power tends to corrupt, and absolute power corrupts absolutely."

1889: Indian Territory in Oklahoma opened to settlement.

1889: Flooding in Johnstown, Pennsylvania, kills thousands.

1889: The 986-foot (300.5-m) Eiffel Tower, part of the Paris exposition, becomes the tallest structure in the world. It will remain so until the Chrysler Building surpasses it in 1930.

1889: Discontented southern farmers merge their farm organizations to form the Southern Alliance.

1891: Construction of Trans-Siberian Railway begins. Meanwhile, crop failures across Russia lead to widespread starvation.

1895: Guglielmo Marconi pioneers wireless telegraphy, which in the next three decades will make possible the use of radio waves for commercial broadcasts and other applications.

1899: Polish-born German socialist Rosa Luxemburg rejects the argument that working conditions in Europe have improved and that change must come by reforming the existing system. Rather, she calls for an overthrow of the existing power structure by means of violent international revolution.

Event and Its Context

Between the First and Second International

Socialism had been transformed in the years since the end of the First International. The early 1870s were a time of severe reaction against socialism in the wake of the defeat of the Paris Commune in 1870. French socialism, which had been the mainstay of the International, was in disarray, with most of its leaders killed or in exile. The hopes for a socialist revolution, which had seemed imminent at the end of the 1860s, were receding. In response, the socialist movement entered a new stage of development. The experience of the Paris Commune had convinced many socialists of the need for the creation of organized and disciplined mass proletarian parties, if the capitalist system was to be overthrown. Karl Marx and Friedrich Engels also felt that the time was not right to maintain an international organization, partly because they feared that the anarchists would dominate it. Instead, they believed that development and consolidation of socialist organizations in each country would prove the key to the progress of their cause.

Therefore, the 1870s and 1880s was a period of refocus for the workers' movement, especially in the face of an international economic depression. Unemployment, wages, and working conditions became major concerns as employers tried to squeeze more productivity out of workers. In response, trade unions organized to protect their workers and attempt to improve wages and working conditions. Despite the depression, industrialization continued at a ferocious pace and the numbers of the urban proletariat increased as a result. This growing population provided fertile soil for the growth of socialist ideals. By the end of the 1880s, socialism was no longer a theory restricted to a few isolated adherents but the basis of a mass political movement in some countries.

The German Example

The rise of socialism was most apparent in Germany, which provided the blueprint for the organization of socialist political parties worldwide. In 1875 the Gotha agreement unified the two main groups of German socialism and created the Socialist Workers Party, which later became the Social Democratic Party (SPD). Wilhelm Liebknecht and August Bebel headed the SPD. They had been involved in the First International, had strong ties to Marx and Engels, and were widely respected in the socialist movement. Under their leadership, an organized and disciplined working-class political movement developed in Germany. In 1890 the Social Democrats won 19.7 percent of the vote in the German general elections, an unprecedented achievement in attracting mass working-class support. What makes this even more remarkable is that it occurred after a decade of persecution by the German government. In 1878 the German parliament passed the repressive Anti-Socialist Laws, which made almost any kind of socialist activity illegal. Rather than stamping out socialism, however, the Anti-Socialist Laws contributed to its strength by creating among the German workers a sense of alienation and hostility toward the state. As a result of the persecution, which led to thousands of arrests, the German SPD was characterized by a sense of discipline and unity that was contrasted sharply with the fragmentary nature of the movement in other countries. This cohesion gave the SPD enormous influence in the Second International.

Moves Toward International Socialism

The focus of socialist action in the 1870s and 1880s was firmly on the national level. Yet the dream of international socialism did not fade completely in these years. Remnants of the First International continued to hold congresses until 1881. These, however, were not genuinely representative of international socialism. In 1877 the organization held a congress in Ghent, Belgium, to attempt to reignite the international socialist movement. This included representatives from most countries, but it was scuttled by conflicts between the anarchists and other socialists. In 1881 another Socialist Congress held in Chur, Switzerland, failed to attract enough support. Those who desired an international socialist movement were forced to admit that the time was not right.

However, the desire for an international organization to represent the concerns of the worker also came from other directions. The labor union movement was interested in developing contact between unions in different countries. Coordinated international action on issues of protective labor legislation was of particular concern. The unions wanted to put pressure on governments to pass laws to regulate hours and conditions. The French and British labor movements held meetings during the 1880s to discuss the establishment of an international organization. It was eventually agreed that there would be a congress in Paris on 14 July 1889, timed to coincide with the centenary of the storming of the Bastille during the French Revolution. The initial impetus for the meeting, therefore, came from the leaders of the union movement, rather than from the socialist political parties. The nature of the French socialist movement, however, meant that the circumstances of the proposed congress were to change.

French Socialism

The situation in French socialism contrasted sharply with the unity of the Germans. After the Paris Commune, socialism in France was shattered. It revived, however, starting in the late 1870s. In 1879 the Marxist *Parti Ouvrier Française*, led by Jules Guesde, formed in an attempt to create an organization based on the German model. Conditions, however, were very different in France. The majority of urban workers were employed in small workshops rather than in large-scale industrial factories. Therefore, Marxism, with its emphasis on a mass urban proletariat of factory workers, did not have the same appeal to French workers. France had its own tradition of socialist theorists whose followers competed with the Marxists for the support of the French worker. There was also more opportunity in the French Republic for coordination with bourgeois radical parties to gain reforms that would benefit workers. This was at odds with the Marxist principles of Guesde, who rejected any compromise with the bourgeoisie, the class enemy of the workers.

Because of these differences, a group led by Paul Brousse split from the French Marxists and founded a new party, which came to be known as the Possibilists. They stressed the possibility of immediate reforms through alliances with other parties and resented the attempt to impose German socialist theory upon the French situation. The Possibilist links to the French labor movement made them the logical choice to lead the organization of the 1889 congress. Although the Possibilists invited all the socialist parties of Europe, the French Marxists boycotted the event and organized their own congress to coincide with that of the Possibilists. Attempts to reach a compromise failed, and both conferences proceeded in an atmosphere of great confusion. Numerically, the Possibilist conference was stronger, with about 600 delegates to the Marxist 400. The Marxists triumphed, however, because the delegates at their conference included the most prestigious names in world socialism. More important, they had the support of the Marxist German SPD, which represented the strongest working class movement in the world. In the power struggle over the leadership of the international workers' movement, it became apparent that momentum lay with the leaders of the Marxist socialist parties. The Second International was established.

The Founding Congress

Despite the confusion, the spirit at the Marxist Congress was one of optimism. William Liebknecht and the Frenchman Edouard Vaillant, a veteran of the Paris Commune, were elected joint presidents of the Congress, a move that represented the solidarity between German and French socialism. Delegates gave reports on the history and present state of the socialist movement in their respective countries. It was apparent that enormous progress had been made since the collapse of the First International. Socialist workers' parties were developing in almost every country in Europe, despite opposition and persecution. The education and organization of the workers was taking place all over the world, and the delegates looked forward with confidence to the eventual downfall of capitalism. There was little discussion in 1889, however, of the nature and form of organization of the Second International. This was in sharp contrast to the First International, which had laid out rules and set up the general council as the executive body of the International at its outset. Instead, for its first 11 years, the Second International had no executive council to represent it between congresses. Unlike the tightly centralized First International, this structure emphasized the autonomy of the national parties.

The Anarchist Problem

During the course of the founding congress, conflict with the anarchists again became a concern. Although the term *anarchist* covered a wide variety of positions and beliefs, adherents were generally revolutionaries who pressed for social transformation through direct violent action against the state. The Marxist parties were also based in revolutionary ideology, but they focused upon organized political action to achieve power for the working class and eliminate the capitalist system. Therefore, one of the resolutions of the 1889 congress committed socialist parties to work toward achieving manhood suffrage. In those countries in which the working man had the vote, socialists were to continue participating in elections with the aim of acquiring political power. The anarchists ridiculed this approach and rejected the leadership of the socialist political parties as sham revolutionaries, an accusation that was not entirely without substance. The anarchists therefore disrupted proceedings at both the Marxist and Possibilist congresses in 1889 by shouting over the other delegates with revolutionary slogans and insults until the anarchists eventually had to be ejected. This was only a temporary measure, and anarchist antics again disturbed the proceedings at the next congress in 1891. Partici-

pants at the 1893 Zurich congress eventually voted that membership should be limited to those parties that acknowledged the necessity of political action. This motion effectively excluded anarchists from the Second International.

May Day

Another key concern at the founding congress was the question of international action on labor legislation. Most of the delegates were particularly interested in this issue because it directly affected the lives of the workers whom they claimed to represent. As a result, the Congress passed a resolution in favor of campaigning in support of the eight-hour workday and improved working conditions. This led to the most significant decision reached by the Congress, in terms of the impact it had on workers worldwide. In 1888 the American Federation of Labor decided to nominate 1 May as an annual day of mass demonstrations and strikes in support of the eight-hour day. The resolution passed by the Second International to support worldwide participation in the May Day protests took the American campaign and transformed it into an international phenomenon. This call for internationally coordinated action was significant because for the first time it made international socialism a reality in the minds of workers.

The impact of the first international May Day protests in 1890 was muted, however, because the instructions from the Second International had not been explicit about how the day should be marked. The resolution stated that the actions taken by the workers in support of the eight-hour day should be "by means and along the lines appropriate to their respective countries." This meant that it was up to the socialist parties in each country to decide what to do, an indication that the influence of the Second International was subordinate to national leadership. The resolution had been drafted with the concerns of the Germans in mind, as they were wary of any actions that might adversely affect their chances for the repeal of the Anti-Socialist Laws. Therefore, despite the commitment to international solidarity on this issue, May Day was marked in different ways in each country. Nationwide strikes and violent protests occurred in France on 1 May, whereas in most of Germany, action was restricted to meetings held on the first Sunday in May. Some socialists in other countries were disappointed at the German attitude, because they felt that an important opportunity to demonstrate international solidarity and strike a blow at the capitalist system had been lost. May Day remained a topic for debate in the Second International throughout the 1890s.

War

The other major resolution passed by the Second International at the founding congress concerned war between the imperial powers. In 1889 this was not of immediate concern, but it was to become the most pressing issue over the next 25 years, and it eventually brought about the disintegration of the Second International. The congress passed a resolution condemning the national armies and calling for them to be replaced with peoples' militias. The socialists believed that the aggressive war mongering of the imperial governments was against the interests of the working class all over the world. The party stance was that it was necessary to disband the national armies to ensure that the working class would not be used as cannon fodder for imperial expansion. Leaving national defense up to workers' militias would ensure that wars would be fought in self-defense rather than for capitalist imperial gain. The basic assumption of the socialists was that as socialism was an international movement, the spread of socialist thought would prevent the outbreak of war between nations. However, the optimistic belief that international workers' solidarity was stronger than nationalist militarism was to be dashed in the events surrounding the beginning of World War I.

The most immediate achievement of the founding of the Second International was that it broke the isolation of the national socialist parties. The meeting provided support and encouragement for the smaller socialist parties, who could look to the strength and success of larger national parties, such as the SPD, for inspiration. The discussions at the Congress had revealed common problems and concerns across the socialist movement, and it had provided a forum for the international resolution of those issues. With the agreement on May Day, the Second International laid the basis for international socialist action, encouraging workers to see beyond their narrow local or national concerns and to engage directly with workers worldwide, which fostered an increased sense of class consciousness. However, the Second International also indicated that internationalism did have limits, and that in many cases, national concerns were to take precedence. In the long term, the founding of the Second International was significant because it heralded the domination of the socialist movement by Marxist ideology, as opposed to the reformist position of the Possibilists or the anarchist approach. In particular, the ideology and methods of the SPD dominated the first congress and most of those that followed.

Key Players

Bebel, August (1840–1913): Leader of the German Social Democratic Party, with Wilhelm Liebknecht. Bebel was well respected in international socialism and was enormously popular among the German workers. His support for the Second International helped to ensure its success, and he became one of its most dominant figures.

Brousse, Paul (1854–1912): French socialist and leader of the Possibilists, who split from the French Marxists. The Possibilists were open to achieving reform by working with bourgeois radicals. Their links with the union movement meant they were originally in charge of organising an international workers congress in Paris in 1889. This was eventually overshadowed by the congress that was organized by the French Marxists.

Guesde, Jules (1845–1922): Leader of the French Marxist Party. Guesde was a doctrinaire Marxist with close ties to the German leaders. His opposition to reform through co-operation with other political parties caused a split in the French socialist movement. Under his leadership, the Marxists boycotted the Possibilist Congress in 1889 and organized their own.

Liebknecht, Wilhelm (1826–1900): Leader of German Social Democratic Party, with August Bebel. Liebknecht had been involved in attempts to reestablish international socialism in the early 1880s and was committed to the success of the Second International. He was elected the joint president of the first congress in Paris in 1889.

See also: *American Federation of Labor; Eight-hour Day Movement; First International; Paris Commune; Red International of Labor Unions.*

BIBLIOGRAPHY

Books

Braunthal, Julian. *History of the International, 1864–1914.* London: Thomas Nelson and Sons Ltd., 1966.

Cole, G. D. H. *A History of Socialist Thought.* Vol. III, Part 1, *The Second International, 1889–1914.* London: Macmillan; New York: St. Martin's Press, 1953–1960.

Foster, William Z. *History of the Three Internationals.* Westport, CT: Greenwood Press, 1968.

Joll, James. *The Second International, 1889–1914.* London: Weidenfeld and Nicolson, 1955.

Lindemann, Albert S. *A History of European Socialism.* New Haven and London: Yale University Press, 1983.

ADDITIONAL RESOURCES

Books

Cole, G. D. H. *A History of Socialist Thought.* Vol. II, *Marxism and Anarchism, 1850–1890.* London: Macmillan; New York: St. Martin's Press, 1953–1960.

Miller, Susanne and Heinrich Potthoff. *A History of German Social Democracy: From 1848 to the Present.* Leamington Spa, UK; Hamburg, Germany; and New York: Berg Publishers, 1986.

—Katrina Ford

Second Reform Act

Great Britain 1867

Synopsis

The Second Reform Act was part of a process of British electoral reform that dated back to the First Reform Act of 1832 and continued into the later part of the nineteenth century. Before 1867 eligibility to vote in the general elections for Members of Parliament (MPs) was based largely upon the value of housing, which prevented low-income people from voting in most areas. Radical groups campaigned throughout the 1860s to extend the franchise to the working class. However, it was rivalry between the main British political parties, the Conservatives and the Liberals, that eventually resulted in reform. With the passing of the Second Reform Act, the male urban working class became a significant part of the political nation for the first time.

John Bright. © Archive Photos Inc. Reproduced by permission.

Timeline

1851: China's T'ai P'ing ("Great Peace") Rebellion begins under the leadership of schoolmaster Hong Xiuquan, who believes himself the younger brother of Jesus Christ. He mobilizes the peasantry against the Manchu emperors in a civil war that will take 20 to 30 million lives over the next 14 years.

1857: Start of the Sepoy Mutiny, an unsuccessful revolt by Indian troops against the British East India Company. As a result of the rebellion, which lasts into 1858, England places India under direct crown rule.

1863: Opening of the world's first subway, in London.

1867: Dual monarchy established in Austria-Hungary.

1867: Maximilian surrenders to Mexican forces under Benito Juarez and is executed. Thus ends Napoleon III's dreams for a new French empire in the New World.

1867: Establishment of the Dominion of Canada.

1867: United States purchases Alaska from Russia for $7,200,000.

1867: Meiji Restoration in Japan ends 675 years of rule by the shoguns.

1867: Karl Marx publishes the first volume of *Das Kapital.*

1871: U.S. troops in the West begin fighting the Apache nation.

1874: As farm wages in Britain plummet, agricultural workers go on strike.

1877: Great Britain's Queen Victoria is proclaimed the empress of India.

Event and Its Context

The Reform Movement before 1866

The First Reform Act of 1832 had been intended as the final solution to the issue of electoral reform. Many people recognized, however, that the inequities of the old electoral system had not been solved by the legislation. The political establishment was hostile to demands for radical political and social reform. Nevertheless, the wish for further moderate reform remained an undercurrent in the political scene throughout the period leading up to the 1860s. From time to time, MPs proposed moderate reform bills, but none attracted enough support to be passed.

From the 1860s, the vague desire for further reform began to gather momentum. Political events overseas, such as the unification of Italy, provided a focus for the activities of British radicals. In 1864, when the Italian nationalist leader Garibaldi visited London, local labor formed the London Workingmen's Garibaldi Association in his honor. From this emerged the Reform League, which was inaugurated in 1865 and led by Edmond Beales. This was a mainly working-class organization, which at its height comprised over 400 branches and 60,000 members, making it the largest working-class movement in Britain since Chartism. Many of those active in the league were associated with the trade union movement and the First International. Older radicals, including many Chartists, also joined the league.

The Reform League cooperated with the middle-class Reform Union, which had been established in 1864 and was led by the Radical MP John Bright. The aims of the two organizations were different. The Reform League campaigned for manhood suffrage, but the Reform Union wanted household suffrage, which would give the vote to every man in charge of a household. Although earlier generations of working- and middle-class radicals had tended to see their interests as antagonistic, however, in the 1860s they were willing to compromise to achieve agreement on the question of electoral reform. This was a result of the changing nature of working-class radicalism in mid-Victorian Britain. Compared to the heightened tensions and class conflict of earlier decades, this period was characterized by a greater sense of social stability and cohesion. As a result, many middle-class reformers felt that certain sections of the working class demonstrated the values of hard work and respectability that were so important to Victorian middle-class culture. The challenge for parliamentary exponents of reform was to adjust the voting qualifications to enfranchise this part of the working class without giving the vote to the lowest segments of society. This contrast between the deserving respectable working class and the undeserving dangerous poor framed the debate about reform.

The Reform Crisis, 1866–1867

In May 1866 W. E. Gladstone, Liberal Chancellor of the Exchequer, introduced another reform bill into Parliament. The bill was moderate and would have only increased the amount of people entitled to vote by about 400,000. The efforts of Gladstone and the Prime Minister Lord Russell, however, failed to pass the bill. A group of right-wing Liberals, fearful of the consequences of increased working-class participation in politics, sided with the Conservatives and refused to support the bill. Robert Lowe, one of the leaders of this group, characterized the working class as violent, ignorant, and generally unfit to take part in the politics of the nation. He was convinced that they would use their vote to attack the upper orders of society. The bill was defeated in June and the government resigned, which allowed formation of a minority Conservative government led by Lord Derby and Benjamin Disraeli.

In response, the reform movement exploded into action. In June and July, mass protests occurred in London, culminating in a call for a national demonstration in Hyde Park on 23 July. The meeting was banned, but a large crowd broke down the railings and invaded the park, skirmishing with police. Although many observers were frightened by the Hyde Park riots, clearly there was never any threat to the social order. The aims of the radical leaders centered on parliamentary reform rather than social revolution.

Mass demonstrations occurred throughout the country over the next few months. The Radical MP John Bright embarked upon a national tour, speaking at Reform League rallies all over the country to hundreds of thousands of people. Many working-class people were deeply offended at being described as drunken and violent by the enemies of reform. As a result, the mass rallies emphasized the respectability and discipline of the independent working-class man and his fitness for the franchise. Nationwide agitation carried the message to Parliament that the issue of reform was not going to go away.

Disraeli's Gamble

The legislation that was eventually passed in 1867, however, was the product of party politics in Parliament. Disraeli recognized an opportunity to divide further the Liberal opposition and humiliate Gladstone, who was now the Liberal leader. He therefore proposed reform legislation that was far more radical than anything the Liberals had proposed. For the first time, voting in the borough electorates was to be based upon household suffrage. Adult males who were heads of urban households would be entitled to vote. When the bill was first presented to Parliament in March 1867, however, it included many restrictions. The most significant was that only those men who paid their taxes directly would be eligible to be included on the voting registers. As many poorer people paid their taxes with their rent through their landlords, a practice known as compounding, they would not be included on the register. The restriction would have prevented a large portion of urban working-class men from voting.

Over the next few months, in a remarkable piece of political maneuvering, Disraeli gathered support for the bill. He convinced his Conservative colleagues that the bill was necessary if they were to stay in power, while simultaneously appealing to the radical members who supported reform. Deals that occurred as part of the campaign removed most of the initial restrictions so as to admit the lower sections of society into the political nation for the first time. Crucially, Hodgkinson's amendment outlawed the practice of compounding, meaning that everyone had to pay their taxes in person, making them eligible to vote. This change alone made an extra 500,000 people eligible to vote in England and in Wales.

Some of the Conservative MPs may have supported the bill because they believed that the lowest sections of the working

Benjamin Disraeli. The Library of Congress.

class were more likely to be conservative, as they were more influenced by attitudes of deference to their superiors. Nobody could be sure, however, how the working classes were going to use their vote. It was, as Disraeli said, a leap in the dark. The Conservatives had been shut out of power for most of the past three decades and so had nothing to lose; they were willing to make concessions to stay in power and defeat the liberal leaders. Gladstone, as leader of the Liberal Party, the traditional reform party, was in the humiliating position of having to oppose a Conservative Reform Bill that was more radical than anything he had proposed.

Radical Reform

The Reform Bill that passed into law had been shorn of most of its initial restrictions and was far more radical than anyone could have foreseen. The bill abolished the 10 pound per annum housing qualification so that in the English and Welsh borough electorates, the numbers of voters increased from approximately 500,000 in 1866 to 1.25 million as of the 1868 election. In the counties, where the voting qualification for leaseholders had been lowered from 50 to 12 pounds per annum, the increase was not as marked. The proportion of men who could vote in Britain, not including Ireland, increased from one-fifth to one-third, according to estimates. The bulk of working-class men could then participate in the political life of the nation.

The impact that they could have on the makeup of the British Parliament, however, was limited in many ways. Although debate had focused on voting eligibility, the Reform Act also effected changes to the distribution of Parliament seats throughout the country. These changes were very conservative. The bill created only 19 new seats in the large urban areas that housed most of the new voters, and 25 new seats went to the more conservative counties. Although the numbers of working-class voters increased, they were contained in areas that had proportionally fewer seats than other areas. The continued dominance of smaller, more conservative constituencies helped to mute the influence of working-class voters.

In the long term, the worst fears of those who opposed reform were not realized. It was apparent in the next two elections that the working class did not vote along class lines, largely because there was no political movement to represent the specific interests of the workers. The Reform League faded after 1867 because of problems with funding and organization. The established parties remained firmly in control. In particular, the Liberal Party dominated working-class political activity; the first working-class MPs were Liberal, rather than representatives of an independent working-class party. Without an organized and independent working-class political movement, the radical impact of the enfranchisement of the working class would be limited.

Key Players

Beales, Edmond (1803–1881): Radical barrister and leader of the Reform League. Beales's support for universal manhood suffrage shocked many middle- and upper-class observers. However, Beales was a reformer, not a revolutionary, and wanted peaceful change within the existing social and political framework.

Bright, John (1811–1889): Radical member of Parliament and leader of the middle-class Reform Union, Bright campaigned for moderate reform measures throughout the 1860s. He cooperated with the working-class Reform League, but he did not believe that all working-class men should be granted the vote.

Disraeli, Benjamin (1804–1881): Conservative chancellor of the Exchequer, later to be Conservative leader and prime minister. Disraeli's desire to keep the Conservatives in power by dividing and humiliating the Liberals determined the nature and timing of the Second Reform Act.

Gladstone, William Ewart (1809–1898): Liberal leader and later prime minister. The defeat of the Reform Bill proposed by Gladstone in 1866 resulted in the Liberal government's resignation. The minority Conservative government that came to power eventually passed the Second Reform Act, despite Gladstone's opposition.

See also: *Chartist Movement; First International.*

BIBLIOGRAPHY

Books

Cowling, Maurice. *1867: Disraeli, Gladstone and Revolution. The Passing of the Second Reform Act.* Cambridge: Cambridge University Press, 1967.

Finn, Margot C. *After Chartism: Class and Nation in English Radical Politics, 1848–1874.* Cambridge: Cambridge University Press, 1993.

Harrison, Royden. *Before the Socialists: Studies in Labour and Politics, 1861–1881.* London: Routledge & Kegan Paul, 1965.

Smith, F.B. *The Second Reform Bill.* London and New York: Melbourne University Press, 1966.

Walton, John K. *The Second Reform Act.* London: Metheun, 1987.

Wright, D.G. *Democracy and Reform, 1815–1885.* London: Longman, 1970.

ADDITIONAL RESOURCES

Books

Biagini, Eugenio F. *Liberty, Retrenchment and Reform: Popular Liberalism in the Age of Gladstone, 1860–1880.* Cambridge: Cambridge University Press, 1992.

Hoppen, K. Theodore. *The Mid Victorian Generation, 1846–1886.* Oxford: Clarendon Press, 1998.

Tholfsen, Trygve R. *Working Class Radicalism in Mid-Victorian England.* London: Croom Helm, 1976.

—Katrina Ford

Settimana Rossa: *See* **Red Week.**

Shanghai May Fourth Movement

China 1919

Synopsis

A massive general strike paralyzed the city of Shanghai in June 1919. A reaction to the May Fourth Movement that had started a month earlier in Beijing, the labor strife in Shanghai marked the beginning of the modern Chinese labor movement. The May Fourth Movement, which began as a protest against the terms of the Versailles Treaty that ended World War I, first attracted students in support of the Beijing events. As the students in Shanghai began to organize and protest, they reached out to other sectors of the city. In particular, they sought ties with Shanghai's merchants and workers. What started as a student strike soon developed into a massive general strike in the city. The May Fourth Movement and subsequent events marked the commencement of an unsettled period for residents of Shanghai and other Chinese cities. The country's urban inhabitants became increasingly aware of global events. The working class united, despite traditional divisions, to fight inflation, warlord rule, and national humiliation.

Timeline

1900: China's Boxer Rebellion, which began in the preceding year with attacks on foreigners and Christians, reaches its height. An international contingent of more than 2,000 men arrives to restore order, but only after several tens of thousands have died.

1907: U.S. markets experience a financial panic.

1912: *Titanic* sinks on its maiden voyage, from Southampton to New York, on 14 April. More than 1,500 people are killed.

1915: At the Second Battle of Ypres, the Germans introduce a terrifying new weapon: poison gas.

1917: The intercepted "Zimmermann Telegram" reveals a plot by the German government to draw Mexico into an alliance against the United States in return for a German promise to return the southwestern U.S. territories taken in the Mexican War. Three months later, in response to German threats of unrestricted submarine warfare, the United States on 6 April declares war on Germany.

1919: Formation of the Third International (Comintern), whereby the Bolshevik government of Russia establishes its control over communist movements worldwide.

1919: Treaty of Versailles signed by the Allies and Germany but rejected by the U.S. Senate. This is due in part to rancor between President Woodrow Wilson and Republican Senate leaders, and in part to concerns over Wilson's plan to commit the United States to the newly established League of Nations and other international duties. Not until 1921 will Congress formally end U.S. participation in the war, but it will never agree to join the League.

1919: Ratification of the Eighteenth Amendment, which prohibits the production, sale, distribution, purchase, and consumption of alcohol throughout the United States.

1919: In India, Mahatma Gandhi launches his campaign of nonviolent resistance to British rule.

1919: In Italy, a former socialist of the left named Benito Mussolini introduces the world to a new socialism of the right, embodied in an organization known as the "Union for Struggle," or Fasci di Combattimento. Composed primarily of young war veterans discontented with Italy's paltry share of the spoils from the recent world war (if not with their country's lackluster military performance in the conflict), the fascists are known for their black shirts and their penchant for violence.

1921: As the Allied Reparations Commission calls for payments of 132 billion gold marks, inflation in Germany begins to climb.

1925: European leaders attempt to secure the peace at the Locarno Conference, which guarantees the boundaries between France and Germany, and Belgium and Germany.

1929: On "Black Friday" in October, prices on the U.S. stock market, which had been climbing wildly for several years, suddenly collapse. Thus begins the first phase of a world economic crisis and depression that will last until the beginning of World War II.

Event and Its Context

The May Fourth Movement Begins

The May Fourth Movement of 1919 began in Beijing as a protest against the governments of both China and Japan. Students in that city took to the streets to voice their disapproval of the terms of the Versailles Treaty at the end of World War I. In particular, the Chinese students were upset because the treaty would hand over China's Shandong province to Japan. Before the war, Germany had concessions in Shandong that it had acquired in the nineteenth century. During the war, Japan had joined the Allies and then seized the German holdings. To make matters worse, the Japanese government issued the Twenty-One Demands to China in 1915. Although the Chinese warlord government rejected some of the demands, it allowed Japan to keep Shandong. In 1917 the European powers agreed to Japan's claim in exchange for taking naval action against the Germans. Furthermore, China declared war in Germany in hopes of reacquiring Shandong and even sent thousands of Chinese workers to Europe. Then in 1918 China made a secret agreement that allowed Japan to keep the conceded territory.

When the agreement became public knowledge, the protesters blamed the government for such national humiliation. Still upset about the loss to Japan in the Sino-Japanese War in 1894–1895, many Chinese thought that losing Shandong to Japan was further proof of their country's malaise. Many were hopeful that in light of Woodrow Wilson's call for self-determination after the war, decades of foreign domination in China would come to an end. Students from 13 schools in Beijing met, made a number of resolutions protesting the agreement, and called for a demonstration. Some 3,000 demonstrators gathered in Tianamen Square. Later the protest became violent, as the students attacked a government official and set the home of another on fire. In response, the government arrested numerous students. The demonstrations in Beijing sparked a nationalist sentiment throughout China, and the protest movement quickly spread to other parts of the country.

The Movement Spreads to Shanghai

News of the events in Beijing reached Shanghai within a day of their occurrence. Many in China's largest city, particularly students, expressed their solidarity with the Beijing protesters and demanded the release of the arrested students and the dismissal of certain government officials. On 7 May thousands of Shanghai residents attended a citizen's meeting. The next day, students resolved to form a union with representatives from all of the major schools in the city. They formally founded the Student Union of the Middle Schools and Institutes of Higher Learning on 11 May, with more than 12,000 students from 61 schools. In addition, they organized the Shanghai Student Volunteer Corps for the Defense of Shandong.

On 19 May the student union leaders resolved that they should strike and also send representatives to other cities to persuade students to join the strike. They originally scheduled the strike for 22 May. They postponed the strike date, however, due to mediation by teachers and the Association of Education. When the Shanghai students learned that the government in Beijing was not going to meet the demands of students there, they went on strike on 26 May. More than 20,000 students from more than 70 schools participated in the strike.

More than in other Chinese cities, the students in Shanghai were concerned about relations with the merchants and the working class. On 27 May the students decided to dispatch representatives to meet with Shanghai's merchant societies and to establish a labor department. Soon, Shanghai became the center of the movement and students from other cities gathered there. On 31 May a memorial meeting attracted 100,000 people.

At a 1 June meeting, merchants promised support for the protest movement. On 2 June authorities began to make arrests in Shanghai. Starting on 5 June 1919, the city was paralyzed by protest activities. In the early morning, students took to the streets. Then, shopkeepers closed their doors to business, first in the Chinese section of the city and later in the French Concession and the International Settlement. By the afternoon, with the exception of some foreign firms, stores throughout Shanghai were all closed. Others soon joined in, including street vendors and even workers in the city's red-light district. The police attempted unsuccessfully to force merchants to reopen their shops. In general, the strike was peaceful, although there were some confrontations with the police and some 100 students were arrested on the first day.

The shopkeepers' action was followed by a massive strike of some 60,000 workers in the city. Because the working class in Shanghai was less organized than the merchants, the workers were slower to respond. The strike started among the workers in the Japanese-owned cotton mills. By the afternoon of 5 June, already some 20,000 workers in these Japanese mills were on strike. It is not surprising that these workers were the first to react, as they had first-hand experience with Japanese imperialism and exploitation. Soon the workers' strike spread to the shipyards, utilities, printing, tobacco, and transportation industries.

The shutdown of the country's largest city and industrial center forced the government to take action. Indeed, Lu Yung-hsiang, the military governor of Shanghai, urged the Beijing government to do something about the demands of the protesters. The Chinese government issued a public apology, released arrested students, fired several government officials involved in the Paris peace talks, and refused to sign the Versailles Treaty. The strike in Shanghai ended on the afternoon of 12 June. When it was confirmed that the Beijing government had dismissed the officials, the Shanghai protesters celebrated with parades and fireworks.

Worker Organization and Participation

Worker organization and participation in the strike took a variety of forms. Among the artisans, both native-place associations and guilds played key roles. Native-place associations served the various migrant communities living in Shanghai. These associations acted as employment agencies for new arrivals and provided welfare when needed. Sometimes, these groups also sponsored cultural events or constructed a temple to a local deity. The associations might also build schools, provide savings and loan facilities, and provide for burials. In general, however, they served to give the Shanghai migrant population a sense of belonging.

In the events of 1919, the Ningbo native-place association played a particularly active role. This was in part due to its members' economic concerns, as members were worried about the competition of Japanese imports. Furthermore, the Ningbo migrants had a confrontation with the French a half century earlier, and the 1919 activities were in a way an outgrowth of their nationalist feelings.

Guilds and early unions also played a role in organizing workers in the 1919 protest movement. For example, the metalworkers' guild helped to organize skilled mechanics from the railroads, the waterworks, and various other industries. Also taking an active role were the printers from the Sincere Comrades Society at the Commercial Press. Painters and construction workers were among the other workers to organize and strike. Even the guild of the ginseng dealers donated the funds collected at its annual celebration for its patron deity.

Other groups, in addition to the skilled workers, took part in the June 1919 strike. Foremen at factories helped to organize unskilled laborers. In particular, the foremen in the foreign-owned cotton mills encouraged strikers and formed an organization to promote Chinese-made products. Gangsters from Shanghai's Green and Red gangs also contributed to the strike. Leading gangsters ordered thieves and pickpockets to join the work stoppage. They also ordered beggars not to beg during the strike, and even some prostitutes joined the strike by singing patriotic songs at night rather than soliciting customers.

Aftermath of the Strike

Once the strike was over, some workers were interested in maintaining the organization and cooperation that had been prevalent during the work stoppage. On 12 June 1919 some 2,000 workers met to plan future worker organization. As was the case in many parts of the world in the years following World War I, there was a wave of working-class organization and activity in Shanghai and other Chinese cities. In part, this activity reflected immediate economic concerns such as high inflation. In addition, Chinese workers had been exposed to European working-class ideologies and forms of protest and organization. For example, during the war, some 10,000 Chinese workers went to work in European factories to replace those who had gone off to war. While in Europe, some learned to read and write and became used to a higher standard of living. These workers were also exposed to labor organization and nationalism. When they returned to Chinese cities such as Shanghai, they were more conscious of workers' rights and the kinds of demands that could be made of management and the government. This situation led to increased unionization and a wave of strikes in Shanghai. In 1918 there had been only about 24 strikes in the city; by 1927 there were well over 200 work stoppages in China's largest city.

The May Fourth Movement and the events surrounding it had many consequences beyond the labor movement in Shanghai. Eventually, at the 1922 Washington Conference, Japan gave up its claim to Shandong province. The movement marked an important break with the past. It was an important influence on many Chinese intellectuals, many of whom became disillusioned with the West and moved toward more radical views and the Communist Party, which was formed in Shanghai in 1921, in part as an outgrowth of the events of 1919.

Key Players

Shao Li-tzu: Shao was a newspaper editor and a professor at Futan University in Shanghai. When he learned of the May Fourth events in Beijing, he attempted to organize students in Shanghai to support the Beijing students. A member of the Guomindang Party, Shao led to the start of the Shanghai protests and strikes.

Tuan His-peng: A member of the Guomindang Party, Tuan was a student from Beijing. He went to Shanghai as a representative of the Beijing student movement. In Shanghai he helped to organize students and convince other groups to join the strike. After the strike, Tuan was selected as the leader of the National Students' Union.

Yu Yung-hsiang: Yu was the military governor of Shanghai in 1919. Although he proclaimed martial law in the Chinese section of the city, he also called an emergency meeting on 7 June to bring together students, merchants, and other groups in hopes of avoiding a major conflict. Yu also urged the Beijing government to address the student demands once he saw the scope of the Shanghai strike.

See also: *Chiang Kai-shek Purges Communists; Shanghai May Thirtieth Movement.*

BIBLIOGRAPHY

Books

Chen, Joseph T. *The May Fourth Movement in Shanghai: The Making of a Social Movement in Modern China.* Leiden, The Netherlands: E. J. Brill, 1971.

Chesneaux, Jean. *The Chinese Labor Movement, 1919–1927.* Stanford, CA: Stanford University Press, 1968.

Harrison, James Pinckney. *The Long March to Power: A History of the Chinese Communist Party, 1921–1972.* New York: Praeger Publishers, 1972.

Perry, Elizabeth. *Shanghai on Strike: The Politics of Chinese Labor.* Stanford, CA: Stanford University Press, 1993.

Van de Ven, Hans. *From Friend to Comrade: The Founding of the Chinese Communist Party, 1920–1927.* Berkeley and Los Angeles: University of California Press, 1991.

—Ronald Young

Shanghai May Thirtieth Movement

China 1925

Synopsis

In early 1925 both the working class and the Chinese elite in Shanghai began to agitate against the presence of foreigners in the city. In May the situation became tense when a Japanese foreman killed a Chinese worker. On 30 May several thousand residents of Shanghai marched to protest the killing. Police responded by firing into the crowds, killing 10 people and injuring dozens more. This event prompted the city's workers, merchants, and students to unite in what is sometimes called the May Thirtieth Movement. The result of the movement was a general strike in the city that virtually shut down Shanghai. However, the unity of the various groups did not last, as the merchants ended their strike in late June. The workers continued to strike until September, by which time they had reached compromises with Shanghai's foreign interests.

Timeline

1910: Introduction of neon lighting.

1915: A German submarine sinks the *Lusitania,* killing 1,195, including 128 U.S. citizens. Theretofore, many Americans had been sympathetic toward Germany, but the incident begins to turn the tide of U.S. sentiment toward the Allies.

1920: Bolsheviks eliminate the last of their opponents, bringing an end to the Russian Civil War. By then, foreign troops, representing a dozen nations that opposed the communists, have long since returned home.

1922: Inspired by the Bolsheviks' example of imposing revolution by means of a coup, Benito Mussolini leads his blackshirts in an October "March on Rome" and forms a new fascist government.

1923: Conditions in Germany worsen as inflation skyrockets and France, attempting to collect on coal deliveries promised at Versailles, marches into the Ruhr basin. In November an obscure political group known as the National Socialist German Workers' Party attempts to stage a coup, or putsch, in a Munich beer hall. The revolt fails, and in 1924 the party's leader, Adolf Hitler, will receive a prison sentence of five years. He will only serve nine months, however, and the incident will serve to attract attention for him and his party, known as the Nazis.

1925: Wyoming Democrat Nellie Tayloe Ross becomes the first woman governor elected in the United States.

1925: European leaders attempt to secure the peace at the Locarno Conference, which guarantees the boundaries between France and Germany, and Belgium and Germany.

1925: In Tennessee, John T. Scopes is fined for teaching evolution in a public school. There follows a highly publicized trial at which famed attorney Clarence Darrow represents the defense, while the aging Democratic populist William Jennings Bryan argues for the state. The "Scopes Monkey Trial" symbolizes a widening divisions between rural and urban America, and though the court decides in favor of the state, it is clear that the historical tide is turning against the old agrarian order symbolized by Bryan—who dies during the trial.

1925: Released from Landsberg Prison, Adolf Hitler is a national celebrity, widely regarded as an emerging statesman who offers genuine solutions to Germany's problems. This year, he publishes the first volume of *Mein Kampf* (My Struggle), which he dictated in prison to trusted confederate Rudolf Hess. The second and final volume of Hitler's opus, a mixture of autobiography, "history," and racial rant, will appear two years later.

1928: Sixty-five nations sign the Kellogg-Briand Pact, outlawing war.

1930: Naval disarmament treaty signed by the United States, Great Britain, France, Italy, and Japan.

1935: Italians invade Ethiopia, and the response by the League of Nations—which imposes sanctions but otherwise fails to act—reveals the impotence of that organization.

Event and Its Context

Events Leading up to the Strike

In the weeks and months leading up to the general strike in Shanghai, there was growing unhappiness among both the Chinese working class in the city and among the elite. The Chinese business elite in Shanghai were upset because of a number of newly proposed laws, and they reacted through their general chamber of commerce. In particular, they were displeased with proposals for higher wharfage fees and press control.

At the same time, worker agitation had begun in the city. As early as February 1925 workers staged strikes against Shanghai's Japanese-owned cotton mills. Worker activity continued in the coming months. More strikes took place in May, and some of the workers formed the West Shanghai Workers' Club. This club, which was led by Liu Hua and Sun Liang-hui, served as a union for the cotton mill workers. The confrontation escalated on 15 May, when a fight broke out between a Japanese foreman and a Chinese worker named Ku Cheng-hung. The Japanese foreman killed Ku, outraging the Chinese laboring class. The workers held a memorial service for Ku on 24 May that drew some 5,000 people. In addition to Ku's fellow workers, student groups in Shanghai also lent their support.

The West Shanghai Workers' Club, students, and members of the Communist Party scheduled a demonstration for 30 May to protest the killing. Several thousand Shanghai residents took part in the march. The protesters soon clashed with police. Without warning, the police fired into the crowd, causing 10 deaths and more than 50 injuries.

In response to the police violence, Shanghai residents held a meeting on 31 May at the offices of the general chamber of commerce. Workers, students, and merchants attended the meeting. All three groups agreed to stage a strike in protest of the 30 May police action. Furthermore, among other demands, they called for a boycott of foreign banks and demanded compensation for the families of the victims of the 30 May incident.

The Strike Begins

The strike began on 1 June and was coordinated by the newly created Shanghai General Union, which had links to the Communist Party. By 4 June some 74,000 strikers were participating. By 13 June the number of strikers had grown to about 160,000. Most affected by the strike were foreign-owned firms in Shanghai, especially those owned by the Japanese and British. Foreign authorities in the city responded with force. They mobilized the Volunteer Corps, the foreign defense force, and declared martial law. They also brought gunboats up the Huangpu River and closed down Shanghai University. There were numerous violent clashes. In the first few days of the strike, more than 60 people lost their lives.

In response to the violent reaction of the foreign authorities, the strikers became even more determined. An action committee, made up of the Shanghai General Union, the Shanghai Students' Federation, the National Students' Federation, and the federated shopkeepers associations, met on 7 June. Together they formed a new group known as the Shanghai Workers', Merchants', and Students' Federation. At a mass demonstration by 20,000 people on 11 June, the new groups ratified a 17-point program. They repeated some of the earlier demands, such as compensation for the victims of 30 May. However, they now went much further and made additional demands on Shanghai's foreign authorities. They demanded that changes be made in the status of the city's International Settlement, such as abolishing the Volunteer Corps; allowing for freedom of speech, assembly, and press in the International Settlement; withdrawing of foreign armed forces; and abolishing extraterritoriality. Thus, the demands of Shanghai residents had gone beyond economic concerns and had acquired a political tone.

The Role of the Shanghai General Union

As the strike progressed, the General Union played the most significant role. Formed on 31 May after the violent clash with police the previous day, the General Union soon had control of much of the city's working class. It established branches in the main working-class areas of Shanghai and encouraged the formation of unions among different trades such as postal workers, printers, and streetcar employees. It also distributed a bulletin several times a week. Furthermore, the General Union helped to organize pickets throughout the city so as to inhibit the use of strikebreakers and to impede the transport of Japanese goods in Shanghai.

The General Union was also important because it was able to collect money for a strike fund to provide for the striking workers. It obtained funds from a variety of sources. Students made donations to the striking workers. The General Union made collections in the Chinese-owned factories where work continued. International labor organizations such as the Red International of Labor Unions provided money to the striking Shanghai workers as did the government at Canton, and the warlord government of the north supplied financial aid to the workers. Finally, the Shanghai elite donated to the strike effort because they generally supported the political demands of the movement and also saw it as a way of squeezing out foreign competition.

The Strike Weakens

Early in the strike there was much solidarity among the various sectors of Shanghai's society, but by the end of June there was much less enthusiasm and unity. The first to abandon the movement were the Chinese bourgeoisie and merchants. They began to make compromises with the authorities of the International Settlement. Once they had achieved what they wanted, the merchants ended their strike on 25 June.

The Shanghai General Union continued its struggle despite the defection of the merchants. However, its efforts were hampered by the action of the city's Municipal Council. At the suggestion of a manager at one of the British-owned cotton mills, the municipal leaders cut off the electricity to the Chinese-owned factories, where work had continued. They did this in hopes of increasing the number of strikers and therefore placing a strain on the General Union's strike fund. In turn, this would weaken the resolve of the workers' movement. In addition, this strategy would pressure the Chinese mill owners not to support the strike, as it would now affect their operations. The move seemed to be successful, as the number of strikers increased by about 20,000 and the Chamber of Commerce began to withdraw its aid to the striking workers.

Once the elite Chinese abandoned the movement, the strikers also lost much of their support from Chinese authorities. By July the military authorities of Shanghai began to complain about the fact that the strike was disturbing public order in the city. Furthermore, they ordered the registration and inspection of the city's unions.

There was also some dissension among the workers of Shanghai. Some accused the General Union of prolonging the strike for its own political purposes and the personal ambitions of some of its leaders. The split among the workers began to pit those who supported the Communist Party against those who opposed its policies. In particular, the anticommunist Federation of Labor Organizations (FLO) began to challenge the Shanghai General Union. In fact, on 22 August a group of armed men attacked the headquarters of the General Union, wounding a number of strikers, destroying property and documents, and stealing money. The attack was generally attributed to the FLO.

The End of the Strike

Because of all of these problems, the strikers began to seek a compromise that would not be seen as capitulation. Their compromise proposal included several issues. The General Union called for the reinstatement of workers and strike pay equal to one-third of their normal pay. It also demanded punishment for those responsible for the 30 May incident and compensation for the families of the victims of the confrontation. In addition, the strikers demanded the recognition of all unions affiliated with the Shanghai General Union, a 10 percent wage increase, and guarantees against poor treatment and unfair dismissal of workers. Thus, by this point, the workers were more concerned with the economic concerns than with the political matters that they had earlier added to their list of demands.

The desire for a compromise among the participants in the strike movement soon led to an agreement with the Japanese interests in the city. The Japanese consul-general in Shanghai met with representatives of the General Union and agreed on compensation for the family of Ku Cheng-hung. The Japanese also recognized the General Union as the representative of worker interests in the city. In addition, the Japanese authorities promised to prevent the ill treatment of Chinese workers. Thus, by the end of August, workers were back on the job in the Japanese-owned mills in Shanghai.

At the same time that the compromise was reached with the Japanese, a number of other workers started new strikes. On 17 August postal workers struck. On 22 August the workers at the city's Commercial Press also walked off the job. Finally, on 29 August the employees of the China Bookshop went on strike. All of these workers were affiliated with the General Union, and all won recognition, wage increases, and other benefits. The agitation also spread to the railroad workers, who obtained wage increases without having to resort to a strike.

The problem with these additional strikes was that they were directed at Chinese firms rather than those owned by foreign interests. Thus, these actions hurt the workers' relationships with the elite Chinese of Shanghai as well as with the city's authorities, who become much less tolerant of the movement as a result. On 19 September, for example, the police announced that all labor organizations in the city were considered to be illegal until the government in Beijing announced its promised trade union legislation. The General Union and its affiliates were shut down, as was the Federation of Workers, Merchants, and Students. This action by the Chinese authorities brought the strike wave to an end. By the end of September the strikers had made an agreement with the British mill owners, and then by early October almost all work resumed in Shanghai.

Key Players

Ku Cheng-hung (?–1925): Ku was a Chinese worker in a Japanese-owned factory in Shanghai. On 15 May 1925, after some of the workers broke down the gates of the factory and wrecked some of the machinery, Ku got into a fight with a Japanese foreman and was killed. Ku's death led to demonstrations against the foreign presence in Shanghai and marked the beginning of the May Thirtieth Movement and the general strike that accompanied it.

Liu Hua (?–1925): A printer by trade, Liu became a leader of the Shanghai labor movement. He was one of leaders of the West Shanghai Workers Club. He was influential in organizing the protests of 30 May 1925 and became the president of the Shanghai General Union that was created as a result of the May Thirtieth Movement. In November 1925 Liu was arrested and executed.

See also: *Shanghai May Fourth Movement.*

BIBLIOGRAPHY

Books

Chesneaux, Jean. *The Chinese Labor Movement, 1919–1927.* Stanford, CA: Stanford University Press, 1968.

Harrison, James Pinckney. *The Long March to Power: A History of the Chinese Communist Party, 1921–1972.* New York: Praeger Publishers, 1972.

Perry, Elizabeth. *Shanghai on Strike: The Politics of Chinese Labor.* Stanford, CA: Stanford University Press, 1993.

—Ronald Young

Sherman Antitrust Act

United States 1890

Synopsis

The Sherman Antitrust Act of 1890 was Congress's first attempt to curb the monopolistic practices of large corporations, trusts, and other forms of business organization. In the following decades, however, the Sherman Act was often used as a tool against organized labor. Employers argued successfully before the courts that union activities were an illegal restraint of trade of the kind that the act was designed to curtail.

President Theodore Roosevelt. The Library of Congress.

Timeline

1870: Beginning of Franco-Prussian War. German troops sweep over France, Napoleon III is dethroned, and France's Second Empire gives way to the Third Republic.

1876: Four-stroke cycle gas engine introduced.

1880: South Africa's Boers declare an independent republic, precipitating the short First Anglo-Boer War.

1883: Foundation of the League of Struggle for the Emancipation of Labor by Marxist political philosopher Georgi Valentinovich Plekhanov marks the formal start of Russia's labor movement. Change still lies far in the future for Russia, however: tellingly, Plekhanov launches the movement in Switzerland.

1886: Bombing at Haymarket Square, Chicago, kills seven policemen and injures numerous others. Eight anarchists are accused and tried; three are imprisoned, one commits suicide, and four are hanged.

1888: Serbian-born American electrical engineer Nikola Tesla develops a practical system for generating and transmitting alternating current (AC), which will ultimately—

and after an extremely acrimonious battle—replace Thomas Edison's direct current (DC) in most homes and businesses.

1890: Police arrest and kill Sioux chief Sitting Bull, and two weeks later, federal troops kill over 200 Sioux at Wounded Knee.

1890: Alfred Thayer Mahan, a U.S. naval officer and historian, publishes *The Influence of Sea Power Upon History, 1660–1783,* which demonstrates the decisive role that maritime forces have played in past conflicts. The book will have an enormous impact on world events by encouraging the major powers to develop powerful navies.

1893: Henry Ford builds his first automobile.

1896: First modern Olympic Games held in Athens.

1900: Establishment of the Commonwealth of Australia.

Event and Its Context

Background: The Second Industrial Revolution

United States history from the end of the Civil War to the beginning of World War I (1865–1914) is largely the history of the second Industrial Revolution. The first Industrial Revolution, dating back to the late 1700s and extending roughly through the first half of the nineteenth century, was based on new technologies imported from Europe, such as large spinning and weaving mills and coal-fired furnaces for the production of iron.

Industrial development in the United States remained on hold during the Civil War, Reconstruction, and the harsh depression of the 1870s. Once these passed, however, the nation was poised for a second Industrial Revolution, one whose effects dwarfed those of the first. Three major developments made the second Industrial Revolution possible. First was the completion of communications and transportation networks—railroads, the telegraph system, and the steamship—making possible the movement of raw materials and finished goods in high volumes. The second was the development of electricity, which provided industry with a cheap, flexible source of power and revolutionized chemical and metallurgical processes. Finally, the application of science to manufacturing created an array of new consumer and industrial products from major corporations whose names remain familiar today: the Aluminum Company of America (Alcoa), Remington, Burroughs, McCormick Harvester (now International Harvester), Borden, Heinz, Campbell, Du Pont, Dow Chemical, Monsanto. These companies' products were transforming American life.

The Rise of the Capitalist

Science and technology provided the know-how. Equally important, though, were the business skills of a new class of entrepreneurs, whose names, too, remain familiar today: John D. Rockefeller in oil, Cornelius and William Vanderbilt in the railroad industry, Andrew Carnegie in steel, and Jay Gould and J. Pierpont Morgan in finance. These men and others amassed enormous fortunes investing in large, capital-intensive enterprises that churned out new or greatly improved products often at a fraction of the cost of similar products a generation earlier. In the early 1870s, for example, the cost of producing a gallon of kerosene was a nickel; by the mid-1880s the cost had fallen to half a cent. Over a 20-year period from 1880 to 1900, the cost to make a ton of steel fell from $65 to $17. The Aluminum Company of America produced what had previously been a precious metal for a mere 35 cents a pound. In 1865 freight rates on the railroads were about 2 cents per ton-mile; by 1900 that figure had fallen to about .75 cents per ton-mile.

Although many of the industrialists who built these mighty enterprises became prominent philanthropists, the public took a dim view of their efforts. This view was given a name in 1934 with the publication of Matthew Josephson's book *Robber Barons*. In the late nineteenth and early twentieth centuries, the public and legislators were observing with alarm the sheer, unbridled economic power of corporations, trusts, pools, trade associations, and similar business combinations. Business leaders in such industries as oil, sugar, whiskey, tobacco, and industrial machinery were learning that by cooperating rather than competing, they could eliminate smaller competitors, control output and the supply of products, establish market territories, raise prices to maximize profits, and impose penalties on members who violated the anticompetitive policies of the combination. Perhaps the most notable example was John D. Rockefeller's Standard Oil. Rockefeller believed that the American economic system was in disarray; to succeed, a modern corporation needed dependable supplies of raw materials, access to capital and credit, reliable transportation, and expansive markets. Accordingly, he ruthlessly bought out smaller competitors in the oil industry, and those he could not buy he forced out of business. Similar patterns emerged in the railroad and other industries. The result was an industrial system that denied freedom of entry to the smaller competitor, or that drove the competitor out of business. And, as William Vanderbilt famously exclaimed, "The public be damned!"

The Sherman Antitrust Act

To curb the predatory monopolistic practices of corporations and trusts, Congress passed the Sherman Antitrust Act in 1890. Section 1 of the act made illegal "Every contract, combination, . . . or conspiracy, in restraint of trade or commerce among the several States." Section 2 specified that "every person who shall monopolize, or attempt to monopolize . . . any part of the trade or commerce among the several States, or with foreign nations," shall be guilty of a misdemeanor.

The Sherman Act was a noble failure. By not defining what constituted a "trust" or a "monopoly," it gave the courts little guidance, so early suits against the sugar and whiskey trusts were thrown out of court, although the courts did order the dissolution of Rockefeller's Standard Oil trust. The administration of Theodore Roosevelt (1901–1909) had somewhat more success, and Roosevelt won a reputation as a "trust-buster" by breaking up the Northern Securities railroad trust and others. The reaction of big business, predictably, was one of outrage that its liberties had been infringed. And in the generally conservative, pro-business climate that prevailed at the time, the courts tended to agree. To close some of the Sherman Act's loopholes, President Woodrow Wilson asked for new legisla-

tion. The result was the 1914 Clayton Act, which among other practices prohibited pricing agreements that restrained trade. Again, though, the courts' enforcement of the act was at best tepid.

The Sherman Act and Organized Labor

The Sherman Act failed specifically to mention labor unions. Thus, it remained an open question whether Congress intended unions to be subject to the act and whether their activities in some circumstances could be construed as "combinations . . . in restraint of trade or commerce." A federal court in Louisiana offered an early answer to this question in 1893, when, in *United States v. Workingmen's Amalgamated Council,* it issued an injunction against a group of unions—a tool employers frequently sought and won in their efforts to thwart organized labor during these years—and declared that Congress's intent was to "include combinations of labor, as well as capital; in fact, all combinations in restraint of commerce, without reference to the character of the persons who entered into them." Similarly, a federal court in *United States v. Agler* (1897), ruling on a suit brought in the wake of the Pullman railroad strike of 1894, asserted its authority under the Sherman Act to "apply the restraining power of the law for the purpose of checking and arresting all lawless interference with . . . the peaceful and orderly conduct of railroad business between the States."

The irony is apparent. The purpose of the Sherman Act was to restrain big business. It failed to do so. But it did stifle organized labor in the early decades of the twentieth century, when employers repeatedly argued in court that certain union activities, in particular the secondary boycott, violated the Sherman Act because they restrained interstate commerce. When some of these cases finally made their way to the Supreme Court, the High Court agreed. In a series of landmark cases, including *Danbury Hatters* (1908), *Gompers v. Bucks Stove and Range Co.* (1911), the *Coronado Coal Company* cases (1922 and 1925), and *Bedford Cut Stone Company v. Journeymen Stone Cutters Association* (1927), the Court turned the Sherman Act and, later, the Clayton Act against union activities.

Two of these cases in particular stand out. The first was *Danbury Hatters*; officially, the case was *Loewe v. Lawlor,* but it took on the name of the location of the Loewe and Company hat factory in Danbury, Connecticut. The case arose in 1902 when the United Hatters of North America attempted to organize workers at the Loewe plant and ultimately called about 250 workers out on strike. When the strike did not have its desired effect, the union adopted a different tactic: it called for a nationwide boycott. The union pressured retailers and wholesalers to stop carrying Loewe hats, and it urged the public not to buy from any store that sold the company's products. So successful was the boycott that the company claimed that in one year it lost $85,000.

Accordingly, the company sued the union and its members in 1903, alleging a violation of the Sherman Act. Five years later, the Supreme Court overturned a court of appeals ruling in the union's favor and said that the union's activities, particularly its use of a secondary boycott, were in fact a restraint of trade within the meaning of the Sherman Act. Thus, the *Danbury Hatters* case removed from labor's hands one of its most effective tools, the "secondary boycott," or pressure on one firm to persuade it to stop doing business with another firm.

If the *Danbury Hatters* decision was a sharp blow to labor, the *Bucks Stove* decision three years later was nearly a knockout punch. The Bucks Stove and Range Company refused to recognize the Molders and Foundry Workers Union of North America, an affiliate of the American Federation of Labor (AFL), as the bargaining agent for its workers. Accordingly, the AFL placed the company's name on its newspaper's "unfair" and "We Don't Patronize" lists, pressured retailers not to carry the company's products, and threatened to boycott those that did. It also urged the public not to buy Bucks Stove products. The union's actions were successful, and sales at the company dropped.

In response, the company filed suit against the officers of the AFL, including its president, Samuel Gompers. The court of appeals granted an injunction against the AFL, but Gompers and the other officers violated the injunction and continued to include the company's name on its "unfair" and "We Don't Patronize" lists and to publicize the boycott in speeches, editorials, and other publications. After the court found the union officials guilty of contempt, they appealed to the Supreme Court. In its decision, the Court addressed the question of whether the Sherman Act was applicable to the case. Citing *Loewe v. Lawlor,* the Court declared that Sherman was applicable and that any boycott or blacklist promoted by printed matter or by words violated the act. In reaching its decision, the Court pointed to the "vast power" of labor unions, with their "multitudes of members." It distinguished between the "right of speech" of a single individual and the "verbal acts" of a multitude that can come under court scrutiny as much as "the use of any other force whereby property is unlawfully damaged." Any "property" that faced "irreparable damage" such as lost profits because of labor union activities could appropriately be protected by the courts through the issuance of an injunction.

It was not until 1940, in *Apex Hosiery Co. v. Leader,* that the Supreme Court nullified these earlier decisions by ruling that a labor strike carried out to further the interests of the union conducting it, even if the effect of the strike is to reduce the amount of goods in interstate commerce, is not a violation of the Sherman Antitrust Act.

Key Players

Gompers, Samuel (1850–1924): Gompers was born to Dutch-Jewish immigrants in London, where he began his working life at age ten as a cigar maker. He immigrated to the United States in 1863 and in 1886 was elected vice president of the Cigarmakers' International Union. That year he was a founder of the American Federation of Labor and served as its president from 1886 to 1895, then from 1896 to 1924. In 1919 Gompers was appointed to the American delegation at the Paris Peace Conference following World War I. His autobiography, *Seventy Years of Life and Labor,* was published in 1925.

Rockefeller, John D. (1839–1937): A high school dropout who eventually gave away $550 million of his fortune, Rockefeller was born in Richford, New York, and began his career as a bookkeeper in Cleveland. He entered the oil business in 1863, and by 1870 his business had expanded to include the Standard Oil Company of Ohio. By the end of the decade Standard Oil dominated the refining, transportation, and sales of petroleum.

Roosevelt, Theodore (1858–1919): Roosevelt, the twenty-sixth president of the United States, was a Harvard graduate who enjoyed an active career in public service. He was a member of the state assembly, head of the U.S. Civil Service Commission, president of the New York City police commission, assistant secretary of the navy, and governor of New York. As vice president, he assumed the presidency when William McKinley was assassinated in 1901. He was known for his aggressive foreign policy and for championing progressive reform at home. He ran again for the presidency against his successor, William Howard Taft, under the banner of the Progressive, or Bull Moose Party in the 1912 election won by Woodrow Wilson.

See also: *American Federation of Labor; Clayton Antitrust Act; Coronado Coal v. UMWA; Gompers v. Bucks Stove; Pullman Strike.*

BIBLIOGRAPHY

Books

Koretz, Robert F. *Statutory History of the United States: Labor Organization.* New York: Chelsea House, 1970.

Northrup, Herbert R., and Gordon F. Bloom. *Government and Labor.* Homewood, IL: Richard D. Irwin, 1963.

Taylor, Benjamin J., and Fred Witney. *Labor Relations Law,* 3rd ed. Englewood Cliffs, NJ: Prentice-Hall, 1979.

Articles

Jones, Edgar A., Jr. "The Right to Picket—Twilight Zone of the Constitution." *University of Pennsylvania Law Review* (June 1954): 997+.

"Labor Picketing and Commercial Speech: Free Enterprise Values in the Doctrine of Free Speech." *Yale Law Journal* (April 1982): 960+.

McNatt, E. B. "Labor Again Menaced by the Sherman Act." *Southern Economic Journal* 6, no. 2 (1939).

Pope, James Gray. "The Thirteenth Amendment versus the Commerce Clause: Labor and the Shaping of American Constitutional Law, 1921–1957." *Columbia Law Review* (January 2002): 112+.

Timbers, Edwin. "The Problems of Union Power and Antitrust Legislation." *Labor Law Journal* 16, no. 9 (1965).

—Michael J. O'Neal

Shoemakers' Strike

United States 1860

Synopsis

The New England Shoemakers' Strike was the largest pre–Civil War labor event in the United States. Between February and April 1860, over 20,000 workers (including both men and women) from all over New England struck both for higher wages and the concession that workers would have an active voice in salary and labor decisions. Though it had some success with the wage issue, the strike gained nothing in terms of the latter demand. Several factors influenced this outcome, including the factory owners' ability to send work to out-of-town laborers (thus bypassing the need for the local, striking labor), and the fact that winter was fast approaching and the strikers needed their lost wages to buy provisions. The strike's historical importance lies not so much in concessions gained or not gained, but rather in the fact of its sheer existence, in which successful worker organization led to the first regional strike in the United States.

Timeline

1841: Act of Union joins Upper Canada and Lower Canada, which consist of parts of the present-day provinces of Ontario and Quebec respectively.

1845: Publication of *The Raven and Other Poems* by Edgar Allan Poe.

1849: Harriet Tubman escapes from slavery in Maryland. Over the next eight years, she will undertake at least 20 secret missions into Maryland and Virginia to free more than 300 slaves through the so-called Underground Railroad.

1853: Commodore Matthew Perry arrives in Japan, and the United States forces the Japanese to permit American trade.

1856: British inventor Henry Bessemer introduces his process for producing steel cheaply and efficiently.

1858: British explorer John Hanning Speke locates Lake Victoria, which he correctly identifies as the source of the Nile.

1860: South Carolina secedes from the Union.

1860: *Maleska: The Indian Wife of the White Hunter* by Anne S. W. Stephens is the first "dime novel." The publisher, Beadle & Adams of New York City, will over the next few years produce hundreds of such books, many of which chronicle the adventures of Deadwood Dick and Nick Carter.

1860: Louis Pasteur pioneers his method of "pasteurizing" milk by heating it to high temperatures in order to kill harmful microbes.

1862: Major Civil War battles include Shiloh, Second Bull Run (Manassas), and Antietam. During the latter battle, 17 September is the bloodiest day in American history, with nearly 5,000 dead and more than 20,000 wounded.

1866: Introduction of the Winchester repeating rifle.

1869: Black Friday panic ensues when James Fisk and Jay Gould attempt to control the gold market.

Event and Its Context

On 22 February 1860 an excited crowd of nearly 10,000 people gathered to watch a parade in the town of Lynn, Massachusetts. It was, not coincidentally, the birthday of George Washington, and those gathered in anticipation knew that the parade would share a philosophical, though not overt, connection to America's first president. The marchers were striking shoemakers, and the spectators their sympathizers. The marchers gathered in Central Square led by their chosen marshal, Willard Oliver, a politically active watchmaker, at around 10:00 A.M. The Lynn Cornet Band playing "Hail, Columbia" headed up the procession of 3,000 striking workers, who carried banners emblazoned with numerous mottoes, including "As men, we do this day unite to pack our kits and strike for rights; our prize is fair and our aim is just—that you'll assent we hope and trust."

The marchers received encouragement from well-wishers who packed the town. Patriotic feeling ran high, and the marchers' spirits were bolstered by the show of support—though that support was by no means unanimous. The marchers, who were "most orderly," nonetheless jeered at one nonsupportive boss whom they found working in his shop, with cries of "scab," "kick him out," and "for shame."

The strikers gathered again at 12:30 P.M. in Central Square to listen to speeches, which shared common threads: the determination to preserve the artisan tradition in New England, and the need for men to provide for their families. The executive strike committee based its platform on these two morally irreproachable stances. The excited crowds met again at 3:00 P.M. for more speeches and reports.

Flushed with a feeling of triumph, the organized shoemakers of Lynn nonetheless had no idea that they had begun what would become known as the New England Shoemakers' Strike. Though both the procession and the strike it inaugurated carried with them a feeling of spontaneity, they were in reality anything but spontaneous. The strike actually had roots as far back as the Panic of 1857 and in the rise of industrial sewing machines; both events had caused severe rifts between workers and the owners who paid them.

By the late 1820s, a number of factors, including the abandonment of the Puritans' negative view of profiteering and certain strictures on the economy, had caused a philosophical shift regarding capitalism. This new outlook allowed factories in small cities and villages to dramatically increase their rates of production, at least initially. The period 1820–1860 was marked by an economy that was given to fits and starts. A healthy economy and demand for goods caused rapid increases in the number of workers, which in turn caused a period of almost feverish growth; inevitably, this was followed by a "panic," which suppressed the demand for goods and caused unemployment and poverty for the workers. Between 1830 and 1836, Lynn manufacturers increased production of goods by two-thirds; a depres-

Procession of striking women shoemakers, Lynn, Massachusetts. © Hulton/Getty Images. Reproduced by permission.

sion began in 1837 and lasted until 1844, severely restraining production growth. After rebounding, the economy and rate of production strengthened (at a somewhat feverish rate), only to be hit with another depression in 1857. This latter depression caused the virtual cessation of shoe production in Lynn and severe poverty as shoemakers throughout the town were let go. Moreover, industrialization was taking hold, and shoemakers were experiencing its consequences in the form of lower wages. Factory owners embraced automation as a more cost-effective means of production. In short, mechanized binding, made possible by sewing machines, was on the rise. The shoemakers had not willingly accepted this innovation and sent a delegation to one shop where a sewing machine had been installed to request that the operator cease running it. The shoemakers' concern reflected that the cost of one sewing machine was only one-third to one-half of a shoe binder's annual wages.

In November 1857 at a meeting at Lyceum Hall, businessmen and politicians were not prepared for the workers' reactions to the businessmen's suggestion of public relief for their struggling companies. Winter, a time of reduced demand for their goods and therefore reduced income, was coming on, but the suggestion of charity was insulting and did little to ease strained relations between workers and bosses. At a second meeting, the workers made their own suggestions, one of which was that the shoe manufacturers continue to give them at least some work until demand for shoes once again rose; another was

that the owners distribute 10 percent of their profits equally among their workers. The owners instead insisted that public relief was necessary, and the public debate seems to have ended there. Hostility between workers and owners, however, was still very much alive, and the distressed economy did little to improve their relationship.

In the spring of 1859, in an uncertain economy bolstered by mistrust toward manufacturers and a revulsion at the idea of receiving charity, the shoemakers formed the Lynn Mechanics Association and began publishing the *New England Mechanic*, which enabled them to organize New England's largest strike. In the winter of 1860, after three years of frustrated livelihood paired with resentment toward both sewing machines and the manufacturers, the workers had had enough and organized the New England Shoemakers' Strike. Though it was by no means the first strike in Lynn, it was unique in its sheer numbers and scope. Estimates indicate that at least 20,000 people struck—half the employees in New England and one-third of the 60,000 workers employed in Massachusetts factories. From Marblehead to Swampscot, workers laid down their tools and hoisted banners as they took to the streets.

The chief goal of the strike, at least at the beginning, was to secure higher wages for shoe bottomers. Though the striking workers presented a united front to the world, the movement was actually rife with opposing views and goals. Chief among the disagreements were the issues of men versus women and factory workers versus home workers. The strike committee wisely associated the strike with George Washington, the artisan tradition, and the duty of men to provide for their families. These associations, along with the cheerful banner-waving parades, gathered tremendous support for shoemakers and other workers alike. When it became apparent that some factory owners were determined to continue with business as usual, some of the strikers decided to take matters into their own hands and use force to gain their objective. The first three days of the strike were characterized by several incidents of mob assaults on "scabs," confrontations with city officials, and public drunkenness that threatened the carefully crafted image of moral Republicanism.

On 25 February, while many of the Lynn shoemakers were in a meeting, William Eaton, a "scab," was seen taking home a basket of work from a manufacturer. He was set upon by an indignant mob. Though both the mayor and the city marshal tried to intervene, the crowd paid them little attention. Alonzo Draper, a member of the strike committee, came on the scene, and finally the crowd released the unfortunate man and dispersed. Another mob attacked a policeman stationed at the depot. Crowds attacked several wagons that contained packages of shoe goods, on one occasion dispersing when the driver brandished a pistol. Throughout the day the crowds seized boxes and goods, and uneasy chaos prevailed. This was not at all the atmosphere desired by the executive strike committee, and they called a meeting that evening to remind strikers of their purpose. In spite of resolutions to the contrary passed at the meeting, by the next afternoon several more incidents had occurred, and the mayor swore in about 100 special policemen. The executive committee formed its own police from among the strikers to work with the mayor's appointees and reiterated its vow of noninterference with shipments. The relationship between city officials and strikers, who before had seen themselves as closely allied by community ties, had already been damaged. In the minds of strikers, the violence caused the officials to ally with the shoe bosses.

This belief was only reinforced when the mayor, responding to an appeal by manufacturers, called in the Lynn light infantry militia. Meanwhile, manufacturers persuaded their friends in city government to contact the state attorney general, the sheriff of Essex county, a major general in the state militia, and the city officials and police chiefs of Boston and South Danvers. As a result, detachments of Boston and South Danvers police were dispatched along with the militia, and the next morning the citizens of Lynn realized that they were living under martial law. At the end of the third day of the strike, the outside police and militia forces left, and there was no more major violence.

During the six weeks of the strike, there were a total of five processions through Lynn itself, with each procession having at least 1,000 people in it. During the procession on 7 March, more than 800 women marched. The largest procession occurred on 16 March. Participants numbered some 6,000 men and women from Lynn and other towns that were sympathetic to the cause. Members of volunteer fire departments, militia companies, and community music groups such as the Lynn Cornet Band all joined in the procession. Many who joined the parade were not strikers themselves; the purpose of the gathering was to demonstrate to the bosses and to themselves the solidarity of not only the striking workers, but that of the entire community. This solidarity extended to at least some of the bosses: several had decorated their buildings for the first procession, just as many had willingly pledged to the strike fund.

The executive strike committee had successfully marketed the strike to the region as both a defense of the artisan tradition against the evils of soulless automation, and as a defense of the family wage. Though these selling points had bought quite a lot of support for the strike, not everyone was entirely pleased with its objectives; among the disenchanted were machinists and unmarried "shop girls" who relied only on themselves for their living.

A great deal of the women's involvement in the strike was carefully considered and manipulated by the men of the executive committee. Knowing that female workers had struck successfully in nearby Marblehead, Draper had suggested on 21 February, prior to the start of the strike, that they should include women in the action. The committee did not pursue this course until after the moral position of the men's strike was called into question by violence and drunkenness that had stimulated criticism by the press. The strike committee needed to reestablish its moral authority, and it believed that the association of women with the strike would reinforce to sympathizers the values of home, family, and the artisan tradition that had originally garnered so much support for its cause.

The executive committee decided that women should boycott owners who did not support higher wages for the shoe bottomers. At a meeting on 23 February, the committee told the men to encourage their wives, girlfriends, and daughters to attend a meeting that night. When Draper addressed the women, he categorized their concerns only in terms of the men's concerns, assuming that they were one in the same. The women called attention to the fallacy of this assumption when they interrupted to point out that not all of them were married or engaged. Draper tried to persuade the women to strike and departed in a flush of excitement to inform the waiting men. During the lively discussion that followed, the participants decided to appoint committees to garner additional local support and draw up a list of wage demands, and to organize other women shoe workers in the shoe towns of Essex County (Marblehead, Newburyport, and Danvers). Their third decision shocked the executive committee: far from remaining passive and taking orders, the women also decided to strike to raise the wages of women workers.

The women's second meeting convened on 27 February in Liberty Hall with nearly 2,000 women attending. The women had agreed to boycott owners who were not sympathetic to the male strikers' goals; the strike committee believed that higher men's wages were the women's only goal. The purpose of the meeting was address the price lists being created for use in bargaining with owners. Two factions, the shop girls and the home workers, formed the heart of the discussion. The committee responsible for determining prices had not considered the fact that wages for home workers should naturally be higher, as the latter bought their machines, threads, and all other materials. Severe jealousies and rivalries appear to have existed on both sides, as reporters witnessed the shrieking match that erupted between the groups. Oliver, who chaired the meeting, attempted to gain cooperation by reminding the participants of their higher purpose. He became disgruntled when the factory girls criticized the recommended wages as too low and argued for striking to increase wages for all women workers, regardless of whether they worked in homes or factories. Clara Brown, a 21-year-old factory girl who emerged as a leader of this group, effectively seized control of the meeting with her persuasive argument, and in the end, the women voted (though not unanimously) to strike for higher wages for men and women. The next order of business was whether or not the women should join the male strikers in the next parade, scheduled for 7 March. Contention on this point as well finally ended with a vote by a small majority to participate. The women ended the meeting with the decision to send out canvassing committees to find more striking women and to report female "scabs" who were still working and had refused to join the strike. Oliver and Mary Damon (speaking for the home workers) insisted on another meeting the next night to reconsider the issue of women's wages.

On 28 February at Lyceum Hall, 2,000 women met for their third official meeting. Draper again addressed the meeting to persuade them that it was more important for their husbands to get higher wages than it was for them. One woman spoke up to remind him that not all of them had husbands, and was greeted with laughter by the crowd. Draper reminded the women that the men had garnered widespread support in 14 towns and effectively urged the women not to mess things up for the men. Oliver then read two wage lists, one a high wage list, and one prepared by the home workers who were closely allied with the men's strike. Debate again broke out between Clara Brown for the factory girls and Damon for the home workers. Brown made an impassioned speech, exhorting the women to hold out for higher wages. Her eloquence carried the day. Oliver, no doubt peeved that he had lost control of the meeting and that the high wage list was once again endorsed, then announced that he no longer thought the women should participate in the 7 March parade. The women ignored him and voted unanimously to march.

Oliver, Damon, and the executive strike committee refused to accept the women's decision in regard to the high wage list and altered the list to their own liking. The list was printed and circulated as the official list. The enraged shop girls confronted them at the fourth and final meeting of the women workers on 2 March. James Dillon, president of the strike committee, replaced Oliver, who had been implicated in the list scandal, as meeting chair. Dillon played on the women's love of their families, convincing them that to strike for themselves was indecent. Many of the home workers truly felt this way and viewed the unmarried shop girls as selfish individualists. Though Clara Brown argued the case for women's wages, the women yielded to the pressure to change their votes: more than 1,700 reversed their decision to support the strike for women's higher wages. The executive committee and the home workers had won, and the chance to change the status of all women workers was lost.

The strike, which ended in mid-April 1860, had won for some the higher wages that were one of the goals but failed to secure a collective voice for wage determination. Had the strike continued for a longer period of time or if factory owners had been unable to secure labor outside of Lynn, perhaps then the strikers would have won this concession. Workers were facing a complete loss of wages and could not afford to continue. Practical needs outweighed philosophical desires. The relationship with manufacturers was no better than before. The independent-minded Lynn shoemakers would not soon forget or forgive the factory owners and town leaders for bringing in the military to squash what they viewed as their Jeffersonian-given right to protest.

Key Players

Dillon, James: Vice president of the Lynn Mechanics' Association; chairman of the strike committee.

Draper, Alonzo (1835–1865): Born in Brattleboro, Vermont, Draper appears to have been a dabbler, claiming no particular occupation. He worked for a time for his father-in-law at the Leverett Street jail and also taught writing, bookkeeping, and French at various times. Though he himself was not a shoemaker nor even employed in a factory, it was he who established both the *New England Mechanic* newspaper and the Lynn Mechanics Association. At one point he also had political aspirations, hoping to be elected to the state legislature. It is unclear how or why Draper managed to acquire and maintain so much influence over the workers in Lynn when he himself was not one of them.

Oliver, William: President of women's strike movement.

———

BIBLIOGRAPHY

Books

Blewett, Mary H. *Men, Women, and Work: Class, Gender, and Protest in the New England Shoe Industry, 1780–1910.* Urbana and Chicago: University of Illinois Press, 1988.

Dawley, Alan. *Class and Community: The Industrial Revolution in Lynn.* Cambridge, MA: Harvard University Press, 1976.

Faler, Paul, G. *Mechanics and Manufacturers in the Early Industrial Revolution: Lynn, Massachusetts, 1780–1860.* Albany: State University of New York Press, 1981.

Periodicals

"The Bay State Strike—Movement Among the Women—Acts and Proceedings of Employers and Workmen." *New York Times,* 25 February 1860.

"The Massachusetts Strike." *New York Times,* 9 March 1860.

"The Massachusetts Strike: State of the Movement at Lynn—Mass Meeting of the Strikers at Lyceum Hall." *New York Times,* 2 March 1860.

"The Massachusetts Strike: The Females Afoot—Mistakes of the Strikers." *New York Times,* 3 March 1860.

"The Shoemakers' Riots: Follies of the Strikers—Threatening Letters, A. C." *New York Times,* 25 February 1860.

"The Shoemakers Still Striking—The Hemmers and Stitchers in the Field—Feminine Spirit Aroused." *New York Times,* 1 March 1860.

"The Strike of the Massachusetts Shoemakers." *New York Times,* 24 February 1860.

—Kimberley Barker

Shop Steward Movement Originates

Great Britain 1898–1900

Synopsis

Shop stewards, or workshop-based union representatives, originated among skilled male workers in the shipbuilding and engineering industries at the end of the nineteenth century. Their functions gradually developed from dues collectors and union representatives to workers' direct representatives who handled a wide range of concerns with employers, who increasingly officially recognized them for that purpose.

Steward organization mushroomed during the World Wars, when stewards built their own independent organizations to challenge official union policy. Their initial concern was the defense of skilled workers, but technological change rendered arguments based on skill increasingly untenable. This circumstance produced increasing steward organization among less skilled workers and women. World War I saw the election of the first women shop stewards.

The steward system spread into many other industries, especially after 1945. Dockers and later public sector stewards led many important disputes in the postwar period. Starting in the early 1980s, many large workplaces closed, which left public sector stewards in the majority. Nevertheless, the steward tradition of direct representation at the point of production was sustained. During the twentieth century the use of the term *shop steward* moved from an obscure description understood only by skilled engineers into common English usage.

Timeline

1882: British forces invade and take control of Egypt.

1894: French army captain Alfred Dreyfus, a Jew, is convicted of treason. Dreyfus will later be cleared of all charges, but the Dreyfus case illustrates—and exacerbates—the increasingly virulent anti-Semitism that pervades France.

1899: Start of the Second Anglo-Boer War, often known simply as the Boer War.

1899: Polish-born German socialist Rosa Luxemburg rejects the argument that working conditions in Europe have improved, and that change must come by reforming the existing system. Rather, she calls for an overthrow of the existing power structure by means of violent international revolution.

1899: Aspirin introduced.

1900: Establishment of the Commonwealth of Australia.

1900: The first zeppelin is test-flown.

1900: Sigmund Freud publishes *The Interpretation of Dreams.*

1900: German physicist Max Planck develops Planck's constant, a cornerstone of quantum theory.

1902: Second Anglo–Boer War ends in victory for Great Britain. It is a costly victory, however, resulting in the loss

of more British lives (5,774) than any conflict between 1815 and 1914. The war also sees the introduction of concentration camps, used by the British to incarcerate Boer civilians.

1906: Founding of the British Labour Party.

1909: William Cadbury's *Labour in Portuguese West Africa* draws attention to conditions of slavery in São Tomé and Principe.

Event and Its Context

Origins

Shop stewards first appeared in the engineering industry between 1898 and 1900. Their origins lay in two central realities. The first was the tradition of minimal intervention or laissez-faire by the British state in economic activity, which left many potential workplace issues open to local negotiation. The second was serious weakening of the main union, the Amalgamated Society of Engineers (ASE) in 1898. Employers, increasingly affected by intensified international competition, wished to increase the rate of technological change, reduce relative labor costs, and assert their "right to manage." Employers perceived the main obstacle to these goals as the controls exercised by the ASE. The ASE resisted piece working, systematic overtime, and the "dilution" of their skills by new machinery and the non-apprenticed workers who operated them. The large engineering employers sought to break these restrictions through a symbolic confrontation. In 1897–1898 the engineering employers successfully locked out ASE members and imposed their "Terms of Settlement" on the union. The terms of settlement created a "Procedure for the Avoidance of Disputes" that tied the national union's hands. The terms also had major implications for daily life in the workshops, especially the introduction of piecework, which the union had always resisted.

The union had been seriously weakened and took measures to strengthen its workshop presence. Previously, district committees had received information on workshop events from members. The union then decided to formalize these reports and to change their rules to allow the appointment or election of shop stewards who would be responsible to district committees.

The First Shop Stewards' Movement: World War I

Initially, shop stewards did little more than collect union dues and report on problems to the district committees. The stewards were not recognized for bargaining purposes by employers but became vocal within the union before 1914. Increasingly, union members elected stewards to represent them. In some districts, the steward system began to develop independently of established union structures. In Scotland stewards played a major role in strikes and constituted an effective means for district committees to evade the control of the national executive committee. Soon, many factories had sizeable bodies of stewards who themselves elected a chief steward or convenor. At that time, however, no national organization of stewards existed independent of their union.

World War I brought dramatic developments. The ASE executive was co-opted by the state into the war machine, and "dilution" accelerated in the workshops as war production grew. Many ASE members felt that their national and often their local union bodies were powerless to deal with their growing problems and that workshop representation had to be developed.

In 1914–1919 stewards led a wave of strikes to maintain their privileged position in the industry and their immunity as skilled men from conscription. This brought, for the first but not the last time, action from government and criticism from the media. Nevertheless, stewards built local committees like the powerful Clyde Workers' Committee (CWC). Arthur Mac-Manus, an experienced steward and socialist, headed the CWC, which published its own newspaper, *The Worker*. These committees federated into the National Shop Stewards' and Workers' Committee Movement, which was independent of the ASE. In Sheffield another socialist, Jack Murphy, wrote the movement's theoretical statement, *The Workers' Committee* (1917), which advocated an encompassing system of workplace representation and support for official union leaders when they represented workers and independent action when they did not. General unions of nonapprenticed workers, such as the Workers' Union, expanded their membership and appointed their own stewards, some of whom were women.

By 1919 the employers felt compelled to recognize the role of shop stewards in a national agreement. Stewards thus became part of the formally agreed mechanism of industrial relations. Peace brought widespread unemployment, however, and restored the employers' power. In 1920 the ASE led a defensive merger of engineering unions and formed the Amalgamated Engineering Union (AEU). In 1922 the employers again locked out engineering workers and withdrew the recognition they had given stewards in 1919.

The Interwar Years: From Near Extinction to Revival

Effective shop steward organization was largely extinguished between 1922 and 1935. Many leading stewards continued their activity in political senses, often in the newly formed Communist Party of Great Britain (CPGB). The shop stewards' movement, not any British political party, contributed most to early discussions in the international communist movement. Communists, often articulate and resourceful individuals, played a prominent part as leading shop stewards for the next half century, though the great majority of stewards did not share their politics.

Steward activity revived with rearmament and increased demand for labor. Semi-skilled workers in the mass production industries led developments. The General Workers' Union (TGWU), successor to the Workers' Union, led a successful strike at the American-owned Pressed Steel factory in Oxford. AEU shop stewards were already operating in the booming aircraft industry and in 1935, conducted a strike in Hawker's factories. They built a network of shop stewards, the Aircraft Shop Stewards National Council, which later broadened to become the Engineering and Allied Trades National Council (E&ATSSNC), which published their own newspaper, *The New Propellor*. The E&ATSSNC national secretary for the war years was the CPGB member Len Powell. The organization existed until 1960.

World War II: Engineers at War

World War II brought the election of many more stewards. Employers felt compelled to recognize formally the stewards' right to operate. Because the AEU did not admit women until 1943, the TGWU made great headway in recruiting them and appointed many women shop stewards to represent women who were flooding the arms factories. A central difference with World War I was the opposition to strikes, after the invasion of the Soviet Union, of the CPGB-dominated E&ATSSNC, though there was a rising strike rate during the war. Although some stewards remained dues-collectors, many broadened their roles as they helped solve workers' complex housing, shopping, childcare, and transport problems. Nevertheless, gaps remained in steward coverage even in 1945 with the return of peace.

Extension in and Beyond Engineering

Between 1945 and the mid-1970s, steward representation became dense in engineering as daily arguments on piecework bargains developed in a tight labor market. Large numbers of workers took on the task of representing others, often representing work groups as small as 20.

The war, and particularly the post-1945 period, saw the shop steward system spread well beyond the engineering and shipbuilding industries. The docks and construction industries elected many stewards. Most large engineering factories, docks, and construction sites now had large "Joint Shop Stewards' Committees," sometimes with over 100 stewards electing convenors. By the late 1950s shop stewards started to move into public awareness as they had in 1914–1918. In 1959 the Boulter brothers' film, *I'm All Right Jack*, appeared. It portrayed the senior shop steward and communist Fred Kite (played by Peter Sellers) as a comically ridiculous and eventually pathetic figure and a cynical manipulator of his members. Stewards and their unions, some argued, were a cause of Britain's relative economic decline and their activities should be restricted. This type of criticism continued until the end of the twentieth century, although workers continued to elect stewards to deal with their workplace problems.

Stewards were prominent in the Liaison Committee for the Defence of Trade Unions (LCDTU) between 1966 and 1979. The LCDTU, under the leadership of Kevin Halpin, an AEU steward, led the strike movements that defeated the Conservative government's Industrial Relations Act in the early 1970s. Yet by the mid-1980s, many shop stewards' committees had been demolished by Margaret Thatcher's Conservative government. Even more significant than political and legal initiatives against them was the decimation of the main workplaces in which they had been located. Although only vestigial steward representation survived in the private sector in the 1990s, steward organization grew in the public sector. Trade unions such as the National Union of Public Employees (NUPE), a previously centralized union led by paid officials, reorganized in the 1970s and developed a steward organization. By 2000 NUPE's successor, UNISON, soon developed into Britain's largest union with probably the largest single group of stewards. In 1900 the typical steward had been a skilled engineering craftsman concerned with "dilution" of the craft or piecework. By 2000 his equivalent was a woman hospital or local authority worker concerned with flexible working systems, childcare, training, and low pay. Surveys conducted in the 1990s showed that roughly two-thirds of public sector workers had stewards. Where they existed, membership satisfaction with union membership was much higher than elsewhere.

Key Players

Halpin, Kevin (1927–): A skilled engineering worker and AEU member. Halpin was an AEU convenor for Briggs Bodies and Ford and a CPGB member. Victimized in 1962, he later worked in ship repair and London Transport. Halpin was chairperson and spokesperson for the Liaison Committee for the Defence of Trade Unions starting in 1970.

MacManus, Arthur (1889–1927): Born in Glasgow of Fenian stock. An Amalgamated Society of Engineers (ASE) member, he was also a member of the Socialist Labour Party starting in 1906. He was a steward at Singers, Barr and Stroud, Albion Motor Works, and elsewhere. He was founder and leader of the Clyde Workers' Committee in 1915–1916. Deported from the Clyde by the government in March 1916, he was president of the National Shop Stewards' and Workers' Committee Movement from 1916 to 1921. He became chairperson of the political bureau of the Communist Party of Great Britain (CPGB) and was a member of the executive committee of the Communist International from 1922 until his death in 1927.

Murphy, J. T. "Jack" (1888–1966): Born in Manchester, he started work at Vickers Brightside works in Sheffield at the age of 13. Murphy was an ASE member and a member of the Socialist Labour Party. By 1917 he was leader of the National Shop Stewards' and Workers' Committee Movement and had published his influential work *The Workers' Committee*. He was a shop stewards' delegate to the second Congress of the Communist International, a founder of the Red International of Labour Unions and was a prominent figure in the international communist movement in the 1920s.

Powell, Len (1901–?):Born in London, Powell was a skilled engineering worker and member of the Amalgamated Engineering Union (AEU). He joined CPGB in 1926 and worked at the Lancashire Dynamo and Crypto Company in Harlesden where he was involved in publication of a factory newspaper. Powell became honorary secretary of the Engineering and Allied Trades National Council (E&ATSSNC) in 1940.

See also: *Amalgamated Society of Engineers.*

BIBLIOGRAPHY

Books

Croucher, Richard. *Engineers at War, 1939–1945*. London: Merlin Press, 1982.

Darlington, Ralph. *The Dynamics of Workplace Unionism: Shop Stewards' Organization in Three Merseyside Plants*. London: Mansell, 1994.

Hinton, James S. *The First Shop Stewards' Movement*. London: Weidenfeld and Nicholson, 1973.

Jefferys, James B. *The Story of the Engineers, 1800–1945*. New York: Johnson Reprint Corporation, 1970.

Wrigley, Chris A., ed. *A History of British Industrial Relations, 1939–79: Industrial Relations in a Declining Economy*. Cheltenham. UK: Edward Elgar, 1996.

ADDITIONAL RESOURCES

Periodicals

Croucher, Richard. "The Coventry Toolroom Agreement, 1941–1972, Part 1: Origins and Operation." *Historical Studies in Industrial Relations* 8 (autumn 1999): 1–41.

———. "The Coventry Toolroom Agreement, 1941–1972, Part 2: Abolition." *Historical Studies in Industrial Relations* 9 (spring 2000): 37–70.

—Richard Croucher

Silk Workers' Revolts

France 1831, 1834

Synopsis

At the beginning of the July Monarchy, in the industrial French city of Lyon, the silk workers had a very hard life. In addition to backbreaking work, they were largely dependent on the fluctuations of the silk market and on the price of labor as fixed by the merchants. In 1831 they revolted against the merchants' tyranny and compelled the prefect state's representative to arbitrate the conflict. The government harshly repressed the uprising, as with the one that broke out later in 1834. Both times, workers from other industries joined the *canuts*, or silk weavers, in support of their protests.

Historians interpret the silk workers' riots in Lyon as the first modern strikes of the industrial era. The canuts' strikes foreshadowed many social struggles in industrialized countries that followed.

Timeline

1809: Progressive British industrialist Robert Owen proposes an end to employment of children in his factories. When his partners reject the idea, he forms an alliance with others of like mind, including the philosopher Jeremy Bentham.

1813: Jane Austen publishes *Pride and Prejudice.*

1818: Donkin, Hall & Gamble "Preservatory" in London produces the first canned foods.

1824: Ludwig van Beethoven composes his Ninth Symphony.

1829: Greece wins its independence after a seven-year war with Turkey.

1831: Unsuccessful Polish revolt against Russian rule.

Silk workers' revolt, Lyon, France, 1834. © Getty Images. Reproduced by permission.

1834: British mathematician Charles Babbage completes drawings for the "analytic engine," a forerunner of the modern computer that he never builds.

1834: American inventor Cyrus H. McCormick patents his reaper, a horse-drawn machine for harvesting wheat.

1835: American inventor and painter Samuel F. B. Morse constructs an experimental version of his telegraph, and American inventor Samuel Colt patents his revolver.

1837: Coronation of Queen Victoria in England.

1841: Act of Union joins Upper Canada and Lower Canada, which consist of parts of the present-day provinces of Ontario and Quebec, respectively.

1846: American inventor Elias Howe patents his sewing machine.

Event and Its Context

The silk workers' riots in Lyon in 1831 and 1834 may be the first real industrial struggle in the history of France. Lyon is located at the confluence of two rivers, the Sâone and the Rhône, about 200 miles north of Marseille. The town had been on international trade roads since the time of the Roman Empire. In the 1830s Lyon was the second largest city in France

with a population of 134,000 within the walls and another 175,000 in the neighboring manufacturing communities of Croix-Rousse, Guillotière, and Vaise.

Lyon had been world renowned for the quality of its silk work since the fifteenth century. According to the Silk Law of 1744, the *Fabrique* consisted of the merchants—who were called "makers" even though they did not make anything—and the weavers—or the *canuts*, as they were called at the time. The merchants held the capital and supplied the weaver masters with the raw silk. The canuts were alone in bearing the costs associated with the weaving looms. Largely dependent on the price of labor as fixed by the merchants, the masters were more like wage-earners than craftsmen. Accordingly, they were highly vulnerable to slumps in silk prices.

The dispersion of the *Fabrique* and the topography of the town explain why the workers did not live at the center of the silk trade but rather in outlying suburbs beyond the tollhouses, where rents and food were cheaper. For example, in Croix-Rousse and Guillotière, weavers' families (about 52,000 workers) lived and worked in dark shops where they spent 16 to 18 hours a day with the windows continually closed to prevent damage to the precious silk. This dense working-class community was peculiar to Lyon but atypical in nineteenth-century France: factories were normally located in rural environments. The extreme poverty of the canuts seemed so scandalous be-

Silk workers' revolt, Lyon, France, 1834. © Getty Images. Reproduced by permission.

cause it contrasted with the luxury of the silk pieces made by them for the enjoyment of the rich.

Most of the time, the canut masters gave shelter to the journeymen they employed. Ultimately, their common and precarious existence generated a feeling of solidarity between the two groups and led to the founding of many friendly societies by the canuts. At the time, those societies were tolerated but they had no legal status.

Silk master weaver Pierre Charnier created the first such society in 1827; one year later, two of Charnier's companions, Bouvery and Joseph Masson-Sibut, seceded to establish the Société du Devoir Mutuel along with 14 other master weavers. Like many other mutual aid societies that existed in France before the Second Empire, this one had the dual purpose of mutual aid and cooperative defense. The members pooled their resources so as to provide support to each other in the event of misfortunes such as illness, the death of a loved one, or disability. Young members could also learn the silk trade from older ones.

This society was famous for its involvement in schemes to establish a minimum price for silk products. Since the eighteenth century, this has been a traditional demand of the weavers. Nonetheless, the merchants lowered the prices in the late 1820's under the pretext of an increase in English silk production. In fact, the future of the silk industry in Lyon was not threatened at all. Its high quality was well known far beyond the borders of France, especially in the North American market.

The 1831 Riot

In 1831 three days of revolutionary violence—*Les Trois Glorieuses*—in Paris led to the establishment of the July Monarchy. Meanwhile, in Lyon the weavers' condition worsened with low wages and cost of living increases. Protests rose up

when the Saint-Simonians, Utopian socialists, denounced worker exploitation in lectures that were closely followed by the workers.

The new bourgeois government led by Louis-Philippe did not live up to the workers' expectations. When a general strike was imminent on 25 October 1831, the prefect Louis Bouvier-Dumolart established a board of conciliation to supervise a minimum tariff for silk products. The board, which brought together merchants and canuts, was essentially a reestablishment of a previous committee, *les Prud'hommes*, that had been instituted by Napoleon in 1806 for the same purpose. The masters Falconnet, Bouvery, and Pierre Charnier assisted in creating the tariff.

The events in Lyon drew a lot of attention from the liberal Parisian newspapers, which criticized the board on the grounds that it would contradict the theory of free contract between employer and employee. Critics also thought that prefect Bouvier-Dumolart was too lenient with the weavers. Although he risked running afoul of public opinion, he went on with his strategy of conciliation. The momentary victory, however, quickly became anger in the working-class suburbs as most of the merchants refused to honor the rate. Some of them went so far as to stop placing orders with the weavers.

The canuts reacted with a strike on 21 November. An uprising followed when workers from other industries joined the protest. The protesters carried black and red flags that bore slogans like "work and bread." Jean-Claude Romand's famous motto, "To live working or to die fighting," became the rallying cry. Luckily for the workers, the National Guard was made up of masters in the working-class suburbs of Croix-Rousse and Guillotière. The guard was sympathetic to the workers' cause and, ultimately, did not confront the 30,000 strikers in the streets. After four days of turmoil, including bloody street fights, the insurrectionists besieged the town hall, established a temporary committee of 16 canuts, and announced the election of an intertrade working council. The arrival of a regiment of 20,000 soldiers led by the Duke of Orleans ended the canuts' social experiment. The National Guard of Lyon was dismissed and Dumolart was replaced by a less conciliatory prefect.

Although he had crushed the riot, Louis-Philippe's government was careful not to add fuel to the fire. One year later, the leaders' trial in Riom ended in a dismissal.

Unlike other cities in France, repression in Lyon did not cause the destruction of the working-class movement, which relied on two structures. The first, *L'Echo de la Fabrique*, was a newspaper written and edited by workers that began publishing in October 1831. The canuts, unlike workers from most other trades, were literate for the most part. The weekly paper's extensive coverage of the riot argued strongly for the unification of workers from all trades. The second structure, the still secret *Société du Devoir Mutuel*, grew stronger when it added new members from the *Société des ferrandiniers*. With more than 1,200 journeyman members in 1833, this group was essentially a union that had to keep a friendly society façade for legal purposes because unions were forbidden at the time.

Although the Saint-Simonians became closer to the workers after 1831, they eventually lost their influence on the movement as the influence of the Republicans increase. A new bill against popular meetings convinced many workers to join them. Among the weavers, the idea spread that social justice could only be realized within a new republican political system.

The 1834 Revolt

In February 1834 the canuts took to the streets again when merchants announced a price reduction for silk products. *La Sociéé du Devoir Mutuel* called for and led the protest. In April the movement grew stronger as the leaders were arrested and judged. Workers searched the town for weapons and built barricades. For a second time in a few years, black and red flags flew over the hills of Lyon.

Unfortunately for the workers, they could no longer rely on the sympathies of the National Guard, as it had been suppressed in 1831. During the week of 9 April, which became known as "the week of blood," soldiers violently suppressed the Croix-Rousse insurgents. Not even children and the elderly were spared. Ultimately, there were approximately 200 civilian and 130 military deaths.

Working conditions had motivated the insurrection of 1831. In 1834 the uprising took a political turn inspired by Republican values and so had national scope. Riots broke out in other cities: Saint-Etienne, Vienne, Grenoble, Marseille, Chalon-sur-Saône and, of course, Paris. The National Army was merciless toward the insurgents. On 4 May 1834 the state banned *L'Echo de la Fabrique*, the last remaining symbol of the Canuts' struggles.

The national press commented widely on the events in Lyon. In December 1831 a reporter of the very bourgeois *Journal des Débats* saw a reflection of "the infighting which takes place in the society between the propertied class and the non-propertied class." In *Le Globe*, Saint-Simonist Michel Chevalier called the situation "a blatant symbol of the industrial situation in France."

The Lyon workers' protests, and the opposition they faced from the contemptuous merchants, served as an example for proletarian struggles in the nineteenth and twentieth centuries. However, the canuts were highly skilled and worked in a traditional environment. They were not like the proletarian workers of the following decades who were usually rural migrants that formed the miserable and undereducated labor force of major industries.

The canuts appear as mythical figures in the works of romantic writers such as Stendhal and Victor Hugo, as well as in the songs of the Parisian singer Aristide Bruant, whose famous refrain was sung in Parisian cabarets until the First World War: *"We are the canuts, We are walking naked."*

Little wonder that, a few decades later, Pierre Proudhon as well as the Commune of Paris (1871) took their inspiration from the canuts' resolutely federalist statements.

Key Players

Bouvier-Dumolart, Louis (1780–1855): Dumolart started his career as prefect under the first Empire. He served in several departments before being nominated in the Rhone in May 1831. During the first canuts' riot of November 1831, he tried to pacify the strikers when he enforced a minimum tariff for silk products. Critics thought he was too indulgent toward the insurgents, and he was dismissed at the end of the uprising. In December 1831 he gave the press a report of his correspondence with the government during the events.

Charnier, Pierre (1795–?): Weaver master. Charnier founded the first friendly society, the *Société de Surveillance et d'Indications Mutuelles* of Lyon in 1827. He was a royalist and Catholic. During the uprising of 1831, he participated actively in the negotiations with the prefect Bouvier-Dumolart for the establishment of a tariff for silk products. Charnier's companions were critical of his political links. After the riot of 1831, he went to Paris to deliver a report of the events of Lyon to Prime Minister Jean-Paul-Pierre Casimir-Perier.

Masson-Sibut, Joseph: Master Masson-Sibut assisted Charnier in the management of the friendly society created in 1827. Masson-Sibut despised Charnier's authoritarianism and so he left the organization. With Bouvery, another dissident mutuellist, they created *la Société du Devoir Mutuel* and the newspaper, *L'Echo des Fabriques* a few years later. Masson-Sibut wrote a pamphlet about the circumstances of the riot of 1831.

Romand, Jean-Claude: This silk worker was one of the leading strikers in 1831. He coined the phrase,"to live working or to die fighting," and authored the book " *Confessions d'un Malheureux*" (1846). At the trial of Riom, Romand was sentenced to two years' imprisonment for his participation in the riot and was condemned to five years of hard labor for having stolen a loaf of bread.

Soult, Jean-de-Dieu Nicolas, Duke of Dalmatie (1769–1851): Starting during the French Revolution, Soult distinguished himself on many battlefields in Europe. As the minister of the war, he was responsible for the repression of the 1831 riot. Following this, he was promoted to prime minister in 1832.

See also: *Paris Commune.*

BIBLIOGRAPHY

Books

Bezucha, Robert. *The Lyon Uprising of 1834: Social and Political Conflict in the Early July Monarchy.* Cambridge, MA: Harvard University Press, 1974.

Froment Pierre. Fernand Rude. *Le mouvement ouvrier à Lyon de 1827 à 1832.* Paris: Anthropos, 1969. Original work published 1944.

Moissonnier, Maurice. *Les Canuts: Vivre en travaillant ou mourir en combattant.* Paris: Messidor/Editions Sociales, 1988.

Montfalcon, Jean-Baptiste. *Histoire des insurrections de Lyon en 1831 et 1834, d'après des documents authentiques.* Toulouse, France: Eche, 1979. Original work published 1834.

Perdu, Jacques. *La révolte des Canuts (1831–1834).* Paris: Spartacus, 1974.

Rude, Fernand. *C'est nous les Canuts.* Paris: Maspéro, 1977.

———. *Les révoltes des Canuts 1831–1834.* Paris: (Re)Découverte, 2001. Original work published 1982.

Willard, Claude, ed. *La France ouvrière, des origines à 1920*, Vol. 1. Paris: Editions Sociales, 1993.

Other

Budde, Erika. "Silk in Lyon." *Silk Circa 1840.* Northampton Silk Project Web Site [cited 20 September 2002]. <www.smith.edu/hsc/silk/papers/budde.html>.

ADDITIONAL RESOURCES

Books

Maitron, Jean. *Dictionnaire Biographique du Mouvement Ouvrier Français, le Maitron.* Paris: Les Editions de l'Atelier, since 1964.

—Patricia Toucas-Truyen

Sinclair Publishes *The Jungle*

United States 1906

Synopsis

Upton Sinclair published *The Jungle* in 1906 as a socialist argument against wage slavery. Instead of generating interest in socialism, his exposure of the unsafe and unclean aspects of the Chicago meatpacking industry fueled reform and helped ensure the passage of the Pure Food and Drug Act of 1906 and the Meat Inspection Act. The novel remains an important one for historical as well as literary reasons and is one of a handful of books in the Muckrakers' canon.

Upton Sinclair. AP/Wide World Photos. Reproduced by permission.

Timeline

1886: Bombing at Haymarket Square, Chicago, kills seven policemen and injures numerous others. Eight anarchists are accused and tried; three are imprisoned, one commits suicide, and four are hanged.

1891: Construction of Trans-Siberian Railway begins. Meanwhile, crop failures across Russia lead to widespread starvation.

1896: Nobel Prize established.

1902: Second Anglo-Boer War ends in victory for Great Britain. It is a costly victory, however, resulting in the loss of more British lives (5,774) than any conflict between 1815 and 1914. The war also sees the introduction of concentration camps, used by the British to incarcerate Boer civilians.

1904: The ten-hour workday is established in France.

1906: After disputes resulting from the presidential election in Cuba, various Cuban parties invite the United States, under the 1901 Platt Amendment (which limits the terms of Cuban independence), to restore order. American troops begin a three-year occupation of the country.

1906: German neurologist Alois Alzheimer identifies the degenerative brain disorder that today bears his name.

1906: An earthquake, the worst ever to hit a U.S. city, strikes San Francisco on 18 April. It kills some 2,500 people, leaves another 250,000 homeless, and destroys more than $400 million worth of property.

1906: Founding of the British Labour Party.

1908: The Tunguska region of Siberia experiences a strange explosion, comparable to the detonation of a hydrogen

Inside cover, *The Jungle* by Upton Sinclair. © Bettmann/ Corbis. Reproduced by permission.

bomb, whose causes will long be a subject of debate. Today many scientists believe that a comet caused the Tunguska event.

1912: *Titanic* sinks on its maiden voyage, from Southampton to New York, on 14 April. More than 1,500 people are killed.

1916: Battles of Verdun and the Somme on the Western Front. The latter sees the first use of tanks, by the British.

Event and Its Context

Sinclair's Background

Born in Baltimore, Maryland, on 20 September 1878, Sinclair was the only child of an alcoholic father and a teetotaling, deeply religious mother. His family moved to New York around 1886, and his mother educated Sinclair at home until age 10. After his graduation in 1897 from the College of the City of New York, he continued his education at Columbia University with the intention of becoming a lawyer. Destitute while in

school, he supported himself by selling puzzles, stories, and other items to magazines and newspapers. He wrote mostly fiction at first, publishing adventure stories for the Street and Smith company and then self-publishing his first novel, *Springtime and Harvest*, in 1901. That same year, he married Meta Fuller, who later gave birth to a son, David.

A chance meeting in 1902 with Leonard D. Abbot, a young socialist, led to Sinclair's introduction to socialism and to meeting several prominent members of the Socialist Party of America. As Sinclair biographer William A. Bloodworth noted, "It took Sinclair several years to grasp the proletarian and reformist aspects of socialism. However, from the beginning, it appears that he understood the way in which many socialists accepted socialism as the culmination of Christianity." Sinclair quickly embraced this mixture of political philosophy with theology. Over the next two years he mingled with the socialist elite, and in the winter of 1902–1903 wrote a short novel, *A Captain of Industry*, from a neosocialist perspective. The work, published in 1906, was unsophisticated fiction and ineffective socialist propaganda.

Sinclair's next book, *Manassas* (1904), about a southern family in the antebellum period and the abolitionist movement just prior to the Civil War, drew on history for its source material. Though it was another weak attempt at fiction, the book was important for Sinclair for several reasons. An improvement over previous efforts, it demonstrated to Sinclair that he could develop a better story when relying extensively on facts and historical data. It signaled the transition from his earlier work, which emphasized imagination rather than reality, and from being a hack writer to a competent one. His research helped him connect the earlier abolitionist crusade with the Progressive movement. He envisioned socialism at the vanguard of political reform. To aid this cause, he turned to exposing the unforgiving reality of the human condition in a contemporary setting in the slaughterhouses of Chicago's stockyards district, which he would call "Packingtown."

Muckrackers and the Beef Trust

By the time Sinclair settled on the topic of how the slaughterhouses in Chicago had created wage slaves of the workers, social and political conditions made his timing ripe for success. Muckraking articles, often serialized in mainstream magazines such as *The World's Work* and *Cosmopolitan*, had created a stir against several trusts, or monopolies, that controlled entire industries. Muckraker journalists such as Lincoln Steffens and Ida Tarbell, whose major works, *The Shame of the Cities* and *History of the Standard Oil Company,* respectively, appeared in 1901. The Muckrakers—so named by Theodore Roosevelt because they, like the Man with the Muckrake in *Pilgrim's Progress*, looked down at the filth and ignored the celestial crown—exposed and attempted to correct graft and corruption in both government and business.

For years, beginning with the "embalmed meat" scandals during the Spanish-American war, muckrakers had been attacking the so-called Beef Trust, focusing attention not only on the unhealthy food but also the monopolistic business practices and corrupt political connections. Theodore Roosevelt, hero of the war in Cuba and governor of New York, testified before a Senate investigating committee in 1899 that he would as soon eat his old hat as the canned goods shipped under government contract to the soldiers fighting in Cuba. Yet, despite the newspaper articles and Senate testimony, there had been very little public outcry against the Beef Trust. The meatpackers managed public relations better than most other businessmen of the era, arranging sham tours to carefully manicured parts of their plants and advertising their virtues. *Cosmopolitan* and other magazines lavished positive articles on the packers. Even the appearance of a series of muckraking articles in 1904 about the trust failed to have any effect.

Meanwhile, Dr. Harvey Wiley had been laying much of the practical groundwork for reforming the beef industry. As chief of the Bureau of Chemistry in the United States Department of Agriculture since 1886, Wiley had been investigating the adulteration of foodstuffs for several years before Sinclair visited Chicago in 1904. In 1902 Wiley began showing through experiments on humans the unhealthful effects of the dyes, boric acid, benzoic acid, and other preservatives used by unscrupulous businessmen and consumed by an ignorant public. Wiley and his associates conducted the basic scientific research that proved necessary for Congress to pass the Pure Food and Drug Act, but it would take the explosive work of Sinclair to push a recalcitrant U.S. House of Representatives into action.

Sinclair and the Chicago Stockyards

Before heading for Chicago in November of 1904 to start his research, Sinclair divided his time between reading about standard socialist theory and philosophy and developing an audience by writing for mass publication journals. In the summer of 1904 Sinclair officially joined the Socialist Party of America. He became a regular contributor to *Appeal to Reason*, a weekly populist-socialist journal published in Kansas. The foremost socialist voice in the country, the magazine had an established circulation in the hundreds of thousands. The *Appeal* introduced Sinclair to a large and sympathetic audience. He wrote a series of articles about the unsuccessful strike in the Chicago meat packing industry that took place that same summer. He informed his readers that the Beef Trust was hardly interested in responding to union demands under the present capitalist system and that socialism was absolutely necessary to combat the problem. He incorporated the strike into his next book, *The Jungle*.

Though *Manassas* was selling poorly, the favorable reviews of the book garnered Sinclair enough publicity to have the mainstream *Collier's* publish two of his articles. One article was an explanation of the aims of the Socialist Party in the upcoming election: to educate Americans about social injustice and to thereby open the door to economic democracy and to avoid revolution. The other article, "Our Bourgeois Literature," argued that as long as workers were being exploited, society could achieve "neither political virtue, nor social refinement, nor true religion, nor vital art." The article signaled Sinclair's break from the idealistic writing that informed his earlier novels and his move toward literature that would help alleviate the conditions workers faced under capitalism. To agitate for change in American culture from the bottom up, he decided to deal specifically with lower-class life and practical politics.

Sinclair approached the publisher of *Manassas* with his idea for a new novel that "would be intended to set forth the breaking of human hearts by a system which exploits the labor of men and women for profits." The publishing house, Macmillan, gave him an advance of $500. The editor of *Appeal to Reason* matched that offer for the serial rights to the novel if he would produce one as good as *Manassas* but one that would deal with present-day wage slavery instead of chattel slavery.

Sinclair devoted seven weeks in Chicago to gathering factual information and personal impressions, spending nearly all of his waking hours at the task. He interviewed a wide variety of people about conditions in the packing plants and the political corruption in Chicago, including lawyers, doctors, laborers, and social workers. His socialist affiliation won him invitations into the homes of laborers for interviews. He toured the plants as an official visitor and as a disguised worker. He met a correspondent for *Lancet*, the prominent British medical journal, who provided him with detailed information about slaughterhouse conditions. What he saw made a disturbing, lifelong impression on him. He returned home and began the difficult task of turning facts and impressions into a novel.

A Brief Summary and Analysis of *The Jungle*

The story of Jurgis Rudkus and his Lithuanian relatives in the first two-thirds of the novel follows the classic naturalistic pattern of inevitable downward spiral toward anarchy and doom. The book opens with the marriage celebration of Jurgis and his 16-year-old bride, Ona Lukoszaite, a lavish celebration they can not afford but feel compelled to stage so as to maintain connections to their heritage. The celebration is marred by the emergence of differences between older men and women and the younger people who have turned their backs on their cultural heritage. The party lasts into the early hours of the morning. Despite the prodigious amounts of alcohol consumed and lack of sleep, the guests and even the bridal couple must still prepare to head for work or risk losing their jobs.

Though Jurgis is a Lithuanian immigrant, Sinclair portrayed him as a stereotype of the American dreamer: he is a strong believer in the work ethic and trusts that his hard work will deliver to him and his family greater and greater material rewards; he goes to night school to learn English and becomes an American citizen; and he purchases a home and provides for his extended family. Yet for all his efforts, Jurgis struggles mostly in vain. The hopeful and hardworking immigrants are ground down by American industry. Their American dream turns into a nightmare.

The strain to exist overwhelms the family. Every able-bodied member of the family must work. When Ona gives birth to their son, her premature return to work makes her sick. When Jurgis injures himself and has to miss work to convalesce, he loses his job at the packing plant and has to take one at a fertilizer plant. The poor pay forces Ona to prostitute herself clandestinely. When Jurgis attacks the man who forced her into prostitution, he lands in jail for 30 days. Upon his release he finds his house has been repossessed, and then he watches as his wife dies of a miscarriage. Despite the devastation, he must still provide for his family, so he takes a job first in a harvester plant and then in a steel mill. He returns home from work one day to find that his son has drowned in a mud puddle in the unpaved streets of the stockyards district. He then flees Packingtown and the pain it has caused him, taking odd jobs in the countryside

Meatpacking plant, Chicago, Illinois. © Bettmann/Corbis. Reproduced by permission.

and spending his wages in saloons and brothels living a life of "wild rioting and debauchery" in an attempt to forget his sorrows.

Jurgis finally returns to Chicago and takes a job digging tunnels beneath the city. Another injury forces him to become a beggar. A chance encounter with the son of a packer reveals that wealth produces no greater rewards of family and a sense of community—the wealthy son is no happier than Jurgis. Jurgis soon finds himself working for the corrupt Democratic political machine and as a strikebreaker in the packing plants. After another stint in jail for again attacking the man who forced his dead wife into prostitution, Jurgis reaches his emotional nadir.

While wandering the streets and trying to figure out how keep from losing his humanity—his concern for others—in a social and economic system that only seems to produce helplessness and sorrow for him, he stumbles into a political meeting where the speaker is discussing socialism.

Jurgis is stirred by what he hears. The masters of the wage slaves, he is told, "do nothing to earn what they receive, they do not even have to come for it. . . . The whole of society is in their grip, the whole labor of the world lies at their mercy. . . . They own not merely the labor of society, they own the governments." As the speaker continues, Jurgis undergoes what can be described best as a religious conversion to socialism. "The whole world had been changed for him—he was free, he was free! . . . He would be a man, with a will and a purpose." Enraptured, Jurgis meets with the speaker afterwards and learns more about socialism, finds a good job, and begins living a better and enlightened life. The serialized version of the story concludes with the Socialist Party having made substantial gains in the election of 1904, but Jurgis is hauled off to jail on election night for having jumped bail earlier. This final stab at social injustice in America was omitted from the book version. The book version ends on the upbeat note of a postelection rally at which a socialist speaker declares that in the next election, "Chicago Will Be Ours!"

Up until the late stages of the story, Sinclair achieved his goal of writing a kind of *Uncle Tom's Cabin* of wage slavery. Jurgis suffers as a result of working in the slaughterhouses and other dangerous jobs, has lost everything of value to him, and is at a point of great despair. Sinclair had effectively set the stage for his hero to find that socialism is the solution to his—and to society's—ills. But in the last third of the novel, from the political meeting through the conclusion, Sinclair diverges from the naturalistic style and gets bogged down as he attempts to convey his political message through the various incidents and discussions that engage Jurgis. When Sinclair shifts the focus from Jurgis to the various lectures and speeches, the book becomes little more than a political treatise in a narrative form. The two sections and styles do not easily coexist. Nonetheless, the work succeeded far more than Sinclair anticipated.

Reaction to *The Jungle*

Sinclair's effort had a huge impact on the reading public. Though the book's dedication had declared, "To the Workingmen of America," Sinclair's original intentions of a prosocialist political tract that exposed unseemly wage slavery became lost in the uproar caused by the book's lurid descriptions of the abysmal working conditions and complete lack of quality control in the stockyards. As Sinclair noted, "I aimed at the public's heart and by accident I hit it in the stomach." Macmillan decided not to publish the story, fearing that many of the scenes in the packing plants were possibly libelous. Doubleday, Page, and Company verified the facts by sending investigators of its own and published the book in 1906. To capitalize on the growing anger over contaminated food, the company advertised the novel as "a searching exposé of . . . the flagrant violations of all hygienic laws in the slaughter of diseased cattle . . . and the whole machinery of feeding a nation." Sinclair became world famous, and book sales earned him enough money to lift him permanently out of poverty.

The book also launched Sinclair into active reform politics. He requested that President Roosevelt order an investigation of sanitary conditions in the Chicago packing plants and agitated for passage of the Pure Food and Drug Act and Meat Inspection Act, which had been stalled in the U.S. Congress for months. Roosevelt threatened to make his own secret investigation report public to coerce Congress into passing the more stringent Senate version of the bill that he favored. Undeterred, the House emasculated the Senate version, and Roosevelt leaked part of the report to the press to force the issue. The confirmation of Sinclair's claims caused a sharp drop in American meat sales in Europe, and the packers and their representatives caved in.

Roosevelt agreed to have the government pay for the meat inspectors but insisted on civil service status for inspectors and the government's right to stop approving meat in plants that refused to act on its suggestions. A new federal agency, the Food and Drug Administration (FDA), was created to carry out the laws. With it, the scope of federal administrative rule was extended and the whole concept of a national duty and power to police and protect the public was enlarged. Though the laws did not have all the provisions for which Sinclair had hoped, in the end Sinclair, Roosevelt, and Wiley could all claim credit for the legislative victory.

Key Players

Roosevelt, Theodore (1858–1919): A lifelong civil servant, war hero, and author, Roosevelt became the youngest president ever upon William McKinley's assassination in 1901. With the passage of laws such as the Pure Food and Drug Act, Roosevelt strengthened the executive branch by using the progressive agenda during his two terms. He ran for a third term in office in 1912 on the Progressive Party ticket but lost.

Sinclair, Upton (1878–1968): Sinclair wrote other novels that exposed social evils, including *King Coal* (1917), *Oil!* (1927), *Boston* (on the Sacco-Vanzetti Case, 1928), and *Little Steel* (1938). An ardent socialist, Sinclair was in and out of the American Socialist Party but was defeated as the Democratic candidate for governor of California in 1934. *World's End* (1940) is the first of a cycle of 11 novels that deal with world events since 1914 and feature the fictional Lanny Budd as hero; the third, *Dragon's Teeth* (1942), won a Pulitzer Prize. Many of Sinclair's more than 80 books have been widely translated.

Wiley, Harvey W. (1844–1930): Food chemist, born near Kent, Indiana. He was professor of chemistry at Purdue (1874–1883), then became chief of the chemical division of the U.S. Department of Agriculture, a position he held for 30 years. His main interest was in improving purity and reducing food adulteration. Conflicts over enforcement of the Pure Food and Drug Act led to his resignation in 1912, but he continued as an active propagandist on food purity until his death. He also served as professor of agricultural chemistry at George Washington University from 1899 to 1914.

See also: *Socialist Party of the U.S.*

BIBLIOGRAPHY

Books

Bloodworth, William A., Jr. *Upton Sinclair.* Boston: G. K. Hall & Co., 1977.

Gould, Lewis L. *The Presidency of Theodore Roosevelt.* Lawrence: The University Press of Kansas, 1991.

Harris, Leon. *Upton Sinclair, American Rebel.* New York: Thomas Y. Crowell Company, 1975.

Morris, Edmund. *Theodore Rex.* New York: Random House, 2001.

Sinclair, Upton. *The Lost First Edition of Upton Sinclair's* The Jungle. Edited with an Introduction by Gene DeGruson. Atlanta, GA: Peachtree Publishers, 1988.

ADDITIONAL RESOURCES

Books

Harbaugh, William Henry. *Power and Responsibility: The Life and Times of Theodore Roosevelt*. New York: Farrar, Straus and Cudahy, 1961.

Miller, Walter James. *Upton Sinclair's* The Jungle: *A Critical Commentary*. New York: Monarch Press, 1983.

Mowry, George Edwin. *The Era of Theodore Roosevelt and the Birth of Modern America, 1900–1912*. New York: Harper & Row, 1958.

Roosevelt, Theodore. *Autobiography*. New York: Charles Scribner's Sons, 1913.

—James G. Lewis

Social Security Act

United States 1935

Synopsis

The creation of the Social Security Act represented a sea change in how Americans addressed issues relating to poverty, infirmity, and aging. Traditionally, the family or community volunteerism supported populations facing these issues. Before 1929 war veterans had been the only recipients of national public assistance.

Prior to the depression, resources such as accurate statistic studies were limited or nonexistent. As a result, the scope of the problems and conditions surrounding poverty were not well documented or understood. Activism and popular protest in reaction to the newly available information greatly influenced the Social Security Act legislation. Many of those who advocated for the passage of the Social Security Act were average citizens.

Although contemporary connotations of "social security" typically are synonymous with old age pensions, at its inception the Social Security Act was an umbrella for various programs including unemployment insurance, old age insurance, and mothers' aid.

Timeline

1920: League of Nations, based in Geneva, holds its first meetings.

1925: European leaders attempt to secure the peace at the Locarno Conference, which guarantees the boundaries between France and Germany, and Belgium and Germany.

1930: Naval disarmament treaty signed by the United States, Great Britain, France, Italy, and Japan.

1933: Newly inaugurated U.S. President Franklin D. Roosevelt launches the first phase of his New Deal to put depression-era America back to work.

1935: Germany annexes the Saar region after a plebiscite. In defiance of Versailles, the Nazis reintroduce compulsory military service. The Allies do nothing, and many western intellectuals maintain that it is only proper for Germany to retake its own territory and begin building up its army again.

1935: Italians invade Ethiopia, and the response by the League of Nations—which imposes sanctions but otherwise fails to act—reveals the impotence of that organization.

1935: Second phase of New Deal begins with the introduction of social security, farm assistance, and housing and tax reform.

1938: The U.S. Fair Labor Standards Act establishes a minimum wage.

1940: Hitler's troops sweep through Western Europe, annexing Norway and Denmark in April, and in May the Low Countries and France. At the same time, Stalin—who in this year arranges the murder of Trotsky in Mexico—takes advantage of the situation to add the Baltic republics (Latvia, Lithuania, and Estonia) to the Soviet empire, where they will remain for more than half a century.

1945: April sees the death of three leaders: Roosevelt passes away on 12 April; the Italians execute Mussolini and his mistress on 28 April; and Hitler (along with Eva Braun, propaganda minister Josef Goebbels, and Goebbels's family) commits suicide on 30 April.

1950: North Korean troops pour into South Korea, starting the Korean War. Initially the communists make impressive gains, but in September the U.S. Marines land at Inchon and liberate Seoul. China responds by sending in its troops.

Event and Its Context

Need, Poverty Preceded Depression

The Great Depression was undoubtedly America's period of greatest need. Some estimates indicated that one-third of the nation lived in substandard housing and needed food, clothing, and regular medical care. To provide these necessities, the government instituted welfare programs during the New Deal. Often referred to as the Second New Deal, the Social Security Act was among the second round reform legislation that was passed during the Roosevelt administration.

Finding adequate solutions for poverty in the United States was compounded by widespread belief that anyone who needed assistance was either not working hard enough or suffered from a fatal character flaw, even moral turpitude. The reasons behind poverty are complex, and the picture is often complicated by the fact that the poor—including children, the disabled or mentally ill, and the very old—are sometimes unable to care for or speak for themselves.

Early American welfare programs were local. State governments provided extremely limited reimbursement for services, if at all. City and county agencies offered some public assistance, but custom dictated that family members were obligated to assist other family members in times of need. This remained the practice even with federal intervention. In 1937 an estimated two-thirds of all states legally required relatives to support their poorer relations. Private agencies, notably churches, filled the gap. The system was far from ideal.

So entrenched were beliefs about welfare and its stigma that the term "relief" was often used in the Great Depression. This distinguished this form of aid from charity or a gift of assistance for which no work was demanded in return for the assistance. Programs of public assistance vary and include means-tested relief (aid provided to people who demonstrate that they do not have the means to provide for themselves and who meet specific criteria to qualify for that aid) and social insurance (entitlement programs such as old age pensions and unemployment insurance).

The Herbert Hoover administration implemented small social programs, but it was not until Franklin D. Roosevelt was sworn into office in January 1933 that substantive changes commenced. Despite opposition to the creation of a welfare state, Roosevelt reiterated that government assistance was a temporary help. "Continued dependence upon relief induces a spiritual and moral disintegration fundamentally destructive to the national fiber," he said. "To dole out relief in this way is to administer a narcotic, a subtle destroyer of the human spirit."

As Roosevelt stated in his June 1934 message to Congress, "Security was attained in the earlier days through the interdependence of members of families upon each other and of the families within a small community upon each other. The complexities of great communities and of organized industry make less real these simple means of security. Therefore, we are compelled to employ the active interest of the Nation as a whole through government in order to encourage a greater security for each individual who composes it."

Social Security remains the most acceptable and controversial federal assistance program. Steve Forbes, magazine publisher and sometime presidential candidate in the 1990s, called the public foment for Social Security "one of the most remarkable grass-roots movements in American history . . . an epochal bill."

Old Age Insurance

The act's keystone was provisions for old age insurance. Americans wanted a means to insure themselves against poverty, particularly in their old age. They needed government assistance and a comprehensive program. The public saw this particular as relatively conservative because it was funded by taxing employers and employees and not publicly subsidized. Workers aged 65 and older would receive an individual pension based on their own financial contributions. Pensions were not to be paid before 1942.

Since 1929 various movements, including Upton Sinclair's End Poverty in California, had wrestled with these concepts. The federally conceived plan was for workers' contributions to fund their own pensions. Their contributions would be available

Social Security poster. © Bettmann/Corbis. Reproduced by permission.

after retirement or as unemployment insurance in the form of Social Security. Most view the program as very practical and cost-effective because Americans, rather than the government, would be paying for their own assistance.

Dr. Francis Townsend, an unemployed physician, propelled the debate on providing pensions for the elderly. His Old-Age Revolving Pension Plan, commonly called the Townsend Plan, was first made public in 1933. This plan proposed to resolve financial problems for the elderly by giving a $200 per month pension to those older than 60. He founded his nonprofit organization, Old Age Revolving Pensions, Ltd., in 1934 to promote the plan; soon after its founding, 500,000 Townsend Club members throughout the United States were espousing the plan.

Economists balked at the plan as "unworkable and impossibly expensive." By 1935, however, these clubs had millions of members and increasing political power. There is some lingering debate over the numbers of members and supporters, but club members deluged congressional leaders and other politicians with correspondence exhorting them to enact Townsend's program.

President Franklin Delano Roosevelt signs Social Security Bill, spectators from left, Rep. Robert L. Doughton, Sen. Robert F. Wagner, Secretary of Labor Frances Perkins, Sen. Pat Harrison, and Rep. David J. Lewis, Washington, D.C. © Bettmann/Corbis. Reproduced by permission.

The Townsend camp often found allies in other national movements, including the Share Our Wealth program instituted by Louisiana senator Huey P. Long, who, it was said, typically received as much mail from the public as the president. Many of Long's ideas about income redistribution were in his book, *Every Man a King*. Another conservative reactionary of the era was Father Charles Coughlin, whose radio shows attacked capitalists as often as he railed against Jews and communists. Several alternate plans gathered support, including the General Welfare Federation Plan, San Diego Income Idea, and Ham and Egges.

The Roosevelt administration was demonstrably threatened by the Townsend movement. Labor Secretary Frances Perkins said that the debate "both drove us and confused the issue." Edwin E. Witte, director of the Committee of Economic Security, is said to have called the Townsend Plan "a terrific menace which is likely to engulf our entire economic system" and might result in demands for "extravagant, gratuitous pensions." Witte also reputedly fueled the campaign designed to discredit Townsend. "All told," wrote author Linda Gordon, "many hours went into studying and damning his proposal."

Among those working with the cabinet to draft the old age pensions section were Barbara Armstrong, J. Douglas Brown, and Murray Latimer. Perkins referred to them as "wild horses." Regardless of their colorful reputations, they did assist in the development of the framework for old age insurance. The plan provided secure old age for many Americans but excluded agricultural workers and domestics, which left two-thirds of all African Americans without any safety net in times of unemployment or in their old age.

Creating Aid for Children

Aid to Dependent Children (ADC) was a noncontroversial part of the Social Security package. Building on decades of work by the U.S. Children's Bureau, which had been founded in 1912, social reformers pressed the Roosevelt administration to provide meaningful assistance for poor mothers and their dependent children. This portion of the bill was designed to support motherhood; however, crafting this support network was not a simple task.

In this era, men worked outside the home, and their wives typically were the family caregivers. Beginning at the turn of the century, aid had been available to widows with children. Single mothers had some relief, starting in the 1920s, with the creation of mothers' aid pensions, which were enacted in 42 states.

Single women, even those widowed with young children, faced the stigma that was attached to taking a hand-out. Plus, once that pride had been swallowed, there were strings attached. Moral fitness was often a prerequisite for aid. Relatively few women were judged morally sufficient to be granted this sorely needed help.

Representatives of the U.S. Children's Bureau, including Grace Abbott, Katharine Lenroot, and Martha Eliot, were instrumental in helping to craft the language of ADC legislation. They were cautious about minimizing their aid requests. The agency had been the target of Red-baiting and funding cuts. This bill needed to pass and was therefore initially weaker than advocates may have desired. Witte and Perkins ultimately sacrificed the bill during the tangles in Congress. To ensure the passage of the entire Social Security bill, Congress cut key portions of the Aid to Dependent Children Act.

The intent of this program was to assist dependent children in single-parent families, and was thus approached differently from the other Social Security Act programs. Most notably, state and local governments, rather than the federal government, were responsible for administering it. The bill was weak and did not put an end to means and moral testing as some advocated. In 1950 the program became what is now known as Aid to Families of Dependent Children (AFDC).

Unemployment Insurance

Because the direction given to the framers of Social Security was that a program of social insurance was to be a first defense against poverty with public assistance a secondary defense, the creation of unemployment insurance and the policies surrounding it received the greatest attention, according to Arthur Altmeyer, assistant secretary of the Department of Labor in the Roosevelt Administration. Roosevelt was unwavering in his mandate that work be found for those able to work and relief stopped.

The technical board of the Committee on Economic Security issued a report that conveyed three possibilities: a solely federal system, a cooperative system with federal subsidies, and a cooperative plan based on the Wagner-Lewis unemployment insurance bill. The board did not clearly support one over the other. There was no consensus and members' opinions shifted even while the bill was still being created. Harry Hopkins, director of the Federal Emergency Relief Administration (FERA), proposed that there be no more discussion of a federal plan. The committee decided to support the Wagner-Lewis framework, which advocated a federal-state tax offset plan. The president later announced his support for a federal-state plan.

The creation of unemployment insurance legislation was fraught with obstacles. As it passed through body after body, it was frequently amended. Senator Robert M. La Follette's suggestion became a permanent amendment that granted discretion to each state to institute the type of unemployment program it deemed appropriate. The president's suggestions that employers should pay into a pooled fund were ignored.

Constitutionality Concerns

There was concern that the Supreme Court would declare all or some portions of these programs unconstitutional, so the framers took great care in crafting the legislation. The fear was not unwarranted. From January 1935 through May 1936, the Supreme Court declared eight laws within the New Deal as unconstitutional. The timidity of those shaping the legislation may have hindered some programs, particularly ADC, from being more potently effective. In retrospect, the bill was regarded as far too conservative.

The initial legislative package also included public works programs and national medical insurance. Vehement opposition from big business and the medical community quickly eliminated these programs. The administration received suggestions and comments from all quarters including business, social workers, medical professionals, politicians in various parties both left and right, and the public. AFL support vacillated. William Green, the union's president, reportedly "made so many suggestions for improving the bill that he seemed to be against it."

Social workers who protested the end of FERA, which was scheduled to be replaced in 1935 by the Works Progress Administration, also caught the administration's attention. The protesters' timing, coming as the Social Security Act was under consideration, was said to have helped greatly in its eventual passage.

The varying demands and lobbying by Townsend and Long supporters served to propel the bill forward. The bill represented a national shift in how entitlement was defined for the purpose of public assistance. Ultimately, the administration seemed willing to compromise—or sacrifice—pieces of the concept just to get the act passed. It took six months to write the bill and another seven before it passed through Congress.

The president signed the Social Security Act on 14 August 1935. Since that time, Social Security has expanded with the addition of new programs, beginning with federal minimum wage and child labor laws (1938) and disability insurance (1956). Witte's diaries, which detailed the minutia of the creation of the Social Security Act of 1935, became the book, *The Develop-*

ment of the Social Security Act. Another lasting impact of the events surrounding the passage of the Social Security Act is the acknowledgement of the power of the ongoing pensioners' lobby by politicians. It is worth noting that these programs bear little resemblance to the contemporary Social Security programs.

Key Players

Altmeyer, Arthur J. (1891–1972): Born in Wisconsin, Altmeyer first came to Washington, D.C., as the director of the Labor Compliance Division of the National Recovery Administration in 1933. He became assistant secretary of the Department of Labor in the Roosevelt administration and technical board chair, President's Cabinet Committee on Economic Security. He was a pivotal member of team that researched and developed legislation that would become the United States Social Security program. He was appointed to head the Social Security Board and served in that position from 1937 to July 1946.

Coughlin, Father Charles Edward (1891–1979): Born in Ontario, Canada, Coughlin was a Roman Catholic priest based in Michigan and was well known for his criticism of Roosevelt's New Deal policies. His ideas were popularized through radio broadcasts that he began in 1930.

Cummings, Homer Stillé (1870–1956): United States' attorney general between 1933 and 1939, he served as a member of the Committee on Economic Security, which developed legislation that would become the United States Social Security program.

Hopkins, Harry Lloyd (1890–1946): As Federal Emergency Relief administrator, he became a member of the Committee on Economic Security. He was active in various roles throughout the Roosevelt administration.

Long, Huey (1893–1935): The controversial populist governor of Louisiana and United States senator, Long was critical of Roosevelt. He advocated a radical income redistribution known as the Share-Our-Wealth Plan. He had discussed running for president in 1936. He was assassinated in September 1935.

Morgenthau, Henry, Jr. (1891–1967): As secretary of the U.S. Treasury, he served as a member of the Committee on Economic Security, which had been created to develop legislation that would become the Social Security program. Morgenthau, born in New York, was a longtime Roosevelt advisor and confidant.

Perkins, Frances (1882–1965): The first female Cabinet officer in the United States government, Perkins served as secretary of labor during the Roosevelt administration. She was first a social worker, which informed her government career. She was instrumental in developing policies that would become the United States Social Security program.

Sinclair, Upton Beall, Jr. (1878–1968): Best known as the author of works such as *The Jungle*, Sinclair created End Poverty in California (EPIC), a reform program that also enabled him to run, although unsuccessfully, for governor.

Van Kleeck, Mary Abby (1883–1972): Born in New York, Van Kleeck criticized New Deal programs, saying they weakened both workers and unions. She was best known in her capacity as director of the Russell Sage Foundation department of industrial studies. She advocated socialism and also wrote on industrial socialization.

Wallace, Henry Agard (1888–1965): Secretary of agriculture during the first two of the four Roosevelt administrations, he was also a member of the Committee on Economic Security, which was created to develop legislation that would become the United States Social Security program. He later became vice president under Roosevelt during the third term.

Winant, John Gilbert (1889–1947): Member of the Committee on Economic Security, he was the first chairman of the Social Security Board. He was tireless in his support for Social Security. Winant resigned from the Social Security Board so that he could defend the act.

Witte, Edwin Emil (1887–1960): A labor economist, Witte was appointed executive director of the Committee on Economic Security. He was at the crux of debates regarding the constitutionality of federal Social Security programs and funding issues. He continued as an advisor in the Social Security Administration.

See also: *Stock Market Crash.*

BIBLIOGRAPHY

Books

Altmeyer, Arthur J. *The Formative Years of Social Security: A Chronicle of Social Security Legislation and Administration, 1934–1954.* Madison: The University of Wisconsin Press, 1966.

Gordon, Linda. *Pitied but Not Entitled: Single Mothers and the History of Welfare.* New York: Free Press, 1994.

Graham, Jr., Otis L., and Meghan Wander, eds. *Franklin D. Roosevelt, His Life and Times: An Encyclopedic View.* Boston: G. K. Hall & Co., 1985.

Handlin, Oscar and Lilian Handlin. *Liberty and Equality: 1920–1994.* New York: HarperCollins Publishers, 1994.

Katz, Michael B. *In the Shadow of the Poorhouse: A Social History of Welfare in America.* New York: Basic Books, Inc., 1986.

Lubove, Roy. *The Struggle for Social Security, 1900–1935.* Cambridge, MA: Harvard University Press, 1968.

Olasky, Marvin. *The Tragedy of American Compassion.* Washington, DC: Regnery Publishing, 1992.

Patterson, James T. *America's Struggle Against Poverty: 1900–1980.* Cambridge, MA: Harvard University Press, 1981.

Watkins, T. H. *The Hungry Years: A Narrative History of the Great Depression in America.* New York: Henry Holt and Company, 1999.

Witte, Edwin E. *The Development of the Social Security Act.* Madison: The University of Wisconsin Press, 1962.

Periodicals

Davies, Gareth, and Martha Derthick. "Race and Social Welfare Policy: The Social Security Act of 1935."

Political Science Quarterly 112, no. 2 (summer 1997): 217–235.

"FDR and the New Deal." *The Economist* 353, no. 8151 (25 December 1999): 49.

Forbes, Steve. "Backhanded Godfather." *Forbes* 159, no. 1 (13 January 1997): 259.

Hutchison, Elizabeth D., and Leanne W. Charlesworth. "Securing the Welfare of Children: Policies Past, Present, and Future." *Families in Society: The Journal of Contemporary Human Services* 81, no. 6 (November 2000): 576.

Jacoby, Sanford. "Downsizing in the Past." *Challenge* 41, no. 3 (May–June 1998): 100–112.

Lopez, Eduard A. "Constitutional Background to the Social Security Act of 1935." *Social Security Bulletin* 50, no. 1 (January 1987): 5–11.

Manza, Jeff. "Political Sociological Models of the U.S. New Deal." *Annual Review of Sociology*, Annual 2000: 297.

—Linda Dailey Paulson

William Dudley Haywood. The Library of Congress.

Socialist Party of America

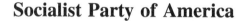

United States 1901

Synopsis

The Socialist Party of America was born in 1901 when the Socialist Labor Party and Socialist Democratic Party of America (SDPA) combined. SDPA leader Eugene V. Debs, a 1900 presidential candidate, was the socialists' perennial candidate for two decades. The party attracted many of the era's leading intellectuals with its call for social reforms and hundreds of thousands of workers with its support for radical labor causes. Party membership rose to more than 150,000 within a decade. In addition to civil rights demands, the party defended improved labor conditions, housing, and welfare legislation. The onset of World War I, the Russian Revolution, and a government offensive against the radical left were severe blows to the party. Even so, Debs managed to win nearly a million votes from prison in the 1920 presidential election. Although the party never displaced the major parties, the socialists would see many of their causes eventually embraced by the mainstream parties.

Timeline

1901: U.S. President William McKinley is assassinated by Leon Czolgosz, an Anarchist. Vice President Theodore Roosevelt becomes president.

1904: Beginning of the Russo-Japanese War, which lasts into 1905 and results in a resounding Japanese victory. In Russia, the war is followed by the Revolution of 1905, which marks the beginning of the end of czarist rule; meanwhile, Japan is poised to become the first major non-Western power of modern times.

1907: U.S. markets experience a financial panic.

1911: Turkish-Italian War sees the first use of aircraft as an offensive weapon. Italian victory results in the annexation of Libya.

1913: Two incidents illustrate the increasingly controversial nature of the arts in the new century. Visitors to the 17 February Armory Show in New York City are scandalized by such works as Marcel Duchamp's cubist *Nude Descending a Staircase,* which elicits vehement criticism, and theatergoers at the 29 May debut of Igor Stravinksy's ballet *Le Sacré du Printemps* (*The Rite of Spring*) are so horrified by the new work that a riot ensues.

1914: On 28 June in the town of Sarajevo, then part of the Austro-Hungarian Empire, Serbian nationalist Gavrilo Princip assassinates Austrian Archduke Francis Ferdinand and wife Sophie. In the weeks that follow, Austria declares war on Serbia, and Germany on Russia and France, while Great Britain responds by declaring war on Germany. By the beginning of August, the lines are drawn, with the Allies (Great Britain, France, Russia, Belgium, Serbia, Montenegro, and Japan) against the Central Powers (Germany, Austria-Hungary, and Turkey).

1915: Turkey's solution to its Armenian "problem" becomes the first entry in a long catalogue of genocidal acts undertaken during the twentieth century. Claiming that the Armenians support Russia, the Turks deport some 1.75 million of them to the Mesopotamian desert, where between 600,000 and 1 million perish.

Socialist Party campaign poster, Eugene V. Debs for President; Ben Hanford for Vice President, 1904. © Corbis. Reproduced by permission.

1916: Battles of Verdun and the Somme on the Western Front. The latter sees the first use of tanks, by the British.

1917: In Russia, a revolution in March (or February according to the old Russian calendar) forces the abdication of Czar Nicholas II. By July, Alexander Kerensky has formed a democratic socialist government, and continues to fight the Germans, even as starvation and unrest sweep the nation. On 7 November (25 October old style), the Bolsheviks under V. I. Lenin and Leon Trotsky seize power. By 15 December, they have removed Russia from the war by signing the Treaty of Brest-Litovsk with Germany.

1918: Upheaval sweeps Germany, which for a few weeks in late 1918 and early 1919 seems poised on the verge of communist revolution—or at least a Russian-style communist coup d'etat. But reactionary forces have regained their strength, and the newly organized Freikorps (composed of unemployed soldiers) suppresses the revolts. Even stronger than reaction or revolution, however, is republican sentiment, which opens the way for the creation of a democratic government based at Weimar.

1919: Treaty of Versailles signed by the Allies and Germany, but rejected by the U.S. Senate. This is due in part to rancor between President Woodrow Wilson and Republican Senate leaders, and in part to concerns over Wilson's plan to commit the United States to the newly established League of Nations and other international duties. Not until 1921 will Congress formally end U.S. participation in the war, but it will never agree to join the League.

Event and Its Context

Origins of American Socialism

The United States in 1900 was no stranger to socialist ideals. Socialistic utopian movements appeared throughout American history, and the utopian ideals of pre-Marxist European socialists such as Charles Fourier gained American adherents in the mid-1800s. The late nineteenth century, most remembered for its industrialists, also brought greater class consciousness and struggle among workers who felt exploited by the wage system. Against a backdrop of strikes, unemployment, wage reduction for unskilled and semiskilled laborers, and general economic unrest, American working-class intellectuals found inspiration in works such as Karl Marx's *Das Kapital* and *The Communist Manifesto*. In 1871 and 1872 American sections of the International Workingmen's Association (later known as the First International, a precursor to the Socialist International) formed, but they died out in 1876 after disputes between Marx and the anarchists. A time when American workers were forming associations such as the Knights of Labor was also a time of widespread immigration from Europe, where socialist and labor union activities were suffering a level of repression sufficient to inspire workers to emigrate. According to Eunice Minette Schuster's 1931–1932 study, "Native American Anarchism," industrial conditions met by immigrants to the U.S. in the last quarter of the nineteenth century "were favorable to Socialist and Anarchist propaganda."

American socialism's first foray into party politics began in 1877. Dissatisfied with American Federation of Labor (AFL) leader Samuel Gompers's eschewal of political action, Daniel De Leon split with the AFL to found the Socialist Labor Party (SLP); the new party largely comprised exiled German worker groups, though De Leon established complete control by the 1890s. In 1897 trade unionist Eugene V. Debs founded the Social Democratic Party of America (SDPA); a fiery orator who had already gained credibility among the working class for his role in the American Railway Union and the Pullman Strike of 1894, Debs brought rapid growth to the party. His presidential run of 1900 (with running mate Job Harriman) reaped 87,814 votes and encouraged the various groups and individuals who had campaigned for him to convene the following year.

Unity Convention

On 29 July 1901 socialists met at the Masonic Hall in Indianapolis for a "Unity Convention." In an attempt to forge a united socialist voice and a series of demands, the meeting attracted socialists from all walks of life: progressive intellectuals, Christian socialists, Jewish labor activists, and members of the AFL and Knights of Labor. Some had agrarian backgrounds. Others were members of the SLP or had been converted to socialism through Edward Bellamy's utopian bestseller *Looking Backward*. In the end, the SDPA merged with an anti-De Leonist faction of the SLP led by Morris Hillquit. With Debs as its leader, the Socialist Party of America was born.

"As a rule, large capitalists are Republicans and small capitalists are Democrats, but workingmen must remember that they are all capitalists," Debs wrote in his 1900 essay, "Outlook for socialism in the United States." Members of both major parties, he said, were "politically supporting their class interests, and this is always and everywhere the capitalist class."

Though some delegates thought that making specific demands might lead to the acceptance of a softer kind of capitalism, the convention came up with a list of immediate demands. These included public ownership of utilities, transportation, communications, monopolies and trusts; workers' compensation and insurance; reduced hours and higher wages; a public system of industries; equal political and civil rights for all men and women; greater application of proportional representation and resources such as the referendum, initiative or recall; and

universal education, with books, clothing, and food for everyone under age 18.

In a neutral stance toward the eastern and Chicago groups, the party established its first office in St. Louis, with Leon Greenbaum as national secretary. Within three years, the party had roughly 16,000 members nationwide; by 1904, socialists were winning seats in local government. That year, Debs was the Socialist Party's candidate for president. Running with Benjamin Hanford as vice presidential candidate, he multiplied almost fivefold his 1900 election results with a total of more than 400,000 votes.

Wobbly Alliance

In 1905 Debs and other Socialist Party members helped found the Industrial Workers of the World (IWW, or "the wobblies"), a decision that would spark divisions in the party for the next eight years. "The trades-union movement is today under the control of the capitalist class. It is preaching capitalist economics," Debs told delegates to the IWW's founding convention in Chicago on 29 June 1905.

As a mosaic of radical movements, this "One Big Union" included anarchists such as Lucy Parsons, trade unionists such as Mother Jones, and syndicalists such as William D. "Big Bill" Haywood. Debs's differences with Haywood were an important source of tension within the Socialist Party; despite agreement on the need for the working class to defend itself, Debs came to believe that the wobblies advocated violence and resigned in 1906. Other party members stayed active in the IWW, and Haywood remained on the Socialist Party's national committee. In a 1911 speech, Haywood criticized evolutionary socialism and advocate direct action. This divergence from the electoral approach led to Haywood's expulsion from the national committee (via mail vote) and in his followers abandoning the party in 1913.

Electoral Advances

In 1908 Debs and Hanford once again declared their quest for the White House. This time Debs and his entourage toured the country in a special campaign train known as the "Red Special," accompanied by the "Red Special Band." Debs addressed enthusiastic crowds at dozens of daily stops. That year they won more than 420,000 votes.

By 1912 the party boasted well over 100,000 members and had 1039 dues-paying members in public office; this included 56 mayors and more than 300 aldermen. In 1910 Victor L. Berger represented a Milwaukee district as the first socialist member of the U.S. House of Representatives. Although Debs's chances of beating Democrats or Republicans in a presidential race were minimal, his campaigns brought into the national dialogue issues including child labor, civil rights, and universal suffrage that otherwise might have been ignored. As Debs said, "I'd rather vote for what I want and not get it, than for what I don't want and get it." That year Debs and running mate Emil Seidel won nearly 900,000 votes; at about 6 percent of that year's total, it would be the pinnacle of the Socialist Party's electoral success. By 1913 the socialist journal *Appeal to Reason* hit a circulation of more than 760,000 and featured contributors like Jack London, Upton Sinclair, Helen Keller, and Mother Jones.

In 1916 Allan Benson was the party's presidential candidate; George R. Kirkpatrick was his running mate. The result was a significant drop from Debs's 900,000-vote showing in 1912, to less than 600,000. Debs declined the presidential nomination to run for Congress at a time when the United States began to consider going to war.

War in Europe, War on Activists

World War I was the beginning of the end for much of the socialist leadership. When the government of Woodrow Wilson entered the war in 1917, the Socialist Party met in St. Louis to condemn the action (140 votes to 5, with 31 "centrist" votes). The government quickly reacted against those who criticized the war or resisted the draft, convicting of treason Socialist Party officers like Irwin St. John Tucker, J. Louis Engdahl, and Adolph Germer (national executive secretary). Victor Berger was charged with violating the Espionage Act, yet was reelected to Congress while out of prison on appeal; the House refused to seat him despite his electoral victory, and he was thereafter sentenced to 20 years in prison.

Debs's turn came on 16 June 1918, when he made a speech in Canton, Ohio, condemning war and comparing the capitalists on Wall Street to the Kaiser's men. According to Debs, working-class men "shed their blood and furnish their corpses," yet never have a voice in declaring war or making peace. "It is the ruling class that invariably do both," he declared. On 14 September, Debs was convicted of violating the Espionage Act and sentenced to 10 years in prison. After a failed appeal in April 1918, he entered the federal penitentiary at Moundsville, West Virginia; he was later moved to the Atlanta Penitentiary.

The government persecution of suspected anarchists and communists continued in 1919, just two years after the Russian Revolution. That year, more than 10,000 were arrested on unsubstantiated charges of plans for revolution. Although most were released, the government deported some 248 activists (including Emma Goldman and Alexander Berkman) to Russia.

From the Jailhouse to the White House

In 1920, with Debs still in prison, the Socialist Party of America once again nominated him for president. Debs accepted and ran with Chicagoan Seymour Stedman. Debs's prisoner status was used prominently: one popular campaign button portrayed him in prison stripes with the slogan "For President Convict No. 9653." Another poster said, "From Atlanta Prison to the Whitehouse, 1920." His program called for better conditions for workers, welfare and housing legislation, and for making more people eligible to vote. That year Debs received almost 920,000 votes, his highest total ever. Despite the increase in actual votes over 1912, Debs's share accounted for only 3.5 percent of 1920 voters. He was pardoned in 1921, though prison time had seriously deteriorated his health.

Given the Red Scare and the assault on leftists, people began to fear subscribing to leftist publications; by November 1922 the *Appeal to Reason* ceased publication, followed by *The Call* in 1923. In the 1924 elections, the Socialist Party became a key endorser of the Progressive Party headed by Senator Robert La Follette, which won more than 4.8 million votes. The Socialist Party revived in 1928 with Norman Thomas, who ran for president six times, as its key candidate.

Key Players

Berger, Victor (1860–1929): An immigrant from Austria-Hungary, Berger was a founding member of the American Socialist Party. In 1910 he became the first socialist in the U.S. Congress, where he championed the idea of old age pensions.

Debs, Eugene Victor (1855–1926): Debs was a trade unionist from Terre Haute, Indiana, who led the foundation of the American Railway Union and the Socialist Party of America. He ran for president five times and was twice imprisoned for his political activism.

Haywood, William Dudley (1869–1928): "Big Bill" Haywood was a Utah-born miner and union activist who joined the American Socialist Party in 1901 and helped found the Industrial Workers of the World (IWW) in 1905. His preference for direct action over electoral politics made him the leader of the party's radical left and put him at odds with Debs. He was ousted from the party in 1913.

Hillquit, Morris (1869–1933): Born in Riga, Russia, as Moses Hilkowitz, he immigrated to the United States at age 17 and worked for the Socialist Labor Party, established the United Hebrew Trades, and helped Debs found the American Socialist Party. A lawyer by trade, Hillquit was the party's leading theoretician.

See also: *American Federation of Labor; First International; Industrial Workers of the World; Knights of Labor; Pullman Strike; Russian Revolutions; Second International.*

BIBLIOGRAPHY

Periodicals

Schuster, Eunice Minette. "Native American Anarchism, a Study of Left-Wing American Individualism." *Smith College Studies in History* 17, nos. 1–4. (October 1931–July 1932).

Other

Debs, E.V. "Outlook for Socialism in the United States." *International Socialist Review.* September 1900 [cited 28 September 2002]. <http://www.marxists.org/archive/debs/works/1900/outlook.htm>.

———. "Speech at the Founding Convention of the Industrial Workers of the World." Industrial Workers of the World Founding Convention Minutes. Chicago, 29 June 1905 [cited 28 September 2002]. <http://www.marxists.org/archive/debs/works/1905/iwwfound.htm>.

Official Site of the Eugene V. Debs Foundation. "Eugene V. Debs—Political activist" [cited 28 September 2002]. <http://www.eugenevdebs.com/pages/polit.html>.

Zeidler, Frank P. *History of the Socialist Party.* Milwaukee: Socialist Party of Wisconsin, 18 July 1991.

ADDITIONAL RESOURCES

Other

Eugene V. Debs Internet Archive [cited 28 September 2002].
    <http://www.marxists.org/archive/debs/>.

—Brett Allan King

Socialist Unity Party of Germany

East Germany 1946

Synopsis

In 1946 East German Communists and Socialists merged
into a single left-wing party, the *Sozialistische Einheitspartei
Deutschlands* (Socialist Unity Party of Germany, SED). Originally, the new party pursued a relatively open and independent
policy that included de-Nazification, political pluralism, and
state intervention in the economy. Starting in 1947, however,
tensions increased between the Western powers and the Soviet
Union. As a result of these tensions, Germany divided into two
antagonistic states in 1949, and the SED became a cold-war organization that exchanged political flexibility for postwar confrontation.

Timeline

1926: Britain paralyzed by a general strike.

1931: Financial crisis widens in the United States and Europe,
which reel from bank failures and climbing unemployment levels. In London, armies of the unemployed riot.

1936: The election of a leftist Popular Front government in
Spain in February precipitates an uprising by rightists
under the leadership of Francisco Franco. Over the next
three years, war will rage between the Loyalists and
Franco's Nationalists. The Spanish Civil War will prove
to be a lightning rod for the world's tensions, with the
Nazis and fascists supporting the Nationalists, and the
Soviets the Loyalists.

1941: Japanese bombing of Pearl Harbor on 7 December
brings the United States into the war against the Axis.
Combined with the attack on the Soviet Union, which
makes Stalin an unlikely ally of the Western democracies, the events of 1941 will ultimately turn the tide of
the war.

1946: Winston Churchill warns of an "Iron Curtain" spreading
across Eastern Europe.

1946: Three months after the first meeting of the United Nations General Assembly in London in January, the all-
but-defunct League of Nations is officially dissolved.

1946: At the Nuremberg trials, twelve Nazi leaders are sentenced to death, and seven others to prison.

1946: Building of the first true electronic computer, the Electronic Numerical Integrator and Computer (ENIAC).

**Walter Ulbricht. © Hulton-Deutsch/Corbis-Bettmann.
Reproduced by permission.**

1951: Six western European nations form the European Coal
and Steel Community, forerunner of the European Economic Community and the later European Union.

1956: Elvis Presley appears on Ed Sullivan's *Toast of the
Town,* where he performs "Hound Dog" and "Love Me
Tender" before a mostly female audience. Nationwide,
54 million people watch the performance, setting a new
record.

1961: President Eisenhower steps down, warning of a "military-industrial complex" in his farewell speech, and 43-
year-old John F. Kennedy becomes the youngest elected
president in U.S. history. Three months later, he launches an unsuccessful invasion of Cuba at the Bay of Pigs.

Event and Its Context

Founding of the SED

The Red Army entered Berlin on 2 May 1945, and the
Wehrmacht surrendered on 8 May. On 9 June the Soviets established a military government in the Soviet-occupied zone of
Germany. Its *Order Number Two* of the following day contem-
plated the legalization of anti-Fascist parties. The Communist

Party of Germany (KPD) became legal that day, followed by the Social-Democratic Party of Germany (SPD), the Liberal Party (LDP), and the Christian-Democratic Union (CDU).

The circumstances of the fight against the common enemy, Nazism, allowed the German Communists to experience the advantages of collaboration with other political forces. On 14 April 1945 the KPD participated in the establishment of a "United Front of anti-Fascist Democratic Parties," the *Antifabloc,* which included Socialists, Christian Democrats and Liberals, and immediately took control of local governments and public services.

The KPD's politics of anti-Fascist fronts demanded a flexible political line in the confrontation of non-Marxist democratic forces. On 11 June the Communists issued a statement in which they declared their intent to postpone revolution until after a period of de-Nazification and democratization of German society.

Together with restoration of democracy, the second cornerstone of KPD policy during the immediate postwar period consisted of beginning a process of unity with the SPD. On 19 June 1945 both parties signed an agreement on unity of action for a program of de-Nazification, trade union unity, nationalization of key economic sectors, agrarian reform, and the establishment of a parliamentary republic.

The SPD welcomed the policy of unity of action with the Communists. The KPD's proposal of unity, however, inspired a bitter debate within the SPD: Leading Socialists such as Kurt Schumacher in the non-Soviet occupied zones of Germany opposed unity, and East German figures such as Otto Grotewohl agreed to the establishment of a single left-wing party in Germany. Between 5 and 7 October 1945, an all-Germany meeting of the SPD took place in Wennigsen (Niedersachsen). The meeting culminated in the independence of the eastern and western SPD organizations. This opened the door to Grotewohl's agenda for the Soviet zone. A joint conference of 30 Communists and 30 eastern Socialists convened in Berlin on 20 and 21 December of 1945 to discuss the issue of unification.

The "Conference of the Sixty Ones," as it would be called thereafter, agreed to a process of unity that began in February 1946 on both the regional and local levels. On 19–20 April 1946 the eastern KPD and SPD organizations met in two separate congresses of unity. The process culminated in a joint congress that took place on 21 and 22 April. The meeting's principle outcome was the decision for the merger of the KPD and SPD into a new unitary party, the Sozialistische Einheitspartei Deutschlands (SED).

The New Party

The congress of unity elected the Socialist Grotewohl and the Communist Wilhem Pieck as cochairs of the SED. The rest of the party's politburo comprised six Socialists and six Communists, including ex-SPD members Erich Gniffke and Max Fechner, and ex-KPD members Anton Ackermann and Walter Ulbricht.

Together with the carefully balanced composition of the leadership, another distinctive characteristic of the SED was the enormous size of its membership. In April 1946 the ranks had swelled to 1,300,000 members (600,000 Communist and 680,000 Socialists), in Saxony, Saxony-Anhalt, Thüringen,

Mecklenburg, Brandenburg, and East Berlin, an area with a population of 19 million. The party developed a powerful propaganda apparatus that included the *Deutsche Volkszeitung, Einheit,* and *Neues Deutschland* newspapers, and the *Neuer Weg* publishing house. This, combined with the support of the USSR, soon made the SED the strongest political organization in the Soviet-occupied zone of Germany. In the municipal elections held in September 1946, the party accrued 19 percent of the vote but made a relatively weak showing in the larger cities. By October, however, SED votes had risen to 50 percent, and the party triumphed over regional governments in Saxony, Thüringen, and Mecklenburg.

Another important tool in the consolidation of the SED as the hegemonic political force of the Soviet-occupied part of Germany was the gamut of party-controlled mass organizations that were established between 1946 and 1949: the Freie Deutsche Gewerkschaftsbund (Federation of Free German Trade Unions), a unitary trade union that comprised Communists, Socialists, and Christian Democrats, had been founded in February 1946. In its second congress of April 1949, however, the SED won almost all of the leadership posts. The Freie Deutsche Jugendliche (Free German Youth), the Demokratische Frauenbund Deutschlands (Women's Democratic League of Germany), and organizations such as the Kulturbund zur Demokratischen Erneuerung Deutschlands (Democratic Cultural Alliance for the Renewal of Germany) followed similar processes.

The SED After 1947: Cold War and Stalinism

In 1946 the SED platform did not differ substantially from those of the KPD and SPD in 1945. Party theoreticians argued that the establishment of socialism in Germany had to consider the country's particularities and, accordingly, it should follow a different course from that in the Soviet Union, which consisted in bringing the bourgeois revolution to a conclusion before taking up the task of building a proletarian society.

This was also the policy of the Soviet military government from 1945 to 1948. It developed the thesis of anti-Fascist unity and people's fronts formulated in the 1935 VII World Congress of the Third International in the face of the spreading of Fascist regimes. The USSR made clear, however, that it would not tolerate anti-Communist political forces in its jurisdiction. The Soviets agreed to the legalization of nonleftist parties such as the CDU and the LDP, but they exercised a tight control on these parties and vetoed Christian-Democrat and liberal politicians who were hostile to SED hegemony. Eventually, this led to the CDU and the LDP becoming mere puppets, with the task of providing the military government and, later, the German Democratic Republic with a mask of political flexibility.

The democratic shortcomings in the Soviet-occupied zone of Germany increased after 1947. By then, the Fascist menace had faded away, and disagreements about German and European politics at large began between the allies and the Soviet Union and its diverse political parties. That year, the French and the Italian Communists were ejected from their respective governments of national unity. The situation worsened in 1948: in March, the USSR quit the all-Germany allies' governing board, the "Control Council." In June, Soviet representatives also abandoned the military government of Berlin and began a blockade on the western part of the city; the Allies decided on the economic division of the country by issuing a new currency, the Deutsche Mark, in their jurisdiction. The process from anti-Nazi collaboration to cold-war confrontation consummated in May 1949, when the Federal Republic of Germany and the German Democratic Republic were proclaimed.

In 1943 Stalin dissolved the Third International in response to Allied pressures on the USSR. In September 1947, however, the first meeting of Cominform, a board of information among the European Communist parties, convened in Poland to discuss the course of the international situation. This signaled a turning point in the policy of alliances on anti-Nazism that international communism had pursued to that point. The new coordinated strategy of confrontation partly abandoned the earlier politics of democratic fronts and political pluralism.

The SED was not an exception to these politics. In 1947 the party proposed the establishment of a new coordinating body of anti-Fascist forces, the Volkskongreßbewegung (Congress of People's Movements). The Antifa-bloc had pursued a program of de-Nazification and stressed the autonomy of its party members. The Volkskongreßbewegung, in contrast, had a more assertive political scope and operated, de facto, as the embryo of the German Democratic Republic.

The first party conference of January 1948 consummated the conversion of the SED into a cold-war Marxist political force. The members approved an organizational structure defined as *demokratischer Zentralismus* that made the SED a hierarchical organization. In addition, the conference decided to take up the fight against "opportunist" parties and began a policy of open confrontation with the West German Socialists. Finally, the membership acknowledged the guiding role of the Soviet Union, thus signaling the end of any attempt to establish an original "German road to socialism."

Key Players

Grotewohl, Otto (1894–1964): Leader of the German Social Democratic Party in the Soviet-occupied zone. Grotewohl was elected cochair of the SED following the April 1946 merger of the KPD and the SPD. He was prime minister of the GDR from 1949 to 1964.

Pieck, Wilhelm (1876–1960): Leader of the German Communist Party. Pieck joined the Social-Democrats in 1895 and participated in the foundation of the KPD in 1918. Together with Grotewohl, Pieck cochaired the SED from 1946 to 1954. He was president of the GDR from 1949 to 1960.

Ulbricht, Walter (1893–1973): Ulbricht joined the SPD in 1912 and the KPD in 1919. He was elected member of the German Parliament in 1928. After Hitler's rise to power in 1933, Ulbricht went into exile in the Soviet Union; he returned to Germany in 1945. Thereafter he was regarded as Moscow's man in Germany. Ulbricht was elected member of the politburo of the SED in 1946 and presided over the GDR from 1960 to 1973.

BIBLIOGRAPHY

Books

Rausch, Heinz, ed. *DDR, das politische, wirtshaftliche und soziale System.* Munich, Germany: Bayerische Landeszentrale für Politische Bildungsarbeit, 1998.

Ross, Corey. *Constructing Socialism at the Grass-roots: The Transformation of East Germany, 1945–1965.* Basingstoke, England: Macmillan, 2000.

Stariz, Dietrich and Weber, Hermann, *Einheits Fronts, Einheits Partei: Kommunisten und Sozialdemokraten in Ost- und Westeuropa, 1944–1948.* Cologne, Germany: Verlag Wissenschaft und Politik, 1989.

Various Authors. *Geschichte der SED, Abriß, Politbüro des ZK der SED and Institut für Marxismus–Leninismus.* Berlin: Dietz Verlag, 1978.

Periodicals

Ackermann, Anton. "Gib es Einer Besonderen Deutschen Weg Zum Sozialismus?" *Einheit,* 9 February 1946.

Benser, Günter. "Mit Welchen Sozialismusvorstellungen war die SED angetreten?" *Hefte zur DDR-Geschichte,* n. 60. Gesellschaftswissenschaftliches Forum e.v., 1999.

—Juan José Gomez Gutiérrez and Valeria Bruschi

Solidarity Emerges

Poland 1980

Synopsis

With major uprisings in 1956, 1968, 1970, and 1976 and the presence of a socially conscious Roman Catholic Church, Poland was the most restive of the Soviet satellites during the cold war. Faced with a drastically declining standard of living and the continued repression of civil liberties in the late 1970s, the country once again tipped toward unrest, even as the nation seemed united in pride over the election of Karol Wojtyla as Pope John Paul II on 16 October 1978. A year after the Pope's June 1979 visit to Poland, a strike wave erupted to protest the government's announcement of new price hikes. By the end of July 1980, 150 factories had shut down; the following month, the major shipyards along the Baltic Coast in Gdansk and Gdynia were occupied by strikers as well. In addition to improved wages and benefits, the strikers' demands included an end to censorship in the press and government interference in trade unions. A new, industry-wide union, Solidarity, emerged as the national coordinator of the strike, and its leader, Lech Walesa, as the primary voice of the opposition. By the end of the year Solidarity claimed a membership of 10 million Poles from all walks of life. By the end of the decade, when it finally confirmed its power by winning the country's first free elections of the postwar era, Solidarity signaled an end to the Soviet Bloc and, eventually, the cold war itself.

Lech Walesa. AP/Wide World Photos. Reproduced by permission.

Timeline

1955: Signing of the Warsaw Pact by the Soviet Union and its satellites in Eastern Europe.

1956: Workers revolt against communist rule in Poland, inspiring Hungarians to rise up against the Soviets. Soviet tanks and troops crush these revolts.

1968: After Czechoslovakia adopts a more democratic, popular regime, Soviet and Warsaw Pact forces invade to crush the uprising.

1978: Pope Paul VI dies and is succeeded by Pope John Paul I, who dies after just 34 days in office. He is in turn succeeded by Karol Cardinal Wojtyla of Poland, the first non-Italian pontiff in centuries, who becomes Pope John Paul II.

1980: In protest of the Soviet invasion of Afghanistan, President Carter keeps U.S. athletes out of the Moscow Olympics. Earlier, at the Winter Games in Lake Placid, New York, the U.S. hockey team scored a historic—and, in the view of many, a symbolic—victory over the Soviets.

1985: A new era begins in the U.S.S.R. as Konstantin Chernenko dies and is replaced by Mikhail Gorbachev,

who at 54 years old is the youngest Soviet leader in decades.

1986: An accident at the Chernobyl nuclear reactor in the Ukraine kills 31 workers and ultimately leads to the deaths of some 10,000 people. The Soviet government attempts to cover up the problem rather than evacuate the area.

1989: Tens of thousands of Chinese students rally for democracy in Beijing's Tiananmen Square. Protests go on for nearly two months, until government troops and tanks crush the uprising. Thousands are killed.

1989: The Iron Curtain begins to crumble, most dramatically in Berlin, where massive protests erupt at the hated Wall on 9 November. Two days later, for the first time in 28 years, the Wall is opened between East and West. The following month, on Christmas Day, the people of Romania execute the dictator Ceausescu and his wife.

1990: Communists in the Soviet Union and Yugoslavia relinquish their monopoly on power. Communist rule also ends in Nicaragua, where the Sandinistas surrender control after Violetta Chamorro wins election as president. East and West Germany reunite, and in Poland, former dissident leader Lech Walesa becomes president.

1993: European nations sign the Maastricht Treaty, which creates the European Union.

1999: In March, NATO begins air strikes against Yugoslavia to stop Serb-led attacks on ethnic Albanians in the Kosovo region.

Event and Its Context

The 1970s were turbulent times in Poland. Like other European countries, it experienced major student-led protests in 1968; in Poland, the demands focused on democracy, cultural freedom, and an end to Soviet interference in Polish affairs. The demonstrations were brutally suppressed and the state engaged in a period of hysterical anti-Semitism to deflect criticism from the regime. The tension never completely diminished. In December 1970 another round of protests against price hikes broke out, this time led by workers at the Lenin Shipyards in Gdansk. After the Gdansk workers marched on the headquarters of the ruling Polish United Workers Party (*Polska Zjednoczona Partia Robotnicza*, PZPR), rioting erupted and management forces drove the workers out of the shipyard by force. In nearby Gdynia, police acted on rumors of sabotage and opened fire on workers who were on their way to the shipyard on the morning of 17 December 1970, killing 13 of them. More died in an uprising in Szczecin that same day.

As smaller strikes broke out around Poland in December 1970, party leader Wladyslaw Gomulka was finally forced out of power after 14 years. Gomulka had come to power during the Polish October of 1956, when he represented destalinization for the PZPR and for Poland. Then seen as hopelessly autocratic and out-of-touch, he was unceremoniously dumped in favor of Edward Gierek. Gierek, who prided himself as a former miner with the common touch, quickly promised a new round of re-

Striking shipyard workers, Gdansk, Poland. © Georges Merillon/Getty Images. Reproduced by permission.

forms, beginning with a price freeze and wage raises. Over the next few years, Gierek redirected the economy to produce more consumer goods and import more western technology. Between 1970 and 1975, per capita wages rose by 40 percent and many Poles indulged in foreign vacations, bought automobiles, and built private houses with the proceeds. The shortage of goods even sent seven million Poles on shopping trips to neighboring East Germany to buy basic supplies in 1974.

With the worldwide energy crisis, however, the Polish economy went into an abrupt tailspin after 1975. With few options available to ease the crisis, Gierek's administration announced drastic price increases on 24 June 1976. Strikes immediately broke out around the country, with thousands of people in Radom converging on the PZPR's headquarters in protest. After the party's offices were ransacked, the police put an end to the demonstration; four lives were lost. The day after the announcement of price increases, Gierek's prime minister withdrew them.

The Workers' Defense Committee (KOR) and the Church

The June 1976 fiasco over price increases proved to be a decisive humiliation for the regime. In response, a group of in-

tellectuals including Jacek Kuron and Adam Michnik formed the Workers' Defense Committee (*Komitet Obrony Robotnikow*, or KOR). Kuron and Michnik realized that the fragmented responses of the intellectuals in 1968 and workers in 1970 had proved counterproductive. They hoped that KOR would build unity among the two groups. Founded to agitate for the release of imprisoned workers and to publicize cases of police brutality, KOR began to publish *Robotnik* (*The Worker*) in September 1977. The newsletter soon expanded to 12 pages and runs of 20,000 copies nationwide. Many of KOR's members also began giving informal talks and lectures around the country as part of a Flying University program. KOR did not maintain a guiding ideology, which gave it a flexibility that allowed it to adapt to the rapidly changing political scene and incorporate members from across the political spectrum.

The Roman Catholic Church also served as a focal point for opposition to the government. Poland's primate, Cardinal Stefan Wyszynski, had fought to keep the church independent from the regime; under his leadership, the church spoke with unrivaled moral authority in the country. The elevation of Poland's Karol Wojtyla to Pope on 16 October 1978 conferred upon the

Strikes in Poland Since the End of Communism

A 2002 study by Rafa Towalski of the Foundation Institute of Public Affairs showed that strikes in Poland declined considerably after the end of communist rule in the early 1990s. Since the communist government had outlawed free organizations of workers, this gave particular moral impetus to the actions of Solidarity in the 1980s, and after communism ended, strikes increased. After 1994, however, the number of work stoppages dropped.

During the first two years of the 1990s, the number of strikes was relatively high—no doubt because of the lifting of communist restrictions—but it did not rise above 305 strikes in 1991. In May 1991 the new democratic government passed an act regulating strikes. The 1991 act forbade strikes that put the public health and security at stake but generally permitted work stoppages in situations where attempts to resolve grievances by other means had been exhausted.

In the two years following the passage of the act, the number of strikes in Poland increased dramatically, rising to 7,443 in 1993. The period from 1994 on, however, saw a precipitous drop. Except for 1999, which experienced a huge number (920) of strikes—most of them by teachers—1994 was the last year when strikes numbered in the triple digits. In 2001 the total number of work stoppages was just 11.

Towalski attributed the decline to a weakening in the role of trade unions, as well as to changes in the views of union members. Unions, she noted, tended to cooperate with management more often than not. Furthermore, union leaders came to regard the strike as a less than effective weapon, and one whose excessive use could cause detriment both to employees and to the companies that provided them with employment.

Source: *European Industrial Relations Observatory.* <http://www.eiro.eurofound.ie>.

—Judson Knight

church an even greater presence in the country. Pope John Paul's first visit to his homeland in June 1979 was a transforming moment for the nation, and his words in support of human rights and dignity empowered the opposition movements.

The Growth of Solidarity

On 1 July 1980, the government announced price hikes on meat; as in 1976, the news was met with a series of strikes across the country. Through July 1980 at least 150 factories struck for higher wages to compensate for inflation; by the end of the month, the economic demands were accompanied by demands for an end to censorship and interference by the government in trade union governance. With KOR as the coordinating body, the strike wave slowly coalesced into a national protest

against the government. The defining moment of the strikes occurred on 14 August 1980, when workers at the Lenin Shipyard in Gdansk occupied the site to protest the firing of crane driver Anna Walentinowicz, who had been dismissed for her constant criticism of the shipyard's management. Lech Walesa, an unemployed electrician who had been fired repeatedly for staging commemorations of the 1970 shipyard protests, emerged as the spokesman for the strikers. By the next day, the rest of Gdansk's shipyards were also shut down; workers in Gdynia joined the protesters. By mid-August 1980 the shipyard strikers announced that they had formed an independent trade union, Solidarity (*Solidarnosc*), and demanded to negotiate with the government over wages, working conditions, censorship, and free trade unionism.

Possibly fearing widespread violence that could lead to a Soviet invasion, Gierek decided to negotiate with Solidarity. The resulting 31 August 1980 Gdansk Agreement—one of three accords that ended the strikes—recognized the right of workers to form independent trade unions and to declare strikes. It also agreed to limit censorship only to protect state secrets; the regime further agreed to broadcast Sunday Mass on state radio each week. Among the economic gains for workers under the new system were increases in the minimum wage and improvements in health services, maternity leaves, and pensions.

As the first recognition of an independent trade union, the Gdansk Agreement was a breakthrough for opposition movements in the Soviet Bloc. Yet Solidarity and the government continued to clash over the implementation of the agreement during 1980 and 1981 at a time when the Polish national economy continued its downward slide. The constant threat of Soviet intervention also played upon tensions between Solidarity and Stanislaw Kania, who took over as the leader of PZPR when Gierek suffered a heart attack in September 1980. Within Solidarity—which grew to include ten million members, or one out of every four adult Poles by the end of 1980—disagreements cropped up over the future of the movement. Many of its members were dismayed by Walesa's call for moderation and patience and urged immediate confrontation with the regime in 1981.

Martial Law

General Wojciech Jaruzelski, commander-in-chief of Poland's armed forces, took over as PZPR leader in October 1981. On 13 December he put the country under martial law as security forces arrested most of Solidarity's leadership. The sudden coup, taken with the suspension of civil liberties in Poland, outraged the international community. By the time martial law was lifted in July 1983, however, Walesa had received the Nobel Peace Prize, Pope John Paul II had made a second visit to Poland, and Solidarity had regrouped its momentum against the government. In October 1984, when leading opposition figure Father Jerzy Popieluszko was murdered by secret police from the interior ministry, hundreds of thousands of Poles turned out for the funeral. After the murder of Father Popieluszko, Jaruzelski's government had little, if any, remaining popular support.

Although Jaruzelski later insisted that his declaration of martial law was undertaken only to prevent a Soviet invasion, the power of the Soviet Union had eroded enough by the late 1980s that the threat was no longer so grave. By 1988, with its economic crisis unabated, the Polish government finally felt compelled to negotiate directly with Solidarity in the face of a renewed strike wave. Secret talks between interior minister Czeslaw Kiszczak and Walesa began in late August 1988 and continued in earnest in February 1989. The resulting Round Table Agreement of April 1989 announced that the offices of President and Senate would be reestablished under free elections. The agreement specified that the parliament (Sejm) would hold 35 freely elected seats and 65 seats would be reserved for PZPR representatives. When the elections took place on 4 June 1989, an overwhelming number of voters chose to cross off the names of PZPR's nominees, and only five of them received enough votes to gain office; in effect, Polish citizens elected almost all Solidarity's candidates in the first round of voting, and clearly rejected the PZPR nominees. A second round of voting on 18 June filled the PZPR's quota of seats, but the damage had been done. On 3 July 1989 Soviet leader Mikhail Gorbachev issued a statement through an envoy that Poland was free to decide its own political future. In August 1989 a coalition government named Tadeusz Mazowiecki as prime minister, the first noncommunist to lead a Soviet Bloc nation. Confirming the end of the country's domination by one party, in January 1990 the PZPR held its final congress. Poland's Communist Party, which had ruled since 1945, was no more.

The fall of the Berlin Wall on 9 November 1989 symbolized for many the end of Communist rule in Eastern Europe, but its downfall had been initiated and sustained after 1980 by Solidarity's leading role as an opposition movement. By the end of 1989 Communist Party leaders had ceded power in Czechoslovakia, East Germany, and Hungary, and the various governments had promised democratic reforms in Bulgaria, Romania, and Yugoslavia. The Soviet Republics of Estonia, Latvia, and Lithuania stated their demands for independence from the Soviet Union. In December 1991 the Soviet Union itself officially ceased to exist. For all of the tumult in its political history, then, Poland had served as the leader of the transition into democracy for the entire region.

The country also led efforts to transform the economy along free-market lines. After taking office in 1989, Mazowiecki immediately announced economic reforms that the press labeled "shock treatment." These reforms were intended to jump start a free-market economy in Poland. Although the immediate effects were indeed painful for many Poles, for the majority of Polish citizens, the presence of Jacek Kuron as minister of labor lent credibility to the government's efforts. In the first presidential elections in 1990, Walesa swept into office for a five-year term. The first free elections in the Sejm in 1991 produced a left-wing coalition of the Left Democratic Alliance (the successor party to the PZRP) and the Polish Peasant Party. Although the coalition butted heads with Walesa during his term in office from 1990–1995, the country made a successful transition into the free market, with the gross national product and per capita income in Poland both growing after 1994.

Key Players

Jaruzelski, Wojciech (1923–): Jaruzelski suffered deportation during the Soviet Union's occupation of Poland in World War II but joined the Polish Communist Army in 1943. He became a general at age 33 and Defense Minister in 1968. Jaruzelski was named prime minister in February 1981 and later became chief of the Communist Party. He served as president of Poland in July 1989 and was defeated in the first free elections for president in November 1990. Since leaving office, Jaruzelski has maintained that he fought to keep the Soviets from invading Poland even as he ruled the country's Communist Party.

John Paul II, Pope, nee Karol Wojtyla (1920–): Karol Wojtyla survived World War II working as a laborer and resumed his studies in theology after the war. He completed his doctorate in 1948. After his ordination, he worked as a parish priest in Krakow and later taught at the Catholic University in Lublin. He was named a Bishop in 1958 and was elevated to Cardinal in 1966. His election as Pope of the Roman Catholic Church in October 1978 came as a surprise, as pontiffs of the previous 455 years had all been Italian. As Pope John Paul II, his visits to Poland in 1979, 1983, and 1987 lent symbolic strength to political reform movements against the Communist regime.

Kuron, Jacek (1934–): Kuron led student protests at Warsaw University in the 1950s and was subsequently sentenced to a three-and-a-half year term in prison for writing an "open letter" with Karol Modzelewski in 1965 that attacked the Communist Party. Kuron was jailed again for participating in the demonstrations of 1968. He helped to form the Workers' Defense Committee (KOR) in 1976 to help bridge the gap between intellectuals and workers. In early 1979 Kuron was a leader of the "Flying University" program of informal lectures to build support for the opposition and remained a leading critic of the government through its transition away from communism.

Michnik, Adam (1946–): The son of communist intellectuals, Michnik was expelled from Warsaw University for taking part in the 1968 protests. He later finished his degree in history at Adam Mickiewicz University and helped found the Workers' Defense Committee (KOR) in 1976. Jailed from 1981 to 1984, and again from 1985 to 1986, Michnik continued to serve as an advisor of Solidarity, most notably during its Round Table discussions with the government in 1989. Elected to the lower house of the Sejm in 1989, Michnik was a cofounder of *Gazeta Wyborcza* as an independent, national daily newspaper.

Walesa, Lech (1943–): Trained as an electrician, Walesa had taken part in the 1970 protests that ended in bloodshed and compiled a lengthy police file for organizing his fellow workers in job protests in the 1970s. In 1979 he helped to found the Solidarity trade union movement and emerged as a leader in the Gdansk shipyard strikes in August 1980. Walesa received the Nobel Peace Prize in 1983. A round–table agreement in April 1989 between Solidarity and the Polish government signaled a transition away from the one-party system that had ruled the country under the communists. In the first free elections in postwar Poland, Walesa was elected President and took office in December 1990. He served as President until 1995.

Wyszynski, Cardinal Stefan (1901–1981): Ordained as a Catholic priest in 1924, Wyszynski served in the underground resistance during World War II. In 1946 he was appointed Bishop of Lublin and in 1949 became the primate of Poland and archbishop of Gniezno and Warsaw. Named a Cardinal in 1953, Wyszynski was jailed by Poland's communist rulers for speaking out against government interference in church affairs and the spiritual life of the nation. Wyszynski was jailed for three years and was released after Wladyslaw Gomulka came to power in 1956. Wyszynski remained a voice of the opposition until his death in 1981.

See also: *Poznan Workers' Riots; USSR Collapse.*

BIBLIOGRAPHY

Books

Asherson, Neal. *The Struggles for Poland.* New York: Random House, 1987.

Garton Ash, Timothy. *History of the Present: Essays, Sketches, and Dispatches from Europe in the 1990s.* New York: Vintage, 1999.

———. *The Magic Lantern: The Revolution of '89 Witnesses in Warsaw, Budapest, Berlin, and Prague.* New York: Random House, 1990.

———. *The Polish Revolution.* New York: Charles Scribner's Sons, 1983.

Goodwyn, Lawrence. *Breaking the Barrier: The Rise of Solidarity in Poland.* New York: Oxford University Press, 1991.

Lukowski, Jerzy, and Hubert Zawadzki. *A Concise History of Poland.* Cambridge: Cambridge University Press, 2001.

Ost, David. *Solidarity and the Politics of Anti-Politics: Opposition and Reform in Poland Since 1968.* Philadelphia: Temple University Press, 1990.

Rosenberg, Tina. *The Haunted Land: Facing Europe's Ghosts After Communism.* New York: Random House, 1995.

Walesa, Lech. *A Way of Hope: An Autobiography.* New York: Henry Holt and Company, 1987.

———. *The Struggle and the Triumph: An Autobiography.* New York: Arcade Publishing, 1992.

Zamoyski, Adam. *The Polish Way: A Thousand-Year History of the Poles and Their Culture.* New York: Franklin Watts, 1988.

—Timothy G. Borden

Steel Seizure Case

United States 1952

Synopsis

On 8 April 1952 President Harry Truman ordered Secretary of Commerce Charles Sawyer to seize control of the U.S. steel industry to avert a strike that, Truman believed, would threaten the nation's security during the Korean conflict. The steel industry immediately brought suit in federal district court. The litigation culminated in *Youngstown Sheet and Tube Co. v. Sawyer* (1952), a landmark case in which the U.S. Supreme Court ruled that the president's action was unconstitutional. In the wake of the Court's decision, the steel industry was returned to private hands and the steelworkers walked off their jobs for nearly eight weeks. *Youngstown Sheet and Tube* and the events before and after it are generally referred to collectively as the *Steel Seizure Case.*

Timeline

1932: Charles A. Lindbergh's baby son is kidnapped and killed, a crime for which Bruno Hauptmann will be charged in 1934, convicted in 1935, and executed in 1936.

1937: Stalin uses carefully staged show trials in Moscow to eliminate all rivals for leadership. These party purges, however, are only a small part of the death toll now being exacted in a country undergoing forced industrialization, much of it by means of slave labor.

1942: Signing of the Declaration of the United Nations in Washington, D.C.

1945: On 7 May, Germany surrenders to the Allied powers. Later in the summer, the new U.S. president, Harry Truman, joins Churchill and Stalin at Potsdam to discuss the reconstruction of Germany. (Churchill is replaced in mid-conference by Clement Attlee as Labour wins control of the British Parliament.)

1947: Establishment of the Marshall Plan to assist European nations in recovering from the war.

1949: Soviets conduct their first successful atomic test. This heightens growing cold war tensions, not least because the sudden acquisition of nuclear capabilities suggests that American spies are passing secrets.

1952: Among the cultural landmarks of the year are the film *High Noon* and the book *The Invisible Man* by Ralph Ellison.

1952: George Jorgenson travels to Copenhagen and returns as Christine Jorgenson. (This is not the first sex-change operation; however, it is the first to attract widespread attention.)

1955: Signing of the Warsaw Pact by the Soviet Union and its satellites in Eastern Europe.

1957: Soviets launch *Sputnik,* the world's first artificial satellite. This spawns a space race between the two superpowers.

1962: As the Soviets begin a missile buildup in Cuba, for a few tense days in October it appears that World War III is imminent. President Kennedy calls for a Cuban blockade, forcing the Soviets to back down and ultimately diffusing the crisis.

1967: Racial violence sweeps America's cities, as Harlem, Detroit, Birmingham, and other towns erupt with riots.

Event and Its Context

The Dispute

The steel seizure dispute pitted the United Steelworkers of America against the entire steel industry. The United Steelworkers represented about 1.1 million members, about 650,000 of them engaged in the basic steel industry at an average hourly wage of $1.88. The steel industry comprised 253 companies that made about 2.1 million tons of steel a week, or 109 million tons per year. About 650,000 stockholders received $320 million in dividends in 1951 out of after-tax industry profits of $690 million.

The controversy began in December 1951 when the union asked for a wage increase in its 1952 contract. Management responded that it could not grant the wage increase unless the government raised the ceiling on steel prices. These and other prices were set by the government to curb inflationary pressures after World War II—a time when both labor and industry sought to make up for lost ground after the wage and price controls imposed during the war. These pressures were increasing as a result of the Korean conflict, but the executive branch was determined to check them. Under the president was the Office of Defense Mobilization, which in turn encompassed the Economic Stabilization Agency (ESA), whose mandate was to control inflation. To carry out its mandate, the ESA directed the activities of two wage and price control agencies: the Wage Stabilization Board (WSB) and the Office of Price Stabilization (OPS).

In March 1952 the WSB, after protracted negotiations with the steelworkers' union and management, worked out a package that would have granted the union a wage increase of 17.5 cents an hour in three steps through June 1953, plus 5.1 cents per hour in fringe benefits—a proposal the union accepted. Management, however, rejected it, arguing that the government had breached its own wage control line, thereby setting a precedent for other unions, which would demand similar wage increases, further increasing the cost of making steel. The steel industry argued that it would have to increase the price of steel by $12 over the average price of $110 per ton: $6 would offset the direct wage increase, and $6 would be needed to pay for increased costs that would come about as suppliers raised prices in response to their unions' wage demands.

For its part, the government argued that the wage package would merely allow the wages of steelworkers to catch up with those of workers in other industries—$1.98 for autoworkers and $2.24 for coal miners, for example. Further, the government maintained that the steel industry could pay the increase out of its profits. Under OPS rules, an industry was not entitled to a price increase unless its profits fell to 85 percent of its best three years from 1946 through 1949; the steel industry's profits were nearly double that, having risen from about $11 per ton in 1947–1949 to over $19 in 1952. The $12 price increase, less the $4–5 per ton cost of the wage settlement, would leave the industry with a profit of $26 or $27 per ton. In his speech announcing the seizure on 8 April 1952, Truman, who believed that the union's demands were reasonable, called management's position "about the most outrageous thing I ever heard of . . . they want to double their money on the deal."

President Harry S Truman signs Foreign Aid Assistance Act, later known as Truman Doctrine. © Hulton Archive/ Getty Images. Reproduced by permission.

The Political Climate

The political climate in early 1952 was a difficult one, both for the president and for the nation. Looming over every presidential decision was the Korean conflict, which was about to enter its third year and had cost the nation 128,000 casualties. Peace talks at Panmunjom were stalemated; alarming reports of communist troop buildups were circulated; riots plagued communist prisoner of war camps. On the domestic front, the war unsettled the American economy, led to an unpopular draft, produced uneven wage and price controls, and fueled inflation. Both the American public and the nation's allies opposed expansion of the war effort.

Truman faced political opposition everywhere he turned. Senator Joseph McCarthy charged that the government, the universities, and the media were "honeycombed with Communists," and the conviction of Julius and Ethel Rosenberg for passing atomic secrets to the Soviets was upheld on appeal. Truman, despite his exemplary record of opposing communist expansion, faced a barrage of charges that the Democratic administration was "soft on communism." In 1952 a coalition of Republicans and southern Democrats in Congress opposed more of the president's legislative proposals than they had in any previous year, while at the same time leveling charges of tax fraud and influence peddling against members of the administration. Frustrated, the president announced in March 1952 that he would not seek reelection.

Battle lines were drawn on the economic front as well. Truman, the haberdasher from Missouri, the "Little Warrior," was at heart prolabor, although some of his actions did not seem to have the interests of labor at heart. Early in his administration, in 1946 in particular, he was concerned about postwar inflation, so he opposed the wage demands of the unions and even threat-

Philip Murray with David McDonald listens to President Harry S Truman's radio broadcast announcing the government would seize the steel plants involved in threatened national strike, 1952. AP/Wide World Photos. Reproduced by permission.

ened to draft striking railroad workers that year. As the election of 1948 approached, one of Truman's most important constituents—the nation's unions and their workers—were bolting from the Democratic camp.

Truman rebuilt his bridges to labor, though, by his opposition to the Labor Management Relations Act of 1947, generally referred to as the Taft-Hartley Act after its congressional sponsors. The act was designed to roll back some of the gains made by labor during the New Deal administration of Truman's predecessor, Franklin D. Roosevelt. The act made closed shops illegal and outlawed secondary boycotts. It allowed states to pass right-to-work laws, enabling them to regulate the number of union shops. It gave the president the power to order an 80-day cooling-off period to halt any strike that threatened the nation's security or safety. It required unions to register and file financial reports, and it required union leaders to take an oath that they were not communists. Truman believed that the bill was punitive, so he vetoed it, but the Republican-controlled 80th Congress overrode his veto. The Taft-Hartley Act drew the labor unions into the political process, and their members over-

whelmingly voted for Truman in his 1948 upset victory over Thomas Dewey.

All of these tensions—war, the economy, politics—led to widespread labor unrest in 1952. That year more strikes occurred than in any year since 1946, with over a half million workers in coal, construction, oil, and other industries walking off their jobs. Labor and management each laid the blame for the nation's stalemate in Korea—and the blood of American troops—at the other's doorstep. In this context, a strike loomed in the nation's most strategic industry, steel.

On 3 April, Philip Murray, president of the United Steelworkers of America, sent a note to the presidents of the steel companies, saying, "You are hereby notified that since a mutually satisfactory agreement has not been reached . . . a strike has been called at the plant of your company . . . effective 12:01 A.M., April 9, 1952." In light of this announcement, the White House had three possible courses of action. One was to invoke the Taft-Hartley law's provision for an 80-day cooling-off period—in effect, an injunction—against the union. Truman, however, was reluctant to take this step, for the union had already deferred its strike for more than three months at the government's request. Additionally, he did not want to alienate Murray, his political ally, by invoking a provision of a law that he, Truman, had vigorously opposed and, in fact, whose repeal he had urged in his 1948 presidential campaign. The second course was to grant some kind of price concession to the industry, perhaps in the $5.50 to $6.50 a ton range.

Truman, however, believed that only a third course of action was open to him—seizure. In his view, Taft-Hartley was designed to settle peacetime labor problems. Wartime labor disputes came under the purview of the Defense Production Act of 1950, which said that it was "the intent of Congress, in order to provide for effective price and wage stabilization . . . and to maintain uninterrupted production, that there be effective procedures for the settlement of labor disputes affecting national defense." Secretary of Commerce Sawyer reported to the president that a shutdown of the steel industry would curtail ship and airplane production and inhibit the nation's ability to make good on its promises to provide allies with war material under the Mutual Defense Assistance Program; Oscar Chapman, secretary of the interior, noted that a steel shutdown would lead to disruption in the oil, gas, coal, and electric industries, all of which relied on steel. All of this, Truman believed, would give succor to the Soviets, who might be tempted to launch further aggression in the belief that U.S. war-making capacity was debilitated.

A Constitutional Crisis

Truman believed in a strong presidency. In a speech on 8 May 1954, he stated that the powers of the president "which are not explicitly written into the Constitution are the powers which no President can pass on to his successor. They go only to him who can take and use them. . . . For it is through the use of these great powers that leadership arises." These views, however, flew in the face of the Constitution's separation of powers among the executive, the legislature, and the judiciary. Specifically, Article II of the Constitution states, "The executive Power shall be vested in a President" and that "he shall take Care that the Laws be faithfully executed." Further, Article II identifies the president as the "Commander in Chief of the Army and Navy of the United States." Truman interpreted these provisions to give him broad inherent powers, including the power to seize the steel industry.

Over the doubts of some members of his administration about the legality of seizure, Truman made his own announcement in a speech delivered at 10:30 P.M. on 8 April—that under Executive Order 10340 the government would "take possession" of the steel mills and keep them operating. Prepared for this step, the companies appeared at 11:30 the next morning in the Federal District Court for the District of Columbia, where Judge Alexander Holtzoff denied the companies' motion for a temporary injunction. On 10 April four of the companies applied to District Judge David A. Pine to schedule a hearing on the matter as soon as possible. Pine obliged, and after hearing arguments, ruled on 29 April that the president's action was devoid of legal justification and issued a preliminary injunction. The union called an immediate strike. The government then filed an application in the U.S. Court of Appeals for the District

of Columbia to stay the injunction, and after a hearing on 30 April, the court granted the stay. With a little bit of breathing room, the government then applied to the U.S. Supreme Court for a writ of certiorari, which the Court granted on 3 May. Given the urgency of the matter, oral arguments before the Court were scheduled for 12 May, giving the government a little over a week to prepare its 175-page brief.

The essence of the government's brief was, first, that the district court had erred in granting injunctive relief; second, that it had erred in reaching and deciding the constitutional issues on a motion for a temporary injunction; and third and most important, that the president had the constitutional authority to take possession of the plaintiffs' steel mills to avert an imminent nationwide halt in steel production. The brief argued that it was not necessary to find a specific clause in the Constitution that gave the president this authority; rather, a reading of history shows that the president had always had such authority, derived inherently from the grants of power in Article II of the Constitution *taken together*. Lincoln, for example, had seized the rail and telegraph lines between Washington and Annapolis during the Civil War; Woodrow Wilson had seized the Smith and Wesson Company for failing to comply with an order of the National War Labor Board during World War I; and Franklin Roosevelt, on at least a dozen occasions, had seized companies threatened by strikes that would weaken the national defense.

The core of the industry's response in its brief was that the president did not have the power to seize private property when Congress had provided a remedy—the Taft-Hartley Act—for dealing with precisely the kind of situation presented in this case. The industry did not dispute that the government has the authority to seize private property in certain circumstances. Its contention was that in this case the wrong branch of government—the executive rather than the legislature—had done so: "The taking of private property by an officer of the United States for public use, without being authorized, expressly or by necessary implication, to do so by some act of Congress, is not the act of the Government."

The Supreme Court's Ruling

The Supreme Court voted quickly on the case, in a conference on 16 May. It did not render its decision, though, until 2 June, when, by a vote of 6 to 3, the Court rejected the government's position and affirmed the judgment of the district court. Justice Hugo Black delivered the opinion of the Court, writing, "There is no statute that expressly authorizes the President to take possession of property as he did here. Nor is there any act of Congress . . . from which such a power can fairly be implied." He went on to say that "the power of Congress to adopt such public policies as those proclaimed by the [executive] order is beyond question. . . . The Constitution does not subject this lawmaking power of Congress to presidential or military supervision or control."

Thus, *Youngstown Sheet and Tube Co. v. Sawyer* entered into the annals of landmark Supreme Court cases bearing on the balance of power among the branches of the U.S. government, a balance that had been upset by the steady accretions to executive power during the Great Depression of the 1930s, the war years of the 1940s, and the early cold war years of the late 1940s and early 1950s. Constitutional scholars point out, how-

Striking steelworkers marching down Broadway Street to Gary Works, U.S. Steel Corporation, Gary, Indiana, 1952. AP/WideWorld Photos. Reproduced by permission.

ever, that the case was not definitive. Seven justices issued separate opinions, the decision of the majority did not appeal to an authoritative precedent, many of the justices relied on dissenting opinions from previous cases in arriving at their conclusions, and the Court generally disregarded the facts showing that the president was acting in an emergency.

The Aftermath

The Supreme Court's decision triggered an immediate strike that shut down the steel industry for 53 days. In the weeks that followed, Congress debated a number of proposals for leg-

islation to end the strike, but passed none of them. On 26 June the House voted to request the president to invoke the Taft-Hartley Act, but the president refused, praising the union and charging that the steel industry was engaged in a conspiracy against the public interest. On 14 July the Chrysler Corporation shut down all of its assembly lines, and steel shortages forced the army to shut down its shell-making plant—the nation's largest—in St. Louis. Finally, on 24 July the White House announced that a settlement had been reached granting the union a 16-cent hourly wage increase and fringe benefits amounting to 5.4 cents per hour. The companies won a $5.20 per ton price increase.

Key Players

Black, Hugo (1886–1971): Black was born in Harlan, Alabama, and began his career as a lawyer, police court judge, and county prosecutor. He was elected to the U.S. Senate in 1927 and became an active supporter of Franklin Roosevelt's New Deal legislation. Roosevelt rewarded him with an appointment to the Supreme Court in 1937, where he served until 1971. Despite his brief membership in the Ku Klux Klan as a youth, he was a vigorous champion of civil rights.

Murray, Philip (1886–1952): Murray was born in Scotland, where he worked as a coal miner before immigrating to the United States in 1902. He rose through the ranks of the United Mine Workers and served as the union's vice president from 1920 to 1941. With John L. Lewis he founded the Committee of Industrial Organizations (CIO) in 1935. Murray succeeded Lewis as its president, an office he held from 1940 to 1952.

Sawyer, Charles (1887–1979): Sawyer was born in Cincinnati, Ohio. He was lieutenant governor of Ohio from 1933 to 1935 and ran unsuccessfully for governor in 1938. From 1944 to 1945 he served as both U.S. ambassador to Belgium and U.S. minister to Luxembourg. In 1948 he was appointed secretary of the U.S. Commerce Department, where he served until 1953. Today, Sawyer is perhaps most remembered for having proclaimed the first National Secretaries' Week (1–7 June 1952).

Truman, Harry S (1884–1972): Born in Lamar, Missouri, Truman, after running a clothing store in Kansas City, began his political career in a succession of county offices, including that of presiding judge on the county court. He was elected to the U.S. Senate in 1935, where he served until he became Franklin Roosevelt's new vice president in 1944. On Roosevelt's death in 1945, Truman became the nation's 33rd president.

See also: *Taft-Hartley Act; United Steelworkers of America.*

BIBLIOGRAPHY

Books

Marcus, Maeva. *Truman and the Steel Seizure Case: The Limits of Presidential Power.* New York: Columbia University Press, 1977.

Westin, Alan F. *The Anatomy of a Constitutional Law Case.* New York: Macmillan, 1958.

Other

"Steel Seizure (A): Supplement." Case Studies in Public Policy Management. Harvard University, John F. Kennedy School of Government [cited 15 October 2002]. <www.ksgcase.harvard.edu/case.htm?PID=309>.

Youngstown Sheet and Tube Company v. Sawyer. 343 U.S. 579 (1952).

—Michael J. O'Neal

Steelworkers Experimental Agreement

United States 1973

Synopsis

After decades of using nationwide strikes as a collective bargaining tool, the United Steelworkers of America (USWA) in 1973 entered into an "Experimental Negotiating Agreement" with the major U.S. steel companies. Under this agreement, the union forfeited the right to strike nationwide in favor of binding arbitration. The steel companies on their part agreed to a yearly 3 percent wage increase and to end stockpiling products. This was the first time a key labor union and an entire industry agreed on their own to settle bargaining conflicts through arbitration. The agreement occurred at a time of growing foreign competition in the steel industry. Despite the perception of increased job security, some rank and file USWA members criticized the secrecy with which the agreement was enacted. The agreement preceded a major depression in the steel industry.

Timeline

1958: China's Mao Zedong proclaims the Great Leap Forward, a program of enforced rapid industrialization that will end a year later, a miserable failure.

1963: Assassination of President Kennedy in Dallas on 22 November.

1968: Communist victories in the Tet offensive mark the turning point in the Vietnam War, and influence a growing lack of confidence in the war, not only among America's youth, but within the establishment as well.

1973: Signing of peace accords in Paris in January ends the Vietnam War.

1973: As the Watergate scandal grows, White House advisers H. R. Haldeman and John D. Ehrlichman resign, and Nixon fires counsel John Dean. Later, Vice President Spiro Agnew resigns. Then, in the October "Saturday Night Massacre," Attorney General Elliot L. Richardson resigns, and Nixon fires special prosecutor Archibald Cox and Deputy Attorney General William D. Ruckelshaus.

1973: Overthrow of Chile's Salvador Allende, the only freely elected Marxist leader in history, who dies in the presidential palace. According to supporters of the new leader, General Augusto Pinochet, Allende committed suicide; but Allende's supporters maintain that he was killed by Pinochet's troops.

1973: Attacked in October, during their Yom Kippur religious festival, the Israelis defeat the combined forces of Egypt, Syria, Iraq, and Jordan. Three weeks later, Arab nations impose an oil embargo on the United States to punish it for its continued support of Israel.

1973: United States launches Skylab, its first space station.

1973: Completion of the twin towers of the World Trade Center in New York City, built at a cost of $750 million.

National Duquesne Works, United States Steel, Duquesne, Pennsylvania. AP/Wide World Photos. Reproduced by permission.

The 110-story buildings are the world's tallest, but by year's end they will be eclipsed by the Sears Tower in Chicago.

1978: More than 900 members of the People's Temple, led by Jim Jones, kill themselves in Jonestown, Guyana. Also dead is Congressman Leo Ryan, who was visiting the Guyana compound and was presumably murdered.

1983: A Soviet fighter plane shoots down a Korean Air Lines 747 that had strayed into Soviet airspace. All 269 passengers, including 61 Americans (among them U.S. Congressman Larry McDonald), are killed.

1988: A terrorist bomb aboard a Pan Am 747 explodes over Lockerbie, Scotland, killing 259 people on the plane and 11 more on the ground.

Event and Its Context

Striking Tradition

From its beginning, the United Steelworkers of America used the threat of strike as their main leverage in collective bar-

Workers at U.S. Steel's Clairton Coke Works, Pittsburgh, Pennsylvania. AP/Wide World Photos. Reproduced by permission.

gaining with the steel companies. By stopping both production and shipping, the union was able to create financial pressure on the companies to bring them to the negotiating table. From the end of World War II through 1959, USWA members joined in simultaneous strikes nationwide. Often exempted from these strikes were a handful of smaller companies that were allowed to continue operation on the condition that they would accept the agreement reached with the major steel companies. Contract negotiations during this postwar period were accompanied by four major steel strikes. The last one, in 1959, was the longest in USWA history, lasting 116 days (before a Taft-Hartley injunction was granted) and affecting 540,000 workers; strikers questioned changing labor conditions and the steel industry's prerogative to abolish unilaterally the standard work practices. With the threat of steel imports, however, the balance of power began to shift away from the unions; the threat of nationwide strike was losing its earlier effectiveness.

As steel industry experts Garth Mangum and Scott McNabb noted in their book *The Rise, Fall and Replacement of Industry-wide Bargaining in the Basic Steel Industry,* the 1959 strike "planted the seeds of eventual dissolution" of industry-wide collective bargaining. The event nonetheless would "not have been pivotal had it not been for its interaction with product-market and technological developments just then emerging in the worldwide steel industry." During the 1959 strike, U.S. customers began importing steel from Europe and Japan. There were no more nationwide strikes after 1959, but the mere threat of one hurt U.S. steelworkers in the marketplace. In the 1960s two major strikes drove domestic buyers to seek foreign steel and domestic manufacturers to stockpile steel. It became increasingly apparent to the union that it needed alternatives to the industry-wide strike.

Experimental Negotiating Agreement

In the late 1960s U.S. steel production faltered. The 1970s brought economic recession and labor unrest. Rather than resorting to the industry-wide strike, the USWA and the major producers of Big Steel entered a ground-breaking agreement. In 1972 USWA President I. W. Abel addressed the union convention, declaring that the time had arrived for the steel industry to sit down with the USWA to explore the "practical advantages and social benefits of smoothing out the production cycle so that, once and for all, we can get rid of the needless boom and slump that now attends our contract negotiations."

In 1973, under Abel's leadership, labor and management wrought the so-called Experimental Negotiating Agreement (ENA), which brought voluntary and final arbitration for unresolved bargaining issues facing the industry in the 1974 negotiations. In exchange for agreements governing job security for steelworkers, the USWA pledged an end to industry-wide lockouts or strikes (though individual plants could address grievances over unresolved local agreements by striking). Moreover, steel companies agreed to end the practice of stockpiling. From that point on, industry-wide issues would be submitted to binding arbitration. After the successful conclusion of the 1974 negotiations, the parties agreed that the ENA would also apply to contract negotiations for 1977. As in 1974, the USWA and the steel companies' coordinating committee would in 1977 and 1980 agree in advance to automatic wage increases of at least

3 percent annually. Moreover, a one-time bonus of $150 was awarded to every worker hired as of 1 August 1974. In addition to wage increases, workers would receive cost-of-living increases based on the rate of inflation. This was to occur regardless of the companies' financial outlook; the increases were derived not from increases in steel company productivity, but rather from national increases in productivity. As a result, the real wages of steelworkers between 1970 and 1980 grew by 29 percent. A precedent in labor history, the ENA marked the first time that a whole industry and a major union agreed to binding arbitration as a means of settling disputes. The 1974 agreement also continued the joint advisory committees on productivity, which were responsible for improving productivity at individual plants. In keeping with the agreement section on "Employment Security and Plant Productivity Committees," committees were to promote the use of American steel, promote harmonious relations at plants, and achieve "prosperity and progress" for the firm and its employees.

At the time, American steel companies were selling all the steel they could produce, so the goal of undisrupted supply seemed a win-win solution. Although both the steel companies and the USWA were attuned to the threat of foreign competitors, the industry counted on a protectionist strategy. Under the list-price system, the big steel companies (generally led by U.S. Steel) published lists that kept steel prices high enough to ensure both high wages and big profits. Most companies followed the price lists, thus allowing a declining industry to show profits even with inefficient, outdated furnaces. Rather than innovate to fight the challenge of foreign steel imports, the steel industry hoped to keep it at bay by lobbying the government for Voluntary Restraint Agreements and similar measures designed to curb steel imports. High U.S. steel prices nonetheless "begged foreign competitors to enter the field."

This alliance between Big Steel and the USWA limited the goals and actions of both parties. Although the steel companies temporarily respected the wages and benefits that had been negotiated with the steelworkers' union, the USWA leadership limited its "ability, willingness, and preparedness" to challenge management plant closings began in the late 1970s. The "unspoken conditions" of the ENA arguably included an unwillingness to discuss true market conditions and thus precluded USWA leadership from questioning the business sense behind plant closures. Moreover, challenging Big Steel "would undermine the joint contention of the steel corporations and the USWA that cheap imports were to blame for industry woes."

Labor's Temporary Gain, Industry's Loss

This unprecedented labor agreement called the ENA proved to be temporary relief for workers in a declining industry that was increasingly threatened by foreign competition. Although the ENA helped prevent strikes and their consequences, some historians contend that wage and benefit gains among American steelworkers contributed to the industry's loss of efficiency and massive decline in the early 1980s. Steel wages rose 179 percent from 1972 to 1982, but productivity did not keep pace. Big Steel, whose productivity grew at a slower rate than that of overseas competitors, faced growing threats from increased productivity abroad. In 1975 Japan surpassed the United States in steel productivity. Where U.S. firms took 10.9 man-hours to make one ton of steel (a modest drop from the 13.1 hours needed in 1964), the Japanese could produce the same quantity in 9.2 hours (a spectacular improvement over the 25.2 hours required in 1964). The higher costs generated by domestic plants thus brought more imports. Moreover, massive integrated steel mills in the United States faced domestic challenges in the phenomenal growth of mini-mills. Rising from a mere 3 percent share of the U.S. market in 1960, mini-mills (which were generally more efficient and boasted greater output per man-hour) would capture 18 percent of the U.S. market share by 1982.

In the late 1970s and early 1980s, the economic downturn and problems facing Big Steel led to massive mill closures and unemployment for hundreds of thousands of steelworkers. Although management took the blame for weak growth in productivity (they had invested millions in outdated, disappearing technology such as the open-hearth furnace), unions were also seen as a factor. As unions fought harder for "featherbedding" rules to provide workers with seniority and greater short-term security, they were criticized for hurting the long-term economic health of employers by inhibiting use of new technology and making the workplace less efficient. Steelworkers at integrated mills found in the ENA temporary relief from a changing market, but both industry and the union were blamed for failing to tie compensation to productivity.

The steel industry's ENA nonetheless served as the touchstone for other unions, and automatic wage increases became a common goal for big-labor contracts. Soon major contracts started including inflation indexing and cost-of-living allowances. As in the steel industry, these raises were automatic (regardless of the financial health of the companies), and union members came to expect them. "At some point, items like indexing and [cost-of-living allowances] became rituals," one labor lawyer later recalled. "We didn't even think of them as contract gains anymore—they were just rights."

Despite perceived gains for steelworkers, not everyone working in the mills was happy with the ENA. Some rank-and-file members of the USWA began to challenge the ENA, charging the union leadership with secretly signing away their right to strike. The ENA, they claimed, surrendered their right to strike before a new three-year contract (1974–1977) had been concluded and ratified, thus stripping the rank and file of their only bargaining tool: the right to leave a job. In 1974 lawyers for the Center for Constitutional Rights represented the workers against this "clear violation of union democracy." The suit of *Aikens et al. v. Abel et al.* was dismissed. The judicial approval of antidemocratic methods prompted the USWA and the steel companies to extend the ENA to cover the 1977–1980 contract negotiations. At this point, the dissenters abandoned the pursuit of their goals in the courtroom and pursued it in the shops.

The 1980s brought a major depression to the American steel industry. More than half the jobs in U.S. steel and iron mines were eliminated. After Big Steel companies dissolved their coordinating committees in 1985, workers at U.S. Steel and Wheeling Pittsburgh experienced lock-outs that lasted months, with the companies unsuccessfully attempting to force pay cuts. Steel companies opened their books to the USWA to prove losses, and most contracts from 1985 to 1987 included cuts. With some companies' financial straits demanding greater

sacrifices than others, wages and benefits at most companies were unequal for the first time in nearly four decades.

Key Players

Abel, Iorwith Wilbur (1908–1987): Abel was an American rolling mill worker and leader of the United Steelworkers of America USWA. He was USWA district director for Canton, Ohio (1942–1952). He later served as third president of the USWA (1965–1977) at the time of the Experimental Negotiating Agreement with steel companies.

See also: *Taft-Hartley Act; United Steelworkers of America.*

BIBLIOGRAPHY

Periodicals

Easterbrook, Gregg. "Voting for Unemployment." *The Atlantic Monthly*, May 1983. <http://www.theatlantic.com/issues/83may/eastrbrk.htm>.

Other

Camp, Scott D., and Westby, David L. "Variation in Worker Protest to Plant Closings: An Extension of the Resource Mobilization Perspective." Paper presented at ASA meeting, Los Angeles, 1994 [cited 22 October 2002]. <http://members.aol.com/scamp6131/sdc_dlw.pdf>.

Center for Constitutional Rights. *CCR Highlights.* "1972–1974" [cited 22 October 2002]. <http://www.ccr-ny.org/about/history04.asp>

"A Retrospective of Twentieth-Century Steel." *New Steel.* November 1999 [cited 22 October 2002]. <http://www.newsteel.com/features/NS9911f2.htm>.

Reynolds, Joy K. "Steel Industry Bargaining." Review of *The Rise, Fall and Replacement of Industrywide Bargaining in the Basic Steel Industry* by Garth L. Mangum and R. Scott McNabb. *Monthly Labor Review Online* 121, no. 5 (May 1998) [cited 22 October 2002]. <http://www.bls.gov/opub/mlr/1998/05/bookrevs.htm>.

United Steelworkers of America, AFL/CIO-CLC. "Workers' Contract Negotiations in the Steel Industry of the United States." 1990, 1996 [cited 22 October 2002]. <http://www.uswa.org/resources/steelnet3.html>.

ADDITIONAL RESOURCES

Books

Mangum, Garth L., and R. Scott McNabb. *The Rise, Fall and Replacement of Industrywide Bargaining in the Basic Steel Industry.* New York: M. E. Sharpe, 1997.

—Brett Allan King

Stock Market Crash

United States 1929

Synopsis

The 1920s are often generalized as a decade of post-war affluence and good times. In reality, however, there was great economic disparity worldwide, which was one of many economic and political factors that precipitated the Great Depression of the 1930s. Nevertheless, the stock market crash of 1929 is the hallmark event frequently said to have brought about these economic hard times.

Various United States economic policies in the 1920s, including tariffs and reparations, decreased the international market for American goods, contributing to economic woes in the U.S. In addition, the nation's productive capacity was greater than its capacity to consume. This prompted credit expansion, which increased public debt. Other credit mechanisms existed that also allowed increased stock market speculation and buying on margin. Those who bought stocks on margin ultimately had to make good on their loan by paying cash or selling the stock, and many opted to sell because of inadequate funds. The federal government had attempted to stem speculative buying, but with little effect.

The stock market crash began Tuesday, 29 October, and continued to fluctuate for the next two weeks. Politicians and financiers expected the economy to self-correct as it had during previous cycles, but it did not, and the effects lasted for years. As *Time* magazine pointed out, in retrospect the blame has been attributed variously to "greedy speculators, Wall Street manipulators, gold merchants, and a carnival of other scapegoats."

John Pierpont Morgan, Jr. The Library of Congress.

Timeline

1914: On the Western Front, the first battles of the Marne and Ypres establish a line that will more or less hold for the next four years.

1919: Treaty of Versailles signed by the Allies and Germany, but rejected by the U.S. Senate. This is due in part to rancor between President Woodrow Wilson and Republican Senate leaders, and in part to concerns over Wilson's plan to commit the United States to the newly established League of Nations and other international duties. Not until 1921 will Congress formally end U.S. participation in the war, but it will never agree to join the League.

1924: In the United States, Secretary of the Interior Albert B. Fall, along with oil company executives Harry Sinclair and Edward L. Doheny, is charged with conspiracy and bribery in making fraudulent leases of U.S. Navy oil reserves at Teapot Dome, Wyoming. The resulting Teapot Dome scandal clouds the administration of President Warren G. Harding.

1927: Charles A. Lindbergh makes the first successful solo nonstop flight across the Atlantic and becomes an international hero.

1929: The Lateran Treaty between the Catholic Church and Mussolini's regime establishes the Vatican City as an independent political entity.

1929: Edwin Hubble proposes a model of an ever-expanding universe.

1931: Financial crisis widens in the United States and Europe, which reel from bank failures and climbing unemployment levels. In London, armies of the unemployed riot.

1933: Newly inaugurated U.S. president Franklin D. Roosevelt launches the first phase of his New Deal to put depression-era America back to work.

1935: Second phase of New Deal begins with the introduction of social security, farm assistance, and housing and tax reform.

1941: Japanese bombing of Pearl Harbor on 7 December brings the United States into the war against the Axis. Combined with the attack on the Soviet Union, which makes Stalin an unlikely ally of the Western democracies, the events of 1941 will ultimately turn the tide of the war.

1944: Creation of International Monetary Fund and World Bank at Bretton Woods Conference.

New York Stock Exchange Building, 24 October 1929. AP/Wide World Photos. Reproduced by permission.

Event and Its Context

Numerous significant events preceded the stock market crash. Some economists trace the start of these events to 1928. Just six months prior to the crash, the stock market was at a record high; by 29 October, the market was down 40 percent, and it lost 11.5 percent in a single day. That day was Tuesday, 29 October, commonly called "Black Tuesday." The previous Thursday had been a record day for the market, with a record of 13 million shares traded. This was four times the previous record. The Dow had fallen 20 percent that day but rallied the following day. More bad news on Monday, 28 October, sent the Dow down 13.5 percent, but the market did not recover.

One factor said to have led to the crash was the ability of investors to buy on margin. Buying on margin is a type of loan enabling people to buy stock against possible future profits, and such loans were notoriously easy to obtain. There were reports of working men and women obtaining margin loans with very little collateral. Stocks were easily purchased for about 10 percent cash. There were some three million investors about this time, many of whom were new and inexperienced and purchased stocks based on tips and bad advice. By enabling speculation and bad trading, these loans caused average working people to lose their savings when the market fell. They also adversely affected banks.

John W. Poole addresses crowd of depositors after shareholders start run on bank. © Hulton-Deutsch Collection/Corbis. Reproduced by permission.

It is also telling that the actual number of stock market investors in 1929 is widely debated. In *Panic on Wall Street*, Robert Sobel says that corporations were reporting 20 million investors. A more realistic number provided by the United States Treasury chief actuary, Joseph McCoy, is three million, which did not include speculators. Sobel says that these figures are difficult to calculate, because many people had more than one—as many as twelve or more—active brokerage accounts. In 1929 there were about 120 million brokerage accounts. The number of margin accounts was about 600,000.

The Market Crashes

There were warnings prior to the crash, but they were largely ignored. Political and financial leaders repeatedly pronounced the national economy "absolutely sound." Share prices had climbed unusually high in an 18-month period and reached a historic high on 3 September 1929. Days later Roger Babson—a statistician some considered eccentric—addressed the National Business Conference. He told them, "Sooner or later, a crash is coming, and it may be terrific." Benjamin Strong,

When Companies Go Bankrupt

Following the 1929 stock market crash, numerous American companies went bankrupt, putting thousands upon thousands of workers on the street. In later years, federal and state governments put in place measures to prevent another devastating crash, as well as safety nets to protect workers if something of that nature did occur.

Though no crash since 1929 has been nearly as severe, the events that attended the economic boom at the end of the late 1990s left a great number of workers without jobs. Starting in 2001, companies that had profited during the boom by falsifying earnings information began to shut their doors, and in many cases executives left their offices in handcuffs. Given the declarations of bankruptcy in those cases, workers might have been forced to give up any hope of collecting on promised benefits, but conditions had changed a great deal since 1929.

After the once-great telecommunications giant WorldCom went bankrupt amid charges of executive corruption in July 2002, the Ex-WorldCom Employee Assistance Fund, with the help of the AFL-CIO, initiated legal proceedings to ensure that former employees received benefits due to them. On 1 October 2002 the U.S. Bankruptcy Court for the Southern District of New York ruled that nearly 9,000 laid-off employees should receive the full severance, commissions, health care, paid vacation, and other benefits that WorldCom owed them. This followed a 3 September judgment whereby the AFL-CIO and laid-off workers from Enron, another bankrupted former giant, won a historic $34 million severance pay agreement.

Source: "Judge Rules WorldCom Workers Will Get Full Severance and Other Benefits." *AFL-CIO*. <http://www.afl-cio.org/news/2002/1002_worldcom.htm>.

—Judson Knight

Before the closing bell sounded on Wednesday, 23 October, 2.6 million shares had sold in the final hour of trading.

When the exchange opened the next day, trading became even more frantic. As stocks were being dumped, prices plunged. According to a *Time* magazine account, "Outside in the streets, people began drifting toward the pillared exchange building and assembling there as though it were some royal palace where a king lay dying." The crowd was in shock. Some reportedly stormed the visitors' gallery to see firsthand what was transpiring on the floor. "They screamed as they noted the large declines," wrote Sobel, "others wept, or looked upon the tumult as through it were the end of the world. At 11 A.M. the gallery was closed, to keep the hysterical and the morbid from the scene."

More than $9.5 billion in paper value was lost during the first two hours of trading. By noon, several bankers assembled at J. P. Morgan to discuss the situation, including representatives of Chase National, Guaranty Trust, Bankers Trust, and First National. These men were in charge of more than $6 billion in assets. They created a pool with which they would purchase stocks to buoy the market financially, hoping to reverse the market's fortunes. The amount said to be involved varies widely—between $20 million and $240 million, though the more likely figure is between $20 and $30 million. The pool purchases were made soon after the meeting ended. Richard Whitney, acting exchange president, purchased 10,000 shares of U.S. Steel. Cheers reportedly arose from the floor. Traders knew it was an attempt to shore market confidence. Whitney made several other above-market purchases of blue-chip stocks, and some ultimately gained. At closing, more than 13 million shares of stock were traded; stocks were only twelve points below those of the previous day.

Although this day is marked as the start of economic problems, the problem lingered for weeks. The demonstration of confidence by bankers had been a temporary fix. There were discussions about closing the market, but it was decided to allow operations to continue in the hope that the market would self-correct. Other recessions and poor markets had corrected with time; why would this be any different? The market continued to yo-yo. It was 13 November when the market reached its low. Between September and November, the stock market lost $30 billion in value.

Consumer Attitudes and the Federal Reserve System

In the late 1920s the global economy was still recovering from World War I. In the United States this era was also marked by a shift in consumer attitudes. New products, notably automobiles and electrical appliances, were available. New forms of credit were also becoming available, allowing people to purchase goods on the installment plan, which changed savings habits as well. American consumers also had greater personal disposable income. In 1919 disposable income was 4.64 percent; it was 9.34 percent by 1929.

Ironically, consumption was down dramatically. Terms for buying on installment were changed to encourage people to purchase, but thrift was a concept so ingrained in most people and so equated with morality that luxury spending remained rare. As Oscar Wells, former president of the American Bankers' Association observed, "Since the war particularly, we have

chair of the Federal Reserve Bank of New York, was also concerned and repeatedly advised the Federal Reserve Bank to raise its interest rates to restrain out of control speculation.

These opinions, however, were counter to those of most United States economists, including those from august institutions such as Stanford and Princeton universities. They stated publicly that stock prices would continue to rise. As Sobel says, this was exactly what the public wanted to hear. "There were few bears on Wall Street, and fewer still on university campuses throughout the nation."

By October 1929 the economic signs could not have become any clearer. Home building was down appreciably; farming was in bad shape and had been for years; automobile sales and industrial production were down; and stocks were down, prompting brokers to initiate margin calls. Those who had purchased stocks on credit had to give their brokers cash. If they did not have the cash by the deadline, the stocks would be sold.

taught that thrift is an attribute, greatly to be sought after. There is no consistency in preaching this doctrine on the one hand and, on the other, of encouraging an indulgence in buying on the installment plan at a cost ranging from fifteen to forty percent for the privilege."

Fingers are frequently pointed in the direction of the Federal Reserve system, which had been operational only since 1914. Officials saw the economy contracting, but they did not adopt policies to halt the recession. Had they been more proactive, a total economic collapse might have been avoided; this is a point that has been debated frequently. Federal Reserve officials were divided as to what would help the economy. They eventually believed that the buildup of installment credit during the 1920s was a key factor in precipitating the downward cycle. Although economic scholars have presented new views about the causes of the Great Depression, some economists including John Kenneth Galbraith believe that the crash was to blame. Other economists now say that the Great Depression was triggered not by the crash but by devotion to the gold standard and other federal monetary policies.

The gold standard had just been resumed after World War I and was still shaky. Currency throughout the world was tied to gold, which was deemed the critical factor in the international economy. Regulating the economy while keeping the gold standard meant that both prices and wages had to fall. Moreover, the United States was not the only country trying to preserve the gold standard. Between 1923 and 1928 there was a worldwide attempt to restore the gold standard, and this strategy was generally seen as the key to a stable international monetary system. It was also hoped that it would spur international trade and speed global economic recovery, which had begun tentatively in 1924.

Folktales Versus Reality

There is no question that the stock market crash of 1929 assumed mythical proportions, particularly in retrospect. One persistent myth concerns distraught brokers and investors who supposedly took their lives, jumping out of office buildings as fortunes were lost. Demographics, however, clearly refute this. Between 15 October and 13 November 1929, the suicide rate in Manhattan was lower than it had been the previous year.

"Wild were the rumors of ruin and suicide," according to one *Time* report of the day. "It has always remained part of American legend that Black Thursday featured stockbrokers leaping from skyscraper windows, but specific instances are hard to find." One such inconclusive report involved the president of Union Cigar, who either jumped or tumbled off a hotel ledge. His company stock had dropped from 113 to 4. The actual number of suicides between 24 October 1929 and 1 January 1930 was eight, two of which were on Wall Street. According to *American Demographics,* "less than one percent of suicides in the U.S. between October and December 1929 were because of the stock market crash."

Another common myth actually fueled stock speculation. Stories circulated about some working person—often a shoeshine boy or waitress—getting a hot stock tip. Once they had invested their savings in a certain stock, they were able to make millions. Author Robert Sobel says that, rather than distorting events, it is more appropriate to consider the crash as "destined

to become a symbol for the reality of 1930 and the decade that followed, and that one should take care not to confuse the symbol with the reality."

Worldwide Depression

The Great Depression, supposedly triggered by the crash, did not occur solely in the United States but was a global depression, the effects of which could be felt throughout the Americas and Europe. European nations, still recovering from World War I, were particularly affected. The crash has been said to have precipitated numerous economic and political problems worldwide. The poor German economy, for example, contributed to the unchecked political ascendance of Adolf Hitler. Banking problems in Germany and Austria as well as the United States also contributed to further worldwide monetary woes. Domestically, there were an estimated 16 million people unemployed. The stock market would continue falling. Declines in unemployment, production, and prices continued.

The Federal Reserve, however, raised interest rates in 1928 and 1929 in attempts to halt market speculation. Conditions in 1929, coupled with federal economic policies, triggered a recession as well as an economic snowball effect. Corporations cut spending, followed by cuts in production, which meant that employment was cut back. This also meant that consumers were spending less. With demand for consumer goods off, the economy continued to contract. "The Federal Reserve slashed the money supply at a time when it should have expanded it," says Paul Ormerod. And George Selgin wrote, "Indeed, government errors were so extensive as to make one wonder whether the depression was inevitable, and whether it would have earned the epithet 'Great' had governments limited themselves to a classical 'hands-off' approach."

Key Players

Babson, Roger: One of the few people to publicly state the stock market was headed for problems, his views were in the minority. He did, however, correctly predict there would be a crash.

Hoover, Herbert (1874–1964): Born in Iowa, Hoover studied engineering at Stanford University. He had served as secretary of commerce under both Warren G. Harding and Calvin Coolidge. Hoover had just become president at the time of the stock market crash.

Mellon, Andrew W. (1855–1937): Secretary of the Treasury (1921–1932), Mellon was influential in shaping government financial polices.

McCoy, Joseph: McCoy was chief actuary of the United States Treasury at the time of the stock market crash.

Morgan, John Pierpont, Jr. (1867–1943): Head of J. P. Morgan & Company, Morgan's business was at the crux of the United States and world economy. The firm had issued bonds for various nations in the Americas and Europe between 1917 and 1928. He was also on the several committees influential in determining war reparations. At the time of the crash, it was in the offices of J.P. Morgan & Company that bankers met to form a financial pool in an attempt to halt the crash. Ironically, Morgan was not in the country at the time of the stock market crash.

Norris, George W.: Governor of the Philadelphia Federal Reserve Bank (1920–1936), Norris was very vocal in the debates about installment credit.

Simmons, E. H. H.: President of the New York Stock Exchange at the time of the crash.

Strong, Benjamin (1872–1928): Born in Fishkill, New York, Strong was involved in the financial industry throughout his life. He was president of the Bankers' Trust Company when the Federal Reserve system was created in 1914. He was appointed governor of the Federal Reserve Bank of New York. Strong was concerned about how federal policies contributed to recessions. Although he died the year prior to the crash, Strong had been very influential in domestic and international finance. He was perceived abroad as the head of the Federal Reserve system.

Whitney, Richard (1888–1974): Acting president of the stock exchange at the time of the market crash, he is often credited with helping stabilize the panicked market by purchasing shares of U.S. Steel. Whitney was actually the exchange's vice president; the body's president was out of the country in October 1929. He was president of the exchange after this and served four terms. Whitney was found guilty of malfeasance in 1938. He served three years at Sing Sing Prison.

Young, Roy A.: Young started his banking career in Michigan. The Federal Reserve Bank of Minneapolis hired him in 1917. He was governor of the bank, but resigned to become a governor on the Federal Reserve Board in 1927. Young was most concerned about the effect speculation would have on the economy and frequently advised President Herbert Hoover to take decisive actions to control it.

See also: *National Industrial Recovery Act; Wagner Act.*

BIBLIOGRAPHY

Books

Foner, Eric and John A. Garraty, eds. *The Reader's Companion to American History.* Boston: Houghton Mifflin, 1991.

Garraty, John A. *The Great Depression: An Inquiry into the Causes, Course, and Consequences of the Worldwide Depression of the Nineteen-Thirties, As Seen by Contemporaries and in the Light of History.* New York: Doubleday, 1987.

Nishi, Dennis, ed. *The Great Depression.* San Diego: Greenhaven, 2001.

Sobel, Robert. *Panic on Wall Street: A History of America's Financial Disasters.* Washington, DC: Beard, 1999.

Periodicals

Dwyer, Victor. "Look Back in Anger: Pierre Berton Finds Villainy in the 1930s." *Maclean's* 103, no. 37 (10 September 1990): 79–80.

Edmondson, Brad. "Dying for Dollars." *American Demographics* 9, no. 10 (October 1987): 14–15.

Friedrich, Otto. "Once Upon a Time in October . . . A Jazz-Age Tale of Shattered Illusions and Vanished Fortunes." *Time* 130, no. 18 (2 November 1987): 54–55.

Kubik, Paul J. "Federal Reserve Policy During the Great Depression: The Impact of Interwar Attitudes Regarding Consumption and Consumer Credit." *Journal of Economic Issues* 30, no. 3 (September 1996): 829–842.

Norton, Rob. "Lessons of the Great Depression." *Fortune* 136, no. 4 (18 August 1997): 36.

O'Brien, Patrick. "The Economic Effects of the Great War." *History Today* 44, no. 12 (December 1994): 22–29.

Ormerod, Paul. "How to Stop a Great Depression." *New Statesman* 127, no. 4406 (9 October 1998): 11–12.

Selgin, George. "The Great Depression: An International Disaster of Perverse Economic Policies." *Southern Economic Journal* 65, no. 3 (January 1999): 653–656.

Svaldi, Aldo. "1929 The Crash." *Denver Business Journal* 51, no. 12 (12 November 1999): 27.

—Linda Dailey Paulson

Strike Ban Lifted

France 1864

Synopsis

On 25 May 1864 the French *Corps Legislatif* passed the Coalitions Law, effectively granting French workers the right to strike. The law revised earlier legislation that had classified the formation of workers' coalitions, or labor unions, as a criminal offense. For most of the early nineteenth century, French governments had regarded strikes, and indeed most forms of labor organization, as a serious transgression against the rights of industry. However, during the Second Empire, the government embarked upon a program of liberal reform, which made it look more kindly upon the requests of workers to be granted the right to strike. The 1864 change in the law was part of an attempt on the part of Napoleon III to woo the laboring classes and secure the Second Empire on a broad base of popular support. The law was not successful in this sense, as it failed to win the workers' gratitude and loyalty; instead, it contributed to an increase in labor agitation and militancy. Nevertheless, the law was a significant shift in the attitude of French authorities towards the rights of workers and stimulated the development of trade union activity in the later nineteenth century.

Timeline

1844: Samuel Laing, in a prize-winning essay on Britain's "National Distress," describes conditions in a nation convulsed by the early Industrial Revolution. A third of the population, according to Laing, "hover[s] on the verge of actual starvation"; another third is forced to labor in "crowded factories"; and only the top third "earn[s] high wages, amply sufficient to support them in respectability and comfort."

Napoleon III.

1849: Elizabeth Blackwell becomes the first woman in the United States to receive a medical degree.

1854: In the United States, the Kansas-Nebraska Act calls for decisions on the legality of slavery to be made through local votes. Instead of reducing divisions, this measure will result in widespread rioting and bloodshed and will only further hasten the looming conflict over slavery and states' rights.

1857: Start of the Sepoy Mutiny, an unsuccessful revolt by Indian troops against the British East India Company. As a result of the rebellion, which lasts into 1858, England places India under direct crown rule.

1860: Louis Pasteur pioneers his method of "pasteurizing" milk by heating it to high temperatures in order to kill harmful microbes.

1862: Victor Hugo's *Les Misérables* depicts injustices in French society, and Ivan Turgenev's *Fathers and Sons* introduces the term *nihilism.*

1864: General William Tecumseh Sherman conducts his Atlanta campaign and his "march to the sea."

1864: Founding of the International Red Cross in Geneva.

1864: George M. Pullman and Ben Field patent their design for a sleeping car with folding upper berths.

1866: Austrian monk Gregor Mendel presents his theories on the laws of heredity. Though his ideas will be forgotten for a time, they are destined to exert enormous influence on biological study in the twentieth century.

1870: Beginning of Franco-Prussian War. German troops sweep over France, Napoleon III is dethroned, and France's Second Empire gives way to the Third Republic.

1873: The gold standard, adopted by Germany in 1871 and eventually taken on by all major nations, spreads to Italy, Belgium, and Switzerland. Though the United States does not officially base the value of its currency on gold until 1900, an unofficial gold standard dates from this period, even as a debate over "bimetallism" creates sharp divisions in American politics.

Event and Its Context

Antiunion Laws

The history of labor legislation in nineteenth-century France began with the Le Chapelier Law of 1791. Intended to buttress the liberty of industry that had been established with the abolition of the trade corporations, the law forbade any citizens from acting together in the interests of their profession. While this was intended to prevent both employers and workers from forming coalitions, in practice it was used almost exclusively to prevent workers from organizing. In the Napoleonic Era additional legislation was implemented to prevent workers from organizing for economic or political reasons. A law enacted on 22 Germinal, Year XI (11 April 1803) specifically banned workers from organizing with the aim of challenging established wages or hours of work. This ban was reconfirmed in 1810 by Articles 414, 415, and 416 of the Napoleonic Penal Code, which also increased the penalty for leading a strike from two years to five. Workers' mutual aid societies were also technically illegal but were tolerated during the Napoleonic and Restoration period. In 1834, in response to waves of strikes following the radicalization of workers after the 1830 revolution, the July Monarchy passed more repressive laws making any gathering of more than 20 people potentially illegal. (*July Monarchy* refers to the Restoration government of France, 1830–1848. It was charged with preserving the principles of the French Revolution, which began in July 1789, while simultaneously restoring and maintaining civil order.) For the first half of the nineteenth century, most attempts by workers to organize were regarded as an attack on the rights of industry. Therefore, workers had little recourse to protest against exploitation or unfair work practices. The state had at its disposal a formidable arsenal of legal regulations designed to prevent workers from organizing.

Labor in the Second Empire

Louis Napoleon (Napoleon III) had an interest in the problems of labor dating back to the 1830s. He concluded that the support of the workers was crucial to the success of Bonapartism. During the 1848 revolution, he had received the support of democrats and republicans and even briefly convinced the socialist theorist Louis Proudhon of his commitment to social change. However, after the coup d'etat in 1851, the Second Empire was dependent on the traditional elites, who supported Napoleon III as a bulwark against the workers and the extreme left.

The brief toleration of labor organization that occurred during the Second Republic was replaced with repression and surveillance by an authoritarian regime, which alienated the workers. However, Napoleon remained committed to projecting an image of himself as a populist ruler. Convinced that the July Monarchy had foundered because it had alienated the workers, he wanted the regime to show concern for the problems of the laboring classes. To this end, government propaganda attempted to convince the workers of the benefits of the Second Empire. The regime tried to present itself as an impartial judge in industrial disputes, and local administrators were instructed to act neutral in labor disputes, to the extent that some major industrial companies accused local prefects of siding with workers. The government showed itself to be willing to intervene in the market to help soften the impact of economic fluctuations. It also provided financial aid to workers' mutual aid societies, as long as these concentrated on self-help rather than economic or social agitation. The extensive public works of the era, such as Baron Hausmann's redesign of inner city Paris, were also touted by the regime as beneficial to the workers, although the thousands made homeless by the project may have disagreed.

Despite these efforts, the working classes remained suspicious of the regime. It was apparent that they needed more than paternal gestures of good will to win them over. Many workers were openly discussing topics such as the right to strike and form trade unions. It was these kinds of issues that the Second Empire needed to address, if it was to be seen as responsive to the concerns of the laboring classes. The regime's need to gain the trust of the workers became more urgent as its support from other sources dropped away. This was demonstrated in poor election results for the government in the late 1850s and early 1860s. Free trade policies and support of the nationalist cause in Italy had alienated much of the Second Empire's support. In response, the emperor embarked upon a concerted policy of liberalization and reconciliation with the left. Serious overtures towards the laboring classes began around 1860, when the emperor's liberal cousin, Prince Napoleon, set up a worker's discussion group that came to be known as the *Palais Royal*. While this group helped produce Bonapartist propaganda aimed at the workers, it also served as a channel through which the regime could become acquainted with issues that concerned the workers. The group was closely involved with the organization of a workers' delegation to the 1862 London exposition, which was supported by the government.

In this atmosphere of greater concern for the grievances of the workers, strikes became more widely tolerated. The case of the 1862 printers' strike highlighted the changing attitudes. Several printers who struck for a wage increase were charged under the antiunion laws. The liberal lawyer Armand Levy defended their case. Nine workers were convicted of violating the laws against strikes, but Napoleon III personally intervened to grant clemency to the men. This indicated both the emperor's intent to appear as the champion of the workers and the regime's softening attitude towards strikes. From 1862 the government-authorized newspaper, *L'Opinion Nationale,* began a campaign calling for a repeal of the ban on strikes. The right to strike was regarded by many left-wing liberals as a natural corollary of the liberalization of trade. The 1860 Cobden-Chevalier commercial treaty with Great Britain opened France up to a more competitive economic environment. The ensuing expansion of industry created the possibility of greater exploitation and hardship for workers. Unless the government was willing to prevent this by intervening more actively in the complicated arenas of wages, hours, and working conditions, allowing the workers permission to strike seemed the easiest way to normalize labor relations.

The 1864 Coalitions Law

Therefore, the desire to win over the workers and left-wing sections of society resulted in a government investigation into the legalization of strikes. The liberal politician Emile Ollivier was appointed as the head of the committee appointed to consider the matter. The resulting legislation was a product of Ollivier's research into the English Combination Act of 1825, which had legalized strikes in certain circumstances. The Coalitions Law of 1864 modified Article 414, 415, and 416 of the penal code. By removing the word "coalition" from the category of actions regarded as criminal, the amendment effectively recognized the legal right of workers to strike. However, certain acts associated with coalition remained punishable crimes. These acts included the use of "violence, coercion, threats or fraudulent maneuvers" in the attempt to bring about a strike, or the use of fines, prohibitions, or bans in plans to prevent people from working. This meant that while workers were allowed to strike, there were severe limits on the methods that they could use to organize strikes, and they were prevented from taking any actions against strikebreakers.

Consequences

Napoleon III's hopes of achieving reconciliation with the left through the reform failed. The legislation received a mixed reception and was attacked by both the left and the right for a variety of reasons. Predictably, representatives of industry were opposed to the change in legislation, arguing that granting workers the right to strike would result in an increase in strikes and disruption to industry. However, the workers and left-wing liberal supporters of the right to strike were not satisfied either. They had sought a straight repeal of the antiunion laws and were not impressed with the reservations and provisos that Ollivier had written into the legislation. While the act of organizing itself may have no longer been a punishable offense, too many actions associated with strikes were still regarded as crimes. In particular, the definition of the vague term *fraudulent maneuvers* as criminal offenses caused concern, as authorities could interpret almost any activity associated with striking as a fraudulent maneuver. In addition, the right to strike was somewhat hollow without the accompanying right to hold public meetings. Without this right, trade union organization was subject to police harassment, and only spontaneous strike activity was technically legal. This placed a limit on the extent of labor organization, although the regime did become broadly tolerant of workers' meetings and organizations. Changes to the laws of association in 1868 allowed union meetings under certain conditions, but trade unions were not officially legalized in France until 1884.

Despite the continued restrictions, it is generally agreed by historians that the legislation did lead to an increase in strikes. Instead of normalizing labor relations and reconciling the workers with the government, however, the mid-to-late 1860s saw a rise in industrial militancy, as workers took the opportunity to organize and press their demands for better wages, hours, and working conditions. After so many years of authoritarian repression, the liberalization of the Second Empire was interpreted not as a gesture of reconciliation, but rather as a sign of weakness that invited exploitation. Government officials complained of the ingratitude of the workers in abusing the right to strike granted them by a benevolent emperor. However, many French workers felt that improvements in wages and conditions would have to be torn from recalcitrant employers rather than bestowed upon them. This controversy provided a major stimulus to the development of the French labor movement.

Key Players

Levy, Armand (1827–1891): Liberal lawyer and journalist during the French Second Empire. Levy had been a revolutionary opposed to Napoleon III but moved closer to the regime in the early 1860s. He defended several printers charged with breaking the laws against strikes and contributed to the newspaper campaign seeking the repeal of laws against workers' coalitions.

Napoleon III (1808–1873): Louis Napoleon, nephew of Napoleon Bonaparte and emperor of the French Second Empire. Louis Napoleon's desire to win the workers' support was the main impetus behind the 1864 Coalitions Law, which effectively granted French workers the right to strike.

Ollivier, Emile (1825–1913): Liberal lawyer, responsible for drafting the 1864 legislation. Originally a republican, Ollivier alienated liberal colleagues by collaborating with the government in the drafting of the legislation.

See also: *June Days Rebellion; Paris Commune.*

BIBLIOGRAPHY

Books

Kulstein, David I. *Napoleon III and the Working Class.* Los Angeles: Ward Ritchie Press, 1969.

Magraw, Roger. *A History of the French Working Class.* Vol. 1, *The Age of Artisan Revolution, 1815–1871.* Cambridge, MA: Blackwell, 1992.

Price, Roger. *Napoleon III and the Second Empire.* London: Routledge, 1997.

Shorter, Edward and Charles Tilly. *Strikes in France.* New York: Cambridge University Press, 1974.

Zeldin, Theodore. *Emile Ollivier and the Liberal Empire of Napoleon III.* Oxford, England: Clarendon Press, 1963.

ADDITIONAL RESOURCES

Books

Judt, Tony. *Marxism and the French Left: Studies in Labour and Politics in France, 1830–1981.* Oxford, England: Clarendon Press, 1986.

Magraw, Roger. *France, 1815–1914: The Bourgeois Century.* New York: Oxford University Press, 1983.

—Katrina Ford

Strike Wave

Italy 1919

Synopsis

Beginning in 1919, Italy was devastated by social, economic, and political problems. Real wages had fallen over 35 percent, shortages had developed in a wide variety of consumer goods, and prices had risen sharply. In spite of Italy having been on the winning side in World War I, it was nonetheless losing its struggle for postwar readjustment with respect to high inflation, out-of-control debt, and increasing unemployment. In the two years following the war, the Italian government was unable to turn around the nation's political and social problems with practical goals and effective policies. Workers in both industry and agriculture were actively seeking change, in some cases even resorting to violence.

The Italian Socialist Party (PSI), which eventually became the Italian Communist Party, was a labor party that reflected the class consciousness and rebelliousness of the Italian working class. Some of the party's militant leaders joined with Italy's first enduring trade union, the General Confederation of Labor (CGL) in 1919 to incite the already unruly workers and peasants to the edge of revolution. During 1919 three overriding issues confronted the already-volatile labor community: length of the workday; inflation and shortages; and wage increases. The inability of the government to address these issues adequately led to a series of massive strikes that spread throughout the country.

Timeline

1900: China's Boxer Rebellion, which began in the preceding year with attacks on foreigners and Christians, reaches its height. An international contingent of more than 2,000 men arrives to restore order, but only after several tens of thousands have died.

1907: U.S. markets experience a financial panic.

1912: *Titanic* sinks on its maiden voyage, from Southampton to New York, on 14 April. More than 1,500 people are killed.

1915: At the Second Battle of Ypres, the Germans introduce a terrifying new weapon: poison gas.

1917: The intercepted "Zimmermann Telegram" reveals a plot by the German government to draw Mexico into an alliance against the United States in return for a German promise to return the southwestern U.S. territories taken in the Mexican War. Three months later, in response to German threats of unrestricted submarine warfare, the United States on 6 April declares war on Germany.

1919: Formation of the Third International (Comintern), whereby the Bolshevik government of Russia establishes its control over communist movements worldwide.

1919: Treaty of Versailles signed by the Allies and Germany but rejected by the U.S. Senate. This is due in part to rancor between President Woodrow Wilson and Republican Senate leaders, and in part to concerns over Wilson's plan to commit the United States to the newly established League of Nations and other international duties. Not until 1921 will Congress formally end U.S. participation in the war, but it will never agree to join the League.

1919: Ratification of the Eighteenth Amendment, which prohibits the production, sale, distribution, purchase, and consumption of alcohol throughout the United States.

1919: In India, Mahatma Gandhi launches his campaign of nonviolent resistance to British rule.

1919: In Italy, a former socialist of the left named Benito Mussolini introduces the world to a new socialism of the right, embodied in an organization known as the "Union for Struggle," or Fasci di Combattimento. Composed primarily of young war veterans discontented with Italy's paltry share of the spoils from the recent world war (if not with their country's lackluster military performance in the conflict), the fascists are known for their black shirts and their penchant for violence.

1921: As the Allied Reparations Commission calls for payments of 132 billion gold marks, inflation in Germany begins to climb.

1925: European leaders attempt to secure the peace at the Locarno Conference, which guarantees the boundaries between France and Germany, and Belgium and Germany.

1929: On "Black Friday" in October, prices on the U.S. stock market, which had been climbing wildly for several years, suddenly collapse. Thus begins the first phase of a world economic crisis and depression that will last until the beginning of World War II.

Event and Its Context

Prewar State of Labor

Early in the twentieth century, Italy experienced a long-delayed industrial upsurge of the sort previously experienced by the United States, England, France, and Germany. Unfortunately, Italy's industrialization was slowed by a poorly developed social, economic, and political structure. During that period, labor unrest was also a continuing cause of economic malaise.

Prior to World War I, Italian labor unions had been ineffective in improving workers' wages and working conditions. This rather lethargic labor movement became more quiescent during the war: labor disputes were relatively peaceful and few in number. Indeed, the yearly average of Italian industrial workers who went on strike during World War I was 146,000, as compared to 385,000 workers who had struck in prewar 1913. The average for agricultural strikers was 17,000 during the war, down from 80,000 in 1913.

Postwar State of Labor

In 1918 Italy began its readjustment to the end of World War I. Even though Italy had sided with the victors (United States, Britain, France), it was seen as an insignificant ally, having sided with the opposition (Germany, Austria) up until the time of its entrance into the war in May 1915. Moreover, Italy's allies felt it had not played a decisive part in the war, and the country's postwar influence was considered minimal because its army had been nearly destroyed. This large loss of men and material wealth left Italy deeply debt-ridden and burdened with an escalating cost of living.

Tens of thousands of Italian wartime workers, along with returning veterans, found that they were unemployed due to reduced peacetime demand for goods. In addition, inflation sent prices dramatically upward. Workers reacted by blaming existing institutions and by initiating violent strikes. The Italian labor movement began to stir to action as workers demanded more say about their living and working conditions.

Dominant Labor and Political Organizations

The major Italian labor union in the early twentieth century was the General Confederation of Labor (CGL). Its two principal bodies were the national craft and industrial unions, known as category federations; and the local chambers of labor. The category federations attempted to improve the basic rights and welfare of workers. However, they remained largely ineffective, unorganized, and small in size. Their reach was limited to areas of the more industrialized North, and even then only in a few trades and industries. The chambers of labor had greater working-class appeal. They secured labor services, provided local employment centers, and coordinated the employment of seasonal workers. The chambers also initiated various kinds of workers' insurance and self-help projects and assumed leadership in the areas of contract demands and strikes. The chambers were able to coordinate activities over broad geographical areas, so their leaders often held positions of political importance. They dominated the labor movement with their revolutionary political actions.

In spite of their broad influence, the category federations and chambers of labor—along with the CGL—experienced problems both individually and collectively. Such problems included disagreement over political alignments (despite a public policy of political neutrality), poor performance in collecting membership dues (resulting in inadequate strike funds), and an inability to secure collective bargaining contracts.

The Italian Socialist Party (PSI) emerged as the dominant political force from 1918 to 1920. During this time the PSI, with leaders such as Antonio Gramsci, issued revolutionary manifestos and proclamations and delivered speeches that incited workers. It rejected the foundations of democratic society and promised the establishment of a dictatorship of the proletariat. However, the PSI only agitated and never developed a plan for organizing society.

Massive Strikes in 1919

Beginning in 1919 strikers and demonstrators swarmed throughout Italy. After hearing about communist-inspired revolts in Russia, Germany, and Hungary, and other social changes that were sweeping across Europe, the Italian people grew tired of waiting for prosperity. Peasants claimed uncultivated lands, and workers occupied plants in northern Italy. The Italian government tried to satisfy worker demands by creating a national system of employment offices, establishing compulsory unemployment insurance, and setting new standards for factory hygiene. At the same time, employers granted wage increases. Suddenly in 1919 real wages rose rapidly from their lowest point in 1918. These advances in buying power brought millions of workers into the chambers of labor and the category federations. CGL membership jumped from 249,000 in 1918 to 1,150,000 in 1919.

Three Major Problems

Three major problems developed in quick succession and helped to fuel the massive Italian strikes of 1919. These problems centered on the length of the workday; inflation and shortages; and wage increases.

At the beginning of 1919, the CGL began a campaign for the eight-hour workday, along with other tangible goals such as increased wages and obligatory social insurance. The CGL asserted that the reduced workday would allow businesses to employ more workers as soldiers returned home. Employers were fearful that such a measure would damage the country's welfare by lowering productivity. However, with overriding worker support, the CGL successfully convinced leading industrialists. These business leaders assumed responsibility for introducing the eight-hour workday in their plants. On 20 February 1919 the Federation of Metallurgical Workers (FIOM) and employees of the metallurgical industries signed the first eight-hour day agreement. Eventually, the eight-hour workday was accepted throughout Italy. Although employees greeted the shortened workday, it placed employers on the defensive when it came to further union demands.

Many demonstrations and riots occurred because of food shortages and the rising prices of consumer goods. Between June and early July 1919, violence had spread throughout the country. In the regions of Emilia-Romagna, Tuscany, and Marche, revolution frequently appeared. Rioters looted warehouses, stores, and cooperatives and took over government offices. An angry mob occupied Florence; strikes closed down activities at Ancona, Bologna, and Palermo (in Sicily); and riots broke out in the industrial centers of Milan, Rome, and Naples. Government forces were uncertain about whether they could control the violence.

By early July the government announced a series of measures to ease the food shortage, turning over to municipal authorities the power to requisition and distribute food. With a lack of focus and leadership on the part of the demonstrators, this action returned most of the country to normalcy. However, during 20 and 21 July 1919, a strike closed down almost the entire economy as the socialist trade union protested the intervention of the Allied armies in Russia. Eventually, the strike turned more festive than revolutionary. Nevertheless, the food riots and July strikes made a deep impression on the Italian populace. The yearlong strikes made it appear that Italy was heading toward a Bolshevik-type revolution similar to those in Russia, Hungary, and Bavaria. However, the aimlessness and the apparent lack of determination of the strikers in the face of opposition indicated that most workers were not seriously committed to a revolution.

In the months immediately after the war, industrial companies were willing to grant concessions to labor organizations to avoid disruption of their efforts to convert quickly from military to civilian production. This prompted massive strikes as workers took advantage of the situation. As additional drives for wage increases began in the summer of 1919, unions began to encounter considerably more resistance from employers than they had only a few months earlier. The most dramatic dispute was in the metallurgical industry. Because the industry set wages and dominated the councils of the employers association, it also set the pattern for resistance to worker demands. The refusal of the metallurgical employers in the northern Lombardy, Liguria, and Emilia-Romagna regions to grant wage concessions prompted a strike in August. The strike lasted for two months and resulted in a settlement favorable to the workers.

Also during August, unions in other industries experienced greater resistance to wage demands, and strikes began in numerous industries and regions of Italy. Overall, the strikes were successful in obtaining significant wage concessions. During 1919, real wages nearly recovered to prewar levels.

Other 1919 Upheavals

A local strike at the Fiat automobile plant in Turin, which began in April 1919, eventually spread throughout the northern region of Piedmont and involved 500,000 workers. Streetcars, railways, public services, and many commercial establishments closed down, as did the entire manufacturing industry of the region. Similar massive protests continued at Forlì on 30 June 1919, later expanded to La Spezia, and then spread to Florence and the other major cities of Tuscany and Emilia-Romagna. On 6 July 1919 mobs damaged or destroyed more than 200 shops in Rome, Naples, and Milan. People throughout Italy were protesting the high cost of living and the perceived ill-gotten gain of war profiteers. During this turmoil federal authorities often could not bring in troops because the soldiers supported the protesters. The government decided to let the turmoil play itself out, which it did in early July.

Workers grew increasingly distrustful of traditional unions because those unions could not unite effectively and because they collaborated with the political system. Union workers basically had three complaints:

- Lack of rank-and-file participation: The typical in-plant organization was the "internal commission" that the rank-and-file activists criticized as basically a union oligarchy, making decisions without the participation of the majority of workers.

- Divisions between union members and nonmembers: Though unions had existed in Italy for some time, union membership was always voluntary; with the result that the workers' collective power was diminished during disputes.

- Divisions by craft and ideology: Oftentimes, different unions represented workers with different types of jobs (such as blue- and white-collar), further weakening the power of labor.

A growing rift between workers and the leaders of the Italian labor movement led to the emergence of new grassroots organizations. This took two main forms. First was the movement for grievance committees (*commissioni interne*), which was independent of the established trade union hierarchy and was promoted by worker activists of the CGL unions. The second form was the emergence and growth of a dissident union, the Italian Syndicalist Union (USI or *Unione Sindacale Italiana*).

In July, FIOM rallied to gain acceptance of grievance committees within factories. During a meeting in November 1919, FIOM leaders reaffirmed their claim that unions must discuss directly with industry, or through grievance committees, all questions concerning wages and the distribution of work. Grievance committees were seen as an effective way to resolve labor issues and to place the ablest of workers in direct contact with the employer, so that they could be trained for eventual operation of the country's factories. Radicals saw grievance committees as a means to gain control of the factories and agitated for their spread throughout industry.

The movement for worker control grew throughout 1919, as measured, for example, by the rapid growth of the USI. New independent shop councils emerged during this period in Milan, which was Italy's biggest city and main commercial center, primarily as a result of USI efforts. The USI mobilized workers with direct action such as strikes, violence, and sabotage, acting on the belief that social transformation could be achieved through "active" strikes in which workers continued production under their own control. This type of organization was often called revolutionary trade unionism or revolutionary syndicalism and advocated control of government and industry by trade unions. Unfortunately, the heavily burdened Italian worker gained few benefits from these USI-inspired actions, but instead endured more repression from public authorities and employers.

Aftereffects of 1919

In 1920 and 1921 widespread labor strikes, riots over high food prices, peasant land occupations, and tax revolts swept Italy. Taking advantage of the chaos, Benito Mussolini, who had organized his Italian Combat Bands (*Fasci Italiani di Combattimento*) in 1919, offered eager industrialists and landlords the services of his armed squads of "Black Shirts" as strikebreakers. Acting sometimes with the complicity of the government, the fascist gangs also destroyed trade unions and socialist groups. Mussolini went on to become prime minister and dictator of Italy from 1922 to 1943, and his ensuing rule crushed the revolutionary labor movement.

Key Players

Gramsci, Antonio (1891–1937): Gramsci studied at the University of Turin in Italy. He joined a local Turin Socialist Party chapter and contributed a regular column to its newspaper, *Aventi!* In 1917 Gramsci was elected secretary of the Turinese socialist chapter. He helped to found *L'Ordine Nuovo*, a weekly (and eventually a daily) review of socialist culture. Gramsci helped the Italian communists separate from the Italian socialists in 1921. He was elected to the Chamber of Deputies in the mid-1920s. While a member of the chamber, Gramsci denounced Benito Mussolini and his fascist supporters. The fascists arrested Gramsci in 1926 and sentenced him to 20 years in prison. Although extremely ill while in prison, he wrote many books and other materials. Gramsci wrote *Prison Notebooks*, which established him as one of Italy's major Marxist philosophers.

See also: *Red Week, Italy.*

─────────────

BIBLIOGRAPHY

Books

Chabod, Federico. *A History of Italian Fascism*. New York: Howard Fertig, 1975.

Ebenstein, William. *Fascist Italy*. New York: American Book Company, 1939.

Goodstein, Phil H. *The Theory of the General Strike from the French Revolution to Poland*. Boulder, CO: East European Monographs, 1984.

Haider, Carmen. *Capital and Labor Under Fascism*. New York: AMS Press, 1968.

Haimson, Leopold H., and Charles Tilly. *Strikes, Wars, and Revolutions in an International Perspective: Strike Waves in the Late Nineteenth and Early Twentieth Centuries*. Cambridge, UK: Cambridge University Press, 1989.

Knox, MacGregor. *Common Destiny: Dictatorship, Foreign Policy, and War in Fascist Italy and Nazi Germany*. London: Cambridge University Press, 2000.

Roberts, David D. *The Syndicalist Tradition and Italian Fascism*. Chapel Hill: The University of North Carolina Press, 1979.

—William Arthur Atkins

Strike Wave

United States 1945–1946

Synopsis

In 1945 and 1946 the largest strike wave in U.S. history occurred when two million workers walked off their jobs at different times during the year. In some cities the strikes even led to general strikes as workers protested for union recognition and wage and benefit increases. In Stamford, Connecticut, workers poured into the city on 3 January 1946 to show their support for strikers at the Yale and Towne metal works; the show of solidarity helped to force the company to enter into collective bargaining with International Association of Machinists. In Rochester, New York, municipal workers enlisted the help of approximately 35,000 members of the American Federation of Labor and Congress of Industrial Organizations for a general strike on 28 May 1946. The action forced the city of Rochester to meet most of the strikers' demands and prevented management from firing those who had gone out on strike. In the longest general strike, 100,000 workers in Oakland, California, essentially shut the city down from 2 to 5 December 1946. The success of these general strikes, combined with the thousands of other work stoppages in 1946, led to a backlash against labor that culminated in the passage of the Taft-Hartley Act in 1947. Among its provisions was a ban on secondary or "sympathy" strikes that essentially outlawed general strikes.

Harry S Truman. © Hulton Archive/Getty Images. Reproduced by permission.

Timeline

1926: Britain paralyzed by a general strike.

1931: Financial crisis widens in the United States and Europe, which reel from bank failures and climbing unemployment levels. In London, armies of the unemployed riot.

1936: The election of a leftist Popular Front government in Spain in February precipitates an uprising by rightists under the leadership of Francisco Franco. Over the next three years, war will rage between the Loyalists and Franco's Nationalists. The Spanish Civil War will prove to be a lightning rod for the world's tensions, with the Nazis and fascists supporting the Nationalists, and the Soviets the Loyalists.

1941: Japanese bombing of Pearl Harbor on 7 December brings the United States into the war against the Axis. Combined with the attack on the Soviet Union, which makes Stalin an unlikely ally of the Western democracies, the events of 1941 will ultimately turn the tide of the war.

1946: Winston Churchill warns of an "Iron Curtain" spreading across Eastern Europe.

1946: Three months after the first meeting of the United Nations General Assembly in London in January, the all-but-defunct League of Nations is officially dissolved.

1946: At the Nuremberg trials, twelve Nazi leaders are sentenced to death, and seven others to prison.

1946: Building of the first true electronic computer, the Electronic Numerical Integrator and Computer (ENIAC).

1951: Six western European nations form the European Coal and Steel Community, forerunner of the European Economic Community and the later European Union.

American Federation of Labor v. Watson and the Closed Shop

In *American Federation of Labor v. Watson* (327 U.S. 582, 1946), the AFL brought suit against Florida Attorney General J. Tom Watson and others on the grounds that an amendment to the Florida constitution violated the First and Fourteenth Amendments, as well as the contract clause of Article I, Section 10, of the U.S. Constitution. In addition, the suit alleged, the Florida statute was at odds with provisions in the National Labor Relations Act and the Norris–La Guardia Act. The amendment, adopted by Florida's legislature in 1944, stated that "The right of persons to work shall not be denied or abridged on account of membership or non-membership in any labor union, or labor organization; provided, that this clause shall not be construed to deny or abridge the right of employees by and through a labor organization or labor union to bargain collectively with their employer."

At issue was the provision that "The right . . . to work shall not be denied or abridged on account of . . . non-membership in any labor union." In the AFL's view, the law thus outlawed any agreement requiring membership in a labor organization—the so-called closed shop. Various AFL unions had been designated as the collective-bargaining representatives of numerous employees in Florida, and most of these unions employed closed-shop agreements, maintaining that this was the most effective means of protecting workers' rights.

A district court held that the Florida constitutional amendment did not violate federal law, but the U.S. Supreme Court overturned the decision of the lower court. Writing for the majority, Justice William O. Douglas noted in part that "from the viewpoint both of the appellant unions and the appellant employers the disruption in collective bargaining which would be occasioned by holding closed-shop agreements illegal would be so serious as to make it futile to attempt to measure the loss in money damages."

Source: *American Federation of Labor v. Watson* (327 U.S. 582), 1946

—Judson Knight

1956: Elvis Presley appears on Ed Sullivan's *Toast of the Town*, where he performs "Hound Dog" and "Love Me Tender" before a mostly female audience. Nationwide, 54 million people watch the performance, setting a new record.

1961: President Eisenhower steps down, warning of a "military-industrial complex" in his farewell speech, and 43-year-old John F. Kennedy becomes the youngest elected president in U.S. history. Three months later, he launches an unsuccessful invasion of Cuba at the Bay of Pigs.

Event and Its Context

Labor had gained a great deal during World War II. In exchange for a "no-strike" pledge, every new worker hired into a union shop during the war had to join the union. The agreement boosted membership in the AFL and CIO unions to 15 million in 1945. After the war, however, wages fell behind price increases for most consumer goods. Between 1945 and 1946, inflation reached 16 percent while the wages of industrial workers increased by just 7 percent. In an attempt to avert a series of strikes over the wage issue, President Harry S Truman convened a labor-management conference in November 1945 to establish a framework for postwar collective bargaining. The conference failed to reach its goal, largely because of disagreements over labor's place in managerial affairs.

The UAW-GM Strike

Although many union leaders used their leverage primarily to bargain for improvements on wages and benefits, others sought to implement a broad range of policies through collective bargaining. One of the most influential leaders in the latter group was Walter Reuther of the United Automobile Workers union (UAW). A UAW vice president at the time of the war's conclusion, Reuther also headed the union's General Motors (GM) bargaining division. Reuther was therefore the union's leading negotiator at the first postwar bargaining talks with GM, which began in October 1945. After talks between the UAW and GM broke down, the union called a strike on 21 November 1945. The strike lasted 113 days—the longest of any of the big strikes of 1945 and 1946—and illuminated many of the fundamental issues of postwar labor relations.

In addition to asking GM for a 30 percent wage raise, Reuther's chief demand was that the company hold the line on the prices of its final product. Because GM was the largest and most profitable of the Big Three auto makers, Reuther believed that it could easily afford the wage hike without increasing the sticker price on its automobiles. As for the massive wage hike, it was necessary to counter wartime inflation, which had increased the cost of living by about one-third. Although GM was willing to discuss wages and benefits with the UAW, its leadership drew the line at allowing the union to look at its books or having input into managerial decisions. The real issue in the dispute, then, was whether or not a union would go beyond its established role in collective bargaining and gain a voice in decisions that previously had been made solely under the discretion of management.

In early December 1945 President Truman directed a special committee to look into the issues of the strike. The report, issued on 10 January 1946, seemed to support Reuther's argument that GM could afford a wage increase without passing the costs on to consumers, although it recommended a wage hike of just 19.5 cents per hour. The two parties continued to negotiate for another two months before finally agreeing to the board's recommended wage increase and some minor changes in the contract language. The strike, which ended on 15 March 1946, marked the last time that the UAW would try to gain a say in managerial affairs under its collective bargaining agreements. From 1946 onward the UAW and other unions would bargain over wages, benefits, work hours, and work conditions, but not about production decisions.

The Steelworkers' Strike

In total, 25 percent of union members went out on strike in 1946. In addition to the GM strike, among the most significant actions were strikes by 200,000 electrical workers, 260,000 meat packers, and 750,000 steelworkers. Under the leadership of Philip Murray, the United Steelworkers of America (USWA) had gone out on strike on 21 January 1946 to secure higher wages. Unlike Reuther, however, Murray did not view collective bargaining as a vehicle for achieving broader social or economic gains for America as a whole. When the USWA received an offer of an 18.5 cents per hour increase in wages, Murray accepted the offer and ended the USWA strike on 15 February 1946. Just days after the settlement the steel industry received permission from the Office of Price Administration (OPA)—a federal agency set up during World War II to set prices and stop wartime inflation—to increase the price of steel by more than five dollars a ton. The price increase seemed to justify Reuther's argument that corporations would pass the wage costs to consumers and thereby fuel inflation. Reuther was also disillusioned by Murray's refusal to speak out against the steel industry's action. Reuther also realized that the USWA's settlement left the UAW in a vulnerable bargaining position, as its strike had lasted almost three months by the time the USWA settled.

The GM and steel industry strikes illuminated the crucial issue of the postwar labor movement: Should unions attempt to gain a voice in management, or should they be limited to bargaining over wages and benefits during contract talks? Reuther, who viewed the labor movement as a vehicle for social and economic change, fell into the first category. Murray, who held a bread-and-butter vision of unionism, was skeptical of such far-reaching plans. In the end Murray's vision would predominate in postwar collective bargaining.

The General Strikes

The automobile and steel industry strikes of 1945 and 1946 were only two of the largest strikes in the immediate postwar era. The period also witnessed several citywide general strikes in 1946, beginning with Stamford, Connecticut, during the first week of January 1946. Workers at the city's Yale and Towne company had joined the International Association of Machinists (IAM) during the war, and the company was determined to oust the union as soon as possible. When contract talks opened in March 1945, Yale and Towne's management demanded an end to the closed shop, or one in which all workers were compelled to join the union. The company also rejected the IAM's request for a 30 percent wage increase; instead, Yale and Towne offered no wage increase at all.

After several months of negotiation, the IAM finally called for a strike, which began on 7 November 1945. The next day strikers prevented Yale and Towne's president, W. Gibson Carey, from entering the factory. After the Stamford Police declined to intervene in several more confrontations, Carey asked the governor of Connecticut to send in a state police force. The arrival of the state police in late December 1945 resulted in a new round of confrontations and the arrest of some strikers and their supporters. To protest against the violence and detentions, the IAM called for a citywide demonstration in Stamford on 3 January 1946. An estimated 10,000 people took part in the protest, which brought the city to a standstill. It also brought Yale and Towne to the bargaining table with a proposed wage increase, the first one the company had offered in the negotiations. Talks dragged on for several more weeks until state and federal mediators forged an agreement between the IAM and Yale and Towne on 5 April. The IAM declared the final contract a victory over the company, as it followed most of the union's recommendations on wages, benefits, and grievance procedures.

The 28 May 1946 general strike in Rochester, New York, began as a protest by municipal workers against the policies of City Manager Louis V. Cartwright, whom they charged with antiunionism. On 15 May, Cartwright had fired 489 municipal employees who had tried to unionize. He subsequently fired 61 city truck drivers who walked off the job to protest the initial firings. After 5,000 demonstrators streamed into Rochester on 23 May in support of the workers, Cartwright agreed to rehire all of those who had been dismissed. His continued refusal to concede union recognition, however, prompted the strike's leaders to call for a citywide strike by Rochester's 35,000 AFL-CIO members. As in Stamford, the 28 May 1946 general strike in Rochester shut down the city and immediately brought in state mediators to resolve the crisis. After one day of talks, Rochester's city officials finally agreed to grant union recognition to its municipal employees and to rehire all of the striking workers.

The largest of the general strikes occurred in Oakland, California, between 2 and 5 December 1946. The action began when department store workers called a strike in November 1946. The Teamsters union immediately declared that none of their members would deliver goods to any department store under a strike. On 2 December 1946 strikers confronted nonunion trucks that were headed to Hastings department store in downtown Oakland and stopped the shipment. In response, about 250 Oakland police officers arrived to help the nonunion trucks through the picket lines. The participation of the police in breaking the strike outraged many Oakland workers, who immediately began walking off the job throughout the city. By the end of the day, strike supporters had convinced most stores to close down; bars that remained open were asked only to serve beer instead of liquor. As the general strike gained momentum, about 100,000 Oakland workers participated by leaving their jobs, manning picket lines, and self-policing the strike zone.

The virtual takeover of Oakland by striking workers demonstrated the power of working-class solidarity. Yet the grassroots nature of the Oakland strike worried some union leaders, who feared that their ability to direct the strike had been lost. On 5 December 1946 the AFL Central Labor Council of Oakland called for an end to the general strike in return for an agreement by the city's police department not to send guards to protect nonunion trucks. The announcement quickly sapped the drive of the strikers, and they slowly began to trickle back to work. Although the incident did not achieve many tangible gains for Oakland's workers, it did give momentum to the election of four prolabor candidates to the City Council in the next municipal elections.

Backlash Against Labor

As in the period after World War I, the labor unrest of 1945 and 1946 had a significant impact on the nation's political life.

In the midst of the largest strike wave in American history, Republican candidates in the fall 1946 elections seized upon the issue as proof of a radical influence on the nation's unions and their members. The red-baiting tactic—a precursor to more extreme attacks on the left—later became commonplace during the cold war as some Republicans linked liberalism to communism. The Republicans were so successful in their campaign that they took control of both houses of Congress in 1946 by reminding voters that the turmoil of the postwar period had occurred under Democratic control.

Some Democrats also adopted a more hostile tone toward labor. This group included President Truman, who had asked Congress for the power to draft into the armed services all striking workers of the Railway Brotherhoods who refused to go back to work in May 1946. Truman had also alienated many labor supporters by sending in federal agents to take over mining operations during a United Mine Workers (UMW) strike in March 1946. Subsequent negotiations helped the UMW to gain pensions and a health-care fund paid out of royalties collected on each ton of coal produced.

The most enduring political change wrought by the 1945–1946 strikes was the passage of the Taft-Hartley Act of 1947. Sponsored by isolationist and antilabor senator Robert A. Taft of Ohio, the law essentially outlawed boycotts or sympathy strikes and made general strikes illegal. The law also forced labor unions to oust any leader who would not take an anti-Communist pledge, permitted states to pass "open shop" legislation, and authorized federal injunctions against strikes that affected public health and safety. Designed to prevent the events of 1946 from ever happening again, the Taft-Hartley Act was denounced by many labor leaders as a "slave labor law." Supporters of the act countered that the law merely adjusted the balance between labor and management, which had been off course since the New Deal.

The political fallout from the 1945–1946 strikes also spelled the end of the New Deal as Democrats lost control of Congress in 1946. After Congress stripped the OPA of most of its price-setting powers, President Truman vetoed the legislation, effectively killing the agency. He later passed a limited version of an OPA, but by the end of 1946 almost all of the price controls had been removed. Labor supporters had slightly better luck in gaining passage of the Full Employment Act of 1946, which committed the federal government to ensuring maximum employment even though it failed to mandate specific measures to achieve that goal. The Full Employment Act was one of the few prolabor pieces of legislation that emerged from Truman's administration. As a result, Truman, who lost much of labor's support after his threat to draft strikers in March 1946, barely retained enough union support to gain reelection as president in 1948.

Union officials also had problems adjusting to the postwar framework of labor relations. In some cases they found it difficult to get their members back to work. They also faced a host of unauthorized work stoppages, or "wildcat" strikes, that demonstrated the tenuous hold that the unions maintained over the workplace after World War II. Unions in other cities were also torn apart by the choices they were forced to make. After the Taft-Hartley Act's ban on Communists in the labor movement went into effect, many unions lost some of their most capable leaders.

As in the era after World War I, strikers in the post–World War II period were immediately confronted with a backlash against labor. In both instances workers and their unions were labeled as radicals and local and state police forces were called in to prevent violence. Both periods also gave way to a more conservative political era in which state and federal governments passed antiunion legislation. The crucial difference between the two eras of labor unrest, however, is that unions did not collapse under the weight of official repression or employer violence after World War II. By 1946 most employers had made at least a grudging peace with organized labor, even if they disagreed with the ambitious goals of labor leaders such as Walter Reuther.

Key Players

Murray, Philip (1886–1952): Vice president of the United Steelworkers (USWA) of America from 1920 to 1940, Murray helped found the Steel Workers Organizing Committee (SWOC) in 1936 and served as its chairman. He was elected president of the Congress of Industrial Organizations in 1940 and held the position through the postwar strikes. At the time of the 1946 steel strike, the USWA had about 750,000 members.

Reuther, Walter Philip (1907–1970): As the UAW's vice president during the 1945–1946 GM strike, Reuther provided leadership to the striking workers. Although GM refused to meet Reuther's demands to grant wage increases without raising the cost of their products, the strike made him into a national spokesman on labor issues. Elected president of the UAW in 1946, Reuther held the position until his death in 1970.

Taft, Robert A. (1889–1953): In a lengthy political career, Taft served in the Ohio State Legislature for several terms and represented Ohio in the U.S. Senate beginning in 1936. One of the most stubborn opponents of the New Deal, Taft was also an isolationist who opposed America's entry into World War II and its international engagements afterwards. Taft lent his name to the Taft-Hartley Act of 1947, which outlawed general strikes and secondary boycotts and allowed companies to sue unions for breach of contract.

Truman, Harry S (1884–1972): After assuming the presidency from Franklin D. Roosevelt in 1945, Truman faced the demands of concluding World War II while preparing for reconversion. His decision to allow the Office of Price Administration to lapse in 1946 riled many workers who feared the effects of postwar inflation, and his intervention in the GM and steel strikes of 1945 and 1946 raised complaints on both sides of the bargaining table.

See also: *American Federation of Labor; Congress of Industrial Organizations; Taft-Hartley Act; United Steelworkers of America.*

BIBLIOGRAPHY

Books

Amberg, Stephen. "The CIO Political Strategy in Historical Perspective: Creating a High-road Economy in the Postwar Era." In *Organized Labor and American Politics, 1894–1994: The Labor-Liberal Alliance*, edited by Kevin Boyle. Albany: State University of New York Press, 1998.

Boyle, Kevin. *The UAW and the Heyday of American Liberalism, 1945–1968.* Ithaca, NY: Cornell University Press, 1995.

Fones-Wolf, Elizabeth A. *Selling Free Enterprise: The Business Assault on Labor and Liberalism, 1945–1960.* Urbana: University of Illinois Press, 1994.

Lichtenstein, Nelson. *Labor's War at Home: The CIO in World War II.* Cambridge: Cambridge University Press, 1982.

———. *The Most Dangerous Man in Detroit: Walter Reuther and the Fate of American Labor.* New York: Basic Books, 1995.

Lipsitz, George. *Rainbow at Midnight: Labor and Culture in the 1940s.* Urbana: University of Illinois Press, 1994.

—Timothy G. Borden

Strikes of Journeymen and Workers

France 1840

Synopsis

During the summer of 1840, strike waves brought industry in Paris to a standstill. Tens of thousands of workers from across the trades were involved at the height of the strikes in late August and early September. The strikers demanded higher wages and better working conditions. Profound changes had occurred in the way work was organized, adversely affecting the Parisian artisans. In response, the journeymen of Paris organized to protect their livelihood. In terms of what concessions the workers gained from employers, the strikes were a failure. Strikes were illegal under laws against coalitions of workers, and the army was brought in. The government did not deal with the strikers' grievances. However, the strikes did have some far-reaching consequences. The harsh repression further alienated the workers from a regime that seemed more interested in the protection of capital than the rights of labor. The strikes also encouraged workers from different trades to recognize their common grievances. The failure of the strike led people to seek alternative ways to address the problems of wages and working conditions. This was the beginning of a decade of labor organization and activity leading up to the 1848 revolution.

Timeline

1815: Napoleon returns from Elba, and his supporters attempt to restore him as French ruler, but just three months later, forces led by the Duke of Wellington defeat his armies at Waterloo. Napoleon spends the remainder of his days as a prisoner on the island of St. Helena in the south Atlantic.

1824: French engineer Sadi Carnot describes a perfect engine: one in which all energy input is converted to energy output. The ideas in his *Reflections on the Motive Power of Fire* will influence the formulation of the Second Law of Thermodynamics, which shows that such a perfect engine is an impossibility.

1826: French inventor Joseph-Nicéphore Niepce makes the first photographic image in history.

1830: French troops invade Algeria, and at home, a revolution forces the abdication of Charles V in favor of Louis Philippe, the "Citizen King."

1833: British Parliament passes the Slavery Abolition Act, giving freedom to all slaves throughout the British Empire.

1837: Coronation of Queen Victoria in England.

1838: As crops fail, spawning famine in Ireland, Britain imposes the Poor Law. Designed to discourage the indigent from seeking public assistance, the law makes labor in the workhouse worse than any work to be found on the outside, and thus has the effect of stimulating emigration.

1839: Invention of the bicycle in Scotland.

1843: First known reference to cigarettes, in a list of products controlled by a French monopoly.

1844: Exiled to Paris, Karl Marx meets Friedrich Engels.

1845: From Ireland to Russia, famine plagues Europe, killing some 2.5 million people.

1852: France's Second Republic ends when Louis Napoleon declares himself Napoleon III, initiating the Second Empire.

Event and Its Context

The Problems of Labor

Several decades of economic and political change lay behind the 1840 strikes. The majority of workers in France for most of the nineteenth century did not work in large factories but in small workshops, usually with only a few employees. However, processes associated with industrialization and modernization still adversely affected these workers. Prior to the nineteenth century, trade corporations or guilds had controlled each trade with regulations about production. Conflict between journeymen and the masters who employed them was not unusual, but there was a sense that everyone had the interests of the trade as a whole in mind. Work took place within the context of a trade community, rather than as separate individuals in a free labor market.

However, one of the most important effects of the French Revolution was the abolition of the corporate organizations. The corporations no longer had any legal basis for the control of the trades, and anyone could practice whatever trade they liked, with no restraint on how they organized their work. Most artisans continued to practice their trade much as they had before. Nevertheless, gradual transformations did occur. These changes were particularly significant in the tailoring trades. Some entrepreneurs saw the opportunity to increase production by making changes to the way work was organized. By cutting the process of making a garment into a series of separate simple tasks, they were able to decrease the level of skills required. This division of labor meant that they could employ more unskilled workers, often women and children, and pay them much less than a skilled journeyman tailor. Other innovations in the organization of work, such as subcontracting, putting-out work, and piecework all became more common and drove down the cost of labor. The main impetus behind these changes was the development of *confection,* or ready-to-wear clothing. Previously, most tailoring was *bespoke,* or made-to-order. However, ready-to-wear clothing boomed in the early nineteenth century, until by 1848 it accounted for 40 percent of the clothing market in Paris. Aimed at the lower-middle-class market, the emphasis was upon quantity rather than quality, which encouraged an increased division of labor and standardized production.

Inevitably, these changes had an impact across the whole trade. Large numbers of low-skilled, poorly paid workers caused wages to fall. Master tailors dropped their prices to compete with the larger operations and therefore pushed their labor costs as low as possible. Inevitably, this caused conflict with the journeymen they employed. More work was required to maintain standards of living, and the working day lengthened. Work became more irregular and uncertain as merchants got rid of workers or stopped ordering from subcontractors during the slow months. Overall, the picture in the tailoring trade was one of declining work standards, declining standards of living, and declining control. Many journeymen and masters lost the battle to survive as independent artisans and were forced into the ranks of the unskilled workers. Most found that the skills on which their identity and dignity rested had declining value in a free labor market. These changes were mirrored in many other trades, as artisans struggled to maintain their status as skilled, independent craftsmen.

With the July Revolution in 1830, many workers hoped that their grievances would be addressed by the new regime. However, it quickly became apparent that the new regime was not sympathetic to their problems. The government made it clear that in matters of industrial disputes, it was not going to intervene to introduce regulations in support of the artisans' demands. In response to strike waves and labor unrest in the early 1830s, repressive laws were passed in 1834, which made any gathering exceeding 20 people potentially illegal. This buttressed existing laws that declared strikes and most kinds of workers organizations illegal. However, workers' organizations did exist, and in fact multiplied during the 1830s and 1840s. Secret journeymen societies, known as *compagnonnoges,* survived from the eighteenth century. Mutual aid societies for workers also developed in this period. Ostensibly, these were for the arrangement of workers' insurance against sickness and death. However, they also organized strikes and collected funds for the support of strikers and their families. In defiance of the state, workers organized in an attempt to defend themselves against what they perceived as unjust work practices.

The 1840 Strikes

Since the strike waves of the early 1830s, there had been relative calm. However, a number of factors conspired to cause upheaval in 1840. The political situation was particularly unstable at this time, with the government in the throes of an extended ministerial crisis. France also came dangerously close to war with England in 1840, owing to disputes over foreign policy issues in the Middle East. Taking advantage of this uncertainty, the republican movement began a campaign of banquets during the summer of 1840, organizing meetings where speakers called for universal suffrage and the organization of labor. Along with this political uncertainty and activity, economic factors were also crucial. The period 1837–1839 was characterized by an economic downturn, which had resulted in high unemployment and high food prices in Paris. However, a good harvest in the spring of 1840 had eased the economic situation, and a slight recovery occurred. Since workers had more bargaining power with employers during periods of recovery, the strike wave began at this point.

The strikes began in March, when journeymen tailors placed an interdict on several masters. This was a traditional tactic designed to control pay rates by threatening to cut off a master's supply of skilled workers. They were led by the journeyman tailor Andre Troncin, who had connections to the republican movement. In response to the journeymen's demands, the masters went to the Parisian authorities and gained permission to impose the *livret* upon the journeymen tailors. The *livret* was a notebook each worker had to carry that listed his work history, including any record of striking or other labor agitation. It effectively blacklisted any worker involved in strikes. Traditionally, the *livret* had not been used in the tailoring trade, and by imposing it on the journeymen, the masters were attempting to prevent their protest. Starting from 1 July 1840, all journeymen tailors were to carry the *livret* or risk arrest.

Workingmen of all trades had a common grievance against the *livret*, and this issue was crucial in spreading the strike movement to other trades. A "communist" banquet, held on 1 July 1840, was significant in bringing together workers from various trades and contributing to the growth of a broad strike movement. Throughout July the strike wave continued to spread across the trades. Martin Nadaud, a building mason involved in organizing the strike in the building trade, described the builder's program as simple: to increase daily wages, eliminate overtime, and abolish supplementary tasks that might be forced upon workers by their employers. The strike wave reached its peak at the beginning of September. Estimates of the numbers of workers involved range from 30,000 to 100,000, but there is no doubt that most of the Parisian trades were affected, and industry in the city was brought to a halt. The strikers organized street demonstrations and mass meetings, and there were reports of intimidation and violence against strikebreakers. Workingmen's groups, supported by donations from workers outside Paris, organized kitchens to feed the strikers and their families.

At this point the state stepped in to restore order. The strikers' demands were focused on economic grievances. However, the government feared that the republican movement would exploit the situation to further its own political agenda. Therefore, the army was brought in to repress the strikes. Hundreds of arrests were made, and there were violent street clashes. By 10 September 1840 the strikes were effectively over. The government blamed the strikes on foreign agents, provocateurs, republicans, and Bonapartists and ignored the legitimate grievances that workers had regarding conditions in the trades. Several of the leaders received prison terms; Andre Troncin was sentenced to five years in prison for his part in leading the tailors' strikes. The strikes were a failure in that the workers did not gain any concessions from their employers or recognition from the state.

Consequences

However, the experience of the strikes certainly had an influence on the attitudes of the workers. The government's actions in using troops to repress the strikes further alienated the workers from the regime. In his account of the aftermath of the repression, Martin Nadaud comments on the bitterness felt by many working people and their antipathy towards the government for its insensitivity towards their grievances. The experience sharpened the workers' sense of the role that the state played in supporting and encouraging the industrial changes that were adversely affecting them. Because of these events and realizations, many workers understood that merely striking for better wages and conditions would be futile. The masters who directly employed them were often victims of the same processes of change and could do little to improve what they offered their workers. What was required was a reorganization of production to protect the livelihood of the workers. From 1840 forward, a variety of socialist ideas about producers' associations, the joint ownership of the means of production, and the reorganization of work became more widely discussed among Parisian workers. The strikes also contributed to a burgeoning sense of class consciousness, because they encouraged workers to see beyond narrow trade concerns and recognize their common experience of exploitation. Therefore, the failure of the strikes contributed to a general radicalization of French workers during the 1840s leading up to the 1848 revolution.

Key Players

Nadaud, Martin (1815–1898): Parisian building mason involved in organizing the strikes in the building trade in Paris in 1840. Nadaud's memoirs outline the working conditions for members of the building trade in the 1830s and 1840s and indicate the bitterness caused by the government's harsh repression of the strikes.

Troncin, Andre (1802–1846): Parisian journeyman tailor. Troncin had been involved in the strike movement of the early 1830s and was connected to the republican movement. He was one of the leaders of the tailoring strikes in 1840, which sparked the strike wave. Troncin was imprisoned for five years for his role in the strikes and died soon after his release from prison.

See also: *June Days Rebellion; Revolutions in Europe.*

BIBLIOGRAPHY

Books

Aguet, Jean Pierre. *Les Grèves Sous La Monarchie de Juillet 1830–1847.* Geneva, Switzerland: Librarie E. Doz, 1954.

Johnson, Christopher H. "Economic Change and Artisan Discontent: The Tailors' History 1800–1848." In *Revolution and Reaction: 1848 and the Second French Republic,* edited by Roger Price. London, England: Croom Helm, 1975.

Magraw, Roger. *A History of the French Working Class.* Vol. 2, *The Age of Artisan Revolution, 1815–1871.* Cambridge, MA: Blackwell, 1992.

Sewell, William Hamilton. *Work and Revolution in France: The Language of Labor from the Old Regime to 1848.* Cambridge, England: Cambridge University Press, 1980.

Shorter, Edward, and Charles Tilly. *Strikes in France, 1830–1968.* New York: Cambridge University Press, 1974.

Mark Traugott, ed. *The French Worker. Autobiographies from the Early Industrial Era.* Berkeley CA: University of California Press, 1993.

ADDITIONAL RESOURCES

Berenson, Edward. *Populist Religion and Left-Wing Politics in France 1830–1852.* Princeton, NJ: Princeton University Press, 1984.

Judt, Tony. *Marxism and the French Left: Studies in Labour and Politics in France, 1830–1981.* Oxford, England: Clarendon Press, 1986.

Magraw, Roger. *France, 1815–1914: The Bourgeois Century.* New York: Oxford University Press, 1983.

Moss, Bernard H. "Parisian Producers' Associations (1830–1851): The Socialism of Skilled Workers." In *Revolution and Reaction: 1848 and the Second French Republic,* edited by Roger Price. London, England: Croom Helm, 1975.

—Katrina Ford

Sweeney Elected President of AFL-CIO

United States 1995

Synopsis

In its 40-year history, the AFL-CIO had never had an election contest until John J. Sweeney successfully challenged the interim president, Thomas Donahue, in October 1995. The election was preceded by another first. Lane Kirkland, president of AFL-CIO since 1979, was forced to retire in June 1995. He left under pressure from labor leaders who included both Sweeney and AFL-CIO secretary-treasurer Donahue, who would have

been Kirkland's chosen successor in a normal uncontested election. The unions' depressed state, a condition that had developed during Kirkland's tenure, precipitated the unhappy circumstance. Unions lost clout and membership, which dropped from 22 percent of the workforce in 1979 to 15.5 percent by 1995. Prior to his election to the top post of the AFL-CIO, Sweeney had been president of the Service Employees International Union (SEIU), the fastest growing union with a membership of 1.1 million in 1995.

Timeline

1976: United States celebrates its bicentennial.

1980: In protest of the Soviet invasion of Afghanistan, President Carter keeps U.S. athletes out of the Moscow Olympics. Earlier, at the Winter Games in Lake Placid, New York, the U.S. hockey team scored a historic—and, in the view of many, a symbolic—victory over the Soviets.

1986: Seven astronauts die in the explosion of the U.S. Space Shuttle *Challenger* on 28 January.

1991: The United States and other allies in the UN force commence the war against Iraq on 15 January. By 3 April the war is over, a resounding victory for the Allied force.

1993: Muslim extremists carry out a bombing at the World Trade Center in New York City on 26 February, killing six and injuring thousands.

1995: The Aum Shinrikyo cult carries out a nerve-gas attack in a Tokyo subway, killing eight people and injuring thousands more.

1995: Bombing of the Alfred P. Murrah Federal Building in Oklahoma City, Oklahoma, kills 168 people. Authorities arrest Timothy McVeigh and Terry Nichols.

1995: Yugoslav forces step up their offensives in Bosnia and Croatia and conduct campaigns of "ethnic cleansing" to rid areas of non-Serb elements. By December, however, a Bosnia peace treaty will be signed.

1995: After a lengthy and highly publicized trial charged with racial animosity, a Los Angeles jury takes just four hours to declare O. J. Simpson not guilty of the murders of Nicole Brown and Ronald Goldman. In a 1997 civil trial, he will be found guilty and fined $33 million.

1995: A Jewish extremist assassinates Israeli Prime Minister Yitzhak Rabin. In elections the following May, Benjamin Netanyahu becomes the new Israeli leader.

1998: In the midst of the Monica Lewinsky scandal, terrorists affiliated with Saudi millionaire and Muslim extremist Osama bin Laden bomb U.S. embassies in Kenya and Tanzania, killing hundreds of people. President Clinton orders air strikes on terrorist camps in Afghanistan and an alleged chemical-weapons factory in the Sudan, but the action—which many observers dismiss as a mere tactic to take attention off the scandal—is ineffective and wins limited support.

2001: On the morning of 11 September, terrorists hijack four jets, two of which ram the twin towers of the World Trade Center in New York City. A third plane slams into the Pentagon in Washington, D.C., and a fourth crashes in an empty field in Pennsylvania. The towers catch fire and collapse before an audience of millions on live television. The death toll is approximately three thousand.

Event and Its Context

The Kirkland Legacy

By the time Lane Kirkland took over for George Meany as president of the AFL-CIO in 1979, the labor movement was already running into employer offensives against unions. In 1981, following failed efforts to reach a contract agreement, the Professional Air Traffic Controllers Organization (PATCO), a union affiliate of the AFL-CIO, went on strike. Labor suffered a serious setback when President Ronald Reagan fired most of the nation's air controllers, enforcing a 1955 government regulation that denied federal employees the right to strike. Not only were 11,359 air traffic controllers fired, but Reagan then decertified their union. The PATCO fiasco contributed to the rapid decline in union membership in the 1980s and 1990s.

In 1986 Kirkland said of predictions of the demise of the American unions that they would endure by committing themselves to "work within the system." Actually, Kirkland had no grassroots experience. Following service in the merchant marine during World War II, he studied at Georgetown University, where he graduated from the School of Foreign Service. Kirkland went directly to work for the AFL. In 1960 he was chosen to be executive assistant to AFL-CIO president Meany. He rose to the number two position of secretary-treasurer in 1969.

Kirkland became known as a "labor statesman" and was more concerned with the role of the AFL-CIO as a model for aspiring free trade unions behind the Iron Curtain than the local state of affairs. He was recognized for his tireless advocacy on behalf of Poland's Solidarity movement. At a memorial for Kirkland after his death in 1999, Polish president Lech Walesa said, "I never had enough opportunity to thank Lane Kirkland for his enormous contribution for our struggle for a better world."

As admirable as were Kirkland's global efforts, he was out of touch with the decline of unions within the United States and unwilling to admit to the problems. He, like Meany before him, saw the role of AFL-CIO senior management as the voice of labor to the federal government with institutional authority regarding labor's "foreign policy." AFL-CIO management officials were well positioned for that role in an impressive location very close to the White House.

Kirkland was coming up for reelection in 1995 when leaders of 11 of the largest unions announced their opposition to his policies and suggested that he resign. As if to document his failures, workers at Bridgestone-Firestone in Decatur, Illinois, had just voted to return to work after a 10-month strike without having received a single concession from management. The rise of Republican congressional power under Newt Gingrich and the loss of any hope for the prolabor legislative effort that had been initiated under President Bill Clinton—the Commission on the

John J. Sweeney. Photograph by Kathy Willens. AP/Wide World Photos. Reproduced by permission.

Future of Worker-Management Relations (the Dunlop Commission)—were other factors behind the opposition to Kirkland and his policies. Labor leaders were looking for a "new voice" who would put money into organizing at the grassroots to rebuild the American union movement.

Sweeney the Candidate

John Sweeney headed the "New Voices for American Workers" ticket with a platform that called for a shift in union priorities to massive additional resources and energy for both active organizing and political action. The movement sought to revitalize the labor movement by rebuilding a strong social movement using rank-and-file mobilization and ongoing involvement. Sweeney had the record to lead the movement. He rose through the ranks to become president of the Service Employees' International Union (SEIU) in 1980. Between 1980 and 1995 the SEIU's membership almost doubled, bringing it to 1.1 million.

Social movement unionism has had a checkered past, although successful social movements in the 1930s produced some of the best growth years for unions. The SEIU used the 1930s' methods of rank-and-file participation to contact prospective members. The movement included making contacts with community and church groups to create an environment that brought in members and kept local pressure on employers who might try to intimidate recruits. However, in 1995 organizing activities faced a much more complex world. Labor unions were facing the challenges of organizing a diverse workforce at home and an expanding global economy that included transnational competition for jobs.

Sweeney spoke at a press conference of the need to recreate a labor movement "that will improve the lives of working people, not just protect them from current assaults. Our members need to see a labor movement that is a powerful voice on behalf of their interests and unorganized workers need to see a movement that can make their lives better." He set organizing the unorganized at the top of an eight-point New Voices platform. Sweeney said he would allocate "at least $20 million to organize over a short period of time." He was planning to accomplish the party goals "by creating a strong grassroots political voice for working people . . . that promotes a clear agenda for workers' rights."

On diversity, the New Voices 1995 platform called for a labor movement that "speaks for and looks like today's workforce" and opens "new opportunities for women, minorities and young people." Sweeney's union could boast of a very successful effort to organize largely immigrant Latino workers in California in a promotion dubbed *Justice for Janitors*. The SEIU's local Justice for Janitors campaign in the Los Angeles area won a contract that included health benefits and paid vacation in addition to a wage of up to $6.80 an hour for its 8,000 Latino workers from a major building cleaning contractor in 1990. It also led to the signing up of 30,000 building cleaners across the country between 1990 and 1995, bringing the total membership in Justice for Janitors up to 180,000.

Running Mates

Sweeney's running mates included Richard Trumka for the position of secretary-treasurer and a female candidate, Linda Chavez-Thompson, for a new position as executive vice president. Trumka was president of the United Mine Workers of America, and Chavez-Thompson was an area vice president of the American Federation of State, County, and Municipal Employees. The Donahue slate also included a female candidate, Barbara Easterling, who was selected to succeed Donahue as AFL-CIO secretary-treasurer when Kirkland resigned. When Donahue boasted of having a female on his slate, Sweeney countered that he not only had a female, but a female of color. Sweeney pledged to bring "many new public faces and voices" into the labor movement.

Linda Chavez-Thompson is a Mexican American, born in Lubbock, Texas. The daughter of a sharecropper, she started her labor career at the age of 10, picking cotton for 30 cents an hour. Before the Sweeney election, no woman or Hispanic had ever held such a high office in the AFL-CIO. At the time, women represented 40 percent of the union workforce and Hispanics 8 percent. She identified minority recruitment as one of her goals.

Sweeney the President

In October 1995 Sweeney won the election by a wide margin to become president of the AFL-CIO, a federation of 78 unions. He started immediately to live up to his campaign goals by increasing organizing expenditures. Sweeney also began working to improve labor's image and to incorporate more women and minorities. He proposed to change the role of the more than 600 Central Labor Councils (CLCs), the diverse constituency groups that include the Coalition of Black Trade, the Coalition of Labor Union Women, the Labor Council for Latin American Advancement, and more. Sweeney charged the CLCs to become "the building blocks and foundation of our revitalized movement."

Top staff positions went to younger and more aggressive unionists. In 1996 Sweeney oversaw the launching of the very successful Union Summer program, a four-week educational internship program of the AFL-CIO that teams students with community activists to develop skills for union organizing drives and campaigns for workers' rights and social justice. The program includes visiting workers in their neighborhoods, participating in direct union actions, and educating the public to rally support for worker's rights issues.

There is no one measure for success of the revitalization campaign begun with the election of Sweeney as president of the AFL-CIO. However, where the slippage of the number of union members compared to the total workforce had been a big factor in the 1995 election, there was some good news at the end of 1999. Union membership grew by over 265,000 that year, the largest single year of growth since the 1970s, just before the start of the decline.

Key Players

Chavez-Thompson, Linda (1944–): Chavez-Thompson is the first woman and the first Hispanic to be elected an officer in the AFL-CIO. In 1993 she was elected to the AFL-CIO Executive Council. In 1995 she was elected to the newly created position of executive vice president, making her the highest ranking woman in the union labor movement at that time.

Kirkland, J. Lane (1922–1999): Kirkland was president of the AFL-CIO from 1979 until his forced retirement in 1995. During his tenure as president, he oversaw the return of the United Auto Workers (1981), the Teamsters (1988), and the United Mine Workers (1989) to the AFL-CIO roster. The Professional Air Traffic Controllers Organization (PATCO) strike that occurred in 1981 contributed to the decline of the union movement, and the percentage of union membership in the workforce declined during Lane's time as president.

Meany, George (1894–1980): Meany was president of the AFL-CIO from the time the two organizations merged in 1955 to 1979, when he retired. He rose through the ranks to become president of the AFL in 1952. During his tenure as president of the AFL-CIO, Meany was not interested in promoting union organizing drives to gain membership as long as uniform wage benefits remained in the well-organized industries.

Sweeney, John J. (1934–): In 1995 Sweeney rose from the ranks to be elected president of the AFL-CIO in the first contested election ever held by the organization. At that time, he was in his fourth term as president of the Service Employees International Union (SEIU), where he had seen the membership double to 1.1 million between 1980 and 1995.

Trumka, Richard L. (1949–): Trumka was elected secretary-treasurer of the AFL-CIO in 1995. Prior to that, he served on the AFL-CIO Executive Council, starting in 1989. When he was elected secretary-treasurer in 1995, Trumka was in his third term as president of the United Mine Workers

(UMW). At the UMW, Trumka had led two major coal strikes.

See also: *AFL, CIO Merge; PATCO Strike.*

BIBLIOGRAPHY

Books

Katz, Harry C., and Richard W. Hurd. *Rekindling the Movement: Labor's Quest for Relevance in the 21st Century.* Ithaca, NY: Cornell University Press, 2001.

Lichtenstein, Nelson. *State of the Union: A Century of American Labor.* Princeton, NJ: Princeton University Press, 2001.

Periodicals

Bernstein, Aaron. "A New Deal at the AFL-CIO?" *Business Week*, 30 October 1995.

———. "Can a New Leader Bring Labor Back to Life?" *Business Week*, 3 July 1995.

Graff, James L., et al. "The Battle to Revive the Unions." *Time*, 30 October 1995.

Regan, Mary Beth. "Shattering the AFL-CIO's Glass Ceiling." *Business Week*, 13 November 1995.

Other

AFL-CIO Web site [cited 11 September 2002]. <http://www.aflcio.org/>.

ADDITIONAL RESOURCES

Buhle, Paul. *Taking Care of Business: Samuel Gompers, George Meany, Lane Kirkland, and the Tragedy of American Labor.* New York: Monthly Review Press, 1999.

Sweeney, John J. *America Needs a Raise: Fighting for Economic Security and Social Justice.* Boston: Houghton Mifflin Company, 1996.

—M. C. Nagel

Syndicalist Movement

Worldwide 1890s–1920s

Synopsis

Between the 1890s and the 1920s, a distinctive group of social movements known variously as revolutionary syndicalist, anarcho-syndicalist, and industrial unionist developed in many parts of Europe, the United States, Latin America, and Australia. However, in juxtaposition to the craft unionism prevalent in the United States and England, syndicalism was a form of labor unionism that aimed to overthrown capitalism through

Pierre-Joseph Proudhon. The Library of Congress.

revolutionary, industrial class struggle and to build a social order free from economic or political oppression. Unlike most socialists who organized workers' parties, the syndicalists concentrated on organizing the working class through unions. Unions served a dual function, acting both as the organizers of class warfare and as the nuclei of the postrevolutionary society. The emancipation of the working class was to be achieved by direct action and the general strike, not by parliamentary pressure or political insurrection designed to lead to state socialism; the aim was control of both the economy and society by workers.

It is far beyond the scope of this entry to explicate every regional and ideological tendency of the syndicalist movement. Rather, emphasis is placed on events in France, as it is the birthplace of both syndicalism and the movement's ideological forefather, Pierre-Joseph Proudhon. However, it is worth noting that in the United States the Industrial Workers of the World (IWW) or "Wobblies" were established in 1905; the Spanish Confederación Nacional del Trabajo (CNT), in 1910; and the Italian Unione Sindacale Italiana, in 1912.

In 1922 the syndicalists set up their own International Workingmen's Association based in Berlin. When the International was established, the Unione Sindacale Italiana had 500,000 members; the Federación Obrera Regional Argentina, 200,000 members; the Portuguese Confederação General dos Trabalhadores, 150,000 members; and the German Freie Arbeiter-Union Deutschlands, 120,000 members. There were smaller organizations in Chile, Uruguay, Denmark, Norway, Holland, Mexico, and Sweden.

In this entry the term "syndicalism" will be substituted for what is more accurately termed "revolutionary syndicalism." The word *syndicat* is the French equivalent of the English trade union, while *revolutionary syndicalism* explicitly means transferring control of production to workers' unions and abolishing

Georges Sorel. The Library of Congress.

formal government by means of a revolutionary general strike. While the latter is a more precise term, the former will be used for the sake of succinctness.

Timeline

1881: U.S. President James A. Garfield is assassinated in a Washington, D.C., railway station by Charles J. Guiteau.

1886: Bombing at Haymarket Square, Chicago, kills seven policemen and injures numerous others. Eight anarchists are accused and tried; three are imprisoned, one commits suicide, and four are hanged.

1890: Alfred Thayer Mahan, a U.S. naval officer and historian, publishes *The Influence of Sea Power Upon History, 1660–1783,* which demonstrates the decisive role that maritime forces have played in past conflicts. The book will have an enormous impact on world events by encouraging the major powers to develop powerful navies.

1894: War breaks out between Japan and China. It will end with China's defeat the next year, marking yet another milestone in China's decline and Japan's rise.

1898: Bayer introduces a cough suppressant, derived from opium. Its brand name: Heroin.

1899: Polish-born German socialist Rosa Luxemburg rejects the argument that working conditions in Europe have improved, and that change must come by reforming the existing system. Rather, she calls for an overthrow of the existing power structure by means of violent international revolution.

1901: U.S. President William McKinley is assassinated by Leon Czolgosz, an anarchist. Vice President Theodore Roosevelt becomes president.

1904: Beginning of the Russo-Japanese War, which lasts into 1905 and results in a resounding Japanese victory. In Russia, the war is followed by the Revolution of 1905, which marks the beginning of the end of czarist rule; meanwhile, Japan is poised to become the first major non-western power of modern times.

1905: Russian Revolution of 1905. Following the "bloody Sunday" riots before the Winter Palace in St. Petersburg in January, revolution spreads throughout Russia, in some places spurred on by newly formed workers' councils, or soviets. Among the most memorable incidents of the revolt is the mutiny aboard the battleship *Potemkin.* Suppressed by the czar, the revolution brings an end to liberal reforms, and thus sets the stage for the larger revolution of 1917.

1908: The U.S. Supreme Court, in the Danbury Hatters' case, rules that secondary union boycotts (i.e., boycotts of nonunion manufacturers' products, organized by a union) are unlawful.

1909: William Cadbury's *Labour in Portuguese West Africa* draws attention to conditions of slavery in São Tomé and Principe.

1918: Upheaval sweeps Germany, which for a few weeks in late 1918 and early 1919 seems poised on the verge of communist revolution—or at least a Russian-style communist coup d'etat. But reactionary forces have regained their strength, and the newly organized Freikorps (composed of unemployed soldiers) suppresses the revolts. Even stronger than reaction or revolution, however, is republican sentiment, which opens the way for the creation of a democratic government based at Weimar.

Event and Its Context

Historical Beginnings of Syndicalism in France

A brief historical overview tracing the contributing factors to the development of French syndicalism within the context of the larger working-class movement is useful to understanding the movement as it took shape at the dawn of the twentieth century. The *compagnonnages* of journeymen dated from the fifteenth century and were organized around a guild structure. They also directed strikes and boycotts in defense of their economic interests. When all citizens were given the right to combine freely in 1790, workers quickly took advantage of the law by organizing trade unions. After a plethora of strikes, the government passed the Le Chapelier law in 1791, forbidding all combinations for the purpose of changing existing labor conditions. Workers responded by forming underground *sociétés de résistance*. Following decades of successive foment and repression, including the revolution of 1848, the right to form unions and strike was restored by Napoleon III (1808–1873), who ruled France as emperor from 1852 to 1871. *Chambres Syndicats Ouvriéres,* later known as *syndicats,* were formed in bakeries, print shops, and newer occupations, including metallurgy.

Beginning with the French Revolution of 1789, some agitators had urged revolution for its own sake, without great concern for what would come next. Adolphe Blanqui was the leading advocate of this approach during much of the nineteenth century; from the Blanquist tradition came many syndicalist leaders, notably Victor Griffuelhes, the head of the *Confédération Générale du Travail* (CGT), the primary organization of the syndicalists in France, during the early twentieth century. Finally, by about 1900, syndicalism benefited from an influx of revolutionary anarchist leaders; disenchanted with the failures of anarchism's tactic of "propaganda by the deed," they began to advocate less violent forms of resistance, primarily the general strike.

Proudhon and the Intellectual Foundation of Syndicalism

The most significant intellectual forerunner of syndicalism was Pierre-Joseph Proudhon, the artisan who made France's greatest contribution to socialist thought. Proudhon's thinking dominated French labor movements in the third quarter of the nineteenth century, and he was in many ways syndicalism's logical precursor.

French workers participated in the creation of the International Workingmen's Association, which came to be known as the First International, in London in 1864. The bulk of delegates from the French section, eventually the largest national section in the First International, were Proudhonists who supported workers' activity in the economic realm through the formation of unions, cooperatives, and mutual banks, rather than party activity. As anarchists, they placed great emphasis on spontaneous action, voluntarism, federalism, and *ouvrierisme* (control of the class struggle without the aid of intellectuals). This placed the syndicalists in direct opposition to the Marxist program of nationalization of industry, electoral activity, and the centralization of both the First International and the state.

At the Basel Congress of 1869, a Proudhonian delegate advocated the concentration of the energies of the First International upon the formation of unions, or *syndicats*. First, he noted, "they are the means of resisting exploitation in the present," and secondly, "the groupings of different trades in the city will form the commune of the future." Once this commune was formed, "the government will be replaced by federated councils of *syndicats,* and by a committee of their respective delegates regulating the relation of labor—this taking the place of politics."

Appeal of Syndicalism to Diverse Groups

The intellectual underpinnings of syndicalism meant that the movement stemmed from and had particular appeal for a number of key groups. The groups can be defined in different though somewhat overlapping ways. Syndicalism attracted many workers raised in a trade-union tradition. Union traditions in this period were strengthened by Proudhonism, which distrusted political methods. Part of syndicalism, then, was a pure and simple trade unionism, with all means of production in the hands of the workers themselves.

The syndicalist approach also had special appeal to craftsmen. Artisans like printers and carpenters had the longest trade-union traditions in France. The syndicalist stress on local organization and producers' control of their own work appealed to even older artisanal traditions; vaguely and in obviously radical language, syndicalism seemed to suggest something like a restoration of idealized guilds. Emphasis on small size and participant control of economic organization in the interests of economic justice and equality certainly recalled the guild tradition; Proudhon's thought had intellectualized this artisanal heritage.

Syndicalism had particular resonance to workers in Paris, partly because of the city's unusually intense revolutionary tradition, which included, in the glorification of the Paris Commune of 1871, hostility to the whole apparatus of central government and vigorous attachment to the Jacobin notion of direct democracy. Furthermore, the professions most open to syndicalism, notably the building trades, were, on the whole, the same as those that had provided the bulk of the men who manned the barricades in 1830 and 1848. These sources gave the movement real strength.

Social, Political, and Economic Factors Encourage Development of Syndicalism

The massacre of about 20,000 Communards during the French government's destruction of the Paris Commune in May 1871 completely changed the nature of the working-class movement and socialism. Government repression of the Com-

285

mune destroyed confidence in the Proudhonist notion, dear to many workers, that emancipation would occur through peaceful evolution. Also, the Commune threw the nascent syndicalist movement into a temporary eclipse. With most of the French militants either dead or in exile, unionism was forced into a period of moderation.

In addition to these social and political factors, there were also economic circumstances that pushed French workers towards syndicalism. First, unusual radicalism was induced by unusual economic hardship in this period; and second, radicalism took a syndicalist form because of the peculiar artisanal structure of French manufacturing.

France was less completely industrialized than either Germany or Britain, and her firms were smaller. This structure in turn encouraged a labor movement whose organization and goals were both highly decentralized. Workers could not easily establish a tightly organized union movement because factories were small and dispersed, and tight organization was unnecessary because their employers too, were individualistic and weakly organized. Finally, large numbers of workers were artisans and sought a movement that would express their hopes for a local, producer-controlled economy. French artisans faced something of a crisis at the end of the nineteenth century, aside from specific developments in wages or levels of employment. Mechanization spread to almost all trades, often for the first time. At the same time, the size of companies in the traditional trades increased.

Development of the *Bourses du Travail*

There were also legal factors to consider. Syndicalism began to emerge in the 1880s after passage of the Waldeck-Rousseau Law (1884) legislated the right of workers to associate. Because of the defeat of the Commune in 1871 and subsequent repression, French labor movements of all sorts had ground to a halt in the 1870s. The trade unions that existed before the 1884 law were mainly local, isolated, and rather conservative. Then, with the possibilities that the 1884 law afforded, the first important associations of unions arose on a local basis. That is, unions from various professions, like printing and baking, grouped in a citywide federation, a *bourse du travail* ("trades council"); national federations in the same profession followed more slowly. The *bourse du travail* movement, which federated very loosely at the national level in the 1890s, both reflected and furthered a syndicalist tendency. In 1892 a national confederation of *bourses du travail* was formed, and by 1895 the anarchists, led by Fernand Pelloutier and Émile Pouget, had acquired positions of leadership.

As with the *compagnonnages,* the *bourses* served as employment offices and fraternal organizations, providing temporary and migrant workers with clean beds, baths, and food. They were also cultural centers in that they compiled libraries and offered vocational classes for the local unions. In addition, the *bourses* quickly became the chief center for organizing trade unions. These unions were usually affiliated by profession. Under the sheltering umbrella of the local *bourses,* however, the unions tended to take on a more regional characteristic, organizing into a federation, with the federations subsequently forming into the *Fédération des Bourses du Travail* (FBT).

The head of the *bourse du travail* movement, Fernand Pelloutier, was the first real articulator of syndicalist ideas. In the late 1890s, the FBT set up a general strike committee. (Even earlier, in the late 1880s, general labor congresses had accepted the idea of a general strike to destroy capitalist society.) The *bourse du travail* movement ebbed after 1900 and soon merged with the CGT, which had begun in 1895. There were numerous splits in the revolutionary workers' movement between advocates of the general strike and their opponents.

But the CGT, though organized mainly on the basis of national industrial unions, had itself been captured by syndicalism. The statutes of the CGT in 1903 included an effective if somewhat muted declaration of syndicalism: "[The CGT] assembles, outside of any political tendency, all workers who are conscious of the struggle necessary for the disappearance of wage work and the employer class."

Merger of the FBT and the CGT

Although the FBT was a strong organization, particularly under Pelloutier's leadership, another organization ultimately came to absorb it. With all the factions still jockeying for control, another national congress was convened in 1895. Included in the delegations were *bourse* leaders, those who supported the general strike, and militants from the radical *Parti Ouvrier Socialiste Révolutionaire* (PSOR). The time had come, delegates agreed, to organize a stronger national committee in order to coordinate labor activities. The new organization was named *Confédération Générale du Travail* (CGT). Its task was to serve as a kind of clearinghouse of labor activity between *syndicats* and *bourses* on the local, regional, and national levels.

The CGT was housed in Paris but held congresses in various parts of the country. Delegates to the administrative council and to the congresses were to be elected by the individual organizations. The duties of the national council were to carry out propaganda and coordinate strikes. More importantly, every *bourse,* local union, and trade federation adhering to the CGT, regardless of the number of members in its organization, had one vote. So, by 1900 syndicalism attracted many French workers, and for a variety of reasons. The suppression of the Commune had embittered many workers and proved to them that the republican government was bourgeois and repressive. Long after the 1870s it was easy to see the government in this role. The French government, for all its commitment to political radicalism, was harsher and less sympathetic to workers than most other European states.

Partly because of the sense that politics had deceived them, French workers were suspicious of other political remedies. They were further disillusioned by French socialism as exemplified by Jules Guesde and the *Parti Ouvrier Socialiste,* which was authoritarian and inflexible. Its Marxist doctrine emphasized disciplined organization and a general disdain of strikes that displeased many French workers. In rebellion against Guesdist control of labor congresses and their increasing efforts to take over the union movement, French workers began introducing resolutions for a general strike in the 1880s. The CGT was formed when a general strike resolution in 1894 led to the collapse of the Guesdist *Fédération Nationale du Syndicats.* All of this activity simply widened the breach with socialism, for the Guesdists did not believe that strikes, whether general or partial, could have any significant success.

The syndicalist movement waned in numbers and influence following World War I. Despite its philosophical opposition to Marxism, the Soviet interpretation of communism lured many syndicalists toward that camp. The material advances being obtained by trade unionism in western European countries outside of France also tended to attract French workers. Some aspects of syndicalist thought still influence contemporary anarchists. Even the richest and most stable governments falter in their resolve to ameliorate long-term social problems, assuring that syndicalist and anarchist thought will retain its attraction for workers and citizens concerned with these issues.

Key Players

Griffuelhes, (Jean) Victor (1874–1922): Griffuelhes was a CGT organizer who supported a shift in the union from craft unionism to industrial unionism. He was also union secretary and coauthor of the Charter of Amiens that made syndicalism the official doctrine of the CGT. His reputation was undermined due to allegations that he misappropriated union funds.

Pelloutier, Fernand (1867–1901): As a young journalist, Pelloutier moved from republicanism to socialism but left the *Parti Ouvrier Français* after the Guesdists rejected the general strike. Widely regarded as the father of anarchosyndicalism, he wrote numerous articles in *Les temps nouveaux* from 1895 to 1901 and was founder and editor of *L'ouvrier des deux mondes*. He authored *L'organisation corporative et l'anarchie* and *Histoire des bourses du travail: origine—institutions—avenir,* which was published posthumously.

Pouget, Jean-Joseph Émile (1860–1931): Anarchist, antimilitarist, and editor. On 8 March 1883 he led a series of attacks on three bakeries with the Communard Louise Michel during a demonstration of the Parisian Unemployed. He was editor of *Le père peinard* and *La sociale*. An organizer of the textile employees union, he became a leading member of the CGT in 1895. In 1900 he founded the CGT publishing organ, *La voix du peuple,* with Fernand Pelloutier. Major works include *Gréve générale réformiste et gréve générale révolutionaire,* and *Comment nous ferons la revolution* with Emile Pataud.

Proudhon, Pierre-Joseph (1809–1865): Proudhon was an editor of *Le représentant du peuple,* its successor *Le peuple,* and *La voix du peuple.* He was a social theorist regarded by many as the father of anarchism. His widely read pamphlet, *What Is Property?* condemned the abuses of private property and embraced anarchism. After the revolution of 1848, he was elected a member of the constituent assembly and unsuccessfully attempted to establish a national bank for reorganization of credit in the interest of the workers. Proudhon left a great mass of literature that influenced the French syndicalist movement. His most important books include *System of Economic Contradictions; or The Philosophy of Poverty* and *De la justice dans la révolution et dans l'église* (Of Justice in the Revolution and in the Church). Proudhon was also a contemporary of Karl Marx and Mikhail Bakunin. In 1846 he took issue with Marx over the organization of the socialist movement, objecting to Marx's authoritarian and centralist ideas. Shortly afterward, when Proudhon published his *Système des contradictions économiques, ou philosophie de la misère* (System of Economic Contradictions: or, The Philosophy of Poverty), Marx attacked him bitterly in a book-length polemic, *La misère de la philosophie.*

Sorel, Georges (1847–1922): An engineer, social philosopher, and writer, Sorel was one of the primary exponents of revolutionary syndicalism. His best-known work, *Réflexions sue la violence,* became an exemplary text of syndicalism. His ideological commitments were disparate, ranging from support for French monarchism to the Bolshevik Revolution.

See also: *Confédération Générale du Travail; First International; Industrial Workers of the World; Paris Commune.*

BIBLIOGRAPHY

Books

Bourgeois, Nicolas. *Les théories du droit international chez Proudhon, le fédéralisme et la paix.* Paris, France: M. Rivière, 1927.

Jackson, J. Hampden. *Marx, Proudhon, and European Socialism.* New York: Collier Books, 1962.

Hoffman, Robert Louis. *Revolutionary Justice: The Social and Political Theory of Pierre-Joseph Proudhon.* Urbana, IL: University of Illinois Press, 1972.

Hyams, Edward. *Pierre-Joseph Proudhon: His Revolutionary Life, Mind, and Works.* New York: Taplinger, 1979.

Jennings, Jeremy. *Syndicalism in France: A Study of Ideas.* New York: St. Martin's Press, 1990.

Maitron, Jean, ed. *Dictionnaire biographique du mouvement ouvrier français.* Vols. 10–15. Paris: Editions Ouvrièrs, 1974.

Mitchell, Barbara. *The Practical Revolutionaries: A New Interpretation of the French Anarchosyndicalists.* New York: Greenwood Press, 1987.

Pelloutier, Fernand. *Histoire des bourses du travail: origine—institutions—avenir.* Paris: Schleicher Freres, 1902.

Proudhon, Pierre-Joseph. *Idée Générale de la révolution au XIXe siècle.* Paris: Rivière, 1851.

———. *La révolution sociale demontrée par le coup d'état du 2 décembre 1851.* Paris: Garnier Freres, 1852.

———. *Oeuvres complètes de P.-J. Proudhon.* Paris: Lacroix, 1866–1876.

———. *Selected Writings of Pierre-Joseph Proudhon.* ed. Stewart Edwards, trans. Elizabeth Fraser. New York: Anchor Books, 1969.

———. *The Principle of Federation.* Toronto: University of Toronto Press, 1979.

Ridley, Frederick F. *Revolutionary Syndicalism in France: the Direct Action of its Time.* Cambridge, England: Cambridge University Press, 1970.

Ritter, Alan. *The Political Thought of Pierre-Joseph Proudhon.* Princeton, NJ: Princeton University Press, 1969.

Spargo, John. *Syndicalism, Industrial Unionism, and Socialism.* New York: B.W. Huebsch, 1913.

Stearns, Peter N. *Revolutionary Syndicalism and French Labor: A Cause Without Rebels.* New Brunswick, NJ: Rutgers University Press, 1971.

Vandervort, Bruce. *Victor Griffuelhes and French Syndicalism, 1895–1922.* Baton Rouge, LA: Louisiana State University Press, 1996.

Woodcock, George. *Pierre-Joseph Proudhon.* London, England: Routledge & Paul, 1956.

—Evan Daniel

T

Taff Vale Case

Great Britain 1900–1901

Synopsis

The Taff Vale case centered on a brief but bitterly fought strike waged by the Amalgamated Society of Railway Servants (ASRS) against the management of the Taff Vale Railway Company in South Wales in August 1900. The company took the ASRS to court and was awarded £23,000 in damages and £19,000 costs. This ruling threatened to destroy the unions' ability to wage effective strike action; the need for political redress led to a sharp increase in the rate of trade union affiliations to the Labour Representation Committee (renamed the Labour Party in 1906). The Trades Disputes Act of 1906 overturned the court decision by legalizing peaceful picketing and restoring union immunity against actions for damages caused by strikes.

Timeline

1880: Cattle drives up the Chisholm Trail in the western United States reach their peak.

1890: Congress passes the Sherman Antitrust Act, which in the years that follow will be used to break up large monopolies.

1896: U.S. Supreme Court issues its *Plessy v. Ferguson* decision, which establishes the "separate but equal" doctrine that will be used to justify segregation in the southern United States for the next half-century.

1900: China's Boxer Rebellion, which began in the preceding year with attacks on foreigners and Christians, reaches its height. An international contingent of more than 2,000 men arrives to restore order, but only after several tens of thousands have died.

1900: Sigmund Freud publishes *The Interpretation of Dreams.*

1900: German physicist Max Planck develops Planck's constant, a cornerstone of quantum theory.

1901: Guglielmo Marconi makes the first successful transmission and reception of a radio signal.

1901: U.S. President William McKinley is assassinated by Leon Czolgosz, an anarchist. Vice President Theodore Roosevelt becomes president.

1901: Austrian-American immunologist Karl Landsteiner identifies A, B, and O blood types.

1903: Henry Ford establishes the Ford Motor Company.

1907: U.S. markets experience a financial panic.

1911: Turkish-Italian War sees the first use of aircraft as an offensive weapon. Italian victory results in the annexation of Libya.

Event and Its Context

The Industrial Context

The roots of the Taff Vale case lay in the particular nature of the railway industry and in the evolving character of the trade union movement in the late nineteenth century. Public safety concerns and industry's economic significance meant that the railways were subject to stringent government regulation. Parliament had limited employees' hours of service and in 1888 and 1894 stipulated uniform schedules of charges for railway services. Rising costs and increased competition in the 1890s led to a squeeze on profits and strengthened the companies' resistance to union demands. Railway managers also believed that union demands infringed upon their responsibility for railway safety. Many railway companies prided themselves on offering high wages and fringe benefits but, whereas company paternalism resented the disruption that was threatened by union activists, in the view of union members, such paternalism slid easily into authoritarianism. As profit margins fell in the 1890s, the Railway Companies' Association agreed on concerted action to oppose union recognition and to maintain services and income in the event of strike action. Many companies subscribed to the National Free Labour Association that was formed in 1893 to supply nonunion labor to strike-affected industries.

Traditionally, trade unionism had been a weak force in the railway industry. In 1890 only 13 percent of the railway workforce (48,000 out of a total of 381,000 workers) were union members. The railway unions, however, shared in the general upsurge of union membership and militancy that occurred between 1889 and 1891. In August 1890 an eight-day strike against the Taff Vale Railway Company achieved reduced hours, a guaranteed weekly wage, and *de facto* union recognition.

Although Taff Vale management respected the letter of the agreement, the arrival of Ammon Beasley as general manager in 1891 signaled a new, more combative phase in union-management relations. Beasley came from the Great Western Railway with a reputation as a harsh disciplinarian, and he refused further bargaining with the railway unions. The company itself, long the beneficiary of a profitable local monopoly on coal transport, was suffering increased competition and declining profits.

The genesis of the Taff Vale dispute offers, therefore, a cameo of the wider patterns of industrial relations that were operating within Britain at the time. The brief success of the ASRS in the 1890 dispute and its subsequent forced retreat reflected contemporary developments in the broader union movement. Union growth and militancy, symbolized by the 1889 Dock Strike, resulted in employer backlash in the 1890s. The creation of employers' confederations; the establishment of the National Free Labour Association; and lock-outs directed against bastions of union power in the cotton, coal, and engineering sectors in 1893 and 1897–1898 all signified a new-

Ramsay MacDonald. The Library of Congress.

found determination among British industrialists to assert their power at a time of growing concerns over the competitiveness of British industry. Newspaper campaigns, notably in *The Times*, bolstered the position of the industrial power base by criticizing union power and obstructionism. A series of legal cases, most notably *Lyons vs. Wilkins* in 1896, which greatly restricted picketing rights, also seemed to reflect "Establishment" hostility to trade unionism.

The Taff Vale Strike

The situation at Taff Vale came to a head in 1900. The railwaymen's bargaining position has been strengthened by the Boer War (reservists had been called up, and the company was an important supplier of coal to the navy). James Holmes, a militant local organizer of the ASRS, took the opportunity to challenge the power of the Beasley, who was known as the "Taff Vale dictator," in an open letter in the September 1899 edition of the ASRS's *Railway Review*. The letter berated the craven attitude of local railwaymen. A mass meeting calling for improved conditions followed, but the subsequent strike ballot was indecisive. In June 1900 Holmes disseminated a circular to the workforce, which was well received in part because of the alleged victimization of John Ewington, a Taff Vale signalman and union activist who had been relocated 16 miles to a new place of work. On 19 August a mass meeting of the ASRS's Pontypridd branch voted for immediate strike action. Against Holmes' powerful local leadership, Richard Bell, the more moderate General Secretary of the ASRS, was unable to contain

what he felt to be a precipitate move and he was sent to Taff Vale to take charge of the dispute. The union's national committee narrowly gave official sanction to the strike by a vote of seven to five. The 350 signalmen, guards, and brakemen who originated the strike were reinforced by drivers and firefighters until some 800 workers were involved in the dispute.

The strike itself was bitterly fought. The company maintained surveillance of union meetings and kept files on strike ringleaders. It also contacted the National Association of Free Labour, which supplied 197 workers to take the place of those on strike. The unions dissuaded one-third of these from taking employment, but Beasley was careful to ensure that those who did work signed contracts of employment. Union members picketed and took additional direct action to prevent the Company from operating. Strikers greased the railway tracks to prevent traffic and on one occasion diverted onto a siding and detained a carriage containing blackleg labor. Local courts issued 400 summonses against the strikers. The company also secured an injunction against Holmes, who had published an article in the local press that was critical of the replacement workers. Taff Vale was able to maintain a level of passenger service, but its freight operations were effectively halted, causing a loss of some £20,000 in revenue.

Nevertheless, the balance of power lay with the employers. The strikers returned to work on 1 September, believing the scab, or blackleg, workers would be dismissed and a Conciliation Board established to adjudicate issues of dispute. In practice, management was less conciliatory—blackleg workers retained their employment and, although most strikers were allowed back, they returned in humiliating circumstances. The company did drop some summonses for intimidation but charges of criminal damage and assault were allowed to stand.

The Taff Vale Case

The ultimate significance of the Taff Vale case to the British labor movement was the company's determination to pursue the union for damages. In the initial hearing, Justice Farwell held that the unions were indeed corporations that were liable for the unlawful conduct of their officials and members. This was overturned in the Court of Appeal, but in July 1901 the House of Lords, the highest court in the land, upheld and reaffirmed the original ruling. The five law lords concurred with the Lord Chancellor, Lord Halsbury, that Parliament, having legalized trade unions as corporate bodies, must have intended them to be suable under the law. Politics and class prejudice played a part in these decisions, which also reflected a widespread antipathy within the legal establishment to the unions' unique legal immunities.

Beasley sought damages against the union for "having conspired to induce the workmen to break their contracts, and also for having conspired to interfere with the traffic of the company by picketing and other unlawful means." Beasley's case against the ASRS reached the courts in December 1902 and the Company was awarded £23,000 in damages plus £19,000 in costs.

Impact of the Decision

The Lords' decision was a bombshell to the British union movement and its implications were stark: the courts had in effect abolished the unions' right to strike or, at any rate, their

James Keir Hardie addresses crowd, Trafalgar Square, London, England. © Hulton/Getty Images. Reproduced by permission.

right to strike effectively and without crippling financial cost. Though a few union leaders initially held that the ruling might have some beneficial impact in curbing the "hotheads" of the movement, most realized that legislation overturning the verdict was essential if the union movement hoped to retain any power to influence industrial relations. A significant decline in industrial action between 1903 and 1907 seems to reflect fears of the Judgment's implications.

The Conservative Government set up a Royal Commission to investigate but made it clear that it had no intention of reforming the law to the unions' benefit. The Liberal Party appeared to lack either the ability or the will to secure redress. In these circumstances, Keir Hardie, Ramsay MacDonald, and other leaders of the Labour Representation Committee (LRC), which was formed in 1900 as an amalgamation of socialist and trade union interests seeking to secure independent labor representation in Parliament, were quick to argue the LRC's essential role. Trade union affiliations to the LRC rose sharply. Between 1900 and mid-1901, 41 unions had joined the LRC, for a total membership of 353,070; between February 1902 and February

1903, 127 additional unions joined, bringing the LRC's membership to 847,315. At this point, 49 unions were affiliated to the LRC, representing some 56 percent of the membership of the Trades Union Congress (TUC).

A Liberal landslide in the 1905 General Election secured the conditions for legislative reform. The Royal Commission's Majority Report in 1906 proposed the legalization of peaceful picketing and the protection of the unions' welfare funds. The general and strike funds, however, would remain vulnerable to legal action. The Labour Party greeted this limited reform, which had been endorsed by the new Liberal government, with hostility. Protest by Labour Members of Parliament (MPs) and sympathetic Liberals, coordinated by David Shackleton, led the government to backtrack. It agreed to take over a bill that had been tabled by the Labour Party along lines suggested by the TUC. The Trades Disputes Act of 1906 granted complete immunity to union funds from legal actions for damages and affirmed rights of peaceful picketing. This act remained the essential charter of trade union rights until the reforms of Margaret Thatcher in the 1980s.

Key Players

Bell, Richard (1859–1930): Born in South Wales, he began work on the railways at age 16. He became an organizing secretary for the ASRS in 1893 and its general secretary in 1898. He served as Labour MP for Derby from 1900 to 1910 but remained essentially a Liberal in his politics. He worked for the Government Board of Trade from 1910 to 1920.

Hardie, James Keir (1856–1915): Hardie began work in Glasgow at age eight. He became a miner at 11 years of age but was later dismissed for his role in organizing a union and strike. He became secretary of the Scottish Miners' Federation and, having abandoned Liberalism, was elected Britain's first socialist MP in 1892. A founding member of the Independent Labour Party in 1893, Hardie was a leading figure in the formation of the LRC in 1900 and Labour's parliamentary leader between 1906 and 1908.

MacDonald, Ramsay (1866–1937): The illegitimate son of a Scottish maidservant. An early member of the Fabian Society and Independent Labour Party, he became the secretary of the Labour Representation Committee. MacDonald was a Labour MP (1906–1918 and 1922–1931 and National Labour MP from 1931 to 1937) and was elected Labour leader in 1922. He served as prime minister in 1924 and 1929–31. MacDonald was an increasingly "respectable" moderate who opposed the 1926 General Strike and became leader of a "National" coalition government from 1931 to 1935.

Shackleton, David (1863–1938): A Lancashire weaver who rose to become president of the Amalgamated Weavers' Association from 1906 to 1910. A member of the TUC's Parliamentary Committee (1904–1910), an MP (1902–1910), and a member of Labour's Executive Committee (1903–1905), Shackleton was important as a trade union moderate who built support for the Labour Party. He worked in labor-related civil service positions from 1910 to 1925.

BIBLIOGRAPHY

Books

Clegg, H. A, Alan Fox, and A. F. Thompson. *A History of British Trade Unions since 1889.* Volume I, *1889–1910.* Oxford: Clarendon Press, 1964.

Periodicals

Alderman, Geoffrey. "The Railway Companies and the Growth of Trades Unionism in the Late Nineteenth and Early Twentieth Centuries." *The Historical Journal* 14, no. 1 (1971): 129–152.

Harvey, Charles, and Jon Press. "Management and the Taff Vale Strike of 1900." *Business History* 42, no. 2 (2000): 63–86.

McCord, Norman. "Taff Vale Revisited." *History* 78 (June 1993): 243–260.

ADDITIONAL RESOURCES

Books

Adelman, Paul. *The Rise of the Labour Party, 1880–1945.* 3rd ed. London, New York: Longman, 1996.

Bealey, Frank, and Henry Pelling. *Labour and Politics, 1900–1906: A History of the Labour Representation Committee.* Westport, CT: Greenwood Press, 1982.

Browne, Harry. *The Rise of British Trade Unions, 1825–1914.* London: Longman, 1979.

Pelling, Henry. *A Short History of the Labour Party.* 11th ed. New York: St. Martin's Press, 1996.

—John Boughton

Taft-Hartley Act

United States 1947

Synopsis

The Taft-Hartley Act was characterized by labor unions at the time of its passage as "the slave-labor law," and many of its congressional proponents thought that the law would inhibit the power of labor unions. Many historians today, however, argue that the act merely codified practices that the National Labor Relations Board (NLRB) was implementing at the time. The passage of this law signaled a change in governmental attitudes toward labor, with real restrictions being placed upon the activities of labor unions. Secondary boycotts and the closed shop were outlawed; states were allowed to pass "right-to-work" laws, which in turn prevented unions from compelling workers that they represented from becoming members of the union; and the president was given the power to proclaim a "cooling-off" period in disputes that he deemed to be a threat to national safety or health. Perhaps most importantly, passage of the Taft-Hartley Act signaled to labor unions that they would never be considered an equal partner with government and business.

Timeline

1926: Britain paralyzed by a general strike.

1931: Financial crisis widens in the United States and Europe, which reel from bank failures and climbing unemployment levels. In London, armies of the unemployed riot.

1936: The election of a leftist Popular Front government in Spain in February precipitates an uprising by rightists under the leadership of Francisco Franco. Over the next three years, war will rage between the Loyalists and Franco's Nationalists. The Spanish Civil War will prove to be a lightning rod for the world's tensions, with the Nazis and fascists supporting the Nationalists, and the Soviets the Loyalists.

1941: Japanese bombing of Pearl Harbor on 7 December brings the United States into the war against the Axis.

Combined with the attack on the Soviet Union, which makes Stalin an unlikely ally of the Western democracies, the events of 1941 will ultimately turn the tide of the war.

1946: Winston Churchill warns of an "Iron Curtain" spreading across Eastern Europe.

1946: Three months after the first meeting of the United Nations General Assembly in London in January, the all-but-defunct League of Nations is officially dissolved.

1946: At the Nuremberg trials, twelve Nazi leaders are sentenced to death, and seven others to prison.

1946: Building of the first true electronic computer, the Electronic Numerical Integrator and Computer (ENIAC).

1951: Six western European nations form the European Coal and Steel Community, forerunner of the European Economic Community and the later European Union.

1956: Elvis Presley appears on Ed Sullivan's *Toast of the Town,* where he performs "Hound Dog" and "Love Me Tender" before a mostly female audience. Nationwide, 54 million people watch the performance, setting a new record.

1961: President Eisenhower steps down, warning of a "military-industrial complex" in his farewell speech, and 43-year-old John F. Kennedy becomes the youngest elected president in U.S. history. Three months later, he launches an unsuccessful invasion of Cuba at the Bay of Pigs.

Event and Its Context

Workers' Rights and the National Labor Relations Act

Passage of the National Labor Relations Act in 1935, better known as the Wagner Act, signaled a slight shift in governmental attitudes towards union organizing. In the spring and summer of 1934, more than half a million workers went out on strike, which caused Congress to seek mechanisms for greater labor stability in the United States. Such stability had long been the objective of the United States government's attitude towards labor-management relations. For much of the previous 50 years, however, the government had left this regulation to the courts, which tried to achieve this aim through court injunctions and restrictive interpretations of legislative acts, both of which benefited management in its ongoing struggle with labor.

Workers first earned the right to bargain collectively when the National Industrial Recovery Act became law in 1933; however, that act was declared unconstitutional in 1935. The Wagner Act reestablished the right of workers to collective bargaining, and it created the National Labor Relations Board (NLRB), an administrative agency. The NLRB had two functions: to supervise union representation elections and to stop unfair labor practices on the part of employers, employees, and unions. This often meant that the NLRB decided, in the midst of conflicting claims, which union would represent workers in a particular establishment. What constituted unfair labor practices was left open-ended, but the NLRB was given the power to investigate charges and the means to encourage informal settlements, as well as to instigate quasijudicial proceedings that could be enforced by the U.S. Court of Appeals.

Strike Wave of 1945–1946

This new activist bent on the part of the state in favor of labor unions was extremely disturbing to American business leaders, as well as to Republican and conservative Democratic politicians in Washington, D.C. Not until after the end of World War II, however, was the political atmosphere conducive to amending the Wagner Act in management's favor. In 1945 and 1946 a wave of strikes occurred across the United States. The United Auto Workers struck General Motors; the United Steel Workers struck U.S. Steel; and the United Electrical Workers struck General Electric. Besides these massive work stoppages, general strikes occurred in Pittsburgh, Pennsylvania; Oakland, California; and Stamford, Connecticut. With millions of workers and citizens affected, the strike wave had two significant results. First, probusiness forces were sufficiently frightened that they searched for common ground to restrict the power of labor. Second, workers were so discouraged that voter turnout in the 1946 congressional elections was very low. Consequently, the Republican Party took control of both the House and the Senate in 1947.

Legislative Efforts to Amend the National Labor Relations Act

In the first two weeks of the first session of the Eightieth Congress, 21 bills were introduced in the Senate, and 37 in the House, that dealt with labor unions and collective bargaining. By early February 1947, Congressman Fred Hartley (1902–1969) of New Jersey was leading hearings on four of these bills in the Committee on Education and Labor. The four bills in committee were those submitted by representatives Case of South Dakota, Hoffman of Michigan, Landis of Indiana, and Smith of Virginia. At the same time, legislative aides and representatives from business and industry, in particular members of the National Association of Manufacturers, were drafting a committee bill, H.R. 3020. H.R. 3020 was based on bills submitted by Case and Smith in 1946 to amend the Wagner Act. (These amendments had previously passed the House in 1940 but never became law.) Prominent features of H.R. 3020 included proposals to restructure the NLRB, outlaw industry-wide bargaining, grant private employers direct access to injunctive relief, and promulgate an employee "bill of rights" that would require extensive government intervention in the internal affairs of unions. Moreover, prescriptive procedures to be followed in collective bargaining were minutely outlined. Minority members of the committee from the Democratic Party protested their limited input in drafting the bill, but it passed the House by a large majority on 17 April.

In the Senate the Committee on Labor and Public Welfare began hearings in late January on two bills introduced by Senator Joseph Ball (1905–1993) of Minnesota. Parts of Ball's two bills were incorporated into the committee bill, S.R. 1126, but the committee bill did not incorporate all of Ball's key provisions. Consequently, Ball and committee chair Robert A. Taft (18891–1953) of Ohio, along with two other members of the committee, recommended amendments to the committee bill during the floor debate, two of which were accepted. The Senate version of the bill, which according to most observers was far less severe than the House version, was passed on 14 May. A considerable amount of publicity appeared calling on the House manager to retreat from some of the more extreme provisions, which might prevent passage of the needed legislation, since any resultant legislation needed to be approved by President Truman or be able to prevail over his veto.

Provisions of the Taft-Hartley Act

Unlike the Wagner Act that it modified, the Taft-Hartley Act was an omnibus bill of four titles. Title I contained most of the modifications to the Wagner Act. It changed the administrative structure of the National Labor Relations Board, as well as some of the procedures of the board as it was described in the Wagner Act. Taft-Hartley changed the definition of "employee" to exclude supervisors (in response to management fears over the proliferation of foremen's unions in the postwar period), and emphasized the rights of employees to decline to participate in collective activity. Title I also attempted to define "good faith" in collective bargaining, and therefore what would constitute an unfair labor practice, and it required both parties to give notice of any intention to terminate or modify their contract. Section 9 of Title I required unions to register with the secretary of labor and to file annual financial reports. Moreover, all officers of unions were required to sign affidavits proclaiming that they were not members of the Communist Party in order to use any of the NLRB apparatus. (This provision is the only part of the Taft-Hartley Act to be eventually overturned, owing to its blatant unconstitutionality.) Finally, Title I restricted state jurisdiction over labor relations except in union security matters, and it banned the closed shop (which required that employees in an establishment belong to the union before they could be hired to work there) within the area of federal jurisdiction. It also required the majority of employees in a unit to approve any attempt to negotiate a union-shop contract.

Title II endorsed enhanced federal aid to conciliation, mediation, and voluntary arbitration, encouraged labor and management to develop grievance procedures for the settlement of disputes, and outlined procedures for the restraint of strikes considered to present a threat to the national interest. Title III declared certain categories of union and employer behavior illegal and established procedures to regulate union welfare funds, to facilitate private suits for damages arising from breach of contract, and to restrict political fund expenditures by unions. Finally, Title IV provided for joint committees of Congress to study and produce reports on problems affecting friendly labor relations and productivity.

Passage of Taft-Hartley caused a firestorm of protest among both leaders and the rank and file in the labor movement. Massive rallies were held in a number of cities in opposition to the law, including the UAW stronghold of Detroit, where a rally organized by the UAW was attended by approximately 200,000 workers. Most of the unions failed to capitalize upon the willingness of their members to protest the passage of this piece of legislation and transform it into an effective political action. In the face of this massive grassroots protest, however, President Truman promptly vetoed the bill.

President Truman's Position on Taft-Hartley

Truman had done very little work with Congress to try to work against passage of antilabor legislation, however. The Congress of Industrial Organizations (CIO) led "Operation Dixie," the attempt to organize both black and white workers in the South. "Operation Dixie" so frightened segregationist Democrats in the region that they had joined the resurgent Republican Party to pass Taft-Hartley. Truman had very little influence over these recalcitrant Democrats in either legislative body, and he chose to expend none of it in attempting to convince members not to override his veto of the bill, which was accomplished on 23 June 1947. Truman's opposition to Taft-Hartley seems to have been mere political expediency, since he did not hesitate to use the emergency powers granted to him against the United Mine Workers when they walked out on strike in October 1947. He had also threatened to nationalize the steel industry temporarily in 1946 in order to end the strike by the United Steelworkers Union. Like many other liberals of the time, Truman seems to have believed that the labor movement had grown too powerful and needed some restrictions.

Union Actions in the Wake of Taft-Hartley

Although most union leaders in the CIO initially resisted Taft-Hartley, leaders of larger unions quickly realized that parts of the new law could be used to their advantage. They used the noncommunist clause to rid labor unions of Communist Party members, insisting that all local leaders make the pledge, resign their positions, or leave the CIO umbrella. Many CIO unions had members who were communists, and these members were often found in leadership positions, not only because of the cell structure of the Communist Party but also because they were often dedicated, hard-working union members. Some of these unions—most prominently the United Electrical Workers—did in fact leave the CIO over this issue. The CIO then formed rival unions and undertook organizing "raids" to steal these members back. These efforts meant that much less time and money was spent trying to organize unorganized workers, however, and promptly killed much of the momentum in those organizing drives. This backlash particularly affected the CIO, which saw its numbers quickly stagnate; by 1955 the CIO merged with the AFL, and the industrial unions of the CIO rapidly became junior partners in the craft-union-oriented organization.

While in many ways Taft-Hartley simply codified the direction that the labor movement was headed, it still had a debilitating effect on the movement. Except where unions like the United Mine Workers were able to negotiate contract language stating otherwise, Taft-Hartley effectively outlawed the wildcat strike, one that is not authorized by either national or international officers. This in turn led unions to discipline members who participated in wildcat strikes, even if those strikes were caused by failure of management to live up to certain conditions of a contract. In practice, workers continued to participate in wildcat strikes whenever they felt conditions warranted such action, and unions were still able to protect many members who participated and negotiated issues that brought on these strikes. However, such union protection was generally extended to strikers only after they had agreed to go back to work under the existing conditions.

This trend toward institutionalizing bureaucracy in the labor movement continued even as Taft-Hartley was amended.

In 1951 legislation that allowed unions to negotiate union-shop agreements with employers without previously polling employees became law. This was a great advantage for union treasuries and staff but further removed the local union from the members that it represented. In the short term, this provision allowed unions to stabilize their finances; however, by making union dues just another payroll checkoff over which laborers had no control, it gave the rank and file the impression that the union was merely one more faceless entity sucking off a portion of a worker's check.

Legacy of the Taft-Hartley Act

By accepting the limitations imposed by Taft-Hartley, labor unions also gave up any hope of contesting control of the workplace. This left issues like the pace of work and automation solely within the purveyance of management, to the detriment of workers and, eventually, their unions. This was particularly devastating for unions that relied upon control of the shop floor to protect members' jobs. The prime example of workers injured by being replaced by technology was the Typographical Workers Union (ITU). Before Taft-Hartley became law, the ITU had negotiated contracts that guaranteed members the retention of their jobs, even when the task they performed was taken over by a machine. Taft-Hartley's clause forbidding "featherbedding"—the retention of union members whose jobs have been replaced through technology—meant this protection no longer existed. Therefore, machines replaced many ITU members, and the union became a shell of its former self. Walther Reuther of the United Automobile Workers initially welcomed the introduction of technology to the workplace, with the promise of shorter workweeks for members, but he quickly became disenchanted when it became apparent that instead of shorter workweeks for everyone, fewer workers would work for the same amount of time. In fact, when a plant manager pointed out to Reuther that the robots in the factory would pay no union dues, Reuther retorted that they would buy no automobiles, either. With labor unions restricted in the role that they could play by Taft-Hartley, however, there was little Reuther or any other labor leaders could do about the situation. The result of Taft-Hartley has been to roll back the gains labor made under the Wagner Act and to ensure that labor remains the junior partner in the management-labor partnership.

Key Players

Hartley, Fred A., Jr. (1902–1969): Hartley was a representative from New Jersey when he became the House sponsor of the Taft-Hartley Act. The House version of the bill was much more severe than the Senate's, and Hartley was instrumental in working out the compromise for the legislation. Hartley was not reelected to the House in 1948.

Murray, Philip (1886–1952): Murray was the second president of the Congress of Industrial Organizations (CIO), succeeding his mentor in the United Mine Workers Union, John L. Lewis. Murray was adamantly opposed to passage of the Taft-Hartley Act, but after passage of the law he used the anticommunist clause to rid the CIO of communists and other leftists.

Reuther, Walter (1907–1970): Reuther, president of the United Automobile Workers (UAW) from 1946 to his death in an airplane crash in 1970, utilized discontent among rank-and-file membership against communist and communist-sympathizing leadership, and then used the anticommunist clause in Taft-Hartley to rid the union of most of the opposition to his leadership.

Taft, Robert A. (1889–1953): Taft was known as "Mr. Republican" during much of his time in the U.S. Senate. Taft was concerned with labor's influence in the political and economic policies of the country, and saw the Taft-Hartley Act as "equalizing" the imbalance that occurred because of the New Deal. Despite efforts to unseat Taft after passage of the act, he remained a member of the Senate until his death in 1953, although his bid for the presidential nomination from his party was spoiled in 1948 and 1952 because of the opposition this stirred in the labor movement.

See also: *AFL, CIO Merge; Congress of Industrial Organizations; National Industrial Recovery Act; Strike Wave, United States; Wagner Act.*

BIBLIOGRAPHY

Books

Halern, Martin. *UAW Politics in the Cold War Era.* Albany, NY: State University of New York Press, 1988.

Lipsitz, George. *A Rainbow at Midnight: Labor and Culture in the 1940s.* Urbana: University of Illinois Press, 1994.

Tomlins, Christopher L. *The State and the Unions: Labor Relations, Law, and the Organized Labor Movement in America, 1880–1960.* New York: Cambridge University Press, 1985.

Periodicals

Lichtenstein, Nelson. "Taft-Hartley: A Slave Labor Law?" *Catholic University Law Review* 47 (1998): 763–789.

—Gregory M. Miller

Tailors' Strike

United States 1827

Synopsis

In 1827 journeymen tailors in Philadelphia, Pennsylvania, went out on strike to protest the discharge of several colleagues who had demanded higher wages from their employer. After the tailors picketed, the employer took them to court on the theory that their actions constituted a conspiracy to harm commerce and the interests of third parties. The jury found the journeymen guilty, setting back early efforts of trade unions to take collective economic action to protect their interests.

The Danbury Hatters' Case

In the early 1900s, the "Danbury Hatters' Case" made legal history when the U.S. Supreme Court ruled that a manufacturer could sue a union for boycotting its goods. This set a precedent for years of federal interference in the activities of labor.

In the Danbury Hatters' Case, or *Loewe v. Lawlor* (208 U.S. 274), the plaintiffs included Dietrich Loewe, a Danbury, Connecticut, hat manufacturer whose firm was engaged in the sale of hats in a number of states across the country. With about $400,000 in annual revenues, Loewe's company employed some 160 men in a nonunion shop. The United Hatters of North America, affiliated with the American Federation of Labor (AFL), initially attempted to force Loewe to employ union labor. Most of his employees, impressed by the union's promises, went on strike, and Loewe responded by hiring scabs.

At that point the Hatters took advantage of the larger numbers represented by the AFL. Whereas the United Hatters had about 9,000 members scattered across half a dozen states and Ontario, the AFL represented some 1.4 million workers in the United States and Canada. Using this considerable clout, they organized a successful nationwide boycott of Loewe's hats.

Loewe initiated his suit in 1902, and by 1908 it had reached the U.S. Supreme Court. At issue was the question of whether the union had unlawfully combined to restrain trade in violation of the Sherman Antitrust Act. The Court ruled that it had, and held the union liable for treble damages to be paid to Loewe. Seven years later, in another case (235 U.S. 522), the Court upheld a lower court's ruling, allowing Loewe to collect damages.

Thus, ironically, the Sherman Antitrust Act—designed to go after big businesses—was wielded against labor instead. To help pay fines, the union organized a "Hatter's Day," during which members were asked to submit an hour's pay. The precedent established in *Loewe v. Lawlor* would not be overturned until the 1930s, with the passage of new labor-friendly legislation.

Source: Karen Orren. "The Danbury Hatters' Case." In *Labor Law in America: Historical and Critical Essays,* edited by Christopher L. Tomlins and Andrew J. King. Baltimore: Johns Hopkins University Press, 1992.

—Judson Knight

Timeline

1802: Beethoven publishes his "Sonata quasi una fantasia," later nicknamed the "Moonlight Sonata."

1805: Britain's Royal Navy, commanded by Admiral Horatio Nelson, defeats the French at Trafalgar, thereby putting an end to Napoleon's hopes of dominating the seas.

1810: German art publisher Rudolph Ackerman invents the differential gear, which enables wheeled vehicles to make sharp turns.

1815: Congress of Vienna establishes the balance of power for post-Napoleonic Europe, and inaugurates a century of British dominance throughout most of the world.

1820: In the Missouri Compromise, Missouri is admitted to the Union as slave state, but slavery is prohibited in all portions of the Louisiana Purchase north of 36°30' N.

1821: Mexico declares independence from Spain.

1823: U.S. President James Monroe establishes the Monroe Doctrine, whereby the United States warns European nations not to interfere in the political affairs of the Western Hemisphere.

1825: Opening of the New York Stock Exchange.

1826: French inventor Joseph-Nicéphore Niepce makes the first photographic image in history.

1828: Election of Andrew Jackson as president begins a new era in American history.

1830: French troops invade Algeria, and at home, a revolution forces the abdication of Charles V in favor of Louis Philippe, the "Citizen King."

1836: In Texas's war of independence with Mexico, the defenders of the Alamo, among them Davy Crockett and Jim Bowie, are killed in a siege. Later that year, Texas wins the Battle of San Jacinto and secures its independence.

Event and Its Context

A Changing Economy

The Philadelphia tailors' strike was one piece in a mosaic of labor unrest in the early nineteenth century. This unrest was the result of distinct changes taking place in the American economy, changes that were a harbinger of the nation's growing industrial might throughout the century. During the colonial period, most of the nation's workers were farmers, and even in 1820, farming supported 72 percent of the population, while only 12 percent earned their living in manufacturing. A crafts worker during this time normally began his career as an apprentice and then worked as a journeyman until he became an independent master craftsman. As such he was a worker, an employer, a capitalist, a merchant, and an entrepreneur all rolled into one. To such a worker, home and factory were often the same.

As the nation expanded in the late eighteenth and early nineteenth centuries, these "retail" crafts workers and small, localized manufacturing concerns on the eastern seaboard were unable to keep pace with growing demand for their products, largely because they often lacked the capital to expand their operations. This need gave rise to a new class of entrepreneur, the merchant-capitalist, usually an affluent man who had access to capital and credit, was able to buy raw materials in bulk and therefore lower their costs, and understood the larger markets in which he operated.

This accumulation of capital laid the groundwork for the emergence of the factory system, whose birth can be dated to

1791 at a cotton-spinning factory in Pawtucket, Rhode Island, and that later spread to such places as Boston, Massachusetts, and the area around Paterson, New Jersey, and Philadelphia, Pennsylvania. From the standpoint of labor, the chief effect of the factory system was to divide and specialize the functions that formerly had been combined in the colonial-era master craftsman. Now, the merchant-capitalist worried about capital and markets; workers in the factories provided muscle and skill to transform raw materials into finished goods.

Those workers quickly discovered, however, that their employers, faced with competition from other employers in other areas, had to cut costs to the bone in order to survive. One way they did so was to cut wages, particularly during unstable economic times, such as the embargoes connected with the Napoleonic Wars, the War of 1812, and the postwar depression that inevitably followed from 1815 to 1820. To protect their interests, house painters, carpenters, printers, hatmakers, weavers, masons, and members of other trades began to organize, bargain for higher wages, and go out on strike when their demands were not met. It should be noted, though, that during this period unskilled workers—often women and children—lacked the clout to organize, so the nation's earliest trade unions were formed to protect the interests principally of skilled craftsmen, most of whom were men.

Conspiracy

In response, employers began to form associations of their own to hold down wages and thwart the activities of the unions. Anticipating the approach of their twentieth-century counterparts, they frequently turned to the courts, though instead of seeking injunctions, the favored twentieth-century tool, they argued at common law that the unions were guilty of unlawful conspiracy. Between 1806 and 1842 at least 17 such cases were tried in the courts. Early on, from 1806 to 1815, six of these cases were directed at cordwainers' (shoemakers) unions and collectively are referred to as the Cordwainers' Conspiracy Cases.

The most famous of these cases was the first, against the Philadelphia cordwainers, in 1806. The position taken by the employers was essentially that when union pressure succeeded in raising wages, products became more expensive. Higher costs reduced the demand for products and caused unemployment in the community. Unions, therefore, injured the community, suppressed commerce and trade, and hurt the interests of other workers. Further, nonunion workers were injured by the activities of unionists who refused to work with them because employers either had to discharge nonunion workers or face a strike by union members. In ruling against the union, the court concluded, "A combination of workmen to raise . . . wages . . . [occurs for two reasons]: One is to benefit themselves . . . the other is to injure those who do not join the society. The rule of law condemns both." Thus, the court declared organizing to increase wages illegal.

The public outcry that followed this decision had an impact on later judgments. In a similar trial involving the New York cordwainers in 1809, the court insisted that unionism itself was not illegal. But the court did call into question the *means* the workers used: they could not use means "of a nature too arbitrary and coercive, and which went to deprive their fellow citizens of rights as precious as any they contended for." Similarly, in an 1815 trial of Pittsburgh cordwainers, the court declared, "Where diverse persons confederate together by direct means to impoverish or prejudice a third person, or to do acts prejudicial to the community," they are guilty of an unlawful conspiracy. The court went on: it was illegal to conspire "to compel an employer to hire a certain description of persons"; "to prevent a man from freely exercising his trade in a particular place"; and "to compel men to become members of a particular society, or to contribute toward it," or to "compel men to work at certain prices."

The Cordwainers' Conspiracy Cases, combined with the depression following the War of 1812, all but crushed the budding labor union movement. When better times returned in the early 1820s, expanding markets increased the demand for labor. Once again, however, employers often found themselves having to cut wages to meet the prices of the competition—this at a time when a factory worker took home as little as $7 or $8 after a week of 12- and even 14-hour days. In 1821 labor began to reorganize as housepainters, stonemasons, ships' carpenters, hatters, weavers, cabinetmakers, and tailors; even unskilled laborers and women began to join "associations" and "societies." Like the earlier unions, they pressed for higher wages and often relied on the "turnout," or strike, as their principal weapon.

Though records are sparse, these unions apparently enjoyed some success, for once again employers turned to the courts, and the 1820s saw six more conspiracy trials. The first of this new crop of cases was *Commonwealth v. Carlisle* in 1821—though the case represented a turnabout, for it was the union that accused the employer, Master Ladies' Shoemakers, of conspiring to *reduce* wages. The Pennsylvania Supreme Court ruled that it was lawful for the "masters" to combine to restore wages to their "natural level." But again, the court focused less on the object of the combination than on the means used to attain that object. In the second of these cases, the 1823 trial of the New York hatters, the court took a similar position. It focused not on whether a combination to raise wages was an illegal conspiracy but on whether the hatters conspired to injure a third person, in this instance to deprive a nonunion worker of his livelihood by coercion and intimidation. Records for a third case, against the tailors' union in Buffalo, New York, are incomplete, but an 1824 newspaper account of the trial suggests that the issues were similar. A strikebreaker "was stigmatised by an appropriate name, and rendered too infamous to be allowed to labour in any shop where his conduct should be known." The doctrine that emerged from these cases—that the means a union adopted to press its demands could be unlawful—had important consequences for the Philadelphia tailors' case in 1827.

The Philadelphia Tailors' Strike

The Philadelphia shop of Robb and Winebrenner manufactured women's clothing. For most of the clothing, tailors worked under a fixed-wage scale. But the shop also manufactured women's riding clothes made out of pongee, a thin, light fabric composed of raw silk. For this type of work, there was no fixed-wage scale, as there was for heavier fabrics. The tailors that worked with pongee were paid at a lower rate, so they demanded to be paid at the higher rate paid for work on heavier materials. Their demand got them discharged, and in protest the shop's journeymen tailors went out on strike. The methods they adopted seem startlingly modern. They picketed the shop, accosted strikebreakers and urged them not to work for the company, and persuaded other companies not to do work for Robb and Winebrenner. Sporadic violence erupted, and Robb and Winebrenner took the tailors to court.

Significantly, the judge, in his instructions to the jury, declined to consider whether a combination to raise wages was illegal, calling the proposition "bad law." Instead, he directed the jury's attention to the issue of intimidation and coercion: "Direct your attention to the sole inquiry, how far the combination charged and the overt acts are calculated to affect the rights of innocent third persons." He further noted, "[Do not] . . . examine the question as to the right to combine to raise wages; which has never been decided on in the United States." In a blow to labor associations, the jury found the actions of the strikers illegal. While unions themselves remained technically legal, they were stripped of their most effective weapons: picketing, circulation of strikebreaker lists, and secondary boycotts.

The Aftermath

In spite of the setbacks of the 1820s conspiracy cases, organized labor continued to grow throughout the 1830s. Several hundred local unions sprang up not only in eastern seaboard cities but also in cities and towns farther inland. The first federation of labor unions, the National Trades Union, was formed in New York City in 1834. In 1836 the New York tailors struck, and after they were found guilty of conspiracy, New York City workers erupted in fury and staged a rally that drew 27,000 people. But the legal status of unions remained precarious, particularly since the courts often backed a new tool used by employers' associations to break the unions, the blacklist.

In 1842 the union movement finally found some relief in court. In Massachusetts a group of shoemakers were convicted in a lower court of conspiracy because they refused to work beside nonunion workers. They appealed to the state Supreme Judicial Court, and in its landmark decision in *Commonwealth v. Hunt,* the court affirmed the legality of unions and union activity. It held that union members could lawfully agree not to work for an employer who used nonunion labor and that union efforts to raise wages were lawful even if they reduced employer profits or increased the prices of goods.

See also: *National Trades Union.*

———

BIBLIOGRAPHY

Books

Commons, John R., et al. *History of Labour in the United States.* New York: Macmillan, 1936.

Perlman, Selig. *A History of Trade Unionism in the United States.* New York: Macmillan, 1922.

Rayback, Joseph G. *A History of American Labor.* New York: Macmillan, 1959.

Wright, Chester Whitney. *Economic History of the United States.* New York: McGraw-Hill, 1949.

Periodicals

Nockleby, John T. "Two Theories of Competition in the Early 19th Century Labor Cases." *American Journal of Legal History* (October 1994).

Witte, Edwin E. "Early American Labor Cases." *Yale Law Journal* 35 (1926): 825–837.

—Michael J. O'Neal

Taylor and "Scientific Management"

United States 1878–1911

Synopsis

As industrialism expanded in the United States following the Civil War, the essence of the labor movement was the struggle for control of the workplace between workers, who were holding fast to their craft skills, and management. One of the most famous figures to participate in this struggle was Frederick Winslow Taylor, who rose from his position as an apprentice sweeping out a foundry in Philadelphia to become the proponent of "scientific management," which combines ruthless industrial efficiency with social gospel, and instigated the genesis of the "science" of management itself.

Although Taylor is most popularly associated with "Taylorism," the practice of time-and-motion studies, this vulgar depiction fails to do justice to the enormous scope of his work, of which the efficiency studies were a small part. His intent was to revolutionize—his term!—the way in which work was organized with a goal of prosperity and industrial harmony.

Timeline

1894: War breaks out between Japan and China. It will end with China's defeat the next year, marking yet another milestone in China's decline and Japan's rise.

1895: German engineer Rudolf Diesel invents an engine capable of operating on a type of petroleum less highly refined, and therefore less costly, than gasoline.

1896: U.S. Supreme Court issues its *Plessy v. Ferguson* decision, which establishes the "separate but equal" doctrine that will be used to justify segregation in the southern United States for the next half-century.

1897: Establishment of the Zionist movement under the leadership of Theodor Herzl.

1898: United States defeats Spain in the three-month Spanish-American War. As a result, Cuba gains its independence, and the United States purchases Puerto Rico and the Philippines from Spain for $20 million.

1899: Start of the Second Anglo-Boer War, often known simply as the Boer War.

1900: China's Boxer Rebellion, which began in the preceding year with attacks on foreigners and Christians, reaches its height. An international contingent of more than 2,000 men arrives to restore order, but only after several tens of thousands have died.

1901: Guglielmo Marconi makes the first successful transmission and reception of a radio signal.

1903: Anti-Jewish pogroms break out in Russia.

1905: Albert Einstein presents his special theory of relativity.

1906: An earthquake, the worst ever to hit a U.S. city, strikes San Francisco on 18 April. It kills some 2,500 people, leaves another 250,000 homeless, and destroys more than $400 million worth of property.

Event and Its Context

Born into a wealthy family in Philadelphia, Frederick Winslow Taylor took a position as a foundry apprentice in 1873, in the midst of the Panic of 1873. The cutting of metal, which he first witnessed in this foundry, became one of his life's obsessions. Taylor immediately noticed two elements of the work process that disturbed him for the remainder of his life and which he committed himself to eliminating.

The first was *soldiering*, a derogatory term for Taylor, by which workers carefully controlled their output. In his congressional testimony in 1912, Taylor maintained that higher productivity led to higher employment, but the workers of the late nineteenth century believed the reverse: they were careful not to finish work too quickly to avoid both running out of work and working too hard. He called this control by an individual *natural soldiering* and termed shop-wide organization *systematic soldiering*. Taylor devoted his life to eliminating these organizing principles from business practice.

Taylor also took on the *rule-of-thumb*, a haphazard practice of organizing the work that gave individual workers enormous control. Production processes had never been subjected to what Taylor called "scientific" scrutiny; work simply continued as it always had, depending upon the inclinations of individual workers. Workers determined machine speeds and the methods—or "feed"—of cutting metal. Foremen were responsible for many functions, including assigning work, disciplining workers, and resolving production delays, but had virtually no direct control over the individual worker.

Taylor saw enormous wastes in the process. Machinists did all of the work on a particular piece, from the unskilled work of setting up the piece to the semiskilled work of grinding their own tools to the skilled work of actually making a cut. They searched for parts in what Taylor called "a leisurely fashion" and often had to wait for other machines to finish. In short, there was no system, and the principles of science, utilizing thoroughly documented experiments, was wholly lacking.

Taylor most resented and directed of all of his work toward the control that workers exerted over the process and ultimately over productivity. In *Scientific Management*, a three-part volume summing up his work, he stated "As was usual then [1879] and in fact is still usual [1911] in most of the shops in this coun-

Frederick Winslow Taylor. © Bettmann/Corbis. Reproduced by permission.

try, the shop was really run by the workmen, and not by the bosses. The workmen together had carefully planned just how fast each job should be done, and they had set a pace for each machine throughout the shop, which was limited to about one-third of a good day's work."

In 1878, Taylor accepted a position at Midvale Steel. He told the workers that "he was now on the side of management, and that he proposed to do whatever he could to get a fair day's work out of the lathers." In the autumn of 1880, his determination to increase productivity prompted him to conduct a series of systematic experiments in metal cutting. He found almost immediately that cooling the cutting tools with a water spray could increase cutting speed by 40 percent.

By February 1884, Taylor had complete authority over the machine shop and set about transforming its organization. He began to time workers with a stopwatch as they worked. He created "instruction cards," which noted each motion and each decision that workers had passed along informally to each other. Taylor recorded these work process decisions for the foreman and for use in instructing new workers. Taylor's "scientific" calculations guided performance and time spent on each task. The result was increased productivity and, most importantly, a transfer of control of the work process to management.

Taylor also worked to simplify each observed production step. Although his immediate goal was increasing productivity, in this way, he contributed to the deskilling of the work place.

Taylor noted the shift in responsibility to the foreman and worked to streamline the job by assigning its traditional duties into five categories: instruction-card clerk, time clerk, inspector, traditional gang-boss, and shop disciplinarian.

For the next decade at Midvale, Taylor experimented and recorded every aspect of the work process and sought to eliminate breakdowns and inefficiencies. In a futile gesture intended to engage worker support, he created a set of differential rates, which promised to pay workers higher rates for increased productivity, an improvement over the simple piece-rate structure.

The goal of the American Society of Mechanical Engineers (ASME) was to gather technical information. In 1886, Henry Robinson Towne, of Yale and Towne lock maker, presented a paper called *The Engineer as Economist*, which has been called "the founding document of the new science of management" because it talked to engineers about the practices of shop management. Taylor adopted and consistently adhered to the tenets set forth in Robinson's paper by using technical improvements to change production organization, deskill certain work tasks, and strengthen management control.

One of Taylor's evaluations involved the system of belts that drove the machines. He measured the life of each belt and its dimensions to determine which ones lasted longest at the highest speeds. He compiled his experimental results in his first public pronouncement, *Notes on Belting*, which he read in December 1893 at the annual meeting of ASME. In June 1895 Taylor presented a second paper for ASME, called *A Piece-Rate System: A Step Toward Partial Solution of the Labor Problem*.

Taylor left Midvale in 1889 and spent years trying to convince other manufactures to adopt scientific management, which, as he conceived it, was a total system of administering the work process and not just isolated pieces such as time-study. Close to the tumult of the Homestead and Pullman strikes, Taylor proposed using "science" to create industrial harmony. He stated "the ordinary piece-rate system involves a permanent antagonism between employers and men" and proposed a "scientific" pay system that "renders labor unions and strikes unnecessary." When this paper was reprinted in *Engineering Magazine*, Taylor became—after 22 years of experimentation—an overnight sensation.

In spring of 1898, Bethlehem Steel hired Taylor to manage Machine Shop No. 2, the largest in the world, which produced enormous cannons for the Spanish-American War. Calling Bethlehem Steel "a case study in inefficiency," he began to transform the work place in every area, installing "scientific management," or "Taylorism," as it was then known, over the objections of both workers and managers.

Working with metallurgist Maunsell White, Taylor began experiments on the heat-treating of tool steel, and eventually determined that heating the tool steel to a temperature of 2,200 degrees provided maximum efficiency and allowed cuts that were 100 percent faster and 40 percent deeper; with this single improvement, a cannon tube that had previously required 72 hours to cut could be finished in 22 hours. Taylor and White applied for a patent and showcased their efforts at the Centennial Exhibition in Paris in 1900. This exposure made Taylor's "scientific" approach world famous and led to the publication *The Art of Cutting Metal*, which first appeared at the ASME meeting in November 1906.

Carl Barth signed on at Bethlehem to develop mathematical formulas for calculating job rates and became another of Taylor's protégés. Barth's contributions including devising a special slide rule that allowed management to predict accurately the amount of time needed for each process and eliminate the rule-of-thumb that had previously dominated production speeds.

The final achievement at Bethlehem involved the famous experiments on shoveling, with a laborer named Henry Noll, later disguised by Taylor as "a man named Schmidt." Taylor set out to evaluate the process of loading pig iron on freight cars, which led to later experiments on shovel sizes and design. This effort illustrated that Taylorism could apply to even the most unskilled job.

In June 1903 Taylor presented a comprehensive summary of "Taylorism" called *Shop Management* as his final important paper presented at an annual ASME meeting. Although the presentation focused on technical exhibits and diagrams, Taylor also set forth his social theory that some workers would appreciate the social and economic benefits of "scientific management," whereas others, "either stupid or stubborn, can never be made to see that the new system is as good as the old; and these, too, must drop out."

As unionism grew after the turn of the century, however, so did organized opposition to Taylorism. The proposed introduction of "scientific management" at the Watertown, Massachusetts, arsenal in 1911 provoked both a walkout of the men and a congressional hearing, whose edited transcript provides the fullest expression of Taylor's views. A time study, initiated in February 1911, caused individual opposition, shop-wide work stoppages, petitions, discharges, extensive meetings and national publicity—all over the topic of Taylorism.

As a result, the House of Representatives authorized a "Special Committee to Investigate the Taylor and Other Systems of Shop Management," at which Taylor testified on 25 January 1912. Living as a consultant of sorts, Taylor had not been confronted directly with the moral implications of scientific management. Over the years he had forced his system through unorganized workplaces. The House committee included Congressman William B. Wilson, a former coal miner from Pennsylvania, who would be appointed as the first secretary of labor in 1913 by President Woodrow Wilson. William Wilson not only challenged Taylor for three days on his system, but also called shop workers to testify about the effects of "scientific management."

The congressional hearing was a pointed attack on "scientific management" and on Taylor personally. Taylor, however, saw it as an opportunity to proclaim the essence of his theory in its broadest and most socially ambitious form, as a progressive, even revolutionary, principle and to denounce managers or critics who took only pieces of his grand vision. He stated that "scientific management is not any efficiency device, not a device for securing efficiency . . . ." and declared that it constituted a "complete mental revolution" on the part of workers and management alike, from business owners to shop foremen, toward both workers and work processes.

Taylor spent the last years of his life as a management consultant, working on various projects—developing the perfect grass for putting greens, for example—and died in Philadelphia on 21 March 1915 of pneumonia. He is buried in the West Laurel Hill Cemetery across the Schuylkill River from the Midvale Steel works.

Consequences

Taylor believed that close examination of and the application of "science" to the work process would allow factories literally to hum with harmony and to produce greater wealth and increased employment.

Efficiency became a key word in modern vocabulary and a significant issue in the disputes between organized labor and management. Over time, management goals of increased productivity at the lowest possible costs eclipsed Taylor's additional goals of improving conditions for workers. "Taylorism" became identified with "Fordism" and the creation of simple and repetitive tasks, industrial duplication on an enormous scale, and the creation of the modern assembly line.

Counter-Taylorism developed originally in the European auto industry, as recognition that workers had the intelligence and insight to contribute to the work process. With self-managed work groups, the modern assembly plant was once again transformed but in 2000, when the International Labor Organization published an article called "A Comeback for Taylorism?" that described the revival of the regimented work place.

Taylor really helped create the science of management as a separate and distinct area of life and of academic concentration. Peter Drucker, known popularly as "a management guru"—that is, one who studies how management should function—received a Presidential Medal of Honor from President George W. Bush in the summer of 2002. The award in its way also honored Taylor. Although Drucker spent more than 50 years refining management practices, it was Taylor who invented "management" as a "science."

Key Players

Taylor, Frederick Winslow (1856–1915): Dedicated his life to transforming industrial practices in all areas, allowing management to have absolute control over the workplace. He introduced the practice of "scientific" evaluation to work processes. Known popularly for "Taylorism," which includes time-and-motion study, he created management as a distinct class and topic of study.

See also: *Homestead Lockout; Panic of 1873; Pullman Strike.*

BIBLIOGRAPHY

Books

Braverman, Harry. *Labor and Monopoly Capital: The Degradation of Work in the Twentieth Century.* Foreword by Paul M. Sweezy. New York: Monthly Review Press, 1974.

Kanigel, Robert. *The One Best Way: Frederick Winslow Taylor and the Enigma of Efficiency.* New York: Viking, 1997.

Nelson, Daniel. *Managers and Workers: Origins of the New Factory System in the United States, 1880–1920.* Madison: University of Wisconsin Press, 1975.

Taylor, Frederick Winslow. *Scientific Management Comprising Shop Management: The Principles of Scientific Management and Testimony Before the Special House Committee.* Foreword by Harlow S. Person. New York: Harper, 1947. Original work published 1911.

Periodicals

Kempe, Martin. "A Comeback for Taylorism? Report from Germany." *World of Work* (March 2000): 18–20.

Other

Samuel C. Williams Library, Steven Institute of Technology. Special Collections: F. W. Taylor Collection [cited 2 August 2002]. <http://taylor.lib.stevens-tech.edu/>.

KQED Public Broadcasting Web site. Stopwatch: "Frederick Winslow Taylor and the 'Taylorization' of America." [cited 2 August 2002]. <http://www.kqed.org/tv/indieproducers/stopwatch/stopwatch2.html>.

—Bill Barry

Taylor Law

United States 1967

Synopsis

The Taylor Law is the common name for New York State's Public Employee Fair Employment Act, Article 14 of the New York State Civil Service Law, which was enacted in 1967. It is named for the chairman of the commission that proposed it. The Taylor Law replaced the Condon-Wadlin Act of 1947, which forbade public employees from striking but made no alternative provisions for settling labor disputes, which effectively left most public employees with few legal options. The Taylor Law was first considered and enacted following a massive, illegal strike of New York City transit workers in 1966, which, among other things, destroyed any impression that the Condon-Wadlin Act did any good whatsoever.

The Taylor Law is to New York State's public sector what the National Labor Relations Act (NLRA) is to most private sector employees in the United States. Its relatively liberal provisions are probably in part responsible for New York State having such a high overall unionization rate (as of 2001, it had the highest in the country). It maintains Condon-Wadlin's prohibition on strikes but establishes NLRA-style procedures to settle labor disputes.

The Taylor Law, among many other initiatives that New York has come to take for granted, was mainly the child of Governor Nelson Rockefeller, and it was almost named after him instead of George Taylor, the famed labor academic who led the gubernatorial committee that created it.

Timeline

1947: Great Britain's Labour government nationalizes coal mines.

Nelson Rockefeller. The Library of Congress.

1952: Among the cultural landmarks of the year are the film *High Noon* and the book *The Invisible Man* by Ralph Ellison.

1957: Integration of high schools in Little Rock, Arkansas, with the aid of federal troops.

1962: As the Soviets begin a missile buildup in Cuba, for a few tense days in October it appears that World War III is imminent. President Kennedy calls for a Cuban blockade, forcing the Soviets to back down and ultimately diffusing the crisis.

1967: Biafra secedes from Nigeria.

1967: Arabs attack Israel, launching the Six-Day War, which results in an Israeli victory. Israel now occupies a number of formerly Arab-held territories, most notably the Old City of Jerusalem. In the years that follow, the Israelis will be forced to give up much of the territory, which stretches to the borders of Egypt. Their continued possession of the Jordan River's West Bank will provide a cause for enduring controversy with their Arab neighbors and with the newly mobilized Palestinian minority.

1967: Racial violence sweeps America's cities, as Harlem, Detroit, Birmingham, and other towns erupt with riots.

1967: The Beatles' *Sgt. Pepper's Lonely Hearts Club Band* tops the list of releases for a year that will long be remembered as a high point of rock history. Among the other great musical events of the year are releases by the Jimi Hendrix Experience, the Doors, and Jefferson Airplane; also, the Monterey Pop Festival marks the debut of Hendrix and Janis Joplin.

1967: Assisted by a team of surgeons, South Africa's Christiaan Barnard performs what is considered the world's first successful human heart transplant, though the patient dies 18 days later.

1972: In June police apprehend five men attempting to burglarize Democratic Party headquarters at the Watergate Hotel in Washington, D.C.

1977: Newly inaugurated U.S. President Jimmy Carter pardons Vietnam draft dodgers.

1982: Israeli troops invade Lebanon in an attack on the Palestine Liberation Organization (PLO).

Event and Its Context

Before 1967, public employee labor relations in New York State was informed by ideas that combined elements of democratic theory, the Civil Service merit system, and Hobbesian notions of the sovereignty of the state. In brief, the current outlook was that public employees' salaries and terms and conditions of employment were best determined by the normal political process. Most held that it would be abhorrent for public employees to negotiate formally or bargain over terms and conditions of employment, as do private sector employees, let alone to have use of the strike weapon. Failing negotiation or strikes, the only legal option left to public employees was thus to lobby the state legislature or the relevant local legislative body, as would any other interest group, or to bargain in an informal and "under the table" manner. The current political climate held that even the act of forming organizations was at least legally questionable, though of course it happened anyway. New York State's largest public employee union, the Civil Service Employees' Association, traces its origins to the pre-Taylor Law era when it was a combination lobbying group and professional association.

Despite their illegality, public employee strikes in New York did happen periodically. In response to a strike by teachers in Buffalo in 1946, the New York's state legislature codified the antistrike common law into the Condon-Wadlin Act in 1947. The act officially forbade strikes by public employees and further provided that public employees who engaged in such actions forfeited their employment. Later attempts to weaken the Condon-Wadlin Act's penalties failed.

Despite, or because of, its harshness, the Condon-Wadlin Act was heralded in many quarters. Governors of several other states wrote to New York State Governor Thomas Dewey and expressed interest in enacting similar legislation in their own states. The law was also praised in legal circles for codifying the sacred common law principles that had always prevented public employees from negotiating collectively. Organized labor tended to decry the law on the grounds that it violated the democratic rights of public employees, but their tone was often defeatist. After all, it was *already* illegal for public employees to strike. In a sense, the new law changed nothing.

The Condon-Wadlin system held for 20 years, though relatively few commentators appear to have ever thought that it worked. The act was resented by labor, proved almost impossible for management to enforce (it is usually regarded as impractical to fire simultaneously a significant portion of any given workforce), and in effect banned strikes without creating a legal alternative to them.

As stated, although strikes were illegal, labor tensions had of course not simply gone away, and neither had the semilegal public employee negotiations that had always occurred under the guise of lobbying before the passage of the act. (Starting in 1954, New York City had experimented with a private sector-style negotiating system, enacted pursuant to a series of mayoral executive orders.) By the late 1960s the weight of experience, empirical evidence, and the general mood of the country conspired to return public sector labor issues to the active political agenda. At that time, the governor of New York was Nelson Rockefeller.

Although Rockefeller appears to have expressed an interest in addressing public sector labor relations as early as 1965, it was a 1966 strike by New York City transit employees that truly brought the issue front and center. The strike was extremely disruptive to the city's economy and drove home the failures of the Condon-Wadlin system.

In 1966 Governor Rockefeller formed the Taylor Commission, led by famous labor academic and mediator George W. Taylor, from the Wharton School at the University of Pennsylvania. Taylor was 65 years old at the time and was only six years away from his death. The credentials of the other members of the commission, E. Wright Bakke, David L. Cole, John T. Dunlop, and Frederick H. Harbison, were almost as impressive as Taylor's. The paper that the commission published on 31 March 1966, widely known and cited as the "Taylor Report," is considered a landmark in the field of labor relations. The Taylor Report adamantly defended both the right of public employees to form unions and to negotiate the terms and conditions of employment, and the right of the state to ban public employee strikes. The basic recommendations of the committee were simple, though of course the details were more complex. In brief, the committee recommended:

- The repeal of the Condon-Wadlin Act
- The retention of the Condon-Wadlin Act's prohibition on public employee strikes and the enactment of appropriate penalties for public employees found to be engaged in strikes or strike-like activity
- The establishment of a new law that gave public employees the explicit right to form unions and negotiate collectively under NLRA-style rules
- A requirement that public employers negotiate with these duly established and certified organizations
- The creation of a Public Employment Relations Board (PERB) to enforce the new law and serve in a similar capacity to the National Labor Relations Board (NLRB)

The Taylor Report led directly into a piece of legislation that Rockefeller allowed to be called the "Taylor Act," though it was and is formally known as the New York State Public Employees' Fair Employment Act. Following a failed attempt to enact the law in 1966, wherein the New York State Assembly held up the measure in favor of an older bill on the topic, the Taylor Act was signed into law (Chapter 392 of the Laws of 1967) within days of its formal introduction in 1967. The act still stands today, albeit in amended form (New York State Civil Service Law, Article 14).

George W. Taylor. AP/Wide World Photos. Reproduced by permission.

The Taylor Act made many noted improvements over the Condon-Wadlin Act and mainly followed the recommendations of the Taylor Committee. Although it retained the Condon-Wadlin Act's prohibition on public employee strikes, threats to strike, and strike-like actions (and, indeed, to this very day, that portion of the Taylor Law remains notably harsh), it enacted more realistic penalties that consisted mainly of forfeiting of income rather than forfeiting employment.

Perhaps surprisingly, the Taylor Act was by and large decried in labor circles. Some unions referred to it as the "Slave Labor Act" and refused to endorse any labor relations reform law that did not grant to public employees the right to strike. Organized labor was rather ineffectual on this issue. Opposition to the Taylor Act had no more impact on its passing than had opposition to the Condon-Wadlin Act on that bill's eventual repeal.

The Taylor Act has been amended several times since its passage, almost always with a pro-labor bent. For example, the state legislature added unfair labor practices of both labor and management in 1969. The specific list of practices mirrors almost exactly the parallel provisions of the NLRA. The state began to allow binding arbitration for local police and fire employees in 1974, and has since permitted it for other public safety and law enforcement employees. The Triborough Amendment of 1982 required that the provisions of an expired contract remain in effect until a new contract was negotiated. PERB's consistent refusal to be limited by NLRB precedents is reflected in PERB's administrative innovations to the act.

The act's infamously harsh penalties for striking, though still less harsh than those provided by the Condon-Wadlin Act, are not often enforced; typically, a union will demand a waiver of strike penalties as part of the final bargaining agreement. A violent and savage 1979 strike by New York State's corrections officers put the strike prohibition to the test. For the most part, however, regardless of early dire predictions by some commentators, the Taylor Law has succeeded in deterring public employee strikes, especially since the 1982 enactment of the Triborough Amendment. Threats to strike are, however, still fairly common, especially among teachers and New York City transportation workers.

Organized labor in New York State, almost exclusively under the banner of the powerful New York State AFL-CIO, has warmed to the Taylor Law over the years. The AFL-CIO's Taylor Law Task Force in 2001 issued an interim report on proposed amendments to the law that recommended only modest revisions. The report praised the law as a whole. Rarely do major Taylor Law reform proposals make their way onto the agenda of the New York State Legislature.

Key Players

Rockefeller, Nelson (1908–1979): Rockefeller was born into privilege, and his pursuit of public service was puzzled over by his famous family. He served as governor of New York from 1959 until 1973 and as vice president of the United States under Ford from 1974 to 1977. His record as governor is considered mixed.

Taylor, George W. (1901–1972): Taylor's presence affected both labor relations and its study. His reputation was already secure by the time he was called on to head up the Taylor Committee. In 1995 the United States Department of Labor inducted him into the Labor Hall of Fame. He has been called "Industrial Peacemaker."

See also: *Wagner Act.*

BIBLIOGRAPHY

Books

Donovan, Ronald. *Administering the Taylor Law: Public Employee Relations in New York.* Ithaca, NY: ILR Press, 1990.

Lefkowitz, Jerome, ed. *Public Sector Labor and Employment Law.* New York: New York State Bar Association, 1988.

Levine, Louis, Robert Helsby, Melvin Osterman, Joseph Zimmerman, and Milton Musicus. "Transformation of the Workplace." In *Rockefeller in Retrospect: The Governor's New York Legacy,* edited by Gerald Benjamin and T. Norman Hurd. Albany, NY: The Nelson A. Rockefeller Institute of Government, 1984.

New York State. Governor's Committee on Public Employee Relations (Taylor Committee). *Final Report of the Governor's Committee on Public Employee Relations (Taylor Committee Report).* Albany, NY: New York State, 1966.

New York State. Public Employment Relations Board. *Rules of Procedure.* Albany, NY: New York State, 1997.

New York State. Public Employment Relations Board. *Mandatory/Nommandatory Subjects of Negotiation.* Albany, NY: New York State, 1997.

New York State. Public Employment Relations Board. *What Is the Taylor Law? And How Does It Work?* Albany, NY: New York State, 1998.

New York State AFL-CIO. *Interim Report of the Task Force on Taylor Law Reform.* Albany, NY: New York State, 2001.

Persico, Joseph E. *The Imperial Rockefeller: A Biography of Nelson A. Rockefeller.* New York: Simon and Schuster, 1982.

Root, Oren. *Persons and Persuasions.* New York: W. W. Norton and Company, Inc., 1974.

Underwood, James E. and William J. Daniels. *Governor Rockefeller in New York: The Apex of Pragmatic Liberalism in the United States.* Westport, CT: Greenwood Press, 1982.

Volans, Tamar. "The Public Employment Relations Board: Administration of the Taylor Law." *New York State Senate Research Service: Issues in Focus* #98–30. Albany, NY: New York State Senate, 1998.

Periodicals

Kheel, Theodore W. "The Taylor Law: A Critical Examination of its Virtues and Defects." 20 *Syracuse Law Reviews* 181 (fall 1968).

King, Bernard T. "The Taylor Act—Experiment in Public Employer–Employee Relations." 20 *Syracuse Law Review* 1 (fall 1968).

McHugh, William F. "New York's Experiment in Public Employee Relations: The Public Employees' Fair Employment Act." 32 *Albany Law Review* 58 (1967).

Peterson, Andrew A. "Deterring Strikes by Public Employees: New York's Two-For-One Salary Penalty and the 1979 Prison Guard Strike." *Industrial and Labor Relations Review* 34, no. 4 (July 1981): 545–562.

Rains, Harry H. "New York Public Employee Relations Laws: Pros and Cons on Proposed Amendments—Stalemate Procedures, Strikes, and Penalties." *Labor Law Journal* (May 1969): 264–288.

Shils, Edward B. "George W. Taylor: Industrial Peacemaker." *Monthly Labor Review.* (December 1995): 29–34.

Zimmer, Lynn and James B. Jacobs. "Challenging the Taylor Law: Prison Guards on Strike." *Industrial and Labor Relations Review* 34 no. 4 (July 1981): 531–544.

Other

New York State AFL–CIO. 1998–2002 [cited 15 August 2002]. <http://www.nysaflcio.org>.

New York State Governor's Office of Employee Relations. Updated 8 August 2002 [cited 15 August 2002]. <http://www.goer.state.ny.us/>.

New York State Public Employment Relations Board. [cited 15 August 2002]. <http://www.perb.state.ny.us/>.

—Steven Koczak

Teamsters Union

United States 1903

Synopsis

The International Brotherhood of Teamsters—today named formally the International Brotherhood of Teamsters, Chauffeurs, Warehousemen, and Helpers of America—was established in 1903 from the merger of the Team Drivers' International Union and the Teamsters' National Union of America. Formed in a cauldron of controversy and dissension, the union throughout its history has remained a relatively loose confederation of local affiliates that retain considerable autonomy.

Timeline

1883: Foundation of the League of Struggle for the Emancipation of Labor by Marxist political philosopher Georgi Valentinovich Plekhanov marks the formal start of Russia's labor movement. Change still lies far in the future for Russia, however: tellingly, Plekhanov launches the movement in Switzerland.

1893: Henry Ford builds his first automobile.

1899: Start of the Second Anglo-Boer War, often known simply as the Boer War.

1903: Anti-Jewish pogroms break out in Russia.

1903: Henry Ford establishes the Ford Motor Company.

1903: Russia's Social Democratic Party splits into two factions: the moderate Mensheviks and the hard-line Bolsheviks. Despite their names, which in Russian mean "minority" and "majority," respectively, Mensheviks actually outnumber Bolsheviks.

1903: Polish-born French chemist Marie Curie becomes the first woman to be awarded the Nobel Prize.

1903: One of the earliest motion pictures, *The Great Train Robbery,* premieres.

1903: United States assumes control over the Panama Canal Zone, which it will retain until 1979.

1903: Wright brothers make their first flight at Kitty Hawk, North Carolina. Though balloons date back to the eighteenth century and gliders to the nineteenth, Orville Wright's twelve seconds aloft on 17 December mark the birth of practical human flight.

1906: Founding of the British Labour Party.

1913: Two incidents illustrate the increasingly controversial nature of the arts in the new century. Visitors to the 17 February Armory Show in New York City are scandalized by such works as Marcel Duchamp's cubist *Nude Descending a Staircase,* which elicits vehement criticism, and theatergoers at the 29 May debut of Igor Stravinsky's ballet *Le Sacré du Printemps* (*The Rite of Spring*) are so horrified by the new work that a riot ensues.

Samuel Gompers. AP/Wide World Photos. Reproduced by permission.

Event and Its Context

Early Teamsters

The modern-day image of a Teamster is that of a long-haul truck driver carrying goods from manufacturing and distribution centers to cities and towns across the United States. Clearly, the development of the highway system and motorized vehicles in the early twentieth century revolutionized the nature of hauling and transportation. "Teamsters," though, were originally the owners and drivers of "teams" of horses and mules that moved people and goods in an era when "horsepower" referred not to the muscle of an engine but literally to the hauling capacity of a horse.

Little is known about early teamster labor groups. During the colonial period, some teamsters on the eastern seaboard formed loose associations, and similar associations in such western cities as San Francisco date back to around 1850. These early associations were more in the nature of guilds than labor organizations, for most of their members were driver-owners; that is, they owned their own teams and were self-employed, in much the same way that today's Teamster might own his (and increasingly, her) own rig while performing work for others or as part owner of a joint business venture. Thus, in contrast to mines or manufacturing plants, it was not always easy to clearly distinguish employers from employees. The team drivers' primary concern was not wages and working conditions but "drayage" rates, or the rates they could charge for their services.

The distinction between employer and employee became somewhat sharper as the nineteenth century progressed, but only somewhat. The more successful teamsters, who often began with a single team of horses they drove themselves, frequently acquired several teams and hired others—often men who had failed as owner-drivers—to drive them. These drivers, who worked for wages, would seem to have been ripe for unionization efforts, but at least four obstacles stood in the way. First, teamsters performed a wide range of work; some were garbage collectors, others delivered milk, still others provided "taxi" services, while in the West some hauled coal or ore. Organizational efforts were difficult given this range of activities and employers. A second factor was the size of drayage operations. Most were small, consisting of the owner and perhaps as many as a half a dozen teams or as few as one or two. Unlike large manufacturing facilities or mining operations that often employed hundreds or even thousands of workers, small drayage enterprises were scattered throughout cities and towns. Third, a principal requirement for being a teamster was size, brawn, and a stubborn, often combative nature needed to handle a team of fractious animals and to perform hard, physical labor under difficult and unpredictable conditions. For this reason, particularly in the East, Teamsters were often recruited from the bar-brawling Irish American community. These men were perceived, rightly or wrongly, as immune to organizational efforts, so few such efforts were made. The final obstacle was that while owners typically hired others to drive teams, the owners themselves often worked side by side with their employees driving one of the teams they owned. Thus, while a distinct class of teamster employees was beginning to emerge, the distinction between employer and employee remained blurry.

The Team Drivers' International Union

Although some local teamsters unions were formed during the late nineteenth century, the first international union was formed on 27 January 1899, as an affiliate of the American Federation of Labor (AFL). In preparation for the federation's 1899 convention, AFL president Samuel Gompers invited a number of local teamster unions to attend with the purpose of organizing an international union. Nine locals, affiliates of the Team Drivers' International Union (TDIU) that had been formed a year earlier, sent delegates to the convention and applied for a charter, which the AFL executive committee granted. Headquartered in Detroit, the new AFL affiliate at first had 18 local chapters and about 1,200 members. Membership was officially restricted to drivers who owned no more than six teams, but in practice few owner-drivers were excluded, and the TDIU was dominated by team owners.

Almost immediately, dissension arose. Because of the six-team limit, the TDIU became in effect an employer cartel. It was able to use its bargaining power to increase drayage rates, but little of the increased revenue found its way into the pockets of employees in the form of higher wages. Particularly vocal in its dissatisfaction with this state of affairs was the Chicago affiliate, one of the TDIU's largest and the one most zealous in protecting its autonomy. Matters came to a boil at the union's 1902 convention in Toledo, Ohio, where the Chicago delegates pressed to lower the "per capita tax," a form of membership dues, to keep the national union weak. Their failure to get the reduction, combined with their resentment over the domination

of the union by owner-drivers, led the group to secede from the union and form the Teamsters' National Union of America (TNU). Other locals joined them, and soon membership in the TNU swelled to over 18,000, even though no owner-driver who hired others was allowed to join.

The TNU wielded considerable clout. In Chicago, for instance, coal drivers mounted a successful strike against Marshall Field and his downtown department store. Field had announced that he was going to heat the store with more economical natural gas rather than coal, cutting into the profits of the coal team owners and potentially throwing employees out of work. After months of struggle, Field gave in and replaced the store's gas heating equipment with coal-burning equipment; when other stores and office buildings in Chicago followed suit, the coal drivers' jobs remained secure.

The Chicago union was also successful in improving working conditions for its drivers. At that time, workweeks of 70 hours were the norm, and 100-hour weeks, with half days on Sunday, were not uncommon. The union abolished Sunday work, reduced the workday to ten and a half hours, and successfully pressured for time-and-a-half pay for work before 6:00 A.M. and after 6:00 P.M. Additionally, milk drivers had commonly been required to put in 80-hour weeks during the winter and 100-hour weeks during the summer, with afternoon milk deliveries each day. The union succeeded in imposing a winter workday of 8:00 A.M. to 5:00 P.M. and abolishing the late-afternoon delivery in the summer. The union refused to bend despite statistics cited by union opponents that the absence of afternoon deliveries was increasing the infant death rate in Chicago.

Formation of the IBT

The delegates at the AFL's 1902 convention in New Orleans, eager to bring the TNU back into the fold, passed a resolution instructing Gompers to try to smooth relations between the AFL and the dissident union. Accordingly, Gompers assembled a committee to bring representatives from the TDIU and the TNU together in Niagara Falls, New York, in August 1903. After extensive bargaining, the committee was able to resolve the differences between the two unions, and on 22 August 1903 the AFL granted a charter to the merged unions, now called the International Brotherhood of Teamsters (IBT). In bringing about the reconciliation, the AFL committee made two major concessions to the TNU: it lowered the per capita tax from 25 cents to 15 cents, and it restricted membership to those owning no more than one team. Anyone who owned even just a second team was considered an employer and thus ineligible for membership. That month, the IBT held its first convention, and in October it moved its headquarters to Indianapolis, Indiana. Under the leadership of President Cornelius Shea, the new union began operations with 50,000 members and a war chest of $25,000.

The Aftermath

The formation of the IBT would seem to have ended dissension, but as events turned out, the dissension was just beginning. The IBT was not a single entity with a common strategy and shared mission but rather a confederation of smaller local affiliate unions, and these affiliates continued to feud both with one another and with the international union. In particular, the powerful Chicago Teamsters remained reluctant to cede power to a national organization. In 1905, in violation of their contract, they took part in a sympathy strike with garment workers against the Montgomery Ward company. Shea and several other Chicago Teamsters officials were arrested and charged with conspiracy for their part in the strike. Sensing the union's vulnerability, many employers—members of the Chicago Employers' Association—broke contracts with the local unions and threatened that if a single driver walked off the job or refused to haul goods for Montgomery Ward, all of the drivers would be locked out. In this climate of conflict, membership in the union plunged and a battle began over the IBT leadership. When Shea was barely reelected at the IBT's 1906 convention, a number of local affiliates in Chicago, Joliet, St. Louis, San Francisco, New York, and elsewhere seceded and formed a rival organization, the United Teamsters of America. Thus, the IBT opened its 1907 convention with a sharply reduced membership roll, almost no money, and mounting debts. Some harmony was restored when Daniel J. Tobin, an unknown Boston driver, unseated Shea by a mere 12 votes, and many of the dissident units rejoined the IBT. However, 17 Chicago locals refused to return to the fold and instead formed the Teamsters' and Helpers Union of Chicago and Vicinity, which survived as an independent union until 1934.

As if the chaotic political environment was not enough, the IBT was plagued with corruption in its early days. Many of the teamsters unions that had existed before the formation of the IBT, particularly in big cities such as New York, Detroit, St. Louis, and, of course, Chicago, had been hijacked by corrupt officials. Some of these unions carried on virtually no trade union activities, instead devoting their energies to fraud, extortion, treasury looting, racketeering, and even kidnapping and murder. Employers' associations routinely bribed union officials to strike against competing firms, refuse to work for firms attempting to enter an industry, agree to "sweetheart" contracts, or call off threatened strikes. Extortion was an even bigger problem. The union would simply threaten to not deliver goods unless the business owner paid union officials a bribe, and few business owners, faced with such a choice, refused.

This was the culture that Tobin inherited in 1907, and he found himself almost powerless to change it. At 150 pounds, he was in the unenviable position of trying to work his will on physically strong men more inclined to settle disputes with their fists than with discussion, negotiation, and compromise. Indeed, Tobin was nearly beaten to death in New York by local officials outraged by his efforts to enforce an IBT executive board decision, though he survived and remained president of the IBT until 1952. Understandably, however, he was thereafter reluctant to meddle in local union matters. The result, which is still reflected in the Teamsters' make-up and culture today, is a union that is an umbrella organization for a loose confederation of powerful, autonomous local affiliates.

Key Players

Gompers, Samuel (1850–1924): Gompers was born to Dutch-Jewish immigrants in London, where he began his working life at age ten as a cigar maker. He immigrated to the United States in 1863 and in 1886 was elected vice president of the Cigarmakers' International Union. That year he was a founder of the American Federation of Labor and served as its president from 1886 to 1895, then again from 1896 to 1924. In 1919 Gompers was appointed to the American delegation at the Paris Peace Conference following World War I. His autobiography, *Seventy Years of Life and Labor,* was published in 1925.

Tobin, Daniel Joseph (1875–1955): Tobin was born in Ireland, but he and his brother immigrated to the United States in 1889. He began his career as a sheet metal worker, but in 1894 he took a job as a driver for the Boston streetcar company. In the late 1890s he bought a team and wagon and delivered meat and dairy goods and won a contract to sprinkle Boston's streets. In 1900 he joined the Team Drivers' International Union, and in 1903 he attended the Niagara Falls conference that led to the formation of the Teamsters Union. In addition to his long tenure as Teamsters president (1907–1952), he served as AFL treasurer, a member of the AFL executive council, and vice president of the AFL's building trades department.

See also: *American Federation of Labor.*

BIBLIOGRAPHY

Books

Fink, Gary M., ed. *Labor Unions.* The Greenwood Encyclopedia of American Institutions. Westport, CT: Greenwood Press, 1977.

Garnel, Donald. *The Rise of Teamster Power in the West.* Berkeley: University of California Press, 1972.

Perlman, Selig, and Philip Taft. *History of Labor in the United States, 1862–1932.* Vol. 4, *Labor Movements.* New York: Macmillan, 1935.

Witwer, David Scott. *Corruption and Reform in the Teamsters Union.* Urbana: University of Illinois Press, 2003.

—Michael J. O'Neal

Ten-Hour Day Movement

United States 1820s–1850s

Synopsis

The 10-Hour Movement began among skilled craftsmen in the major East Coast cities of the United States in the early 1820s. Workers' early efforts were unevenly successful in the short term and, with the exception of the building trades in New York City, uniformly unsuccessful in the long term. In the 1830s the movement spread as skilled workers organized across

Martin Van Buren. AP/Wide World Photos. Reproduced by permission.

crafts to form community trades unions. These organizations saw some successes, but only among skilled workers in particular crafts and cities. In 1840 President Martin Van Buren ordered the 10-hour day for workers employed on federal projects. In the early 1840s interest in the 10-hour day spread to noncraft workers. By the mid-1840s the 10-hour day was a central demand of the new "Labor Reform" societies that attempted to organize industrial workers across skill levels and genders. Labor Reformers petitioned for and won state legislation for the 10-hour workday in seven states. These laws, however, proved to be loophole-ridden and did little to change the actual hours of labor for most workers. In the 1850s sectional politics led northern merchant-capitalists to embrace the 11-hour day, the adoption of which effectively quelled the 10-Hour Movement.

Timeline

1820: In the Missouri Compromise, Missouri is admitted to the Union as slave state, but slavery is prohibited in all portions of the Louisiana Purchase north of 36°30' N.

1821: Mexico declares independence from Spain.

1823: U.S. President James Monroe establishes the Monroe Doctrine, whereby the United States warns European nations not to interfere in the political affairs of the Western Hemisphere.

1825: Opening of the New York Stock Exchange.

1826: French inventor Joseph-Nicéphore Niepce makes the first photographic image in history.

1828: Election of Andrew Jackson as president begins a new era in American history.

1831: Young British naturalist Charles Darwin sets sail from England aboard the H.M.S. *Beagle* bound for South America, where he will make discoveries leading to the formation of his theory of evolution by means of natural selection.

1835: American inventor and painter Samuel F. B. Morse constructs an experimental version of his telegraph, and Samuel Colt patents his revolver.

1838: As crops fail, spawning famine in Ireland, Britain imposes the Poor Law. Designed to discourage the indigent from seeking public assistance, the law makes labor in the workhouse worse than any work to be found on the outside, and thus has the effect of stimulating emigration.

1842: Scientific and technological advances include the development of ether and artificial fertilizer; the identification of the Doppler effect (by Austrian physicist Christian Johann Doppler); the foundation of biochemistry as a discipline; and the coining of the word *dinosaur*.

1846: The United States declares war on Mexico, and adds California and New Mexico to the Union.

1851: Britain's Amalgamated Society of Engineers applies innovative organizational concepts, including large contributions from, and benefits to, members, as well as vigorous use of direct action and collective bargaining.

1852: Publication of *Uncle Tom's Cabin* by Harriet Beecher Stowe. Though far from a literary masterpiece, it is a great commercial success, with over half a million sales on both sides of the Atlantic. More important, it has an enormous influence on British sentiments with regard to slavery and the brewing American conflict between North and South.

1856: British inventor Henry Bessemer introduces his process for producing steel cheaply and efficiently.

1859: American abolitionist John Brown leads a raid on the federal arsenal at Harpers Ferry, Virginia. His capture and hanging in December heighten the animosities that will spark the Civil War 16 months later.

Event and Its Context

The Early Movement: The 1820s

The early 10-Hour Movement emerged in New York City, Philadelphia, and Boston in the 1820s. All were centers of the rising merchant and capitalist classes and had large and active artisan populations. The struggle over hours was twofold. First, it was a conflict between masters and journeymen to control the latter's free time. The household labor system in which masters and journeymen worked and lived together had been breaking down and masters struggled to retain control over the time and lives of their workers. Second, it was a conflict between merchant-capitalists and workers. As time rather than task became the dominant method of measuring work, control of the hours

Workers May pole offering, May Day, 1894. © Hulton/Getty Images. Reproduced by permission.

of labor came to mean control over labor itself to both the employers and the employed.

Workers in the building trades formed the core of 10-hour activists during this period. In 1825 Boston carpenters struck for the 10-hour day. Their protest was easily met by a combination of masters who refused to hire 10-hour agitators and merchants and capitalists who would not contract with master carpenters who employed such journeymen. The *Columbian-Central* reported that merchant-capitalists issued a resolution that they were prepared "to suspend, if necessary, building altogether," so as to put down the strike. Carpenters went back to work in Boston without achieving the 10-hour day.

In 1827 the movement gained momentum in Philadelphia from the speeches and pamphlets of William Heighton, who wrote as "An Unlettered Mechanic." Heighton argued that capitalists were stealing the extra labor of working men and that in order to be good citizens of the Republic, working men needed shorter hours to allow time for education about public affairs. This reasoning resonated with Philadelphia carpenters and 600 of them went on strike for 10 days in support of the 10-hour day. The strike was unsuccessful, but they rebounded the next year, along with the city's bricklayers, and won the 10-hour day for at least a season. Organized through the Workingmen's Party for political action, Philadelphia's workers elected officeholders with the backing of the Jacksonian Democratic Party. Despite their political origins as elected officials the Workingmen's Party, candidates failed to produce legislation for shorter hours.

The only city that enjoyed solid success was New York City. Carpenters there had enjoyed the 10-hour day since the early part of the century. In 1829, however, their customary hours came under attack from employers who wanted to increase the number of working hours to 11 per day. This threat spawned a massive reaction among skilled workers who believed the change in hours would create unemployment. Craftsmen rallied together to form the New York Workingmen's Party. Hours in New York's shops remained at 10 hours per day.

Trades Union Activism: The 1830s

The 10-hour demand continued to be central to the labor movement in the Northeast as skilled workers continued to strike into the 1830s. New organizations that were more broadly conceived to include workers from a variety of trades and drawn from a larger geographic area developed in the name of the 10-hour day.

Seth Luther, a New England carpenter, was a pivotal player in the new organizing efforts. Luther traveled around northern New England in 1832 delivering lectures calling for the 10-hour day. His lecture, "Address to the Working-Men of New England," argued for the unity of skilled workers and factory operatives in pursuit of the 10-hour day. Although his speech, and later pamphlet, failed to inspire such a union of skilled and unskilled workers, it did spur the creation of the New England Association of Farmers, Mechanics, and Other Working Men. Under the banner of this new organization, machinists and workers in the building trades made vigorous efforts in March and April to secure the 10-hour day, but were unsuccessful. Strikers went out in Lowell, Rochester, Fall River, South Bos-

ton, Wheeler's Point, and Taunton, Massachusetts; Bath, Maine; Providence, Rhode Island; and even as far away as Utica, New York; Louisville, Kentucky; and Detroit, Michigan. Boston and New Bedford, Massachusetts, were the sites of the largest strikes.

In 1834 the Boston Trades' Union (BTU) formed. Modeled on a similar group in New York City, the BTU was more strongly organized along trade lines than the New England Association had been. This trade orientation, however, did not limit the unionists to discussion on issues related to skilled workers alone. At the National Trades' Union meeting in August 1834, six city Trades Union representatives met; their discussion about hours included the condition of female factory operatives and resulted in a resolution that noted the damaging effects that long hours had on child laborers.

The publication of the "Ten-Hour Circular" in 1835 incited a new wave of strikes centered on the hours issue. In part authored by Seth Luther, the circular summed up the arguments for the 10-hour day. It argued for 10 hours on the basis of natural rights, religious rights, bodily necessity, mental necessity, intellectual need, and republican virtue. It showed how employers' arguments about long hours of work keeping workers from drunkenness and sinfulness were a lie. Employers made such arguments in the summer when they wanted workers on the job from sunrise to sunset, but felt no such interest in workers' morals in the winter when there was much less work. In Boston, union members went out on strike for two months, but to no avail. The union collapsed and workers went back to their jobs under the old system.

The strike in Boston and the publication of the "Ten-Hour Circular" in Philadelphia inspired the already agitated workforce in the latter city to form a general citywide strike of all working men. Workers who had been thinking of their struggles over piece-rates as wage issues came to define them as hours issues. They argued that they should make enough in piece rate to make a living wage working a 10-hour day. The strikers petitioned the city's Common Council, which responded with a law mandating the 10-hour day for all city workers. Private employers followed suit and workers in Philadelphia won the 10-hour day. The success in Philadelphia became the model for skilled workers in other cities. Not every city or trade won the 10-hour day, but advances were made by several groups of workers in cities in the Northeast.

Although 1835 brought great albeit uneven success for skilled workers in achieving a shorter work day, unskilled workers were largely unaffected. Industrial workers were also involved in labor activism in this period, but their issues differed from those of skilled workers. Workers in textile mills in places like Lowell, Massachusetts, and Dover, New Hampshire, struck against wage reductions, speed ups, and stretch outs. Turn outs involved mostly women workers who saw wages, not hours, to be their most important issue. The Panic of 1837 dampened union activity in the late 1830s but did not undo the gains that the unions had made in securing shorter hours among some skilled laborers. The depression, however, delayed efforts to spread the 10-hour day to all skilled and unskilled laborers until the early 1840s.

The Federal 10-Hour Law: 1840

On 31 March 1840 President Martin Van Buren issued an executive order mandating that all manual workers employed on government contracts would be required to work only 10 hours per day. This order brought government manual labor in line with the hours of government clerical labor; government offices were open eight hours per day in winter and 10 in summer under an 1836 federal law. Workers happily received this order. In particular, shipwrights who worked in the Navy Yards were pleased with the act. Their shortened hours inspired other shipyard workers to organize for the 10-hour day with great success in Maine, Connecticut, and Massachusetts.

Historians have not come to a definitive explanation for why Van Buren issued this order. Early interpretations focused on labor activism among workers and point to the example of workers in the Philadelphia Navy Yard who successfully petitioned President Andrew Jackson for shorter hours in 1836. However, the dissolution of the National Trades Union in 1837 and the generally weak state of organized labor, despite local and state efforts, seem to undermine that argument. Other historians have advanced the position that the executive order stemmed from an effort to secure the votes of workers to the Democratic Party. Skilled workers had long made the argument that a reduction in the number of hours worked was necessary to ensure that workers would be able to participate fully as citizens of the Republic. These egalitarian sentiments meshed well with Jacksonian ideals of democracy.

Labor Reform Movement: 1840s

The 10-Hour Movement changed in the 1840s. Whereas 10-hour agitators in the 1820s and 1830s had been mainly male skilled workers striking against masters and merchant-capitalists, in the 1840s this was not the case. Not only did the demographics of the protesters change, but the manner and objects of their protests were transformed as well.

In 1840s the 10-Hour Movement attracted the attention of factory workers and unskilled laborers, many of whom were female textile workers. Operatives formed organizations to protest the long hours of labor which could run from twelve and half to fifteen hours a day. The Lowell Female Labor Reform Association (LFLRA), founded by Sarah G. Bagley and a small group of Lowell operatives in 1845, was the center of hours activism in New England. The association grew rapidly as Bagley and British activist John C. Cluer toured New England, assisting mill workers in other cities in forming their own Labor Reform Associations. Associations all over New England corresponded with and encouraged each other through the pages of the LFLRA's newspaper, the *Voice of Industry*, which Bagley edited.

Women were major players in the 1840s movement, but they did not act alone. Men also took part in these struggles. In 1844 the New England Workingmen's Association (NEWMA) formed. Unlike its predecessors in the 1830s, the NEWMA was organized by community rather than by trade except in large cities and included significant numbers of industrial workers. Despite its name, the NEWMA welcomed both men and women and tried to make hours an issue that would unite all laborers. Women's participation was so strong that the group's name was changed to the Labor Reform League in 1846.

Strikes against the corporations had been the major weapons of mill workers in the 1830s. In the 1840s they employed the petition. Aimed at the state legislature, rather than at mill owners, petitions called for the state to exercise its power over the corporations that it had chartered. The reasoning was that because the state could form the corporation, it could also establish operating parameters within which the corporations would have to act if they proposed to maintain the legal benefits of incorporation. In making the case for reduced hours for women and children, petitioners particularly emphasized the deleterious health effects of mill work by pointing to the short meal breaks, bad air, and pollution from lamps during winter evenings. In making the case for the 10-hour day for men, reformers emphasized the need for education in public affairs and the securing of the rights of citizenship to working men. These gender differences highlight both how labor reform included but differentiated between men and women. Women needed protection while men were exercising their rights.

Massachusetts was the epicenter of Labor Reform activism. In 1845 petitioners won the attention of the Massachusetts state legislature, which established a Special Committee to Investigate Labor Conditions. Unfortunately for the reformers, the chairman of the committee was William Schouler, a Whig newspaperman who had run a smear campaign against activist John Cluer. The committee interviewed several women workers from Lowell, Sarah Bagley among them. Despite the workers' consistent testimony that long hours were detrimental to health, both mental and physical, the committee found that legislation on the matter was not needed.

Unlike Massachusetts, many states did respond to the petitions of mill workers and set limits on the hours of labor. New Hampshire was the first to enact such a law, passing its statute in 1847. State laws followed in Pennsylvania and Maine (1848), Ohio (1852), Rhode Island and California (1853), and Connecticut (1855). These laws, however, changed nothing. The 10-hour rule, according to the laws, applied only to those who had not made some other contract or arrangement with an employer. Lawmakers argued that this protected free labor from government interference with private contracts. For employers, the solution to the 10-hour law was clear: upon employment have workers sign a contract that requires them to adhere to the "customary hours" of labor. Many workers had, in fact, signed such contracts before the laws took effect.

Labor Reform was part of a constellation of reform movements, along with temperance and antislavery, that swept the United States in the 1840s as associational life proliferated. Yet, despite the affinities Labor Reform shared with other reform movements, it fizzled out in the late 1840s due to the effects of economic depression and corporate blacklisting.

The 11-Hour Day: 1850s

The hours question emerged in the 1850s as part of the national struggle over slavery. Although factory workers had compared themselves to slaves in talking about the oppressiveness of long hours, their condition as "free" workers who could contract their labor of their own volition made them into a political enigma in the emerging national debate. Traditionally supported by Democrats, the 10-hour issue was also given attention by Free Soilers and Republican ex-Whigs.

Strike activity increased over the 10-hour issue in the first few years of the 1850s. Some workers won concessions to the 11-hour day from employers who belonged to parties seeking workers' votes. By the mid-1850s, however, the issue had become a political hot potato. Democrats did not want to endorse it because any sort of national legislation would conflict with their states' rights stance. Republicans shunned it because it confused the issue of free labor. Ultimately, the 10-hour demand was removed from politics as widespread adoption of the 11-hour day effectively ended the movement.

Key Players

Bagley, Sarah G. (1806–?): Bagley worked in the Lowell mills for eight years. As the editor of the *Voice of Industry* and organizer of the Lowell Female Labor Reform Association, she was an outspoken advocate of women's rights and the 10-hour day. In 1845 she was elected as an officer of the New England Workingmen's Association.

Cluer, John C. (1806–1886): Cluer was an English weaver with a background as a temperance agitator, land reformer, and Chartist. A charismatic speaker, he arrived in the United States in 1845 and traveled around New England preaching the 10-hour day to textile workers. He was the victim of a smear campaign waged by William Schouler, a supporter of the mill owners.

Heighton, William (1800–1873): Heighton was an English cordwainer who immigrated to Philadelphia, Pennsylvania. In 1827 he wrote a pamphlet under the pseudonym "An Unlettered Mechanic," that animated the 10-Hour Movement in East Coast cities. In his pamphlet he argued that the 10-hour day was needed so that workers would have time to educate themselves and act as good citizens in the Republic. He also argued that workers were exploited by capitalists who paid them less in wages than the value that their work produced.

Luther, Seth (1799–1846): Luther was a carpenter who lectured widely on the 10-hour day. In 1832 he wrote and delivered a speech that was later issued as a pamphlet titled, "Address to the Working-Men of New England," in which he called for unity between skilled craftsmen and factory operatives under the banner of the 10-Hour Movement. He also helped produce the influential "Ten Hour Circular" (1835), which summed up the arguments for the 10-hour day.

Schouler, William (1814–1872): Schouler was a procorporation Whig who published the Lowell *Courier*. He also funded the procorporation Lowell *Offering*, a magazine that was published to showcase the dignity of the mill girls and the beneficial environment and working conditions offered to them. As a representative to the Massachusetts legislature, Schouler acted as chairman of the 1845 Special Committee to Investigate Labor Conditions. The committee found that there was no legislation needed to protect workers.

Van Buren, Martin (1782–1862): Van Buren was a lawyer, the eighth president of the United States, and a career politician who spent eight years each in the U.S. House and Senate. In 1840 he passed an executive order that mandated a 10-hour day for workers on federally funded projects.

See also: *Dover Textile Strike; Eight-hour Day Movement; Factory Girls' Association; Workingmen's Party (1828).*

BIBLIOGRAPHY

Books

Dublin, Thomas. *Women at Work: The Transformation of Work and Community in Lowell, Massachusetts, 1826–1860.* New York: Columbia University Press, 1979.

Dulles, Foster Rhea. *Labor in America: A History.* 3rd ed. New York: Thomas Y. Crowell Company, 1966.

Langenfelt, Gösta. *The Historic Origin of the Eight Hours Day: Studies in English Traditionalism.* Stockholm: Almqvist and Wiksell, 1954.

Murolo, Priscilla, and A. B. Chitty. *From the Folks Who Brought You the Weekend: A Short, Illustrated History of Labor in the United States.* New York: The New Press, 2001.

Murphy, Teresa Anne. *Ten Hours' Labor: Religion, Reform, and Gender in Early New England.* Ithaca, NY, and London: Cornell University Press, 1992.

Roediger, David R., and Philip S. Foner. *Our Own Time: The History of American Labor and the Working Day.* Contributions to Labor Studies, Number 23. New York, Westport, CT, and London: Greenwood Press, 1989.

Seldon, Bernice. *The Mill Girls: Lucy Larcom, Harriet Hanson Robinson, Sarah G. Bagley.* New York: Atheneum, 1983.

Wallace, Anthony F. C. *Rockdale: The Growth of an American Village in the Early Industrial Revolution.* New York: Alfred A. Knopf, 1978.

Zonderman, David A. *Aspirations and Anxieties: New England Workers and the Mechanized Factory System, 1815–1850.* New York and Oxford: Oxford University Press, 1992.

ADDITIONAL RESOURCES

Books

Frankfurter, Felix, assisted by Josephine Goldmark. *The Case for the Shorter Workday: The Supreme Court of the United States, October Term 1915. Franklin O. Bunting v. The State of Oregon. Brief for the Defendant in Error,* vols. I and II. New York: National Consumers' League, 1915.

Kleene, Gustav Adolph. *History of the Ten-Hour Day in the United States.* Ph.D. diss., University of Pennsylvania, 1896.

Luther, Seth. "An Address to the Working-Men of New England." Boston, 1832. In *Religion, Reform and Revolution: Labor Panaceas in the Nineteenth Century,* edited by Leon Stein and Philip Taft. New York: Arno, 1969.

Periodicals

Thompson, E. P. "Time, Work-Discipline and Industrial Capitalism." *Past and Present* 38 (December 1967): 56–97.

—Kimberly F. Frederick

Texas and New Orleans Railroad Company et al v. Brotherhood of Railway and Steamship Clerks et al

United States 1930

Synopsis

The growth of unionism in the railway industry has been a tempestuous affair, marked with victories and tragedies. Railroad employees have been fighting for their rights since the industry's beginning. These efforts are a reaction to the harsh and deadly work environment the workers have had to endure. Injuries and death are common, as are poor wages and long hours. As early as 1855, workers organized into labor unions to protect their labor rights. Several hundred workers were even injured and killed while striking against wage cuts. Despite opposition from employers, railway employees continued to fight for better working conditions and pay.

One major victory came on 20 May 1926 with the passing of the Railway Labor Act (RLA). The act originally was designed to ensure workers the right to unionize and engage in collective bargaining. The act further prohibited employers from discriminating against employees for being involved in union activities.

RLA was both a success and a failure. Employers remained, for the most part, opposed to unionism and found different ways to manipulate union influence in the railway industry. For example, the Texas and New Orleans Railroad Company (NOR) essentially created its own "union" and intimidated and coerced their employees into joining it. The company's control of the union and its representatives served the company's interests, not those of the employees. In turn, the employees had already nominated the Brotherhood of Railway and Steam Clerks (Brotherhood) to serve as their labor representatives. Management of the Texas and New Orleans Railroad Company refused to deal with these representatives and continued to force its employees to leave the union. An alleged violation of the Railway Labor Act prompted the Brotherhood and railway company to enter into an extensive legal battle that proceeded from the district court up to the Supreme Court. At each level, the courts found in favor of the Brotherhood. Unfortunately, the victory was, in part, a hollow one. Although RLA spelled out specific rules of behavior, enforcing them was another matter. This case did, however, inspire legislators to amend RLA so that its language and penalties were strengthened, thus increasing its effectiveness.

Timeline

Event and Its Context

The Railway Labor Act

For much of America's history, the economy has been based on the success of the railroad industry, with its ability to ship people and commodities to all corners of the country. The industry has also witnessed some of the greatest changes in labor relations. From the earliest days, railway employees commonly faced dangerous work environments and injuries during the course of their duties. In addition, employees faced regular wage cuts and long hours. Their walkouts met stiff resistance, both from employers and the government. Railroad company management solicited assistance from federal troops, as well as local and state militia, to suppress strikes and rioting. It was not uncommon for these face-offs to result in strikers being killed or injured, such as in 1877, when over 100 employees were killed while protesting a 10 percent wage reduction.

Therefore, it is not hard to understand why unionism gained acceptance among railway workers. Under public pressure, legislators slowly began to make changes to improve labor conditions in the railroad industry. The first changes focused on safety, such as the Safety Appliance Act of 1893, the Federal Employers Liability Act of 1908, and the Accident Reports Act of 1910. Although some legislation, such as the Sherman Antitrust Act of 1890, attempted to hinder unionism's growth in the railway industry, unionism continued to progress.

On 20 May 1926 the government passed the Railway Labor Act (RLA). RLA required employers to engage in collective bargaining and prohibited them from discriminating against employees on the basis of union involvement. RLA also enforced its rulings under penalty of law. According to David Moberg in a 2001 article in the *Progressive Media Project*, "the [RLA] was designed to minimize transportation disruptions while recognizing the right of workers to organize and negotiate contracts. It set up a multistage procedure of mediation, 'cooling off' periods, and the establishment of presidential 'emergency boards' to investigate disputes and push settlements." The National Mediation Board could intervene to promote proper mediation.

To the common observer, the railway workers now possessed a powerful legal tool in their fight for improved labor relations. On the surface, this was true, but as the employees of the Texas and New Orleans Railroad Company would soon discover, RLA contained hidden problems.

The Brotherhood v. the Texas/New Orleans Railroad Company

Beginning in 1918, the railway clerks of the Texas and New Orleans Railroad (NOR) Company had authorized, by majority, the Brotherhood of Railway and Steamship Clerks (Brotherhood) to serve as their arbitrators in all matters of labor. The Texas and NOR Company continued to recognize the Brotherhood as the legitimate representatives for their employees, even after the union entered an application for an employee wage increase on November 1925. The railroad company denied this application. In response, the Brotherhood filed a petition with the National Mediation Board, asking the board to intervene and prompt the company to engage in wage negotiations.

In essence, the Texas and NOR Company decided not to recognize the Brotherhood after all. Even as the petition to the United States Board of Mediation came under consideration, the company created its own union of railway clerks, naming it the Association of Clerical Employees–Southern Pacific Lines. This "union" consisted of company-appointed representatives, many of whom where officers in the company and favored the company's interests more than those of the employees. In addition to the formation of its company-controlled union, the Texas and NOR Company began a campaign of in-

timidation and coercion. Employees found themselves being influenced to join the Association of Clerical Employees–Southern Pacific Lines, nominate the Association to act as their official labor representative, and abandon the Brotherhood. In some cases, the company offered favors and rewards to certain employees, subtly influencing the negotiations toward the corporate side. Should the employees not proceed as the company wished, it would revoke the favors. In other cases, the company used direct intimidation to attempt to force its employees to sign with the Association or face possible termination.

Citing this to be a violation of RLA, the Brotherhood took the Texas and NOR Company to court. During the proceedings, the company stated that it had acted in proper accordance with the law, as the majority of employees had authorized the Association of Clerical Employees–Southern Pacific Lines to be their designated representative. As such, the company could not recognize the Brotherhood of Railway and Steamship Clerks nor its request for a wage increase. After the final hearing, the district court found the railroad company in contempt and ordered the Texas and NOR Company to disband the Association of Clerical Employees and reinstate the Brotherhood as the proper labor representatives. This injunction then transferred to the circuit court of appeals, which found that the district court had acted appropriately in its authority and upheld the injunction.

The case did not end there. It went to the Supreme Court on 1 May 1930 (281 U.S. 548). Once more the Texas and NOR Company declared its innocence of all charges and asked for the dismissal of the injunctions that had been placed upon it. The company's attorneys argued that the company's actions were lawful and that the district court decision violated the company's First and Fifth Amendment rights under the Constitution, with freedom of speech and property issues being the key components of the controversy. Pointing to the First Amendment protection of freedom of speech, the Texas and NOR Company claimed it was within its rights to discuss union representation with its employees and that the restrictions placed on it by RLA and district court were unfair. It also questioned the district court's decision to order it to compensate terminated employees with back pay, because it claimed it had the right to terminate employees for any reason. Furthermore, it claimed that the injunction of the district court that had been placed against the company was invalid according to section 20 of the Clayton Act.

In turn, the Brotherhood's attorneys demonstrated to the Court the company's gross violations of RLA. Perhaps the most damning evidence against the Texas and NOR Company took the form of a letter from H. M. Lull, the company's executive vice president, to A. D. McDonald, the company's president. Dated 24 May 1927, after the Brotherhood's petition to the National Mediation Board, the letter detailed the possible results for the company should the wage increase issue go to arbitration. Lull referred to a similar case in which the railway clerks on lines west of El Paso were awarded a payroll increase of $340,000 per annum. Lull explained that to the best of his knowledge the Brotherhood did not represent the majority of employees. According to the United States Supreme Court, 281 U.S. 548, Lull further wrote that "it is our intention, when handling the matter in mediation proceedings, to raise the question of the right of [the Brotherhood] to represent these employees and if arbitration is proposed, we shall decline to arbitrate on the basis that the petitioner does not represent the majority of the employees." Lull anticipated that this approach would allow them to settle with employees for no more than $75,000 per annum. Obviously, the company's interests would be best served by not dealing with the Brotherhood, which, despite Lull's explanation, did represent the majority of railway clerks. Further evidence revealed that the Texas and NOR Company engaged in intimidation and coercion to promote its Association. On 26 May 1930 the Supreme Court upheld the findings of the district court and circuit court of appeals. It made a clear distinction between freedom of speech and unlawful coercion.

The Texas and NOR Company was found guilty of violating RLA, but the legislation did not provide for punishment. In other words, although the Supreme Court could say that the Texas and NOR Company was in the wrong, it could do little else but restore the status quo and require that any egregious behavior be stopped. The legislation had been designed to encourage fairness in labor negotiations, but it did not detail enforcement. Companies such as Texas and NOR were expected to conduct business according to RLA more or less out of good faith. With no legal consequences to back it up, RLA remained ineffectual. Amendments to the law were obviously required.

RLA after 281 U.S. 548

Since the landmark legal case in 1930, RLA has been enhanced by several amendments. For example, the act has been extended to cover airlines as well as railroads. In addition, amendments govern the selection of employee representatives and the arbitration, mediation, and negotiation processes. The most important change was the strengthening of the law's enforcement policy. Employers can be criminally prosecuted for RLA violations and face imprisonment (for up to six months) and fines of $20,000 per day that the employer fails to comply with obligations outlined under RLA.

Key Players

Lull, H. M.: Executive vice president of the Texas and New Orleans Railroad Company, Lull wrote a letter detailing the plan to manipulate labor negotiations to the company's advantage. This letter, which revealed the company's willing violation of RLA, became a key point during the court action that followed.

See also: *Railroad Strike of 1877; Railway Labor Act.*

BIBLIOGRAPHY

Periodicals
Moberg, David. "On 75th Anniversary of Railway Labor Act, We Need to Protect Workers' Rights." *The Progressive Media Project,* 16 May 2001.

Other
Etters, Ronald M. The Railway Labor Act: An Outline. 2002 [cited 26 September 2002]. <http://www.gmu.edu/departments/law/drc/RLAOutline.htm>.

Findlaw for Legal Professionals. Laws: Cases, Codes, and Regs. *Texas and New Orleans Railroad v. Brotherhood of Railway and Steamship Clerks.* 281 U.S. 548 (1930). 2002 [cited 26 September 2002]. <http://laws.lp.findlaw.com/getcase/us/281/548.html>.
Texas and New Orleans Railroad Company et al. v. Brotherhood of Railway and Steamship Clerks et al., 281 U.S. 548; 50 S. Ct. 427; 74 L. Ed. 1034 (1930).
United States Department of Justice. 2454 The Railway Labor Act (RLA)—45 U.S.C. 151, *et seq.* 2002 [cited 26 September 2002]. <http://www.usdoj.gov/usao/eousa/foia_reading_room/usam/title9/crm02454.htm>.
United Transportation Union. About UTU. *Rail Strikes Marked Early Days as Workers Organized Unions.* 2002 [cited 26 September 2002]. <http://www.utu.org/worksite/history/strikes.htm>.

—Lee Ann Paradise

Tompkins Square Rally

United States 1874

Synopsis

On the morning of 13 January 1874, some 7,000 unemployed New Yorkers gathered in Tompkins Square in New York City to demand public aid and employment during a time of economic depression. The Committee of Safety, a group of socialists, trade union leaders, and labor reformers, called the meeting after one with city leaders in late December failed. The press and the police were on high alert and denounced the committee as a body of vagabonds and communists. The police force was set on swiftly dispersing the meeting. Men, women, and children scattered when the police suddenly charged into the crowd and started indiscriminately clubbing people. Several German socialists decided to resist the police action and engaged in fights. When the square had been cleared, Police Commissioner Abram Duryee ordered mounted police to forcefully disperse all people from the side streets. By dusk, Tompkins Square was calm and 46 workers were in jail.

Timeline

1854: Republican Party is formed by opponents of slavery in Michigan.

1859: American abolitionist John Brown leads a raid on the federal arsenal at Harpers Ferry, Virginia. His capture and hanging in December heighten the animosities that will spark the Civil War sixteen months later.

1864: General William Tecumseh Sherman conducts his Atlanta campaign and his "march to the sea."

1867: Establishment of the Dominion of Canada.

1870: Beginning of Franco-Prussian War. German troops sweep over France, Napoleon III is dethroned, and

France's Second Empire gives way to the Third Republic.

1872: The Crédit Mobilier affair, in which several officials in the administration of President Ulysses S. Grant are accused of receiving stock in exchange for favors, is the first of many scandals that are to plague Grant's second term.

1874: As farm wages in Britain plummet, agricultural workers go on strike.

1874: Discovery of gold in the Black Hills of South Dakota.

1874: Norwegian physician Arrnauer Gerhard Henrik Hansen discovers the bacillus that causes leprosy. This marks the major turning point in the history of an ailment (now known properly as Hansen's disease) that afflicted humans for thousands of years and was often regarded as evidence of divine judgment.

1876: General George Armstrong Custer and 264 soldiers are killed by the Sioux at the Little Big Horn River.

1882: The Chinese Exclusion Act, a treaty between the United States and China, provides for restrictions on immigration of Chinese workers.

1884: Chicago's Home Life Insurance Building, designed by William LeBaron Jenney, becomes the world's first skyscraper.

Event and Its Context

The Committee of Safety

In scope, the Tompkins Square "riot" was a minor incident, but it revealed much about class divisions in urban America. At a time of rapid and often bewildering change, Americans of all walks of life struggled to cope with forces outside their control. The workers' demand for public responsibility in times of hardship was a response to the depression, but after 13 January, the Tompkins Square rally became a symbol of class antagonism in a supposedly classless America.

Once described by *Harper's Weekly* as "the grand plebeian plaza of New York City," Tompkins Square is situated in the northern part of Manhattan's Lower East Side, a working-class district inhabited by a large immigrant population of mostly Irish and German workers. The panic of September 1873 caused a widespread economic depression that wreaked havoc among working people in the cities. By the winter of 1873–1874, one-fourth of New York's workforce had lost their jobs, and hunger and homelessness were spreading at an alarming rate.

Reformers, labor leaders, and socialists immediately lashed out at the financial system and the "moneyocracy." They demanded that New York provide public works, relief for distressed families, and an end to winter-time evictions. A meeting at the Cooper Institute on 11 December 1873 appointed a 50-member Committee of Safety that included German, French, Irish, and American delegates. The committee's task was to organize the unemployed in ward clubs and set up a meeting with city leaders. After the latter refused to meet, the committee

Peter J. McGuire. © Getty Images. Reproduced by permission.

called for a large rally in the 10-acre park in Tompkins Square on 13 January, followed by a march on City Hall. They also demanded that the city make available $100,000 to a Labor Relief Bureau. The committee received permission from the Department of Parks and the Police Board to meet in Tompkins Square, but the latter strictly prohibited any demonstration near City Hall, a decision that flew in the face of free assembly according to labor leaders such as John Swinton and Peter J. McGuire.

From the start, the mainstream press and most well-to-do New Yorkers vilified the Committee of Safety. Despite its no-violence pledge, some leaders such as McGuire made it clear that, unless relief was forthcoming, workers had the right to take food. Such a program was radical and perceived as a threat by respectable society. The press too was particularly eager to discredit the workers' plea. The Paris Commune of 1871 formed the backdrop for the formation of an anti-labor attitude and anxiety among the public. Newspapers printed stories of allegedly smuggled weapons and jewelry to aid the communists in America. At the same time, public opinion branded the jobless as lazy, undeserving, and dangerous.

The Committee of Safety also struggled to maintain unity among the disaffected workers themselves. When the 13 January rally was announced, a rival organization captained by bricklayer Patrick Dunn dismissed the event and criticized the committee for being dominated by socialists. He quickly scheduled a gathering in Union Square for 5 January. Despite the impatience of the workers, committee member McGuire was able to persuade them to support the initial gathering on the 13th. In the days leading up to the rally, the committee streamlined its organization and won the support of the Société de la Commune, a small group of French radicals.

Confusion prevailed on the day before the rally. After appealing unsuccessfully to New York Governor John A. Dix, the Committee of Safety accepted the alternate parade route offered by the Police Board (from Tompkins to Union Square). Later in the evening, however, the committee canceled the Union Square march and focused solely on the Tompkins Square gathering. Meanwhile, the Police Board expressed second thoughts and in a last minute decision forced the Parks Department to cancel the permit to meet in Tompkins Square. No announcements were made to the committee or ward clubs, and no placards were posted in Tompkins Square to inform the workers.

Dispersing the Crowd

By 10 A.M. on 13 January 1874, several thousand workers and their families had assembled in Tompkins Square. Huddled together, they braved freezing temperatures and conversed in different languages about the effects of the meeting. In the northeast corner, 1,200 members of the German 10th Ward Workingmen's Association arrived while committee members moved about the silent mass delivering news sheets. Several hours earlier the Police Board had mobilized a sizeable army of officers: some 1,600 men assumed positions in the area between Tompkins Square and City Hall.

When the crowd had swelled to 7,000, Police Commissioner Abram Duryee, flanked by officers with drawn batons, marched into the crowd and raised the tension level of an otherwise uneventful gathering. Duryee urged everyone to go home, but without warning, the police charged into the throng with excessive force and left dozens wounded. Several German workers resisted and attacked the officers. Among them was Joseph Höfflicher, who hit a patrolman with his cane while Christian Mayer used a hammer. Justus H. Schwab, a socialist saloonkeeper, further defied authorities by marching onto the square holding a red flag while chanting the Marseillaise. Soon they were all apprehended and within minutes the square was empty and sealed off. Duryee then ordered the surrounding streets swept clean of thousands of people who fled in panic or jumped into cellar ways to escape the horsemen. The clubbing lasted for hours, and the mêlée spread to streets leading to City Hall. Astonished by this brutality, members of the Committee of Safety called on Mayor William Havemeyer for protection from the police, but to no avail.

By the end of the day, 46 workers were jailed including 24 Germans and 10 native-born Americans. The rest consisted of French, Polish, Italian, Irish, and Swedish immigrants. The German resisters, however, fared worse: Höfflicher and Mayer were imprisoned on assault and battery charges, and Schwab was accused of inciting to riot and "waving a red flag."

The conduct of the police unleashed strong emotions on both sides of the class divide. Organized labor and many radical groups attacked the police and city authorities for their behav-

ior, which, in their opinion, had no place in a democracy. German socialists contended that even in despotic monarchies one would not encounter such fierceness. A few liberal papers such as the *New York Sun* and the *New York Graphic* condemned the police riot as a serious violation of civil liberties. They interpreted the suppression as an attack on republican values and institutions.

Despite the vigor of these arguments, the overwhelming majority of public opinion applauded the actions of the police and the city leaders. Major papers felt relieved that an imminent danger by the foreign element had been firmly quelled. Again, the memory of the Paris Commune was invoked by such print media as the *Philadelphia Inquirer* and *Harper's Weekly*. Others were furious at the labor leaders for corrupting American hospitality and for abusing the precious gift of free speech. The public's hostility effectively crippled the movement for relief.

The Aftermath

Immediately following the debacle, police detectives launched an early example of a "red scare." They shadowed labor organizations as well as socialist meetings, which kept workers from attending them. The police set up a smear campaign when they warned against church burnings and bomb attacks by foreign communists. When the police found a useless pile of grenades that had been acquired by a French patriot for his government during the war with Prussia but never shipped, the police presented it as new evidence of a French communist connection. Most likely these actions reflected a desire on the part of the law enforcement community to justify their behavior on the 13th.

The labor and reform community also launched an ambitious campaign to oust the Police Board. Again, German workers and free thinkers played a crucial role, as evidenced by John Swinton's praise for their exemplary role in the fight for workers' rights. Eventually, a protest meeting convened at Cooper Institute on 30 January. With the exception of John Swinton's address, all speeches were in German. Everybody denounced the double standard practiced by police when dealing with meetings of workers as opposed to those by captains of industry, and Swinton eloquently defended the principle of free speech. In February petitions circulated against the police and labor proponents solicited affidavits from witnesses. Still, the workers lacked broad public support. The campaign slowly withered away. By March the Tompkins Square incident had faded from the minds of the middle and upper classes.

One last hope arose when the petitioners, represented by Swinton and two Germans, were allowed to plead their case before the New York State Assembly's Committee on Grievances in Albany on 25 March 1874. Swinton's speech reminded the lawmakers of the sanctity of free speech and respect for dissenting opinions. His appeal was later published as a pamphlet called *The Tompkins Square Outrage*.

During the summer, socialists in New York organized a campaign to free Christian Mayer, who had just been sentenced to an additional six months in prison. A group calling itself the Committee of Citizens, which included Swinton and many German trade unionists, formed to plan another Tompkins Square rally for 31 August. This rally proceeded in an orderly fashion. On this occasion Governor Dix decided to pardon Mayer. The meeting itself attracted little attention, but for some it signified a vindication of the January affair. In the end, however, the Police Board remained intact.

On the surface the Tompkins Square affair seems to have been merely a matter of over-zealous police officers, but it also reveals the fault line of the classes in an urban society unaccustomed to the process of industrialization and the effects of free-wheeling capitalism. Urban life fostered extreme antagonism between patrician urbanites and the swelling masses around them. Urban workers, many of them foreign, fought as much for their dignity as for bread. Like other Americans, urban workers resisted the whims of a global economy and its leaders and struggled to maintain control over their own lives.

Key Players

Havemeyer, William F. (1804–1874): Wealthy businessman and mayor of New York. As a member of Tammany Hall and an able manager, Havemeyer was elected mayor in 1845 and again in 1848, after which he returned to private life. After the Tweed scandals he made a comeback as Republican mayor in 1872.

McGuire, Peter J. (1852–1906): Labor activist of Irish immigrant parents. McGuire attending courses at Cooper Union and became a journeyman carpenter. His involvement in the Tompkins Square campaign cast him in the spotlight of labor activism. He founded the United Brotherhood of Carpenters and Joiners and helped establish Labor Day as a national holiday in 1882.

Schwab, Justus H. (1847–1900): German-American socialist and beginning in 1880 an anarchist. He owned a First Street saloon, which became famous as the meeting place of international radicalism. He was a founding member of the New York Social-Revolutionary Club that invited Johann Most for a lecture tour in the United States in 1882.

Swinton, John (1829–1901): A labor leader and journalist, Swinton was apprenticed as a printer, immigrated to Canada in 1843, and arrived in New York in 1850. He was active in the abolitionist movement before entering journalism as a writer for the *New York Times* and *Sun*. The Tompkins Square affair started his career as an activist. In 1883 he launched his own *John Swinton's Paper*, but he later returned to the *Sun* as editor until his death.

See also: *Panic of 1873; Paris Commune.*

BIBLIOGRAPHY

Books

Burrows, Edwin G. and Wallace, Mike. *Gotham: A History of New York City to 1898*. New York: Oxford University Press, 1999.

Swinton, John. *The Tompkins Square Outrage*. Appeal of John Swinton, addressed to the Legislature, through the Committee on Grievances, and delivered in the Assembly chamber at Albany, 25 March 1874.

Periodicals

"Defeat of the Communists." *New York Times* (14 January 1874).

Gutman, Herbert G. ''The Tompkins Square 'Riot' in New York City on January 13, 1874: A Re-Examination of Its Causes and its Aftermath." *Labor History* 6, no. 1 (winter 1965): 44–70.

"A Tompkins Square Rioter Sentenced." *New York Times* (23 January 1874).

ADDITIONAL RESOURCES

Books

Auble, Arthur G. "The Depressions of 1873 and 1882 in the United States." Ph.D. diss., Harvard University, 1949.

Feder, Leah H. *Unemployment Relief in Periods of Depression: A Study of Relief Measures Adopted in Certain American Cities, 1857–1932*. New York: Arno Press, 1936.

Gompers, Samuel. *Seventy Years of Life and Labor*. 2 vols. New York: E.P. Dutton, 1925.

Lynch, Denis Tilden. *The Wild Seventies*. New York, London: Appleton–Century, 1941.

Pinkerton, Allan. *Strikers, Communists, Tramps, and Detectives*. New York: G. W. Carleton & Co., 1878.

Ringenback, Paul T. *Tramps and Reformers 1873–1916: The Discovery of Unemployment in New York*. Westport, CT: Greenwood Press, 1973.

Periodicals

Cherry, George L. "American Metropolitan Press Reaction to the Paris Commune of 1871." *Mid-America* 32 (January 1950): 3–12.

Other

United Brotherhood of Carpenters and Joiners of America, Union History. "The Story of a Remarkable American and Trade Unionist" [cited 15 August 2002]. <http://www.carpenters.org/history/>.

—Tom Goyens

Trade Union Formation and Suppression

Japan 1890–1900

Synopsis

As Japan industrialized, many attempts were made to set up unions and a labor movement of one kind or another. In 1890 Takano Fusataro and his Japanese colleagues set up a study group in the United States known as the Japanese Knights of Labor. Once back in Japan in July 1897, they established the Society to Promote Trade Unions, which was a form of trade union school.

In December 1897 the Metalworkers' Union was formed, and in March 1898 the Japan Railway Company followed suit. Tokyo printers, ship carpenters, plasterers, furniture-makers, and doll-makers subsequently organized other unions. By 1899 problems were already appearing. The number of industrial workers had declined, some workers were losing interest, and the number of strikes was declining. Moreover, Takano was no longer coordinating matters at the society. The organizational and social barriers to worker unity were also quite strong and were exacerbated by worker ignorance and crucially by the strategic and tactical naiveté of the fledgling movement.

Government repression dealt the final blow. General harassment of unionists took its toll, and then in 1900 the government passed the Public Peace Police Law, which outlawed all labor agitation. This act of repression inaugurated the infamous "Dark Ages" of Japanese labor history.

Timeline

1881: U.S. President James A. Garfield is assassinated in a Washington, D.C. railway station by Charles J. Guiteau.

1886: Bombing at Haymarket Square, Chicago, kills seven policemen and injures numerous others. Eight anarchists are accused and tried; three are imprisoned, one commits suicide, and four are hanged.

1890: Alfred Thayer Mahan, a U.S. naval officer and historian, publishes *The Influence of Sea Power Upon History, 1660–1783,* which demonstrates the decisive role that maritime forces have played in past conflicts. The book will have an enormous impact on world events by encouraging the major powers to develop powerful navies.

1894: War breaks out between Japan and China. It will end with China's defeat the next year, marking yet another milestone in China's decline and Japan's rise.

1898: Bayer introduces a cough suppressant, derived from opium. Its brand name: Heroin.

1899: Polish-born German socialist Rosa Luxemburg rejects the argument that working conditions in Europe have improved, and that change must come by reforming the existing system. Rather, she calls for an overthrow of the existing power structure by means of violent international revolution.

1901: U.S. President William McKinley is assassinated by Leon Czolgosz, an anarchist. Vice President Theodore Roosevelt becomes president.

1904: Beginning of the Russo-Japanese War, which lasts into 1905 and results in a Japanese victory. In Russia, the war is followed by the Revolution of 1905, which marks the beginning of the end of czarist rule; meanwhile, Japan is poised to become the first major non-western power of modern times.

1905: Russian Revolution of 1905. Following the "bloody Sunday" riots before the Winter Palace in St. Petersburg in January, revolution spreads throughout Russia, in some places spurred on by newly formed workers' councils, or soviets. Among the most memorable incidents of the revolt is the mutiny aboard the battleship

Potemkin. Suppressed by the czar, the revolution brings an end to liberal reforms, and thus sets the stage for the larger revolution of 1917.

1908: The U.S. Supreme Court, in the Danbury Hatters' case, rules that secondary union boycotts (i.e., boycotts of nonunion manufacturers' products, organized by a union) are unlawful.

1909: William Cadbury's *Labour in Portuguese West Africa* draws attention to conditions of slavery in São Tomé and Principe.

1918: Upheaval sweeps Germany, which for a few weeks in late 1918 and early 1919 seems poised on the verge of communist revolution—or at least a Russian-style communist coup d'etat. But reactionary forces have regained their strength, and the newly organized Freikorps (composed of unemployed soldiers) suppresses the revolts. Even stronger than reaction or revolution, however, is republican sentiment, which opens the way for the creation of a democratic government based at Weimar.

Event and Its Context

Historical Background of the Japanese Labor Movement

The origins of the labor movement in Japan could be said to lie in the "social reform" that was awakened by two interrelated processes in Japan just before and during the Meiji era (1868–1912).

First, in 1853 Commodore Matthew Perry arrived with gunboats from the United States to force Japan to open its ports to Western products. The presence of industrial and military power—so starkly combined as they were in the image of Perry's black ships—first shocked, then galvanized Japan. The subsequent Meiji Restoration, the Civilization and Enlightenment Movement of the 1870s, and the Freedom and Popular Rights Movement of social reform in the 1880s all reflected specific Japanese responses to changes needed in its social and political structures. These were intended to keep Japan from buckling under the strain of Western imperial pressure. The culmination of this complex process was the establishment of the first parliament and constitutional monarchy in Asia proper: the Imperial (Meiji) Constitution promulgated in 1889 and the Diet (parliament), which began in 1890.

The second impetus was the onset of Japan's state-led industrialization and its route to economic modernity. Because the Japanese state needed to catch up with the West, it employed a distinctive pattern of development in the modern era, called the "developmental state model."

Japan's situation was not entirely unique. As the Japanese socialist Karl Kiyoshi Kawakami once wrote in regard to social democracy (echoing the Fabian socialists), so could it be said of the modern Japanese labor movement, namely that social democracy is the product of the Industrial Revolution. "Wherever the Industrial Revolution has been set on foot, we find the antagonism between the *bourgeoisie* and the *proletariat*, and with it we hear the cry of social democracy. It is only natural that in Japan, where the Industrial Revolution is fairly on its way,

Socialism has found disciples." As this suggests, the early stages of industrialization had specific social consequences. Conflict of interest between owners and workers began to appear in the form of workers' protests and eventually the adoption of tactics such as the strike.

All the processes set in motion from the Meiji Restoration onward eventually led to an awareness of social problems in the modern sense and to the consequent striving for change by different social groups employing different tactics, strategies, and ideologies. The Japanese labor movement in this period made diverse attempts to provide its own solutions to the problems at hand.

Early Beginnings of the Labor Movement

The main underlying cause of the development of the labor movement lies in the modernization and industrialization fostered by the Meiji oligarchs who ruled Japan after the Restoration of 1868. Acutely aware of the link between military power and the level of industrialization of a nation, they embarked upon an ambitious policy of *fukoku kyohei* (developing a rich country and a strong military). Crucial to its success was the nurturing of a sound economic, financial, and institutional foundation, including accumulation of capital, managerial and technical skills, and the right kinds of businesses for the modern industrial age. As private initiative was not always strong in the early Meiji era, the state was often involved and helped shape the transformation of the economy. In tune with its own interests, it concentrated on heavy industry and communication facilities, thus strengthening the recently founded forces of the military and navy. Slowly but surely, industrialization and capitalism took hold of various sectors of the Japanese economy leading up to and beyond the Sino-Japanese War of 1894–1895. During the war with China, the number of factories grew, the volume of corporately subscribed capital expanded, and the total of industrial workers rose significantly. Despite these massive changes from the Tokugawa era, Japan's industrialization was meager compared with that of the advanced Western nations. This was the perhaps unpropitious context in which Takano Fusataro and his colleagues were to begin their tentative steps toward building a labor movement in Japan.

The First Steps in the Development of the Labor Movement

The labor movement in Japan can be traced back to the left wing of the Freedom and Popular Rights Movement. Oi Kentaro, one of the left-wing leaders of the movement, was one of the first in Japan to plead on behalf of the laboring classes, which meant mainly the peasantry, tenant farmers, and groups such as miners. Oi discussed policies for popular welfare and the like in his publications and founded such organizations as the Laborers' Union and the Popular Suffrage Advocating League to try to kick start a labor movement.

As had been the case during industrialization in the West, there were benign capitalists in Japan who sympathized with the predicament of labor. Sakuma Teiichi was one of them. He was even dubbed by Takano Fusataro "the Robert Owen of Japan" because of his pro–working-class sympathies. Sakuma owned the Shueisha Printing House and tried to help the newly founded Printers' Union in 1884. Despite failure in this, he went on to help with the formation of the Laborers' Union.

In 1889 a league of ironworkers was organized under the guiding hand of Ozawa Benzo and others. The intention was to found a cooperative-style iron factory, but the factory only lasted for a few years.

All the previous examples are entirely preparatory in comparison with what happened in 1890 in America. While Samuel Gompers was laying the foundations for the American Federation of Labor (AFL) in 1886, Takano arrived in San Francisco. Four years later, Takano and his colleagues Jo Tsunetaro, Sawada Hannosuke, and other Japanese workers organized a study group, the Japanese Knights of Labor, in the United States. The group's aim was to return to Japan and prepare their countrymen for the social problems that were bound to arise from the country's ever-advancing shift toward an industrial economy. Takano returned to Japan in 1896. Once Jo and Sawada had returned in late 1896, they re-formed their study group. One of the first things that the group undertook was the writing and distribution of a pamphlet titled *A Summons to the Workers* to factory employees in Tokyo.

The group organized public meetings at which Sakuma Teiichi, Takano, and others spoke on labor issues. Funding problems hampered their success. Japan had entered a recession and strikes continued, but the group decided to persevere despite the difficulties of the economic situation. Around this time, the group invited Katayama Sen, the settlement house director, to get involved. Shimada Saburo, Matsumura Kaiseki, Suzuki Junichiro (a professor of economics), and Sakuma Teiichi (the progressive capitalist owner of a large printing house in Tokyo) also backed the project.

The Establishment of the Society to Promote Trade Unions

In June 1897, at a public meeting in Kanda, 47 people responded to the call to establish an association to promote the formation of trade unions. The Society to Promote Trade Unions was founded in early July 1897. It concentrated on educating workers about labor problems; the workers in turn would pass on this knowledge to other workers. The society coordinated the activities of various existing trade unions. It focused mainly on skilled workers, which limited the membership. Takano had learned this lesson in America from the failure of the Knights of Labor and its policy of centralization and industrial unionism. Takano's perception of the situation was that it would be difficult to develop a mass labor movement even in the United States. Thus, he believed that the federation and craft unionism of the AFL were better suited to Japanese conditions, especially in light of the powerful sense of hierarchy that dominated the Japanese social context of the time. Artisans and mechanics, for example, were very conscious of their social status and were thus loath to cross feudal class lines (a holdover from Tokugawa times) or to identify themselves with what was in terms of status the virgin territory of the category of the modern industrial worker.

Formation of the Metalworkers' Union

Given the orientation of the society and the nature of the skilled trades, it came as no surprise when the Metalworkers' Union was formed on 1 December 1897. With over 1,000 members, this was the first significant modern trade union in Japan.

Katayama was heavily involved in the formation process and became both one of the secretaries of the union as well as the editor of *Labor World*, the union journal, the first issue of which appeared on the same day the union was founded.

The Great Railway Strike

In 1898 a strike broke out at the largest railway company in Japan as a result of worker dissatisfaction with working conditions. Firemen and engineers began to organize secretly, were betrayed, and then finally were dismissed by the company. The dismissal signaled the workers, who had prepared ahead of time, to strike, and they did so starting on 24 February 1898. The strike lasted only a few days before the company caved in and met worker demands. This victory encouraged the railroad men to form a union; they forced the company to recognize it and founded a closed shop.

In 1898 *Labor World* reported 15 strikes involving about 7,000 workers on the Japan Railway. In addition, two old guilds were revived and reorganized into modern unions: the Ship Carpenters' Union and the Wood Sawyers' Union. After four years, the Metalworkers' Union had 5,400 members. If the revived unions were included, according to Katayama, the unions could boast at one stage almost 20,000 members.

Reasons for the Decline of the Movement

Accounts differ as to why the labor movement did not continue to grow after its initial successes. Although some commentators place most of the blame for the collapse of the movement on external reasons such as the heavy repression and interference by the police and the state, others emphasize the internal stresses and strains of the movement and the tactical, strategic, and ideological failings of particular leaders. Clearly a combination of these factors is the most plausible.

The suppression of the labor movement gained force when the Public Peace Police Law was passed in February 1900 during the spring session of the Imperial Diet. This measure prevented the working class from establishing any kind of union. Any agitation against employers and landowners became illegal and subversive from that time forth. The implications of this law were profound. Employees could not ask for higher wages or shorter hours without violating the law. Workingmen could not organize, because the law forbade it, with a threat of fines or hard labor. The focus solely on skilled workers doomed the movement to very small numbers and created a split in the ranks of a weak working class. Some have further argued that workers lost interest in the movement as repression mounted and the hopes of the leaders did not seem to be coming to fruition. The number of strikes fell sharply in 1899, dropping from 43 in 1898 to only 15 the following year. Strategic faults were also noticeable, one of which was the tendency of AFL-style decentralization to produce fractures in the overall solidarity of the labor movement. Minimal coordination by the Society to Promote Trade Unions, attributable to Takano's absence from late 1898 until the summer of 1899, worsened this lack of solidarity. The historical legacy of worker timidity, servility, and ignorance meant that workers were resistant to change. The newness of the union phenomenon meant that union promoters were frequently mistaken for just another brand of extortion, the latest form of worker exploitation by labor racketeers.

Finally, leaders such as Takano himself as well as Katayama have been criticized for different kinds of tactical, strategic, and ideological flaws. Takano's ideological and tactical proximity to the Association for the Study of Social Policy (not least via his brother, Iwasaburo) as well as to the AFL (via contact with Gompers) made him very wary of any labor involvement in politics. He was very much a moderate politically, as he thought it unwise to antagonize Japanese employers and the state, whether for ideological or more pragmatic reasons. Even the pamphlet *A Summons to the Workers* provides a good sense of his use of chauvinistic motifs to woo nationalistic workers, employers, and the Japanese state. The downside to this orientation was that workers who saw their interests ignored by employers and the state clearly had no time for proemployer unions. There were no concrete benefits. Moreover, the leadership often counseled them not to strike, but rather to use, in Takano's words, "peaceful and conservative methods as represented in pure and simple trade unionism." On the other hand, Katayama Sen has been criticized for using the trade union to hasten the millennium and draw the wrath of the police and the state.

The Reaction to Repression

The reaction of the movement to the devastating blow of the new legislation is revealing. Rather than contesting the questionable legality of this move and radicalizing, it largely and very respectably moved on to what it saw as the next task within the bounds of the legal status quo. This meant that workers were limited to founding associations for universal suffrage. Although this was a worthy goal as well, it was inadequate in light of the fact that the labor problem had broadened. It was rapidly turning into the old question of how best to combat an authoritarian state and the Japanese employers, both of whose interests were entirely opposed to those of the ordinary working masses. The labor movement could not run away from this issue but sooner or later had to face it or merely succumb with a whimper. The shifting of this conflict to the political realm simply transferred the same problem elsewhere. It did not constitute a resolution of it.

Key Players

Jo, Tsunetaro (1863–1904): One of the founders of the Knights of Labor in the U.S. He distributed Takano's pamphlet to workers in Tokyo. He was a shoemaker, who on returning to Japan in 1893 set up a shoemakers' association. Later he moved to Tokyo to help Takano in his union activities.

Kanai, Noburu (1865–1933): A founding member of the Association for the Study of Social Policy and a professor at Tokyo Imperial University.

Katayama, Sen (1859–1933): Born in what later became Okayama Prefecture, Katayama went to America and graduated from Grinnell College in 1892. From 1892 to 1894 he attended Andover Theological Seminary, and in 1895 he studied at Yale Divinity School. He became a Christian and later a socialist. He returned to Japan in 1896 and became a director of Kingsley Hall, the settlement house, involving himself in countless social causes. Takano convinced him to help in the labor movement, and in December 1897 he became very influential in the movement as editor of *Labor World*, the journal of the Metalworkers' Union. Later he helped organize the Japanese Communist Party.

Kuwata, Kumazo (1868–1932): Like Kanai, a founding member of the Association for the Study of Social Policy and a professor at Tokyo Imperial University. He was an aristocratic Diet member.

Sawada, Hannosuke (1868–?): One of the founders of the Japanese Knights of Labor and a distributor of Takano's pamphlet to workers in Tokyo. He was a tailor. In 1895 he tried to organize tailors in Tokyo. He also assisted Takano in his efforts at union organization.

Takano, Fusataro (1868–1904): Born in Nagasaki, Takano went to the United States in 1886, as Samuel Gompers was laying the foundations for the American Federation of Labor (AFL). Although not a founder of the Japanese Knights of Labor in San Francisco in 1890 (reconstituted in Japan in 1897), Takano became its most important member. A journalist by profession, he wrote a pamphlet, *A Summons to the Workers*, which was distributed to factory workers in Tokyo in 1897. Takano was also the key organizer in the establishment in July 1897 of the Society to Promote Trade Unions, which was essentially a school to assist the formation and growth of unions and to educate workers about them.

Takano, Iwasaburo (1871–1949): The younger brother of Fusataro and a founding member of the Association for the Study of Social Policy, he later became a professor at Tokyo Imperial University. He supported his brother's union drive. Later he became a famous social scientist and founded the Ohara Social Sciences Research Institute.

See also: *American Federation of Labor.*

BIBLIOGRAPHY

Books

Abe, Isoo. "Socialism in Japan." In *Fifty Years of New Japan*, vol. 2, compiled by Shigenobu Okuma. English version edited by Marcus Huish. London: Smith, Elder & Co., 1910.

Banno, Junji. *The Establishment of the Japanese Constitutional System.* Translated by J. A. A. Stockwin. London and New York: Routledge, 1992.

Crump, John. *The Origins of Socialist Thought in Japan.* London: Croom Helm, 1983.

de Bary, Wm. Theodore, et al. *Sources of Japanese Tradition*, vol. 2. New York: University of Columbia Press, 1964.

Gordon, Andrew. *The Evolution of Labor Relations in Japan: Heavy Industry, 1853–1955.* Cambridge, MA, and London: Council on East Asian Studies, Harvard University Press, 1988.

Halliday, Jon. *A Political History of Japanese Capitalism.* New York: Pantheon Press, 1975.

Hane, Mikiso. *Modern Japan: A Historical Survey.* 2nd ed. Boulder, CO: Westview Press, 1992.

Ike, Nobutaka. *The Beginnings of Political Democracy in Japan.* Baltimore, MD: John Hopkins Press, 1950.

Katayama, Sen. *The Labor Movement in Japan.* Chicago: Charles H. Kerr and Company Cooperative, 1918.

Kawakami, Karl Kiyoshi. *The Political Ideas of Modern Japan.* Tokyo, Japan: Shokwabo, 1903.

Kublin, Hyman. *Asian Revolutionary: The Life of Sen Katayama.* Princeton, NJ: Princeton University Press, 1964.

Lockwood, William. *The Economic Development of Japan: Growth and Structural Change, 1868–1938.* Princeton, NJ: Princeton University Press, 1954.

Marsland, Stephen. *The Birth of the Japanese Labor Movement: Takano Fusataro and the Rodo Kumiai Kiseikai.* Honolulu, HI: University of Hawaii Press, 1989.

Morris-Suzuki, Tessa. *A History of Japanese Economic Thought.* London and New York: Routledge, 1989.

Notehelfer, Fred. *Kotoku Shusui: Portrait of a Japanese Radical.* Cambridge, MA: Cambridge University Press, 1971.

Scalapino, Robert. *The Early Japanese Labor Movement: Labor and Politics in a Developing Society.* Berkeley: Institute of East Asian Studies, University of California, 1983.

Smith, Thomas C. *Political Change and Industrial Development in Japan: Government Enterprise, 1868–1880.* Stanford, CA: Stanford University Press, 1955.

Stead, Alfred. *Great Japan.* New York: John Lane, 1906.

Sugihara, Shiro, and Tanaka Toshihiro, eds. *Economic Thought and Modernization in Japan.* Cheltenham, UK, and Northampton, MA: Edward Elgar, 1998.

Tsurumi, Patricia. *Factory Girls: Women in the Thread Mills of Meiji Japan.* Princeton, NJ: Princeton University Press, 1990.

Wray, Harry, and Conroy, Hilary. *Japan Examined: Perspectives on Modern Japanese History.* Honolulu, HI: University of Hawaii Press, 1983.

Yanaga, Chitoshi. *Japan Since Perry.* New York: McGraw Hill, 1949.

Periodicals

Katayama Sen. "Labor Problem Old and New." *Far East* 2 (1897).

Kublin, Hyman. "The Japanese Socialists and the Russo-Japanese War." *Journal of Modern History* 22 (1950).

———. "Takano Fusataro: A Study in Early Japanese Trades-Unionism." *Proceedings of the American Philosophical Society* 103, no. 4 (August 1959).

Redman, H. Vere. "Sen Katayama." *Contemporary Japan* 2 (1934).

—Nik Howard

Trades and Labor Congress of Canada

Canada 1883

Synopsis

First meeting in Toronto in 1883, the Trades and Labor Congress of Canada (TLC) was the first long-standing labor central in Canada. TLC formed within the larger context of a developing national political economy—the recent confederation of the former British North American colonies into one nation in 1867, the rise of large-scale manufacturing enterprises, and the concomitant formation of a working class. The organization was an expression of the growing call for labor unity and political independence emanating from the turbulent trade union and Knights of Labor (KOL) agitation and struggles of the 1870s and 1880s.

Timeline

1863: Opening of the world's first subway, in London.

1869: Completion of the first U.S. transcontinental railway.

1873: Typewriter introduced.

1876: Four-stroke cycle gas engine introduced.

1878: Thomas Edison develops a means of cheaply producing and transmitting electric current, which he succeeds in subdividing so as to make it adaptable to household use. The value of shares in gas companies plummets as news of his breakthrough reaches Wall Street.

1881: In a shootout at the O.K. Corral outside Tombstone, Arizona, Wyatt, Virgil, and Morgan Earp, along with "Doc" Holliday, kill Billy Clanton, Frank McLowry, and Tom McLowry. This breaks up a gang headed by Clanton's brother Ike, who flees Tombstone. The townspeople, however, suspect the Earps and Holliday of murder. During the same year, Sheriff Pat Garrett shoots notorious criminal William Bonney, a.k.a. Billy the Kid, in Fort Sumner, New Mexico.

1883: Brooklyn Bridge completed.

1883: Foundation of the League of Struggle for the Emancipation of Labor by Marxist political philosopher Georgi Valentinovich Plekhanov marks the formal start of Russia's labor movement. Change still lies far in the future for Russia, however: tellingly, Plekhanov launches the movement in Switzerland.

1883: *Life* magazine begins publication.

1885: Belgium's King Leopold II becomes sovereign of the so-called Congo Free State, which he will rule for a quarter-century virtually as his own private property. The region in Africa, given the name of Zaire in the 1970s (and Congo in 1997), becomes the site of staggering atrocities, including forced labor and genocide, at the hands of Leopold's minions.

1889: Indian Territory in Oklahoma opened to settlement.

1893: Henry Ford builds his first automobile.

Event and Its Context

The Trades and Labor Congress of Canada (TLC) dates to the 1870s, when Canadian workers agitated for a shorter working day. Marked by the considerable expansion of manufacturing, the rise of significant urban populations and markets, the beginnings of a national railway, and the political and administrative consolidation of the Canadian Confederation, the 1870s also witnessed the first concerted attempts at national labor mobilization. Struggles for a shorter working day in Canada vaulted onto the national stage in 1872. Inspired by similar protests that had shook Britain and the United States in the 1860s, skilled craftsmen in central Canada's burgeoning industrial cities—Hamilton, Montreal, Toronto—forged a network of "Nine-Hour Leagues" to agitate for a shorter working day. The leagues developed a strategy of mass agitation and staged industrial conflict to back up their demand for the nine-hour day. Hamilton machinist James Ryan, the leading spokesperson and agitator in the Nine-Hours movement, established the Canadian Labor Protective and Mutual Improvement Association (CLPMIA). The CLPMIA also sought to provide a political voice for labor, drawing representatives from the key industrial centers of southern Ontario and Montreal. However, the autonomous craft union components that comprised the Nine-Hours movement were ultimately unable to agree on concerted strike action. Consequently, employers were able to isolate and defeat the first strike in Hamilton, which eventually put an end to the movement, although a select few of the most highly skilled workers won a reduced workday.

The struggle for a shorter workday nonetheless provided an important ideological precedent to the efforts by labor to organize around political and economic demands beyond the narrow confines of craft or industry. Citywide trade associations and assemblies sprouted up in the 1870s in the key industrial centers of the main provinces of Ontario and Quebec. A layer of pro-working-class intellectuals, dubbed "brainworkers" by historians such as Phillips Thompson, J. L. Blain, and George Wrigley, used their positions as activists, editors, journalists, and lecturers to popularize sharp critiques of the capitalist system, encourage united working-class struggle, and articulate alternative versions of society. Popular newspapers such as the *Ontario Workman* in Toronto and the *Northern Journal* in Montreal publicized labor's message on a wider basis. A growing cadre of working-class leaders, who looked to independent representation to advance labor's political aims, coalesced around the city-based assemblies and, building on the example of the short-lived CLPMIA, formed another central labor body in 1873, the Canadian Labor Union (CLU). Reluctant to break from the patronage politics of the mainstream parties, the CLU remained committed to political reforms that promoted the interests of labor such as an end to prison and child labor, legal rights for unions, and trade policies that created employment. In 1872 and 1874 the first explicitly working-class-supported candidates won political office at the federal and Ontario provincial level, respectively. Strike activity escalated in many industries in the first half of the decade, the previously aloof engineers were brought into the labor fold, and, as severe economic depression in the closing years of the 1870s spawned large-scale unemployment, workers across trade and skill lines joined together to protest the jobs crisis.

The process of labor unity would receive a critical boost with the coming of the Noble and Holy Order of the Knights of Labor (KOL) to Canada in 1875. In its 30-year history, the Canadian KOL built impressive support in the major cities of Canada as well as many smaller towns and villages, including numerous industrial towns and cities in the French-speaking province of Quebec. As in the United States, the KOL combined workplace struggle around economic issues with rich political and cultural ideas and practices borrowed from religious brotherhoods, political reform groups, and fraternal orders. As Gregory S. Kealey and Bryan D. Palmer have demonstrated, the KOL stood for inclusive working-class unity and buttressed their initiatives for labor reform on a complex amalgam of oppositional culture and ideological alternatives to capitalist exploitation and oppression. Moreover, the KOL promoted labor unity among all elements of the working class and organized women workers. The organization tackled questions of national chauvinism, especially anti-Irish sentiments, although regional Knights' organs retained racist stereotypes of and organized against immigrant Chinese workers. Yet, most importantly in terms of political organization and unity, the KOL spurred efforts to mobilize workers through independent politics.

Throughout the 1880s, the KOL, many of whose members also belonged to locals of international craft unions based in the United States, organized political reform associations in various cities and marshaled support for a diverse body of labor candidates at the local, provincial, and federal level. The KOL won impressive shares of the vote and elected numerous alderman and mayors. Increasing arguments for greater workplace unity among the various craft locals and the KOL accompanied developments in the formal political theater. It was KOL leaders and leading craft unionists, such as Daniel O'Donoghue, Alfred Jury, and Charles March, who would build on their base in the urban trades' councils, especially the well-organized Toronto Trades and Labor Council (TTLC), to found the first permanent central labor body in 1883, the TLC.

The TLC first met in Toronto in 1883 as the Canadian Labor Congress and soon after renamed itself. The TLC mounted consistent lobbying campaigns at the provincial and federal levels for factory legislation, increased male working-class suffrage, more resources for the public education system, equal pay for women workers, and a reduced workday. It also agitated against immigrant workers, especially the Chinese, who were seen as unsavory pawns used by capitalists to lower wages and undermine unions. Anti-immigration policies would form a common thread in the early trade union movement in Canada. The TLC was active in supporting working-class political candidates and passed resolutions eight separate times between 1883 and 1899 for independent working-class political representation. In the 1890s it worked in concert with populist groups, such as the Single Tax Association and the Patrons of Industry, to advance a farmer-labor populist agenda.

Until the twentieth century, the TLC was dominated by trade unions from the large urban centers, especially Toronto, yet there was minority participation from delegates outside the large cities. Unlike the bitter divide between the KOL and the AFL in the United States, the TLC was a much more homogenous body: delegates were accepted from the KOL and purely local unions as well as from the international craft unions, who worked together to advance a common labor agenda. Indeed, KOL delegates, including the first two women to participate in a TLC convention in the 1880s, Elizabeth Wright of St. Thomas and Emma Witt of Toronto, often constituted a clear majority of delegates in the TLC conventions of the nineteenth century. Various KOL members also served as presidents of the TLC throughout the period, demonstrating the order's continuing influence in working-class communities long after the power of the KOL south of the border had waned.

By the late 1890s, however, the international unions increased their influence in the TLC as the KOL gradually declined. The TLC of the twentieth century largely rejected independent political organization and opted for purely economic trade unionism consistent with the philosophy of the American Federation of Labor, even if socialist and other rank-and-file militants within the craft unions continued to raise broader political concerns until the mid-twentieth century. In 1953 the TLC merged with the industrial union central, the Canadian Congress of Labor, to form the Canadian Labour Congress, the main organized labor central in Canada today.

Key Players

Jury, Alfred Fredman (1848–1916): Jury was a Toronto tailor who figured prominently in the Nine-Hours movement of the 1870s and in the KOL and the TTLC. He was a founding member and leading activist in the TLC during the 1880s. He later worked for the federal Department of the Interior, where he was responsible for organizing the sea passages of orphan children to Canada for Dr. Barnardo's Homes, a settlement scheme designed to bring British orphans to live in Canada.

March, Charles (1849–1908): March was a long-time Toronto trade unionist and labor reformer who helped initiate the TLC. He served as the first president of the labor central.

O'Donoghue, Daniel (1844–1907): O'Donoghue, an Irish immigrant who came to Canada at the age of eight, is considered the "father of Canadian trade unionism." He was a long-time member of the International Typographical Union (ITU), the Knights of Labor (KOL), and a leading political activist in the early Canadian trade union movement. Founding member, secretary, and later president of the Ottawa Trades Council, formed in the wake of the Nine-Hours movement in the 1870s, he also participated in the Canadian Labor Union (CLU) in the 1870s. O'Donoghue became one of the first elected labor politicians in Canada, winning a seat in the Ontario provincial legislature in 1874. After moving to Toronto, he continued to play a key role in the ITU, the KOL and the Toronto Trades and Labor Council (TTLC), and later helped create the TLC. He ended his career as an inspector for the federal Department of Labor, investigating and publicizing workplace conditions across the country.

Thompson, T. Phillips (1844–1933): Thompson was the most prominent of the pro-working-class intellectuals who emerged in the course of the early Canadian trade union movement. He wrote and lectured extensively on trade unions, working-class politics, and the KOL from the 1870s to the 1890s and, in the twentieth century, was active in the

Socialist Party of Canada. His book, *The Politics of Labor*, is the definitive contemporary statement of working-class radicalism in the late nineteenth century.

See also: *American Federation of Labor; Knights of Labor.*

BIBLIOGRAPHY

Books

Babcock, Robert. *Gompers in Canada: A Study in American Continentalism Before the First World War.* Toronto: University of Toronto Press, 1974.

Forsey, Eugene. *Trade Unions in Canada, 1812–1902.* Toronto: University of Toronto Press, 1982.

Kealey, Gregory S., and Bryan D. Palmer. *Dreaming of What Might Be: The Knights of Labor in Canada.* Toronto: Cambridge University Press, 1982.

Palmer, Bryan D. *Working-Class Experience: Rethinking the History of Canadian Labour, 1800–1991.* Toronto: McClelland and Stewart, 1992.

—Sean Purdy

Thomas Hughes.

Trades Union Act

Great Britain 1871

Synopsis

The British government appointed a royal commission in 1867 to hear evidence from employers and leading trade unionists on the question of trades (labor) unions and to make recommendations. The outcome was legalization of such organizations so that they had a recognized status and could protect their funds. Three of the commission's eleven members signed a minority report that was more favorable to the unions than the majority one; the law was based on the minority report. The Liberal government of Prime Minister William Gladstone brought in the Trades Union bill in February 1871. It included "criminal provisions" that prescribed penalties for any form of picketing; those clauses were eventually embodied in a separate measure, the Criminal Law Amendment Act. Both this and the Trades Union Act became law in June of the same year. The existence of a second act made it easier for trade unionists and their supporters to focus on repeal of the objectionable parts of the law while leaving the statutory legalization intact. Further measures later improved the position of the unions, but 1871 stands as the legal watershed.

Timeline

1851: Britain's Amalgamated Society of Engineers applies innovative organizational concepts, including large contributions from, and benefits to, members, as well as vigorous use of direct action and collective bargaining.

1853: Crimean War begins in October. The struggle, which will last until February 1856, pits Russia against the combined forces of Great Britain, France, Turkey, and Sardinia-Piedmont. A war noted for the work of Florence Nightingale with the wounded, it is also the first conflict to be documented by photojournalists.

1861: Unification of Italy under Sardinian king Victor Emmanuel II.

1864: Foundation of the International Red Cross in Geneva.

1867: Dual monarchy established in Austria-Hungary.

1871: Franco-Prussian War ends with France's surrender of Alsace-Lorraine to Germany, which proclaims itself an empire under Prussian king Wilhelm, crowned Kaiser Wilhelm I.

1871: U.S. troops in the West begin fighting the Apache nation.

1871: Boss Tweed corruption scandal in New York City.

1871: Chicago fire causes 250 deaths and $196 million in damage.

1873: Financial panic begins in Vienna and soon spreads to other European financial centers as well as to the United States.

1876: Alexander Graham Bell introduces the telephone.

1880: Completion of Cologne Cathedral, begun 634 years earlier. With twin spires 515 feet (157 m) high, it is the tallest structure in the world, and will remain so until 1889, when it is surpassed by the Eiffel Tower. (The previous record for the world's tallest structure lasted much longer—for about 4,430 years following the building of Cheops's Great Pyramid in c. 2550 B.C.)

Event and Its Context

By the third quarter of the nineteenth century, attitudes on both sides of the capital-labor division in Britain were shifting and modifying. On the one hand, "new unionism" meant that large amalgamated organizations would seek to be perceived not as a threat but as a force for progress, fulfilling useful functions in a benevolent fashion. On the other, some enlightened proprietors and manufacturers advocated conciliation and arbitration rather than reacting repressively against any attempts by workers to better their lot. Influential thinkers and writers likewise endorsed a more sympathetic approach on both moral and rational grounds. The existing restrictions on what were coming to be seen as legitimate, necessary activities appeared inappropriate, more so when a new stratum of voters (composed particularly of urban artisans) gained a political voice that was conferred by the 1867 Reform Act.

The Perceived Problem

At the same time, labor engaged in confrontations, strikes, and lockouts that shattered the industrial peace. In 1866 the Sheffield outrages, which involved arson and violent intimidation against nonunion workers, tarnished the unions' public image and led to calls for an inquiry. Meanwhile in the courts, in the case of *Hornby v. Close* (1867), the Boilermakers' Society was unable to seek redress when a local official absconded with funds. This decision resulted because the society's purpose had been judged unlawful, in spite of its having gone through a registration process. Advocates for the trade unionists attempted to address the anomalies in the unions' legal position in an ad-hoc fashion, using new or amended acts of Parliament.

The Search for a Solution

Against this backdrop, the royal commission that had been appointed early in 1867 by the Conservative government had the task of studying trade unionism in general and seeking a long-term solution. Although the government would not go so far as to appoint a working man (women, of course, were not considered), the commission's 11 members included two who were regarded as allies of the trade unionists: their nominee, writer and barrister Frederic Harrison, and "interested Member of Parliament (MP)" Thomas Hughes. Several employers, notably J. A Roebuck, MP for Sheffield, also served, along with two Lords, Elcho and Lichfield.

Hostile witnesses denounced "restrictive practices," but sympathy for union aims and agreement with their general outlook was apparent in much of the evidence that was heard by the commission. Robert Applegarth of the carpenters union, who also attended as observer on behalf of the unions, and William Allan of the engineers union were influential witnesses. They and three other union leaders had been working together in the group known to historians as the *Junta*. The Junta's tactics were to focus attention on the big unions, functioning in an organized way and exerting control over their finances and members. An alternative view might have been heard if Thomas Connolly, president of the stonemasons, had not been excluded from meetings at an early stage after an unfortunate public speech; he was the representative nominated by the group organized by George Potter, editor of the labor paper *The Bee-Hive*, known as a militant advocate of strike action. The others did not

necessarily abdicate a class position but made an effort to portray strikes as a last resort. Allan, for example, maintained that there was an inevitable divergence of interests between employers and workers, as the former sought the cheapest labor and the latter the highest wages possible.

The case for working with rather than against the union leaders was put cogently from the bosses' point of view by A. J. Mundella, a successful hosiery manufacturer who had pioneered arbitration as well as improving hours, wages, and conditions in his Nottingham firm. He described the unions as standing between the ordinary workers and the employers, an influence for moderation and progressive change. Parallel arguments were put forth by the workers' representatives, who emphasized respectability and responsibility and claimed to improve working people's characters as well as lives. A consensus was emerging that the existence of unions should be recognized and regulated. Such far-from-radical organs of the national press as *The Times* and *The Economist* of London printed moderate or favorable comments. The outcome of the commission was accordingly not implacable opposition to the idea of unions, but its eventual report was too restrictive to be acceptable to three of its members, even after some modification. In the end there were majority and minority reports; the latter, which was to be the more significant, was signed by Harrison, Hughes, and Lichfield.

Changing the Law

Acceptance of the commission's recommendations was not a foregone conclusion, and it was only when faced with the prospect of Mundella and Hughes introducing their own measure in Parliament that the incoming Liberal government of Gladstone put forth a Trades Union bill. This provided for the registration of trade unions that had seven or more members subscribing to union rules. Because of the 1825 Combination Act and their dubious position in law, many unions had been calling themselves Friendly Societies and registering as such, especially since the enactment of the Friendly Societies Act of 1855. In 1869 the list of such societies included engineers, machinists, millwrights, smiths, carpenters, and bricklayers. The 1855 act, like the Companies Act and others, would not apply to trades unions, which were enabled to obtain similar status, legal recognition, and protection of funds through a similar procedure and on the same terms but on a separate register. Notably, however, trade union members remained liable to criminal prosecution if they took direct action in the course of a dispute. The *Annual Register* for 1871 related that in February the Trades Union bill showed how the doctrine of restraint of trade had been gradually turned to the disadvantage of workers and their societies. Optional registration with protection of accounts was to allow protection of the legitimate interests of workmen, and civil disabilities were to be swept away. The bill not only retained certain offenses, however, but punished some of them more forcefully. Practices seen as essential to effective industrial action could lead to imprisonment, with "molestation and obstruction" defined to include deliberate work slowdowns or hiding tools, for example. Attempts to have the "criminal" clauses deleted only succeeded to the extent of having them taken out of the Trades Union bill and enacted as part of a separate piece of legislation, the Criminal Law Amendment Act.

The cause of labor won the main point, however: "Trades Unions not criminal" reads the unequivocal marginal note to the first clause of the Trades Union Act, which states that the purpose of these organizations was not to be deemed unlawful so as to render any member liable to prosecution for conspiracy or otherwise. The second clause specified that trade unions were "not unlawful for civil purposes" and thus their agreements and trusts were not to be interpreted as "void or violable." Some agreements were not enforceable as contracts in law, but were not unlawful either. The bill defined a trade union, in inevitably gendered language, as a "combination" that regulated relations between workmen and masters, workmen and workmen, or masters and masters, or that imposed restrictive conditions on conduct of trade or business such as would formerly have been deemed in restraint of trade.

The twin acts were passed on 30 June 1871. Their separation made it possible to demand repeal of the obnoxious aspects of the law while leaving intact the basic legalization measure. This effort became a preoccupation of labor law activists over the next few years, during which several groups of workers suffered prosecution and imprisonment. Disillusionment with the Liberal stance on the issue lost them votes, and it was under a new government, Benjamin Disraeli's Tories (and after another royal commission), that labor secured the desired amendments to the legislation. In the mid-1870s different acts placed employers and workmen on the same terms with regard to civil contracts, legalized peaceful picketing, ended the specific criminalization of collective actions, and extended protection of union funds.

Lasting Significance of the 1871 Act

In spite of the limitations of the outcome, the 1871 act stands clearly not as a final solution, but as the definitive landmark in the continuing process of legalization of unions. The Trades Union Act, and the process that led to it, may be seen too as setting a pattern for industrial relations in Britain, with large, powerful unions integrated into the country's public life. The leadership of this type of workers' organization had gained access to the corridors of power, thereby distancing themselves from the shop floor and from any more revolutionary aspirations that might appear among the rank and file.

Key Players

Allan, William (1813–1874): Allan was general secretary of the Amalgamated Society of Engineers from 1850 to 1874 and was instrumental in its formation as a national "new model" union. He was a member of the London Trades Council and its "Junta" of trade union leaders and of the Labour Representation League (1869).

Applegarth, Robert (1834–1924): General secretary of the Amalgamated Society of Carpenters and Joiners from 1862 to 1871, Applegarth was the dominant personality in the "Junta" and was active in forming the Conference of Amalgamated Trades (1867). He was appointed to a royal commission on the Contagious Diseases Act in 1871.

Harrison, Frederic (1831–1923): A Liberal-Radical barrister, writer, and founding member of the London Positivist Society (1867), Harrison was regarded as an ally of trade unionists and often gave legal advice to unions in dispute. In 1889 he was appointed to the new London County Council. His books include *The Philosophy of Common Sense* (1907).

Hughes, Thomas (1822–1896): Hughes trained as a lawyer and was elected as a Radical Member of Parliament for Lambeth, London, in 1865. He served on royal commissions on trade unions and labor laws. His Christian Socialist outlook led him to support reforms and workers' education, self-help, and cooperation. He achieved literary fame with his best known book, *Tom Brown's Schooldays* (1857).

Mundella, Anthony John (1825–1897): Born in Leicester, of Italian-Welsh parents, Mundella was an industrialist who introduced reforms and set up a labor conciliation board for the Nottingham hosiery industry in 1860. He became a Liberal politician and minister in the Department of Education and the Board of Trade.

Potter, George (1832–1893): Editor of the labor journal *The Bee-Hive*, founded in 1861. Potter challenged the dominance of the "Junta" group in the trade union movement. As president of the London Working Men's Association, he opened the Trades Union Congress in 1868. He ran for Parliament in 1874 and 1886 but was not elected.

See also: *Second Reform Act.*

BIBLIOGRAPHY

Books

Browne, Harry. *The Rise of British Trade Unions, 1825–1914*. London: Longman, 1979.

Checkland, Sydney G. *The Rise of Industrial Society in England, 1815–1885*. Harlow, Essex, UK: Longman, 1964.

Fraser, W. Hamish. *A History of British Trade Unionism, 1700–1998*. London/Basingstoke, UK: Palgrave Macmillan, 1999.

Gosden, Peter H. J. H. *The Friendly Societies in England, 1815–1875*. Manchester, UK: Manchester University Press, 1961.

Harrison, Royden. "The Positivists: A Study of Labour's Intellectuals." In Royden Harrison, *Before the Socialists: Studies in Labour and Politics, 1861–1881*. Toronto: Toronto University Press, 1965.

Hunt, Edward H. *British Labour History, 1815–1914*. London: Weidenfeld & Nicolson, 1981.

Pelling, Henry. *A History of British Trade Unionism*. 4th edition. Harmondsworth, Middlesex, UK: Penguin Books, 1987.

Perrin, Bryn. *Trade Union Law*. London: Butterworth & Co., 1985.

Other

The Trades Union Congress Web site. "History of TUC, Part 1: Early Victories. Section: The TUC's First Victories" [cited 29 August 2002]. <http://www.tuc.org.uk/the_tuc/>.

ADDITIONAL RESOURCES

Books

Briggs, Asa. "Robert Applegarth and the Trade Unions." In Asa Briggs, *Victorian People*. Harmondsworth: Penguin Books, 1965.

Webb, Sidney, and Beatrice Webb. *The History of Trade Unionism, 1866–1920*. London: Longman Green & Co, 1920.

Periodicals

Potter, George. "Trades' Unions, Strikes and Lock-outs: A Rejoinder." *Contemporary Review* 17 (1871): 529.

—Elizabeth A. Willis

Trades Union Congress

Great Britain 1868

Synopsis

What remains the largest campaigning pressure group on behalf of workers' conditions, pay, and rights in the United Kingdom, the Trades Union Congress (TUC), was founded in Manchester in 1868. A voluntary association of unions, it gave a formal, national voice to previously disparate regional and sectional trade unions. Besides defending the precarious legal status of the unions in mid-nineteenth-century Britain and pressuring the government to adopt legislation favorable to the TUC's interests and to those of its members, the TUC also had a political function. Early leading figures like Henry Broadhurst were Liberals, but the TUC also played a decisive role in the founding (and funding) of the Labour Party in 1900. The TUC reached its peak in the late 1970s with more than 12 million affiliated trade union members, but it has remained at the helm of the British trade union movement despite a decline in membership since then.

Timeline

1851: China's T'ai P'ing ("Great Peace") Rebellion begins under the leadership of schoolmaster Hong Xiuquan, who believes himself the younger brother of Jesus Christ. He mobilizes the peasantry against the Manchu emperors in a civil war that will take 20 to 30 million lives over the next 14 years.

1857: Start of the Sepoy Mutiny, an unsuccessful revolt by Indian troops against the British East India Company. As a result of the rebellion, which lasts into 1858, England places India under direct crown rule.

1863: Opening of the world's first subway, in London.

1867: Dual monarchy established in Austria-Hungary.

1867: Maximilian surrenders to Mexican forces under Benito Juarez and is executed. Thus ends Napoleon III's dreams for a new French empire in the New World.

1867: Establishment of the Dominion of Canada.

1867: United States purchases Alaska from Russia for $7.2 million.

1867: Meiji Restoration in Japan ends 675 years of rule by the shoguns.

1867: Karl Marx publishes the first volume of *Das Kapital.*

1871: U.S. troops in the West begin fighting the Apache nation.

1874: As farm wages in Britain plummet, agricultural workers go on strike.

1877: Great Britain's Queen Victoria is proclaimed the empress of India.

1882: The Chinese Exclusion Act, a treaty between the United States and China, provides for restrictions on immigration of Chinese workers.

1884: Chicago's Home Life Insurance Building, designed by William LeBaron Jenney, becomes the world's first skyscraper.

Event and Its Context

Unions in Britain Between the 1850s and 1870s

In the decades after the defeat of Chartism in 1848, the mood of trade unionism was one of moderation and compromise. Its voice was quiet but never silent. The voice of organized labor was more to the fore than that of political radicalism. The "new model" unions were epitomized by the Amalgamated Society of Engineers, formed in 1851, which brought together a variety of skilled craft trades in a national organization, with professionally trained officials. Moderate in outlook, the new model unions (like Robert Applegarth's Amalgamated Society of Joiners and Carpenters) aimed to secure a permanent presence for unions, rather than see them continue to function as fleeting strike organizations. Leaders such as Applegarth and William Allan, the Engineers' secretary, believed they could press their claims more effectively with employers only after these conditions had been established.

Trades councils, local associations of trade unions, were another important development during this period. Trades councils claimed to voice the concerns or interests of a broad section of workers, although larger unions like the Engineers were often not represented. The London Trades Council (LTC) was formed in 1860. Because of the diverse nature of artisan trade unions in London and the presence of national officials like Applegarth and Allan, the LTC was the nearest the trade union movement had to a national voice. Radical George Odger, the LTC secretary, along with Applegarth, Allan, and Edwin Coulson of the Bricklayers' Union, were later dubbed the "junta" by Sidney and Beatrice Webb in their study of trade unionism.

The influence of the junta was contested by George Potter, the voice of radical, small London trades and artisans, in his newspaper the *Bee-Hive*. Titled after Cruickshank's 1840 cartoon critique of the structure of British society—workers at the base, royals at the top—the *Bee-Hive* was the LTC's official paper. Its militant outlook concerned the junta, although not because they were disinterested in radical causes; on the contrary, they welcomed Garibaldi to London, favored the North in the American Civil War, and most saw the extension of the franchise to working men as a means to advance union interests. Most (though not Allan, whose union barred him from "political" activity) were thus active in the Reform League, of which George Howell was secretary. The passing of the 1867 Reform Act focused the attention of leading unionists on using Parliament as means of reform.

The Union Question

There was much to reform. The existing Master and Servant Act meant employees (unlike employers) could still be liable to criminal prosecution and prison for any breach of contract. The Glasgow Trades Council led the campaign to amend this, which a select committee duly did in 1867. The legal case *Hornby v. Close* had thrown into doubt union control of their funds. The court declared that unions were not covered by the 1855 Friendly Society Act (to recover funds from defaulting officers), as they were still technically illegal organizations, acting (potentially) in restraint of trade. Besides their legal and financial standing, the public profile of unions was at issue following the "Sheffield Outrages" of 1866, when unionists in the cutlery trade used violence (including blowing up one workman's house) against nonunion labor. In 1867 the government appointed the Royal Commission on Trade Unions.

For the junta and Applegarth (the first witness), the commission represented an opportunity to secure the legal and financial status of the unions and legitimize their standing in the public mind. To this end they emphasized the responsible activities of the new model unions—Applegarth, for instance, stressed that unions played a minimal role in controlling the volume of apprenticeships. The commission also called into question who spoke for the unions: the Conference of Amalgamated Trades (as the LTC had been retitled) appointed a representative (the barrister Frederic Harrison), but Potter's rival Conference of Trades was also asked to send an observer.

The unions had supporters on the commission, such as Harrison and, Thomas Hughes, the Liberal MP for Lambeth, but there were also opponents. The commission's majority report recommended that unions register under the Friendly Societies aegis, but it also proposed stringent supervision of the unions (for example over their strike funds). A minority report rejected any need for such supervision.

Creation of the TUC

Union leaders, anxious to ensure that government legislation resulting from the commission was favorable and that the union lobby spoke with a clear, unified voice, renewed their efforts to create a national union forum. Various attempts—like a conference of 138 delegates at Sheffield in 1866—had floundered. What succeeded in creating the TUC was a call in February 1868 from the Trades Councils of Manchester and Salford for a congress to be held that following May. The aim of the congress was to create a discussion forum for trade unionism, in part modeled on the National Social Science Association, a middle-class association in which Harrison and Hughes participated and in which the unions had received a reasonable hear-

George Howell. © Hulton/Getty Images. Reproduced by permission.

ing. Although the junta did not attend, Potter did. Among the subjects discussed was "the necessity of an annual congress." The congress was at this stage not a permanent, annual body.

What gradually gave it permanency was the lobbying by labor leaders of the government's legislation. This granted unions legal rights under the Friendly Societies, without interference, but retained measures making unionists liable to criminal prosecution and on picketing. The unions managed to split the Liberals' legislation into the 1871 Trade Union Act (with which they were happy) and Criminal Law Amendment Act (against which they continued to campaign). Partly successful in its lobbying and with Applegarth resigning from the Carpenters' Union in 1871, the leadership passed to the TUC—or more particularly to the small, parliamentary committee appointed by the congress as a permanent, national union voice.

The Impact

George Howell was the first secretary of the TUC's parliamentary committee. With attempts to reform the criminal liability law thwarted by the Liberals, Howell raised the issue (and his old cause) of getting workers elected as MPs. In 1874 miners Alexander McDonald and John Burt were the first two trade unionists to sit as MPs (known as *Lib-Labs,* in light of their alliance with the Liberals). Though skeptical of Benjamin Disraeli's new Conservative government elected that year, the new government would prove to fulfill the TUC's goal, replacing the Master and Servant Act with the Employer and Workmen Act in 1875, which reduced charges for breach of contract from criminal to civil. Disraeli's government did enact legislation covering hours and conditions and legalized peaceful picketing. In 1875 Howell was succeeded by Henry Broadhurst, a moderate Liberal (and MP for Stoke from 1880) who worked closely with Gladstone and cemented the TUC's links with the Liberals.

The TUC's formation in 1868 marked an attempt to secure the presence of trade unions in British society and to generate some order in a fragmented union movement. Though in essence a defensive measure, it coincided with a period of sharp growth in union membership, though this reversed in the latter 1870s. Despite the advances made between 1867 and 1875, the TUC was ensured a hefty workload due to legal issues, intimidation, the struggle to establish new unions among the unskilled, and the organization of women (who first attended the congress in 1875). The influence of the TUC extended beyond Britain: it served as the model for the American Federation of Labor. Although the TUC was not always an effective national voice, a Scottish TUC was formed in 1897, the Scottish Trades Councils having been partly excluded from the TUC.

Ernest Bevin, the Transport and General Workers' leader and British foreign secretary (1945–1951), claimed Labour was "born from the bowels of the TUC." This may be true, but Labour's parentage was also to be found, like that of the TUC, in the confused strands of nineteenth-century British labor law.

Key Players

Applegarth, Robert (1834–1924): Born in Hull, East Yorkshire, Applegarth was the leading figure in the so-called trade union junta of the London Trades Council. A carpenter, as general secretary of the Amalgamated Society of Joiners and Carpenters (1862–1871), he presided over a tenfold expansion in membership and created the "new model" of trade unions. Though a moderate, Applegarth supported the Reform League (for extending the vote) and was chief advocate of the Minority Report of the Royal Commission on Trade Unions. In 1871 he was the first labor leader appointed to the Royal Commission on Contagious Diseases by William Gladstone's Liberal government. Later a successful businessman, he rejected Lloyd George's offer of a Companionship of Honour in 1917.

Howell, George (1833–1910): Born in Wrington, Somerset, Howell was the first secretary of the TUC's parliamentary committee (1871–1905). He was a shoemaker and bricklayer who mixed with Chartists and was a Methodist and temperance advocate. Campaigning for a nine-hour workday and as secretary of the Reform League (from 1865), he joined the London Trades Council executive in 1861. He agreed not to stand working-class radical candidates against Liberals in 1868 and was later the Liberal-Labour MP for Bethnal Green (1885–1895).

Potter, George (1832–1893): Born in Kenilworth, Warwickshire, Potter published and edited the radical, prostrike *Bee-Hive* in the 1860s and 1870s. His London Men's Working Association and its 1867 Conference of Trades were chief rivals to the London junta. A carpenter, Potter achieved notoriety in the 1859 building trade lock-out. Despite financial problems (it was rescued by Liberals in the late 1860s), the *Bee-Hive* gave Potter a basis of support: he was one of two London delegates at the founding congress in 1868 and became president of the TUC in 1871 and chaired its parliamentary committee.

See also: *Amalgamated Society of Engineers.*

———————

BIBLIOGRAPHY

Books

Fraser, W. Hamish. *A History of British Trade Unionism, 1700–1998.* New York: St. Martin's Press, 1999.

Martin, R. *TUC: The Growth of a Pressure Group, 1868–1976.* Oxford: Clarendon Press, 1980.

Musson, A. E. *The Congress of 1868.* Basingstoke: Macmillan, 1955.

———. *British Trade Unions 1800–75.* London: Macmillan, 1972.

Pelling, H. *A History of British Trade Unionism.* London: Macmillan, 1963.

Webb, Sidney, and Beatrice Webb. *History of Trade Unionism.* New York: Longmans, Green and Co., 1902.

Periodicals

McCready, H. W. "British Labour and the Royal Commission on Trade Unions, 1867–9." *University of Toronto Quarterly* XXIV (1955).

———. "British Labour's Lobby, 1867–1875." *Canadian Journal of Economic and Political Science* XXII (1956).

ADDITIONAL RESOURCES

Summary Description of the Papers of the Trade Unions Congress. Modern Records Centre, Warwick University (cited 21 January 2003). <http://www.warwick.ac.uk/services/library/mrc/ead/292col.htm>.

Trade Unions Congress online (cited 21 January 2003). <http://www.tuc.org.uk/index.cfm>.

TUC Library Collections. University of North London. Updated 20 November 2002 (cited 21 January 2003). <http://www.unl.ac.uk/library/tuc/>.

—Lawrence Black

Tragic Week

Argentina 1919

Synopsis

La Semana Trágica ("The Tragic Week") witnessed the deaths of more than 100 protesters in Buenos Aires, Argentina, after a general strike was quashed with machine guns by the army and by employers' private vigilante groups. The event dealt a blow to the moderate labor policies of the Radical Party administration under Hipólito Yrigoyen, who had previously refrained from using state force to end strikes. Under pressure from right-wing nationalist groups, Yrigoyen was unable to carry out his party's program of political and economic reform and instead resorted to massive spending schemes to gain popular support. Yrigoyen was later ousted during his second term in office by a military coup, which ended an era of constitutionally elected presidents dating back to 1862. La Semana Trágica

Juan Domingo Perón. © Hulton/Getty Images. Reproduced by permission.

was thus a decisive event that turned Argentina back from its path toward democratization and economic modernization and paved the way for the military-populist government of Juan Domingo Perón in 1946.

Timeline

1900: China's Boxer Rebellion, which began in the preceding year with attacks on foreigners and Christians, reaches its height. An international contingent of more than 2,000 men arrives to restore order, but only after several tens of thousands have died.

1907: U.S. markets experience a financial panic.

1912: *Titanic* sinks on its maiden voyage, from Southampton to New York, on 14 April. More than 1,500 people are killed.

1915: At the Second Battle of Ypres, the Germans introduce a terrifying new weapon: poison gas.

1917: The intercepted "Zimmermann Telegram" reveals a plot by the German government to draw Mexico into an alliance against the United States in return for a German promise to return the southwestern U.S. territories taken in the Mexican War. Three months later, in response to German threats of unrestricted submarine warfare, the United States on 6 April declares war on Germany.

1919: Formation of the Third International (Comintern), whereby the Bolshevik government of Russia establishes its control over communist movements worldwide.

1919: Treaty of Versailles signed by the Allies and Germany but rejected by the U.S. Senate. This is due in part to rancor between President Woodrow Wilson and Republican Senate leaders, and in part to concerns over Wilson's plan to commit the United States to the newly established League of Nations and other international duties. Not until 1921 will Congress formally end U.S. participation in the war, but it will never agree to join the League.

1919: Ratification of the Eighteenth Amendment, which prohibits the production, sale, distribution, purchase, and consumption of alcohol throughout the United States.

1919: In India, Mahatma Gandhi launches his campaign of nonviolent resistance to British rule.

1919: In Italy, a former socialist of the left named Benito Mussolini introduces the world to a new socialism of the right, embodied in an organization known as the "Union for Struggle," or Fasci di Combattimento. Composed primarily of young war veterans discontented with Italy's paltry share of the spoils from the recent world war (if not with their country's lackluster military performance in the conflict), the fascists are known for their black shirts and their penchant for violence.

1921: As the Allied Reparations Commission calls for payments of 132 billion gold marks, inflation in Germany begins to climb.

1925: European leaders attempt to secure the peace at the Locarno Conference, which guarantees the boundaries between France and Germany, and Belgium and Germany.

1929: On "Black Friday" in October, prices on the U.S. stock market, which had been climbing wildly for several years, suddenly collapse. Thus begins the first phase of a world economic crisis and depression that will last until the beginning of World War II.

Event and Its Context

After securing its independence from Spanish rule in 1816, Argentina rivaled the United States as the country with the greatest potential for economic development in the nineteenth century. Its capital and largest city, Buenos Aires, served as an important transportation and shipping center for the southern cone of the Western Hemisphere. *La pampa*, a flat grassland extending across the country's midsection, held one of the most productive soils in the world and was an ideal environment for cattle ranching. By the end of the century, these factors combined to make Argentina a major exporter of grain, beef products, and wool. Between 1880 and 1890 its shipping traffic rose from 2.1 million tons to 7.7 million tons. Foreign investment from Britain, France, and the United States developed the country's infrastructure, while a surge of immigrants from Europe, particularly from Spain and Italy, provided the labor. In the 1880s alone, over 850,000 immigrants arrived in Argentina

from Europe; an additional 1.6 million immigrants joined them between 1900 and 1914. With the gross domestic product growing by an average of 6 percent per year between 1890 and World War I, the remark to be "as rich as an Argentine" became a stock phrase in France, where many of the cattle barons vacationed.

Although Argentina had cast off Spanish rule in 1821, many of the forces that shaped the country's colonial period continued to dominate its development even after independence. Almost all of the country's economic and political power remained in the hands of the cattle barons, who made their wealth off of *la pampa* but lived in Buenos Aires. Also known as the "oligarchs," the country's political elite forestalled reforms such as universal suffrage, which could have democratized the republic. Further, the elites' interest in trade and export typically coincided with the interests of foreign capital, thereby linking Argentina's fate to outside forces that sometimes destabilized the country. The dominance of the cattle-based economy also prevented Argentina from developing a sizeable manufacturing base, because local capitalists had little incentive to invest outside of the lucrative livestock market. Above all else, the continued presence of the military in Argentine politics stunted its democratization and regularly contributed to domestic instability.

Calls for Reform

Argentina's vulnerabilities to world market forces were demonstrated with the onset of World War I in 1914. That year, net migration to Argentina dropped for the first time since 1891, and inflation staggered the economy. Adding to the tension, a pivotal shift had occurred in the nation's government. After the introduction of universal and compulsory suffrage for male citizens under the 1912 Sáenz Peña Law, the Radical Party under Hipólito Yrigoyen came to power in 1916, promising to reform Argentine politics along more democratic lines.

Hipólito Yrigoyen was born in Buenos Aires in 1852 and worked as a lawyer. In the 1890s he was drawn into the reformist politics of the Unión Cívica Radical (Radical Party), an offshoot of the Unión Cívica de la Juventud (Youth Civic League), founded in 1889. Although Yrigoyen's leadership style was unassuming—giving rise to his nickname, "El Pelduo" (the armadillo)—in 1896 he assumed control of the Radical Party after the suicide of its founder, Leandro N. Alem. Yrigoyen attempted to overthrow the government in an abortive coup in 1905 but gradually used the party as a platform for institutional change. Largely because of the Radical Party's efforts, the country adopted the Sáenz Peña Law, which provided for a secret ballot, universal suffrage for all male citizens, and more thorough reviews of voter registration lists. Argentina's political elite allowed reforms, because they assumed that they would easily dominate the new, more democratic system. Their assumption proved wrong, and the Radical Party grew in strength after universal suffrage was introduced. In 1916 Yrigoyen captured the presidency by a one-vote margin in the electoral college.

In part, Yrigoyen's political agenda in office followed his party's populist roots, with an emphasis on expanding state subsidies for farmers and increasing the public sector. In a bid to win middle-class support by awarding patronage jobs to the party's supporters, Yrigoyen increased public spending by 50 percent between 1918 and 1922, to 614 million pesos. Yrigoyen also faced a restive working class during his first term as president. Although Argentina remained neutral during World War I, the war threw the nation's economy into chaos. Unemployment in Buenos Aires exceeded 19 percent in 1917; in former times, the largely immigrant working class of the city would return to Europe during hard times, but because of the war they were stranded in Argentina.

The end of the war brought an upswing in the economy, but inflation, which had increased food prices by 50 percent during the war, continued to erode purchasing power. Yrigoyen's mismanagement of the economy threatened to undermine the support he had won from the nation's workers for his moderate stance on labor disputes. One of Yrigoyen's first acts as president had been to offer arbitration in a maritime workers' strike in Buenos Aires. His refusal to use police force to break the strike was a significant departure from past policies.

The Bloody Week

Along with other trade unions seeking relief from post-World War I economic pressures, metallurgical workers in the capital announced their intention to go on strike in December 1918. During the first week of January 1919, the workers followed through on their declaration. The strike quickly turned violent, and an officer was killed in one of the first battles between the strikers and the Buenos Aires police force. Another confrontation left five people dead; all of the victims were apparently bystanders to the strike's violence. After the two fatal run-ins, a general strike was called for 9 January 1919 to coincide with the funerals of some of the previous days' victims.

Over the next few days, a series of demonstrations and counter-demonstrations rocked Buenos Aires. Rioting strikers burned automobiles in the streets, while other groups marched to protest the general strike itself. As the violence escalated, Yrigoyen failed to act decisively, and the army intervened by sending troops with machine guns to face the strikers. One such battalion was led by Juan Domingo Perón, who at the time was a young lieutenant in the army. Under Perón's orders, as many as 100 strikers were gunned down. After the strike was quashed, the violence continued in the hands of vigilante groups, many of them set up by antiunion employers eager for revenge. In addition to hunting down strike leaders, the groups invaded the city's Jewish quarter to beat and kill Russian Jews, who were labeled suspicious in the wake of the Russian Revolution. The week of violence became known as "La Semana Trágica" in Argentina, while international observers called it the "Bloody Week."

In light of the Yrigoyen administration's initial hesitation in reacting to the strike, the oligarchy increased its opposition to Yrigoyen. In 1919 the Liga Patriótica Argentina (Argentine Patriotic League) was formed as a nationalistic, antiunion, and anticommunist organization, and by the end of the year it claimed 833 brigades with 20,000 members across Argentina. A majority of the league's members were drawn from the landowning upper class, and although it contained some Radical Party members, it served as a pressure group against Yrigoyen. With the support of British interests, the Asociación Nacional del Trabajo (National Labor Association) also stepped up its efforts as an antiunion force by intervening in strikes and

publishing antiunion material. Because of these efforts, trade union membership rapidly declined from its peak of over 68,000 members in 1920 to fewer than 27,000 dues-paying members the following year.

The Infamous Decade and Perónism

Yrigoyen managed to finish his first term in 1922 under increasing hostility from the elite, leaving behind an economy sliding into recession. In the 1920s Argentina's economy remained subject to instability, a fact that Yrigoyen used to make a political comeback to the presidency in 1928, with promises of renewed prosperity. The global depression at the beginning of Yrigoyen's second term sent his popularity plummeting. The league renewed its criticism of democracy, labor unions, and the opening of once elite institutions such as the nation's universities to the middle and lower classes. In September 1930 the military, under General José F. Uriburu, overthrew Yrigoyen in a coup. Although civilian government was ostensibly restored in restricted elections in 1932—from which the Radical Party was banned—the military remained in power for the rest of the "Infamous Decade," as the 1930s came to be known.

Argentina's competing trends of populism and militarism in politics came together after World War II in the commanding figure of Juan Domingo Perón. The minister of war in the closing days of the conflict, Perón survived a military coup by competing officers in October 1945 and won the presidential election in May 1946. Like Yrigoyen, Perón expanded the public sector and state-sponsored welfare projects to ensure popular support for his regime, yet depended on the military to suppress dissent. Three years into his second term in 1955, Perón was deposed in a military coup, largely a result of the country's declining economic fortunes. Along with Yrigoyen, Perón was the dominant figure in Argentine politics in the twentieth century and demonstrated the country's difficulties in implementing democratic reforms.

Key Players

Alem, Leandro N. (1842–1896): A major political figure in the final decades of the nineteenth century, Alem founded the Unión Cívica de la Juventud (Youth Civic League) in 1889. The group gave rise to the Unión Cívica Radical (Radical Party), led by Hipólito Yrigoyen. Alem committed suicide in 1896.

Perón, Juan Domingo (1895–1974): Perón began his military career in 1915 and rose to the rank of colonel at the end of 1941. Taking part in a military coup in June 1943, Perón became minister of war and was elected to the presidency in May 1946. He ruled until 1955, when he was overthrown in a military coup; he returned to power one year before his death in 1974.

Yrigoyen, Hipólito (1852–1933): A lawyer, professor, and head of the Radical Party after 1896, Yrigoyen was the most important politician of his generation. Elected to the presidency in 1916, he served until 1922. His first term was marked by an inability to manage the competing demands of the working class and the country's elite. Yrigoyen was returned to office in the election of 1928 but was deposed in a military coup in 1930.

See also: *Peron Elected President.*

BIBLIOGRAPHY

Crassweller, Robert. *Perón and the Enigmas of Argentina.* New York: Norton, 1987.

Lewis, Paul H. *The Crisis of Argentine Capitalism.* Chapel Hill, NC: University of North Carolina Press, 1990.

Page, Joseph. *Perón: A Biography.* New York: Random House, 1983.

Rock, David. *Argentina 1516–1987: From Spanish Colonization to Alfonsín.* Berkeley: University of California Press, 1987.

—Timothy G. Borden

Transport Workers' Strike

Worldwide 1911

Synopsis

On 14 June 1911 dockworkers in Britain, Belgium, the Netherlands, and the East Coast of the United States went on strike. It was probably the first internationally organized strike. In Britain it developed into a general strike of transport workers. The demands and the tactics of the trade unions that participated in the strike differed from country to country and sometimes from port to port. In addition to two general demands, the participants made diverse local demands. The various unions conducted decentralized negotiations, which contributed to the disparate course of the conflict and its resolution. In some cases it ended within a few days; in others it continued for a matter of months. Due in part to increasingly favorable economic conditions, in most cases the conflict ended in triumph for the strikers.

Timeline

1891: Construction of Trans-Siberian Railway begins. Meanwhile, crop failures across Russia lead to widespread starvation.

1896: First modern Olympic Games held in Athens.

1901: U.S. President William McKinley is assassinated by Leon Czolgosz, an anarchist. Vice President Theodore Roosevelt becomes president.

1904: Beginning of the Russo-Japanese War, which lasts into 1905 and results in a resounding Japanese victory. In Russia the war is followed by the Revolution of 1905, which marks the beginning of the end of czarist rule; meanwhile, Japan is poised to become the first major non-Western power of modern times.

1911: Turkish-Italian War sees the first use of aircraft as an offensive weapon. Italian victory results in the annexation of Libya.

1911: In China revolutionary forces led by Sun Yat-sen bring an end to more than 2,100 years of imperial rule.

1911: Revolution in Mexico, begun the year before, continues with the replacement of the corrupt Porfirio Diaz, president since 1877, by Francisco Madero.

1911: Ernest Rutherford at the University of Manchester correctly posits that the atom contains a positively charged nucleus surrounded by negatively charged electrons. (Discovery of the protons that give the nucleus its positive charge, and of the neutrons that, along with protons, contribute to its mass, still lies in the future.)

1911: Norwegian explorer Roald Amundsen and his team of four other Norwegians are the first men to reach the South Pole, on 14 December. A month later, a group of British explorers led by Robert F. Scott will reach the Pole, only to die of starvation soon afterward.

1915: A German submarine sinks the *Lusitania,* killing 1,195, including 128 U.S. citizens. Theretofore, many Americans had been sympathetic toward Germany, but the incident begins to turn the tide of U.S. sentiment toward the Allies.

1919: Formation of the Third International (Comintern), whereby the Bolshevik government of Russia establishes its control over communist movements worldwide.

1919: Treaty of Versailles signed by the Allies and Germany but rejected by the U.S. Senate. This is due in part to rancor between President Woodrow Wilson and Republican Senate leaders, and in part to concerns over Wilson's plan to commit the United States to the newly established League of Nations and other international duties. Not until 1921 will Congress formally end U.S. participation in the war, but it will never agree to join the league.

Event and Its Context

By the end of the nineteenth century, the labor market for seamen was already international in scope. North Americans, Britons, Continental Europeans, Indians, and sailors of other nationalities worked alongside one another on ships sailing the North Atlantic. The trade unions in the individual countries could respond in two ways: by trying to exclude foreigners from those ships registered in their country, or by trying to recruit those foreigners as union members. The first option was problematic because it was in the interests of the powerful ship owners to have a multinational labor force because it was easier to discipline and could be used to keep wages low. Seamen's unions often opted for the second approach. This was true of the seamen's union of the world's largest maritime nation at the time, Great Britain. The National Seamen's and Firemen's Union of Great Britain and Ireland (NSFU) was founded in 1887 under the leadership of Havelock Wilson. Initially, the NSFU attempted to exclude foreigners, but within a few years it had changed its policy. Later, Wilson wrote, "There was once upon a time when I was foolish enough to believe that the foreigners were the great curse of the British seamen. I have got past that stage many, many years ago, and I believe that a foreigner has equally as much right to live in the world as a Britisher. The only point is that I want that foreigner not to undersell my labour and I want him to be as competent to do the work as I would do it myself."

Starting in 1890 the NSFU opened branches or agencies in other ports, including Copenhagen, Hamburg, New York, and Rotterdam. In 1896, when the high cost of maintaining such an extensive network became clear, Wilson took the initiative to establish the International Federation of Ship, Dock and River Workers, which in turn became the International Transport Workers' Federation (ITF) in 1898. The ITF's main objective was to promote the development of trade unions in all ports, and thereby continue the international work of the NSFU on a larger scale. This task was made easier because, independently of the ITF, dockers and longshoremen in many ports began to organize themselves during this period. Establishment of international federations was not restricted to employees; employers did the same. At the end of 1909 ship owners from Britain, Belgium, France, Germany, the Netherlands, the United States, and Scandinavia founded the International Shipping Federation (ISF), the main objective of which was to undermine the seamen's unions. Within the ISF, British ship owners, represented by the Shipping Federation, were the most dominant force.

The cooperation engendered between transport workers in the North Atlantic region on the one hand and many of their employers on the other formed the backdrop to the international strike of 1911. The idea of an international seamen's strike had been around for many years, but plans really only began to take shape when Havelock Wilson and his colleague from the United States, Andrew Furuseth of the International Seamen's Union, raised the matter at the ITF congress in Copenhagen in August 1910. The economic recession of 1908–1909 had ended and unemployment was beginning to decline again. The upturn in the economic cycle strengthened the negotiating position of the transport workers. The Dutch and the Belgians were sympathetic to an international strike, but the Germans and the Austrians believed that their unions were still too weak to undertake successfully such a venture. Those who supported the strike action convened in Antwerp on 14 March 1911; seamen's unions from Belgium, Britain, Denmark, the Netherlands, Norway, and Sweden attended. Attendees set up an international committee with Wilson as chairman. They proffered two general demands: an end to the "demeaning" practice of medical examinations performed by doctors employed by the ship owners, and improved quarters aboard ships. The participants agreed that negotiations in any one country would be terminated if they discovered that strikebreakers from that country were being used elsewhere. The international employers' organization was issued an ultimatum.

Only the Danish ship owners reached a settlement. They made several significant concessions in exchange for an eight-year collective agreement on pay and conditions. The ISF declined to respond. With the date having been secretly agreed upon as of 1 May, the strike began on 14 June 1911 in Britain, Belgium, and the Netherlands. U.S. seamen were not represented on the strike committee, but nonetheless they organized a number of strikes in Atlantic ports. The demands and the tactics of the unions differed from country to country and sometimes from port to port. In addition to the two general demands, the unions made a number of local demands. Decentralized negotiations produced different resolutions in different locales.

In the United States, both Furuseth and Wilson had tried to canvass support, but backing for the strike was disappointing. By 15 June news of the strike in Europe had filtered through to East Coast ports. In the days that followed, strikes began at a number of shipping lines (including Morgan, Clyde, Mallory, Old Dominion, and Savannah), most of which ended in victory for the strikers within two weeks. The demands of the U.S. unions tended to be somewhat racist in character, unlike those of the British NSFU; U.S. unions wanted to exclude foreigners (especially blacks and the Chinese) rather than force them to become members.

In Antwerp, Belgium, a defense committee was set up several days before the strike began. Several organizations joined the committee, including the national trade-union confederation, the national Labor Party, and several local unions. The number of strikers increased steadily, and by 21 June it had reached 600, including 200 foreigners. On 22 June, English ship owners made a series of concessions that were also favorable to Belgian seamen, and the unions lifted the strike against English shipping lines. However, the strike against the recalcitrant Belgian ship owners turned increasingly bitter. On 27 June the longshoremen announced that they would begin a sympathy strike if employers did not concede to the seamen's demands within 48 hours. The ship owners' organization relented (only one major line, the Red Star Line, was not a member). The strikers achieved several successes, including agreement on the length of the working day and the establishment of a municipal labor exchange in an effort to end the activities of subcontractors (known as "crimps").

In the Netherlands strikes broke out in the two largest ports, Rotterdam and Amsterdam. A social-democratic trade union represented Rotterdam's seamen; their brethren in Amsterdam had a syndicalist union. The two unions were hostile toward one another and so failed to coordinate their protests. On 11 July the Rotterdam union reached a settlement with the employers that recognized the union and granted a wage increase to 2,300 out of the 3,000 seamen on condition that they would make no further wage demands for the next three years. In Amsterdam the number of seamen participating in the strike continued to increase, from 200 on 14 June to 1,500 by 18 July. The longshoremen began to join the strikers on 22 June, but to no avail. The large numbers of strikebreakers imported from outside Amsterdam (and from Germany) and the repressive measures by the police and army created major difficulties for the strikers. On 26 July the longshoremen withdrew their support, and on 9 August the seamen too were forced to accept defeat.

The strike in Britain was the largest and most complex. The seaman, as in the other countries, were the first to join. On 14 June they held public meetings in London, Cardiff, Bristol, Southampton, Hull, Glasgow, Grimsby, Dublin, and Manchester. The NSFU handed out flags bearing the text, "War Is Now Declared: Seamen Strike Hard and Strike for Liberty on 14th June 1911." A wave of protests spread across the country, and more and more crews left their ships. The longshoremen were quick to join. On 16 June longshoremen in Goole, Glasgow, Southampton, and Newcastle threw in their lot with the seamen, followed on 19 June by those in Hull, and on 20 June by those in Manchester and Liverpool. The support of the longshoremen was a factor in the 28 June decision of the recently founded National Transport Workers' Federation to back the seamen. On 17 August railway workers in many parts of the country walked out to protest long hours and low wages. The strike spread to other occupations. In some cases, even though their own demands had been conceded, workers continued to strike in solidarity with those from other trades who had joined the strike later and had so far failed to achieve their aims. As a whole, the wave of strikes made an uncoordinated impression. Many protests and negotiations had a local character. Sometimes, the conflict finished in one city before it had even peaked in another. The degree of repression shown by the authorities also differed from city to city. In many towns police and troops intervened, most savagely in Liverpool on 13 August ("Bloody Sunday"), when a brutal attack on demonstrators by police and mounted troops left 350 people injured. The strike eventually ended on 24 August. Apart from the railway workers, most of the strike participants achieved significant concessions, which ranged from wage increases and the abolition of the "ticket" (a certificate of good conduct for sailors) to union recognition.

Key Players

Furuseth, Andrew (1854–1938): Merchant seaman, born in Norway; president of the North American International Seamen's Union from 1908 until his death.

Wilson, Joseph Havelock (1858–1929): Founder of the National Amalgamated Sailors' and Firemen's Union of Great Britain and Ireland in 1887. Wilson was several times a liberal labor Member of Parliament. He opposed the British General Strike of 1926.

BIBLIOGRAPHY

Books

Lee, H. W. *The Great Strike Movement of 1911 and Its Lessons.* London: Twentieth Century Press, 1911.

Marsh, Arthur, and Victoria Ryan. *The Seamen: A History of the National Union of Seamen, 1887–1987.* Oxford: Malthouse Press, 1989.

Taplin, Eric. *The Dockers' Union: A Study of the National Union of Dock Labourers, 1889–1922.* New York: St. Martin's Press, 1985.

Periodicals

Mogridge, Basil. "Militancy and Inter-union Rivalry in British Shipping, 1911–1929." *International Review of Social History* 6 (1961): 375–412.

Sneevliet, Henk. "De Stakingen in het Transportbedrijf." *De Nieuwe Tijd* 16 (1911): 769–791, 834–856, 971–994.

—Marcel van der Linden

Triangle Shirtwaist Fire

United States 1911

Synopsis

On 25 March 1911 the worst industrial fire in the history of American capitalism killed 146 employees of the Triangle Shirtwaist Factory in New York City. Still listed in annual almanacs because of its ferocity, the fire breathed new life into labor organizations and crusades for greater industrial regulatory power, especially by the state. Factory owners did not face scrutiny alone as the city's politicians, business community, and bureaucrats also faced public condemnation for the lack of safety precautions to prevent such a disaster. Cries of "who will protect the working girl" had resounded for years under the protectionist ideal of the Progressive Era as young immigrant women flooded the city's industrial factories. The very use of the term "girl" conjured images of childish, immature people who needed the protection of a "stronger" entity. Functioning simultaneously in a capitalist and patriarchal state, labor laws allowed women to participate in the paid labor force while defining their primary function in familial terms as reproducers of the race. In the wake of the fire, the state legislature organized the New York Factory Investigating Committee (FIC) to guaranteeing safety standards in the city's factories. Commenting on the new powers assumed by the state, FIC member Frances Perkins commented, "The Triangle fire was the first day of the New Deal."

Timeline

1891: Construction of Trans-Siberian Railway begins. Meanwhile, crop failures across Russia lead to widespread starvation.

1896: First modern Olympic Games held in Athens.

1901: U.S. President William McKinley is assassinated by Leon Czolgosz, an anarchist. Vice President Theodore Roosevelt becomes president.

1904: Beginning of the Russo-Japanese War, which lasts into 1905 and results in a resounding Japanese victory. In Russia the war is followed by the Revolution of 1905, which marks the beginning of the end of czarist rule; meanwhile, Japan is poised to become the first major non-Western power of modern times.

1911: Turkish-Italian War sees the first use of aircraft as an offensive weapon. Italian victory results in the annexation of Libya.

1911: In China revolutionary forces led by Sun Yat-sen bring an end to more than 2,100 years of imperial rule.

1911: Revolution in Mexico, begun the year before, continues with the replacement of the corrupt Porfirio Diaz, president since 1877, by Francisco Madero.

1911: Ernest Rutherford at the University of Manchester correctly posits that the atom contains a positively charged nucleus surrounded by negatively charged electrons. (Discovery of the protons that give the nucleus its posi-

Triangle Shirtwaist Company destroyed by fire, New York City, 1911. AP/Wide World Photos. Reproduced by permission.

tive charge, and of the neutrons that, along with protons, contribute to its mass, still lies in the future.)

1911: Norwegian explorer Roald Amundsen and his team of four other Norwegians are the first men to reach the South Pole, on 14 December. A month later, a group of British explorers led by Robert F. Scott will reach the Pole, only to die of starvation soon afterward.

1915: A German submarine sinks the *Lusitania,* killing 1,195, including 128 U.S. citizens. Theretofore, many Americans had been sympathetic toward Germany, but the incident begins to turn the tide of U.S. sentiment toward the Allies.

1919: Formation of the Third International (Comintern), whereby the Bolshevik government of Russia establishes its control over communist movements worldwide.

1919: Treaty of Versailles signed by the Allies and Germany but rejected by the U.S. Senate. This is due in part to rancor between President Woodrow Wilson and Republican Senate leaders, and in part to concerns over Wilson's plan to commit the United States to the newly established League of Nations and other international

duties. Not until 1921 will Congress formally end U.S. participation in the war, but it will never agree to join the league.

Event and Its Context

The Fire

The Asch building housed the Triangle Shirtwaist Factory on the top three floors of a 10-story building. Completed in 1901, the building billed itself as fireproof, although its height of 135 feet allowed it legally to contain wooden trim, window frames, and floors, which would have been required to be metal or concrete had the building been 15 feet taller. In 1910 H. F. J. Porter told the *New York Times* that "one man whom I advised to install a fire alarm replied to me. 'Let 'em burn. They're a lot of cattle, anyway.'" Factories often occupied buildings that had been intended originally for the display and storage of goods rather than their manufacture. Owners preferred upper stories (to save on lighting bills) and buildings with high ceilings, as state law required each worker to have 250

Members of International Ladies' Garment Workers Union in front of poster depicting Triangle Shirtwaist Company fire, New York City. AP/Wide World Photos. Reproduced by permission.

cubic feet of air. The Triangle Factory contained somewhere around 5 to 600 total workers that day, but the elevators held only 15 to 20 passengers at one time, and the fire escape opened into a closed court and dangled above the ground. During the course of the fire, the escape stairs warped and twisted into a tangled mess. Addressing the inadequate fire escape, Arthur MacFarlane wrote in *McClure's Magazine,* "Out of nearly six hundred, this 'good and sufficient means of egress' (to quote the Building Code again) saved fewer than twenty."

Although the cause of the fire remains unknown, by-product material from making shirtwaists littered the factory's floors. These rags, which were collected six times a year, had last been removed two months earlier and had weighed over a ton at that point. Alongside these remnants stood barrels containing oil to lubricate the sewing machines. At the time of the fire, workers found that the window openings to the fire escape had rusted shut. A fire drill had never been performed in the building. Doors in the building opened inward. As firefighters arrived, the water from their fire hoses reached only the seventh floor and thus proved useless to those trapped in the factory on

the upper floors. Aerial ladders also reached only to the area between the sixth and seventh floors. As the fire grew, dozens jumped to their deaths as flames engulfed them. The ninth floor door was locked as the owners often locked doors to prevent workers from taking breaks during work hours and to prevent them from stealing. Firefighters found 19 bodies melted against this particular door. Because it was fireproof, the building itself suffered little damage, and the fire department had the fire under control within 20 minutes of its outbreak. The day after the fire, a writer for the *New York Times* commented, "The building was fireproof. It shows hardly any signs of the disaster that overtook it. The walls are as good as ever, as are the floors: nothing is worse for the fire except the furniture and 141 [sic] of the 600 men and girls that were employed in its upper three stories."

History of the Shirtwaist Workers

The history of the Shirtwaist workers perhaps makes the huge death toll of the fire even more damning. Shirtwaists, paired with tailored skirts, had become the standard fashion for women in the early twentieth century, and Triangle owners Isaac Harris and Max Blanck owned the largest firm in the business. They hired operators who then contracted out for factory workers. There was no fixed rate of pay for workers, and the company itself dealt only with its contractors. Despite this arrangement, gathering workers under the same roof had proved conducive to collective action by workers. Eighteen months before the fire, a spontaneous walkout by 400 garment employees led to the "uprising of the 20,000" in New York City. For three months, tens of thousands of women participated in this general strike. In the end, the strikers gained shorter work hours and higher wages along with some safety reforms, but industry owners refused to recognize their union. At the Triangle Shirtwaist Factory, for example, workers gained a 52-hour work week and a 12 to 15 percent increase in wages, but the union remained the key to assuring lasting reform. Rose Schneiderman played a central role in organizing this strike, giving a riveting speech insisting that workers needed both bread and roses. She continued to organize women workers throughout the 1910s at the grassroots level. In 1919 half of all women's garment workers participated in trade unions. Over the next two decades, Schneiderman increasingly focused on lobbying for and shaping labor legislation. In 1926 she served as president of both the national and New York Women's Trade Union League. Although not a middle-class reformer herself, she met Frances Perkins while working with the Factory Investigating Commission that was established after the fire, and in the 1930s Perkins, herself the first woman to become secretary of labor, helped secure Schneiderman a high-level government appointment.

Victims of the fire included members of the International Ladies Garment Workers' Union. Their Local 25 had frequently rallied against the very working conditions that led to the fire.

Aftermath of the Fire

Following the fire, the *Sun* described the bodies as "charred and dripping." The city set up temporary morgues to house them. Many of these working women, mainly recent Italian and Jewish immigrants, had been their family's breadwinners. As outrage brewed, the workers and their supporters began looking for people to blame. The Women's Trade Union League organized the first protest meeting following the fire. Its meeting the day after the fire included representatives from 20 leading labor and civic organizations. A week later, the city held a funeral procession for the unclaimed dead. Over 120,000 people participated. On 2 May a mass meeting at the Metropolitan Opera House protested factory conditions, and its participants included New York Governor John Dix. Rose Schneiderman again made a fiery speech that compared factory conditions to torture devices of the Inquisition. She lamented, "The life of men and women is so cheap and property is so sacred." The fire solidified her role as a highly effective labor leader for decades to come. Suffrage meetings began to stress self-protection in industry and argued that the vote would protect workers against factory owners who locked doors and against complacent voters, be they male or nonindustrial workers.

In the fire's aftermath, the "shirtwaist kings" and owners of the Triangle Shirtwaist Factory, Isaac Harris and Max Blanck, were indicted on manslaughter charges. The judge charged the jury that they could not find the defendants guilty unless the jurors believed the proprietors knew that the ninth floor door was locked. In December, despite parading through a group of 300 women chanting "murderers," the jury acquitted the two owners of any criminal wrongdoing. One member of the all-male jury commented to a newspaper reporter that many of the women probably panicked and thereby caused their own deaths. Twenty-three families later sued Harris and Blanck in a civil suit; and the families eventually received $75 each in 1913. That same year, a general sessions court fined Blanck $20 for keeping a door in another factory locked. The Triangle owners themselves eventually collected around $200,000 in insurance in the fire's aftermath.

The fire pushed issues of unsafe factories and immigrant exploitation into the public consciousness for quite possibly the first time. The Triangle fire exposed the deplorable conditions of New York factories. Investigators found 14 with no fire escapes, 65 with only a ladder, and nearly 500 with a sole fire escape as the only available fire exit. The fire also destroyed the traditional barriers against factory legislation. The commissions established and legislation passed in the fire's wake laid the groundwork for a welfare state with the state itself wielding wide authority to regulate and patrol industrial practices. Arthur McEvoy has argued that although the owners were not convicted at trial because the public did not connect the owners' control of the workplace with the victims' death, the fire began to change the public's mind over time. This prompted the eventual evolution of a mindset that held factory owners responsible for industrial safety. In such a climate, the public increasingly viewed "accidents" at work as a social problem worthy of both public redress and state intervention. Such a change in attitude is particularly important in the garment industry, which had a reputation as nonhazardous because it was seen as domestic work done mainly by women as an extension of the home. The role of labor organizations such as the International League of Garment Workers' Union cannot be overstated as they led the public battle for labor reform and kept those issues in the public eye long enough to be politically effective.

In the wake of the fire, New York passed the Sullivan-Hoey law in October 1911. This law established the Bureau of Fire Prevention and expanded both the power and the duties of the fire commissioner. It charged the bureau with ridding factories of fire hazards, and these measures mandated that doors must open outward, required that doors be unlocked during working hours, made sprinklers mandatory for businesses employing more than 25 people above the ground floor, and made fire drills mandatory in buildings without sprinklers. The state conducted five years of hearings on these matters and created a five-member Industrial Board, which was abolished in 1915 in favor of a newly structured Industrial Commission over the New York State Department of Labor. The commission had the authority to administer labor laws, workmen's compensation, and the state insurance fund. The state gave a newly created Building Department city-wide jurisdiction to mandate the removal and condemnation of unsafe buildings. The commission also established a system of penalties for department employees accepted bribes or performed inadequately.

The Factory Investigating Commission

In the summer following the fire, the New York legislature created the nine-member Factory Investigating Commission

(FIC). The FIC consisted of two state senators, three Assembly members, and four governor-appointees and included Senator Robert Wagner, Al Smith, Samuel Gompers (president of the American Federation of Labor), and Mary Dreier (the New York Women's Trade Union League president). Established to investigate the city's sweatshop conditions, it ultimately produced 25 new laws. Between 10 October and 21 December 1911, the FIC collected over 3000 pages of testimony from more than 200 witnesses. The FIC helped to establish legislation for factory fire control, sanitation conditions, and regulations regarding child and female employment. New York's state codes became some of the most advanced in the nation in the 1910s. Leon Stein, in a retrospective look at the FIC's legacy decades after the fire, maintained that these laws overhauled the state Department of Labor and turned its attention to hazards beyond fire, such as reducing the work week for women and children, applying industrial laws to canneries for the first time, and restricting the work of women immediately after childbirth.

The FIC also gathered vast amounts of data, which confirmed the consistent low wages paid to women workers. Only a few years earlier, in a 1908 ruling on *Muller v. Oregon,* the Supreme Court empowered states to use their police power to restrict the number of hours women worked in industry. Previously, state legislatures had continually struck down both maximum hour and minimum wage laws as denying workers' property rights and interfering with their individual liberty. The Consumers' League first began the minimum wage movement in hopes that merchants would voluntarily establish minimum wages for women in the 1890s. By 1913, however, nine states had passed minimum wage legislation. The FIC's data itself has been cited as the most formidable array of facts ever gathered by a minimum wage inquiry. Its inquiries and public hearings also helped fuel the state's campaign to regulate working conditions. Their figures showed that over half of all women employed in shirt manufacturing and over 60 percent of women in retail trades made less than $400 per year in a city whose subsistence-level standard of living was simultaneously calculated at just under $500 per year. These calculations were made for individuals, and many of these women's wages supported their entire family. The investigation concluded that productivity and profits did not significantly determine wages and noted that native female workers consistently received higher wages than immigrant women.

Businessmen adamantly opposed minimum wage legislation and argued that they would lead to higher unemployment, price increases, and relocations of businesses to other states in which no such legislation was in effect. They also argued that established minimums would become maximums in practice and would leave workers with no incentive to increase production.

Social workers and civic leaders usually favored minimum wage legislation, arguing chiefly that minimum standards would not only guarantee a certain standard of living but that it would also regularize employment. Progressives used the push for the minimum wage to illustrate how it could expand participatory democracy. They argued that wage boards would be established to set the minimum wages; the boards would consist of a variety of interested people, ranging from employer and employee representatives to representatives of the public interest. Some tagged such proposals as socialism intent on abolishing private industry and employment. Labor leaders themselves often divided over the issue of minimum wages. Samuel Gompers, for example, consistently opposed minimum wages, arguing both that minimums would become maximums and that the lack of enforcement would render the legislation useless. He eventually resigned from the FIC because of his opposition to the minimum wage.

The Rise of the State

As the commission worked on labor legislation, it increasingly lobbied for the state to assume the responsibility to protect workers. During the FIC's existence from 1911 to 1915, historian Thomas Kerr has argued, the FIC established a trajectory for state protection and labor legislation that continued to influence the minimum wage movement through the 1930s on both a state and, ultimately, a national level. Although the FIC was unsuccessful in securing wage laws during its existence, its wage investigation helped fuel the growing minimum wage debates throughout the nation. In 1933 a minimum wage law passed under the National Industrial Recovery Act, only to be struck down a few years later when the Supreme Court ruled against it. In response, however, the United States Congress passed the Fair Labors Standard Act in 1938, which established a flat minimum wage rate of 25 cents an hour in certain industries, to be increased to 40 cents within seven years. The FIC and its extensive wage study injected labor reformers' arguments concerning minimum wage into the public debate, and in the 1930s it continued to influence the debate as those who had once served on the commission moved into national politics and applied their ideas nationally under Franklin D. Roosevelt's administration.

The Legacy

The FIC ultimately rewrote New York's labor and factory codes in 13 volumes of reports between 1911 and 1915. New York's codes became a model for all other states until the New Deal, when Roosevelt enacted similar national legislation. The FIC and state regulatory power thus began as a very specific response by the state to a popular movement, yet it eventually gained national predominance by the time of the New Deal. During the 1930s the federal government's workplace safety measures and organizations served as the forerunners for the Occupational Safety and Health Administration (OSHA) in operation today.

Historian William Greider, however, has suggested that little has changed in urban industrial work for immigrant women and that the main differences in modern sweatshops are simply the names and the faces of new immigrants. In a 1990s study of New York and Los Angeles garment factories, over 60 percent violated minimum wage or overtime laws. In 1991 a fire engulfed an Imperial Food Products factory in North Carolina. Most of its workers were both women and immigrants. The factory lacked sprinklers, fire alarms, and marked fire exits. The fire injured over 50 people and killed 25. Investigators found most of the dead piled against locked doors. Although the conditions resembled the Triangle fire, the immediate aftermath did not. The company faced charges on 54 instances of "willful" safety violations, and owner Emmet Roe received a 20-year prison sentence. The company went bankrupt.

Key Players

Dix, John (1860–1928): Governor of New York at the time of the Shirtwaist Factory fire, Democrat Dix served in the state's highest office between 1911 and 1913.

Dreier, Mary (1875–1963): A social reformer and activist, Dreier helped form the Women's Trade Union League and served as an FIC member.

Gompers, Samuel (1850–1924): Gompers served as the American Federation of Labor's first president and, with the exception of a single year, retained the office until his death. He was the leading spokesman for the labor movement in the early twentieth century.

Perkins, Frances (1882–1965): Perkins worked at Hull House and served as the executive secretary of the New York Consumers' League. In 1929 then-New York governor Franklin D. Roosevelt appointed her the industrial commissioner of New York to direct the enforcement of factory and labor laws. In 1933 Roosevelt appointed her secretary of labor, the first woman appointed to the U.S. Cabinet.

Schneiderman, Rose (1884–1972): A Polish immigrant, Schneiderman initially worked in a factory stitching linings into caps. She became a prominent labor organizer and served as the WTUL's sole organizer on the East Coast during the 1910s. In the 1930s she served as a National Recovery Administration official and was a member of Roosevelt's brain trust.

See also: *Fair Labor Standards Act; Muller v. Oregon; National Industrial Recovery Act; Occupational Safety and Health Act (OSHA).*

―――――――

BIBLIOGRAPHY

Books

Baker, Elizabeth. *Protective Labor Legislation.* New York: Columbia University Press, 1925.

Downey, Fairfax. "Burnt Sacrifice: Triangle Shirtwaist Factory Fire, New York 1911." In Fairfax Downey, *Disaster Fighters.* New York: G. P. Putnam's Sons, 1938.

Jensen, Frances. *The Triangle Fire and the Limits of Progressivism.* Ph.D. Diss. University of Massachusetts at Amherst, 1996.

Lehrer, Susan. *Origins of Protective Labor Legislation for Women, 1905–1925.* Albany: State University of New York Press, 1987.

McClymer, John. *The Triangle Strike and Fire.* Orlando, FL: Harcourt Brace, 1998.

McEvoy, Arthur F. *The Triangle Shirtwaist Factory Fire of 1911: Social Change, Industrial Accidents, and the Evolution of Commonsense Causality.* Chicago: American Bar Association, 1994.

Mitelman, Bonnie. "Rose Schneiderman and the Triangle Fire." In *The Way We Lived: Essays and Documents in American Social History,* edited by Frederick Binder and David Reimers. Lexington, MA: D. C. Heath and Company, 1988.

Orleck, Annelise. *Common Sense and a Little Fire: Women and Working-class Politics in the U.S., 1900–1965.* Chapel Hill: University of North Carolina Press, 1995.

Perry, Elizabeth. *Belle Moskowitz: Feminine Politics and the Exercise of Power in the Age of Alfred Smith.* New York: Routledge, 1992.

Stein, Leon. *The Triangle Fire.* Ithaca, NY: Cornell University Press, 1962.

Periodicals

Kerr, Thomas. "The New York Factory Investigating Commission and the Minimum Wage Movement." *Labor History* 12, no. 3 (1971): 373–391.

Other

Rosa, Paul. "The Triangle Shirtwaist Fire." The History Buff Library page [cited 17 August 2002]. <www.historybuff.com/library/refshirtwaist.html>.

The Triangle Factory Fire. Kheel Center at the Cornell University Library, in collaboration with UNITE! 2002 [cited 17 August 2002]. <www.ilr.cornell.edu/trianglefire>.

Yaz, Gregg. *The Triangle Shirtwaist Fire of 1911.* "Leap for Life, Leap of Death." California State University, Northridge. 2002 [cited 17 August 2002]. <www.csun.edu/~ghy7463/mw2.html>.

ADDITIONAL RESOURCES

Books

Lewellyn, Chris. *Fragments from the Fire: The Triangle Shirtwaist Company Fire of March 25, 1911.* New York: Penguin Books, 1987.

—Melissa Ooten

Truax v. Corrigan

United States 1921

Synopsis

In *Truax v. Corrigan* the U.S. Supreme Court invalidated an Arizona law that prohibited the state courts from issuing injunctions against labor unions involved in disputes with employers over the terms and conditions of employment. The case was a setback for organized labor in its efforts to seek legislation that would allow peaceful picketing and boycotts without the interference of the courts.

Timeline

1906: Founding of the British Labour Party.

1911: Revolution in Mexico, begun the year before, continues with the replacement of the corrupt Porfirio Diaz, president since 1877, by Francisco Madero.

William Howard Taft. The Library of Congress.

1916: Battles of Verdun and the Somme on the Western Front. The latter sees the first use of tanks, by the British.

1918: The Second Battle of the Marne in July and August is the last major conflict on the Western Front. In November, Kaiser Wilhelm II abdicates, bringing an end to the war.

1921: As the Allied Reparations Commission calls for payments of 132 billion gold marks, inflation in Germany begins to climb.

1921: Canadian scientists Frederick Banting and Charles Herbert Best isolate insulin, an advance that will alter the lives of diabetics and greatly reduce the number of deaths associated with the disease.

1921: Washington Disarmament Conference limits the tonnage of world navies.

1921: In a controversial U.S. case, Italian-born anarchists Nicola Sacco and Bartolomeo Vanzetti are tried and convicted of armed robbery and murder. Despite numerous protests from around the world, they will be executed six years later.

1924: V. I. Lenin dies, and thus begins a struggle for succession from which Stalin will emerge five years later as the undisputed leader of the Communist Party, and of the Soviet Union.

1928: Discovery of penicillin by Alexander Fleming.

1931: Financial crisis widens in the United States and Europe, which reel from bank failures and climbing unemployment levels. In London, armies of the unemployed riot.

1936: Germany reoccupies the Rhineland, while Italy annexes Ethiopia. Recognizing a commonality of aims, the two totalitarian powers sign the Rome-Berlin Axis Pact. (Japan will join them in 1940.)

Event and Its Context

The Injunction in Labor Disputes

The Sherman Antitrust Act of 1890 was designed chiefly to curb monopolistic business practices, but an unintended outcome of the act was that it was used against organized labor. In effect, the courts repeatedly held—in such cases as *Danbury Hatters* (officially *Loewe v. Lawler*, 1908) and *Gompers v. Bucks Stove and Range Company* (1911)—that trade unionism violated antitrust law because certain of its tactics constituted an illegal restraint of trade. Although trade unionism remained technically legal, the only weapons that it had to influence the outcome of labor disputes were held to be illegal.

Employers quickly learned that they had a potent weapon in their arsenal against labor: the injunction. The courts routinely granted injunctions to halt the activities of organized labor, including picketing and secondary boycotts. In the early twentieth century, organized labor mounted a campaign to get both the federal and state judiciaries out of labor disputes by curbing the use of injunctions. The American Federation of Labor (AFL), which at the time was the only federation of labor unions in existence in the United States, spearheaded this effort. Although the AFL wanted federal legislation, it concentrated much of its effort on getting anti-injunction statutes passed in the states, largely because the use of injunctions on the state level had predated their use in the federal courts. The AFL, however, met with only moderate success. By 1914 only six states had passed laws limiting the power of state courts to issue injunctions in labor disputes. In four of these states— California, Oklahoma, Massachusetts, and Montana—the legislation regulated specific aspects of the labor injunction. Two states, however—Kansas and Arizona—passed more sweeping laws that actually tried to halt judicial interference in labor disputes by prohibiting injunctions. It was this type of law that the AFL hoped to see in each state and at the federal level.

The AFL thought that it had finally gotten its wish in 1914 with the passage of the Clayton Act. Among other provisions, the act specifically stated that the federal courts could not restrain unions from engaging in peaceful picketing, strikes, and employer boycotts. The act also spelled out the circumstances in which a temporary restraining order might be issued against the activities of organized labor. The act required the court to notify the union that such an order would be issued unless there was an imminent danger of irreparable injury to property for which there was no other remedy at law. In the event that a restraining order was issued, it expired in 10 days. Employers seeking a restraining order had to post a bond that would indemnify the union if it was later determined that the union's activities were lawful. The act further required that any injunction that was issued had to specify in detail the union activities that were enjoined.

Armed with the Clayton Act, the AFL redoubled its efforts to get similar legislation passed in each of the states, for the Clayton Act would apply only to labor actions that affected interstate commerce. Again, its success was moderate: only five states passed laws modeled on the Clayton Act, and no state passed such a law after 1921, because in that year the U.S. Supreme Court ruled, in *Truax v. Corrigan*, that the 1913 Arizona anti-injunction law was unconstitutional. Actually, a pair of cases the Court ruled on that year—*Truax* and *American Steel Foundries v. Tri-City Central Trades Council*—rendered the Clayton Act impotent as it pertained to labor injunctions, for the Court reasoned that the injunction provisions of the Clayton Act were superseded by the restraint-of-trade provisions of the Sherman Antitrust Act.

A Setback for Labor

The High Court telegraphed the position it would take in *Truax* in *American Steel Foundries*, when it sharply curtailed the ability of unions to picket. In particular, the Court limited the number of picketers, attempted to control conduct on the picket line, and prevented picketing by workers who were not directly involved in the labor dispute. Although the Court did not rule directly on the constitutionality of the Clayton Act, it effectively negated the protections afforded to organized labor under the act.

Then just weeks later, on 19 December 1921, the Court dealt a death blow to state anti-injunction legislation when it ruled on the *Truax* case. The plaintiffs were the owners of a restaurant, the English Kitchen, in Brisbee, Arizona. In 1916 a dispute arose between the owners and the defendants' union over the terms and conditions of employment as they affected the restaurant's employees. When the restaurant refused to accede to the employees' demands, they went on strike. They picketed the restaurant, displayed banners, denounced the restaurant as "unfair" to labor, advertised the strike, and attempted to induce the restaurant's patrons to stay away. Their actions were successful; daily receipts at the restaurant fell to less than half of what they had been before the strike. Consequently, the restaurant went to county court to seek both a temporary and a permanent injunction against the union, claiming that the picketing, boycott, and other activities would bring irreparable harm to the business and that it had no other remedy at law because of the insolvency of the strikers. The basis of the restaurant's claim was that the employees' actions violated the Fourteenth Amendment to the Constitution by depriving the restaurant of its property without due process of law and by denying the plaintiffs equal protection. The county court dismissed the complaint, and the state supreme court, citing the 1913 statute, affirmed the lower court's ruling. The restaurant appealed to the U.S. Supreme Court, which, by a 5 to 4 vote, reversed the decision of the Arizona Supreme Court, in the process declaring the Arizona statute prohibiting injunctions unconstitutional.

Chief Justice William Howard Taft delivered the majority opinion. In his decision he made two fundamental arguments. First, he agreed with the plaintiffs that both the union's activi-

Supreme Court Justice Louis D. Brandeis walking with his daughter, Elizabeth. © Bettmann/Corbis. Reproduced by permission.

ties and the 1913 Arizona anti-injunction statute deprived the restaurant of property without due process of law: "a law which operates to make lawful such a wrong as is described in plaintiff's complaint deprives the owner of the business and the premises of his property without due process and cannot be held valid under the Fourteenth Amendment." Second, Taft declared that the statute was unconstitutional because it denied employers equal protection under the law. Specifically, Taft said, the statute provided the employees with a right that their employers did not enjoy: "The necessary effect of [the Arizona law] is that the plaintiffs would have had the right to an injunction against such a campaign as that conducted by the defendants, if it had been directed against the plaintiffs . . . in any kind of a controversy which was not a dispute between employer and former employees."

Among the four dissenters were two giants in the history of jurisprudence, Justices Oliver Wendell Holmes and Louis Brandeis, whose dissenting opinions frequently evolved into mainstream legal doctrine in later years. It was Brandeis who delivered the most elaborate dissent in *Truax*. He stressed that the Arizona legislature, acting through the legislative process, did not act unreasonably when it passed an anti-injunction statute, and thus the plaintiffs were not deprived of due process of law. Further, he said, changing social needs and conditions necessitated the statute, for as labor unions attempted to press their demands, the injunctive process stacked the deck in favor of employers in labor controversies.

The Aftermath

For more than a decade, no state passed an anti-injunction bill. The courts in those states that had such a law on the books, following the Supreme Court's lead in *Truax*, interpreted them in such a way as to render them worthless to the labor movement. In 1927 Congress, increasingly recognizing the essential role of collective bargaining in resolving labor disputes, began to fashion a federal anti-injunction bill, the Norris–La Guardia Act, which was finally passed by overwhelming majorities in 1932. The act curtailed judicial involvement in labor disputes. Accordingly, it denied the federal courts the power to enjoin peaceful picketing or strikes regardless of their purpose, and it narrowly defined the process and the circumstances under which an injunction against labor might be issued when the law did not forbid it. The question that remained was, in light of Court decisions such as that in *Truax*, would the act pass constitutional muster?

The first test case, *Senn v. Tile Layers Protective Union*, came in 1938. The case involved the tile-laying union in Wisconsin. In 1931 Wisconsin had passed an anti-injunction statute whose provisions closely paralleled those of the Norris–La Guardia Act, which had been the subject of widespread public discussion and debate for years before its passage. Thus, observers felt that if in *Senn* the Court upheld the Wisconsin statute, it would in effect be ratifying the Norris–La Guardia Act. By a vote of 5 to 4, the Court upheld the constitutionality of the Wisconsin law in 1938. In a minor historical irony, it was Justice Brandeis who delivered the majority opinion. In a very real sense his dissenting opinion in *Truax* became the majority opinion and a key precedent 16 years later. In the wake of the Court's decision in *Senn*, some states passed what were called "Little Norris–La Guardia Acts" to protect workers who were not covered by the federal law. The court injunction as a tool to hamper efforts by labor to press its demands was finally blunted.

Key Players

Brandeis, Louis D. (1856–1941): Brandeis, one of the judiciary's most distinguished scholars and the first Jew to be appointed to the U.S. Supreme Court, was born in Louisville, Kentucky. From 1879 to 1916 he maintained private law practices in St. Louis, then in Boston. In 1916 President Woodrow Wilson nominated him to the U.S. Supreme Court, where he served until 1939. Brandeis is perhaps best known for his belief that in rendering their decisions judges must take into account not only the strict letter of the law but also current social and economic conditions.

Taft, William Howard (1857–1930): Born in Cincinnati, Ohio, Taft enjoyed a long and distinguished career. In 1892 he became a federal circuit judge, but in 1900 he gave up that position when President Theodore Roosevelt appointed him civil governor of the Philippines, then secretary of war in 1904. As Roosevelt's anointed successor, Taft was elected president in 1908, but he lost the 1912 election to Woodrow Wilson. In 1913 Taft took a faculty position at the Yale law school, which he left in 1921 when President Warren Harding appointed him chief justice of the Supreme Court, where he served until a month before his death.

See also: *American Federation of Labor; Clayton Antitrust Act; Gompers v. Bucks Stove; Norris–La Guardia Act.*

BIBLIOGRAPHY

Books

Taylor, Benjamin J. *Arizona Labor Relations Law*. Tempe: Arizona State University, Occasional Paper No. 2, Bureau of Business and Economic Research, College of Business Administration, 1967.

Taylor, Benjamin J., and Fred Witney. *Labor Relations Law*, 3rd ed. Englewood Cliffs, NJ: Prentice-Hall, 1979.

Periodicals

Jones, Edgar A., Jr. "The Right to Picket—Twilight Zone of the Constitution." *University of Pennsylvania Law Review* (June 1954): 997.

"Labor Picketing and Commercial Speech: Free Enterprise Values in the Doctrine of Free Speech." *Yale Law Journal* (April 1982): 960.

Pope, James Gray. "The Thirteenth Amendment versus the Commerce Clause: Labor and the Shaping of American Constitutional Law, 1921–1957." *Columbia Law Review* 102 (January 2002): 112.

Other

American Steel Foundries v. Tri-City Central Trades Council, 257 U.S. 184 (1921).

Senn v. Tile Layers Protective Union, 301 U.S. 468 (1938).

Truax v. Corrigan, 257 U.S. 312 (1921).

—Michael J. O'Neal

U

Union Federations Split Along Ideological Lines

South America 1900–1920

Synopsis

By the late nineteenth century, workers in some South American countries had begun to organize. European ideologies such as anarchism, syndicalism, and socialism influenced the continent's labor movements. A growing number of trade unions appeared, particularly in countries such as Argentina, Chile, and Brazil. In most cases, union leaders attempted to unify their organizations into national confederations. However, in all cases, such countrywide organizations had a precarious existence and often split along ideological lines.

Timeline

1882: British forces invade, and take control of, Egypt.

1894: French army captain Alfred Dreyfus, a Jew, is convicted of treason. Dreyfus will later be cleared of all charges, but the Dreyfus case illustrates—and exacerbates—the increasingly virulent anti-Semitism that pervades France.

1899: Start of the Second Anglo-Boer War, often known simply as the Boer War.

1899: Polish-born German socialist Rosa Luxemburg rejects the argument that working conditions in Europe have improved, and that change must come by reforming the existing system. Rather, she calls for an overthrow of the existing power structure by means of violent international revolution.

1899: Aspirin introduced.

1900: Establishment of the Commonwealth of Australia.

1900: The first zeppelin is test-flown.

1900: Sigmund Freud publishes *The Interpretation of Dreams*.

1900: German physicist Max Planck develops Planck's constant, a cornerstone of quantum theory.

1902: Second Anglo–Boer War ends in victory for Great Britain. It is a costly victory, however, resulting in the loss of more British lives (5,774) than any conflict between 1815 and 1914. The war also sees the introduction of concentration camps, used by the British to incarcerate Boer civilians.

1906: Founding of the British Labour Party.

1909: William Cadbury's *Labour in Portuguese West Africa* draws attention to conditions of slavery in São Tomé and Principe.

Event and Its Context

The Formation of Working-class Organizations in Latin America

Workers in South American countries began to organize starting as early as the 1840s, when some formed mutual aid societies and others carried out utopian experiments. During this formative period, which lasted until World War I, the conditions in many of the region's countries produced a much larger working class. South America became increasingly integrated into the world economy as exports grew and foreign investment increased. In turn, urban populations increased, the service sector expanded, and some industry appeared. These conditions fostered a bigger and increasingly more organized working class.

Workers in a number of South American countries became more militant and began to organize on a larger scale in the late nineteenth century. Earlier forms of organization had not led to any real improvements in the conditions of the working classes, and these failures prompted the change in approach. In many cases, these early labor movements drew on the experiences and ideologies of the working classes in other countries as an increasing number of European immigrants brought their working-class ideologies with them. In countries such as Argentina, Brazil, and Chile, workers looked to European ideologies such as anarchism, syndicalism, and socialism. By the early twentieth century, many workers had formed unions, federations, and confederations.

Working-class Ideologies in Latin America

Several main European working-class ideologies appeared in South America in the late nineteenth and early twentieth centuries. Anarchism, anarcho-syndicalism, syndicalism, and socialism all influenced labor movements throughout Latin America. Proponents of these ideologies agreed that capitalists exploited the laboring classes. However, they differed as to how to improve the condition of working-class people. In addition, the differences were sometimes blurred or strayed from their original positions.

Anarchists could be found throughout much of Latin American during this period, although there was a great deal of diversity among them. Some remained true to the anarchist ideology and thus viewed trade unions as merely reformist rather than revolutionary. Instead, these anarchists relied on small affinity groups to attract workers to a revolution that would destroy the state and private property, marking the start of a new society. Other anarchists became somewhat more pragmatic and joined trade unions in hopes of making their struggles more revolutionary.

As was the case elsewhere in the world, an anarcho-syndicalist movement appeared in South America in the late 1800s and would play an even larger role than anarchism. Sometimes referred to as "revolutionary syndicalism," this current was a reaction to what many saw as a socialist movement that was too moderate and reformist, as well as to the perceived ineffectiveness of the anarchists. This ideology adapted a number of anarchist ideals to the realties of industrial capitalism. Like the anarchists, the anarcho-syndicalists were a diverse group. However, at the core of the ideology was the tenet of direct action. Trade unions would lead this struggle against the capitalist class, and anarcho-syndicalists would not allow for compromise with the bourgeois state. Workers would rely on tactics such as strikes, sabotage, and boycotts rather than seeking gains through the state and traditional politics. The main weapon of the anarcho-syndicalist was the general strike that would paralyze the economy. Anarcho-syndicalists opposed electoral politics and sought to take over the state. At the core of a new society would be the trade unions that brought down the state. In reality, however, some anarchist groups did allow workers to make short-term demands that would improve their immediate conditions.

A distinct syndicalist movement also developed, particularly in Argentina. Similar to anarcho-syndicalism in many ways, the key difference for syndicalists was their dedication to securing more immediate economic gains. In addition, the syndicalists were more willing to negotiate and collaborate with the state if they thought this approach would serve the interests of their union members.

Socialism also played a role in the South American labor movement, although on a limited basis. Most Latin American socialists were similar to European Social Democrats. Thus, although the Latin American socialists believed in long-term goals, they stressed immediate results within the existing system. They encouraged legal and peaceful means, such as electoral participation to effect reforms. They generally believed that trade unions should be subordinate to political parties. Socialists had difficulty making inroads in many Latin American countries because of the size and composition of the working class. The nature of the state and electoral politics in the region also served to limit the influence of socialism. In Argentina, where socialism played the most significant role, the socialists were largely reformist and had weak links to the labor movement. Elsewhere, particularly in northern Chile, socialists were less reformist.

The Labor Movement in Argentina

In 1890 Argentine labor leaders attempted to form the *Federación Obrera Argentina* (FOA), the country's first national labor confederation. Socialist leaders, mainly immigrants, were largely responsible for organizing the FOA. However, the confederation was often inactive, and on several occasions labor leaders attempted to revive the organization. Finally, in 1901 they permanently established the *Federación Obrera Regional Argentina* (FORA). This organization comprised 27 unions in the capital, Buenos Aires, as well as in the interior of the country. Although FORA still did not control the majority of Argentine unions, it was the largest such confederation in all of Latin America. However, ideological differences soon caused a split in the FORA. After the organization's 1902 congress, socialists and other nonanarchists withdrew from the organization, leaving the anarchists in control of the organization.

Anarchism first appeared in Argentina in the 1880s among Italian and Spanish immigrants. The ideology became especial-

ly strong after 1899 when the resumption of the gold standard in the country ended increases in real wages and caused rents to rise. Argentine anarchists renounced their traditional individualism and began organizing unions. Anarchism had a great appeal to many Argentine workers, and some 20,000 workers in Buenos Aires belonged to the federation, representing about 5 percent of the city's total working class. Anarchism's simple conflict ideology and philosophy of action attracted many workers; others favored the utopian and even millenarian aspects of the ideology. On a number of occasions during the first decade of the twentieth century, there were great anarchist struggles, often taking the form of a general strike. Massive demonstrations and street battles with police were often the result. This situation sometimes prompted government crackdowns, which ranged from declaring a state of siege to laws such as the Law of Residence (1902) and the Law of Social Defense (1910). In 1910 anarchists threatened to sabotage Argentina's centennial celebrations. This threat led to attacks on anarchists and their organizations. The anarchists never fully recovered from this repression, nor did they succeed in implementing their social revolution.

In 1903 many of socialists who had left the FORA formed a new group known as the *Unión General de Trabajo* (UGT). Early Argentine socialists were the best organized in Latin America. Led by Juan B. Justo, they had formed the Socialist Party in the 1890s and were at first active among the working classes. Increasingly, however, many workers felt that the socialists were too reformist and did not represent their interests. Therefore, the UGT soon took on a syndicalist bent. By the time of the UGT's third congress in 1905, syndicalists clearly dominated the organization, and Argentine socialists deemphasized their role among the working classes.

In 1909 the syndicalists formed yet another new organization known as the *Confederación Obrera Regional Argentina* (CORA). They were unhappy with other organizations as they felt that the socialists were too moderate and the anarchists were ineffective. The syndicalists were particularly strong among the port workers of Buenos Aires. They gained influence by staging limited strikes that resulted in immediate economic gains.

In 1914 the FORA and the CORA united. By the following year, the syndicalists had taken control of the new group, which would be known as FORA IX, after the ninth congress. This caused the anarchists to withdraw from the newly combined organization. Instead, the anarchists formed the FORA V, so named because they adhered the anarchist ideals of the fifth congress of 1905.

During the government of Hipolito Yrigoyen (1916–1923), the syndicalists and the state engaged in some cooperative efforts. The syndicalists supported Yirgoyen's Radical Party, and in exchange, the government withheld police action against certain strikes. By 1918 the syndicalist-led FORA had some 80,000 members in the capital of Buenos Aires, about 20 to 25 percent of the city's workers. There were also violent confrontations in this period, most notably the "Tragic Week" massacre in January 1919.

The Labor Movement in Chile

There was no national labor federation in Chile until just before World War I, despite at least five attempts to create one.

Members of certain trades managed to create their own federations, such as typographers, breadmakers, and shoemakers. There was also a certain level of provincial organization. For example, workers in Santiago and Tarapacá created federations.

Despite the lack of a national labor organization, the first decade of the twentieth century did see a series of labor conflicts in Chile. In 1903 a maritime workers strike in Valparaíso resulted in rioting, and the government brought in the navy to suppress the movement. There were also walkouts in the northern nitrate fields. In 1907 government troops massacred miners in Iquique.

Although a national federation came late in Chile, other forms of working-class organization existed earlier. During the early twentieth century resistance societies appeared in certain trades, particularly in the cities of Santiago and Valparaíso. Anarchism and anarcho-syndicalism influenced these societies. Among the most significant actions taken by such groups was the 1903 Valparaíso maritime strike, which encountered violence that resulted in some 100 deaths. Between 1905 and 1907 many new societies appeared in the two cities and there were more than 75 strikes.

In the northern mining region of the country, there appeared organizations known as *mancomunales*. These groups combined the functions of mutual aid societies and trade unions. They were based on geography rather than trade, joining skilled and unskilled workers in the nitrate and transport industries. The mancomunales were well organized and militant. Yet by 1907 heavy repression and economic crisis virtually ended both the mancomunales and the resistance societies until World War I.

Chile's first national labor organization appeared in 1909. Known as the *Gran Federación Obrera de Chile* (GFOCh), the federation was conservative in its early years. The GFOCh collaborated with the government and sought reforms such as security against sickness, death, and unemployment. It also fought for a minimum wage and eight-hour workday. At first the federation was organized along a loose federal structure, with national, departmental, and local councils. Later the organization became more centralized. After 1917 it was known simply as FOCh.

If anarchist and anarcho-sydicalist ideology dominated the early resistance societies in Chile, socialism also made inroads in the labor movement. In 1912 Luis Emilio Recabarren founded the *Partido Oberero Socialista* (POS), which was much less reformist than its Argentine counterpart. The POS had a significant working-class following, especially in the North. However, the POS had minimal success in elections.

Socialists also played an important role in the changing focus of the FOCh. At the 1919 FOCh convention, the socialists had clearly come to dominate the organization. No longer a reformist federation that largely served as a mutual aid society, the FOCh had become a revolutionary group that opposed capitalism. Indeed, in 1921 the FOCh joined the Red International of Labor Unions.

Other workers joined a Chilean affiliate of the Industrial Workers of the World (IWW) of the United States. Following the anarcho-syndicalist model, the Chilean IWW opposed the government and capitalism. It favored direct action such as strikes, boycotts, and sabotage. Some 9,000 workers joined the IWW, mainly in Santiago and in several port cities. The IWW was especially strong among maritime, bakery, masonry, and leatherworkers.

The Labor Movement in Brazil

In Brazil, the labor movement grew in the 1890s, and by the first decade of the twentieth century workers in major cities had become active. The first citywide general strike took place in Rio de Janeiro in 1905. Some 40,000 strikers shut down the city for 20 days and gained some concessions. There was a general strike in São Paulo in 1906, although authorities brutally put it down. Workers in São Paulo struck again in 1907, with some acquiring an eight-hour day. These gains did not last, however, as many unions disappeared in an economic downturn that affected the country.

The first workers' congress in Brazil met in 1906, with representatives from 28 organizations. The delegates passed resolutions that generally represented the anarcho-syndicalist position. They agreed to form the *Confederacão Operária Brasileira* (COB). Led by the Edgard Leuenroth, the COB lived a precarious existence. Although the COB helped to exchange information and coordinate labor activities, it did not play a major role. Furthermore, the early anarcho-syndicalist movement in Brazil was less extreme than its Argentine counterpart, using the general strike less often and allowing for collective bargaining with management. In 1913 delegates to the second workers' congress reaffirmed the anarcho-syndicalist position of the COB.

The anarcho-syndicalists in Brazil continued to play a role over the next several years, exemplified by their participation in the 1917 general strike in São Paulo. The strike started as a work stoppage at a large textile factory where workers demanded higher wages. The strike soon spread to other factories, especially after the police killed one demonstrator. The dead worker's funeral procession sparked a general strike in the city that involved some 45,000 workers. Indeed, civil authorities lost control of the city for a time and some looting took place. Anarcho-syndicalists workers formed the *Comitê de Defesa Proletária* (CDP). The group composed a list of relatively moderate demands that in general were not consistent with anarcho-syndicalist ideology, which paved the way for some middle-class support. The committee used a group of supporters to conduct negotiations with the government. The CDP obtained a 20 percent increase in wages and the promise of other reforms. This victory for labor led to even more organizing. Labor agitation spread to the interior of the state and to Rio de Janeiro. At the same time, it led to increased oppression, as the government closed unions, arrested and deported many leaders, and declared a state of siege in 1918. In turn, this situation produced internal divisions in Brazilian labor over strategy and tactics. By 1920 the period of labor expansion had largely come to an end.

A growing split in the Brazilian labor movement occurred in the 1920s. Some reformist unions appeared, especially in Rio de Janeiro and often encouraged by the government. At the same time, many anarcho-syndicalists changed their earlier strategy and came to reject all political participation and strikes for short-term gains. Greatly influenced by the Bolsheviks and the Russian Revolution, the anarcho-syndicalists remained dominant in São Paulo. However, their influence greatly declined elsewhere in the country.

Although there was no significant socialist party in Brazil during the early twentieth century, the Brazilian Communist Party was founded in 1922. It was formed by many former anarcho-syndicalists and had some influence in many unions in Rio de Janeiro. Soon a struggle for control of the labor movement developed between the anarcho-syndicalists and the communists. In 1926 the communists created an electoral front known as the *Bloco Operário e Camponês* (BOC), which elected several candidates. The communists also created a short-lived national trade union confederation in 1929 called the *Confederacão Geral do Trabalhadores do Brazil*. By the end of the 1920s, communists dominated the Brazilian labor movement.

Key Players

Justo, Juan B. (1865–1928): Argentine doctor and politician. Justo was the founder of the Argentine Socialist Party, the best organized in the region. In its early years, the Socialist Party played an active role among Argentine workers. Justo founded the socialist worker newspaper *La Vanguardia* in 1894. He served as both a deputy and senator in Argentina's national legislature.

Leuenroth, Edgard (1881–1968): A Brazilian labor leader who was instrumental in organizing the country's first labor confederation, the *Confederacão Operária Brasileira* (COB). An anarcho-syndicalist, Leuenroth also edited a number of working-class newspapers in Brazil. He was jailed several times for his participation in labor activities.

Recabarren, Luis Emilio (1876–1924): Chilean typographer and labor leader. Recabarren edited several working-class newspapers in the northern nitrate mining region of the country. He was a leading figure in the *Partido Democático* and was elected to the Chilean congress in 1906. He later felt that the *Partido Democrático* was too conservative and formed the *Partido Obrero Socilaista* (POS) in 1912. Recabarren was exiled in Argentina from 1916 to 1918. Upon his return to Chile, he gained control of the country's main labor confederation. In 1924 he committed suicide.

See also: *Anarchists Lead Argentine Labor Movement; Longshoremen and Miners Strikes; Organized Labor Established; Tragic Week, Argentina.*

BIBLIOGRAPHY

Books

Alexander, Robert J. *Organized Labor in Latin America.* New York: The Free Press, 1965.

Godio, Julio. *Historia del Movimiento Obrero Latinoamericano.* 2nd ed. Caracas, Venezuela: Nueva Sociedad, 1983.

Gómez, Alfredo. *Anarquismo y Anarcosindicalismo en América Latina.* Barcelona: Ibérica de Ediciones y Publicaciones, 1980.

Hall, Michael, and Hobart Spalding. "The Urban Working Class and Early Latin American Labour Movements, 1880–1930." In *The Cambridge History of Latin America, 1870–1930*, edited by Leslie Bethell. Cambridge, MA: Cambridge University Press, 1986.

Poblete Troncoso, Moisés, and Ben G. Burnett. *The Rise of the Latin American Labor Movement.* New York: Bookman Associates, 1960.

Rock, David. *Argentina, 1516–1987: From Spanish Colonization to Alfonsín.* Berkeley and Los Angeles: University of California Press, 1989.

Spalding, Hobart. *Organized Labor in Latin America: Historical Case Studies of Workers in Dependent Societies.* New York: New York University Press, 1977.

—Ronald Young

Union Label Movement

United States 1874

Synopsis

The union label movement began in 1874. The first union label was white, to distinguish cigars made by white union men from those produced by Chinese immigrants. From these ignoble beginnings, the union label became one of several weapons in efforts to end sweatshops and child labor and to improve the working conditions of laborers in the United States. The union label movement continued in the twenty-first century with similar aims: to end sweatshops, slavery, and child labor, conditions that still existed globally.

Timeline

1854: Republican Party is formed by opponents of slavery in Michigan.

1859: American abolitionist John Brown leads a raid on the federal arsenal at Harpers Ferry, Virginia. His capture and hanging in December heighten the animosities that will spark the Civil War sixteen months later.

1864: General William Tecumseh Sherman conducts his Atlanta campaign and his "march to the sea."

1867: Establishment of the Dominion of Canada.

1870: Beginning of Franco-Prussian War. German troops sweep over France, Napoleon III is dethroned, and France's Second Empire gives way to the Third Republic.

1872: The Crédit Mobilier affair, in which several officials in the administration of President Ulysses S. Grant are accused of receiving stock in exchange for favors, is the first of many scandals that are to plague Grant's second term.

1874: As farm wages in Britain plummet, agricultural workers go on strike.

1874: Discovery of gold in the Black Hills of South Dakota.

1874: Norwegian physician Arrnauer Gerhard Henrik Hansen discovers the bacillus that causes leprosy. This marks the major turning point in the history of an ailment (now known properly as Hansen's disease) that afflicted humans for thousands of years and was often regarded as evidence of divine judgment.

1876: General George Armstrong Custer and 264 soldiers are killed by the Sioux at the Little Big Horn River.

1882: The Chinese Exclusion Act, a treaty between the United States and China, provides for restrictions on immigration of Chinese workers.

1884: Chicago's Home Life Insurance Building, designed by William LeBaron Jenney, becomes the world's first skyscraper.

Event and Its Context

The radio and television jingle, "Look for the Union Label," created by Paula Green for the International Ladies' Garment Workers' Union (ILGWU) in 1975, has been a familiar musical reminder to many Americans to buy union-made goods. Labels differentiate union-made from non–union-made products, enabling consumers to decide by whom and under what conditions the goods and services they purchase are produced. The union label allows consumers to lend material support to labor's fight to improve working conditions and to support businesses that engage in fair labor practices.

The union label movement is an outgrowth of a broader union labor movement. In the 1800s workers organized in trade unions to improve their terms of employment through collective bargaining and legislation. During the Progressive Era (1890s–1920s), the labor movement expanded precipitously in response to the deteriorating conditions of many American workers as immigrant-employing sweatshops, fatal disasters, and the use of low-wage child and convict slave labor rapidly increased.

The union label movement, which began in the 1870s, expanded the labor movement's arsenal of tools and its self-conception of workers. It broadened the meaning of the union laborer to include union consumer. According to the *Union Label Advocate*, "You as the consumer are the employer of labor, and if you have to work for wages see to it that your hard earned money is not expended to support employers who do not recognize any organization of the men they employ." If workers successfully organized the collective purchasing power of union members and supporters, a powerful prounion message would be sent to businesses. In effect, to "look for the union label" was viewed as an act of solidarity with workers that rewarded union-friendly businesses while maintaining a "peaceful boycott" against those selling goods and services produced by workers who were unprotected by the collective bargaining process.

Early Labels: 1874–1900

In 1874 union cigar makers in San Francisco pasted white "union made" labels on cigar boxes to indicate that they had been made by white men. Union members did this to protect

Florence Kelley. The Library of Congress.

white workers from competition from Chinese immigrant cigar makers, whose produce was driving down prices and wages. The San Francisco union claimed that Chinese immigrant-produced cigars were made by sickly workers who labored in unsanitary conditions and who were satisfied with wages that were below the "American standard." Appealing to 1870s Pacific Coast anti-Chinese public sentiment, cigar makers promoted their white label as a way that consumers could help white working men maintain living wages in decent shops and drive their nonwhite competitors back to China. The positive public response to this message spurred sales of cigars and thus smoothed businesses' acceptance of the union label. In 1875 St. Louis cigar makers adopted the San Francisco makers' practice but with a red label to symbolize solidarity.

At the 1880 International Cigar Makers' annual meeting, attendees raised concerns about competition from immigrant workers, prison labor, and tenement sweatshops. Prompted by the California cigar makers' success and unable to decide between white and red, the delegates voted to adopt a blue union label. The union agreed to deliver labels to any requesting manufacturer who operated in compliance with union hour and wage rules and to set aside funds to promote sales of union-made cigars.

At their national convention in 1885, a second union, United Hatters of North America, established an identifying label for their men's hats. In 1891 the International Typographical Union began to use a union label or "bug." The union bug met with early success. By 1897, 40 city councils had passed ordinances requiring union labels on all municipal printing. By the turn of the century, numerous unions representing garment workers to iron molders all were using union labels. The Barbers' Union issued union shop cards to barbers who employed union members.

White labels frequently were used to prey on the health fears of American consumers. White indicated the "sanitary conditions" under which an item was produced. If appeals to ethics or solidarity failed to motivate consumers to check labels, fears of tuberculosis succeeded. In the 1890s garment factories in Massachusetts had to be licensed by the board of health. If a garment was not factory-made, it was required to bear a "tenement made" tag.

The union label was also used as an organizing tool. The American Federation of Labor (AFL) supported the use of identifying labels as emblems of unionism. Unions promised to promote the products of manufacturers and business that permitted union labeling. Some businesses allowed use of labels as requested by unionized employees in exchange for promotion. Unions convinced other employers of the promotional value of labels. These employers received labels conditional on organizing current employees and committing to subsequent union hiring. Several unions (for example, the Cigar Makers, the Boot and Shoe Workers) preferred to use labeling agreements as a "peaceful" method of organizing that avoided employer-employee conflict.

The union label movement was initially so successful that fraudulent use or imitation of union label symbols became an immediate problem. By 1895, 25 states had enacted criminal and civil laws to protect union labels from counterfeit or allowed labels to be registered as trademarks. Despite these efforts however, conditions under which union labels could be used went unmonitored and were loosely enforced.

Progressive Era: Label Promotion

In the Progressive Era, numerous social clubs and improvement societies supported labor's agenda by sponsoring strike benefits, labor legislation, and regular lectures and discussions. One such organization, the Social Reform Club of New York, founded in 1894, promoted the union label movement among middle- and upper-class purchasers, characterizing it as a way to help the working classes help themselves.

Labor leaders understood that predominantly male union members made few household purchases. Consequently, women became the focus of union label purchasing promotion. In 1909 the AFL created its Union Label and Service Trades Department, which sponsored formation of local union label leagues to promote label shopping. In 1910 Pauline Newman, an ILGWU label promoter, recommended going beyond male union members and promoting union labels to socially minded women. After making her case in newspapers, Newman was invited to promote label purchasing to audiences in society clubs, women's clubs, and churches.

In tandem with the union label, another label movement with similar aims formed. In 1899 Florence Kelley helped to establish the National Consumer's League (NCL) to secure maximum hours, minimum wages, and improved working conditions for women and children. The NCL introduced a "white label" that could only be used by employers that met their stan-

dards. The NCL and its local chapters asked consumers to boycott goods not bearing its label of approval.

Union Labels in the Twentieth Century

Despite efforts to educate consumers about buying union-made products, the label movement experienced mixed results. Even label advocates themselves did not always adhere to the use of labeled products. For example, Alice Dodge Wolfson, a delegate from Stenographers, Bookkeepers, Accountants, and Office Employee's Union Local 14965 attended a 1935 AFL meeting. At the end of a speech by I. M. Ornburn, head of the Union Label and Service Trades Department, admonishing all to buy union-label products, Wolfson stood up and demanded to know why there was no Stenographer's Union label on the copies of his speech distributed to the audience.

Between the Great Depression and the 1970s, organized labor's battle for better working conditions yielded a series of victories in the U.S. Congress. In 1933 the National Industrial Recovery Act (NIRA) gave organized labor an ongoing role in setting legally enforceable labor standards on an industry-by-industry basis. It also gave workers the right to organize and to bargain collectively with employers. Employers who satisfied NIRA conditions were permitted to display the Blue Eagle Label, a universal label indicating conformity to fair labor practices. However, the U.S. Supreme Court in *Schechter Poultry v. United States* (1935) struck down the NIRA as unconstitutional.

Congress responded to the *Schechter Poultry* decision by enacting a series of new statutes, each targeted at improving the welfare of laborers. The Wagner Act (1935) established the rights of workers to organize and bargain collectively and created the National Labor Relations Board. The Fair Labor Standard Act (FLSA, 1938) instituted national minimum wages and maximum hours and ended the lawful use of child labor. The Occupational Safety and Health Act (1970) sought to ensure workplace safety. As organized labor focused its efforts during this period on the legislative arena, it did not expend as much effort as in the past on promoting consumer awareness of union labels.

In the 1970s, however, interest in union labels was revived when the onset of globalization increased the level of competition between American-made goods and those made in foreign sweatshops by nonunion labor. In this new context, union labels again came to symbolize the American labor movement's struggle to maintain fair labor standards in global labor and product markets. At the same time, globalization threatened to reverse many of the gains achieved by organized labor during the twentieth century. The ability to outsource overseas dramatically increased industry's bargaining power. As manufacturers subcontracted or moved their operations overseas, union organizers were less likely to follow as they did after World War II, when manufacturers relocated from the organized North to the unorganized South. Further, federal labor laws such as the Wagner Act and the FSLA did not follow American manufacturers overseas. Thus, American manufacturers often were able to lower their production costs by relying on sweatshop conditions and child labor in countries with lax labor laws.

At the beginning of the twenty-first century, organized labor's loss of both bargaining power and legislative protection had the potential to reinvigorate the union label movement. Although manufacturers in the global economy were often able to evade both U.S. laborers and U.S. laws, they could not operate profitably without appealing to the vast U.S. markets for their products. Thus, U.S. consumers constituted a key point through which organized labor could continue to exert pressure on manufacturers. If large numbers of U.S. consumers could be persuaded to look for the union label before purchasing goods, then manufacturers would gain an incentive to re-engage in collective bargaining with labor unions so as to satisfy those consumers. Some steps were taken in this direction. The 1980s and 1990s, for instance, saw the formation of numerous antisweatshop organizations such as Global Exchange, United Students Against Sweatshops, National Labor Committee, and Workers Right Consortium.

Although the perceived meaning of union labels varied, one tenet of the movement remained consistent: by buying union, consumers could help their fellow workers maintain decent jobs with fair wages. In the twenty-first century, these goals became international.

Key Players

Kelley, Florence (1859–1932): Philadelphia-born daughter of U.S Congressman William D. Kelley. She received a law degree from Northwestern University and joined reformers at Chicago's Hull House. She was a founder of the National Consumer League.

Newman, Pauline (circa 1890–1986): Born in Lithuania and came to the United States in 1901. Newman was employed by New York's Triangle Shirtwaist Factory as a child. By 1910 she was an organizer, activist, and ILGWU union label promoter.

See also: *American Federation of Labor; Wagner Act.*

BIBLIOGRAPHY

Books

Brooks, John Graham. "The Trade Union Label." In *Making of America*, edited by Robert La Follette. Chicago: John D. Morris and Company, 1905.

Glickman, Lawrence B. *A Living Wage: American Workers and the Making of Consumer Society*. Ithaca, NY: Cornell University Press, 1997.

Marot, Helen. *American Labor Unions*. New York: Henry Holt and Company, 1914.

Mitchell, John. *Organized Labor: Its Problems, Purposes and Ideals and the Present and Future of American Wage Earners*. Philadelphia: American Book and Bible House, 1903.

Tyler, Gus. *Look for the Union Label: A History of the International Ladies' Garment Workers' Union*. Armonk, NY: M. E. Sharpe, 1995.

Periodicals

Kelley, M. E. J. "Union Label." *North American Review* 165 (July 1897).

The Union Label Advocate (March 1920).

ADDITIONAL RESOURCES

Other

Union Services Directory [cited 7 October 2002]. <www.union-label.com/directory.htm>.

Wolfson, Alice Dodge/Charlie Potter, and Beth Friend. "Right After That They Walked Out": Alice Wolfson recalls the Origins of the CIO. Interview by the Oral History of the American Left, Tamiment Library, NYU for the public radio program, *Grandma Was an Activist*. History Matters Web site [cited 8 October 2002]. <http://historymatters.gmu.edu/d/130/>.

—Linda Dynan

Unions Plan Merger

United States 1995

Synopsis

The three largest industrial unions in North America announced their intent to merge in July 1995. The United Auto Workers (UAW), the United Steelworkers (USW), and the International Association of Machinists (IAM) pledged to unite their roughly two million members by the year 2000. In a Unity Statement the three unions explained that they could jointly "better win a secure and prosperous future for working men and women in the global economy of the twenty-first century." By July 1999 the merger plans as announced in 1995 were called off.

Timeline

1976: United States celebrates its bicentennial.

1980: In protest of the Soviet invasion of Afghanistan, President Carter keeps U.S. athletes out of the Moscow Olympics. Earlier, at the Winter Games in Lake Placid, New York, the U.S. hockey team scored a historic—and, in the view of many, a symbolic—victory over the Soviets.

1986: Seven astronauts die in the explosion of the U.S. Space Shuttle *Challenger* on 28 January.

1991: The United States and other allies in the UN force commence the war against Iraq on 15 January. By 3 April the war is over, a resounding victory for the Allied force.

1993: Muslim extremists carry out a bombing at the World Trade Center in New York City on 26 February, killing six and injuring thousands.

1995: The Aum Shinrikyo cult carries out a nerve-gas attack in a Tokyo subway, killing eight people and injuring thousands more.

1995: Bombing of the Alfred P. Murrah Federal Building in Oklahoma City, Oklahoma, kills 168 people. Authorities arrest Timothy McVeigh and Terry Nichols.

1995: Yugoslav forces step up their offensives in Bosnia and Croatia and conduct campaigns of "ethnic cleansing" to rid areas of non-Serb elements. By December, however, a Bosnia peace treaty will be signed.

1995: After a lengthy and highly publicized trial charged with racial animosity, a Los Angeles jury takes just four hours to declare O. J. Simpson not guilty of the murders of Nicole Brown and Ronald Goldman. In a 1997 civil trial, he will be found guilty and fined $33 million.

1995: A Jewish extremist assassinates Israeli Prime Minister Yitzhak Rabin. In elections the following May, Benjamin Netanyahu becomes the new Israeli leader.

1998: In the midst of the Monica Lewinsky scandal, terrorists affiliated with Saudi millionaire and Muslim extremist Osama bin Laden bomb U.S. embassies in Kenya and Tanzania, killing hundreds of people. President Clinton orders air strikes on terrorist camps in Afghanistan and an alleged chemical-weapons factory in the Sudan, but the action—which many observers dismiss as a mere tactic to take attention off the scandal—is ineffective and wins limited support.

2001: On the morning of 11 September, terrorists hijack four jets, two of which ram the twin towers of the World Trade Center in New York City. A third plane slams into the Pentagon in Washington, D.C., and a fourth crashes in an empty field in Pennsylvania. The towers catch fire and collapse before an audience of millions on live television. The death toll is approximately 3,000.

Stephen P. Yokich. © UPI/Corbis-Bettmann. Reproduced by permission.

Event and Its Context

Background on Union Mergers

Union mergers are not new. Samuel Gompers, founder and first president of the American Federation of Labor (AFL), promoted union mergers to conserve resources and to eliminate jurisdictional disputes. Mergers reduce costly duplication of expenses, provide larger strike funds, increase collective bargaining power, and heighten organizing ability. Larger unions also have greater resources for political action. Diminished in a merger are the local history and culture of small unions.

Union membership reached its peak in the United States in 1979 and began to decline thereafter. Membership decreased by more than four million between 1979 and 1995. Some of the areas that were particularly hard hit were the primary metals, automobiles, and aerospace equipment manufacturing, which were represented by the three unions: United Auto Workers (UAW), United Steel Workers (USW), and the International Association of Machinists (IAM).

The fortieth anniversary of the merger between the AFL and the Congress of Industrial Organizations (CIO) occurred in 1995. The AFL-CIO, a federation of autonomous labor unions, had a constitution that encouraged mergers. From the time of the AFL-CIO merger until 1995 there were 133 mergers among unions, although not all of the mergers were within the AFL-CIO. Between 1975 and 1995, half of the mergers were between

AFL-CIO members and 35 percent of the mergers were between AFL-CIO affiliates and independents. The rest were between independents.

When unions that are essentially equal in size unite to form a new entity, it is described as amalgamation. When a small union merges with a large union, as is the most common form of merger, it is called absorption. If the unions each retain their own identity within the merger, it is described as an affiliation.

After January 1985, the IAM was involved in four mergers, the UAW in two, and the USW in three. All these mergers were with small unions. There is no information readily available on how many mergers were started but never completed. However, experts believe that far more mergers are begun than are completed. Information surfaces on failed mergers if the proposal makes it as far as a convention and the members reject it. Such was the case with a proposed megamerger between the National Education Association (NEA) and the American Federation of Teachers (AFT) that had been discussed intermittently for 30 years before a merger agreement was finally taken to the membership in 1998 and voted down. At the beginning of the twenty-first century, state and local groups continued to negotiate a merger.

International Association of Machinists

To understand what is involved in a merger of the proportions proposed in 1995, one has to look first at the individual unions. The IAM, with a membership over 700,000, started in 1888 when 19 machinists met in a locomotive pit in Atlanta, Georgia, and voted to form a trade union. In 1895 the IAM joined the AFL and moved its headquarters to Chicago. In 1936 aerospace workers joined IAM and the membership grew to 130,000. By 1995 IAM represented workers in auto and auto parts, wood and paper, electronics, construction, and general manufacturing industries, although most of the membership came from the defense and aerospace industry. About 40,000 IAM members were Canadian.

The organization of the IAM was somewhat different from that of both the UAW and USW. In the IAM much of the power and authority was decentralized, held in the local and district lodges, a structure that traces back to its origin as a craft union. The local lodges kept 50 percent of the dues, and 2.5 percent went into a strike fund. The International (called the Grand Lodge) elected officers by a membership referendum. In 1995 George Kourpias was president of the union, but he was due to retire before the merger would be completed.

United Auto Workers

In 1995 the UAW also had a membership of over 700,000 including 4,000 Canadians. Both the CIO and the UAW were formed in 1935. The UAW was chartered originally with the AFL but soon changed affiliation to the CIO. A Canadian regional office opened in 1937. The UAW had significant success in organizing and bargaining in the auto industry in the 1930s and 1940s. After recruiting aerospace membership throughout the 1930s and 1940s, the UAW added an aerospace department in 1943.

Walter Reuther was elected president of the UAW in 1946. He led the UAW to become a member of the AFL-CIO when the two groups merged in 1955, but because of disagreements over social issues, organizing unorganized workers, and international labor and foreign policies, he also led the UAW to withdraw from the AFL-CIO in 1968. In 1981 the UAW rejoined the labor federation.

Although most UAW members worked in the auto, auto parts, and truck industries, there was a considerable membership in the agricultural implement, aerospace, and defense industries. In 1986 the majority of the Canadian members formed their own union, the Canadian Auto Workers (CAW).

The political structure of the UAW was centralized, with significant authority given to the international and regional levels. The local share of the UAW dues was 38 percent; 30 percent went to a strike fund. Every three years the union elected its president in a vote of delegates at an international convention. Stephen Yokich became UAW president in 1995.

United Steelworkers

The United Steelworkers grew out of a 1936 CIO group, the Steel Workers Organizing Committee (SWOC). When most of the basic steelworkers were organized by the SWOC in 1942, they changed the name to United Steelworkers. By 1995 the union had a membership of over 600,000, partly accrued in mergers of industries in the production and fabrication of other metals. About 170,000 of the members were Canadian.

The USW had a centralized structure much like that of the UAW, except that the members elected the international officers by referendum. The local share of the dues was 44 percent; the strike fund received 7 percent. In 1995 George Becker was president of the USW.

Ten Merger Issues

A megamerger such as the one as proposed by the IAM, UAW, and USW has the obvious advantage of scale in bargaining and political action, but there are at least 10 issues that can interfere and take time to resolve, if they can be resolved at all. The issues are: 1) The method of electing national officers: IAM and USW elected by a secret ballot referendum, and the UAW elected by a vote of delegates at a convention. 2) Members of the executive board and election procedures: The UAW and USW had similar structures for their executive board, but IAM was different; the selection process was different in all three unions. 3) The distribution of decision-making power: The UAW and USW had a centralized system, but IAM was more regional; the power granted to the union president was also different in each of the unions. 4) The process by which members and officers exercise their rights of appeal of the actions of the national union, a right assured by the Labor-Management Reporting and Disclosure Act (LMRDA), was different in the UAW than in both the IAM and the USW: the UAW had a unique public review board made up of distinguished academics; the IAM and USW involved delegates to the national convention in the appeal process. 5) The rights of retirees were different in each of the three unions: Retirees had full voting rights only in the UAW; IAM retirees had some voting rights, and UAW retirees had none. 6) The dues structure was different in each of the three unions: Although the amount of dues collected was similar, the local share and the strike fund share were very different. 7) The compensation for international officers was different in all three unions: The IAM president received the most at about $130,000 per year, and the USW president received just over $100,000. 8) The net assets of the three unions were different: the UAW had about five times the assets of either the IAM or UAW at over $950 million, compared to about $190 million for each of the other two. 9) The headquarters and education centers were different for each of the three unions: Although it was conceivable that all three locations could be used to some degree, to do so would cut into the economy produced by a merger. 10) Who will become president of the merged entity? This and the name given to a newly formed union introduced the issues of union loyalty, history, and culture.

Aftermath of the Merger Announcement

At the time that the intent to merge was announced, the unions formed three committees to initiate the process. These included an international president's committee to study all issues related to the merger, a finance committee of the secretary-treasurers of the three unions to examine the financial aspects, and a constitution committee composed of vice presidents and other necessary staff. In 1996 the unions added a 54-member general membership advisory committee. In spite of these efforts, the unions were unable to complete the merger. On 25 June 1999 the unions' leaders announced that the merger plan had failed. The differences in the issues were too great to be reconciled.

Key Players

Becker, George (1928–): Becker, a second-generation steelworker, rose through the ranks to become president of the United Steelworkers in 1993. He was elected for a second term in 1997. Becker had been a vice president of the union for two terms before being elected president. He grew up across the street from a steel mill in Illinois.

Gompers, Samuel (1850–1924): Gompers was born in London, England, but immigrated to the United States when he was 13 years old. Gompers was a cigar maker and became active in the Cigarmaker's Union. He then became involved in the Federation of Trades and Labor Unions and was chairman of it when its name was changed to the American Federation of Labor (AFL) in 1886. Gompers supported union mergers.

Kourpias, George J. (1932–): Kourpias served as an International Association of Machinists (IAM) district president, a Grand Lodge representative, and a national vice president before he was elected president of IAM in 1989. He served as president of IAM until 1997. Kourpias was also elected to the AFL-CIO executive council in 1989.

Yokich, Stephen P. (1935–2002): Yokich was a third-generation UAW member. He was elected president of the UAW in 1995. He was well respected in the UAW for his skill in collective bargaining.

See also: *AFL, CIO Merge.*

BIBLIOGRAPHY

Books

Katz, Harry C., and Hurd, Richard W. *Rekindling the Movement, Labor's Quest for Relevance in the 21st Century.* Ithaca, NY: Cornell University Press, 2001.

Periodicals

Clark, Paul F., and Lois S. Gray. "Assessing the Proposed IAM, UAW, and USW Merger: Critical Issues and Potential Outcomes." *Journal of Labor Research* 21, no. 1 (winter 2000): 65–81.
"Union Merger Called Off?" *Cleveland Plain Dealer,* 25 June 1999.
Verespej, Michael A. "Megaunions: Mega-headaches?" *Industry Week* 244, no. 16 (4 September 1995): 71–73.
Williamson, Lisa. "Union Mergers: 1985–94 Update." *Monthly Labor Review* (February 1995): 18–24.

ADDITIONAL RESOURCES

Books

Lichtenstein, Nelson. *State of the Union: A Century of American Labor.* Princeton, NJ: Princeton University Press, 2001.

Periodicals

Garland, Susan B. "Breath of Fire or Last Gasp?" *Business Week* (14 August 1995): 42.

Hauser, Thomas. "E. Pluribus Union." *The Nation* (28 August–4 September 1995): 190.

—M. C. Nagel

United Automobile Workers of America

United States 1935

Synopsis

During the Great Depression of the 1930s, the U.S. automobile industry experienced labor relations troubles with its workers. In the midst of these struggles, the United Automobile, Aircraft, and Vehicle Workers of America was formed. It eventually evolved into one of the most powerful unions in labor history: the United Automobile Workers of America (UAW).

Officially designated today as the United Automobile, Aerospace, and Agricultural Implement Workers of America, the UAW was formed in 1935 as a part of the Committee for Industrial Organization (hereafter called the "Committee") within the American Federation of Labor (AFL). The UAW soon became disenchanted with the lack of interest shown by AFL leadership with respect to organizing workers in the mass-production industries, especially the automobile industry. As part of the dissolution of the Committee from the AFL, the UAW and other discouraged industrial unions separated from the AFL in 1936. They eventually reunited under the auspices of the Committee, which by then was known by the more familiar title of the Congress of Industrial Organizations (CIO). Growing out of an initial discontent with its inability to represent automobile workers, the UAW eventually became a dominant force as one of the largest labor unions in North America.

Timeline

1920: League of Nations, based in Geneva, holds its first meetings.

1925: European leaders attempt to secure the peace at the Locarno Conference, which guarantees the boundaries between France and Germany, and Belgium and Germany.

1930: Naval disarmament treaty signed by the United States, Great Britain, France, Italy, and Japan.

1933: Newly inaugurated U.S. President Franklin D. Roosevelt launches the first phase of his New Deal to put depression-era America back to work.

1935: Germany annexes the Saar region after a plebiscite. In defiance of Versailles, the Nazis reintroduce compulsory military service. The Allies do nothing, and many western intellectuals maintain that it is only proper for Germany to retake its own territory and begin building up its army again.

1935: Italians invade Ethiopia, and the response by the League of Nations—which imposes sanctions but otherwise fails to act—reveals the impotence of that organization.

1935: Second phase of New Deal begins with the introduction of social security, farm assistance, and housing and tax reform.

1938: The U.S. Fair Labor Standards Act establishes a minimum wage.

1940: Hitler's troops sweep through Western Europe, annexing Norway and Denmark in April, and in May the Low Countries and France. At the same time, Stalin—who in this year arranges the murder of Trotsky in Mexico—takes advantage of the situation to add the Baltic republics (Latvia, Lithuania, and Estonia) to the Soviet empire, where they will remain for more than half a century.

1945: April sees the death of three leaders: Roosevelt passes away on 12 April; the Italians execute Mussolini and his mistress on 28 April; and Hitler (along with Eva Braun, propaganda minister Josef Goebbels, and Goebbels's family) commits suicide on 30 April.

1950: North Korean troops pour into South Korea, starting the Korean War. Initially the communists make impressive gains, but in September the U.S. Marines land at Inchon and liberate Seoul. China responds by sending in its troops.

Event and Its Context

The Parent AFL

The AFL was established as a labor union in 1886 with Samuel Gompers elected as the founding president. It began with 25 national craft unions (each composed of members of a single occupation such as carpenters or electricians) and a total of about 140,000 members. By 1900 the AFL had about one million members. The AFL was almost exclusively organized according to worker skills or occupations. These traditional *craft* jurisdictions were popular during the early years of unionization, but as companies began to mass-produce goods, semi-skilled and unskilled workers greatly increased in number, and the *industrial* jurisdictions began to gain popularity. The inability of the AFL to change with a changing environment caused it enormous internal problems, as was clearly the case with its relationship to the automobile industry.

In 1920 a semi-industrial union called the United Automobile, Aircraft, and Vehicle Workers, with about 45,000 members and affiliated with the AFL, began to develop alongside the burgeoning automobile industry. However, in 1921 the union was expelled from the AFL for unrestricted industrial unionism (that is, not organizing along craft lines). James O'Connell, president of the Metal Trades Department within the AFL, again raised this sensitive issue of industrial organizing in 1925 when he asked the question as to the possibility of organizing workers in the automobile industry. At this time the automobile industry, part of the mass-production sector, was one of the

John L. Lewis. U.S. Information Agency.

largest industries in the United States, with over half a million unorganized (that is, nonunion) workers.

Industrial Versus Craft

O'Connell stated that the "automobile industry [was] so highly and scientifically specialized as to produce a jumble of jurisdictional claims and disputes that would be almost impossible" to unravel. Hotly debated arguments within the AFL divided the members along jurisdictional lines: how would the highly mechanized, repetitive operations performed by the workers in the automobile industry be divided?

Some factions wanted the AFL divided along industrial lines (where all the workers in a particular industry would belong to one union), others wanted the workers organized into federal labor unions (and later further divided into appropriate international unions), while still others wanted the workers (especially the small groups of skilled workers such as machinists, painters, and upholstery workers) divided by skills (as in a craft union). Not much was accomplished at this time, other than the continuing rift that was developing between the majority craft unions and the minority industrial unions of the AFL.

In 1927 AFL president William Green appointed Paul K. Smith as the director to lead the Automobile Organizing Campaign in order to organize workers in the automobile industry into local unions directly affiliated with the AFL. However, Smith found resistance due to the general indifference of the automobile workers (who were more concerned with increasing unemployment) and due to the hostility of the industry leaders (who did not want union workers). In June 1933 not a single union of automobile workers was affiliated with the AFL, and the efforts to organize the automobile workers were shelved. The automobile workers were said to feel hopeless about the overbearing bureaucracy within the AFL.

Samuel Gompers. AP/Wide World Photos. Reproduced by permission.

Favorable Actions Geared Toward Automobiles

In the early 1930s, as the depression continued throughout the United States, the U.S. National Recovery Administration submitted a code of fair competition to the automobile industry. It basically stated that employers were to bargain collectively with chosen representatives of their employees and that discrimination against their employees would not be tolerated on the grounds of union affiliation. As a result, the automobile workers began to look more favorably towards the AFL. The AFL begrudgingly granted the right of local automobile unions to form a national body. Thus, at the 1934 AFL convention, a resolution was granted to admit automobile workers.

By June 1934 the number of automobile workers' unions within the AFL had reached 106. At about that same time, delegates from the local unions met in Detroit, Michigan, and formed the National Council of Automobile Workers' Unions, while the federal government established the Automobile Labor Board in order to conduct collective bargaining between automobile employers and employees. During this convention, the Executive Council of the AFL reported that a local union was now established in every major automobile plant in the United States.

Founding of the United Automobile Workers

During the first quarter of 1935, the AFL decided to grant a national charter to automobile workers. The International Union, United Automobile Workers (UAW), held its founding convention on 26 August 1935 in Detroit. With deep divisions

from members of the fledgling union as to whom to elect as president, AFL president William Green ultimately appointed Francis J. Dillon—who was the automobile organizer for the AFL—as the first president of the UAW. Edward Hall was appointed as secretary-treasurer, and Homer Martin, vice president. The workers protested the appointments, wanting to elect their own leaders. Green gave them a choice—Dillon or nothing—and they reluctantly chose Dillon.

At first, organizing efforts in the automobile industry were slow and the tiny UAW had very little influence. But the rank-and-file members, with little help from Green and Dillon, organized at a dramatic pace. In 1935 the UAW represented no more than 20,000 automobile workers out of a total automobile-industry workforce of around 445,000 workers. However, the UAW was gaining momentum due to the discontent and unrest (caused by the depression) among the automobile workers.

The AFL grew rapidly in the last half of the 1930s as union organization was encouraged and protected by President Franklin Roosevelt's New Deal legislation. The New Deal improved opportunities for trade union growth, but it also raised the issue of whether the AFL should organize by occupation (skilled craftsmen) or by industry (semiskilled and unskilled industrial workers).

Twenty-one resolutions concerning various activities of industrial unions were submitted to the AFL convention from 7 to 19 October 1935 in Atlantic City, New Jersey. John L. Lewis, president of the United Mine Workers of America (UMWA); Charles P. Howard, president of the International Typographical Union; and David Dubinsky, president of the International Ladies' Garment Workers Union, stated at the convention that it was the obligation of the AFL to organize the unorganized workers in the industrial field. They criticized the AFL for not meeting the "present-day needs" of its members. The minority report, for those favoring the industrial workers, stated, "The fact that after fifty-five years of activity and effort we have enrolled under the banner of the A. F. of L. approximately 3,5,000,000 of members of the 39,000,000 of organizable workers is a condition that speaks for itself. . . . Industrial organization is the only solution." Lewis continued the attack on the AFL by reporting on the dismal organizing record of the AFL for the past year. Fisticuffs even broke out between various leaders over the volatile issue of the industrial workers.

Committee for Industrial Organization

On 9 November 1935 Lewis, Howard, Dubinsky, and Sidney Hillman (president of the Amalgamated Clothing Workers) led the formation of the Committee for Industrial Organization within the AFL. This action was in response to years of frustration at not being able to properly organize industrial workers within the AFL. With seven founding unions, the Committee's purpose was to organize workers rapidly, notably workers in mass production industries. A majority of the unions within the AFL challenged the Committee's efforts to organize these previously nonunionized, unskilled workers into existing or new industrial unions. For the next year, bickering within the AFL over the actions of the Committee continued.

On 27 April 1936 in South Bend, Indiana, the UAW held its second convention. In its first year, UAW membership had increased 50 percent to 30,000. At the convention, Dillon relinquished his job when Homer Martin was elected president by a unanimous vote. Young, enthusiastic leaders emerged during this time including Richard T. Frankensteen, Robert C. Travis, and the three Reuther brothers—Walter, Roy, and Victor. Although the UAW was wary of hurting its relationship with the AFL, on 2 July 1936 the UAW formalized its belief in industrial unionism by affiliating with the Committee, while still a member of the AFL.

On 23 November 1936 the national AFL convention was held in Tampa, Florida. Fights once again broke out between leaders of the craft and industrial unions. The old craft faction that had earlier agreed to organize the mass-production industries into industrial unions now went back on its commitment. During this time, the Executive Council of the AFL agreed to immediately dissolve the Committee after its members perceived continued Committee activities as a challenge to the supremacy of the AFL. The members of the Committee challenged the statement, stating that they had no intentions of interfering with or obstructing the ordinary functions of the AFL. Lewis also emphasized the good results that the Committee had achieved with respect to organizing the unskilled and semiskilled workers. During ensuing discussions, Lewis stated that the Committee wished to remain a member of the AFL but insisted that it continue to be allowed to organize the mass-production industries.

Despite these efforts, the AFL suspended the ten unions affiliated with the Committee: the United Mine Workers of America; Amalgamated Clothing Workers of America; International Union, Mine, Mill, and Smelter Workers; International Ladies' Garment Workers Union; United Textile Workers of America; Federation of Flat Glass Workers; Amalgamated Association of Iron, Steel, and Tin Workers; International Union, United Automobile Workers; Oil Field, Gas Well, and Refinery Workers of America; and United Rubber Workers of America.

Amidst all of the trouble brewing between the Committee and the AFL, the UAW was still a small, struggling organization just barely organizing automobile workers. However, at the end of 1936 the UAW called a strike against the General Motors Corporation (GM) in Flint, Michigan. The strike began as a small walkout of 7,000 workers at the Cleveland, Ohio, Fisher body plant but quickly spread to the other plants in Detroit and Flint (both in Michigan) and subsequently to all the GM plants in Indiana, Ohio, Georgia, and Missouri. The strike was finally ended in February 1937 with the assistance of Michigan governor Frank Murphy and UMWA president (and Committee member) Lewis. In all, 140,000 workers went out on strike out of a total force of 150,000 workers. With such widespread grievances from its employees, GM recognized the UAW as the union representing its workers. Further strike action and union organizing actions throughout the year eventually allowed the UAW to be accepted as the industry's recognized bargaining agent. The GM strike is generally considered as one of the most important employer-employee conflicts of the 1930s, and it heightened the status of the UAW considerably. At the end of 1937, the expanded UAW contained 375,000 members.

With such organizational victories, the executive officers of the Committee authorized that certificates of affiliation be issued to national, international, state, regional, and city central bodies and local groups that joined its organization. This action

showed the AFL that the Committee was functioning as a rival. By December 1937 negotiations between the Committee and the AFL had collapsed.

In 1938 the AFL leadership, during its Denver, Colorado, convention, expelled the unions that formed the Committee, revoking the charters of all Committee affiliates. As a direct result, Lewis led the expelled unions, including the UAW, out of the AFL and formally established a new federation: the Congress of Industrial Organizations (CIO). The purpose of the newly established CIO, with Lewis as president, was to encourage and promote the organization of the unorganized workers in mass-production industries and other similar industries. The CIO rapidly developed into a full competitor with the AFL, and the UAW increased its union-building clout in the automobile industry.

Aftermath

By the twenty-first century the UAW was an internationally known union that represented a diverse group of workers in almost all sectors of the economy. It represented workplaces ranging from international corporations, small manufacturers, and state and local governments to universities and colleges, hospitals, and non-profit organizations. By 2003 the UAW had over 710,000 active members and over 500,000 retired members. It was affiliated with the reunited American Federation of Labor-Congress of Industrial Organizations (AFL-CIO) and was organized into more than 950 local unions in the United States, Canada, and Puerto Rico.

As one of the largest unions in North America, the UAW has been at the forefront of collective bargaining, winning such benefits as worker pensions, a cost-of-living wage escalator clause, an unemployment benefit providing a laid-off member with nearly 90 percent of income for one year, and a health security program. The UAW was the first union to successfully bargain for an employer-paid health insurance plan for industrial workers.

In addition to the UAW's bargaining success, it has always consisted of leaders who fought for economic and social rights for its members. The UAW has been actively involved in promoting civil rights legislation and developing affirmative action programs. The UAW has been influential in forming national politics and has played an important role in passing such important legislation as Medicare and Medicaid, the Employee Retirement Income Security Act, the Occupational Safety and Health Act, the Family and Medical Leave Act, the Voting Rights Act, the Fair Housing Act, and the Civil Rights Restoration Act.

Key Players

Dillon, Francis J. (1887–?): Dillon completed a pattern-maker apprenticeship that resulted in employment at a number of pattern shops in Ohio and Indiana. He later served as a business agent and a member of the general executive board for the Pattern Makers League in Indianapolis, Indiana, and Cleveland, Ohio. Dillon served as an automotive organizer in Flint and Detroit, Michigan, for the American Federation of Labor (AFL). He was the first president of the United Automobile Workers (UAW), serving from August 1935 to

April 1936, and subsequently served as its national representative and organizer.

Gompers, Samuel (1850–1924): Gompers was an American labor leader who was the founding president of the American Federation of Labor (AFL) in 1886 and remained its president (except in 1895) until his death in 1924.

Lewis, John L. (1880–1969): Lewis helped to organize industrial workers of the United States through the Congress of Industrial Organizations in the 1930s, and later helped to create some of the country's leading labor unions, including the United Steelworkers of America, United Automobile Workers, and the Communication Workers of America. He was president of the United Mine Workers of America from 1920 to 1960.

Martin, Warren Homer (1902–?): Martin was the second president of the UAW (from 1936 to 1939). He was a former minister, having graduated from William Jewell College in Missouri.

See also: *AFL, CIO Merge; American Federation of Labor; Committee for Industrial Organization; Congress of Industrial Organizations; Ford-UAW Contract; Ford-UAW SUB Agreement; GM Recognizes UAW; GM-UAW Landmark Contracts.*

BIBLIOGRAPHY

Books

Austin, Aleine. *The Labor Story: A Popular History of American Labor, 1786–1949.* New York: Coward-McCann, Inc., 1949.

Beard, Mary. *A Short History of the American Labor Movement.* New York: Greenwood Press, 1968.

Dulles, Foster Rhea, and Melvyn Dubofsky. *Labor in America: A History,* 5th ed. Arlington Heights, IL: Harlan Davidson, Inc., 1984.

Lorwin, Lewis L., with assistance from Jean Atherton Flexner. *The American Federation of Labor.* Washington, DC: The Brookings Institution, 1933.

Morris, James O. *Conflict Within the AFL: A Study of Craft Versus Industrial Unionism, 1901–1938.* Ithaca, NY: Cornell University Press, 1958.

Stolberg, Benjamin. *The Story of the CIO.* New York: Arno and The New York Times, 1971.

Taft, Philip. *The A. F. of L. from the Death of Gompers to the Merger.* New York: Harper and Brothers, 1959.

Periodicals

Automotive News (1948 Almanac issue), 7 June 1948, p. 74.

Fine, Sidney. "President Roosevelt and the Automobile Code." *Mississippi Valley Historical Review* (June 1958).

—William Arthur Atkins

United Fruit Company Strike

Colombia 1928

Synopsis

In 1928 workers in the Colombian banana zone in the Department of Magdalena went on strike against the United Fruit Company. Workers in the region had been organizing for a decade, creating unions such as the *Unión Sindical de Trabajadores del Magdalena* (USTM). In 1928 the leaders of the USTM presented the company with a list of demands that ranged from wage increases to the abolition of company stores. When the company refused to meet these demands, the workers went on strike in November 1928. With the strike unresolved in early December, the government sent in army troops who massacred hundreds and perhaps thousands of strikers who were peacefully gathering for a march in the town of Ciénaga. The massacre, made famous in novel *One Hundred Years of Solitude* by Nobel Prize–winning author Gabriel García Márquez, had profound political consequences in Colombia, as it damaged the reputation of the ruling Conservative Party and contributed to a victory by the Liberal Party in the 1930 elections.

Timeline

1914: On the Western Front, the first battles of the Marne and Ypres establish a line that will more or less hold for the next four years.

1919: Treaty of Versailles signed by the Allies and Germany, but rejected by the U.S. Senate. This is due in part to rancor between President Woodrow Wilson and Republican Senate leaders, and in part to concerns over Wilson's plan to commit the United States to the newly established League of Nations and other international duties. Not until 1921 will Congress formally end U.S. participation in the war, but it will never agree to join the League.

1924: In the United States, Secretary of the Interior Albert B. Fall, along with oil company executives Harry Sinclair and Edward L. Doheny, is charged with conspiracy and bribery in making fraudulent leases of U.S. Navy oil reserves at Teapot Dome, Wyoming. The resulting Teapot Dome scandal clouds the administration of President Warren G. Harding.

1927: Charles A. Lindbergh makes the first successful solo nonstop flight across the Atlantic and becomes an international hero.

1929: The Lateran Treaty between the Catholic Church and Mussolini's regime establishes the Vatican City as an independent political entity.

1929: On "Black Friday" in October, prices on the U.S. stock market, which had been climbing wildly for several years, suddenly collapse. Thus begins the first phase of a world economic crisis and depression that will last until the beginning of World War II.

1929: Edwin Hubble proposes a model of an ever-expanding universe.

1931: Financial crisis widens in the United States and Europe, which reel from bank failures and climbing unemployment levels. In London, armies of the unemployed riot.

1933: Newly inaugurated U.S. president Franklin D. Roosevelt launches the first phase of his New Deal to put depression-era America back to work.

1935: Second phase of New Deal begins with the introduction of social security, farm assistance, and housing and tax reform.

1941: Japanese bombing of Pearl Harbor on 7 December brings the United States into the war against the Axis. Combined with the attack on the Soviet Union, which makes Stalin an unlikely ally of the Western democracies, the events of 1941 will ultimately turn the tide of the war.

1944: Creation of International Monetary Fund and World Bank at Bretton Woods Conference.

Event and Its Context

The Creation of the United Fruit Company

The United Fruit Company was one of the first large multinational corporations to operate in the Western Hemisphere. The company was formed in the late nineteenth century, and by 1910 the "great white fleet" of United Fruit had more than 100 steamers that shipped goods from Latin American countries. United Fruit had several positive effects on Latin America. The company built hospitals, schools, and ports. It constructed water and sanitation facilities. The company also operated hundreds of miles of railroads in the region. United Fruit's business activities created jobs and generated tax revenue.

At the same time, United Fruit also had numerous negative effects in the region, and for many in Latin America, the company would soon come to represent the economic imperialism of the United States. United Fruit owned hundreds of thousands of acres of land in Latin America, of which only a small portion was actually cultivated. The company did not abide competition and often ruined rival planters. United Fruit management sometimes became involved in politics, bribing officials and even helping to overthrow governments. United Fruit generally opposed organized labor and exploited consumers.

The United Fruit Company in Colombia

United Fruit became involved in Colombia after 1900, particularly in the Department of Magdalena around the city of Santa Marta. The company's purpose there was to produce bananas for the international market. In 1901 the company exported about 250,000 bunches of bananas from Santa Marta; by 1929 it exported 10 million bunches, making Colombia the third largest banana producer after Jamaica and Honduras.

Once a sparsely populated area, the banana zone began to attract workers once United Fruit arrived. At first the company tried to import workers from the Caribbean. When this failed,

Jorge Eliécer Gaitán. The Library of Congress.

the company began to offer wages that were higher than those found in most of the rest of the country. These wages led to internal migration, with some 90,000 workers arriving in the region by 1928. Soon a large, landless proletariat existed in the banana zone. Most workers performed their jobs on a piecework basis through a labor contracting system. The company employed relatively few workers directly, which allowed United Fruit to ignore issues such as social security laws. At the same time, most workers were paid in scrip that was redeemable only at company stores. The situation caused resentment against the company among many workers.

Early Labor Organization in the Banana Zone

The 1928 strike against the United Fruit Company was the culmination of increasing worker organization in the banana zone. The first significant wave of labor activity in the region came between 1918 and 1920. The end of World War I had brought with it a revival of trade. As early as 1918, workers in the banana zone struck, affecting United Fruit plantations, its railroad operation, and its banana shipments. In the early 1920s United Fruit workers formed "Workers' Societies" to negotiate with the company. In 1924 dockworkers in the region called a strike and attempted to form a union. However, the government called in the military and declared the action illegal, forcing the workers to abandon their attempt to organize. Later, some

3,000–4,000 workers joined the *Sociedad Unión*, a union associated with the company. Members of this organization agreed not to make demands on the company.

The Creation of the USTM

Many of those who joined the *Sociedad Unión* also joined the *Unión Sindical de los Trabajadores del Magdalena* (USTM). Several Italian and Spanish immigrants who had been influenced by anarcho-syndicalism formed this new union in 1926. This organization was independent of company control and could make demands on United Fruit, unlike the *Sociedad Unión*. The USTM not only organized the workers in the city of Santa Marta, but also the agricultural workers who labored on the plantations. It also attempted to establish links with workers elsewhere in the country.

Two important changes took place in 1928. First, in April and August, dock and railroad workers received wage increases from United Fruit. These gains increased the prestige of the USTM and gave workers more confidence in their union. A second important development was that the leadership of the USTM had been taken over by socialists from the *Partido Socialista Revolucionaria* (PSR), which was the Colombian section of the Third International. Led by Raúl Mahecha and Alberto Castrillón, the PSR was an umbrella organization for unions and peasant leagues from the region and would play a leading role in the events of 1928.

Planning the 1928 Strike

Mahecha and Castrillón, along with José Russo, formed the USTM's executive committee, which began planning the activities to be taken against the United Fruit Company as the union gained support among the workers. In October 1928 Mahecha drew up a petition with a list of demands that the USTM would present to the company. These demands included social security for the workers, the right to collective bargaining, wage increases, and the abolition of the hated company stores. On 6 October delegates at a plenary session accepted the demands. On 28 October the union presented the demands to the company, which rejected them. In the meantime, on 19 October some 30 union members were arrested during a meeting. Despite such repression, the union moved forward, especially after a local labor inspector declared that the demands were within the law.

The 1928 Strike

The USTM leadership then declared a strike for 11 November. Some 30,000 workers participated in the strike. Picketing workers disrupted transportation in the region. Despite the fact that authorities had arrested some 400 workers by the end of November, the strikers succeeded in preventing trains of strikebreakers from reaching their destinations. The strike greatly affected the company's operations, as this was the time of the year's second major harvest. United Fruit Company ships were forced to go to Jamaica to acquire cargoes. Unable to attract enough strikebreakers, the company even offered to pay the workers for the days they missed during the strike if they would return to work.

Tensions increased in December, as national troops arrived and the Colombian president assigned General Carlos Cortés Vargas to bring the situation under control. On 3 December the

armed forces posted notices that regulations regarding public order would be more strictly enforced. Troops shot one worker who attempted to remove one of the notices. On 4 December strikebreakers left Santa Marta under armed escort. Picketing workers blocked many of the strikebreakers, although the replacement workers did cut some bananas on the plantations.

On the night of 4 December, the striking workers met in the town of Ciénaga to plan a march to Santa Marta in order to present their demands to the governor and the company. The USTM urged workers to gather in Ciénaga on 5 December. That afternoon, the USTM executive committee received a message that company and government officials were on their way to Ciénaga to agree to the strikers' demands. When they later learned that the officials were not coming, the gathering crowd grew angry and even took over one of the company trains that had been used to transport strikebreakers. A spontaneous rally occurred. The workers insisted that the planned march would indeed take place. In the meantime, thousands of men, women, and children gathered in the square in front of the train station in Ciénaga.

The Massacre

At about midnight, the military arrived in Ciénaga. General Cortés Vargas had received a declaration of a state of siege from Bogotá and brought his troops to confront the strikers. Armed troops lined the square while Cortés Vargas read the state of siege declaration and ordered the crowd to disperse. The workers refused and Cortés Vargas repeated his order. When the crowd still refused to disperse, the general gave the order to fire. The troops killed many in the crowd, and the survivors fled the scene.

It is unclear exactly how many people died in the confrontation. When government officials arrived in the morning, there were only eight bodies in the square. Decades later, however, a mass grave was discovered near the sight. Rumors indicated that many corpses had been loaded on trains, taken to the coast, and dumped into the sea. Newspaper accounts of the incident reported that several hundred people perished. Survivors of the massacres estimate the number of dead at about 2,000.

Clashes between workers and troops continued for several days as the strikers sought a measure of revenge. The state of siege continued, and civil liberties were suspended. Soon, the worker organization was destroyed. In January and February 1929 military tribunals tried more than 100 strikers. These tribunals convicted 30 workers and sentenced them to between four months and 25 years in prison, although some sentences were later commuted.

Despite the harshness with which the strike ended, the workers did gain some concessions from the company. United Fruit agreed to a gradual increase in wages, although no time frame was set. The company also promised to build hospitals and schools, as well as to improve the sanitation of worker housing.

The Political Consequences of the Strike and Massacre

The massacre of the striking banana workers had important political consequences in Colombia. The event served to discredit the ruling Conservative Party in the eyes of many Colombians. In particular, Liberal Party member Jorge Eliécer Gaitán used the massacre to paint the Conservative government as a mere puppet of United States capitalism that would even kill its own people to satisfy foreign investors. In 1930 the Liberal Party won the presidential elections after 30 years of Conservative rule. Gaitán himself used the events to increase his own political popularity, although his career was cut short when he was assassinated in 1948.

Key Players

Castrillón, Alberto: A printer from Bogotá, Castrillón was a member of the *Partido Socalista Revolucionaria* (PSR) and one of the key leaders of the 1928 strike against United Fruit. After a trip to Moscow in early 1928, he returned to Colombia, where he was arrested in July of that year. Castrillón was released in August and ordered to leave the country. However, he stayed to work with the *Unión Sindical de Trabajadores del Magdalena* (USTM). After the 1928 strike, he was tried and sentenced to 10 years in prison.

Gaitán, Jorge Eliécer (1898–1948): Colombian politician who rose to fame by attacking the Conservative Party's handling of the 1928 strike against the United Fruit Company. A member of the opposition Liberal Party, he made numerous speeches criticizing the Conservative government's willingness to kill its own people so as to protect the interests of a foreign company. Gaitán's efforts helped his Liberal Party win the 1930 elections. Gaitán himself ran for president in 1946 but lost because of a split in his party. He was assassinated in 1948.

Mahecha, Raúl (1884–1940): The son of a lawyer, Mahecha spent his life organizing Colombian workers. He played a key role in the 1911 strike movement among the transport workers on the Magdalena River. He was also the leader of a 1924 strike in Barrancebermeja. In April 1928 he was arrested for planning a strike in the banana zone but was later released. He then was one of the main organizers of the 1928 strike against United Fruit.

BIBLIOGRAPHY

Books

Brungardt, Maurice P. "The United Fruit Company in Colombia." In Henry C. Dethloff and C. Joseph Pusateri, *American Business History: Case Studies*. Arlington Heights, IL: Harlan Davidson, 1987.

Gómez, Alfredo. *Anarquismo y anarcosindicalismo en América Latina*. Barcelona, Spain: Ibérica de Ediciones y Publicaciones, 1980.

LeGrand, Catherine. "Living in Macondo: Economy and Culture in a United Fruit Company Banana Enclave in Colombia." In Gilbert Joseph, et al., *Close Encounters of Empire: Writing the Cultural History of U.S.-Latin American Relations*. Durham, NC: Duke University Press, 1998.

McGreevey, William. *An Economic History of Colombia, 1845–1930*. Cambridge, MA: Cambridge University Press, 1971.

Randall, Stephen J. *Colombia and the United States: Hegemony and Interdependence*. Athens, GA, and London: University of Georgia Press, 1992.

Rippy, J. Fred. *The Capitalists and Colombia*. New York: The Vanguard Press, 1931.

Safford, Frank, and Marco Palacios. *Colombia: Fragmented Land, Divided Society*. Oxford and New York: Oxford University Press, 2002.

White, Judith. *The United Fruit Company in the Santa Marta Banana Zone, Colombia: Conflicts of the '20s*. Ph.D. Dissertation, Oxford University Press, 1971.

Periodicals

LeGrand, Catherine. "Colombian Transformations: Peasants and Wage Laborers in the Santa Marta Banana Zone." *The Journal of Peasant Studies* 11, no. 4 (1984): 178–200.

—Ronald Young

United Mine Workers of America

United States 1890

Synopsis

The United Mine Workers of America (UMWA) is an industrial labor union that was formed in 1890 by the joining of the National Progressive Union of Miners and Mine Laborers and the Knights of Labor Trade Assembly No. 135. The UMWA had established itself as a formidable opponent to mine owners and operators by the end of its first decade of operations.

UMWA membership includes American and Canadian miners and workers in the coal and coal-related industries. The UMWA has made sustained efforts throughout its existence to bring about collective bargaining for its members. Its purpose is to win from management a wide variety of labor guarantees, such as continuity of employment, fair wages, and health and safety rules. When collective bargaining efforts failed, the UNWA often staged strikes to gain concessions from mine owners and operators. The UMWA also improved the living conditions of its members who lived in company-owned towns and who were exposed to extreme occupational hazards inherent to their jobs.

Timeline

1870: Beginning of Franco-Prussian War. German troops sweep over France, Napoleon III is dethroned, and France's Second Empire gives way to the Third Republic.

1876: Four-stroke cycle gas engine introduced.

1880: South Africa's Boers declare an independent republic, precipitating the short First Anglo-Boer War.

1883: Foundation of the League of Struggle for the Emancipation of Labor by Marxist political philosopher Georgi Valentinovich Plekhanov marks the formal start of Russia's labor movement. Change still lies far in the future for Russia, however: tellingly, Plekhanov launches the movement in Switzerland.

1886: Bombing at Haymarket Square, Chicago, kills seven policemen and injures numerous others. Eight anarchists are accused and tried; three are imprisoned, one commits suicide, and four are hanged.

1888: Serbian-born American electrical engineer Nikola Tesla develops a practical system for generating and transmitting alternating current (AC), which will ultimately—and after an extremely acrimonious battle—replace Thomas Edison's direct current (DC) in most homes and businesses.

1890: U.S. Congress passes the Sherman Antitrust Act, which in the years that follow will be used to break up large monopolies.

1890: Police arrest and kill Sioux chief Sitting Bull, and two weeks later, federal troops kill over 200 Sioux at Wounded Knee.

1890: Alfred Thayer Mahan, a U.S. naval officer and historian, publishes *The Influence of Sea Power Upon History, 1660–1783,* which demonstrates the decisive role that maritime forces have played in past conflicts. The book will have an enormous impact on world events by encouraging the major powers to develop powerful navies.

1893: Henry Ford builds his first automobile.

1896: First modern Olympic Games held in Athens.

1900: Establishment of the Commonwealth of Australia.

John Mitchell. The Library of Congress.

Event and Its Context

Two hundred coal miners met in Columbus, Ohio, in 1890 and altered the history of laborers and labor unions. The formation of the United Mine Workers of America (UMWA) brought together a remarkable group of men who were characterized by their common dedication, wisdom, and militancy. The labor union they formed eventually redefined the labor movement, not only for miners in the United States but also for workers all over the world.

Coal Is King

During the last half of the nineteenth century, coal was the most important natural resource mined in the United States. Between 1890 and 1900 the amount of coal mined in the United States nearly doubled, and it continued to do so from 1900 to 1910. Coal prices also experienced an upward spiral, although less so that the amount mined. Historians generally agree that coal powered the U.S. Industrial Revolution, a transformation that turned the country's economy into the largest and most productive in the world. The supply and demand for coal, however, often was inconsistent with the wages paid to the miners who dug the coal.

Supply and Demand

During this period of time, anthracite ("hard") and bituminous ("soft") coal were the principal resources for three important uses: the heating of homes, the powering of the expanding railroad system, and the supplying of the iron and steel industry. The uncoordinated growth of the coal industry occurred wherever scattered supplies of coal could be found, especially if the supply was conveniently located near a railroad line, navigable river, or metropolitan area.

Mines produced excess supplies of coal as demand continued to increase. The number of men employed in the coal industry increased from less than 200,000 in 1890 to more than 600,000 in 1920, mostly due to the increased number of mines in operation throughout the country. The number of mines rose from 2,500 in 1895 to 5,600 in 1914.

The miners' wages were the primary cost of coal production, and because mine owners wished to lower their costs, miners were constantly forced to accept reduced salaries. This was compounded by irregular work schedules and company-sponsored towns and stores that usually kept the workers in debt to the owners.

Unions That Came Before

During the early nineteenth century, mine owners implemented few safety and health rules for the workers. Because of this, horrible accidents frequently claimed hundreds of lives. At the same time, there was no limit to the number of hours that workers labored, no minimum wages, and no compensation for accidents. Some two million children worked in and around the mines. To combat the lack of benefits, low wages, numerous accidents, child labor, harsh conditions, unfair treatment, and other inequities, mineworkers turned to labor unions, first at the local and regional levels, and gradually at the national level.

Mineworkers had been organized into local unions in the United States since the year 1849. In that year coal miner John Bates organized a local union in the anthracite coal area of Pennsylvania. Low wages contributed to his organizing actions, as did the actions of others across the country who despaired over the rights of mineworkers. These first feeble attempts to organize the miners were no match for the well-organized mine owners. These efforts, however, ultimately led to the formation of the UMWA.

American Miners' Association

Near the end of 1860, the work of Welshman Thomas Lloyd and Englishman Daniel Weaver attracted the interest of mineworkers of southern Illinois and northern Missouri in a national union. This union, founded on 28 January 1861 as the American Miners' Association, was the first national union of mineworkers organized in the United States. It is usually credited with the beginning of the modern American labor movement. The union only lasted for a few years; it dissolved in 1868 after an unsuccessful strike weakened the organization beyond repair. Local unions continued to organize in Illinois, Indiana, Pennsylvania, Ohio, Maryland, and other coal-producing states, but because of a lack of unifying effort no national union came about.

Miners' National Association

In 1873 an industrial congress convened in Cleveland, Ohio, to find ways whereby local unions could act together for the betterment of conditions for mineworkers. Conflicts between labor and management were difficult for isolated local unions to resolve successfully. Eventually, a united effort was necessary for the mounting wrongs committed against miners. The principle result from that meeting was a call for a national union. The Miners' National Association of the United States of America was formed with John Siney as its president.

Other Unions

Other important unions during this timeframe were the Miners' and Laborers' Benevolent Association (founded in 1868 as the Workingman's Benevolent Association), the Amalgamated Association of Miners of the United States (founded in 1883), and the National Federation of Miners and Mine Laborers (founded in 1885). Each short-lived union died for a variety of disheartening reasons, including ineffectual strikes, union rivalries, disputes within unions, and depressed economic conditions.

Immigration of British Isle Miners

Approximately 60,000 experienced miners from the British Isles came to the United States around the time of the Civil War (from 1861 to 1865). They arrived in response to a great demand for skilled labor in the postwar industrial era and because of low wages and overproduction in the United Kingdom. British immigrant miners used the same methods of cutting, blasting, and loading coal as they had used earlier in England. English workers brought over an independent work ethic that had worked in their homeland. Miners would often leave the mine whenever they had earned enough money to satisfy their immediate needs. The mine owners attempted to break this habit that kept wages at high levels and reduced their profits. The un-

John McBride. AP/Wide World Photos. Reproduced by permission.

skilled immigrants from Italy, Hungary, Poland, and Greece joined the skilled British workers that immigrated to the United States. The influx of unskilled workers helped owners keep wages low. These men formed the backbone of the coal mining industry.

The Need for Unions

Arguments over control of miners' rights, such as number of work hours and wage levels, started the need for unions. In the nineteenth century there were no laws regulating the working conditions of miners. Miners were paid by the number of loads of coal taken from the earth, not by the preparatory work necessary to extract the coal, such as blasting to find coal, building timber supports for inside the mines, and clearing rocks and debris from the tracks of mine cars. Miners had little control over the price they received for a load, and the company controlled the town in which the miners lived. In the end, the miners were always in debt to the company, unable to better their condition.

Local groups of activists organized meetings to protest low pay, dangerous working conditions, child labor, lack of health care for work-related illnesses, and lack of safety rules. Regional bodies formed with more formal structure, complete with membership dues and some type of benefit system. Finally, na-

Miners working three miles underground, Pennsylvania. © Bettmann/Corbis. Reproduced by permission.

tional trade unions formed as a result of the efforts of these smaller organizations. The local and regional bodies had little success against the mighty mine owner; but the national unions had better luck, at least over the long run.

Formation of the UMWA

The founding convention of the UMWA probably represented about 17,000 coal miners and laborers belonging to two rival organizations: the National Progressive Union of Miners and Mine Laborers and the National Trade Assembly #135 of the Knights of Labor. These two unions had been competing for membership of miners. Because wage rates were radically different from state to state, the battle for miners was waged on a statewide basis. The need to gain level wages across the country forced the two unions to merge.

Constitution

The original constitution that was adopted by its founding delegates spelled out how the UMWA would attempt to improve the conditions of its members, and listed specific grievances that confronted miners. Specifically, its purpose was to:

- Secure a fair weekly wage compatible with the dangers associated with mining
- Assure wages were paid with legally recognized money (not company-sponsored "scrip")
- Minimize the hazards related to mining
- Guarantee the eight-hour day
- Abolish child labor (those under the age of 14 or without a reasonable education)
- Prevent unfair dealings by the coal companies and their operators (including private police forces employed in coal fields)

The UMWA statement of policy pledged "to use all honorable means to maintain peace between ourselves and employers; adjusting all differences, as far as possible, by arbitration and conciliation, that strikes may become unnecessary."

Wages

The most important objective for the UMWA was no doubt the wage policy. It was often generally characterized as "more and more—now." Specifically, though, the goals of the UMWA with regards to wage policy were:

- Consistent improvement of the economic status of miners in relation to workers in other industries

- Stabilization of wage rates during times of downward cyclical markets

- Fair competitive relationships among mine owners in localized coal-producing areas of the country

- Use of wage agreements that did not give competitive advantage to any geographical area, so members would have an equal opportunity to work anywhere in the country

Only a national union was in a position to succeed at obtaining such a wage policy. Although the UMWA announced and tried to achieve these stated goals during its first fledgling years as a union, its primary goal was simply to survive. It had yet to achieve recognition from the mine owners, and it had yet to achieve a stable organization with its members working together for the common good of all.

Other Policies

The UMWA concerned itself with policies that affected its overall membership in a general way; it also addressed concerns of lesser scope. For example, despite many racist beliefs of the time, the UMWA established a nondiscrimination policy that miners should be hired and compensated without regard to race, religion, or national origin. It specifically drew attention to men of African descent. At a time when the rights of African Americans were mostly restricted, this uncompromising position was forward-looking. The UMWA leadership realized that discriminatory practices were ethically wrong, but, just as important in their view, such practices limited its membership roster. The eventual success of the UMWA was based partially on a large, unsegregated membership.

Fred Ball, a union president in a West Virginia coal town in the early 1900s, aptly expressed the united nature of the UMWA when he said, "I call it a darn solid mass of different colors and tribes blended together, woven, bound, interlocked, tongued and grooved and glued together in one body." The fact remained that the mine operators continued to work *all* miners as if they were slaves, regardless of who they were. The union tried to abolish that slavelike system and attempted to more fairly balance the power between the corporate owners and the workers.

Within a few years of the founding of the UMWA the scope of its charter expanded. Craftsmen who worked indirectly in and around the mines, such as blacksmiths, could disrupt the work of the miners when they struck. As a result, the UMWA adopted a policy called the Scranton Declaration of December 1901 by which the union was able to organize all workers in and around the mines.

President Rae (1890–1892)

The initial membership of the UMWA consisted almost entirely of native-born or British immigrant miners from the states running east from Illinois to West Virginia, and south to Alabama. They elected Knights of Labor leader John B. Rae as president on 25 January 1890, marking the formal unification of organized miners into the United Mine Workers of America. The 17,000 charter members of the founding UMWA rapidly grew to 53,000 within a year.

When Rae took office, he inherited several strikes that eventually failed because of economic conditions at the time. The resulting losses drained the new union's treasury as Rae tried to coordinate better benefits for his members, among them the eight-hour workday. At the 1892 convention, Rae refused to run for reelection after learning that the miners were not ready for another concerted drive for shorter work hours.

Establishment at End of First Decade

During the first decade of the UMWA's existence, differences occurred between the subgroups within the union and with mineworkers who were not yet in the union. The unions that merged to form the UMWA still existed within the national union, and internal strife occurred as the UMWA tried to coordinate the various factions. Mine operators rarely recognized the union, and efforts to centralize decision-making and coordinate activities rarely succeeded. Coordination among the miners did grow slowly as communications improved. The creation of the *UMW Journal* in February 1891 provided an effective way to trade information. Solidarity grew as miners saw that similar conditions and complaints occurred throughout the industry. It was not until the end of its first decade that the UMWA became a strong and established national union able to bargain effectively with mine owners.

John McBride took over as president of the United Mine Workers of America in 1892. Membership was only 20,000 at the time, and the treasury held only $10,000. The union had a dismal record of defeats. The UMWA sank to its worst level in 1893 when a depression hit the United States. The coal industry's two primary markets—railroads and industry—drastically reduced demand, leaving only the home heating market as a viable income source. By 1894, when McBride left the presidency, membership was down to 13,000, a decline of more than 40 percent within a year.

With McBride as president, the UMWA called for a strike to raise wages that had declined because of an abundance of workers and a lack of demand for coal. About 100,000 men stopped work on 21 April 1894, and eventually 180,000 of the country's 193,000 bituminous coal miners joined the stoppage. The strike helped to consolidate the union, garnered needed national attention, and increased membership.

Economic difficulties in the nation and continued internal strife kept the union from substantial advancement during the years of president Phil Penna (1894–1896). The UMWA was in trouble, as were many unions of that day, but Penna was enthusiastic about his job and was able to raise the spirits of the miners. Nevertheless, conditions worked against the union, as the whole country became economically oppressed, with many families on the verge of starvation. At the end of Penna's term, membership had declined further to under 10,000, and the union's treasury held less than $300. In 1896 a disheartened Penna resigned to become labor commissioner for the Indiana coal operators.

In 1896 Michael Ratchford became president with the UMWA at an extremely low point in its brief history. Because wage rates continued to decline as the country barely returned to economic normalcy, Ratchford called a national strike for miners on 4 July 1897. Fearing that the U.S. government would institute an injunction against the union for restraint of trade,

Ratchford cautiously proceeded with the strike in hopes of driving up wages and reinstituting interstate bargaining. Around 150,000 miners eventually joined the 12-week strike, along with strong support from Samuel Gompers of the American Federation of Labor. The strike was successful, mainly because an upturn in coal demand coincided with the end of the depression and a return to economic prosperity. Many coal owners eventually agreed to a 20 percent wage increase, with a promise to meet for an interstate conference. In an era when union victories were rare, this achievement helped to strengthen labor with regard to labor-management relations in the coal industry.

Historians claim that this strike was a major turning point in the history of the UMWA. The struggle by American mineworkers that ended with victory prompted thousands of mineworkers to return to the union. As a result, Ratchford gained a national reputation as a great labor statesman. Union membership rapidly increased to 34,000, and the treasury contained $11,000.

John Mitchell became president of the UMWA in 1898 and remained its boss until his retirement in 1908. He was the first president to serve an extended term. Mitchell was responsible for increasing membership (from 34,000 to 300,000 workers) across the country and into Canada, centralizing the power of the national union while expanding the democratic nature of the union; improving wages and working conditions, and promoting collective bargaining. Under Mitchell's leadership, the UMWA finally won the fight for an eight-hour workday. Mitchell maintained that the interests of labor and capital coincided. During Mitchell's tenure mine owners benefited from a relatively peaceful labor force, uninterrupted production, and a decline in competition (which meant higher profits for them). Union miners benefited from higher wages, more regular work, protection against favoritism and discrimination, and assurance that their grievances would be heard.

Turning Point

The turning point for the UMWA came in January 1898, at the end of Ratchford's watch, when an interstate conference convened in conjunction with the UMWA convention. Coal mine owners at this time realized that extensive competition was threatening their livelihood. Operators agreed with the union that a stable and competitive wage rate was important to the industry and the workers alike. At this time, owners also realized the need for a union to control nonunion workers who were threatening certain markets. The mine owners, for the first time, collectively recognized the UMWA. It was at this conference (and at another one in 1902 during Mitchell's tenure) that collective bargaining became an accepted principle in the coal mining regions of Illinois, Indiana, Ohio, and western Pennsylvania. This joint agreement, complete with the newly created collective bargaining agreement, was the major event that allowed the UMWA to expand and eventually made the United Mine Workers of America one of the largest labor unions in the world.

In the history of North American labor, the United Mine Workers of America has occupied a prominent position of undeniable leadership. The UMWA led the struggle to establish industrial health and safety laws and collective bargaining in the United States. Its principles and policies, along with the de-termination of its leaders, have been a testament to working families of coal miners since its formation in 1890.

Key Players

McBride, John: McBride, from Ohio, served as vice chairman at the UMWA founding convention in 1890. He was UMWA president from 1892 to 1894, succeeding Rae to become its second president. His father had been a loyal trade unionist, and McBride followed his father's lead, working the mines starting at 15 years of age. He was a charter member of Lodge No. 15 of the Miners and Laborers Benevolent Association and was its secretary until the lodge merged into the Miners' National Association. In 1882 he helped organize the Ohio Miners' Amalgamated Association and became its president. In 1889 he became president of the Miners' National Progressive Union. Mc-Bride resigned the UMWA to become president of the American Federation of Labor.

Mitchell, John (1870–1919): Mitchell, from Illinois, was vice president of the UMWA before becoming the fifth UMWA president in 1898, and continued as president until 1908. Under Mitchell's leadership, UMWA's membership rose from 34,000 to 300,000 members. Two of Mitchell's greatest accomplishments was bringing together diverse cultural and ethnic groups within the union and acquiring a long-lasting contract for his workers that guaranteed an eight-hour workday and a minimum wage. Mitchell was the key figure in spreading the UMWA across the United States and into Canada and in modernizing and democratizing the union's structure. Mitchell was known for seeking out peaceful reconciliations to labor disputes.

Penna, Phil H.: Penna, from Indiana, was the third UMWA president, serving from 1894 to 1896. Previous to this, Penna was the UMWA's vice president under McBride. The lowest point for the union occurred during Penna's reign, due mostly to poor economic conditions in the country that lead to unemployment and to the low wages that ensued. Membership in the UMWA declined to 10,000 near the end of his term. Penna unhappily left to become labor commissioner for the Indiana coal operators.

Rae, John B.: Rae, from Pennsylvania, was the first president of the UMWA, serving from 1890 to 1892. Born in Scotland, Rae had been a miner from early childhood and believed strongly in trade unions. He had become involved with the Knights of Labor in Pennsylvania and was one of the organizers of the National Trade Assembly No. 135. Rae was present when the United Mine Workers of America was founded, having been chosen to preside over the convention, previous to being elected its first president.

Ratchford, Michael: Ratchford, from Ohio, was the fourth UMWA president, serving from 1896 to 1898. During his tenure UMWA membership expanded rapidly to 40,000 members, and the union attained agreement for the eight-hour workday on 1 April 1898. During his presidency, Ratchford called the first meeting of what later was known as the Annual Joint Conference of Coal Miners and Operators of Illinois, Indiana, Ohio, and Western Pennsylvania. Many historians state that the conference was a major stabilizing factor for the union during the next 30 years. It was the first national agreement that any important industry in the country had made with its workers. Ratchford resigned to accept a position on the United States Industrial Commission.

See also: *Bituminous Coal Strike; Knights of Labor; Workingman's Benevolent Association.*

BIBLIOGRAPHY

Books

Baratz, Morton S. *The Union and the Coal Industry.* Port Washington, NY: Kennikat Press, 1955.

Corbin, David. *Life, Work, and Rebellion in the Coal Fields.* Urbana and Chicago: University of Illinois Press, 1981.

Evans, Chris. *History of United Mine Workers of America from the Year 1860 to 1890.* Indianapolis, IN: Allied Printing, 1918.

Fox, Maier B. *United We Stand: The United Mine Workers of America 1890–1990.* United Mine Workers of America, 1990.

Laslett, John H. M., ed. *The United Mine Workers of America: A Model of Industrial Solidarity?* University Park, PA: The Pennsylvania State University Press, 1996.

Richards, Elizabeth Levy Tad. *Struggle and Lose, Struggle and Win: The United Mine Workers.* New York: Four Winds Press, 1977.

—William Arthur Atkins

Matewan and Mingo County, 1920

The setting of the 1987 motion picture *Matewan* is Mingo County, in West Virginia's coal-mining country, during a 1920 conflict between unions and mine owners. Today this part of West Virginia, along the Kentucky border, is economically depressed from the gradual decline of the coal-mining industry, but in 1920, the people of Mingo faced other problems. In that year, when the miners attempted to start a union, the coal companies responded by bringing in scabs—and since the scabs were black and Italian, this only heightened animosity among the white Protestant coal miners.

Yet as *Matewan* shows, eventually the working men found common cause under the leadership of union activist and former Wobbly Joe Kenehan (Chris Cooper). Based on an actual incident, *Matewan* includes a number of real figures from the Mingo County of 1920: Sid Hatfield (David Strathairn), Cabell Testerman (Josh Mostel), C. E. Lively (Bob Gunton), and Few Clothes Johnson (James Earl Jones).

Two matters of trivia should be noted. First, filming of the movie took place in Thurmond, a ghost town about 150 miles east of Matewan. Abandoned along with the mines, Thurmond had the authentic look of a West Virginia coal-mining town of the 1920s. Also notable is the last name of Sid Hatfield, a policeman who became a hero of the miners for his defense of them. (He was gunned down by company detectives in 1921.) Though Mingo is part of the same area from which the famous feuding Hatfields and McCoys came, Sid Hatfield apparently was not related to *the* Hatfields.

Source: John Sayles. *Thinking in Pictures: The Making of the Movie Matewan.* Boston: Houghton-Mifflin, 1987.

—Judson Knight

United Mine Workers Strike

United States 1919

Synopsis

When a large number of coal miners in the Belleville subdistrict of Illinois struck briefly in early July 1919 to protest the jailing of labor activist Tom Mooney, they were fined under the terms of their union contract. When the subdistrict's coal operators declined to return those fines, miners ignored local union officials' pleas and voted to stop work altogether. The contract providing for the fines had been drawn up under the so-called Washington Agreement that addressed the economic pressures of World War I and extended until 1 April 1920. The strike spread despite union officials' moves to stop it. When the United Mine Workers' (UMW) national convention convened the following month in Cleveland, the 2,000 delegates present voted to strike on 1 November if a new contract providing for a 30-hour workweek and 60 percent wage increase were not negotiated by then. When no such contract was forthcoming, 425,000 coal miners nationwide went on strike. Almost imme-

diately, the government took steps to end the strike. President Woodrow Wilson declared the strike unlawful, and federal troops were ordered into the minefields of several states. In response to an 8 November federal court order, acting UMW President John L. Lewis ordered the miners back to work. The miners, however, continued the strike for nearly a month. When President Wilson proposed an immediate wage increase of 14 percent and an arbitration panel to consider further demands, miners finally returned to work. Unhappy with the eventual settlement, the miners staged a number of wildcat work stoppages into 1920, and all work had stopped in Illinois and Indiana by the summer of 1920. Labor unrest in coal mining country continued on and off into 1923.

Timeline

1900: China's Boxer Rebellion, which began in the preceding year with attacks on foreigners and Christians, reaches its height. An international contingent of more than

2,000 men arrives to restore order, but only after several tens of thousands have died.

1907: U.S. markets experience a financial panic.

1912: *Titanic* sinks on its maiden voyage, from Southampton to New York, on 14 April. More than 1,500 people are killed.

1915: At the Second Battle of Ypres, the Germans introduce a terrifying new weapon: poison gas.

1917: The intercepted "Zimmermann Telegram" reveals a plot by the German government to draw Mexico into an alliance against the United States in return for a German promise to return the southwestern U.S. territories taken in the Mexican War. Three months later, in response to German threats of unrestricted submarine warfare, the United States on 6 April declares war on Germany.

1919: Formation of the Third International (Comintern), whereby the Bolshevik government of Russia establishes its control over communist movements worldwide.

1919: Treaty of Versailles signed by the Allies and Germany but rejected by the U.S. Senate. This is due in part to rancor between President Woodrow Wilson and Republican Senate leaders, and in part to concerns over Wilson's plan to commit the United States to the newly established League of Nations and other international duties. Not until 1921 will Congress formally end U.S. participation in the war, but it will never agree to join the League.

1919: Ratification of the Eighteenth Amendment, which prohibits the production, sale, distribution, purchase, and consumption of alcohol throughout the United States.

1919: In India, Mahatma Gandhi launches his campaign of nonviolent resistance to British rule.

1919: In Italy, a former socialist of the left named Benito Mussolini introduces the world to a new socialism of the right, embodied in an organization known as the "Union for Struggle," or Fasci di Combattimento. Composed primarily of young war veterans discontented with Italy's paltry share of the spoils from the recent world war (if not with their country's lackluster military performance in the conflict), the fascists are known for their black shirts and their penchant for violence.

1921: As the Allied Reparations Commission calls for payments of 132 billion gold marks, inflation in Germany begins to climb.

1925: European leaders attempt to secure the peace at the Locarno Conference, which guarantees the boundaries between France and Germany, and Belgium and Germany.

1929: On "Black Friday" in October, prices on the U.S. stock market, which had been climbing wildly for several years, suddenly collapse. Thus begins the first phase of a world economic crisis and depression that will last until the beginning of World War II.

Event and Its Context

What began as a relatively fleeting series of strikes cutting across a number of industries triggered several years of labor strife in America's coal fields. During the week of 4 July 1919, unions across the country staged strikes to protest the arrest of San Francisco–based radical labor activist Tom Mooney on grounds that many found questionable. The strikes were widespread among coal miners in the Belleville subdistrict of southeastern Illinois, not far from St. Louis.

When their next paychecks arrived, Belleville area miners who had participated in the strikes discovered that they had been fined for their participation in these work stoppages. Their existing contract, which had been drawn up under the so-called Washington Agreement, levied a fine of one dollar per day on any miner who went on strike. The Washington Agreement took effect in 1917, the year the United States entered World War I, and was intended to help deal with pressures imposed by the war on the domestic economy. Labor contracts negotiated under the agreement all carried penalty clauses with fines and firings for workers who participated in work stoppages. The agreement strictly limited the size of wage increases that could be granted under contracts negotiated while the agreement was in effect. Although World War I ended in the fall of 1918, the agreement was scheduled to remain in force until 1 April 1920. This rankled workers in many industries who saw themselves falling behind financially as price increases exceeded the wage hikes that could be negotiated under the agreement. Harry Garfield, head of the United States Fuel Administration under President Wilson, administered the agreement.

Furious about the fines, Belleville area miners demanded that the mine owners return the fine monies. When the miners heard that the owners had refused to do so, the miners demanded that local union officials call a meeting to discuss the situation. When union officials declined to do so, workers held an impromptu meeting of their own and voted a resolution declaring the fines for participating in the Mooney work stoppages illegal and unjustified. They also voted to stop work in protest. Despite the efforts of local UMW officials to nip the strike in the bud, the work stoppages quickly spread to other mining operations in the region. The UMW called a meeting of miners in the district in the hope they could win approval of a couple of resolutions, one of which called upon miners to return to work and fight through regular channels to win changes in policy. The other resolution was essentially a statement of general union policy reflecting the strong socialist tradition of Illinois miners. The policy resolution passed overwhelmingly at the union meeting, attended by nearly 2,000 area miners. However, the resolution to end the strike was voted down, and the miners instead decided to try to spread the strike even further.

Although the Illinois miners initially went on strike to protest the Mooney fines, the rationale for the action was soon broadened to include a demand for a new labor contract with no penalty clause and a new wage scale. The attempts of local UMW officials to end the strike were uniformly unsuccessful. In desperation, Frank Farrington, president of the UMW's Illinois district, sent out this appeal to all member miners across the state: "Our union is facing a crisis. The elements of destruction are at work. The issue is: Shall the forces of defiance and rebellion prevail and stab our union to death, or shall reason and orderly procedure dominate the affairs of the United Mine Workers of America?" After Farrington's appeal failed to sway the striking miners, the UMW sought to undercut the effects of the strike by supplying strikebreakers so that the struck mines could be reopened. Further, union members loyal to the local leadership were sworn in as special deputy sheriffs to arrest striking miners. In many cases, these deputies were paid directly from the union coffers. The tactics used by union leaders to try to break the strike angered strikers, who now resolved to continue until all of the UMW's state officers had resigned their jobs.

Having failed to bring the insurgent miners back under their control through other means, Illinois UMW officials next sought to reassert their authority at the state UMW convention. They passed a resolution to end the strike on the grounds that bargaining on a new contract was scheduled to begin shortly. To win approval for their plan, however, union leaders agreed to adopt the contract demands of the striking miners. The strikers' demands became the basis for the rank-and-file program at the national UMW convention one month later. At that convention in Cleveland, Ohio, the face-off between union leaders and the rank and file transferred to the national stage. Despite resistance from union leaders, delegates to the national convention voted overwhelmingly to seek a new contract calling for a 60 percent wage increase and a 30-hour workweek. They also set a strike date of 1 November if management had refused to negotiate such a contract by that date.

Overwhelmed by the will of the rank and file, UMW leaders were forced to begin negotiations with coal operators to seek a new contract. When they were unable to hammer out a satisfactory agreement by 1 November, 425,000 miners went on strike. The federal government mobilized immediately to end the massive work stoppage. President Wilson said the strike was "not only unjustifiable but unlawful." Attorney General A. Mitchell Palmer convinced a federal judge to issue an injunction barring UMW leaders from taking any action to further the strike. The judge also ordered the union's pension fund sequestered. Federal troops were moved into the coal fields of New Mexico, Oklahoma, Pennsylvania, Utah, and Washington. One week after the strike began, the federal court ordered UMW leaders to rescind the strike order and direct the miners to return to work. Acting UMW President John L. Lewis complied and announced the rescission of the strike call, declaring, "We are Americans, we cannot fight our government."

Miners were not persuaded by Lewis's patriotic plea for a return to work. They continued the strike for more than a month and were gratified when they saw the effects of their work stoppage on the national economy. A number of schools were forced to close for lack of heat, railroad operations were cut back sharply, numerous factories closed, and the federal government began rationing coal. Even after President Wilson had proposed an immediate wage hike of 14 percent and the convening of an arbitration board to consider other demands, the miners resisted the urgings of the UMW leadership to end the strike. Finally, after another powerful plea from Lewis, the miners began to return to work in mid-December, although there were holdouts in some mining regions.

Although the miners had returned to work in late 1919, all was not well on the coal industry's labor front. In his report to

the UMW's national convention in January 1920, Lewis explained that the obvious determination of the federal government to end the strike was a major factor in the decision by union leaders to accept the settlement plan proposed by President Wilson. Philip Murray, president of UMW District 5, moved that the Lewis report be accepted by affirmation, suggesting that such a vote would prove delegates' loyalty to the union, its officers, and the country. Critics of the settlement argued that they should not move so quickly. A delegate from District 12 in Illinois contended that it was better to go to jail to defend one's rights than to back down on a matter of principle. He also called for the ouster of Lewis from the union's presidency. In the end, the report was approved by a lopsided vote of 1,639 to 231, but it was clear that there were pockets of dissent within the union.

The underlying unhappiness of the rank and file became increasingly apparent in the early years of the new decade. In mid-1920, 85,000 miners in the anthracite coal fields struck. Despite earnest efforts by UMW leaders to bring an early end to the strike, it continued for nearly a month. In May 1920 a strike broke out in Mattewan, West Virginia, over the firing of members of a new union. The strike spread throughout Mingo County, West Virginia, and into nearby Pike County, Kentucky. Attempts to bring the strike to an end sparked violence. In April 1922 the UMW ordered strikes in both anthracite and bituminous coal fields. Some 75,000 nonunion miners in and around the Connellsville coke region of Pennsylvania joined in the strike with the union miners. In July the federal government moved to reopen the nation's mines. President Warren Harding told coal operators to resume operations, pledging the full support of the U.S. government. The governors of Ohio and Pennsylvania ordered state troops to the mines, and union strikers finally accepted a settlement, abandoning the nonunion miners in Pennsylvania to their fate. Those miners continued to strike for a total of 16 months but were finally starved out.

After 1923 an uneasy peace settled over the coal industry, at least for a couple of decades, but it was probably attributable less to any particular satisfaction among rank-and-file miners than an end to the post-World War I coal boom amid increasing competition from other energy sources. As the coal industry weakened, the clout of the UMW declined accordingly.

Key Players

Garfield, Harry Augustus (1863–1942): Born in Hiram, Ohio, Garfield was the first son of James Abram Garfield, future president of the United States. He served the administration of President Woodrow Wilson as wartime fuel administrator, presiding over the decision to extend the so-called Washington Agreement after the World War I until 1 April 1920. It was this decision that initially triggered the United Mine Workers strike of 1919. Both before and after this period of public service, Garfield served as president of Williams College in Massachusetts.

Lewis, John L. (1880–1969): The son of Welsh immigrants, Lewis was born in the coal mining town of Cleveland, Iowa. After completing all but his final year of high school, he went to work in the mines and by 1901 had been elected secretary of a UMW local. He quickly worked his way up through the ranks of union leadership and become an AFL organizer in 1911. He returned to the UMW as its statistician in 1917. A year later he was named acting vice president and in 1919 became acting president. The year after the 1919 strike, Lewis was elected UMW president, a position he held until his retirement in 1960.

Wilson, Thomas Woodrow (1856–1924): A native of Staunton, Virginia, Wilson began his career as an academic, teaching political science at Bryn Mawr, Wesleyan, and Princeton. In 1902 he was named president of Princeton, and in 1910 he was persuaded to run as the Democratic candidate for governor of New Jersey. He won handily and proved himself both a masterful administrator and politician. In 1912 he was elected president of the United States. Wilson declared the 1919 strike of the UMW unlawful. He is perhaps best remembered for his role in creating the League of Nations, for which he later received the Nobel Peace Prize.

See also: *United Mine Workers of America.*

BIBLIOGRAPHY

Books

Brecher, Jeremy. *Strike!* Rev. ed. Cambridge, MA: South End Press, 1997.

Dictionary of American Biography, Suppl. 3: 1941–1945. New York: Scribner, 1973.

Dictionary of American Biography, Suppl. 8: 1966–1970. New York: American Council of Learned Societies, 1988.

Carson, Thomas. *Gale Encyclopedia of U.S. Economic History.* Farmington Hills, MI: Gale Group, 1999.

Other

Marcus, Irwin, Eileen Mountjoy Cooper, and Beth O'Leary. "The Coal Strike of 1919 in Indiana County and Its Aftermath." IUP Libraries Special Collections and Archives. *Coal Dust: The Early Mining Industry of Indiana County.* 26 July 2000 [24 September 2002]. <http://www.lib.iup.edu/spec_coll/articles/coalstrike1919.html>.

ADDITIONAL RESOURCES

Books

Laslett, John H. M., ed. *The United Mine Workers of America: A Model of Industrial Solidarity?* State College: Pennsylvania State University Press, 1996.

Long, Priscilla. *Where the Sun Never Shines: A History of America's Bloody Coal Industry.* St. Paul, MN: Paragon House, 1989.

—Don Amerman

United States Joins International Labor Organization

United States 1934

Synopsis

After 15 years on the sidelines of the League of Nations and its sister organization, the International Labor Organization (ILO), the United States entered the ILO in 1934. Although the United States continued to show antipathy toward the League of Nations and Republican presidents shunned the ILO, the arrival of President Franklin D. Roosevelt (FDR) and his New Deal measures fostered a change of attitude. Labor Secretary Frances Perkins convinced Roosevelt to seek congressional approval to join the ILO. New Hampshire governor John Winant become the ILO's first American director general, and the United States quickly became an influential member of the organization, with key leadership roles over the coming decades.

Timeline

1919: Formation of the Third International (Comintern), whereby the Bolshevik government of Russia establishes its control over communist movements worldwide.

1924: In the United States, Secretary of the Interior Albert B. Fall, along with oil company executives Harry Sinclair and Edward L. Doheny, is charged with conspiracy and bribery in making fraudulent leases of U.S. Navy oil reserves at Teapot Dome, Wyoming. The resulting Teapot Dome scandal clouds the administration of President Warren G. Harding.

1929: On "Black Friday" in October, prices on the U.S. stock market, which had been climbing wildly for several years, suddenly collapse. Thus begins the first phase of a world economic crisis and depression that will last until the beginning of World War II.

1931: Financial crisis widens in the United States and Europe, which reel from bank failures and climbing unemployment levels. In London, armies of the unemployed riot.

1934: Austrian chancellor Engelbert Dollfuss, who aligns his nation with Mussolini's Italy, establishes a fascist regime in an attempt to keep Austria out of the Nazi orbit. Austrian Nazis react by assassinating Dollfuss.

1934: Dionne sisters, the first quintuplets to survive beyond infancy, are born in Canada.

1937: Japan attacks China, and annexes most of that nation's coastal areas.

1939: After years of loudly denouncing one another (and quietly cooperating), the Nazis and Soviets sign a non-aggression pact in August. This clears the way for the Nazi invasion of Poland, and for Soviet action against Finland. (Stalin also helps himself to a large portion of Poland.)

1942: Axis conquests reach their height in the middle of this year. The Nazis control a vast region from Normandy to the suburbs of Stalingrad, and from the Arctic Circle

John Gilbert Winant. © Hulton/Getty Images. Reproduced by permission.

to the edges of the Sahara. To the east, the Japanese "Co-Prosperity Sphere" encompasses territories from China to Burma to the East Indies, stretching deep into the western Pacific.

1945: April sees the death of three leaders: Roosevelt passes away on 12 April; the Italians execute Mussolini and his mistress on 28 April; and Hitler (along with Eva Braun, propaganda minister Josef Goebbels, and Goebbels's family) commits suicide on 30 April.

1949: Establishment of North Atlantic Treaty Organization (NATO).

Event and Its Context

History of the ILO

The International Labor Organization (ILO) was founded in 1919 under the Treaty of Versailles, which established the League of Nations. The ILO's goal was to advance social and economic justice and ensure adequate human rights for working people worldwide. Ironically, although the United States was not among the 42 founding members of the ILO, the organization's founding conference was held in Washington, D.C. Samuel Gompers, president of the American Federation of Labor

(AFL), presided over the conference and helped draft the ILO constitution. In a lengthy speech to delegates, Gompers hailed this attempt by workers as a measure that might enable them to engage productively in "the work of going further every hour of every day . . . of pressing forward the claims of labor for a higher and better life, for more freedom, for more justice."

The ILO's governing body was conceived as a tripartite entity representing governments, labor unions, and employers. British convention delegates, who cited industrial nations' successful mobilization of labor and capital in industrialized nations during World War I, successfully proposed this model at the convention. Gompers spoke out against the proposal based on his view of society as the sum of two groups: "the employed and the employing." Gompers, a former socialist, cooperated with Europe's labor unions but defended the idea that American unions should shun party affiliations and social movements and deal exclusively with concrete issues such as better working conditions, wages, and benefits. In 1919–1920 the U.S. Congress rejected entry both into the League of Nations and into the ILO.

Given that the U.S. Senate failed to ratify the Treaty of Versailles and Republican presidents were critical of both the ILO and the League of Nations, the United States could not take part in the new organization. Even without the participation of this key industrial nation, the ILO nonetheless prospered in its early years, becoming an effective and dynamic organization. In its first three years of existence, the organization adopted 16 conventions and 18 recommendations dealing with key labor issues. These included the eight-hour workday and the 48-hour workweek, night work for women and young people, maternity benefits, and protection for maritime and farm workers. When governments opposed ILO standards and rights, the ILO took them before the International Court of Justice, which recognized the body's authority in cases heard between 1922 and 1926. Research programs commissioned experts to perform extensive firsthand field research, conduct studies, and create a database, all of which served to reinforce the authority status granted by the International Court. Although the growing resistance of some governments to the labor organization's work slowed down lawmaking activities, the membership continued its outreach to less advanced economies in Asia, Africa, and Latin America. In 1930 the Forced Labor Convention (one of the ILO's "core" conventions) called for an end to forced or compulsory labor in all its forms.

Changing Attitudes

In the United States, sentiments toward the ILO began to change. Years of economic depression, the departure of Republicans from the White House, and the advent of Roosevelt's New Deal paved the way for entry into the international organization. In its 1932 and 1933 conventions, the AFL reversed its earlier stance to pass resolutions supporting U.S. entry into the ILO. Even so, the union was not united on the issue of membership. Favoring negotiation over legislative protections, a dissident faction argued that any conventions voted by the ILO were likely to be a lot weaker than the ones that American unions already had or should achieve through collective bargaining.

The election of FDR had brought a new, prolabor message to the White House. For some, evidence of Roosevelt's concern for the plight of American workers came with his appointment of Frances Perkins, a social reformer known for her fight for improved workplace conditions, as secretary of labor in 1933. Perkins, as well as Commissioner of Labor Statistics Isador Lubin, had long been supportive of U.S. membership in the ILO. In June of that year, Congress moved further toward the ILO agenda with approval of the National Recovery Act, which aimed to eliminate child labor, limit workweek hours, and raise industrial wages. In 1934, with the Roosevelt administration continuing to push for economic recovery and improved worker conditions, Perkins convinced the president to present Congress with legislation authorizing him to apply for ILO membership. Perkins worked actively to mobilize congressional support, arguing that ILO standards would support the goals of the New Deal. On 19 June 1934 the Senate and the House of Representatives approved Joint Resolution 43, which gave approval for the United States to enter the ILO. The resolution authorized the president to accept memberships for the United States but not to assume obligation under the League of Nations covenant. On 22 June the International Labor Conference adopted a resolution inviting the American government to accede to the ILO. On 20 August, Roosevelt accepted the invitation.

Entry of the United States

Despite continued antipathy toward the League of Nations, the United States entered the ILO in 1934. The 1919 conven-

tion, nonetheless, was not a priority for either the federal government or the American public and was not ratified. Even so, Americans would hold leading roles in the organization for the greater part of the next half century. ILO membership would also serve as a means to monitor closely the League of Nations. Although the U.S. government would not officially enter the world organization, numerous Americans served on its committees.

In October 1934 Roosevelt contacted John G. Winant, third-term governor of New Hampshire, and asked him to consider representing the United States as its first representative to the ILO. Despite his Republican affiliation, Winant was a supporter of FDR and the New Deal and was sympathetic to ILO goals of improving the living conditions of workers worldwide. He had already had indirect contact with international labor as an officer of the American Association for Labor Legislation, one of the U.S. bodies pushing for social insurance. Harold Butler, the British director general of the ILO, embraced the idea with the goal of grooming Winant to succeed him. Although New Hampshire Republicans wanted Winant to run for the Senate in 1936 and many in the GOP saw him as presidential material, the governor was most interested in pursuing the cause of peace and economic justice internationally. In April 1935 Winant sailed to Europe to become the assistant director of the ILO. After just four months in Geneva, Winant was asked by Roosevelt to return to the United States to take on the post of chairman of the newly established, three-member, bipartisan Social Security Board (SSB). Winant accepted and returned to head the SSB in October. Winant had nonetheless done in four months what he could not achieve in New Hampshire in a decade: he got the ILO Conference to accept the 40-hour workweek as an international standard. In 1936 he took up his post as assistant director of the ILO and showed particular interest in the elaboration of social security programs worldwide. In 1939 Winant succeeded Butler to become the ILO's third director general (and the first American in that position). He served in that post until 1941.

The birth of Social Security in the United States had direct ties to the ILO. Winant was both ILO deputy director and chairman of the SSB. Grace Abbott, who served on Roosevelt's Council on Economic Security from 1934 to 1935 and helped plan the Social Security system, also served as the American delegate to the ILO in 1935 and 1937. The ILO provided technical support in designing U.S. Social Security legislation.

Despite the U.S. role in the ILO, many Americans continued to fight against membership. Some of those were isolationists who saw no reason to yield to a global organization. Others saw the ILO as a threat to freedom-of-contract provisions in the U.S. Constitution.

In 1944, the ILO met in Philadelphia to reaffirm its authority and plan its postwar agenda; the Philadelphia declaration revised the 1919 constitution but reaffirmed the ILO's original mission. The United States continued to play an active role in the ILO, though the cold war at times made it a challenge to maintain the ILO's global character. Although the League of Nations had been dissolved, the ILO survived to join the United Nations system in 1946. American leadership returned with David A. Morse, who served as director general from 1948 to 1970. The Soviet Union (which joined the ILO in 1934) halted participation in 1937 and did not resume until 1954. The United States, in protest over the perceived immunity of Soviet-bloc nations to criticism of their own working conditions and over the deterioration of the ILO's tripartite structure, withdrew temporarily in 1977. When ILO leadership had taken measures to return to its founding principles, the United States returned in 1980 and continued to support the organization. By the end of the century, the ILO had adopted more than 180 conventions and 190 recommendations.

Key Players

Abbott, Grace (1878–1939): An American social worker who specialized in child welfare and immigrant living conditions, Abbott served as a member of President Franklin D. Roosevelt's Council on Economic Security (1934–1935) and as U.S delegate to the ILO in 1935 and 1937.

Gompers, Samuel (1850–1924): Gompers was an English-born American labor leader. As head of the American Federation of Labor, he chaired the committee that drafted the ILO constitution at its founding convention in 1919.

Perkins, Frances (1882–1965): Perkins was an American social reformer who lobbied for better working conditions. Roosevelt appointed her secretary of labor in 1933, making her the first woman in U.S. history to hold a cabinet position. She pushed for U.S. entry into the ILO and helped design the Social Security system. She served until 1945 (longer than any other secretary of labor), resigning to head the U.S. delegation to the ILO conference in Paris.

Winant, John Gilbert (1889–1947): A former governor of New Hampshire, Winant was the first chairman of the Social Security Board. He was deputy director of the ILO (1935–1938) and later served as the organization's third director general, the first American to hold that position (1939–1941).

BIBLIOGRAPHY

Books

McHenry, Robert, ed. "Abbott, Grace." In *Her Heritage: A Biographical Encyclopedia of Famous American Women*. Interactive Multimedia. Cambridge, MA: Pilgrim New Media, 1994.

Other

AFL-CIO Culture and History. "Frances Perkins (1880–1965)" [cited 24 October 2002]. <http://laborday.aflcio.org/gallery/perkins.cfm>.

DeWitt, Larry. "John G. Winant: The First Chairman of the Social Security Board." Social Security Administration. May 1999 [cited 24 October 2002]. <http://www.ssa.gov/history/mywinantarticle.html>.

Geneva Briefing Book. "The Briefing Book on International Organizations in Geneva" [cited 24 October 2002]. <http://www.genevabriefingbook.com/chapters/ilo.html>.

International Labor Organization [cited 24 October 2002]. <http://www.ilo.org>.

Legal Information Institute. "International Labor Organization: Membership." U.S. Code Collection. Title 22, Chapter 7, Sec. 271 [cited 24 October 2002]. <http://liimirror.warwick.ac.uk/uscode/22/271.html>.

Perlman, Mark. "U.S. International Labour Standards Policy." Review of *Defining Global Justice: The History of U.S. International Labor Standards Policy* by Edward C. Lorenz (Notre Dame, IN: University of Notre Dame Press, 2001). International Association of Labor History Institutions. *IALHI News Service*. 15 March 2002 [cited 24 October 2002]. <http://www.ialhi.org/news/i0203_4.html>.

Rosen, Sumner M. "CU Labor Seminar." International Labor Organizations, Global Policy Forum, Social and Economic Policy. 18 September 2000 [cited 24 October 2002]. <http://www.globalpolicy.org/socecon/inequal/labor/history.htm#5>.

Social Security Administration. "Frances Perkins" [cited 24 October 2002]. <http://www.ssa.gov/history/fperkins.html>.

U.S. Department of Labor. "Be Ye Steadfast. The Life and Work of Frances Perkins" [cited 24 October 2002]. <http://www.dol.gov/opa/frances/frances.htm>.

VanGrasstek, Craig. "U.S. Law and Policy on the Linkage Between Labor Rights and Trade." *Washington Trade Reports*. Information and Analysis for a Global Market. 2000 [cited 24 October 2002]. <http://www.washingtontradereports.com/LaborRights.htm>.

—Brett Allan King

United States v. United Mine Workers of America

United States 1947

Synopsis

In 1947 the U.S. Supreme Court upheld a federal district court decision fining the United Mine Workers of America $700,000 and its president, John L. Lewis, $10,000 for contempt of court. The case, which arose out of the union's defiance of a federal district court injunction against a 1946 coal strike, was the culmination of Lewis's contentious relationship with the federal government during the 1940s.

Timeline

1932: A "Bonus Army" of unemployed veterans marches on Washington, D.C. Many leave after Congress refuses their demands for payment of bonuses for wartime service, but others are forcibly removed by General Douglas MacArthur's troops. Also participating are two other figures destined to gain notoriety in the next world war: majors Dwight D. Eisenhower and George S. Patton.

1937: In the middle of an around-the-world flight, Amelia Earhart and her plane disappear somewhere in the Pacific.

Tom C. Clark. Collection of the Supreme Court of the United States.

1942: Establishment of the women's military services in the United States.

1947: Great Britain's Labour government nationalizes coal-mines.

1948: Israel becomes a nation.

1949: Establishment of North Atlantic Treaty Organization (NATO).

1950: North Korean troops pour into South Korea, starting the Korean War. Initially, the communists make impressive gains, but in September the U.S. Marines land at Inchon and liberate Seoul. China responds by sending in its troops.

1951: Julius and Ethel Rosenberg are convicted and sentenced to death for passing U.S. atomic secrets to the Soviets.

1954: The French military outpost at Dien Bien Phu falls to the communist Vietminh. France withdraws after decades of trying to suppress revolt; meanwhile, the United States pledges its support for the noncommunist government in the South.

1956: Elvis Presley appears on Ed Sullivan's *Toast of the Town,* where he performs "Hound Dog" and "Love Me Tender" before a mostly female audience. Nationwide,

54 million people watch the performance, setting a new record.

1961: President Eisenhower steps down, warning of a "military-industrial complex" in his farewell speech, and 43-year-old John F. Kennedy becomes the youngest elected president in U.S. history. Three months later, he launches an unsuccessful invasion of Cuba at the Bay of Pigs.

Event and Its Context

Background

United States v. United Mine Workers of America is the name of a specific legal case, but it equally denotes the combative relationship between the autocratic president of the United Mine Workers of America (UMWA), John L. Lewis, and the federal government.

Lewis, who first descended into the coal mines at age 16, rose to acting president of the UMWA in 1919. The following year he was elected to the presidency, a post he held until 1960. In 1933 he launched an aggressive membership drive for the UMWA, which had been losing members throughout the 1920s, and rebuilt it into a powerful union. Additionally, he served as president of the Congress of Industrial Organizations (CIO) from 1936 to 1940, and from that position was able to force union recognition and collective bargaining on two of the nation's industrial giants, U.S. Steel and General Motors. By the late 1930s Lewis was regarded as one of the nation's most creative and influential labor leaders—although to his critics he was "Cunning John," "Lewis the Dictator," "Old Ironjaw," and "The Eyebrow," the last in reference to his trademark bushy eyebrows.

At heart Lewis was a Republican, and in the early 1930s he actually served as chair of the Republican Party's National Labor Committee. In 1932, though, he joined the Democratic Party, believing that the party and its standard bearer, Franklin D. Roosevelt, were allies of organized labor; Lewis actively supported Roosevelt's New Deal legislation. By the 1940 presidential campaign, however, Lewis believed that the president was taking labor for granted, and in a public breakup he threw his support to Republican Wendell Willkie. After the CIO rank and file rejected his advice and returned Roosevelt to the presidency, Lewis, in disgust, resigned the presidency of the CIO and thereafter concentrated his efforts on building his power base within the UMWA.

"Damn Your Coal-Black Soul!"

During World War II Lewis lost whatever support he had enjoyed from the American public and began to lay the groundwork for his contempt charge in 1946. Coal was a resource vital to the war effort, yet on the eve of America's entry into the war, Lewis called the mineworkers out on strike—to embarrass the president, many thought. Then, concerned about the loss of real wages in the coal industry brought about by the demands of the war, he led workers out on a second wartime strike in 1943, which prompted Roosevelt to seize the coal industry. Fevered negotiations involving the UMWA, the mine operators, Secretary of the Interior Harold Ickes, and the National War Labor

Board finally led to a settlement, but not before 500,000 workers had walked off their jobs.

The American public was incensed against the union and its "holdup" tactics. In Congress, conservatives and liberals alike denounced Lewis for subverting the national interest during war. News of the coal strike competed with stories from the war on the front pages of the nation's newspapers. Rumors circulated that Lewis was a Nazi collaborator. Even CIO leaders denounced Lewis as a self-serving demagogue out for revenge against the president. An editorial in the military newspaper *Stars and Stripes* exclaimed, "Speaking for the American soldier, John L. Lewis, damn your coal-black soul!" This line virtually became a national chant. Lewis made gains for miners during the war, but the price he paid was increasing isolation from other labor leaders and former political allies.

Post–World War II Turmoil

The public mood took a sharp antilabor turn in the months and years following the war. As the nation demobilized, Americans expected that the privations of the war years would come to an end. Instead the nation faced shortages and inflation in part because labor, which in general had remained quiet during the war, sought to recoup some of its sacrifices. Particularly disturbing was the wave of strikes in the 12 months following the end of the war: 200,000 General Motors employees, 300,000 meat packers, 180,000 electrical workers, 750,000 steel workers—in sum, 4,630 work stoppages involving five million workers. Americans' simmering antilabor sentiment accorded well with the efforts of Harry Truman's administration to curb the power of organized labor.

In this context the coal strike of 1946 was the last straw. The sequence of events began on 2 March when Lewis announced that he wanted to reopen negotiations with the coal operators and that a labor dispute existed. In talks through March, Lewis focused more on health and safety issues than on economic demands and pressed for a health and welfare fund, although some observers interpreted his recital of mining accidents and lack of sanitation in the mining camps as a cynical ploy designed to win back sympathy from the public. On 1 April the union's contract expired and the miners walked out, but negotiations continued for 10 more days until a frustrated Lewis left the bargaining table.

Throughout the spring the nation burned its coal reserves down to a dangerous level, the steel industry cut production by half, and auto plants in Detroit closed. Congress introduced various punitive bills that would have restricted the right to strike. On 10 May, Lewis announced a two-week truce, but when negotiations collapsed in mid-May, Truman ordered Secretary of the Interior Julius A. Krug to seize the mines. On 29 May, Lewis and Krug signed an agreement that provided workers with retirement and medical funds as well as a wage increase and a promise to enact a federal mine safety code. Confidence ran high that the dispute was settled.

That confidence was premature. Throughout the summer and early fall, the mines were still in the hands of the government, and efforts to get producers on board with the agreement were meeting with resistance, particularly in the South. Then on 21 October, Lewis sent shock waves through the nation when, invoking a provision that he claimed was part of the 29

May agreement, he informed Secretary Krug that he wanted to reopen negotiations. Resentfully, the Truman administration agreed, and on 11 November, Lewis presented demands for a reduction in hours, a hefty wage boost, and an increase in coal companies' contributions to the welfare and retirement fund. The administration wanted to avert a strike but did not want to agree to inflationary wage increases, so on 17 November, with the Lewis-Krug agreement about to expire on 20 November, Truman announced that he would "fight John L. Lewis on all fronts." The drama grew as he ordered the Solid Fuel Administration to freeze all coal in transit and the Office of Defense Transportation to order the railroads to cut their use of coal. On 18 November, Judge T. Alan Goldsborough of the U.S. District Court for the District of Columbia granted Attorney General Tom Clark's request for an injunction against the strike.

Contempt

Strictly speaking, Lewis did not call for a strike. He simply remained silent as the 20 November deadline came and went. Hearing of the injunction, 33,000 workers walked off their jobs prematurely. Then at midnight on 20 November, the entire bituminous coal industry shut down. Again, an atmosphere of crisis pervaded the nation. The *New York Times* proclaimed that 25 million workers could be idled as a result of the strike. To save electricity, plans were even made to shut off the lights illuminating the Capitol Dome in Washington, D.C., prompting the Committee on American History to ask, "Are we going to darken it for John L. Lewis?"

Lewis was in a corner, and he knew it. He hired an FBI agent-turned-private eye to dig up dirt on Judge Goldsborough. As he worked to find some way out of the crisis, he was summoned to district court on 25 November to answer contempt charges. On 3 December, Judge Goldsborough rejected the defendants' claim that the injunction violated the Clayton and Norris–La Guardia Acts and held that the government, despite the acts, had the power to obtain and enforce a labor injunction when its purpose was to avoid potential public calamity.

Then, Judge Goldsborough turned to the defendants and administered a tongue-lashing. He referred to Lewis's actions as "an evil, demonic, monstrous thing that means hunger and cold and unemployment and destitution and disorganization of the social fabric." Apocalyptically, he went on, "Unless those who are directing the affairs of this union are corrected, they will destroy the union, because if the worst should come to the worst . . . and it is a question of the destruction of this union or the preservation of this Republic, the Republic is going to be preserved." Goldsborough noted that in his view Lewis should be imprisoned, but the government, not wanting to turn Lewis into a martyr, had asked instead for a fine. Accordingly, the court fined the union $3.5 million and Lewis $10,000.

Lewis appealed to the U.S. Supreme Court, but he knew he was defeated. On 7 December he called off the strike. The Supreme Court heard the case on 14 January 1947, and in its decision on 6 March upheld the fine against Lewis, though it reduced the fine against the union to $700,000.

Aftermath

The crisis brought into public focus the intensely personal feud between Lewis and Truman, one that often led to public sniping. After Truman, in response to a proposal that he appoint Lewis ambassador to Moscow, quipped that he would not make Lewis the dogcatcher of the country, the *New York Times* published Lewis's rejoinder: "The President could ill afford to have more brains in the Dog Department than in the Department of State, and from this standpoint, his remarks to you are eminently justified."

On one level, the crisis represented a humiliation for Lewis and a corresponding boost to Truman, who had long been trying to emerge from Roosevelt's shadow. On another level, though, the case had important consequences for the balance of power between the federal government and private enterprise. The government won the battle and reaffirmed its power to seize an industry and force a union to negotiate a contract. The UMWA may have won the war, for in 1947 events came full circle when a contract finally was negotiated that gave miners a $3 per day increase in wages and benefits, lowered the workday from nine to eight hours, and established a welfare and retirement fund similar to that worked out in the Lewis-Krug agreement.

Key Players

Clark, Tom C. (1899–1977): Clark, born in Dallas, Texas, became assistant U.S. attorney general in 1943 and attorney general under Truman in 1945. In 1949 the president appointed him to the U.S. Supreme Court (1949–1967).

Goldsborough, Thomas Alan (1877–1951): Born in Greensboro, South Carolina, Goldsborough worked as a lawyer until he was elected as a Democrat to the U.S. House of Representatives in 1921. He served until 1939, when he was appointed an associate justice of the U.S. District Court for the District of Columbia, where he served until his death.

Krug, Julius Albert (1907–1970): Krug was born in Madison, Wisconsin. He served as President Truman's secretary of the interior from March 1946 to December 1949.

Lewis, John L. (1880–1969): Born in the coal mining town of Cleveland, Iowa, Lewis began working in the coal mines at age sixteen. He became president of the United Mine Workers of America in 1920 and held the position until his retirement in 1960.

Truman, Harry S (1884–1972): Born in Lamar, Missouri, Truman, after running a clothing store in Kansas City, began his political career in a succession of county offices, including that of presiding judge on the county court. He was elected to the U.S. Senate in 1935, where he served until he became Franklin Roosevelt's new vice president in 1944. On Roosevelt's death in 1945, Truman became the nation's 33rd president.

See also: *Congress of Industrial Organizations; Strike Wave: United States; United Mine Workers of America.*

BIBLIOGRAPHY

Books

Dubofsky, Melvyn, and Warren Van Tine. *John L. Lewis: A Biography.* New York: New York Times Books Co., 1977.

Zieger, Robert H. *John L. Lewis: Labor Leader.* Boston: Twayne, 1988.

Other

United States v. United Mine Workers of America. 70 F. Supp. 42; 67 S.Ct. 677.

—Michael J. O'Neal

United Steelworkers of America

United States 1942

Synopsis

On 22 May 1942 the Steel Workers Organizing Committee (SWOC), a group established by the Congress of Industrial Organizations (CIO) to organize the largest nonunion industry in the United States, adopted its first constitution at its convention in Cleveland, Ohio. In so doing, the organization became the United Steelworkers of America (USW). SWOC President Philip Murray continued in the same role in the new union. Future USW president David J. McDonald took the post of secretary-treasurer. The convention set up the locals in geographic districts, authorized a biennial international constitutional convention, and required officers and district directors to be voted in every four years. The new union inherited all of the old contracts that had been signed by SWOC.

Like the SWOC before it, the USW was organized on a top-down basis. No local could call a strike without the approval of the international. The president had the power to appoint the union's entire staff. The international received three times as much from dues as did the locals. This made the union financially strong but conservative compared to the SWOC.

Timeline

1921: Washington Disarmament Conference limits the tonnage of world navies.

1925: European leaders attempt to secure the peace at the Locarno Conference, which guarantees the boundaries between France and Germany, and Belgium and Germany.

1931: Financial crisis widens in the United States and Europe, which reel from bank failures and climbing unemployment levels. In London, armies of the unemployed riot.

1936: Germany reoccupies the Rhineland, while Italy annexes Ethiopia. Recognizing a commonality of aims, the two totalitarian powers sign the Rome-Berlin Axis Pact. (Japan will join them in 1940.)

1941: German troops march into the Balkans, conquering Yugoslavia and Greece. (Bulgaria and Romania, along with Hungary, are aligned with the Nazis.)

1941: In a move that takes Stalin by surprise, Hitler sends his troops into the Soviet Union on 22 June. Like his hero

Napoleon, Hitler believes that by stunning Russia with a lightning series of brilliant maneuvers, it is possible to gain a quick and relatively painless victory. Early successes seem to prove him right, and he is so confident of victory that he refuses to equip his soldiers with winter clothing.

1941: Japanese bombing of Pearl Harbor on 7 December brings the United States into the war against the Axis. Combined with the attack on the Soviet Union, which makes Stalin an unlikely ally of the Western democracies, the events of 1941 will ultimately turn the tide of the war.

1941: The United States initiates the Manhattan Project to build an atomic bomb and signs the Lend-Lease Act, whereby it provides aid to Great Britain and, later, the Soviet Union.

1941: Great films of the year include *The Maltese Falcon, Sullivan's Travels, Meet John Doe, How Green Was My Valley,* and a work often cited as one of the greatest films of all time: Orson Welles's *Citizen Kane.*

1946: Winston Churchill warns of an "Iron Curtain" spreading across Eastern Europe.

1951: Introduction of color television.

1956: First aerial testing of the hydrogen bomb at Bikini Atoll. The blast is so powerful—the equivalent of 10 million tons of TNT—that it actually results in the infusion of protons to atomic nuclei to create two new elements, einsteinium and fermium, which have atomic numbers of 99 and 100, respectively.

John L. Lewis. U.S. Information Agency.

Event and Its Context

The transformation of SWOC into the USWA is the story of a temporary organizing campaign that consolidated its gains to become a stable union. SWOC had won a huge victory when it convinced the United States Steel Corporation, or "Big Steel," to recognize it without a strike in March 1937, but it lost the "Little Steel" strike against U.S. Steel's largest competitors later that same year. (Little Steel was a loose conglomeration of half a dozen steel manufacturers, including Bethlehem Steel and Republic Steel, all led by staunch antiunion entrepreneurs.) If SWOC had been unable to grow, the gains it had made might have vanished. Renewal of the U.S. Steel contract with SWOC in February 1938 without a wage cut helped the cause, but as long as Little Steel remained nonunion, SWOC's existence was not secure.

Philip Murray and many of his aides came from John L. Lewis's United Mine Workers of America (UMW). As the SWOC tried to establish itself, its leaders looked to the UMW as their model for how to operate. For instance, in October 1937 a special convention adopted a series of rules designed to centralize power at the top, in the same manner as had been used at the UMW. Before U.S. Steel's decision to recognize SWOC, the committee had been a loosely organized rank-and-file-driven organization. Henceforth, SWOC would be run from the top as with any bureaucratic union. In fact, SWOC was more autocratic than bureaucratic because it had no provisions for internal government. It had been created by an agreement with the defunct Amalgamated Association of Iron, Steel, and Tin Workers. It had to answer only to the CIO, and after the U.S. Steel agreement John L. Lewis left SWOC pretty much alone. Not until it adopted a constitution and changed its name would ordinary steelworkers have any say over the direction of their organization, and even then it was not much.

The biggest problem faced by the SWOC at this time was lack of funds. At a time when it needed as many people as possible organizing steelworkers, precious manpower and resources had to go toward collecting dues from those who had already joined. Things got so bad that secretary-treasurer McDonald had to resort to dues picketing, or having intimidating-looking members stand by the gates of plants and shake down workers for the money they owed the union as they entered.

In this situation, SWOC could grow and stabilize without help from the government. President Franklin Roosevelt, however, did not give SWOC the help it expected. This is best illustrated by Roosevelt's response to the Memorial Day Massacre, which took place during the Little Steel Strike. "A plague on both your houses," he told a press conference, condemning labor and management alike. That comment, along with other issues, led to John L. Lewis's decision to break with Roosevelt before the 1940 presidential election. This in turn led Lewis to resign the presidency of the CIO. Murray replaced him in this position, and by 1942 the two union leaders had broken ties completely. Lewis went so far as to throw Murray out of the UMW.

With no help from Roosevelt, the committee looked to the National Labor Relations Board (NLRB) for help. In the months following the Little Steel strike, SWOC's legal department filed a huge number of complaints under the National

Philip Murray. The Library of Congress.

Labor Relations Act, alleging, among other things, that firms such as Republic Steel and Bethlehem Steel had refused to bargain in good faith. SWOC also established itself within the industry by winning representation elections held under NLRB auspices despite management's vehement objections to elections, let alone the committee. Through July 1939, SWOC won 81 of 122 NLRB elections. In 39 elections in which its opponent was an independent union or a former company union, SWOC won 22.

On 18 October 1938 the NLRB ruled that Republic Steel had to reinstate workers who had been unlawfully discharged during the Little Steel Strike and pay them wages lost since the date of their termination. This decision would eventually affect 7,000 employees and cost the company $2 million in back pay. Republic Steel appealed the ruling through every legal channel. When the United States Supreme Court refused to take the case in April 1940, company president Tom Girdler finally agreed to abide by the decision. In addition to the legal costs of fighting the NLRB, Republic Steel paid an additional $350,000 in 1945 to settle claims filed by strikers and the families of strikers who were killed or injured during the 1937 dispute. The money made by Republic Steel during World War II, however, made these costs much easier to bear, and does much to explain why Republic Steel recognized the committee.

The desire to complete new government defense contracts also explains why other firms that made up Little Steel settled as the buildup accelerated. SWOC won an NLRA-inspired case against Youngstown Sheet and Tube on 17 February 1941. On 25 July 1941 Republic Steel, Inland Steel, and Youngstown Sheet and Tube agreed to abide by the results of an NLRB cross-check of SWOC membership at their plants to avoid representation elections. The board certified that SWOC held ma-

jorities at each company. A new contract with U.S. Steel signed in April 1941 that had much better terms for union members also helped SWOC considerably.

In February 1941 Bethlehem Steel's management agreed to let employees at its Lackawanna, New York, plant vote on their collective bargaining agent after a successful 39-hour strike. This inspired a strike at South Bethlehem in March. When state and local police tried to disperse strikers, serious violence (but no casualties) resulted. As part of the settlement, South Bethlehem agreed to let its workers vote for their bargaining agent as well. Between May and September of that year, SWOC won elections at all of Bethlehem Steel's facilities.

SWOC had won recognition from all of Little Steel by mid-to-late 1941, but this does not mean that Little Steel signed contracts with the committee. Collective bargaining between SWOC and Little Steel began in September 1941. During the course of these negotiations, the United States entered World War II. In January 1942 the government created a new National War Labor Board (NWLB) to prevent strikes at companies involved in the war effort. The World War I version of the board had to depend on the power of public opinion to force companies to comply with its decisions, but the new NWLB had the full backing of the U.S. government. Furthermore, the new NWLB had the power to determine wages throughout the economy and to grant "union security" to organized labor. Union security consisted of two important contract provisions: maintenance-of-membership and dues check off. Maintenance-of-membership automatically enrolls new hires in the union. Workers enrolled in this manner during World War II could quit after a short time, but very few ever chose to do so. Dues check off means that union dues are automatically subtracted from an employee's paycheck (thereby saving union officials the time and expense of collecting dues from each member individually). SWOC believed it needed union security to survive.

The impasses between Little Steel and the USW led to the 16 July 1942 Little Steel decision by the NWLB. This decision not only determined the terms for collective bargaining between these two parties, it also determined how the board would set wage levels for all of American industry during the war. The NWLB granted the USWA both maintenance-of-membership and dues check off. Both these provisions helped the union immensely. Maintenance-of-membership helped SWOC grow from 373,000 members in 1941 to 733,000 members in 1946. Thanks to the dues check off provision of the Little Steel decision, the union's treasury grew sevenfold between May 1942 (right before the Little Steel decision) and November 1943. The union also had to continue to abide by the no-strike pledge that the AFL and the CIO had made on behalf of their member unions at the beginning of the war; in the patriotic climate of that time, SWOC leaders never even considered going back on that pledge. The maintenance-of-membership and dues check off provisions of the Little Steel decision were more responsible for the institutionalization of the steelworkers union than any other factor.

The results of the wage portion of the Little Steel decision were more ambiguous. The union had wanted a wage increase of 12.5 cents per hour over wages at the start of the war. The most recent prewar wage gain had been devoured completely by inflation. The committee calculated that steelworkers on average received over $6 less than other defense employees because they worked shorter hours than their peers. This explains why so many steelworkers left to seek jobs in other defense industries during the war. Management countered that such a wage increase for steelworkers would be inflationary because the cost would be passed on to other industries that used steel in their products.

The Little Steel decision gave union members a wage increase of 17.3 cents per hour. Of the difference between the union's demand and what it got, 3.2 cents represented what the union needed to catch up to the national inflation rate that had governed prices since the NWLB had starting considering the dispute. The board tacked on 2.3 cents more because inflation in steel towns exceeded the national average. The committee was happy that it had made up the difference between what its members had once earned in real terms and what it needed to maintain that difference, but the standard of living for most steelworkers before the war had been low. The union was concerned that it would have trouble getting wages raised during the rest of the war. Another cause for concern was that the decision did not address wage inequalities that existed between steelworkers. SWOC (and later the USW) would spend the remainder of the war trying to achieve wage increases above the caps set by the Little Steel formula.

Little Steel still objected to union recognition on philosophical grounds, and management abided by the decision only because of the war emergency. To defy an activist government at that point might have led to hostile publicity and an armed takeover of their facilities, as happened at Montgomery Ward in April 1944. Therefore, the antiunion executives who ran Little Steel swallowed their pride and signed union contracts.

The NWLB's Little Steel formula set the standard by which the board decided all future wage cases that came before it. Unions from any industry whose complaints came before the board would be guaranteed a wage increase of 15 percent over what its members had earned on 1 January 1941. The board could award larger gains if it detected inequalities or injustices. For instance, the NWLB tried to guarantee equal pay between men and women if they performed equal work. In most instances, however, the unions in future cases had the same reaction as had SWOC: gratitude for the pay raise tempered by concern about what they would do when wartime inflation consumed the gain. Only an NWLB complaint could lead to a government-mandated wage increase, and the board had too many complaints before it to ensure that workers' wages kept pace with inflation. To make matters worse, SWOC's success before the NWLB only encouraged more unions to file.

Buoyed by the organizing victories of the late 1930s and early 1940s, steelworkers expected to have greater influence over both the conditions under which they labored and the production process itself. Instead, they were disturbed to find that their employers still wanted to treat them as nothing but one of many factors of production. Before the war began, SWOC leadership took the initiative to establish a better working relationship with the industry. Beginning in 1938, the union established cooperation programs at some 50 small, financially troubled metal-fabricating firms that were willing to cede some shop floor control to the union so as to increase production efficiency. Two SWOC staffers, Harold Ruttenberg and Clinton Gol-

den, provided the intellectual force behind these efforts to get labor and management to work together to confront the problems of the industry. By early 1940 they had convinced the union to make cooperation a central tenet of the union. In a 1941 address to the CIO convention, Philip Murray proposed a series of "Industry Councils" to give labor a voice in planning for all defense areas. Although most industries rejected such arrangements outright, steel firms agreed to implement the plan under the strain of the wartime emergency and the threat of government intervention. By 15 March 1944 there were 451 of these committees throughout the iron and steel industry, representing some 719,530 workers.

Union officials tried to use these committees to show management ways that production might be improved, but little came from these recommendations because management never took the committees seriously. Although some of these bodies helped decrease absenteeism and raise productivity, they disappeared soon after the end of the war. This reconfirmed to most employees that management would not cooperate with labor unless they were so compelled by outside forces. Stung by this rebuke, the USW would become as enthusiastic about cooperating with management as management was about cooperating with the union.

In 1946 the USW struck the entire industry to protect the wage and union security gains that it had won in the years preceding its formation and during the war. The union won this struggle because President Harry Truman's administration decided to allow the industry to raise the price of steel, thus making union gains easier for management to swallow. The concession, however, led to a wage spiral that contributed to four more nationwide strikes in the next 13 years and to the eventual collapse of the entire industry.

Key Players

Lewis, John L. (1880–1969): UMW president and founder of the Congress of Industrial Organizations. Deeply involved in SWOC's early history, his opposition to Franklin Roosevelt led him to curtail his involvement after the 1940 presidential election.

McDonald, David J. (1902–1979): SWOC secretary-treasurer who succeeded Murray as president of the USWA in 1952.

Murray, Philip (1886–1952): Handpicked by John L. Lewis to be SWOC president, Murray was also the first USW president and succeeded Lewis as CIO president in 1940. Cautious but successful, he was responsible for many of the policies that helped stabilize the union.

See also: *Congress of Industrial Organizations; Memorial Day Massacre; United Mine Workers of America; U.S. Steel Recognizes Steel Workers Organizing Committee.*

BIBLIOGRAPHY

Books

Clark, Paul, Peter Gottlieb, and Donald Kennedy, eds. *Forging a Union of Steel.* Ithaca, NY: ILR Press, 1987.

Hoerr, John. *And the Wolf Finally Came.* Pittsburgh, PA: University of Pittsburgh Press, 1988.

Seidman, Joel. *American Labor from Defense to Reconversion*. Chicago: University of Chicago Press, 1953.

Ulman, Lloyd. *The Government of the Steelworkers' Union*. New York: Wiley, 1962.

—Jonathan Rees

United Tailoresses Society

United States 1825

Synopsis

Early nineteenth-century women by no means humbly accepted their lot without complaint despite the social restraints placed on them. Long before the Suffrage Act granted them the right to vote, women had been fighting for their rights on many levels. Of great importance were their rights in the workplace. Unfortunately, although the union movement had begun by 1820, labor activists typically ignored women and their plight. It was not until they stood up for themselves that unions finally took notice. One group that led the way in gaining public recognition was the United Tailoresses Society of New York. Protesting against unfair wages and deplorable conditions, the Tailoresses brought to light the truth about the textile and clothing industry. This act of bravery in the face of overwhelming opposition would inspire working women for decades to come.

Timeline

1800: Italian physicist Alessandro Volta develops the voltaic cell, an early form of battery.

1803: English chemist and physicist John Dalton develops the first modern form of atomic theory.

1808: First performances of Beethoven's Fifth and Sixth symphonies.

1812: Napoleon invades Russia in June, but by October, his army, cold and hungry, is in retreat.

1818: Donkin, Hall & Gamble "Preservatory" in London produces the first canned foods.

1825: British Parliament enacts a law permitting workers to join together in order to secure regulation of wages and hours; however, other provisions in the law effectively deny the right to strike.

1826: French inventor Joseph-Nicéphore Niepce makes the first photographic image in history.

1828: Election of Andrew Jackson as president begins a new era in American history.

1829: Greece wins its independence after a seven-year war with Turkey.

1829: Overturning of the last of the "penal laws" imposed by the English against the Catholics of Ireland since 1695.

1830: French troops invade Algeria, and at home, a revolution forces the abdication of Charles V in favor of Louis Philippe, the "Citizen King."

1831: Young British naturalist Charles Darwin sets sail from England aboard the H.M.S. *Beagle* bound for South America, where he will make discoveries leading to the formation of his theory of evolution by means of natural selection.

Event and Its Context

Women and Labor in 1820

In the early nineteenth century, women possessed little power and even fewer rights. American society expected them to remain at home, raise children, and avoid political thinking. At the same time, economic conditions were forcing an increasing number of lower- and middle-class women out of the home and into the workplace. Once there, these women faced harsh work conditions and unfair labor practices. Even so, society expected them to be proper and restrained regardless of their circumstances. Meanwhile, men were allowed to act in their own best interests, even so far as to protest against adversity in the workplace. Unionists and social activists typically ignored working women, who faced ridicule for speaking out against employers and working conditions. Despite the restraints imposed by society, many women refused to stay quiet and unassuming. Although legal "equality" would remain almost a century in their future, American working women made sure their voices were heard. The nation soon knew of their struggle and their displeasure with the labor community.

Perhaps the greatest inspiration for early nineteenth-century female activists came from the American Revolution. During the conflict for independence, women had played vital roles in the revolutionary effort. The Daughters of Liberty, for example, became involved in enforcing the nonimportation agreements and passing resolutions. In addition to their supportive role during the War of Independence, women such as Deborah Sampson Gannett actually fought as soldiers. Having grown up hearing of these acts of female heroism told by their mothers and grandmothers, many early nineteenth-century women had the revolutionary spirit in their blood. This spirit would serve them well in their own revolution in the pursuit of social change and improvements in workplace conditions. The first true sign of this spirit of activism appeared in Pawtucket, Rhode Island.

By the 1820s women had become the core of the workforce in the textile industry. Their numbers far outweighed those of men: in some mills women comprised more than 85 percent of the employees. Most of these women came from rural communities, often having been lured to the cities by the corporate agents. The women were placed in the lowest level jobs, and the men held all of the supervisory and skilled positions. The women received a predetermined wage, whereas the men were allowed to negotiate for their salaries. Much of the time, women earned less than half that of their male counterparts. Shifts commonly ran 12 or 13 hours, and sometimes longer during the summer months. The appalling work conditions were typically hazardous and unsanitary. Employers were infamous for locking shut the workroom windows to maintain the humidity, which prevented damage to the threads. As a result, workers constantly fainted from heat exhaustion. Disciplinary actions came without warning or mercy for "infractions" as simple as "questionable character." As the companies also controlled the women's boarding houses, activities outside the mill could result in termination, eviction, or reduction in pay.

Before 1824 the most common incidents of activism against the tyrannical conditions were work stoppages and acts of personal defiance. Most of these ended without success with the women being fired or disciplined for their efforts. In May 1824, however, approximately 100 female weavers joined male workers in a protest against wage cuts and an extension of work hours. The event sent a ripple of shock throughout New England as it went completely against the beliefs of the time. Unfortunately, the female weavers were forced to return to work under the employer's provisions only a week later. Their voices, however, had been heard by other female textile workers. Between 1824 and 1837 women participated in or led at least 12 other mill strikes. Few won their demands, but word of their efforts spread throughout the nation. In December 1828 the first all-women strike took place in Dover, New Hampshire, at the Cocheco Mill. Some 340 women from the mill protested the inception of new rules that banned talking, introduced a "blacklist," and fined employees 12.5 cents for being one minute late to work. After the public protest, the strikers eventually succeeded in having the rules rescinded. The example of the Dover women inspired a relatively unknown group of woman laborers in New York to take action. The United Tailoresses Society of New York would follow in the Dover women's footsteps and catch the public's attention with one of the most famous strikes in the New York textile industry.

Tailoresses and Their Struggle

As women struggled for better working conditions in the factories, another group of female laborers, the seamstresses, had begun to organize. Forced into the workplace by personal circumstances, thousands of women took positions in the clothing industry. In the early nineteenth century, a huge demand for ready-made clothing had developed in Boston, New York, and Philadelphia. Although the industry served the needs of the U.S. Army and Navy, most of the demand came from southern slave owners who required cheap, sturdy pants and shirts. Much of the garment construction process was performed in tiny stores, which were nicknamed "slop shops" because of their typically squalid, waterfront locations. Most seamstresses, however, worked out of their homes. In both cases, the women faced grueling hours of labor, which sometimes meant working 15 or 16 hours a day. These horribly long workdays stemmed from the fact that the seamstresses were paid by the piece, not the hour. In Philip Foner's book *Women and the American Labor Movement*, one such tailoress explained, "Think of a poor woman, confined to her seat fifteen hours out of twenty-four to make a pair of . . . pantaloons, for which she receives only twenty-five cents. And indeed, most of them are not able to make a pair in much less than two days." Employers regularly found fault with the work and reduced the women's pay by half or withheld it entirely. A proponent of the tailoresses, Matthew Carey, a Philadelphia publisher and activist, expressed his disgust and shock

at the indignities these women suffered for their trade. In one of his editorials discussed in Foner's *Women and the American Labor Movement*, Carey said, "I have known a lady [who would] pay thirty or forty dollars on a bonnet, and fifty for a shawl; yet make a hard bargain with a seamstress . . . who had to work at her needle . . . for thirteen or fourteen hours to make a bare livelihood for herself." During this time, some of the women's committees contacted Carey to inform him that his already grim portrayals of the industry were actually understatements of the truth. The realities were actually far harsher. On average, tailoresses made $1.12 a week. Rent required two-thirds of their weekly salary, leaving these women with hardly more than 40 cents for all of life's other necessities, including food and clothing. In some cities, such as New York, rents were even higher. Considering this, it is easy to understand why many women were forced to resort to begging, stealing, and even prostitution.

Frustrated and desperate, the tailoresses realized that they needed to take action to implement change. In New York a group of tailoresses came together to do just that. What began as a simple meeting of the minds transformed into one of the first trade unions for women, the United Tailoresses Society (UTS) of New York. Following in the steps of the female strikers of Dover in 1828, the tailoresses' union would soon lead one of New York's, if not the nation's, most notable labor protests.

The United Tailoresses Society

In 1825 several tailoresses began weekly meetings to discuss the plights of their trade, the horrors of their work situations, and their possible means for recourse. They banded together in self-protection in the face of poor wages and dangerous conditions. That same year the weekly meetings led to the adoption of a full-fledged association. The women formed committees to draft a constitution and outline how they could achieve change for their fellow tailoresses and seamstresses. The UTS gained prompt attention when its secretary, Lavinia Wright, added the issue of women's rights to the discussions. A woman ahead of her time, Wright believed that women should have the right to vote and to participate in the legislature. The organization's outspoken views on the subject stirred up public ridicule. The *Boston Evening Transcript* was one of the leaders in defaming the UTS's public stance on women's issues. According to John Andrews and W. D. P. Bliss's *History of Women in Trade Unions*, the *Transcript* criticized "Wright's 'clamorous and unfeminine' declarations of the personal rights of women . . . 'which it is obvious a wise Providence never destined her to exercise.'" Despite the constant criticism and slanderous reports, the UTS continued to meet and publicize the plight of their members.

Perhaps inspired by the Dover strike of 1828, the UTS members also began to consider the option of striking to obtain their goals. The participants had come to recognize that they would have to stand up publicly for their rights. They had already won some societal support from labor presses such as the New York *Daily Sentinel*. They continued their discussions on how to proceed for several years. Then, in June 1831 the union's representatives presented employers with a list of minimum wages for their services. Should the employers not agree to these proposed wages, members of the UTS would engage in a general strike. Not surprisingly, employers refused to accept the demands. In response, 1600 tailoresses went on strike.

The public reaction to the UTS strike was a mixture of ridicule and support. The employers argued that wage increases were a ludicrous notion, as women, by virtue of their gender, did not have to support families as men did. To provide them with a "man's wage" therefore made little sense. Much of the commercial press agreed with this belief. The UTS's secretary responded publicly that many women were indeed the sole supporters of their families and did not receive adequate compensation to do so; yet unmarried men spent their higher wages on no one but themselves. The New York *Daily Sentinel* and other labor newspapers offered an open discussion of how the tailoresses might prevail in their efforts. Some correspondents asked the male trade unions to boycott tailors who refused to comply with the UTS's wage demands. Others pleaded for the male trade unions and the clergy to spearhead the collection of support funds from the public for the striking women.

This show of emotional support, however, never translated to financial support. Very soon the UTS members found themselves facing the harsh reality of no money. Despite the public outcry for help, the male trade unions and clergy refused to lend their aid to the UTS. The employers remained steadfast to their refusal of a wage increase of any kind. By 25 July 1831 the women of the UTS had voted to return to work. Before they did so, they addressed the public, promising to continue their fight against wage inequality and poor labor conditions in the tailoring industry. Unfortunately, their defeat appeared to be a permanent one. The last documented account of the UTS's activities came on 5 September 1831, when the New York *Daily Sentinel* printed what amounted to little more than a meeting announcement.

After the Strike of 1831

Although the UTS had failed in achieving its goals, the concept of unionism for women remained strong in the tailoring and textile industries. Cities outside of New York responded more favorably to the union activities of tailoresses during the subsequent years. When the Female Union Society of Tailoresses and Seamstresses of Baltimore threatened to strike on 1 October 1833, for example, they received assurances of support from the city's journeymen tailors. In June 1835 Matthew Carey spoke at a workingwomen's convention in Philadelphia and urged them onward in their efforts toward labor organization. The same meeting witnessed the formation of the first citywide women's trade federation, the Female Improvement Society for the City and County. This trend continued over the following years. Many from this new generation of female trade unions succeeded where the UTS had failed. Tailoresses won wage increases and better working conditions and slowly advanced the labor rights of their fellow laborers.

Key Players

Carey, Matthew (1760–1839): An Irish immigrant, Carey became a publisher and well-known advocate for the "American System." He campaigned for several years to improve labor conditions and wages for women, specifically those involved in the tailoring industry.

Waight, Lavinia: Waight held the position of secretary in the United Tailoresses Society. Her speeches and writing about inequality and the difficulties faced by female workers of her time served to raise social conscience.

See also: *Dover Textile Strike; Lowell Industrial Experiment; Pawtucket Textile Strike.*

BIBLIOGRAPHY

Books

Andrews, John, and W. D. P. Bliss. *History of Women in Trade Unions.* New York: Arno Press, 1974.

Foner, Philip. *Women and the American Labor Movement.* New York: Macmillan Publishing Co., 1979.

Other

Colman, David M. "A History of the Labor Movement in the United States." Iowa Federation of Labor, AFL-CIO. November 2000 [cited 17 October 2002]. <http://www.iowaaflcio.org/history_book.htm#Chapter%202>.

Henry, Alice. "The Trade Union Woman." In *Bread and Roses: Poetry and History of the American Labor Movement*, edited by Jim Zwick. 2002 [cited 17 October 2002]. <http://www.boondocksnet.com/editions/tuw/tuw01.html>.

Lane Memorial Library. "The Lowell, Massachusetts Turnout of 1834. 2002 [cited 17 October 2002]. <http://www.hampton.lib.nh.us/children/homework/lowellturnout1834.htm>.

—Lee Ann Paradise

United Textile Workers of America

United States 1901

Synopsis

The founding of the United Textile Workers of America (UTWA) in 1901 came about for several reasons. At the turn of the century, the progress of textile unionism remained extremely slow. This was worsened by the radical manufacturing shift from the North, specifically New England, to the southern states, such as Alabama, the Carolinas, Georgia, and Virginia. The poor reaction to unionism in the South further hindered the movement in the textile industry. It was not until the Knights of Labor began their attempts to organize workers in the mid-1880s that progress was truly made. Slowly, craft and textile unions began to form, mostly in New England and the Middle States. Even so, the Knights failed to make real headway with regard to the textile industry and eventually disbanded. In 1891 the American Federation of Labor (AFL) attempted to amalgamate many of these craft and textile unions by founding the National Union of Textile Workers (NUTW). The NUTW, however, remained ineffectual because of its poor financial and membership strength. After pressure began to mount on the AFL, the federation held conferences and a convention to develop a new amalgamated confederation of textile unions. In November 1901 the parties reached a compromise and founded the UTWA. Although it would face many of the same difficulties experienced by its predecessor, the UTWA became a strong union whose influence would be felt in the textile industry for decades to come.

Timeline

1881: U.S. President James A. Garfield is assassinated in a Washington, D.C., railway station by Charles J. Guiteau.

1886: Bombing at Haymarket Square, Chicago, kills seven policemen and injures numerous others. Eight anarchists are accused and tried; three are imprisoned, one commits suicide, and four are hanged.

1891: French troops open fire on workers during a 1 May demonstration at Fourmies, where employees of the Sans Pareille factory are striking for an eight-hour workday. Nine people are killed—two of them children—and 60 more are injured.

1894: Thousands of unemployed American workers—a group named "Coxey's Army" for their leader, Jacob S. Coxey—march on Washington, D.C. A number of such marches on the capital occurred during this period of economic challenges, but Coxey's march was the only one to actually reach its destination.

1897: In the midst of a nationwide depression, Mrs. Bradley Martin, daughter of Carnegie Steel magnate Henry Phipps, throws a lavish party at New York's recently opened Waldorf-Astoria Hotel, where she has a suite decorated to look like Versailles. Her 900 guests, dressed in Louis XV period costumes, consume 60 cases of champagne.

1899: Polish-born German socialist Rosa Luxemburg rejects the argument that working conditions in Europe have improved and that change must come by reforming the existing system. Rather, she calls for an overthrow of the existing power structure by means of violent international revolution.

1901: U.S. President William McKinley is assassinated by Leon Czolgosz, an anarchist. Vice President Theodore Roosevelt becomes president.

1901: Austrian-American immunologist Karl Landsteiner discovers A, B, and O blood.

1901: Guglielmo Marconi makes the first successful transmission and reception of a radio signal.

1903: Russia's Social Democratic Party splits into two factions: the moderate Mensheviks and the hard-line Bolsheviks. Despite their names, which in Russian mean "minority" and "majority," respectively, Mensheviks actually outnumber Bolsheviks.

1907: At the Second Hague Peace Conference, 46 nations adopt 10 conventions governing the rules of war.

1911: Turkish-Italian War sees the first use of aircraft as an offensive weapon. Italian victory results in the annexation of Libya.

Event and Its Context

A Time for Change

In 1793 British mechanic Samuel Slater completely changed the American textile industry with the introduction of the first successful water-powered textile mill in Pawtucket, Rhode Island. He also introduced organizational methods that would spawn the American Industrial Revolution. Corporal punishment, child labor, and company housing and stores were common practices in the Slater Mill. These methods quickly became so commonplace in the industry they were named the Rhode Island System. Therefore, it is ironic that another dramatic change in the textile industry also took place in Pawtucket: the first labor strike in an American textile mill. In 1824 the workers of Pawtucket mills walked out to protest the simultaneous reduction of wages and increase in work hours. This strike also saw female employees joining their male coworkers in protest, which was unprecedented. What began in Pawtucket would in many ways lead to the founding of the United Textile Workers of America (UTWA) almost 80 years later.

The seeds of unionism were undoubtedly sown by the poor work conditions prevalent in the textile industry. Of all their complaints, low pay and long hours were the usual cause for most worker protests. As late as 1899, the average pay remained $5 per week for textile workers (if they were lucky). This does not take into account the many wage cuts caused by fluctuations in the economy at the time. Management also expected employees to work between 12 and 14 hours a day, five days a week. Sometimes there was an additional 10-hour shift expected on Saturdays. These long hours only increased the dangers of an already perilous work environment. Exhausted workers commonly lost fingers or pieces of scalp to the machinery. Because the textile mills owned the workers' homes and controlled their access to food and goods, employees could be thrown into the street or starved at the first sign of complaint. In many cases, strikers were simply replaced with immigrant workers.

Even against overwhelming odds, textile workers continued to fight for a better life. Although there were far more failures than successes, victories still occurred. These victories, no matter how small, sparked the flame of unionism in America's textile industry. This flame, however, would remain dim in the turbulent times before the founding of the UTWA in 1901.

The Trials of Textile Unionism

The growth of union memberships in the textile industry remained stunted for several reasons. Among the obstacles were low wages, low skill requirements, the predominance of immigrant workers, and even the unions themselves. Unions tended to ignore the lower-paid workers in favor of the highly skilled and thus higher paid workers. Because most textile workers earned low wages, the unions abandoned a large pool of potential members. This large population of low-skilled workers also limited the source of effective leadership, which furthered the union's preference for the highly skilled. Conservative union leadership also ignored female workers, despite their active role in unionism. The large numbers of immigrant workers further hampered membership growth because of prejudice and poor communication, which kept the workers unorganized and divided. Because of the different crafts and the industries' geographical extent, numerous unions formed. These scattered unions were constantly at odds, often for ideological or political reasons, thus hindering unionism even further.

This general disorganization would continue to hamper the textile industry until the latter part of the nineteenth century. It became obvious from the continuing struggles and reemergence of unions, however, that there was momentum for the movement. Something needed to be done to foster and maintain the existence of unionism. The Knights of Labor, founded in 1869, would help push the textile industry down this road in the mid-1880s.

One Step Forward, Two Steps Back

The Knights of Labor wished to unify all laborers, skilled and unskilled, into a single labor organization. The ranks of the Knights of Labor swelled quickly and local assemblies for textile workers formed. By 1886 more than 25,000 textile workers were members of the Knights. Despite this, the Knights had little success in improving labor conditions and preventing craft partisanship. The Knights' slow dissolution after 1886 left several textile and trade assemblies struggling in its wake, as well as southern textile workers with little unification. The concept of unionism still remained, albeit unattended.

The American Federation of Labor (AFL) realized that to inspire comprehensive unionism in the textile industry they needed to find a middle ground between the Knights of Labor and the separatist craft unions. A single organization of skilled workers might be able to accomplish that goal. With that belief in mind, the AFL chartered the National Union of Textile Workers (NUTW) in 1891. This first attempt at amalgamation brought together several textile unions from New England and the Middle States. However, the membership numbers remained low and most organizations refused to join. Despite its strong start, the NUTW would also suffer several setbacks, as had the Knights before it. In 1895 a socialist victory drove off most of NUTW's New England membership. Individualism remained rampant and craft unions continued to break off through the NUTW's history. Defeats, such as the action at Cone Mills of Greensboro, North Carolina, in 1900, continued to weaken the union further. By 1901 the NUTW was foundering.

In spite of its failures, the NUTW brought about positive change for the future. In many ways, it laid the groundwork for the founding of the UTWA and became a blueprint from which to build. More important, the NUTW launched a very successful campaign in the South. Strikes in the South, including the key 1898 strike in Augusta, Georgia, revived workers' interest in unionism. Led by Prince W. Greene, several new textile organizations began to form. Greene went to the AFL to apply for affiliation. In turn, the AFL incorporated these fledgling unions with the NUTW. The campaign that ensued resulted in the southern workers suddenly having the majority vote in the weakened NUTW. This foothold in the South would serve the AFL well during the formation of the UTWA.

Getting It Right: The Founding of the United Textile Workers of America

Although the NUTW remained weak at the turn of the century, an economic shift in the textile industry from the North to the South was taking place. Newer technology along with lower manufacturing costs and taxes would soon lead to the South's domination of the textile industry. Samuel Gompers, president of the AFL, quickly recognized the new opportunity for the amalgamation of textile unions. Because of the economic shift, New England textile workers found themselves facing serious wage reductions. F. Ray Marshall's book, *Labor in the South*, quotes Gompers as saying that the wage cuts "may well prove a blessing in disguise." He believed the result was "to arouse the inactive spirit of the [New England] textile workers" and to revive the need for "the organization of the textile workers in the South." Because Prince W. Greene of the NUTW had already launched a successful campaign in the South, the opportunity to accomplish the latter remained strong. The next logical step was to bring together all of the parties.

The AFL led the way in accomplishing this goal. Middle State independents were beginning to strengthen; many of these had previously broken off from the NUTW. In 1900 the National Federation of Textile Operatives established a loose alliance of craft unions in New England and eventually brought about the founding of the American Federation of Textile Operatives (AFTO). Although a diverse amalgamation of craft unions, the AFTO believed their federation did not yet have the strength to accomplish all of their goals. In addition, their desire to draw southern unions into their ranks so as to gain dominance over the industry immediately brought them into conflict with the NUTW. Both sides appealed to the AFL, which stepped in as a mediator.

Still holding to the principle of amalgamation, the AFL convinced the AFTO and the NUTW to begin negotiations to merge their organizations into one entity. Several conferences between the two unions followed as they began to work out the details of unification. On 19 November 1901, the AFL held a convention in Washington, D.C., and brought together the AFTO and the NUTW. During that time, the obstacles of craft unionism began to fall. The differences that had once prevented other attempts at amalgamation were, for the most part, settled. Finally, an entity that represented all crafts and textile workers, both skilled and unskilled, came into being. The AFTO and NUTW disbanded and reformed into a single union that was officially named the United Textile Workers of America.

Under the presidency of John Golden, the UTWA survived through the years, regardless of the troubles it faced. Unlike its predecessors, the UTWA maintained solidarity by adapting to the rapidly changing textile industry. In 1902 its membership was 10,600 among 185 local unions. By 1920 its ranks would increase to around 100,000 (serving approximately 3 percent of the industry's workforce). Over the next 20 years, the organization would undergo several changes in membership and even name, but the UTWA remained a bastion of unionism for textile workers in the United States. In 1995 the UTWA merged with the United Food and Commercial Workers Textile and Garment

Council, thus continuing its proud heritage of unionism and amalgamation.

Key Players

Golden, John: A Lancashire spinner, Golden became the president of the United Textile Workers and a member of the board of directors for the Militia of Christ, a Catholic organization against radial unionism. He was a strong proponent of southern unionism and was criticized harshly for his role as conciliator during the Lawrence, Massachusetts, strike of 1912.

Gompers, Samuel (1850–1924): Born in London, Gompers's harsh life motivated him to help improve working conditions. He became the first president of the American Federation of Labor in 1886 and played a vital role in the formation of the International Labor Organization. During that time, Gompers worked to correct the disparities between the northern and southern textile industries.

Greene, Prince W.: Born in Columbus, Georgia, Greene brought several southern craft unions into the National Union of Textile Workers in 1898. He became the president of the National Union of Textile Workers between 1898 and 1900, then served as secretary-treasurer until the merger with the United Textile Workers of America in 1901.

See also: *American Federation of Labor; Knights of Labor; Pawtucket Textile Strike.*

BIBLIOGRAPHY

Books

Daniel, Clete. *Culture of Misfortune*. Ithaca, NY: Cornell University Press, 2001.

Foner, Eric, and John A. Garraty, eds. *The Reader's Companion to American History*. Boston: Houghton Mifflin, 1991.

Hutchins, Grace. *Labor and Silk*. New York: International Publishers, 1929.

Marshall, F. Ray. *Labor in the South*. Cambridge: Harvard University Press, 1967.

Mitchell, George S. *Textile Unionism and the South*. Chapel Hill: University of North Carolina Press, 1931.

Simon, Bryant. "Choosing Between the Ham and the Union: Paternalism in the Cone Mills of Greensboro, 1925–1930." In *Hanging by a Thread: Social Change in Southern Textiles*, edited by J. Leiter, M. Schulman, and R. Zingraff. Ithaca, NY: ILR Press, 1991.

Zieger, Robert H. *Organized Labor in the Twentieth-Century South*. Knoxville: University of Tennessee Press, 1991.

Other

Eckilson, Erik. "Samuel Slater: Father of the Industrial Revolution." 2002 [cited 20 September 2002]. <http://www.geocities.com/~woon_heritage/slaterhist.htm>.

Tucker, Barbara M. "My History Is American History." American History Files: Textile Industry. 2000 [cited 20 September 2002]. <http://www.myhistory.org/historytopics/articles/textile_industry.html>.

—Lee Ann Paradise

U.S. Government Seizes Railroads

United States 1917–1920

Synopsis

The nation's railroads were under government control during World War I. Some 360,000 miles of track and more than two million workers were directed by the United States Railroad Administration (USRA) from 26 December 1917 until the passing of the Transportation Act of 1920 on 28 February 1920. The act, also known as the Cummins-Esch Law, remanded operation of the railroads to private control on 1 March 1920. Railroads benefited from regulatory control, functioned efficiently, and prospered from construction and infrastructure improvements. Additionally, the government guaranteed a six-month profit after the transfer and agreed to dispense more than $530 million in federal funds to the railroads. The act was President Woodrow Wilson's final victory for comprehensive federal railroad regulation, which he implemented to lend stability and rationale to the industry. Further, the act permitted railroads joint use of facilities and allowed traffic agreements between railroads that previously had been illegal under the Sherman Antitrust Act (1890) and the Clayton Act (1914).

Timeline

1898: United States defeats Spain in the three-month Spanish-American War. As a result, Cuba gains it independence, and the United States purchases Puerto Rico and the Philippines from Spain for $20 million.

1903: Russia's Social Democratic Party splits into two factions: the moderate Mensheviks and the hard-line Bolsheviks. Despite their names, which in Russian mean "minority" and "majority," respectively, Mensheviks actually outnumber Bolsheviks.

1908: Ford Motor Company introduces the Model T.

1911: Revolution in Mexico, begun the year before, continues with the replacement of the corrupt Porfirio Diaz, president since 1877, by Francisco Madero.

1914: On 28 June in the town of Sarajevo, then part of the Austro-Hungarian Empire, Serbian nationalist Gavrilo Princip assassinates Austrian Archduke Francis Ferdinand and wife Sophie. In the weeks that follow, Austria declares war on Serbia, and Germany on Russia and France, while Great Britain responds by declaring war on Germany. By the beginning of August, the lines are drawn, with the Allies (Great Britain, France, Russia, Belgium, Serbia, Montenegro, and Japan) against the Central Powers (Germany, Austria-Hungary, and Turkey).

1916: Battles of Verdun and the Somme on the Western Front. The latter sees the first use of tanks, by the British.

1918: The Second Battle of the Marne in July and August is the last major conflict on the Western Front. In November, Kaiser Wilhelm II abdicates, bringing an end to the war.

1919: Formation of the Third International (Comintern), whereby the Bolshevik government of Russia establishes its control over communist movements worldwide.

1920: In the United States, the U.S. Department of Justice launches a campaign to track down and deport communists, anarchists, and other radicals, as well as those suspecting of being left-leaning revolutionaries. Raids are also used for the purpose of rooting out and deporting illegal aliens.

1922: Inspired by the Bolsheviks' example of imposing revolution by means of a coup, Benito Mussolini leads his blackshirts in an October "March on Rome" and forms a new fascist government.

1926: Britain paralyzed by the general strike.

1930: Collectivization of Soviet agriculture begins, and with it one of the greatest crimes of the twentieth century. In the next years, as Soviet operatives force peasants to give up their lands, millions will die either by direct action, manmade famine, or forced labor. Overseas, however, and particularly among intellectuals and artists of the West, Soviet collectivization and industrialization are regarded as models of progress for the world.

Event and Its Context

Prior to World War I, railroads were largely unregulated and in disrepair. The increasing costs of expansion, maintenance, materials, and labor burdened rail carriers at a time when small profits prevented them from reinvesting capital into the industry. Rail carriers could not increase rates to improve their profits because the Interstate Commerce Commission (ICC) tightly controlled passenger and freight rates. The need for government subsidy of the industry arose when profits significantly dropped between 1911 and 1913. Rail companies anticipated a general rate increase, though the ICC, which attempted to keep rail transportation costs comparable with the shipping industry, successfully repelled it. Although the newly stimulated war economy brought temporary prosperity in 1915 and 1916 via increased freight business, the effects were short-term.

Railroads' War Board

Wartime control of railroads by governments was both immediate and a standard procedure among America's European enemies. Slow to intervene in operations, the U.S. government delayed involvement in the matter until several months into the war. However, to address the wartime operations of the rail transportation industry, railroad presidents converged on Washington five days after President Woodrow Wilson's declaration of war. They formed a five-member executive committee known as the Railroads' War Board (RWB). The five members were Howard Elliott of the New York, New Haven and Hartford Railroad; Hale Holden, president of the Chicago, Burlington and Quincy Railroad; Julius Kruttschnitt of the Southern Pacific Company; Samuel Rea, president of the Pennsylvania Railroad; and Fairfax Harrison, president of Southern Railway. There were two ex-officio members, E. E. Clark of the ICC and Daniel Willard of the Council of National Defense. The General

Committee was divided into six geographic regions and also included several subcommittees: Commission on Car Service, Military Equipment Standards, Military Transportation Accounting, Military Passenger Tariffs, Military Freight Tariffs, Materials and Supplies, and Express Transportation. Responsible for synchronizing federal and private resources to combat the industry's escalating costs and fight the war on the home front, their efforts proved largely ineffective for several reasons.

The RWB's cooperative efforts at cannibalizing each other's railways and rationing the use of the railroads failed, although it was initially successful on a small scale. The two objectives that the RWB worked to realize were resolving the national boxcar shortage and alleviating rail congestion by prioritizing rail traffic. Boxcars that had clogged eastern terminals were redistributed among the railways. Empty cars were removed from surplus and incorporated into lines experiencing shortages, and dilapidated cars were scrapped for metal. Passenger service on the eastern seaboard was interrupted when the RWB appropriated locomotives and passenger cars for wartime use. The redistribution measures targeted specific locations for short-term solutions. The RWB addressed the prioritization of rail traffic by jointly using terminals and rails, which violated the Sherman Antitrust Act. Overall, the railway infrastructure could not bear the added traffic on its meager terminal, passing, and double tracks.

The RWB faced additional problems in 1916 including the threat of a general strike and an exceptionally harsh winter. Wages for skilled rail workers failed to remain competitive with those of similarly skilled jobs in other industries. Trainmen left the railroads for higher pay or often were conscripted into the military, thus causing many railways to operate with skeleton crews and imperiling efficient operation. Manpower shortages were estimated as high as 25 percent on some lines. Labor unions and railroad management could not come to terms on increased wages for railroad employees.

Army Appropriation Act of 1916

Wilson avoided a general railroad strike in September 1916 by passing the Adamson Act, which shortened the workday from 10 hours to eight hours with no reduction in pay for trainmen and enginemen. A major victory for labor unions and workers, management perceived the act as a threat to capitalism. Additionally, Wilson sanctioned the restructuring and extension of the ICC. Wilson and the ICC disagreed over the terms of the Adamson Act. Under the guise of neutrality due to the upcoming election, Wilson appointed General George W. Goethals and two other men to the ICC to study the effect of the eight-hour day upon rail workers and recommend changes to him and to Congress. In their report to Congress in December 1916, the committee demanded that the ICC be strengthened and requested the authority to assume control of the railroads in the event of war. Congress granted their request with the Army Appropriation Act of 1916, which granted the president the right to assume control of private railroads during war. Besides railroads, the act authorized government control of coastwise steamship lines, inland waterways, and telephone and telegraph companies. All were seized in the interest of national security and all parties abided compensatory agreements. The

ICC expanded and the federal government formally took control of the nation's railroads in August 1917. The ICC formed regional groups that would address new problems that were anticipated as a result of the change.

The winter of 1916–1917 dealt another blow to the RWB's plans for wartime mobilization. Steam engines could not be kept operable in the inadequate facilities that most railroads had not maintained or expanded during the lean years prior to the war. Most roundhouses and engine shops could not accommodate the locomotives, which had increased in size to accommodate the new longer and heavier trains. Further, the Justice Department began an investigation of the RWB for antitrust violations.

William McAdoo and the U.S. Railroad Administration

When management proved deficient and failed to effect improvements in the performance of the nation's rail transportation, President Wilson requested that Congress grant authority for setting of railroad rates to the newly formed United States Railroad Administration (USRA). The Federal Railroad Control Act that was passed by Congress March 1918 legalized this move. The act limited the ICC's association with the USRA to a reviewing capacity and mandated that governance be returned to the companies no later than 21 months after the end of the war. William Gibbs McAdoo was appointed director general of the USRA. McAdoo, who was Wilson's son-in-law, was also secretary of the treasury. The USRA comprised several divisions: Division of Finance and Purchasing, Division of Operation, Division of Traffic, Division of Labor, Division of Public Service and Accounting, Division of Capital Expenditures, and Division of Inland Waterways. Like the RWB, the USRA divided the railroads by geographic region. The three divisions were Eastern, Western, and Southern. The Eastern Division was subdivided 1 June 1918 into the Allegheny Region and the Pocahontas Region. The directors appointed to each region were presidents of primary railway systems. The USRA developed a permit system that ensured prioritization of war industry freight.

Antitrust and antipooling laws were suspended so as to bring control of the railroads under the government. The USRA's immunity to these laws allowed the organization to distribute traffic along the shortest routes, impose traffic priorities to federal and private shippers, raise rates, and raise wages to persuade workers to remain in their jobs. The USRA created seven major regions in which federal officers were partnered with private executives.

McAdoo called for railroad managers to streamline operations. He required that redundant services be discontinued, especially passenger service, which drained wartime traffic of efficiency. Those cutbacks released additional locomotives for freight service and lightened rail traffic.

McAdoo created a Railroad Wage Commission to investigate wages and recommend changes. He proposed an increase in wages in January 1918, and the commission agreed. Congress granted him the authorization to raise wages in May. McAdoo made the increase retroactive to 1 January 1918. Although the Adamson Act of 1916 shortened the work day and maintained wages, trainmen and enginemen were the only railway workers that the Act covered. All railway workers benefit-

ed from McAdoo's wage increase. Though the workday remained lengthy, railway workers were finally being paid time and a half for more than eight hours of work. Better compensation attracted new workers who eagerly filled more than 100,000 slots that railroads were required to fill in response to McAdoo's provisions. With permission implicit in the Federal Control Act, the USRA inflated rates by 25 percent to fulfill the promise of improved wages.

Though pleased by McAdoo's responsiveness to their demands, rail workers continually clamored for higher wages. To address concerns of the workers, McAdoo created a Division of Labor, composed equally of management and union members, which was to watch over working conditions. Three Railway Boards of Adjustment were responsible for representing those in the operating crafts, shop crafts, and other allied employees. Number One included engineers, firemen, trainmen and conductor; they were the operating crafts. Number Two included machinists, boilermakers, blacksmiths, electricians, sheet metal workers, and carmen; the shop crafts. Number Three included clerks, telegraphers, switchmen, and maintenance-of-way workers. The USRA further appeased workers by following the Division of Labor's suggestion that rail workers should be entitled to trade union membership. Once the government recognized the survival of the trade unions and cemented their position between the workers and railroad management, labor organizations gained power and affirmed their influence on the industry.

The War Ends

The USRA formed a Division of Capital Expenditures to solicit capital improvements for urgent projects. Funding of requests depended on whether the project served the war effort. The division set priorities for improvements and determined that roundhouses and shops were the most important, with improvements to passing and yard tracks, signals, and fuel stations following closely. The USRA was initially responsible for financing the projects, but railroads often paid for improvements from their own revenue. Just as the effects of the USRA's policies were being felt along the nation's railways, the war ended in November 1918. Labor unions lobbied for nationalization of railroads because workers had greatly benefited from government intervention and regulation of wages and working conditions. McAdoo, whose dual position as director general of the USRA and secretary of the treasury afforded him a strategic political position during the war, was prepared to extend the federal control for five years. Congress debated the matter for 16 months, but ultimately returned control of the railroads to private ownership. McAdoo resigned his position in January 1918, and his assistant Walker D. Hines assumed command of the USRA. Somber upon McAdoo's resignation, workers believed that nationalization of the railroads would ensure wage increases, further benefits, and regulated working conditions.

Although the railroads were under government control, ownership of individual systems had remained in the private sector. Critics of this arrangement accused Wilson of promoting a socialist agenda. Wilson realized the importance of the rail transportation industry to the growth of the country and supported the development of a strong national rail infrastructure prior to World War I. He advocated strongly for the railroads and relied upon the initiatives of railroad leaders because other matters consumed the objectives of his administration.

Railroad owners claimed that the government returned the railroads with a deficit and complained that making national agreements with labor unions had undermined their autonomy in setting wages. USRA's maintenance of the railroads had proven insufficient as well. Under Hines's administration, the USRA spent modest amounts on railroad improvements. Hines was unwilling to increase categorically the value of the railroads. He was frugal with government expenditures and slowed maintenance to a minimum so that railroads saw no increase in value while under the control of the USRA. The government was not obligated to improve the value of the railroads but did compensate owners for deferred maintenance after figures were calculated. Revenues generated during the war covered expenses for that duration but they fell short by some $642 million from what Congress had guaranteed to private owners.

Although McAdoo had ingratiated himself with labor organizations because of his advocacy of higher wages for workers, Hines bore the brunt of railroad owners' wrath because he institutionalized the gains that workers had made during the war. Once the war ended, other private industries retracted benefits that workers had gained during the labor shortages. Hines brokered national agreements between labor unions and railroad companies and managed to give workers a small increase. Hines's strategies contributed to the difficulty of the transition from federal to private control. Struggling with rigid work rules for decades afterward, railroad management fared poorly when technological change came to the industry and render those rules obsolete. Charged with dismantling the USRA, Hines was diverted from his responsibilities by a rash of unauthorized strikes. Workers demanded increased wages to offset the cost of living that had increased following the war. Focusing its resources on pacifying striking laborers, the USRA was regarded as unnecessary after the passage of the Transportation Act of 1920.

Key Players

Elliott, Howard: President of Northern Pacific Railroad as of 23 October 1903. A graduate of Harvard College, Elliott began his work in the railroad industry by carrying a chain with a surveying corps. He was responsible for moving the general manager's headquarters from St. Joseph to St. Louis. Elliott was a director of the St. Louis World's Fair. He became vice president of the Great Burlington System headquartered in Chicago.

Hines, Walker Downer (1870–1934): Born in Kentucky, Hines studied law at the University of Virginia and worked in the law offices of the Louisville and Nashville Railroad. He was assistant director of the United States Railroad Administration (USRA, 1917–1919) then succeeded William McAdoo as director general. Hines resigned from the position on 15 May 1920.

Holden, Hale (1869–1940): Born in Missouri and of English descent, Holden was a lawyer and the youngest executive of any rail system. He was president of Chicago, Burlington and Quincy and a spokesman for the industry during the strike that was averted by the passage of the Adamson Act.

He was a member of the Railroads War Board, and McAdoo invited him to head the USRA. Though Holden declined, he served two months in an advisory capacity to the director general. He was a vice president and director of the American Railway Association (1919–1924).

McAdoo, William Gibbs (1863–1941): Born in Georgia, McAdoo was a lawyer, political leader, and secretary of the treasury. He actively promoted Woodrow Wilson for the presidency in 1912 and was given a cabinet post. The Federal Reserve System was begun during McAdoo's administration of the Department of the Treasury, and he was its first chairman. He also managed the financing of American participation in World War I and served as director general of railroads during the period of government operation during World War I (1917–1919).

See also: *Clayton Antitrust Act.*

BIBLIOGRAPHY

Books

Davis, Colin. "United States Railroad Administration." In *The U. S. in the First World War: An Encyclopedia*, edited by Anne Cipraino Venzon. New York: Garland Publishing, 1995.

Hines, Walker D. *War History of the American Railroads.* New Haven, CT: Yale University Press, 1928.

Kolk, Gabriel. *Railroads and Regulation, 1877–1916.* Princeton, NJ: Princeton University Press, 1965.

Thompson, Gregory L. "Railroad Transportation Services." In *The U. S. in the First World War: An Encyclopedia*, edited by Anne Cipraino Venzon. New York: Garland Publishing, 1995.

ADDITIONAL RESOURCES

Books

Cunningham, William J. *American Railroads: Government Control and Reconstruction Policies.* Chicago: Shaw, 1922.

Godfrey, Aaron A. *Government Operation of the Railroads: Its Necessity, Success and Consequences, 1918–1920.* Austin, TX: San Felipe Press, 1974.

Kerr, K. Austin. *American Railroad Politics, 1914–1920.* Pittsburgh, PA: University of Pittsburgh Press, 1969.

Meyer, Balthasar Henry. *Railway Legislation in the United States.* New York: Arno Press, 1973.

Saunders, Richard. *The Railroad Mergers and the Coming of Conrail.* Westport, CT: Greenwood Press, 1978.

Summers, Harrison Boyd, and Robert E. Summers (compilers). *The Railroad Problem: With Reference to Government Ownership.* New York: H. W. Wilson Company, 1939.

—Rebecca Tolley-Stokes

U.S. Steel Defeats the Amalgamated Association

United States 1901

Synopsis

After the Amalgamated Association of Iron, Steel, and Tin Workers (AAISTW, or the Amalgamated Association) strike was defeated in the aftermath of the Battle of Homestead (the gun battle between members of the Amalgamated Association and Pinkerton agents during the 1892 strike at the Carnegie Mill in Homestead, Pennsylvania), the union still held onto a precarious position in the iron and steel industry. This limited position was itself practically eliminated by the ill-conceived strike in 1901, when after a three-month strike the union was defeated by United States Steel and forced to withdraw from most of the mills owned by the steel trust.

Timeline

1881: U.S. President James A. Garfield is assassinated in a Washington, D.C., railway station by Charles J. Guiteau.

1886: Bombing at Haymarket Square, Chicago, kills seven policemen and injures numerous others. Eight anarchists are accused and tried; three are imprisoned, one commits suicide, and four are hanged.

1891: French troops open fire on workers during a 1 May demonstration at Fourmies, where employees of the Sans Pareille factory are striking for an eight-hour workday. Nine people are killed—two of them children—and 60 more are injured.

1894: Thousands of unemployed American workers—a group named "Coxey's Army" for their leader, Jacob S. Coxey—march on Washington, D.C. A number of such marches on the capital occurred during this period of economic challenges, but Coxey's march was the only one to actually reach its destination.

1897: In the midst of a nationwide depression, Mrs. Bradley Martin, daughter of Carnegie Steel magnate Henry Phipps, throws a lavish party at New York's recently opened Waldorf-Astoria Hotel, where she has a suite decorated to look like Versailles. Her 900 guests, dressed in Louis XV period costumes, consume 60 cases of champagne.

1899: Polish-born German socialist Rosa Luxemburg rejects the argument that working conditions in Europe have improved and that change must come by reforming the existing system. Rather, she calls for an overthrow of the existing power structure by means of violent international revolution.

1901: U.S. President William McKinley is assassinated by Leon Czolgosz, an anarchist. Vice President Theodore Roosevelt becomes president.

1901: Austrian-American immunologist Karl Landsteiner discovers A, B, and O blood.

John Pierpont Morgan. The Library of Congress.

1901: Guglielmo Marconi makes the first successful transmission and reception of a radio signal.

1903: Russia's Social Democratic Party splits into two factions: the moderate Mensheviks and the hard-line Bolsheviks. Despite their names, which in Russian mean "minority" and "majority," respectively, Mensheviks actually outnumber Bolsheviks.

1907: At the Second Hague Peace Conference, 46 nations adopt 10 conventions governing the rules of war.

1911: Turkish-Italian War sees the first use of aircraft as an offensive weapon. Italian victory results in the annexation of Libya.

Event and Its Context

The Amalgamated Association was established in 1876 by the merger of three labor unions that had formed in the earlier history of the industry: the Sons of Vulcan, the Heaters' and Rollers' Union, and the Roll Hands' Union. The new union thrived in these early years of the iron industry; by 1891 the Amalgamated Association claimed over 24,000 members, making it one of the largest unions in the American Federation of Labor (AFL). The leadership of the Amalgamated Association concentrated on creating uniformity in the wage scales of members, which in turn helped mill owners to anticipate production costs. This did not prevent bitter disputes from breaking out between management and labor, but management tolerated the union for this reason. The membership of the Amalgamated Association was concentrated almost entirely west of the Allegheny Mountains; most of the iron mills in the Ohio Valley and in Illinois were organized, but none east of Pittsburgh were unionized.

Technological advances in the field began to undermine the position of the union, particularly the shift to the production of steel, as the union had accomplished little organization in that part of the industry. The union was also quick to accommodate mill owners when they claimed that technological advances led to increases in productivity; most famously, the Amalgamated Association accepted a reduction of wages for its members at the Homestead Works in 1889 because of the introduction of new machinery at the mill that reduced the workload for members (and also eliminated several hundred jobs)—before the famous strike there of 1892. After the Battle of Homestead, the Amalgamated Association lost most of its membership in the mills that produced raw steel as well as in the mills that turned out rods and wire products. The union managed to hold on in those factories that turned out finished steel products, particularly sheet steel, tin plate, and steel hoops. It was in these remaining mills that the Amalgamated Association came into conflict with the monolithic United States Steel.

The formation of U.S. Steel, the first billion-dollar corporation in the United States, came at the climax of a period of business consolidations in the steel industry. Companies in several branches of the industry had consolidated in the years before the formation of U.S. Steel and were able to dominate their markets. U.S. Steel, under the direction of financier J. P. Morgan, was then able to merge these steel companies under a holding company under Morgan's control. Each of these companies controlled their particular segment of the steel industry but operated under a variety of different conditions; in particular, some of the companies operated with union workers and some without unions. The preference of most of the managers of the subsidiaries of U.S. Steel was to run their businesses nonunion. In fact, much of the work within these divisions was being directed away from union plants and into nonunion plants, which meant that union members were losing jobs to nonunion members. The Amalgamated Association was aware of the antiunion preference of many of the divisions of U.S. Steel and was determined to prevent this "whip-sawing" effect upon the mills with which they had contracts. The leadership of the Amalgamated Association adopted the goal of winning union contracts in all of the mills of the subsidiaries. A sense of urgency informed these efforts, as the officers felt compelled to act before the size and coordination of divisions made U.S. Steel impregnable to unionization efforts. Management of the steel trust was moving in a parallel direction, hoping to stave off unionization efforts long enough to stockpile enough product to wait out a potential strike down the road several months.

The executive committee of U.S. Steel agreed to sign new contracts with the union, but only for those mills that the Amalgamated Association had already organized. This policy was then passed down to the various divisions. When the negotia-tions between the divisions and the Amalgamated Association opened, however, the implementation of the policy was less than perfect. The Amalgamated Association opened negotiations with two divisions of U.S. Steel, the American Sheet Steel Company and the American Tin Plate Company. American Tin Plate initially attempted to rid itself of the union in mills that the Amalgamated Association had already organized. In the midst of negotiations, however, the division shifted positions and offered to allow the Amalgamated Association to organize all of its mills if American Sheet Steel would do the same. American Sheet Steel, however, remained true to the prescribed bargaining strategy and refused to allow the Amalgamated Association to organize its unorganized mills.

The Amalgamated Association, reaching this impasse, called a strike of the workers they represented on 1 July 1901. The Amalgamated Association was initially able to exploit the divisiveness of the two subsidiaries against them and especially against U.S. Steel management. The American public had a long-standing mistrust of monopolies, and a company that controlled 40 percent of the nation's steel-making capacity was a large target for such mistrust. The Amalgamated Association hoped to pressure the subsidiaries by using the mistrust of the parent corporation. This was an effective strategy, particularly because the formation of the trust was fairly new and upper management (particularly Judge Elbert Gary) decided that U.S. Steel was particularly vulnerable to such an attack. The executive committee of U.S. Steel forced the antiunion sheet mill managers to offer contracts to the Amalgamated Association in all but five plants.

At this point, the leadership of the Amalgamated committed a serious blunder. Confident that the union would soon win contracts in all of the plants, the union rejected management's offer. The union based this confidence upon the fact that not only had sheet steel workers enthusiastically entered the strike, but also that they had been joined by hoop steel workers in many plants as well. The Amalgamated Association therefore sent out a call for all tin plate workers to join the strike on 15 July. In the meantime, the union leadership traveled to New York City to negotiate with J. P. Morgan. Amalgamated Association president T. J. Shaffer and secretary John Williams were the primary union negotiators with Morgan. They found Morgan congenial but unyielding. They returned to Pittsburgh with an offer for contracts with all mills that had already been unionized at the end of June 1901. The executive board of the Amalgamated Association rejected this deal. The entire board then traveled to New York with the counterproposal of union contracts for all mills on strike at the time. Morgan rejected this proposal and accused Shaffer and Williams of bad faith bargaining because they had not prevailed upon fellow board members to agree to the earlier offer.

At this juncture, the union decided to raise the stakes rather than accept less than their goal of company-wide unionization. The executive committee of the Amalgamated Association called on workers in basic steel (that is, turning ore into steel) to join the strike. Membership of the Amalgamated Association in basic steel was small, and few answered the call of a union that had largely ignored them since the failure of the Homestead strike. With the continuation of work in the basic steel plants, workers in the finishing mills witnessed their jobs being taken over by strikebreakers. This development was a severe blow to the morale of union members, who had long clung to the belief that the job skills they possessed made them indispensable to the company.

The union responded to this development by asking the executive committee of the AFL to call out associated unions in mining and railroading, which the executive committee of the AFL refused to do. President Schaffer accused AFL president Samuel Gompers of betraying the union, a charge that did nothing to further the union's strike effort. An agreement to end the strike was not reached until 14 September, and the terms were very unfavorable to the union. The only mills that the Amalgamated Association retained were those that had remained out on strike, so the Amalgamated Association was only able to retain a token presence in the industry. In less than 20 years, the largest union in the AFL had been reduced to a mere shadow presence.

Key Players

Gompers, Samuel (1850–1924): Gompers was the first president of the American Federation of Labor (AFL). Gompers was a proponent of "bread-and-butter" unionism—getting union members contracts that rewarded them financially, above all. Gompers was not a strong proponent of social unionism or of using strikes for any other purpose than gaining better wages.

Morgan, John Pierpont (1837–1913): Succeeded his father at the head of J. S. Morgan and Company and was the guiding force behind the formation of the U.S. Steel Company, the first company in the U.S. to have a billion dollars in assets. Morgan and his company controlled the financial status of the entire country. He loaned the U.S. government gold in 1895 and assumed a major role in the Panic of 1907. Although Morgan often came under withering public criticism, this had no effect upon his business dealings.

Shaffer, T. J. (1853–1892): President of the Amalgamated Association of Iron, Steel, and Tin Workers at the time of the 1901 strike against U.S. Steel. Shaffer badly miscalculated both the strength of his union and the resolve of U.S. Steel to resist unionization of its entire operation. The result of these miscalculations was the greatly diminished importance of the Amalgamated Association.

See also: *American Federation of Labor; Homestead Lockout.*

BIBLIOGRAPHY

Books

Brody, David. *Steelworkers in America: The Nonunion Era.* Cambridge, MA: Harvard University Press, 1960.

Couvares, Francis. *The Remaking of Pittsburgh: Class and Culture in an Industrializing City, 1877–1919.* Albany: State University of New York Press, 1984.

Robinson, Jesse. *The Amalgamated Association of Iron, Steel, and Tin Workers.* Baltimore, MD: Johns Hopkins University Press, 1920.

Strouse, Jean. *Morgan: American Financier.* New York: Random House, 1999.

—Gregory M. Miller

U.S. Steel Recognizes the Steel Workers Organizing Committee as an Official Bargaining Agent

United States 1937

Synopsis

On 2 March 1937 the United States Steel Corporation, throughout its history a fierce opponent of organized labor, signed a preliminary agreement recognizing the Steel Workers Organizing Committee (SWOC) as a legitimate bargaining agent for employees who were members of that organization. The two parties signed a formal contract on 17 March. These agreements were the culmination of secret talks between Congress of Industrial Organizations (CIO) president John L. Lewis and U.S. Steel chairman Myron Taylor. The agreement was the first victory for SWOC in its efforts to represent the entire steel industry. That violence was not used to prevent unionization made the victory even more surprising. The agreement with U.S. Steel led directly to many other steel firms recognizing SWOC, even though the so-called Little Steel firms, large competitors of U.S. Steel, continued to resist unionization until after World War II began.

Timeline

1922: Publication of James Joyce's novel *Ulysses* and T. S. Eliot's poem *The Waste Land*—works that will transform literature and inaugurate the era of modernism.

1927: American inventor Philo T. Farnsworth demonstrates a working model of the television, and Belgian astronomer Georges Lemaître proposes the Big Bang Theory.

1932: In German elections, Nazis gain a 37 percent plurality of Reichstag seats, raising tensions between the far right and the far left. On a "bloody Sunday" in July, Communists in Hamburg attack Nazis with guns, and a fierce battle ensues.

1937: Italy signs the Anti-Comintern Pact, signed by Germany and Japan the preceding year. Like the two others before it, Italy now withdraws from the League of Nations.

1937: Japan attacks China and annexes most of that nation's coastal areas.

1937: Stalin uses carefully staged show trials in Moscow to eliminate all rivals for leadership. These party purges, however, are only a small part of the death toll now being exacted in a country undergoing forced industrialization, much of it by means of slave labor.

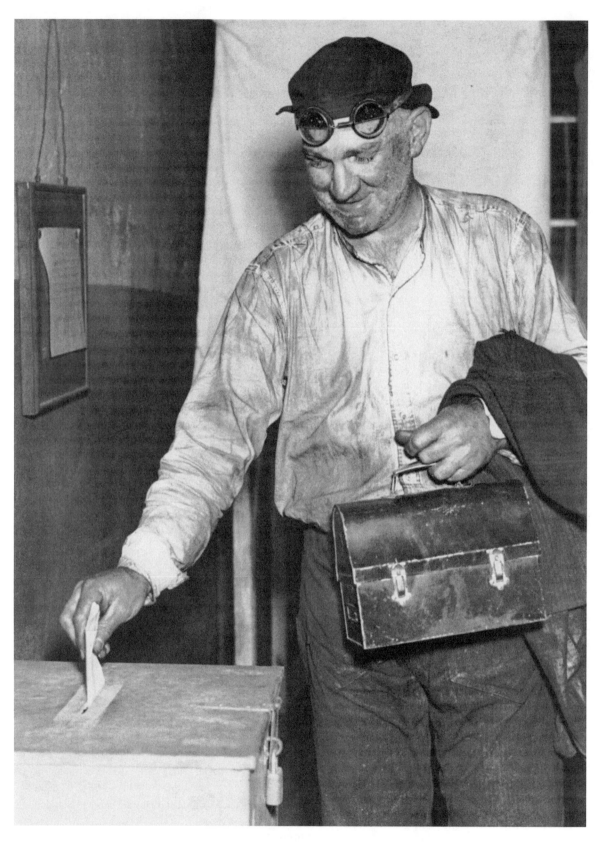

Open-hearth steel worker votes on union representation issue, Jones and Laughlin Steel Company plant, Alquippa, Pennsylvania. © Bettmann/Corbis. Reproduced by permission.

National Labor Relations Board supervises steel workers' vote on union representation, 1937. © UPI/Corbis-Bettmann. Reproduced by permission.

1937: In the middle of an around-the-world flight, Amelia Earhart and her plane disappear somewhere in the Pacific.

1937: Crash of the *Hindenburg* in Lakehurst, New Jersey, kills 36 and ends the brief era when rigid airships promised to be the ocean liners of the skies.

1937: Pablo Picasso paints his famous *Guernica* mural dramatizing the Nationalist bombing of a town in Spain. Thanks to artists and intellectuals such as Picasso and Ernest Hemingway, the Loyalists are winning the battle of hearts and minds, even if they are weaker militarily, and idealistic young men flock from America to join the

"Abraham Lincoln Brigade." Yet as George Orwell later reveals in *Homage to Catalonia,* the lines between good and evil are not clear: with its Soviet backing, the Loyalist cause serves as proxy for a totalitarianism every bit as frightening as that of the Nationalists and their German and Italian supporters.

1942: Axis conquests reach their height in the middle of this year. The Nazis control a vast region from Normandy to the suburbs of Stalingrad, and from the Arctic Circle to the edges of the Sahara. To the east, the Japanese "Co-Prosperity Sphere" encompasses territories from

China to Burma to the East Indies, stretching deep into the western Pacific.

1947: Establishment of the Marshall Plan to assist European nations in recovering from the war.

1952: Among the cultural landmarks of the year are the film *High Noon* and the book *The Invisible Man* by Ralph Ellison.

Event and Its Context

The talks that culminated in the March accord began after a chance encounter between Taylor and Lewis in the dining room of the Mayflower Hotel in Washington, D.C., on 9 January 1937. Taylor, worried about the future of the industry, had been thinking about the wording of a possible compromise between U.S. Steel and the CIO since the previous summer. Therefore, when Lewis quietly suggested a meeting, Taylor offered to see him the next day. This led to a lengthy series of conferences that eventually resulted in a contract. Even though Lewis was making front-page news every day because of the sit-down strike in Flint, Michigan, the media did not know about these talks until after the initial agreement became public. However, the leaders of U.S. Steel's competitors did; they had been told about the talks early in the negotiation process. They did not like this development but could do little about it. Lewis told almost nobody about his talks with Taylor. His presence at U.S. Steel's New York headquarters would not have been surprising because he had been elected a collective bargaining representative for some of their "captive mines" (those wholly owned by a steel company) in 1933. Nevertheless, to preserve their secrecy, most of the negotiations between the two men occurred at Taylor's New York townhouse.

The 2 March agreement covered workers in U.S. Steel's Carnegie-Illinois Steel subsidiary only, although the parties signed nearly identical agreements covering other subsidiaries in the weeks following the 3 March announcement. The initial agreement had five sections. The first section stated that the Carnegie-Illinois Steel Corporation recognized SWOC as the collective bargaining agent for its employees who belonged to the Amalgamated Association of Iron, Steel, and Tin Workers (the union SWOC had effectively taken over at its formation in 1936). Management also recognized and agreed not to interfere with the right of employees to join the union. In return, SWOC agreed not to intimidate or coerce employees. Section Two of the agreement increased wages by 10 cents an hour for all Carnegie-Illinois employees. Section Three formally established an 8-hour workday and a 40-hour workweek. It also mandated time-and-a-half pay for all hours worked over that total. Section Four laid out a procedure for establishing a working committee to negotiate issues like working conditions and dispute arbitration. The last section set the length of the contract. It ran for about a year, until 28 February 1938.

As far as U.S. Steel was concerned, the wording of Section One made the agreement palatable. SWOC's willingness to limit its bargaining rights to those employees who had joined the organization meant that, in principle, the new agreement might not alter labor policy at all. Interested employees could theoretically continue to bargain with U.S. Steel through the company union. This group of organizations in 1933 had been established to satisfy government-imposed collective bargaining requirements in the National Industrial Recovery Act (NIRA) and, later, in the National Labor Relations Act (NLRA). In management circles, they were known as employee representation plans (ERPs). U.S. Steel believed it could maintain its own ERPs to counter the power of the union. It voluntarily recognized SWOC in order to maintain the principle of choice between an inside and an outside union, even though it could have probably fought the union and won. Management was more concerned about defending the principle of allowing workers not to choose SWOC than it was about keeping its works completely union-free.

The Taylor-Lewis agreement shocked the business world. The press, the public, and industry observers had been expecting an all-out war between U.S. Steel and SWOC. Instead, the agreement not only assured the survival of trade unions in a critical industry, it also served as a catalyst to the organization of other industries. Although the decision of General Motors to recognize the United Auto Workers a week earlier is remembered because of the dramatic sit-down strikes that preceded it, the U.S. Steel agreement is impressive because it was achieved without violence and with minimal government coercion.

Reaction in the mills to the Taylor-Lewis agreement also surprised everyone, even the union. So many employees joined SWOC in the weeks following the agreement that its membership almost doubled and, in practice, the open shop ceased to exist. Even so, SWOC did not have complete control over U.S. Steel's employees. As late as September 1937, only 44 percent of its workers were SWOC members. Nevertheless, the union did have enough members to become the only viable union in the shops.

With management's encouragement, some former employee representatives tried to create alternatives to SWOC. In January 1937 employees in the Chicago area created the Steel Employees Independent Labor Organization. By that summer, dues made this organization self-supporting. It even had offices, a lodge hall, a full-time president, and an attorney. Nevertheless, the group eventually disappeared because it never won a contract. A group in the Pittsburgh area created the American Union of Steel Workers in the days following the preliminary accord between SWOC and U.S. Steel. This organization attracted considerable media attention when it sent a letter to William Green, president of the American Federation of Labor (AFL), asking for his assistance. Nothing came of this effort either.

The final blow to these company unions came after the U.S. Supreme Court upheld the constitutionality of the NLRA in April 1937. The NLRA included the first permanent language that recognized the right of workers to join unions of their own choosing and provisions against company-dominated labor organizations. In response to the decision, U.S. Steel withdrew all financial support for the ERP and stopped providing facilities for elections and other company union activities. At that point, SWOC had no rivals for the loyalty of U.S. Steel's employees. This guaranteed it a strong base of support for its campaign to organize the rest of the steel industry.

Explanations of why U.S. Steel settled with SWOC are several. First and foremost, historians focus on successful efforts by trade union sympathizers to take over U.S. Steel's company unions. These organizations had some success in limiting reform early in their history because management used them as a vehicle for making small changes to improve workers' lives. Nevertheless, many U.S. Steel employees wanted greater changes than those management offered through the ERPs.

The first moves toward complete independence among U.S. Steel's ERPs appeared shortly after the passage of the NLRA. Seeing the law as legal cover for collective action, employee representatives worked to make their company unions more independent. In August 1935 workers at U.S. Steel's South Works in Chicago voted to organize themselves. Soon after, it had a dues-paying membership of between 1,300 and 1,500 people. (It eventually grew to some 3,000 members before affiliating with SWOC in July 1936.) In September 1935 the employee representatives in U.S. Steel's multiplant American Sheet and Tin Plate subsidiary held a convention in New Castle, Pennsylvania. At first, management tried to stop the gathering, but when it became apparent that the convention would be held anyway, U.S. Steel paid for the whole meeting, including the travel expenses of the delegates. On the first day, delegates heard speeches from company executives. Then the representatives voted to exclude management from the two remaining days of the meeting. During these meetings, the delegates passed resolutions asking for a 15 percent wage increase, an increase in the minimum monthly pension, and vacations with pay.

On 26 January 1936, 80 delegates from the nine original Carnegie Steel plants, meeting at the Fort Pitt Hotel in Pittsburgh, Pennsylvania, voted to establish a permanent central committee of employee representatives from throughout U.S. Steel's plants in the Pittsburgh area. Representatives from five plants showed up at the Central Committee's first March meeting to demand both its recognition as the collective bargaining unit for the Pittsburgh area and compulsory arbitration. Around the same time, the company unions at Gary, Indiana; Duquesne and McKeesport, Pennsylvania; and the Edgar Thomson Works in Braddock, Pennsylvania, made similar demands on management.

After it formed on 3 June 1936, SWOC encouraged union sympathizers to join the ERPs so they could accelerate this existing movement for reform. For example, SWOC assistance helped bring about a 10 percent wage increase before U.S. Steel had even recognized the union. On 25 August 1936 employee representatives from both the Chicago and Pittsburgh districts of U.S. Steel's Carnegie-Illinois met in Pittsburgh. They drew up a list of demands for management that included a 25 percent wage increase. Despite the discontent that this action suggests, only a few of the employee representatives wanted to affiliate with SWOC at that time. On 6 November 1936, after months of continued agitation by employee representatives who sympathized with SWOC, U.S. Steel finally agreed to grant its workers an across-the-board 10 percent wage increase. This concession backfired when SWOC took credit for pressuring management into making this decision. Whether or not this claim was true, there is no doubt that SWOC's long-running

campaign for higher wages at U.S. Steel gave it enormous legitimacy when management finally gave in on this issue.

Furthermore, the wage concession did not stop employee representatives from participating in interplant conferences and demanding further concessions. On 22 November 1936 employee representatives from the Cleveland-Youngstown, Ohio, area held their first joint conference. Their demands included a $5 per day minimum and a further $1.24 per day increase for some employees. On 20 December, 244 employee representatives from 42 firms throughout the eastern United States met in Pittsburgh and joined SWOC at the same time. At this point, these haphazard gatherings of employee representatives merged to become the CIO Representative Council. More defections by workers and employee representatives came in the weeks following this meeting, until the Taylor-Lewis agreement eliminated the risk of joining and created a flood of applicants for the new union.

Despite SWOC's success at steering company unions to its side, the importance of this effort to Myron Taylor's actions are probably overrated. U.S. Steel's employee representatives, although an important and influential constituency, could not make up for the absence of SWOC members among the rest of the workers in the mills. To believe that winning over an employee representative was like organizing rank-and-file steelworkers is the equivalent of believing that representatives in the company unions actually represented the constituencies that elected them. At the time of the Taylor-Lewis agreement, only 18 percent of U.S. Steel employees had joined the union. Nevertheless, SWOC took credit for the actions of independent-minded employee representatives whether or not participants had joined the union. In this way, SWOC created an impression of strength that did not really exist.

If SWOC was trying to deceive U.S. Steel about the extent of its strength, the ruse failed. U.S. Steel had been keeping close watch on SWOC's progress since 1936, and it never saw the union as a serious threat. Corporate spies told management that the union's membership figures were inflated and that the employee representation plans were checking further growth. Even acknowledging gains in late 1936–1937, SWOC membership was not keeping up with the growth of the workforce brought about by increased employment to meet the demands of a rebounding market for steel. Therefore, the SWOC campaign alone could not have forced U.S. Steel to the bargaining table.

Had U.S. Steel decided to fight SWOC, it probably would have won. However, Taylor's style was to compromise rather than fight. He was part of a new generation of steel executives. He had not started out in the steel business, and his attitude toward unions was not colored by old prejudices. In his only public statement on the settlement, Taylor said he wanted to avoid a costly strike at a time when business was beginning to enter a sustained recovery. Rather than absorb the cost of fighting the union, Taylor wanted to pass on that cost to his competitors. His predecessor at the helm of U.S. Steel, Elbert Gary, would have fought the union, no holds barred, no matter the consequences.

An unheralded reason that might have influenced Taylor to settle with the union was the possibility of government intervention. The NLRA of 1935 had created a set of rules for collective bargaining that companies in every industry had to follow. The act also created the National Labor Relations Board

(NLRB) to enforce the rules. Most antiunion corporate executives refused to comply with the act until the U.S. Supreme Court declared it constitutional. These executives assumed the Court would invalidate the act, but they were wrong. Taylor, on the other hand, bucked conventional wisdom in predicting the NLRA would survive the Court's scrutiny. Because SWOC had filed a complaint against U.S. Steel under the NLRA in November 1936, Taylor feared the NLRB might force him to recognize SWOC as the exclusive bargaining agent for U.S. Steel employees. Under Section One of his agreement with Lewis, management recognized SWOC as the bargaining agent for its members only. In theory, this meant U.S. Steel's company union could compete with SWOC for membership. Before the agreement was signed, this would have seemed advantageous to management. However, SWOC's popularity among rank-and-file employees made the distinction irrelevant as soon as the Taylor-Lewis agreement became public.

The Taylor-Lewis agreement marked the beginning of the end of the steel industry's nonunion era. The industry had effectively fended off trade unions since the Homestead Lockout in 1892. Now, having established a foothold in U.S. Steel, the unions would never let go. Large independent companies continued to resist SWOC, notably during the Little Steel Strike of 1937, but SWOC's legal maneuvers to protect the rights guaranteed its members by the NLRA eventually forced most of these companies to recognize outside unions. Only when the industry itself began to collapse in the 1970s did the union presence in the steel industry begin to recede.

Key Players

Lewis, John L. (1880–1969): President of the United Mine Workers and the Congress of Industrial Organizations. His secret talks with Myron Taylor led to the surprise announcement that U.S. Steel would recognize SWOC without a fight.

Murray, Philip (1886–1952): Head of the Congress of Industrial Organizations. Murray ran the organizing campaign against U.S. Steel that helped bring it into talks for a compromise.

Taylor, Myron (1874–1959): Chairman of the United States Steel Corporation. Unlike the earlier generation of steel executives, Taylor was willing to recognize outside trade unions because he believed such action would be best for business.

See also: *Congress of Industrial Organizations; GM Recognizes UAW; National Industrial Recovery Act; Wagner Act.*

BIBLIOGRAPHY

Books

Clark, Paul, Peter Gottlieb, and Donald Kennedy, eds. *Forging a Union of Steel.* Ithaca, NY: ILR Press, 1987.

Galenson, Walter. *The CIO Challenge to the AFL.* Cambridge: Harvard University Press, 1960.

Stolberg, Benjamin. *The Story of the CIO.* New York: Viking, 1938.

—Jonathan Rees

USSR Collapse

USSR 1991

Synopsis

Beginning under Nikita Khrushchev from 1953 to 1964 and throughout the period after his resignation as general secretary, the USSR stagnated. The leaders of this totalitarian regime had a thirst for power but questionable ability. The economy suffered from lack of investment, and the government's reaction to general dissatisfaction was to counter with repressive measures. Though many historians agree that Yuri Andropov, general secretary from 1982 to 1984, was a reformer, his only achievement was to promote younger, more liberal communists on to the Politburo. The fact that the Politburo elected the conservative former KGB officer Konstantin Chernenko as Andropov's successor, however, highlights the fact that the liberal element lacked decisive influence. By the time of Chernenko's death, 13 months after Andropov, many of the "old guard" Brezhnevites had also died. This allowed Mikhail Gorbachev, a Leninist reformer, to be elected with the unanimous support of the Politburo, a decision met with euphoria among the Communist Party membership. Gorbachev inherited a state that was in virtual collapse. His reforms, intended to reinvigorate communism, actually dealt the USSR its deathblow. As a political and civil society developed and the various nationalities within the Soviet Union demanded independence, it was clear that the state was fragmenting. In an attempt to reverse this situation, in 1991 a group of communists attempted to remove Gorbachev from office. The coup's failure marked the end of communist rule. As it had been a century earlier, the only alternative to instituting change was to allow the Russian people to bring about change from below.

Timeline

1968: After Czechoslovakia adopts a more democratic, popular regime, Soviet and Warsaw Pact forces invade to crush the uprising.

1975: U.S. *Apollo* and Soviet *Soyuz* spacecraft link up in space.

1979: More than a year after Afghan communists seized control of their nation, Afghanistan is in disarray, and in December, Soviet tanks roll in to restore order, as they once did in East Germany, Poland, Hungary, and Czechoslovakia. This time, however, the task of suppressing the local populace will not prove so easy: little do the Soviets know that they are signing on for a decade-long war from which they will return in defeat.

1983: A Soviet fighter plane shoots down a Korean Air Lines 747 that had strayed into Soviet airspace. All 269 passengers, including 61 Americans (among them U.S. Congressman Larry McDonald), are killed.

1989: The Iron Curtain begins to crumble, most dramatically in Berlin, where massive protests erupt at the hated Wall on 9 November. Two days later, for the first time in 28 years, the Wall is opened between East and West. The following month, on Christmas Day, the people of Romania execute the dictator Ceausescu and his wife.

1991: The United States and other allies in the UN force commence the war against Iraq on 15 January. By 3 April the war is over, a resounding victory for the Allied force.

1991: South African Parliament repeals the laws establishing the system of Apartheid.

1991: After a stormy confirmation battle in which Professor Anita Hill accuses the appointee of sexual harassment, the U.S. Senate approves the appointment of Clarence Thomas to the Supreme Court.

1991: In December the last three U.S. hostages held in Lebanon are freed.

1994: Russian troops invade Chechnya to stop its attempted secession from the Russian Federation. The Russians will soon depart, but in 1999 will return with an even larger force.

1999: Longtime Russian President Boris Yeltsin steps down, and Vladimir Putin is elected to replace him.

Event and Its Context

Perestroika and Glasnost

Mikhail Gorbachev was elected within 11 hours of Chernenko's death, an unprecedentedly swift transition. With the backing of a number of liberals and the sponsorship of Andrei Gromyko, elder statesman of the Soviet Union, Gorbachev's accession seemed inevitable. Historians suggest that there was a consensus surrounding the need for reform. Culture Minister Pyotr Demichev supported him, saying Gorbachev had "a feeling for the new." Foreign Minister Eduard Shevardnadze declared Gorbachev's accession was "something the whole country and the entire party are expecting." Clearly public opinion backed Gorbachev's vision for the USSR. His statement that "we can't go on living like this anymore" was indicative of the mood in the Soviet Union. Furthermore his plan to redesign Marxist-Leninism to suit the requirements of modern Russia, eventually outlined in Perestroika, enjoyed the support of the Communist Party of the Soviet Union (CPSU).

The CPSU was, however, the obstacle to reform. The majority of Gorbachev's supporters favored cosmetic and superficial restructuring that would not alter the power relations from which they benefited. These inconsistencies also prevailed in Gorbachev's thinking. On the 70th anniversary of the October Revolution, he at once condemned and applauded Joseph Stalin: on the one hand Stalin was the shameless perpetrator of genocide, and on the other he was the defender of socialism. Gorbachev's approach combined modest reforms with "business as usual."

Debate centered on the "capitalization of society" and introduction of market economics, which Gorbachev rejected. *Perestroika* (reconstruction) was a program of democratization that reestablished the CPSU as the vanguard of the people. The USSR remained a totalitarian state, but with a more responsive

Mikhail Gorbachev. The Library of Congress.

government. This ignored the obvious conclusion that democratization was possible only with the dissolution of the totalitarian, bureaucratic model of government. Gorbachev, however, refused to permit political competition or to create completely new institutions for governing Russia.

Glasnost (openness), however, allowed the people to voice such ideas and to establish competing groups. Alternative thinking became widespread, and CPSU meetings attracted fewer delegates and membership plummeted. Effectively, by 1987, the CPSU was in a position to melt away despite being the instrument of government.

Gorbachev sidelined the domestic difficulties to concentrate on his world image. In October 1989 the USSR abandoned the Brezhnev Doctrine and allowed the Warsaw Pact nations freedom from Soviet influence. In March, Gorbachev withdrew Soviet troops from Afghanistan, which made him popular with Western governments. In December 1990 he was awarded the Nobel Peace Prize. With his award of *Time Magazine* Man of the Year, he was the most popular world figure in opinion polls during the period from 1988 to 1990. In the USSR, however, Dmitri Volkogonov, deputy director of the Political Department of the Soviet Army, a subdepartment of the Central Committee, argued that Gorbachev was viewed as the "little-respected leader of a bankrupt party." His attachment to the ideology of Marxist-Leninism led him to hinder the progress he had instituted.

The Coup

Between 1989 and 1990 the "velvet revolution" swept across the former Soviet satellite states, and democracy dis-

Boris Yeltsin. © Reuters/Corbis-Bettmann. Reproduced by permission.

placed communism. At the same time the USSR was also moving toward a transformation into a union of sovereign states that would be closer to the European Union model than that established under Stalin. These trends exacerbated tensions between the competing factions within the CPSU. The reformists, nominally led by Chairman of the Supreme Soviet Boris Yeltsin, were happy to cede power and stand for election. The conservatives, however, were highly fearful of the place they might have in a post-communist Russia. Gorbachev's attempts to appease both sides actually appealed to no one. The conservative communists had only one chance to retain their grip on power and to keep the USSR intact, and that would involve decisive action against Gorbachev and the reformers.

Although the timing of the attempted coup was, perhaps, too late, the CPSU had enormous power still at its disposal. The military, the police, and the KGB all had primary loyalty to the CPSU, and the leaders of each institution were loyal communists. The announcement that a treaty was to be signed with ceding Soviet republics on 20 August 1991 triggered a revolt. The mastermind of the coup was KGB chief Vladimir Kriuchkov; the leader, for the sake of legitimacy, was Gennadii Ianaev, Gorbachev's vice president. Under the assumption that Gorbachev would acquiesce to their demands, on 18 August a delegation went to his *dacha* on the Crimea to ask for his resignation. His refusal created panic among the plotters, and they attempted to oust him by force.

Over the night of 18 August the military seized government buildings in Moscow and arrested all of the reformers that they could find. At 6 A.M. on 19 August, Moscow Radio broadcast an appeal for the support of the Soviet people. The appeal, made in the name of the CPSU, claimed that the action was necessary because Gorbachev's policies had failed and made the USSR ungovernable.

Boris Yeltsin was instrumental in defeating the coup. Despite being Gorbachev's bête noire, Yeltsin opposed any move that would undermine what Gorbachev had achieved. Yeltsin also understood that the public mood, including among the troops, was ambivalent to the CPSU, which gave him a strong position from which to fight. On hearing the radio broadcast, Yeltsin made his way immediately to the White House. He navigated through the lines of tanks and dared the soldiers to arrest him. Standing astride the gun barrel of a tank, he demanded that Gorbachev be restored to the presidency, called a general strike in support of democratization, and asked the soldiers and people to pledge their loyalty to an elected government. Following the initial confusion, the majority of troops rallied to Yeltsin. Sporadic fighting ensued but by 21 August, at the cost of only three lives, the coup was defeated. Though Gorbachev was able to return to Moscow as the victor, the glory belonged, as did public support, to Yeltsin. Effectively, the Soviet Union and the CPSU were no more.

The Collapse of Communism and the USSR

The republic's leaders, fearing another coup, rushed to declare their independence from Russia, thus backing Yeltsin's declaration. Though Gorbachev attempted to utilize his skills as a negotiator to prevent a complete break up, he was thwarted. The instability of politics in Russia, the former hub of control, and the beliefs that the republics could govern themselves successfully, led them to secede. Within Russia, also, he was blamed for the ills of society. His attachment to Marxist-Leninism was seen as the cause for the failure to arrest economic collapse. The Minsk Declaration accepted that the Commonwealth of Independent States had superseded the USSR; by 21 December 1991 it had the support of 14 former Soviet republics, with only the Baltic States and Georgia choosing complete independence from Russia.

On 31 December, Gorbachev resigned as president. Six days earlier he had declared in a televised speech that under his leadership "Society . . . has been emancipated politically and spiritually," but warned the people that their task now was to "learn how to use that liberty." Political power passed to Yeltsin, who in October 1991 had been granted emergency powers to implement economic reforms by decree. Though the transition of power was undemocratic, the fact that Yeltsin enjoyed a large popular mandate indicated that he would have won a presidential election. Yeltsin and his successor, Vladimir Putin, showed no adversity to subverting the democratic process when necessary. Russia finally became democratic according to scales set by the United Nations. Regular elections and a fairly smooth transition to capitalism allowed significant progress and made Russia a partner in the world order. The inequalities and class system that have been consequences of marketization have led some to hark back to the "good old days of communism," but in general there are few who miss Soviet communism. Within Russia, and across the world, the CPSU is synonymous with repression, brutality, and stagnation.

Key Players

Gorbachev, Mikhail (1931–): Lifelong communist and leader of the Soviet Union, 1985–1991. He is perhaps best remembered for his role in ending the Cold War; within Russia, however, he is vilified as the man who destroyed communism or the man that kept it alive for too long. His *Memoirs* (1995) is an unrivalled document of Soviet history.

Yeltsin, Boris (1931–): The first democratically elected leader of Russia. A former engineer and loyal communist, he recognized that the problems of the Soviet Union could not be solved by the Communist Party. He charted his life and ideas in *Against the Grain* (1990) and *The Struggle for Russia* (1994).

See also: *Russian Revolutions.*

————————

BIBLIOGRAPHY

Books

Aron, Leon. *Boris Yeltsin: A Revolutionary Life.* London: Harper Collins, 2000.

Gorbachev, Mikhail. *Perestroika.* London: Collins, 1987.

————. *Memoirs.* London: Transworld Publishers, 1995.

Lewin, Moshe. *The Gorbachev Phenomenon: A Historical Interpretation.* London: Hutchinson Radius, 1998.

Sheehy, Gail. *Gorbachev: A One-man Revolution.* London: Mandarin, 1991.

Volkogonov, Dmitri. *The Rise and Fall of the Soviet Empire.* London: Harper Collins, 1998.

—Darren G. Lilleker

W

Wages and Hours Act: *See* **Fair Labor Standards Act.**

Wagner Act

United States 1935

Synopsis

The National Labor Relations Act of 1935, known popularly as the Wagner Act, was New Deal legislation designed to maintain industrial production by preventing labor strife. It protected the right of workers to organize and bargain collectively with their employers or to refrain from all such activity. The act generally applied to all businesses involved in interstate commerce except agriculture. The enforcement arm of the act was the National Labor Relations Board (NLRB), which conducted secret-ballot elections to determine whether employees sought union representation. The NRLB also investigated and remedied unfair labor practices by employers and unions. Shortly after the adoption of the statute, several companies challenged its constitutionality, including the Jones and Laughlin Steel Corporation of Aliquippa, Pennsylvania. This steel company, which had discharged workers because of their union activity and to discourage membership in the union, challenged the act as an attempt to regulate all industry that thereby usurped the reserved powers of the states. In a 1937 decision, the Supreme Court declared the act to be constitutional and the right to organize to be fundamental.

Timeline

1920: League of Nations, based in Geneva, holds its first meetings.

1925: European leaders attempt to secure the peace at the Locarno Conference, which guarantees the boundaries between France and Germany, and Belgium and Germany.

1930: Naval disarmament treaty signed by the United States, Great Britain, France, Italy, and Japan.

1933: Newly inaugurated U.S. President Franklin D. Roosevelt launches the first phase of his New Deal to put depression-era America back to work.

1935: Germany annexes the Saar region after a plebiscite. In defiance of Versailles, the Nazis reintroduce compulsory military service. The Allies do nothing, and many western intellectuals maintain that it is only proper for Germany to retake its own territory and begin building up its army again.

1935: Italians invade Ethiopia, and the response by the League of Nations—which imposes sanctions but otherwise fails to act—reveals the impotence of that organization.

1935: Second phase of New Deal begins with the introduction of social security, farm assistance, and housing and tax reform.

1938: The U.S. Fair Labor Standards Act establishes a minimum wage.

1940: Hitler's troops sweep through Western Europe, annexing Norway and Denmark in April, and in May the Low Countries and France. At the same time, Stalin—who in this year arranges the murder of Trotsky in Mexico—takes advantage of the situation to add the Baltic republics (Latvia, Lithuania, and Estonia) to the Soviet empire, where they will remain for more than half a century.

1945: April sees the death of three leaders: Roosevelt passes away on 12 April; the Italians execute Mussolini and his mistress on 28 April; and Hitler (along with Eva Braun, propaganda minister Josef Goebbels, and Goebbels's family) commits suicide on 30 April.

1950: North Korean troops pour into South Korea, starting the Korean War. Initially the communists make impressive gains, but in September the U.S. Marines land at Inchon and liberate Seoul. China responds by sending in its troops.

Event and Its Context

Although the United States had experienced serious economic downturns in the past, nothing approached the economic catastrophe that was the Great Depression. Following the stock market crash of 1929, the economy continued to worsen throughout the early 1930s, affecting almost every person in the country. Resentment against the economic system rose, and much of the prestige of business disappeared. In this climate, President Franklin Delano Roosevelt embarked on a frenetic mission to fix the economy with his New Deal programs.

A common belief had developed among Roosevelt administration officials and the general public that an increase in mass purchasing power would permit full production and lead to full employment. The organization of labor and collective bargaining would create this buying power by balancing the so-far unrestrained power of the corporations. It appeared to be good public policy to take measures to promote greater equality of bargaining power in order to increase wages.

National Industrial Recovery Act

Amid a flurry of optimistic projections, Congress passed the National Industrial Recovery Act (NIRA) in 1933. NIRA established economic planning agencies, including the National Recovery Administration (NRA). This agency encouraged labor and business to collaborate on codes of "fair practice" to stabilize the economy and, through section 7(a) of the NIRA, guaranteed the right of workers to bargain collectively through independent unions and to enjoy, under the codes of fair competition, minimum standards for wages, hours, and working conditions. NIRA stimulated an upsurge in trade union membership, but the lack of enforcement provisions and the administrators' disagreements about the section's requirements ensured that few employers were willing to recognize and bargain with the unions.

By the end of 1933, the failure of the NRA was already becoming clear. Labor representatives had participated in the construction of fewer than 10 percent of the 557 NRA codes and had begun to deride the agency as the "National Run Around." Large companies obeyed the codes when it was in their interest to do so and ignored them when convenient. Employers remained free to spy on, interrogate, discipline, discharge, and blacklist union members. A great strike wave in 1933 and 1934 that included citywide general strikes and factory takeovers offered ample evidence that the act had not created peace in the workplace. These violent confrontations occurring between workers trying to form unions and the police and private security forces defending the interests of antiunion employers led many Americans to suspect that revolution was near. In 1935 the NRA finally died when the Supreme Court declared it unconstitutional in *Schechter Poultry Company v. United States* on the grounds that Congress had delegated legislative authority to the executive branch.

Introduction of the National Labor Relations Act

In 1935 Roosevelt presented Congress with a series of reforms that would constitute the Second New Deal, but these programs did not include any measures to help workers organize. The paternalistic Roosevelt, not a strong supporter of unions, worried that labor's militant new spirit would accelerate the violent confrontations of 1933–1934. He preferred instead that workers rely on his social programs. Concern about his survival in the upcoming 1936 elections also led the president to resist measures that might antagonize business interests. Meanwhile, in 1934 Robert Wagner, a Democratic senator from New York with a long history as a friend of labor, had introduced the NLRA bill to protect the rights of workers to organize and bargain collectively. Wagner had played a leading role in drafting the NIRA and had insisted on the inclusion of section 7(a).

When complaints about the NRA had grown loud, Roosevelt established a seven-member National Labor Board with New Deal supporter Wagner as the chair. Although it set up rules providing that a majority of workers in any plant could bargain for all workers, that secret elections be held to determine bargaining units, and that good faith efforts be made to secure agreements, the board had no power to enforce its decisions. These enforcement difficulties led Wagner to ignore Roosevelt administration opposition and introduce the NLRA on 28 February 1934.

The Wagner bill was based on the theory that continuing strikes interrupted and slowed the flow of interstate commerce and thereby harmed the general welfare. In a speech on the Senate floor, Wagner argued that it would also raise purchasing power through its provisions. The bill stated that employees shall have the right to self-organization; to form, join, or assist labor organizations; to bargain collectively through representatives of their own choosing; and to engage in other concerted

activities for the purpose of collective bargaining or other mutual aid and protection. The bill contained the teeth that the NIRA had lacked in the form of an enforcement arm. It provided for a permanent labor board to prevent unfair labor practices that interfered with the right of employees to organize or discriminated against union members. This National Labor Relations Board (NLRB), composed of employers, employees, and members of the public, would have the power to arbitrate labor disputes as well as prevent unfair labor practices.

Roosevelt sabotaged the bill in 1934, wavered in 1935, and supported it unequivocally only after the Supreme Court had gutted his recovery program and overturned the NIRA. The bill's proponents included the American Federation of Labor (AFL), a few professors, and Frances Perkins, the head of the Department of Labor and the only administration official who spoke on behalf of the bill. Chief opposition to NLRA came from chambers of commerce and manufacturer's associations throughout the country as well as the conservative Liberty League. The National Manufacturers Association (NAM) insisted that the bill was constitutionally void on the grounds that manufacturing and production were not a part of interstate commerce, that the bill interfered with liberty of contract as guaranteed by the Fifth Amendment, and that it violated the Fifth Amendment by conferring judicial power on an administrative agency whose procedures violated due process of law.

The NLRA received Senate approval on 16 May 1935, passed the House of Representatives on 19 June 1935, and was signed by Roosevelt on 5 July 1935. Hope of avoiding greater labor unrest may have led some members of Congress to vote for the bill. In late August 1935 Roosevelt appointed the members of the NLRB. J. Warren Madden, a professor of law at the University of Pittsburgh, served as chair. The rest of the board consisted of John M. Carmody, a member of the National Mediation Board, and Edwin M. Smith, a former member of the National Labor Board. Charles Fahy, former chair of the Petroleum Labor Board and assistant solicitor of the Department of Labor, served as general counsel.

Key Provisions of the NLRA

Sections 7, 8, and 9 of the NLRA would have the greatest impact upon labor and would prompt businesses to file Supreme Court challenges to the law. Section 7 defines the right of employees to unionize and bargain collectively. It protects such activities as filing grievances, on-the-job protests, picketing, and strikes. Section 8 defines employer unfair labor practices by making five types of conduct illegal: employer interference, restraint, or coercion directed against union or collective activity; employer domination of unions; employer discrimination against employees who take part in union or collective activities; employer retaliation for filing unfair labor practice charges or cooperating with the NLRB; and employer refusal to bargain in good faith with union representatives. Threats, warnings, and orders to refrain from protected activities are forms of interference and coercion that violate section 8. Disciplinary actions, such as suspensions, discharges, transfers, and demotions also break the law. Failures to supply information, unilateral changes, refusals to hold grievance meetings, and direct dealings with employees constitute further violations. Although this section focuses heavily on unfair business practices, it also pro-

**Western Pennsylvania miners and steel workers celebrate the upholding of the Wagner Act, Farrell, Pennsylvania.
© AP/Wide World Photos. Reproduced by permission.**

hibits union unfair labor practices, which include failure to provide fair representation to all members of the bargaining unit. Women and African Americans had traditionally experienced union discrimination, and this provision protects these groups. Section 9 provides that unions, if certified or recognized, are the exclusive representatives of bargaining unit members. It prohibits the adjustment of employee grievances unless a union representative is given the opportunity to be present and establishes procedures to vote on union representation.

Jones and Laughlin

The NLRA immediately created a wave of anger in the business community. Several companies prosecuted under the act challenged its legality in federal court. Among the protesting businesses were the Fruehauf Trailer Company of Detroit (for discharge of employees for belonging to the AFL); the Friedman-Harry Marks Clothing Company in Richmond (for discharge of employees for attending a organizational meeting of the Amalgamated Clothing Workers); the Associated Press (for discharge of an employee who had attempted to bargain collectively); the Washington, Virginia, and Maryland Coach

Company (for discharge of employees who had requested union recognition), and the Jones and Laughlin Steel Company.

Headquartered in Pittsburgh, Pennsylvania, Jones and Laughlin had a large plant in nearby Aliquippa that became the object of the NLRB prosecution. Vertically integrated with 19 subsidiaries, it owned and operated ore, coal, and limestone properties; lake and river transportation facilities; and terminal railroads located at its manufacturing plants. The fourth largest steel and pig iron company in the nation, Jones and Laughlin employed 33,000 men mining ore, 44,000 men mining coal, 4,000 men quarrying limestone, 16,000 men manufacturing coke, 343,000 men manufacturing steel, and 83,000 men transporting its product. The company had about 10,000 employees in its Aliquippa plant, which was located in a community of about 30,000 persons.

Following the *Schechter* decision, Jones and Laughlin resumed efforts to prevent unionization. In June 1935 the company held elections for representatives under its employee representation plan at its Aliquippa plant. All of its other plants in Michigan, Minnesota, Pennsylvania, and West Virginia operated on an open-shop basis. Harry Phillips, president of the local Beaver Valley Lodge No. 200, which was affiliated with the Amalgamated Association of Iron, Steel and Tin Workers of America, joined with other union officials in urging employees to boycott the formation of this company-run union. The company pressured employees to vote by sending company police to the homes of workers and discharging 20 employees for refusing to participate. In July, Jones and Laughlin began to fire the active members of the Amalgamated Association. Several were officers and others were leaders of particular groups. Of the dismissed employees, two were motor inspectors, one was a tractor driver, three were crane operators, one was a washer in the coke plant, and three were laborers. Phillips, the union head, was fired for failing to answer a whistle while in the restroom. Marlin Dunn, a charter member of the union, lost his job for leaving his crane keys on a bench in violation of company rules, and union vice president Angelo Volpe was terminated for operating his crane in response to head signals from his helper rather than the mandated hand signals. When the union complained about these dismissals, Jones and Laughlin replied that all the men had been fired for cause. The union filed a charge of unfair labor practice with the NLRB on 28 January 1936.

When the Jones and Laughlin case came before the NLRB in March 1936, the company officials raised many of the arguments first presented by the NAM. They tried to establish that only raw materials entered the Aliquippa plant and only manufacturing operations took place within the plant. The company's attorney then moved for dismissal on the grounds that the NLRB lacked jurisdiction over manufacturing enterprises. The attorney representing the NLRB countered by introducing evidence showing the interstate nature of the company's operations. The board also introduced testimony by experts in labor relations who argued that a substantial proportion of strikes were caused by the refusal of employers to recognize the right of employees to organize and bargain collectively. On 9 April the NLRB found Jones and Laughlin guilty of unfair labor practices, ordered it to reinstate the 10 fired employees with back pay for time lost, and mandated the posting for 30 days of no-

tices that the corporation would not discharge or discriminate against members of the labor union. Jones and Laughlin refused to comply. The NLRB responded by filing a petition of enforcement in the Fifth Circuit Court of Appeals in New Orleans in the belief that this court would favor the board in the expected appeal by the company.

Jones and Laughlin appealed. In a surprise decision, the Fifth Circuit denied the NLRB's petition on 15 June on the grounds that the board had no jurisdiction over a labor dispute in a steel plant engaged only in manufacture, since the Constitution does not grant the right to regulate employer-employee relations in production or manufacture. The NLRB now appealed to the Supreme Court, and oral arguments began 9 February 1937. Jones and Laughlin argued that that if the discharged men had to be rehired, then all freedom of contract and right to manage a business would be lost.

The company's argument failed. On 12 April 1937 the Supreme Court reversed the appeals court in a 5–4 decision read by Chief Justice Charles Evans Hughes. Justices Hughes, Louis Brandeis, Benjamin Cardozo, Harlan Stone, and Owen Roberts found that Jones and Laughlin had indeed fired the workers for engaging in union activity. They also found the NLRA to be constitutional because it aimed to reach only what burdened or obstructed interstate commerce rather than to influence such commerce. They declared the steel company guilty of unfair labor practices that ignored a "fundamental right" of workers. Stating that employees had as much right to organize themselves as Jones and Laughlin had to organize its business, the Court added in strong language that the company's coercive and discriminatory activities were the "proper subject for condemnation by competent legislative authority." The four dissenting justices, George Sutherland, Pierce Butler, James McReynolds, and Willis Van Devanter, cited grounds of commerce and due process. The power of Congress to regulate industry and the relationships of employers to employees had been sustained.

Impact of *Jones and Laughlin*

The successful prosecution of the *Jones and Laughlin* case ensured the survival of the NLRA and galvanized union organizing. The number of complaints presented to the NLRB rose by 100 percent, and successful union campaigns began in the automobile, steel, electrical, manufacturing, and rubber industries. Membership in U.S. labor unions soared: by 1941 there were two and a half times as many Americans in unions as had been the case in 1935. By 1945 union membership reached 35 percent of the workforce.

Key Players

Roosevelt, Franklin Delano (1882–1945): After defeating Herbert Hoover for the presidency in 1932, Roosevelt developed the New Deal to bring the nation out of the Great Depression. The experimental programs of the New Deal did not rely on any particular formula for relief but simply offered hope of improvement. Roosevelt's laws would transform the role of the federal government in the workings of the nation's economy.

Wagner, Robert Ferdinand, Sr. (1877–1953): As a New York State senator, the German-born Wagner gained a reputation for being a friend to labor as chair of the Factory Investigating Commission, appointed after the tragic 1911 Triangle Fire. He helped push through the most effective worker's compensation law in the nation as well as new laws prescribing safety and sanitary conditions in the workplace, restricting child labor, and limiting the hours of working women. Wagner served a brief stint as a state court judge who refused to issue injunctions against striking workers and made history by enjoining an employer from breaching a union contract. He entered the United States Senate in 1927 and took a leading role in constructing the New Deal.

See also: *National Industrial Recovery Act; Stock Market Crash.*

BIBLIOGRAPHY

Books

Aikin, Charles, ed. *National Labor Relations Board Cases.* New York: John Wiley, 1939.

Bernstein, Irving. *A Caring Society: The New Deal, the Worker, and the Great Depression.* Boston: Houghton Mifflin, 1985.

Cortner, Richard C. *The Wagner Act Cases.* Knoxville: University of Tennessee Press, 1964.

Gross, James A. *The Making of the National Labor Relations Board: A Study in Economics, Politics and the Law.* Albany: State University of New York Press, 1974.

Millis, Harry A., and Emily Clark Brown. *From the Wagner Act to Taft-Hartley: A Study of National Labor Policy and Labor Relations.* Chicago: University of Chicago Press, 1950.

National Labor Relations Board. *Legislative History of the National Labor Relations Act, 1935.* Washington, DC: United States Government Printing Office, 1948.

ADDITIONAL RESOURCES

Books

Huthmacher, J. Joseph. *Senator Robert F. Wagner and the Rise of Urban Liberalism.* New York: Atheneum, 1968.

—Caryn E. Neumann

Wagner-Peyser Act

United States 1933

Synopsis

The Wagner-Peyser Act of 1933 declared that its purpose was "To provide for the establishment of a national employment system and for cooperation with the States in the promo-

tion of such system, and for other purposes established a nationwide system of public employment offices." The key function of the act was to provide (1) federal matching funds for the operation of state employment offices, (2) federal supervision of operations, (3) state administration of services, and (4) employment services to veterans. It was amended in 1998 as part of the Workforce Investment Act, P.L. 105-220, which required that public employment services be provided as a component of the "One-Stop" delivery system of the states. Its state-related funds were used to provide three different methods of labor exchange services to job seekers and employers: self-service, facilitated self-help service, and staff-assisted service.

Timeline

1918: Influenza, carried to the furthest corners by returning soldiers, spreads throughout the globe. Over the next two years, it will kill nearly 20 million people—more than the war itself.

1922: Publication of James Joyce's novel *Ulysses* and T. S. Eliot's poem *The Waste Land*—works that will transform literature and inaugurate the era of modernism.

1928: Discovery of penicillin by Alexander Fleming.

1930: Discovery of Pluto.

1933: Hitler becomes German chancellor, and the Nazi dictatorship begins. A month later, the Reichstag building burns, a symbol of the new regime's contempt for democracy. (Though a Dutch communist is punished for the crime, the perpetrators were almost certainly Nazis.) During this year, virtually all aspects of the coming horror are manifested: destruction of Jewish-owned shops and bans on Jewish merchants; elimination of political opposition (including the outlawing of trade unions); opening of the first concentration camps (and the sentencing of the first Jews to them); book-burning; and the establishment of the first racial purity laws.

1933: Germany and Japan withdraw from the League of Nations.

1933: Newly inaugurated U.S. president Franklin D. Roosevelt launches the first phase of his New Deal to put depression-era America back to work.

1933: Twenty-First Amendment repeals Prohibition.

1933: Even as Stalin's manmade famine rages in the Ukraine, the new administration of President Roosevelt formally recognizes the USSR.

1936: The election of a leftist Popular Front government in Spain in February precipitates an uprising by rightists under the leadership of Francisco Franco. Over the next three years, war will rage between the Loyalists and Franco's Nationalists. The Spanish Civil War will prove to be a lightning rod for the world's tensions, with the Nazis and fascists supporting the Nationalists, and the Soviets the Loyalists.

1938: The U.S. Fair Labor Standards Act establishes a minimum wage.

1943: Worn down by two Russian winters, the Germans begin to fall back. In January, the siege of Leningrad (which

Robert Ferdinand Wagner. The Library of Congress.

at more than 800 days is the longest in modern history) is broken, and a month later, the German 6th Army surrenders at Stalingrad.

Event and Its Context

It took the United States government about 150 years and several aborted attempts to establish a permanent federal employment service for American citizens. The first state regulation of private employment agencies occurred in 1848. A year later Wisconsin and Minnesota required licensing of private employment agencies, and soon other states enacted similar licensing laws. The state of Ohio established the first state employment agency in 1890. The entry of the federal government into employment offices occurred in 1907 when the Bureau of Immigration and Naturalization opened employment offices to aid people in obtaining jobs.

The World War I Era

The first real advancement toward the eventual establishment of a federal employment service for all American citizens occurred in 1914 in response to conditions surrounding World War I. War in Europe drastically reduced the number of immigrants arriving in the United States. As a result, the Federal Bureau of Immigration became an employment service for the growing number of unemployed workers in the United States. As the country became directly involved in World War I, the federal government needed a coordinated system to match people with war-related jobs.

Beginning around 1917, to deal with the masses of people needing jobs, along with unskilled workers beginning to immigrate to metropolitan areas, the U.S. Congress organized the Vocational Education Program. This action was a turning point in federal employment assistance because prior to this legislation the federal government felt that worker education, training, and any such related help was the responsibility of the states. At the same time, however, the states felt that such responsibility was in the hands of local communities. Consequently, little in the way of government-sponsored action was accomplished prior to passage of this legislation.

In January 1918 the United States Employment Service (USES) was established as a unit in the Department of Labor. In its first year of operation, more than 10 million job seekers made applications for jobs, and the USES referred about 6 million people to jobs. By the time World War I ended in 1918, decreasing funds and considerable opposition to its functions ended its brief existence (at least for the time being).

First Federal Bill

Although no longer functioning, the war-related work of the USES highlighted the need for a permanent and effective national employment service. In 1919 a group of state and federal employment officers, labor leaders, and other influential people recommended the establishment of a comprehensive public employment service based on cooperation between the various state governments and the federal government. Consequently, Congress passed the Kenyon-Nolan bill, but it failed to become law.

During the postwar depression of 1920, the government enacted the Vocational Rehabilitation Act to assist returning veterans and others in finding employment. Although somewhat limited in scope during this time, this measure marked the beginning of the federal involvement in employment assistance. A conference on unemployment convened in 1921 at the urging of Secretary of Commerce Herbert Hoover to discuss the need for an active national employment service to replace the defunct, temporary wartime USES. Little was actually accomplished at this meeting; in fact, little was accomplished during the next 10 year in the areas of unemployment and federal employment services (largely due to a subsequent 1920s economic expansion and the high level of employment that resulted).

The dire economic events that occurred in 1929 changed the perception of employment services. When the U.S. stock market crashed in October of that year and triggered the Great Depression, there was an immediate need for a federal employment service. With unemployment impacting one-fourth of the country's workforce—more than 12 million people—the need for employment assistance was greater than was possible on the local and state levels. The Wagner Act of 1931 contained provisions for a cooperative federal-state employment service very much similar to that contained in the Kenyon-Nolan bill of 1918. The bill passed both the House of Representatives and the Senate, but because it was perceived as competing with rather than helping other community services, it was later vetoed.

The Wagner-Peyser Act

In 1933 the federal government implemented a number of programs to assist people with employment. Unfortunately, some of them were later found to be unconstitutional, and most were only temporary in nature. However, one signaled a new direction for permanent employment assistance. The enactment of the Wagner-Peyser Act, which was approved by President Franklin D. Roosevelt on 6 June 1933, established a national employment service in the United States. The law authorized the federal government to cooperate with the states in establishing and maintaining public employment services. Its functions were to develop a national system of public employment offices, furnish information on employment opportunities, and maintain a system for dealing with labor among the states. The act reestablished the USES as a division of the Department of Labor.

Under the Wagner-Peyser Act, each state received funds that were allocated for the planning and administration of a labor program that could deal effectively with the needs of both employers and job seekers. The act appropriated $1.5 million for its first fiscal year with approximately $1.1 million reserved for subsidies to state offices that were affiliated with the federal service and that conformed to standards laid down by the federal service. The appropriation for the second fiscal year (ending 30 June 1935) was $3.7 million, of which about $165,000 was expended for services in the District of Columbia; $200,000 was granted for Veterans' Placement Service; and the bulk of the monies, $3 million, was reserved for the states.

President Roosevelt appointed Frances Perkins on 4 March 1933, as U.S. secretary of labor. Perkins made recommendations to Congress, suggesting such measures as a permanent unemployment service, a mediation service, unemployment insurance, low cost housing, worker safety, old-age insurance, higher wages, an end to child labor, and the right of workers to organize. Perkins was instrumental in the passage and later in the application of the Wagner-Peyser Act.

Although unemployment insurance was not directly a part of the Wagner-Peyser Act of 1933 and the federal/state employment service that resulted, it is worth noting as an important follow-up to the act in terms of worker security. The need for unemployment insurance had been evident for a long time. Massachusetts had introduced the concept in 1916, and over 180 legislative proposals for unemployment compensation had followed in 28 states over the following 18 years. Only the state of Wisconsin, however, actually adopted such a program. The federal Social Security Act of 1935 also established the unemployment insurance program, which provided for the first time a defense against the effects of unemployment by assisting the individual and the local community.

The Wagner-Peyser Act required that all federal and state positions for public service be filled based on merit. For this reason, the USES prepared a manual, *Specifications for Positions in State Employment Services*, to establish national uniform requirements for like positions in the various states and to equalize salaries in each type of work position throughout the country. A national advisory council was appointed to help the USES determine and elucidate its policies, maintain neutrality between employers and labor, and place efficiency ahead of political considerations. Similar state and local advisory councils were established on an as-needed basis.

By August of 1934, 19 of the 48 states and the District of Columbia, as well as the U.S. territories of Hawaii and Alaska (along with a total of 167 local offices) were associated with the USES in the service of unemployment compensation and public employment services. Each state received federal subsidies after it signed a formal, written agreement that bound the state to compliance with federal regulations and standards, including selection and training of personnel, supervision of salaries, standardized record systems, and premises used for offices.

The charter of the USES strengthened and improved in efficiency throughout the years as employment services integrated with unemployment compensation. Although the procedures and purposes of employment service and unemployment compensation are not identical, each presents a distinct step in one extended process.

Since the 1960s Congress has passed several acts that have expanded the scope of services offered by the USES, including the Area Redevelopment Act (1961), the Manpower Development and Training Act (1962), the Vocational and Educational Act (1963), the Economic Opportunity Act (1964), the Job Training Partnership Act (1982), and the Economic Dislocation and Worker Adjustment Assistance Act (1988). Since 1979 the USES also has provided employers with tax credits for hiring disadvantaged workers.

The USES in Modern Times

According to a February 1995 report by the Government Accounting Office, there were at least 163 federal employment and training programs in existence at the time. Fourteen federal departments administered these programs. The USES maintained over 1,700 local public employment offices in the states and territories, which provided about 3.2 million workers with jobs annually. Although the names of these offices varied, with the use of such titles as Employment Services, Employment Security Commission, Job Service, One-Stop Center, or Workforce Development Center, the mission of each was identical: to assist job seekers in finding jobs, to assist employers in locating qualified workers, and to provide job training and related services.

The United States Public Employment Service evolved throughout the latter half of the twentieth century into a series of public services as the U.S. Congress created new programs to serve specific target audiences and to address changing labor market conditions. At the beginning of the twenty-first century, the U.S. Employment Service represented a solid foundation for a vast, publicly supported workforce development system.

Key Players

Perkins, Frances (1882–1965): Perkins was born in Boston, Massachusetts, and graduated from Mount Holyoke College in 1902. She received her master's degree in sociology from Columbia University in 1910. In 1910 she became leader of the New York Consumer's League and lobbied for better working conditions and shorter hours of work. President Franklin D. Roosevelt appointed Perkins as secretary of labor in 1933. She held the position for 12 years, longer than any other secretary of labor. Perkins was the first woman to hold a cabinet position in the United States. As secretary of labor she played a critical role in New Deal legislation. Her most important contribution is generally considered her work as chairwoman of the President's Committee on Economic Security. In this position she was involved in all the preliminary work that eventually resulted in the Social Security Act of 1935.

Peyser, Theodore Albert (1873–1937): Peyser was born in Charleston, West Virginia. He worked at various occupations in the West Virginia area before moving to Cincinnati, Ohio, in 1893 to become a traveling salesman. Peyser moved to New York City in 1900 and worked in the life insurance business. He was elected as a Democratic representative from the state of New York to the 73rd, 74th, and 75th Congresses and served from 4 March 1933 until his death in 1937.

Wagner, Robert Ferdinand (1877–1953): Wagner graduated from the New York City College in 1898 and the New York Law School in 1900. He was a Democratic state legislator from New York in 1904 and was elected to the New York State senate in 1908. Wagner took a particular interest in industrial working conditions and developed sympathy for the emerging trade union movement. In 1919 Wagner became a justice of the New York Supreme Court, holding this position until 1926, at which time he was elected to the United States Senate. During his first term, Wagner failed in his attempts to persuade Congress to pass legislation to help trade unions and the unemployed. President Franklin D. Roosevelt appointed Wagner in 1933 as the first chairman of the National Recovery Administration, and he eventually became an important figure in the Roosevelt administration. He was instrumental in drafting such legislation as the National Industrial Recovery Act, the Federal Emergency Relief Administration, and the Social Security Act. Wagner sponsored the National Labor Relations Act (or the Wagner Act), which in 1935 established the federal government as the regulator and ultimate arbitrator in labor disputes. It is widely regarded as the single most important piece of labor legislation enacted in the United States in the twentieth century. The intent of the Wagner Act was to eliminate interference by employers when workers attempt to organize into a union.

See also: *Perkins Becomes Secretary of Labor; Stock Market Crash.*

BIBLIOGRAPHY

Books

Commons, John R. "United States Employment Service" and "The Wagner-Peyser Act." In *Historical Dictionary of the New Deal: From Inauguration to Preparation for War,* edited by James S. Olson. Westport, CT: Greenwood Press, 1985.

Other

Bane, Frank. "Promoting Job Security." *Social Security Bulletin* 1, no. 6 (June 1938) [cited 27 September 2002]. <http://www.ssa.gov/history/bane638.html>.

Biographical Directory of the United States Congress. "Peyser, Theodore Albert, 1873–1937" [cited 27

September 2002]. <http://bioguide.congress.gov/scripts/biodisplay.pl?index=P000281>.

Employment and Training Administration, United States Department of Labor. "United States Department of Labor Program Highlights" [cited 27 September 2002]. <http://www.doleta.gov/uses/proghigh.asp>.

Gross, Robert. Interstate Conference of Employment Security Agencies. "New Range of Services of the Public Employment Service in the United States, Given the New Challenges of the Labor Market" [cited 27 September 2002]. <http://members.aon.at/wapes/public/en/congress/gross.htm>.

New Mexico Department of Labor. History: Workforce Investment Act. "History and Background: Early Federal Programs—The Great Society" [cited 27 September 2002]. <http://www.wia.state.nm.us/WIA_history.html>.

Social Security Administration. Social Security Pioneers. "Francis Perkins" [cited 27 September 2002]. <http://www.ssa.gov/history/fperkins.html>.

Spartacus Educational. "Robert Wagner" [cited 27 September 2002]. <http://www.spartacus.schoolnet.co.uk/USARwagner.htm>.

United States Department of Labor. United States Employment Service. "The Employment and Workforce Information Service" [cited 27 September 2002]. <http://www.workforcesecurity.doleta.gov/employ.asp>.

Virginia Employment Commission (VEC). "Wagner-Peyser Act of June 6, 1933" [cited 27 September 2002]. <http://www.vec.state.va.us/docs/generaldocs/documents/wagner_peyser/act.doc>.

—William Arthur Atkins

Walsh-Healy Act: *See* **Public Contracts Act.**

Washington Union Shop Law

United States 1973

Synopsis

The Washington Federation of State Employees (WFSE) helped to initiate and pass the Union Shop Bill that became law in the state of Washington on 20 March 1973. A union shop agreement is a clause of a collective bargaining agreement whereby an employer hires persons without regard to their membership or nonmembership in a labor union that represents its employees, with the provision that the person hired must become a member of the union after a specified period. This union shop law for civil service employees was the first of its kind in the United States.

Timeline

1958: China's Mao Zedong proclaims the Great Leap Forward, a program of enforced rapid industrialization that will end a year later, a miserable failure.

1963: Assassination of President Kennedy in Dallas on 22 November.

1968: Communist victories in the Tet offensive mark the turning point in the Vietnam War, and influence a growing lack of confidence in the war, not only among America's youth, but within the establishment as well.

1973: Signing of peace accords in Paris in January ends the Vietnam War.

1973: As the Watergate scandal grows, White House advisers H. R. Haldeman and John D. Ehrlichman resign, and Nixon fires counsel John Dean. Later, Vice President Spiro Agnew resigns. Then, in the October "Saturday Night Massacre," Attorney General Elliot L. Richardson resigns, and Nixon fires special prosecutor Archibald Cox and Deputy Attorney General William D. Ruckelshaus.

1973: Overthrow of Chile's Salvador Allende, the only freely elected Marxist leader in history, who dies in the presidential palace. According to supporters of the new leader, General Augusto Pinochet, Allende committed suicide; but Allende's supporters maintain that he was killed by Pinochet's troops.

1973: Attacked in October, during their Yom Kippur religious festival, the Israelis defeat the combined forces of Egypt, Syria, Iraq, and Jordan. Three weeks later, Arab nations impose an oil embargo on the United States to punish it for its continued support of Israel.

1973: United States launches Skylab, its first space station.

1973: Completion of the twin towers of the World Trade Center in New York City, built at a cost of $750 million. The 110-story buildings are the world's tallest, but by year's end they will be eclipsed by the Sears Tower in Chicago.

1978: More than 900 members of the People's Temple, led by Jim Jones, kill themselves in Jonestown, Guyana. Also dead is Congressman Leo Ryan, who was visiting the Guyana compound and was presumably murdered.

1983: A Soviet fighter plane shoots down a Korean Air Lines 747 that had strayed into Soviet airspace. All 269 passengers, including 61 Americans (among them U.S. Congressman Larry McDonald), are killed.

1988: A terrorist bomb aboard a Pan Am 747 explodes over Lockerbie, Scotland, killing 259 people on the plane and 11 more on the ground.

Event and Its Context

The Washington Federation of State Employees

On 8 November 1960 the civil service initiative (Initiative 207) for the state of Washington passed by the wide margin of 606,511 to 471,730. At about the same time, the Washington Federation of State Employees (WFSE) was acting to combat workplace discrimination, which occurred frequently with regard to the civil service employees of the state of Washington.

During the 1960s the WFSE organized many bargaining units and negotiated several employer-employee contracts. The union, however, still faced many barriers that were applied to civil service employees throughout the state. These early civil rights actions eventually led to passage of a law that allowed the union shop for civil service employees in the state of Washington.

Preliminary Civil Service Rights and the Victories of the WFSE

In December 1961 the executive board of the WFSE created a union civil rights committee whose express purpose was to ensure that state laws prohibiting discrimination in employment and promotion because of age, national origin, race, and religion, were observed to the fullest extent of the law. During the next 15 years and beyond, the WFSE committee actively pursued the enactment of important laws for the civil service employees of the state of Washington. As the result of a 1962 convention resolution from Olympia Local 443, WFSE won passage in 1963 of House Bill 6, which for the first time allowed the state, when sufficient funds were available, to pay some of the premiums for the state employee medical insurance. Additional state health benefits were realized in 1965.

In 1967 the WFSE secured passage of legislation amending the civil service law. The Public Employees Collective Bargaining Law of 1967 broadly expanded the union's authority to bargain collectively. With enactment of this law, state managers were for the first time forced to deal with a union and, in essence, to share power with an officially appointed bargaining agent of its employees. It also required the state to engage in collective bargaining with the employees and to deal with them on an equal basis. Although the law removed several barriers to union organizing and bargaining, it still left the actual establishment of wages, benefits, and other economic issues in control of the Washington state legislature.

The WFSE achieved steady progress in the early 1970s. In 1971 the WFSE secured passage of unemployment coverage; in 1972, a Public Assistance contract; and in 1973, an executive order (EO 71-04) guaranteeing the rights of state employees (in agencies under the jurisdiction of the governor) to union representation. The 1973 institutions law gave the state's public sector employees the opportunity to have an active voice in determining their working conditions, as well as the manner in which each employee's work was to be performed. Larry Goodman, the director of field services within the WFSE, stated in the mid-1990s that the 1973 institutions law proved to be a model law, one that did not change fundamentally for two decades.

The Union Shop Law

By the early 1970s, the leaders of the WFSE became aggravated by workers who refused to join the union but still were able to enjoy the benefits gained by the union. The majority of the state's civil service employees were of the opinion that whether or not one was a member of the union, that employee still received all the increased benefits that had been won by the union. In 1972 Executive Director Norm Schut began the slow process of attaining approval for a union shop law from the state legislature and the state governor. The purpose of the bill would be to require a union shop for civil servants. In other words, it was a mechanism mandating that all employees who are within a particular bargaining unit and covered by a collective bargaining agreement must join the exclusively recognized employee organization and must pay dues and initiation fees after a specified period of employment. The bill did not require a group of civil service employees to be represented by a union, but only stated that *if* a union represented a group, then all employees within that group must join the union.

Schut helped modify the bill to overcome objections from such groups as the Seventh Day Adventist Church, the National Civil Service League, and the Washington Public Employees Association. Even so, the governor vetoed a portion of the bill. Political columnist Mike Layton wrote of Shut's work, "Schut . . . shepherded the bill through the Legislature with all the care of a Scottish sheep dog bringing home the ewes."

On 31 January 1973 a bipartisan group of politicians from the Washington state House of Representatives sponsored the Union Shop Bill 489. Representatives Barden, Cessarelli, Charette, Paris, Perry, and Thompson took the proposal to the floor of the House on 15 February 1973, where it was debated and passed on the following day by a vote of 69 to 27. It was soon debated in the Senate of Washington state, where it passed by a vote of 34 to 15 on 27 February 1973. It became law on 20 March 1973.

Aftereffects

Within a year, membership of the WFSE/AFSCME rose to 13,700 union members (from 5,000 members in 1973) as union members in several bargaining units voted to create union shops. The Buildings and Grounds workers in the Department of General Administration voted in the first union shop on 26 October 1973. Less than two weeks later, physical plant workers at Western Washington State College in Bellingham voted in the first WFSE/AFSCME union shop in higher education.

Conclusion

The union shop law in the state of Washington, the first state to allow the union shop for civil service employees, allowed the WFSE to organize and develop a stable membership. WFSE president Howard Jorgenson noted at the time that he considered the union shop law the greatest accomplishment by the union in more than 20 years.

Key Players

Schut, Norm: Schut was the executive cirector of the Washington Federation of State Employees (WFSE)—an affiliate of the American Federation of State, Civil, and Municipal Employees (AFSCME) of the American Federation of Labor–Congress of Industrial Workers (AFL-CIO).

BIBLIOGRAPHY

Other

Heitman, Herrick. "State Library." Washington Secretary of State [cited 6 December 2002]. <http://www.statelib.wa.gov>.

Municipal Research and Services Center of Washington. *Association of Capitol Powerhouse Engineers, Appellant,* v. The State of Washington, et al, Respondents. 27 October 1977 [cited 6 December 2002]. <http://www.mrsc.org/mc/courts/supreme/89wn2d/89wn2d177.htm>.

Washington Federation of State Employees. "A Brief History of WFSE/AFSCME's First 50 years, 1943–1993" [cited 6 December 2002]. <http://www.wfse.org/hist1.htm>.

———. "Homepage of WFSE" [cited 6 December 2002]. <http://www.onevoice-wfse.org/>.

———. "Marching to the Future: The First 50 years of WFSE/AFSCME." Originally published in November 1993 *WFSE/AFSCME Washington State Employee* [cited 6 December 2002]. <http://www.wfse.org/hist4.htm>.

—William Arthur Atkins

Watsonville Canning Strike

United States 1985–1987

Synopsis

Latina workers within Watsonville, California's frozen food processing industry walked out on 9 September 1985 after their employers radically cut their base pay and benefits, citing competition from right-to-work states and Latin American processors able to pay lower wages. The International Brotherhood of Teamsters, the union representing these workers, held out for 18 months. The union typically had a decent relationship with area employers. Edward T. Console, owner of Watsonville Canning and Frozen Foods, had signed the industry's first union contract with the Teamsters in 1949, which established industry wage patterns, but by 1985 they were in a bitter battle. Union representatives saw this strike as not only important for the women on strike in Watsonville, but also as a barometer for labor throughout the country. Unions were in decline and this strike was viewed as a predictor of labor's future health. Ultimately, the union and the company settled, but the damage to the local food processing industry was profound. Despite boycotts, there was such a market glut that consumers never felt affected by the strike. Competition was so fierce that plants ultimately closed.

Timeline

1965: Arrest of the Rev. Martin Luther King, Jr., and more than 2,600 others in Selma, Alabama. Three weeks later, in New York City, Malcolm X is assassinated.

1975: U.S. *Apollo* and Soviet *Soyuz* spacecraft link up in space.

1980: Beginning of the eight-year Iran-Iraq War, destined to be the costliest conflict in the twentieth century's second half.

1982: Argentina invades the Falkland Islands, a British possession, and Great Britain strikes back in a 10-week war from which Britain emerges victorious.

1985: A new era begins in the USSR as Chernenko dies and is replaced by Mikhail Gorbachev, who at 54 years old is the youngest Soviet leader in decades.

1985: In a year of notable hijackings by Muslim and Arab terrorists, Shi'ites take a TWA airliner in June, Palestinians hijack the Italian cruise ship *Achille Lauro* in October, and fundamentalists take control of an Egyptian plane in Athens in November.

1986: Seven astronauts die in the explosion of the U.S. space shuttle *Challenger* on 28 January.

1986: An accident at the Chernobyl nuclear reactor in the Ukraine kills 31 workers and ultimately leads to the deaths of some 10,000 people. The Soviet government attempts to cover up the problem rather than evacuate the area.

1986: In November the scandal variously known as Iran-Contra, Irangate, and Contragate breaks, when it is revealed that the Reagan administration agreed to sell arms to Iran in exchange for hostages, and to divert the funds from the arms sales to support the anti-Sandinista Contras in Nicaragua.

1987: Iran-Contra hearings continue for much of the year, making a household name of such figures as Oliver North and his secretary, Fawn Hall.

1992: Former Panamanian leader General Manuel Noriega is convicted on drug charges in a U.S. court and sentenced to 40 years in prison.

2002: The U.S. economy, already suffering with the end of the technology boom in 2000 and the drop in stock prices following the 11 September terrorist attacks, is not helped by revelations of malfeasance on the part of corporate executives. Some of these former business leaders are led away from their offices in handcuffs, and huge corporations such as Enron and WorldCom are forced into bankruptcy as a result of illegal accounting practices.

Event and Its Context

Workers Strike to Keep Wages

Workers at two large frozen food processing plants—Watsonville Canning and Frozen Foods and Richard A. Shaw—went on strike on 9 September 1985, because their base pay and benefits had been drastically reduced. Most were Latina. Company owners said they had to cut pay to compete, as cheaper products flooded the domestic market. Other unionized plants negotiated settlements.

Watsonville, California, the so-called frozen vegetable capital of the world prior to the strike, packed than 40 percent of the United States' frozen broccoli, brussels sprouts, green peppers, and spinach, much of it grown along the Pacific Coast and inland in the Salinas Valley. Watsonville Canning processed produce for both Birds Eye and supermarket private labels. At its peak, the plant processed 140 million pounds of produce annually. It and the Richard A. Shaw Company together handled 80 percent of all the frozen food processed in Watsonville. The California industry employed about 3,000 workers, and the reported number of striking workers varied widely. Workers' pay had been previously cut by 40 cents per hour, and by July 1985 union employees were paid $5.85 an hour. Other companies were reportedly paying much more than Watsonville Canning in employee benefits. Prior to the strike, union workers earned $7.06 hourly.

Teamsters Local 912, which represented the cannery workers, was formed in 1952. Richard King headed the local from its inception. Teamsters for a Democratic Union, a reform faction within the union membership formed in September 1976, pressed the local to strike, and the workers walked out at all city canneries. In a 28 October 1985 "final offer," workers turned down a $5.05-per-hour wage proposal by a vote of 800–1. Shaw settled after four months. The 900 union employees agreed to a 17 percent pay cut. After union members at another cannery agreed in July 1986 to accept proposed pay cuts, $5.85 per hour became the standard industry wage.

The 18-month holdout took a great economic toll on the Watsonville strikers. With pride, the phrase is repeated in various prounion strike accounts: No striker scabbed. Strikers were provided with a $55-per-week strike benefit in return for picketing or other union work. In addition to losing their paychecks—about $250 per week mid-season—workers' benefits ended. Few had food stamps or other welfare support. Local food banks and family members filled the gap. Those who had savings lost them. About 16 months into the strike, assistance such as groceries had tapered significantly. Some women lost their cars and furniture, but they continued to hold out for a better contract. Some workers found other jobs that allowed them to picket night or weekends. Company executives hired replacement workers who earned $5.16 per hour. Police accompanied strikebreakers bused to Watsonville; those who had cars found them vandalized at the shift's end. Scabs typically worked a few weeks before quitting.

Union Politics Muddy the Situation

Confusing matters further, Jackie Presser, president of the Teamsters, had forced M. E. "Andy" Anderson from office in 1984. Anderson had been vice president of the international union and head of the Western Conference of Teamsters. Anderson supported the company during the strike as a labor relations consultant. He was a friend of owner Mort Console as well. According to the *Los Angeles Times*, "union negotiators were stunned when they saw Anderson sitting with company officials at the last bargaining session a few weeks ago. It was the first they knew of his role with the company." Anderson submitted that the union was trying to destroy the company. Company officials blamed Presser for instigating the strike as revenge against Anderson. Representatives of both the Teamsters and Teamsters for a Democratic Union said these charges were ridiculous.

Teamsters for a Democratic Union helped draw attention to the strike and helped raise funds. The group asked for weekly meetings for the duration of the strike. They urged the union to increase strike benefits from $55 to $100 per week. The Teamsters estimated the strike cost the union more than $5 million. It was, however, viewed by key union officials as having the potential to revitalize the flagging national labor movement. Richard King, the representative for the union local, told the *New York Times* very early in the strike that both employers and unions throughout the country were closely watching events in Watsonville. "If we lose the strike," he said, "it would have one hell of a bad effect on labor. The Teamsters are a strong union in California, and California is a strong labor state. If we lose here, companies all over the country would try what they're trying to do here."

Race and Gender in Negotiations

Ethnicity was a factor throughout the strike. The employers and the local city officials were Anglo in a city inhabited by a Latino majority. Most growers were Anglo men. An estimated 85 percent of all strikers were Latina. The head of the local was a white man who did not speak Spanish. Many of the striking workers were also single mothers. Discrimination was a factor, according to union representatives, in how the union-company negotiations progressed. During the strike, a jury awarded a former Watsonville Canning employee $135,000 on grounds of discrimination. This ethnic and cultural divide would solidify support by the Chicano and Mexican communities, and the success of the strike is attributed to this solidarity. As Frank Bardacke explained in an article in *El Andar,* "Strike defections are not just questions of morale. When a company can win back a significant minority of its experienced workers, those workers and raw scabs can restore production to a high enough level to wear down a strike. Throughout the strike at Watsonville Canning . . . the whole packaging operation was a shambles, forcing the company to pack by hand or to bulk pack and send its product to other companies to be repacked. . . . When all the Wats Can mechanics went on strike, the supervisors, management personnel and even out-of-town experts could not get the plant into good working order."

Support from other unions helped immensely, including that from the United Farm Workers as well as organizations attuned to Latino issues, such as the League of United Latin American Citizens and the Mexican American Political Association. The attitude among strikers was that you could not cross the picket line and still continue to live in Watsonville. This was not out of fear but pride. Despite the hardships, friendships were forged under pressure. Some grocers extended credit to strikers while merchants declined to cash scab checks. By one account, "so many turkeys were donated by the community in the 1985 Thanksgiving turkey drive that the food committee had enough frozen turkeys left over to serve turkey enchiladas at strike events months later." Violence during the strike included attacks on replacement workers entering the plant. They were reportedly pelted with rocks. Fires caused an estimated $2 million in property damage. One of these destroyed a packing shed.

Watsonville Canning, idled by the strike, owed growers an estimated $7 million and Wells Fargo Bank an additional $18 million. The bank had loaned the company $23 million during the strike. The Teamsters exerted pressure on the bank by announcing a vote requesting that the union withdraw its $800 million from the bank. As the union prepared to close its accounts, Wells Fargo foreclosed on the company.

In September 1986 the California Department of Food and Agriculture announced it was investigating the company. With help from Wells Fargo Bank, new ownership was found for the failing company. With new ownership in February 1987, negotiations commenced immediately. Union officials approved the initial agreement, but workers thought the medical benefits were inadequate for most. The union cut strike benefits, announcing the end of the strike. The workers, however, went back on strike. Several women launched a hunger strike to draw attention to their demands. Within five days, the growers' consortium relented. In addition to meeting their demands for medical benefits for all workers, they also granted seniority rights and striker amnesty. A three-year contract with a base hourly pay of $5.85 was accepted 11 March, by a vote of 543 to 21. Both sides were elated. By March 1987 the growers who were still owed money formed Norcal Frozen Foods.

The plant opened with a skeletal staff rehired on a seniority basis. Although the new owners provided the plant with plenty of produce and business, other customers had struck deals with other packaging facilities during the strike. The company did not survive.

Key Players

Anderson, M. E. "Andy": Formerly vice president of the Teamsters international union as well as head of the Western Conference of Teamsters, Anderson was a "labor relations consultant" during the strike.

Console, Edward T.: Owner of Watsonville Canning who signed the frozen food processing industry's first union contract with the Teamsters in 1949. This agreement established the industry wage pattern.

Console, Mort: Owner of Watsonville Canning during the stike. The company was the nation's largest frozen vegetable processor at the time of the strike. He closed the plant under a huge debt burden.

Gill, David L.: A third-generation farmer based in King City, California, and a 1973 graduate of California Polytechnic State University San Luis Obispo, Gill was president of Gilco Produce Co. during the Watsonville Canning strike. He was one of the growers to whom Watsonville Canning and Frozen Foods owed money. He became president of Norcal Frozen Foods.

King, Richard: At the time of the strike, King had been the Teamsters local president since its inception in 1952. He retired in December 1985.

Lopez, Sergio: Upon the retirement of Richard King in December 1985, Lopez was elected to head Teamsters Local 912.

Presser, Jackie (1926–1988): Born in Cleveland, Ohio, Presser headed the International Brotherhood of Teamsters at the time of the Watsonville Canning strike. He had been the union's national president since 1983. Some thought the strike was the result of a power struggle between Presser and M. E. ""Anderson, who had left the union in 1984.

Shaw, Richard A.: owner of Richard A. Shaw, Inc., one of the two frozen food processing plants involved in the Watsonville strike. His company settled with the union four months into the labor action.

See also: *International Brotherhood of Teamsters.*

———————

BIBLIOGRAPHY

Books

Craft, Donna, and Terrance W. Peck, eds. *Profiles of American Labor Unions.* Detroit: Gale Research, 1998.

Moody, Kim. *An Injury to All: The Decline of American Unionism.* New York: Verso, 1988.

Periodicals

Bardacke, Frank. "The Workers, United." *El Andar,* October 1995.

Bernstein, Harry. "Labor: Ex-Teamster Leader Bolsters Union's Foes." *Los Angeles Times,* 10 September 1986, p. 1.

Brandt, Richard. "A Fight for Survival on Cannery Row." *Business Week: Industrial/Technical Edition,* 30 March 1987, p. 90B.

Brecher, Jeremy. "Labor History: Resisting Concessions," *Z Magazine,* May 1998.

"Concessions at Issue in Strike of Food Plants." *New York Times,* 20 October 1985, Sec. 1, p. 28.

Erlich, Reese. "California Teamsters Election Tests Influence of Women, Hispanics." *Christian Science Monitor,* 10 December 1985, p. 8.

———. "Canning-plant Workers Say Discrimination Is Behind Wage Cuts." *Christian Science Monitor,* 4 November 1985, p. 6.

Lindsey, Robert. "Eating Patterns Affect Packers Strike." *New York Times,* 1 January 1987, Sec. 1, p. 14.

———. "Packing Plant Strike: Arduous Battle to Survive." *New York Times,* 27 January 1987, Sec. 1, p. 14.

Tirschwell, Peter M. "Frozen Out by Free Trade." *Journal of Commerce* (1 March 1996): 1.

"Workers Vote 543–521 to End Bitter Eighteen-Month Strike at Frozen Food Plant." *Los Angeles Times,* 12 March 1987, Part 1, p. 24.

Zonana, Victor F. "Eighteen-Month Strike at Food Plant May End." *Los Angeles Times,* 4 March 1987, Part 1, p. 24.

ADDITIONAL RESOURCES

"Santa Cruz, a Century—The 1980s: Community's Latinos Shake Political Stick." *Santa Cruz Sentinal* (22 January 2003). <http://www.santacruzsentinel.com/extra/century/82/>.

—Linda Dailey Paulson

Weavers' Revolt

Silesia 1844

Synopsis

In June 1844 disturbances and riots occurred in the Prussian province of Silesia, a major center of textile manufacturing.

Crowds of weavers attacked homes and warehouses, destroyed machinery, and demanded money from local merchants. In response, the Prussian army was called to restore order in the region. In a confrontation between the weavers and troops, shots were fired into the crowd, killing 11 people and wounding others. The leaders of the disturbances were arrested, flogged, and imprisoned. The uprising was a result of severe social and economic distress in the region. Due to competition from overseas markets, the Silesian textile industry was in decline. This, combined with the impact of population growth, threatened to force the income of the Silesian weavers to below subsistence levels. In many ways the Silesian weavers' revolt was a traditional response to poverty and hunger. However, some of the weavers' words and actions seemed to indicate a changing understanding of their position in society. Because of this event has gained enormous significance in the history of the German labor movement. In particular, Karl Marx regarded the uprising as evidence of the birth of a German workers' movement. The weavers' rebellion served as an important symbol for later generations concerned about poverty and oppression in German society.

Timeline

1822: German composer Franz Schubert introduces his Eighth ("Unfinished") Symphony.

1828: Election of Andrew Jackson as president begins a new era in American history.

1834: American inventor Cyrus H. McCormick patents his reaper, a horse-drawn machine for harvesting wheat.

1837: Coronation of Queen Victoria in England.

1842: Scientific and technological advances include the development of ether and artificial fertilizer; the identification of the Doppler effect (by Austrian physicist Christian Johann Doppler); the foundation of biochemistry as a discipline; and the coining of the word *dinosaur.*

1844: Samuel Laing, in a prize-winning essay on Britain's "National Distress," describes conditions in a nation convulsed by the early Industrial Revolution. A third of the population, according to Laing, "hover[s] on the verge of actual starvation"; another third is forced to labor in "crowded factories"; and only the top third "earn[s] high wages, amply sufficient to support them in respectability and comfort."

1844: Exiled to Paris, Karl Marx meets Friedrich Engels.

1844: American inventor Charles Goodyear patents his process for "vulcanizing" rubber.

1846: Height of the Irish potato famine.

1846: Discovery of the planet Neptune.

1850: German mathematical physicist Rudolf Julius Emanuel Clausius enunciates the Second Law of Thermodynamics, stating that heat cannot pass from a colder body to a warmer one, but only from a warmer to a colder body. This will prove to be one of the most significant principles of physics and chemistry, establishing that a perfectly efficient physical system is impossible, and that all physical systems ultimately succumb to entropy.

1853: Commodore Matthew Perry arrives in Japan, and the United States forces the Japanese to permit American trade.

Event and Its Context

The Uprising

In January and April 1844, weavers from the Silesian towns of Langenbielau and Peterswaldau petitioned the government to intervene in setting prices in the textile industry. With the support of the authorities, the weavers hoped to prevent local merchants from further dropping the prices they paid for the weavers' work. However, the government failed to respond to their grievances. Unrest gradually increased over the spring and early summer, as the weavers' resentment towards the merchants continued to simmer. Finally, the situation came to a head on the evening of 3 June, when several weavers gathered outside the home of the Zwanziger family of merchants in Peterswaldau. The Zwanzigers had attracted attention in the community for their rapid accumulation of wealth and harsh exploitation of the local weavers. With songs and chants, the weavers insulted the Zwanzigers, accusing them of being devils who preyed on the poor. As a result of the demonstration, one of the weavers was beaten and handed over to police.

This incident seemed to serve as a catalyst for the broader mobilization of the local population. Another local weaver, Karl Müller, called for all the weavers to band together and demand the release of the prisoner, threatening physical violence to those who did not join in. The weavers set out on a march through the local villages to gather supporters for their confrontation with the merchant and police.

By the afternoon of 4 June, a large crowd had gathered outside the Zwanziger's dwelling. The leaders called for the release of the prisoner, as well as higher pay and a "present" from the Zwanzigers to atone for the suffering of the weavers. This demand was a traditional part of premodern social protest and reflected the accepted customs of traveling journeymen, who often asked for "presents" from members of the community in which they were seeking work. When these demands were not met, the crowd began to attack the house, and the family was forced to flee to Breslau for safety. The local police were powerless in the face of such a large and angry crowd, and the weavers proceeded to destroy the Zwanziger's house and property. They also attacked the warehouse and factory, destroying bales of cotton, yarn, account books, and other business documents, as well as the machinery in the factory. The house and property of a neighboring merchant were spared, as he was known to treat the weavers more humanely, and he acquiesced to the crowd's demand for a present. This scene was repeated several times at the homes of other merchants in the area.

The next day, 5 June, a crowd reported to number in the thousands gathered at the home of the merchant Dierig in the town of Langenbielau. As people lined up to receive money from the merchant's representatives, troops arrived. In the ensuing confrontation, the soldiers fired shots, resulting in the deaths of 11 people; more were reported wounded. In response, the crowd attacked the soldiers, and the troops were forced to retreat until reinforcements arrived from neighboring towns. By 6 June, with the arrival of more troops and artillery, authorities were able to regain control, and the revolt was effectively over. Several of the leaders were arrested and later imprisoned.

Economic Decline and Social Distress

The grievances of the weavers centered on their exploitation by local merchants who controlled the textile trade. They were particularly concerned by the low prices they received for their work. The weavers, many of whom had come from generations of relatively well-off independent craftsmen, were facing impoverishment as their incomes slipped below subsistence levels. What lay behind this problem was several decades of change in the Silesian textile industry. The region had been a center of textile, particularly linen, manufacturing since the sixteenth century. Local feudal lords had established the industry among their serfs in cooperation with foreign merchants. Silesian linen was exported to markets in Holland, England, and Spain, as well as to their colonies. In time the economy of the whole region came to depend heavily on the linen trade.

However, from the late eighteenth century, several factors led to the decline of linen manufacturing in Silesia. The demand for Silesian linen dropped as it faced increased competition from the development of linen industries in Ireland and Scotland. English cotton also became a popular and cheap alternative to linen, particularly in the tropical climates. Because of the development of mechanized factory production in the British textile industry, Silesian producers found it increasingly difficult to compete. By contrast, centralized factory production and technology such as power looms were still rare in protoindustrial Silesia. Domestic weavers, who bought the raw materials from merchants and sold back the finished product, generally worked in their homes or in small workshops. The persistence of feudal social and economic arrangements in Silesia prevented the development of more efficient systems of production. The export of Silesian linen declined rapidly in the 1830s and 1840s, and the economy of the region stagnated.

This process of economic decline had a shattering effect on the local population. While cotton manufacturing in the region did expand in these decades, the only way for the merchants to remain competitive in the international market was by keeping labor costs low. This was made possible by oversupply in the labor market. The German region had experienced a period of sustained population growth during the eighteenth and nineteenth centuries. As industrialization had not yet reached levels where factories could absorb this increase in people, unemployment and underemployment reached chronic levels. Weavers coming out of the declining linen and wool industries compounded the problem. The merchants were able to exploit the ready supply of weavers desperate for work by pushing prices down even further.

The weavers were in an impossible situation. As the merchants had a monopoly on access to the markets for the weavers' work, the weavers had no choice but to accept the prices that they were offered. The weavers also had the additional economic pressure of feudal obligations, being still forced to pay seignorial dues in many places. Some weavers were forced into debt, having to borrow money in order to buy the raw materials with which they worked. This helps explain why the weavers destroyed account books and business documents during the uprising. For those with resources, immigration to America was a popular option during this period. Those unable to leave faced a dismal future. The situation became increasingly desperate in the 1840s, as the failure of the potato crop caused food prices to skyrocket. Widespread starvation occurred in what has been called the last great subsistence crisis in European society.

Reaction

The weavers' uprising sent shock waves across the region. It contributed to growing concerns about the problem of "pauperism" in society. In the 1840s contemporary social debate focused on the poverty, crime, and disorder that seemed on the verge of engulfing respectable society. Economic hardship and social unrest reached epidemic proportions, as German society struggled to cope with its expanding population. There was a sense among social observers that the nature and scale of these problems was much more serious than in previous generations. The hunger and desperation of such a large mass of the population was regarded as a sign that there was something fundamentally wrong with European society. Newspapers published article after article offering analysis and solutions to "the social problem" and issue of the organization of labor. In this concern and agitation lay the seeds of the 1848 revolutions.

The Silesian weavers symbolized this sense of social crisis. While the violence and bloodshed undoubtedly alarmed most people, there was also considerable sympathy for their desperate situation. The weavers' revolt quickly became a popular theme in contemporary art and literature, as artists and writers exploited the pathos of the weavers' desperate plight. In particular, the well-known German romantic poet Heinrich Heine brought the despair and anger of the weavers to a wider European audience with his poem "The Silesian Weavers," written in the months immediately after the event.

In Heine's poem the desperation of the weavers is seen as a catalyst for social revolution. For many political radicals, the weavers' uprising was an example of the inadequacy of the existing political system to deal with the growing social crisis. However, for the members of the fledgling socialist movement,

the event acquired particular significance in terms of their theories about the confrontation between workers and the bourgeoisie in capitalist society. The description of the uprising by the journalist Wilhelm Wolff encouraged this interpretation, influenced as it was by his developing socialist beliefs. Published in June 1844 and based upon eyewitness accounts, it caused a sensation in Germany and became the most influential account of the revolt. Wolff was the son of Silesian peasants and had already been imprisoned for his involvement in radical politics. His account of the uprising was clearly shaped by his sympathy for the situation of the weavers, as well as his antipathy towards the merchants who exploited them. In interviews with workers at the time of the uprising, Wolff emphasized how many others shared the grievances of the weavers. This seemed to suggest the potential for broader solidarity among the workers.

Wolff later became involved in the Communist League, led by Karl Marx and Friedrich Engels. For Engels and Marx, the weavers' uprising was also very important, because it supported their developing theories about capitalism and class conflict in society. Engels reported on the uprising in his capacity as German correspondent for the English newspaper the *Northern Star*. He attributed it to the suffering of the weavers, caused by the consequences of competition from products produced in the English factory system. For his English audience, Engels emphasized the common exploitation of the Silesian weavers and the textile workers of Lancashire and Yorkshire. The consequences of the factory system were oppression and toil for the many, riches and wealth for the few, in all parts of the world.

Karl Marx welcomed the uprising as evidence of the maturation of the workers' movement in Germany. He believed that an understanding of themselves as a distinct class, in conflict with the bourgeois merchants, lay behind the weavers' actions. Therefore, this was a confrontation between labor and capital. According to Marx, "the Silesian rebellion starts . . . with an understanding of the nature of the proletariat. . . . [N]ot . . . one of the French and English insurrections has had the same theoretical and conscious character." In Marx's view the three-day uprising was more significant than either the Chartist disturbances in England during the 1840s or the French silk-weavers' strikes in Lyon during the 1830s. Because of Marx's interpretation, the Silesian uprising acquired enormous significance in the history of the labor movement in Germany.

It also served as a potent symbol of resistance to oppression and exploitation for subsequent generations. Artists on the left who were concerned about the poverty and suffering of the working classes used the theme of the weavers' uprising as a way to express their social criticism. Fifty years after the event, the German playwright Gerhart Hauptmann shocked audiences with his starkly realistic play, *The Weavers,* based upon Wolff's account. First performed in 1893, the play was banned by authorities in Wilhelmine Germany. Faced with an expanding socialist movement, the government was naturally antagonistic to a sympathetic portrayal of social protest. Hauptmann's play inspired the German artist Käthe Kollwitz, who created a series of prints from 1893 to 1897, *The Weavers' Uprising*. Her powerful images eloquently expressed the despair and anger of the weavers, echoing the poverty and desperation of the working class in 1890s Germany. The tale of the weavers' uprising had the power to move new generations still grappling with problems of social distress and oppression among the working class.

Transitional Labor Protest

Marx and his fellow socialists interpreted the weavers' uprising as the birth of a self-conscious workers' movement in Germany. However, the significance of the event in these terms was overstated. The uprising was part of a wave of social unrest that swept Germany during the 1840s, a time of intense social crisis and economic breakdown. As with many other incidents of protest in this era, the weavers were spontaneously rebelling against the poverty that threatened to overwhelm them. Some of their actions, such as their demands for gifts from the merchants to alleviate their suffering, suggest that the weavers were still operating within older systems of social values and relations. The weavers did not have a sense of themselves as members of a distinct class in conflict with another class. Instead, they acted as members of a community, intent on punishing those who had transgressed certain rules regarding the value of their work. Their actions in targeting the houses of specific merchants, while leaving intact the homes of others, showed that they were not antagonistic to the merchants as a class, but only to certain individuals whose behavior they perceived as exploitative. Nor is there any evidence that the weavers had any alternative social vision, or suggested any reorganization of production to redistribute profits more fairly. This was not the birth of a social movement but was rather a spontaneous expression of economic distress.

Nevertheless, some historians have regarded the weavers' uprising as an example of transitional social protest. While certainly retaining much of the character of earlier generations of social protest, the weavers were acting as workers, rather than as members of a traditional craft or guild. Rather than demanding the restoration of traditional rights, as was often the case in earlier examples of strikes and protests, the weavers' main grievance focused on better recompense for their labor, foreshadowing the demands of workers in the modern labor movement. In mobilizing their community against the merchants, the weavers stood on the boundary between a world of craft and communal attitudes to work and a new understanding of conflict between the forces of labor and capital.

Key Players

Heine, Heinrich (1797–1856): German romantic poet who became influenced by socialist ideas. Heine's poem "The Silesian Weavers" helped bring the Silesian weavers' revolt to the attention of a European audience. It was hailed by Karl Marx as "an intrepid battle cry."

Marx, Karl (1818–1883): Founder of modern socialist theory. Marx interpreted the Silesian weavers' revolt as the birth of the German workers' movement. This gave the uprising lasting significance in the history of the German labor movement.

Wolff, Wilhelm (1809–1864): German journalist and political radical. Wolff's account of the Silesian weavers' revolt is the most influential description of the event. Wolff later met Karl Marx and Friedrich Engels, becoming a cofounder of the Communist League upon its inception in 1847. Wolff

returned to Silesia in 1848 and was heavily involved in the left wing of the revolution. Marx dedicated the first volume of *Das Kapital* to Wolff.

See also: *Silk Workers' Revolts.*

BIBLIOGRAPHY

Books

Berger, Stefan. *Social Democracy and the Working Class in Nineteenth and Twentieth Century Germany.* New York: Longman, 1999.

Kisch, Herbert. "The Textile Industries in Silesia and the Rhineland: A Comparative Study in Industrialization (with a Postscriptum)." In *Industrialization before Industrialization. Rural Industry in the Genesis of Capitalism,* edited by Peter Kriedte, Hans Medick, and Jürgen Schlumbohm. Cambridge, England: Cambridge University Press, 1981.

Kocka, Jürgen. "Problems of Working-Class Formation in Germany: The Early Years, 1800–1875." In *Working-Class Formation: Nineteenth-Century Patterns in Western Europe and the United States,* edited by Ira Katznelson and Aristide R. Zolberg. Princeton, NJ: Princeton University Press, 1986.

Sheehan, James. *German History, 1770–1866.* Oxford, England: Clarendon Press, 1989.

Tilly, Charles, Louise Tilly, and Richard Tilly. *The Rebellious Century, 1830–1930.* Cambridge, MA: Harvard University Press, 1975.

Wolff, Wilhelm. "Das Elend und der Aufruhr in Schlesien 1844." In *The Revolutions of 1848–49,* translated and edited by Frank Eyck. Edinburgh, Scotland: Oliver & Boyd, 1972.

Other

Marx and Engels: Major Works 1844 [cited 26 October 2002]. <www.marxists.org/archive/marx/works/1844/>.

ADDITIONAL RESOURCES

Books

Geary, Dick. *European Labour Protest, 1848–1939.* London, England: Croom Helm, 1981.

Grebing, Helga. *History of the German Labour Movement.* Leamington Spa, Warwickshire, England: Berg Publishers, 1985.

—Katrina Ford

Charles H. Moyer, William Dudley Haywood, and Charles Pettibone of Western Federation of Miners. © Corbis. Reproduced by permission.

Western Federation of Miners

United States 1893

Synopsis

In reaction to the use of federal troops to break a strike of unionized miners of nonferrous metals in Idaho, miners' unions from five western states formed the Western Federation of Miners (WFM), an industrial union of wage earners (miners and smelter workers) in and around the mines. The WFM endorsed the class struggle in the preamble to its constitution and engaged in labor strikes in which the mining corporations used troops to defeat the union miners. The WFM created the Western Labor Union and its successor, the American Labor Union, as competitors to the more conservative, craft union-dominated American Federation of Labor. The WFM endorsed the Populists in 1896 and the newly formed Socialist Party in 1900, and in 1905 the WFM took a leading role in the founding of the Industrial Workers of the World, an organization committed to industrial syndicalism. In 1916 the WFM changed its name to the International Union of Mine, Mill, and Smelter Workers and adopted the more conciliatory language of bread-and-butter unionism.

Timeline

1893: Henry Ford builds his first automobile.

1898: United States defeats Spain in the three-month Spanish-American War. As a result, Cuba gains it independence, and the United States purchases Puerto Rico and the Philippines from Spain for $20 million.

1900: China's Boxer Rebellion, which began in the preceding year with attacks on foreigners and Christians, reaches its height. An international contingent of more than 2,000 men arrives to restore order, but only after several tens of thousands have died.

1903: Polish-born French chemist Marie Curie becomes the first woman to be awarded the Nobel Prize.

1908: Ford Motor Company introduces the Model T.

1913: Two incidents illustrate the increasingly controversial nature of the arts in the new century. Visitors to the 17 February Armory Show in New York City are scandalized by such works as Marcel Duchamp's cubist *Nude Descending a Staircase,* which elicits vehement criticism, and theatergoers at the 29 May debut of Igor Stravinksy's ballet *Le Sacré du Printemps* (*The Rite of Spring*) are so horrified by the new work that a riot ensues.

417

1914: On the Western Front, the first battles of the Marne and Ypres establish a line that will more or less hold for the next four years. Exuberance is still high on both sides but will dissipate as thousands of German, French, and British soldiers sacrifice their lives in battles over a few miles of barbed wire and mud. The Eastern Front is a different story: a German victory over Russia at Tannenberg in August sets the stage for a war in which Russia will enjoy little success, and will eventually descend into chaos that paves the way for the 1917 revolutions.

1918: The Second Battle of the Marne in July and August is the last major conflict on the Western Front. In November, Kaiser Wilhelm II abdicates, bringing an end to the war.

Event and Its Context

Early Labor Unionism

The earliest miners in the American West were prospectors and placer miners in search of quick riches that seemed possible from the California gold rush in 1849 through the 1860s. Many of those who stayed in the West after their dreams evaporated found employment in the deep shaft mines that began to develop in California in the 1850s and spread throughout the West in the following decades. The miners' resentment of their lost independence coupled with the shared dangers of underground mining produced a strong sense of solidarity. Starting with the first hard rock miners' union in 1863 at Nevada's rich Comstock Lode, hard rock men pushed for a uniform wage for all underground workers. As one of the earliest successful American industrial unions, the local miners' union was often a formidable force in small mining towns. They were especially effective when middle-class shopkeepers and professionals, who were dependent upon workers' wages, threw their support to the miners' union during conflicts with mining corporations that were financed by eastern and European capital. The miners also voted for city officials, including law enforcement, who were friendly to labor.

In reaction to the miners' community support, major mining corporations used their influence at the state level to exert judicial and military powers against miners' unions. This occurred most dramatically in 1892, when mining companies in the Coeur d'Alene mining district of northern Idaho convinced the state government to request U.S. Army troops to break a strike by miners who opposed a wage reduction. The military rounded up hundreds of union members and imprisoned them in an open stockade known as the "bull pen." Edward Boyce, who would become president of the WFM, and 11 other union miners who were incarcerated for contempt of court, came together to devise a plan for a federation of local miners' unions.

The Birth of the Western Federation of Miners

In May 1893, 40 delegates from 15 miners' unions met in Butte, Montana, home to the Butte Miners' Union (which was America's largest local labor union during the 1890s), to found the Western Federation of Miners (WFM). The preamble to its constitution called for moderate labor measures—safety legislation, decent wages, and arbitration. Even a moderate union met strong opposition from mining companies. In 1894 mine owners in Colorado's Cripple Creek mining district increased the workday from eight to nine hours. The miners waged a successful strike in great part because Governor Davis Waite, a Populist whom the miners had supported, used the state militia to disperse the company's gunmen.

Edward Boyce, one of the architects of the WFM and a member of its executive board, was elected president in 1896. He affiliated the WFM with the American Federation of Labor (AFL) in the belief that membership would strengthen the miners' position. At Leadville, Colorado, in 1896, local officials swore in strikebreakers as National Guard troops and enlisted them to break the strike. When the Leadville miners went on strike, Boyce asked for financial assistance. After the AFL neglected to provide assistance, Boyce took the WFM out of the eastern-dominated amalgamation of trade unions. In 1898 Boyce played a significant role in the Salt Lake City convention that founded the Western Labor Union as a regional competitor to the AFL. In 1899 federal troops broke a strike in the Coeur d'Alene district where Boyce had served as the recording secretary of the Wardner Miners' Union and as a strike leader in the 1892 defeat.

A significant increase in mergers of American corporations occurred between 1898 and 1902. The metal mining and smelting industries reflected this merger movement with the creation of the Phelps Dodge Copper Company, the American Smelting and Refining Company, and the Amalgamated Copper Company (owned primarily by Standard Oil executives), which dominated the industry and the western communities where they extracted and processed ore.

Colorado Labor Wars

Miners supported labor friendly candidates, especially from the Populist Party. In 1899 the Colorado legislature enacted an eight-hour workday, but the Colorado Supreme Court struck it down. In 1902 Colorado voters passed a referendum to amend the state constitution to include the eight-hour day, but the legislature failed to pass the legislation.

In addition to the political battle, Colorado experienced a struggle that became known as the "Colorado labor wars" (1901–1903), between the WFM and mining corporations. In 1901 the Telluride miners' union struck to protect the eight-hour day. The owners' backed down, but the WFM wanted mine owners to recognize the union. After a violent confrontation, Vincent St. John, president of the Telluride Miners' Union, negotiated a ceasefire. The governor refused the companies' request for troops. The miners returned to work with the eight-hour day intact, but without union recognition.

The WFM attempted to organize smelter workers at Colorado City in the Cripple Creek district during 1902. Over the next two years, the governor ignored local officials and at the companies' request intermittently sent the state militia to stifle the union's organizing drive, suspended *habeas corpus*, and allowed the arrest and deportation of union members. Charles Moyer, a South Dakota smelter worker and president of the WFM, was jailed and denied *habeas corpus*, which precipitated his advocacy of socialism and broad-based radical unionism. Local citizens' alliances intimidated union sympathizers. The

WFM called off the strike in 1904. The mining companies also used the militia, martial law, arrests and deportations, and Citizens' Alliances to defeat the WFM, in 1903–1904, at Idaho Springs and San Juan in Colorado.

Left-wing Unionism

In the meantime, the WFM moved further to the political left as membership reached its highest point of 30,000 out of 200,000 employed in the metalliferous mining industry. The *Miners' Magazine*, a WFM weekly founded in 1900, denounced corporations, capitalism, and the government. In 1902 the Western Labor Union (WLU) changed its name to the American Labor Union as part of an unsuccessful attempt to organize workers in the East, and the WFM and WLU endorsed the Socialist Party. In 1905 the WFM took the lead in founding the Industrial Workers of the World (IWW), an industrial union built on the syndicalist principles of direct action and opposition to time contracts with employers. By the end of 1905, the IWW had 50,000 members, of which 27,000 belonged to the WFM.

In December 1905 a dynamite explosion murdered Frank Steunenberg, a former governor of Idaho who was disliked by the miners for his role in defeating the WFM during the Coeur d'Alene strike of 1899. Upon the testimony of Henry Orchard, a man of suspect character; the court extradited WFM president Moyer; WFM secretary Bill Haywood; and George Pettibone, a small businessman who had been a leader in the Coeur d'Alene strike of 1892, and charged them with Steunenberg's murder. Famous attorney Clarence Darrow helped achieve acquittals for Haywood and Pettibone and dropped charges for Moyer. The long trial was costly, however, and deprived the WFM and the nascent IWW of leadership during a crucial period.

The IWW's second convention of 1906 split the organization into two factions: one led by Charles O. Sherman, which most WFM members followed, and the other led by Daniel DeLeon and William Trautmann. Goldfield, Nevada, became the battlefield of IWW factions within the WFM. Here Vincent St. John, a WFM delegate to the IWW convention and former WFM local president, led an IWW local affiliated with the DeLeon-Trautmann faction that opposed time contracts and conciliatory relationships with employers. St. John organized nonminers in Goldfield and brought them into the WFM local, which forced it into local, nonmining labor disputes. Business leaders eventually convinced Nevada's governor to call in federal troops to stop the turmoil. This signaled the end for the IWW and WFM locals in Goldfield and set the stage for the national WFM to cut all fiscal and organizational ties with the IWW in 1908. The WFM rejoined the AFL in 1911.

Death of the WFM

In 1913–1914 the WFM, which had been organizing copper miners in Michigan's upper peninsula, became involved in a bitter nine-month strike against poor working conditions, low wages, and company control of daily life. Company gunmen shot Moyer and the strike was eventually crushed. The action depleted WFM's treasury. When an internal struggle destroyed the Butte Miners' Union in 1914, the WFM lost its most reliable source of income. The WFM had fewer than 17,000 members

in 1916 when it changed its name to the International Union of Mine, Mill, and Smelter Workers.

For over 20 years, the WFM confronted Gilded Age mining corporations whose wealth and political connections often enlisted the aid of the courts and the military to break labor strikes. The extreme violence and oppression transformed a moderate industrial union into a leading radical labor organization that repudiated the conservative trade unionism of the AFL and embraced socialism and syndicalism to fight the class struggle.

Key Players

Boyce, Edward (1863–1941): Boyce emigrated from Ireland and worked as a hard rock miner, planning the formation of the Western Federation of Miners (WFM) while imprisoned for his leadership of Coeur d'Alene strike of 1892. He served as WFM president (1896–1902), pushing for the formation of the Western Labor Union and support of the Socialist Party.

Haywood, William Dudley (1869–1928): Haywood held various WFM offices, played a major role in the Telluride and Cripple Creek strikes, and chaired the founding convention of the Industrial Workers of the World in 1905. He was jailed in 1906 for the murder of a former Idaho governor but was acquitted in 1907. He was expelled from the WFM in 1908.

Moyer, Charles H. (1893–1929): Moyer served as president of WFM from 1902 until dissolution of WFM in 1916 and continued as president of the International Union of Mine, Mill, and Smelter Workers until 1926. He was jailed for the murder of a former Idaho governor in 1906 and acquitted in 1907. He participated in the formation of the Industrial Workers of the World (IWW), took WFM out of the IWW in 1908, and rejoined the AFL in 1911.

O'Neill, John M. (c. 1857–1936): O'Neill, a college-educated journalist, edited the *Miners' Magazine* (1901–1910), the WFM's weekly publication, and made it a vehicle for radical unionism and socialism. He was a delegate to the first IWW convention, but by 1910 advocated rejoining the AFL.

St. John, Vincent (1876–1929): St. John led the Telluride Miners' Union in the 1901 and 1903 strikes, helped to found the IWW, and was a leader of the faction that supported revolutionary industrial unionism. As a member of the IWW executive board, he organized workers in Goldfield, NV, an action that contributed to the WFM's withdrawal from the IWW. He served as IWW general secretary–treasurer (1908–1915).

See also: *American Federation of Labor; Industrial Workers of the World; People's Party; Socialist Party of America.*

BIBLIOGRAPHY

Books

Jensen, Vernon H. *Heritage of Conflict: Labor Relations in the Nonferrous Metals Industry up to 1930*. Ithaca, NY: Cornell University Press, 1950.

Laslett, John H. M. *Labor and the Left: A Study of Socialist and Radical Influences in the American Labor Movement, 1881–1924.* New York: Basic Books, 1970.

Perlman, Selig, and Philip Taft. *History of Labor in the United States, 1896–1932. Vol. 4: Labor Movements.* New York: Macmillan, 1935.

Wyman, Mark. *Hard Rock Epic: Western Miners and the Industrial Revolution, 1860–1910.* Berkeley: University of California Press, 1979.

ADDITIONAL RESOURCES

Books

Brown, Ronald C. *Hard-Rock Miners: The Intermountain West, 1860–1920.* College Station: Texas A&M University, 1979.

Byrkit, James W. *Forging the Copper Collar: Arizona's Labor-Management War of 1901–1921.* Tucson: University of Arizona, 1982.

Calvert, Jerry W. *The Gibraltar: Socialism and Labor in Butte, Montana, 1895–1920.* Helena: Montana Historical Society Press, 1982.

Cash, Joseph H. *Working the Homestake.* Ames: Iowa State University, 1973.

Conlin, Joseph R. *Big Bill Haywood and the Radical Union Movement.* Syracuse, NY: Syracuse University Press, 1969.

Dubofsky, Melvin. *We Shall Be All: A History of the Industrial Workers of the World.* Chicago: Quadrangle Books, 1969.

Emmons, David M. *The Butte Irish: Class and Ethnicity in an American Mining Town, 1875–1925.* Urbana: University of Illinois Press, 1989.

Jameson, Elizabeth. *All That Glitters: Class, Conflict and Community in Cripple Creek.* Urbana: University of Illinois Press, 1998.

Lankton, Larry. *Cradle to Grave: Life, Work and Death at the Lake Superior Copper Mines.* New York: Oxford University Press, 1991.

Larson, Robert W. *Populism in the Mountain West.* Albuquerque: University of New Mexico, 1986.

Lingenfelter, Richard E. *The Hardrock Miners: A History of the Mining Labor Movement in the American West, 1863–1893.* Berkeley: University of California Press, 1974.

Malone, Michael P. *The Battle for Butte: Mining and Politics on the Northern Frontier, 1864–1906.* Seattle: University of Washington Press, 1981.

Mellinger, Philip J. *Race and Labor in Western Copper: The Fight for Equality, 1896–1918.* Tucson: University of Arizona Press, 1995.

Paul, Rodman. *Mining Frontiers of the Far West, 1848–1880.* New York: Holt, Rinehart, and Winston, 1963.

Smith, Robert W. *The Coeur d'Alene Mining War of 1892: A Case Study of an Industrial Dispute.* Gloucester, MA: Peter Smith, 1968.

Suggs, George G. Jr. *Colorado's War on Militant Unionism: James H. Peabody and the Western Federation of Miners.* Detroit, MI: Wayne State University Press, 1972.

Wright, James Edward. *The Politics of Populism: Dissent in Colorado.* New Haven: Yale University Press, 1974.

—Paul A. Frisch

Widowed Mother's Fund Association

United States 1909

Synopsis

In the early twentieth century, thousands of widowed and abandoned mothers became trapped in a horrifying catch-22 situation: to feed their families in an age when charities were overburdened and the government provided no relief for destitute children, they had no choice but to work outside the home (almost invariably in jobs that were at best subsistence level), yet by working outside their homes they risked having their children taken by the state and placed in orphanages. In 1909 a group comprising mainly wealthy Jewish women formed the Widowed Mother's Fund Association specifically to help fatherless families in New York City remain together. The association and its founders were instrumental in obtaining the first government funding for dependant children in peacetime.

Timeline

1889: Flooding in Johnstown, Pennsylvania, kills thousands.

1893: Wall Street stock prices plummet on 5 May, precipitating a market collapse on 27 June. In the wake of this debacle, some 600 banks and 15,000 other businesses fail. The nationwide depression will last for four more years.

1898: Bayer introduces a cough suppressant, derived from opium. Its brand name: Heroin.

1902: The *Times Literary Supplement,* a weekly review of literature and scholarship, begins publication in London.

1905: Russian Revolution of 1905. Following the "bloody Sunday" riots before the Winter Palace in St. Petersburg in January, revolution spreads throughout Russia, in some places spurred on by newly formed workers' councils, or soviets. Among the most memorable incidents of the revolt is the mutiny aboard the battleship *Potemkin.* Suppressed by the czar, the revolution brings an end to liberal reforms, and thus sets the stage for the larger revolution of 1917.

1909: Robert E. Peary and Matthew Henson reach the North Pole.

1909: Founding of the National Association for the Advancement of Colored People (NAACP) by W. E. B. Du Bois and a number of other prominent black and white intellectuals in New York City.

1909: William Cadbury's *Labour in Portuguese West Africa* draws attention to conditions of slavery in São Tomé and Principe.

1911: Revolution in Mexico, begun the year before, continues with the replacement of the corrupt Porfirio Diaz, president since 1877, by Francisco Madero.

1915: A German submarine sinks the *Lusitania,* killing 1,195, including 128 U.S. citizens. Theretofore, many Americans had been sympathetic toward Germany, but the incident begins to turn the tide of U.S. sentiment toward the Allies.

1919: Formation of the Third International (Comintern), whereby the Bolshevik government of Russia establishes its control over communist movements worldwide.

Event and Its Context

Hannah Bachman Einstein, a first generation American, was the wife and the daughter of two of the wealthiest German-Jewish businessmen in New York City, but her dedication to the plight of indigent families was not the least bit superficial. Active in charitable outreach since childhood, she had already headed numerous Jewish women's benevolent societies by the time she became the first woman to serve on the board of United Hebrew Charities (UHC), one of the best funded and efficiently run philanthropic societies in the world. Eager to understand fully the problems of the desperate women who filled her office every day, she undertook extensive field research and embarked on what was (for a middle-aged, turn-of-the-century, wealthy Ashkenazi society matron) considered an eccentric act by undertaking formal sociology training at Columbia University.

As Russian pogroms and European anti-Semitism escalated, the flood of penniless Jewish immigrants filing through Ellis Island increased exponentially. Fred Baur, superintendent of the Department of Charities for the City of New York at this time, estimated that impoverished Jewish families, who had previously accounted for only 10 percent of the handouts from Manhattan charities, now received 60 percent of charitable contributions, and the number was rising. As more families lost their breadwinners to death, injury, or desertion, the number of Jewish mothers who were unable to care for their children multiplied, and Einstein herself estimated that she encountered at least 300 children in danger of being placed in orphanages every week.

The Hebrew Orphan Asylum, built in 1855 when the entire Jewish population of New York was only 15,000, was far beyond capacity, as were most of the other private and public orphanages in the city. In most cases, the children housed at the orphanages had at least one living parent but had been given up voluntarily or else forcibly removed from their homes because of their families' inability to provide for them. Most orphanages were completely privately funded and in 1909 many still, in a page from Dickens, required older children to work in factories and sweatshops to pay their own upkeep.

UHC provided pensions to hundreds of widowed and abandoned wives so that they could avoid having their children committed. UHC administered more than $100,000 per year in aid,

but the explosion in Jewish immigration finally exhausted even their resources. They were forced to remove the names of many pensioners from their rolls beginning in 1908. The result was the separation of yet more Jewish families.

Although she never stated the reason for her beliefs, Hannah Einstein did not feel that UHC was doing all within its power to meet the crisis. On Wednesday, 28 April 1909, she resigned the vice presidency of the organization and in an interview with *The New York Times* announced her intention to form a society dedicated solely to helping widowed mothers "in one way or another . . . [to] try to get them work, paying their rent for them until we can help them in better ways."

The first meeting of the society was held at Einstein's home on Thursday, 13 May 1909. The agenda was a discussion of the association's missions and how they would be achieved. The Widowed Mother's Fund Association (WMFA) was incorporated that summer by Supreme Court Justice Blanchard with Einstein as president and Mrs. Daniel Guggenheim (from the millionaire mining family), Mrs. Randolph Guggenheimer, Annette Kohn, Olivia Leventritt, Mrs. Taylor Phillips, and Mrs. Jefferson Seligman as its first board of directors. The same month, Einstein began a major appeal to charities, philanthropists, and private citizens to raise the $100,000 she felt was needed to carry out the WMFA's work.

Within the first nine months, the WMFA received gifts ranging from $500 to $2,500 from wealthy Jewish families in New York City and gained 5,000 members who each paid $1 per year in dues. The association established an office where widowed mothers, who did not have to be Jewish (though most who called on this charity were), could come for assistance. Having evidently separated amicably, Einstein and the UHC soon operated jointly so as to share information and avoid duplicate efforts. In its first year of existence, the organization had more than 500 pensioners.

Members of the board and the many female volunteers of the WMFA went out into the community to find employment opportunities, organize baby-sitting services, and help in other ways to attain the WMFA's aims. Einstein realized that the charity she formed would never be large enough to reach all who needed assistance. Her decades of observation and education convinced her that government funding was the only real hope for indigent families, and she became one of the new century's most impressive and effective lobbyists.

Admirable as her cause was by modern standards, Einstein met fierce opposition. Ironically, her most vocal opponents were the very orphanages and relief agencies whose overburdening she had tried to alleviate. The early twentieth century was a time of sharp division and heated debate between those who believed the government should assist the poor and those who believed that only private charities should fill this role. Many charities indignantly rejected the idea of "outdoor" help from public funds. A 1908 conference that met to debate government support of indigent children resulted in argument and deadlock as the sides refused to compromise or even enter rational dialogue.

Sociologist Frank Dekker Watson was a leader of the pro-government welfare faction and condemned charities for helping struggling mothers, arguing that until charities stopped taking the state slack government would never provide as they should. On the other extreme was Otis Bannard, head of New York's Charity Organization Society, who cited government pensions as tantamount to socialism and the first step on a slippery slope to anarchy. Still others in both camps echoed the sentiments of influential humanitarian Josephine Howell (herself a widowed mother during the Civil War) and argued that aid for widows was admirable but that aid for deserted wives, even mothers, would, like legalized abortion, encourage wanton immorality. Einstein had to fight a war on several fronts.

Writer Sophie Irene Loeb became Einstein's staunchest ally. Though Jewish, Loeb had little else in common with Einstein: Russian-born, divorced, and working class in background, she supported herself as a columnist for the *New York Evening World* and used her editorials to personalize the plights of separated families and bring them to a mass audience. When Einstein was appointed chair of the State Commission on Relief for Widowed Mothers, Loeb undertook extensive research on her behalf, initially in New York City and later throughout the United States and Europe, to investigate government and private welfare organizations. She returned more convinced than ever of the need for and viability of state-funded "widow's pensions." Her detailed reports and *World* editorials won popular support for the Child Welfare Law of 1915. This act was the first state-funded support for underprivileged children other than those of veterans killed in war. Though it still did not provide support for their mothers, the $100,000 it allotted for needy children allowed the dollars of the Widowed Mothers' Fund and other charities to go much further.

Loeb became, prior to women's suffrage, one of the most powerful women officials in New York. She used her position as president of the New York City Child Welfare Board to increase city funding for indigent families to $4.5 million per year by 1922. The WMFA, relieved somewhat of having to meet the most base needs of those who came to it for help, was able to change its focus. Einstein's new aim was to allow single mothers to remain at home as full-time homemakers, for "to nurture the family requires a commitment of every hour . . . but achieves the ultimate social good."

Einstein and Loeb continued to work together and separately in national lobbies to improve and expand pensions. By 1929, the year both women died, only four states had not passed legislation for mothers' pensions. Many states had extended coverage to include the families of disabled parents, motherless families, or indigent childless women (though most included strict clauses that disallowed women deemed of low moral character from receiving full benefits). The WMFA was ultimately reabsorbed into the United Jewish Charities as government welfare and the widespread entry of women into the professions eradicated much of its need. Even so, the WMFA was a benchmark in the private management of social neglect and a springboard to legislation that saved thousands of families from separation.

Key Players

Einstein, Hannah Bachman (1862–1929): A mother of two who was married at 19 to a very successful wool merchant, Einstein was one of the founders of the Reform synagogue Temple Emanu-El long before joining United Hebrew Charities (UHC). Her study of criminology and sociology convinced her that poverty and broken homes were the twin roots of social evil and she dedicated her life to their eradication. She held many influential public and private offices in her life, including presidency of the New York State Child Welfare Boards, but she was proudest of the Widowed Mother's Fund Association and remained its president until her death.

Loeb, Sophie Irene (1876–1929): Born in Rovno, Russia, Loeb was herself reared as a fatherless child in Pittsburgh, Pennsylvania. Already a career writer when she met Hannah Einstein in 1909, she wrote a book in 1920 titled *Everyman's Child,* part autobiography and part social credo, in which she detailed her fight for child welfare legislation. Loeb served on several boards, including the National Institute of Social Sciences, but her main work was as an independent lobbyist for children and, later in her life, as an advocate of Zionism.

BIBLIOGRAPHY

Periodicals
Chambers, Clarke A. "Toward a Redefinition of Welfare History." *Journal of American History* 73 (September 1986): 407–433.
Gordon, Linda. "Social Insurance and Public Assistance: the Influence of Gender in Welfare Thought in the United States from 1890–1935." *American Historical Review* 97 (February 1992): 19–54.
"Hebrew Charities Drop Old Pensioners." *New York Times*, 3 May 1909, p. 3, col. 2.
"Helping Widowed Mothers." *New York Times*, 18 January 1910, p. 18, col. 1.
"Needs $100,000 For Charity: Widowed Mothers' Fund Association Sends Out a Call for Help." *New York Times*, 26 July 1909, p. 4, col. 4.
"Widowed Mothers Fund Incorporated." *New York Times*, 8 July 1909, p. 16, col. 5.

Other
Olasky, Marvin. "Excitement of a New Century." Olasky.com Archives [cited 8 October 2002]. <http://www.olasky.com/Archives/toac/08%20(Word5).pdf>.

ADDITIONAL RESOURCES

Other
Brody, Seymour. "Hannah Bachman Einstein: Leader in Social Welfare and Jewish Philnthropy" [sic]. *Jewish Heroes and Heroines in America, 1900 to World War II, A Judaica Collection Exhibit.* Florida Atlantic University Libraries [cited 8 October 2002]. <http://www.fau.edu/library/bro49.htm>.

—Jonathan Darby

Wisconsin Unemployment Insurance

United States 1932

Synopsis

A landmark in the development of American social insurance, the Wisconsin Unemployment Insurance Act of 1932 had roots in the social and political reform movements of the early twentieth century. Conceived and promoted by John R. Commons and his students at the University of Wisconsin, the law was an expression of their distinctive approach to labor legislation, which stressed the prevention of social ills such as unemployment through the creation of financial incentives, in this case for steady, full-time work. Their first campaigns, in 1921 and 1923, failed, ironically, because Wisconsin employers remained skeptical of their arguments. With the onset of the depression in 1930, Commons's students made their bill more conservative to blunt employer resistance and mobilized public interest in unemployment insurance as an antipoverty measure. The bill ultimately passed the legislature in early 1932 and went into effect in 1934. Its immediate effect was to make unemployment insurance politically acceptable and to popularize the idea of prevention, which was incorporated in much of the state legislation of the following years. The Wisconsin law thus demonstrated the impact of Commons and his followers on the movement for social insurance and economic security.

Timeline

1917: Russian revolutions.

1922: Inspired by the Bolsheviks' example of imposing revolution by means of a coup, Benito Mussolini leads his blackshirts in an October "March on Rome," and forms a new fascist government.

1927: Charles A. Lindbergh makes the first successful solo nonstop flight across the Atlantic and becomes an international hero.

1929: On "Black Friday" in October, prices on the U.S. stock market, which had been climbing wildly for several years, suddenly collapse. Thus begins the first phase of a world economic crisis and depression that will last until the beginning of World War II.

1932: When Ukrainians refuse to surrender their grain to his commissars, Stalin seals off supplies to the region, creating a manmade famine that will produce a greater death toll than the entirety of World War I.

1932: A "Bonus Army" of unemployed veterans marches on Washington, D.C. Many leave after Congress refuses their demands for payment of bonuses for wartime service, but others are forcibly removed by General Douglas MacArthur's troops. Also participating are two other figures destined to gain notoriety in the next world war: majors Dwight D. Eisenhower and George S. Patton.

1932: In German elections, Nazis gain a 37 percent plurality of Reichstag seats, raising tensions between the far right

Elizabeth Brandeis with her father, Supreme Court Justice Louis D. Brandeis. © Bettmann/Corbis. Reproduced by permission.

and the far left. On a "bloody Sunday" in July, Communists in Hamburg attack Nazis with guns, and a fierce battle ensues.

1932: Charles A. Lindbergh's baby son is kidnapped and killed, a crime for which Bruno Hauptmann will be charged in 1934, convicted in 1935, and executed in 1936.

1935: Second phase of New Deal begins with the introduction of social security, farm assistance, and housing and tax reform.

1937: Italy signs the Anti-Comintern Pact, signed by Germany and Japan the preceding year. Like the two others before it, Italy now withdraws from the League of Nations.

1942: Axis conquests reach their height in the middle of this year. The Nazis control a vast region from Normandy to the suburbs of Stalingrad, and from the Arctic Circle to the edges of the Sahara. To the east, the Japanese "Co-Prosperity Sphere" encompasses territories from China to Burma to the East Indies, stretching deep into the western Pacific.

1947: Establishment of the Marshall Plan to assist European nations in recovering from the war.

John R. Commons. AP/Wide World Photos. Reproduced by permission.

Event and Its Context

In 1932 Wisconsin became the first American state to adopt a system of unemployment insurance. The law was a response to the Great Depression and to the startling rise in unemployment. Its specific features, however, and the willingness of the legislature to consider it several years before unemployment insurance had gained support in other states reflected events in the reform community and in Wisconsin during the preceding decades. Thus, the 1932 law was the product of an extended effort to create a suitably American form of social insurance, together with the political opportunities created by the economic crisis of the early 1930s.

Until the twentieth century, unemployed workers were often viewed as unemployables, misfits, or unfortunates who could not or would not work in good times or bad. Charity, provided by private religious or philanthropic groups, was widely viewed as the appropriate response. The severe depression of the mid-1890s, and the lesser recessions of 1914–1915 and 1920–1922, however, demonstrated to all but the most heartless observers that able-bodied, hard-working individuals could lose jobs and face extreme hardship. Unemployment, then, could result from individual failure and deficiency but was more commonly a consequence of inadequate opportunity, especially in recession periods.

There were two responses. In most western European countries, governments introduced benefit programs to compensate unemployed workers for their losses. This approach proved to be expensive and in some cases self-defeating. Particularly in the chaotic aftermath of World War I, costs skyrocketed and a growing number of workers (at least to American observers) seemed content to accept their benefits and remain unemployed. Many Americans viewed the European programs as failures:

they perpetuated the problem that they were supposed to solve and converted the able-bodied unemployed into unemployables. European experiences thus reinforced American doubts about the feasibility and value of social insurance.

The second response proved to be more fruitful. If unemployment (and certainly mass unemployment) was a sign of a broken economy, then the economy, rather than the individual victim, ought to command the attention of reformers and policymakers. By the mid-1910s, American reformers had devised a comprehensive plan for addressing such problems. The plan included four complementary measures. First were more numerous and efficient public employment offices, so unemployed workers could quickly learn what was available. Second was counter-cyclical public works planning designed to increase expenditures and create jobs in times of rising unemployment and then to reduce them in more prosperous periods. Third was employment regularization by private employers, who would be encouraged (perhaps with financial incentives) to plan their operations to avoid seasonal hiring and firing. The final measure was unemployment insurance to assist the residual group of unemployed workers—a residual that, if everything else worked, would only be a fraction of the usual total.

John R. Commons

The most important creator and promoter of these ideas was John R. Commons, a prominent economics professor at the University of Wisconsin. Commons was a historian and theoretician, a founder of the institutional school of economics, a critical figure in the development of labor legislation, and an enormously influential teacher whose students addressed practical problems as government administrators and reformers. A socialist in his earlier career, Commons had concluded by 1904, when he arrived at Wisconsin, that meaningful change was only possible within the established economic system. He set out to find conservative ways to bring about far-reaching reforms. One of his principal targets was unemployment.

Commons and other reformers established an advocacy organization, the American Association for Labor Legislation (AALL), in 1906. Two years later he installed a former student, John B. Andrews, as executive director. Under Andrews, the AALL became the single most influential force in promoting labor legislation and took the lead in publicizing the unemployment measures noted above. The Association's initial focus was workers compensation, the first widely adopted American social insurance program. Commons was deeply involved in the drafting and implementation of the early Wisconsin law (1909–1911) and became fascinated with one of its features, experience rating, which adjusted the employers' taxes to the volume of claims. By reducing claims through accident prevention, employers could reduce their taxes and presumably increase their profits. Accident prevention thus served the interests of workers and employers alike. Commons believed that the same idea could be applied to hazards such as unemployment. Preventing job losses would be more important than the actual benefits paid to unemployed workers. Writing about workers compensation in the 1910s, he argued that "insurance and compensation are secondary." The system "is much better described as a kind of social pressure brought to bear upon all employers in order to make them devote as much attention to the prevention of accidents . . . as they do to the manufacture and sale of their products." Substitute the word unemployment for accidents and this would be Commons's formula for unemployment insurance in the 1920s and 1930s.

The Wisconsin Bills

The first real opportunity to promote unemployment insurance came in 1920–1921 as cutbacks in government spending produced a severe recession and rising unemployment. With public concern growing and politicians eager to do something, Commons and Andrews seized the opportunity to promote unemployment insurance. Their efforts marked the beginning of a campaign that continued for a decade and made Wisconsin a pioneer. Although the AALL continued to agitate for the four programs and succeeded in enlisting wide support for public works planning and employment regularization, it had little success in promoting unemployment insurance except in Wisconsin.

Apart from Commons and his graduate students, the other critical reason for Wisconsin's role was the state's unorthodox labor movement. Although affiliated with the conservative American Federation of Labor (AFL), the Wisconsin State Federation of Labor reflected the influence of Milwaukee's powerful German socialist movement, which dominated the city's politics. Milwaukee socialists believed in activist government and a variety of worker-oriented benefit programs. At a time when most AFL leaders were becoming more conservative and distrustful of the state (opposing social insurance, for example, on the grounds that it undercut collective bargaining), Wisconsin unionists were enthusiastic proponents of a welfare state, even on a small scale. In their minds, collective bargaining and state programs such as Commons's unemployment insurance plan were complementary and mutually supporting.

In 1920 the state federation appointed a committee to work with Commons in drawing up an unemployment insurance bill. The unionists readily accepted Commons's emphasis on prevention and low benefit payments; their only objection was to a proposal for employee contributions, which Commons agreed to eliminate. The result was a business-friendly bill based on the workers compensation system that provided incentives for systematic operations and paid meager benefits ($1.50 per day for a maximum of 13 weeks). State senator Henry Huber, a leader of the legislature's progressive Republican faction, introduced the bill on 4 February 1921.

Commons spearheaded the campaign for support in nonlabor circles. With assistance from the AALL, he employed a graduate student to stump the state. He personally spoke to a variety of employer groups, denying that the bill had anything to do with "relief" or "socialistic agitation" and argued that only employers and businesses could prevent unemployment. Judicious revisions (reducing the benefit to $1.00 per day, for example) and the letters and petitions generated by this effort forced the state senate to consider the bill. When representatives of the leading employer groups strongly opposed it, senate conservatives united to defeat it by a narrow vote.

Commons and the union leaders mounted another campaign for unemployment insurance in 1923. They enlisted the groups that had backed them in 1921 and brought in leading employers who had embraced employment regularization to

buttress their arguments that unemployment was preventable. Commons wrote that the Huber bill reflected a "business-like way" of dealing with unemployment and that the "business man is the dynamic factor. . . . He is the Captain of Industry." The "Captains of Industry," however, remained wary. The state manufacturers association agreed to support a legislative study if the reformers would drop the bill. At the last minute, however, the association reneged on the agreement and left Commons and his allies empty-handed.

After 1923 interest in unemployment insurance waned as prosperity reduced the number of unemployed and the severity of their distress. Commons's allies introduced versions of the Huber bill in 1925, 1927, and 1929, but they received little attention.

The Groves Bill

An alarming rise in layoffs and plant closings after 1929 (by some measures Wisconsin was the most severely affected of the Midwestern states) reawakened interest in unemployment and, in Wisconsin, the campaign for unemployment insurance. The political alignments of the 1920s remained largely unchanged, and a new group of activist students took on the mantle of the earlier reformers. Notable among them were Elizabeth Brandeis, daughter of Louis Brandeis, the famous jurist, and her husband, Paul Raushenbush. Brandeis and Raushenbush were influenced by the elder Brandeis's ideas about the strategic role of the business firm and were willing to go beyond Commons in making prevention the centerpiece of the new bill.

Brandeis, Rauschenbush, and Harold Groves, another former Commons student who had been elected to the legislature, devised a new bill during the summer of 1930. In an effort to lessen employer opposition, they scrapped the mutual insurance fund and experience rating—the prevention mechanism that Commons and Andrews had advocated—in favor of individual unemployment reserves. Under this plan, each employer would contribute to a state account that would pay benefits to that firm's employees. When the account reached $75 per worker, the contributions would cease. As workers drew on the account (the maximum benefit was $10 per week), the employer would resume contributions. The reserves were similar to the unemployment funds that a handful of companies had introduced in the 1920s as part of their regularization efforts. Their shortcomings were obvious: there was no sharing of risks and employees would be dependent on their employers. Groves introduced the new bill in February 1931.

The Groves bill generated new controversies. Employers continued to attack any compulsory plan, and John Andrews and Wisconsin's labor leaders were skeptical of the reserves plan. The state federation of labor broke with the academics and endorsed a new version of the Huber bill. This dissension allowed opponents to block any action during the regular legislative session. The reformers did persuade the legislature to authorize a study of the competing approaches, to be completed by November, when it would return for a special session.

During the summer Commons and his students launched a campaign to raise public awareness of unemployment insurance and pressure the legislature. Although the growing number of jobless workers made this assignment relatively easy, the severity of the depression also made it difficult to finance the campaign. Finally, Brandeis and Raushenbush decided that they personally would provide the money. They also agreed that the appeal would be for unemployment insurance and not for a specific measure.

These developments helped to bridge the differences in the reformers' ranks. Commons endorsed the reserves idea and Andrews agreed to cooperate. The union leaders also concluded that any system was better than none. In the meantime, the students mobilized a variety of interest groups, including the politically powerful farm organizations. By the fall of 1931, the employers were the only hold-outs.

In November, the legislature's study committee reported in favor of unemployment reserves—with the employer members vigorously dissenting—and set the stage for the dramatic special session. In response to employer objections that a voluntary effort would be preferable, the governor, a strong supporter, proposed and won approval of an amendment suspending the law if 200,000 workers were covered by voluntary plans by 1 June 1933, a concession that he viewed—correctly—as meaningless. The lower house then passed the Groves bill on 21 December. The senate was at first evenly divided, but public pressure persuaded several undecided senators to support the bill. The two houses reconciled minor differences and the Governor signed it on 28 February 1932.

The Wisconsin Act went into effect in 1934 (employers succeeded in delaying it for a year) with Paul Raushenbush as state administrator. Qualified workers began to receive benefits the following year. When President Roosevelt's Committee on Economic Security drafted a nationwide plan, which became the unemployment insurance section of the Social Security Act (1935), it included the reserves idea as an option for state consideration, but only one other state—Nebraska—adopted it. Whether the act actually prevented unemployment became a subject of extended controversy. After 1934 many Wisconsin employers supported the system, but mostly, it seemed, because it was less expensive than other approaches.

The Wisconsin Act was a significant departure for state government and a symbolically important step toward an American welfare state. It emphasized the continuity of the social reform impulse and the continuing appeal of unemployment prevention (via experience rating, rather than reserves), which was incorporated into most of the state legislation. In retrospect, it is clear that a nationwide system of unemployment insurance was no more inevitable in the 1930s than was a national health insurance system. Unemployment insurance became a reality when it did largely because a spirited group of Wisconsin activists, working in conjunction with the unorthodox state labor movement, kept the idea alive for more than a decade and responded to a changing political environment.

Key Players

Andrews, John B. (1880–1943): After receiving a Ph.D. from the University of Wisconsin (1908), Andrews became executive director of the new American Association for Labor Legislation and served in that position until his death. A prominent advocate of labor legislation, he was also the author of numerous books and articles (e.g., with Commons, *Principles of Labor Legislation* in 1916) on the subject.

Brandeis, Elizabeth (1896–1984): Daughter of U.S. Supreme Court Justice Louis Brandeis, Elizabeth Brandeis absorbed his ideas on the importance of small, competitive businesses. She studied under Commons at the University of Wisconsin, was co-author of the fourth volume of his famous *History of Labour in the United States* (1935), and taught at the University for the rest of her career. With husband Paul Raushenbush, she was a creator, promoter, and vigorous defender of the Wisconsin Act.

Commons, John R. (1862–1945): A central figure in the American progressive reform movement, Commons attended Johns Hopkins University as a graduate student in the late 1880s but failed to receive a degree. After failing at several college teaching positions, he became a prominent investigator of societal problems and received an appointment at the University of Wisconsin in 1904. Working with his graduate students, he promoted labor reforms and social insurance and wrote *History of Labour in the United States* (1918–1935), his seminal work. Many of his students became activists and reformers.

See also: *American Association for Labor Legislation; American Federation of Labor; Social Security Act.*

BIBLIOGRAPHY

Books

Berkowitz, Edward, and Kim McQuaid. *Creating the Welfare State: The Political Economy of Twentieth Century Reform.* Lawrence: University Press of Kansas, 1992.

Moss, David A. *Socializing Security: Progressive Era Economists and the Origins of American Social Policy.* Cambridge: Harvard University Press, 1996.

Nelson, Daniel. *Unemployment Insurance: The American Experience, 1915–1935.* Madison: University of Wisconsin Press, 1969.

Patterson, James T. *America's Struggle Against Poverty in the Twentieth Century.* Cambridge: Harvard University Press, 2000.

—Daniel Nelson

Women in Industry Service

United States 1918

Synopsis

During spring 1917 the United States began shipping thousands of men overseas to fight in World War I. This immediate strain on the U.S. labor force created problems for industry, which became overburdened by wartime production requirements. The War Labor Administration, a division of the U.S. Department of Labor, worked to resolve these problems in part by replacing male workers with female ones. Realizing that

Women seeking better working conditions picket in front of the White House, Washington D.C., 1917. National Archives and Records Administration.

women's labor issues needed to be addressed specifically, as well as to prevent them from disrupting wartime production, the Department of Labor created the Women in Industry Service (WIS) in 1918.

This cooperative-based bureau was run by women for women. Most of its policy suggestions for addressing women's labor issues were later implemented. Although the end of the war in November 1918 meant the return of men to industry, the WIS succeeded in bringing governmental attention to the rights of women laborers. The WIS operated until 1920, when Congress granted the bureau permanent status through public law;

the organization then became known as the U.S. Women's Bureau. As the only federal organization devoted to the welfare of working women, the Women's Bureau became a powerful advocate for their rights, conducting industry research and helping to shape public policy regarding their welfare.

Timeline

1898: United States defeats Spain in the three-month Spanish-American War. As a result, Cuba gains it independence, and the United States purchases Puerto Rico and the Philippines from Spain for $20 million.

1903: Russia's Social Democratic Party splits into two factions: the moderate Mensheviks and the hard-line Bolsheviks. Despite their names, which in Russian mean "minority" and "majority," respectively, Mensheviks actually outnumber Bolsheviks.

1910: Revolution breaks out in Mexico and will continue for the next seven years.

1914: On 28 June in the town of Sarajevo, then part of the Austro-Hungarian Empire, Serbian nationalist Gavrilo Princip assassinates Austrian Archduke Francis Ferdinand and wife Sophie. In the weeks that follow, Austria declares war on Serbia, and Germany on Russia and France, while Great Britain responds by declaring war on Germany. By the beginning of August, the lines are drawn, with the Allies (Great Britain, France, Russia, Belgium, Serbia, Montenegro, and Japan) against the Central Powers (Germany, Austria-Hungary, and Turkey).

1916: Battles of Verdun and the Somme on the Western Front. The latter sees the first use of tanks, by the British.

1918: The Bolsheviks execute Czar Nicholas II and his family. Soon civil war breaks out between the communists and their allies, known as the Reds, and their enemies, a collection of anticommunists ranging from democrats to czarists, who are known collectively as the Whites. In March, troops from the United States, Great Britain, and France intervene on the White side.

1918: The Second Battle of the Marne in July and August is the last major conflict on the Western Front. In November, Kaiser Wilhelm II abdicates, bringing an end to the war.

1918: Upheaval sweeps Germany, which for a few weeks in late 1918 and early 1919 seems poised on the verge of communist revolution—or at least a Russian-style communist coup d'etat. But reactionary forces have regained their strength, and the newly organized Freikorps (composed of unemployed soldiers) suppresses the revolts. Even stronger than reaction or revolution, however, is republican sentiment, which opens the way for the creation of a democratic government based at Weimar.

1918: Influenza, carried to the furthest corners by returning soldiers, spreads throughout the globe. Over the next two years, it will kill nearly 20 million people—more than the war itself.

1921: As the Allied Reparations Commission calls for payments of 132 billion gold marks, inflation in Germany begins to climb.

1925: European leaders attempt to secure the peace at the Locarno Conference, which guarantees the boundaries between France and Germany, and Belgium and Germany.

Event and Its Context

Regulating Labor During Wartime

On 4 March 1913 the bill establishing the U.S. Department of Labor (DOL) was signed by President William Howard Taft.

In part, the creation of the DOL resulted from the Progressive movement at the turn of the century, which called for better working conditions and environmental conservation through private and government actions. More directly, its creation can be traced to the social reform advocates who called for a federal department that would give organized labor a presence in the president's cabinet. In 1915 numerous employment offices were set up by the DOL throughout the United States; by 1917 they had placed more than 250,000 people in jobs.

The United States entered World War I in April 1917, necessitating the government's prompt attention to any labor problems that might affect wartime production levels. Labor disputes were common, as worker shortages and higher production demands increased union power. The DOL was charged with implementing the nation's war labor programs and policies. Secretary of Labor William B. Wilson convinced President Woodrow Wilson to appoint a commission to investigate labor problems, and a national war labor policy was developed based on the commission's findings. To ensure that the policy was implemented properly, the War Labor Administration (WLA) was created with Secretary Wilson at its helm. In 1918 the War Labor Board was established as part of the WLA; comprising leaders from industry and organized labor, the board made recommendations to Secretary Wilson regarding labor disputes and promoted their peaceful resolution. The WLA also encompassed the War Labor Policies Board, which was designed to maintain consistent labor policies among government contract agencies and thereby eliminate any disruptions to the war effort.

As government agencies expanded and industries feverishly tried to replace their male workers who had been sent to war, a shift occurred in female employment. Although some women entered the workforce for the first time during the war effort, the number of female laborers did not increase dramatically. Instead, according to the historian Ross Paulson, for the most part "women came from other industries into the war industries, not from the ranks of the unemployed." Most of the women who took positions associated with the war effort had factory experience; another large group came from the restaurant and domestic service industries. There were additional employment opportunities for African American women, as white women fled domestic service or low-paying industrial jobs for higher paying ones in the war industry. However, hiring discrimination against African American women continued. This was also true for immigrant women—some employers felt it was their patriotic duty to hire U.S. workers over those from other countries.

Regardless of their race or ethnicity, most working women did not face a rosy employment situation. Men were usually chosen for the best jobs at the highest pay. After working a 10-hour day, women then faced numerous domestic chores at home. The women who were able to join unions often found that they were not equally represented and their specific needs were not understood. Many tragic events, such as the Triangle Shirtwaist Company fire in 1911 that took the lives of 146 women and girls in New York City, brought the deplorable work conditions of factory women into the public eye, making work safety a primary concern for many social reformers.

Establishing the Women in Industry Service

The Women in Industry Service (WIS) was established as part of the DOL in July 1918 to address the labor issues of women separately from those of men, specifically as they related to the war effort. The bureau's main purpose, as instructed by Secretary Wilson, was to "develop standards and policies to insure the effective employment of women while conserving their health and welfare." Two experts on women's employment, Mary Abby van Kleeck and Mary Anderson, were appointed as the WIS's first director and assistant director, respectively. Van Kleeck and Anderson kept in close contact with other DOL divisions that worked on issues relating to women in industry.

To develop a consistent program that best addressed the needs of women in industry, the new bureau cooperated with all state departments of labor that dealt on any level with the problems faced by working women. The Council on Women in Industry, comprised of female representatives from every division of the DOL, was founded to help coordinate these efforts. Subjects discussed by the council included safeguards for establishing new occupations for women, regulation of night work under war conditions, enforcement of state labor laws, and equal pay for equal work.

Although the WIS ultimately compiled a formal policy outlining several key issues regarding women's employment during the war, many of the program's elements were not implemented, as World War I ended only four months after the bureau's creation. However, some action was taken with regard to each of the recommendations. In the meantime, the War Labor Policies Board added clauses to government contracts requiring compliance with state labor laws and worked with the WIS to develop a cooperative effort between national and state agencies regarding the enforcement of the clauses.

In addition, the WIS conducted a survey in Niagara Falls, New York, that focused on the occupational health hazards faced by women employed in chemical industries. A committee made up of representatives from the Surgeon General's Office of the U.S. Army, U.S. Public Health Service, and New York Industrial Commission discussed the survey results and together with the WIS made recommendations for improved labor conditions including sanitary safety. The WIS also discussed with several labor organizations the need to control night work for women's safety and health.

In October 1918 the WIS presented to the secretary of labor and the War Labor Policies Board a tentative draft of standards to be used to govern the employment of women in industry; the standards were met with approval and were only somewhat modified on 25 October. This was a huge accomplishment not only for the WIS as a whole, but also specifically for its director, van Kleeck, who was instrumental in developing the draft.

The standards, which addressed issues such as equal pay for equal work and reasonable work hours, were used as the basis for a reconstruction program after the end of the war. Copies of the program were broadly distributed to the state departments of labor as well as to numerous organizations that took an active interest in the welfare of working women, making the program an official part of the public discourse in December 1918. On 11 November 1918 the WIS had submitted a memorandum to the chairman of the War Labor Policies Board addressing some of the employment challenges women faced during the readjustment period and suggesting that all attempts be made to lessen unemployment and "reinstate the largest number of women in normal occupations for which they are adapted." The memo included a direct call for the permanent status of working women to be recognized and for protective legislation to be implemented, addressing their welfare as wage earners. More subtly, the memo promoted the idea that women should be part of the decision-making process affecting their professional lives.

WIS Becomes the Women's Bureau

By 1919 Anderson had assumed the WIS director's role. The decision was made to continue the organization's temporary status with funding until 30 June 1920, and joint committee hearings were held to discuss making the organization's status permanent. In keeping with the maternalist environment of the day, Congressman P. P. Campbell argued, "There are physical differences that the women understand, which make it important that provision be made in all industries of the country for the methods under which women work and for accommodation while employed, which make it not only wise but humane that women shall have charge of this sort of thing."

From dealing with women who were out in the trenches, Anderson knew there was a need for a permanent federal agency to champion the interests of working women. For example, in 1919 Anderson received a frantic telegram detailing the struggle women faced at a Joliet, Illinois, steel plant. According to the historian Alice Kessler-Harris, the women workers had supported their male colleagues in a recent strike, only to have the union try to force them to give up their jobs, claiming the work was too physically demanding for women. With stories like this becoming more and more frequent, it seemed evident to Anderson and other social reformers that women workers needed ongoing representation at the federal level.

On 5 June 1920 Congress passed a bill that gave the WIS permanent status through public law and renamed the organization as the U.S. Women's Bureau. As outlined by statute (41 Stat. L., 987), the bureau's functions are "to formulate standards and policies which shall promote the welfare of wage-earning women, improve their working conditions, increase their efficiency, and advance their opportunities for profitable employment." The Women's Bureau also was given authorization to investigate and report to the DOL on "all matters pertaining to the welfare of women in industry" and to bring the special needs of women to the nation's attention.

In the 1920s the Women's Bureau performed numerous investigations concerning working women through field studies and surveys. The surveys covered topics such, labor legislation, postwar wages, opportunities for women in government service, industrial training for women, the employment of women streetcar conductors, and a comparison of the family responsibilities of men and women. Using census information from 1910 to 1920, the bureau analyzed changes in women's occupational status and completed a report on "a physiological basis for the shorter working day for women." Conducting research and preparing reference materials were fundamental aspects of the Women's Bureau in the 1920s, and continued to be critical elements of the bureau's work throughout the twentieth century.

With a reputation as a Progressive social reformer, Anderson seemed above partisan politics, cooperating with both sides to form key alliances and achieve the bureau's goals. The Women's Bureau was actively engaged in the exchange of information between state and national agencies, and by 1923 was performing numerous problem-solving investigations. In 1922 the bureau's groundbreaking research on the experiences of African American working women led to greater social awareness and recommendations for change. Its investigations on how women felt about protective legislation helped to form public policy and to identify the social mindset. The bureau's research showed that state-based legislative changes held greater appeal to women than ones sanctioned by the unions alone. For example, after the passage of a law in Massachusetts limiting work hours, one Women's Bureau agent noted, "The girls felt that legislation establishing a 48-hour week was more 'dignified' and permanent than one obtained through the union as it was not so likely to be taken away."

As an advocate for fair wages and reasonable work hours, the Women's Bureau played a significant role in ensuring women's work was regulated by the Fair Labor Standards Act of 1938, which established minimum wage levels and work hour limits for the first time. During World War II the Women's Bureau fought successfully for broader job opportunities and training as well as for better pay and work conditions for the new female workforce. According to the historian Kathleen Laughlin, the "backstage maneuvering [by the Women's Bureau] around established bureaucratic constraints to promote the women's economic agenda in the postwar years led to center stage feminist advocacy by the 1970s."

Given the social climate of the 1920s and 1930s, Anderson walked a legislative tightrope that paradoxically embraced both equal rights legislation for women workers and maternalist policies that protected women due to perceived gender-based differences. Ironically, the maternalist arguments long used to keep women in their place were effectively spin-doctored to achieve legislation that benefited working women. Nonetheless, some historians who apply gender analysis to policy formation from the Progressive Era to World War II "trace the source of women's inequality to 'maternalists,'" claiming that such viewpoints only served to "stall organized campaigns for women's rights until the 1960s." Interestingly, some modern-day benefits for working women, such as maternity leave, successfully embrace elements of both the maternalist and equal rights theories.

As the only federal organization dedicated to the welfare of working women, the Women's Bureau has been and continues to be an extremely valuable and influential organization, especially with regard to forming public policy and making women aware of their rights in the workplace.

Key Players

Anderson, Mary (1872–1964): The Swedish-born Anderson obtained her first permanent job as a shoe stitcher in Illinois. An active unionist, she was elected as the president of the women's stitchers union and later joined the Women's Trade Union League through which she developed a close friendship with its president, Margaret Dreier Robins. With their keen understanding of union politics,

Anderson and Robins were loyal allies during the garment industry strikes. Serving as the director of the Women's Bureau from 1920 to 1944, Anderson earned a reputation for reliable fact-finding and extremely effective advocacy for women workers.

van Kleeck, Mary (1883–1972): The daughter of a minister, van Kleeck received her bachelor's degree from Smith College in 1904. She first worked as a social researcher, investigating New York City's female factory workers. Having served for decades as the director of the Russell Sage Foundation's department of industrial studies, van Kleeck was instrumental in bringing about legislative reform designed to improve working conditions. An authority on women's employment, van Kleeck played a key role in setting the War Labor Policies Board standards for women in industry and served as the first director of the Women in Industry Service.

See also: *Department of Labor; National War Labor Board.*

BIBLIOGRAPHY

Books

Kessler-Harris, Alice. "Where Are the Organized Women Workers?" In *A Heritage of Her Own: Toward a New Social History of American Women,* edited by Nancy F. Cott and Elizabeth H. Pleck. New York: Simon and Schuster, 1979.

Laughlin, Kathleen A. *Women's Work and Public Policy: A History of the Women's Bureau, U.S. Department of Labor, 1945–1970.* Boston: Northeastern University Press, 2000.

Paulson, Ross Evans. *Liberty, Equality, and Justice: Civil Rights, Women's Rights, and the Regulation of Business, 1865–1932.* Durham, NC: Duke University Press, 1997.

Weber, Gustavus A. *The Women's Bureau: Its History, Activities, and Organization.* Baltimore: Johns Hopkins Press, 1923.

Other

"Start-up of the Department and World War I, 1913–1921." U.S. Department of Labor, Office of the Secretary [cited 3 February 2003]. <http://www.dol.gov/asp/programs/history/dolchp01.htm>.

U.S. Statutes at Large. 41: 987.

"WB—An Overview, 1920–2002." U.S. Department of Labor, Women's Bureau [cited 3 February 2003]. <http://www.dol.gov/wb/info_about_wb/interwb.htm>.

                                                           —Lee Ann Paradise

Women's Trade Union League: *See* **National Women's Trade Union League.**

Workers' Congress

Mexico 1876

Synopsis

The first workers' congress in Mexico began on 5 March 1876 in Mexico City. Delegates to the convention named the new organization *Congreso Obrero Permanente* (Permanent Working Congress) with the hope that they would be able to unite all workers of Mexico. The next 30 years heralded the early beginnings of industrialization in Mexico and the parallel rise in the burgeoning labor movement. Many labor organizations formed at this time with the purpose of helping Mexican workers advance their rights after a history of struggle against repressive governmental and capitalistic groups. Unfortunately, many of these early labor organizations ultimately folded.

Timeline

1856: Gustave Flaubert publishes *Madame Bovary.*

1861: Emancipation of the serfs in Russia.

1867: Maximilian surrenders to Mexican forces under Benito Juarez and is executed. Thus ends Napoleon III's dreams for a new French empire in the New World.

1869: Completion of the first U.S. transcontinental railway.

1872: The Crédit Mobilier affair, in which several officials in the administration of President Ulysses S. Grant are accused of receiving stock in exchange for favors, is the first of many scandals that are to plague Grant's second term.

1874: Discovery of gold in the Black Hills of South Dakota.

1876: General George Armstrong Custer and 264 soldiers are killed by the Sioux at the Little Big Horn River.

1876: Alexander Graham Bell introduces the telephone.

1876: Four-stroke cycle gas engine introduced.

1878: Opening of first commercial telephone exchange, in New Haven, Connecticut.

1882: Agitation against English rule spreads throughout Ireland, culminating with the assassination of chief secretary for Ireland Lord Frederick Cavendish and permanent undersecretary Thomas Burke in Dublin's Phoenix Park. The leader of the nationalist movement is Charles Stewart Parnell, but the use of assassination and terrorism—which Parnell himself has disavowed—makes clear the fact that he does not control all nationalist groups.

1886: Bombing at Haymarket Square, Chicago, kills seven policemen and injures numerous others. Eight anarchists are accused and tried; three are imprisoned, one commits suicide, and four are hanged.

Porfirio Díaz. The Library of Congress.

Event and Its Context

Political Background: The 1850s and 1860s

The Mexican labor movement, especially in the mining, railroad, textile, and tobacco industries, led to the beginning of the first workers' congress in Mexico in 1876. The Mexican movement can be traced back to the late 1850s (although its roots probably go back much further) and to the rule of Emperor Maximilian from 1863 to 1867.

Mexican president Ignacio Comonfort enacted a new liberal constitution that reestablished a federal form of government in 1857—providing for liberties such as individual rights (including labor rights), male suffrage (that is, male voting rights), and freedom of speech. After a period of civil disturbance known as the War of the Reform from 1858 to 1860, Benito Pablo Juárez, a liberal from a minority political faction, overpowered his opposition and was elected president in 1861. He set about trying to establish order in the financially troubled country. One thing that Juárez did was to suspend interest payments on foreign loans incurred by preceding governments. Taking offense at such action, the French emperor Napoleon III, with the support of English and Spanish leaders, persuaded Maximilian in 1863 to accept the crown of Mexico in order to protect their financial interests. Backed by French troops, Juárez was removed (temporarily, it turned out) from power and Maximilian was installed as the country's ruler. Around 1866 the United States, which objected to France's intervention, began pressuring the French to leave. When they withdrew in 1867, Maximilian refused to go with them. After that, republican forces under Juárez quickly regained control of Mexico in 1867 (and held power until 1872), under what was called the Restored Republic. Captured by the republicans at Querétaro, Maximilian was tried by court-martial and shot in June 1867. Juárez died in office in 1872 and was succeeded by Sebastián Lerdo de Tejada, head of the Mexican supreme court, who remained in power until 1876.

Labor Organizations

Under the political conditions of the mid-1850s to the mid-1870s, the country struggled with political unrest and uncertainty. The economy was dormant, with little opportunity for Mexican workers to improve their working conditions. Manufacturing, except for a struggling cotton textile industry and a few other minor factories, was generally confined to artisans producing specialized goods, such as silver jewelry, by hand for local markets. The 1850s saw the rise of mutualist organizations (worker benevolent societies) such as the *Sociedad Particular de Socórros Mutuál* (or Particular Society of Mutual Aid), which was founded in October 1864 with the support of such anarchist leaders as Santiago Villanueva, Francisco Zalacosta, and José María González. The primary purpose of these societies was to improve the economic and social conditions of their members, which included craftsmen such as shoemakers, tailors, and carpenters. The organizations also established savings funds for their members for medical expenses, unemployment compensation, and pensions. The labor movement began to change at this time, shifting focus from providing help and cooperating with employers to one of revolution as militant organizers spread the word about miserable working (and living) conditions throughout Mexico.

Most artisan mutualist societies did not promote strikes. However, several strikes occurred during this time and disrupted the nation's industrial environment, as workers, especially in the textile and mining industries, tried whatever means they could to improve their meager existence, especially with regard to wages. The influence of anarchist leaders such as Plotino C. Rhodakanaty guided the strike activities of artisans (and sometimes students, common laborers, and intellectuals). On 10–11 June 1865 strikes began at the textile mills of San Ildefonso and La Colmena, near Mexico City. On 19 June 1865, 25 armed representatives of the government fired upon the San Ildefonso strikers. Several of the strikers were wounded and about 25 were jailed. The strikes in both cities failed with respect to worker demands. In July 1868 workers at La Fama Montaneasa in the Federal District that surrounds Mexico City carried out a successful strike in which they gained improved working conditions.

Mutualist and Cooperative Societies in the 1870s

By the early 1870s numerous mutualist and cooperative societies had been formed among such Mexico City artisans as carpenters, shoemakers, tailors, and among mill workers at various Federal District cotton textile factories. By the mid-1870s the number of members of such organizations in Mexico City alone was estimated at between 8,000 and 10,000 workers. The 1870s were much better for organizing labor than the two previous decades. Although the strike was not the preferred method of effecting change during this time, several strikes, mostly for

wages, did occur. Miners at Real del Monte in Hidalgo struck from August 1872 to January 1873 and were able to secure an acceptable settlement. However, the government later deported a number of miners because of their labor activities.

On 16 September 1870 leading Mexico City artisans, including Santiago Villanueva, established a national labor federation that involved several mutualist organizations. The new federation was called the *Gran Círculo de Obreros de México* (Great Circle of Workers of Mexico, or the "Circle"). The stated purpose of the Circle was to improve the social and economic condition of the working class. By 1875 the Circle had established 28 branches in 12 states and the Federal District, including locals in several cotton textile mills. Total membership was about 2,000 workers. Hoping then to establish a national labor congress, the Circle asked labor delegates to meet in the spring of 1876.

At a convention in Mexico City on 5 March 1876, 35 delegates (of the eventual total of 73) representing numerous diverse labor groups attended the first Permanent Working Congress (*Congreso Obrero Permanente*) for the purpose of uniting Mexican workers. The delegates elected officers, organized committees, and determined its business operations. Its objectives included support for adult and child education, founding of artisan-run businesses, the right to operate as the agent for all Mexican workers, and the right to establish wages based on industry or region. The new organization viewed the strike as a legitimate way to achieve its purposes and even went so far as to declare that its members should be free from the "yoke of capitalism." These strong words came from the anarchist-led members of the congress.

Labor during the Porfiriato

The regime of Mexican president Porfirio Díaz from November 1876 to 1911 (with a temporary break from 1880 to 1884), was known as the *Porfiriato*. This administration led the way to broad industrialization. The regime stabilized Mexico's finances, and the country experienced dramatic economic development. Foreign investors, especially American, put capital into mineral resources, and mining, textile, and other key industries expanded; railroad and telegraph lines were constructed; and foreign trade expanded. Along with these developments came the formation of labor unions. On the other hand, foreign investors removed much of the country's wealth, and much of the land was redistributed to a small number of landowners. During Díaz's long rule, he forcibly suppressed social discontent, which created several factors that restricted the growth of unions. The unions that developed were usually numerically small, ideologically diverse organizations that were widely scattered throughout the country. These factors in combination greatly hindered such organizations from gaining strength among laborers.

Numerous conflicting political groups slowed the progress of unions. Such groups as the anarcho-syndicalists, anarchists, utopian socialists, Christian democrats, communists, mutualists, and progovernment reformists vied for the attention of the Mexican workers, especially among the peasants, the lower middle class, and the rapidly growing sector of blue-collar laborers. Most damaging to these early unions was the power that Díaz and his technical staff held over the workers and the general populace of Mexico. Díaz's technical organization, known as the "scientists" ("*científicos*"), was determined to maintain a peaceful environment in the nation's mines, factories, farms, and transportation centers. Díaz was adamant that foreign investors, so important in reshaping Mexico's industrial base, would view their manufacturing sector as conducive to profits. Díaz did not want a repeat of Mexico's first 50 years of independence, which was plagued with political turmoil and few industrial advances. (Mexico had been proclaimed a republic with the full name United Mexican States, or *Estados Unidos Mexicanos*, in 1824.)

In 1876 Díaz and the Mexican government established the Large Confederation of Associations of Workers of the Mexican Republic (GCATRM). It endorsed trade unionism, established producers' and consumers' cooperatives, and focused on creating a stable working-class. Professor Stephen Niblo, who studied the economy surrounding the *Porfiriato* rule, stated that due to these prolabor stands early in the presidency, most workers and artisans believed Díaz would improve their working situation.

However, Díaz was not as supportive of the labor movement as was hoped. By the late 1880s Díaz reversed his decision about labor unions as he was unable to tolerate the often abusive and violent opposition generated by the workers' organizations. The Mexican government shut down the union newspapers, persecuted union leaders, and forcibly ended strikes. Several violent demonstrations—such as the ones at the Cananea copper mine in Sonora (1906), the Río Blanco-Orizaba textile mill in Veracruz (1907), and throughout the railroad industry (1907–1908)—were quickly terminated by violent counterattacks from the police and military troops.

The congress called its second conference at the end of 1879 in Mexico City. The delegates promised to provide financial support for strikes, to fight for wage increases, and to better the conditions of rural workers. However, with pressure from an increasingly hostile government and internal discord, the congress broke up in the spring of 1880. Although various labor groups remained active through 1882, the government increased its repressive campaign against all labor groups with the arrest, incarceration, and execution of several labor leaders. In the 1880s various groups attempted to reorganize the mutualist movement, but all failed.

Conclusion

Although Mexico's first working congress was short-lived, the early strikes by Mexican workers showed an intense interest in better working conditions and wages. However, the era was also marked by the ability and willingness of the Mexican government and the country's industrial community to squash the independent labor movement. Political and economic dissatisfaction were leading rapidly to "the year of the strikes" in 1906 and to the Mexican workers' revolution of 1910. Although this revolution produced improvements to working conditions, the labor movement in Mexico continues today in its long struggle for better wages and working conditions.

Key Players

Díaz, Porfirio (1830–1915): Díaz, whose full name was José de la Cruz Porfirio Díaz, was a Mexican soldier and states-

man. He entered the army and served in three wars: the Mexican War (1846–1848), the Civil War (1858–1860), and the Patriotic War (1863–1867). In 1867 and 1871 Díaz was an unsuccessful candidate for the presidency of Mexico. In 1876 he overthrew the government of President Sebastián Lerdo de Tejada and became president the following year. Under the Mexican constitution, he could not serve two consecutive terms, so Díaz gave up the presidency in 1880. He was reelected in 1884, secured passage of an amendment to the constitution permitting successive presidential terms, and remained in power until 1911.

Rhodakanaty, Plotino Constantino (1828–?): Rhodakanaty was a scholar, crusader, and political activist. Arriving in Mexico in the early 1860s, he became a teacher at the Colegio de San Ildefonso in Mexico City. He was one of the first advocates of anarchist doctrine and founded the first anarchist working-class organizing group in Mexico. Rhodakanaty had a tremendous impact on the labor movement in Mexico during the 1860s through the 1880s.

Villanueva, Santiago (1838–1872): Villanueva began work in a cabinet shop at a young age to help his poor parents. He eventually became a master woodcarver. While attending medical school, he came into contact with Francisco Zalacosta and Plotino Rhodakanaty. Villanueva spent most of the rest of his life organizing urban workers and popularizing anarchism. He coordinated the unionization effort in the Valley of Mexico.

Zalacosta, Francisco (1844–c1882): Zalacosta joined a group of students studying under Plotino C. Rhodakanaty while he was in preparatory school in Mexico City. Zalacosta was one of Rhodakanaty's most ardent disciples and played an important role in the Mexican labor movement of the late nineteenth century.

See also: *Cananéa Strike.*

BIBLIOGRAPHY

Books

Anderson, Rodney D. *Outcasts in Their Own Land: Mexican Industrial Workers, 1906–1911*. DeKalb: Northern Illinois University Press, 1976.

Clark, Marjorie Ruth. *Organized Labor in Mexico*. New York: Russell & Russell, 1973.

Grayson, George W. *The Mexican Labor Machine: Power, Politics, and Patronage*. Significant Issues Series, XI, no. 3. Washington, DC: The Center for Strategic and International Studies, 1989.

Hart, John M. *Anarchism and the Mexican Working Class, 1860–1931*. Austin and London: University of Texas Press, 1978.

Niblo, Stephen Randall. *The Political Economy of the Early Porfiriato: Politics and Economics in Mexico, 1876 to 1880*. Ph.D. Diss., Northern Illinois University, 1972.

—William Arthur Atkins

Working Women's Protective Union

United States 1863

Synopsis

Just five years after its creation in 1863, the Working Women's Protective Union (WWPU) had established itself as a champion of working women. The WWPU did not consider organizing women to strike as one of its purposes. Rather, it focused its activities on forcing employers to pay women their agreed-upon wage and acted primarily as a resource for job training and legal defense and as an employment center. Though the WWPU was often criticized for not attempting to increase wages or supporting important labor legislation, it was considered a model for like-minded groups; representatives from across the United States and Europe traveled to New York City to study its structure so that they might create similar organizations. Interestingly, working women had no real power in the administration of the organization and acted in only an advisory capacity. The day-to-day running of the union was in the hands of middle- and upper-class women concerned with the plight of working women. Major decisions were made by those members who could contribute $25 or more, though even they were led by a group of powerful, wealthy men who served as advisors to the organization. Working women's unions modeled on this pattern existed in large cities all over the United States. Twenty-seven years into its mission, the WWPU had collected over $41,000 for 12,000 women and typically received over 10,000 applications for job placement. Though not a union in the way many had come to expect, the WWPU was indeed a union in the truest sense of the word, and its formation occurred at a time when just such an advocate was desperately needed.

Timeline

1843: First known reference to cigarettes, in a list of products controlled by a French monopoly.

1848: Women's Rights Convention in Seneca Falls, New York, launches the women's suffrage movement.

1852: Publication of *Uncle Tom's Cabin* by Harriet Beecher Stowe. Though far from a literary masterpiece, it is a great commercial success, with over half a million sales on both sides of the Atlantic. More important, it has an enormous influence on British sentiments with regard to slavery and the brewing American conflict between North and South.

1856: Gustave Flaubert publishes *Madame Bovary*.

1859: In Belgium, Jean-Joseph-étienne Lenoir builds the first practical internal-combustion engine.

1861: Within weeks of Abraham Lincoln's inauguration, the Civil War begins with the shelling of Fort Sumter. Six states secede from the Union, joining South Carolina to form the Confederate States of America (later joined by four other states) and electing Jefferson Davis as presi-

Moses Yale Beach. The Library of Congress.

dent. The first major battle of the war, at Bull Run or Manassas in Virginia, is a Confederate victory.

1863: President Lincoln issues the Emancipation Proclamation, freeing all slaves in Confederate territories, on 1 January. Thus begins a year that sees the turning point of the Civil War, with decisive Union victories at Gettysburg, Vicksburg, and Chattanooga. Thereafter, the Confederacy is almost perpetually on the defensive, fighting not to win but to avoid losing.

1863: French forces occupy Mexico City, and formerly exiled Mexican leaders declare their nation an empire under Austria's Archduke Maximilian, brother of Emperor Franz Josef. The real power, however, is Emperor Napoleon III of France.

1863: Opening of the world's first subway, in London.

1865: Civil War ends with the surrender of General Robert E. Lee to General Ulysses S. Grant at Appomattox, Virginia. More than 600,000 men have died and the South is in ruins, but the Union has been restored.

1867: Maximilian surrenders to Mexican forces under Benito Juarez and is executed. Thus ends Napoleon III's dreams for a new French empire in the New World.

1873: Financial panic begins in Vienna, and soon spreads to other European financial centers, as well as to the United States.

Event and Its Context

In November 1863 a man named Daniel Walford visited the editor of the *New York Sun*, Moses Beach. Walford was president of the Workingmen's Association and a mechanic who met thousands of working women and knew of their terrible living conditions. Many were starving, working for pittances that their employers often refused to pay them. The poorest of the poor, these women had no power to affect their work lives, and Daniel Walford was determined to help them. With his own money, Walford rented the Bowery's Military Hall for a mass meeting at which sewing women might meet to discuss their situation. He asked the editor of the newspaper to attend and report the results. The editor agreed, and what he reported in the *New York Sun* galvanized the conscience of an entire city.

On the night of the meeting, Military Hall was filled to capacity with hundreds of sewing women. Hoop-skirt makers, photographers, press feeders, silver burnishers, shirt makers, vest makers, and umbrella sewers had all come in the hopes of some relief. Among those in attendance were about six men, including an ex-chief of police and a dry goods merchant; each man had been specially invited by Daniel Walford. At first it seemed that the meeting would not begin as the women, already nervous, milled about and had no idea of how to proceed. One woman approached the gentlemen present and asked them to preside. The dry goods merchant obliged, and so the meeting began. As the women shared the details of their everyday lives, it quickly became apparent that action must be taken. That very night a committee of working women and powerful, concerned citizens was formed. The next week they met to name themselves (they chose the "Workingwomen's Union") and to appoint a committee to write a constitution. Over the next few weeks they also took lengthy testimony from thousands of women. Among the information gathered from the interviews were stories of women who worked 10 hours per day to support sick husbands and children for 12.5 cents per day. The testimony led to the gut-wrenching realization that the average pay was $2 to $3 per week (at a time when housing alone could not be obtained for less than $3 per week). The committee heard countless stories of women who were robbed of their wages when employers, knowing the women had no recourse, refused to pay them. All of these stories made the more prominent citizens determined to do something; the only problem was that no one could decide what course of action to take. At last, one committee member suggested that ensuring payment for the women upon completion of work was their most promising course of action. It was endorsed by the heartfelt cry of one woman, "Oh, if we could always get paid for our work, we could get along!" This decided the primary mission of the WWPU.

The first draft of the organization's constitution, presented on 24 November, offered membership without price to any working woman, excepting household servants. The constitution also suggested the creation of a board of delegates to be elected by and represent each shop. Although these suggestions passed unanimously, they were not to stay in place. A committee of "Presidents of Societies" and men who had contributed heavily to union funds held a meeting, and on 16 December they presented their suggestions, which greatly altered the original constitution. These "suggestions" included changing the name to the "Working Women's Protective Union" and providing reserved membership and decision-making power only to those who contributed $25 or more. These changes led to the replacement of the board of delegates with a 12-member council of working women who had only advisory powers.

To achieve their goal of helping women collect the wages that were owed to them, prominent New York attorneys offered their services free of charge. It became increasingly difficult for employers to deny women their agreed-upon wages for finished work. When an employer refused to pay, the woman spoke with the superintendent and then, if the superintendent thought the complaint worthy of prosecution, filed a complaint with the WWPU's legal representatives on "Complaint Day" (one designated day per week in the offices of the WWPU). Organization delegates then questioned the woman and her witnesses. If the complaint was judged to be valid, the WWPU served the offender with notice that allowed three days to answer. The complaint, signed by the WWPU superintendent, notified the offender that the claimant had filed for a given amount of pay and asked for a response that would provide "any just cause why she should not receive this money." After three days without a response, the notification advised, the organization "shall assume that you admit the debt, and the claim will be placed in court for collection."

If the WWPU did not receive an answer to the complaint in the three-day window, the next step was to deliver a legal summons for the offender to appear in court. If he was found guilty or failed to appear, the judge automatically awarded in favor of the plaintiff and ordered the defendant to pay the wages owed plus all costs related to the court appearance. Some of these fraudulent bosses went to prison, and all at least were embarrassed in the business community. Not all employers just accepted a guilty judgment, of course. Many chose to appeal the decisions and demanded retrials. If the defendant chose to appeal to the state court level, he might find himself facing a bill 20 times the amount of the original complaint plus court costs. As word of the WWPU's legal successes grew, many delinquent employers chose to settle out of court rather than face those inflated costs.

By 1890 the WWPU had collected more than $41,000 for 12,000 women who otherwise would have had no recourse. It also lobbied for a law that penalized employers who refused to pay their workers. This law was passed, and there is no doubt that it greatly aided the WWPU in achieving more than 20,000 (out of 27,292 grievances) out-of-court settlements in its first 15 years of existence. Additionally, the union was able to discourage employers from deducting money from owed wages for supposedly imperfect work. As it did not hesitate to pursue prosecution in these cases, employers soon realized that such behavior was pointless, as the women were no longer without recourse.

The union's secondary purpose was to train women for work. The WWPU had the farsighted goal of training women for new occupations so that overcrowding (and thus unemployment) was less likely to occur. Seamstresses who worked by hand, for example, receiving training in the use of sewing machines, which increased their production and earning potential. It took a skilled seamstress 14 hours to hand sew a shirt; use of a sewing machine cut production time to one hour. Obviously the offer of training was invaluable. The WWPU taught women skills in seven different branches of mechanical labor.

Hand in hand with training women came the union's third purpose: job placement. In its first year, the WWPU placed 3,500 women, and by 1870 it received over 10,000 applications for work each year.

Yet another resource the WWPU made available to working women was a 4,000-volume library, endowed by the donations of middle-class citizens. For a nominal fee, women could borrow books. Although the *Boston Daily Evening Voice* praised this effort, it also remarked that the WWPU should be about the business of establishing and maintaining acceptable wages for the women they championed. Until then, it stated, the working women "will have but little time and not much money to patronize their library."

The WWPU did not have the goal of organizing women workers. Although it lobbied for better hours and higher wages, the union did not see itself as a militant organization that would encourage women to strike. Whether this decision came from the wish not to see women go hungry or because strikes would interfere with the comfortable economies upon which the union's volunteers themselves depended is not clear. In any case, only once in its history did the WWPU actively cooperate with a trade union when, in 1864, it endorsed a letter from the Working Women's Union of New York to then Secretary of War Edwin McMasters Stanton. It also made use of its friends in the press, asking them to publish the letter and reveal that women were being paid a mere 6 cents for each army shirt they made.

Chief Justice Charles P. Daly was named the first president or WWPU, and Mrs. Catherine Brooks offered her services as the lady superintendent. The WWPU was staffed and supported mostly by middle- and upper-class women who were moved by the plight of the working poor. Positions on its boards and committees were almost exclusively held by men. Many wealthy women also hoped to save working women from a life of prostitution, as that occupation became for many the only means to avoid starvation.

Reinforcing the fact that this was not a labor union, officers were not elected, working women never acted in any decision-making capacity, and there were no dues to pay. The WWPU instead relied on "the voluntary donations of those who approve the helping of those who help themselves, and defending the otherwise defenseless."

The WWPU, with its obvious successes, was a model for those hoping to establish such organizations. Working women's unions based on the WWPU also formed in Chicago, Boston, Philadelphia, Indianapolis, Detroit, and St. Louis. The National Women's Trade Union League also owes its establishment to the WWPU. In 1873 Emma Paterson, wife of a unionist cabinetmaker, visited New York from her native England and was impressed by the organization and activities of several organizations, including the WWPU. When she returned to England in 1874, she worked to establish the Women's Protective and Provident League, later known as the British Women's Trade Union League. In 1903 the American William English Walling observed the dynamic activities of this organization during a visit to England. Upon returning to America, he met with inter-

ested parties, who announced a meeting regarding the formation of such a union at the American Federation of Labor convention that same year. This organization became the National Women's Trade Union League. The WWPU was dissolved in 1894.

Key Players

Beach, Moses Yale (1800–1868): Beach moved to New York City in 1834 to work for his brother-in-law as manager of the mechanical department of the *New York Sun*. In 1838 Beach bought out his brother-in-law to become editor and full owner of the newspaper. Known for his obsession with speed in gathering news, Beach routinely used riders on horseback, carrier pigeons, and a boat sent specifically to meet ships arriving from Europe to gather the latest news. His greatest competitor was the *New York Herald*. Beach was key in the formation of the New York Associated Press and the Harbor Association; the purpose of both organizations was to speed the gathering and delivery of news. Beach was the first of the American editors to publish a European edition of his paper, which he called the *American Sun*. By the time Beach retired from journalism in 1848, the popular *New York Sun* had a circulation of 50,000.

Daly, Charles Patrick (1816–1899): After working as a sailor, Daly studied law at Columbia University and was admitted to the bar of New York in 1837. In 1843 he became a member of the New York Assembly. In 1844 he was appointed a judge of the court of common pleas, an office that he held until 1886. He wrote 16 volumes of law reports and a book about the first settlement of Jews in the United States. He served as a member of several scientific societies including the American Geography Society, of which he was president in 1864.

See also: *National Women's Trade Union League.*

BIBLIOGRAPHY

Books

Foner, Philip S. *Facts of American Labor: A Comprehensive Collection of Labor Firsts in the United States.* New York: Holmes and Meir, 1984.

———. *Women and the American Labor Movement: From Colonial Times to the Eve of World War I.* New York: The Free Press, 1979.

Henry, Alice. *Women and the Labor Movement.* New York: Arno and *The New York Times*, 1971.

Johnson, Allen, ed. *Dictionary of American Biography*, Vol. 2: *Barsotti-Brazer.* New York: Charles Scribner's Sons, 1929.

Kessler-Harris, Alice. *Out to Work: A History of Wage-Earning Women in the United States.* New York and Oxford: Oxford University Press, 1982.

Weiner, Lynn Y. *From Working Girl to Working Mother: The Female Labor Force in the United States, 1820–1980.* Chapel Hill: University of North Carolina Press, 1985.

Wertheimer, Barbara Mayer. *We Were There: The Story of Working Women in America*. New York: Pantheon Books, 1977.

Working Women's Protective Union: Twenty-Five Years History, 1863–1888. New York: Working Women's Protective Union, 1888.

—Kimberley Barker

Workingman's Benevolent Association

United States 1868

Synopsis

Part labor union and part advocate of nonviolent change, the Workingman's Benevolent Association (WBA) represented the demands of miners in the American North for better labor standards. Founded by John Siney, an Irish immigrant, in 1868, the Workingman's Benevolent Association originally presented a less violent front than its sister organizations, including the "Molly Maguires." The association focused on arbitrating the bitter confrontation between its components, namely the coal miners of Pennsylvania, specifically the Saint Clair region, and the owners of companies such as the Reading Railroad who were attempting to consolidate control over the anthracite (hard) coal fields in eastern Pennsylvania in the mid-to-late nineteenth century.

Timeline

1848: Revolutions rock Europe, and Marx and Engels publish the *Communist Manifesto.*

1853: Crimean War begins in October. The struggle, which will last until February 1856, pits Russia against the combined forces of Great Britain, France, Turkey, and Sardinia-Piedmont. A war noted for the work of Florence Nightingale with the wounded, it is also the first conflict to be documented by photojournalists.

1859: In Belgium, Jean-Joseph-étienne Lenoir builds the first practical internal-combustion engine.

1861: Within weeks of U.S. President Abraham Lincoln's inauguration, the American Civil War begins with the shelling of Fort Sumter. Six states secede from the Union, joining South Carolina to form the Confederate States of America (later joined by four other states) and electing Jefferson Davis as president. The first major battle of the war, at Bull Run or Manassas in Virginia, is a Confederate victory.

1864: Foundation of the International Red Cross in Geneva.

1866: Prussia defeats Austria in the Seven Weeks' War.

1868: Ratification of the Fourteenth Amendment to the U.S. Constitution, which grants civil rights to African Americans.

1868: Spain decrees that all children born to slaves in Puerto Rico will be free.

1870: Beginning of Franco-Prussian War. German troops sweep over France, Napoleon III is dethroned, and France's Second Empire gives way to the Third Republic.

1873: The gold standard, adopted by Germany in 1871 and eventually taken on by all major nations, spreads to Italy, Belgium, and Switzerland. Though the United States does not officially base the value of its currency on gold until 1900, an unofficial gold standard dates from this period, even as a debate over "bimetallism" creates sharp divisions in American politics.

1874: As farm wages in Britain plummet, agricultural workers go on strike.

1878: Russo-Turkish War, begun in 1877, ends with the defeat of Turkey, which ceases to be an important power in Europe. The Treaty of San Stefano concluding the war is revised by the Congress of Berlin, which realigns the balance of power in southeastern Europe.

Event and Its Context

The legacy of the Workingman's Benevolent Association is not just the story of its founder, John Siney, but also the story of the immigrant miners who composed its membership. Composed mostly of immigrants from England, Ireland, Wales, and the German states who had immigrated to the Pennsylvania coal regions, the backgrounds of the association's members were so diverse that they often united only for the purpose of accomplishing a particular task. Most of the Welsh and English immigrants to Saint Clair had already gained valuable skills from working in the richest coal districts of the British Isles, so they often moved into the more skilled and therefore more highly paid positions in the mines. Their Irish counterparts, many of whom had fled Ireland during the Potato Famine (1845–1849), lacked advanced training; their farming backgrounds provided little in the way of skills needed for mining. There were even variations among the Irish immigrants; those from the southern and eastern counties, such as Kilkenny, were more skilled than their comrades from the northern and western counties. The former would eventually become associated with the more violent backbone of the miner's movement, the Molly Maguires, which created conflicts with their less-skilled former countrymen. German immigrants, on the other hand, had more in common with the English and Welsh and often became artisans.

This background directly influenced the formation of the Workingman's Benevolent Association. Coal miners were constantly in harm's way due to exposure to the gases from the coal piles and the threat of the explosion of the mines. Furthermore, the collapse of the tunnels deep within the mines was a constant danger. In addition to these occupational hazards, a disease common to miners, known as "black lung disease" or "miner's asthma," caused by inhalation of matter in the cold and damp environment of the mines, led to work-related illnesses and early death. Without proper health care and given the lack of provisions for ailing miners, many miners had only their families to rely on. The mining operations, known as collieries, rarely supplied tools and supplies for their miners; rather, the miners could purchase supplies at the company store, with the cost deducted from their already meager weekly wages. Each of these hardships led to complaints, and the grievances eventually led to the formation of various mining associations. The first coal mining union, the Bates Union, formed in 1849 by John Bates, a native of Saint Clair, called for the first regional strike against the fixed price of coal. When merchants in Philadelphia and New York refused to pay the high prices, the coal masters refused to ship the coal.

The success of the Bates Union was questionable. It led to the formation of the first fairly effective miner's union, Siney's Workingman's Benevolent Association (WBA). Organized to protect the families of the injured workers and to improve working conditions, the WBA attempted to represent all miners, regardless of ethnic background. Nevertheless, the attempts at inclusion failed miserably; the combination of ethnic unrest and the corruption of mine owners led to violence, something that Siney had attempted to avoid by advocating a nonviolent stance. On the subject of violence, Siney commented, "By rules of the association all acts of violence are strictly forbidden, and any member found guilty of such will not only be expelled from the association, but from the county also." With this statement, Siney summarized his advocacy of a strict adherence to social law and order. Siney had immigrated to the anthracite mining regions of Pennsylvania in 1863 at the age of 32, immediately following the death of his first wife. An immigrant from England (although born in Ireland), Siney had been president of the local bricklayer's union and well trusted in England. His diligence as leader of the WBA led to the creation of the first mine safety inspection laws in the United States, even though these laws were not regularly enforced. Siney also spent time in negotiations for the first minimum wage opportunities for working miners, as well as the first instances of collective bargaining among miner's associations. The union locals in the Schuylkill area of Pennsylvania also organized local food cooperatives and libraries to both feed and educate members of their communities.

Angered by the decrease in wages in the post–Civil War era and the price fixing by mining cooperatives, Siney spent months traveling among the miners in the Saint Clair area, listening to their complaints, and attempting to gain insight into their problems. In a meeting on 23 July 1868 in Walker's Hall, Siney presented a resolution he had drafted calling for an eight-hour workday; this was the first public recognition of Siney's efforts and would be the first of many such speeches for Siney. In a letter dated 2 December 1868 and published in *The Pottsville Standard*, a local newspaper, Siney explained the purpose of the WBA: "The object of the Workingman's Benevolent Association is to unite in one band of brotherhood all who earn their bread by hard toil—more especially the miners and laborers of Pennsylvania." He noted that "benevolence is not sectional," and proposed that the members become united so as to offer support across the region. He argued that "the great danger in the business we follow" had made miners "outcast from all other benevolent societies" and stated that they must band together so that their fate would not be passed to their children.

The WBA represented a small success for miners, but any advances were limited by the market; if the market for coal continued to expand, then the WBA could continue to be successful. Politics soon interfered, however, particularly as the United States entered a depression in the mid-1870s, and greed took over and fueled the desire to monopolize the coal industry. When the combination of the union's ability to keep both coal prices and wages somewhat high became too much for the corporations to handle, the Philadelphia and Reading Railroad, which hauled coal from the Pennsylvania region, increased rates, thereby destroying smaller companies. Led by Franklin B. Gowen, president of the Reading Railroad, and with the suspected use of Pinkerton's National Detective Agency, the move to undermine the efforts of the WBA began in 1873, after the last of the smaller operators were forced out of business. Gowen essentially controlled the state police as well with the establishment of the Coal and Iron Police, which represented his petition of the government and the money he used to "buy" government silence. Siney—one of the last labor leaders to fight the self-made mine operators and the first labor leader to fight the burgeoning leaders of the anthracite mining movement, including Gowen—was essentially caught in the middle. He had gained national attention in August of 1869 when he attended the National Labor Union meeting in Philadelphia, and Susan B. Anthony championed his cause. She offered to run a weekly column in her New York–based paper, *The Revolution*, to express the interests of the miners. This led to Siney's own editorship of his new paper, *The Workingman*, a weekly four-page newspaper that debuted on 5 April 1873. All of this media attention made Siney the target of union-busters such as Franklin Gowen.

By 1874 the WBA had begun its downward spiral, focusing less on matters of principle and more on a slightly more forceful approach. The United States was in the midst of a full depression, with one-third of the workers in Pennsylvania alone unemployed. Gowen took advantage of this crisis to begin stocking up on coal and cutting wages, which, in turn, led to the "Long Strike" of 1875. Beginning in January, the strike lasted until June and completely undermined all of Siney's efforts at ethnic cohesiveness. In addition to the blow caused by unemployment, the Irish mine workers felt that the English and Welsh mine workers were given preferential treatment, which created discord that resulted in a crime spree associated with the Molly Maguires and a turn in public opinion against the WBA. The strike failed; the coal operators reopened the mines in May and offered protection to those who wished to return. Because the WBA had been unable to negotiate a "return-to-work" offer prior to the reopening, its leadership counseled workers to return to the mines and accept any type of protection, which resulted in a violent rejection of WBA protocol. Protests and demonstrations, violent at times, occurred throughout June. The miners actually shut down nine mines in the course of their demonstrations. The press scorned WBA's efforts with comments such as, "Let the leaders of these riots be hunted down and arrested. If [they] will learn tolerance only by being shot down, it is better to shoot them down than to let them shoot others." The WBA attempted to fight such slander in *The Workingman*, but fought a losing battle, as it was forced to admit that some miners had committed acts of violence in violation of the philosophy behind the WBA. The efforts of the WBA, although passive, had garnered national attention but forced Siney into an early retirement with a spiraling depression. Siney died in poverty at the age of 48 in 1879 and was buried in St. Mary's Cemetery near his adopted town of Saint Clair.

Siney's efforts for his beloved WBA did not go unnoticed, however. After the violence of the Molly Maguires subsided, the WBA lived on the formation of the United Mine Workers of America, whose first Pennsylvania chapter formed in 1890.

Key Players

Siney, John (1831–1879): An Irish immigrant to the United States, Siney founded the Workingman's Benevolent Association in 1868 to protect the rights of coal miners in Pennsylvania. An advocate for miners in Pennsylvania politics until his death, he was credited with nationally publicizing the abuses of miners, particularly in the fight between corporations and labor unions.

See also: *Eight-hour Day Movement; Molly Maguires; National Labor Union; Potato Famine; United Mine Workers of America.*

BIBLIOGRAPHY

Books

Dewees, F. P. *Molly Maguires: The Origin, Growth, and Character of the Organization.* Philadelphia: J. B. Lippincott and Company, 1877.

Kenny, Kevin. *Making Sense of the Molly Maguires.* New York: Oxford University Press, 1998.

Pinkowski, Edward. *John Siney: The Miner's Martyr.* Philadelphia: Sunshine Press, 1963.

Other

Lutz, Valerie Ann. "Immigrants in the Coal Region." *The Old Country in the New World* [cited 3 October 2002]. <http://www.amphilsoc.org/library/exhibits/wallace/immigrants.htm>.

—Jennifer Harrison

Workingmen's Party

United States 1828

Synopsis

The Workingmen's Party was formed in Philadelphia in 1828. The organization's primary goal was to gain equality for the working man of America through political means. Branches

George Henry Evans. The Library of Congress.

soon began in New York and Boston. The major platform of the party was education for all and an end to the divisions between the rich and the poor. The party was not successful and disintegrated by 1832. The Workingmen's Party laid the groundwork for future political labor-based organizations.

Timeline

1803: German pharmacist Friedrich Wilhelm Adam Saturner isolates an opium derivative, to which he gives the name *morphine.*

1808: First performances of Beethoven's Fifth and Sixth symphonies.

1813: Jane Austen publishes *Pride and Prejudice.*

1818: British surgeon James Blundel performs the first successful blood transfusion.

1823: U.S. President James Monroe establishes the Monroe Doctrine, whereby the United States warns European nations not to interfere in the political affairs of the Western Hemisphere.

1826: Invention of friction or "Lucifer" matches in England.

1828: Election of Andrew Jackson as president begins a new era in American history.

Andrew Jackson. The Library of Congress.

1829: Greece wins its independence after a seven-year war with Turkey.

1831: Unsuccessful Polish revolt against Russian rule.

1834: American inventor Cyrus H. McCormick patents his reaper, a horse-drawn machine for harvesting wheat.

1837: Coronation of Queen Victoria in England.

1839: England launches the First Opium War against China. The war, which lasts three years, results in the British gaining a free hand to conduct a lucrative opium trade, despite opposition by the Chinese government.

Event and Its Context

The Party Begins

In 1827 in Philadelphia, carpenters went out on strike in an attempt to shorten their workday to 10 hours. Workers from other trades went out on strike in support of the carpenters. William Heighton was a shoemaker who had urged his colleagues to strike in support of the carpenters. He was instrumental in the formation later that year of the Mechanics Union of Trade Associations (MUTA), the first central labor body. One of MUTA's unifying themes was the disparity between the wealthy and the working poor. The organization's preamble focused on the evils of the capitalist system that allowed some to grow wealthy off of the backs of those who labored in abject poverty while working for the wealthy. The preamble suggested

---

Major Third-Party Movements in American History

Listed below are a few—though far from all—of the third parties that have made an impact in American history, along with the year of their founding. Most rose and fell in a matter of months or just a few years, whereas others, such as the principal socialist and communist parties, still exist.

Antimasonic Party (1827)

Workingmen's Party (1828)

Free Soil Party (1848)

Know-Nothing Party (1852)

Equal Rights Party (1872)

Prohibitionist Party (1872)

"Greenback" Party (1875)

Workingmen's Party (1876; became Socialist Labor Party in 1877)

People's Party (1892)

Socialist Party USA (1900)

Progressive ("Bull Moose") Party (1912)

Communist Party of the United States of America (1919)

Farmer–Labor Party (1919)

States' Rights Democratic Party (1948)

Progressive Party (1948)

Libertarian Party (1971)

Reform Party (1995)

Green Party of the United States (1996)

Source: *Directory of U.S. Political Parties.*
<http://www.politics1.com/parties.htm>.

—Judson Knight

---

that, left unchecked, the disease of capitalism would eventually destroy those at the top as the market became flooded with too many products and too few consumers. The only way to circumvent such a disaster was to recognize the laborers and reward them with fair wages, fair hours, and the respect to which they were entitled.

In 1828 a political labor party appeared when MUTA supported the emergence of the "Republican Political Association of the Workingmen of the City of Philadelphia," otherwise known as the "Workingmen's Party." The focus of the Workingmen's Party was the advancement and enrichment of working men's work and private lives. The group included the unions of many individual groups such as bricklayers, painters, and journeymen.

Working-class men in 1828 did not have reason to hope for an advance in their socioeconomic standing. They found themselves at odds with legal statutes that enforced debtors' prisons.

They were not able to obtain a reasonable education because there was no public school system to which they or their children might go. Technological advances brought about the rise of the factory system, which meant low wages and unsafe working conditions. The gap between the rich and the poor was growing rapidly. The men who formed and joined the Workingmen's Party sought to bring about change through political action.

The party wrote a statement expressing its demands. The Philadelphia party's newspaper, *Mechanics Free Press*, published the statement, which was, in format and title, the *Declaration of Independence*. This declaration, written by George Evans, a former member of MUTA and at that time a member of the Workingmen's Party, outlined the party's agreed-upon agenda. The overall goal was to raise the esteem in which these laborers were held. The agenda included the demand for a 10-hour day, universal male suffrage, the eradication of debtors' prisons, the end of the militia system, a lien law to protect them in the event of the death or bankruptcy of their employer, the end of all chartered monopolies, plus a strong commitment to the equal access of quality education regardless of financial means.

The Workingmen's Party had to fight for its political existence from the start. According to historian John Commons and colleagues in *History of Labour in the United States*, professional politicians and "legitimate" political machines tried to break up the party by attempting to prevent it meetings. When they could not prevent the meetings, the professional politicians tried to disband them. The meetings continued despite the politicians' best efforts.

The Voice of the Party

Philadelphia's *Mechanics Free Press* newspaper was started by labor activist William Heighton as a way to circumvent the politics of the major city press at the time and provide a voice for the working-class man. The *Press* became a vehicle for the critique of the city's corrupt political, social, and moral views toward the working class. The paper also served as a call to arms to mobilize the city's entire working-class population to vote as a bloc for candidates who were committed to helping working men achieve their goals. The paper demanded that the rich and powerful come to terms with the working men of the city, who were on the rise and seeking equal treatment in all arenas. It reiterated the agenda as set forth in the Workingmen's *Declaration of Independence*.

Politically, Philadelphia was at odds with itself. The Federalists' had a strong hold, and the Republicans were split into two factions, the Adamites and Jacksonians. The Federalist-Adamite group was heading toward a single political faction known as the Federal-Republican Party. The members of this party were predominantly lawyers and aristocrats; in 1828 the party controlled the city of Philadelphia. The other faction, the Jacksonians, whose members were predominantly bank managers and office managers, controlled Philadelphia County. In 1828 the Workingmen's Party nominated one ticket for the city and one for the county. Only eight of all of those nominated were from the Workingmen's ticket alone; the rest were from the other two parties. Most of the Workingmen's candidates were working men themselves. Thus they earned the nickname *Workies*.

The Workingmen's Party campaigned vigorously and spread its message via the press. Although none of the strictly Workingmen's candidates won, the Federalist and Jackson nominees who were on the Workingmen's ticket won 300 to 600 more votes than those who were not on the Workingmen's ticket. In 1829 the Workingmen's Party achieved tremendous success in the election after it combined with the anti-Jackson faction.

In 1829 the party organized clubs and urged all laborers to take necessary steps to ensure that they could vote legally. They named the candidates that they endorsed early and won 20 seats in the election that year.

New York Chapter

In 1829 a New York Workingmen's Party appeared and held its first meeting on 19 October. In the meeting, members decided to follow in Philadelphia's footsteps and run Workingmen's candidates on a separate political ticket. The agenda for the New York branch of the party was similar to Philadelphia's, even down to the adoption of the *Declaration of Independence*. New York's *Working Man's Advocate*, which emulated the format and tone of the Philadelphia *Mechanics Free Press*, published the declaration with an added paragraph to address specifically the problems of working men in New York. The key difference in New York was that there the mechanics had already earned the right to a 10-hour day.

The New York branch sought to gain equal access to land for all men, no matter their income. They also sought direct election of mayors, compensation for jurors and witnesses, civil service reform, the end of capital punishment, free trade, and a pension for veterans of the Revolutionary War.

The *Advocate* published a piece by the Workingmen's Party on 31 October 1829 that went beyond the concepts put forth in the *Declaration* by specifically outlining the detailed workings of the party. The article explained the motivations behind the formation of the Association of Working Men. It promised to name and hold responsible those who were the cause of the working men's oppression and outlined in detail how this would be done. The article reiterated the party's commitment to promoting a system of public education and discussed the party's decision to stay out of all religious matters. Religion, according to this article, was to be between men and their makers.

In the spring of 1829 some New York companies threatened to revoke the 10-hour day that had been granted to machinists because of a sluggish economy. Thomas Skidmore, a city machinist and labor activist, provoked machinists throughout the city to organize large demonstrations whose sole purpose was to tell employers that the laborers would not give up their 10-hour day. At the end of this short-lived struggle, the laborers maintained their 10-hour day. The association appointed a committee of 50 men to help the laborers maintain this right.

Skidmore assumed the helm of the "Committee of Fifty," and with the 10-hour workday intact, they turned their heads to other issues. Skidmore's solution to the inequities visited upon working men was to see that every working man had access to land ownership. As it was, the financially well-off had a monopoly on land, and working men rarely owned any. Joseph G. Rayback, in *A History of American Labor*, asserted that the

Committee of Fifty was the reason that the New York Working-men's Party turned to politics to address its needs in the 1829 election.

The party wanted to see its representatives elected in every office, including in the state legislature in Albany, and to make itself known to as many people and political parties as possible, in an effort to see to the rise of the working man. The party had great success in the fall election of 1829. Every candidate on the Workingmen's ticket, according to Rayback in *A History of Labor*, received a minimum of 6,000 of the 21,000 votes that were cast.

The strong showing of support for the Workingmen's Party at the polls had an effect on professional politics of the time. Seeing the number of votes to be gained and the strength of this segment of voters, some of the professional politicians began to incorporate labor concerns into their own platforms, most specifically the fight for a 10-hour day. Jacksonian Democrats, popular among Workingmen's Party members, were the most likely to embrace the needs and concerns of labor. *The Mechanics Free Press* reported that both of the major political parties placed signs on their carriages that read, "The Working Man's Ticket," in an attempt to capture the labor vote.

The success of labor candidates is credited by author Edward Pessen, in an article written for the fall 1963 edition of *Labor History*, as being part of a shift in voting habits of people who formerly had voted for the Republican Party. After this election, the party split into three separate factions. The Sentinel or Advocate wing came to embrace the Democratic platform and was absorbed into the Jacksonian organization after a resounding defeat in the 1830 elections. Men who were not of the working class infiltrated the party to gain political advantage, yet they had no commitment to the working man once elected. This was one reason that the party began to splinter.

Another reason for the development of factions was that party leadership was split on an appropriate direction for the union. Skidmore, agrarian and believer that equal access to land would solve the inequities of the working men's lives, pushed for land reform as a singular platform. In his 1829 publication *The Rights of Man to Property*, he argued for a new constitution that would allow the state to take back all personal property and redistribute it on an egalitarian basis. Without land, he argued, the poor owned only one thing: their own labor. Skidmore compared this labor to slavery. He went on to warn that technology was creating labor-saving devices and processes that could eventually lead to the working man's extinction, if all he owned was indeed his own labor. Using the steam engine as an example, Skidmore claimed that it was not the device itself that would injure the poor, but the lack of receiving any benefit from it that hurt them. The problem, in essence, was that the minority controlled the majority of resources. Life would not be fair to workers until the day that all of the resources had been redistributed to everyone over the age of majority.

Members of the Workingmen's Party were not interested in long-range solutions. With support for Skidmore's ideas being so low, he and a few others separated from the group and began the Equal Rights Party.

Henry Evans and Robert Dale Owens were both strong proponents of equal access to education as being the way out of poverty for the working class. Evans and Owens hoped to see the state take custody of children by sending them to boarding schools where they would receive not only education but food and clothing as well. This, they believed, would give the children a step up in the world. Fanny Wright, a feminist and education advocate, was also involved with the Evans and Owens faction. Noah Cook and Henry G. Guyon both preached about a public school system that would keep families intact and yet allow children to receive a decent education. These two trains of thought led to further disintegration among the proeducation faction specifically and the Workingmen's Party as a whole.

Another factor working against the Workingmen's Party was the harassment of people by organizations such as the Tammany Hall political machine. Other "legitimate" politicians and newspapers as well painted the party as group of no-goods just looking to stir up trouble and laughed at the concerns of party members. The nay-sayers targeted individual leaders, such as Fanny Wright, who had run a commune called Nashoba, which was devoted to racial and sexual equality and was ripe for the nasty innuendos and accusations of the "legitimate" press. All of this had a demoralizing effect on the party and hindered the ability of the membership to remain solid.

Other States Come Aboard

The Boston *Advocate* of September 1830 and the Boston *Courier* of 11 and 28 August 1830 stated that a Workingmen's Party meeting was held in Boston in the summer of 1830. This meeting raised candidates to be run on behalf of the party, as they had in New York and Philadelphia. The articles described the men in attendance as coming from work and looking every bit the part of a working man.

In New London, Connecticut, three Workingmen's candidates were elected to the state legislature in 1830. That year, Workingmen's Party candidates also carried the day in Newark, New Jersey. Similar groups became active in Pennsylvania, Vermont, and Ohio towns. Scholars disagree on which groups were actually offshoots of the Philadelphia party and which groups were formed with goals that were not directly political.

In the end, the Workingmen's Party, committed to change through political candidates, disintegrated as the Federalist and Democratic parties along with the major newspapers of the day set out to destroy them. This did not mean that the working class did not achieve any gains. In Philadelphia, laborers saw the passage of an act guaranteeing a 10-hour day. By 1834 Pennsylvania began experimenting with public educational facilities that would be open to people from all socioeconomic groups and eliminated jail time for debtors. The party newspapers served to help advance the goals of the working class by shaping public policy and uniting the workers.

A book published in 1831, Stephen Simpson's *The Working Man's Manual*, contained rhetoric about the great importance of education that went back to the days of ancient Greece and Rome in an effort to make his argument that education, above all else, was the answer to the dilemma of the working man.

In New York, by 1832, the Workingman's Party was virtually laid to rest when former members distanced themselves from the party and an overwhelming number of working men voted for the Democratic candidate, Andrew Jackson.

Key Players

Evans, George Henry (1805–1856): Evans was born in England and immigrated to New York as a teenager. He became an activist during the depression of 1819. An advocate of the free-soil movement, Evans became active in 1829 in the Working Man's Party. He started the party newspaper, *The Working Man's Advocate*.

Jackson, Andrew (1767–1845): President of the United States (1829–1837). While Jackson was in office, the one American political party separated into two, the Democratic Republicans (Democrats) and the Republicans or Whigs. Many members of the Workingmen's Party deserted it to support Jackson and the Democrats, who came to be seen as friendly to labor.

Owens, Robert Dale (1771–1858): Owens opened the Institute for the Formation of Character, a school that offered free education to all members of the community. He was a strong advocate of a public education system that would educate everyone and thus change society for the betterment of all. He was actively involved in the New York Workingman's Party.

Wright, Fanny (1795–1852): Wright was a Scottish woman who became enamored with America and bought 2,000 acres of land in Tennessee, where she began a community called Nashoba. Devoted to ending slavery, universal suffrage, socialism, and free education for everyone, Wright worked with many people including Robert Dale Owens. Owens and Wright both became involved in the New York Workingmen's Party. Wright was elected to the New York Assembly on the Workingman's ticket.

See also: *Mechanics Union of Trade Associations; Ten-hour Day Movement.*

BIBLIOGRAPHY

Books

Commons, John R., David J. Saposs, Helen L. Sumner, E. B. Mittelman, H. E. Hoagland, John B. Andrews, and Selig Perlman. *History of Labour in the United States*, Vol. 1. New York: The Macmillan Company, 1921.

Hugins, Walter Edward. *Jacksonian Democracy and the Working Class: A Study of the New York Workingmen's Movement, 1829–1837*. Stanford, CA: Stanford University Press, 1960.

Rayback, Joseph G. *A History of American Labor*. New York: The Macmillan Company, 1959.

Sorge, Friederich A. *Friedrich A. Sorge's Labor Movements in the United States: A History of the American Working Class from Colonial Times to 1890*. Westport, CT: Greenwood Press, 1977.

Tyler, Gus. *The Labor Revolution: Trade Unions in a New America*. New York: The Viking Press, 1966.

Periodicals

Garrison, Frank. "To Unionists, 'Scab' Is Truly a Four Letter Word." *BMWE Journal* 106, no. 9 (October 1997).

Pessen, Edward. "The Workingmen's Movement of the Jacksonian Era." *The Mississippi Valley Historical Review* 43, no. 3 (December 1956): 428–443.

Other

Hieghton, William. "Memorial on the U.S. Congress: On the Land Question." Lause's Links. *Mechanics' Free Press*, 25 October 1828, p. 1, cols. 3, 4 [cited 12 September 2002]. <http://www.geocities.com/CollegePark/Quad/6460/doct/830PWland.html>.

Illinois Labor History Society. "The Working Man's Declaration of Independence" [cited 20 September 2002]. <http://www.kentlaw.edu/ilhs/doc29.html>.

IWB Online. "Andrew Jackson and the Origins of Democracy." 23 September 1996 [cited 2 September 2002]. <http://www.wsws.org/public_html/prioriss/iwb9-23/andre.htm>.

Kelling, Karla. "The Labor and Radical Press 1820–Present: An Overview and Bibliography" [cited 20 September 2002]. <http://faculty.washington.edu/gregoryj/laborpress/Kelling.htm>.

The National Archives Learning Curve. "Fannie Wright" [cited 12 September 2002]. <http://www.spartacus.schoolnet.co.uk/REwright.htm>.

Oberlin College Web site. "Preamble to the Mechanics Union of Trade Association" [cited 12 September 2002]. <http://www.oberlin.edu/~gkornbl/Hist258/MechanicsUnion.html>.

San Diego State University's College of Education. "Organization by Workingmen of an Association for the Protection of Industry and for the Promotion of National Education, 1829." *Working Man's Advocate*, 31 October 1829 [cited 20 September 2002]. <http://edweb.sdsu.edu/people/DKitchen/new_655/workers.htm>

Skidmore, Thomas. "The Rights of Man to Property." Lauses's Links [cited 21 September 2002]. <http://www.geocities.com/CollegePark/Quad/6460/doct/829RMP.html>.

—Beth Emmerling

Workingmen's Party of the United States

United States 1876

Synopsis

The Workingmen's Party of the United States (WPUS), organized 19–22 July 1876, was the first nationwide socialist organization in the United States. Although it lasted less than two years before splitting into irreconcilable factions, it was an important seed-bed for future developments of the American labor movement in that it embraced trade unionism, labor journalism, worker education, struggle for social reform, socialism, and electoral activity.

One and a Quarter Centuries of the Socialist Labor Party

Formed in 1876, the Workingmen's Party of the United States changed its name to the Socialist Labor Party (SLP) in 1877. One and a quarter centuries later, it was still extant, and like its much larger Republican and Democrat rivals, it had its own Web page (<http://www.slp.org>). Yet like many another socialist party in America, after rising to prominence in the latter part of the nineteenth century and the first half of the twentieth, it had faded into obscurity after World War II.

The party had lost members in 1901, when more moderate socialists split off to form the Socialist Party USA (SPUSA). (These are just two among dozens of "socialist" parties representing political gradations from trade unionism to Maoism.) The SPUSA was destined to gain much greater prominence than the SLP: in 1912, SPUSA presidential candidate Eugene V. Debs earned 900,000 votes, a staggering 6 percent of the total popular vote—a truly impressive showing for a third party in America, and especially a socialist one.

Though overshadowed by the SPUSA, the SLP continued to field presidential candidates until 1976, when the last SLP presidential candidate earned just 9,600 votes. Thereafter, the party abandoned presidential races, which are costly for candidates at the margins. Still, a small remnant of the faithful held on, and the party fielded a handful of candidates for local office, primarily in New Jersey.

The party newspaper, started in 1991, still functions, and the Web site keeps alive the ideas of Daniel De Leon (1852–1914). Though he did not found the SLP, De Leon, a law professor at Columbia, was a seminal figure in the development of its ideology, and SLP members place his ideas on a par with those of Marx and Engels.

Source: *Directory of U.S. Political Parties.* <http://www.politics1.com/parties.htm>.

—Judson Knight

Timeline

1856: Gustave Flaubert publishes *Madame Bovary.*

1861: Emancipation of the serfs in Russia.

1867: Maximilian surrenders to Mexican forces under Benito Juarez and is executed. Thus ends Napoleon III's dreams for a new French empire in the New World.

1869: Completion of the first U.S. transcontinental railway.

1872: The Crédit Mobilier affair, in which several officials in the administration of President Ulysses S. Grant are accused of receiving stock in exchange for favors, is the first of many scandals that are to plague Grant's second term.

1874: Discovery of gold in the Black Hills of South Dakota.

1876: General George Armstrong Custer and 264 soldiers are killed by the Sioux at the Little Big Horn River.

1876: Alexander Graham Bell introduces the telephone.

1876: Four-stroke cycle gas engine introduced.

1878: Opening of first commercial telephone exchange, in New Haven, Connecticut.

1882: Agitation against English rule spreads throughout Ireland, culminating with the assassination of chief secretary for Ireland Lord Frederick Cavendish and permanent undersecretary Thomas Burke in Dublin's Phoenix Park. The leader of the nationalist movement is Charles Stewart Parnell, but the use of assassination and terrorism—which Parnell himself has disavowed—makes clear the fact that he does not control all nationalist groups.

1886: Bombing at Haymarket Square, Chicago, kills seven policemen and injures numerous others. Eight anarchists are accused and tried; three are imprisoned, one commits suicide, and four are hanged.

Event and Its Context

The WPUS formed as the result of the merger of several organizations: the North American remnants of the International Workingmen's Association (Karl Marx was a primary leader of the First International chapter of this group, which had among its members Friedrich Sorge, Carl Speyer, and Otto Weydemeyer); the Social–Democratic Workingmen's Party of North America (which included Adolph Strasser, Peter J. McGuire, George Schilling, Thomas J. Morgan, and Albert Parsons), and two smaller groups, the Workingmen's Party of Illinois and the Social Political Workingmen's Party of Cincinnati. The influence of Marx was obvious within the WPUS, but there were other influences as well, including the ideas of the late German socialist leader, Ferdinand Lassalle, and the analyses and agitation for the eight-hour workday by the U.S. working-class intellectual, Ira Steward.

Ethnic Diversity, Class Unity

The WPUS reflected the fact that the United States was a multicultural "nation of nations." The party had two official weekly German-language papers—the Chicago *Verbote* (Herald), edited by Conrad Conzett, and the New York *Arbeiter–Stimme* (Labor's Voice), edited by Otto Walster, to serve the organization's large number of German–American members. (Germans were the largest immigrant group in the U.S. at this time, followed by the Irish.) The party's official English-language weekly, the *Labor Standard*, was edited by J. P. McDonnell, a former Irish Fenian who later served for a time as secretary to Karl Marx in the First International. At least 21 other newspapers around the U.S. supported the WPUS, of which 12 were German, 7 English-language, 1 Bohemian, and 1 Swedish. In its first year, the WPUS had about 3500 members in 55 sections grouped by nationality: 33 German, 16 English-language, 4 Bohemian, 1 Scandinavian, and 1 French. By the following summer the WPUS had doubled its membership to 7,000, with 82 sections (of which 23 were English-language).

The WPUS favored working-class unity transcending racial and ethnic divisions. Yet there is evidence of prejudice among some of the members in California toward imported Chinese laborers and in Missouri toward African American workers. Nor was there an appreciation in the organization of the catastrophe wrought by the Republican Party's final betrayal of Reconstruction and black rights in the South. The organization was divided over whether women workers should be organized into trade unions or instead be driven back to their "rightful place" in the home, so as not to compete with male labor. On the other hand, the WPUS did have a small number of African American members (most prominently Peter H. Clark of Cincinnati) and women members (generally concentrated in "women's clubs" or, in German, *frauenverein*), and one of its founding documents proclaimed the organization's adherence to "perfect equality of rights of both sexes."

Labor Action, Diverging Perspectives

Another founding document asserted that "in this country the ballot box has long ago ceased to record the popular will, and only serves to falsify the same in the hands of professional politicians," adding that "the organization of the working people is not yet far enough developed to overthrow this state of corruptions." It concluded that workers should "abstain from all political movements for the present and to turn their back on the ballot box," and should instead concentrate on organizing workers into trade unions to provide a strong basis for future labor politics: "Let us bide our time! It will come!" The WPUS would eventually founder on precisely this issue.

The decisive event in the short life of the WPUS was what has been appropriately tagged "the great labor uprising of 1877," a wave of militant labor insurgencies and street battles that swept through many cities as part of a nationwide strike of railway workers. In many cities, WPUS members apparently played no part in the upsurge, but organized support meetings and rallies in others (most notably in Boston, Cincinnati, Louisville, Newark, New York City, Paterson, San Francisco). In Chicago's general strike WPUS leaders Philip Van Patten, George Schilling, and Albert Parsons were arrested for their efforts to draw the spontaneous outburst into more organized channels. In St. Louis such WPUS stalwarts as Albert Currlin and Peter Lofgreen (who later assumed prominence as a writer under the name Laurence Gronlund) played a central role in a general strike that for a brief period put workers in control of that city, which was then dubbed by the newspapers as "the St. Louis Commune." The result was a flood of new members who were determined to help advance the struggle of labor against capital.

By 1877 a sharp political divided the WPUS. Some historians have emphasized a so-called Marxist vs. Lassallean conflict in the WPUS. Lassalle had rejected the value of trade union organizing (because the so-called iron law of wages would supposedly prevent working-class gains under capitalism), and called instead for the development of a socialist party that would vote capitalism out of existence. Marx insisted that trade union gains could be made and that such gains would provide experience, organization, and a power base for organizing a successful labor party. The use of "Marxist" and "Lassallean" labels, however, does not correspond to how the combatants actually identified the divisions. The split had little to do with views on the value of trade unionism but focused instead on whether socialists should also be engaging in socialist election campaigns.

In the autumn of 1877, the working-class ferment in many U.S. cities encouraged many WPUS sections to run candidates and rewarded them with amazingly high vote totals. In Louisville, the WPUS took 8,850 out of 13,578 votes cast, sending five out of seven candidates to the Kentucky state legislature. Vote totals in other cities: Chicago, 7,000; Cincinnati (where African American socialist Peter Clark ran ahead of the entire ticket) 9,000; Buffalo, 6,000; Milwaukee, 1,500; New York, 1,800; Brooklyn, 1,200; New haven, 1,600; and Detroit, 800. The rush to the ballot box, in contradiction to the WPUS founding documents, led to a split at the end of 1877. A substantial minority—including Friedrich Sorge, Otto Weydemeyer, Carl Speyer, J.P. McDonnell, Adolph Strasser, a young Samuel Gompers, and others—left the WPUS to concentrate on union organizing that began with the International Labor Union and eventually evolved into the American Federation of Labor. The majority renamed the WPUS the Socialistic Labor Party, later simply the Socialist Labor Party (SLP).

Socialist Labor Party

Despite its initial successes, the SLP failed to become a significant electoral force. This failure was accentuated by the counterattack from the two major capitalist parties, Democrats and Republicans (both of which projected themselves as the "true" party of labor). It proved especially difficult to compete successfully against another electoral alternative, the Greenback-Labor, whose platform called for monetary reforms, particularly the increase of paper currency to promote better circulation of money, which was conceived as a way to erode the power of financial business interests. In 1878, combining "greenbackism" with a variety of other reforms and strongly prolabor rhetoric, the Greenback-Labor Party polled more than a million votes nationwide and elected 14 congressmen.

The lure of this proved too strong for the SLP, which was led by its national secretary Phillip Van Patten, prominent German-American stalwart Adolph Douai, Peter J. McGuire, and others into the Greenback-Labor presidential campaign of 1880. General James B. Weaver, a Greenback congressman from Iowa, was the presidential candidate. The SLP unsuccessfully backed the eminent life-long U.S. socialist John F. Bray (whose writings were cited favorably in Marx's *Capital*) for the vice-presidential slot. The socialists' choice was rejected in favor of Texas radical B. J. Chambers, and their distinctive orientation was swamped in the welter of diverse reforms and panaceas. What's more, the wind was going out of the Greenbackers' sails and the national ticket received little more than 300,000 votes.

This led to another split in 1881, with more revolutionary elements bolting from the SLP to help create the anarchist-influenced International Working People's Association (IWPA), which tended toward a revolutionary antistatist interpretation of Marx's ideas more than toward traditional anarchist theory. The Chicago wing of this organization gained an especially large following and a foothold in the labor movement. IWPA's leaders were at the head of the massive movement for the eight-hour workday on the first May Day, in 1886, but shortly thereafter were victimized and falsely condemned for murder in the wake of the violent Haymarket Affair.

SLP membership dropped below 3000 by 1883, and its demoralized American-born national secretary, Van Patten, abandoned the party in the wake of a personal scandal. A rapid succession of national secretaries (all foreign-born) in the years that followed reflected the party's disarray, although some of its members maintained influence among the larger and more vital Knights of Labor and AFL. In 1886–87, in a major effort to establish its relevance on the U.S. political scene, the SLP allied with various trade union activists and labor reformers (particularly "single-tax" advocate Henry George) to run a United Labor Party campaign in various cities. Once again, substantial vote totals in some localities failed to bring victories, and the electoral alliances dissolved. By 1890, hindered by consequent drift and demoralization, the SLP fell under the sway of intellectual Daniel De Leon's rigid interpretation of Marxism, its pre-1890 history of "fusion and confusion" being rejected by most remaining party stalwarts. By 1901 some of the SLP's members had broken away to join the new Socialist Party of America, which bypassed the older organization.

Key Players

Clark, Peter H. (1829–1925): Grandson of William Clark of the Lewis and Clark expedition. Before the Civil War Clark was a prominent African American abolitionist and founding member of the Republican Party. He worked as a teacher and had been active in the National Labor Union and in efforts to establish consumer cooperatives. For several years a leading socialist in Cincinnati, he later gravitated to the Democratic Party.

Douai, Adolph (1819–1888): Douai moved to the U.S. after the defeat of the 1848 revolution in Germany. He became an antislavery activist and pioneer of the kindergarten movement, as well as a prominent writer and editor in the socialist movement.

Gompers, Samuel (1850–1924): Prominent in the Cigar Makers Union, Gompers became the long-time (1886–1924) and increasingly conservative president of the American Federation of Labor and a spokesman for the "pure and simple union" orientation that had been developed initially by his colleague Adolph Strasser. In his later years Gompers became an outright opponent of socialism (though he never lost his admiration for Karl Marx, whose outlook he viewed as consistent with his own "pure and simple" unionism).

Gronlund, Laurence (1846–1899): Under the name of Peter Lofgreen, Danish-born Gronlund (who worked at various times as a teacher, a clerk, and a journalist) was a leader of the St. Louis WPUS. He was later author of the first substantial popularization of Marxist ideas in the U.S., the 1884 classic *The Cooperative Commonwealth*. After drifting out of the SLP, he became a leading activist in the Nationalist Clubs initiated by Edward Bellamy, author of the best-selling utopian novel *Looking Backward*.

McDonnell, J. P. (1840–1906): An Irish revolutionary, ex-Fenian, and former secretary to Karl Marx in the First Inter-

national, McDonnell became prominent in socialist and labor politics upon his arrival in the U.S. in the 1870s. He remained editor of the *Labor Standard* after it disaffiliated from the WPUS, was prominent in various labor reform efforts, and became the leader of the New Jersey Federation of Trades and Labor Unions from its founding in 1883 until his death in 1906.

McGuire, Peter J. (1852–1906): An American-born worker whose initial involvement in socialist politics was as a member of the First International. McGuire left the SLP in the 1880s to become a founder and general secretary of the Brotherhood of Carpenters and Joiners and a founder of the AFL. He is often credited for being involved in the creation both of Labor Day (1882) and May Day (1886), although—as with Gompers—his socialist commitments faded with the passage of time.

Morgan, Thomas J. (1847–1912): A stalwart of Chicago socialism for three decades and leading activist in the Machinists union who later secured a law degree. Morgan became a leader of the strong socialist current in the AFL. In 1893 he submitted a political program for adoption by the AFL, calling for an independent labor party based on the unions plus "the collective ownership by the people of all means of production and distribution." The adoption of this platform was prevented only by the strenuous efforts of Samuel Gompers and his allies. Morgan continued to play an important role in the SLP until he left with others to help form the Socialist Party of America.

Parsons, Albert (1848–1887): Parsons was a Confederate war veteran in Texas who fell in love with and married a woman of color (Lucy Gonzales, at least partly African American, perhaps also Indian and Mexican). Parsons subsequently became a Radical Republican; with the collapse of Reconstruction in Texas, he fled with his wife to Chicago where they both become active in radical labor activities. Active in the Typographical Workers union, he was blacklisted after 1877 when he became a full-time labor and socialist activist. Editor of the revolutionary paper *The Alarm* in the 1880s, and a leader of the radical wing of the eight-hour movement, he was victimized as one of the Haymarket martyrs and executed in 1887.

Schilling, George (1850–1938): Initially a cooper by trade, active in socialist politics for many years, Schilling ran for mayor of Chicago on the SLP ticket in 1881. He was involved in the Knights of Labor, the eight-hour movement, and the Chicago Trades and Labor Assembly. He was prominent in the defense of the Haymarket defendants. In the 1890s he become an aide to Democratic Governor John Peter Altgeld (under whom he served as secretary of the Illinois Labor Department), and was active in Chicago's "single-tax" club.

Sorge, Friedrich (1827–1906): Sorge was a music teacher who emigrated to the United States after the defeat of the 1848 Revolution in Germany. He joined the Communist Club in New York City in 1858, engaged in an extensive correspondence with Marx and Engels, and became a central figure in the North American sections of the International Workingmen's Association (the First International). After its dissolution Sorge became a founder of the WPUS then left it to focus on helping to build the International Labor Union. In the 1890s he wrote a classic history, *Labor Movement in the United States*, which was serialized in the German Marxist journal *Neue Zeit*.

Strasser, Adolph (1851–1910): President of the Cigar Makers Union and a founder of the AFL, Strasser shifted sharply away from his socialist orientation in 1883 with the articulation of the "pure and simple" union orientation, which rejected "ultimate ends" in favor of "day-to-day" struggles to attain "immediate objects" (higher wages, a shorter workday, better working conditions) that can be realized in a few years. In later years he left the labor movement to enter the real estate business.

Weydemeyer, Otto: Son of Joseph Weydemeyer (a hero of the 1848 Revolution in Germany and of the Civil War in the U.S.), and like his father close to Karl Marx, Otto Weydemeyer was a leading member of the International Workingmen's Association (the First International). He was the first to translate into English portions of *Capital*, which was initially published as a series of articles in the *Labor Standard*, then as a pamphlet for U.S. workers.

See also: *American Federation of Labor; Eight-hour Day Movement; First International; Haymarket Riot; Socialist Party of America.*

BIBLIOGRAPHY

Books

Avrich, Paul. *The Haymarket Tragedy*. Princeton, NJ: Princeton University Press, 1984.

Buhle, Mary Jo. *Women and American Socialism, 1870–1920*. Urbana: University of Illinois Press, 1983.

Buhle, Mary Jo, Paul Buhle, and Dan Georgakas, eds. *Encyclopedia of the American Left*. Urbana: University of Illinois Press, 1992.

Commons, John R. et al. *History of Labor in the United States*, Vol. 2. New York: Macmillan, 1918.

De Leon, Solon, ed. *The American Labor Who's Who*. New York: Hanford Press, 1925.

Fine, Nathan. *Labor and Farmer Parties in the United States, 1828–1928*. New York: Rand School of Social Science, 1928.

Foner, Philip S. *The Great Labor Uprising of 1877*. New York: Monad Press, 1977.

———. *History of the Labor Movement in the United States*, Vol. 1. New York: International Publishers, 1947.

———. *The Workingmen's Party of the United States, A History of the First Marxist Party in the Americas*. Minneapolis: MEP Publications, 1984.

Girard, Frank, and Ben Perry. *The Socialist Labor Party 1876–1991, A Short History*. Philadelphia: Livra Books, 1991.

Hillquit, Morris. *History of Socialism in the United States*. New York: Funk and Wagnalls, 1910.

Johnpoll, Benard K., with Lillian Johnpoll. *The Impossible Dream: The Rise and Decline of the American Left*. Westport, CT: Greenwood Press, 1981.

Kaufman, Stuart Bruce. *Samuel Gompers and the Origins of the American Federation of Labor*. Westport, CT: Greenwood Press, 1973.

Marx, Eleanor, and Edward Aveling. *The Working-Class Movement in America*. Edited by Paul Le Blanc. Amherst, NY: Humanity Books, 2000.

McNeill, Lydia. "Peter Humphries Clark." In *Encyclopedia of African–American Culture and History*, Vol. 2. Edited by Jack Salzman, David Lionel Smith, and Cornell West. New York: Simon and Schulster/Macmillan, 1996.

Quint, Howard H. *The Forging of American Socialism*. Indianapolis, IN: Bobbs-Merrill Co., 1953.

Sorge, Friedrich A. *Labor Movement in the United States*. Edited by Philip S. Foner and Brewster Chamberlin. Westport, CT: Greenwood Press, 1977.

ADDITIONAL RESOURCES

Other
Labor Standard, 1876–1878 (on microfilm).
George A. Schilling Papers, Illinois State Historical Library.
Socialist Labor Party Papers (on microfilm).

—Paul Le Blanc

World Federation of Trade Unions

France 1945

Synopsis

A wave of popular internationalism and union self-confidence following the defeat of fascism in World War II led to the founding of the World Federation of Trade Unions (WFTU) in Paris in 1945. Other influencing factors arose from the interests of the allied nations. Although the All Union Central Council of Trade Unions (AUCCTU) was self-admittedly a "transmission belt" for the Soviet state, in the West there had been increasingly intense collaboration between the unions, industry, and the governments during the war. There was a definite assumption in the labor movement that the unions would play a role in economic reconstruction and in the establishment of liberal or social democracies in the liberated countries. There was a similarly widespread assumption that such national corporatism (the functional cooperation of labor, capital, and state in economic and political modernization) would be reflected in the new United Nations (1946). Even at the founding of the WFTU, however, there was evidence of traditional union divisions (communist v. social democratic, left v. right, political v. economic, nationalist v. internationalist, imperial v. colonial). Elements of the overlapping capitalist/communist bloc divide that led to the cold war split in international unionism just four years later were already present as well.

Vicente Lombardo Toledano. The Library of Congress.

Timeline

1925: In Tennessee, John T. Scopes is fined for teaching evolution in a public school. There follows a highly publicized trial at which famed attorney Clarence Darrow represents the defense, while the aging Democratic populist William Jennings Bryan argues for the state. The "Scopes Monkey Trial" symbolizes a widening divisions between rural and urban America, and though the court decides in favor of the state, it is clear that the historical tide is turning against the old agrarian order symbolized by Bryan—who dies during the trial.

1930: Collectivization of Soviet agriculture begins, and with it one of the greatest crimes of the twentieth century. In the next few years, as Soviet operatives force peasants to give up their lands, millions will die either by direct action, manmade famine, or forced labor. Overseas, however, and particularly among intellectuals and artists of the West, Soviet collectivization and industrialization are regarded as models of progress for the world.

1935: Second phase of New Deal begins with the introduction of social security, farm assistance, and housing and tax reform.

1940: Hitler's troops sweep through western Europe, annexing Norway and Denmark in April, and in May the Low Countries and France. At the same time, Stalin—who in this year arranges the murder of Trotsky in Mexico—takes advantage of the situation to add the Baltic republics (Latvia, Lithuania, and Estonia) to the Soviet empire, where they will remain for more than half a century.

1945: At the Yalta Conference in February, Roosevelt, Churchill, and Stalin make plans for Germany after its by now inevitable surrender.

1945: April sees the death of three leaders: Roosevelt passes away on 12 April; the Italians execute Mussolini and his mistress on 28 April; and Hitler (along with Eva Braun, propaganda minister Josef Goebbels, and Goebbels's family) commits suicide on 30 April.

1945: On 7 May, Germany surrenders to the Allied powers. Later in the summer, the new U.S. president, Harry Truman, joins Churchill and Stalin at Potsdam to discuss the reconstruction of Germany. (Churchill is replaced in mid-conference by Clement Attlee as Labour wins control of Parliament.)

1945: United States drops atomic bombs on the Japanese cities of Hiroshima and Nagasaki in early August, and a month later, on 2 September, Japan surrenders.

1945: Establishment of the United Nations on 24 October.

1950: U.S. Senator Joseph McCarthy launches his campaign to root out communist infiltrators.

1955: African and Asian nations meet at the Bandung Conference in Indonesia, inaugurating the "non-aligned" movement of Third World countries.

1960: Congo, along with several other African nations, becomes independent. But as the province of Katanga secedes, and pro-Soviet prime minister Patrice Lumumba disappears (he is later murdered), the country devolves into civil war. Soon UN troops will arrive to restore order.

Event and Its Context

Labor and Political Economy Background

Whereas labor had long been mobilized and incorporated into the Soviet state, the need for war production in the United Kingdom and the United States spurred recovery from the Great Depression and actually improved living conditions (rationing, fixed prices, full employment), raised working-class importance within the wartime culture, and drew new population sectors into the industrial working class (symbolized in the United States by the "Rosie the Riveter" recruiting poster for women workers). This intensified incorporation into the nation state was supplemented by involvement in "the good war" and notions of sympathy, identity, or solidarity with workers and nations abroad. In the occupied countries of Europe, wartime deprivation, brutal Nazi repression, and involvement in passive or active resistance movements similarly raised labor demands for economic advancement and even sociopolitical transformation. These movements often had a simultaneously national-democratic and internationalist character. In the colonial and semicolonial worlds of Africa, Asia, and Latin America, increased agricultural and industrial production, and the sometimes direct involvement in the war of workers (as second-class soldiers or merchant seamen), similarly raised nationalist (anticolonial, anti-imperialist) and internationalist consciousness among workers. The "workers in uniform" of the Allied powers often witnessed the misery of the occupied and colonized, which produced contradictory feelings of national or racial superiority and anticolonial sympathy. At the end of the war, British soldiers in Egypt, India, and elsewhere revealed themselves to be markedly prolabor. Demonstrations and (near) mutinies helped to undermine renewed British imperial ambitions and upper-class self-confidence.

Union Background

Between the two wars, the major national (European, American, Soviet) unions had had complex and frequently changing relations of cooperation and conflict. These were heavily marked by the formal split of the traditional union internationals brought about by World War I and the Russian Revolution of 1917. They were even more heavily influenced by the decision of the Soviet Union and its communist allies elsewhere to create a highly centralized Third International (Comintern) with a complete array of subordinate organizations, including the Red International of Labor Unions (RILU, or Profintern). The RILU made a major appeal to the colonized areas in Africa, Asia, and Latin America, thereby challenging widespread western union racism and collaboration with imperial states. Meanwhile, the western unions were increasingly incorporated into the International Labor Organization (ILO), a body for which they had originally fought but that the western states had then conceded precisely because of western labor unrest and the threat of the Soviet model. Cooperation between the communist and social-democratic (and other social-reformist unions internationally) was impeded by the centralized nature of the first and the pluralistic nature of the second.

Thus, the western unions were not only divided by national differences and rivalries (Europeans v. North Americans) but by the confederations of national union centers (such as the International Federation of Trade Unions, IFTU) versus those of the older and more grounded, industrially specific, confederations, the International Trade Secretariats (ITSs). In the West, different ideological traditions (e.g., socialist, religious) also militated against effective international union solidarity. The spread of fascism in the West further deprived international unionism of major national contingents (Germany, Italy, Spain, Austria, and then others).

The war-heightened class, democratic, and international consciousness led to renewed efforts for international and cross-ideological trade union unity. This was largely facilitated by the profound incorporation of the unions into the national economies and polities, combined with the wartime coalition of the Allies. Trade union leaders were not only involved at the highest public national levels. They were sometimes granted diplomatic roles in or were involved with clandestine military intelligence operations within Nazi-occupied Europe.

Directly following the Nazi attack on the Soviet Union, the British Trades Union Congress, with the collaboration of the British government, began negotiations to create an Anglo-Russian Trade Union Council (1941). In February 1945 London hosted a World Trade Union Conference, addressed to unions of the 38 United Nations, including the left-nationalist Confederación de Trabajadores de América Latina (CTAL). The new organization permitted attendance of more than one federation per country. The conservative American Federation of Labor (AFL) opposed this conference, while the progressive Congress of Industrial Organizations (CIO) supported it.

The founding congress of the World Federation of Trade Unions (WFTU) took place in Paris in October 1945. It was much inspired by both union and state notions of a new world order and was organized in the spirit of both the communist Popular Front and the U.S. New Deal; 346 delegates represented some 64 million unionists. Unions of the colonial and semicolonial countries were for the first time heavily represented at an international union conference. Foremost, perhaps, was the major continental confederation of this group of countries, the CTAL. The congress claimed to represent 90 percent of the world's unionists. It declared itself against every form of fascism, against war and its causes, for the right of self-determination, and against colonialism, discrimination, and racism. It favored the extension of union rights, the improvement of working and living conditions, and the limitation and liquidation of monopolies.

For both the CIO and the AUCCTU, the creation of the WFTU was a way to break out of their previous international isolation. The Trades Union Congress (TUC) had doubts, the AFL was opposed, and the ITSs were strongly resistant to being reduced to departments of the WFTU. The WFTU hoped to become a member of the UN General Assembly. Meanwhile, the new world order was turning into the cold war order. The breaking point came with the U.S. Marshall Plan offer to Europe, which the communists and other leftists saw as establishing U.S. economic hegemony over Europe and as a major anti-Soviet initiative. The Soviets had considerable power within the secretariat of WFTU through Louis Saillant, procommunist general secretary of the French Confédération Générale du Travail (CGT). The AFL was maneuvering on the fringes through Irving Brown, later revealed to be a major Central Intelligence Agency (CIA) collaborator in the international union movement. Cold war policies and ideology played back into the national unions, with both the TUC and the CIO moving away from the WFTU. By 1949 the international trade union movement was split on the lines of the cold war blocs and on the oppositions of communist and reformist ideology.

According to Tony Carew, "There was an irresistible wave of grass roots enthusiasm for a grand trade union alliance" but the tangible achievements of the WFTU and the approach of dealing exclusively with the labor movement through national centers failed to inspire the membership. The WFTU agenda became the concern of "a tiny elite of national leaders and officials" and as a result its demise passed almost unnoticed. "The essential weakness of the WFTU was that it failed . . . to develop a genuine trade union role."

This epitaph is true enough, even if the WFTU continues a shadow existence today, a decade or more after the collapse of the state socialism to which it subordinated itself.

Key Players

Citrine, Walter (1887–1983): Born into a Liverpool, England, working-class family, he became an electrical worker and a union and Independent Labour Party activist. He rose through the union ranks, becoming assistant general secretary (1924), then general secretary of the Trades Union Congress (1924–1946). He wrote extensively, including reports of official trips to Russia and Finland and two volumes of memoirs. His best-known work is his *ABC of Chairmanship*. He was continually involved in national-level industrial relations and held government and semi-governmental posts beginning in World War II. He was president of the International Federation of Trade Unions (1928–1945) and president of the WFTU (1945–1946). He became a peer in 1946 and served on the National Coal Board, the Electricity Council, the Atomic Energy Authority, and other boards.

Saillant, Louis (1910–1974): A furniture worker, Saillant became active as a socialist within the *Confédération Générale du Travail* in the 1930s; he was involved in street struggles and suffered beatings and imprisonment. An active member of the French underground during World War II, he was coresponsible for the reunification of the previously divided CGT. He was CGT's representative in the National Council of the Resistance, of which he became president. He also gained a seat in the Consultative Assembly that recreated the French Republic. He was general secretary of the WFTU, 1945–1969; though he resided in France, he remained active in the CGT when the WFTU moved to Czechoslovakia. He received a number of French state and communist awards. Although not a member of the Communist Party, he remained identified with communist unionism and Soviet communism until the Soviet invasion of Czechoslovakia in 1968, which he, along with the overwhelming majority of the WFTU secretariat, temporarily condemned.

Toledano, Vicente Lombardo (1894–1968): An almost-forgotten figure of international unionism, Toledano was the most prominent Marxist union leader and politician in the history of Mexico. He was possibly the most prominent "southern" unionist in the history of the international trade union movement. Toledano graduated in law in 1919, taught at his university, and received a Ph.D. from it in 1933. He simultaneously followed an extremely varied union, political, and journalistic career, and founded a Workers University that continues his tradition. He was early associated with the Mexican Regional Confederation of Trade Unions (CROM) and its political expression, the Mexican Labor Party (PLM). He was a parliamentary deputy in Congress (1926–1928) and later joined the Institutional Revolutionary Party (PRI). In the 1930s he moved to the left, eventually becoming general secretary of the Confederation of Workers of Mexico (CTM). He came to prominence under the reformist regime of Cardenas (1934–1940), a radical-nationalist variant on the Roosevelt regime in the United States. Toledano was founder and president of the radical CTAL (1938–1961). As such he had intense contacts with the CIO in the United States, which was prepared at one time to grant him some kind of sovereignty over Latin American unions. He had a prominent position within the International Labor Organization (1944), was present at the World Trade Union Conference in London (1945), and vice president of the WFTU (1945–1963). An independent Marxist, Toledano moved to the left as Mexico moved to the right after World War II, and thus lost political and union influence nationally and internationally.

See also: *American Federation of Labor; Confederación de Trabajadores de América Latina; Confédération Générale du Travail; Congress of Industrial Organizations; International Federation of Trade Unions; International Labor Organization; Red International of Labor Unions.*

BIBLIOGRAPHY

Books

Carew, Tony. "A False Dawn: The World Federation of Trade Unions." In *The International Confederation of Free Trade Unions*, edited by Marcel van der Linden. Bern, Switzerland: Peter Lang, 2000.

Lane, Thomas, ed. *Biographical Dictionary of European Labor Leaders*. 2 vols. Westport, CT: Greenwood, 2000.

McShane, Denis. *International Labour and the Origins of the Cold War*. Oxford: Oxford University Press, 1992.

Silverman, Victor. *Imagining Internationalism in American and British Labor, 1939–49*. Urbana: University of Illinois Press, 2000.

Weiler, Peter. *British Labour and the Cold War*. Stanford, CA: Stanford University Press, 1988.

Periodicals

Saville, Richard. "Politics and the Labour Movement in the Early Cold War." *Our History Journal*, no. 15 (1990): 27–35.

Other

Hyman, Richard. "The International Labor Movement on the Threshold of Two Centuries: Agitation, Organization, Bureaucracy, Diplomacy." London: Industrial Relations Department, London School of Economics, 2002.

Waterman, Peter. "Union Internationalism 1939–45: Limits of the Bureaucratic Corporatist Imagination." The Hague: Global Solidarity Dialogue, 2000.

—Peter Waterman

Protesters, World Trade Organization meeting, Seattle, Washington, 1999. © Getty Images. Reproduced by permission.

World Free Trade Conference Demonstrations

United States 1999

Synopsis

The World Trade Organization's week-long Third Ministerial meeting in Seattle, Washington, in November 1999 was the focus of protests by groups interested in a wide range of issues, including labor topics such as banning child labor and creating a global equitable minimum wage. International unions were most interested in drawing attention to the lack of worker rights. The event drew between 40,000 and 60,000 protesters from about 100 different nations and representing more than 700 organizations. Unusual alliances were forged during the event, including some between traditional foes such as environmental groups and union organizations. To date, it is still premature to label the event as either an uncharacteristic gathering spawned by millennial concerns or a significant demonstration of popular global concerns. The legacy of the Seattle demonstrations remains uncertain.

Timeline

1978: Terrorists kidnap and kill former Italian premier Aldo Moro. In Germany, after a failed hijacking on behalf of the Red Army Faction (RAF, better known as the Baader-Meinhof Gang), imprisoned RAF members commit suicide.

1984: Indian army occupies Sikh Golden Temple in Amritsar in June, and four months later, two Sikh bodyguards of Prime Minister Indira Gandhi assassinate her. Gandhi is succeeded by her son, Rajiv, who will later be assassinated himself.

1989: Tens of thousands of Chinese students rally for democracy in Beijing's Tiananmen Square. Protests go on for nearly two months, until government troops and tanks crush the uprising. Thousands are killed.

1992: Four Los Angeles police officers are acquitted in April on federal civil rights charges stemming from the 1991 beating of motorist Rodney King, an incident captured on videotape. Following the announcement of the verdict, Los Angeles erupts with rioting and looting.

1995: The Aum Shinrikyo cult causes a nerve-gas attack in a Tokyo subway, killing eight people and injuring thousands more.

Protesters, World Trade Organization meeting, Seattle, Washington, 1999. © Hulton/Getty Images. Reproduced by permission.

1999: Though the U.S. House of Representatives has voted along party lines in December to impeach President Bill Clinton on two charges—perjury and obstruction of justice—the vigor has gone out of the entire case by the time it reaches the Senate, which acquits him of all charges on 12 February.

1999: In March, NATO begins air strikes against Yugoslavia to stop Serb-led attacks on ethnic Albanians in the Kosovo region.

1999: School shootings have been in the U.S. news for several years, but no incident attracts as much attention—or results in as many deaths—as the massacre at Columbine High School in Littleton, Colorado, where two students kill 13 others before turning their guns on themselves. Later in the year, there are several other non-school shooting sprees, including one in Atlanta's Buckhead financial district that kills nine.

1999: A custody battle erupts around five-year-old Cuban refugee Elián González, whose father wants to take him back to Cuba. On 22 April of the following year, federal troops raid the home of his Miami relatives and reunite him with his father.

2000: Stock drop on 25 February marks the beginning of the end of several years' worth of prosperity, much of it buoyed by the boom in technology companies. By April, signs are clear that the boom is over.

2001: The Clinton administration ends with scandal and controversy, as Clinton issues a series of pardons, including ones for billionaire fugitive Marc Rich and a group of Puerto Rican terrorists.

2002: The U.S. economy, already suffering with the end of the technology boom in 2000 and the drop in stock prices following the 11 September terrorist attacks, is not helped by revelations of malfeasance on the part of corporate executives. Some of these former business leaders are led away from their offices in handcuffs, and huge corporations such as Enron and Worldcom are forced into bankruptcy as a result of illegal accounting practices.

_____

The Persistence of Slavery in 1999

The end of plantation slavery in the New World during the second half of the nineteenth century had seemed to mark the end of slave labor as an institution. Then, of course, the twentieth century brought the rebirth of slave labor in a grotesque new form through the totalitarian systems of Soviet Russia and Nazi Germany. Yet with the collapse of communism that began in 1989, it seemed possible once again to believe that a new day had dawned. As in the late nineteenth century, however, this optimism may have been premature, as a glance at several articles from 1999 illustrates.

In the *South China Morning Post* in August, Huw Watkin described the growth of sex slavery—in particular, prostitution and the selling of "mail-order brides"—in China and Southeast Asia. Just the previous week, reports had emerged that some 12,000 young Vietnamese women had "married" (the quotation marks were Watkin's) Taiwanese men between 1996 and 1998 with the help of intermediaries. Nearly half of the women, whose families received up to $12,000, said they agreed to be married off for economic reasons. According to a Vietnamese UNICEF representative, "False marriages and mail-order brides are often used as camouflage to bring women to work in overseas brothels, and the victims of this sort of trafficking find it difficult to argue in court that they are, in fact, victims."

Indian professor Vijay Prashad, writing in *Dollars and Sense* in September, cited the extensive use of child labor in countries of South Asia such as India and Pakistan—nations with which the United States and other Western governments had economic and political ties. Though President Bill Clinton had denounced child labor before the International Labor Organization in Geneva in June, Prashad maintained, the United States continued to support overseas companies that together employed some 250 million children under the age of 15.

Finally, the All Africa News Agency reported in December on perhaps the most astonishing phenomenon of all: the persistence of old-fashioned chattel slavery, in which people—specifically, black Africans—were literally bought and sold into lifetimes of service, just as Africans five centuries before had been. As part of the civil war in the Sudan, black villages were subjected to raids in which people were herded away into slavery. Many were subjected to forced conversion to Islam, as well as beatings, rape, and public execution, and those who survived were sold into slavery like Africans five centuries earlier.

Source: Huw Watkin, "Rise in Women Forced to Work as Sex Slaves," *South China Morning Post,* 11 August 1999; Vijay Prashad, "Calloused Consciences: The Limited Challenge to Child Labor," *Dollars and Sense,* September 1999, p. 21; All Africa News Agency, "Humanitarian Group Buys Freedom for 4,300 Sudanese," Africa News Service, 3 December 1999.

—Judson Knight

Event and Its Context

Background to the Meeting and Protests

The World Trade Organization (WTO) was chartered on 1 January 1995 as part of the Uruguay Round Agreements of the General Agreement on Tariffs and Trade (GATT). The WTO consists of 135 member states. Since its formation, the aims of the group were questioned by those who thought its members were grossly overstepping discussions of trade. They were not addressing basic labor issues. Rather than protecting citizens internationally, the organization appeared to be upholding corporate interests. As an example, nations attempting to ban imports from a particular country based on poor labor conditions could face WTO sanctions.

The Seattle conference was the third meeting of member states and global leaders. Well before the Seattle event, activists of various stripes had begun protesting outside other WTO summits as well as at meetings of other international political-economic groups including the G-7, International Monetary Fund, and Asia Pacific Economic Cooperation. These activists were associated with a potpourri of groups, including nongovernmental organizations, labor unions, students, religious groups, and anarchists, with a wide variety of viewpoints.

Because these groups had no singular common cause, the protest issues have not been consolidated around a single group of specific economic or related political issues. The concerns are diverse: ecology, human rights, genetically engineered foods, and debt relief for third-world nations. Some acknowledge that this fragmentation has its advantages in that organizations that wish to be involved need not sacrifice their core issues to participate.

One of the most unusual alliances to emerge was between labor and environmentalists. Although traditional enemies, these groups had worked together previously, for example to defeat international plans for the Multilateral Agreement on Investments. Discussions between labor and environmentalists had begun in 1997. The unions' primary concern was the desire for trade rules and sanctions designed to protect internationally recognized labor rights. This includes fundamental issues such as the right to organize and protection of worker rights, issues that united the AFL-CIO and global labor federations. Unlike environmentalists, labor interests do not want to eliminate the WTO, but they want these types of multinational political organizations to provide basic social justice across the globe.

There are several examples of these types of alliances being forged prior to Seattle. Steelworkers and Earth First!, for example, united against corporations such as Maxxam on issues related to logging. The Paper, Allied, Industrial, Chemical and Energy Workers and Oil, Chemical and Atomic Workers allied with environmentalist organizations such as Greenpeace and Friends of the Earth to fight major corporations in the oil and chemical industries. One organizer noted that some unions have attacked others, such as the Steelworkers, for engaging in dialogue with the environmentalists, as environmental regulations often result in job elimination. The United Mine Workers, for example, view reduction of carbon emissions as bringing about an end to coal mining and thus have worked to shape labor policy on climate change.

These issues also spurred the formation of groups such as Unions for Jobs and the Environment, whose members include unions such as the UMW, the United Food and Commercial Workers, and the Teamsters. Unions in other industrial nations—International Confederation of Free Trade Unions, the European Trade Union Confederation, and the Communications, Energy and Paperworkers of Canada—have also been interested in these issues.

Protesters Converge on Seattle

The WTO's Third Ministerial meeting convened in Seattle on 30 November 1999 at the Seattle Convention Center. The week-long protest in Seattle brought together groups interested in labor rights, environmental protection, and other issues germane to the global economy. Labor issues of concern included the elimination of child labor and initiating an equitable minimum wage. The protests attracted, by various estimates, between 40,000 and 60,000 people. They represented more than 700 organizations. Protesters were from the United States and about 100 other nations.

The whole idea behind these demonstrations was to inject other views and voices into the political and corporate discussions about the global economy. The international unions were most interested in drawing attention to the lack of worker rights. They contended that so-called free trade agreements such as the North American Free Trade Agreement (NAFTA) created rules designed to protect the interests of corporations but not of workers and citizens. Author and environmentalist Paul Hawken called the Seattle demonstrations "the most striking expression of citizens struggling against a worldwide corporate-financed oligarchy." Some contended that organizations like the WTO and its member nations wanted to create a blueprint for global capitalism that catered to corporate rights at the peril of human rights and healthy communities.

During the Seattle protests, the AFL-CIO and other unions were part of a coalition including environmentalists, labor groups, religious organizations, and consumer groups. *Time* magazine characterized Seattle as particularly well chosen for the protest, saying the Pacific Northwest city, "with its unionist past, grungy youth-culture present, and ever-Green future, is an anarchist hotbed."

Demonstrations were organized using new technologies such as e-mail, the Internet, and cellular telephones. The Direct Action Network served in a coordinating capacity to bring together diverse groups such as the Ruckus Society, Third World Network, and the Rainforest Action Network. Hawken called protestors "organized, educated, and determined" and stated that they were "human rights activists, labor activists, indigenous people, people of faith, steel workers, and farmers. They were forest activists, environmentalists, social justice workers, students, and teachers. And they wanted the World Trade Organization to listen." The ground rules: no violence, no weapons, and no drugs or alcohol.

Those in the Seattle streets the last week of November met law enforcement agents clad in riot-gear and carrying tear gas and pepper spray, even rubber bullets. In addition to the Seattle Police Department, the United States Secret Service, the FBI, and the Central Intelligence Agency were also reportedly on hand. Some protestors blocked a pre-convention cocktail reception on 29 November as well as the convention center on the morning of 30 November before police arrived. A group of 2,000 people started marching to the convention center at 7 A.M. to block traffic. Cordons of law enforcement attempted to prevent more protestors from blocking entrances to the meeting area.

Police and protestors alike had also staked out the Paramount Theater, site of a planned opening meeting. Police blocked the theater with city buses. Protestors gathered outside the bus corral. Reportedly only few of the 5,000 official WTO delegates, and none of the scheduled speakers, were able to enter.

As the initial events of the meeting were coming to a halt, Direct Action Network organizers continued to coordinate groups throughout downtown Seattle to prevent WTO delegates from moving about the city. The network mobilized about 10,000 people who were divided into groups with various functions. There were several designated as being willing to be arrested. As groups were hit with pepper spray, others moved in to take their place. During this same period, a labor march took place apart from the Direct Action rally. Some of the labor marchers joined the other demonstrators near the convention center.

Later in the day on 30 November, the U.S. government threatened to cancel the meeting if downtown Seattle were not secured. Local officials responded by calling a curfew and establishing "no protest" zones. Seattle was declared under civil emergency. An estimated 1,500 protestors remained downtown. At nightfall, frustrated police used tear gas against residents and protestors without discrimination. The authorities called in the National Guard to help. Anarchists and locals intent on vandalism entered downtown after dark. The organized anarchists attacked specific multinational businesses identified for their track record on specific issues. These included Fidelity Investments, Starbucks, and The Gap. The anarchist group comprised a fraction of those participating, but their actions attracted most of the media coverage.

The protests continued through the week as the WTO attempted to resume its meetings. Late on 4 December, the meeting was suspended. Another labor-led march took place as the meeting closed.

Aftermath

Even years after the WTO meeting in Seattle, it remains unclear whether this event was an uncharacteristic gathering spawned by millennial concerns or a significant demonstration of popular global concerns. This issue and its impacts on history and society both are still being debated.

Immediately after the Seattle meetings, pundits were mixed on the effectiveness of the protests. Some said that global trade politics would be forever altered even while decrying the attendant property damage. There were, as author Naomi Klein pointed out in *The Nation*, serious problems with the perceptions of the protestors "as tree-wearing, lamb-costumed, drum-beating bubble brains." Complicating the continuity of the movement was the lack of central organization needed to conduct follow-up protests. "This is the flip side of the persistent criticism that the kids on the street lack clear leadership—they lack clear followers too," stated Klein.

Despite this disorganization and the seeming lack of ideological cohesion, "The victory in Seattle has emboldened labor, environmental, and other anti-WTO forces to redouble their efforts," according to a *Business Week* article published in December 1999. Among the post-Seattle protests in which labor groups such as the AFL-CIO participated were an antisweatshop vigil in Manhattan and attempts to block China's membership in the WTO.

Other issues besides the demonstrations hampered meaningful progress in the WTO meeting. Observers contend that the novelty of the WTO plus the large numbers of participants in the talks are two major impediments to progress. The issues involved are also too complex to discuss thoroughly in a few days' time.

Business Week also observed that the Seattle debacle convinced some policymakers and business leaders that the public may be wary of globalization and the changes that attend it and reported that David L. Aaron, United States undersecretary of commerce, stated, "A lot of people have the sense that global corporations can't be controlled, that we have lost our cities and towns to chain stores that are the same everywhere, and that we have lost the guarantee of a job and security for life." The impact of this observation may be evident in President Bill Clinton's statement to the press that he wanted enforceable labor standards as a condition of free trade. Clinton's comments angered WTO members as well as international business leaders. Labor and environmental issues continue unresolved.

As Klein noted, this type of popular uprising is not likely to catch the establishment unprepared in the future. Law enforcement across the United States and other nations have now subscribed to e-mail lists in which these types of protests might be publicized. Some police departments have made sizeable investments in equipment and training to protect their cities against such protests.

David Moberg, writing in *The Nation*, observed that if the unlikely coalitions between unions and environmentalists are sustained, "it's ultimately an issue of labor and environment together, the people against the corporations."

Key Players

Barshefsky, Charlene (1950–): United States trade representative who was cochair of the WTO meeting in Seattle. She was to have given the opening address in Seattle but was reportedly unable to get out of her hotel a block from the convention center.

Becker, George: President of the United Steelworkers of America at the time of the Seattle WTO summit.

Chavez-Thompson, Linda (1944–): Born in Lubbock, Texas, Chavez-Thompson was executive vice president of the AFL-CIO at the time of the Seattle protests. Chavez-Thompson is the first person of color to serve on the union's executive council. She began her union career in the Laborers' International Union and the American Federation of State, County and Municipal Employees (AFSCME), AFL-CIO. She has been the national vice president of the Labor Council for Latin American Advancement, AFL-CIO, since 1986.

Dolan, Mike: Principal Seattle protest organizer.

Hyde, David: Student leader of the Seattle protests.

Nova, Scott: Director, Citizens Trade Campaign.

Roddick, Anita (1942–): Chief executive officer and founder of the Body Shop, a United Kingdom–based company noted for its progressive policies. Roddick was reportedly on the streets during the WTO meeting, assisting protestors who had been injured by police pepper spray.

Schell, Paul (1937–): Seattle mayor during the WTO protests.

Sweeney, John J. (1934–): President of the AFL-CIO at the time of the Seattle trade talks.

Wallach, Lori M.: Trade lawyer and director of Public Citizen's Global Trade Watch. She founded the Citizens Trade Campaign and is also a member of the International Forum on Globalization.

Yokich, Stephen P. (1935–): Born in Detroit, Michigan, Yokich was UAW president at the time of the Seattle protests. A third-generation UAW member, he reportedly participated in his first strike at 22 months of age when he walked a picket line with his mother. He served in the United States Air Force and was a tool-and-die worker, which is when he became active in the UAW.

See also: *North American Free Trade Agreement.*

BIBLIOGRAPHY

Books

Wallach, Lori, and Michelle Sforza. *The WTO: Five Years of Reasons to Resist Corporate Globalization.* New York: Seven Stories Press, 1999.

Periodicals

Butkiewicz, Jerry. "WTO's Seattle Summit Reveals New Age of Activism." *San Diego Business Journal* 21, no. 8 (21 February 2000): 51.

"Free Trade Needs a Nod from Labor." *Business Week,* 22 November 1999, p. 150.

Hawken, Paul. "Journal of the Uninvited N30." *Whole Earth* (spring 2000): 28.

Klein, Naomi. "The Vision Thing: Were the DC and Seattle Protests Unfocused, or are Critics Missing the Point?" *The Nation,* 10 July 2000, p. 18.

Krantz, Michael. "How Organized Anarchists Led Seattle into Chaos." *Time,* 13 December 1999, p. 38.

Malone, Scott. "Marchers Rail Against Sweatshops, Child Labor." *Women's Wear Dailey,* (10 December 1999): 20.

Moberg, David. "For Unions, Green's Not Easy." *The Nation,* 21 February 2000, p. 17.

"The New Radicals: Seattle Wasn't Exactly the '60s, but, Along with the Tear Gas, There is a Whiff of a Very '90s Radicalism in the Air. Behind the New Face of Protest." *Newsweek,* 13 December 1999, p. 36.

"The Seattle Protestors Got it Right." *Business Week,* 20 December 1999, p. 25.

Weissman, Robert. "Democracy Is in the Streets." *Multinational Monitor* 20, no. 12 (December 1999): 24.

"What Really Sabotaged the Seattle Trade Talks." *Business Week,* 7 February 2000, p. 26.

"Whose World is it, Anyway?" *Business Week*, 20 December 1999, p. 40.

—Linda Dailey Paulson

World War II Labor Measures

United States 1941–1945

Synopsis

The political economy of wartime is unlike any other economic cycle. Raw materials, money, production and shipping capacity, agricultural goods, management skills, and labor are consumed by the war, and the home front must be adequately supplied and protected from destructive inflation. Extensive government intervention is required to deploy resources in the national interest. World War II was an extraordinary series of events marked, more than anything else, by change. United States involvement varied in form and intensity during the war. President Franklin Delano Roosevelt's administration set up several wartime agencies to meet shifting military and civilian strategic needs. As employment rose from 44,482,000 in 1938 to a wartime peak of 65,370,000 in 1944, Roosevelt created the National War Labor Board (NWLB) to facilitate labor's war effort. The NWLB modified the impact of industrial disputes; it controlled wages, which, in turn, checked inflation and slowed the wasteful turnover of workers; it helped coordinate national war mobilization; and it created publicly acceptable outlets for industrial demands.

Timeline

1921: As the Allied Reparations Commission calls for payments of 132 billion gold marks, inflation in Germany begins to climb.

1925: Released from Landsberg Prison, Adolf Hitler is a national celebrity, widely regarded as an emerging statesman who offers genuine solutions to Germany's problems. This year, he publishes the first volume of *Mein Kampf* (My Struggle), which he dictated in prison to trusted confederate Rudolf Hess. The second and final volume of Hitler's opus, a mixture of autobiography, "history," and racial rant, will appear two years later.

1931: Financial crisis widens in the United States and Europe, which reel from bank failures and climbing unemployment levels. In London, armies of the unemployed riot.

1936: The election of a leftist Popular Front government in Spain in February precipitates an uprising by rightists under the leadership of Francisco Franco. Over the next three years, war will rage between the Loyalists and Franco's Nationalists. The Spanish Civil War will prove to be a lightning rod for the world's tensions, with the Nazis and fascists supporting the Nationalists, and the Soviets the Loyalists.

Franklin Delano Roosevelt. The Library of Congress.

1941: The United States initiates the Manhattan Project to build an atomic bomb and signs the Lend-Lease Act, whereby it provides aid to Great Britain and, later, the Soviet Union.

1942: By executive order of the U.S. president, some 120,000 Japanese Americans are placed in West Coast internment camps.

1943: To offset the costs of war, the U.S. government introduces income tax withholding—which it claims to be a temporary measure.

1944: Creation of International Monetary Fund and World Bank at Bretton Woods Conference.

1945: At the Yalta Conference in February, Roosevelt, Churchill, and Stalin make plans for Germany after its by now inevitable surrender.

1950: United States begins developing the hydrogen bomb.

1955: Over the course of the year, a number of key items are added to the pantheon of American culture: the 1955 Chevrolet, the first of many classic models; Tennessee Williams's *Cat on a Hot Tin Roof*; Marilyn Monroe's performance in *The Seven-Year Itch*; Disneyland; and Bill Haley and the Comets' "Rock Around the Clock."

1961: U.S. President Eisenhower steps down, warning of a "military-industrial complex" in his farewell speech, and 43-year-old John F. Kennedy becomes the youngest elected president in U.S. history. Three months later, he launches an unsuccessful invasion of Cuba at the Bay of Pigs.

Event and Its Context

World War II came relatively slowly to the United States and was met by attitudes framed during New Deal management of the Great Depression. Powerful antistate interests decried the growth of government regulation and intervention. Influential liberals had worked hard to modify business's influence on the national economy. War mobilization depended on both big business and big government but, even more, it depended on the national workforce. Roosevelt used all his political skill to create a working consensus between all three. A mixture of government subsidies, low-cost loans, tax breaks, commercial freedom, and guaranteed profits encouraged business, but massive mobilization, both for military and war production purposes, destabilized workers in the predominantly antilabor business milieu. Hoping to avert the danger of ongoing dispute, Roosevelt made two great adjustments to the wartime labor market. He created the National War Labor Board (NWLB) to mediate and arbitrate in disputes that interfered with the war effort, and he used wage controls to stabilize the workforce. These measures brought organized labor into a policy-making relationship with government and business.

The United States in Neutrality

Although President Roosevelt proclaimed a limited national emergency on 8 September 1939 (five days after Britain and France declared war on Germany) and an unlimited national emergency on 27 May 1941, it was not until the Japanese attacked Pearl Harbor that the United States embraced all-out war. Before the 7 December air raid, union leaders (among others) resisted active war, fearing it would erode the improved working conditions and union rights that had been hard-won and hard-kept through the 1930s. However, as the war progressed, their attitudes changed. Philip Murray had replaced John L. Lewis as head of the Congress of Industrial Organizations (CIO), and his experience on Pennsylvania's Regional Labor Board in World War I led him to seek an institutional role for labor in the war effort. William Green, president of the American Federation of Labor (AFL), agreed with him and, although they did not always see eye to eye, together they encouraged Roosevelt's often-stated commitment to preserve labor conditions.

Lend-lease agreements with the United Kingdom, the Soviet Union, and other Western allies intensified the problems of earlier industrial mobilization. The vast numbers of workers recruited into war-related industries were frequently mobile, previously unemployed, young, and inexperienced: a volatile mix. War industries such as aircraft production were also young, and the war's demand for more units and improved designs pressured the inadequate facilities and unavailable or unsuitable labor. Erratic working conditions deteriorated under inexperienced leaders. Manufacturers seemed to be raking in easy prof-

William Green. The Library of Congress.

its, paid for by labor, and workers wanted a larger share. Their agitation was fuelled by the belief that war contracts would not continue beyond the immediate future and that when they were finished, mass unemployment, which still afflicted 15 percent of the workforce in 1940, would return. Unanticipated changes in War Department requirements exacerbated the situation. Large plants hoarded workers in the hopes of winning lucrative contracts or discarded them as war needs veered wildly from one commodity to another. Enterprises such as automotive firms achieved notoriety by making record sales of civilian goods while falling behind in defense production. Many people became convinced that war production was less urgent than the government claimed. It is not surprising that workers could not see the overall shortage of labor that lay just over the horizon. Even the War Department, dipping into the seemingly bottomless pool of unemployed workers, still denied the need for a concerted labor procurement program.

In June 1940 Roosevelt pledged that the United States would rearm itself and become the "arsenal of democracy," but labor disputes at significant war-supply plants showed that sectional interests could undermine his aims. Thus, starting in mid-1940, labor-management relations were identified as a significant political arena requiring state intervention. Seeking a compromise position that would not set disputes rolling throughout industry, the National Defense Advisory Commission promised in August 1940 that it would require defense contractors to comply with the full raft of state and local labor laws. Several influential contractors ignored these requirements, and strikes, disputes, and slowdowns marked the winter of 1940–1941,

Removed by the Seat of His Pants

One of the more memorable photographs from the U.S. home front during World War II depicted soldiers physically carrying Montgomery Ward president Sewell Avery from his offices in Chicago. At that time Ward's, which finally closed its doors in 2001 after 129 years of business, was a major retail outlet, and Avery's defiance of National War Labor Board directives was a thorn in President Roosevelt's side.

Avery had been an outspoken opponent of FDR since the earliest days of the New Deal, and neither patriotism nor wartime pressures—nor even the company's inflated profits, a result of increased government spending during the war—did anything to dampen this animosity. By defying the NWLB rulings on enforcement of a closed shop and higher wages for union workers, Avery eventually pushed Roosevelt to take the extreme step of sending in the army. The result, in April 1944, was Avery's removal—quite literally, by the seat of his pants—from Montgomery Ward offices in Chicago.

Even after this, Avery remained fervent in his opposition to the Roosevelt administration. Finally, at Christmastime in 1944, something even more unusual than his forced removal occurred: Roosevelt ordered the army to take over operation of seven Montgomery Ward stores. Only with the end of the war did these return to private operation.

Source: "Montgomery Ward vs. the NWLB." *Boss of the Waterfront: Wayne Morse and Labor Arbitration.* http://libweb.uoregon.edu/speccoll/mss/morse/Panel-5Extra.html.

—Judson Knight

drawing accusations from government bodies and the public that strikers were sabotaging the war effort. The National Labor Relations Board (NLRB) and the Department of Labor Conciliation Service, the two federal bodies dedicated to controlling industrial unrest, could not control the mix of bad management and worker resentment in war production plants and mines.

Spring 1941 brought the war closer to the United States as German submarines began to haunt North Atlantic shipping lanes. Desperate to increase the rate of mobilization while defusing industrial discord and protecting labor rights, Roosevelt created the National Defense Mediation Board (NDMB; Executive Order 8716, 19 March 1941), a federal government, business, and labor combination, to mediate disputes that Secretary of Labor Frances Perkins believed threatened national defense. The board's strength was that it could hear evidence from all sides of industrial disputes, but it was weakened by the dual union situation and by the fact that union representatives tended to be officials rather than elected leaders. This undermined their authority even among their own members. In a situation so grave that Roosevelt declared a state of unlimited national emergency on 27 May 1941, the board's most significant weakness was that its deliberations could lead only to recommendations.

Establishment of NWLB

The Japanese attack on Pearl Harbor jolted the nation. America was in the war. A few days later, fearing that Congress might legislate unpalatable labor control, Roosevelt called a national conference of union, employer, and government representatives. There, the unions pledged "no strikes," the management pledged "no lock-outs," and all agreed that disputes should be settled by peaceful mediation backed up by a Mediation Board with teeth. Roosevelt converted the NDMB into the NWLB, comprising four representatives (chosen by the president) from each of the three sectors, and extended its mediation role to conciliation and arbitration in labor disputes that might interrupt "the effective prosecution of the war." The board, under Chairman Lloyd K. Garrison, sought to meet this aim by institutionalizing preexisting employer-union relationships. When a dispute appeared troublesome, the board, participating as a third-party, assisted in the initial workplace collective bargaining. If that failed and the U.S. Conciliation Service could not help, the board formally heard the case and arbitrated a settlement. The board's decisions were enforced not by the courts but by the president. The major sanction was public opinion, but later in the war, in extreme cases of noncompliance, the Labor Disputes Act of 25 June 1943 authorized the president to seize a recalcitrant employer's plant or sequester funds and cancel union preference deals to discipline a union. The NWLB, empowered to deal only with *organized* labor, encouraged union membership—which grew from 10.5 million in December 1941 to nearly 15 million by war's end—and supported the War Production Board in its demand that employers accept unions or be denied government contracts.

Initially, the board operated in Washington, D.C., receiving only advice from regional offices, but in January 1943 the 12 regional offices became Regional War Labor Boards, exercising considerable autonomy in resolving local disputes. In addition, the NWLB established several special tripartite industry bodies to deal on a national level with particular industries and sectional interests. Its extensive structure allowed the NWLB to settle nearly 20,000 wartime disputes affecting about 12 million workers and approve about 415,000 wage agreements.

The War Manpower Commission

Acquisition officers distributed contracts and situated defense works in areas where industrial workers were already concentrated. Thus by 1942 densely industrialized districts were suffering serious labor scarcity while some regions experienced continued local unemployment. Roosevelt's resolve to maintain a free labor market weakened. Deciding that available labor should be allocated according to centrally determined priorities rather than by the free competition of employers, the president created the War Manpower Commission (WMC; EO 9139) in April. Paul McNutt, the Federal Security Administrator, chaired the commission, which comprised representatives from the Departments of War, Agriculture, Labor, and Navy, the Federal Security Agency, the War Production Board, Selective Service System, and Civil Service Commission. Despite McNutt's mixed industrial reputation, his belief that a free labor market was fundamental to the capitalist system and American democracy encouraged management and both Green and Murray to support his appointment.

By the end of 1942, the commission had created several committees responsible for particular groups of workers and specialized workforce training. Notable among them was the Management-Labor Policy Committee (MLPC), an advisory body established in May 1942. Unlike the WMC, the MLPC included representatives of both labor and management. McNutt relied heavily on its recommendations when trying to increase mobilization without sparking further industrial dispute. Another significant WMC body was the Women's Advisory Committee, established in August 1942 under the chair of Margaret A. Hickey, to advise on all matters specific to women and children under 18 years old doing war work.

The commission was doomed to only partial success. Responsible for mediating labor-management relationships and supervising the military Selective Service System, it was enormously influential but, despite periodic reorganization, it remained powerless to set military recruitment rates or civilian employment priorities.

Wartime Wage Adjustments

Wage control was an important aspect of business-labor mediation. Although wage increases were frequently negotiated as resolutions to labor disputes, the NWLB attempted to control inflation by limiting wage rises. It established four principles. Wages could be raised only to meet the cost of living, to correct inequities and inequalities, to raise substandard rates, and to aid the war. Government intervention in wage rates in general, rather than in specific cases, offended workers at several levels, not least because they occurred when, at last, industrial conditions favored high wages. Management was willing to pay rather than risk industrial dispute and could shift the expense to the government under the cost-plus-expenses guarantees of their contracts.

General wage adjustments were instituted for two predominant reasons. First, having voluntarily agreed not to strike during the war, the unions were forced to turn to the NWLB for wage revision. Second, as production capacity expanded and war contractors found themselves desperate for labor, wage competition encouraged turnover. Piracy, or the practice of poaching workers from other plants by offering higher wages, became common, frequently disrupting production. Further, many pirated workers were hoarded (even when not engaged in essential work) with the hope that contracts would come. This uncoordinated recruitment aggravated problems associated with inadequate housing, transport, and even food and clothing supplies in the receiving areas. These conditions were particularly hard for workers to understand in an environment in which late conversion to war work produced visible pockets of localized unemployment even in 1942.

Many officials, equating labor peace with productivity, preferred to blame the overall labor shortfall on labor's behavior. Absenteeism and turnover rates were exaggerated in media reporting, and this, combined with the inflation surge of early 1942, made Congress even more anxious about wage increases. Roosevelt was increasingly pressured to freeze wages. He set up the Wage Adjustment Board in May 1942. Composed of representatives of federal contracting agencies and labor unions, it

administered the wage stabilization agreement of 22 May 1942, which froze some government wage rates at July 1942 levels. Public and union members of the NWLB were sympathetic to wage demands but were also aware that wage rises added to inflationary pressure. The board tried to contain wage rates through the "Little Steel Formula," a wage stabilization agreement that arose out of attempts to revise pay scales at smaller steel-works. This formula, which combined preexisting norms with cost-of-living compensation, slowed inflationary wage creep but it could not control labor piracy, absenteeism, rapid turnover, or social troubles. Furthermore, unionists resented it because it kept wages well behind cost-of-living rises and some of its provisions were both hard to define and unevenly applied. By the Stabilization Act of 2 October 1942, Congress directed the president to stabilize the economy by freezing wages and prices at 15 September levels (plus inflation). This put wage adjustments under direct government control. Roosevelt responded with a limited extension of the NWLB's authority to stabilize wages and salaries.

Strikes and labor shortages greeted 1943, and Roosevelt's management of the tripartite production partnership faltered. Secretary of Labor Perkins did not believe that wages encouraged worker turnover, but significant labor mandarins such as McNutt and James Francis Byrnes argued that varying wage rates did indeed cause workers to change jobs. Roosevelt concurred and moved to "hold the line" by freezing wages and prices and authorizing McNutt to freeze labor movement. Beginning with Executive Order 9238 of 8 April 1943, the president made several largely unsuccessful attempts to ease worker agitation and end piracy by wage stabilization. The Wage Stabilization Division of the NWLB was to process all requests for wage readjustment, remove wage anomalies, and raise unacceptably low wages. By June 1943 the board had abandoned the Little Steel Formula in favor of the "bracket principle." This method, which recognized the prevailing occupational rates in specific labor market areas, had two main advantages: it automatically avoided gross wage anomalies, and its simplicity allowed for speedy processing of new and old disputes and requests. Wage stabilization remained so unpopular that some union leaders resigned from government committees.

In early May coal miners, whose conditions and wages were deplorable, began another highly publicized strike. National opinion polarized. On 27 May, Roosevelt returned mobilization control to the president by creating the Office of War Mobilization under Byrnes, his right-hand man.

The president moved just too late. Overriding his energetic veto, Congress—with military support—easily passed the War Labor Disputes (Smith-Connally) Act on 25 June 1943. This act modified the NLRB, severely curtailing unions' right to strike and greatly increasing state powers of intervention. In the next two years, the army occupied at least 25 strike-bound plants.

Transfer to Peace

On 19 September 1945 the NWLB was transferred to the Department of Labor. It was terminated in December by the same Executive Order (9672) that created the National Wage Stabilization Board, which, for the next year, maintained the NWLB's role in the settling of wages and salaries and carried on a much-limited dispute arbitration role.

TABLE 1

Work Stoppages in the United States, 1940-45

Year	Number	Average duration (days)	Workers involved (thousands)
1940	2,508	20.9	577
1941	4,288	18.3	2,360
1942	2,968	11.7	840
1943	3,752	5.0	1,980
1944	4,956	5.6	2,120
1945	4,750	9.9	3,470

SOURCE: United States Department of Labor Handbook of Labor Statistics, Washington, D.C.

Conclusion

Assessment of the NWLB's achievements are mixed. Strike action diminished in 1942, but the reduction can be attributed to simple patriotism. In the months between Pearl Harbor and the turning of the Pacific War at battles such as Coral Sea and Midway, even the most persuasive isolationists were quieted, if not silenced. The United States was in palpable danger. Committed also to the war in North Africa and Europe, the entire nation was called to the war effort, and every aspect of life was touched by new or augmented government powers. Nowhere were those powers more evident than at work, where workers were initially restrained. However, disorganized mobilization, directed by commercial interests rather than nationally determined priorities, unsettled workers who felt entitled to demand a fair share of what they saw as a temporary bonanza. The fact that strikes increased after the sudden slow-down of 1942 indicates that a significant number of workers believed that Roosevelt's measures were insufficient to protect their interests. After the war, Garrison reported to the president that the board had settled 17,807 disputes involving 12,300,000 employees and had received 415,000 applications for wage adjustment involving 26,300,000 employees. This achievement clearly reduced the disruptive potential of industrial strife. It is important to note that, although 1943 saw a dramatic rise in the number of strikes, only a remarkably low 0.15 percent of available man hours were lost. Strike rates remained high until the end of the war, but strike duration was usually fleeting.

The NWLB's major achievement was that it institutionalized industrial disputes and dictated the rules by which they should be fought. It regulated labor dissent into state-managed pathways and created in the American mind a concept of what became known as "responsible unionism." Although union membership grew by about two-thirds during the war (combined membership of the AFL and CIO was about 15 million by August 1945), it was membership in a state-approved style of unionism. In addition, the NWLB ensured that wartime disputes are remembered as a criticism of labor rather than as a criticism of management or employers.

Key Players

Byrnes, James Francis (1882–1972): Born in Charleston, South Carolina, Byrnes was a journalist and lawyer. He served in all three branches of the federal government. In 1942 he resigned his position as associate justice of the Supreme Court to become director of the Office of Economic Stabilization, where he wielded more power than any other public official and earned the sobriquet "assistant president." As war organization expanded, Byrnes directed the Office of War Mobilization (1943–1944) and the Office of War Mobilization and Reconversion (1944–1945). His assiduous checking of war spending saved the country as much as $15 billion.

Garrison, Lloyd Kirkham (1897–1991): A Harvard law graduate who, turning to public service, was appointed first chairman of the old National Labor Relations Board in 1934 and helped start the National War Labor Board (NWLB) while serving as dean of the University of Wisconsin Law School. He is best remembered for his groundbreaking defense of civil rights and the environment, particularly the preservation of Storm King Mountain on the Hudson River.

Green, William (1870–1952): Born in Coshocton, Ohio, Green was a coal miner for 20 years then entered labor politics through leadership positions in the United Mine Workers of America (of which he was a founding member) and AFL, in which he succeeded Samuel Gompers as president in 1924. He served in the Ohio senate for 28 years and edited the *American Federationist*. His argument with Lewis over craft unionism versus industrial unionism led Lewis to split the AFL and found the CIO.

Hickey, Margaret Anne (1902–1994): A journalist and lawyer born in Kansas City, Missouri, Hickey became sympathetic to women's problems. Her community service and government advisory work during the depression introduced her to Perkins, who recommended her for appointment to the Women's Advisory Committee, set up to assist in bringing about five million women into the wartime workforce.

McNutt, Paul V. (1891–1955): Born in Franklin, Indiana, McNutt became law professor, governor of Indiana, and U.S. high commander of the Philippines before being appointed federal security administrator in 1939.

Murray, Philip (1886–1952): A Scottish immigrant to western Pennsylvania, Murray rose to leadership in mining and steel unions and served on Pennsylvania's Regional Labor Board in World War I. He replaced Lewis as head of the CIO in 1940.

Perkins, Frances (1882–1965): Born in Boston, Massachusetts, Perkins graduated from the University of Pennsylvania and Columbia University. A social reformer who was active in labor politics, she became the first female member of cabinet when Roosevelt appointed her secretary of labor in 1933.

Roosevelt, Franklin Delano (1882–1945): Born in Hyde Park, New York, Roosevelt graduated from Harvard University and Columbia Law School. Entering politics as a Democrat, Roosevelt became the 32nd president, serving a record four terms. Elected first in 1932, Roosevelt encouraged

Congress to enact sweeping reform and relief measures that ameliorated the effects of the Great Depression. As a war president, Roosevelt used all his wily political skills to hold a huge and diverse nation in a loose war-winning consensus. He died before tasting the victory that was only a few weeks away.

See also: *No-strike Pledge, World War II.*

BIBLIOGRAPHY

Books

Atleson, James B. *Labor and the Wartime State: Labor Relations and Law During World War II.* Urbana and Chicago: University Of Illinois Press, 1998.

Brinkley, Alan. *The End of Reform: New Deal Liberalism in Recession and War.* New York: Alfred A. Knopf, 1985.

Fairchild, Byron and Jonathan Grossman. *The Army and Industrial Manpower.* Washington, DC: Office of the Chief of Military History, Department of the Army, 1959.

Fairris, David. *"Shopfloor Matters": Labor-Management Relations in Twentieth-Century American Manufacturing.* London and New York Routledge, 1997.

Fleming, Thomas. *The New Dealers' War: FDR and the War Within World War II.* New York: Basic Books, 2001.

Flynn, George Q. *The Mess in Washington: Manpower Mobilization in World War II.* Westport, CT: Greenwood Press, 1979.

Freeman, Joshua B. *Working Class: New York Life and Labor Since World War II.* New York: The New Press, 2000.

Hart, Scott. *Washington at War: 1941–1945.* Englewood Cliffs, NJ: Prentice-Hall, 1970.

Hooks, Gregory. "The United States of America: The Second World War and the Retreat from New Deal Era Corporatism." In *Organising Business for War: Corporatist Economic Organisation During the Second World War,* edited by Wyn Grant, Jan Nekkers, and Frans Van Waarden. New York and Oxford: Berg, 1991.

Jeffries, John W. *Wartime America: The World War II Home Front.* Chicago: Ivan R. Dee, 1996.

Lichtenstein, Nelson. *Labor's War at Home: The CIO in World War II.* New York: Cambridge University Press, 1982.

———. *State of the Union: A Century of American Labor.* Princeton, NJ: Princeton University Press, 2002.

Lichtenstein, Nelson, and Howell John Harris. *Industrial Democracy in America: The Ambiguous Promise.* Washington, DC: Woodrow Wilson Center Press and Cambridge University Press, 1993.

Metz, Harold W. *Labor Policy of the Federal Government.* Washington, DC: The Brookings Institution, 1945.

National Labor Relations Board 60th Anniversary Committee. *The First Sixty Years: The Story of the National Labor Relations Board, 1935–1995.* Washington, DC: United States Government Publication, 1995.

Rockoff, Hugh. "The United States: From Ploughshares to Swords." In *The Economics of World War II: Six Great Powers in International Comparison,* edited by Mark Harrison. Cambridge, UK: Cambridge University Press, 1998.

Smith, R. Elberton. *The Army and Economic Mobilization.* Washington, DC: Center of Military History, United States Army, 1985.

Tolliday, Steven, and Jonathan Zeitlin, eds. *Shop Floor Bargaining and the State.* New York: Cambridge University Press, 1987.

Wilks, Stephen, and Maurice Wright, eds. *Comparative Government-Industry Relations: Western Europe, the United States, and Japan.* Oxford: Clarendon Press, 1987.

Witney, Fred. *Wartime Experiences of the National Labor Relations Board, 1941–1945.* Urbana: University of Illinois Press, 1949.

Zieger, Robert H. *American Workers, American Unions.* Baltimore, MD, and London: The Johns Hopkins University Press, 1986, 1994.

Other

U.S. National Archives and Records Administration (NARA) Web site. Guides to Archival Holdings (cited 13 November 2002). <http://www.archives.gov/facilities/co/denver/holdings.html>.

—Carol Fort

GLOSSARY

GLOSSARY

Affirmative action: An attempt to overcome the effects of discrimination by allocating jobs and resources to members of groups that have historically been disadvantaged, such as African Americans, Latinos, and women. This policy has been voluntarily adopted by a number of unions, businesses, and institutions despite charges that it encourages reverse discrimination against white males.

Apprentice: An assistant to a master craftsman who is taught a trade in exchange for room and board. Terms of apprenticeship generally terminated at age 21 for males and age 16–18 for females. Upon completion of the term, apprentices would become journeymen.

Arbitration: A proceeding held by an independent third person or panel for two parties with a legal dispute. The parties present their arguments and evidence to an arbitrator who in turn decides how to resolve the case.

Bargaining in good faith: Practice in which management must confer with a union by participating in a number of conferences, displaying a good attitude toward the union, and making counteroffers. Good faith bargaining does not require management to agree to anything to which a reasonable person may object under the circumstances.

Blackballed: To exclude from social, professional, or commercial participation. It derives from the practice of using a black ball as a negative ballot.

Blacklisted: To list as deserving of suspicion and punishment and ban from employment.

Blue collar: Refers to employees who perform manual labor, typically in manufacturing or construction.

Bolshevik: A Russian term that originally applied to the communist revolutionary followers of Vladimir Lenin and that has since come to describe all radicals who oppose capitalism.

Bourgeois: A well-educated prosperous group; also categorized as middle class.

Boycott: To refrain from using, buying, or dealing with certain products or services to express protest or coerce action.

Chartism: A British working-class movement established in 1836 to achieve social and economic reform through changes in the English constitution. Chartists sought votes for all men, equal electoral districts, abolition of the requirement that members of Parliament be property owners, payment for service in Parliament, annual general elections, and the secret ballot.

Check weighman: A worker employed and paid by miners to ensure that they receive accurate wages for work performed. The check weighman balances the scales, sees that the coal is properly weighed, and verifies that a correct account of the weigh is kept.

Civil service: Institution in which government jobs are assigned on the basis of merit instead of political reasons.

Closed shop: Work atmosphere in which a company agrees to hire only those who belong to a union.

Collective bargaining: An agreement negotiated between a labor union and an employer that sets forth the terms of employment for the employees who are members of that labor union. This type of agreement may include provisions regarding wages, vacation time, working hours, working conditions, and health insurance benefits.

Communitarian: A philosophy that posits that individuals profit by working with others instead of in opposition to them.

Company town: A settlement that is controlled by one company and is typically exploitative of workers. It includes company-owned houses rented to employees, company-owned stores that typically charge exorbitant prices and accept only company scrip, a company-owned bank, and company-hired police and service workers.

Debt peonage: A type of involuntary servitude that mandates labor until a debt is repaid.

Equal Rights Amendment: A proposed amendment to the United States Constitution that states that equality of rights under the law shall not be denied or abridged by the United States or by any state on account of gender.

Filial preference: A practice of favoring the sons or nephews of union members when assigning work.

Fordism: A type of high-volume mass production of cheap goods, pioneered by automobile tycoon Henry Ford, in which unions are suppressed and worker loyalty is maintained by offering a higher real standard of living.

Gold standard: The use of gold as the standard value for the money of a country.

Jim Crow: A system of laws and actions in the United States that designated blacks as inferior to whites, thereby justifying segregation and disfranchisement of African Americans. The policy became entrenched and particularly strong in the South after the end of Reconstruction in 1877 and remained in force until federal enforcement of civil rights protections in the 1950s and 1960s.

Journeyman: A worker who has become skilled in a trade by serving an apprenticeship and is employed in a business owned by another.

Labor exchange: A service that matches job seekers with employers.

Laissez faire: A philosophy that holds that the individual is best served by private enterprise free from government restrictions. Under this system, all citizens theoretically have fair and equal opportunity and the economy self-regulates to punish inefficient businesses.

Lockout: An action taken by an employer for the purpose of compelling employees to agree to terms and conditions of employment. Lockouts may include the closing of all or part of a place of employment, a suspension of work, or a refusal to continue to employ workers.

Majority shareholder: A single shareholder or organized group of shareholders with control over more than half of a firm's outstanding shares.

Maquiladora: An assembly plant owned by a foreign-based company but located in Mexico to benefit from duty-free entry of goods and low prevailing wages. Parts are assembled at the factory and then exported back to the company's home country for sale.

Master: A craftsman who has completed an apprenticeship and, after serving as a journeyman, has founded a business.

Nationalization: Government ownership of a company or industry.

Open shop: Work atmosphere in which a company is free to hire workers regardless of whether they belong to a union.

Owenism: A type of socialism that attempted to create an alternative to capitalism by establishing communities in which all people would be equal and would work for the benefit of the entire settlement. Founded by Robert Owen, it had a number of adherents in the United States and Great Britain in the first part of the nineteenth century.

Perónism: An Argentine populist movement created by Juan Domingo Perón that gave workers political power as well as favored status in negotiations with business owners.

Piecework: A payment system in which an agreed sum of money is paid in exchange for a specified unit of work. Money piecework, the most common form, attaches a price to each piece of work. Time piecework gives a worker a fixed time to do a job but offers the same pay if the job is finished earlier.

Pink collar: Refers to workers in industries that are female-dominated such as nursing or secretarial work.

Populist: A form of political thought that promotes the interests and concerns of the common people rather than the rich or the politically powerful.

Protective labor legislation: Laws designed to protect the health of female workers by limiting hours worked, banning night work, and restricting the type of work that can be performed.

Proudhonism: A nonviolent and nationalistic form of socialism that aims to reform capitalism by placing more authority in the hands of individuals and less in the hands of government. The name comes from the nineteenth-century French theorist and anarchist Pierre Joseph Proudhon.

Right-to-work: A legal statute that bans enforcement of the union shop.

Scab: Any person who takes the place of a worker whose work has ceased as the result of a lockout or strike.

Secondary boycott: An attempt to boycott a third party or to coerce it into joining an ongoing boycott. Workers instituting a boycott may refuse to patronize firms that continue to deal with the initially boycotted party or strike an employer in order to force the business to join the boycott of another firm.

Serf: A peasant who is bound to the land and cannot leave it without the permission of the land's owner, a noble. Serfs are subject to the jurisdiction of the lord's court in any dispute.

Sharecropper: A poor farmer in the southern United States, often African American, who tills the land in return for supplies and a share of the crop, generally about half. Variations in sharecropping ranged from cash rental to debt peonage.

Shop stewards: Laborers who are chosen to be union representatives at the place of work by other union members. They are lay officials of the union but are not union employees.

Short-term disability: A temporary injury or illness that prevents a worker from working for a period that is generally from 13 to 26 weeks.

Sit-down strike: Strike in which workers come to their place of work but refuse to work or to go home.

Slowdown: Protest action in which workers deliberately slow their pace of work so as to reduce productivity and thereby place pressure on the employer to meet certain worker demands.

Social Darwinism: A belief, based loosely on Charles Darwin's theory of evolution, that only the strongest and fittest survive in the world of business. It justified the suppression of workers as an acceptable part of the natural order.

Social Gospel: A theory, formulated by steel magnate Andrew Carnegie, that the rich have a duty to use their wealth to advance social progress.

Social Security: A pension program funded by payroll taxes to provide assistance to retired elderly persons, the disabled, and dependent children.

Stretch-out: An attempt by factory managers to increase production by improving efficiency through the use of faster machines and the tying of wages to production quotas that only the quickest employees can meet.

Strike: Any concerted stoppage of work by employees including picketing, slowdowns, and failing to report for work. A stoppage by reason of the expiration of a collective-bargaining agreement is considered to be a strike.

Strikebreaker: Any person who takes the place of an employee whose work has ceased as a direct consequence of a lockout or strike as well as any person who attempts to end a strike through the use of violence or intimidation.

Sweating: A system of labor under which workers toil for long hours in poor and dangerous conditions for low wages.

Sweatshop: A shop or factory where workers are subject to extreme exploitation, including hazardous working conditions, arbitrary discipline, low wages, and denial of dignity and basic human rights.

Sympathy strike: A secondary strike expressing solidarity with another strike and involving employees of other businesses or of the same employer but at another production unit.

Syndicalist union: Workers who join together on the basis of class instead of trade to promote an economic system in which industries are owned and managed by the workers.

Tariff: A tax imposed on imported or exported goods.

Taylorism: System of management that removes control of the workplace from workers by designating the exact process and tools to be used to complete a task and the amount of time required for completion. Also known as scientific management, it is based on time and motion studies conducted by Frederick W. Taylor.

Trust: A means of centralizing control of an entire industry and eliminating competition. Stockholders turn over their shares to trustees who have voting control in several companies and issue dividends to the stockholders.

Unemployment insurance: Type of insurance that provides temporary income support to laid-off workers.

Unfair labor practices: Attempts by businesses to restrict the legal rights of employees including interfering with the for- mation of a union, refusal to bargain with a union, and discharging of employees who testify about unfair labor practices. Unfair practices by unions include threats to employees who are not members of the union and attempts to intimidate workers.

Union shop: Work atmosphere in which all workers must join the union before or at the end of a probationary period, not less than 30 days. Employees are required to remain in the union for the duration of their contract or until the union is terminated.

Utopian movement: An attempt to better the lives of all people by remaking society and such institutions as the family through the establishment of new communities.

Yellow-dog contract: An employment agreement, once widely used to block unionization efforts, in which a worker agrees not to join a union. Any subsequent attempt to organize workers can be regarded as a breach of contract.

Wildcat strike: An unauthorized work stoppage while a contract is still in effect.

Worker's compensation: A no-fault system in which an injured employee does not have to prove that an injury was caused by the negligence of another to receive compensation.

Work-in: Workers refuse to leave the place of work and continue working, in spite of management instructions not to do so.

GENERAL CHRONOLOGY

GENERAL CHRONOLOGY

1776:
Signing of the Declaration of Independence.

1789:
French Revolution begins with the storming of the Bastille.

1793:
Eli Whitney patents his cotton gin—a machine that, by making cotton profitable, spurs the expansion of slave labor in the southern United States.

1801:
United Kingdom of Great Britain and Ireland is established.

1803:
Administration of President Thomas Jefferson negotiates the Louisiana Purchase from France, whereby the United States doubles its geographic size, adding some 827,000 square miles (2,144,500 sq km)—all for the price of only $15 million.

1812:
Napoleon invades Russia in June, but by October, his army, cold and hungry, is in retreat.

1815:
Napoleon returns from Elba, and his supporters attempt to restore him as French ruler; but just three months later, forces led by the Duke of Wellington defeat his armies at Waterloo. Napoleon spends the remainder of his days as a prisoner on the island of St. Helena in the south Atlantic.

1818:
In a decisive defeat of Spanish forces, soldier and statesman Simón Bolívar leads the liberation of New Granada, which includes what is now Colombia, Panama, Venezuela, and Ecuador. With Spanish power now waning, Bolívar becomes president and virtual dictator of the newly created nation of Colombia.

1820s–1850s:
Struggle for a 10-hour workday in the United States.

1823:
Industrial organization experiment begun in Lowell, Massachusetts.

1825:
Opening of the New York Stock Exchange.

1830:
French troops invade Algeria, and at home, a revolution forces the abdication of Charles V in favor of Louis Philippe, the "Citizen King."

1834:
Abolition of slavery in the British Empire.

1836:
In Texas's war of independence with Mexico, the defenders of the Alamo, among them Davy Crockett and Jim Bowie, are killed in a siege.

1839:
England launches the First Opium War against China. The war, which lasts three years, results in the British gaining a free hand to conduct a lucrative opium trade, despite opposition by the Chinese government.

1845:
From Ireland to Russia, famine plagues Europe, killing some 2.5 million people.

1848:
Revolutions rock Europe, and Marx and Engels publish the *Communist Manifesto*.

1850:
U.S. Congress passes a series of laws, known collectively as the Compromise of 1850, to address growing divisions over slavery and the disposition of territories acquired in the Mexican War.

1853:
Crimean War begins in October. The struggle, which will last until February 1856, pits Russia against the combined forces of Great Britain, France, Turkey, and Sardinia-Piedmont. A war noted for the work of Florence Nightingale with the wounded, it is also the first conflict to be documented by photojournalists.

1860s–1900s:
Struggle for an eight-hour workday in the United States.

1861:
Within weeks of President Abraham Lincoln's inauguration, the American Civil War begins with the shelling of Fort Sumter in Charleston harbor.

1863:
President Lincoln issues the Emancipation Proclamation, freeing all slaves in Confederate territories, on 1 January. Thus begins a year that sees the turning point of the Civil War, with decisive Union victories at Gettysburg, Vicksburg, and Chattanooga.

1864:
International Working Men's Association, later known as the First International, is formed in London.

1865:
U.S. Civil War ends with the surrender of General Robert E. Lee to General Ulysses S. Grant at Appomattox, Virginia. More than 600,000 men have died and the South is in ruins, but the Union has been restored. A few weeks after the Confederate surrender, John Wilkes Booth shoots President Lincoln while the latter attends a performance at Ford's Theater in Washington, D.C.

1865:
Beginning of Reconstruction, a 12-year period during which federal troops occupy the former states of the Confederacy. This era also sees the passing of the Thirteenth, Fourteenth, and Fifteenth amendments to the Constitution, which end slavery and extend the civil rights of all Americans, particularly former slaves.

1870:

Beginning of Franco-Prussian War. German troops sweep over France, Napoleon III is dethroned, and France's Second Empire gives way to the Third Republic. The war ends in the next year with France's surrender of Alsace-Lorraine to Germany, which proclaims itself an empire under Prussian king Wilhelm, crowned Kaiser Wilhelm I.

1871:

Parisians establish the Commune, a revolutionary government that controls the capital—similar revolts break out in other cities—for about two months. In the end, the Third Republic suppresses the Commune with a brutality exceeding that of the Reign of Terror.

1873:

Panic of 1873, followed by a nationwide depression, wipes out most labor unions in the United States.

1876:

Alexander Graham Bell introduces the telephone.

1881:

President James A. Garfield is assassinated in a Washington, D.C., railway station by Charles J. Guiteau.

1885:

Belgium's King Leopold II becomes sovereign of the so-called Congo Free State, which he will rule for a quarter-century virtually as his own private property. The region in Africa, given the name of Zaire in the 1970s (and Congo in 1997), becomes the site of staggering atrocities, including forced labor and genocide, at the hands of Leopold's minions.

1886:

Formation of the American Federation of Labor.

1889:

Second International formed.

1890s–1920s:

Rise of syndicalism in Europe.

1890:

Congress passes the Sherman Antitrust Act, which in the years that follow will be used to break up large monopolies.

1890:

United Mine Workers of America formed.

1895:

Brothers Auguste and Louis Lumière show the world's first motion picture—*Workers Leaving the Lumière Factory*—at a café in Paris.

1898:

United States defeats Spain in the three-month Spanish-American War. As a result, Cuba gains its independence, and the United States purchases Puerto Rico and the Philippines from Spain for $20 million.

1900:

China's Boxer Rebellion, which began in the preceding year with attacks on foreigners and Christians, reaches its height. An international contingent of more than 2,000 men arrives to restore order, but only after several tens of thousands have died.

1904:

Beginning of the Russo-Japanese War, which lasts into 1905 and results in a Japanese victory. In Russia, the war is followed by the Revolution of 1905, which marks the beginning of the end of czarist rule; meanwhile, Japan is poised to become the first major non-Western power of modern times.

1905:

Formation of the Industrial Workers of the World.

1910:

Revolution breaks out in Mexico, and will continue for the next seven years.

1911:

Triangle Shirtwaist Company fire in New York City kills 146 workers, mostly women, and leads to the establishment of the New York Factory Investigating Commission.

1913:

Two incidents illustrate the increasingly controversial nature of the arts in the new century. Visitors to the 17 February Armory Show in New York City are scandalized by such works as Marcel Duchamp's cubist *Nude Descending a Staircase,* which elicits vehement criticism, and theatergoers at the 29 May debut of Igor Stravinksy's ballet *Le Sacré du Printemps* (*The Rite of Spring*) are so horrified by the new work that a riot ensues.

1913:

U.S. Department of Labor established.

1914:

On 28 June in the town of Sarajevo, then part of the Austro-Hungarian Empire, Serbian nationalist Gavrilo Princip assassinates Austrian Archduke Francis Ferdinand and wife Sophie. In the weeks that follow, Austria declares war on Serbia, and Germany on Russia and France, while Great Britain responds by declaring war on Germany. By the beginning of August, the lines are drawn, with the Allies (Great Britain, France, Russia, Belgium, Serbia, Montenegro, and Japan) against the Central Powers (Germany, Austria-Hungary, and Turkey).

1915:

A German submarine sinks the *Lusitania,* killing 1,195, including 128 U.S. citizens. Theretofore, many Americans had been sympathetic toward Germany, but the incident begins to turn the tide of U.S. sentiment toward the Allies.

1916:

Battles of Verdun and the Somme on the Western Front. The latter sees the first use of tanks, by the British.

1917:

The intercepted "Zimmermann Telegram" reveals a plot by the German government to draw Mexico into an alliance against the United States in return for a German promise to return the southwestern U.S. territories taken in the Mexican War. Three months later, in response to German threats of unrestricted submarine warfare, the United States on 6 April declares war on Germany.

1917:

In Russia, a revolution in March (or February according to the old Russian calendar) forces the abdication of Czar Nicholas II.

By July, Alexander Kerensky has formed a democratic socialist government, and continues to fight the Germans, even as starvation and unrest sweep the nation. On 7 November (25 October old style), the Bolsheviks under V. I. Lenin and Leon Trotsky seize power. By 15 December, they have removed Russia from the war by signing the Treaty of Brest-Litovsk with Germany.

1918:

The Second Battle of the Marne in July and August is the last major conflict on the Western Front. In November, Kaiser Wilhelm II abdicates, bringing an end to the war.

1918:

Upheaval sweeps Germany, which for a few weeks in late 1918 and early 1919 seems poised on the verge of communist revolution. But reactionary forces regain strength and suppress the revolts. Even stronger than reaction or revolution, however, is republican sentiment, which opens the way for the creation of a democratic government based at Weimar.

1918:

Influenza, carried to the furthest corners by returning soldiers, spreads throughout the globe. Over the next two years, it will kill nearly 20 million people—more than the war itself.

1919:

Treaty of Versailles signed by the Allies and Germany but rejected by the U.S. Senate. This is due in part to rancor between President Woodrow Wilson and Republican Senate leaders, and in part to concerns over Wilson's plan to commit the United States to the newly established League of Nations and other international duties. Not until 1921 will Congress formally end U.S. participation in the war, but it will never agree to join the league.

1922:

Inspired by the Bolsheviks' example of imposing revolution by means of a coup, Benito Mussolini leads his blackshirts in an October "March on Rome," and forms a new fascist government.

1923:

Conditions in Germany worsen as inflation skyrockets, and France, attempting to collect on coal deliveries promised at Versailles, marches into the Ruhr basin. In November, an obscure political group known as the National Socialist German Workers' Party attempts to stage a coup, or putsch, in a Munich beer hall. The revolt fails, and in 1924 the party's leader, Adolf Hitler, will receive a prison sentence of five years. He will only serve nine months, however, and the incident will serve to attract attention for him and his party, known as the Nazis.

1924:

V. I. Lenin dies, and thus begins a struggle for succession from which Josef Stalin will emerge five years later as the undisputed leader of the Communist Party, and of the Soviet Union.

1927:

Charles A. Lindbergh makes the first successful solo nonstop flight across the Atlantic and becomes an international hero.

1929:

On "Black Friday" in October, prices on the U.S. stock market, which had been climbing wildly for several years, suddenly collapse. Thus begins the first phase of a world economic crisis and depression that will last until the beginning of World War II.

1930:

Collectivization of Soviet agriculture begins, and with it one of the greatest crimes of the twentieth century. In the next years, as Soviet operatives force peasants to give up their lands, millions will die either by direct action, manmade famine, or forced labor.

1933:

Hitler becomes German chancellor, and the Nazi dictatorship begins. During this year, virtually all aspects of the coming horror are manifested: opening of the first concentration camps (and the sentencing of the first Jews to them); the establishment of the first racial purity laws; destruction of Jewish-owned shops and bans on Jewish merchants; elimination of political opposition (including the outlawing of trade unions); and book-burning.

1933:

In the United States, newly inaugurated president Franklin D. Roosevelt launches the first phase of his New Deal to put depression-era America back to work.

1935:

Formation of the Committee for Industrial Organization within the American Federation of Labor.

1936:

The election of a leftist Popular Front government in Spain in February precipitates an uprising by rightists under the leadership of General Francisco Franco. Over the next three years, war will rage between the Loyalists and Franco's Nationalists. The Spanish Civil War will prove to be a lightning rod for the world's tensions, with the Nazis and fascists supporting the Nationalists, and the Soviets the Loyalists.

1937:

AFL expels CIO over charges of dual unionism or competition. A year later, the CIO, heretofore the Committee for Industrial Organization, becomes the Congress of Industrial Organizations, with John L. Lewis as president.

1938:

Fair Labor Standards Act creates a $0.25 minimum wage and time-and-a-half for hours over 40 per week.

1939:

After years of loudly denouncing one another (and quietly cooperating), the Nazis and Soviets sign a non-aggression pact in August. This clears the way for the Nazi invasion of Poland, which results in a declaration of war by France and Great Britain.

1941:

Two events occur that will ultimately turn the tide of the war. On 22 June, Hitler invades the Soviet Union, and on 7 December, the Japanese bomb Pearl Harbor. Thus the Soviet Union and the United States are brought into the fighting on the side of the Allies.

1941:

First-ever union-shop agreement, between the United Auto Workers and Ford Motor Company. Also in 1941, the AFL and CIO announce a no-strike pledge for the duration of the war.

1943:

Worn down by two Russian winters, the Germans begin to fall back. In January, the siege of Leningrad (which at more than 800 days is the longest in modern history) is broken, and a month later, the German Sixth Army surrenders at Stalingrad.

1943:

President Roosevelt signs an executive order creating a Committee on Fair Employment Practices to eliminate employment discrimination in war industries.

1944:

Allies land at Normandy on 6 June, conducting the largest amphibious invasion in history.

1945:

On 7 May, Germany surrenders. Four months later, the United States drops atomic bombs on the Japanese cities of Hiroshima and Nagasaki. On 2 September, Japan surrenders.

1946:

Largest strike wave in U.S. history occurs, as pent-up labor troubles are unleashed by the end of wartime controls.

1948:

Israel becomes a nation, and a war with neighboring Arab countries ensues. In Eastern Europe, Stalin places a blockade on areas of Berlin controlled by the Western democracies, and communists seize control of Czechoslovakia—adding yet another communist government to a growing sphere of Soviet influence.

1949:

CIO anticommunist drive leads to the expulsion of two unions at its annual convention. Nine other unions are expelled by mid-1950.

1950:

North Korean troops pour into South Korea, starting the Korean War. A conflict with no clear victors, the war ends with an armistice establishing an uneasy peace between South Korea and North Korea.

1955:

AFL and CIO reunite, with George Meany as first president.

1956:

Workers revolt against communist rule in Poland, inspiring Hungarians to rise up against the Soviets. Soviet tanks and troops crush these revolts.

1961:

President Eisenhower steps down, warning of a "military-industrial complex" in his farewell speech, and 43-year-old John F. Kennedy becomes the youngest elected president in U.S. history. Three months later, he launches an unsuccessful invasion of Cuba at the Bay of Pigs.

1962:

As a result of an executive order by President Kennedy, federal employees' unions are given the right to bargain collectively with government agencies.

1963:

Assassination of President Kennedy in Dallas.

1964:

Congress approves the Gulf of Tonkin resolution, giving President Johnson broad powers to prosecute the by now rapidly escalating war in Vietnam.

1964:

Civil Rights Act prohibits discrimination in employment based on race, color, religion, sex, or national origin.

1968:

Communist victories in the Tet Offensive mark the turning point in the Vietnam War, and influence a growing lack of confidence in the war, not only among America's youth but within the establishment as well. At home, Martin Luther King Jr. and Robert Kennedy are assassinated.

1970:

President Nixon sends U.S. troops into Cambodia on 30 April. Four days later, National Guardsmen open fire on antiwar protesters at Kent State University in Ohio. By 24 June, antiwar sentiment is so strong that the Senate repeals the Gulf of Tonkin resolution. On 29 June, Nixon orders troops back out of Cambodia.

1970:

Congress passes the Occupational Safety and Health Act (OSHA).

1973:

Signing of peace accords in Paris in January ends the Vietnam War.

1974:

On 30 July, the House Judiciary Committee adopts three articles of impeachment against President Nixon for his role in the Watergate break-in and the subsequent cover-up. Rather than undergo a lengthy trial, Nixon on 8 August becomes the first president in U.S. history to resign. His successor, Gerald Ford, pardons him in September.

1979:

After years of unrest, the Shah of Iran leaves the country, and Islamic fundamentalist revolutionaries under the leadership of Ayatollah Ruhollah Khomeini take control. Conditions in neighboring Afghanistan, meanwhile, are approaching anarchy until, on Christmas Day 1979, Soviet troops arrive to restore order. Thus begins a ten-year war—one of the twentieth century's most vicious—that will help bring an end to the Soviet empire.

1980:

Formation of Solidarity in Poland, the first significant labor union within the communist bloc.

1981:

Most U.S. air-traffic controllers are fired by President Ronald Reagan, who then de-certifies their union in response to an illegal strike.

1985:

A new era begins in the USSR as Konstantin Chernenko dies and is replaced by Mikhail Gorbachev, who at 54 years old is the youngest Soviet leader in decades.

1989:

The Iron Curtain begins to crumble, most dramatically in Berlin, where massive protests erupt at the hated Berlin Wall on 9 November. Two days later, for the first time in 28 years, the wall is opened between East and West. The following month, on Christmas Day, the people of Romania execute the dictator Ceausescu and his wife.

1991:

The United States and other members of the United Nations attack Iraq on 15 January. By 3 April, the war is over, a resounding victory for the Allied force.

1992:

Passage of North American Free Trade Agreement.

1993:

European nations sign the Maastricht Treaty, which creates the European Union.

1997:

Financial crisis sweeps east Asia. The crisis, which will continue into 1998, foreshadows the end of the economic boom in the United States in 2000.

1999:

Demonstrations at World Free Trade Conference in Seattle highlight a growing antiglobalization movement.

2000:

In the most disputed presidential election in U.S. history, Democrats demand a recount after initial tabulation of votes in Florida shows a narrow victory for Republican candidate George W. Bush. The battle goes on for five weeks and involves numerous recounts and court injunctions, until the U.S. Supreme Court puts an end to recounts and declares Bush the winner.

2001:

On the morning of 11 September, terrorists hijack four jets, two of which ram the twin towers of the World Trade Center in New York City, which later collapse. A third plane slams into the Pentagon in Washington, D.C., and a fourth crashes in an empty field in Pennsylvania.

READING LIST

READING LIST

Adelman, Paul. *The Rise of the Labour Party, 1880–1945*. 3rd ed. London, New York: Longman, 1996.

Aldrich, Mark. *Safety First: Technology, Labor and Business in the Building of Work Safety, 1870–1939*. Baltimore, MD: Johns Hopkins University Press, 1997.

Alexander, Robert Jackson. *Organized Labor in Latin America*. New York: The Free Press, 1965.

Altmeyer, Arthur J. *The Formative Years of Social Security: A Chronicle of Social Security Legislation and Administration, 1934–1954*. Madison: The University of Wisconsin Press, 1966.

Amberg, Stephen. *The Union Inspiration in American Politics: The Autoworkers and the Making of a Liberal Industrial Order*. Philadelphia: Temple University Press, 1994.

Anderson, Rodney. *Outcasts in Their Own Land: Mexican Industrial Workers, 1906–1911*. De Kalb: Northern Illinois University Press, 1976.

Andrews, Gregg. *Shoulder to Shoulder? The American Federation of Labor, the United States, and the Mexican Revolution, 1910 to 1924*. Berkeley: University of California, 1991.

Andrews, John B., and W. D. P. Bliss. *History of Women in Trade Unions*. New York: Arno Press, 1974.

Aptheker, Herbert. *American Negro Slave Revolts*. New York: Columbia University Press, 1943.

Aranzadi, Dionisio. *Collective Bargaining and Class Conflict in Spain*. London: Weidenfield and Nicholson, 1972.

Archer, Julian P.W. *The First International in France 1864–1872: Its Origins, Theories, and Impact*. Lanham, MD: University Press of America, 1997.

Arnesen, Eric. *Brotherhoods of Color: Black Railroad Workers and the Struggle for Equality*. Cambridge, MA: Harvard University Press, 2001.

Ashby, Joe C. *Organized Labor and the Mexican Revolution Under Lazaro Cardenas*. Chapel Hill: The University of North Carolina Press, 1967.

Atleson, James B. *Labor and the Wartime State: Labor Relations and Law During World War II*. Urbana and Chicago: University of Illinois Press, 1998.

Austin, Aleine. *The Labor Story: A Popular History of American Labor 1786–1949*. New York: Coward-McCann, Inc., 1949.

Ayusawa, Iwao F. *A History of Labor in Modern Japan*. Honolulu: East-West Center Press, Hawaii University, 1966.

Babcock, Robert. *Gompers in Canada: A Study in American Continentalism Before the First World War*. Toronto: University of Toronto Press, 1974.

Badger, Anthony. *The New Deal: The Depression Years, 1933–1940*. New York: Hill and Wang, 1989.

Baily, Samuel L. *Labor, Nationalism, and Politics in Argentina*. New Brunswick, NJ: Rutgers University Press, 1967.

Barkan, Joanne. *Visions of Emancipation: The Italian Workers' Movement Since 1945*. New York: Praeger Publishers, 1985.

Bates, Beth Tompkins. *Pullman Porters and the Rise of Protest Politics in Black America, 1925–1945*. Chapel Hill: University of North Carolina Press, 2001.

Beard, Mary. *A Short History of the American Labor Movement*. New York: Greenwood Press, 1968.

Beechert, Edward D. *Working in Hawaii: A Labor History*. Honolulu: University of Hawaii Press, 1985.

Beinin, Joel, and Zachary Lockman. *Workers on the Nile: Nationalism, Communism, Islam, and the Egyptian Working Class, 1882–1954*. Princeton, NJ: Princeton University Press, 1987.

Belchem, John. *Industrialization and the Working Class: The English Experience, 1750–1900*. Brookfield, VT: Gower, 1990.

Bendiner, Burton. *International Labour Affairs: The World Trade Unions and the Multinational Companies*. Oxford: Clarendon Press, 1987.

Berger, Stefan. *Social Democracy and the Working Class in Nineteenth and Twentieth Century Germany*. New York: Longman, 1999.

Berkowitz, Edward, and Kim McQuaid. *Creating the Welfare State: The Political Economy of Twentieth Century Reform*. Lawrence: University Press of Kansas, 1992.

Bernstein, David E. *Only One Place of Redress: African Americans, Labor Regulations, and the Courts, from Reconstruction to the New Deal*. Durham, NC: Duke University Press, 2001.

Bernstein, Irving. *Turbulent Years: A History of the American Worker, 1933–1941*. Boston: Houghton Mifflin, 1970.

———. *A Caring Society: The New Deal, the Worker, and the Great Depression*. Boston: Houghton Mifflin, 1985.

Bird, Stewart, Dan Georgakas, and Deborah Shaffer. *Solidarity Forever: An Oral History of the IWW*. Chicago: Lake View Press, 1985.

Black, Lawrence. *The Political Culture of the Left in Britain, 1951–1964: Old Labour, New Britain?* Houndmills, Basingstoke, Hampshire; New York: Palgrave, 2002.

Blackwell, William L. *The Industrialization of Russia: An Historical Perspective*. New York: Thomas Y. Crowell Company, 1970.

Blatz, Perry K. *Democratic Miners: Work and Labor Relations in the Anthracite Coal Industry, 1875–1925*. Albany: State University of New York Press, 1994.

Blewett, Mary H. *Men, Women, and Work: Class, Gender, and Protest in the New England Shoe Industry, 1780–1910*. Urbana: University of Illinois Press, 1988.

———. *The Last Generation: Work and Life in the Textile Mills of Lowell, Massachusetts, 1910–1960*. Amherst: University of Massachusetts Press, 1990.

———. *We Will Rise in Our Might: Workingwomen's Voices from Nineteenth-Century New England*. Ithaca, NY: Cornell University Press, 1991.

———. *Constant Turmoil: The Politics of Industrial Life in Nineteenth-Century New England*. Amherst: University of Massachusetts Press, 2000.

Bonnell, Victoria E. *Roots of Rebellion: Workers' Politics and Organizations in St. Petersburg and Moscow, 1900–1914*. Berkeley: University of California Press, 1983.

Bookchin, Murray. *The Spanish Anarchists: The Heroic Years, 1868–1936*. Edinburgh, Scotland; San Francisco: AK Press, 1997.

Boris, Eileen, and Nelson Lichtenstein. *Major Problems in the History of American Workers*. Lexington, MA: D. C. Heath and Company, 1991.

Bortz, Jeffrey, and Stephen Haber, eds. *The Mexican Economy, 1870–1930: Essays on the Economic History of Institutions, Revolution, and Growth*. Stanford, CA: Stanford University Press, 2002.

Boyle, Kevin. *The UAW and the Heyday of American Liberalism*. Ithaca, NY: Cornell University Press, 1995.

Brass, Tom, and Marcel van der Linden, eds. *Free and Unfree Labour: The Debate Continues*. Bern, Switzerland; New York: Peter Lang, 1997.

Braunthal, Julius. *History of the International*, Vol. 2: *1914–1943*. New York: Praeger, 1967.

Braverman, Harry. *Labor and Monopoly Capital: The Degradation of Work in the Twentieth Century*. Foreword by Paul M. Sweezy. New York: Monthly Review Press, 1974.

Briggs, Vernon M., Jr. *Immigration and American Unionism*. Ithaca, NY: Cornell University Press, 2001.

Briggs, Vernon M., Jr., Walt Fogel, and Fred H. Schmidt. *The Chicano Worker*. Austin: University of Texas Press, 1977.

Brody, David. *Steelworkers in America: The Nonunion Era*. Cambridge, MA: Harvard University Press, 1960.

———. *In Labor's Cause: Main Themes in the History of the American Worker*. New York: Oxford University Press, 1993.

Brown, Ronald C. *Hard-Rock Miners: The Intermountain West, 1860–1920*. College Station: Texas A&M University, 1979.

Buckley, Ken, and E. L. Wheelwright. *No Paradise for Workers: Capitalism and the Common People in Australia, 1788–1914*. Melbourne: Oxford University Press, 1988.

Buhle, Mary Jo. *Women and American Socialism, 1870–1920*. Urbana: University of Illinois Press, 1983.

Buhle, Mary Jo, Paul Buhle, and Dan Georgakas, eds. *Encyclopedia of the American Left*. Urbana: University of Illinois Press, 1992.

Buhle, Paul. *Taking Care of Business: Samuel Gompers, George Meany, Lane Kirkland, and the Tragedy of American Labor*. New York: Monthly Review Press, 1999.

Burstein, Paul. *Discrimination, Jobs, and Politics: The Struggle for Equal Employment Opportunity in the United States Since the New Deal*. Chicago: University of Chicago Press, 1985.

Buse, Dieter K., and Juergen C. Doerr, eds. *Modern Germany: An Encyclopedia of History, People, and Culture, 1871–1990*. New York: Garland, 1998.

Bush, Gary. *Political Role of International Trade Unions*. New York: St. Martin's Press, 1983.

Byrkit, James W. *Forging the Copper Collar: Arizona's Labor-Management War of 1901–1921*. Tucson: University of Arizona, 1982.

Castañeda, Jorge G. *Utopia Unarmed: The Latin American Left After the Cold War*. New York: Alfred A. Knopf, 1993.

Chan, Sucheng, ed. *Entry Denied: Exclusion and the Chinese Community in America, 1882–1943*. Philadelphia: Temple University Press, 1991.

Chapman, Stanley David. *The Cotton Industry in the Industrial Revolution*. London: Macmillan, 1972.

Chesneaux, Jean. *The Chinese Labor Movement, 1919–1927*. Stanford, CA: Stanford University Press, 1968.

Chinoy, Ely. *Automobile Workers and the American Dream*. 1955. Reprint, Urbana: University of Illinois Press, 1992.

Christie, Robert. *Empire in Wood: A History of the Carpenters' Union*. Ithaca, NY: Cornell University Press, 1956.

Claeys, Gregory. *Machinery, Money, and the Millennium: From Moral Economy to Socialism, 1815–1860*. Princeton, NJ: Princeton University Press, 1987.

Clark, Paul, Peter Gottlieb, and Donald Kennedy, eds. *Forging a Union of Steel*. Ithaca, NY: ILR Press, 1987.

Clegg, H. A, Alan Fox, and A. F. Thompson. *A History of British Trade Unions Since 1889*. 3 vols. Oxford: Clarendon Press, 1964–1994.

Cochran, Bert. *Labor and Communism: The Conflict that Shaped American Unions*. Princeton, NJ: Princeton University Press, 1977.

Cohen, Lizabeth. *Making a New Deal: Industrial Workers in Chicago, 1919–1939*. Cambridge: Cambridge University Press, 1990.

Cole, G. D. H. *A History of Socialist Thought*. 3 vols. London: Macmillan; New York: St. Martin's Press, 1953–1960.

Collier, Ruth Berins, and David Collier. *Shaping the Political Arena: Critical Junctures, the Labor Movement and Regime Dynamics in Latin America*. Princeton, NJ: Princeton University Press, 1991.

Collins, Henry, and Chimen Abramsky. *Karl Marx and the British Labour Movement, Years of the First International*. London: Macmillan, 1965.

Commons, John R., et. al. *History of Labour in the United States*. 3 vols. New York: Macmillan, 1918–1935.

Conquest, Robert. *Kolyma: The Arctic Death Camps*. New York: The Viking Press, 1978.

———. *The Harvest of Sorrow: Soviet Collectivization and the Terror-famine*. London: Hutchinson, 1986.

Cook, Maria Lorena. *Organizing Dissent: Unions, the State, and the Democratic Teachers' Movement in Mexico*. University Park: Pennsylvania State University Press, 1996.

Couvares, Francis G. *The Remaking of Pittsburgh: Class and Culture in an Industrializing City, 1877–1919*. Albany: State University of New York Press, 1984.

Cowherd, Raymond. *The Humanitarians and the Ten Hour Movement in England*. Boston: Baker Library, 1956.

Craton, Michael. *Sinews of Empire: A Short History of British Slavery*. Garden City, NY: Anchor Books, 1974.

Croucher, Richard. *Engineers at War 1939–1945*. London: Merlin Press, 1982.

Crump, John. *The Origins of Socialist Thought in Japan*. London: Croom Helm, 1983.

Daniel, Cletus. *Chicano Workers and the Politics of Fairness: The FEPC in the Southwest, 1941–1945*. Austin, TX: University of Texas Press, 1991.

Darlington, Ralph. *The Dynamics of Workplace Unionism: Shop Stewards' Organization in Three Merseyside Plants*. London: Mansell, 1994.

Davis, Mike. *Prisoners of the American Dream: Politics and Economy in the History of the U.S. Working Class*. London: Verso, 1986.

Dawley, Alan. *Class and Community: The Industrial Revolution in Lynn.* Rev. ed. Cambridge, MA: Harvard University Press, 2001.

Department of Research and Investigations of the National Urban League. *Negro Membership in American Labor Unions.* New York: Negro Universities Press, 1969.

De Shazo, Peter. *Urban Workers and Labor Unions in Chile, 1902–1927.* Madison: University of Wisconsin Press, 1983.

Deslippe, Dennis A. *"Rights, Not Roses": Unions and the Rise of Working-Class Feminism, 1945–1980.* Urbana: University of Illinois Press, 2000.

Dickerson, Dennis C. *Out of the Crucible: Steelworkers in Western Pennsylvania, 1875–1980.* Albany: State University of New York Press, 1986.

Dollinger, Sol, and Genora Johnson. *Not Automatic: Women and the Left in the Forging of the Auto Workers Union.* New York: Monthly Review Press, 2000.

Drescher, Seymour. *The Mighty Experiment: Free Labor Versus Slavery in British Emancipation.* New York and Oxford: Oxford University Press, 2002.

Dublin, Thomas. *Women at Work: The Transformation of Work and Community in Lowell, Massachusetts, 1826–1860.* New York: Columbia University Press, 1979.

———. *Farm to Factory: Women's Letters, 1830–1860.* New York: Columbia University Press, 1981.

———. *Transforming Women's Work: New England Lives in the Industrial Revolution.* Ithaca: Cornell University Press, 1994.

———. *When the Mines Closed: Stories of Struggles in Hard Times.* Ithaca, NY: Cornell University Press, 1998.

Dubofsky, Melvyn. *We Shall Be All: A History of the Industrial Workers of the World.* Chicago: Quadrangle, 1969.

———. *The State and Labor in Modern America.* Chapel Hill: University of North Carolina Press, 1994.

Dubofsky, Melvyn, and Warren Van Tine. *John L. Lewis: A Biography.* Urbana: University of Illinois Press, 1986.

———. *Labor Leaders in America.* Urbana: University of Illinois Press, 1987.

Dulles, Foster Rhea, and Melvyn Dubofsky, eds. *Labor in America: A History.* 5th ed. Arlington Heights, IL: Harlan Davidson, Inc., 1984.

Duncan, Robert, and Arthur McIvor, eds. *Militant Workers: Labour and Class Conflict on the Clyde, 1900–1950.* Edinburgh: John Donald, 1992.

Dye, Nancy Schrom. *As Equals and as Sisters: Feminism, the Labor Movement, and the Women's Trade Union League of New York.* Columbia: University of Missouri Press, 1980.

Edwards, P. K. *Strikes in the United States: 1881–1974.* New York: St. Martin's Press, 1981.

Epstein, J. and Thompson, Dorothy, eds. *The Chartist Experience: Studies in Working-Class Radicalism and Culture, 1830–60.* London and Basingstoke: Macmillan Press, 1982.

Epstein, Melech. *Jewish Labor in the U.S.A., 1882–1952.* New York: KTAV Publishing House, 1969.

Esenwein, George R. *Anarchist Ideology and the Working-class Movement in Spain, 1868–1898.* Berkeley: University of California Press, 1989.

Fairris, David. *"Shopfloor Matters": Labor-Management Relations in Twentieth-Century American Manufacturing.* London and New York Routledge, 1997.

Fay, Charles R. *Life and Labour in the Nineteenth Century.* Cambridge, U.K.: The University Press, 1947.

Ferriss, Susan, and Ricardo Sandoval. *A Fight in the Fields: Cesar Chavez and the Farmworkers Movement.* New York: Harcourt Brace, 1997.

Figes, Orlando. *A People's Tragedy: The Russian Revolution, 1891–1924.* London: Jonathan Cape, 1996.

Filtzer, Donald. *Soviet Workers and Stalinist Industrialization: The Formation of Modern Soviet Production Relations, 1928–1941.* Armonk, NY: M. E. Sharpe, Inc., 1986.

Fine, Sidney. *Sit-Down: The General Motors Strike of 1936–37.* Ann Arbor: University of Michigan Press, 1969.

Fink, Gary M., ed. *Biographical Dictionary of American Labor.* Westport, CT: Greenwood Press, 1984.

Finley, Joseph E. *The Corrupt Kingdom: The Rise and Fall of the United Mine Workers.* New York: Simon and Schuster, 1972.

Finn, Margot C. *After Chartism: Class and Nation in English Radical Politics 1848–1874.* Cambridge: Cambridge University Press, 1993.

Fishback, Price V. *Soft Coal, Hard Choices: The Economic Welfare of Bituminous Coal Miners, 1890–1930.* Oxford: Oxford University Press, 1992.

Fitzpatrick, Sheila. *The Russian Revolution, 1917–1932.* Oxford: Oxford University Press, 1982.

Flynn, Ralph J. *Public Work, Public Workers.* Washington, DC: The New Republic Book Company, Inc., 1975.

Foner, Eric. *Reconstruction: America's Unfinished Revolution, 1863-1877.* New York: Harper and Row Publishers, 1988.

———. *Free Soil, Free Labor, Free Men: The Ideology of the Republican Party Before the Civil War.* Oxford: Oxford University Press, 1995.

Foner, Philip S. *History of the Labor Movement in the United States.* New York: International Publishers, 1947.

———. *Women and the American Labor Movement: From Colonial Times to the Eve of World War I.* New York: The Free Press, 1979.

———. *Women and the American Labor Movement: From World War I to the Present.* New York: The Free Press, 1980.

———. *Organized Labor and the Black Worker (1619–1981).* 2nd ed. New York: International Publishers, 1982.

Foner, Philip S., and Ronald L. Lewis, eds. *Black Workers: A Documentary History from Colonial Times to the Present.* Philadelphia: Temple University Press, 1989.

Fones-Wolf, Elizabeth A. *Selling Free Enterprise: The Business Assault on Labor and Liberalism, 1945–1960.* Urbana: University of Illinois Press, 1994.

Forsey, Eugene. *Trade Unions in Canada, 1812–1902.* Toronto: University of Toronto Press, 1982.

Frank, Dana. *Purchasing Power: Consumer Organizing, Gender, and the Seattle Labor Movement, 1919–1929.* New York: Cambridge University Press, 1994.

Fraser, Steven. *Labor Will Rule: Sidney Hillman and the Rise of American Labor.* New York: Free Press, 1991.

Fraser, W. Hamish. *A History of British Trade Unionism, 1700–1998.* London/Basingstoke, U.K.: Palgrave Macmillan, 1999.

Freeland, Robert. *The Struggle for Control of the Modern Corporation: Organizational Change at General Motors, 1924–1970.* New York: Cambridge University Press, 2000.

Freeman, Joshua B. *Working Class: New York Life and Labor Since World War II.* New York: The New Press, 2000.

Friedman, Allen, and Ted Schwarz. *Power and Greed: Inside the Teamsters Empire of Corruption.* New York: Watts, 1989.

Friedman, Gerald. *State-making and Labor Movements: France and the United States, 1876–1914.* Ithaca, NY: Cornell University Press, 1998.

Friedman, Lawrence M. *Your Time Will Come: The Law of Age Discrimination and Mandatory Retirement.* New York: Russell Sage Foundation, 1984.

Frisch, Michael H., and Daniel J. Walkowitz, eds. *Working-Class America: Essays on Labor, Community, and American Society.* Urbana: University of Illinois Press, 1983.

Fry, Eric, ed. *Common Cause: Essays in Australian and New Zealand Labour History.* Sydney, Wellington, NZ: Allen and Unwin, 1992.

Gabin, Nancy F. *Feminism in the Labor Movement: Women and the United Auto Workers, 1935–1975.* Ithaca, NY: Cornell University Press, 1990.

Galenson, Walter. *The CIO Challenge to the AFL: A History of the American Labor Movement, 1935–1941.* Cambridge: Harvard University Press, 1960.

Garnel, Donald. *The Rise of Teamster Power in the West.* Berkeley: University of California Press, 1972.

Garon, Sheldon M. *The State and Labor in Modern Japan.* Berkeley: University of California Press, 1987.

Garton Ash, Timothy. *The Magic Lantern: The Revolution of '89; Witnesses in Warsaw, Budapest, Berlin, and Prague.* New York: Random House, 1990.

Geary, Dick. *Labour and Socialist Movements in Europe Before 1914.* New York: St. Martin's Press, 1989.

Gillman, Howard. *The Constitution Besieged: The Rise and Demise of Lochner Era Police Powers Jurisprudence.* Durham, NC: Duke University Press, 1993.

Gitelman, Howard M. *Legacy of the Ludlow Massacre: A Chapter in American Industrial Relations.* Philadelphia: University of Pennsylvania Press, 1988.

Glickman, Lawrence B. *A Living Wage: American Workers and the Making of Consumer Society.* Ithaca, NY: Cornell University Press, 1997.

Gluckstein, Donny. *The Nazis, Capitalism and the Working Class.* London: Bookmarks, 1999.

Goldberg, Arthur J. *AFL-CIO: Labor United.* New York: McGraw-Hill Co., 1956.

Golden, Miriam. *Labor Divided: Austerity and Working-Class Politics in Contemporary Italy.* Ithaca, NY, and London: Cornell University Press, 1988.

Goode, Bill. *Infighting in the UAW: The 1946 Election and the Ascendancy of Walter Reuther.* Westport, CT: Greenwood Press, 1994.

Goodstein, Phil H. *The Theory of the General Strike from the French Revolution to Poland.* Boulder, CO: East European Monographs, 1984.

Goodwyn, Lawrence. *The Populist Moment: A Short History of the Agrarian Revolt in America.* New York: Oxford University Press, 1978.

Gordon, Andrew. *The Evolution of Labor Relations in Japan: Heavy Industry, 1953–1955.* Cambridge, MA: Harvard University Press, 1985.

———. *The Wages of Affluence: Labor and Management in Postwar Japan.* Cambridge, MA: Harvard University Press, 1998.

Goswami, Dharani. *Trade Union Movement in India: Its Growth and Development.* New Delhi, India: People's Publishing House, 1983.

Goulden, Joseph C. *Meany, The Unchallenged Strong Man of American Labor.* New York: Atheneum, 1972.

Graham, Helen, and Paul Preston, eds. *The Popular Front in Europe.* New York: St. Martin's Press, 1987.

Grayson, George W. *The Mexican Labor Machine: Power, Politics, and Patronage.* Significant Issues Series, XI, no. 3. Washington, DC: The Center for Strategic and International Studies, 1989.

Grebing, Helga. *History of the German Labour Movement.* Leamington Spa, Warwickshire: Berg Publishers, 1985.

Greene, Victor R. *The Slavic Community on Strike: Immigrant Labor in Pennsylvania Anthracite.* Notre Dame, IN: University of Notre Dame Press, 1968.

Gregory, Charles O. *Labor and the Law.* New York: W. W. Norton and Co., 1961.

Griffin, Larry J., and Marcel van der Linden, eds. *New Methods for Social History.* Cambridge, U.K.; New York: Cambridge University Press, 1999.

Gross, James. *Broken Promise: The Subversion of U.S. Labor Relations Policy, 1947–1994.* Philadelphia: Temple University Press, 1995.

Grossman, Jonathan. *William Sylvis, Pioneer of American Labor: A Study of the Labor Movement During the Civil War.* New York: Octagon Books, 1973.

Grunwald, Joseph, and Kenneth Flamm. *The Global Factory: Foreign Assembly in International Trade.* Washington, DC: Brookings Institution, 1985.

Gutman, Herbert G. "Trouble on the Railroads, 1873–1874." In *Work, Culture and Society in Industrializing America: Essays in American Working-class and Social History.* New York: Vintage Books, 1977.

Haimson, Leopold H., and Charles Tilly. *Strikes, Wars, and Revolutions in an International Perspective: Strike Waves in the Late Nineteenth and Early Twentieth Centuries.* Cambridge: Cambridge University Press, 1989.

Halpern, Martin. *UAW Politics in the Cold War Era.* Albany: State University of New York Press, 1988.

Halpern, Rick, and Roger Horowitz. *Meatpackers: An Oral History of Black Packinghouse Workers and Their Struggle for Racial and Economic Equality.* New York: Monthly Review Press, 1999.

Hanagan, Michael P. *The Logic of Solidarity: Artisans and Industrial Workers in Three French Towns, 1871–1914.* Urbana: University of Illinois Press, 1979.

———. *Nascent Proletarians: Class Formation in Postrevolutionary France.* Oxford, U.K.; Cambridge, MA: Basil Blackwell, 1989.

Harris, Howell J. *The Right to Manage: Industrial Relations Policies of American Business in the 1940s.* Madison: University of Wisconsin Press, 1982.

Harris, William H. *The Harder We Run: Black Workers Since the Civil War*. New York: Oxford University Press, 1982.

Harrison, James Pinckney. *The Long March to Power: A History of the Chinese Communist Party, 1921–1972*. New York: Praeger Publishers, 1972.

Harrison, Royden. *Before the Socialists: Studies in Labour and Politics, 1861–1881*. London: Routledge and Kegan Paul, 1965.

Harsin, Jill. *Barricades: The War of the Streets in Revolutionary Paris, 1830–1848*. New York: St. Martin's Press, 2002.

Hart, John Mason. *Anarchism and the Mexican Working Class, 1860–1930*. Austin: University of Texas Press, 1978.

Hawkins, Carroll. *Two Democratic Labor Leaders in Conflict: The Latin American Revolution and the Role of the Workers*. Lexington, MA: D. C. Heath and Company, 1973.

Herling, John. *Right to Challenge: People and Power in the Steelworkers Union*. New York: Harper and Row, 1972.

Hickey, S. H. F. *Workers in Imperial Germany: The Miners of the Ruhr*. Oxford: Clarendon Press, 1985.

Hill, Herbert. *Black Labor and the American Legal System: Race, Work, and the Law*. Madison, WI: University of Wisconsin Press, 1985.

Hindley, Donald. *The Communist Party of Indonesia, 1951–1963*. Berkeley: University of California Press, 1964.

Hindman, Hugh. *Child Labor: An American History*. Armonk, NY: M. E. Sharpe, 2002.

Hinshaw, John, and Paul Le Blanc, eds. *U.S. Labor in the Twentieth Century: Studies in Working-class Struggles and Insurgency*. Amherst, NY: Humanity Books, 2000.

Hobbs, Sandy, Jim McKechnie, and Michael Lavalette. *Child Labor: A World History Companion*. Santa Barbara, CA: ABC-CLIO, 1999.

Honey, Michael K. *Southern Labor and Black Civil Rights: Organizing Memphis Workers*. Urbana, IL: University of Illinois Press, 1993.

Horowitz, Daniel. *The Italian Labor Movement*. Cambridge, MA: Harvard University Press, 1963.

Horowitz, Roger. *Negro and White, Unite and Fight! A Social History of Industrial Unionism in Meatpacking, 1930–1990*. Urbana: University of Illinois Press, 1997.

Hugins, Walter. *Jacksonian Democracy and the Working Class: A Study of the New York Workingmen's Movement, 1829–1837*. Palo Alto, CA: Stanford University Press, 1960.

Hutchinson, E. P. *Legislative History of American Immigration Policy, 1798–1965*. Philadelphia: University of Pennsylvania Press, 1981.

Jacoby, Sanford M. *Employing Bureaucracy: Managers, Unions, and the Transformation of Work in American Industry, 1900–1945*. New York: Columbia University Press, 1985.

James, Wilmont G. *Our Precious Metal: African Labour in South Africa's Gold Industry, 1970–1990*. Bloomington and Indianapolis: Indiana University Press, 1992.

Jaynes, Gerald David. *Branches Without Roots: Genesis of the Black Working Class in the American South, 1862–1882*. New York: Oxford University Press, 1986.

Judt, Tony. *Marxism and the French Left: Studies in Labour and Politics in France, 1830–1981*. Oxford: Clarendon Press, 1986.

Katz, Harry C. and Richard W. Hurd. *Rekindling the Movement: Labor's Quest for Relevance in the 21st Century*. Ithaca, NY: Cornell University Press, 2001.

Kawanishi, Hirosuke, ed. *The Human Face of Industrial Conflict in Postwar Japan*. London and New York: Kegan Paul International, 1999.

Kearney, Richard C. *Labor Relations in the Public Sector*. New York: Marcel Dekker, 1984.

Kersten, Andrew Edmund. *Race, Jobs, and the War: The FEPC in the Midwest, 1941–1946*. Urbana, IL: University of Illinois Press, 2000.

Kessler Harris, Alice. *Out to Work: A History of Wage-Earning Women in the United States*. New York: Oxford University Press, 1982.

———. *A Woman's Wage: Historical Meanings and Social Consequences*. Lexington: University of Kentucky Press, 1990.

———. *In Pursuit of Equity: Women, Men, and the Quest for Economic Citizenship in Twentieth-Century America*. New York: Oxford University Press, 2001.

Kirstein, Peter N. *Anglo over Bracero: A History of the Mexican Worker in the United States from Roosevelt to Nixon*. San Francisco: R and E Research Associates, 1977.

Kiser, George C., and Martha Woody Kiser. *Mexican Workers in the United States: Historical and Political Perspectives*. Albuquerque: University of New Mexico Press, 1979.

Kochan, Thomas A., et al. *The Transformation of Industrial Relations*. New York: Basic Books, 1986.

Kofas, Jon F. *The Struggle for Legitimacy: Latin American Labor and the United States*. Tempe, AZ: Center for Latin American Studies, Arizona State University, 1992.

Koh, Tommy, and Marcel van der Linden, eds. *Labour Relations in Asia and Europe*. Singapore: Asia-Europe Foundation, 2000.

Kornbluh, Joyce L. *Rebel Voices: An IWW Anthology*. Chicago: Charles H. Kerr, 1988.

Kushner, Sam. *Long Road to Delano: A Century of Farmworkers' Struggle*. New York: International Publishers, 1975.

LaBotz, Dan. *The Crisis of Mexican Labor*. New York: Praeger, 1988.

———. *Mask of Democracy: Labor Suppression in Mexico Today*. Boston: South End Press, 1992.

Lane, Thomas. *Solidarity or Survival? American Labor and European Immigrants, 1830–1924*. Westport, CT: Greenwood Press, 1987.

Lankton, Larry. *Cradle to Grave: Life, Work, and Death at the Lake Superior Copper Mines*. New York: Oxford University Press, 1991.

Large, Stephen S. *Organized Workers and Socialist Politics in Interwar Japan*. Cambridge, MA: Cambridge University Press, 1981.

Larson, Simeon. *Labor and Foreign Policy: Gompers, the AFL and the First World War*. Rutherford, NJ: Fairleigh Dickinson University Press, 1975.

Laslett, John H. M. *Labor and the Left: A Study of Socialist and Radical Influences in the American Labor Movement, 1881–1924*. New York: Basic Books, 1970.

————, ed. *The United Mine Workers of America: A Model of Industrial Solidarity?* University Park, PA: The Pennsylvania State University Press, 1996.

Laughlin, Kathleen A. *Women's Work and Public Policy: A History of the Women's Bureau, U.S. Department of Labor, 1945–1970.* Boston: Northeastern University Press, 2000.

Le Blanc, Paul. *A Short History of the U.S. Working Class, from Colonial Times to the Twenty-First Century.* Amherst, NY: Humanity Books, 2000.

Lehrer, Susan. *Origins of Protective Labor Legislation for Women, 1905–1925.* Albany: State University of New York Press, 1987.

Lens, Sidney. *Strikemakers and Strikebreakers.* New York: E.P. Dutton, 1985.

Letwin, Daniel. *The Challenge of Interracial Unionism: Alabama Coal Miners, 1878–1921.* Chapel Hill, NC: University of North Carolina Press, 1998.

Levenstein, Harvey A. *Labor Organizations in the United States and Mexico: A History of Their Relations.* Westport, CT: Greenwood Publishing, 1971.

Levine, Louis. *The French Labor Movement.* Cambridge: Harvard University Press, 1954.

Licht, Walter. *Working for the Railroad: The Organization of Work in the Nineteenth Century.* Princeton, NJ: Princeton University Press, 1983.

————. *Industrializing America: The Nineteenth Century.* Baltimore, MD: The Johns Hopkins University Press, 1995.

Lichtenstein, Nelson. *The Most Dangerous Man in Detroit: Walter Reuther and the Fate of American Labor.* New York: Basic Books, 1995.

————. *State of the Union: A Century of American Labor.* Princeton, NJ: Princeton University Press, 2001.

Lindemann, Albert S. *A History of European Socialism.* New Haven, CT, and London: Yale University Press, 1983.

Lingenfelter, Richard E. *The Hardrock Miners: A History of the Mining Labor Movement in the American West, 1863–1893.* Berkeley: University of California Press, 1974.

Lipsitz, George. *Rainbow at Midnight: Labor and Culture in the 1940s.* Urbana: University of Illinois Press, 1994.

Lombardi, John. *Labor's Voice in the Cabinet: A History of the Department of Labor from Its Origin to 1921.* New York: Columbia University, 1942.

Long, Priscilla. *Where the Sun Never Shines: A History of America's Bloody Coal Industry.* New York: Paragon Books, 1991.

Lovell, John Christopher. *Stevedores and Dockers: A Study of Trade Unionism in the Port of London, 1870–1914.* London: Macmillan 1969.

Lynd, Staughton, ed. *We Are All Leaders: The Alternative Unionism of the Early 1930s.* Champaign: University of Illinois Press, 1996.

Madison, Charles A. *American Labor Leaders: Personalities and Forces in the Labor Movement.* New York: Frederick Unger Publishing, 1962.

Magraw, Roger. *A History of the French Working Class.* Vol. 2: *The Age of Artisan Revolution, 1815–1871.* Cambridge, MA: Blackwell, 1992.

Mangum, Garth L., and R. Scott McNabb. *The Rise, Fall and Replacement of Industrywide Bargaining in the Basic Steel Industry.* New York: M. E. Sharpe, 1997.

Marsh, Arthur, and Victoria Ryan. *The Seamen: A History of the National Union of Seamen, 1887–1987.* Oxford: Malthouse Press, 1989.

Marshall, F. Ray. *Labor in the South.* Cambridge: Harvard University Press, 1967.

Marsland, Stephen. *The Birth of the Japanese Labor Movement: Takano Fusataro and the Rodo Kumiai Kiseikai.* Honolulu, HI: University of Hawaii Press, 1989.

Martin, Benjamin. *The Agony of Industrialization: Labor and Industrialization in Spain.* Ithaca, NY: ILR Press, 1990.

Marx, Eleanor, and Edward Aveling. *The Working-Class Movement in America,* edited by Paul Le Blanc. Amherst, NY: Humanity Books, 2000.

Mason, Timothy W. *Social Policy in the Third Reich: The Working Class and the National Community.* Providence, RI: Berg, 1993.

Matthiessen, Peter. *Sal Si Puedes (Escape if You Can): Cesar Chavez and the New American Revolution.* Berkeley: University of California Press, 2000.

Mayer, Henry. *All on Fire: William Lloyd Garrison and the Abolition of Slavery.* New York: St. Martin's Press, 1998.

McCartin, Joseph A. *Labor's Great War: The Struggle for Industrial Democracy and the Origins of Modern American Labor Relations, 1912–1921.* Chapel Hill: University of North Carolina Press, 1997.

McClain, Charles, ed. *Chinese Immigrants and American Law.* New York: Garland Publishing, 1994.

McGrath, Robert C., Jr. *American Populism: A Social History, 1877–1898.* New York: Hill and Wang, 1993.

McLaurin, Melton A. *The Knights of Labor in the South.* Westport, CT: Greenwood Press, 1978.

McMurry, Donald L. *The Great Burlingtion Strike of 1888: A Case Study in Labor Relations.* Cambridge: Harvard University Press, 1956.

McShane, Denis. *International Labor and the Origins of the Cold War.* Oxford: Clarendon, 1992.

McVey, Ruth. *The Rise of Indonesian Communism.* Ithaca, NY: Indonesia Project, Southeast Asia Program, Cornell University Press, 1965.

Mehta, B. L. *Trade Union Movement in India.* Delhi, India: Kanishka Publishing House, 1991.

Mellinger, Philip J. *Race and Labor in Western Copper: The Fight for Equality, 1896–1918.* Tucson: University of Arizona Press, 1995.

Middlebrook, Kevin J. *The Paradox of Revolution: Labor, the State, and Authoritarianism in Mexico.* Baltimore, MD: The Johns Hopkins University Press, 1995.

Miller, Susanne and Heinrich Potthoff. *A History of German Social Democracy: From 1848 to the Present.* Leamington Spa, U.K.; Hamburg, Germany; and New York: Berg Publishers, 1986.

Milner, Susan. *The Dilemmas of Internationalism: French Syndicalism and the International Labour Movement, 1900–1914.* Oxford, U.K.: Berg, 1990.

Montgomery, David. *Beyond Equality: Labor and the Radical Republicans, 1862–1872.* New York: Alfred A. Knopf, 1967.

————. *The Fall of the House of Labor: The Workplace, the State, and American Labor Activism, 1865–1925.* New York: Cambridge University Press, 1987.

Montgomery, David, and Marcel van der Linden, eds. *August Sartorius von Waltershausen: The Workers' Movement in the United States, 1879–1885.* Cambridge, U.K.; New York: Cambridge University Press, 1998.

Moody, J. Carroll, and Alice Kessler-Harris, eds. *Perspectives on American Labor History: The Problems of Synthesis.* Dekalb: Northern Illinois University Press, 1989.

Moody, Kim. *An Injury to All: The Decline of American Unionism.* New York: Verso, 1988.

Moore, Joe. *Japanese Workers and the Struggle for Power, 1945–1947.* Madison: University of Wisconsin Press, 1983.

Moreno, Paul D. *From Direct Action to Affirmative Action: Fair Employment Law and Policy in America, 1933–1972.* Baton Rouge: Louisiana State University Press, 1997.

Morgan, Carol E. *Women Workers and Gender Identities, 1835–1913: The Cotton and Metal Industries in England.* London: Routledge, 2001.

Morgan, David. *The Socialist Left and the German Revolution.* Ithaca: Cornell University Press, 1975.

Morgan, Roger. *The German Social Democrats and the First International 1864–1872.* Cambridge: Cambridge University Press, 1965.

Morris, Richard B., ed. *A History of the American Worker.* Princeton, NJ: Princeton University Press, 1983.

Moses, John A. *Trade Unionism in Germany from Bismarck to Hitler, 1869–1933.* Vol. 1: *1869–1918.* London: George Prior Publishers, 1982.

Moss, David A. *Socializing Security: Progressive-Era Economists and the Origins of American Social Policy.* Cambridge, MA: Harvard University Press, 1996.

Munck, Ronaldo. *Argentina from Anarchism to Peronism: Workers, Unions and Politics, 1855–1985.* London: Zed Books Ltd., 1987.

Murolo, Priscilla and A. B. Chitty. *From the Folks Who Brought You the Weekend: A Short, Illustrated History of Labor in the United States.* New York: The New Press, 2001.

Murphy, Teresa Anne. *Ten Hours' Labor: Religion, Reform, and Gender in Early New England.* Ithaca, NY, and London: Cornell University Press, 1992.

Murray, R. Emmett. *The Lexicon of Labor.* New York: New Press, 1998.

Nelson, Bruce. *Workers on the Waterfront: Seamen, Longshoremen, and Unionism in the 1930s.* Urbana, IL: University of Illinois Press, 1988.

Nelson, Daniel. *American Rubber Workers and Organized Labor, 1900–1941.* Princeton, NJ: Princeton University Press, 1988.

———. *Farm and Factory: Workers in the Midwest, 1880–1990.* Bloomington: Indiana University Press, 1995.

———. *Managers and Workers: Origins of the Twentieth Century Factory System in the United States, 1880–1920.* Madison: University of Wisconsin Press, 1995.

———. *Shifting Fortunes: The Rise and Decline of American Labor, from the 1820s to the Present.* Chicago: Ivan R. Dee, 1997.

Nolan, Melanie. *Breadwinning: New Zealand Women and the State.* Christchurch, New Zealand: Canterbury University Press, 2000.

Northrup, Herbert R., and Gordon F. Bloom. *Government and Labor.* Homewood, IL: Richard D. Irwin, 1963.

Norwood, Stephen H. *Strikebreaking and Intimidation: Mercenaries and Masculinity in Twentieth-Century America.* Chapel Hill: University of North Carolina Press, 2002.

Nove, Alec. *The Soviet Economic System.* London: Allen & Unwin, 1977.

———. *An Economic History of the USSR, 1917–1991.* London: Penguin, 1992.

Novkov, Julie. *Constituting Workers, Protecting Women: Gender, Law, and Labor in the Progressive Era and New Deal Years.* Ann Arbor, MI: University of Michigan Press, 2001.

O'Brien, Ruth Ann. *Workers' Paradox: The Republican Origins of New Deal Labor Policy, 1886–1935.* Chapel Hill, NC: University of North Carolina Press, 1998.

Oestreicher, Richard Jules. *Solidarity and Fragmentation: Working People and Class Consciousness in Detroit, 1875–1900.* Urbana: University of Illinois Press, 1986.

O'Farrell, Brigid, and Kornbluh, Joyce L. *Rocking the Boat: Union Women's Voices, 1915–1975.* New Brunswick, NJ: Rutgers University Press, 1996.

O'Neill, Colleen. *Making a Living and Working Elsewhere: Navajo Workers in the Twentieth Century.* Lawrence: University Press of Kansas, forthcoming.

O'Neill, Colleen, and Brian C. Hosmer, eds. *Native Pathways: American Indian Economies and Culture in the Twentieth Century.* Boulder: University of Colorado Press, forthcoming.

Orleck, Annelise. *Common Sense and a Little Fire: Women and Working-class Politics in the U.S., 1900–1965.* Chapel Hill: University of North Carolina Press, 1995.

Palmer, Bryan D. *Working-Class Experience: Rethinking the History of Canadian Labour, 1800–1991.* Toronto: McClelland and Stewart, 1992.

Patterson, James T. *America's Struggle Against Poverty in the Twentieth Century.* Cambridge: Harvard University Press, 2000.

Paulson, George E. *A Living Wage for the Forgotten Man: The Quest for Fair Labor Standards, 1933–1941.* London: Associated University Presses, 1996.

Paulson, Ross Evans. *Liberty, Equality, and Justice: Civil Rights, Women's Rights, and the Regulation of Business, 1865–1932.* Durham, NC: Duke University Press, 1997.

Peffer, William. *Populism: Its Rise and Fall.* Lawrence: University Press of Kansas, 2000.

Pelling, Henry. *A History of British Trade Unionism,* 3d ed. New York: Penguin, 1976.

———. *A Short History of the Labour Party.* 11th ed. New York: St. Martin's Press, 1996.

Perry, Elizabeth. *Shanghai on Strike: The Politics of Chinese Labor.* Stanford, CA: Stanford University Press, 1993.

Pessen, Edward. *Most Uncommon Jacksonians: The Radical Leaders of the Early Labor Movement.* Albany: State University of New York Press, 1967.

Phillips, G. A. *The General Strike: The Politics of Industrial Conflict.* London: Weidenfeld and Nicolson, 1976.

Poblete Troncoso, Moisés, and Ben G. Burnett. *The Rise of the Latin American Labor Movement.* New York: Bookman Associates, 1960.

Posusney, Marsha Pripstein. *Labor and the State in Egypt: Workers, Unions and Economic Restructuring.* New York: Columbia University Press, 1997.

Preis, Art. *Labor's Giant Step, Twenty Years of the CIO.* New York: Pathfinder Press, 1972.

Prothero, Iorwerth. *Radical Artisans in England and France, 1830–1870.* Cambridge: Cambridge University Press, 1997.

Radosh, Ronald. *American Labor and the United States Foreign Policy: The Cold War and the Unions from Gompers to Lovestone.* New York: Random House, 1969.

Raman Rao, A. V. *Indian Trade Unions.* Honolulu: University of Hawaii Industrial Relations Center, 1967.

Reichard, Richard W. *From the Petition to the Strike: A History of Strikes in Germany, 1869–1914.* New York: Peter Lang Publishing, 1991.

Renshaw, Patrick. *The Wobblies: The Story of Syndicalism in the United States.* Garden City, NY: Doubleday & Co., Inc., 1967.

Rice, John, ed. *British Trade Unionism, 1750–1850: The Formative Years.* London: Longman, 1988.

Richardson, Reed C. *The Locomotive Engineer, 1863–1963: A Century of Railway Labor Relations and Work Rules.* Ann Arbor: University of Michigan Press, 1963.

Roberts, David D. *The Syndicalist Tradition and Italian Fascism.* Chapel Hill: The University of North Carolina Press, 1979.

Rockenbach, Leslie. *The Mexican-American Border: NAFTA and Global Linkages.* New York: Routledge, 2001.

Ross, Corey. *Constructing Socialism at the Grass-roots: The Transformation of East Germany, 1945–1965.* Basingstoke, England: Macmillan, 2000.

Roth, Bert. *Trade Unions in New Zealand.* Wellington, NZ: Reed Education, 1973.

Roy, Andrew. *A History of the Coal Miners of the United States.* Westport, CT: Greenwood Press, 1970.

Rule, John. *The Labouring Classes in Early Industrial England, 1750–1850.* New York: Longman, 1986.

Ruotsila, Markku. *British and American Anticommunism Before the Cold War.* London, U.K., and Portland, OR: Frank Cass, 2001.

Safford, Frank, and Marco Palacios. *Colombia: Fragmented Land, Divided Society.* Oxford and New York: Oxford University Press, 2002.

Salomon, Larry R. *Roots of Justice: Stories of Organizing in Communities of Color.* Berkeley, CA: Chardon Press, 1998.

Sass, Steven A. *The Promise of Private Pensions: The First Hundred Years.* Cambridge, MA: Harvard University Press, 1997.

Saxton, Alexander. *The Indispensable Enemy: Labor and the Anti-Chinese Movement in California.* Berkeley: University of California Press, 1995.

Scalapino, Robert. *The Early Japanese Labor Movement: Labor and Politics in a Developing Society.* Berkeley: Institute of East Asian Studies, University of California, 1983.

Schlesinger, Stephen, and Stephen Kinzer. *Bitter Fruit: The Story of the American Coup in Guatemala.* Cambridge, MA: Harvard University Press, 1999.

Schneider, Dorothy, and Carl J. Schneider. *The ABC–CLIO Companion to Women in the Workplace.* Santa Barbara, CA: ABC-CLIO, 1993.

Schneider, Michael. *A Brief History of the German Trade Unions.* Bonn, Germany: J.H.W Dietz, 1991.

Sewell, William Hamilton. *Work and Revolution in France: The Language of Labor from the Old Regime to 1848.* Cambridge, England: Cambridge University Press, 1980.

Sheehan, James J., ed. *Industrialization and Industrial Labor in Nineteenth-century Europe.* Major Issues in History. New York: Wiley, 1973.

Shorter, Edward, and Charles Tilly. *Strikes in France, 1830–1968.* New York: Cambridge University Press, 1974.

Silverman, Victor. *Imagining Internationalism in American and British Labor, 1939–1949.* Urbana: Illinois University Press, 2000.

Singer, Daniel. *Prelude to Revolution: France in May 1968.* New York: Hill and Wang, 1970.

Skocpol, Theda. *Protecting Soldiers and Mothers: The Political Origins of Social Policy in the United States.* Cambridge, MA: Belknap, 1992.

Smelser, Neil J. *Social Change in the Industrial Revolution: An Application of Theory to the Lancashire Cotton Industry, 1770–1840.* London: Routledge and Paul, 1959.

Smith, William C. *Second Empire and Commune: France, 1848–1871.* 2nd ed. London and New York: Longman, 1996.

Sosnick, Stephen H. *Hired Hands: Seasonal Farm Workers in the United States.* Santa Barbara, CA: McNally and Loftin, 1978.

Sovern, Michael. *Legal Restraints on Racial Discrimination in Employment.* New York: The Twentieth Century Fund, 1966.

Spalding, Hobart. *Organized Labor in Latin America: Historical Case Studies of Workers in Dependent Societies.* New York: New York University Press, 1977.

Sperber, Jonathan. *The European Revolutions, 1848–1851.* Cambridge, MA: Cambridge University Press, 1994.

Stearns, Peter N. *Revolutionary Syndicalism and French Labor: A Cause Without Rebels.* New Brunswick, NJ: Rutgers University Press, 1971.

Steedman, Mercedes, Peter Suschnigg, and Dieter K. Buse. *Hard Lessons: The Mine Mill Union in the Canadian Labour Movement.* Toronto, Canada; Niagara Falls, NY: Dundurn Press, 1995.

Stein, Leon, ed. *Out of the Sweatshop: The Struggle for Industrial Democracy.* New York: Quadrangle/New York Times, 1977.

Steinfeld, Robert J. *Coercion, Contract, and Free Labor in the Nineteenth Century.* New York: Cambridge University Press, 2001.

Stockton, Frank T. *The International Molders Union of North America.* Baltimore: Johns Hopkins University Press, 1921.

Stone, Richard D. *The Interstate Commerce Commission and the Railroad Industry: A History of Regulatory Policy.* New York: Praeger, 1991.

Storrs, Landon R.Y. *Civilizing Capitalism: The National Consumers' League, Women's Activism, and Labor Standards in the New Deal Era.* Chapel Hill, NC: University of North Carolina Press, 2000.

Stover, John F. *American Railroads.* Chicago: University of Chicago Press, 1997.

Stranahan, Patricia. *Underground: The Shanghai Communist Party and the Politics of Survival, 1927–1937*. Lanham, MD: Rowan and Littlefield Publishers, Inc., 1998.

Stromquist, Shelton. *A Generation of Boomers: The Pattern of Railroad Labor Conflict in Nineteenth-Century America*. Urbana: University of Illinois Press, 1987.

Taft, Philip. *The AFL in the Time of Gompers*. New York: Harper, 1957.

———. *The AFL from the Death of Gompers to the Merger*. New York: Harper and Brothers, 1959.

———. *Organized Labor in American History*. New York: Harper & Row, 1964.

Tallion, Paul Michel. *Culture, Politics, and the Making of the Railroad Brotherhoods, 1863–1916*. Ann Arbor, MI: University Microfilms, 1997.

Tariq, Ali, and Susan Watkins. *1968: Marching in the Streets*. New York: Free Press, 1998.

Tax, Meredith. *The Rising of the Women: Feminist Solidarity and Class Conflict, 1880–1917*. New York: Monthly Review Press, 1980.

Taylor, Albion Guilford. *Labor Problems and Labor Law*. New York: Prentice Hall, 1938.

Taylor, Benjamin J., and Fred Witney. *Labor Relations Law*, 3rd ed. Englewood Cliffs, NJ: Prentice-Hall, 1979.

Terrell, John U. *The United States Department of Labor: A Story of Workers, Unions, and the Economy*. New York: Meredith, 1968.

Thompson, E. P. *The Making of the English Working Class*. New York: Pantheon Books, 1964.

Thompson, Willie. *The Communist Movement Since 1945*. Oxford, U.K.: Blackwell, 1998.

Thorpe, W. *"The Workers Themselves": Revolutionary Syndicalism and International Labour, 1913–1923*. Dordrecht: Kluwer Academic Publishers, 1989.

Tilly, Charles. *European Revolutions, 1492–1992*. Oxford, U.K.: Basil Blackwell, 1993.

Tolliday, Steven, and Jonathan Zeitlin, eds. *Shop Floor Bargaining and the State*. New York: Cambridge University Press, 1987.

Tomlins, Christopher L. *The State and the Unions: Labor Relations, Law, and the Organized Labor Movement in America, 1880–1960*. New York: Cambridge University Press, 1985.

Tone, Andrea. *The Business of Benevolence: Industrial Paternalism in Progressive America*. Ithaca, NY: Cornell University Press, 1997.

Trattner, Walter I. *Crusade for the Children: A History of the National Child Labor Committee and Child Labor Reform in America*. Chicago: Quadrangle Books, 1970.

Traugott, Mark. *Armies of the Poor: Determinants of Working-class Participation in the Parisian Insurrection of June 1848*. Princeton, NJ: Princeton University Press, 1985.

Tsurumi, Patricia. *Factory Girls: Women in the Thread Mills of Meiji Japan*. Princeton, NJ: Princeton University Press, 1990.

van der Linden, Marcel. *Transnational Labour History: Explorations*. Burlington, VT: Ashgate, 2002.

van der Linden, Marcel, and Jan Lucassen, eds. *Racism and the Labour Market: Historical Studies*. Bern, Switzerland; New York: P. Lang, 1995.

van der Linden, Marcel, and Richard Price, eds. *The Rise and Development of Collective Labour Law*. Bern, Switzerland; New York: P. Lang, 2000.

van der Linden, Marcel, and Jürgen Rojahn, eds. *The Formation of Labour Movements, 1870–1914: An International Perspective*. Leiden, Netherlands; New York: E.J. Brill, 1990.

van der Linden, Marcel, and Wayne Thorpe, eds. *Revolutionary Syndicalism: An International Perspective*. Hants, England: Scolar Press, 1990.

van der Linden, Marcel, and Lex Heerma van Voss, eds. *Class and Other Identities: Gender, Religion and Ethnicity in the Writing of European Labor History*. New York: Berghahn Books, 2002.

van der Walt, Lucien. *The IWW, Revolutionary Syndicalism and Working Class Struggle in South Africa, 1910–1921*. Durban, South Africa: Zabalaza Books, n.d.

van Holthoon, Frits, and Marcel van der Linden, eds. *Internationalism in the Labour Movement, 1830–1940*. Leiden, Netherlands; New York: E.J. Brill, 1988.

Vargas, Zaragosa. *Proletarians of the North: A History of Mexican Industrial Workers in Detroit and the Midwest, 1919–1933*. Berkeley: University of California Press, 1993.

———. *The Union Makes Us Strong: Mexican American Workers, Unionism, and the Struggle for Civil Rights, 1929–1945*. Princeton, NJ: Princeton University Press, forthcoming.

Voss, Kim. *The Making of American Exceptionalism: The Knights of Labor and Class Formation in the Nineteenth Century*. Ithaca, NY: Cornell University Press, 1993.

Waldrep, G. C., III. *Southern Workers and the Search for Community*. Champaign: University of Illinois Press, 2000.

Walker, Ivan L., and Ben Weinbren. *2000 Casualties: A History of the Trade Unions and the Labour Movement in the Union of South Africa*. Johannesburg, R.S.A.: The South African Trade Union Council, 1961.

Walsh, John, and Garth Mangum. *Labor Struggle in the Post Office*. New York: M. E. Sharpe, Inc., 1992.

Ward, John Trevor. *The Factory Movement, 1830–1855*. New York: St. Martin's Press, 1962.

Weiler, Peter. *British Labour and the Cold War*. Stanford, CA: Stanford University Press, 1988.

Weir, Robert E. *Beyond Labor's Veil: The Culture of the Knights of Labor*. University Park, PA: Pennsylvania State University Press, 1996.

———. *Knights Unhorsed: Internal Conflict in a Gilded Age Social Movement*. Detroit: Wayne State University Press, 2000.

Wertheimer, Barbara M. *We Were There: The Story of Working Women in America*. New York: Pantheon Books, 1977.

Wikander, Ulla, Alice Kessler-Harris, and Jane Lewis, eds. *Protecting Women: Labor Legislation in Europe, the United States, and Australia, 1880–1920*. Urbana: University of Illinois Press, 1995.

Wilentz, Sean. *Chants Democratic: New York City and the Rise of the American Working Class, 1788–1850*. New York: Oxford University Press, 1984.

Williams, Roger L. *The French Revolution of 1870–1871*. New York: Norton, 1969.

Wilson, Francis. *Labour in the South African Gold Mines, 1911–1969*. Cambridge, MA: Cambridge University Press, 1972.

Wise, David A. *Pensions, Labor, and Individual Choice*. Chicago: University of Chicago Press, 1985.

Witwer, David Scott. *Corruption and Reform in the Teamsters Union*. Urbana: University of Illinois Press, 2003.

Wood, Alan. *The Origins of the Russian Revolution, 1861–1917*. 2nd ed. London: Routledge, 1993.

Woodward, Llewellyn. *The Age of Reform: England, 1815–1870*, 2nd ed. Oxford: Oxford University Press, 1962.

Wyman, Mark. *Hard Rock Epic: Western Miners and the Industrial Revolution, 1860–1910*. Berkeley: University of California Press, 1979.

Young, John D. *The Very Bastards of Creation: Scottish International Radicalism, 1707–1995*. Glasgow: Clydeside Press, 1997.

Zieger, Robert. *The CIO, 1935–1955*. Chapel Hill: University of North Carolina Press, 1995.

Zonderman, David A. *Aspirations and Anxieties: New England Workers and the Mechanized Factory System, 1815–1850*. New York and Oxford: Oxford University Press, 1992.

NOTES ON ADVISERS AND CONTRIBUTORS

AMERMAN, Don. Editor and writer, Saylorsburg, Pennsylvania. Frequent contributor to publications of Gale Group, Rock-Hill Communications, and Charles Scribner's Sons. **Essays:** Brotherhood of Sleeping Car Porters, United States; National Typographical Union, United States; United Mine Workers Strike, United States.

ATKINS, William Arthur. Science and business writer, editor, and consultant, Normal, Illinois. Educational background in business (B.B. and M.B.A.) and physics and mathematics (B.S.). Professional experience in space sciences (U.S. space program), engineering, computer sales and service, teaching, and project management. **Essays:** Abolition of Slavery, United States; American Association for Labor Legislation, United States; American Federation of Labor, United States; Anarchists Lead Argentine Labor Movement, Argentina; Bituminous Coal Strike, United States; Bloody Sunday, Russia; Coal Mine Contract Signed, United States; Colored National Labor Union, United States; European Strike Wave, Europe; Forced Labor, USSR; General Allotment Act, United States; General Trades' Union, United States; Hawaii Collective Bargaining Law, United States; Hot Autumn, Italy; Interstate Commerce Commission, United States; McKees Rocks Strike, United States; Milan Barricade Fights, Italy; National Union of Iron Molders, United States; No-strike Pledge, World War II, United States; Organized Labor Established, Argentina; Power Loom Invented, United States; Red Week, Italy; Strike Wave, Italy; United Automobile Workers of America, United States; United Mine Workers of America, United States; Wagner-Peyser Act, United States; Washington Union Shop Law, United States; Workers' Congress, Mexico.

BARKER, Kimberley. Assistant professor, Russell Library, Georgia College and State University, Milledgeville, Georgia. Research interests include marketing and public relations in academic libraries. **Essays:** Shoemaker's Strike, United States; Working Women's Protective Union, United States.

BARRY, Bill. Director of labor studies, Community College of Baltimore County, Dundalk, Maryland. Teaches the full range of worker education courses, including labor history. **Essays:** Gabriel's Rebellion, United States; Molly Maguires, United States; Taylor and Scientific Management, United States.

BISHOP, Elizabeth A. Teaches in Cairo University's History Department, and at the American University in Cairo. **Essay:** International Confederation of Arab Trade Unions, Egypt.

BLACK, Lawrence. Fulbright visiting professor of British history, Westminster College, Fulton, Missouri. Author of *The Political Culture of the Left in Affluent Britain, 1951–64,* 2003. Coeditor of *Consensus or Coercion?,* 2001 and *An Affluent Society? Britiain's Golden Age Revisited,* 2004. Currently researching postwar British political culture. **Essays:** Dockers' Strike, Great Britain; Trades Union Congress, Great Britain.

BLEWETT, Mary H. Emerita professor of history, University of Massachusetts, Lowell. Author of *Men, Women, and Work: Class Gender, and Protest in the Nineteenth-Century New England Shoe Industry,* 1988; *The Last Generation: Work and Life in the Textile Mills of Lowell, Massachusetts, 1910–1960,* 1990; *We Will Rise in Our Might: Workingwomen's Voices in Nine-teenth-Century New England,* 1991; and *Constant Turmoil: The Politics of Industrial Life in Nineteenth-Century New England,* 2000. **Essay:** St. Crispin Organizations, United States.

BORDEN, Timothy G. Writer and historian, Toledo, Ohio. Author of labor history articles in *Michigan Historical Review, Polish American Studies,* and *Labor History.* Teaches world and U.S. history courses. **Essays:** American Plan, United States; Ford-UAW SUB Agreement, United States; GM-UAW Landmark Contracts, United States; Lodz Uprising, Poland; Mass Strikes, United States; Panic of 1893, United States; Perón Elected President, Argentina; Poznan Workers' Riots, Poland; Solidarity Emerges, Poland; Strike Wave, United States; Tragic Week, Argentina.

BORTZ, Jeffrey. Professor of history, Appalachian State University, Boone, North Carolina. Author of recent articles on Mexican labor in *Labor History, Journal of Latin American Studies, International Review of Social History,* and *The Americas.* Coeditor (with Stephen Haber) of *The Mexican Economy, 1870–1930,* 2002. **Essay:** Mexican Labor Confederations, Mexico.

BOUGHTON, John. Visiting assistant professor of European history, Goucher College, Baltimore, Maryland. Coauthor of IT-learning software on Stalin and the rise of the British Labour Party. **Essays:** Chartist Movement, Great Britain; London Workingmen's Association, Great Britain; Miners' and General Strikes, Great Britain; Osborne Judgment, Great Britain; Peterloo Massacre, Great Britain; Taff Vale Case, United States.

BRUSCHI, Valeria. Has a degree in philosophy from Humboldt University in Berlin, Germany, and translates from German, Spanish, and Greek into Italian for the European Social Forum. **Essay:** General Strike, Spain.

BURNS, William E. Historian. Author of books on prodigies in early modern England, the scientific revolution, and witch hunting. **Essays:** Abolition of Slavery, British Empire; Combination Acts, Great Britain; Factory Act, Great Britain; Repeal of Combination Acts, Great Britain.

BUSE, Dieter K. Professor of history, Laurentian University, Sudbury, Ontario, Canada. Editor of *Modern Germany: An Encyclopedia of History, People and Culture, 1871–1990,* 1998; coeditor of *Hard Lessons: The Mine Mill Union in the Canadian Labour Movement,* 1995. **Essay:** German Revolution, Germany.

CASSANELLO, Robert. Assistant professor of history, Miles College, Fairfield, Alabama. **Essays:** Black Codes, United States; Jim Crow Segregation and Labor, United States; *Muller v. State of Oregon,* United States; National War Labor Board, United States.

COMPAGNON, Olivier. Université Paris I-Sorbonne, France. Historian of modern Latin America and the author of *Jacques Maritain et l'Amérique du Sud,* 2003. **Essay:** Popular Unity, Chile.

CONTREPOIS, Sylvie. Research fellow, Working Lives Research Institute, London, United Kingdom. Member of the "Genres et rapports sociaux" CNRS research unit in Paris,

France. Author of *Syndicats, la nouvelle donne,* 2003. **Essays:** Confédération Générale du Travail, France; General Strike, France.

CROUCHER, Richard. Senior research fellow, International Trade Union Centre, Cranfield University, United Kingdom. Author of *Engineers at War 1939–45;* and historian of the National Unemployed Workers Movement, 1920–1946. **Essays:** Amalgamated Society of Engineers, Great Britain; Shop Steward Movement Originates, Great Britain.

DANIEL, Evan. Graduate student, New School for Social Research, New York City, and junior archivist, Tamiment Library/ Robert F. Wagner Labor Archives, New York University. Author of *Anarchist Labor and the National Liberation Movement in Cuba, 1857–1898,* forthcoming. **Essays:** Barcelona Workers' Rebellion, Spain; Syndicalist Movement, Worldwide.

DARBY, Jonathan. Assistant professor, Ina Dillard Russell Library, Georgia College and State University, Milledgeville, Georgia. Primary research interests are the history of technology and religion. **Essays:** Mechanics' Union of Trade Associations, United States; Widowed Mother's Fund Association, United States.

DARLINGTON, Ralph. Senior lecturer in industrial relations, University of Salford, United Kingdom. Author of *The Dynamics of Workplace Trade Unionism,* 1994; *The Political Trajectory of J. T. Murphy,* 1998; and (with Dave Lyddon) *Glorious Summer: Class Struggle in Britain, 1972,* 2001. **Essay:** Red International of Labor Unions, Russia.

DEFOORT, Hendrik. Cultural heritage coordinator. **Essay:** Charleroi Confrontation Between Miners and the Military, Belgium.

DESLIPPE, Dennis. Lecturer, School of Social Sciences, Australian National University, Canaberra, Australia. Author of *Rights, Not Roses: Unions and the Rise of Working-Class Feminism, 1945–90,* 2000. **Essays:** Coalition of Labor Union Women, United States; Equal Pay Act, United States; National Organization for Women, United States.

DUBLIN, Thomas. Professor of history, State University of New York at Binghamton. Author of *Women at Work: The Transformation of Work and Community in Lowell, Massachusetts, 1826–1860,* 1979, and *When the Mines Closed: Stories of Struggles in Hard Times,* 1998. Coeditor of *Women and Social Movements in the United States.* **Essay:** Lowell Industrial Experiment, United States.

DYNAN, Linda. Independent researcher and scholar, Cincinnati, Ohio. Teaches economics courses on labor issues and health care organization. Has published articles in the same areas. **Essays:** Byrnes Act, United States; Public Contracts Act, United States; Union Label Movement, United States.

EMMERLING, Beth. Writer based in Baltimore, Maryland. **Essays:** Dover Textile Strike, United States; National Labor Union, United States; Workingmen's Party, United States.

ENNIS, Lisa. Assistant professor, coordinator of instruction, and government documents librarian, Russell Library, Georgia College and State University, Milledgeville, Georgia. Teaches a wide variety of classes on information literacy and research skills with particular interests in American social history. **Essays:** Bureau of Labor Established, United States; Hawes-Cooper Act, United States; Mediation Commission, World War I, United States; New Orleans General Strike, United States; Postal Workers' Strike, United States.

FORD, Katrina. Writer based in South Yarra, Victoria, Australia. Contributor to several historical reference works, including *Science and Its Times, Science in Dispute,* and the *Dictionary of Nineteenth Century British Scientists.* **Essays:** Bans on Labor Unions Lifted, Germany; *Communist Manifesto* Published, England; June Days Rebellion, France; Miners' Strike, Germany; National Congress of German Trade Unions, Germany; Paris Commune, France; Second International, France; Second Reform Act, Great Britain; Strike Ban Lifted, France; Strikes of Journeymen and Workers, Paris, France; Weavers' Revolt, Silesia.

FORT, Carol. Visiting research fellow, Department of History, Flinders University of South Australia, Adelaide. Currently working on nineteenth- and twentieth-century political history, especially the development of national employment policies in war time and the development of political identity in settler societies. **Essay:** World War II Labor Measures, United States.

FREDERICK, Kimberly F. Graduate student, American history, Brandeis University, Waltham, Massachusetts. Research interests include labor history, urban planning, and architecture. **Essay:** Ten-Hour Day Movement, United States.

FRISCH, Paul. Professor, dean of the library, Our Lady of the Lake University, San Antonio, Texas. Research interests are American biography and U.S. labor history. **Essays:** Knights Break Color Line, United States; Knights of Labor, United States; Western Federation of Miners, United States.

GANNON, Kevin M. Assistant professor of history, Merrimack College, North Andover, Massachusetts. Teaches a variety of courses in early national and antebellum U.S. history, as well as in Latin American history. Current research centers around states' rights thought and the use of nullification and secession by various actors in the antebellum North. **Essays:** Dorr Rebellion, United States; Equal Rights Party, United States.

GOLD, Roberta. Doctoral candidate in history, University of Washington, Seattle. Completing dissertation on tenant movement in New York City. **Essay:** Seattle General Strike, United States.

GÓMEZ GUTIÉRREZ, Juan José. Editor and art historian. Author of articles on modern art and politics; advisor in municipal cultural politics for Izquierda Unida Group of Councillors between 2000 and 2003, Seville City Council (Spain); advisor in municipal cultural politics for Seville's section of Comisiones Obreras Trade Union, 2003. **Essays:** Hungarian Revolution and Workers Councils, Hungary; Socialist Unity Party of Germany, East Germany.

GOYENS, Tom. Doctoral candidate, University of Leuven, Belgium. Author of articles on the anarchist movement in America, Belgian immigrants, and colonial theater. **Essay:** Tompkins Square Rally, United States.

HANAGAN, Michael. Senior lecturer, New School University, New York City. Author of *The Logic of Solidarity,* 1979, and *Nascent Proletarians,* 1989. Coeditor of *Challenging Authority,* 1998, and *Extending Citizenship, Reconfiguring States,* 1999. **Essays:** Charter of Amiens, France; Herrin Massacre, United States; Potato Famine, Ireland; Revolutions in Europe.

HARRISON, Jennifer. Essay: Workingman's Benevolent Association, United States.

HOLZKA, Jane. LaGuardia Community College, Queens, New York. Teaches courses on U.S. history, urban history, world geography, and sociology. **Essays:** Child Labor Amendment, United States; CIO Expelled From AFL, United States; Fair Labor Standards Act, United States; Philadelphia Plan, United States.

HOROWITZ, Roger. Associate director, Center for the History of Business, Technology, and Society, Hagley Museum and Library, Wilmington, Delaware. Author of *"Negro and White, Unite and Fight!": A Social History of Industrial Unionism in Meatpacking, 1930–1990,* 1997, and *Meatpackers: An Oral History of Black Packinghouse Workers and Their Struggle for Racial and Economic Equality,* 1996 and 1999. **Essay:** Hormel Strike, United States.

HOWARD, Nik. Independent scholar, Leeds, United Kingdom. Author of articles on the origins of socialism in Japan and on asylum and refugee questions. Research interests include the Japanese left and right before World War II. **Essays:** Japanese Labor After World War II, Japan; Japanese Labor Unions Dissolved, Japan; Trade Union Formation and Suppression, Japan.

KANNENBERG, Lisa. Associate professor of history, College of Saint Rose, Albany, New York. Specialist in U.S. history, with particular emphasis on labor, business, and women's history. Currently completing a history of General Electric's labor and community relations policies in Schenectady, New York. **Essays:** CIO Anticommunist Drive, United States; Equal Rights Amendment and Protective Legislation, United States.

KELLING, Karla. Doctoral candidate, University of Washington, Seattle. Dissertation, "'Imprudent Conduct': Women, Work, and the Streets in Nineteenth-Century Philadelphia." **Essays:** Factory Girls' Association, United States; Free Soil Party, United States.

KESSLER-HARRIS, Alice. R. Gordon Hoxie Professor of American History, Columbia University, New York City. Author of *Out to Work: A History of Wage Earning Women in the U.S.,* 1982; *A Woman's Wage: Historical Meanings and Social Consequences,* 1990; and *In Pursuit of Equity: Women, Men, and the Quest for Economic Citizenship in Twentieth Century America,* 2001.

KING, Brett Allan. Writer based in Madrid, Spain. **Essays:** Brotherhood of Locomotive Engineers, United States; Chinese Rail Workers Strike, United States; Clayton Antitrust Act, United States; Eight-hour Day Movement, United States; European Trade Union Confederation, Europe; French Labor, World War II; Industrial Workers of Africa, South Africa; IWW Copper Strike, United States; Luddites Destroy Woolen Machines, Great Britain; March on Washington Movement, United States;

Minimum Wage Movement, United States; Socialist Party of America, United States; Steelworkers Experimental Agreement, United States; United States Joins International Labor Organization, United States.

KOCZAK, Steven. Research analyst, New York State Senate, Albany, New York. Writes on a broad array of topics in the areas of labor, public employees, and pensions. Aside from Senate publications, has also contributed to *The Encyclopedia of Work in America.* **Essays:** Davis-Bacon Act, United States; Employee Retirement Income Security Act, United States; *Lochner v. New York,* United States; Taylor Law, United States.

Le BLANC, Paul. Associate professor and dean of graduate studies at La Roche College, Pittsburg, Pennsylvania. Author of *A Short History of the U.S. Working Class,* 1999; coeditor with John Hinshaw of *U.S. Labor in the Twentieth Century,* 2000. **Essays:** AFL, CIO Merge, United States; Federation of Organized Trades and Labor Unions of the United States and Canada (FOTLU), United States and Canada; International Labor Union, United States; International Ladies Garment Workers Union, United States; Labor Day Established, United States; Lawrence Textile Strike, United States; Meany and Reuther Lead AFL, CIO, United States; Protocol of Peace, United States; Pullman Strike, United States; Railroad Strike of 1877, United States; Workingmen's Party of the United States, United States.

LEE, Andrew H. Tamiment Librarian, New York University, New York City. Editor of *Scottsboro, Alabama: A Story in Linoleum Cuts,* 2002. Moderator of H-LABOR.

LEWIS, James G. Historian, writer, and multimedia producer. Contributor to a wide array of print and on-line reference materials and producer of several CD-ROMs. **Essays:** Anthracite Coal Strike, United States; Department of Commerce and Labor, United States; Sinclair Publishes *The Jungle,* United States.

LEWIS-COLMAN, David. Visiting assistant professor, Department of History, University of Iowa, Iowa City. Teaches courses on social movements, labor and urban politics, African American history, and United States and world affairs. **Essay:** Fair Employment Practice Committee, United States.

LILLEKER, Darren G. Senior lecturer in political communication, Bournemouth Media School, Bournemouth University, Poole, Dorset, United Kingdom. Author of *Against the Cold War,* 2003, and numerous journal articles and chapters covering political science and history. **Essays:** Abolition of Serfdom, Russia; Five-Year Plan, USSR; Red Clyde Strike, Scotland; Russian Revolutions, Russia; USSR Collapse, USSR.

MANNING, Martin. Librarian and writer, U.S. Department of State, Washington, D.C. Contributor to several reference books and coauthor of *Herbal Medicine and Botanical Medical Fads,* 2002. **Essays:** Department of Labor, United States; General Agreement on Tariffs and Trade, Worldwide.

MARCHING, Soe Tjen. Doctoral candidate, Monash University, Melbourne, Australia. Winner of the National Competition for Indonesian Composers in 1998. Teaches Indonesian literature at Melbourne University. **Essay:** Indonesian Communist Party and Trade Unions Suppressed, Indonesia.

McCARTIN, Joseph. Associate professor of history, Georgetown University, Washington, D.C. Author of *Labor's Great War: The Struggle for Industrial Democracy and the Origins of Modern American Labor Relations, 1912–1921,* 1997. **Essay:** Railway Labor Act, United States.

McMULLEN, David Lee. Doctorial candidate in history, University of Aberdeen, Scotland/University of North Carolina at Charlotte. Teaches courses in U.S. history and literature, twentieth-century world history, and writing. **Essay:** Loray Mill Strike, United States.

McQUEEN, Lee. Assistant professor and social sciences reference librarian, Texas A&M University, College Station. Contributor to *The Scribner Encyclopedia of American Lives: The 1960s.* Interests in literacy, Spanish language and literature, and ethnic studies. **Essay:** Colored Farmers' Alliance, United States.

MILLER, Greg. Essays: Chinese Exclusion Act, United States; National Industrial Recovery Act, United States; Pawtucket Textile Strike, United States; Taft-Hartley Act, United States; U.S. Steel Defeats the Amalgamated Association, United States.

MIRRA, Carl. State University of New York at Old Westbury. Teaches American studies. Editor of *Enduring Freedom or Enduring War,* forthcoming. **Essay:** Guatemalan Coup Orchestrated by CIA, Guatemala.

MISNER, Paul. Emeritus professor of theology, Marquette University, Milwaukee, Wisconsin. Areas of interest include history of Christian life and thought, modern European history. Author of *Social Catholicism in Europe,* 1991. **Essay:** Christian Trade Unionists Conference, Switzerland.

NACK, David. Assistant professor, School for Workers, University of Wisconsin-Extension, Madison. Teaches labor education classes on a wide range of subjects and issues, as well as courses in history and labor relations, and has written on American labor and the cold war. **Essay:** National Civic Federation, United States.

NAGEL, Miriam C. Technical analyst and writer, Avon, Connecticut. Author of technical reports for Frost and Sullivan, features and articles for American Chemical Society, entries for textbooks and encyclopedias. Former columnist and feature editor, *Journal of Chemical Education.* **Essays:** General Motors Introduces Team Concept, United States; North American Free Trade Agreement, North America; Occupational Safety and Health Act, United States; PATCO Strike, United States; Sweeney Elected President of AFL-CIO, United States; Unions Plan Merger, United States.

NELSON, Daniel. Emeritus professor of history, University of Akron, Ohio. Author of *Unemployment Insurance, the American Experience,* 1969; *American Rubber Workers and Organized Labor,* 1988; and other books and essays on labor history, industrial relations, and public policy. **Essays:** Burlington Railroad Strike, United States; Goodyear Strike, United States; Introduction, U.S. Labor, 1800–2000; Wisconsin Unemployment Insurance, United States.

NEUMANN, Caryn E. Doctoral candidate and instructor, Ohio State University, Columbus. Former editor of the *Journal of Women's History* and author of the dissertation *Status Seekers: Mainstream Women's Organizations, Civil Rights, and Feminism,* forthcoming. **Essays:** Boston Police Strike, United States; *Liberator* Founded, United States; Ludlow Massacre, Colorado, United States; National Child Labor Committee, United States; Owen Model Communities, Great Britain, United States; Wagner Act, United States.

NEWTON-MATZA, Mitchell. Adjunct instructor, University of St. Francis, Joliet, Illinois, and Roosevelt University, Chicago, Illinois. Author of articles and conference papers on labor and legal history of Chicago and Illinois; legal history during the New Republic; world and U.S. history. Active member of Illinois State Historical Society and Illinois Labor History Society. **Essays:** *Commonwealth v. Hunt,* United States; Haymarket Riot, United States; Norris–La Guardia Act, United States.

NOLAN, Melanie. Senior lecturer, Department of History, Victoria University of Wellington, New Zealand. Coeditor of *Suffrage and Beyond: International Feminist Perspectives,* 1994. Author of *Breadwinning: New Zealand Women and the State,* 2000. Teaches New Zealand and Australian history, labor history, comparative history, historiography, and social history. **Essay:** Maritime Strike, Australasia.

OLIVARES, Jaime Ramon. Houston Community College, Houston, Texas. **Essays:** Cananéa Strike, Mexico; Clifton-Morenci-Metcalf Strike, United States; Confederación de Trabajadores de América Latina, Latin America; Longshoremen and Miners Strike, Chile.

O'NEAL, Michael J. Writer and editor, Moscow, Idaho. Author of five books in the Great Mysteries/Opposing Viewpoints series by Greenhaven Press. **Essays:** AFSCME Strike, United States; *Apex Hosiery Co. v. Leader,* United States; Carlisle Indian School, United States; Civil Rights Act of 1964, United States; *Coronado Coal v. UMWA,* United States; Erdman Act, United States; Gallup Coal Strike, United States; *Gompers v. Bucks Stove,* United States; Guffey Act, United States; Harpers Ferry Raid, United States; Keating-Owen Act, United States; Landrum-Griffin Act, United States; Lloyd-La Follette Act, United States; National Origins Act, United States; People's Party, United States; Sherman Antitrust Act, United States; Steel Seizure Case, United States; Tailors' Strike, United States; Teamsters Union, United States; *Truax v. Corrigan,* United States; *United States v. United Mine Workers of America,* United States.

O'NEILL, Colleen. Assistant professor of ethnic studies, California Polytechnic State University-San Luis Obispo. Author of *Making a Living and Working Elsewhere, Navajo Workers in the Twentieth Century,* forthcoming; coeditor of *Native Pathways, American Indian Economies and Culture in the Twentieth Century,* forthcoming.

OOTEN, Melissa. Doctoral candidate, College of William and Mary, Williamsburg, Virginia. Researches and teaches American history, specializing in twentieth-century race, gender, and popular culture studies. **Essay:** Triangle Shirtwaist Fire, United States.

PARADISE, Lee Ann. Writer and editor, Lubbock, Texas. Contributor to *Science in Dispute.* Technical writer of *Pain*

Medicine: A Comprehensive Review, 2003. **Essays:** Age Discrimination in Employment Act, United States; Federal Employees Gain Union Rights, United States; Hatch Act, United States; La Follette Seamen's Act, United States; National Trades Union, United States; National Women's Trade Union League, United States; Panic of 1873, United States; Perkins Becomes Secretary of Labor, United States; *Texas and New Orleans Railroad Company et al v. Brotherhood of Railway and Steamship Clerks et al*, United States; United Tailoresses Society, United States; United Textile Workers of America, United States; Women in Industry Service, United States.

PAULSON, Linda Dailey. Writer based in Ventura, California. Contributor to various periodicals and reference works including Gale's Biography Resource Center, *The Scribner Encyclopedia of American Lives: The 1960s,* and *Encyclopedia of World Biography.* **Essays:** AFL-CIO Expels Key Unions, United States; Battle of the Overpass, United States; Civilian Conservation Corps, United States; Committee for Industrial Organization, United States; Congress of Industrial Organizations, United States; Ford-UAW Contract, United States; Grape Pickers' Strike, United States; Industrial Workers of the World, United States; March of the Mill Children, United States; Millworkers' Strike, United States; Navajos Occupy Fairchild Plant, United States; Social Security Act, United States; Stock Market Crash, United States; Watsonville Canning Strike, United States; World Free Trade Conference Demonstrations, United States.

PRONO, Luca. Independent scholar, Bologna, Italy. Author of articles and chapters on American working class and communist fiction of the 1930s, Italian neorealism, and gay and lesbian studies. **Essays:** Legalitarian Strike, Italy; Memorial Day Massacre, United States.

PURDY, Sean. Doctoral candidate, Department of History, Queen's University, Kingston, Ontario, Canada. Author of *Radicals and Revolutionaries: The History of Canadian Communism from the Robert S. Kenny Collection* and numerous scholarly articles on the political economy and social history of housing in Canada. **Essay:** Trades and Labor Congress of Canada, Canada.

REES, Jonathan. Assistant professor of history, Colorado State University, Pueblo. Author of *Managing the Mills: Labor Policy in the American Steel Industry During the Nonunion Era.* **Essays:** Great Steel Strike, United States; Homestead Lockout, United States; U.S. Steel Recognizes the Steel Workers Organizing Committee as an Official Bargaining Agent, United States; United Steelworkers of America, United States.

RENTON, David. Senior research fellow, Department of History, Sunderland University, United Kingdom. Author of *Fascism: Theory and Practice,* 1999, and *This Rough Game,* 2001. **Essay:** Forced Labor, Germany.

RUOTSILA, Markku. Docent (adjunct associate professor), Department of History, University of Tampere, Finland. Author of *British and American Anticommunism Before the Cold War,* 2001, and other works. Teaches courses in American and British political, intellectual, and religious history. **Essay:** International Labor Organization, France.

SHAH, Courtney Q. Doctoral candidate, Department of History, University of Houston, Texas. Research interests include history of medicine, labor history, and the Progressive Era. **Essay:** Act to Encourage Immigration, United States.

STRAUS, Emily. Doctoral candidate, Department of History, Brandeis University, Waltham, Massachusetts. Research interests include urban history, working-class history, and history of education. **Essay:** Alliance for Labor Action, United States.

THOMPSON, Willie. Visiting professor of history, Northumbria University, Newcastle upon Tyne, United Kingdom. Author of *The Left in History,* 1997, and *The Communist Movement Since 1945,* 1998. **Essays:** Introduction, International Labor, 1800–2000; Popular Front, France.

TOLLEY-STOKES, Rebecca. Assistant professor, University Libraries, East Tennessee State University, Johnson City. Contributor to *Encyclopedia of Appalachia, Dictionary of American History,* and other reference works. **Essays:** Arbitration Act of 1888, United States; Brotherhood of Railroad Trainmen, United States; U.S. Government Seizes Railroads, United States.

TOUCAS-TRUYEN, Patricia. Independent scholar, La Rochelle, France. Historian at the Groupement national de la coopération, and teaches courses about the history of the social economy at the University of Le Mans (France). Author of *Histoire de la mutualité et des assurances,* 1998, and *L'identité mutualiste,* 2001. **Essay:** Silk Workers' Revolts, France.

van der LINDEN, Marcel. Research director, International Institute of Social History, Amsterdam, the Netherlands. Editor, *International Review of Social History* (Cambridge). Author of books including *Transnational Labour History: Explorations,* 2003. **Essays:** First International, Great Britain; International Federation of Miners, Worldwide; Transport Workers' Strike, Worldwide.

Van DYKE, Michael T. Visiting assistant professor, Department of American Thought and Language, Michigan State University, East Lansing. Completed an online audio gallery about the Flint Sit-Down Strike of 1936–1937, which can be heard at <www.historicalvoices.org/flint>. **Essay:** General Motors Recognizes United Auto Workers, United States.

Van GOETHEM, Geert. Deputy director of the Amsab—Institute of Social History, Gent, Belgium. Author of studies on the history of May Day, the Belgian socialist movement, and international trade unionism. **Essay:** International Federation of Trade Unions, Netherlands.

VARGAS, Zaragosa. Associate professor of history, University of California, Santa Barbara. Author of *Proletarians of the North, A History of Mexican Industrial Workers in Detroit and the Midwest, 1919–1933,* 1993, and *The Union Makes Us Strong, Mexican American Workers, Unionism, and the Struggle for Civil Rights, 1929–1945,* forthcoming.

VIAU, Yanic. Independent scholar, Montreal, Quebec, Canada. Master's degree in comparative history from Universitat Autònoma de Barcelona (Spain). Coauthor of *Jacques-Victor Morin, syndicaliste et éducateur populaire,* 2003. **Essay:** General Strike, Spain.

WALLER, Joel. Essay: Pullman Strike, United States.

WATERMAN, Peter. Retired senior lecturer, Institute of Social Studies, The Hague, Netherlands. Author or editor of numerous articles and books on international labor history and contemporary labor and social movement internationalism. Currently focusing on the World Social Forums and global justice and solidarity movement. **Essays:** CIO Joins, AFL Rejects WFTU, United States; International Confederation of Free Trade Unions, Worldwide; World Federation of Trade Unions, France.

WILLIS, Elizabeth. Independent researcher and writer, London, United Kingdom. Regular contributor to *Medicine, Conflict and Survival.* Author of pamphlet, *Women in the Spanish Revoluton.* **Essays:** Lancashire Textile Strikes, Great Britain; Trades Union Act, Great Britain.

YOUNG, Ronald. Assistant professor of history, Georgia Southern University, Statesboro. Teaches courses in world history and Latin American history. Research interest is in the area of urban history. **Essays:** Agriculture Workers Strike, Italy; All-India Trade Union Congress, India; Bracero Program, United States and Mexico; Calcutta General Strike, India; Chiang Kai-shek Purges Communists, China; Confederación Obrera Pan-Americana, Western Hemisphere; Congress of South African Trade Unions, South Africa; Foran Act, United States; International Transport Workers' Federation, Europe; Maquiladoras Established, Mexico; Miners' Strike, 1922, South Africa; Miners' Strike, 1946, South Africa; Organización Regional Inter-americana de Trabajadores, Western Hemisphere; Salt of the Earth Strike, United States; Shanghai May Fourth Movement, China; Shanghai May Thirtieth Movement, China; Union Federations Split Along Ideological Lines, South America; United Fruit Company Strike, Colombia.

INDEX

INDEX

Red Week (1914), 2:177–181
    strike wave (1919), **2:270–273**
ITF (International Transport Workers'
    Federation) (Europe), **1:481–483**;
    2:335–336
Itliong, Larry, 1:398, 400
ITS. *See* International Trade
    Secretariats
ITU (International Typographical
    Union), **2:31–35**, 90, 295, 349–350
IUE (International Union of Electrical
    Workers), 1:162, 266
IUMMSW. *See* International Union of
    Mine, Mill, and Smelter Workers
Iverson, Peter, 2:48
IWA (Industrial Workers of Africa)
    (South Africa), **1:448–453**
IWMA (International Working Men's
    Association). *See* First International
IWPA (International Working People's
    Association), 2:445–446
IWW. *See* Industrial Workers of the
    World

J

Jackson, Andrew
    Bank of the United States and,
        1:274; 2:30
    biographies, 2:31, 443
    civil service and, 1:548
    illustrations, *2:27, 440*
    National Trades' Union and, 2:29,
        30
    workday length and, 2:311
    Workingmen's Party and, 2:442
Jackson, Helen Hunt, 1:358, 359
Jackson, Patrick Tracy, 2:140
Jackson, Tracy, 1:290
Jacquard, Joseph-Marie, 2:141
Jallianwala Bagh massacre (India,
    1919), 1:42
Jamahiriya, 2:284
Jamaica, 1:6, 8
James, John, 1:18
Janson, Paul, 1:132
Japan
    National Origins Act and, 2:26
    19th-century unionism, **2:318–322**
    1930s union dissolution, **1:495–500**
    postwar labor, **1:493–495**
Japan Federation of Employers'
    Organizations (Nikkeiren), 1:494
Japan Railway Company, 2:319
Japanese Americans, 2:26, 205

Japanese Knights of Labor, 2:318, 320
Jaques, Moses, 1:274
Jarrett, John, 1:53, 112, 309, 310
Jarrett, Vernon, 1:585
Jaruzelski, Wojciech, 2:250, 251
Jáuregui Hurtado, Arturo, 2:74–75
Jaurès, Jean, 1:135, 136
Javits, Jacob K., 1:262, 263
Jefferson, Thomas, 1:351, 415, 416–
    417, 418, 546
Jencks, Clinton, 2:201, 202
Jencks, Virginia, 2:202
Jewish Federation of Labor, 1:479
Jewish immigrants
    International Ladies Garment
        Workers Union and, 1:477, 478,
        479; 2:25
    National Origins Act and, 2:26
    Russian Revolution and, 2:25–26
    Triangle Shirtwaist fire and, 2:339
    Widowed Mother's Fund
        Association and, 2:420–422
Jim Crow laws, 1:194, **500–505**, 584;
    2:41
Jo, Tsunetaro, 2:320, 321
Job Training Partnership Act (1982),
    2:407
John Paul II (Pope), 2:247, 249–250,
    251
Johnson, Albert, 2:26, 27
Johnson, Andrew, 1:85, 88, 243; 2:90,
    91
Johnson, Ethel M., *2:154*
Johnson, Few Clothes, 2:367
Johnson, Fred, 2:48
Johnson, Genora, 1:367
Johnson, Gloria, 1:191, 192
Johnson, Gustave, 2:134
Johnson, Howard M., 1:296
Johnson, Hugh Samuel, 1:594, 595;
    2:14, 15
Johnson, Lyndon B.
    affirmative action and, 2:121, 122,
        123
    age discrimination and, 1:32, 34
    biographies, 1:34, 177, 504
    Bracero program and, 1:99
    Civil Rights Act (1964) and, 1:175,
        176, 504
    illustration, *1:31*
    National Organization for Women
        and, 2:22
    Occupational Safety and Health
        Act and, 2:67, 69

pension benefits and, 1:262
    UAW support for, 1:370–371
    War on Poverty and, 1:38
Johnson-Reed Act. *See* National
    Origins Act
Johnstone, Gordon A., Loray Mill
    Strike and, 1:564
Jones, David R., 1:527
Jones, Ernest, 1:140, 531
Jones, James P., 1:648–649
Jones, Mary Harris "Mother"
    biographies, 1:84, 457, 576, 582
    bituminous coal strike and, 1:83
    illustration, *1:581*
    Industrial Workers of the World
        and, 1:455, 456; 2:243
    Knights of Labor and, 1:519
    Ludlow massacre and, 1:575
    March of the Mill Children and,
        1:580–583, 584
    potato famine and, 2:139
    Socialist Party of America and,
        2:243
*Jones and Laughlin Steel Corporation,
    NLRB v.* (1937), 1:409–410; 2:401
Jones v. Alfred H. Mayer Co. (1968),
    1:176
Jorgenson, Howard, 2:410
Josephson, Matthew, 2:219
Joshi, N. M., 1:42, 43
Jouhaux, Léon, 1:346, 469, 470
*Journeyman Stone Cutters
    Association, Bedford Cut Stone
    Company v.* (1927), 1:65; 2:219
Juárez, Benito Pablo, 2:431, 432
Juchade, Hermann, 1:483
Julian, George, 1:342
June Days Rebellion (France, 1848),
    1:505–507; 2:188
The Jungle (Sinclair), 2:112, **231–236**
Jury, Alfred Fredman, 2:324
Justice for Janitors campaign (AFL-
    CIO), 2:282
Justo, Juan B., 2:346, 348

K

Kádár, Janos, 1:441, *441*, 442, 443
Kamenev, Lev, 2:193
Kamil, Fathi, 1:459, 460
Kanai, Noboru, 2:321
Kania, Stanislaw, 2:250
Kansas, Atkin v. (1903), 2:155
Kansas Exodus (1879), 1:198

Memorial Day massacre and,
1:613; 2:377–378
National Industrial Recovery Act
and, 2:14
Reagan appointees, 1:371
SWOC recognition and, 2:395–396
Taft-Hartley Act and, 2:292, 294
United Automobile Workers and,
1:369
World War II and, 2:458
National Labor Tribune, 1:476
National Labor Union (NLU), **2:15–
19**, 90
African Americans and, 1:196,
197–198, 502–503; 2:17
American Federation of Labor and,
1:51, 52
Colored National Labor Union and,
1:197–198
contract labor and, 1:17
demise of, 1:307; 2:19
Department of Labor creation and,
1:111, 112; 2:15, 18
eight-hour day movement and,
1:301; 2:15, 16, 17, 18, 90
International Labor Union and,
1:475
National Trades' Union and, 2:31
St. Crispin organizations and,
2:199
See also Federation of Organized
Trades and Labor Unions of the
United States and Canada
National Laborer, 1:255
National League, 1:261
National League of Cities v. Usery
(1976), 1:261
National Maritime Union, 1:223
National Mediation Board (NMB),
2:170, 314
National Metal Trades Association,
2:7
National Miners Union (NMU), 1:353,
354; 2:57
National Mobilization Bill (Japan,
1938), 1:498
National Negro Congress, 1:295
National Negro Labor Union, 1:503
National Organization for Women
(NOW), 1:190, 191–192; **2:19–23**
National Origins Act (1924), 1:319;
2:24–27
National Park Service (NPS), 1:180
National Postal Union, 2:133, 135
National Progressive Union of Miners
and Mine Laborers, 1:82; 2:361,
364

National Proletarian Defense
Committee (*Comité Nacional de
Defensa Proletaria*) (CNDP)
(Mexico), 1:617
National Protective Association of the
Brotherhood of Locomotive
Engineers, 1:102
National Railroad Adjustment Board
(NRAB), 2:170
National Railroad Strike. *See* Railroad
Strike (1877)
National Recovery Administration
(NRA), 1:593; 2:14
automobile industry and, 2:356
Goodyear Strike (1936) and, 1:393
Memorial Day massacre and, 1:610
Public Contracts Act and, 2:156
Steel Workers Organizing
Committee and, 1:168
See also National Industrial
Recovery Act
National Revolutionary Party (*Partido
Nacional Revolucionario*) (PNR)
(Mexico), 1:616
National Safety Council, 2:68
National Seamen's and Firemen's
Union of Great Britain and Ireland
(NSFU), 2:334, 335
National Seamen's Union of America.
See International Seamen's Union
National Sharecroppers Fund, 1:194
National Shop Stewards' and
Workers' Committee Movement
(Great Britain), 2:226
National Students' Federation (China),
2:216
National Teachers Association, 1:304
National Textile Workers Union
(NTWU), 1:562, 564, 622
National Trades' Union (NTU), 1:51,
383; **2:27–31**, 298, 311
National Typographical Society
(NTS), 2:32
National Typographical Union. *See*
International Typographical Union
National Union of Iron Molders, **2:35–
38**
National Union of Maritime Cooks
and Stewards, 1:162, 163
National Union of Public Employees
(NUPE) (Great Britain), 2:226
National Union of Railwaymen (Great
Britain), 1:628
National Union of Textile Workers
(NUTW), 2:383, 384
National Union of the Working
Classes (Great Britain), 1:558

National War Labor Board (NWLB)
(World War I), 1:54, 56, 186;
2:38–42, 428
National War Labor Board (NWLB)
(World War II)
creation of, 2:456, 457, 458
equal-pay legislation and, 1:265
racial discrimination and, 1:503,
585–586
Salt of the Earth strike and, 2:201
steel industry and, 2:378–379
wage controls and, 2:459
World War II no-strike pledge and,
2:55–56, 378–379, 458
National Women's Christian
Temperance Union (NWCTU),
1:148
National Women's Party (NWP),
1:268, 270–271, 643; 2:22
National Women's Trade Union
League (WTUL), **2:42–46**
child labor amendment and, 1:148
Coalition of Labor Union Women
and, 1:190
equal-pay legislation and, 1:266
garment industry and, 2:149
Great Uprising (1934) and, 1:624
protective legislation and, 1:269,
270, 271
Triangle Shirtwaist fire and, 2:339
Working Women's Protective
Union and, 2:436
National Workshops (France), 1:506;
2:188
Nationalism
Chile, 1:561
India, 1:42
international labor alliances and,
1:314
Japan, 1:496–497; 2:321
Latin American regional labor
organizations and, 1:212, 214;
2:73
Mexico, 1:127–128
Poland, 1:554
Shanghai May Fourth Movement
and, 2:212, 213
Nationalist Party (*Guomindang*)
(GMD) (China), 1:141–145
Native Americans
Burke Act, 1:360
Carlisle Indian School, 1:128–131
Civilian Conservation Corps and,
1:180
Fairchild Plant occupation, 2:46–49